MW00335071

UNIVERSITY CASEBOOK SERIES®

UNITED STATES ANTITRUST LAW AND ECONOMICS

THIRD EDITION

EINER ELHAUGE
Petrie Professor of Law, Harvard University

444 Cedar Street, Suite 700
St. Paul, MN 55101
1-877-888-1330

Printed in the United States of America

ISBN: 978-1-63459-352-6

SUMMARY OF CONTENTS

TABLE OF CONTENTS

TABLE OF CASES

The principal cases are in bold type.

UNIVERSITY CASEBOOK SERIES®

UNITED STATES ANTITRUST LAW AND ECONOMICS

THIRD EDITION

CHAPTER 1

INTRODUCTION

A. THE FRAMEWORK OF LEGAL ISSUES RAISED BY BASIC ANTITRUST ECONOMICS

How the Basic Economics Explains the Core Legal Concerns. In a world of perfect competition, life is good. Firms can enter and exit markets instantly and without cost, products are homogeneous, and everyone is perfectly informed. Firms are so numerous that none of them is large enough to influence prices by altering output, and all act independently. Supplier competition for sales thus drives prices for products and services down to the costs of providing them. (Costs here should be understood to include capital and risk-bearing costs, and thus incorporates a normal profit that reflects the capital market rate of return necessary to induce investment in firms given the risk level.) Any firm that tried to charge more than costs would be undercut by another firm that would charge less, because they would gain sales whose revenue exceeded costs. Lower cost producers would thus underprice and displace higher cost producers. Their output would be purchased whenever market buyers found that the value of the product to them exceeded its price/cost, but not otherwise.

If demand increased or costs decreased, so that suppliers would earn supranormal profits if their output remained constant, then the existence or prospect of those supranormal profits would induce supplier expansion or entry, increasing supply until it drove prices back down toward costs. If demand decreased or costs increased, so that suppliers would earn substandard profits if their output remained constant, then they would contract or exit the market, shifting any moveable capital to more profitable ventures and reducing supply until prices rose to meet costs. The nice result is to allocate societal resources towards those markets where they can best provide value to buyers. Even nicer, it does not have to be the case that suppliers are omniscient, or even know what they're doing—the market will winnow out those who guess wrong regardless.

In the real world, life is regrettably imperfect. Entry, exit or expansion are costly and take time. Products vary by brand or attributes and information is imperfect. Economies of scale mean many markets cannot sustain a large enough number of firms to leave each without any incentive to consider the effect of its decisions on market prices. But despite such unavoidable realities, typical markets are workably competitive in the sense that they produce results that are fairly close to perfect competition, at least in the long run. In any event, perfect competition provides an aspiration and useful benchmark that helps identify the sort of interferences with market mechanisms that should most concern antitrust law. The economic literature analyzing such issues can be frightfully complicated and mystifying. Luckily, the essential regulatory issues flow in a simple straightforward way from the basics outlined above.

The first major concern is that firms might agree to avoid competing with each other, thus elevating prices above cost and increasing their profits to supracompetitive levels. Price-fixing agreements among competitors constitute a classic example. Similar results can be obtained by agreements to restrict output or divide markets or impede entry. The legal responses to such concerns about agreements to restrict competition will occupy us in Chapter 2.

A second concern is that one firm might individually be large enough to raise prices by reducing output. In the pure case of monopoly, there is only one firm and entry is impossible. Such a monopolist need not worry that, if it raises prices, it will lose business to rivals. Instead, it has incentives to raise prices above costs, up to the point that the extra profits earned from the customers willing to pay the higher price are offset by the profits lost from diminished sales to other customers who aren't willing to pay that price. The result is higher prices, lower output, and many customers who inefficiently do not get the product even though they value it more than it costs to provide. A single buyer, called a monopsonist, raises the parallel problem that it has incentives to suppress prices below competitive levels, which suppresses output from suppliers.

True monopolists are rare. More typical is what economists call a dominant firm, which is a firm that is much larger than the other firms because it has lower costs or a better product. A dominant firm also has incentives to price above cost, but is somewhat constrained by the ability of the other firms to offer the product at their costs. The dominant firm faces what is called the residual demand that results when one subtracts from total market demand the output that the other less efficient firms provide at any given price. The dominant firm effectively faces no competition for this residual demand, and thus has similar incentives to a monopolist to increase prices above its costs. A similar result follows even if rivals are not less efficient, but would have difficulty expanding or entering in response to an increase in prices.

The mere possession of monopoly or dominant power need not, however, be a concern. If a firm makes a better mousetrap, and the world beats a path to its door, it may drive out all rivals and establish a monopoly; but that is a good result, not a bad one. Dominant market power normally reflects the fact that a firm is more efficient because of some cost or quality advantage over its rivals. If a firm has acquired that efficiency advantage through productive investments in innovation, physical capital, or organization, then the additional profits it is able to earn might reasonably be thought to provide the right reward for that investment, especially since any price premium it charges cannot exceed its efficiency advantage over other prevailing market options.

Typically the antitrust laws are instead focused on anticompetitive conduct that is used to obtain or maintain monopoly or dominant market power at levels that were not earned through productive efforts. A dominant firm has incentives to use anticompetitive conduct to exclude rivals from the market, impair rival efficiency, or impede the sort of rival expansion and entry that would drive down prices toward more competitive levels. So does a firm that, while not yet dominant, thinks such anticompetitive conduct will help it obtain dominance. Because a firm that obtains or maintains monopoly or dominant market power can exploit it unilaterally, it also has incentives to engage in such anticompetitive conduct unilaterally, rather than requiring agreement or coordination with rivals. Chapter 3 will address how the law seeks to identify such unilateral anticompetitive conduct and distinguish it from procompetitive unilateral conduct.

Firms with market power might likewise have incentives to enter into agreements with suppliers or buyers to try to exclude rivals, diminish their efficiency, or impede their expansion or entry. Because these agreements are up or down the supply chain, they are generally called "vertical" agreements, in contrast to the "horizontal" agreements entered into by rivals at the same level. They thus involve concerted action but also involve firms who use such vertical agreements to obtain or maintain single firm market power. Chapter 4 addresses these sets of cases.

Firms might also engage in unilateral conduct or vertical agreements that antitrust law fears will impede competition among downstream firms. One form of unilateral conduct that some laws seek to condemn on this score is price discrimination among buyers that distorts their ability to compete downstream. Similar concerns have been raised about vertical agreements to restrain resale by buyers, including agreements to fix the prices that distributors can charge downstream, or to limit where or to whom they can sell. As we will see, legal liability for such conduct or agreements has been the subject of strong economic critique, based mainly on the observation that firms typically have little incentive to impede competition among downstream firms. Such issues will be addressed in Chapter 5.

Chapter 6 then addresses how to prove the existence of an agreement, and addressed a third concern: that some markets have few enough firms that each has an influence on prices and output, and can notice and respond to the actions of each other. If so, then even without an explicit agreement, such firms may be able to coordinate to restrict output and raise prices. This is called oligopolistic coordination. The big difficulty this raises is whether such coordination can be condemned without proof of an agreement, especially when oligopolistic firms cannot avoid knowing that their pricing and output decisions will affect the behavior of other firms.

The final major concern, addressed in Chapter 7, is that rivals might merge or combine into one firm. Horizontal mergers can have anticompetitive effects if the resulting firm has monopoly or dominant market power, or the structure of the rest of the market means the merger will create an oligopoly or exacerbate its ability to coordinate on higher prices. The difficulty is determining when this is the effect of a merger and whether the merger is justified by any greater efficiencies it might create. Vertical mergers between firms up and down the supply chain raise issues similar to vertical agreements that might exclude or impair rival competition. Mergers between firms that are not related horizontally or vertically are called conglomerate mergers, which raise issues if they eliminate potential horizontal competition or enable the merged firm to engage in anticompetitive exclusionary conduct.

Graphing the Basic Economics. The prior section explains the basic relevant economics using simple words. But some might find graphical depictions more helpful. In a competitive market, the situation is represented by Figure 1. The X-axis indicates the market quantity Q. The Y-axis indicates the market price P. The line marked D is the demand curve, which indicates what quantity buyers would demand at each price. As price (P) goes up, the quantity demanded (Q) goes down because making a product more expensive means fewer buyers will find the value of the product worth the price. The line marked MC indicates the marginal cost of production. It generally increases as quantity goes up, mainly because increasing market quantity generally requires bidding away resources from other markets or because seller's plants are operating at output levels where their marginal costs of operation would increase if they made more. The MC curve is also the same as the supply curve, S, which indicates the quantity the market would supply at each price, because in a competitive market suppliers should be willing to supply output at any price that exceeds their marginal cost. If they didn't, then a rival seller would take away the sale at any P > MC because that would be more profitable to the rival than losing that sale.

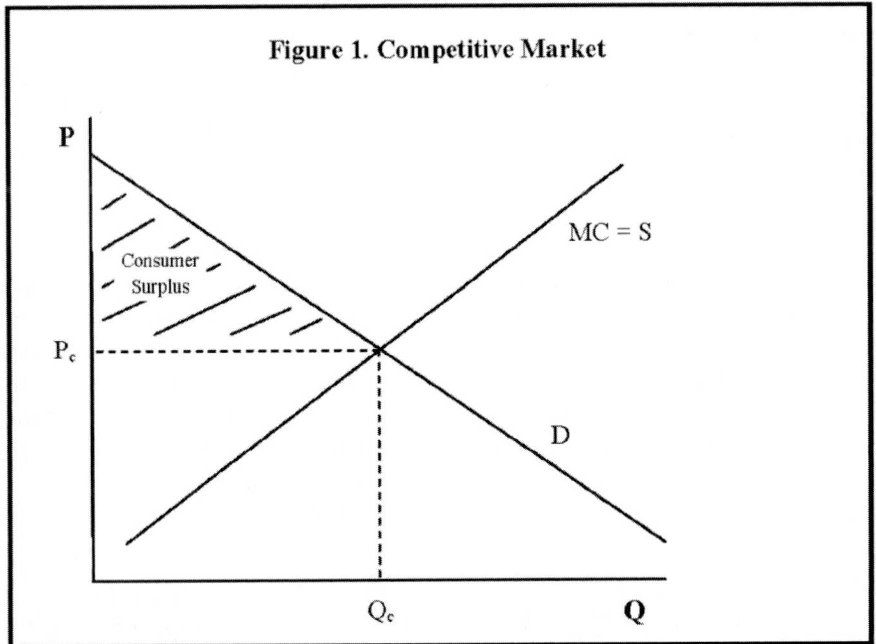

Figure 1. Competitive Market

The intersection of the demand and supply curves is the competitive market equilibrium, where buyer willingness to pay matches supplier willingness to provide, and P_c and Q_c are, respectively, the competitive market price and quantity. If the price dipped below P_c, then quantity supplied would dip below Q_c but that would leave some buyer demand unsatisfied because some buyers are willing to pay a higher price, and thus they would bid up the price until it reached P_c again. If a supplier tried to charge above P_c then the quantity demanded would go below Q_c, but that would leave an opportunity for a rival seller to win sales by charging a lower price. Thus rival sellers would bid down the price until it reached P_c again.

This competitive market equilibrium has many wonderful features. Goods are never provided to buyers if the marginal cost of doing so exceeds the value buyers would put on it, as indicated by buyer willingness to pay. Goods are provided whenever buyer valuation does exceed marginal cost. If demand increases (such as if rainy weather increases the need for umbrellas), then the demand curve will shift to the right (at each price, more quantity demanded), but then a new equilibrium arises, with a higher P_c and Q_c, that again provides the good whenever buyer valuation exceeds market cost. If costs increase (such as if increased metal costs make it more expensive to make umbrellas), then the supply curve will go up, resulting in a higher P_c and lower Q_c, but again the product will be supplied whenever buyer valuation exceeds the new marginal cost. And the whole thing works in reverse if market demand or costs decrease.

Further, only the marginal buyer (the buyer on the demand curve whose willingness to pay just equals P_c) pays a price that equals her valuation of the product. All the inframarginal buyers (buyers on the demand curve to the left of Q_c) value the product more highly than P_c, and thus enjoy a consumer surplus that reflects the difference between their valuation and P_c. The total consumer surplus is the shaded area in Figure 1.

Now suppose that instead of a competitive market, we have a monopoly market with only one supplier. Then the situation will instead reflect Figure 2. The monopolist will not simply increase its output whenever the market price exceeds its marginal cost. The reason is that the monopolist knows that if it increases output to sell to the marginal buyer, it will decrease prices to all its inframarginal buyers as well. Thus, for every increased unit of output, its marginal revenue, marked by the MR curve, is lower than the market price because selling that unit gains it the market price on the marginal unit, but also causes it to suffer a lower price on all the inframarginal units. (In a competitive market, sellers ignore this effect because the inframarginal units are sold to other sellers.) Thus, instead of setting its market output at where price equals marginal cost, a monopolist will maximize profits by setting its market output at where its marginal revenue equals marginal cost, or at Q_m. At this subcompetitive level of output, market demand will lead to a supracompetitive price, P_m.

Figure 2. Monopoly Market

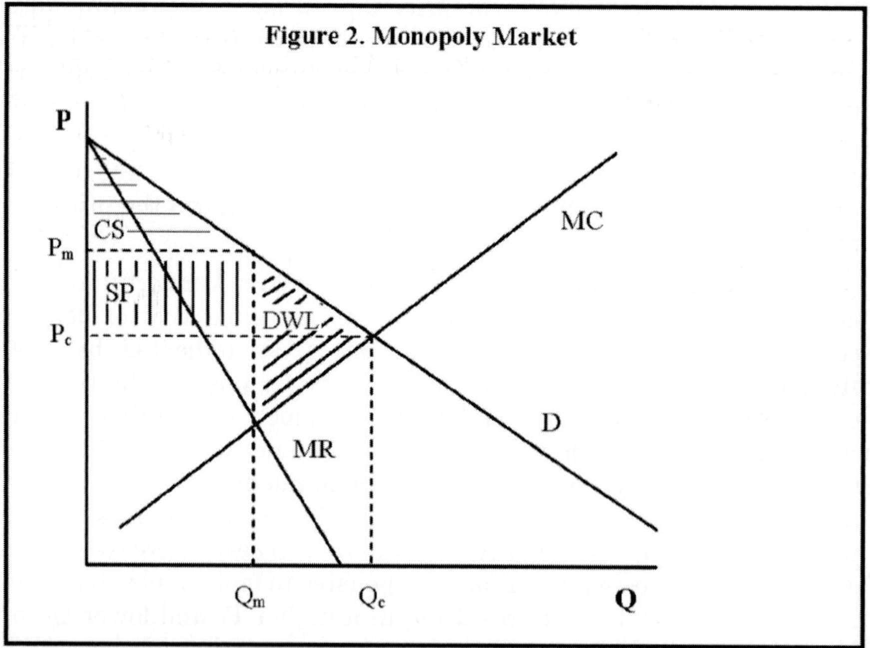

At this monopoly price there will be an allocative inefficiency, called a dead weight loss, which is marked DWL on the graph. This reflects the fact that many buyers who value the product more than it would cost to make it (all the buyers on the demand curve between Q_m and Q_c) would not get it. It is called an allocative inefficiency because it reflects an inefficient allocation of resources. The supracompetitive profits would equal the quantity produced (Q_m) times the difference between P_m and P_c, which is represented by the box marked SP. The consumer surplus would be reduced to the area marked CS on the graph. Thus, the monopoly pricing would both be inefficient and reduce consumer welfare.

In a cartel, rivals agree to make decisions about price or output together, and thus collectively act like a monopolist, maximizing their profits by agreeing to fix a price above the competitive level, or by agreeing to fix an output below the competitive level. Either strategy amounts to the same thing. Both strategies require the cartel members to reach some sort of understanding about how to allocate the market quantity among the various rivals, because all of the sales earn supracompetitive profits and thus every rival will want them.

A dominant firm prices in a way similar to a monopolist, but against a residual demand curve. Suppose, for example, a firm enjoys dominant market power because the rest of the market is capacity-constrained; rivals are making as much as they can and cannot make any more. Then the situation can be illustrated by Figure 3. D_{mkt} indicates overall market demand. At any price, the dominant firm knows that its rivals can produce no more than their capacity cap, marked as Q_{riv}. Thus, the dominant firm faces the residual demand curve, marked D_{res}. Against that residual demand curve, the dominant firm will price just like a monopolist, producing price and quantity P_{dom} and Q_{dom}. If rivals' ability to expand output is not totally blocked, but is limited so that they are more willing to expand supply at higher prices, then Q_{riv} will get larger at higher prices. This will make the residual demand curve flatter, but will not eliminate it unless rivals' supply is perfectly elastic—that is, unless rivals can expand instantly to supply the whole market if prices go above competitive levels. A firm can have such market power even if it does not have a huge share of the market if rival ability to expand output is sufficiently limited.

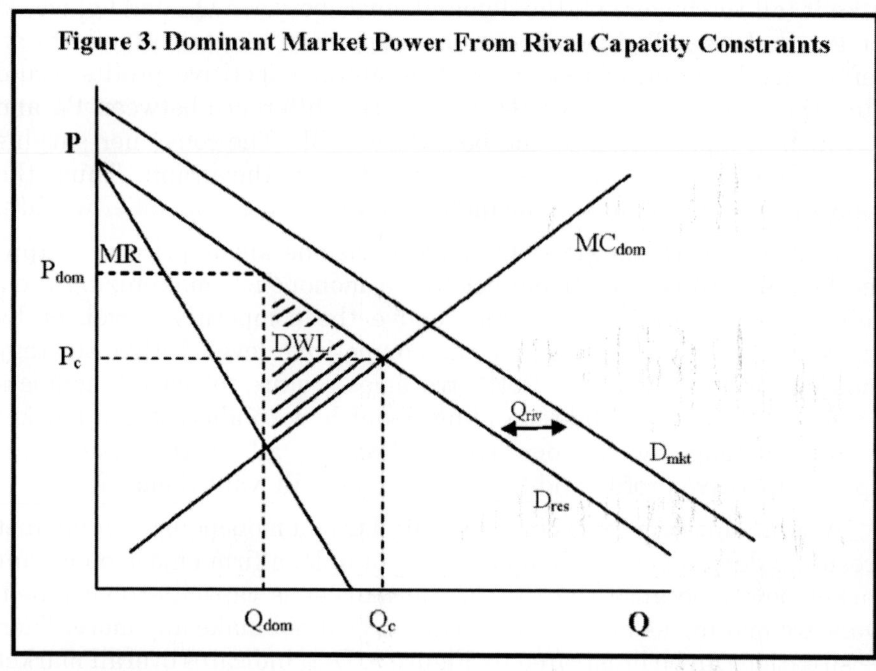

Figure 3. Dominant Market Power From Rival Capacity Constraints

The situation is a bit more complicated, but similar, where a dominant firm enjoys market power because it is more efficient than its rivals. Suppose a dominant firm has marginal costs that are lower than its rivals. Then the situation can be described by Figure 4. We can ascertain the residual demand curve faced by the dominant firm by asking what quantity its rivals would supply at each price given their higher costs, and then subtracting that quantity from the market demand. For example, at price P_A, rivals operating at marginal cost will make enough output to satisfy all market demand, leaving the dominant firm with zero residual demand. At price P_B, rivals will make zero output, so that residual demand equals the entire market demand at that price, or Q_B. For any price between P_A and P_B, the residual demand available to the dominant firm is the line that connects point (P_A, 0) and point (P_B, Q_B). The residual demand at each price reflects the difference between the quantity rivals will supply at that price and the quantity the market would demand at that price, which is the difference between MC_{riv} and D_{mkt}, marked as $\leftrightarrow$ on the graph. Against that residual demand curve, the dominant firm prices just like a monopolist. Again, a firm can have such market power even if it does not have a huge market share.

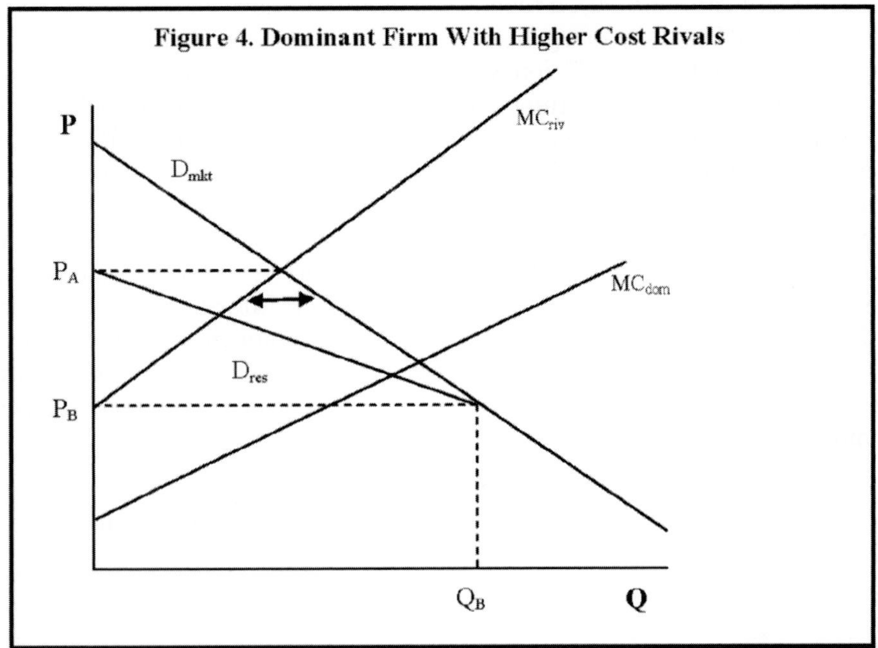

Mere possession of monopoly or market power is not a concern because it may merely indicate the fruits of investment in building more capacity or becoming more efficient than rivals. If a firm lowers its marginal costs, it is said to increase its productive efficiency, and such an increase in productive efficiency can offset any reduction in allocative efficiency. Indeed, in the above cases, buyers are clearly better off if the dominant firm exists or has lower costs, than if it did not, because if it did not then prices would be higher and quantity lower. However, agreements that create cartels that have monopoly or market power are a concern because they create no offsetting efficiencies. Likewise, anticompetitive conduct that restricts rival competitiveness, by limiting their ability to expand output or by raising rival costs, can enhance monopoly or market power without offsetting efficiencies and thus are also an anticompetitive concern.

If there are not many firms, they may be able to coordinate on prices that are above competitive levels without reaching an actual agreement. Such coordination can achieve results similar to monopoly or dominant firm pricing if the coordinating firms collectively have monopoly or market power. Mergers are often condemned because they make such coordination possible or easier. Mergers may also be condemned because they create a firm that will enjoy unilateral market power or because they make it easier for the merged firm to engage in anticompetitive conduct that impairs rival efficiency.

However, mergers and other conduct may create both productive efficiencies and allocative inefficiencies, and sometimes the former might offset the latter. Consider Figure 5. Suppose that before a merger (or some alleged misconduct), a firm is constrained to price at marginal cost, depicted as MC_{pre}. The merger (or conduct) both lowers its marginal costs (increasing productive efficiency) and gives it market power, so it now acts as a monopolist against the demand curve, creating allocative inefficiency. Consider two cases. In case 1, the merger (or conduct) lowers marginal cost all the way down to MC_{post1}. The firm then sets output at where its marginal revenue equals its marginal costs, meaning at Q_{post1}, which results in a price of P_{post1}, which is actually lower than the initial price of P_{pre}. Here enough productive efficiency was passed on to consumers that they are that they are better off after the conduct than before, and the firm is better off since it earns higher profits than before. The merger (or conduct) in case 1 increased both consumer welfare and producer welfare, and thus increased total welfare, which is the combination of the two.

Figure 5. Allocative Inefficiency With Offsetting Productive Efficiency

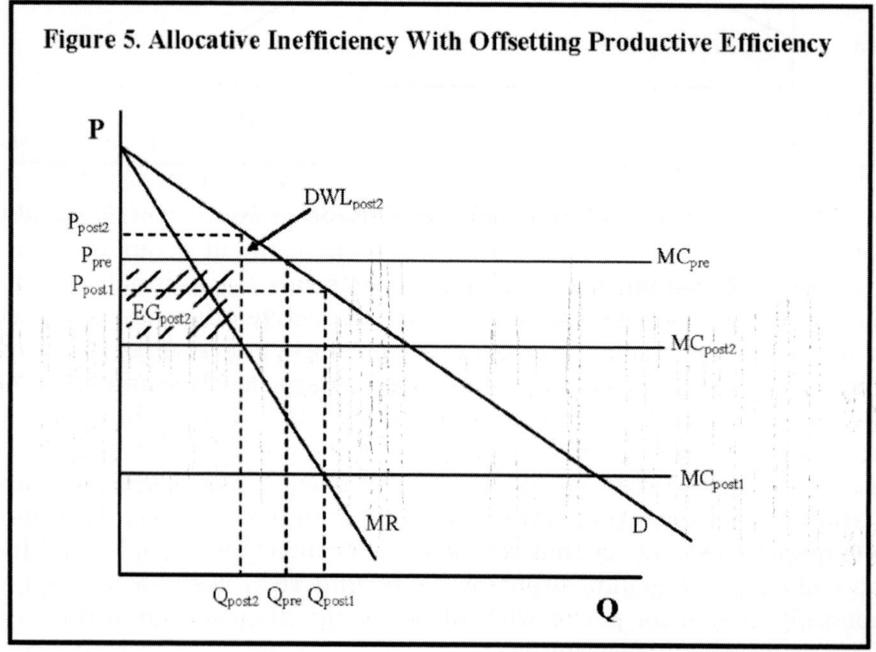

In case 2, the merger (or conduct) lowers marginal cost down somewhat less, to MC_{post2}. The firm then produces Q_{post2}, at a price of P_{post2}, which is actually higher than the initial price of P_{pre}. Now we have conflicting effects. Compared to the initial situation, there is a deadweight loss, indicated by DWL_{post2}, reflecting the fact that output is lower than it was before. However, there is also an efficiency gain, indicated by EG_{post2}, reflecting the fact that costs are lower. If, as here the size of the efficiency gain exceeds the size of the dead weight loss, then there is a net increase in efficiency and total welfare. However, consumer welfare has decreased, not only because of the deadweight loss, but also because buyers pay a higher price on the output they still buy. However, the firm gains both the latter higher prices and the efficiency gain, so the increase to producer welfare exceeds the loss to consumer welfare. Thus, conduct might simultaneously decrease consumer welfare and increase total welfare, raising the issue of which to favor. As we shall see, so far antitrust law generally favors a consumer welfare standard, perhaps on the notion that producers could always convert a total welfare gain into a consumer welfare gain by transferring some of their increased profits back to consumers. But the issue remains controversial, particularly for mergers of firms that mainly export to other nations.

B. AN OVERVIEW OF U.S. ANTITRUST LAWS AND REMEDIAL STRUCTURE

The primary sources of U.S. antitrust law are a handful of statutes enacted by the U.S. Congress. The Sherman Act, enacted in 1890, provides the basic laws condemning (in § 1) anticompetitive agreements and (in § 2) unilateral conduct that monopolizes or attempts to monopolize.[1] Violations of either section constitute a felony that can be criminally prosecuted by the U.S. Department of Justice (DOJ). Other provisions make the Sherman Act enforceable by DOJ actions for injunctive relief, and through private suits brought by injured parties (or by states on their behalf) for treble damages, injunctive relief, and attorney fees.[2]

The 1914 Clayton Act added more specific antitrust laws governing (in § 2) price discrimination in commodities, (in § 3) sales of commodities conditioned on the buyer not dealing with the seller's rivals, and (in §§ 7–8) mergers and interlocking directorates. Clayton Act § 3 remains in its original form, but the provision on price discrimination was amended in 1936 by the Robinson-Patman Act, and the provision on mergers was amended in 1950 by the Celler-Kefauver Act and supplemented in 1976 by the Hart-Scott-Rodino Act, which provides for pre-merger notification to U.S. enforcement agencies.[3] These Clayton Act provisions are not enforceable by criminal penalties, but are otherwise enforceable by the DOJ and private suits in the same way as the Sherman Act.[4] They are also enforceable through prospective cease-or-desist orders by the FTC, unless the conduct occurs in an industry regulated by a special federal agency, in which case the special agency has that authority.[5]

---

[1] *See* 15 U.S.C. §§ 1–2.

[2] *See* 15 U.S.C. §§ 4, 12, 15–15c, 25–26.

[3] *See* 15 U.S.C. §§ 13–14, 18–19.

[4] *See* 15 U.S.C. §§ 12, 15–15c, 25–26. Robinson-Patman Act § 3 imposes criminal penalties up to $5000 and a year in prison for knowingly price discriminating with an anticompetitive purpose, *see* 15 U.S.C. § 13a, but this provision is seldom enforced.

[5] *See* 15 U.S.C. § 21. The special agencies are the Federal Communications Commission, the Federal Reserve Board, the Department of Transportation, and the Surface Transportation Board. *Id.*

The 1914 Congress also enacted FTC Act § 5, which generally prohibits all "unfair methods of competition."[6] (This provision also prohibits unfair or deceptive practices, which are addressed by a separate consumer protection branch of the FTC.) The vagueness of the "unfair" language has been cabined by a 1994 amendment, which provides that the FTC cannot deem conduct "unfair unless the act or practice causes or is likely to cause substantial injury to consumers which is not reasonably avoidable by consumers themselves and not outweighed by countervailing benefits to consumers or to competition."[7] The FTC Act is not enforceable by private suits, nor by the DOJ, nor by any retroactive penalties.[8] Instead, it is enforceable only by the FTC itself, whose only remedy is to issue a prospective order to cease and desist the activity, which is in turn subject to review by the federal courts of appeals.[9] The FTC can also go to court to seek a preliminary injunction pending a final resolution by itself and the courts.[10] Although the FTC may have authority to adopt prospective rules defining the conduct it regards as an unfair method of competition, it has not exercised such authority as a matter of practice.[11]

---

[6] *See* 15 U.S.C. § 45(a).

[7] 15 U.S.C. § 45(n).

[8] *See* 15 U.S.C. § 12 (defining "antitrust laws" enforceable in those ways to exclude the FTC Act); 15 U.S.C. § 56(a) (vesting the FTC with exclusive enforcement authority over the FTC Act with limited exceptions).

[9] *See* 15 U.S.C. § 45.

[10] 15 U.S.C. § 53(b).

[11] The legal issue is surprisingly unsettled. Before 1973, it was seriously doubted that the FTC Act gave the FTC authority to issues substantive rules. *See* K. DAVIS, ADMINISTRATIVE LAW TEXT 130 (3d ed. 1972); Marinelli, *The Federal Trade Commission's Authority to Determine Unfair Practices and Engage in Substantive Rulemaking*, 2 OHIO N.U.L. REV. 289, 295–96 & n.75 (1974). Then, in National Petroleum Refiners Ass'n v. FTC, 482 F.2d 672, 673–78 (D.C.Cir. 1973), Judge Skelly Wright interpreted 15 U.S.C. § 46(g) to give the FTC authority to adopt substantive rules defining "unfair methods of competition" and "unfair and deceptive trade practices." But that was a debatable interpretation because § 46(g) could be read to just authorize creating procedural rules for carrying out the FTC's cease and desist powers. It was also dicta as applied to rules defining "unfair methods of competition" because the case was actually about a rule defining an "unfair and deceptive trade practice," namely the failure to disclose octane levels on gas pumps. The House initially passed a bill that said the FTC had authority to enact rules defining deceptive trade practices but not unfair methods of competition; however, the House compromised with the Senate on a statute that did the former, but did not purport to alter whether or not authority existed to enact rules defining unfair methods of competition. *See* 15 U.S.C. § 57a(2); H.R. Rep. No. 1107, 93d Cong., 2d Sess. 49–50 (1974), reprinted in 4 U.S. Code Cong. & Ad. News 7702, 7727 (1974); S. Rep. No. 1408, 93d Cong., 2d Sess. 32 (1974) (conference report), reprinted in 4 U.S. Code Cong. & Ad. News 7755, 7764 (1974). Thus, it appears there were insufficient legislative votes for either the proposition that the FTC could enact rules defining anticompetitive practices or the proposition that it could not. The FTC rules on its rulemaking procedure seem to carefully limit its rulemaking to deceptive practices (Rule 1.7) or special areas where it has express statutory authority to adopt rules, such as defining whether certain conduct constitutes illegal price discrimination (Rule 1.23–1.24), unless the reference in Rule 1.2.1 to "unlawful trade practices" is intended to cut more broadly. The only substantive rule related to competition that the FTC ever enacted was pursuant to its special authority to define price discrimination under 15 U.S.C. § 13(a), and has since been rescinded. *See* 58 Fed. Reg. 35907–01. The FTC does not appear to have adopted any substantive rule that purported to define "unfair methods of competition" that were not deceptive nor any procedural rule that claims general authority to enact rules defining "unfair methods of competition" that are not deceptive.

The FTC does not have jurisdiction to enforce Sherman Act violations, *see* 15 U.S.C. § 21, but this is of little practical importance in cases seeking injunctive relief because anything that violates the Sherman Act could also be deemed an unfair method of competition actionable under FTC Act § 5.[12] Thus, the DOJ and FTC effectively have concurrent jurisdiction over most industries when seeking injunctive relief. However, especially for mergers, they have adopted a practice of informally dividing their jurisdiction by concentrating on different industries, though an effort to adopt a written agreement that would more precisely define this division was withdrawn in the face of Congressional opposition.[13]

Federal courts have exclusive jurisdiction over federal antitrust claims.[14] Antitrust cases brought by anyone other than the FTC (or special agency) are brought in the U.S. federal district courts for a trial to adjudicate the facts and determine the relevant law,[15] and citations to their opinions are marked "F. Supp." Appeals from decisions of the district courts are generally first brought to the U.S. Courts of Appeals (noted "F.2d" or "F.3d" in citations), which are often called the circuit courts because there is a different one for each region of the country. Most are numbered (e.g., "1st Cir." is New England, "9th Cir." comprises certain West Coast states) except for the D.C. Circuit, which sits in Washington, D.C. and tends to handle appeals from federal agency decisions. Appeals are on questions of law, though this can include such legal questions as whether there was sufficient evidence to support the factual findings and whether those findings suffice to meet the legal standard. Losing parties can then seek review before the U.S. Supreme Court (marked "U.S." in citations), but although that Court was formerly obligated to take any appeal that presented a "substantial" federal question, it now has discretion to decide when to take a case (called taking "certiorari"), which it generally does only when the circuit courts are split on an important relevant legal issue.[16]

---

12 *See* FTC v. Cement Institute, 333 U.S. 683, 689–95 (1948).

13 *See* Baer, Feinstein & Shaheen, *Taking Stock: Recent Trends in U.S. Merger Enforcement*, 18 ANTITRUST 15, 20–21 (Spring 2004).

14 *See* Marrese v. American Academy of Orthopaedic Surgeons, 470 U.S. 373, 379 (1985).

15 At the FTC, the general procedure is instead (1) the five commissioners issue a complaint, (2) that complaint is adjudicated by an administrative law judge (ALJ) within the FTC, (3) that ALJ decision is appealed to the five commissioners who decide whether to issue the cease and desist order, and (4) that FTC decision is appealed directly to the Courts of Appeal, and from there to the Supreme Court where appropriate. *See* 15 U.S.C. §§ 21, 45. The exception is that the FTC must bring a claim for a preliminary injunction to a federal district court, 15 U.S.C. § 53(b), which generally must be done in merger cases to prevent the merger from occurring. At any step along the way, the FTC (like the DOJ) can instead settle with the parties and enter into a consent decree limiting their conduct or merger in some way, which is in fact how the bulk of cases are ultimately handled.

16 Historically, there were special statutes that provided for antitrust trials by 3 judge district courts and direct appeal to the U.S. Supreme Court, which was true in some of the cases in this book. But today direct appeal from district court to the U.S. Supreme Court is exceedingly rare, though possible in extreme cases. *See* 15 U.S.C. § 29.

In addition, many states have their own antitrust statutes. These statutes tend to be less vigorously enforced, in part because they generally borrow U.S. antitrust standards and are usually brought as ancillary claims to U.S. antitrust claims that can be brought only in federal court. Plus, state antitrust enforcement is usually left to the understaffed offices of state attorneys general. However, state antitrust law is free to prohibit conduct that federal antitrust law allows,[17] and in the rare cases where it does so, it can have important effects. And occasionally the state attorneys general indicate a willingness to pursue a case beyond where the federal authorities think is appropriate even under the same antitrust standards, as happened in the Microsoft case where some states did not agree to the U.S.'s settlement and thus continued to pursue the states' claims.

i. Criminal Penalties. The criminal penalties for violating the Sherman Act have changed over time, and currently provide for punishment "by fine not exceeding $100,000,000 if a corporation, or, if any other person, $1,000,000, or by imprisonment not exceeding 10 years, or by both said punishments, in the discretion of the court." *See* 15 U.S.C. §§ 1–2. In addition, general U.S. criminal law allows for an alternative fine equal to twice the defendant's pecuniary gain or the victims' pecuniary loss. *See* 15 U.S.C. § 3571(d).

The Supreme Court has held that defendants can be criminally liable even for rule of reason offenses.[18] However, proving a criminal violation of the Sherman Act requires proving a criminal intent (called *mens rea*), which necessitates proof that the conduct either (1) had "anticompetitive effects" and was "undertaken with knowledge of its probable consequences" or (2) had "the purpose of producing anticompetitive effects . . . , even if such effects did not come to pass."[19] Thus, criminal violations require proof either of an anticompetitive intent or of knowledge that anticompetitive effects were probable and in fact ensued. The Supreme Court has explained that the reason for adding these elements in a criminal suit, even though the same elements would not be required in civil suit alleging a violation under the very same statutory language, was the concern that, compared to civil penalties, criminal penalties would produce greater "overdeterrence" of "procompetitive conduct lying close to the borderline of impermissible conduct."[20]

The Department of Justice (DOJ) brings criminal prosecutions, and indeed most of the DOJ's cases are criminal cases. The DOJ Manual generally limits enforcement to conduct that is clearly unlawful, known to be unlawful, intended to suppress competition, or a repeat offense.[21]

---

[17] *See* California v. ARC America Corp., 490 U.S. 93, 104–05 (1989).

[18] *See* Nash v. United States, 229 U.S. 373, 376–78 (1913).

[19] United States v. United States Gypsum, 438 U.S. 422, 444 & n.21 (1978).

[20] *Id.* at 441.

[21] II PHILLIP E. AREEDA, ROGER D. BLAIR, & HERBERT HOVENKAMP, ANTITRUST LAW ¶ 303, at 29 (2d ed. 2000).

The DOJ does not limit its enforcement to per se violations, and indictments have even been sustained against agreements that other district courts found legal under the rule of reason.[22] But as a matter of practice, virtually all the criminal prosecutions are for patently per se illegal horizontal agreements like price-fixing between unrelated competitors. These cases thus tend to raise few interesting legal issues in their adjudication. More interesting are the enforcement policy implications arising from the facts that the size of criminal penalties and number of criminal cases have both increased over time, that these cases are increasingly focused on foreign-based conspirators, and that the DOJ has had increasing success by offering leniency to the first conspirator who reveals the conspiracy or implicates the other conspirators.

ii. Treble Damages. The most distinctive feature of U.S. antitrust enforcement is that it provides actions for treble damages that mean government enforcement is supplemented, and in many areas dominated, by private suits. "[A]ny person who shall be injured in his business or property by reason of anything forbidden in the antitrust laws" can sue the violator for three times their damages plus litigation costs, including reasonable attorney fees.[23] The requirement of an injury to "business or property" excludes claims for physical injury but includes any claim of monetary injury.[24] If a court concludes the defendant has improperly delayed the antitrust suit, it can also award interest covering the period from the time the plaintiff filed suit to the time of judgment.[25]

Treble damages often sound excessive because, at first cut, single damages should be adequate to deter any conduct whose harm exceeds its benefits. However, in fact treble damages are not as draconian as they sound because they are reduced by the fact that: (a) plaintiffs cannot collect pre-suit interest and usually cannot collect prejudgment interest, (b) plaintiffs have difficulty proving harm from the fact that the anticompetitive overcharge caused them not to buy the product at all (that is, the deadweight loss triangle usually cannot be collected), and (c) in many courts, plaintiffs cannot recover damages for the harmful umbrella effect an overcharge causes by increasing the prices of rivals or substitutes. It has been calculated that the combination of these three factors reduces treble damages to single damages on average.[26] Further, single damages are likely to underdeter anticompetitive conduct because it is often difficult to detect or prove. Some conduct (like a cartel) is hard to detect, but once detected is easy to prove to be anticompetitive. Other

---

[22] *See id.* at 29–30 & n.9.

[23] *See* 15 U.S.C. § 15. "Antitrust laws" are defined to include the Sherman and Clayton Acts (as amended by later acts) but not the FTC Act or Robinson-Patman Act § 3. *See* 15 U.S.C. § 12; Nashville Milk v. Carnation Co., 355 U.S. 373, 378–79 (1958). The former is enforceable just by injunctive claims by the FTC and the latter just by criminal actions by the DOJ, which are rarely brought.

[24] Reiter v. Sonotone Corp., 442 U.S. 330, 339 (1979).

[25] *See* 15 U.S.C. § 15.

[26] *See* Robert H. Lande, *Five Myths About Antitrust Damages,* 40 U.S.F. L. Rev. 651 (2006).

conduct may be easier to detect, but harder to prove it is anticompetitive, such as a tie of some computer software to other software. High litigation costs may also deter many claims. Because expected damages will be the actual damages times the odds of detection and adjudicated punishment, they may well be less than the gains of conduct that inflicts greater costs than benefits.

Damage claims can be brought not only by private parties but by governments injured in their own "business or property," though foreign governments are limited to single damages, unless they themselves were not eligible for foreign sovereign immunity from antitrust claims because they were engaged in commercial activities.[27] In addition, states can bring a treble damages action on behalf of its residents (called a "parens patriae" action) for monetary injuries they suffered from a Sherman Act violation, unless the residents opt out in court filings after receiving notices of the parens patriae action.[28] In such a parens patriae case, the district court can either distribute the damages to the injured parties or deem the damages a civil penalty and deposit them in the state treasury.[29] Few parens patriae are in fact brought, which probably reflects not only the uncertainty of gain to the state treasury but also a provision that makes the state liable for the defendant's attorney fees if the court determines the action was in bad faith.[30]

To prove damages, a party must show: (1) that the antitrust violation was a material but-for cause of its injury; (2) that its injury flowed from the anticompetitive effects of the violation; (3) that the link between the violation and injury was sufficiently direct or proximate; and (4) the amount of damages it suffered from the injury.

(1) Material But-For Causation. Like any plaintiff seeking damages, an antitrust plaintiff must show the violation was the "but-for" cause of its injury. This does not mean the plaintiff must show that the injury definitely would not have occurred but for the violation, nor that other factors did not contribute to the likelihood or extent of that injury. The plaintiff need only show the violation was a "material cause" of its injury or "materially contributed" to that injury.[31] Under this standard, "It is therefore enough that the antitrust violation contributes significantly to the plaintiff's injury even if other factors amounted in the aggregate to a more substantial cause."[32] Lower courts have interpreted

[27] *See* 15 U.S.C. § 15a (authoring federal suits); State of Georgia v. Evans, 316 U.S. 159 (1942) (holding that states are "persons" authorized to sue under the statute); 15 U.S.C. § 15(b) (limiting damage claims of foreign nations).

[28] *See* 15 U.S.C. § 15c.

[29] *See* 15 U.S.C. § 15e.

[30] *See* 15 U.S.C. § 15c(d).

[31] Zenith Radio Corp. v. Hazeltine Research, Inc. (Zenith I), 395 U.S. 100, 114 & n.9 (1969) ("It is enough that the illegality is shown to be a material cause of the injury; a plaintiff need not exhaust all possible alternative sources of injury in fulfilling his burden of proving compensable injury."); Continental Ore v. Union Carbide, 370 U.S. 690, 702 (1962) (enough that violation "materially contributed" to the harm).

[32] II AREEDA ET AL., *supra* note 21, at ¶ 338a, at 317.

this to mean that there need only be a "reasonable probability" defendants' antitrust violation caused plaintiffs' injury; plaintiffs "need not rule out 'all possible alternative sources of injury.' "[33] In short, to show but-for material causation, a plaintiff need only show that, but for the violation, the probability or extent of its injury would have been significantly lower. Just what constitutes "significantly lower" is not clear, but it is clear that the violation does not have to be more than 50% responsible for the probability or extent of injury.

Further, a defendant cannot defeat causation by arguing that it *could* have caused the same injury through lawful conduct.[34] Nor can it defeat causation by arguing that others would have chosen to act in the same way absent an anticompetitive restraint that dictated that choice.[35] The basic rationale is twofold. First, where defendants themselves thought they needed to restrain a certain market choice, it is highly likely that their restraint was in fact necessary to prevent that choice, because defendants are unlikely to adopt restraints that they think have no purpose or effect. Second, any inquiry into whether defendants and others would have engaged in the same conduct absent a restraint that dictated that conduct involves a highly burdensome and counterfactual inquiry into a state of affairs that never existed. Because it is defendants' own fault that this unrestrained state of affairs did not exist, antitrust courts and plaintiffs should not bear the burden on this hypothetical inquiry.

(2) Antitrust Injury. An antitrust plaintiff seeking damages must also show that its injury constituted "*antitrust* injury, which is to say injury of the type the antitrust laws were intended to prevent and that flows from that which makes defendants' acts unlawful. The injury should reflect the anticompetitive effect either of the violation or of anticompetitive acts made possible by the violation."[36] In short, a plaintiff must allege an injury that results from an anticompetitive aspect of the antitrust violation rather than from a procompetitive aspect of the challenged conduct. The basic point of this requirement is to preclude actions by antitrust plaintiffs that would suffer no injury unless the challenged conduct were actually procompetitive.[37]

---

[33] Catlin v. Washington Energy Co., 791 F.2d 1343, 1347 (9th Cir.1986); *see also* Virginia Vermiculite, Ltd. v. W.R. Grace & Co.-Conn., 156 F.3d 535, 539 (4th Cir. 1998); Advanced Health-Care Servs., Inc. v. Radford Community Hosp., 910 F.2d 139, 149 (4th Cir. 1990).

[34] *Virginia Vermiculite,* 156 F.3d at 540; Lee-Moore Oil Co. v. Union Oil Co., 599 F.2d 1299, 1302 (4th Cir.1979); Irvin Indus. v. Goodyear Aerospace Corp., 974 F.2d 241, 245–46 (2d Cir. 1992). *Cf.* In re Cardizem CD Antitrust Litigation, 332 F.3d 896, 914 (6th Cir. 2003) (in Sixth Circuit, defendant can defeat causation by showing that legal conduct *would* have caused the same injury even without any antitrust violation).

[35] *See* United Shoe v. United States, 258 U.S. 451, 462 (1922); X AREEDA, ELHAUGE & HOVENKAMP, ANTITRUST LAW ¶ 1753c, at 294–96 (1996) (collecting cases).

[36] Brunswick Corp. v. Pueblo Bowl-O-Mat, 429 U.S. 477, 489 (1977) (emphasis in original).

[37] *See* Los Angeles Memorial Coliseum v. NFL, 791 F.2d 1356, 1364 (9th Cir. 1986) ("[T]he *Brunswick* standard is satisfied 'on a showing that the injury was caused by a reduction, rather than an increase, in competition flowing from the defendant's acts.' ")

Thus, the Supreme Court has twice found no antitrust injury for rivals challenging horizontal mergers because the mergers would hurt the rival only if they *decreased* market prices to more competitive levels.[38] It has also found no antitrust injury for rivals challenging nonpredatory price-fixing or output restrictions (whether horizontal or vertical) because the challenged agreements would benefit the rival if they raised prices and thus could injure the rival only by bringing prices closer to competitive levels.[39] On the other hand, when a rival is an unwilling participant in the conspiracy and is punished or threatened with punishment for deviating from it, then it does suffer antitrust injury and has standing to sue.[40] Indeed, even a plaintiff that voluntarily agreed to an anticompetitive restraint can bring an antitrust claim if: (a) the plaintiff was injured by the anticompetitive aspects of that restraint or by its enforcement against the plaintiff; and (b) the plaintiff was not equally responsible for the restraint.[41]

This antitrust injury doctrine provides an enormously useful function: it screens out those plaintiffs whose anticompetitive motives make litigation unlikely to benefit consumer welfare. This not only saves litigation costs but also lowers the risk that antitrust courts will mistakenly impose liability that deters procompetitive conduct. Thus, like the *mens rea* requirement in criminal cases, this doctrine is an important part of reducing the overdeterrence of procompetitive conduct that antitrust law inevitably creates given errors or difficulties in distinguishing such conduct from anticompetitive conduct.

(3) Proximate Causation. An antitrust plaintiff seeking damages must also show that its injury was sufficiently direct or proximate. This generally, but not always, precludes antitrust claims by a plaintiff that claims the antitrust violation harmed an intervening party that passed the harm on to it. For example, if an antitrust violation harms a corporation, then its shareholders, employees and creditors cannot bring an antitrust suit. However, the Supreme Court has held that whether it terms an injury "direct" or "indirect" turns not on formalisms, such as whether an intervening party exists, but rather on the application of three policy factors.[42] Those factors are: (1) whether a more directly injured party could bring the same cause of action to vindicate the

---

[38] *See Brunswick*; Cargill, Inc. v. Monfort of Colorado, Inc., 479 U.S. 104 (1986).

[39] Matsushita Electric v. Zenith Radio, 475 U.S. 574, 586 (1986); Atlantic Richfield v. U.S.A Petroleum, 495 U.S. 328 (1990).

[40] *See, e.g.,* NCAA v. Board of Regents, 468 U.S. 85 (1984).

[41] *See* Perma Life Mufflers v. International Parts Corp., 392 U.S. 134, 138–141 (1968); *id.* at 143–48 (White, J., concurring). Because Justice White was the fifth vote for the Court opinion, his concurring opinions would seem to limit language in the Court opinion that suggested a plaintiff could sue even if it were equally responsible.

[42] Associated General Contractors of Cal. v. California State Council of Carpenters, 459 U.S. 519, 536 n.33 (1983) (rejecting the "directness of the injury" test, stating that instead "courts should analyze each situation in light of the factors set forth in the text"); Holmes v. SIPC, 503 U.S. 258, 272 n.20 (1992) (interpreting the antitrust standard for incorporation to RICO cases and concluding, "Thus, our use of the term 'direct' should merely be understood as a reference to the proximate-cause enquiry that is informed by the concerns set out in the text.")

interest in statutory enforcement; (2) whether allowing suit by the indirect party would require complicated apportionment of damages to avoid duplicative damages; and (3) whether indirectness makes the causal inquiry too speculative.[43] The Court interprets these factors to foster, rather than frustrate, enforcement by concentrating the antitrust claim in the hands of the private party with the best incentives to vigorously enforce the statute.[44] The goal is to pick the best plaintiff, not to bar all plaintiffs.

Thus, in *Associated General Contractors,* the Court denied antitrust standing to unions complaining that (a) the defendants had boycotted landowners and general contractors who used unionized subcontractors, (b) who in turn may (to some extent) have declined to use unionized subcontractors, (c) who in turn may have passed on some (unspecified) harm onto unionized employees, (d) who in turn may have passed on some (unspecified) harm to the unions who were the plaintiffs.[45] The Court concluded that this causal chain was too speculative, rife with possibilities for duplicative or hard-to-apportion damages, and that more direct plaintiffs existed. On the other hand, the Court stated that the unionized subcontractors allegedly injured at step (b) would have standing even though they were indirectly injured.[46] Why? Because the three factors were met for those plaintiffs. (1) Although more directly injured, the landowners and general contractors would have had little incentive to sue because they could avoid the harm by declining to use unionized subcontractors. (2) The unionized subcontractors' injury of lost business was distinct from the harm to landowners and general contractors of not being able to choose their preferred subcontractors. (3) The causal connection was not unduly speculative, especially since the harm to the unionized subcontractors was clearly intended and foreseeable.

Likewise, *McCready* found antitrust standing for patients complaining that a conspiracy to withhold coverage for psychologist services in the insurance sold to their employers meant that the patients were unable to obtain reimbursement for psychologist services.[47] Why did the patients have standing even though they did not directly purchase from the defendants? Because they met the three policy factors. (1) No more direct party could sue for these damages because only the patients paid the medical bills.[48] (2) There was no difficulty apportioning

---

43 *Associated General*, 459 U.S. at 538–45; *Holmes*, 503 U.S. at 269, 273 n.20.

44 *See Associated General*, 459 U.S. at 542 (noting that the Court does not deny standing when that is "likely to leave a significant antitrust violation undetected or unremedied" and inquiring into "existence of an identifiable class of persons whose self-interest would normally motivate them to vindicate the public interest in antitrust enforcement."); Kansas v. UtiliCorp, 497 U.S. 199, 214 (1990) ("our interpretation of [Clayton Act] § 4 must promote the vigorous enforcement of the antitrust laws.").

45 459 U.S. at 538–45.

46 *Id.* at 541–42.

47 *See* Blue Shield v. McCready, 457 U.S. 465 (1982).

48 *Id.* at 475, 483.

to avoid duplicative damages since the harm to the patients was distinct from harm to employers or to psychologists, the latter of which could also sue for their separate (also indirect) injury of lost business from other patients who (to avoid losing reimbursement) switched to psychiatrists.[49] (3) Causation was not too speculative (even though the intervening employers could have changed insurers) because the insurance contracts meant the patients' medical costs could be ascertained to the penny.[50]

In *Illinois Brick,* the Supreme Court dealt with a more commonly occurring type of case, a claim that price-fixing injured indirect purchasers because the direct purchasers passed on some of the supracompetitive prices to their downstream customers.[51] The Court concluded that generally the indirect purchasers could not sue, reasoning that the direct purchasers had adequate incentives to sue and that allowing suits by both direct and indirect purchasers would require complicated and difficult inquiries into the extent to which the inflated prices were passed on. Such a complicated and difficult inquiry would increase the evidentiary burdens on plaintiffs and thus discourage statutory enforcement.[52] Thus, it concluded "that the antitrust laws will be more effectively enforced by concentrating the full recovery . . . in the direct [party]."[53] In the same decision, the Court recognized that indirect purchasers may have standing if they bought under pre-existing, cost-plus contracts.[54] Why? Because none of the policy factors indicate that the latter sort of indirect claim should be barred if the direct purchaser has a cost-plus contract that fixes quantity. (1) The more direct party has no incentive to sue because the cost-plus contract meant it suffered no injury. (2) The cost-plus contract also eliminates any difficulty in apportioning to avoid duplicative damages. (3) The cost-plus contract further means causation is not at all speculative.[55] On the other hand,

---

[49] *Id.* at 483.

[50] *Id.* at 475 n.11 & 480 n.17.

[51] Illinois Brick v. Illinois, 431 U.S. 720 (1977).

[52] *See id.* at 737 (rejecting apportionment option because "it would add whole new dimensions of complexity to treble-damage suits and seriously undermine their effectiveness"); *id.* at 745–46 (doctrine concentrating claims in most directly injured party supports "the longstanding policy of encouraging vigorous enforcement of the antitrust laws" because they thus are "not only spared the burden of litigating the intricacies of pass-on but also are permitted to recover the full amount of the overcharge"); *id.* at 732 (trying to trace complex economic adjustments through a second market level would "reduce the effectiveness of already protracted treble-damages proceedings"). *See also McCready*, 457 U.S. at 475 n.11 (task of disentangling overlapping damages would "discourage vigorous enforcement of the antitrust laws by private suit"); *Associated General*, 459 U.S. at 545 (agreeing that apportionment must be rejected because it "undermines the effectiveness of treble-damage suits."); *California*, 490 U.S. at 104 ("*Illinois Brick* was concerned that requiring direct and indirect purchasers to apportion the recovery under a single statute—§ 4 of the Clayton Act—would result in no one plaintiff having a sufficient incentive to sue under that statute.")

[53] *Illinois Brick v. Illinois*, 431 U.S. at 735.

[54] *Id.* at 736.

[55] *See also California*, 490 U.S. at 102 n.6 ("*Illinois Brick* . . . was concerned . . . that at least some party have sufficient incentive to bring suit. Indeed, we implicitly recognized as much in noting that indirect purchasers might be allowed to bring suit in cases in which it would be easy to prove the extent to which the overcharge was passed on to them.").

when the cost-plus contract does not specify the quantity, then the direct purchaser is given standing instead of the indirect purchaser because supracompetitive prices would harm the direct purchaser by reducing output.[56]

In the wake of *Illinois Brick,* many states enacted "*Illinois Brick* repealer" statutes that authorized indirect purchasers to bring suit under state antitrust law. Indeed, this is the main area where state antitrust law differs significantly from federal antitrust law. In *ARC America,* the Supreme Court held that such statutes are not preempted by federal antitrust law, holding that there is no duplication problem necessitating apportionment where damages under state antitrust law might duplicate federal antitrust damages because there is no "federal policy against states imposing liability in addition to that imposed by federal law."[57]

(4) Proving the Amount of Damages. Proving antitrust damages is often very difficult because it requires comparing what actually happened to a but-for world that never occurred. Unless we gain the ability to observe parallel universes, courts can never be certain just what would have happened in the but-for world. The U.S. Supreme Court has responded by adopting a "traditional rule excusing antitrust plaintiffs from an unduly rigorous standard of proving antitrust injury."[58] This traditional rule has two elements. First, proof of injury can be more uncertain in an antitrust case than in other cases. This reflects the practical fact that antitrust damages are inherently more difficult to prove because they rest on counterfactual claims about what would have happened in the market absent defendants' restraint of trade.[59] Second, once the plaintiff establishes the *fact* of antitrust damages (that is, material proximate causation) by a preponderance of the evidence, then it can collect damages even though the *amount* of antitrust damages is uncertain.[60] The rationale for this doctrine is that antitrust defendants should not be permitted to profit from the uncertainty created by their own antitrust violations.[61] It suffices that

[56] *Utilicorp*, 497 U.S. at 220.

[57] *Id.* at 104–05.

[58] J. Truett Payne Co. v. Chrysler Motors Corp., 451 U.S. 557, 565 (1981).

[59] *J. Truett*, 451 U.S. at 566 ("Our willingness to accept a degree of uncertainty in these cases rests in part on the difficulty of ascertaining business damages as compared, for example, to damages resulting from a personal injury or from condemnation of a parcel of land."); *Zenith I*, 395 U.S. at 123 (damages resulting "from a partial or total exclusion from a market . . . are rarely susceptible of the kind of concrete detailed proof of injury which is available in other contexts.")

[60] Story Parchment Co. v. Paterson Parchment Paper Co., 282 U.S. 555, 562 (1931) ("there is a clear distinction between the measure of proof necessary to establish the fact that petitioner had sustained some damage, and the measure of proof necessary to enable the jury to fix the amount. The rule which precludes the recovery of uncertain damages applies to such as are not the certain result of the wrong, not to those damages which are definitely attributable to the wrong and only uncertain in respect of their amount.").

[61] Bigelow v. RKO Radio Pictures, 327 U.S. 251, 265 (1946) ("The most elementary conceptions of justice and public policy require that the wrongdoer shall bear the risk of the uncertainty which his own wrong has created."); *Story Parchment*, 282 U.S. at 563 ("Where the tort itself is of such a nature as to preclude the ascertainment of the amount of damages with

some "reasonable inference" can be made about damages "although the result be only approximate."[62]

In short: "The Court has repeatedly held that in the absence of more precise proof, the factfinder may 'conclude as a matter of just and reasonable inference from the proof of defendants' wrongful acts and their tendency to injure plaintiffs' business, and from the evidence of the decline in prices, profits and values, not shown to be attributable to other causes, that defendants' wrongful acts had caused damage to the plaintiffs.' "[63] In practice, what this typically means is that the antitrust plaintiff first comes forward with (a) evidence showing that it suffered the sort of injury that the proven antitrust violation tends to create and (b) some rough method of approximating the amount of damages it suffered. Although this burden does not require the plaintiff to disprove the possibility that other causal factors also contributed to the injury, the defendant then has an opportunity (and burden) to prove that the other causal factors in fact created all or some portion of the alleged injury. In the typical case involving injured firms claiming lost profits, antitrust defendants usually employ various "blame the victim" arguments that the injured firm would have lost profits anyway because it was poorly managed, poorly located, had a bad product, or was less efficient than other firms in some other way. In cases claiming inflated prices, the defendants will typically argue either that prices actually went down or would have increased anyway because of increased costs or other market factors.

Under this rough-approximation-of-damages standard, the Supreme Court has approved awarding lost profits damages based on assumptions that, absent the antitrust violation, the plaintiff would have (1) acquired the same market share as it had in another nation, (2) made the same profits as another firm, (3) made the same profits as it made in the past, or (4) enjoyed the same prices as it enjoyed in the past.[64] One cannot really know whether, absent an antitrust violation, a firm would have done as well as another or as it did in a different nation, nor that past profits or prices will continue into the future. But such crude assumptions are permitted to deal with the uncertainty caused by defendant's antitrust violation.

---

certainty, it would be a perversion of fundamental principles of justice to deny all relief to the injured person, and thereby relieve the wrongdoer from making any amend for his acts"); Eastman Kodak Co. v. Southern Photo Materials Co., 273 U.S. 359, 379 (1927) ("a defendant whose wrongful conduct has rendered difficult the ascertainment of the precise damages suffered by the plaintiff, is not entitled to complain that they cannot be measured with the same exactness and precision as would otherwise be possible."); *J. Truett*, 451 U.S. at 566 ("Any other rule would enable the wrongdoer to profit by his wrongdoing at the expense of his victim. . . . [I]t does not 'come with very good grace' for the wrongdoer to insist upon specific and certain proof of the injury which it has itself inflicted."); *Zenith I,* 395 U.S. at 124 (same).

[62] *Story Parchment,* 282 U.S. at 563; *J. Truett,* 451 U.S. at 565–66; *Zenith I,* 395 U.S. at 123; *Bigelow*, 327 U.S. at 264.

[63] *Zenith I,* 395 U.S. at 123–24 (collecting cases).

[64] *Zenith I,* 395 U.S. at 124–25; *Bigelow*, 327 U.S. at 259–65; *Kodak*, 273 U.S. at 379; *Story Parchment*, 282 U.S. at 562–66.

Thus, the typical method allowed is to pick some contemporaneous or past baseline where or when markets or firms were not affected by the anticompetitive conduct and assume that any difference between the baseline and reality was caused by the anticompetitive conduct. Unfortunately, contemporaneous or past baselines may be inaccurate because of different costs or demand, because they were also affected by the same anticompetitive conduct, or because the firms in those baselines differ in their efficiency or other features. The past can also be a poor baseline in the typical case where a monopolist is engaging in anticompetitive conduct precisely to slow down the inevitable erosion of a monopoly power it initially earned.[65] In such cases, using a past baseline may falsely suggest the conduct caused no damages even though the conduct did anticompetitively make prices higher than they would have been in the but-for world without that conduct.

Plaintiffs thus often must base their cases on expert projections about what prices or profits would have been but for the anticompetitive conduct in a way that accounts for differences between the but-for world and the posited baseline. One possible method is to run a regression analysis that correlates various features of the market and firms with prices or profit levels to predict what prices or profits would have been but for the anticompetitive conduct, in a way that accounts for differences in market features or firms.[66] Where the claim involves future lost profits, a present value calculation must also be conducted to reduce the stream of future lost profits into a current damage amount.[67]

Often, it is attractive to build a model of how prices are set in the relevant industry, and then use it to predict what but-for prices would have been absent some change caused by the conduct. This can lead to conflicting results because models with different assumptions can lead to quite different results. One promising modern approach, called the New Empirical Industrial Organization (NEIO) approach, is to use empirical analysis to estimate the conduct parameters rather than assume them.[68] In particular, with empirical estimates of (1) the relevant demand-elasticities, (2) seller concentration levels, and (3) producer price-cost margins, one can calculate (4) the extent to which firms in the market act competitively ("the conduct parameter").[69] One could then use such

---

[65] Einer R. Elhauge, *Defining Better Monopolization Standards*, 56 STAN. L. REV. 253, 337–39 (2003).

[66] II AREEDA ET AL., *supra* note 21, at ¶¶ 393, 394b.

[67] *Id.* ¶ 392c.

[68] *See, e.g.*, Timothy F. Bresnahan, *Empirical Methods for Industries with Market Power*, in 2 HANDBOOK OF INDUSTRIAL ORGANIZATION (Richard Schmalensee & Robert Willig eds., North Holland 1989); Timothy F. Bresnahan & Valerie Y. Suslow, *Oligopoly Pricing with Capacity Constraints*, 15/16 ANNALES D'ECONOMIE ET DE STATISTIQUE 267–89 (1989); Jonathan B. Baker & Daniel L. Rubinfeld, *Empirical Methods in Antitrust Litigation: Review and Critique*, 1 AM. L. & ECON. REV. 386, 427–29 (1999).

[69] For example, as we shall see in Chapter 7, the Cournot Model of competition predicts that (without any collusion or coordination), $(P - MC)/P = HHI/\varepsilon$, assuming the products are homogeneous and marginal costs are constant, where P is price, MC is marginal cost, HHI is the sum of squares of the market shares of the firms, and ε equals the absolute value of the

data to calculate the extent to which that conduct parameter changed with the relevant conduct and how much that change affected prices. Or one might calculate the extent to which changes in seller concentration levels might alter prices if the conduct parameter remained constant. Or one might be able to assume, say in a cartel case, that the conduct parameter was at maximum anticompetitive levels, and then calculate one of the other missing variables.

Where a plaintiff can show that prices were inflated by the defendants' anticompetitive conduct, it is entitled to recover the amount of the price overcharge times the quantity it purchased.[70] Notwithstanding arguments that business purchasers should be limited to the lost profits that more accurately measure their injury, they are entitled to recover for the full overcharge because the *Illinois Brick* doctrine concentrates the antitrust claim in their hands rather than allowing indirect purchasers to sue for any overcharge that was passed on downstream. However, this does seem to undercompensate for the total harm inflicted by the violation, which will include not only this overcharge but the deadweight loss caused because the price increase will diminish output and crowd some purchasers out of the market. In theory, a plaintiff should be able to satisfy the requisite standards on causation and damages by showing that it would have bought a greater amount but for the antitrust violation, or (if it purchased nothing) that it would have been a direct purchaser but for the antitrust violation. But proof of that will usually be difficult. This undercompensation problem is to some extent offset by trebling damages.

(5) Allocating Damages Among Defendants. When multiple firms engage in a conspiracy that causes anticompetitive harm, their liability

---

marketwide demand elasticity. In contrast, the Bertrand Model predicts that prices will equal marginal cost even in a duopoly. Finally, monopoly models predict that a cartel (or perfectly coordinating oligopoly) would set prices at $(P - MC)/P = 1/\varepsilon$. Rather, than assuming a particular model is true, one could simply set $(P - MC)/P = HHI(1 + k)/\varepsilon$, where k is the conduct parameter, which could vary from −1 (where the Bertrand prediction holds) to 0 (if Cournot holds) or to positive numbers (where collusion or coordination is true) up to $k = (1 - HHI)/HHI$ (where collusion or coordination is perfect). With a conduct parameter calculated from data rather than assumed by model, one could then calculate what the change in conduct parameter must have been between two periods if one has the data on price, cost, market shares and demand elasticity in the two periods, and then calculate what effect that change in conduct parameter had given current prices, costs and market shares. Or, if one wants to calculate the effects of a merger, one might calculate the current conduct parameter, conservatively assume that it would not be any higher after the merger (i.e., that the merger would not increase the degree of oligopolistic coordination), and then calculate what the change in market prices would be.

Other models can be used to calculate the predicted price effects of a merger if one instead assumes Bertrand competition on differentiated markets. Assuming the merged firms are closest to each other in the relevant product space, one need simply calculate the cross-elasticities of demand between the firms and the aggregate elasticity of the alleged product space using current price-output data, and then (with varying assumptions about the shape of the demand curve) predict the prices that the merged firm would charge, and thus the extent to which those prices would be higher than premerger levels. Using this method, one can even calculate the extent to which a posited decrease in marginal costs would offset any tendency toward increased prices.

[70] *See* Chattanooga Foundry & Pipe Works v. City of Atlanta, 203 U.S. 390, 396 (1906).

is joint and several.[71] This means that, although a plaintiff can sue all the defendant co-conspirators, the plaintiff also has the option to sue just one (or some) of the defendant co-conspirators for the entire amount of the injury resulting from the conspiracy.[72] The plaintiff need not even *name* the co-conspirators in its complaint,[73] though in some cases specificity might be necessary to adequately allege the conspiracy. The fact that the plaintiff actually did not buy from the defendant does not matter as long as the price at which the plaintiff bought was fixed by the conspiracy.[74] Indeed, if the defendant and his co-conspirators fixed prices in a way that caused market prices to rise generally, a plaintiff should be able to recover even if the plaintiff did not buy from a co-conspirator at all, on the ground that the illegal conspiracy did materially contribute to the higher prices the plaintiff paid in a way that directly flowed from the anticompetitive aspects of the conduct. However, the cases are somewhat split on this last point.[75]

The Supreme Court has also held that a defendant cannot even seek contribution from its co-conspirators for their share of the damages caused.[76] This does not mean that a plaintiff can get double recovery by separately suing each defendant for the full amount of its loss. Rather, each defendant is entitled to a defense of payment for any amount previously paid by other co-conspirators.[77] However, the non-contribution rule does create incentives for plaintiffs to settle early with some co-defendants for less than their pro-rata share of damages in order to fund the rest of the litigation and minimize the downside risk, confident that the remaining co-defendants are still on the hook for all other damages. It also creates corresponding incentives for co-defendants to settle early to avoid being the nonsettling defendant left exposed to a disproportionate share of the liability risk.

iii. Injunctive Relief. Claims for injunctive relief to prevent Sherman or Clayton Act violations can be brought not only by the Department of Justice, but also by private parties injured by those violations.[78] The FTC can also seek or impose injunctive relief as noted

---

[71] *See* Texas Industries v. Radcliff Materials, 451 U.S. 630, 646 (1981).

[72] *See* Burlington Indus. v. Milliken & Co., 690 F.2d 380, 392 n.8 (4th Cir. 1982); MacMillan Bloedel Limited v. Flintkote Co., 760 F.2d 580, 584–85 (5th Cir. 1985); In re Uranium Antitrust Litigation, 617 F.2d 1248, 1257 (7th Cir. 1980).

[73] *See Texas Industries*, 451 U.S. at 632–33 (plaintiff complaint allowed to proceed that did not even name who defendant's horizontal co-conspirators were).

[74] *See Chattanooga Foundry*, 203 U.S. at 396 (upholding antitrust verdict against horizontal co-conspirator of actual seller, even though actual seller was not sued). Thus, a plaintiff who alleges it paid retail prices that were fixed by an illegal vertical price-fixing agreement between a manufacturer and dealer can elect to sue just the manufacturer or just the dealer or both. *See* II AREEDA ET AL., *supra* note 21, at ¶ 346h, at 369; VII AREEDA, ANTITRUST LAW ¶ 1459b4, at 186–87 (1986).

[75] *See* II AREEDA ET AL., *supra* note 21, at ¶ 347, at 384–85.

[76] *Texas Industries*, 451 U.S. at 646–47.

[77] *See* Zenith Radio Corp. v. Hazeltine Research, Inc. (Zenith II), 401 U.S. 321, 348 (1971); *Burlington Indus.*, 690 F.2d at 391–92.

[78] *See* 15 U.S.C. §§ 4, 25–26.

above for Clayton and FTC Act violations.[79] "In a Government case the proof of the violation of law may itself establish sufficient public injury to warrant relief."[80] In contrast, a private plaintiff must prove "threatened loss or damage," in other words that the violation threatens to have a material causal link to an injury that would constitute antitrust injury.[81] Thus, two of the elements necessary to prove damages have parallels in private injunctive claims. The other two do not. A private plaintiff seeking injunctive relief need not prove that any causal link is proximate because an injunction poses no danger of duplicative or speculative damages.[82] And obviously the plaintiff seeking injunctive relief need not prove the amount of its damages. Rather, it must generally show the opposite: that damages do not provide it an adequate remedy, which is true whenever some portion of its injury is too difficult to quantify in damages.[83] Thus, a private plaintiff will typically seek damages and injunctive relief in the alternative because denial of the former supports the latter. Often a plaintiff will be able to quantify past but not future damages, in which case it should get a damage award for the past and injunctive relief for the future. Subject to the above limitations, private parties have the same right to seek extraordinary injunctive relief like divestiture as the government does, though district courts are not obligated to order such remedies in every case where the government could obtain it.[84] If a private party "substantially prevails" on a claim for injunctive relief, it is also entitled to have the defendant reimburse its litigation costs and reasonable attorneys' fees.[85]

Injunctive relief should be awarded not only (1) to prevent or undo the anticompetitive conduct but also (2) to undo any anticompetitive effects the conduct had on the market and (3) to deny the defendant the fruits of its antitrust violations.[86] Thus, injunctive relief need not be

---

[79] *See* 15 U.S.C. §§ 21, 45, 53(b).

[80] *See* California v. American Stores, 495 U.S. 271, 295 (1990). However, as shown below, if the government is not simply seeking injunctive relief to prevent or undo the anticompetitive conduct, but also seeks affirmative injunctive relief to undo the anticompetitive effects or force disgorgement of anticompetitive gains, it must show a material causal link between the defendant's conduct and those anticompetitive effects or gains.

[81] *See id.*; 15 U.S.C. § 26; *Cargill*, 479 U.S. at 111 (private plaintiff seeking injunction must prove antitrust injury); *Zenith I*, 395 U.S. at 130 (injunctive "remedy is characteristically available even though the plaintiff has not yet suffered actual injury; he need only demonstrate a significant threat of injury from an impending violation of the antitrust laws or from a contemporary violation likely to continue or recur" to show the requisite causal connection); II AREEDA ET AL., *supra* note 21, at ¶ 337b, 310–13.

[82] *Cargill*, 479 U.S. at 110–111 n.6.

[83] *See* Blue Cross v. Marshfield Clinic, 152 F.3d 588, 591 (7th Cir.1998) (Posner, J.).

[84] *See American Stores*, 495 U.S. at 295–96.

[85] *See* 15 U.S.C. § 26.

[86] *See* United States v. Microsoft, 253 F.3d 34, 103 (D.C.Cir.2001) (en banc) ("[A] remedies decree in an antitrust case must seek to 'unfetter a market from anticompetitive conduct' [and] . . . deny to the defendant the fruits of its statutory violation . . .") (citing Ford Motor v. United States, 405 U.S. 562, 577 (1972), and United States v. United Shoe, 391 U.S. 244, 250 (1968)); Schine Chain Theatres, Inc. v. United States, 334 U.S. 110, 128–29 (1948) (injunctive relief "serves several functions: (1) It puts an end to the combination or conspiracy when that is itself

limited to either prohibiting illegal conduct nor to returning the market to the status quo ante, but can include more affirmative relief to undo anticompetitive effects or gains.[87] District courts have considerable discretion to fashion remedies to achieve these goals, including orders requiring firms to: divest or create companies, share access to physical or intellectual property, enter into contracts or modify them, or refrain from certain businesses or practices even though they are normally legal.[88]

Injunctive relief cannot be punitive in the sense of seeking to inflict hardships on the defendant that are unnecessary to accomplish the above three goals, but it is also true that defendant hardships cannot relegate the plaintiff to injunctive relief that is less effective at accomplishing those three goals.[89] When the injunctive relief sought does not simply seek to prevent or undo antitrust violations, a material causal connection must generally be shown between the anticompetitive conduct and the anticompetitive effects it seeks to undo or the fruits it seeks to take away, even in a suit brought by the government.[90]

Injunctions to undo the conduct's anticompetitive effects can include conduct regulation designed to influence markets far into the future: in *Ford Motor* the Supreme Court awarded injunctive relief designed to affect how the market would look like ten years in the future, and stressed that drafting an antitrust decree by necessity "involves predictions and assumptions concerning future economic and business events."[91] Courts can also modify injunctions many years after trial (whether or not the court expressly retained jurisdiction in the original decree) if subsequent evidence indicates the earlier injunction was not completely effective.[92]

Injunctions to deprive the defendant of the fruits of its anticompetitive conduct should include injunctions ordering the defendant to divest property:

> "if the property was acquired . . . as a result of practices which constitute unreasonable restraints of trade. Otherwise, there would be reward from the conspiracy through retention of its fruits. Hence the problem of the District Court does not end with enjoining continuance of the unlawful restraints nor with dissolving the combination which launched the conspiracy. Its function includes undoing what the conspiracy achieved. . . . [T]he requirement that the defendants restore what they

---

the violation. (2) It deprives the antitrust defendants of the benefits of their conspiracy. (3) It is designed to break up or render impotent the monopoly power which violates the Act.")

87 *See* Professional Engineers v. United States, 435 U.S. 679, 697–98 (1978); United States v. Loew's, 371 U.S. 38, 53 (1962); *Ford Motor*, 405 U.S. at 573 n.8; *American Stores*, 495 U.S. at 283–84.

88 *See* II AREEDA ET AL., *supra* note 21, ¶ 325a, at 248 (collecting cases).

89 *See* United States v. E.I. du Pont de Nemours & Co., 366 U.S. 316, 326–27 (1961).

90 *See Microsoft*, 253 F.3d at 106.

91 405 U.S. at 578.

92 United States v. United Shoe, 391 U.S. 244, 251–52 (1968).

unlawfully obtained is no more punishment than the familiar remedy of restitution."[93]

This language would appear broad enough to authorize the government to bring antitrust claims seeking the disgorgement of any supracompetitive profits causally related to antitrust violations.[94] Although not yet frequently sought as a remedy, the FTC has sought disgorgement as injunctive relief and had its authority to do so upheld,[95] as has the DOJ.[96] Further, the Sherman Act gives the DOJ express authority to obtain forfeiture of any property owned by or pursuant to any antitrust conspiracy that crosses state or national boundaries.[97] This can be done in a civil action rather than criminal prosecution.[98]

Governments and private parties can also obtain preliminary injunctions to prevent conduct from occurring or continuing pending litigation, under the normal standards that balance the likelihood of ultimate success on the merits, the harm the preliminary injunction would cause the defendant, and whether any injury to the plaintiff or public from allowing the conduct would be irreparable later.[99] Such preliminary injunctions are typically the remedy sought in the biggest area of antitrust practice: suits to prevent mergers from occurring.

iv. Consent Decrees and the Interplay Between Public and Private Enforcement. Treble damages compensate for the underdeterrence problems that might otherwise result because it is often hard to detect antitrust violations and costly and risky to bring antitrust actions. The regime is thus often said to enlist "private attorneys general" to aid antitrust enforcement. This can result in tension because private parties often pursue cases that government agencies view as wrongheaded. Further, private suits are an omnipresent factor in judicial interpretation because courts interpreting a U.S. antitrust statute (other than the FTC Act) know that they cannot simply adopt broad interpretations to give disinterested government agencies authority to root out all possible undesirable conduct, confident that they will typically exercise their prosecutorial discretion to avoid bringing cases that involve overinclusive applications of that interpretation. Instead, courts know that any such overinclusive applications will be pursued by private litigants whenever it is profitable to do so. The antitrust injury requirement helps reduce this overdeterrence problem by barring suits by private plaintiffs that could not suffer any injury unless the alleged

---

93 United States v. Paramount Pictures, 334 U.S. 131, 171–72 (1948).

94 *See* II AREEDA ET AL., *supra* note 21, at ¶ 325a, at 245 ("equity relief may include . . . the disgorgement of improperly obtained gains"); Elhauge, *Disgorgement as an Antitrust Remedy*, 76 Antitrust L.J. 79 (2009).

95 *See* FTC v. Mylan Labs., 62 F. Supp. 2d 25, 36–37 (D.D.C. 1999) (collecting cases upholding authority of FTC to seek disgorgement as an injunctive relief).

96 *See* United States v. Keyspan Corp., 2011 WL 338037 (S.D.N.Y. 2011).

97 *See* 15 U.S.C. §§ 6, 11.

98 28 U.S.C. § 2461(a).

99 *See* 15 U.S.C. §§ 4, 25–26, 53(b).

conduct were procompetitive, but it remains a serious problem given the difficulties of accurately sorting out procompetitive conduct. This makes courts inclined to interpret U.S. antitrust statutes more narrowly than they might if the statutes authorized only government suits.

However, government agencies also rely on private enforcement to supplement their efforts. Indeed, sometimes agencies will decline to pursue cases precisely because they believe that the incentives for private suit are adequate, and thus the agencies conclude that they should allocate their scarce resources to those areas where private suits are less likely. Agencies also sensibly focus their energies on cases that have the most general impact, leaving to private litigation issues that are of relevance to a more limited set of parties. Thus, a governmental decision not to bring suit after investigation does not create an adverse inference about private litigation over the same matter. In contrast, if the government obtains a judgment after obtaining testimony, then that judgment has preclusive effect in subsequent private lawsuits, unless the judgment constitutes a consent decree entered before testimony was obtained.[100] The statute of limitations for private suits is also suspended pending the government suit.[101] And even if the government loses its litigation, subsequent parties may be able to benefit from the discovery the government collected. Accordingly, potential plaintiffs often lobby the government agencies to bring the cases first, and defendants often enter into consent decrees in order to avoid adverse effects on subsequent private suits.

To be effective, governmental consent decrees must be approved by courts under the Tunney Act after others have had sixty days notice to comment.[102] The rather vague statutory standard is the court can approve the consent decree only if it determines it is in the "public interest."[103] However, courts cannot review the government's decision to simply dismiss a case without any consent judgment.[104] Nor can a judge refuse to accept a consent decree based on facts that the government's complaint never alleged and were never tested by the adversary process and appeal.[105] Given that the government generally files its complaints and corresponding consent decrees at the same time, this means that the government can generally avoid any meaningful review of pre-litigation settlements by simply tailoring its factual allegations closely to its consent decree relief. Even without these limitations, one suspects that

[100] Although the antitrust statutes state that the prior government judgment only constitutes prima facie evidence of a violation, *see* 15 U.S.C. § 16(a), modern developments in collateral estoppel law give prior litigated judgments (whether in public or private suits) preclusive effect, effectively mooting this provision. *See* II AREEDA ET AL., *supra* note 21, ¶ 319c, at 204.

[101] *See* 15 U.S.C. § 16(i).

[102] *See* 15 U.S.C. § 16(b)–(h).

[103] 15 U.S.C. § 16(e).

[104] *See* In re IBM Corp., 687 F.2d 591, 600–03 (2d Cir. 1982).

[105] *See* United States v. Microsoft Corp., 56 F.3d 1448 (D.C.Cir.1995).

courts would generally approve consent decrees because it is difficult to make a reluctant agency prosecute a case effectively and the courts can hardly take over the prosecution of a case themselves. The main utility of the Tunney Act is to provide better information about such consent decrees and to avoid unintended adverse consequences for other parties or markets that might be caused by the decree's terms.

v. ***Statute of Limitations.*** Whether brought by a private or public actor, antitrust claims seeking injunctive relief have no statute of limitations, but claims seeking damages must be brought within four years from when the claim accrued.[106] However, suits seeking injunctive relief can be barred by the doctrine of laches when suit is unjustifiably delayed, though this doctrine normally does not apply to government suits, and some courts seem drawn to four years as a baseline measure of unjustifiable delay.[107] Criminal antitrust cases fall within the general five-year statute of limitations for criminal prosecutions.[108]

A cause of action "accrues" in a way that begins the limitations period when a defendant commits a violation that injures a plaintiff.[109] That is, *both* requirements must be fulfilled: misconduct and injury. Further, some courts have held that the statute of limitations cannot begin to run until the plaintiff *discovers* his injury.[110]

The limitations period can be tolled not only by a prior government suit, as noted above, but also by three other doctrines.

(1) The Fraudulent Concealment Doctrine. The statute of limitations is tolled during any period where the defendant fraudulently concealed the violation, as long as the plaintiff was unaware of the concealed violation despite due diligence.[111]

(2) The Continuing Conduct Doctrine. When a defendant engages in a continuing series of anticompetitive conduct, then each act that is part of the violation and injures the plaintiff restarts the period of limitations, even though the plaintiff knew the illegality began much earlier.[112] However, although this doctrine allows the plaintiff to sue for conduct that began more than four years ago, it can recover only for injuries suffered from those acts that occurred within the last four years.[113] To illustrate, if defendants engage in a continuous course of horizontal price-fixing from 2000 to 2004, then a plaintiff can bring suit in 2006, even though it knew the price-fixing began in 2000, because each sale at the fixed price restarts the statute of limitations period. However,

---

[106] 15 U.S.C. § 15b.

[107] *See* II AREEDA ET AL., *supra* note 21, at ¶ 320g, 237–39.

[108] 18 U.S.C. § 3282.

[109] *Zenith II,* 401 U.S. at 338.

[110] In re Copper Antitrust Litigation, 436 F.3d 782 (7th Cir. 2006).

[111] *See* II AREEDA ET AL., *supra* note 21, at ¶ 320e, at 231–3.

[112] *See* Klehr v. A.O. Smith Corp., 521 U.S. 179, 189 (1997).

[113] *Id.*

unless some other tolling doctrine applied, the plaintiff could not recover for the inflated prices it paid before 2002.

(3) The Speculative Injury Doctrine. Even if the misconduct and injury have occurred, the statute does not begin to run until the injury becomes sufficiently non-speculative to form the basis for reasonably ascertainable damages.[114] The logic is fairly straightforward: a plaintiff cannot be penalized for delaying suit if an earlier suit would have been barred on the grounds that its damages had not yet become reasonably ascertainable. For example, if the exclusionary conduct started producing injury to rivals in 2000, but the magnitude was not reasonably measurable until 2003, then the limitations period would not start until 2003, and thus a lawsuit could still be brought in 2006 for all injury since 2000.

vi. Class Actions. Antitrust cases are often particularly well-suited for resolution by class action because antitrust aims to protect marketwide competition, not individual firms or buyers, and therefore necessarily requires resolution of issues that are marketwide and thus common to any class of persons in that market. This includes market definition, market power, market shares, foreclosure shares, characterization of the conduct, whether the conduct had anticompetitive effects, whether it had procompetitive effects, whether there was less restrictive alternative, whether it caused injury, whether that injury constituted antitrust injury, and what the total damages were. Because those issues are all common to any class of persons in that market, requiring separate litigation of those issues would be greatly duplicative. Also, where there are many persons in the market, each may lack a sufficient incentive to litigate given their individual stakes and the large costs of antitrust litigation. These problems are worsened by collective action problems that make every person in the market prefer to have others bear the burden of litigation and free ride on those efforts, either by enjoying the benefits of an injunction for the market or through later collateral estoppel in their own damages claim.

One major obstacle to class actions has been finding a common methodology for distributing those total damages among different persons in the market, who may have bought on varying terms or have varying preferences. These problems can be overstated because these variances exist not only in the actual world but also in the but-for world without the anticompetitive conduct, so they generally cancel out using the method of rough approximation allowed to calculate antitrust damages when a violation has been proven.[115] Still, problems with

---

[114] *Zenith II*, 401 U.S. at 339–40.

[115] Suppose, for example, that a monopolist has engaged in anticompetitive foreclosure that has raised market prices, but each buyer pays somewhat different prices because they have varying negotiating ability. This would be no obstacle to measuring classwide damages because that variance in negotiating ability would exist in *both* the actual world and the but-for world, and thus cancels out. That is, suppose each buyer pays a price for the product in the actual world of $P_{actual} + N_i$, where P_{actual} is the average market price in the actual world with the

proving individual damages sometimes causes courts to balk at certifying an antitrust class action on damages under Federal Rule of Civil Procedure 23. However, even in such cases, a class can often be certified on all other issues, including the existence of liability and the appropriateness of injunctive relief, leaving only proof of individual damages to separate trials. In addition, modern economic methods of measuring damages and the increasing computerization of sales data makes it easier and easier to devise common methods for calculating individuated damages from the common market injury. Plaintiffs seeking classwide damages must, however, prove that those damages flow from classwide theories of antitrust liability, rather than from other theories of liability that are not capable of classwide proof.[116]

Another major obstacle is that, when firms contract with buyers (or others), they can require arbitrations of antitrust claims that preclude classwide adjudication, even when doing so makes it financially unfeasible to prove the antitrust claims.[117] Normally, antitrust law solves the collective action problem that buyers acting individually are willing to consent to anticompetitive conduct (such as agreeing to buy at cartel prices or with exclusionary conditions) for a trivial individual discount from the inflated price that results from that anticompetitive conduct, even though the net effect of many buyers doing so is to significantly harm all buyers in the market.[118] Those same collective action problems mean buyers will individually consent to nonclass arbitrations that make it unfeasible to prove antitrust claims for a trivial discount, even though the net effect of many buyers agreeing to nonclass arbitrations is to significantly harm all buyers in the market.[119] It remains to be seen whether the Supreme Court or Congress will cut back on such uses of nonclass arbitration agreements to preclude effective private enforcement of antitrust law.

Even when a private class action cannot be certified under Rule 23, states continue to have the right to bring "parens patriae" actions on behalf of their residents to remedy antitrust violations, which are

defendant's conduct, and N_i reflects the varying negotiating of each of i buyers, being negative for buyers that have the negotiating ability or power to get reductions from the average and positive for buyers who are sufficiently lacking in ability or power that they pay above the average. Such an ability or inability to negotiate for favorable pricing presumably would also hold in the but-for world, and can reasonably be approximated to be about the same in magnitude in both the actual and but-for worlds. Thus, the price the ith buyer pays in the but-for world would be $P_{butfor} + N_i$, where P_{butfor} is the average price each buyer would have paid in the but-for world. The injury to each buyer will accordingly equal: $(P_{actual} + N_i) - (P_{butfor} + N_i) = P_{actual} - P_{butfor}$. Because each buyer's varying negotiating ability or power cancels out, each buyer is injured by the difference in the average price between the actual and but-for worlds. If separate trials were conducted, that would require duplicating this same inquiry about the difference in average prices at each trial.

[116] Comcast Corp. v. Behrend, 133 S.Ct. 1426 (2013).

[117] *American Express v. Italian Colors Restaurant*, 133 S.Ct. 2304 (2013).

[118] Elhauge, *How* Italian Colors *Guts Private Antitrust Enforcement by Replacing It With Ineffective Forms Of Arbitration,* 38 FORDHAM INT'L LAW JOURNAL 771 (2015).

[119] *Id.*

effectively a procedurally simpler form of class action.[120] Where it is too difficult to distribute individuated damages to the injured parties, an antitrust statute allows the problem to be avoided by simply depositing the damages in the state treasury.[121] Another provision specifies that, in a parens patriae action challenging price-fixing, damages can be shown through aggregate statistical methods without need to prove individual damages.[122] Agreeing to preclude classwide arbitration of private suits would not preclude such a parens patriae action by a state, though residents can choose to opt out of that action in a court filing after receiving notice of the parens patriae action, just like they can choose to opt out of private class actions after they are brought.[123]

vii. Personal Jurisdiction and Venue. Antitrust suits against corporations "may be brought not only in the judicial district whereof it is an inhabitant, but also in any district wherein it may be found or transacts business; and all process in such cases may be served in the district of which it is an inhabitant, or wherever it may be found."[124] The latter clause is understood to allow worldwide service of process,[125] but the courts are split on whether that process provision depends on showing venue under the first clause.[126]

If the clauses are independent, then the service of process clause confers personal jurisdiction in any district court, which allows suit to be brought in any district against corporations because a general venue state allows suit in any district that a corporation is subject to personal jurisdiction (and against aliens in any district) as long as they have minimum contacts with the United States.[127] If the process clause does depend on the venue clause, then the worldwide service of process provision applies only if the case is brought in a district where the corporation is an inhabitant, may be found, or transacts business. This "dependent" interpretation does not bar showing venue under the general provisions of 28 U.S.C. §§ 1391, but normal service of process limitations would apply if that is the basis of venue, which usually require a state long-arm statute and minimum contacts with the state in which the district court sits.[128]

---

[120] *See* 15 U.S.C. § 15c.

[121] *See* 15 U.S.C. § 15e.

[122] *See* 15 U.S.C. § 15d.

[123] *See* 15 U.S.C. § 15c.

[124] *See* 15 U.S.C. § 22; Go-Video, Inc. v. Akai Elec. Co., 885 F.2d 1406, 1414–16 (9th Cir. 1989).

[125] *See, e.g., Go-Video*, 885 F.2d at 1413.

[126] *See* Daniel v. American Bd. of Emergency Medicine, 428 F.3d 408, 422–23 (2d Cir. 2005) (collecting the conflicting cases).

[127] *See* 28 U.S.C. § 1391(c)–(d); *Go-Video*, 885 F.2d at 1408–16; Icon Indus. Controls Corp. v. Cimetrix, Inc., 921 F.Supp. 375, 376 (W.D.La.1996); Kingsepp v. Wesleyan Univ., 763 F.Supp. 22, 24–25 (S.D.N.Y.1991) *But see* Cumberland Truck Equipment Co. v. Detroit Diesel Corp., 401 F. Supp. 2d 415 (E.D. Pa. 2005).

[128] *See Daniel,* 428 F.2d at 427.

This split may not matter much, however. Even under the "dependent clause" interpretation, if a defendant is not subject to jurisdiction in any state because it lacks sufficient contacts with any one state, then Federal Rule of Civil Procedure 4(k)(2) allows worldwide service of process based on nationwide contacts. Thus, neither interpretation allows a foreign firm to avoid personal jurisdiction in the United States as long as it has minimum contacts with the nation as a whole. The main effect of the "dependent clause" interpretation is that, in cases where a corporate defendant has minimum contacts with some states and not with others, the plaintiff cannot bring the case in a district located in a state where the defendant has no contacts. But even under the "independent clause" interpretation, if a plaintiff brings a case in such a forum, the defendant should be able to get the case transferred to some district where it does have minimum contacts under the doctrine of forum non conveniens.[129] Thus, under either interpretation, a plaintiff can bring suit in some U.S. district as long as the defendant has minimum contacts with the United States as a whole, but the plaintiff's ability to forum-shop among the districts will be constrained where the defendant has contacts with some states but not others.

Noncorporate antitrust defendants are not subject to any special antitrust service of process provision and are subject either to the general venue provisions or under the antitrust venue provision to suit "in any district court of the United States in the district in which the defendant resides or is found or has an agent." 15 U.S.C. § 15. Antitrust venue thus does not extend to any district in which a noncorporate defendant "transacts business," but it does extend to any district in which such a defendant may be "found." Under the general venue statute, aliens may be sued in any district,[130] subject to ordinary service of process limits, which (as we have seen) allow worldwide service if the alien would not otherwise be subject to suit in any district.

However, for both corporate and noncorporate defendants, if service is only feasible in a foreign nation, then it is only valid if it complies with foreign or international law or is expressly authorized by some other federal law.[131] Thus, theoretically worldwide service of process might be restricted by foreign prohibitions, though this is not usually an obstacle because foreign nations typically want firms to be amenable to service for other purposes.

viii. Limits on Antitrust. Application of U.S. antitrust laws is limited in three ways. First, the statute has been interpreted to exclude certain conduct, like state legislation or petitioning for governmental action, even though it results in fixed prices or other anticompetitive

---

[129] *See* 28 U.S.C. § 1404(a); United States v. National City Lines, 337 U.S. 78 (1949); Capital Currency Exchange v. National Westminster Bank, 155 F.3d 603 (2d Cir. 1998).

[130] 28 U.S.C. §§ 1391(d) ("An alien may be sued in any district.")

[131] *See* Fed. Rule Civ. Proc. 4(f), (h)(2); Prewitt Enterprises, Inc. v. OPEC, 353 F.3d 916 (11th Cir. 2003).

effects. Second, in some areas, federal statutes explicitly or implicitly exempt specific industries or conduct from antitrust liability. Third, the statute requires some trivial effect on interstate commerce, and does not cover foreign restraints that have no substantial effect on U.S. markets.

(1) State Action and Petitioning Immunity. The antitrust statutes have been interpreted not to apply to "state action" on the ground that Congress did not intend to interfere with the traditional state power to regulate markets, even though such regulation often fixes prices, restrains output, and restricts entry.[132] Nor do the antitrust statutes apply to private petitioning efforts that are designed to obtain such anticompetitive government regulation, even though such genuine petitioning efforts might incidentally impose direct anticompetitive effects.[133]

a. STATE ACTION IMMUNITY. Antitrust state action doctrine employs three different tiers of immunity, depending on who has set the terms of the challenged anticompetitive restraint.

1. Top of Three Branches of Government—An anticompetitive restraint is per se immune from antitrust scrutiny if the terms of that restraint were set by the state legislature, the highest state court acting legislatively, or (probably) the governor.[134] However, even though such state efforts are immune from antitrust scrutiny, they do face dormant commerce clause review if they exploit out-of-staters.[135]

2. State Agencies and Municipalities—Public entities that are subordinate to the top levels of state government, like state agencies or municipalities, enjoy antitrust immunity if their restraints are clearly authorized by one of the entities that acts directly for the state (such as the state legislature, supreme court, or governor).[136] The "clear authorization" test is something of a misnomer because it does not require much clarity or authority. As for clarity, it suffices that the agency or municipality has a general regulatory authority whose exercise the state naturally would contemplate would displace competition, even though the state never considered the specific anticompetitive effects or restraint being challenged.[137] As for authority, municipalities and state

---

[132] Parker v. Brown, 317 U.S. 341, 350–52 (1943); *see generally* Elhauge, *The Scope of Antitrust Process,* 104 HARV. L. REV. 667 (1991) (synthesizing the caselaw and explaining its underlying theory).

[133] Eastern R.R. Pres. Conf. v. Noerr Motor Freight, 365 U.S. 127 (1961); *see generally* Elhauge, *Making Sense of Antitrust Petitioning Immunity*, 80 CALIF. L. REV. 1177 (1992).

[134] *See* Hoover v. Ronwin, 466 U.S. 558, 567–69 (1984). The Supreme Court's approach suggests that the actions of state governors will also be per se immune, but it has left the issue open. *See id.* at 568 n.17.

[135] *See* Elhauge, *supra* note 132, at 732.

[136] *See* Southern Motor Carriers Rate Conference, Inc. v. United States, 471 U.S. 48, 57, 60–61, 62–63 (1985); Town of Hallie v. City of Eau Claire, 471 U.S. 34, 38–40, 46–47 & n.10 (1985); *Hoover*, 466 U.S. at 568–69; Community Communications Co. v. City of Boulder, 455 U.S. 40, 50–54 (1982).

[137] *See* FTC v. Phoebe Putney Health Sys., Inc., 133 S. Ct. 1003, 1011–16 (2013); City of Columbia v. Omni Outdoor Advertising, 499 U.S. 365, 372–73 (1991); *Hallie*, 471 U.S. at 41–42; *Southern Motor Carriers*, 471 U.S. at 64; Elhauge, *supra* note 132, at 691–92. If the state is

agencies have been found immune even when their specific restraints were literally *un*authorized because they exceeded the scope of their regulatory authority.[138]

In short, if a disinterested municipality or state agency has been given general regulatory authority, it enjoys antitrust immunity when adopting any regulation that—whether or not actually authorized—has the sorts of anticompetitive effects one would naturally contemplate from the regulatory authority that was granted, whether or not any of the top three branches of government actually considered the specific anticompetitive effects or restraints. The word "disinterested" is included in the last sentence because the caselaw makes clear that even someone that has been formally designated a state official or agent will be deemed a "private" actor (and thus governed by the third tier below) if they operate businesses that are financially interested in the terms of the challenged restraint.[139] More generally, state action immunity may not apply when a municipality or state agency acts as a commercial participant rather than just as a regulator, especially when it furthers the financial interests of its residents by imposing extraterritorial costs.[140]

Although *City of Boulder* might suggest a more narrow immunity because it held that municipal home rule authority did not constitute a sufficiently clear authorization to merit antitrust immunity,[141] a later decision held that municipal regulation of this sort could be subject to review only as unilateral conduct under Sherman Act § 2, thus effectively limiting antitrust review to cases where the municipality had the sort of market power over outsiders that would give it a financial interest in the regulation.[142] Further, the Local Government Antitrust Act of 1984 has eliminated damage claims in cases involving municipal action, thus

---

merely neutral on whether regulation or action that displaces competition should occur, the state does not sufficiently contemplate the displacement of competition to satisfy the clear authorization requirement for state action immunity. *Phoebe Putney*, 133 S. Ct. at 1012; Boulder, 455 U.S. at 55.

[138] *See City of Columbia,* 499 U.S. at 370–72; Elhauge, *supra* note 132, at 692.

[139] North Carolina State Bd. of Dental Examiners v. F.T.C., 135 S.Ct. 1101 (2015) (official state agency created by state statute is deemed private if it is controlled by active market participants and thus also requires active supervision from the state for antitrust state action immunity); Goldfarb v. Virginia State Bar, 421 U.S. 773, 776 & n.2, 789–92 (1975) (state bar controlled by financially interested lawyers treated as private and enjoyed no antitrust state action immunity even though it was a statutorily designated state agency exercising an authority granted by the state); Continental Ore Co. v. Union Carbide & Carbon Corp., 370 U.S. 690, 703 n.11, 706–07 (1962) (financially interested corporation enjoyed no antitrust state action immunity even though the Canadian government had appointed the corporation its official agent and delegated to it "discretionary agency power to purchase and allocate to Canadian industries all vanadium products."); *see also* Allied Tube & Conduit Corp. v. Indian Head, Inc. 486 U.S. 492, 501 (1988) (citing *Goldfarb* and *Continental Ore* for the proposition that "persons with economic incentives to restrain trade" are not state actors who enjoy antitrust state action immunity); Elhauge, *supra* note 132, at 683–91.

[140] *See City of Columbia,* 499 U.S. at 374, 379; City of Lafayette v. Louisiana Power & Light Co., 435 U.S. 389, 403–04 (1978); Elhauge, *supra* note 132, at 732–33.

[141] 455 U.S. 40.

[142] Fisher v. City of Berkeley, 475 U.S. 260 (1986); Elhauge, *supra* note 132, at 734–35.

leaving antitrust review of municipal action that imposes extraterritorial costs out-of-town much the same as dormant commerce clause review of state action that imposes extraterritorial costs out-of-state.[143]

3. Private Actors—Anticompetitive restraints by "private" persons are immune only if those restraints are both (1) clearly authorized and (2) actively supervised by the state, which can include supervision by municipalities or state agencies.[144] As the Court has interpreted the active supervision requirement, it effectively requires evidence that some disinterested state or municipal official exercised substantive control over the terms of the relevant restraint.[145] Mere rubberstamping by a public official does not suffice: the official must make a substantive decision in favor of the restraint's terms.[146] Nor can the substantive approval come after-the-fact: the public official must make the substantive decision before the restraint is imposed on the market.[147] When disinterested public officials do not control the terms of the relevant restraint, then no state action immunity applies even if a state statute explicitly allows or even requires private actors to adopt such restraints.[148] On the other hand, when disinterested public officials do substantively control the terms of the restraint, then antitrust immunity applies whether or not they "conspired" with the regulated private actors.[149]

4. Combining the Three Tiers—Given how the cases define clear authorization and active supervision, one can simplify these complex tiers into one test: "restraints are immune from antitrust review whenever financially disinterested and politically accountable persons control and make a substantive decision in favor of the terms of the challenged restraint before it is imposed on the market."[150]

b. PETITIONING IMMUNITY. Petitioning immunity clearly applies when the complaint is that the petitioning led some disinterested public lawmaker to impose an anticompetitive restraint, even if the petitioner

---

[143] 15 U.S.C. §§ 35–36; Elhauge, *supra* note 132, at 735.

[144] California Retail Liquor Dealers Association v. Midcal Aluminum, Inc., 445 U.S. 97, 105–06 & n.9 (1980); Patrick v. Burget, 486 U.S. 94, 101–03 (1988) (evaluating whether supervision by various state agencies was sufficiently active). An additional prong applies when a facial challenge is brought against a state statute or municipal ordinance. If the state action doctrine does not provide immunity, the statute or ordinance is facially preempted only if it authorizes or mandates conduct that per se violates the antitrust laws. *See Fisher*, 475 U.S. at 264–65; Rice v. Norman Williams Co., 458 U.S. 654, 661 (1982). This prong does not apply when plaintiffs challenge a statute or ordinance as applied. *See Fisher*, 475 U.S. at 270 n.2; *Rice*, 458 U.S. at 662 & nn.7–8.

[145] *Patrick*, 486 U.S. at 101; 324 Liquor Corp. v. Duffy, 479 U.S. 335, 344–45 & n.7 (1987).

[146] FTC v. Ticor Title Insurance Co., 504 U.S. 621 (1992); *Patrick*, 486 U.S. at 100–01.

[147] *See* Elhauge, *supra* note 132, at 714–15.

[148] *See 324 Liquor*, 479 U.S. at 343–45; *Midcal*, 445 U.S. at 105–06; Schwegmann Bros. v. Calvert Distillers Corp., 341 U.S. 384, 389 (1951).

[149] *See City of Columbia,* 499 U.S. at 374–79; Elhauge, *supra* note 132, at 704–06.

[150] Elhauge, *supra* note 132, at 671, 696. Here, "politically accountable" means that the authority of the public official can be traced to an election, appointment by elected officials, or through some chain of appointment starting with elected officials. *Id.* at 671 n.10. A judge is thus politically accountable within the meaning used here.

"conspired" with the lawmaker.[151] In such a case, the petitioning immunity could be deemed derivative of the state action immunity that applies to the challenged restraint. By the same token, petitioning immunity clearly does not apply to efforts to persuade a financially interested market participant to impose an anticompetitive restraint that would not enjoy state action immunity.[152] Nor does petitioning immunity apply if a financially interested market participant imposes the challenged market restraint in order to coerce government action.[153]

The difficulty is with dual effect cases where the same private activity both (a) indirectly helps procure government action and (b) directly restrains trade in a way that would cause anticompetitive effects whether or not the government made a favorable substantive decision. Petitioners are always immune for the former effects given state action immunity,[154] and are also immune for the latter direct effects when they are incidental to genuine petitioning efforts that are valid by the standards of the relevant governmental process.[155] Immunity for the direct effects is thus denied if the alleged input into public decisionmaking was a "sham" in the sense that the activity was not genuinely designed to influence government action,[156] or if the direct effects were inflicted by a restraint that was in fact separate from the valid effort to influence the government and thus was not "incidental" to any such petitioning.[157] Such cases are not true dual effect cases because one of the effects is a sham or the duality does not really exist because the effects are severable.

Even in true dual effect cases, immunity for the direct effects is also denied if the restraint violates the prevailing standards for providing input to the relevant government decisionmaking process.[158] Under the no-holds-barred standards for providing input to the political process, this can protect even deceptive and unethical speech.[159] Under the more stringent standards for providing input into the adjudicative process, immunity can be lost for the direct effects of conduct that violates the

---

[151] *See City of Columbia,* 499 U.S. at 379–84; United Mine Workers v. Pennington, 381 U.S. 657, 660–61, 669–72 (1965).

[152] *See Allied Tube,* 486 U.S. at 501; *Continental Ore,* 370 U.S. at 707–08; Elhauge, *supra* note 133, at 1200–03.

[153] *See* FTC v. Superior Court Trial Lawyers Ass'n, 493 U.S. 411, 421–25, 427 (1990); *Allied Tube,* 486 U.S. at 503; Elhauge, *supra* note 133, at 1206–11, 1237–40.

[154] *See Allied Tube,* 486 U.S. at 499; *Noerr,* 365 U.S. at 135–36; *City of Columbia,* 499 U.S. at 378–79; Elhauge, *supra* note 133, at 1213, 1220, 1240–42.

[155] *See Noerr,* 365 U.S. at 142–44; Elhauge, *supra* note 133, at 1213–37.

[156] Professional Real Estate Investors v. Columbia Pictures Indus., 508 U.S. 49, 58–61 (1993); *City of Columbia,* 499 U.S. at 380; *Allied Tube,* 486 U.S. at 500 n.4, 508 n.10; *Noerr,* 365 U.S. at 144.

[157] Elhauge, *supra* note 133, at 1215–19 (collecting cases).

[158] *See id.* at 1219–21.

[159] *See Noerr,* 365 U.S. at 140–41 & n.20 (stressing that the challenged activity was in widespread use and apparently not prohibited by the laws applicable to lobbying); Elhauge, *supra* note 133, at 1223–26.

legal standards applicable to litigation.[160] This does not mean immunity is lost for the results of a favorable court decision obtained by invalid litigation conduct, just that there is no immunity for the direct effects that flow regardless of whether substantive judicial approval obtained, such as the litigation costs imposed by the process itself.[161] Immunity is also denied to a firm that procures a patent by filing false information with the Patent Office, a holding that can be explained on the grounds that, because the Patent Office does not check the accuracy of filings before issuing a patent, it has effectively delegating factual determinations to the financially interested applicant, thus making this a direct effect of financially interested decisionmaking.[162]

(2) Federal Antitrust Exemptions and Limitations.

a. IMPLIED EXEMPTIONS OR LIMITATIONS. A federal statute enacted subsequent to an antitrust statute is always free to partially repeal the antitrust laws by exempting particular industries. However, important canons of interpretation adopt powerful presumptions against interpreting any federal statute to create an antitrust exemption and for narrowly construing any exemption that does exist.[163]

Absent an explicit antitrust exemption, an antitrust exemption can be "implied only if necessary to make the [non-antitrust statute] work, and even then only to the minimum extent necessary."[164] This test does not require a showing that the specific challenged conduct or rule is necessary for the regulatory scheme to function, but rather a conclusion that the regulatory system could not work properly if antitrust liability could conflict with regulatory determinations about the desirability of the conduct.[165] The doctrine generally denies an exemption if the agency either (a) lacks the power to authorize, require, or prohibit the relevant sort of conduct, or (b) has such power but has not exercised it, unless the decision not to exercise such a power reflects a regulatory judgment to allow the challenged sort of conduct despite consideration of its potential anticompetitive effects.[166]

---

[160] *See Allied Tube,* 486 U.S. at 499–500; California Motor Transp. Co. v. Trucking Unlimited, 404 U.S. 508, 512–13 (1972); *Professional Real Estate*, 508 U.S. at 62–66 (judging whether conduct constitutes an abuse of process under traditional litigation standards).

[161] *See Professional Real Estate*, 508 U.S. at 60–61; *City of Columbia,* 499 U.S. at 380; Elhauge, *supra* note 133, at 1228–29, 1249–50.

[162] Walker Process Equip. Inc. v. Food Mach. & Chem. Corp., 382 U.S. 172 (1965); Elhauge, *supra* note 133, at 1248–50.

[163] E.g., National Gerimedical Hosp. & Gerontology Ctr. v. Blue Cross, 452 U.S. 378, 389 (1981); Group Life & Health Ins. Co. v. Royal Drug Co., 440 U.S. 205, 231 (1979).

[164] Silver v. NYSE, 373 U.S. 341, 357 (1963); *Nat'l Gerimedical*, 452 U.S. at 389.

[165] *See* Gordon v. NYSE, 422 U.S. 659, 662, 683 (1975); United States v. NASD, 422 U.S. 694, 726–28 (1975); *Nat'l Gerimedical*, 452 U.S. at 389.

[166] *See Nat'l Gerimedical*, 452 U.S. at 389–90; *NASD,* 422 U.S. at 726–28; Georgia v. Pennsylvania R.R., 324 U.S. 439 (1945); United States v. Borden, 308 U.S. 188 (1939); Nader v. Allegheny Airlines, 426 U.S. 290, 301 (1976); McLean Trucking Co. v. United States, 321 U.S. 67 (1944). In addition, even without any implicit antitrust exemption, regulators are sometimes held to have primary jurisdiction in the sense that antitrust courts should defer their adjudications until the agency has had a chance to address the issue first, generally either

In *Credit Suisse,* the Court held that federal securities law precludes antitrust law when the two are "clearly incompatible" given "(1) the existence of regulatory authority under the securities law to supervise the activities in question; (2) evidence that the responsible regulatory entities exercise that authority; . . . (3) a resulting risk that the securities and antitrust laws, if both applicable, would produce conflicting guidance, requirements, duties, privileges, or standards of conduct," and that "(4) . . . the possible conflict affected practices that lie squarely within an area of financial market activity that the securities law seeks to regulate."[167] The Court emphasized that the possible conflict need not be a present one: even if the federal securities agency currently prohibits precisely the same conduct that antitrust law prohibits, it suffices for an antitrust exemption that, in the future: (a) the agency could create a conflict by choosing to exercise its regulatory authority differently, or (b) the agency and antitrust courts might interpret or apply their similar prohibitions differently.[168]

This test uses factors similar to those considered by prior implied exemption cases, but goes beyond them to suggest an affirmative test of when an antitrust exemption would be implied. If generalizable beyond securities cases, it indicates that an implied antitrust exemption applies if: (1) a federal non-antitrust agency has an exercised power to regulate the relevant conduct, and (2) current or future agency choices about how to exercise or apply that power might create a risk of a conflict with antitrust standards on conduct that is squarely within the core area covered by the non-antitrust law. Two features indicated, however, that the Court was trying to cabin this implied exemption doctrine a bit. First, the limitation of implied exemption to the core areas covered by non-antitrust laws indicated a potential narrowing of implied exemption law. Second, the Court suggested in several places that the potential-conflict exemption test might be unique to securities law.[169]

One can see why the Court might be worried about applying this standard outside of securities cases. Given the extent of modern federal regulation, it may well be the case that, in most of our economy, some agency has an exercised power to regulate some conduct that might also constitute an antitrust violation. If all such conduct were exempt from antitrust scrutiny, there could well be little left to the antitrust laws.

---

because the agency has an expertise advantage in determining the facts relevant to the antitrust claim or because agency resolution might affect whether an antitrust exemption existed. *See id.* at 301–04; Ricci v. Chicago Mercantile Exch., 409 U.S. 289, 305, 307 (1973); Carnation Co. v. Pacific Westbound Conf., 383 U.S. 213, 222 (1966); Far East Conf. v. United States, 342 U.S. 570, 574–75 (1952). However, other cases have somewhat inconsistently held that agencies should hold off until an antitrust court has addressed the relevant issue. *See* California v. FPC, 369 U.S. 482 (1962). Perhaps the best resolution is that the latter was a merger case brought a federal antitrust agency, which generally both requires a quick decision (and thus makes deferring impracticable) and means the agency in the antitrust suit has an equal or greater claim to expertise.

[167] Credit Suisse Securities v. Billing, 551 U.S. 264, 275 (2007).

[168] *Id.* at 271–73, 278–82.

[169] *Id.* at 269, 275.

Further, usually Congress has authorized the relevant agency to regulate the conduct in some more limited way, or based on more limited standards that are unrelated to competitive concerns. It seems implausible that in all such cases that Congress really meant to oust antitrust review, or that doing so would be socially desirable. Instead, Congress may well have intended to express even more concern about the relevant conduct, by indicating it was undesirable not only under competition standards, but under other normative standards as well. If these concerns prove persuasive, it may be the case that *Credit Suisse* does not generate a new broad general doctrine of implied exemption, but rather has defined a "securities exemption" that, like the labor and insurance exemptions discussed below, is a special exemption doctrine with its own elements that do not extend to other sorts of cases.

The filed rate doctrine differs from an exemption in that it provides only that a party may not collect damages (in antitrust or otherwise) based on an overcharge that reflected a rate filed with and approved by a federal regulator.[170] This doctrine does not provide an exemption because it bars only some damage claims and not others, and bars no claims for injunctive relief or criminal penalties.[171] Unlike with state action immunity, rubberstamp approval by a federal regulator suffices for the filed rate doctrine even absent evidence that the agency considered any anticompetitive conduct.[172] However, a filed rate that the agency either disapproves or lacks authority to regulate can form the basis for an antitrust action.[173] The filed rate doctrine bars only claims that seek damages on the grounds that the rate reflected an overcharge, and thus does not bar claims that seek damages from a requirement to buy the product or service,[174] or from a filed rate that excluded rivals (because it reflected a price squeeze or predatory price) and thus resulted in lost profits to that rival.[175]

U.S. government agencies enjoy sovereign immunity from antitrust liability unless there is a statutory waiver, and even when a general waiver exists, are not deemed "persons" eligible to be defendants under

---

[170] *See* Square D Co. v. Niagara Frontier Tariff Bureau, 476 U.S. 409, 415–420 (1986).

[171] *See id.* at 418–19, 422.

[172] *See* Mississippi Power & Light v. Mississippi, 487 U.S. 354, 374 (1988); *Square D*, 476 U.S. at 417 n.19. Some lower courts have extended the filed rate doctrine to rates approved by state agencies, but it seems unlikely the Supreme Court would approve such an extension because the Court has (1) expressed doubts about the wisdom of this doctrine and adhered to it only because it was statutory precedent that Congress left unaltered, *id.* at 420, 423–24, and (2) denied state action immunity to state agencies that engage in the sort rubberstamp approvals that receive protection under the filed rate doctrine, *see Ticor Title*, 504 U.S. 621.

[173] *See* Litton Sys., Inc. v. American Tel. & Tel. Co., 700 F.2d 785, 820 (2d Cir.1983); Florida Municipal Power Agency v. Florida Power & Light, 64 F.3d 614 (11th Cir. 1995).

[174] *See Litton*, 700 F.2d at 820.

[175] *See* Cost Management Service v. Washington Natural Gas, 99 F.3d 937, 944–45 (9th Cir. 1996); City of Kirkwood v. Union Elec. Co., 671 F.2d 1173, 1178 (8th Cir. 1982).

the antitrust statutes unless the agency statute explicitly provides otherwise.[176]

b. EXPLICIT EXEMPTIONS OR LIMITATIONS. Congress has also frequently enacted explicit exemptions or alterations of antitrust standards. These include exemptions that:

1. Allow those who farm or fish to form cooperatives without those cooperatives being considered agreements in restraint of trade, although the Secretary of Agriculture has authority to enjoin cooperatives that unduly enhance prices.[177] This exemption does not extend to agreements with nonexempt persons, nor to exclusionary conduct by cooperatives against rivals or other nonmembers.[178]
2. Exempt certain mergers and television agreements by sports leagues.[179] Baseball also enjoys a special judicially-created antitrust exemption, other than for conduct that affects the employment of ballplayers,[180] which is instead governed by the labor exemption described below.
3. Immunize charitable gift annuities or charitable remainder trusts.[181]
4. Exempt the medical resident matching program.[182]
5. Provide more generous antitrust standards for mergers and agreements between newspapers when one is a failing firm.[183]
6. Exempt professional review bodies from antitrust damages for actions that are based on the quality of a physician's care and may adversely affect the physician's hospital privileges or society memberships, provided the actions were based on a reasonable belief that they would enhance the quality of health care and were made after reasonable investigation and process.[184]

---

[176] *See* United States Postal Service v. Flamingo Indus. (U.S.A.) Ltd., 540 U.S. 736 (2004). An earlier case had held that the United States was not a "person" who could be an antitrust damages plaintiff or defendant, *see* United States v. Cooper Corp., 312 U.S. 600, 607–09, 614 (1941), and Congress had responded with a statute that did not make the United States a "person" who could sue and be sued, but rather simply gave the United States standing to sue for antitrust damages, *see* 15 U.S.C. § 15a.

[177] *See* 15 U.S.C. § 17, 7 U.S.C. § 291; 15 U.S.C. § 521.

[178] *See* United States v. Borden, 308 U.S. 188, 194, 205 (1939); Maryland & Va. Milk Producers Ass'n v. United States, 362 U.S. 458, 466–68, 471–72 (1960).

[179] *See* 15 U.S.C. §§ 1291–95.

[180] *See* Flood v. Kuhn, 407 U.S. 258, 282 (1972); 15 U.S.C. § 26b.

[181] *See* 15 U.S.C. § 37.

[182] *See* 15 U.S.C. § 37b.

[183] *See* 15 U.S.C. § 1803.

[184] *See* 42 U.S.C. § 11111–12, 11151(9)–(11).

7. Exempt collective rate making that is known and approved by the Interstate Commerce Commission.[185]
8. Exempt shipper conduct that is already prohibited by the Shipping Act of 1984.[186]
9. Exempt agreements that the President finds vital to national defense.[187]
10. Exempt joint research and development that has been approved by the Small Business Administration.[188]
11. Provide more generous antitrust standards for judging bank mergers.[189]

All of these exemptions require examination of the detailed statutory requirements. Two other exemptions require a bit more discussion because of their importance and doctrinal development.

c. STATE-REGULATED INSURANCE ACTIVITIES. The McCarran-Ferguson Act exempts insurance practices that are regulated by state laws unless the practices involve boycotts.[190] To receive this exemption, all of the following three requirements must be met:

1. The Practice Involves the Business of Insurance—To merit this exemption, it is not enough that the defendant is an insurer. Rather, the challenged practice itself must involve the "business of insurance" under a doctrine that considers three factors, all of which are relevant but none of which are determinative: "*first*, whether the practice has the effect of transferring or spreading a policyholder's risk; *second*, whether the practice is an integral part of the policy relationship between the insurer and the insured; and *third*, whether the practice is limited to entities within the insurance industry."[191] Thus, the exemption does not cover insurer practices that are not integral to the transfer or spread of risk, such as (i) health insurer agreements with pharmacies on the prices charged to fill prescriptions, or (ii) insurer peer review of the reasonableness of professional fees or treatment.[192]

2. The Practice Is Regulated by State Laws—The McCarran-Ferguson Act governs more than just antitrust. It states:

---

185 *See* 49 U.S.C. § 10706.

186 *See* 46 U.S.C. § 1706(c)(2).

187 *See* 50 U.S.C. § 2158. *See also* 15 U.S.C. § 640.

188 *See* 15 U.S.C. § 638.

189 12 U.S.C. § 1828(c).

190 *See* 15 U.S.C. §§ 1011–1103; Group Life & Health Ins. v. Royal Drug, 440 U.S. 205, 210 n.4, 220 (1979).

191 Hartford Fire Ins. Co. v. California, 509 U.S. 764, 781–82 (1993); Union Labor Life Ins. Co. v. Pireno, 458 U.S. 119, 129 (1982).

192 *See Group Life*, 440 U.S. 205; *Pireno*, 458 U.S. at 129–31. On similar logic, most courts also hold the exemption inapplicable to insurer decisions to limit or exclude reimbursement for nonphysician services. *See* Virginia Academy of Clinical Psychologists v. Blue Shield, 624 F.2d 476, 484 (4th Cir. 1980); Hahn v. Oregon Physicians Serv., 689 F.2d 840 (9th Cir. 1982). *But see* Health Care Equalization Comm. v. Iowa Med. Socy., 851 F.2d 1020 (8th Cir. 1988).

> "No Act of Congress shall be construed to invalidate, impair, or supersede any law enacted by any State for the purpose of regulating the business of insurance ... unless such Act specifically relates to the business of insurance: *Provided*, That after June 30, 1948, ... the Sherman Act, ... the Clayton Act, and ... the Federal Trade Commission Act ... shall be applicable to the business of insurance to the extent that such business is not regulated by State law."[193]

Read literally, the second clause provides no freestanding antitrust exemption, but rather *limits* the first clause's exemption in cases involving antitrust statutes, which means that an antitrust exemption should require a showing that the antitrust statute would "impair" the state regulation in addition to the factors in the second clause. However, based on certain legislative history, the Supreme Court has traditionally read the second clause as an independent affirmative grant of immunity from federal antitrust law for insurance practices that are regulated by state law.[194] Still, the most recent Supreme Court opinion more accurately describes the second clause as an exception to the first,[195] suggesting that future courts may instead follow the plain meaning of the statute and require a showing of impairment. This would also be more consistent with the statutory canon requiring narrow interpretation of any antitrust exemption, as well as with the full legislative history.[196]

---

[193] 15 U.S.C. § 1012(b).

[194] *See* F.T.C. v. National Casualty Co., 357 U.S. 560, 563 n.3 (1958).

[195] *See Hartford Fire*, 509 U.S. at 780. If it is only an exception, this would narrow the exemption because, in non-antitrust cases, the Court has found such impairment only when the federal claim would directly conflict with state regulation or frustrate a declared state policy. *See* Humana Inc. v. Forsyth, 525 U.S. 299, 311–12 (1999). The main difference is that, unlike the regulated-by-state-law standard, the impairment standard does not preclude federal prohibitions of the same sort of conduct prohibited by state law. For example, state regulation of deceptive insurance practices does not preclude RICO efforts to penalize such deception under the impairment standard, *id.*, but does preclude FTC efforts to penalize such deception under the regulated-by-state-law standard. *See National Casualty*, 357 U.S. at 563.

One might wonder whether reading the second clause as an exception renders it superfluous on the ground that federal antitrust law could never impair state law when the matter is not regulated by state law. But the impairment clause applies to any state law enacted for the "purpose" of regulating insurance whether or not it actually does so. Thus, a plain meaning interpretation would not create superfluity because under it the federal antitrust laws would apply when they impair a state law that has the purpose of regulating insurance but does not actually do so. It is unclear the extent to which such state laws actually exist, but it is not superfluous for Congress to provide for the possibility. In any event, superfluous language in statutes is in fact commonplace, and the canon against superfluous language is not followed when it conflicts with the most sensible reading of statutory language.

[196] Of the legislative history cited in *National Casualty*, the only part that actually supports its statutory reading is that Senator McCarran did state that state regulation would oust federal antitrust liability. *See* 91 Cong. Rec. 1443. However, given the context, he may have simply been assuming a case where the antitrust liability would impair the state regulation, especially since what the Senators mainly had in mind was state regulations authorizing collective ratemaking by insurers subject to state supervision. *See id.* at 1444, 1481, 1484. Other Senators supporting the statute read the language to mere be a "positive declaration" of when antitrust applied notwithstanding the impairment clause, *see id.* at 1444 (Sen. O'Mahoney), or stressed that state regulation would preclude antitrust liability only when the state regulation was "in conflict" with antitrust law or affirmatively "permitted" conduct that would otherwise

Leaving aside the possible future addition of this impairment test, the traditional regulated-by state-law standard does not require proof that the state "effectively" enforces its regulation of the practice as long as the state "authorizes enforcement through a scheme of administrative supervision."[197] This element is also satisfied if the state regulator permits or authorizes the relevant practice, like collective ratemaking, even though the regulator does not substantively control those rates, as long as the practice is open and supervised by the state regulator.[198] Although the occasional court mistakenly thinks it suffices that *insurers* are generally regulated by the state, in fact the test is whether the particular *insurance practice* is regulated by the state in that it either (a) prohibits undesirable instances of the practice and has some system of enforcement, or (b) has made a considered regulatory judgment to permit the practice subject to ongoing public monitoring.[199] This is less rigorous than the state action immunity requirement that the regulator actually substantively approve the terms of any immune restraint, but comes fairly close to the standards for determining whether a federal statute creates an implicit antitrust exemption.

Further, for the McCarran-Ferguson antitrust exemption, the practice must both occur in *and* have effects in the state that regulates the practice; there is thus no federal antitrust immunity for conduct that is regulated by the state in which the insurer exists and committed the practice but has effects in other states.[200] Even if immune from federal antitrust law, insurance practices remain subject to state antitrust law unless it provides otherwise.

3. The Practice Does Not Constitute a "Boycott"—The insurance exemption has an exception which states that nothing in the McCarran-Ferguson Act "shall render the . . . Sherman Act inapplicable to any

---

violate antitrust law, *id.* at 1481 (Sen. Murdock), which is quite similar to the impairment standard. None of the legislative history suggested that the antitrust laws would be deemed inapplicable when they did not conflict with state law or some declared state policy, and thus none of it conflicts with applying the impairment standard to antitrust cases.

[197] *See* St. Paul Fire & Marine Ins. Co. v. Barry, 438 U.S. 531, 551 (1978); *National Casualty*, 357 U.S. at 564–65; Lawyers Title Co. v. St. Paul Title Ins. Corp., 526 F.2d 795, 797 (8th Cir. 1975).

[198] *Group Life*, 440 U.S. at 223; *St. Paul Fire*, 438 U.S. at 548 n.21, 549; *Pireno*, 458 U.S. at 129; Ohio AFL-CIO v. Insurance Rating Board, 451 F.2d 1178, 1181 (6th Cir. 1971).

[199] *See* sources collected in last two notes. The claim that any state regulation of insurers ousts all federal antitrust regulation of nonboycott insurer practices is inconsistent with the statutory text, which makes clear that federal antitrust laws continue to apply "to the extent" insurers are not regulated by states, 15 U.S.C. § 1012(b), rather than "only if" insurers are not regulated by states. This claim is also inconsistent with the legislative history. It was specifically rejected by Senator McCarran, who agreed with Senator White that the federal antitrust laws "shall be applicable to whatever extent the State fails to occupy the ground and engage in regulation. . . . If . . . the state goes only to the point indicated, then these Federal statutes apply throughout the whole field beyond the scope of the State's activity." *See* 91 Cong. Rec. 1444. Senator McCarran even agreed with Senator Barkley that "where States attempt to occupy the field—but do it inadequately—. . . these [federal antitrust] acts still would apply." *Id.*

[200] *See* FTC v. Travelers Health Ass'n, 362 U.S. 293, 297–99 (1960). The Court left open the question whether the exemption might apply if all the states in which the conduct had effects also effectively regulated it. *Id.* at 298 n.4.

agreement to boycott, coerce, or intimidate, or act of boycott, coercion, or intimidation."[201] This creates an interesting interpretive question because a "boycott" is a concerted refusal to deal, and one could think of any agreement in restraint of trade as a concerted refusal to deal on anything other than at the restrained terms. Indeed, in defining the substantive law of antitrust, the Supreme Court has characterized a concerted refusal to deal at less than a fixed price as a "boycott" even though it noted it could also be considered a price-fixing agreement.[202] And yet the McCarran-Ferguson Act was intended to allow insurers to collectively agree on insurance prices and terms (subject to state monitoring) and thus must have been using a more narrow understanding of the word "boycott."

Accordingly, the Supreme Court has held that the "boycott" element of the insurance exemption requires a concerted refusal to deal that went beyond refusing to deal on other than desired terms.[203] This includes an absolute concerted refusal to deal with a party (either entirely or on some transactions) in order to punish that party for its past conduct.[204] It also includes a conditioned refusal to deal that is designed to coerce the party to change its future conduct to meet the condition, but only if the scope of the refusal includes matters "unrelated" or "collateral" to the desired terms in the transaction with the refused party.[205] Under this standard, if a conspiracy sought to sell an insurance product at $10 or only on term *X,* then a concerted refusal to sell that product to any buyer for less than $10 or terms worse than *X* would not be a boycott. But it would be a boycott to have a concerted refusal to sell that product (on nondiscriminatory terms) to buyers based on their *other* transactions (such as with noncomplying sellers) or to refuse to buy or sell some *other* product (on nondiscriminatory terms) to firms that don't buy or sell the first product at $10 or on term *X*.

d. THE LABOR EXEMPTIONS. Without a labor exemption, ordinary union activities like strikes or setting labor prices in collective bargaining agreements would be horizontal boycotts and price-fixing agreements subject to the risk of antitrust liability. To avoid this, Congress has enacted statutes that provide antitrust exemptions for, and bar injunctions against, such ordinary labor union activities as collective refusals to supply labor or agreements not to compete on wages or other employment terms.[206] This explicit statutory exemption protects agreements among labor employees, but not among independent

---

[201] *See* 15 U.S.C. § 1013(b).

[202] *See Trial Lawyers*, 493 U.S. at 422–23, 432–36 & n.19.

[203] *See Hartford Fire*, 509 U.S. at 801–03. Although in substantive antitrust law, the Court sometimes uses "boycott" to refer to those concerted refusals to deal that are per se unlawful, the boycott exception to the insurance exemption does not require that the concerted refusal be per se unlawful. *See St. Paul Fire*, 438 U.S. at 542.

[204] *Hartford Fire*, 509 U.S. at 801.

[205] *Id.* at 801–803, 806, 810–11.

[206] *See* 15 U.S.C. § 17; 29 U.S.C. §§ 52, 101–115.

contractors who collectively engage in boycotts or price-fixing.[207] The explicit statutory exemption extends only to conduct and agreements by employees and their unions, and not to their agreements with non-labor groups.[208]

The Court has also recognized what it calls a "nonstatutory exemption" for agreements between unions and employers, but only to the extent necessary to make the collective bargaining process work.[209] It would be more accurate to call this exemption "implicit" rather than "nonstatutory" given that it is in fact implied from the statute. The Court has interpreted this nonstatutory (implicit) labor exemption to extend even to horizontal agreements among employers on the other side of the same collective bargaining process about the terms they will offer as part of that process or impose if the union does not agree, on the grounds that such immunity is necessary to make multi-employer collective bargaining work.[210] In short, the labor exemption allows the competition model favored by antitrust to be replaced with the model of bilateral collective bargaining between sellers and buyers that is favored by labor law. In the latter type of case, the process is policed by the National Labor Relations Board rather than by antitrust courts.[211]

The nonstatutory (implicit) labor exemption is limited to activities that are legitimately within the collective bargaining process about wages, hours, and other employment terms. Even collective bargaining agreements between union and businesses can lose their immunity when used to suppress competition from a rival business[212] or to restrain competition by employers in their product markets.[213] *A fortiori*, this doctrine offers no immunity when a union and business impose a direct restraint on market competition outside any collective bargaining agreement.[214] Accordingly, the courts have repeatedly held that alleged

---

207 *See* AMA v. United States, 317 U.S. 519, 526–27, 536 (1943) (physicians); United States v. National Ass'n of Real Estate Boards, 339 U.S. 485, 489 (1950) (real estate brokers); Columbia River Packers Ass'n v. Hinton, 315 U.S. 143 (1942) (fisherman). Those employees who are considered managers, which generally includes professionals who have any supervisory responsibilities, are also not eligible to form labor unions and bargain collectively. *See* NLRB v. Health Care & Retirement Corp., 511 U.S. 571 (1994) (licensed practical nurses); FHP, Inc., 274 N.L.R.B. 1141, 1142–43 (1985) (physicians who were HMO employees).

208 United States v. Hutcheson, 312 U.S. 219, 232 (1941).

209 Connell Constr. Co., Inc. v. Plumbers & Steamfitters Local Union No. 100, 421 U.S. 616, 622 (1975); *see also Pennington*, 381 U.S. at 662 (collecting cases); Allen Bradley Co. v. Local Union No. 3, IBEW, 325 U.S. 797, 810 (1945) ("the same labor union activities may or may not be in violation of the Sherman Act, dependent upon whether the union acts alone or in combination with business groups.").

210 *See* Brown v. Pro Football, 518 U.S. 231 (1996).

211 *Id.* at 242.

212 *See Pennington,* 381 U.S. at 662–69 (holding that this lack of immunity applied even when the restraint involves a compulsory subject of collective bargaining).

213 *See id.* at 662–63; Amalgamated Meat Cutters v. Jewel Tea Co., 381 U.S. 676 (1965).

214 *See* A.L. Adams Constr. Co. v. Georgia Power Co., 733 F.2d 853, 855–56 (11th Cir.1984) (no exemption if Agreement was not part of a collective bargaining relationship); C & W Constr. Co. v. Brotherhood of Carpenters, 687 F.Supp. 1453, 1464 (D. Hawai'i 1988) (union-business refusal to deal that was outside any collective bargaining agreement was per se outside the labor exemption).

conspiracies between unions and businesses to suppress competition from another business enjoy no antitrust exemption.[215] For example, *Connell* involved an agreement between a union and general contractor that the general contractor would award subcontracts only to firms that had a contract with the union.[216] The Court held that this was not exempted because it involved a direct restraint on a business market, rather than being part of a collective bargaining agreement limited to the standardization of wages and working conditions.[217] It did not matter that the union's only goal was the legal one of organizing as many subcontractors as possible because the method violated antitrust law.[218] In *Pennington*, the allegation was that the union and large coal operators conspired to exclude small coal operators from the market by imposing an agreed-upon wage on smaller coal operators.[219] The Court concluded that, although those wages were a compulsory subject of bargaining, the agreement to impose those wage levels on other employers outside the bargaining unit stated an antitrust claim.[220]

The inapplicability of the labor exemption does not eliminate the need to prove the nonexempt conduct actually violates antitrust law. Nor does the inapplicability of the nonstatutory exemption to an agreement between unions and employers remove the statutory exemption for agreements among union members. Rather, where the nonstatutory exemption does not apply, the horizontal agreement among union members remains exempt under the statutory exemption and the only issue is whether the union's nonexempt vertical agreement with the employer violates antitrust law. For example, when *Connell* held the nonstatutory labor exemption inapplicable, it remanded for a determination of whether the vertical "agreement between Local 100 and Connell. . . . restrains trade," not whether the horizontal agreement among union members of Local 100 did.[221] Likewise, *Pennington* removed only the nonstatutory exemption for the vertical "agreement between [United Mine Workers] and the large operators," not the statutory exemption for the horizontal agreement among members of United Mine Workers. In cases where the nonstatutory labor exemption does not apply, the situation comes close to treating the union as a single entity, but is distinct from it because any union decision to offer a wage or refuse to deal with an employer would remain immune under the statutory labor exemption even when the union collectively has monopoly power that would, if it were a single business entity, make such decisions

[215] *See Connell Constr.*, 421 U.S. at 623–26; *Pennington,* 381 U.S. at 662–69; *Allen,* 325 U.S. at 809–810; United States v. Employing Plasterers Assn., 347 U.S. 186, 190 (1954); Philadelphia Record v. Manufacturing Photo-Engravers Assn., 155 F.2d 799, 803 (3d Cir. 1946); Gilmour v. Wood, Wire & Metal Lathers Intern., 223 F.Supp. 236, 248 (N.D. Ill. 1963).

[216] 421 U.S. at 618–19.

[217] *Id.* at 623–26.

[218] *Id.* at 625.

[219] 381 U.S. at 664.

[220] *Id.* at 665–69.

[221] 421 U.S. at 637.

reviewable as predatory pricing or unilateral refusal to deals when certain conditions are met.

(3) Effect on U.S. Interstate Commerce. Finally, the U.S. antitrust statutes require some effect on U.S. interstate commerce. This imposes three limitations. First, the restraint or anticompetitive effect must be on "commerce" rather than on some noncommercial activity. Second, the effects of the conduct cannot be limited to one state, but must have some interstate effects. However, the required effect is so trivial that this rarely poses a practical barrier. Third, for foreign restraints, U.S. law requires some substantial effect on U.S. markets or exporters.

a. EFFECT ON COMMERCE. To be covered by U.S. antitrust law, the restraint or anticompetitive effect must be on "commerce," which is to say on some market that involves the sale of goods, services or property in exchange for valuable consideration. A restraint on a donative activity, such as an agreement between two charities that one will provide or solicit donations in the eastern United States and the other in the western United States, would not be a restraint on commerce.[222] This does not mean that charities or nonprofit *entities* are not covered by the antitrust laws. To the contrary, nonprofits are covered whenever they restrain some commercial market, such as providing medical care or college education in exchange for money.[223] Further, even noncommercial activities, like donations or promulgating safety standards, are restraints on commerce if their terms affect some commercial market.[224] However, Congress has enacted specific exemptions for charitable gift annuities and charitable remainder trusts.[225]

b. EFFECT ON INTERSTATE COMMERCE. All of the U.S. antitrust statutes require that the challenged conduct involve or affect interstate commerce.[226] But while this requirement was historically important, it has been narrowly interpreted in a way that makes it practically irrelevant. Even a restraint of a highly local market within one state has the requisite interstate effects as long as lawyers remember to dutifully plead that some sort of business is transacted across state lines by either the defendants or any firms in the market directly affected by the

[222] *See* Dedication & Everlasting Love to Animals v. Humane Society, 50 F.3d 710, 712 (9th Cir. 1995).

[223] *See id.* at 713; *infra* Chapter 2.

[224] *See* American Soc'y v. Hydrolevel, 456 U.S. 556, 560–62 (1982) (nonprofit liable for issuing a letter that, without any financial benefit to the nonprofit, interpreted a safety standard in a way that restrained trade); *Allied Tube*, 486 U.S. at 501 (antitrust rule of reason applies to safety standard setting by disinterested nonprofit associations); *Virginia Vermiculite*, 156 F.3d 535 (donation of land by mining company with restrictive covenants prohibiting its use for mining was an agreement in restraint of commerce); Ozee v. American Council, 110 F.3d 1082, 1093 (5th Cir. 1997) (donation to charity is treated as a commercial transaction when the donor receives an "annuity, substantial tax advantage, and the satisfaction of having given to charity.")

[225] *See* 15 U.S.C. § 37.

[226] *See* 15 U.S.C. §§ 1–2, 12(a), 13, 14, 18, 44–45.

defendant's conduct.[227] It is hard to know how one could ever fail to satisfy this requirement unless one had an odd market where no sellers or buyers ever made interstate sales, purchases, loans, or phone calls. Indeed, at least one prominent judge has concluded that the requirement is so trivial that merely pleading the bare conclusion that interstate commerce was affected should suffice.[228] The U.S. Supreme Court has held the interstate commerce requirement satisfied in a case where the defendants allegedly conspired to deny staff privileges in a Los Angeles hospital to a single surgeon.[229] The Court has also interpreted the Sherman Act to extend to the furthest reaches of congressional power to regulate interstate commerce,[230] which itself covers even a farmer's decision to grow wheat for his farm's own consumption.[231]

c. EFFECT ON U.S. COMMERCE. The U.S. antitrust laws reach extraterritorial conduct as long as it has effects on U.S. commerce or exporters that are direct, substantial, and reasonably foreseeable.[232] Caselaw to this effect was effectively codified in the Foreign Trade Antitrust Improvements Act (FTAIA) of 1982, which stated that the Sherman and FTC Acts "shall not apply to conduct involving trade or commerce (other than import trade or import commerce) with foreign nations unless . . . (1) such conduct has a direct, substantial, and reasonably foreseeable effect" on U.S. commerce or on U.S. exporters and "(2) such effect gives rise to a claim" under the Sherman or FTC Acts.[233] The directness element adds little to damage claims, which (as noted above) must already show directness to show proximate causation. However, it remains important because it effectively adds a proximate causation requirement for non-damage claims against foreign conduct, including those brought by the government. In addition, the FTAIA adds the new requirement (which was perhaps simply assumed in the prior cases where it was always met) that the requisite U.S. effect gives rise to the relevant antitrust claim. This requirement adds little to the typical suit by private plaintiffs operating in the U.S., because they must already prove antitrust injury. But it too is important because it effectively adds

---

[227] *See* Summit Health v. Pinhas, 500 U.S. 322, 329–33 (1991); McLain v. Real Estate Board of New Orleans, 444 U.S. 232, 235–36; 241–46 (1980).

[228] Hammes v. AAMCO Transmissions, Inc., 33 F.3d 774, 778–79 (7th Cir. 1994) (Posner, J.).

[229] *Summit*, 500 U.S. 322.

[230] *Summit,* 500 U.S. at 328–29 & n.8, 332–33; *McLain*, 444 U.S. at 241. Other cases have held that the Clayton Act and Robinson-Patman Act did not go quite so far because they did not apply to any conduct that affected interstate commerce but rather required that the defendants and their activities be "in" interstate commerce, *see* United States v. American Bldg. Maintenance Indus., 422 U.S. 271, 275–84 (1975); Gulf Oil Corp. v. Copp Paving Co., 419 U.S. 186, 194–203 (1974). However, Congress amended Clayton Act § 7 to include persons and conduct affecting interstate commerce, *see* 15 U.S.C. § 15, and amended FTC Act § 5 to include conduct in or affecting commerce, *see* 15 U.S.C. § 45, and the FTC has authority to enforce the Clayton and Robinson-Patman Act. In addition, the Sherman Act likely covers any anticompetitive conduct covered by Clayton Act §§ 3,7, *see infra* Chapters 4, 7.

[231] Wickard v. Filburn, 317 U.S. 111 (1942).

[232] *See* Hartford Fire Insur. v. California, 509 U.S. 764, 796 (1993); Matsushita Elec. Industrial Co. v. Zenith Radio Corp., 475 U.S. 574, 582 n.6 (1986).

[233] *See* 15 U.S.C §§ 6a, 45(a)(3).

the requirement of proving antitrust injury to U.S. commerce or exports in suits brought by a U.S. agency, and requires private plaintiffs to show that their antitrust injury was connected to such U.S. effects. This precludes cases by plaintiffs claiming injuries suffered in foreign nations that were independent of the U.S. effects.[234]

Although the U.S. antitrust statutes can reach any foreign anticompetitive conduct with a direct, substantial, foreseeable effect in the United States, many cases have also held that this authority should not be exercised when it would violate principles of international comity. Some cases have held that this comity doctrine means that courts must weigh the substantiality of the effects in the U.S. against the interests of foreign nations, using a multi-factor balancing test.[235] The Supreme Court has not yet resolved this issue, but has held that comity does not dictate the nonapplication of U.S. antitrust law merely because the extraterritorial conduct is legal in the foreign nation where it occurred, but probably does if the foreign law actually compels that conduct.[236] It has also held that the comity principle can apply categorically, rather than just case by case, justifying a general interpretation of the U.S. antitrust statutes against remedying the independent foreign effects of conduct that also has U.S. effects, because the foreign interest in such cases is much greater than the U.S. interest.[237]

When foreign nations engage in anticompetitive acts, they generally enjoy sovereign immunity from antitrust liability unless they are engaged in a commercial activity.[238] Further, the act of state doctrine precludes litigation that would definitely require declaring a foreign act of state invalid, even when the litigation is against private parties.[239]

---

234 *See* F. Hoffmann-La Roche Ltd. v. Empagran S.A., 542 U.S. 155, 166–75 (2004).

235 Timberlane Lumber v. Bank of America, 549 F.2d 597, 611–15 (9th Cir. 1976); Mannington Mills v. Congoleum Corp., 595 F.2d 1287, 1297 (3d Cir. 1979); *see also* Restatement (Third) of Foreign Relations Law § 403 (1987) (providing a multi-factor balancing test).

236 *See Hartford*, 509 U.S. 764.

237 *Empagran*, 542 U.S. 155.

238 28 U.S.C. §§ 1604–05 (1988); Republic of Argentina v. Weltover, Inc., 504 U.S. 607 (1992) (holding that issuing bonds is a commercial activity).

239 W.S. Kirkpatrick & Co. v. Environmental Tectonics, 493 U.S. 400 (1990).

CHAPTER 2

WHICH HORIZONTAL AGREEMENTS ARE ILLEGAL?

A. RELEVANT U.S. LAWS AND GENERAL LEGAL STANDARDS

Horizontal agreements are agreements between firms who operate at the same market level. Vertical agreements are agreements between firms that are in some supply relation. For example, suppose we have a steel market with two firms that supply steel to two car manufacturers, which in turn sell cars to consumers. Then, an agreement between the two steel suppliers would be a horizontal agreement, as would an agreement between the two car makers. An agreement between a steel supplier and car maker would be a vertical agreement. Where effects at both market levels are relevant, the steel market would be called the upstream market and the car market the downstream market, with the market closest to the ultimate consumer the downstream one. The topic of this chapter shall be horizontal agreements, with vertical agreements deferred until Chapters 4 and 5. Mergers between competitors could be considered horizontal agreements, but raise distinctive issues that will be deferred until Chapter 7. This chapter shall instead focus on agreements between firms that continue to operate separately at the same market level.

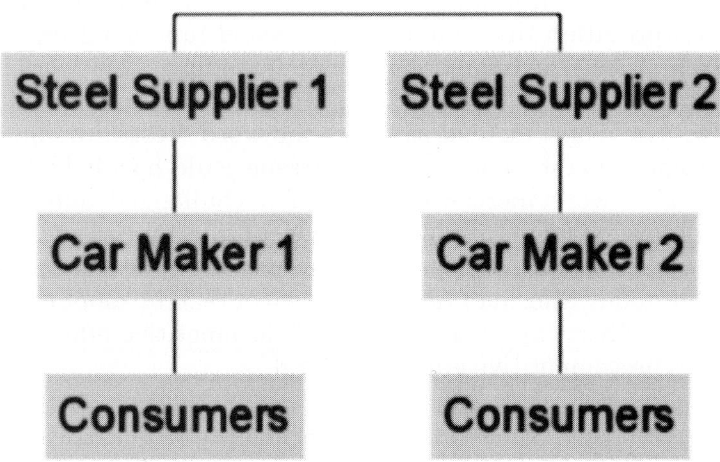

Three statutes cover horizontal agreements. The most important is Sherman Act § 1:

Sherman Act § 1, 15 U.S.C. § 1

> Every contract, combination in the form of trust or otherwise, or conspiracy, in restraint of trade or commerce among the several States, or with foreign nations, is declared to be illegal.

The statute's reference to a "contract, combination in the form of trust or otherwise, or conspiracy" has been interpreted to require some sort of agreement. Just what constitutes an "agreement" will prove to be a big question in many cases, but those issues are deferred until Chapter 6, with this Chapter assuming an agreement has been proven and focusing on the application to horizontal agreements. The statute also contains an interstate commerce requirement (as do all the U.S. antitrust statutes), but as Chapter 1 details, this requirement is trivial to establish for conduct in the U.S., although it technically remains necessary to dutifully plead an effect on interstate commerce in any complaint. When the conduct occurs in foreign nations, it is necessary to make a more serious showing of sufficient effects on U.S. commerce. *See* Chapter 1.

Leaving aside these jurisdictional limits, which rarely affect a case in the U.S., the statute effectively reads: "Every agreement in restraint of trade or commerce is declared to be illegal." The word "every" was the subject of much hand-wringing in the early days of the interpretation of the Sherman Act, with the ultimate judicial resolution being that the word "every" could not be taken literally, otherwise every contract or partnership would be unlawful. Thus, the traditional view was that the statute must instead mean to condemn only "unreasonable" restraints of trade, with an unreasonable restraint being one whose anticompetitive effects outweigh its procompetitive ones.[1] But there is an alternative textual interpretation that could likewise avoid functional irrationality without committing the linguistic violence of reading a new word into the statute and effectively reading the word "every" out. Under this alternative, one could instead say that the word "restraint" inherently suggests some *net* restraint of trade, for trade could hardly be said to be restrained if it were increased. Thus, if a challenged agreement on balance increases competition and trade output, it is not really in restraint of trade at all.[2] Whatever interpretive path one chooses, the fact remains that today Sherman Act § 1 is in effect read to adopt the general standard that "Every agreement whose anticompetitive effects on trade outweigh its procompetitive effects is illegal."

---

1 *See* Standard Oil Co. v. United States, 221 U.S. 1, 59–68 (1911); Chicago Board of Trade v. United States, 246 U.S. 231, 238 (1918); United States v. Topco Associates, 405 U.S. 596, 606–07 (1972); National Soc'y of Prof'l Eng'rs v. United States, 435 U.S. 679, 687–90 (1978); Arizona v. Maricopa County Med. Soc'y, 457 U.S. 332, 342–43 (1982); NCAA v. Board of Regents, 468 U.S. 85, 98, 103 (1984); Texaco Inc. v. Dagher, 547 U.S. 1, 5 (2006).

2 Indeed, language in the old *Standard Oil* case that created the rule of reason does in fact focus on whether an agreement constitutes a "restraint of trade" within the meaning of the statute. 221 U.S. at 63–64.

But while this is the general standard, the U.S. Supreme Court has also held that certain agreements are so likely to be anticompetitive, and so unlikely to have procompetitive effects, that they are condemned "per se," which means without any case-by-case inquiry into their net effect.[3] The following horizontal agreements have been held to be per se illegal: price-fixing,[4] market divisions,[5] output restraints,[6] and boycotts.[7] When an agreement is per se illegal, the Court says it will consider neither any procompetitive justifications the defendant might offer nor whether anticompetitive effects actually occurred.[8]

If a per se rule does not apply, then general "rule of reason" review applies. Under the rule of reason, courts consider on a case by case basis whether the agreement has a plausible procompetitive justification. If it does, then the plaintiff must prove an anticompetitive effect either through direct proof or by showing market power that can be used to infer the anticompetitive effect. If the anticompetitive effect is shown, the defendant must prove the procompetitive justification empirically and that the challenged restraint is the least restrictive means of accomplishing that procompetitive virtue. If that is proven, the court must determine whether the anticompetitive effects outweigh the procompetitive effects.

This way of framing the distinction between per se and rule of reason scrutiny has, however, been eroded by two doctrinal developments. First, the Supreme Court has stated that, even if a horizontal agreement "literally" constitutes price-fixing, an output restraint or a boycott, it will not be deemed to fall within such per se illegal categories when a procompetitive justification in fact exists for the agreement in question.[9] Second, the Court has held that, even if a restraint falls within the rule of reason, it will be condemned summarily as a "naked" restraint if no procompetitive justification is offered for it.[10] This has led some to conclude that the distinction is incoherent. On this view, the rule of reason is really being applied in all cases; it is just that the rule can be

---

[3] Northern Pacific R. Co. v. United States, 356 U.S. 1, 5 (1958); *Topco*, 405 U.S. at 607; *Maricopa*, 457 U.S. at 344–45.

[4] United States v. Socony-Vacuum Oil Co., 310 U.S. 150, 218 (1940); *Northern Pacific*, 356 U.S. at 5; *Maricopa*, 457 U.S. at 345–48; *Dagher*, 547 U.S. at 5.

[5] *Northern Pacific*, 356 U.S. at 5; Palmer v. BRG, 498 U.S. 46 (1990); *Topco*, 405 U.S. at 608–09.

[6] *NCAA*, 468 U.S. at 99–101.

[7] FTC v. Superior Court Trial Lawyers Association, 493 U.S. 411 (1990); Klor's Inc. v. Broadway-Hale Stores, Inc., 359 U.S. 207 (1959); Fashion Originators' Guild of Am. v. FTC, 312 U.S. 457 (1941); *Northern Pacific*, 356 U.S. at 5.

[8] *See Socony-Vacuum*, 310 U.S. at 218, 226 n.59; *Maricopa*, 457 U.S. at 345, 351.

[9] *NCAA*, 468 U.S. at 101–04; Broadcast Music, Inc. v. CBS, 441 U.S. 1, 8–9, 13, 20–21 (1979); Northwest Wholesale Stationers v. Pacific Stationery & Printing, 472 U.S. 284, 294–98 (1985). And even when it has said the per se rule applies and precludes consideration of procompetitive justifications, it has nonetheless gone ahead to consider and reject those justifications. *See Maricopa*, 457 U.S. at 351–54.

[10] FTC v. Indiana Federation of Dentists, 476 U.S. 447, 459 (1986); *NCAA*, 468 U.S. at 109–110; *Professional Engineers*, 435 U.S. at 693–95.

applied quite quickly in cases where no plausible procompetitive justification has been offered. Others have more charitably concluded that what the cases actually stand for is that certain defenses are excluded, such as: (a) the claim that the defendants tried to fix prices or restrict output but lacked the market power to have the anticompetitive effect; or (b) the claim that the fixed prices were reasonable because market prices would be too high or too low.[11]

An alternative way that might offer a clearer way of understanding the pattern of case results is to keep in mind a distinction between horizontal agreements among unrelated firms and those among firms that are in a productive business relationship. When firms are in some business relationship where their joint efforts produce some tangible product or service, then it makes sense to apply some rule of reason to see whether the restraint benefits their ability to produce in a way that outweighs any anticompetitive costs. Indeed, it is hard to see how it could be otherwise since the Supreme Court was driven to adopt the rule of reason precisely to avoid condemning every partnership that might be formed, and yet every partnership could be said to result in the partners fixing prices, restraining output, and boycotting others when the partnership makes decisions about what price, output, suppliers and customers to choose.

In contrast, when firms are unrelated by any productive business collaboration, then the per se rules do have bite, for it is only in cases involving productive joint ventures that the Court has stated that procompetitive justifications can take a restraint out of per se rules. The Court will not listen to claims by unrelated horizontal businesses that their restraints have procompetitive justifications, even though such justifications might exist and suggest market failures that would merit government regulation of price or output. Because restraints among unrelated firms do not involve joint business efforts but rather effective market regulation, disinterested and politically accountable government agencies might be thought per se better suited than financially interested and unaccountable businesses to determine whether the regulation is merited. As we shall see, the pattern of Supreme Court cases largely tracks the above distinction.

The distinction between agreements between productively related and unrelated rivals suggests two sorts of limitations. First, sometimes a productive business collaboration might exist, but the price-fixing agreement in question is unrelated to its advancement, or the productive business collaboration is nothing more than a fig leaf to avoid per se scrutiny. In such cases, the courts generally apply the per se rule, notwithstanding the technical existence of a productive business collaboration.[12] Second, professionals have traditionally engaged in self-

---

[11] *See* Krattenmaker, *Per se Violations in Antitrust Law,* 77 GEO. L.J. 165 (1988).

[12] *See Palmer,* 498 U.S. 46 (fig leaf); *Maricopa,* 457 U.S. at 356–57 (restraint unrelated to advancing procompetitive purposes of joint venture). Similarly, in *Dagher*, the Court rejected

regulation designed to correct the sort of market failures that government agencies normally regulate in nonprofessional business markets. Consistent with this, courts have been less willing to per se condemn professional efforts to self-regulate through horizontal agreements that are not ancillary to any productive business collaboration, but rather have allowed such efforts subject to rule-of-reason review.[13]

Sherman Act § 2 is also relevant. It provides:

Sherman Act § 2, 15 U.S.C. § 2

> Every person who shall monopolize, or attempt to monopolize, or combine or conspire with any other person or persons, to monopolize any part of the trade or commerce among the several States, or with foreign nations, shall be deemed guilty of a felony. . . .

The statute is generally targeted at unilateral conduct and thus does not require proof of an agreement, other than for proving a conspiracy to monopolize. However, agreements or combinations to form a corporation or cartel that exercises monopoly power have long been held to constitute monopolization in violation of § 2 as well as an agreement in restraint of trade that violates § 1.[14] Because any agreement that creates monopoly power would surely also be an agreement in restraint of trade, this adds little to the law on horizontal agreements, but will prove relevant (in Chapter 3) to assessing unsuccessful attempts to form cartel agreements. Further, the provision on conspiracies to monopolize may have different elements than those for agreements in restraint of trade. *See* Chapter 3.

Finally, Federal Trade Commission Act § 5 provides:

Federal Trade Commission Act § 5, 15 U.S.C. § 45

> "Unfair methods of competition in or affecting commerce . . . are hereby declared unlawful."

Although this general prohibition of unfair methods of competition clearly extends beyond horizontal agreements, it does also authorize the FTC to bring actions against any anticompetitive horizontal agreements.

---

application of the per se rule both because there the joint venture was not a "sham," 547 U.S. at 6.n.1, and the challenged agreement involved a core activity of the joint venture rather than one unrelated to the venture, *id.* at 6–8.

[13] *See* California Dental Ass'n v. FTC, 526 U.S. 756 (1999).

[14] *See, e.g.*, United States v. Grinnell Corp., 384 U.S. 563, 576 (1966); American Tobacco Co. v. United States, 328 U.S. 781, 783–84, 808–09, 813–14 (1946); Standard Oil Co. v. United States, 221 U.S. 1, 70–75 (1911); Lorain Journal Co. v. United States, 342 U.S. 143 (1951).

B. HORIZONTAL PRICE-FIXING

United States v. Trenton Potteries

273 U.S. 392 (1927).

■ MR. JUSTICE STONE delivered the opinion of the Court.

Respondents, twenty individuals and twenty-three corporations, were convicted . . . of violating the Sherman Anti-Trust Law. . . . The indictment . . . charged a combination to fix and maintain uniform prices for the sale of sanitary pottery. . . . On appeal, the court of appeals for the second circuit reversed the judgment of conviction on both counts on the ground that there were errors in the conduct of the trial. . . .

Respondents, engaged in the manufacture or distribution of 82 per cent. of the vitreous pottery fixtures produced in the United States for use in bathrooms and lavatories, were members of a trade organization known as the Sanitary Potters' Association. . . . There is no contention here that the verdict was not supported by sufficient evidence that respondents, controlling some 82 per cent. of the business of manufacturing and distributing in the United States vitreous pottery of the type described, combined to fix prices and to limit sales in interstate commerce to jobbers. . . .

The trial court charged, in submitting the case to the jury, that if it found the agreements or combination complained of, it might return a verdict of guilty without regard to the reasonableness of the prices fixed, or the good intentions of the combining units, whether prices were actually lowered or raised or whether sales were restricted . . . since [the] agreements of themselves were unreasonable restraints. . . . In particular the court refused the request to charge the following: "The essence of the law is injury to the public. It is not every restraint of competition and not every restraint of trade that works an injury to the public; it is only an undue and unreasonable restraint of trade that has such an effect and is deemed to be unlawful." . . . [T]he trial judge plainly and variously charged the jury that the combinations alleged in the indictment, if found, were violations of the statute as a matter of law, saying: ". . . the law is clear that an agreement on the part of the members of a combination controlling a substantial part of an industry, upon the prices which the members are to charge for their commodity, is in itself an undue and unreasonable restraint of trade and commerce; . . ." . . .

The question therefore to be considered here is whether the trial judge correctly withdrew from the jury the consideration of the reasonableness of the particular restraints charged.

That only those restraints upon interstate commerce which are unreasonable are prohibited by the Sherman Law was the rule laid down by the opinions of this Court in the *Standard Oil* and *Tobacco* cases. But it does not follow that agreements to fix or maintain prices are reasonable restraints and therefore permitted by the statute, merely because the prices themselves are reasonable. Reasonableness is not a concept of definite and unchanging content. Its meaning necessarily varies in the different fields of the law, because it is used as a convenient summary of the dominant considerations which control in the application of legal doctrines. Our view of what is a reasonable restraint of commerce is controlled by the recognized purpose of the Sherman Law itself. Whether this type of restraint is reasonable or not must be judged in part at least in the light of its effect on competition, for whatever difference of opinion there may be among economists as to the social and economic desirability of an unrestrained competitive system, it cannot be doubted that the Sherman Law and the judicial decisions interpreting it are based upon the assumption that the public interest is best protected from the evils of monopoly and price control by the maintenance of competition.

The aim and result of every price-fixing agreement, if effective, is the elimination of one form of competition. The power to fix prices, whether reasonably exercised or not, involves power to control the market and to fix arbitrary and unreasonable prices. The reasonable price fixed today may through economic and business changes become the unreasonable price of tomorrow. Once established, it may be maintained unchanged because of the absence of competition secured by the agreement for a price reasonable when fixed. Agreements which create such potential power may well be held to be in themselves unreasonable or unlawful restraints, without the necessity of minute inquiry whether a particular price is reasonable or unreasonable as fixed and without placing on the government in enforcing the Sherman Law the burden of ascertaining from day to day whether it has become unreasonable through the mere variation of economic conditions. Moreover, in the absence of express legislation requiring it, we should hesitate to adopt a construction making the difference between legal and illegal conduct in the field of business relations depend upon so uncertain a test as whether prices are reasonable—a determination which can be satisfactorily made only after a complete survey of our economic organization and a choice between rival philosophies. . . .

[U]niform price-fixing by those controlling in any substantial manner a trade or business in interstate commerce is prohibited by the Sherman Law, despite the reasonableness of the particular prices agreed upon. . . .

The charge of the trial court, viewed as a whole, fairly submitted to the jury the question whether a price-fixing agreement as described in the first count was entered into by the respondents. Whether the prices actually agreed upon were reasonable or unreasonable was immaterial. . . .

NOTES AND QUESTIONS ON *TRENTON POTTERIES*

1. ***Why no reasonableness defense?*** Although the Sherman Act only prohibits unreasonable restraints of trade, the Court held in *Trenton Potteries* that defendants could not introduce evidence that the prices they fixed were reasonable. Does this holding make sense?

a. ***Fixed prices always unreasonable on principle?*** In places, the court suggests that any price fixed by horizontal agreement is unreasonable on principle, so that it makes no sense to allow a reasonableness defense for price-fixing. Do judges and juries have any principled criteria for assessing reasonableness other than whether prices were set by competition? They could try to compare prices to marginal costs, but that may be the wrong measure, for reasons elaborated in Chapter 3B. Nor do the antitrust laws demand the substantive outcome of pricing at marginal cost. They demand prices set by a competitive process, which may or may not equal marginal cost.

b. ***Reasonable price defense too administratively difficult?*** The court also indicates that even if principled criteria existed for judging the reasonableness of prices, it would be administratively too difficult for courts to apply it. Why so? Part of the problem is that economic facts like marginal costs are notoriously hard to assess. Further, even if one can assess them accurately, market conditions would be continually changing in ways judges and juries could not monitor in episodic litigations that each take many years to resolve. Adopting a reasonableness standard would also reduce the incentives of the government and private actors to bring antitrust suits because of the increased costs of litigation and the increased uncertainty of winning. Further, such an uncertain rule would adversely affect firms' ability to ascertain and comply with the law because they would have difficulty predicting what judges and juries might conclude was a reasonable price.

c. ***Avoiding the sea of doubt.*** For these reasons of principle and practicality, antitrust courts have generally refused to "set sail on a sea of doubt" of assuming the power to decide that some naked restraints on price competition are reasonable. United States v. Addyston Pipe & Steel Co., 85 F. 271, 283–284 (CA6 1898). Do you think courts are right to take this view?

2. ***Why isn't the lack of any effect a defense?*** The court also refused to any inquiry into "whether prices were actually lowered or raised." Even if defendants should not be allowed the defense that their fixed prices were reasonable, why shouldn't defendants be able to introduce the defense that their restraint had no effect on prices at all? Consider the following reasoning.

Normally the reason to allow an exception to a rule is to prevent the rule from discouraging desirable conduct, which would raise an "overdeterrence" problem because it would mean the law has gone beyond deterring good conduct to deter desirable conduct. Here, however, allowing an ineffective-cartel defense would not prevent the overdeterrence of any desirable conduct because there is nothing procompetitive about a price-fixing cartel, even if it is ineffective. There is thus no social gain from allowing such a defense.

To be sure, if courts could perfectly and costlessly ascertain whether price-fixing agreements had an effect, there would also be no social loss from allowing an ineffectiveness defense. But we do not live in such a world. In reality, courts will sometimes erroneously conclude a cartel had no effect even though it really did, and adjudicating whether a cartel has an effect is costly. Thus, allowing an ineffectiveness defense would increase the underdeterrence of anticompetitive conduct, which is socially harmful.

Accordingly, allowing this defense would not reduce the overdeterrence of procompetitive conduct (and thus would produce no social gain), but would increase the underdeterrence of anticompetitive conduct (and thus produce a social loss). This one-sided tradeoff helps explain why courts have adopted such a categorical rule of condemnation.

One could also infer from the act of price fixing that the defendants must have had the purpose of altering market prices and thought they had the power to have that effect. Firms are usually better placed to decide whether they have the power to have such an effect than judges and juries.

Do you agree that the lack of any effect should not be a defense to price-fixing?

3. ***Why no defense of low market share?*** The decision in *Trenton Potteries* is limited to "price-fixing by those controlling in any substantial manner a trade or business", which means those with a substantial market share. But later cases like United States v. Socony-Vacuum Oil Co., 310 U.S. 150 (1940), make clear that the per se rule against horizontal price-fixing applies no matter what market share the defendants have. Why should price-fixing be condemned even if the defendants comprise a trivial market share, like say 1%?

Part of the problem is that a low market share defense could create underdeterrence when market definition is assessed incorrectly or is too costly to prove. The defendants may argue their market share is 1% based on a broad market definition, but perhaps the true market definition is more narrow, in which case their market share is greater. Further, as we shall see in Chapter 2, market share is an imperfect proxy for a market power to raise prices, so a low market share may not mean an inability to raise prices. Allowing the low-market share defense could thus lead to underdeterrence whenever market definition is assessed incorrectly or is costly to determine or if a low market share mistakenly indicates a lack of power to raise prices.

A low-market share defense would also raises the question of just how low the share threshold should be. If the law allowed the defense when market shares were only 1%, should it also allow it at 10%? 20%? 30%? Whatever line we drew, firms that are close to the line might have market power, resulting in increased underdeterrence problems.

In contrast, allowing a low-market share defense would not produce any reduction in overdeterrence because, even if a low market share made a cartel ineffective, it would not be procompetitive. Thus, allowing a low-market share defense would increase underdeterrence without any offsetting reduction in overdeterrence.

Broadcast Music, Inc. (BMI) v. Columbia Broadcasting System

441 U.S. 1 (1979).

■ MR. JUSTICE WHITE delivered the opinion of the Court.

This case involves an action under the antitrust and copyright laws brought by respondent Columbia Broadcasting System, Inc. (CBS), against petitioners, American Society of Composers, Authors and Publishers (ASCAP) and Broadcast Music, Inc. (BMI), and their members and affiliates. The basic question presented is whether the issuance by ASCAP and BMI to CBS of blanket licenses to copyrighted musical compositions at fees negotiated by them is price fixing *per se* unlawful under the antitrust laws.

I

CBS operates one of three national commercial television networks, supplying programs to approximately 200 affiliated stations and telecasting approximately 7,500 network programs per year. Many, but not all, of these programs make use of copyrighted music recorded on the soundtrack. CBS also owns television and radio stations in various cities. . . .

Since 1897, the copyright laws have vested in the owner of a copyrighted musical composition the exclusive right to perform the work publicly for profit, but the legal right is not self-enforcing. In 1914, Victor Herbert and a handful of other composers organized ASCAP because those who performed copyrighted music for profit were so numerous and widespread, and most performances so fleeting, that as a practical matter it was impossible for the many individual copyright owners to negotiate with and license the users and to detect unauthorized uses. . . . As ASCAP operates today, its 22,000 members grant it nonexclusive rights to license nondramatic performances of their works, and ASCAP issues licenses and distributes royalties to copyright owners in accordance with a schedule reflecting the nature and amount of the use of their music and other factors.

BMI, a nonprofit corporation owned by members of the broadcasting industry,[4] was organized in 1939, is affiliated with or represents some 10,000 publishing companies and 20,000 authors and composers, and operates in much the same manner as ASCAP. Almost every domestic copyrighted composition is in the repertory either of ASCAP, with a total of three million compositions, or of BMI, with one million.

Both organizations operate primarily through blanket licenses, which give the licensees the right to perform any and all of the compositions owned by the members or affiliates as often as the licensees desire for a stated term. Fees for blanket licenses are ordinarily a

---

[4] CBS was a leader of the broadcasters who formed BMI, but it disposed of all of its interest in the corporation in 1959.

percentage of total revenues or a flat dollar amount, and do not directly depend on the amount or type of music used. Radio and television broadcasters are the largest users of music, and almost all of them hold blanket licenses from both ASCAP and BMI. Until this litigation, CBS held blanket licenses from both organizations for its television network on a continuous basis since the late 1940's and had never attempted to secure any other form of license from either ASCAP[5] or any of its members.

... After an 8-week trial, ... the [trial] court dismissed the complaint, rejecting again the claim that the blanket license was price fixing and a *per se* violation of § 1 of the Sherman Act, and holding that since direct negotiation with individual copyright owners is available and feasible there is no undue restraint of trade, illegal tying, misuse of copyrights, or monopolization. ... [T]he Court of Appeals held that the blanket license issued to television networks was a form of price fixing illegal *per se* under the Sherman Act. This conclusion, without more, settled the issue of liability under the Sherman Act, ... and required reversal of the District Court's judgment, as well as a remand to consider the appropriate remedy. ... Because we disagree with the Court of Appeals' conclusions with respect to the *per se* illegality of the blanket license, we reverse. ...

II

In construing and applying the Sherman Act's ban against contracts, conspiracies, and combinations in restraint of trade, the Court has held that certain agreements or practices are so "plainly anticompetitive," and so often "lack ... any redeeming virtue," that they are conclusively presumed illegal without further examination under the rule of reason generally applied in Sherman Act cases. This *per se* rule is a valid and useful tool of antitrust policy and enforcement.[11] And agreements among competitors to fix prices on their individual goods or services are among those concerted activities that the Court has held to be within the *per se* category. But easy labels do not always supply ready answers.

A

To the Court of Appeals and CBS, the blanket license involves "price fixing" in the literal sense: the composers and publishing houses have joined together into an organization that sets its price for the blanket license it sells.[13] But this is not a question simply of determining whether

---

[5] Unless the context indicates otherwise, references to ASCAP alone in this opinion usually apply to BMI as well.

[11] "This principle of *per se* unreasonableness not only makes the type of restraints which are proscribed by the Sherman Act more certain to the benefit of everyone concerned, but it also avoids the necessity for an incredibly complicated and prolonged economic investigation into the entire history of the industry involved, as well as related industries, in an effort to determine at large whether a particular restraint has been unreasonable—an inquiry so often wholly fruitless when undertaken." *Northern Pac. R. Co. v. United States,* 356 U.S. 1, 5 (1958).

[13] CBS also complains that it pays a flat fee regardless of the amount of use it makes of ASCAP compositions and even though many of its programs contain little or no music. We are

two or more potential competitors have literally "fixed" a "price." As generally used in the antitrust field, "price fixing" is a shorthand way of describing certain categories of business behavior to which the *per se* rule has been held applicable. The Court of Appeals' literal approach does not alone establish that this particular practice is one of those types or that it is "plainly anticompetitive" and very likely without "redeeming virtue." Literalness is overly simplistic and often overbroad. When two partners set the price of their goods or services they are literally "price fixing," but they are not *per se* in violation of the Sherman Act. *See United States v. Addyston Pipe & Steel Co.,* 85 F. 271, 280 (CA6 1898), aff'd, 175 U.S. 211 (1899). Thus, it is necessary to characterize the challenged conduct as falling within or without that category of behavior to which we apply the label "*per se* price fixing." That will often, but not always, be a simple matter.

Consequently, . . . "[i]t is only after considerable experience with certain business relationships that courts classify them as *per se* violations. . . ." We have never examined a practice like this one before; indeed, the Court of Appeals recognized that "[i]n dealing with performing rights in the music industry we confront conditions both in copyright law and in antitrust law which are *sui generis.*" And though there has been rather intensive antitrust scrutiny of ASCAP and its blanket licenses, that experience hardly counsels that we should outlaw the blanket license as a *per se* restraint of trade.

B

. . . In separate complaints in 1941, the United States charged that the blanket license, which was then the only license offered by ASCAP and BMI, was an illegal restraint of trade. . . . The case was settled by a consent decree that imposed tight restrictions on ASCAP's operations. . . . Under the amended decree, which still substantially controls the activities of ASCAP, members may grant ASCAP only nonexclusive rights to license their works for public performance. Members, therefore, retain the rights individually to license public performances, along with the rights to license the use of their compositions for other purposes.[15] ASCAP itself is forbidden to grant any license to perform one or more specified compositions in the ASCAP repertory unless both the user and the owner have requested it in writing to do so. ASCAP is required to grant to any user making written

unable to see how that alone could make out an antitrust violation or misuse of copyrights: "Sound business judgment could indicate that such payment represents the most convenient method of fixing the business value of the privileges granted by the licensing agreement. . . . Petitioner cannot complain because it must pay royalties whether it uses Hazeltine patents or not. What it acquired by the agreement into which it entered was the privilege to use any or all of the patents and developments as it desired to use them." *Automatic Radio Mfg. Co. v. Hazeltine Research, Inc.,* 339 U.S. 827, 834 (1950).

[15] [Editor's Note: Although members retained this right to individually license the use of their songs, members of ASCAP or BMI could not license their songs to another performance rights organization. *See* United States v. Broadcast Music, Inc. and RKO General, Inc., 1966 Trade Cas. (CCH) ¶ 71,141, at Consent Decree § VI.A.]

application a nonexclusive license to perform all ASCAP compositions either for a period of time or on a per-program basis. ASCAP may not insist on the blanket license, and the fee for the per-program license, which is to be based on the revenues for the program on which ASCAP music is played, must offer the applicant a genuine economic choice between the per-program license and the more common blanket license. If ASCAP and a putative licensee are unable to agree on a fee within 60 days, the applicant may apply to the District Court for a determination of a reasonable fee, with ASCAP having the burden of proving reasonableness.

The 1950 decree, as amended from time to time, continues in effect, and the blanket license continues to be the primary instrument through which ASCAP conducts its business under the decree. The courts have twice construed the decree not to require ASCAP to issue licenses for selected portions of its repertory. It also remains true that the decree guarantees the legal availability of direct licensing of performance rights by ASCAP members; and the District Court found, and in this respect the Court of Appeals agreed, that there are no practical impediments preventing direct dealing by the television networks if they so desire. Historically, they have not done so. Since 1946, CBS and other television networks have taken blanket licenses from ASCAP and BMI. It was not until this suit arose that the CBS network demanded any other kind of license.

Of course, a consent judgment, even one entered at the behest of the Antitrust Division, does not immunize the defendant from liability for actions, including those contemplated by the decree, that violate the rights of nonparties. . . . But it cannot be ignored that the Federal Executive and Judiciary have carefully scrutinized ASCAP and the challenged conduct, have imposed restrictions on various of ASCAP's practices, and, by the terms of the decree, stand ready to provide further consideration, supervision, and perhaps invalidation of asserted anticompetitive practices. In these circumstances, we have a unique indicator that the challenged practice may have redeeming competitive virtues and that the search for those values is not almost sure to be in vain.[24] Thus, although CBS is not bound by the Antitrust Division's actions, the decree is a fact of economic and legal life in this industry, and the Court of Appeals should not have ignored it completely in analyzing the practice. That fact alone might not remove a naked price-fixing scheme from the ambit of the *per se* rule, but, as discussed *infra,* Part III, here we are uncertain whether the practice on its face has the effect, or could have been spurred by the purpose, of restraining competition among the individual composers. . . .

---

[24] Moreover, unthinking application of the *per se* rule might upset the balancing of economic power and of procompetitive and anticompetitive effect presumably worked out in the decree.

Finally, we note that Congress itself, in the new Copyright Act, has chosen to employ the blanket license and similar practices. Congress created a compulsory blanket license for secondary transmissions by cable television systems . . . 17 U.S.C. App. § 111(d)(5)(A). And the newly created compulsory license for the use of copyrighted compositions in jukeboxes is also a blanket license, which is payable to the performing-rights societies such as ASCAP unless an individual copyright holder can prove his entitlement to a share. § 116(c)(4). Moreover, in requiring noncommercial broadcasters to pay for their use of copyrighted music, Congress again provided that "[n]otwithstanding any provision of the antitrust laws" copyright owners "may designate common agents to negotiate, agree to, pay, or receive payments." § 118(b). Though these provisions are not directly controlling, they do reflect an opinion that the blanket license, and ASCAP, are economically beneficial in at least some circumstances. . . .

III

Of course, we are no more bound than is CBS by the views of the Department of Justice, the results in the prior lower court cases, or the opinions of various experts about the merits of the blanket license. But while we must independently examine this practice, all those factors should caution us against too easily finding blanket licensing subject to *per se* invalidation.

A

As a preliminary matter, we are mindful that the Court of Appeals' holding would appear to be quite difficult to contain. If, as the court held, there is a *per se* antitrust violation whenever ASCAP issues a blanket license to a television network for a single fee, why would it not also be automatically illegal for ASCAP to negotiate and issue blanket licenses to individual radio or television stations or to other users who perform copyrighted music for profit? Likewise, if the present network licenses issued through ASCAP on behalf of its members are *per se* violations, why would it not be equally illegal for the members to authorize ASCAP to issue licenses establishing various categories of uses that a network might have for copyrighted music and setting a standard fee for each described use?

Although the Court of Appeals apparently thought the blanket license could be saved in some or even many applications, it seems to us that the *per se* rule does not accommodate itself to such flexibility and that the observations of the Court of Appeals with respect to remedy tend to impeach the *per se* basis for the holding of liability.[27]

---

[27] The Court of Appeals would apparently not outlaw the blanket license across the board but would permit it in various circumstances where it is deemed necessary or sufficiently desirable. It did not even enjoin blanket licensing with the television networks, the relief it realized would normally follow a finding of *per se* illegality of the license in that context. Instead, as requested by CBS, it remanded to the District Court to require ASCAP to offer in addition to blanket licensing some competitive form of per-use licensing. But per-use licensing by ASCAP,

CBS would prefer that ASCAP be authorized, indeed directed, to make all its compositions available at standard per-use rates within negotiated categories of use. But if this in itself or in conjunction with blanket licensing constitutes illegal price fixing by copyright owners, CBS urges that an injunction issue forbidding ASCAP to issue any blanket license or to negotiate any fee except on behalf of an individual member for the use of his own copyrighted work or works. Thus, we are called upon to determine that blanket licensing is unlawful across the board. We are quite sure, however, that the *per se* rule does not require any such holding.

B

In the first place, the line of commerce allegedly being restrained, the performing rights to copyrighted music, exists at all only because of the copyright laws. Those who would use copyrighted music in public performances must secure consent from the copyright owner or be liable at least for the statutory damages for each infringement and, if the conduct is willful and for the purpose of financial gain, to criminal penalties. . . . Although the copyright laws confer no rights on copyright owners to fix prices among themselves or otherwise to violate the antitrust laws, we would not expect that any market arrangements reasonably necessary to effectuate the rights that are granted would be deemed a *per se* violation of the Sherman Act. Otherwise, the commerce anticipated by the Copyright Act and protected against restraint by the Sherman Act would not exist at all or would exist only as a pale reminder of what Congress envisioned.[32]

C

More generally, in characterizing this conduct under the *per se* rule,[33] our inquiry must focus on whether the effect and, here because it tends to show effect, the purpose of the practice are to threaten the proper operation of our predominantly free-market economy—that is, whether the practice facially appears to be one that would always or almost

---

as recognized in the consent decrees, might be even more susceptible to the *per se* rule than blanket licensing.

The rationale for this unusual relief in a *per se* case was that "[t]he blanket license is not simply a 'naked restraint' ineluctably doomed to extinction." To the contrary, the Court of Appeals found that the blanket license might well "serve a market need" for some. This, it seems to us, is not the *per se* approach, which does not yield so readily to circumstances, but in effect is a rather bobtailed application of the rule of reason, bobtailed in the sense that it is unaccompanied by the necessary analysis demonstrating why the particular licensing system is an undue competitive restraint.

[32] Because a musical composition can be "consumed" by many different people at the same time and without the creator's knowledge, the "owner" has no real way to demand reimbursement for the use of his property except through the copyright laws *and* an effective way to enforce those legal rights. It takes an organization of rather large size to monitor most or all uses and to deal with users on behalf of the composers. Moreover, it is inefficient to have too many such organizations duplicating each other's monitoring of use.

[33] The scrutiny occasionally required must not merely subsume the burdensome analysis required under the rule of reason, or else we should apply the rule of reason from the start. That is why the *per se* rule is not employed until after considerable experience with the type of challenged restraint.

always tend to restrict competition and decrease output, and in what portion of the market, or instead one designed to "increase economic efficiency and render markets more, rather than less, competitive."

The blanket license, as we see it, is not a "naked restrain[t] of trade with no purpose except stifling of competition," but rather accompanies the integration of sales, monitoring, and enforcement against unauthorized copyright use.... ASCAP and the blanket license developed together out of the practical situation in the marketplace: thousands of users, thousands of copyright owners, and millions of compositions. Most users want unplanned, rapid, and indemnified access to any and all of the repertory of compositions, and the owners want a reliable method of collecting for the use of their copyrights. Individual sales transactions in this industry are quite expensive, as would be individual monitoring and enforcement, especially in light of the resources of single composers. Indeed, as both the Court of Appeals and CBS recognize, the costs are prohibitive for licenses with individual radio stations, nightclubs, and restaurants, and it was in that milieu that the blanket license arose.

A middleman with a blanket license was an obvious necessity if the thousands of individual negotiations, a virtual impossibility, were to be avoided. Also, individual fees for the use of individual compositions would presuppose an intricate schedule of fees and uses, as well as a difficult and expensive reporting problem for the user and policing task for the copyright owner. Historically, the market for public-performance rights organized itself largely around the single-fee blanket license, which gave unlimited access to the repertory and reliable protection against infringement. When ASCAP's major and user-created competitor, BMI, came on the scene, it also turned to the blanket license.

With the advent of radio and television networks, market conditions changed, and the necessity for and advantages of a blanket license for those users may be far less obvious than is the case when the potential users are individual television or radio stations, or the thousands of other individuals and organizations performing copyrighted compositions in public.[34] But even for television network licenses, ASCAP reduces costs absolutely by creating a blanket license that is sold only a few, instead of thousands, of times, and that obviates the need for closely monitoring the networks to see that they do not use more than they pay for.[36] ASCAP also provides the necessary resources for blanket sales and enforcement, resources unavailable to the vast majority of composers and publishing houses. Moreover, a bulk license of some type is a necessary consequence of the integration necessary to achieve these efficiencies, and a necessary consequence of an aggregate license is that its price must be established.

---

[34] And of course changes brought about by new technology or new marketing techniques might also undercut the justification for the practice.

[36] To operate its system for distributing the license revenues to its members, ASCAP relies primarily on the networks' records of which compositions are used.

D

This substantial lowering of costs, which is of course potentially beneficial to both sellers and buyers, differentiates the blanket license from individual use licenses. The blanket license is composed of the individual compositions plus the aggregating service. Here, the whole is truly greater than the sum of its parts; it is, to some extent, a different product. The blanket license has certain unique characteristics: It allows the licensee immediate use of covered compositions, without the delay of prior individual negotiations[37] and great flexibility in the choice of musical material. Many consumers clearly prefer the characteristics and cost advantages of this marketable package, and even small-performing rights societies that have occasionally arisen to compete with ASCAP and BMI have offered blanket licenses.[39] Thus, to the extent the blanket license is a different product, ASCAP is not really a joint sales agency offering the individual goods of many sellers, but is a separate seller offering its blanket license, of which the individual compositions are raw material.[40] ASCAP, in short, made a market in which individual composers are inherently unable to compete fully effectively.

E

Finally, we have some doubt—enough to counsel against application of the *per se* rule—about the extent to which this practice threatens the "central nervous system of the economy," *United States v. Socony-Vacuum Oil Co.*, 310 U.S. 150, 226 n. 59 (1940), that is, competitive pricing as the free market's means of allocating resources. Not all arrangements among actual or potential competitors that have an impact on price are *per se* violations of the Sherman Act or even unreasonable restraints. Mergers among competitors eliminate competition, including price competition, but they are not *per se* illegal, and many of them withstand attack under any existing antitrust standard. Joint ventures and other cooperative arrangements are also not usually unlawful, at least not as price-fixing schemes, where the agreement on price is necessary to market the product at all.

---

[37] *See* Timberg, The Antitrust Aspects of Merchandising Modern Music: The ASCAP Consent Judgment of 1950, 19 Law & Contemp.Prob. 294, 297 (1954) ("The disk-jockey's itchy fingers and the bandleader's restive baton, it is said, cannot wait for contracts to be drawn with ASCAP's individual publisher members, much less for the formal acquiescence of a characteristically unavailable composer or author"). Significantly, ASCAP deals only with nondramatic performance rights. Because of their nature, dramatic rights, such as for musicals, can be negotiated individually and well in advance of the time of performance. The same is true of various other rights, such as sheet music, recording, and synchronization, which are licensed on an individual basis.

[39] *See* also Garner, *United States v. ASCAP*: The Licensing Provisions of the Amended Final Judgment of 1950, 23 Bull.Copyright Soc. 119, 149 (1975) ("no performing rights are licensed on other than a blanket basis in any nation in the world").

[40] Moreover, because of the nature of the product—a composition can be simultaneously "consumed" by many users—composers have numerous markets and numerous incentives to produce, so the blanket license is unlikely to cause decreased output, one of the normal undesirable effects of a cartel. And since popular songs get an increased share of ASCAP's revenue distributions, composers compete even within the blanket license in terms of productivity and consumer satisfaction.

Here, the blanket-license fee is not set by competition among individual copyright owners, and it is a fee for the use of any of the compositions covered by the license. But the blanket license cannot be wholly equated with a simple horizontal arrangement among competitors. ASCAP does set the price for its blanket license, but that license is quite different from anything any individual owner could issue. The individual composers and authors have neither agreed not to sell individually in any other market nor use the blanket license to mask price fixing in such other markets. Moreover, the substantial restraints placed on ASCAP and its members by the consent decree must not be ignored. The District Court found that there was no legal, practical, or conspiratorial impediment to CBS's obtaining individual licenses; CBS, in short, had a real choice.

With this background in mind, which plainly enough indicates that over the years, and in the face of available alternatives, the blanket license has provided an acceptable mechanism for at least a large part of the market for the performing rights to copyrighted musical compositions, we cannot agree that it should automatically be declared illegal in all of its many manifestations. Rather, when attacked, it should be subjected to a more discriminating examination under the rule of reason. It may not ultimately survive that attack, but that is not the issue before us today. . . .

NOTES AND QUESTIONS ON *BMI*

1. ***Does this case really involve horizontal price fixing?*** The Supreme Court assumed that this case literally involved horizontal price-fixing. But did it? To be sure, the blanket license terms involved fixing sale prices to the networks, as well as the prices paid to composers (though there was little focus on the latter because the plaintiff was a network). But if, as the Court said, a blanket license "is truly greater than the sum of its parts; it is, to some extent, a different product," then blanket licenses are different product from individual compositions, and fixing the price of blanket licenses is not horizontal price fixing because the composers did not compete in the market for offering blanket licenses. Rather, one could argue that all we have here is a productive joint venture that buys inputs (individual compositions) and combines them to create a different product (blanket licenses) whose price the joint venture unilaterally sets. A joint venture of rubber and steel makers that combined rubber and steel to make automobiles would set a price for those automobiles, but we would not call that "horizontal" price fixing. Compositions are somewhat different because one purchasing the set of them a network wants to use could be functionally equivalent to buying a blanket license, but if one thought the blanket license was truly a different product, one might not categorize the blanket license price as horizontal price-fixing at all.

2. ***Was the position of CBS and the Court of Appeals consistent with the claim that because blanket licenses involved horizontal price fixing, they are per se illegal?*** No. Both CBS and the Court of

Appeals argued that the blanket licenses involved horizontal price fixing and were thus per se illegal. But the Court of Appeals acknowledged that blanket licenses were allowable where necessary or sufficiently desirable, which is not a per se prohibition. CBS argued that the organizations should be directed to license at standard per-use rates rather than negotiated rates, but those per-use rates would also involve price-fixing by the organization and thus be horizontal price fixing under their theory. Thus, both wanted to allow some form of horizontal price fixing, which is inconsistent with their theory that all horizontal price fixing is per se prohibition. The important general lesson for antitrust litigants is that one has to think through what one wants and whether that is consistent with the theory of antitrust liability being proposed.

3. ***What is the meta-test for figuring out when literal horizontal price-fixing is per se illegal?*** Although the Court agreed that the blanket license literally involved horizontal price-fixing, it nonetheless took the position that literal horizontal price-fixing was sometimes per se illegal but sometimes not. This raised the question: what precisely is the court's meta-test for figuring out when literal horizontal price-fixing falls within the per se rule and when it does not?

a. ***Per se rule applies unless horizontal price-fixing is ancillary to productive joint venture?*** Although the Court raised three possible meta-tests, the one that seems decisive is that here the price-fixing restraint was ancillary to a productive rival collaboration and integration of business activities, where "ancillary" means reasonably necessary to advance the procompetitive virtues of the business collaboration. The Court explicitly cited this factor to support its conclusion. This test is also consistent with the Court's reasoning that the per se rule could not apply to all literal horizontal price-fixing because otherwise all partnerships that fix the price of their product (like a law firm partnership that sets its billable rates) would be per se illegal. This test also provides a fairly clean doctrinal test. A horizontal price-fixing agreement between unrelated businesses (i.e., firms that are not related in a productive business collaboration, like the firms in *Trenton Potteries*) is categorically per se illegal. But a horizontal price-fixing agreement that is ancillary to a productive business collaboration is subject to rule of reason analysis. That does not necessarily make such an agreement legal, but it means that categorical condemnation does not apply.

b. ***Per se rule does not apply when horizontal price-fixing involves a "different product"?*** Another factor the Court cited for declining to apply the per se rule, even though it thought the blanket license involved horizontal price-fixing, was that ASCAP and BMI were producing a "different product" from their members. However, this factor cannot be necessary to its meta test because this factor does not explain the Court's conclusion that per se illegality cannot apply to prices set by ordinary partnerships, which often are not offering a different product from their members. Consider law firms, which collectively offer legal services just like their partners do individually. Even though they are not offering a "different product", such partnerships have procompetitive virtues because they enable partners to share expenses and pool resources in a way that can make their product cheaper or better. Indeed, the "different product" rule could be considered a special case of the more general exception for restraints ancillary to productive joint ventures. It applies when the procompetitive benefits of collaboration are so dramatic that they produce an entirely different product. But when a business collaboration produces less dramatic benefits, like making the same product cheaper or higher in quality, it can still procompetitively benefit consumers in a way one would not want to categorically condemn.

c. ***Per se rule does not apply when procompetitive justifications are strong and the anticompetitive effects weak?*** The third possibility suggested by the Court's reasoning is that the per se rule does not apply when, as here, the procompetitive justifications are strong and the anticompetitive effects weak. Many commentators read the Court as adopting this test. But the problem with this interpretation is that a test that examines procompetitive justifications and anticompetitive effects is the same as doing rule of reason analysis. It thus cannot really be part of a meta-test for deciding when a per se rule *precludes* rule of reason analysis inquiry into procompetitive justifications or anticompetitive effects. Although the Court considered the procompetitive justifications, it did so here in a context where the challenged price-fixing restraint was alleged to be reasonably necessary to advance the procompetitive purposes of a productive business collaboration—that is, a joint venture that actually made some business product that it sold—and thus was ancillary to it. This holding does not mean a procompetitive justification can be offered when firms are not related in such a productive business collaboration, but instead are unrelated firms that are just trying to regulate the market in ways that the government could regulate in a more disinterested fashion.

4. ***Why does application of the Court's meta-test indicate that the per se rule should not apply here?*** The Court's opinion not only created a meta-test for determining when literal horizontal price-fixing was per se illegal, but also applied that meta-test to conclude that the per se rule did not apply to blanket licenses at issue in this case. What explains that conclusion?

One factor the Court cited is that negotiation, monitoring, and enforcement costs require a collective organization to negotiate licenses, monitor violations, and bring enforcement actions. It would be too hard for users to find individual composers to negotiate licenses for each song they use and it would be too hard for individual composers to monitor every TV and radio station for usage of their songs and to bring litigation over whatever small damages that usage by one of them would cause.

Although this is true, one might wonder why such collective organization requires a blanket license. Why couldn't each organization instead (or also) allow each composer to post her own price for each song through the organization? One reason is that broadcasters might prefer the convenience of not having to price shop for every song, though that seems contrary to CBS's preference and does not necessarily explain why both per-use and blanket options are not offered. Another reason is that the organization's monitoring costs would be higher for any broadcasters that bought a per-use license because then the organization would have to monitor broadcasters to see what songs they were using. In contrast, the organizations can skip monitoring altogether for broadcasters that buy a blanket license. True, the organizations still need to monitor usage because they pay composers based on usage. But the blanket license makes it easier to monitor usage because the blanket licenses give broadcasters incentives to voluntarily provide accurate data on usage. If broadcasters were instead charged based on usage, they would have incentives to understate their use to avoid higher charges. One could argue that this concern could also addressed by offering both per-use and blanket options, with a surcharge for any extra monitoring costs inflicted by the per-use option, and allow broadcasters to choose between them. But that itself would raise questions about whether the surcharge amount was proportional to any additional monitoring costs.

The above sorts of arguments do not necessarily mean that selling only a blanket license at an organization-fixed price was procompetitive. But they mean that the organization's argument that selling only a blanket license was reasonably necessary to advance the procompetitive purposes of the productive joint venture were at least plausible enough that they had to be seriously considered. That suffices to show that such arguments have to be assessed under the rule of reason, rather than categorically condemning the restraint under the per se rule.

a. Does modern technology change these conclusions? Suppose the advent of the computer and internet provides a cheap, reliable way for determining what compositions every television network has used and for each composer to list the price she wishes to charge for her songs in a way that networks could easily ascertain. Would the case then come out differently? Perhaps so because such a development in technology would mean a blanket license might no longer further the joint venture's procompetitive justifications. This might call for a different result because footnote 34 of the Court's opinion states that "changes brought about by new technology or new marketing techniques might also undercut the justification for the practice." On the other hand, such a change might not justify applying the per se rule as much as it might alter the outcome under rule of reason analysis. Do you think technology has changed sufficiently that this case would come out differently today?

b. Does collective licensing require the restraint that fixes the prices paid to composers for their compositions? Another question is whether collective licensing requires the upstream agreement to pay composers primarily on downstream usage of their songs by buyers of the blanket licenses. *See* n.36. This method does not allow lesser-known composers to compete with their better-known peers by offering a lower price. Because all compositions cost the same to use under a blanket license, broadcasters have incentives to use the most famous composers, thus continuing their fame advantage. This result, one might argue, produces anticompetitive results and distorts the music we hear to concentrate more on pop music. However, if only blanket licenses to buyers are efficient, then lesser-known composers would have no incentive to bid a lower price because that would not affect the extent of their usage. This argument would thus seem relevant only if per-use pricing to buyers were efficient. If it were (or if new technology made it efficient), then any restriction on such price competition by composers would not seem necessary to further the procompetitive purposes of the organizations.

c. ***Does collective licensing also require the restraint that bans members from licensing their songs to rival performance rights organizations?*** It seems far less clear that collective licensing requires the additional restraint that bans members from licensing their songs to rival performance rights organizations. *See* n.15. Indeed, that restraint may be the most anticompetitive aspect of the organizations, though one might also wonder how organizations could price their products if they were offering the identical songs. In any event, because that restraint was not challenged, the Court did not consider it. Should the ban on members from licensing their songs to rival performance rights organizations be deemed lawful?

5. ***How should rule of reason analysis come out on remand?*** The lower court concluded on remand that the ability to negotiate individual licenses with composers eliminated any anticompetitive effect from the blanket license and that therefore it survived rule of reason analysis. Some question this logic because, if the procompetitive justification for the joint ventures is correct, then individual license negotiation, monitoring, and enforcement is not feasible. But eliminating an unfeasible option cannot create an anticompetitive effect.

Indeed, the possibility of direct negotiation exists for every price-fixing cartel because a cartel cannot legally restrict negotiation with individual cartel members. Therefore the mere possibility of individual negotiation cannot suffice to eliminate the anticompetitive effect. The distinction is that here individual negotiation was not feasible. Also, cartels have an unenforceable agreement not to sell below the cartel price, which did not exist here.

If one thought there were anticompetitive effects, then under the rule of reason one would have to consider whether those anticompetitive effects were offset by procompetitive justifications, and part of the latter inquiry would be whether a less restrictive alternative would have been to instead (or also) offer individual composition prices set by composers. This turns on the same factors discussed above regarding this alternative. Only here the issues would be directly analyzed on the merits because the issue is no longer whether the argument that the restraint is reasonably necessary for such a justification is so implausible that per se condemnation should apply. The issue is instead whether the restraint survives rule of reason analysis, which requires direct inquiry into the extent to which the restraint had net anticompetitive effects.

In considering such an alternative, one might argue that if such the alternative were feasible and preferable, the organizations would have already chosen to provide it to compete better in the market for blanket licenses. However, because there are only two organizations in the market, they may not want to adopt policies that would increase price competition.

Nor is likely a third major firm would enter because new firms cannot get meaningful access to compositions, given that the ASCAP and BMI agreements ban composers from licensing their compositions to a rival organization.

6. ***Was there a more promising rule of reason theory?*** Instead of attacking the blanket license, a better line of attack under of the rule of reason may have been to challenge the fact that the organizations grouped all compositions into just two organizations with 75% and 25% of the market respectively. It is not at all clear that the procompetitive justifications for blanket licenses requires grouping them all into only two licenses. One would think that the procompetitive justifications could equally be achieved by having five to ten competing firms offer blanket licenses, which would give us the benefit of blanket licenses along with competitive pricing of those blanket licenses. Such more extensive competition is currently precluded because of the restraint that prohibits composers who license their compositions to one organization from licensing them to rival organizations.

Because the existence of only two firms with blanket licenses creates anticompetitive pricing, they are, as the Court noted, governed by a consent decree under which, if a buyer and organization cannot agree on the price for a blanket license, the district court must determine a reasonable license fee. This approach requires courts to set sail on the sea of doubt of assessing what a reasonable fixed price is, which has proven very difficult. If the procompetitive efficiencies of blanket licenses requires only two organizations, then this difficult sail seems unavoidable. But if blanket licenses could be provided by 5–10 competing firms, then breaking them up under the rule of reason would allow prices for blanket licenses to be set by the competitive market, which would get courts out of the price-setting business.

Arizona v. Maricopa County Medical Society

457 U.S. 332 (1982).

■ JUSTICE STEVENS delivered the opinion of the Court.

The question presented is whether § 1 of the Sherman Act . . . has been violated by agreements among competing physicians setting, by majority vote, the maximum fees that they may claim in full payment for health services provided to policyholders of specified insurance plans. The United States Court of Appeals for the Ninth Circuit held that the question could not be answered without evaluating the actual purpose and effect of the agreements at a full trial. Because the undisputed facts disclose a violation of the statute, we . . . reverse. . . .

II

The Maricopa Foundation for Medical Care is a nonprofit Arizona corporation composed of licensed doctors of medicine, osteopathy, and podiatry engaged in private practice. Approximately 1,750 doctors, representing about 70% of the practitioners in Maricopa County, are members.

The Maricopa Foundation was organized in 1969 for the purpose of promoting fee-for-service medicine and to provide the community with a competitive alternative to existing health insurance plans. The foundation performs three primary activities. It establishes the schedule of maximum fees that participating doctors agree to accept as payment in full for services performed for patients insured under plans approved by the foundation. It reviews the medical necessity and appropriateness of treatment provided by its members to such insured persons. It is authorized to draw checks on insurance company accounts to pay doctors for services performed for covered patients. In performing these functions, the foundation is considered an "insurance administrator" by the Director of the Arizona Department of Insurance. Its participating doctors, however, have no financial interest in the operation of the foundation.

The Pima Foundation for Medical Care, which includes [30–80% of the doctors in Pima County], performs similar functions. For the purposes of this litigation, the parties seem to regard the activities of the two foundations as essentially the same. No challenge is made to their peer review or claim administration functions. Nor do the foundations allege that these two activities make it necessary for them to engage in the practice of establishing maximum-fee schedules.

At the time this lawsuit was filed, each foundation made use of "relative values" and "conversion factors" in compiling its fee schedule. The conversion factor is the dollar amount used to determine fees for a particular medical specialty. . . . The relative value schedule provides a numerical weight for each different medical service—thus, an office consultation has a lesser value than a home visit. The relative value was multiplied by the conversion factor to determine the maximum fee. The fee schedule has been revised periodically. The foundation board of trustees would solicit advice from various medical societies about the need for change in either relative values or conversion factors in their respective specialties. The board would then formulate the new fee schedule and submit it to the vote of the entire membership.[10]

The fee schedules limit the amount that the member doctors may recover for services performed for patients insured under plans approved by the foundations. To obtain this approval the insurers—including self-insured employers as well as insurance companies[11]—agree to pay the doctors' charges up to the scheduled amounts, and in exchange the

[10] The parties disagree over whether the increases in the fee schedules are the cause or the result of the increases in the prevailing rate for medical services in the relevant markets. There appears to be agreement, however, that 85–95% of physicians in Maricopa County bill at or above the maximum reimbursement levels set by the Maricopa Foundation.

[11] Seven different insurance companies underwrite health insurance plans that have been approved by the Maricopa Foundation, and three companies underwrite the plans approved by the Pima Foundation. The record contains no firm data on the portion of the health care market that is covered by these plans. The State relies upon a 1974 analysis indicating that insurance plans endorsed by the Maricopa Foundation had about 63% of the prepaid health care market, but the respondents contest the accuracy of this analysis.

doctors agree to accept those amounts as payment in full for their services. The doctors are free to charge higher fees to uninsured patients, and they also may charge any patient less than the scheduled maxima. A patient who is insured by a foundation-endorsed plan is guaranteed complete coverage for the full amount of his medical bills only if he is treated by a foundation member. He is free to go to a nonmember physician and is still covered for charges that do not exceed the maximum-fee schedule, but he must pay any excess that the nonmember physician may charge.

The impact of the foundation fee schedules on medical fees and on insurance premiums is a matter of dispute. The State of Arizona contends that the periodic upward revisions of the maximum-fee schedules have the effect of stabilizing and enhancing the level of actual charges by physicians, and that the increasing level of their fees in turn increases insurance premiums. The foundations, on the other hand, argue that the schedules impose a meaningful limit on physicians' charges, and that the advance agreement by the doctors to accept the maxima enables the insurance carriers to limit and to calculate more efficiently the risks they underwrite and therefore serves as an effective cost-containment mechanism that has saved patients and insurers millions of dollars. . . . [W]e must assume that the respondents' view of the genuine issues of fact is correct [because the question here is whether the district court was right to enter summary judgment finding liability]. . . .

III

The respondents recognize that our decisions establish that price-fixing agreements are unlawful on their face. But they argue that the *per se* rule does not govern this case because the agreements at issue are horizontal and fix maximum prices, are among members of a profession, are in an industry with which the judiciary has little antitrust experience, and are alleged to have procompetitive justifications. . . .

A

Section 1 of the Sherman Act of 1890 literally prohibits *every* agreement "in restraint of trade." In *United States v. Joint Traffic Assn.*, 171 U.S. 505 (1898), we recognized that Congress could not have intended a literal interpretation of the word "every"; since *Standard Oil Co. of New Jersey v. United States*, 221 U.S. 1 (1911), we have analyzed most restraints under the so-called "rule of reason." As its name suggests, the rule of reason requires the factfinder to decide whether under all the circumstances of the case the restrictive practice imposes an unreasonable restraint on competition.

The elaborate inquiry into the reasonableness of a challenged business practice entails significant costs. Litigation of the effect or purpose of a practice often is extensive and complex. Judges often lack the expert understanding of industrial market structures and behavior to determine with any confidence a practice's effect on competition. And the result of the process in any given case may provide little certainty or guidance about the legality of a practice in another context.

The costs of judging business practices under the rule of reason, however, have been reduced by the recognition of *per se* rules. Once experience with a particular kind of restraint enables the Court to predict with confidence that the rule of reason will condemn it, it has applied a conclusive presumption that the restraint is unreasonable. As in every rule of general application, the match between the presumed and the actual is imperfect. For the sake of business certainty and litigation efficiency, we have tolerated the invalidation of some agreements that a fullblown inquiry might have proved to be reasonable.[16]

Thus the Court in *Standard Oil* recognized that inquiry under its rule of reason ended once a price-fixing agreement was proved, for there was "a conclusive presumption which brought [such agreements] within the statute." 221 U.S., at 65. By 1927, the Court was able to state that "it has . . . often been decided and always assumed that uniform price-fixing by those controlling in any substantial manner a trade or business in interstate commerce is prohibited by the Sherman Law." *Trenton Potteries*. . . .

Thirteen years later, the Court could report that "for over forty years this Court has consistently and without deviation adhered to the principle that price-fixing agreements are unlawful *per se* under the Sherman Act and that no showing of so-called competitive abuses or evils which those agreements were designed to eliminate or alleviate may be interposed as a defense." *United States v. Socony-Vacuum Oil Co.*, 310 U.S. 150, 218 (1940). In that case a glut in the spot market for gasoline had prompted the major oil refiners to engage in a concerted effort to purchase and store surplus gasoline in order to maintain stable prices. Absent the agreement, the companies argued, competition was cutthroat and self-defeating. The argument did not carry the day:

> "Any combination which tampers with price structures is engaged in an unlawful activity. Even though the members of the price-fixing group were in no position to control the market, to the extent that they raised, lowered, or stabilized prices they would be directly interfering with the free play of market forces. The Act places all such schemes beyond the pale and protects that vital part of our economy against any degree of interference. Congress has not left with us the determination of whether or not particular price-fixing schemes are wise or unwise, healthy or destructive. It has not permitted the age-old

[16] . . . The Court made the same point in *Continental T.V., Inc. v. GTE Sylvania Inc.*, 433 U.S. at 50, n.16: "*Per se* rules thus require the Court to make broad generalizations about the social utility of particular commercial practices. The probability that anticompetitive consequences will result from a practice and the severity of those consequences must be balanced against its procompetitive consequences. Cases that do not fit the generalization may arise, but a *per se* rule reflects the judgment that such cases are not sufficiently common or important to justify the time and expense necessary to identify them."

> cry of ruinous competition and competitive evils to be a defense to price-fixing conspiracies. It has no more allowed genuine or fancied competitive abuses as a legal justification for such schemes than it has the good intentions of the members of the combination. If such a shift is to be made, it must be done by the Congress. Certainly Congress has not left us with any such choice. Nor has the Act created or authorized the creation of any special exception in favor of the oil industry. Whatever may be its peculiar problems and characteristics, the Sherman Act, so far as price-fixing agreements are concerned, establishes one uniform rule applicable to all industries alike." *Id.* at 221–222.

The application of the *per se* rule to maximum-price-fixing agreements in *Kiefer-Stewart Co. v. Joseph E. Seagram & Sons, Inc.*, 340 U.S. 211 (1951), followed ineluctably from *Socony-Vacuum:*

> "For such agreements, no less than those to fix minimum prices, cripple the freedom of traders and thereby restrain their ability to sell in accordance with their own judgment. We reaffirm what we said in *Socony-Vacuum*, 310 U.S. at 223: 'Under the Sherman Act a combination formed for the purpose and with the effect of raising, depressing, fixing, pegging, or stabilizing the price of a commodity in interstate or foreign commerce is illegal *per se.*' " 340 U.S., at 213.

Over the objection that maximum-price-fixing agreements were not the "economic equivalent" of minimum-price-fixing agreements, *Kiefer-Stewart* was reaffirmed in *Albrecht v. Herald Co.*, 390 U.S. 145 (1968). . . .

B

Our decisions foreclose the argument that the agreements at issue escape *per se* condemnation because they are horizontal and fix maximum prices. *Kiefer-Stewart* and *Albrecht* place horizontal agreements to fix maximum prices on the same legal—even if not economic—footing as agreements to fix minimum or uniform prices.[18] The *per se* rule "is grounded on faith in price competition as a market force [and not] on a policy of low selling prices at the price of eliminating competition." In this case the rule is violated by a price restraint that tends to provide the same economic rewards to all practitioners regardless of their skill, their experience, their training, or their willingness to employ innovative and difficult procedures in individual cases. Such a restraint also may discourage entry into the market and may deter experimentation and new developments by individual entrepreneurs. It may be a masquerade for an agreement to fix uniform prices, or it may in the future take on that character.

---

[18] It is true that in *Keifer-Stewart*, as in *Albrecht*, the agreement involved a vertical arrangement in which maximum resale prices were fixed. But the case also involved an agreement among competitors to impose the resale price restraint. In any event, horizontal restraints are generally less defensible than vertical restraints. . . .

Nor does the fact that doctors—rather than nonprofessionals—are the parties to the price-fixing agreements support the respondents' position. In *Goldfarb v. Virginia State Bar*, 421 U.S. 773, 788, n.17 (1975), we stated that the "public service aspect, and other features of the professions, may require that a particular practice, which could properly be viewed as a violation of the Sherman Act in another context, be treated differently." The price-fixing agreements in this case, however, are not premised on public service or ethical norms. The respondents do not argue . . . that the quality of the professional service that their members provide is enhanced by the price restraint. The respondents' claim for relief from the *per se* rule is simply that the doctors' agreement not to charge certain insureds more than a fixed price facilitates the successful marketing of an attractive insurance plan. But the claim that the price restraint will make it easier for customers to pay does not distinguish the medical profession from any other provider of goods or services.

We are equally unpersuaded by the argument that we should not apply the *per se* rule in this case because the judiciary has little antitrust experience in the health care industry.[19] The argument quite obviously is inconsistent with *Socony-Vacuum*. In unequivocal terms, we stated that, "[w]hatever may be its peculiar problems and characteristics, the Sherman Act, so far as price-fixing agreements are concerned, establishes one uniform rule applicable to all industries alike." 310 U.S. at 222. We also stated that "[t]he elimination of so-called competitive evils [in an industry] is no legal justification" for price-fixing agreements, *id.* at 220, yet the Court of Appeals refused to apply the *per se* rule in this case in part because the health care industry was so far removed from the competitive model.[20] Consistent with our prediction in *Socony-Vacuum,* 310 U.S. at 221, the result of this reasoning was the adoption by the Court of Appeals of a legal standard based on the reasonableness of the fixed prices,[21] an inquiry we have so often condemned. Finally, the

[19] The argument should not be confused with the established position that a *new per se* rule is not justified until the judiciary obtains considerable rule-of-reason experience with the particular type of restraint challenged. . . .

[20] "The health care industry, moreover, presents a particularly difficult area. The first step to understanding is to recognize that not only is access to the medical profession very time consuming and expensive both for the applicant and society generally, but also that numerous government subventions of the costs of medical care have created both a demand and supply function for medical services that is artificially high. The present supply and demand functions of medical services in no way approximate those which would exist in a purely private competitive order. An accurate description of those functions moreover is not available. Thus, we lack baselines by which could be measured the distance between the present supply and demand functions and those which would exist under ideal competitive conditions." 643 F.2d at 556.

[21] "Perforce we must take industry as it exists, absent the challenged feature, as our baseline for measuring anticompetitive impact. The relevant inquiry becomes whether fees paid to doctors under that system would be less than those payable under the FMC maximum fee agreement. Put differently, confronted with an industry widely deviant from a reasonably free competitive model, such as agriculture, the proper inquiry is whether the practice enhances the prices charged for the services. In simplified economic terms, the issue is whether the maximum fee arrangement better permits the attainment of the monopolist's goal, viz., the matching of marginal cost to marginal revenue, or in fact obstructs that end." *Ibid.*

argument that the *per se* rule must be rejustified for every industry that has not been subject to significant antitrust litigation ignores the rationale for *per se* rules, which in part is to avoid "the necessity for an incredibly complicated and prolonged economic investigation into the entire history of the industry involved, as well as related industries, in an effort to determine at large whether a particular restraint has been unreasonable—an inquiry so often wholly fruitless when undertaken." *Northern Pacific*, 356 U.S. at 5.

The respondents' principal argument is that the *per se* rule is inapplicable because their agreements are alleged to have procompetitive justifications. The argument indicates a misunderstanding of the *per se* concept. The anticompetitive potential inherent in all price-fixing agreements justifies their facial invalidation even if procompetitive justifications are offered for some.[23] Those claims of enhanced competition are so unlikely to prove significant in any particular case that we adhere to the rule of law that is justified in its general application. Even when the respondents are given every benefit of the doubt, the limited record in this case is not inconsistent with the presumption that the respondents' agreements will not significantly enhance competition.

The respondents contend that their fee schedules are procompetitive because they make it possible to provide consumers of health care with a uniquely desirable form of insurance coverage that could not otherwise exist. The features of the foundation-endorsed insurance plans that they stress are a choice of doctors, complete insurance coverage, and lower premiums. The first two characteristics, however, are hardly unique to these plans. Since only about 70% of the doctors in the relevant market are members of either foundation, the guarantee of complete coverage only applies when an insured chooses a physician in that 70%. If he elects to go to a nonfoundation doctor, he may be required to pay a portion of the doctor's fee. It is fair to presume, however, that at least 70% of the doctors in other markets charge no more than the "usual, customary, and reasonable" fee that typical insurers are willing to reimburse in full. Thus, in Maricopa and Pima Counties as well as in most parts of the country, if an insured asks his doctor if the insurance coverage is complete, presumably in about 70% of the cases the doctor will say "Yes" and in about 30% of the cases he will say "No."

It is true that a binding assurance of complete insurance coverage—as well as most of the respondents' potential for lower insurance premiums[25]—can be obtained only if the insurer and the doctor agree in

---

[23] "Whatever economic justification particular price-fixing agreements may be thought to have, the law does not permit an inquiry into their reasonableness. They are all banned because of their actual or potential threat to the central nervous system of the economy." *United States v. Socony-Vacuum Oil Co.*, 310 U.S. 150, 226 n.59 (1940).

[25] We do not perceive the respondents' claim of procompetitive justification for their fee schedules to rest on the premise that the fee schedules actually reduce medical fees and accordingly reduce insurance premiums, thereby enhancing competition in the health insurance

advance on the maximum fee that the doctor will accept as full payment for a particular service. Even if a fee schedule is therefore desirable, it is not necessary that the doctors do the price fixing. . . . [I]nsurers are capable not only of fixing maximum reimbursable prices but also of obtaining binding agreements with providers guaranteeing the insured full reimbursement of a participating provider's fee. . . .

The most that can be said for having doctors fix the maximum prices is that doctors may be able to do it more efficiently than insurers. The validity of that assumption is far from obvious,[28] but in any event there is no reason to believe that any savings that might accrue from this arrangement would be sufficiently great to affect the competitiveness of these kinds of insurance plans. It is entirely possible that the potential or actual power of the foundations to dictate the terms of such insurance plans may more than offset the theoretical efficiencies upon which the respondents' defense ultimately rests.[29]

C

Our adherence to the *per se* rule is grounded not only on economic prediction, judicial convenience, and business certainty, but also on a recognition of the respective roles of the Judiciary and the Congress in regulating the economy. Given its generality, our enforcement of the Sherman Act has required the Court to provide much of its substantive content. By articulating the rules of law with some clarity and by adhering to rules that are justified in their general application, however, we enhance the legislative prerogative to amend the law. The respondents' arguments against application of the *per se* rule in this case therefore are better directed to the Legislature. Congress may consider the exception that we are not free to read into the statute.

IV

Having declined the respondents' invitation to cut back on the *per se* rule against price fixing, we are left with the respondents' argument that their fee schedules involve price fixing in only a literal sense. For this argument, the respondents rely upon *Broadcast Music, Inc.*

---

industry. Such an argument would merely restate the long-rejected position that fixed prices are reasonable if they are lower than free competition would yield. It is arguable, however, that the existence of a fee schedule, whether fixed by the doctors or by the insurers, makes it easier—and to that extent less expensive—for insurers to calculate the risks that they underwrite and to arrive at the appropriate reimbursement on insured claims.

[28] In order to create an insurance plan under which the doctor would agree to accept as full payment a fee prescribed in a fixed schedule, someone must canvass the doctors to determine what maximum prices would be high enough to attract sufficient numbers of individual doctors to sign up but low enough to make the insurance plan competitive. In this case that canvassing function is performed by the foundation; the foundation then deals with the insurer. It would seem that an insurer could simply bypass the foundation by performing the canvassing function and dealing with the doctors itself. . . .

[29] In this case it appears that the fees are set by a group with substantial power in the market for medical services, and that there is competition among insurance companies in the sale of medical insurance. Under these circumstances the insurance companies are not likely to have significantly greater bargaining power against a monopoly of doctors than would individual consumers of medical services.

In *Broadcast Music* . . . the . . . so-called "blanket license" was entirely different from the product that any one composer was able to sell by himself. Although there was little competition among individual composers for their separate compositions, the blanket-license arrangement did not place any restraint on the right of any individual copyright owner to sell his own compositions separately to any buyer at any price. But a "necessary consequence" of the creation of the blanket license was that its price had to be established. . . .

This case is fundamentally different. Each of the foundations is composed of individual practitioners who compete with one another for patients. Neither the foundations nor the doctors sell insurance, and they derive no profits from the sale of health insurance policies. The members of the foundations sell medical services. Their combination in the form of the foundation does not permit them to sell any different product. Their combination has merely permitted them to sell their services to certain customers at fixed prices and arguably to affect the prevailing market price of medical care.

The foundations are not analogous to partnerships or other joint arrangements in which persons who would otherwise be competitors pool their capital and share the risks of loss as well as the opportunities for profit. In such joint ventures, the partnership is regarded as a single firm competing with other sellers in the market. The agreement under attack is an agreement among hundreds of competing doctors concerning the price at which each will offer his own services to a substantial number of consumers. It is true that some are surgeons, some anesthesiologists, and some psychiatrists, but the doctors do not sell a package of three kinds of services. If a clinic offered complete medical coverage for a flat fee, the cooperating doctors would have the type of partnership arrangement in which a price-fixing agreement among the doctors would be perfectly proper. But the fee agreements disclosed by the record in this case are among independent competing entrepreneurs. They fit squarely into the horizontal price-fixing mold. . . .

NOTES AND QUESTIONS ON *MARICOPA*

1. ***Suppose the case had involved naked maximum price-fixing among unrelated firms. Why should maximum price-fixing be within the per se rule, given that lowering prices is good for consumers?*** There are several reasons why maximum price fixing is deemed per se illegal. First, an agreement to a maximum price could really be a target price for a minimum, in which case it likely raises prices. Second, even if a maximum price really does reduce prices, subcompetitive prices are bad for consumers because they lead to subcompetitive levels of output or quality. In other words, consumers would be willing to pay more for the competitive level of output and quality. Thus, pricing above or below competitive levels leads to deadweight loss and harm to consumer welfare. Third, maximum price-fixing that really lowered prices would reduce entry into the regional market by more doctors or by higher-quality doctors, who would choose instead to enter a market where the prices they could charge were higher.

2. ***Why aren't the defendants right that the per se rule should not apply because this a new arrangement with which the Court lacks experience?*** Because there is an important difference between a new arrangement and using an old arrangement in a new industry. Here, horizontal maximum price-fixing was being used in a new industry (medical services), but maximum price-fixing unrelated to a productive collaboration was not a new arrangement with which the Court lacked experience.

3. ***Why is the* Maricopa *case within the per se rule given* BMI*?*** Some might view the Court's holding that the horizontal price-fixing agreement in *Maricopa* was per se illegal as being inconsistent with *BMI* because in both cases the defendants offered procompetitive justifications. However, in *Maricopa*, unlike in *BMI*, the defendant did not even claim that the price-fixing restraint was necessary to advance procompetitive purposes that were ancillary to the relevant productive joint venture. In *BMI*, the defendant made a plausible claim that the procompetitive purposes served by collective monitoring and enforcement may require collective price-setting. In contrast, in *Maricopa*, the defendants made no claim that collective peer review and insurance claim administration may require collective price-setting. *See* p.66. ("No challenge is made to their peer review or claim administration functions. Nor do the foundations allege that these two activities make it necessary for them to engage in the practice of establishing maximum-fee schedules.") Instead, the *Maricopa* defendants advanced procompetitive justifications that were unrelated to their productive business collaboration in peer review and claim insurance administration.

a. ***Why isn't this agreement outside the per se rule because the Foundation offers a "different product"?*** The Court's opinion concluded that the Foundation did not supply a "different product," which rejected a dissent argument that the Foundation was offering a "different product" consisting of "maximum-fee scheduling service". The problem with the dissent's argument is that, by that logic, any price-fixing agreement could be considered a "different product" that offers a minimum or maximum "price-scheduling service." To deserve a "different product" exception, the relevant product or services needs to be adding a market option without taking away any market options already in play. This means that the agreement should create a product or services distinct enough from the original offering that consumers receive benefits that are unavailable in the original product, and that outweigh any anticompetitive concerns. Generally, this requires that the restraint be necessary to the procompetitive purpose of the productive collaboration in creating that distinct product, which is why it seems like a special case of the more general exception.

b. ***Why aren't the defendants right that the per se rule should not apply because they did offer procompetitive justifications (namely, limiting physician charges and insurer risk)?*** As the Court pointed out, this would make little sense because having a per se rule is supposed to make procompetitive justifications inadmissible. If offering a procompetitive justification sufficed to get out of the per se rule, then the per se rule could never exclude procompetitive justifications. The *Maricopa* case is thus consistent with the view that having a procompetitive justification for horizontal price-fixing does not get a defendant out of the per se rule *unless* that the restraint is reasonably necessary to advance the procompetitive virtues of a productive business collaboration. This view also squares *Maricopa* with the result in *BMI*. This interpretation provides a fairly simple rule. Horizontal price-fixing that is not ancillary to a productive joint venture is per se illegal; horizontal price-fixing that is ancillary to a productive joint venture is subject to rule-of-reason review.

However, the *Maricopa* case created some confusion because after holding the justifications inadmissible, the Court nonetheless in the alternative considered them on the merits and rejected them. It concluded that reducing physician charges is not a procompetitive justification because subcompetitive prices are not procompetitive, for the reasons noted above. It also concluded that reducing insurer risk is not a good procompetitive justification because individual insurers could fix maximum fees in their vertical contracts with physicians and do not need horizontal physician agreements to cabin their risk. But one might wonder why the Supreme Court bothered to consider inadmissible justifications in the alternative given that no court can overrule it. Perhaps the explanation is that, while Congress cannot overrule individual case results, it can effectively override Supreme Court precedent with statutory interpretations. To fend off Congressional override, it might have been useful to explain that the justifications being offered were not meritorious.

c. Would rule-of-reason review have required a sail on the sea of doubt? Yes. Because the doctors were basically arguing that maximum price-fixing is desirable when the maximum price is desirable, their claim would have required courts to assess the reasonableness of the prices. One might think a reasonableness inquiry could be avoided by instead simply asking the factual question whether the agreement reduced or increased prices. However, for reasons noted above, a price that is either above *or* below competitive levels would be anticompetitive and harm consumer welfare. This is another reason not to recognize an exception to the per se rule.

Texaco Inc. v. Dagher

547 U.S. 1 (2006).

■ JUSTICE THOMAS delivered the opinion of the Court.

From 1998 until 2002, petitioners Texaco Inc. and Shell Oil Co. collaborated in a joint venture, Equilon Enterprises, to refine and sell gasoline in the western United States under the original Texaco and Shell Oil brand names. Respondents, a class of Texaco and Shell Oil service station owners, allege that petitioners engaged in unlawful price fixing when Equilon set a single price for both Texaco and Shell Oil brand gasoline. We granted certiorari to determine whether it is per se illegal under § 1 of the Sherman Act, for a lawful, economically integrated joint venture to set the prices at which the joint venture sells its products. We conclude that it is not, and accordingly we reverse the contrary judgment of the Court of Appeals.

I

Historically, Texaco and Shell Oil have competed with one another in the national and international oil and gasoline markets. Their business activities include refining crude oil into gasoline, as well as marketing gasoline to downstream purchasers, such as the service stations represented in respondents' class action.

In 1998, Texaco and Shell Oil formed a joint venture, Equilon, to consolidate their operations in the western United States, thereby ending competition between the two companies in the domestic refining and marketing of gasoline. Under the joint venture agreement, Texaco and Shell Oil agreed to pool their resources and share the risks of and profits from Equilon's activities. Equilon's board of directors would comprise representatives of Texaco and Shell Oil, and Equilon gasoline would be sold to downstream purchasers under the original Texaco and Shell Oil brand names. The formation of Equilon was approved by consent decree, subject to certain divestments and other modifications, by the Federal Trade Commission, as well as by the state attorneys general of California, Hawaii, Oregon, and Washington. Notably, the decrees imposed no restrictions on the pricing of Equilon gasoline. . . .

II

. . . Price-fixing agreements between two or more competitors, otherwise known as horizontal price-fixing agreements, fall into the category of arrangements that are per se unlawful. These cases do not present such an agreement, however, because Texaco and Shell Oil did not compete with one another in the relevant market—namely, the sale of gasoline to service stations in the western United States—but instead participated in that market jointly through their investments in Equilon.[1] In other words, the pricing policy challenged here amounts to little more than price setting by a single entity—albeit within the context of a joint venture—and not a pricing agreement between competing entities with respect to their competing products. Throughout Equilon's existence, Texaco and Shell Oil shared in the profits of Equilon's activities in their role as investors, not competitors. When "persons who would otherwise be competitors pool their capital and share the risks of loss as well as the opportunities for profit . . . such joint ventures [are]

[1] We presume for purposes of these cases that Equilon is a lawful joint venture. Its formation has been approved by federal and state regulators, and there is no contention here that it is a sham. As the court below noted: "There is a voluminous record documenting the economic justifications for creating the joint ventures. [T]he defendants concluded that numerous synergies and cost efficiencies would result" by creating Equilon as well as a parallel venture, Motiva Enterprises, in the eastern United States, and "that nationwide there would be up to $800 million in cost savings annually." Had respondents challenged Equilon itself, they would have been required to show that its creation was anticompetitive under the rule of reason. *See Copperweld*.

regarded as a single firm competing with other sellers in the market." *Maricopa*. As such, though Equilon's pricing policy may be price fixing in a literal sense, it is not price fixing in the antitrust sense. *See BMI* ("When two partners set the price of their goods or services they are literally 'price fixing,' but they are not per se in violation of the Sherman Act").

This conclusion is confirmed by respondents' apparent concession that there would be no per se liability had Equilon simply chosen to sell its gasoline under a single brand. We see no reason to treat Equilon differently just because it chose to sell gasoline under two distinct brands at a single price. As a single entity, a joint venture, like any other firm, must have the discretion to determine the prices of the products that it sells, including the discretion to sell a product under two different brands at a single, unified price. If Equilon's price unification policy is anticompetitive, then respondents should have challenged it pursuant to the rule of reason. But it would be inconsistent with this Court's antitrust precedents to condemn the internal pricing decisions of a legitimate joint venture as per se unlawful.[3]

The court below reached the opposite conclusion by invoking the ancillary restraints doctrine. That doctrine governs the validity of restrictions imposed by a legitimate business collaboration, such as a business association or joint venture, on nonventure activities. *See*, e.g., *NCAA*; Citizen Publishing Co. v. United States, 394 U.S. 131, 135–136 (1969). Under the doctrine, courts must determine whether the nonventure restriction is a naked restraint on trade, and thus invalid, or one that is ancillary to the legitimate and competitive purposes of the business association, and thus valid. We agree with petitioners that the ancillary restraints doctrine has no application here, where the business practice being challenged involves the core activity of the joint venture itself-namely, the pricing of the very goods produced and sold by Equilon. And even if we were to invoke the doctrine in these cases, Equilon's pricing policy is clearly ancillary to the sale of its own products. Judge Fernandez, dissenting from the ruling of the court below, put it well:

> "In this case, nothing more radical is afoot than the fact that an entity, which now owns all of the production, transportation, research, storage, sales and distribution facilities for engaging in the gasoline business, also prices its own products. It decided to price them the same, as any other entity could. What could be more integral to the running of a business than setting a price for its goods and services?"

---

[3] Respondents alternatively contend that petitioners should be held liable under the quick look doctrine. To be sure, we have applied the quick look doctrine to business activities that are so plainly anticompetitive that courts need undertake only a cursory examination before imposing antitrust liability. But for the same reasons that per se liability is unwarranted here, we conclude that petitioners cannot be held liable under the quick look doctrine.

See also BMI ("Joint ventures and other cooperative arrangements are . . . not usually unlawful, at least not as price-fixing schemes, where the agreement on price is necessary to market the product at all").

Because the pricing decisions of a legitimate joint venture do not fall within the narrow category of activity that is per se unlawful under § 1 of the Sherman Act, respondents' antitrust claim cannot prevail. . . .

NOTES AND QUESTIONS ON *TEXACO V. DAGHER*

1. ***Wasn't fixing prices for the two brands an unavoidable feature of a legitimate joint venture?*** The Court stressed that, if the joint venture had produced a single brand of gasoline, there would have been no way for it to set different prices. Thus, there was no reason to treat the joint venture differently because it sold two different brands. But the point goes even further. An agreement by unrelated rivals to fix their respective prices is horizontal price-fixing even they do not fix the same price for each rival. Accordingly, even if the joint venture had fixed *different* prices for Texaco and Shell brand gasoline, their agreement would still involve horizontal price-fixing.

Thus, the key distinction here was that the challenged collective price-setting was an *unavoidable* feature of the joint venture to make gasoline, so there was no way to distinguish condemnation of the pricing from condemnation of the joint venture. Moreover, here it was undisputed that the joint venture was procompetitive. *See* n.1. Thus, a simple way to understand the case is that, when a joint venture to offer a product is procompetitive, a court cannot condemn unavoidable features of that joint venture, like setting a price for that product.

2. ***Given this decision, could* BMI *have been resolved on a simpler theory?*** Perhaps, but it depends on how one treats the legal theory in *BMI*. If one thinks the real antitrust theory in *BMI* was that the defendant joint ventures should have collectively monitored and enforced licenses, but let composers set the prices for each distinctive composition, then the claim was that offering a blanket license was not an unavoidable feature of the legitimate productive joint venture in monitoring and enforcement, which explains why further analysis was necessary in *BMI*. On the other hand, given that CBS did not challenge offering a blanket license or having the organization set per-use prices, one could under *Dagher* resolve *BMI* under the simpler theory that, because the joint venture to offer a blanket license was not alleged to be anticompetitive, the agreement to fix the price of its joint product—the blanket license—could not violate the per se rule.

3. ***Were Texaco and Shell a single entity?*** The Court suggests that because Texaco and Shell do not compete in the Western United States, the "pricing policy challenged here amounts to little more than price setting by a single entity." However, it does not seem that the Court meant this literally because the Court concluded that plaintiffs "should have challenged [the price setting] pursuant to the rule of reason." If the Court really thought the joint venture was a single entity, then the correct conclusion would be that it was incapable of agreeing with itself, *see* Chapter 6, which would have made any price-setting per se *legal* under Sherman Act § 1, rather subject to the rule of reason.

Moreover, a single-entity conclusion would face several problems. The firms in fact had not merged and were separate business entities. Indeed, because there was no finding that the Western United States was a properly defined economic market, Texaco and Shell may in fact have been current horizontal competitors. Even if the Western United States were a properly defined market, the firms' agreement not to compete separately in that market would be a per se illegal horizontal market division, as discussed below in Chapter 2.D.

Thus, it seems like the *Dagher* must stand for the more narrow proposition that when a plaintiff makes no claim that a productive joint venture is anticompetitive, the plaintiff cannot challenge unavoidable features of that productive joint venture. Consistent with this conclusion, the Supreme Court later held in *American Needle* held that even when a joint venture's restraint affected a market in which the members had agreed not to compete, the restraint could be an anticompetitive agreement because the participants were *potential* competitors in that market. *See* Chapter 6. When firms are potential competitors in a restrained market, then the restraint can have an anticompetitive effect that would not exist if they were truly merged.

4. ***Do the reasons to reject per se invalidity also support rejecting abbreviated rule of reason scrutiny?*** The Court indicated in footnote 3 that the reasons to reject the per se rule also supported rejecting abbreviated rule of reason scrutiny. As a general proposition, this conclusion is dubious because the per se rule excludes justifications, whereas the abbreviated rule of reason applies only when defendants cannot articulate a plausible justification. There are strong reasons why courts may want to consider justifications (and thus decline to apply the per se rule), but still want to summarily condemn restraints when no plausible justifications are even offered. The Court's statement thus seems limited to special cases, like this one, where the justifications for the joint venture were undisputed and the challenged restraint was a necessary part of that joint venture.

C. HORIZONTAL OUTPUT RESTRICTIONS

Given any particular market demand curve, every output level implies a price and every price implies an output level. Thus, horizontal agreements to restrict output below the competitive level are just the flip side of horizontal agreements to fix prices. Indeed, a horizontal agreement on output production is generally necessary for any price-fixing agreement, otherwise members of the cartel might increase production to gain a greater market share at the cartel price and, if left with unsold product, would be tempted to undercut the cartel price to unload it. Restrictions on output might also well be more effective because they can be easier to verify, more clearly allocate market share among participants, and lead ineluctably to increased market prices while allowing the precise level of those inflated prices to vary with changing market demand. Prominent cartels like OPEC thus often focus on agreements to restrict output rather than fix prices.

Thus, like price-fixing, horizontal agreements to restrict output are typically regarded as per se illegal under U.S. law.[16] Indeed, what is generally considered one of the most famous U.S. cases on horizontal price-fixing was in fact a cartel to take output off the market in order to raise prices.[17] But as with price-fixing, an output restraint might be viewed as reasonably necessary to some productive rival collaboration, such as when a partnership decides how much output to produce. This thus raises issues, similar to those we saw above for price fixing, regarding when an agreement that literally restricts output should nonetheless be characterized as falling outside the per se rule.

NCAA v. Board of Regents of University of Oklahoma

468 U.S. 85 (1984).

■ JUSTICE STEVENS delivered the opinion of the Court. . . .

[The NCAA is an association of colleges that, among other things, sets the rules for collegiate football. It collectively negotiated television rights for college football games with two television networks, CBS and ABC, setting the maximum number of total televised games and the minimum aggregate price each network had to pay college teams, limiting any individual school to no more than six televised games (four nationally televised), and requiring that each network televise at least 82 colleges in each two-year period. The University of Oklahoma and other major football colleges organized the College Football Association (CFA), which signed a contract with NBC that gave them more television appearances and increased their revenue. The NCAA threatened disciplinary action against CFA members, prompting an antitrust suit that resulted in a ruling that the NCAA had violated Sherman Act § 1, which was affirmed by the Court of Appeals.]

II

There can be no doubt that the challenged practices of the NCAA constitute a "restraint of trade" in the sense that they limit members' freedom to negotiate and enter into their own television contracts. In that sense, however, every contract is a restraint of trade, and as we have repeatedly recognized, the Sherman Act was intended to prohibit only unreasonable restraints of trade.

It is also undeniable that these practices share characteristics of restraints we have previously held unreasonable. The NCAA is an association of schools which compete against each other to attract

---

16 *See NCAA*, 468 U.S. at 99–101.

17 *Socony*, 310 U.S. 150.

television revenues, not to mention fans and athletes. As the District Court found, the policies of the NCAA with respect to television rights are ultimately controlled by the vote of member institutions. By participating in an association which prevents member institutions from competing against each other on the basis of price or kind of television rights that can be offered to broadcasters, the NCAA member institutions have created a horizontal restraint—an agreement among competitors on the way in which they will compete with one another. A restraint of this type has often been held to be unreasonable as a matter of law. Because it places a ceiling on the number of games member institutions may televise, the horizontal agreement places an artificial limit on the quantity of televised football that is available to broadcasters and consumers. By restraining the quantity of television rights available for sale, the challenged practices create a limitation on output; our cases have held that such limitations are unreasonable restraints of trade. Moreover, the District Court found that the minimum aggregate price in fact operates to preclude any price negotiation between broadcasters and institutions, thereby constituting horizontal price fixing, perhaps the paradigm of an unreasonable restraint of trade.

Horizontal price fixing and output limitation are ordinarily condemned as a matter of law under an "illegal per se" approach because the probability that these practices are anticompetitive is so high; a per se rule is applied when "the practice facially appears to be one that would always or almost always tend to restrict competition and decrease output." In such circumstances a restraint is presumed unreasonable without inquiry into the particular market context in which it is found. Nevertheless, we have decided that it would be inappropriate to apply a per se rule to this case. This decision is not based on a lack of judicial experience with this type of arrangement,[21] on the fact that the NCAA is organized as a nonprofit entity,[22] or on our respect for the NCAA's historic role in the preservation and encouragement of intercollegiate amateur athletics.[23] Rather, what is critical is that this case involves an industry in which horizontal restraints on competition are essential if the product is to be available at all.

---

[21] While judicial inexperience with a particular arrangement counsels against extending the reach of per se rules, the likelihood that horizontal price and output restrictions are anticompetitive is generally sufficient to justify application of the per se rule without inquiry into the special characteristics of a particular industry.

[22] There is no doubt that the sweeping language of § 1 applies to nonprofit entities, *Goldfarb*, 421 U.S. at 786–787, and in the past we have imposed antitrust liability on nonprofit entities which have engaged in anticompetitive conduct, American Society of Mechanical Engineers, Inc. v. Hydrolevel Corp., 456 U.S. 556, 576 (1982). Moreover, the economic significance of the NCAA's nonprofit character is questionable at best. Since the District Court found that the NCAA and its member institutions are in fact organized to maximize revenues, it is unclear why petitioner is less likely to restrict output in order to raise revenues above those that could be realized in a competitive market than would be a for-profit entity. . . .

[23] While as the guardian of an important American tradition, the NCAA's motives must be accorded a respectful presumption of validity, it is nevertheless well settled that good motives will not validate an otherwise anticompetitive practice.

. . . What the NCAA and its member institutions market in this case is competition itself—contests between competing institutions. Of course, this would be completely ineffective if there were no rules on which the competitors agreed to create and define the competition to be marketed. A myriad of rules affecting such matters as the size of the field, the number of players on a team, and the extent to which physical violence is to be encouraged or proscribed, all must be agreed upon, and all restrain the manner in which institutions compete. Moreover, the NCAA seeks to market a particular brand of football—college football. The identification of this "product" with an academic tradition differentiates college football from and makes it more popular than professional sports to which it might otherwise be comparable, such as, for example, minor league baseball. In order to preserve the character and quality of the "product," athletes must not be paid, must be required to attend class, and the like. And the integrity of the "product" cannot be preserved except by mutual agreement; if an institution adopted such restrictions unilaterally, its effectiveness as a competitor on the playing field might soon be destroyed. Thus, the NCAA plays a vital role in enabling college football to preserve its character, and as a result enables a product to be marketed which might otherwise be unavailable. In performing this role, its actions widen consumer choice—not only the choices available to sports fans but also those available to athletes—and hence can be viewed as procompetitive.

Broadcast Music squarely holds that a joint selling arrangement may be so efficient that it will increase sellers' aggregate output and thus be procompetitive. . . . Respondents concede that the great majority of the NCAA's regulations enhance competition among member institutions. Thus, despite the fact that this case involves restraints on the ability of member institutions to compete in terms of price and output, a fair evaluation of their competitive character requires consideration of the NCAA's justifications for the restraints.

Our analysis of this case under the Rule of Reason, of course, does not change the ultimate focus of our inquiry. Both per se rules and the Rule of Reason are employed "to form a judgment about the competitive significance of the restraint." . . . Per se rules are invoked when surrounding circumstances make the likelihood of anticompetitive conduct so great as to render unjustified further examination of the challenged conduct. But whether the ultimate finding is the product of a presumption or actual market analysis, the essential inquiry remains the same—whether or not the challenged restraint enhances competition. . . .

III

Because it restrains price and output, the NCAA's television plan has a significant potential for anticompetitive effects.[28] The findings of

---

[28] In this connection, it is not without significance that Congress felt the need to grant professional sports an exemption from the antitrust laws for joint marketing of television rights. *See* 15 U.S.C. §§ 1291–1295. The legislative history of this exemption demonstrates Congress'

the District Court indicate that this potential has been realized. The District Court found that if member institutions were free to sell television rights, many more games would be shown on television, and that the NCAA's output restriction has the effect of raising the price the networks pay for television rights. Moreover, the court found that by fixing a price for television rights to all games, the NCAA creates a price structure that is unresponsive to viewer demand and unrelated to the prices that would prevail in a competitive market. And, of course, since as a practical matter all member institutions need NCAA approval, members have no real choice but to adhere to the NCAA's television controls.

The anticompetitive consequences of this arrangement are apparent. Individual competitors lose their freedom to compete. Price is higher and output lower than they would otherwise be, and both are unresponsive to consumer preference. This latter point is perhaps the most significant, since "Congress designed the Sherman Act as a 'consumer welfare prescription.'" Reiter v. Sonotone Corp., 442 U.S. 330, 343 (1979). A restraint that has the effect of reducing the importance of consumer preference in setting price and output is not consistent with this fundamental goal of antitrust law.[34] Restrictions on price and output are the paradigmatic examples of restraints of trade that the Sherman Act was intended to prohibit. At the same time, the television plan eliminates competitors from the market, since only those broadcasters able to bid on television rights covering the entire NCAA can compete. Thus, as the District Court found, many telecasts that would occur in a competitive market are foreclosed by the NCAA's plan.

Petitioner argues, however, that its television plan can have no significant anticompetitive effect since the record indicates that it has no market power—no ability to alter the interaction of supply and demand in the market.[38] We must reject this argument for two reasons, one legal, one factual.

As a matter of law, the absence of proof of market power does not justify a naked restriction on price or output. To the contrary, when there is an agreement not to compete in terms of price or output, "no elaborate industry analysis is required to demonstrate the anticompetitive character of such an agreement."[39] Petitioner does not quarrel with the

---

recognition that agreements among league members to sell television rights in a cooperative fashion could run afoul of the Sherman Act. . . .

[34] . . . ". . . Many games for which there is a large viewer demand are kept from the viewers, and many games for which there is little if any demand are nonetheless televised."

[38] Market power is the ability to raise prices above those that would be charged in a competitive market.

[39] "The fact that a practice is not categorically unlawful in all or most of its manifestations certainly does not mean that it is universally lawful. For example, joint buying or selling arrangements are not unlawful per se, but a court would not hesitate in enjoining a domestic selling arrangement by which, say, Ford and General Motors distributed their automobiles nationally through a single selling agent. Even without a trial, the judge will know that these two large firms are major factors in the automobile market, that such joint selling would

District Court's finding that price and output are not responsive to demand. Thus the plan is inconsistent with the Sherman Act's command that price and supply be responsive to consumer preference. We have never required proof of market power in such a case. This naked restraint on price and output requires some competitive justification even in the absence of a detailed market analysis.

As a factual matter, it is evident that petitioner does possess market power. The District Court employed the correct test for determining whether college football broadcasts constitute a separate market—whether there are other products that are reasonably substitutable for televised NCAA football games. Petitioner's argument that it cannot obtain supracompetitive prices from broadcasters since advertisers, and hence broadcasters, can switch from college football to other types of programming simply ignores the findings of the District Court. It found that intercollegiate football telecasts generate an audience uniquely attractive to advertisers and that competitors are unable to offer programming that can attract a similar audience. These findings amply support its conclusion that the NCAA possesses market power. Indeed, the District Court's subsidiary finding that advertisers will pay a premium price per viewer to reach audiences watching college football because of their demographic characteristics is vivid evidence of the uniqueness of this product.[47] Moreover, the District Court's market analysis is firmly supported by our decision in International Boxing Club of New York, Inc. v. United States, 358 U.S. 242 (1959), that championship boxing events are uniquely attractive to fans[48] and hence constitute a market separate from that for non-championship events.[49] Thus, respondents have demonstrated that there is a separate market for telecasts of college football which "rest[s] on generic qualities differentiating" viewers. It inexorably follows that if college football broadcasts be defined as a separate market—and we are convinced they are—then the NCAA's complete control over those broadcasts provides a

---

eliminate important price competition between them, that they are quite substantial enough to distribute their products independently, and that one can hardly imagine a pro-competitive justification actually probable in fact or strong enough in principle to make this particular joint selling arrangement 'reasonable' under Sherman Act § 1. The essential point is that the rule of reason can sometimes be applied in the twinkling of an eye." P. Areeda, The "Rule of Reason" in Antitrust Analysis: General Issues 37–38 (Federal Judicial Center, June 1981) (parenthetical omitted).

[47] . . . the most analogous programming in terms of the demographic characteristics of its audience is professional football, and as a condition of its limited exemption from the antitrust laws the professional football leagues are prohibited from telecasting games at times that conflict with intercollegiate football. *See* 15 U.S.C. § 1293.

[48] We approved of the District Court's reliance on the greater revenue-producing potential and higher television ratings of championship events as opposed to other events to support its market definition.

[49] For the same reasons, it is also apparent that the unique appeal of NCAA football telecasts for viewers means that "from the standpoint of the consumer—whose interests the statute was especially intended to serve," there can be no doubt that college football constitutes a separate market for which there is no reasonable substitute. Thus we agree with the District Court that it makes no difference whether the market is defined from the standpoint of broadcasters, advertisers, or viewers.

solid basis for the District Court's conclusion that the NCAA possesses market power with respect to those broadcasts. . . .

Thus, the NCAA television plan on its face constitutes a restraint upon the operation of a free market, and the findings of the District Court establish that it has operated to raise prices and reduce output. Under the Rule of Reason, these hallmarks of anticompetitive behavior place upon petitioner a heavy burden of establishing an affirmative defense which competitively justifies this apparent deviation from the operations of a free market. We turn now to the NCAA's proffered justifications.

IV

Relying on *Broadcast Music*, petitioner argues that its television plan constitutes a cooperative "joint venture" which assists in the marketing of broadcast rights and hence is procompetitive. While joint ventures have no immunity from the antitrust laws, as *Broadcast Music* indicates, a joint selling arrangement may "mak[e] possible a new product by reaping otherwise unattainable efficiencies." The essential contribution made by the NCAA's arrangement is to define the number of games that may be televised, to establish the price for each exposure, and to define the basic terms of each contract between the network and a home team. The NCAA does not, however, act as a selling agent for any school or for any conference of schools. The selection of individual games, and the negotiation of particular agreements, are matters left to the networks and the individual schools. Thus, the effect of the network plan is not to eliminate individual sales of broadcasts, since these still occur, albeit subject to fixed prices and output limitations. Unlike *Broadcast Music*'s blanket license covering broadcast rights to a large number of individual compositions, here the same rights are still sold on an individual basis, only in a non-competitive market.

The District Court did not find that the NCAA's television plan produced any procompetitive efficiencies which enhanced the competitiveness of college football television rights; to the contrary it concluded that NCAA football could be marketed just as effectively without the television plan. There is therefore no predicate in the findings for petitioner's efficiency justification. Indeed, petitioner's argument is refuted by the District Court's finding concerning price and output. If the NCAA's television plan produced procompetitive efficiencies, the plan would increase output and reduce the price of televised games. The District Court's contrary findings accordingly undermine petitioner's position. In light of these findings, it cannot be said that "the agreement on price is necessary to market the product at all." *Broadcast Music*. In *Broadcast Music*, the availability of a package product that no individual could offer enhanced the total volume of music that was sold. Unlike this case, there was no limit of any kind placed on the volume that might be sold in the entire market and each individual remained free to sell his own music without restraint. Here production has been limited, not enhanced.[54] No individual school is free to televise its own games without restraint. The NCAA's efficiency justification is not supported by the record. . . .

V

Throughout the history of its regulation of intercollegiate football telecasts, the NCAA has indicated its concern with protecting live attendance. This concern, it should be noted, is not with protecting live attendance at games which are shown on television; that type of interest is not at issue in this case. Rather, the concern is that fan interest in a televised game may adversely affect ticket sales for games that will not appear on television.[56]

Although . . . studies in the 1950's provided some support for the thesis that live attendance would suffer if unlimited television were permitted, the District Court found that there was no evidence to support that theory in today's market. Moreover, as the District Court found, the television plan has evolved in a manner inconsistent with its original design to protect gate attendance. Under the current plan, games are shown on television during all hours that college football games are played. The plan simply does not protect live attendance by ensuring that games will not be shown on television at the same time as live events.

There is, however, a more fundamental reason for rejecting this defense. The NCAA's argument that its television plan is necessary to protect live attendance is not based on a desire to maintain the integrity of college football as a distinct and attractive product, but rather on a fear that the product will not prove sufficiently attractive to draw live attendance when faced with competition from televised games. At bottom the NCAA's position is that ticket sales for most college games are unable to compete in a free market.[60] The television plan protects ticket sales by limiting output—just as any monopolist increases revenues by reducing output. By seeking to insulate live ticket sales from the full spectrum of competition because of its assumption that the product itself is insufficiently attractive to consumers, petitioner forwards a justification that is inconsistent with the basic policy of the Sherman Act. "[T]he Rule of Reason does not support a defense based on the assumption that competition itself is unreasonable."

---

[54] Ensuring that individual members of a joint venture are free to increase output has been viewed as central in evaluating the competitive character of joint ventures.

[56] The NCAA's plan is not even arguably related to a desire to protect live attendance by ensuring that a game is not televised in the area where it is to be played. No cooperative action is necessary for that kind of "blackout." The home team can always refuse to sell the right to telecast its game to stations in the immediate area. The NCAA does not now and never has justified its television plan by an interest in assisting schools in "blacking out" their home games in the areas in which they are played.

[60] Ironically, to the extent that the NCAA's position has merit, it rests on the assumption that football telecasts are a unique product. If, as the NCAA argues, all television programming is essentially fungible, it would not be possible to protect attendance without banning all television during the hours at which intercollegiate football games are held.

VI

Petitioner argues that the interest in maintaining a competitive balance among amateur athletic teams is legitimate and important and that it justifies the regulations challenged in this case. We agree with the first part of the argument but not the second.

Our decision not to apply a per se rule to this case rests in large part on our recognition that a certain degree of cooperation is necessary if the type of competition that petitioner and its member institutions seek to market is to be preserved. It is reasonable to assume that most of the regulatory controls of the NCAA are justifiable means of fostering competition among amateur athletic teams and therefore procompetitive because they enhance public interest in intercollegiate athletics. The specific restraints on football telecasts that are challenged in this case do not, however, fit into the same mold as do rules defining the conditions of the contest, the eligibility of participants, or the manner in which members of a joint enterprise shall share the responsibilities and the benefits of the total venture.

The NCAA does not claim that its television plan has equalized or is intended to equalize competition within any one league.[62] The plan is nationwide in scope and there is no single league or tournament in which all college football teams complete. There is no evidence of any intent to equalize the strength of teams in Division I-A with those in Division II or Division III, and not even a colorable basis for giving colleges that have no football program at all a voice in the management of the revenues generated by the football programs at other schools. The interest in maintaining a competitive balance that is asserted by the NCAA as a justification for regulating all television of intercollegiate football is not related to any neutral standard or to any readily identifiable group of competitors.

The television plan is not even arguably tailored to serve such an interest. It does not regulate the amount of money that any college may spend on its football program, nor the way in which the colleges may use the revenues that are generated by their football programs, whether derived from the sale of television rights, the sale of tickets, or the sale of concessions or program advertising. The plan simply imposes a restriction on one source of revenue that is more important to some colleges than to others. There is no evidence that this restriction produces any greater measure of equality throughout the NCAA than would a restriction on alumni donations, tuition rates, or any other revenue-

62 It seems unlikely, for example, that there would have been a greater disparity between the football prowess of Ohio State University and that of Northwestern University in recent years without the NCAA's television plan. The District Court found that in fact the NCAA has been strikingly unsuccessful if it has indeed attempted to prevent the emergence of a "power elite" in intercollegiate football. Moreover, the District Court's finding that there would be more local and regional telecasts without the NCAA controls means that Northwestern could well have generated more television income in a free market than was obtained under the NCAA regime.

producing activity. At the same time, as the District Court found, the NCAA imposes a variety of other restrictions designed to preserve amateurism which are much better tailored to the goal of competitive balance than is the television plan, and which are "clearly sufficient" to preserve competitive balance to the extent it is within the NCAA's power to do so. And much more than speculation supported the District Court's findings on this score. No other NCAA sport employs a similar plan, and in particular the court found that in the most closely analogous sport, college basketball, competitive balance has been maintained without resort to a restrictive television plan.

Perhaps the most important reason for rejecting the argument that the interest in competitive balance is served by the television plan is the District Court's unambiguous and well-supported finding that many more games would be televised in a free market than under the NCAA plan. The hypothesis that legitimates the maintenance of competitive balance as a procompetitive justification under the Rule of Reason is that equal competition will maximize consumer demand for the product. The finding that consumption will materially increase if the controls are removed is a compelling demonstration that they do not in fact serve any such legitimate purpose.[68] . . . *Affirmed.*

NOTES AND QUESTIONS ON *NCAA*

1. ***Why isn't this agreement per se illegal?*** Given that the agreement here involved horizontal output-fixing, why isn't it per se illegal? The Court stressed that the NCAA had a productive joint venture and that it was undisputed that some agreements were necessary to further the joint venture's procompetitive purposes. In particular, here the product was itself sports competition between college teams, which requires some agreements among competitors, such as on the rules of football competition. However, that does not itself imply any need to agree on television contracts. Nor does it distinguish *Maricopa*, where there was a productive joint venture on peer review and claims administration that clearly required some agreements.

The stronger difference is that the NCAA argued that the output-fixing restraints on television contracts were reasonably necessary to advance the procompetitive purposes of its productive joint venture. Whether the television restraints were actually reasonably necessary is a matter to address under the rule of reason, and indeed the Court rejected that claim in its rule of reason analysis. But the case holding suggests that a plausible allegation of such a connection to a productive joint venture is enough to take the case out of the per se rule. This is the difference from *Maricopa*, where the defendants did not claim their agreement was reasonably necessary to advance the procompetitive purposes of their productive joint venture on

[68] This is true not only for television viewers, but also for athletes. The District Court's finding that the television exposure of all schools would increase in the absence of the NCAA's television plan means that smaller institutions appealing to essentially local or regional markets would get more exposure if the plan is enjoined, enhancing their ability to compete for student athletes.

peer review and claims administration. Instead, in *Maricopa*, the defendants argued a free-standing procompetitive justification unrelated to their joint venture, which amounted to a form of market regulation.

2. ***Why don't "exclusive TV rights" fit within the new product exception?*** The Court rejected the "new product" argument, which rejected a dissent argument that the agreement produced "exclusive TV rights" that were more valuable and thus fit within the "new product" exception of *BMI*. The problem with the dissent's logic is that it would equally suggest that the "new product" exception could cover any output restriction, which could always be described as offering limited rights to that output which make it more valuable. The disagreement between the Court and the dissent also highlights that one problem with a new product exception is that it is difficult to devise a formal rule on what qualifies as a "new product." One could focus on how functionally desirable the new product was, but that seems to just get us back to the point that the new product exception is just a special case of a procompetitive justification that is ancillary to a productive business collaboration. As the *Maricopa* and *NCAA* rejections of "new product" arguments suggest, the new product test articulated in *BMI* has not turned out to be very determinative of how future cases have been resolved.

3. ***Why weren't the NCAA's justifications valid?*** The NCAA did offer various justifications for the output-fixing restraints. Note that because antitrust law limited the NCAA to justifications that were reasonably necessary for its business collaboration, the NCAA could not argue that restraining competition fixed a general market failure. The NCAA had to argue that the restraint made its product—college sports competition—more attractive in some way, such as by making games closer or preserving some attribute (loud crowds or amateur players) that made consumers enjoy the product more. But the Court rejected each of those justifications. Why?

a. ***What is wrong with the justification of protecting live attendance from competition with televised college football?*** If the goal was to protect live attendance at *televised* games by preventing fans from staying home to watch the same game on television, this could be a valid procompetitive justification because empty stadiums would make games less exciting and thus make the product less attractive to television viewers, who are the consumers in the relevant market. However, achieving this goal had a clear less restrictive alternative: teams could individually decide not to televise their games in their region. *See* n.56. If the goal was to protect live attendance at some games by preventing fans from watching *other* games on television, then the Court concluded that goal was anticompetitive on principle because it interfered with free consumer choice between watching one game live versus watching another game on television. There was also no real empirical evidence that the agreement advanced the goal of protecting live attendance, and the agreement was poorly tailored to do so since the NCAA had college games on at the same time as live events all the time.

b. ***What is wrong with the justification of evening out TV revenue/exposure of different schools to increase parity on the football field?*** The Court agreed the parity argument was a legitimate justification because more equal teams are more likely to lead to close games that consumers want to see. But the Court thought the agreement was poorly tailored to advance parity. The Court implicitly seemed to think a less restrictive alternative would be regulating spending by teams on football. However, the Court did not consider the fact that this alternative would restrict output in the input markets, such as in the labor market for college football coaches. Nor would equal spending alter the fact that greater television exposure helps recruits the best athletes. So it is not so clear that alternatives were preferable means to advance parity.

A stronger point may be that the parity argument does not justify grouping so many schools in one division. Because the claim that parity is procompetitive is not about abstract equality but rather about making games closer and thus more exciting for consumers, it only justifies attempting to maintain parity among those teams who play each other. Parity among CFA members could suffice.

Finally, the Court concluded that the NCAA plan did not in fact create parity on the field or in television exposure and revenue, which was a decisive problem with this defense. Increasing regional telecasts probably would have created more parity. *See* n.62.

c. What is wrong with the justification of reducing TV exposure/revenue to protect amateurism? The NCAA also argued that that reducing TV exposure and revenue would protect amateurism. Note that to be procompetitive, this cannot be an argument that amateurism should be protected from competition because amateurism is morally good in some general sense. To be procompetitive, the argument instead has to be college sports has a distinctive attraction to its viewers because of the players' amateur status. This distinctive attraction might, for example, explain why college football is so much more popular with television viewers than minor league baseball. The empirics of the extent to which fans care about amateur status was not developed (and may perhaps have changed in modern times), but the Court seemed to assume it for the sake of argument. The logic of why greater television exposure and college revenue would significantly affect amateurism was also not well explained. The implicit reasoning seems to be that when a lot of fame and money is floating around, it increases the incentives of colleges or their boosters to pay to get the best players, thus ruining their amateur status.

The Court, however, concluded that even if amateurism was important to the attractiveness of the product to its consumers, a less restrictive alternative for preserving amateurism would be greater enforcement of academic eligibility requirements. This logic is decisive if one assumes that enforcing academic eligibility requirements is easy, but what if enforcing them is hard? Given such difficulties, it could be that the restraint significantly aided enforcement of academic eligibility requirements by lowering the gains for evading them, in which case enforcing those requirements alone might not be an alternative that could equally achieve the same goal.

4. If there is no procompetitive justification that does not have a less restrictive alternative, is there any need to inquire into whether defendants had the market power to restrict output? No, because without any procompetitive justification, any net effect of a horizontal output restraint can only be negative. Thus, even if the per se rule does not apply, a "naked" restraint (i.e., one not clothed with a procompetitive justification), can be summarily condemned under the rule of reason without requiring proof of market power or an actual effect on output, as the Court held.

5. If we know output has been restricted, should courts bother to consider evidence on market power or efficiency justifications? If we know output has been restricted, there is also no need to inquire into market power or efficiency justifications because the output restriction means (a) the defendants must have had the market power to restrict output and (b) that the anticompetitive effects on output must have outweighed any procompetitive effects on output, as the Court held.

D. HORIZONTAL MARKET DIVISIONS

Horizontal agreements between unrelated rivals to divide a market are per se illegal. Such market divisions generally involve territorial divisions, where each firm agrees to limit itself to a geographic area different from the other firm. But customers can also be divided in other ways, such as having one rival sell to commercial users and another to regular consumers, or by having firms agree to restrict themselves to different products or lines of commerce. Bid rigging is also a form of market division, where the conspirators agree that only one of them will really bid for each particular job. Similar to the above sections, the question is whether and when horizontal market divisions might be taken out of the per se rule on the grounds that they are incidental to some productive rival collaboration.

Horizontal market divisions can be even more anticompetitive than price-fixing or output-restrictions. They allow cartels to avoid the difficulties of fixing and monitoring prices and output, and of allocating market share among the cartel members. The cartel need simply monitor where or to whom firms are selling. Further, market divisions end all forms of competition between the firms, including on quality and service. Thus, unlike price and output restraints, market divisions cannot be undermined by nonprice competition.

Palmer v. BRG

498 U.S. 46 (1990).

■ PER CURIAM opinion:

In preparation for the 1985 Georgia Bar Examination, petitioners contracted to take a bar review course offered by respondent BRG of Georgia, Inc. (BRG). In this litigation they contend that the price of

BRG's course was enhanced by reason of an unlawful agreement between BRG and respondent Harcourt Brace Jovanovich Legal and Professional Publications (HBJ), the Nation's largest provider of bar review materials and lecture services. The central issue is whether the 1980 agreement between respondents violated § 1 of the Sherman Act.

HBJ began offering a Georgia bar review course on a limited basis in 1976, and was in direct, and often intense, competition with BRG during the period from 1977–1979. BRG and HBJ were the two main providers of bar review courses in Georgia during this time period. In early 1980, they entered into an agreement that gave BRG an exclusive license to market HBJ's material in Georgia and to use its trade name "Bar/Bri." The parties agreed that HBJ would not compete with BRG in Georgia and that BRG would not compete with HBJ outside of Georgia. Under the agreement, HBJ received $100 per student enrolled by BRG and 40% of all revenues over $350. Immediately after the 1980 agreement, the price of BRG's course was increased from $150 to over $400.

. . . [The Court of Appeals held] that per se unlawful horizontal price fixing required an explicit agreement on prices to be charged or that one party have the right to be consulted about the other's prices. . . . [It also held] that to prove a per se violation under a geographic market allocation theory, petitioners had to show that respondents had subdivided some relevant market in which they had previously competed. . . .

In United States v. Socony-Vacuum Oil Co., 310 U.S. 150 (1940), we held that an agreement among competitors to engage in a program of buying surplus gasoline on the spot market in order to prevent prices from falling sharply was unlawful, even though there was no direct agreement on the actual prices to be maintained. We explained that "under the Sherman Act a combination formed for the purpose and with the effect of raising, depressing, fixing, pegging, or stabilizing the price of a commodity in interstate or foreign commerce is illegal per se."

The revenue-sharing formula in the 1980 agreement between BRG and HBJ, coupled with the price increase that took place immediately after the parties agreed to cease competing with each other in 1980, indicates that this agreement was "formed for the purpose and with the effect of raising" the price of the bar review course. It was, therefore, plainly incorrect for the District Court to enter summary judgment in respondents' favor. Moreover, it is equally clear that the District Court and the Court of Appeals erred when they assumed that an allocation of markets or submarkets by competitors is not unlawful unless the market in which the two previously competed is divided between them.

In United States v. Topco Associates, Inc., 405 U.S. 596 (1972), we held that agreements between competitors to allocate territories to minimize competition are illegal:

> "One of the classic examples of a per se violation of § 1 is an agreement between competitors at the same level of the market structure to allocate territories in order to minimize competition. . . . This Court has reiterated time and time again that 'horizontal territorial limitations . . . are naked restraints of trade with no purpose except stifling of competition.' Such limitations are per se violations of the Sherman Act."

The defendants in Topco had never competed in the same market, but had simply agreed to allocate markets. Here, HBJ and BRG had previously competed in the Georgia market; under their allocation agreement, BRG received that market, while HBJ received the remainder of the United States. Each agreed not to compete in the other's territories. Such agreements are anticompetitive regardless of whether the parties split a market within which both do business or whether they merely reserve one market for one and another for the other. Thus, the 1980 agreement between HBJ and BRG was unlawful on its face.

The petition for writ of certiorari is granted, the judgment of the Court of Appeals is reversed, and the case is remanded for further proceedings consistent with this opinion.

■ JUSTICE MARSHALL, dissenting. Although I agree that the limited information before us appears to indicate that the Court of Appeals erred in its decision below, I continue to believe that summary dispositions deprive litigants of a fair opportunity to be heard on the merits and significantly increase the risk of an erroneous decision. I therefore dissent from the Court's decision today to reverse summarily the judgment below.

NOTES AND QUESTIONS ON *PALMER V. BRG*

1. ***Why does this agreement constitute price-fixing when it does not fix a price?*** The Supreme Court held that, even though the agreement did not explicitly fix a price, it constituted horizontal price-fixing because its purpose and effect was to raise prices. Is this purpose-and-effect test consistent with the per se rule against price-fixing that was applied in *Maricopa*? True, a purpose-and-effect test amounts to a (somewhat truncated) form of rule-of-reason inquiry, and per se rules are supposed to categorically condemn agreements without regard to proof of purpose or effect. However, what the combination of *Palmer* and *Maricopa* suggests is that, if a purpose and effect to alter prices exists, an explicit agreement on prices need not be proven, but that if an explicit agreement on prices is proven, such a purpose and effect need not be shown. The latter is thus still a categorical per se rule. Further, the former still means that if a purpose and effect of altering prices is proven, the Court will still not admit justifications that the effect on prices was reasonable.

2. ***How do we know the purpose and effect here was to raise prices?*** The Court believed the revenue-sharing agreement showed a purpose to profit from a price increase and that the actual post-agreement

price increase proved a price effect. However, because the Court decided the case summarily on the petition for certiorari without the benefit of briefing on the merits, it ignored record evidence suggesting that neither of those conclusions was so clearcut. In particular, it ignored the lower court finding that, in 1979, BRG was charging low prices only because it was getting free test-marketed West materials, and HBJ charged low prices to compete with BRG but was losing money. The district court concluded the 1980 price increase was as likely caused by West's decision to stop its free test-market as by the challenged agreement. This evidence and finding undermine the Court's assumption that the plain effect of the agreement was to raise prices. It also gives an independent motive for why BRG wanted to obtain HBJ materials and thus undermines the Court's assumption that the plain purpose was to raise prices.

The agreement could be justified by the agreement to license higher-quality Bar/Bri materials. This licensing could help explain the revenue-sharing, because it makes sense to compensate HBJ to the extent high-quality materials allowed a price increase, and the price increase, because higher-quality materials can be sold at higher prices. The Supreme Court's failure to address these facts suggests that perhaps Justice Marshall was correct that the Court acted precipitously in adjudicating this case summarily without the benefit of briefing on the merits.

3. ***Was the agreement also per se illegal as a horizontal market division?*** Even if this agreement were not deemed horizontal price-fixing, the Court held it was plainly a per se illegal horizontal market division. In doing so, the Court easily rejected the lower court conclusion that the per se prohibition on horizontal market divisions applied only when firms divide and stay in the same market. After all, an agreement to become and stay monopolists in separate markets is even more anticompetitive because it totally eliminates competition in each market. So this part of the lower court reasoning was clearly flawed, which perhaps explains why the Supreme Court treated this as any easy case.

But again there was other evidence that the Supreme Court ignored when it summarily decided the case without the benefit of briefing on the merits. The lower court had found that, at about the same time that BRG lost access to free West materials, the lawyer who had been in charge of HBJ in Georgia had a heart attack, and HBJ had said it decided to leave the Georgia market then, which was months before it reached its agreement with BRG. This evidence suggests that, absent the agreement, BRG and/or HBJ might not have competed in Georgia in 1980, because BRG had personnel but no materials and HBJ had materials but lacked key personnel. They may have been able to better stay in the market by combining BRG's personnel with HBJ's materials. Given this evidence, it is far less clear this agreement should be classified as a horizontal territorial restraint that ended horizontal competition that otherwise would have existed. This evidence also further suggests that the agreement may have had a purpose and effect other than raising prices and reducing competition. Do you think the Supreme Court would have come out the same way if it had taken into account this evidence?

*4. **Why doesn't the relation to a productive business collaboration take this case out of the per se rule?*** Even if the agreement were deemed a horizontal price-fix or market division, one might argue that the agreement should have been deemed outside the per se rule under *BMI* and *NCAA* because the agreement was ancillary to the productive business collaboration of licensing bar review materials. But the Supreme Court did not address this argument or treat the licensing of the materials as a serious motivation. The Court apparently thought that here the putative joint venture was really just a fig leaf to try to escape per se scrutiny of what was really a naked horizontal market division.

*5. **Why wasn't this agreement vertical rather than horizontal?*** Given that the territorial division was part of HBJ's agreement to license bar materials to BRG, the defendants argued below that this agreement should have been characterized as vertical rather than horizontal. A vertical agreement between a supplier and distributor that restricts the territory in which the distributor can do business is subject to rule-of-reason review under U.S. law, even when the supplier chooses to itself distribute in other territories. *See* Chapter 5. The Court did not consider this argument, probably because the Court believed the agreement ended horizontal competition between the only two firms in the market. Moreover, the agreement here might not be deemed reasonably necessary to licensing the copyrighted HBJ materials because it did not limit just BRG's distribution of those materials but also eliminated any competition by BRG outside of Georgia. On the other hand, a supplier might have procompetitive reasons to want its distributor to focus on a particular region, one of which is to focus efforts and resources in one region which would enhance such distribution efforts. *See* Chapter 5.

*6. **Would this case come out the same way if 10 equally-sized firms were left in the Georgia bar review market after the agreement?*** Probably not. If ten equally sized-firms were left in the Georgia bar review market after the agreement, they would likely assure a level of competition that makes it far less likely that the agreement would have an anticompetitive effect, which it turn would make it more likely that the agreement had some procompetitive relation to a collaboration that combined personnel with materials in a way that allowed the joint venture to compete better with other firms in the Georgia market. The fact that the case would likely come out differently with different market shares and structure suggests, in turn, the Court was not really applying a per se test. It is rather a case that looked obvious to the Court because the Court thought the business collaboration was a sham and eliminated competition between the only two firms in the market. This seems more like twinkling-of-an-eye abbreviated rule of reason condemnation than a real per se rule.

In doing so, the Court again ignored record evidence below. The lower court had found there were actually two other bar review firms in the Georgia market: NORD and PMBR. There was no evidence on the record about what happened to those firm's prices from 1979 to 1980. Plaintiffs' expert opined that HBJ or BRG combined had over 80% of University of Georgia law students who took a bar review course in Athens, Georgia in

1979, but the district court held that the expert improperly defined the market as limited to Athens during the winter academic term. The district court concluded the proper market was instead statewide, on which the HBJ-BRG market share was unclear but presumably lower. The existence of these two statewide competitors makes it more likely that the purpose of the agreement may have been procompetitive rather than anticompetitive, though hardly as clear as in the hypothetical where 10 other competitors existed. Might taking this evidence into account have changed the Supreme Court's conclusions?

E. HORIZONTAL AGREEMENTS NOT TO DEAL WITH PARTICULAR FIRMS

Horizontal agreements between unrelated rivals not to do business with another firm are considered per se illegal boycotts under U.S. antitrust law. As with the other per se offenses, the per se rule against boycotts tends not to apply when the rivals are related in a productive rival collaboration that is furthered by the agreement. Rather, a more nuanced analysis is used to determine when it is unlawful for members of a productive rival collaboration to agree to refuse to admit other competitors into their collaboration, or to expel them after they were previously admitted.

But horizontal boycotts do have some consistent thematic differences from other per se offenses such as fixing prices or output or dividing markets. First, boycotts are often aimed at harming particular competitors, rather than competition in general. This raises an issue whether such activity should be condemned by antitrust given that it is often said that antitrust laws aim to protect "competition, not competitors."[18] But such statements are almost always made in the context of rejecting a claim that antitrust law should protect competitors at the expense of competition and efficiency. If competitors are being harmed without any benefit to competition or efficiency, then there seems little reason to tolerate the abuse. This seems especially true when the conduct might create anticompetitive effects that are costly or difficult to ascertain accurately.

Second, boycotts are more likely to have plausible noneconomic justifications, such as punishing particular bad actors. But this also raises a parallel new noneconomic objection: the concern that firms might abuse any extra-governmental power conferred on them by their collective market position to further views that are self-interested, politically unaccountable, and possibly idiosyncratic.

[18] *See, e.g.,* Brooke Group Ltd. v. Brown & Williamson Tobacco Corp., 509 U.S. 209, 224 (1993); Copperweld Corp. v. Independence Tube Corp., 467 U.S. 752, 768 n.14 (1984); Brunswick Corp. v. Pueblo Bowl-O-Mat, Inc., 429 U.S. 477, 488 (1977); Brown Shoe Co. v. United States, 370 U.S. 294, 320 (1962).

1. BOYCOTTS BY UNRELATED RIVALS

Klor's Inc. v. Broadway-Hale Stores, Inc.

359 U.S. 207 (1959).

■ MR. JUSTICE BLACK delivered the opinion of the Court.

Klor's, Inc., operates a retail store on Mission Street, San Francisco, California; Broadway-Hale Stores, Inc., a chain of department stores, operates one of its stores next door. The two stores compete in the sale of radios, television sets, refrigerators and other household appliances. Claiming that Broadway-Hale and 10 national manufacturers and their distributors have conspired to restrain and monopolize commerce in violation of §§ 1 and 2 of the Sherman Act, Klor's brought this action for treble damages and injunction in the United States District Court.

In support of its claim Klor's made the following allegations: . . . Klor's is as well equipped as Broadway-Hale to handle all brands of appliances. Nevertheless, manufacturers and distributors of such well-known brands as General Electric, RCA, Admiral, Zenith, Emerson and others have conspired among themselves and with Broadway-Hale either not to sell to Klor's or to sell to it only at discriminatory prices and highly unfavorable terms. Broadway-Hale has used its "monopolistic" buying power to bring about this situation. . . . The concerted refusal to deal with Klor's has seriously handicapped its ability to compete and has already caused it a great loss of profits, goodwill, reputation and prestige.

The defendants did not dispute these allegations, but sought summary judgment and dismissal of the complaint for failure to state a cause of action. They submitted unchallenged affidavits which showed that there were hundreds of other household appliance retailers, some within a few blocks of Klor's who sold many competing brands of appliances, including those the defendants refused to sell to Klor's. . . . [T]he District Court concluded that the controversy was a "purely private quarrel" between Klor's and Broadway-Hale, which did not amount to a "public wrong proscribed by the (Sherman) Act." On this ground the complaint was dismissed and summary judgment was entered for the defendants. The Court of Appeals for the Ninth Circuit affirmed the summary judgment. It stated that "a violation of the Sherman Act requires conduct of defendants by which the public is or conceivably may be ultimately injured." It held that here the required public injury was missing since "there was no charge or proof that by any act of defendants the price, quantity, or quality offered the public was affected, nor that there was any intent or purpose to effect a change in, or an influence on, prices, quantity, or quality * * *." The holding, if correct, means that unless the opportunities for customers to buy in a competitive market are reduced, a group of powerful businessmen may act in concert to deprive a single merchant, like Klor, of the goods he needs to compete effectively. . . .

We think Klor's allegations clearly show one type of trade restraint and public harm the Sherman Act forbids, and that defendants' affidavits provide no defense to the charges. . . . In the landmark case of *Standard Oil*, this Court read § 1 to prohibit those classes of contracts or acts which the common law had deemed to be undue restraints of trade and those which new times and economic conditions would make unreasonable. . . . The effect . . . the Court said, was to adopt the common-law proscription of all "contracts or acts which it was considered had a monopolistic tendency * * * " and which interfered with the "natural flow" of an appreciable amount of interstate commerce. The Court recognized that there were some agreements whose validity depended on the surrounding circumstances. It emphasized, however, that there were classes of restraints which from their "nature or character" were unduly restrictive, and hence forbidden by both the common law and the statute. As to these classes of restraints, the Court noted, Congress had determined its own criteria of public harm and it was not for the courts to decide whether in an individual case injury had actually occurred.

Group boycotts, or concerted refusals by traders to deal with other traders, have long been held to be in the forbidden category. They have not been saved by allegations that they were reasonable in the specific circumstances, nor by a failure to show that they "fixed or regulated prices, parcelled out or limited production, or brought about a deterioration in quality." *Fashion Originators'. Cf. Trenton Potteries.* Even when they operated to lower prices or temporarily to stimulate competition they were banned. For, . . . "such agreements, no less than those to fix minimum prices, cripple the freedom of traders and thereby restrain their ability to sell in accordance with their own judgment."

Plainly the allegations of this complaint disclose such a boycott. This is not a case of a single trader refusing to deal with another, nor even of a manufacturer and a dealer agreeing to an exclusive distributorship. Alleged in this complaint is a wide combination consisting of manufacturers, distributors and a retailer. This combination takes from Klor's its freedom to buy appliances in an open competitive market and drives it out of business as a dealer in the defendants' products. It deprives the manufacturers and distributors of their freedom to sell to Klor's at the same prices and conditions made available to Broadway-Hale and in some instances forbids them from selling to it on any terms whatsoever. It interferes with the natural flow of interstate commerce. It clearly has, by its "nature" and "character," a "monopolistic tendency." As such it is not to be tolerated merely because the victim is just one merchant whose business is so small that his destruction makes little difference to the economy. Monopoly can as surely thrive by the elimination of such small businessmen, one at a time, as it can by driving them out in large groups. In recognition of this fact the Sherman Act has consistently been read to forbid all contracts and combinations which "tend to create a monopoly," whether "the tendency is a creeping one" or "one that proceeds at full gallop." . . . [R]eversed . . .

NOTES AND QUESTIONS ON *KLOR'S*

1. ***Was it plausible that the manufacturers would horizontally agree to boycott a retailer?*** The agreement that was held per se illegal was the horizontal agreement among those 10 suppliers to stop doing business with Klor's, not the 10 vertical agreements between Broadway-Hale and the 10 suppliers. One might wonder how plausible that horizontal agreement is. After all, the suppliers did not have any incentive to agree to eliminate one of their retailers. The suppliers benefit from increasing retail competition because that tends to lowers retail markups and thus increase sales of the suppliers' goods. Moreover, if each supplier agreed only because of Broadway-Hale's buyer market power, then one could argue that Klor's supply was cut off by a series of 10 vertical agreements and that any horizontal agreement was not necessary to the boycott. However, it is easier to persuade suppliers to go along with such a boycott if they can be assured that their supplier rivals would not be able to gain any advantage by continuing to sell through Klor's. Thus, a series of vertical agreements might not have been quite enough to get the suppliers to go along without a horizontal agreement. Because here the issue was whether to dismiss a complaint, the Court simply accepted the allegation that there was a horizontal agreement among the suppliers to boycott Klor's.

2. ***If this boycott would eliminate only Klor's, does any harm justify per se condemnation?*** A horizontal boycott would clearly harm Klor's. However, consumers would be deprived of just one retailer among hundreds in the area, some within a few blocks. Why then wasn't the district court correct that such a boycott could not create a public harm to market prices, output, or quality that justifies Sherman Act condemnation?

Part of the Court's answer was that eliminating Klor's might be the first step to an "incipient monopoly," but that hardly seems plausible given the number of retailers and one could always condemn any later boycotts that actually create market power under the rule of reason. The Court today generally does not condemn restraints that have no anticompetitive effects because later restraints might create anticompetitive effects.

Another part of the Court's answer was that the harm to a single competitor like Klor's sufficed to show anticompetitive harm. That seems sensible where, as here, there was allegedly zero offsetting procompetitive benefit to consumers. On the other hand, we shall see that the Court commonly invokes the proposition that the antitrust laws protect "competition, not competitors" to refuse to condemn conduct that harms a competitor but benefits consumers. But where there is zero benefit to consumers, this case suggests that harm to individual competitors can suffice for antitrust condemnation.

The final part of the Court's answer was that horizontal boycotts were per se illegal, and thus illegal without any proof of harm to market prices, output, or quality. That part of the argument seems somewhat circular because the question is why horizontal boycotts should be illegal even when they cause no harm to market prices, output, or quality. Perhaps what the Court had in mind was that, to the extent this boycott had *any* effect on market prices, output, or quality, it could only be harmful to consumers given the alleged lack of any procompetitive justification. Eliminating one retailer cannot benefit consumers. But eliminating one retailer might harm consumers slightly. It might even harm consumers significantly if the correct market definition was the local block on Mission Street. Indeed, if Broadway-Hale did not think Klor's was imposing a restraint on Broadway-Hale's prices that other retailers were not, then Broadway-Hale had no reason to organize a boycott to eliminate Klor's. And if Broadway-Hale did think Klor's was imposing some unique restraint on Broadway-Hale's prices, then Broadway-Hale must have thought that being the only retailer on the block would have given it some market power to raise prices.

Moreover, even if the absence of an effect on market prices, output, or quality looked obvious in this case, allowing a no-effect defense would affect other cases, where anticompetitive effects might be more debatable, such as when it seems a closer call whether eliminating one rival would affect prices, output, or quality. Sometimes courts will erroneously conclude that no anticompetitive effects exist when they actually do, and the costs of having to establish anticompetitive effects will discourage bringing cases. Both of those consequences will increase the underdeterrence of boycotts that do impose anticompetitive harms on consumers. This additional underdeterrence is not worth bearing for boycotts that, as alleged here, lack any procompetitive justification and thus raise no overdeterrence concern.

3. ***The importance of putting something on the positive side of the ledger.*** Crucial to the analysis above was that the plaintiff alleged there was zero procompetitive justification and the defendants did not put one forward. This is somewhat of a running theme of antitrust law: if no procompetitive justification is offered, then courts are likely to favor plaintiffs who raise even weak anticompetitive concerns, on the grounds that if the agreement had any effect at all, it would be a net negative. Defendants who put nothing on the positive side of the ledger tend to lose and provoke sweeping opinions contrary to them.

4. ***What if the boycott was motivated by spite?*** As noted above, given the lack of any procompetitive justification, Broadway-Hale had no rational reason to organize a boycott of Klor's unless it thought that the boycott would increase prices. But what if Broadway-Hale was instead motivated by irrational spite? Spite against next-door neighbors is, alas, somewhat common. If spite were the motive, then we cannot necessarily conclude that Broadway-Hale thought that anticompetitive effects were likely. On the other hand, irrational spite is also not socially desirable, so it remains the case that applying per se condemnation creates no overdeterrence concern to offset the underdeterrence concern that would have been raised by creating an exception to the per se rule against horizontal boycotts by unrelated firms.

Fashion Originators' Guild of Am. v. FTC

312 U.S. 457 (1941).

■ MR. JUSTICE BLACK delivered the opinion of the Court.

The Circuit Court of Appeals ... affirmed a Federal Trade Commission decree ordering petitioners to cease and desist from certain practices found to have been done in combination and to constitute "unfair methods of competition" tending to monopoly. . . .

Some of the members of the combination design, manufacture, sell and distribute women's garments—chiefly dresses. Others are manufacturers, converters or dyers of textiles from which these garments are made. Fashion Originators' Guild of America (FOGA), an organization controlled by these groups, is the instrument through which petitioners work to accomplish the purposes condemned by the Commission. The garment manufacturers claim to be creators of original and distinctive designs of fashionable clothes for women, and the textile manufacturers claim to be creators of similar original fabric designs. After these designs enter the channels of trade, other manufacturers systematically make and sell copies of them, the copies usually selling at prices lower than the garments copied. Petitioners call this practice of copying unethical and immoral, and give it the name of "style piracy." And although they admit that their "original creations" are neither copyrighted nor patented, and indeed assert that existing legislation affords them no protection against copyists, they nevertheless urge that sale of copied designs constitutes an unfair trade practice and a tortious invasion of their rights. Because of these alleged wrongs, petitioners, while continuing to compete with one another in many respects, combined among themselves to combat and, if possible, destroy all competition from the sale of garments which are copies of their "original creations." They admit that to destroy such competition they have in combination purposely boycotted and declined to sell their products to retailers who follow a policy of selling garments copied by other manufacturers from designs put out by Guild members. As a result of their efforts, approximately 12,000 retailers throughout the country have signed agreements to "cooperate" with the Guild's boycott program, but more than half of these signed the agreements only because constrained by threats that Guild members would not sell to retailers who failed to yield to their demands—threats that have been carried out by the Guild practice of placing on red cards the names of non-cooperators (to whom no sales are to be made), placing on white cards the names of cooperators (to whom sales are to be made), and then distributing both sets of cards to the manufacturers.

The one hundred and seventy-six manufacturers of women's garments who are members of the Guild occupy a commanding position in their line of business. In 1936, they sold in the United States more than 38% of all women's garments wholesaling at $6.75 and up, and more than 60% of those at $10.75 and above. The power of the combination is great; competition and the demand of the consuming public make it necessary for most retail dealers to stock some of the products of these manufacturers. And the power of the combination is made even greater by reason of the affiliation of some members of the National Federation of Textiles, Inc.—that being an organization composed of about one hundred textile manufacturers, converters, dyers, and printers of silk and rayon used in making women's garments. Those members of the Federation who are affiliated with the Guild have agreed to sell their products only to those garment manufacturers who have in turn agreed to sell only to cooperating retailers.

The Guild maintains a Design Registration Bureau for garments, and the Textile Federation maintains a similar Bureau for textiles. The Guild employs "shoppers" to visit the stores of both cooperating and non-cooperating retailers, "for the purpose of examining their stocks, to determine and report as to whether they contain . . . copies of registered designs. . . ." An elaborate system of trial and appellate tribunals exists, for the determination of whether a given garment is in fact a copy of a Guild member's design. In order to assure the success of its plan of registration and restraint, and to ascertain whether Guild regulations are being violated, the Guild audits its members' books. And if violations of Guild requirements are discovered, as, for example, sales to red-carded retailers, the violators are subject to heavy fines. . . .

If the purpose and practice of the combination of garment manufacturers and their affiliates runs counter to the public policy declared in the Sherman and Clayton Acts, the Federal Trade Commission has the power to suppress it as an unfair method of competition. . . . And among the many respects in which the Guild's plan runs contrary to the policy of the Sherman Act are these: it narrows the outlets to which garment and textile manufacturers can sell and the sources from which retailers can buy; subjects all retailers and manufacturers who decline to comply with the Guild's program to an organized boycott; takes away the freedom of action of members by requiring each to reveal to the Guild the intimate details of their individual affairs; and has both as its necessary tendency and as its purpose and effect the direct suppression of competition from the sale of unregistered textiles and copied designs. In addition to all this, the combination is in reality an extra-governmental agency, which prescribes rules for the regulation and restraint of interstate commerce, and provides extra-judicial tribunals for determination and punishment of violations, and thus "trenches upon the power of the national legislature and violates the statute." . . .

Petitioners, however, argue that the combination cannot be contrary to the policy of the Sherman and Clayton Acts, since the Federal Trade Commission did not find that the combination fixed or regulated prices, parcelled out or limited production, or brought about a deterioration in quality. But action falling into these three categories does not exhaust the types of conduct banned by the Sherman and Clayton Acts. . . . [I]t was the object of the Federal Trade Commission Act to reach not merely in their fruition but also in their incipiency combinations which could lead to these and other trade restraints and practices deemed undesirable. In this case, the Commission found that the combination exercised sufficient control and power in the women's garments and textile businesses "to exclude from the industry those manufacturers and distributors who do not conform to the rules and regulations of said respondents, and thus tend to create in themselves a monopoly in the said industries." While a conspiracy to fix prices is illegal, an intent to increase prices is not an ever-present essential of conduct amounting to a violation of the policy of the Sherman and Clayton Acts; a monopoly contrary to their policies can exist even though a combination may temporarily or even permanently reduce the price of the articles manufactured or sold. For as this Court has said, "Trade or commerce under those circumstances may nevertheless be badly and unfortunately restrained by driving out of business the small dealers and worthy men whose lives have been spent therein, and who might be unable to readjust themselves to their altered surroundings. Mere reduction in the price of the commodity dealt in might be dearly paid for by the ruin of such a class, and the absorption of control over one commodity by an all-powerful combination of capital."

But petitioners further argue that their boycott and restraint of interstate trade is not within the ban of the policies of the Sherman and Clayton Acts because "the practices of FOGA were reasonable and necessary to protect the manufacturer, laborer, retailer and consumer against the devastating evils growing from the pirating of original designs and had in fact benefited all four." The Commission declined to hear much of the evidence that petitioners desired to offer on this subject. As we have pointed out, however, the aim of petitioners' combination was the intentional destruction of one type of manufacture and sale which competed with Guild members. The purpose and object of this combination, its potential power, its tendency to monopoly, the coercion it could and did practice upon a rival method of competition, all brought it within the policy of the prohibition declared by the Sherman and Clayton Acts. . . . Under these circumstances it was not error to refuse to hear the evidence offered, for the reasonableness of the methods pursued by the combination to accomplish its unlawful object is no more material than would be the reasonableness of the prices fixed by unlawful combination. Nor can the unlawful combination be justified upon the argument that systematic copying of dress designs is itself tortious, or should now be declared so by us. In the first place, whether or not given conduct is tortious is a question of state law. . . . In the second place, even if copying were an acknowledged tort under the law of every state, that situation would not justify petitioners in combining together to regulate and restrain interstate commerce in violation of federal law.... *Affirmed.*

NOTES AND QUESTIONS ON *FASHION ORIGINATORS'*

1. ***Is the boycott to prevent dress-design copying per se illegal even if preventing such copying is procompetitive?*** The defendants in this case had a strong procompetitive justification. If firms can copy the dress designs of other firms, there will be fewer original clothing designs because copying decreases incentives to create innovative designs by making it harder for creators to reap profits to cover the investments needed to create those innovative designs. Thus, preventing copying can increase the output of original clothing designs, which would be procompetitive. Indeed, the government often recognizes intellectual property rights (like patents and copyrights) that bar copying in order to avoid the market failure that would otherwise result if new innovations were freely copied by others. The effect of such intellectual property rights on innovation is generally considered procompetitive, and that procompetitive effect can offset the anticompetitive effects of preventing the competitive supply of the innovative product.

However, the Court affirmed the FTC ruling that such a procompetitive justification was inadmissible. This is consistent with the view that having a procompetitive justification—even as here a powerful one often used by the government—does not create any exception to a per se rule. The procompetitive justification must be ancillary to some productive business collaboration. That was not the case here because the members of Fashion Originators were not in any joint business venture to make dresses together. They were simply separate businesses that were combining to try to regulate a market failure on their own. Thus, even if stopping copying is procompetitive, a horizontal boycott to stop copying remains per se illegal.

2. ***Why should the Fashion Originators be barred from advancing the same sort of procompetitive justifications that a government lawmaker could pursue?*** Decisions about whether to create intellectual property rights require a tradeoff between the right's positive effect on increasing incentives to innovate and its negative effect on decreasing competition in the efficient dissemination of new ideas. The Fashion Originators have a financial interest that makes it likely to overweigh the positive effects and underweigh the negative ones. This financial interest seems likely to cause the defendants to protect original clothing designs even though a disinterested government lawmaker would decide the net tradeoff was negative. Here, the federal government may have deliberately decided not to grant patent or copyright protection to original dress designs for precisely this reason. More generally, whenever defendants are offering procompetitive justifications that amount to claims that market failures justify a restraint, government regulation is a more disinterested alternative than private party regulation. In contrast, when the restraints are ancillary to business collaborations, then government regulation is not an alternative because the government generally does not operate businesses.

3. ***Why aren't any concerns with allowing defendants to offer the procompetitive justification of regulating market failures addressed by having antitrust courts review their restraints under the rule of reason?*** One might argue that any concern with allowing defendants to offer the procompetitive justification of regulating market failures is overstated because their restraints would survive rule-of-reason review only if they persuaded antitrust courts that the preventing the copying at issue would create net procompetitive effects. However, allowing such a defense would amount to the court creation of a new species of intellectual property that is enforceable by group boycotts. One might conclude that whether to create new intellectual property rights is the sort of decision better left to legislatures or regulators. A decentralized system of antitrust adjudication about when the procompetitive effects outweighed the anticompetitive ones would make the existence of this new intellectual property right turn on the happenstance of the judge and jury drawn in the antitrust case. This approach would also effectively create a new intellectual property right that was enforceable only when innovators happened to already possess the organized market power to enforce their right through a boycott. Even if the antitrust courts can accurately weigh the costs and benefits of such a proposed intellectual property right, it is hard to see why one would want to give the right only to firms that could enforce it through their own market power.

4. ***If copying is illegal, would the boycott to prevent copying still be per se illegal?*** Although copying dress designs did not violate federal patent or copyright law,[19] the defendants argued that it was a tort that violated state law. The Court held that, even if that were so, the boycott remained per se illegal. What sense does that make? After all, in states that make copying dress designs a tort, the lawmakers seem to have made a disinterested decision that the positive effects of such a ban outweigh the negative ones. The answer is that the boycott also required the defendants to decide (a) whether particular clothing designs were original and copied by others and (b) what penalties should be imposed on violations. The Fashion Originators would thus remain financially biased towards finding originality and copying when it might not exist and to inflict excessive penalties. In other words, the boycott made the defendants an extra-governmental agency that was adjudicating cases and setting penalties, despite a clear conflict of interest. If copying is illegal under state law, there is even less reason for such vigilante justice because the defendants could simply bring actions in state court, which would offer a disinterested forum to adjudicate such claims and set penalties.

5. ***Why is the collective effort to stop copying per se illegal in*** **Fashion Originators** ***but not in*** **BMI?** In *BMI*, the joint venture collectively brought enforcement actions, but neutral lawmakers determined whether and what copying was harmful under copyright law and neutral

---

[19] Although that was the understanding at the time, a recent case indicates that some clothing designs can be copyrighted if they contain a feature that can be perceived as a protected work of art separate from the functional features of the clothing. *See* Star Athletica v. Varsity Brands, 137 S.Ct. 1002 (2017).

courts adjudicated whether such copying occurred and determined the penalties. In *Fashion Originators,* a financially interested private group did both itself. Further, the agreement here was not ancillary to the sort of productive business collaboration the government regulators normally do not provide—it was just a means of private regulation that replaced what government regulators could do. In *BMI*, the agreement was ancillary to a productive joint venture that the government normally does not provide: the defendants were jointly producing a business product that they sold. Here, the firms did not jointly make any product. Their collaboration was just naked market regulation, unrelated to any productive joint venture.

6. ***Why doesn't condemnation require a finding that the boycott had some effect on output, price or quality?*** The Court responded that it suffices that the defendants had the market power to exclude boycotted firms, indicating that harmful effects on the boycotted competitors suffices for condemnation. As noted in the discussion of the *Klor's* case, that answer seems compelling when no procompetitive benefit to consumers is alleged, but here there was an alleged procompetitive benefit. Should that change the result? Part of the answer seems to be no because it is a procompetitive benefit that the government could supply instead. In a sense, government regulation is a less restrictive alternative in this case. But there is also a simpler answer: the procompetitive justification could only be true if the boycott *did* increase prices. After all, if preventing copying did not increase prices for original dress designs, it could not protect the profits of original designers in a way that allowed them to recoup their investments in creating those original designs. The procompetitive justification offered in this case was thus internally inconsistent with the claimed lack of any price effect. This is often a difficulty defendants have. In can be hard to simultaneously argue that a restraint has a procompetitive effect and that it has no effect at all.

2. EXCLUSIONS AND EXPULSIONS FROM A PRODUCTIVE COLLABORATION OF RIVALS

Associated Press v. United States

326 U.S. 1 (1945).

■ MR. JUSTICE BLACK delivered the opinion of the Court.

[Associated Press (AP) had 1,200 newspapers as its members. In addition to collecting news via AP employees, each member furnished AP with any news it had from its area, and AP then distributed the collective results to every member. Each member thus received the local news generated by every other member without having to have staff in each area. AP members comprised 65% of U.S. newspapers and 83% of U.S. circulation. AP bylaws prohibited members from providing news to any other agency or publisher or to any non-member in advance of publication. The AP board of directors could admit without payment any applicant that did not compete with any existing member in a local newspaper market. But if an applicant did compete with an existing member, then under the bylaws the applicant had to not only obtain approval by the AP board but also either (1) obtain that member's permission to join or (2) get the approval of a majority of AP members and pay AP 10% of the total amount paid by members in that area since 1900. The district court granted the government summary judgment and enjoined application of the bylaw that imposed additional hurdles to admitting competing applicants.]

The District Court found that the By-Laws in and of themselves were contracts in restraint of commerce in that they contained provisions designed to stifle competition in the newspaper publishing field. The court also found that AP's restrictive By-Laws had hindered and impeded the growth of competing newspapers. This latter finding, as to the *past* effect of the restrictions, is challenged. We are inclined to think that it is supported by undisputed evidence, but we do not stop to labor the point. For the court below found, and we think correctly, that the By-Laws on their face, and without regard to their past effect, constitute restraints of trade. Combinations are no less unlawful because they have not as yet resulted in restraint. An agreement or combination to follow a course of conduct which will necessarily restrain or monopolize a part of trade or commerce may violate the Sherman Act, whether it be "wholly nascent or abortive on the one hand, or successful on the other." For these reasons the argument, repeated here in various forms, that AP had not yet achieved a complete monopoly is wholly irrelevant. Undisputed evidence did show, however, that its By-Laws had tied the hands of all of its numerous publishers, to the extent that they could not and did not sell any part of their news so that it could reach any of their non-member competitors. In this respect the court did find, and that finding cannot possibly be challenged, that AP's By-Laws had hindered and restrained the sale of interstate news to non-members who competed with members.

Inability to buy news from the largest news agency, or any one of its multitude of members, can have most serious effects on the publication of competitive newspapers, both those presently published and those which, but for these restrictions, might be published in the future. This is illustrated by the District Court's finding that, in 26 cities of the United States, existing newspapers already have contracts for AP news and the same newspapers have contracts with United Press and International News Service under which new newspapers would be required to pay the contract holders large sums to enter the field.[11] The net effect is seriously to limit the opportunity of any new paper to enter these cities. Trade restraints of this character, aimed at the destruction of competition, tend to block the initiative which brings newcomers into a field of business

[11] INS and UP make so-called "asset value" contracts under which if another newspaper wishes to obtain their press services, the newcomer shall pay to the competitor holding the UP or INS contract the stipulated "asset value."

and to frustrate the free enterprise system which it was the purpose of the Sherman Act to protect.

Nor can we treat this case as though it merely involved a reporter's contract to deliver his news reports exclusively to a single newspaper, or an exclusive agreement as to news between two newspapers in different cities. For such trade restraints might well be "reasonable," and therefore not in violation of the Sherman Act. But however innocent such agreements might be, standing alone, they would assume quite a different aspect if utilized as essential features of a program to hamper or destroy competition. It is in this light that we must view this case.

It has been argued that the restrictive By-Laws should be treated as beyond the prohibitions of the Sherman Act, since the owner of the property can choose his associates and can, as to that which he has produced by his own enterprise and sagacity, efforts or ingenuity, decide for himself whether and to whom to sell or not to sell. While it is true in a very general sense that one can dispose of his property as he pleases, he cannot "go beyond the exercise of this right, and by contracts or combinations, express or implied, unduly hinder or obstruct the free and natural flow of commerce in the channels of interstate trade." The Sherman Act was specifically intended to prohibit independent businesses from becoming "associates" in a common plan which is bound to reduce their competitor's opportunity to buy or sell the things in which the groups compete. Victory of a member of such a combination over its business rivals achieved by such collective means cannot consistently with the Sherman Act or with practical, everyday knowledge be attributed to *individual* "enterprise and sagacity"; such hampering of business rivals can only be attributed to that which really makes it possible—the collective power of an unlawful combination. That the object of sale is the creation or product of a man's ingenuity does not alter this principle. *Fashion Originators'*. It is obviously fallacious to view the By-Laws here in issue as instituting a program to encourage and permit full freedom of sale and disposal of property by its owners. Rather, these publishers have, by concerted arrangements, pooled their power to acquire, to purchase, and to dispose of news reports through the channels of commerce. They have also pooled their economic and news control power and, in exerting that power, have entered into agreements which the District Court found to be "plainly designed in the interest of preventing competition."[15]

It is further contended that since there are other news agencies which sell news, it is not a violation of the Act for an overwhelming majority of American publishers to combine to decline to sell their news to the minority. But the fact that an agreement to restrain trade does not

[15] Even if additional purposes were involved, it would not justify the combination, since the Sherman Act cannot "be evaded by good motives. The law is its own measure of right and wrong, of what it permits, or forbids, and the judgment of the courts cannot be set up against it in a supposed accommodation of its policy with the good intention of parties, and it may be, of some good results." Standard Sanitary Mfg. Co. v. United States, 226 U.S. 20, 49.

inhibit competition in all of the objects of that trade cannot save it from the condemnation of the Sherman Act. It is apparent that the exclusive right to publish news in a given field, furnished by AP and all of its members, gives many newspapers a competitive advantage over their rivals. Conversely, a newspaper without AP service is more than likely to be at a competitive disadvantage. The District Court stated that it was to secure this advantage over rivals that the By-Laws existed. It is true that the record shows that some competing papers have gotten along without AP news, but morning newspapers, which control 96% of the total circulation in the United States, have AP news service. And the District Court's unchallenged finding was that "AP is a vast, intricately reticulated organization, the largest of its kind, gathering news from all over the world, the chief single source of news for the American press, universally agreed to be of great consequence."

. . . [The district court had enjoined AP from discriminating against applicants that competed with existing members, which the Supreme Court held was not unduly vague. The Supreme Court also upheld the district court's decision not to enjoin the ban on furnishing news to non-members standing alone, noting that the district court retained jurisdiction to alter that decision if the injunction against discriminatory admissions proved insufficient.]

NOTES AND QUESTIONS ON *ASSOCIATED PRESS*

1. ***What precisely was the illegal agreement?*** The illegal agreement was not the formation of AP because no one was seeking to break up AP, which had the clear procompetitive purpose of achieving economies of scale in newsgathering. The illegal agreement was instead the AP bylaws that discriminated against applicants who competed with members in local newspaper markets, by requiring applicants who did not have a competing member's permission to get the approval of a majority of AP and pay a fee equal to 10% of all AP member fees in the area since 1900. When denying access to a valuable joint venture leaves rivals at a competitive disadvantage, it can have anticompetitive effects in those local markets.

2. ***Could the discrimination against rival applicants have had a procompetitive justification?*** The AP does not seem to have put forth procompetitive justifications for discriminating against rival applicants that might be reasonably related to the joint venture, so the Court did not have occasions to consider them. One problem is that excluding new members seems contrary to the joint venture's core procompetitive purpose of achieving economies of scale, given that more members would increase the scale. Even if at some point having too many members would create diseconomies of scale (like clogging up the newswires), that would not explain why the AP discriminated against only those applicants who happened to compete with existing members.

A more plausible procompetitive justification might be that admitting local rivals would reduce member incentives to invest in getting news scoops because the obligation to share the news with AP would mean their local rivals would get access to those news scoops through AP. Perhaps AP did not pursue this potential justification because it seems to have a less restrictive alternative: the AP could send each newspaper only news that did not come from its local rivals. This alternative would require the additional expense of preparing different AP wires for each city with competing members, but that would justify charging new members only that additional expense, which may bear no relation to 10% of all past local AP fees.

Perhaps the strongest procompetitive justification would be that applicants who compete with existing members add less incremental news because they operate in areas for which AP already gets news from existing members. If so, it might make sense to charge rival applicants more because they contribute relatively less in return. However, this seems hard to quantify and it is not clear why it would bear any relation to 10% of all past local AP fees and the additional procedural burden of getting a majority of AP members to approve the competing applicant.

3. ***Is this case governed by the per se rule against horizontal boycotts?*** In holding "that the By-Laws on their face, and without regard to their past effect, constitute restraints of trade," the Court does hold that proof of anticompetitive effects (including proof of any harm to rival growth) was unnecessary in this case. However, the Court indicated this was true only because AP had market power in news (even though other news sources existed) and that access to AP was valuable enough to give members a "competitive advantage over their rivals." The Court noted that the United Press and International News Service had similar rules that charged more to newcomers who competed with existing members, but the Court did not suggest they were subject to the same antitrust prohibition, probably because they lacked similar market power in news. Moreover, AP offered no explanation for why its discrimination against rivals had a procompetitive justification that was ancillary to AP's productive business collaboration. The opinion thus does not require condemnation when a joint venture lacks market power over such a valuable facility or offers procompetitive justifications for denying access to that facility. But the case does prohibit joint ventures from discriminating against rivals of their members when the joint venture has dominant market power over a valuable facility that confers a competitive advantage and the discrimination against rivals of members was not reasonably necessary to advance the procompetitive justifications for having the joint venture.

4. ***If the Court had instead imposed a general duty on valuable joint ventures to admit rivals of its members, what could that have done to the initial incentives of joint ventures to create valuable facilities or of rivals to create competing facilities?*** A general duty on valuable joint ventures to admit firms that compete with members could reduce the initial incentives to create valuable joint ventures. Just as when firms invest to create patented innovation, a major motivation to create a new joint venture is precisely to gain a competitive advantage over rivals. Further, if valuable joint ventures have a duty to deal, other firms have incentives to decline to join a risky joint venture until they find out whether it turns out to be valuable and then join later. This could deter the creation of the valuable joint venture in the first place, which would harm consumer welfare.

Likewise, such a duty could reduce the incentives of competing firms to form or join a rival joint venture that can duplicate the valuable joint venture sufficiently to compete with it. It is much easier to join an existing valuable facility than to form or join a competing facility that may not work out. Such an incentive effect would be unfortunate because competition would be enhanced if there were vigorous competition not only among newspapers, but also among news agencies.

In theory, both these disincentives can be overcome by setting the price for new members at a level high enough to compensate creators of the joint venture for their investment and risk and to encourage rivals to create their own facilities. But determining the needed price is hard and businesses might reasonably expect that courts would often get it wrong if they were imposing a general duty to deal.

However, the *AP* case does not create a general duty for joint ventures to admit firms that compete with members. It creates a prohibition (in certain conditions) only on discriminating against competitors of members. As long as the joint venture charges the same fee to all applicants, the *AP* rule leaves the joint venture free to charge whatever monopoly price it wants to recover its investment and risk. The desire to avoid paying such a monopoly price would give competitors efficient incentives to create rival news organizations.

Moreover, in *AP,* the Court seemed to think neither of these concerns was strong. The Court suggested that the creation of AP did not involve significant investment or risk because members simply "pooled" their already existing supplies of news. Further, while the existence of UPI and INS showed that forming rival news organizations was certainly possible, they could not duplicate what AP offered because AP had already locked up the lion's share of newspapers and had another bylaw that prevented members from supplying news to anyone but AP. Indeed, given that many towns had only one newspaper that was already signed up by AP, it was not possible for rival newspapers to form a rival news agency that could duplicate the geographic coverage of news offered by AP.

5. Should the by-law requiring members to provide their own news exclusively to AP be illegal? The Court sustained the district court's decision not to enjoin the by-law requiring members to provide their own news exclusively to AP, but did so in part on the ground that the district court retained jurisdiction to enjoin it if need be. This suggests the Court was not sure this bylaw was anticompetitive, but thought it might be. As noted above, this bylaw might prevent efficient competition among new agencies, particularly given that many towns only had one newspaper. But this bylaw might also advance a procompetitive purpose if, without it, other news agencies could free ride off by getting all the AP news from an AP member. Such free-riding would undermine the incentives of AP to invest to compete with rival news agencies. The bylaw may thus have been necessary so that AP was not supplying its service to rival news agencies that were providing a competing service. A prohibition against a joint venture discriminatorily denying its service to rivals of its members does not necessarily prohibit the joint venture from refusing to supply its services to rivals of the joint venture itself.

Northwest Wholesale Stationers v. Pacific Stationery

472 U.S. 284 (1985).

■ JUSTICE BRENNAN delivered the opinion of the Court. . . .

Because the District Court ruled on cross-motions for summary judgment after only limited discovery, this case comes to us on a sparse record. Certain background facts are undisputed. Petitioner Northwest Wholesale Stationers is a purchasing cooperative made up of approximately 100 office supply retailers in the Pacific Northwest States. The cooperative acts as the primary wholesaler for the retailers. Retailers that are not members of the cooperative can purchase wholesale supplies from Northwest at the same price as members. At the end of each year, however, Northwest distributes its profits to members in the form of a percentage rebate on purchases. Members therefore effectively purchase supplies at a price significantly lower than do nonmembers.[2] Northwest also provides certain warehousing facilities. The cooperative arrangement thus permits the participating retailers to achieve economies of scale in purchasing and warehousing that would otherwise be unavailable to them. In fiscal 1978 Northwest had $5.8 million in sales.

Respondent Pacific Stationery & Printing Co. sells office supplies at both the retail and wholesale levels. Its total sales in fiscal 1978 were approximately $7.6 million; the record does not indicate what percentage of revenue is attributable to retail and what percentage is attributable to wholesale. Pacific became a member of Northwest in 1958. In 1974 Northwest amended its bylaws to prohibit members from engaging in both retail and wholesale operations. A grandfather clause preserved Pacific's membership rights. In 1977 ownership of a controlling share of the stock of Pacific changed hands, and the new owners did not officially bring this change to the attention of the directors of Northwest. This failure to notify apparently violated another of Northwest's bylaws.

In 1978 the membership of Northwest voted to expel Pacific. Most factual matters relevant to the expulsion are in dispute. No explanation for the expulsion was advanced at the time, and Pacific was given neither notice, a hearing, nor any other opportunity to challenge the decision. Pacific argues that the expulsion resulted from Pacific's decision to maintain a wholesale operation. Northwest contends that the expulsion resulted from Pacific's failure to notify the cooperative members of the

---

[2] Although this patronage rebate policy is a form of price discrimination, § 4 of the Robinson-Patman Act specifically sanctions such activity by cooperatives. . . .

change in stock ownership. The minutes of the meeting of Northwest's directors do not definitively indicate the motive for the expulsion. It is undisputed that Pacific received approximately $10,000 in rebates from Northwest in 1978, Pacific's last year of membership. Beyond a possible inference of loss from this fact, however, the record is devoid of allegations indicating the nature and extent of competitive injury the expulsion caused Pacific to suffer.

Pacific brought suit . . . The gravamen of the action was that Northwest's expulsion of Pacific from the cooperative without procedural protections was a group boycott that limited Pacific's ability to compete and should be considered *per se* violative of § 1. On cross-motions for summary judgment the District Court rejected application of the *per se* rule and held instead that rule-of-reason analysis should govern the case. Finding no anticompetitive effect on the basis of the record as presented, the court granted summary judgment for Northwest.

The Court of Appeals for the Ninth Circuit reversed . . .

The decision of the cooperative members to expel Pacific was certainly a restraint of trade in the sense that every commercial agreement restrains trade. Whether this action violates § 1 of the Sherman Act depends on whether it is adjudged an *unreasonable* restraint. Rule-of-reason analysis guides the inquiry unless the challenged action falls into the category of "agreements or practices which because of their pernicious effect on competition and lack of any redeeming virtue are conclusively presumed to be unreasonable and therefore illegal without elaborate inquiry as to the precise harm they have caused or the business excuse for their use."

This *per se* approach permits categorical judgments with respect to certain business practices that have proved to be predominantly anticompetitive. Courts can thereby avoid the "significant costs" in "business certainty and litigation efficiency" that a full-fledged rule-of-reason inquiry entails. *Maricopa*. The decision to apply the *per se* rule turns on "whether the practice facially appears to be one that would always or almost always tend to restrict competition and decrease output . . . or instead one designed to 'increase economic efficiency and render markets more, rather than less, competitive.' " *BMI. See also NCAA* ("*Per se* rules are invoked when surrounding circumstances make the likelihood of anticompetitive conduct so great as to render unjustified further examination of the challenged conduct").

This Court has long held that certain concerted refusals to deal or group boycotts are so likely to restrict competition without any offsetting efficiency gains that they should be condemned as *per se* violations of § 1 of the Sherman Act. *See Klor's;* United States v. General Motors Corp., 384 U.S. 127 (1966); Radiant Burners, Inc. v. Peoples Gas Light & Coke Co., 364 U.S. 656 (1961); *Associated Press*; *Fashion Originators';* Eastern States Retail Lumber Dealers' Assn. v. United States, 234 U.S. 600 (1914). The question presented in this case is whether Northwest's decision to expel Pacific should fall within this category of activity that is conclusively presumed to be anticompetitive. The Court of Appeals held that the exclusion of Pacific from the cooperative should conclusively be presumed unreasonable on the ground that Northwest provided no procedural protections to Pacific. . . .

[Silver v. NYSE, 373 U.S. 341 (1963), had held that the Securities Exchange Act provided antitrust immunity to self-regulation by the stock exchange only when the exchange provided procedural protections. But those procedural protections under *Silver* were, the Court held, relevant only to the scope of that regulatory immunity and were not affirmatively imposed by antitrust law.]

. . . [T]he absence of procedural safeguards can in no sense determine the antitrust analysis. If the challenged concerted activity of Northwest's members would amount to a *per se* violation of § 1 of the Sherman Act, no amount of procedural protection would save it. If the challenged action would not amount to a violation of § 1, no lack of procedural protections would convert it into a *per se* violation because the antitrust laws do not themselves impose on joint ventures a requirement of process. . . .

This case therefore turns not on the lack of procedural protections but on whether the decision to expel Pacific is properly viewed as a group boycott or concerted refusal to deal mandating *per se* invalidation. "Group boycotts" are often listed among the classes of economic activity that merit *per se* invalidation under § 1. Exactly what types of activity fall within the forbidden category is, however, far from certain. . . . Some care is therefore necessary in defining the category of concerted refusals to deal that mandate *per se* condemnation.

Cases to which this Court has applied the *per se* approach have generally involved joint efforts by a firm or firms to disadvantage competitors by "either directly denying or persuading or coercing suppliers or customers to deny relationships the competitors need in the competitive struggle." *See, e.g., Silver* (denial of necessary access to exchange members); *Radiant Burners* (denial of necessary certification of product); *Associated Press* (denial of important sources of news); *Klor's* (denial of wholesale supplies). In these cases, the boycott often cut off access to a supply, facility, or market necessary to enable the boycotted firm to compete, *Silver; Radiant Burners*, and frequently the boycotting firms possessed a dominant position in the relevant market. *e.g., Silver; Associated Press; Fashion Originators'*. In addition, the practices were generally not justified by plausible arguments that they were intended to enhance overall efficiency and make markets more competitive. Under such circumstances the likelihood of anticompetitive effects is clear and the possibility of countervailing procompetitive effects is remote.

Although a concerted refusal to deal need not necessarily possess all of these traits to merit *per se* treatment, not every cooperative activity involving a restraint or exclusion will share with the *per se* forbidden boycotts the likelihood of predominantly anticompetitive consequences.

For example, we recognized last Term in *NCAA* that *per se* treatment of the NCAA's restrictions on the marketing of televised college football was inappropriate—despite the obvious restraint on output—because the "case involves an industry in which horizontal restraints on competition are essential if the product is to be available at all."

Wholesale purchasing cooperatives such as Northwest are not a form of concerted activity characteristically likely to result in predominantly anticompetitive effects. Rather, such cooperative arrangements would seem to be "designed to increase economic efficiency and render markets more, rather than less, competitive." *BMI.* The arrangement permits the participating retailers to achieve economies of scale in both the purchase and warehousing of wholesale supplies, and also ensures ready access to a stock of goods that might otherwise be unavailable on short notice. The cost savings and order-filling guarantees enable smaller retailers to reduce prices and maintain their retail stock so as to compete more effectively with larger retailers.

Pacific, of course, does not object to the existence of the cooperative arrangement, but rather raises an antitrust challenge to Northwest's decision to bar Pacific from continued membership.[6] It is therefore the action of expulsion that must be evaluated to determine whether *per se* treatment is appropriate. The act of expulsion from a wholesale cooperative does not necessarily imply anticompetitive animus and thereby raise a probability of anticompetitive effect. Wholesale purchasing cooperatives must establish and enforce reasonable rules in order to function effectively. Disclosure rules, such as the one on which Northwest relies, may well provide the cooperative with a needed means for monitoring the creditworthiness of its members.[7] Nor would the expulsion characteristically be likely to result in predominantly anticompetitive effects, at least in the type of situation this case presents. Unless the cooperative possesses market power or exclusive access to an element essential to effective competition, the conclusion that expulsion is virtually always likely to have an anticompetitive effect is not warranted. Absent such a showing with respect to a cooperative buying arrangement, courts should apply a rule-of-reason analysis. At no time has Pacific made a threshold showing that these structural characteristics are present in this case.

---

[6] Because Pacific has not been wholly excluded from access to Northwest's wholesale operations, there is perhaps some question whether the challenged activity is properly characterized as a concerted refusal to deal. To be precise, Northwest's activity is a concerted refusal to deal with Pacific on substantially equal terms. Such activity might justify *per se* invalidation if it placed a competing firm at a severe competitive disadvantage.

[7] Pacific argues, however, that this justification for expulsion was a pretext because the members of Northwest were fully aware of the change in ownership despite lack of formal notice. According to Pacific, Northwest's motive in the expulsion was to place Pacific at a competitive disadvantage to retaliate for Pacific's decision to engage in an independent wholesale operation. Such a motive might be more troubling. If Northwest's action were not substantially related to the efficiency-enhancing or procompetitive purposes that otherwise justify the cooperative's practices, an inference of anticompetitive animus might be appropriate. But such an argument is appropriately evaluated under the rule-of-reason analysis.

The District Court appears to have followed the correct path of analysis—recognizing that not all concerted refusals to deal should be accorded *per se* treatment and deciding this one should not. The foregoing discussion suggests, however, that a satisfactory threshold determination whether anticompetitive effects would be likely might require a more detailed factual picture of market structure than the District Court had before it. Nonetheless, in our judgment the District Court's rejection of *per se* analysis in this case was correct. A plaintiff seeking application of the *per se* rule must present a threshold case that the challenged activity falls into a category likely to have predominantly anticompetitive effects. The mere allegation of a concerted refusal to deal does not suffice because not all concerted refusals to deal are predominantly anticompetitive. When the plaintiff challenges expulsion from a joint buying cooperative, some showing must be made that the cooperative possesses market power or unique access to a business element necessary for effective competition. Focusing on the argument that the lack of procedural safeguards required *per se* liability, Pacific did not allege any such facts. Because the Court of Appeals applied an erroneous *per se* analysis in this case, the court never evaluated the District Court's rule-of-reason analysis rejecting Pacific's claim. A remand is therefore appropriate for the limited purpose of permitting appellate review of that determination. . . .

NOTES AND QUESTIONS ON *NORTHWEST STATIONERS*

1. ***Why doesn't the per se rule apply?*** In this case, the concerted refusal to deal arguably served the procompetitive purposes of a productive business collaboration that increased economies of scale in purchasing and warehousing and ensuring availability of supply. Nor was there the sort of market power over a needed input that was present in *Associated Press*.

2. ***Why did the Court hold the expulsion here might plausibly be reasonably necessary to advance the procompetitive purpose of the buying association?*** Expelling members standing alone does not further economies of scale in purchasing and warehousing. It reduces them. But the Northwest argued that the expulsion was due to the unreported change in ownership, and the rule requiring disclosure of a change in member ownership might be relevant because the joint venture extends credit to members and thus would reasonably want to ascertain the creditworthiness of its members. To be sure, the plaintiffs argued that this explanation for the expulsion was a pretext, but that would be a matter to decide under the rule of reason. *See* n.7. Moreover, because this argument goes to whether the actual purpose was procompetitive, a court probably would not need to address the justification under the rule of reason absent evidence of actual market power or anticompetitive effects, which the district court found missing here.

3. ***Was there a procompetitive justification for expelling members who also wholesale?*** Northwest argued that the expulsion was due to the unreported change in ownership, not because Pacific was also wholesaling. This is probably because Northwest feared that the *Associated Press* decision banned discrimination against rivals. But discrimination against rivals of the joint venture is very different from discrimination against rivals of members of the joint venture. A joint venture might legitimately want to exclude its own rivals to avoid strategic use of the joint venture's capacity or resources. A rival wholesaler could, for example, strategically buy from Northwest Stationers whenever it had lower prices, but not offer the return benefit to Northwest Stationers. Nor does a rival wholesaler have a very strong argument that it needs access to the joint venture's wholesale facility. One would think the rival wholesaler could compete downstream through its own wholesale supply. The situation here is more like AP refusing to admit UPI, than like AP refusing to admit a newspaper that competes with one of its members. Thus, even if Pacific were right that it was excluded for its wholesale activities, the case probably should have come out the same way.

4. ***Are and should the standards for proving illegality be easier to satisfy for a concerted expulsion or non-admission?*** In practice, *Northwest* sets a looser standard for condemning concerted expulsions than *AP* set for condemning concerted refusals to admit. Both cases require that the concerted refusal be for reasons unrelated to the procompetitive justification for the productive joint venture. But the additional requirements were that *Northwest* required proof of either market power *or* control over an input vital for rival competition, whereas *AP* required *dominant* market power *and* control over an input vital for rival competition. This difference in standards makes sense because it is easier in a case of expulsion (than non-admission) to determine whether a joint venture was discriminating on the basis of rivalry with members because in expulsion cases the previous admission of a rival makes it easier to determine: (a) whether the rival is an appropriate member; (b) whether there are legitimate diseconomies of scale to including more members; and (c) what the terms of membership should be for that rival.

5. ***Should any procedural protections given to expulsion decisions change the competitive analysis?*** As the Court held, any increases in procedural protections provided to expelled businesses should not alter the competitive analysis. A lack of due process would not imply an anticompetitive motive if the joint venture generally denied due process. Competitive businesses often decide on their business relations without elaborate procedures. Nor would giving due process help if an anticompetitive motive drove the decision-making process.

F. ARE SOCIAL WELFARE JUSTIFICATIONS ADMISSIBLE?

Social welfare justifications often exist for restraining unfettered competition. Few, for example, would quarrel with the government ban on baby-selling, even though it does restrain a form of competition. But the questions raised in antitrust law are not whether and when it might be in the public interest for government lawmakers to regulate competition. The questions rather focus on: (1) whether private market actors can be trusted to exercise their collective market power to restrain competition in public interest, and to properly trade off any noncompetitive benefits against competitive ones; (2) whether, if such private actors cannot be trusted, review by antitrust courts of such issues suffices to make sure that private regulation of this sort will be in the public interest; (3) whether it makes sense to instead have such issues resolved by government lawmakers or regulators when the restraints are not ancillary to a productive business collaboration; (4) whether, even if one thinks such private regulation might make sense, the relevant laws permit it or rather reflect a contrary policy judgment; and (5) whether any resolution of the first four issues should be modified when the private actors in question are professionals or nonprofit corporations.

National Society of Professional Engineers v. United States

435 U.S. 679 (1978).

■ MR. JUSTICE STEVENS delivered the opinion of the Court.

This is a civil antitrust case brought by the United States to nullify an association's canon of ethics prohibiting competitive bidding by its members. The question is whether the canon may be justified under the Sherman Act because it was adopted by members of a learned profession for the purpose of minimizing the risk that competition would produce inferior engineering work endangering the public safety. The District Court rejected this justification without making any findings on the likelihood that competition would produce the dire consequences foreseen by the association. The Court of Appeals affirmed. We granted certiorari to decide whether the District Court should have considered the factual basis for the proffered justification before rejecting it. Because we are satisfied that the asserted defense rests on a fundamental misunderstanding of the Rule of Reason frequently applied in antitrust litigation, we affirm.

I

Engineering is an important and learned profession. There are over 750,000 graduate engineers in the United States, of whom about 325,000 are registered as professional engineers. . . . About half of those who are registered engage in consulting engineering on a fee basis. They perform services in connection with the study, design, and construction of all types of improvements to real property—bridges, office buildings, airports, and factories are examples. Engineering fees, amounting to well over $2 billion each year, constitute about 5% of total construction costs. In any given facility, approximately 50% to 80% of the cost of construction is the direct result of work performed by an engineer concerning the systems and equipment to be incorporated in the structure.

The National Society of Professional Engineers (Society) was organized in 1935 to deal with the nontechnical aspects of engineering practice, including the promotion of the professional, social, and economic interests of its members. Its present membership of 69,000 resides throughout the United States and in some foreign countries. Approximately 12,000 members are consulting engineers who offer their services to governmental, industrial, and private clients. Some Society members are principals or chief executive officers of some of the largest engineering firms in the country.

. . . This case does not . . . involve any claim that the National Society has tried to fix specific fees, or even a specific method of calculating fees. It involves a charge that the members of the Society have unlawfully agreed to refuse to negotiate or even to discuss the question of fees until after a prospective client has selected the engineer for a particular project. Evidence of this agreement is found in . . . the Society's Code of Ethics, [which prohibited competitive bidding, defined as submitting price information (other than recommended fee schedules prepared by engineering societies) that would allow clients to compare engineers on price before an engineer was selected. Instead, members had to use] . . . the traditional method, [whereby] the client initially selects an engineer on the basis of background and reputation, not price [and then either negotiates a fee agreement with that engineer or, if unable to do so, selects a new engineer to negotiate with.]

. . . [T]he Society admitted the essential facts alleged by the Government and pleaded [the] . . . defense . . . that the standard set out in the Code of Ethics was reasonable because competition among professional engineers was contrary to the public interest. It was averred that [competitive bidding would: (1) result in engineers offering their services at the lowest possible price, which would cause them to spend insufficient effort and instead design unnecessarily expensive structures; (2) cause buyers to pick engineers purely on price rather than quality, thus endangering public safety.]

. . . The District Court did not . . . make any finding on the question whether, or to what extent, competition had led to inferior engineering work which, in turn, had adversely affected the public health, safety, or welfare. That inquiry was considered unnecessary because the court was convinced that the ethical prohibition against competitive bidding was "on its face a tampering with the price structure of engineering fees in violation of § 1 of the Sherman Act." . . .

II

In Goldfarb v. Virginia State Bar, 421 U.S. 773, the Court held that a bar association's rule prescribing minimum fees for legal services violated § 1 of the Sherman Act. In that opinion the Court . . . said:

> "The fact that a restraint operates upon a profession as distinguished from a business is, of course, relevant in

determining whether that particular restraint violates the Sherman Act. It would be unrealistic to view the practice of professions as interchangeable with other business activities, and automatically to apply to the professions antitrust concepts which originated in other areas. The public service aspect, and other features of the professions, may require that a particular practice, which could properly be viewed as a violation of the Sherman Act in another context, be treated differently. . . ."

Relying heavily on this footnote, and on some of the major cases applying a Rule of Reason . . . petitioner argues that its attempt to preserve the profession's traditional method of setting fees for engineering services is a reasonable method of forestalling the public harm which might be produced by unrestrained competitive bidding. . . .

A. The Rule of Reason

One problem presented by the language of § 1 of the Sherman Act is that it cannot mean what it says. The statute says that "every" contract that restrains trade is unlawful. But, as Mr. Justice Brandeis perceptively noted, restraint is the very essence of every contract; read literally, § 1 would outlaw the entire body of private contract law. Yet it is that body of law that establishes the enforceability of commercial agreements and enables competitive markets—indeed, a competitive economy—to function effectively.

Congress, however, did not intend the text of the Sherman Act to delineate the full meaning of the statute or its application in concrete situations. The legislative history makes it perfectly clear that it expected the courts to give shape to the statute's broad mandate by drawing on common-law tradition. The Rule of Reason, with its origins in common-law precedents long antedating the Sherman Act, has served that purpose. It has been used to give the Act both flexibility and definition, and its central principle of antitrust analysis has remained constant. Contrary to its name, the Rule does not open the field of antitrust inquiry to any argument in favor of a challenged restraint that may fall within the realm of reason. Instead, it focuses directly on the challenged restraint's impact on competitive conditions.

This principle is apparent in even the earliest of cases applying the Rule of Reason, *Mitchel v. Reynolds*[, 24 Eng. Rep. 347 (1711)]. *Mitchel* involved the enforceability of a promise by the seller of a bakery that he would not compete with the purchaser of his business. The covenant was for a limited time and applied only to the area in which the bakery had operated. It was therefore upheld as reasonable, even though it deprived the public of the benefit of potential competition. The long-run benefit of enhancing the marketability of the business itself—and thereby providing incentives to develop such an enterprise—outweighed the temporary and limited loss of competition.

The Rule of Reason suggested by *Mitchel* has been regarded as a standard for testing the enforceability of covenants in restraint of trade which are ancillary to a legitimate transaction, such as an employment contract or the sale of a going business. Judge (later Mr. Chief Justice) Taft so interpreted the Rule in his classic rejection of the argument that competitors may lawfully agree to sell their goods at the same price as long as the agreed-upon price is reasonable. United States v. Addyston Pipe & Steel Co., 85 F. 271, 282–283 (CA6 1898), aff'd, 175 U.S. 211. That case, and subsequent decisions by this Court, unequivocally foreclose an interpretation of the Rule as permitting an inquiry into the reasonableness of the prices set by private agreement.

The early cases also foreclose the argument that because of the special characteristics of a particular industry, monopolistic arrangements will better promote trade and commerce than competition. That kind of argument is properly addressed to Congress and may justify an exemption from the statute for specific industries, but it is not permitted by the Rule of Reason. As the Court observed in *Standard Oil*, "restraints of trade within the purview of the statute . . . [can] not be taken out of that category by indulging in general reasoning as to the expediency or nonexpediency of having made the contracts, or the wisdom or want of wisdom of the statute which prohibited their being made."

The test prescribed in *Standard Oil* is whether the challenged contracts or acts "were unreasonably restrictive of competitive conditions." Unreasonableness under that test could be based either (1) on the nature or character of the contracts, or (2) on surrounding circumstances giving rise to the inference or presumption that they were intended to restrain trade and enhance prices. Under either branch of the test, the inquiry is confined to a consideration of impact on competitive conditions.[16] . . . [T]he inquiry mandated by the Rule of Reason is whether the challenged agreement is one that promotes competition or one that suppresses competition. . . .

There are, thus, two complementary categories of antitrust analysis. In the first category are agreements whose nature and necessary effect are so plainly anticompetitive that no elaborate study of the industry is needed to establish their illegality—they are "illegal per se." In the second category are agreements whose competitive effect can only be evaluated by analyzing the facts peculiar to the business, the history of the restraint, and the reasons why it was imposed. In either event, the purpose of the analysis is to form a judgment about the competitive significance of the restraint; it is not to decide whether a policy favoring competition is in the public interest, or in the interest of the members of

[16] . . . "This standard . . . makes obsolete once prevalent arguments, such as, whether monopoly arrangements would be socially preferable to competition in a particular industry, because, for example, of high fixed costs or the risks of 'cut-throat' competition or other similar unusual conditions."

an industry. Subject to exceptions defined by statute, that policy decision has been made by the Congress.

B. The Ban on Competitive Bidding

Price is the "central nervous system of the economy," *Socony-Vacuum*, and an agreement that "interfere[s] with the setting of price by free market forces" is illegal on its face. United States v. Container Corp., 393 U.S. 333, 337. In this case we are presented with an agreement among competitors to refuse to discuss prices with potential customers until after negotiations have resulted in the initial selection of an engineer. While this is not price fixing as such, no elaborate industry analysis is required to demonstrate the anticompetitive character of such an agreement. . . .

The Society's affirmative defense confirms rather than refutes the anticompetitive purpose and effect of its agreement. The Society argues that the restraint is justified because bidding on engineering services is inherently imprecise, would lead to deceptively low bids, and would thereby tempt individual engineers to do inferior work with consequent risk to public safety and health. The logic of this argument rests on the assumption that the agreement will tend to maintain the price level; if it had no such effect, it would not serve its intended purpose. The Society nonetheless invokes the Rule of Reason, arguing that its restraint on price competition ultimately inures to the public benefit by preventing the production of inferior work and by insuring ethical behavior. As the preceding discussion of the Rule of Reason reveals, this Court has never accepted such an argument.

It may be, as petitioner argues, that competition tends to force prices down and that an inexpensive item may be inferior to one that is more costly. There is some risk, therefore, that competition will cause some suppliers to market a defective product. Similarly, competitive bidding for engineering projects may be inherently imprecise and incapable of taking into account all the variables which will be involved in the actual performance of the project. Based on these considerations, a purchaser might conclude that his interest in quality—which may embrace the safety of the end product—outweighs the advantages of achieving cost savings by pitting one competitor against another. Or an individual vendor might independently refrain from price negotiation until he has satisfied himself that he fully understands the scope of his customers' needs. These decisions might be reasonable; indeed, petitioner has provided ample documentation for that thesis. But these are not reasons that satisfy the Rule; nor are such individual decisions subject to antitrust attack.

The Sherman Act does not require competitive bidding; it prohibits unreasonable restraints on competition. Petitioner's ban on competitive bidding prevents all customers from making price comparisons in the initial selection of an engineer, and imposes the Society's views of the costs and benefits of competition on the entire marketplace. It is this restraint that must be justified under the Rule of Reason, and petitioner's attempt to do so on the basis of the potential threat that competition poses to the public safety and the ethics of its profession is nothing less than a frontal assault on the basic policy of the Sherman Act.

The Sherman Act reflects a legislative judgment that ultimately competition will produce not only lower prices, but also better goods and services. "The heart of our national economic policy long has been faith in the value of competition." *Standard Oil.* The assumption that competition is the best method of allocating resources in a free market recognizes that all elements of a bargain—quality, service, safety, and durability—and not just the immediate cost, are favorably affected by the free opportunity to select among alternative offers. Even assuming occasional exceptions to the presumed consequences of competition, the statutory policy precludes inquiry into the question whether competition is good or bad.

The fact that engineers are often involved in large-scale projects significantly affecting the public safety does not alter our analysis. Exceptions to the Sherman Act for potentially dangerous goods and services would be tantamount to a repeal of the statute. In our complex economy the number of items that may cause serious harm is almost endless—automobiles, drugs, foods, aircraft components, heavy equipment, and countless others, cause serious harm to individuals or to the public at large if defectively made. The judiciary cannot indirectly protect the public against this harm by conferring monopoly privileges on the manufacturers.

By the same token, the cautionary footnote in *Goldfarb* . . . cannot be read as fashioning a broad exemption under the Rule of Reason for learned professions. We adhere to the view expressed in *Goldfarb* that, by their nature, professional services may differ significantly from other business services, and, accordingly, the nature of the competition in such services may vary. Ethical norms may serve to regulate and promote this competition, and thus fall within the Rule of Reason.[22] But the Society's argument in this case is a far cry from such a position. We are faced with a contention that a total ban on competitive bidding is necessary because otherwise engineers will be tempted to submit deceptively low bids. Certainly, the problem of professional deception is a proper subject of an ethical canon. But, once again, the equation of competition with deception, like the similar equation with safety hazards, is simply too broad; we may assume that competition is not entirely conducive to ethical behavior, but that is not a reason, cognizable under the Sherman Act, for doing away with competition.

---

[22] Courts have, for instance, upheld marketing restraints related to the safety of a product, provided that they have no anticompetitive effect and that they are reasonably ancillary to the seller's main purpose of protecting the public from harm or itself from product liability. *See*, e.g., Tripoli Co. v. Wella Corp., 425 F.2d 932 (CA3 1970) (en banc); cf. *GTE Sylvania*.

In sum, the Rule of Reason does not support a defense based on the assumption that competition itself is unreasonable. Such a view of the Rule would create the "sea of doubt" on which Judge Taft refused to embark in *Addyston*, and which this Court has firmly avoided ever since.

III

The judgment entered by the District Court, as modified by the Court of Appeals, prohibits the Society from adopting any official opinion, policy statement, or guideline stating or implying that competitive bidding is unethical. Petitioner argues that this judgment abridges its First Amendment rights. We find no merit in this contention. . . . Just as an injunction against price fixing abridges the freedom of businessmen to talk to one another about prices, so too the injunction in this case must restrict the Society's range of expression on the ethics of competitive bidding. . . . Affirmed.

NOTES AND QUESTIONS ON *PROFESSIONAL ENGINEERS*

1. Does the ban on competitive bidding amount to price-fixing that is per se illegal? The Supreme Court stated that the agreement here "is not price fixing as such." But one could argue that it was. After all, the ban on competitive bidding prevented engineers from offering prices before they were selected *other than* the recommended fee schedules. This agreement thus effectively fixed pre-selection prices at those association-recommended levels. Even though selected engineers could later deviate from those recommended prices, fixing prices during the selection process is still a form of price fixing. To be sure, buyers could always withdraw from their selection of a particular engineer if they were unable to later negotiate a satisfactory fee. But fixing prices during the selection process means buyers cannot get simultaneous competitive price information from engineers and cannot even get it over time without having to incur the additional transaction costs of selecting a series of engineers. Moreover, the fact that the engineers' recommended fees would have already been disclosed before selection makes it hard to negotiate for a post-selection reduction in those fees.

Even if this were not deemed to constitute explicit price-fixing, the defendant's own justification indicated that the clear purpose and effect of the agreement was to alter prices. As the Court emphasized, the offered justification was that, without the agreement, competitive bidding would lead to lower prices that would reduce the quality and safety of engineering. Thus, if ethical rule did not increase prices, it could not further the alleged justification. The defendants' own justification accordingly meant that the purpose and effect of the restraint had to be to keep prices higher, which would satisfy the purpose-and-effect test of *Socony* (later applied in *Palmer*) for deeming an agreement to constitute price fixing even when it does not explicitly fix prices. Consistent with this conclusion, the Court stated that "no elaborate industry analysis is required to demonstrate the anticompetitive character of such an agreement", which is the same sort of language that the Court used to characterize the "per se rule," thus suggesting that the Court was holding horizontal agreements to ban competitive bidding are per se illegal.

However, the Court went on to say that the challenged restraint "must be justified under the Rule of Reason" and to give enough consideration to the offered justification that the Court could rule it was not a cognizable procompetitive justification. The reference to the Rule of Reason is not entirely clear because the Court also characterized the per se rule as one branch of a more general Rule of Reason. But the Court's willingness to consider whether there were cognizable justifications seems inconsistent with a per se rule that makes any justification inadmissible. The summary analysis the Court applied thus seems more like the abbreviated rule-of-reason review that applies when defendants cannot articulate any procompetitive justification for a horizontal restraint. But *Maricopa* also considered justifications after explicitly ruling them inadmissible under the per se rule. Perhaps the Court simply thought it did not have to reach the question whether the case was properly resolved under the per se rule or abbreviated rule of reason because the result was the same either way.

Why isn't it obvious that the per se rule should apply here given that the challenged restraint was not ancillary to any productive business collaboration? After all the Professional Engineers were not engaged in the joint production of any business service; they were rather regulating how unrelated engineers compete with each other. The reason for the Court's caution about whether the per se rule applies appears to reflect the fact that here the challenged restraint was part of a professional canon of ethics. The law has traditionally allowed, and even encouraged, professionals to self-regulate against certain market failures, so *Fashion Originator's* per se ban on private self-regulation of market failures might, if applied to professionals, be too broad and its assumption that government regulation is preferable might be more debatable. Moreover, the Court was willing to accept the possibility that "the nature of the competition" in professional markets might differ from ordinary markets in a way that alters the likely effects of certain restraints. To be sure, *Professional Engineers, Maricopa,* and *Goldfarb* all hold that the direct fixing of prices by professionals remains per se illegal. But *Professional Engineers* suggests that, when professionals adopt ethical restraints that indirectly affect prices, then (unlike other businesses) professionals at least get the chance to offer procompetitive justifications that are not necessarily ancillary to a joint business collaboration.

2. ***Why are only procompetitive justifications cognizable?*** The *Professional Engineers* opinion is most famous for its holding that the Rule of Reason does not admit any possible social welfare justification, but only procompetitive justifications because under the Sherman Act "the inquiry is confined to a consideration of impact on competitive conditions." Thus, the Court held it irrelevant whether the quality produced by competition was socially desirable. The Sherman Act reflects the legislative judgment that the competitive process leads to the best combination of price and quality, allowing buyers to decide for themselves how much they think it is worth paying for any improvement in quality. Nor did the Court think it relevant

whether competitive bidding was desirable. If any set of buyers believed that competitive bidding led to nonoptimal quality, then the competitive process would lead those buyers to individually choose to purchase without it and individual engineering businesses to compete for those buyers by declining to engage in it. But engineers cannot by agreement collectively impose their judgment about the undesirability of competitive bidding on the market, especially since the engineers have a clear financial incentive to favor higher prices regardless of whether the quality improvement is worth it.

3. ***What counts as a procompetitive justification?*** In this case, the challenged agreement reduced independent decisionmaking by competitors by replacing it with one collective approach, and the Court was unwilling to entertain the argument that this made the market better off. But as the Court's discussion of the *Mitchel* case indicates, it does sometimes deem a restraint to have procompetitive effects even though the restraint reduces the number of competitors who make independent decisions. In *Mitchel,* a bakery seller agreed not to compete with the purchaser by opening a new bakery in the same area for a few years. Even if the agreement reduced the number of bakeries competing in that area for some years, that anticompetitive effect was deemed offset by the procompetitive justification that the restraint made the bakery more marketable and thus increased the incentives to invest in developing bakeries that consumers value. Likewise, horizontal mergers necessarily reduce the number of competitors, but are often deemed procompetitive when they create a more efficient firm that offers consumers a better market option. Agreements that improve a market option can thus be procompetitive even though they reduce the number of market options, as long as the improved market option itself is itself subject to a competitive process because it competes with other firms for the business of buyers in a way that leaves those buyers better off according to their own market judgments. In other words, it could be procompetitive to cooperate to improve the market options available in a competitive process in a way that seems likely to improve consumer welfare, but it would not be procompetitive to limit market options based on a rejection of the competitive process itself.

4. ***Could assessing this justification have avoided the sea of doubt?*** Another major problem with the justification offered here is that considering it would have required the Court to assess the reasonableness of the market prices because the premise of the justification was that competitive markets produce the wrong price-quality tradeoffs. The Court would thus have to make its own assessment about which price and quality level was socially desirable for engineering services. Moreover, if the justification that higher prices lead to better quality were admissible, it could be offered in every price-fixing case. The *Palmer* defendants would, for example, have been able to argue that the quality of bar preparation courses will be too low unless prices are fixed high. Even if the Court did not think such arguments contradicted the competitive principle of the Sherman Act, it might well doubt its institutional competence to make such determinations.

FTC v. Indiana Federation of Dentists

476 U.S. 447 (1986).

■ JUSTICE WHITE delivered the opinion of the Court.

[Dental insurers try to contain costs by using x rays and other information to review whether the dental care provided was unnecessary or more expensive than equally effective alternative care. Typically, the initial review is done by lay examiners, who either approve payment or refer the claim to dentists hired by the insurer to make a final determination. Fearing a loss of money and professional independence, the Indiana Dental Association initially organized dentists to agree not to submit x rays to insurers. It stopped doing so under an FTC consent decree, but another group of dentists split off and formed the Indiana Federation of Dentists to continue this denial of x rays.]

Although the Federation's membership was small, numbering less than 100, . . . [it] succeeded in enlisting nearly 100% of the dental specialists in the Anderson area, and approximately 67% of the dentists in and around Lafayette. In the areas of its strength, the Federation was successful in continuing to enforce the Association's prior policy of refusal to submit x rays to dental insurers.

[T]he Federal Trade Commission . . . ruled that the Federation's policy constituted a violation of § 5 . . . [because it] amounted to a conspiracy in restraint of trade that was unreasonable and hence unlawful under the standards for judging such restraints developed in this Court's precedents interpreting § 1 of the Sherman Act. . . . The . . . Court of Appeals for the Seventh Circuit . . . vacated the order. . . . We now reverse. . . .

The policy of the Federation with respect to its members' dealings with third-party insurers resembles practices that have been labeled "group boycotts": the policy constitutes a concerted refusal to deal on particular terms with patients covered by group dental insurance. Although this Court has in the past stated that group boycotts are unlawful *per se,* we decline to resolve this case by forcing the Federation's policy into the "boycott" pigeonhole and invoking the *per se* rule. As we observed last Term in *Northwest Stationers,* the category of restraints classed as group boycotts is not to be expanded indiscriminately, and the *per se* approach has generally been limited to cases in which firms with market power boycott suppliers or customers in order to discourage them from doing business with a competitor—a situation obviously not present here. Moreover, we have been slow to condemn rules adopted by professional associations as unreasonable *per se, see Professional Engineers,* and, in general, to extend *per se* analysis to restraints imposed in the context of business relationships where the economic impact of certain practices is not immediately obvious, *see BMI.* Thus, as did the FTC, we evaluate the restraint at issue in this case under the Rule of Reason rather than a rule of *per se* illegality.

Application of the Rule of Reason to these facts is not a matter of any great difficulty. The Federation's policy takes the form of a horizontal agreement among the participating dentists to withhold from their customers a particular service that they desire—the forwarding of x rays to insurance companies along with claim forms. . . . A refusal to compete with respect to the package of services offered to customers, no less than a refusal to compete with respect to the price term of an agreement, impairs the ability of the market to advance social welfare by ensuring the provision of desired goods and services to consumers at a price approximating the marginal cost of providing them. Absent some countervailing procompetitive virtue—such as, for example, the creation of efficiencies in the operation of a market or the provision of goods and services, *see BMI; Chicago Board of Trade;* cf. *NCAA*—such an agreement limiting consumer choice by impeding the "ordinary give and take of the market place," *Professional Engineers,* cannot be sustained under the Rule of Reason. No credible argument has been advanced for the proposition that making it more costly for the insurers and patients who are the dentists' customers to obtain information needed for evaluating the dentists' diagnoses has any such procompetitive effect.

The Federation advances three principal arguments for the proposition that, notwithstanding its lack of competitive virtue, the Federation's policy of withholding x rays should not be deemed an unreasonable restraint of trade. First, . . . the Federation suggests that in the absence of specific findings by the Commission concerning the definition of the market in which the Federation allegedly restrained trade and the power of the Federation's members in that market, the conclusion that the Federation unreasonably restrained trade is erroneous as a matter of law, regardless of whether the challenged practices might be impermissibly anticompetitive if engaged in by persons who together possessed power in a specifically defined market. This contention, however, runs counter to the Court's holding in *NCAA* that "[a]s a matter of law, the absence of proof of market power does not justify a naked restriction on price or output," and that such a restriction "requires some competitive justification even in the absence of a detailed market analysis." Moreover, even if the restriction imposed by the Federation is not sufficiently "naked" to call this principle into play, the Commission's failure to engage in detailed market analysis is not fatal to its finding of a violation of the Rule of Reason. The Commission found that in two localities in the State of Indiana (the Anderson and Lafayette areas), Federation dentists constituted heavy majorities of the practicing dentists and that as a result of the efforts of the Federation, insurers in those areas were, over a period of years, actually unable to obtain compliance with their requests for submission of x rays. Since the purpose of the inquiries into market definition and market power is to determine whether an arrangement has the potential for genuine adverse effects on competition, "proof of actual detrimental effects, such as a reduction of output," can obviate the need for an inquiry into market power, which is but a "surrogate for detrimental effects." 7 P. Areeda, Antitrust Law ¶ 1511, p. 429 (1986). In this case, we conclude that the finding of actual, sustained adverse effects on competition in those areas where IFD dentists predominated, viewed in light of the reality that markets for dental services tend to be relatively localized, is legally sufficient to support a finding that the challenged restraint was unreasonable even in the absence of elaborate market analysis.

Second, the Federation . . . argues that a holding that its policy of withholding x rays constituted an unreasonable restraint of trade is precluded by the Commission's failure to make any finding that the policy resulted in the provision of dental services that were more costly than those that the patients and their insurers would have chosen were they able to evaluate x rays in conjunction with claim forms. This argument, too, is unpersuasive. Although it is true that the goal of the insurers in seeking submission of x rays for use in their review of benefits claims was to minimize costs by choosing the least expensive adequate course of dental treatment, a showing that this goal was actually achieved through the means chosen is not an essential step in establishing that the dentists' attempt to thwart its achievement by collectively refusing to supply the requested information was an unreasonable restraint of trade. A concerted and effective effort to withhold (or make more costly) information desired by consumers for the purpose of determining whether a particular purchase is cost justified is likely enough to disrupt the proper functioning of the price-setting mechanism of the market that it may be condemned even absent proof that it resulted in higher prices or, as here, the purchase of higher priced services, than would occur in its absence. *Professional Engineers*. Moreover, even if the desired information were in fact completely useless to the insurers and their patients in making an informed choice regarding the least costly adequate course of treatment—or, to put it another way, if the costs of evaluating the information were far greater than the cost savings resulting from its use—the Federation would still not be justified in deciding on behalf of its members' customers that they did not need the information: presumably, if that were the case, the discipline of the market would itself soon result in the insurers' abandoning their requests for x rays. The Federation is not entitled to pre-empt the working of the market by deciding for itself that its customers do not need that which they demand.

Third, the Federation complains that the Commission erred in failing to consider, as relevant to its Rule of Reason analysis, noncompetitive "quality of care" justifications for the prohibition on provision of x rays to insurers in conjunction with claim forms. . . . The gist of the claim is that x rays, standing alone, are not adequate bases for diagnosis of dental problems or for the formulation of an acceptable course of treatment. Accordingly, if insurance companies are permitted to determine whether they will pay a claim for dental treatment on the basis of x rays as opposed to a full examination of all the diagnostic aids available to the examining dentist, there is a danger that they will erroneously decline to pay for treatment that is in fact in the interest of the patient, and that the patient will as a result be deprived of fully adequate care.

The Federation's argument is flawed both legally and factually. The premise of the argument is that, far from having no effect on the cost of dental services chosen by patients and their insurers, the provision of x rays will have too great an impact: it will lead to the reduction of costs through the selection of inadequate treatment. Precisely such a justification for withholding information from customers was rejected as illegitimate in the *Professional Engineers* case. The argument is, in essence, that an unrestrained market in which consumers are given access to the information they believe to be relevant to their choices will lead them to make unwise and even dangerous choices. Such an argument amounts to "nothing less than a frontal assault on the basic policy of the Sherman Act." *Professional Engineers*. Moreover, there is no particular reason to believe that the provision of information will be more harmful to consumers in the market for dental services than in other markets. Insurers . . . are themselves in competition for the patronage of the patients—or, in most cases, the unions or businesses that contract on their behalf for group insurance coverage—and must satisfy their potential customers not only that they will provide coverage at a reasonable cost, but also that that coverage will be adequate to meet their customers' dental needs. There is thus no more reason to expect dental insurance companies to sacrifice quality in return for cost savings than to believe this of consumers in, say, the market for engineering services. Accordingly, if noncompetitive quality-of-service justifications are inadmissible to justify the denial of information to consumers in the latter market, there is little reason to credit such justifications here.

In any event, the Commission did not, as the Federation suggests, refuse even to consider the quality-of-care justification for the withholding of x rays. . . . The Commission was amply justified in concluding on the basis of . . . conflicting evidence that even if concern for the quality of patient care could under some circumstances serve as a justification for a restraint of the sort imposed here, the evidence did not support a finding that the careful use of x rays as a basis for evaluating insurance claims is in fact destructive of proper standards of dental care.

In addition to arguing that its conspiracy did not effect an unreasonable restraint of trade, the Federation appears to renew its argument . . . that the conspiracy to withhold x rays is immunized from antitrust scrutiny by virtue of a supposed policy of the State of Indiana against the evaluation of dental x rays by lay employees of insurance companies. Allegedly, such use of x rays by insurance companies—even where no claim was actually denied without examination of an x ray by a licensed dentist—would constitute unauthorized practice of dentistry by the insurance company and its employees. The Commission found that this claim had no basis in any authoritative source of Indiana law, and the Federation has not identified any adequate reason for rejecting the Commission's conclusion. Even if the Commission were incorrect in its reading of the law, however, the Federation's claim of immunity would fail. That a particular practice may be unlawful is not, in itself, a sufficient justification for collusion among competitors to prevent it. *See Fashion Originators'*. . . . [A]ccordingly, whether or not the policy the Federation has taken upon itself to advance is consistent with the policy of the State of Indiana, the Federation's activities are subject to Sherman Act condemnation. . . . *Reversed.*

NOTES AND QUESTIONS ON *INDIANA DENTISTS*

1. Given that the agreement here is a horizontal boycott between unrelated firms, why isn't it per se illegal? The Court offered three reasons. First, this case did not involve market power like in *Northwest Stationers*. But that case involved a concerted refusal to deal that was plausibly related to a productive joint venture, and when there is no such plausible connection to a productive joint venture, cases like *Klor's* have applied the per se rule without any proof of market power. Second, this case did not involve a secondary boycott that targets third parties to stop them from doing business with rivals. But direct boycotts can also be anticompetitive and there was no secondary boycott in *Klor's*.

The third reason thus seems the decisive one. The Court thought it should hesitate to apply the per se rule to rules adopted by professional associations. One can see the reason for hesitation. Many professional ethical rules not to engage in certain conduct could be characterized as a boycott. For example, a medical ethical canon against offering ineffective snake oil could be characterized as a boycott of snake oil. Such professional self-regulation is so commonly accepted that the Court is not willing to deem all of it per se illegal. Moreover, while here the X-ray boycott furthered the financial interest of dentists, many ordinary professional rules that "boycott" certain products might not.

2. Is the agreement here nonetheless condemned summarily? Yes, even though the per se rule did not apply, the restraint was condemned under the abbreviated rule of reason because it lacked any procompetitive justification. Thus, as with *Professional Engineers,* the difference between ordinary business groups and professional associations is that the latter get the opportunity to offer a procompetitive justification even though their restraint is not ancillary to any productive business collaboration. But the professional associations still lose summarily if they cannot provide a procompetitive justification.

3. If full scale rule of reason applied, could the restraint be condemned without proof of market power? Yes, the Court held, in the alternative, that direct proof of anticompetitive effects obviates any need to prove market power. After all, the whole point of looking at market definition and power is they are a basis to infer likely anticompetitive effects. If anticompetitive effects are proven, then there is no need to inquire into market definition or power. Here, the output of x rays was constrained in many towns, thus the anticompetitive effect was directly proven.

Nor did it matter that it had not been proven that dental prices were altered. To show anticompetitive effects, it sufficed that insurers were denied a market output they wanted—x rays. Whether insurers were right that access to x rays would allow them to lower prices is beside the point. The antitrust laws neither second-guess the wisdom of consumer demand nor allow sellers to do so. If insurers were wrong, and using x rays raised prices, then the market should lead them to stop demanding x rays without any need for a boycott.

4. ***Why isn't the quality-of-care justification procompetitive?*** On principle, the justification was rejected because it involved a claim that informed consumers would make bad choices. Factually, it was rejected on the grounds that insurers represented consumer interests because insurers had to compete for consumer patronage. The latter seems more debatable because agency costs give insurers incentives to increase profits by misusing x-ray information to deny desirable claims. Perhaps the case would come out differently if the insurers did not use dentists to make the denial decisions, because then there would have been more fear the decisions were not being based on sound medical judgment.

5. ***Would it be illegal for a dental association to conclude that some type of dental polish causes health problems and agree to stop using it?*** One could deem such an agreement anticompetitive because it imposes a collective judgment by dentists to deny that type of dental polish to the market, rather than allowing buyers to choose for themselves. However, in Allied Tube & Conduit Corp. v. Indian Head, Inc. 486 U.S. 492, 501 (1988), the Court stated that "When . . . private associations promulgate safety standards based on the merits of objective expert judgments and through procedures that prevent the standard-setting process from being biased by members with economic interests in stifling product competition, those private standards can have significant procompetitive advantages." In this hypothetical, the dental association would lack any financial interest, assuming they do not sell dental polish or gain money off the sales of competing dental polish, and thus their restraint might be deemed procompetitive. *Allied Tube* thus suggests that professionals and other experts have greater ability to regulate their markets when their decisions are not affected by any financial self-interest.

How is the dental polish hypothetical any different from the Indiana Federation of Dentists concluding that x rays will be used in an unsafe manner by insurers and agreeing to stop giving those x rays to insurers? The biggest difference is that the denial of x rays furthered the financial interest of the dentists, and thus they had incentives to deny them even when their provision would be good for consumer welfare. While financially interested actions have to be submitted to the competitive discipline of the market to channel them in socially desirable ways, disinterested self-regulation might arguably merit different scrutiny. Another difference may be that in the dental polish hypothetical, the buyers are ordinary consumers, whereas in

Indiana Dentists the buyers are sophisticated insurers and in *Professional Engineers* the buyers were sophisticated businesses buying engineering services. One might think the latter are better able to make their own judgments and have less need of protection by professional self-regulation.

FTC v. Superior Court Trial Lawyers Ass'n

493 U.S. 411 (1990).

■ JUSTICE STEVENS delivered the opinion of the Court.

[Under the D.C. Criminal Justice Act (CJA), private lawyers were appointed to represent indigent criminal defendants at rates of $30/hr. for court time and $20/hr. for other time. Most such appointments went to about 100 lawyers, called CJA regulars, who derived almost all their income from representing the indigent. Through the Superior Court Trial Lawyers Association (SCTLA), they tried to persuade D.C. to raise the rate to $35/hr., but were unsuccessful. At a SCTLA meeting, the CJA regulars then agreed decided to stop taking cases unless their rates were raised. They also publicized their boycott. D.C. was unable to find other lawyers to accept these cases, and concluded its criminal justice system was on the brink of collapse. D.C. then agreed to raise the rate to $35/hr. and the boycott ended. The Administrative Law Judge (ALJ) found that it was the shortage of lawyers, rather than the publicity, that caused D.C. to capitulate.

The FTC concluded this conduct violated Sherman Act § 1, and thus violated FTC Act § 5, and enjoined future such boycotts. The Court of Appeals held the First Amendment immunized the boycott unless the defendants were on remand found to have market power.]

. . . . Respondents' boycott may well have served a cause that was worthwhile and unpopular. We may assume that the preboycott rates were unreasonably low, and that the increase has produced better legal representation for indigent defendants. Moreover, given that neither indigent criminal defendants nor the lawyers who represent them command any special appeal with the electorate, we may also assume that without the boycott there would have been no increase in District CJA fees. . . . These assumptions do not control the case, for it is not our task to pass upon the social utility or political wisdom of price-fixing agreements.

As the ALJ, the FTC, and the Court of Appeals all agreed, respondents' boycott "constituted a classic restraint of trade within the meaning of Section 1 of the Sherman Act." As such, it also violated the prohibition against unfair methods of competition in § 5 of the FTC Act. Prior to the boycott CJA lawyers were in competition with one another, each deciding independently whether and how often to offer to provide services to the District at CJA rates. The agreement among the CJA lawyers was designed to obtain higher prices for their services and was implemented by a concerted refusal to serve an important customer in the market for legal services and, indeed, the only customer in the market for the particular services that CJA regulars offered. "This constriction of supply is the essence of 'price-fixing,' whether it be accomplished by agreeing upon a price, which will decrease the quantity demanded, or by agreeing upon an output, which will increase the price offered." The horizontal arrangement among these competitors was unquestionably a "naked restraint" on price and output. *See NCAA*.

It is of course true that the city purchases respondents' services because it has a constitutional duty to provide representation to indigent defendants. It is likewise true that the quality of representation may improve when rates are increased. Yet neither of these facts is an acceptable justification for an otherwise unlawful restraint of trade. As we have remarked before, the "Sherman Act reflects a legislative judgment that ultimately competition will produce not only lower prices, but also better goods and services." *Professional Engineers*. This judgment "recognizes that all elements of a bargain—quality, service, safety, and durability—and not just the immediate cost, are favorably affected by the free opportunity to select among alternative offers." *Ibid*. That is equally so when the quality of legal advocacy, rather than engineering design, is at issue.

The social justifications proffered for respondents' restraint of trade thus do not make it any less unlawful. The statutory policy underlying the Sherman Act "precludes inquiry into the question whether competition is good or bad." *Ibid*. Respondents' argument, like that made by the petitioners in *Professional Engineers*, ultimately asks us to find that their boycott is permissible because the price it seeks to set is reasonable. But it was settled shortly after the Sherman Act was passed that it "is no excuse that the prices fixed are themselves reasonable." *See, e.g., Trenton Potteries*. Respondents' agreement is not outside the coverage of the Sherman Act simply because its objective was the enactment of favorable legislation. . . .

The Court of Appeals, however, crafted a new exception to the per se rules, and it is this exception which provoked the FTC's petition to this Court. The Court of Appeals derived its exception from United States v. O'Brien, 391 U.S. 367 (1968). In that case O'Brien had burned his Selective Service registration certificate on the steps of the South Boston Courthouse. He did so before a sizable crowd and with the purpose of advocating his antiwar beliefs. We affirmed his conviction. We held that the governmental interest in regulating the "nonspeech element" of his conduct adequately justified the incidental restriction on First Amendment freedoms. Specifically, we concluded that the statute's incidental restriction on O'Brien's freedom of expression was no greater than necessary to further the Government's interest in requiring registrants to have valid certificates continually available.

However, the Court of Appeals held that, in light of *O'Brien*, the expressive component of respondents' boycott compelled courts to apply the antitrust laws "prudently and with sensitivity," with a "special solicitude for the First Amendment rights" of respondents. The Court of Appeals concluded that the governmental interest in prohibiting boycotts is not sufficient to justify a restriction on the communicative element of the boycott unless the FTC can prove, and not merely presume, that the boycotters have market power. Because the Court of Appeals imposed this special requirement upon the Government, it ruled that per se antitrust analysis was inapplicable to boycotts having an expressive component.

There are at least two critical flaws in the Court of Appeals' antitrust analysis: it exaggerates the significance of the expressive component in respondents' boycott and it denigrates the importance of the rule of law that respondents violated. Implicit in the conclusion of the Court of Appeals are unstated assumptions that most economic boycotts do not have an expressive component, and that the categorical prohibitions against price fixing and boycotts are merely rules of "administrative convenience" that do not serve any substantial governmental interest unless the price-fixing competitors actually possess market power.

It would not much matter to the outcome of this case if these flawed assumptions were sound. *O'Brien* would offer respondents no protection even if their boycott were uniquely expressive and even if the purpose of the per se rules were purely that of administrative efficiency. We have recognized that the Government's interest in adhering to a uniform rule may sometimes satisfy the *O'Brien* test even if making an exception to the rule in a particular case might cause no serious damage. United States v. Albertini, 472 U.S. 675, 688 (1985) ("The First Amendment does not bar application of a neutral regulation that incidentally burdens speech merely because a party contends that allowing an exception in the particular case will not threaten important government interests"). The administrative efficiency interests in antitrust regulation are unusually compelling. The per se rules avoid "the necessity for an incredibly complicated and prolonged economic investigation into the entire history of the industry involved, as well as related industries, in an effort to determine at large whether a particular restraint has been unreasonable." *Northern Pacific*. If small parties "were allowed to prove lack of market power, all parties would have that right, thus introducing the enormous complexities of market definition into every price-fixing case." R. Bork, The Antitrust Paradox 269 (1978). . . .

In any event, however, we cannot accept the Court of Appeals' characterization of this boycott or the antitrust laws. Every concerted refusal to do business with a potential customer or supplier has an expressive component. At one level, the competitors must exchange their views about their objectives and the means of obtaining them. The most blatant, naked price-fixing agreement is a product of communication, but that is surely not a reason for viewing it with special solicitude. At another level, after the terms of the boycotters' demands have been agreed upon, they must be communicated to its target: "We will not do business until you do what we ask." That expressive component of the boycott conducted by these respondents is surely not unique. On the contrary, it is the hallmark of every effective boycott.

At a third level, the boycotters may communicate with third parties to enlist public support for their objectives; to the extent that the boycott is newsworthy, it will facilitate the expression of the boycotters' ideas. But this level of expression is not an element of the boycott. Publicity may be generated by any other activity that is sufficiently newsworthy. Some activities, including the boycott here, may be newsworthy precisely for the reasons that they are prohibited: the harms they produce are matters of public concern. Certainly that is no reason for removing the prohibition.

In sum, there is thus nothing unique about the "expressive component" of respondents' boycott. A rule that requires courts to apply the antitrust laws "prudently and with sensitivity" whenever an economic boycott has an "expressive component" would create a gaping hole in the fabric of those laws. Respondents' boycott thus has no special characteristics meriting an exemption from the per se rules of antitrust law.

Equally important is the second error implicit in respondents' claim to immunity from the per se rules. In its opinion, the Court of Appeals assumed that the antitrust laws permit, but do not require, the condemnation of price fixing and boycotts without proof of market power. The opinion further assumed that the per se rule prohibiting such activity "is only a rule of 'administrative convenience and efficiency,' not a statutory command." This statement contains two errors. The per se rules are, of course, the product of judicial interpretations of the Sherman Act, but the rules nevertheless have the same force and effect as any other statutory commands. Moreover, while the per se rule against price fixing and boycotts is indeed justified in part by "administrative convenience," the Court of Appeals erred in describing the prohibition as justified only by such concerns. The per se rules also reflect a long-standing judgment that the prohibited practices by their nature have "a substantial potential for impact on competition." *Jefferson Parish*. . . .

The per se rules in antitrust law serve purposes analogous to per se restrictions upon, for example, stunt flying in congested areas or speeding. Laws prohibiting stunt flying or setting speed limits are justified by the State's interest in protecting human life and property. Perhaps most violations of such rules actually cause no harm. No doubt many experienced drivers and pilots can operate much more safely, even at prohibited speeds, than the average citizen.

If the especially skilled drivers and pilots were to paint messages on their cars, or attach streamers to their planes, their conduct would have an expressive component. High speeds and unusual maneuvers would help to draw attention to their messages. Yet the laws may nonetheless be enforced against these skilled persons without proof that their conduct was actually harmful or dangerous.

In part, the justification for these per se rules is rooted in administrative convenience. They are also supported, however, by the observation that every speeder and every stunt pilot poses some threat to the community. An unpredictable event may overwhelm the skills of the best driver or pilot, even if the proposed course of action was entirely prudent when initiated. A bad driver going slowly may be more dangerous that a good driver going quickly, but a good driver who obeys the law is safer still.

So it is with boycotts and price fixing. Every such horizontal arrangement among competitors poses some threat to the free market. A small participant in the market is, obviously, less likely to cause persistent damage than a large participant. Other participants in the market may act quickly and effectively to take the small participant's place. For reasons including market inertia and information failures, however, a small conspirator may be able to impede competition over some period of time. Given an appropriate set of circumstances and some luck, the period can be long enough to inflict real injury upon particular consumers or competitors. . . .

Of course, some boycotts and some price-fixing agreements are more pernicious than others; some are only partly successful, and some may only succeed when they are buttressed by other causative factors, such as political influence. But an assumption that, absent proof of market power, the boycott disclosed by this record was totally harmless—when overwhelming testimony demonstrated that it almost produced a crisis in the administration of criminal justice in the District and when it achieved its economic goal—is flatly inconsistent with the clear course of our antitrust jurisprudence. Conspirators need not achieve the dimensions of a monopoly, or even a degree of market power any greater than that already disclosed by this record, to warrant condemnation under the antitrust laws. . . .

The judgment of the Court of Appeals is accordingly reversed insofar as that court held the *per se* rules inapplicable to the lawyers' boycott[19]. . . .

NOTES AND QUESTIONS ON *TRIAL LAWYERS ASS'N*

1. ***Should social welfare justifications be inadmissible even when they involve furthering a constitutional right?*** So the Court held. First, this argument falls into the general principle that defendants cannot argue that prices should be elevated to improve quality. This principle holds

[19] In response to JUSTICE BRENNAN'S opinion, and particularly to its observation that some concerted arrangements that might be characterized as "group boycotts" may not merit *per se* condemnation, we emphasize that this case involves not only a boycott but also a horizontal price-fixing arrangement—a type of conspiracy that has been consistently analyzed as a *per se* violation for many decades. . . .

even when the claim at issue is a constitutionally required level of quality. Second, this justification could not be assessed without inquiring into the reasonableness of prices. Finally, the defendants are financially interested parties, who, as in *Fashion Originators*, might perceive constitutional violations where none existed or impose higher penalties or prices than disinterested courts or regulators would. It is better to leave constitutional issues to adjudication by disinterested judges rather than to private vigilante enforcement by financially-interested market participants.

2. ***Should a boycott be deemed outside of antitrust law or protected by the First Amendment if it was intended to have only a symbolic effect?*** The Court held no. The Court reasoned that a contrary rule would mean defendants could always argue that any boycott had an expressive element, effectively creating a market power exception to the per se rule against boycotts that increases underdeterrence. The Court's emphasis that there was no market power exception to the per se rule against boycotts confirms the prior conclusion in *Klor's*. The Court's holding that the per se rule against boycotts applied also seems to cut back on dicta in *Indiana Dentists* suggesting that the per se rule might be limited to secondary boycotts or generally inapplicable to professionals. To be sure, the Court stressed that the agreement also constituted price-fixing, but the opinion explicitly refers to it as a per se illegal boycott.

3. ***Is it plausible that the defendants lacked market power?*** No, the evidence showed that the boycott led to shortages in output and resulted in increased prices, thus demonstrating direct evidence of anticompetitive effects that necessarily implied a market power to have effects. Although the District of Columbia is a government, it is hardly a monopsonistic purchaser of legal services because it competes with other cities and clients to buy legal services. Even if the District of Columbia were the only buyer, countervailing buyer power is not a defense to an antitrust claim, as discussed next.

Countervailing Power and the Problem of the Second Best

As *Trial Lawyers* indicates, U.S. antitrust law recognizes no exception to its per se rule for cases where a cartel is organized to counteract market power. However, Congress has provided some antitrust exemptions (such as for farmer cooperatives and collective bargaining by labor) that might in part be based on such a theory. One might wonder why the lawyers could not have unionized to qualify for the labor exemption. The answer is that labor law allows unionization only by employees, and the trial lawyers were independent contractors. Even when lawyers and other professionals are employees, they are typically (but not always) deemed supervisors ineligible to unionize. 29 U.S.C. § 152.

Absent such an antitrust exemption, the defense that current prices are unreasonable is inadmissible even if that claim is based on the argument that current prices are uncompetitive. Indeed, this per se rule applies even if the defendants can show that their counterparts on the other side of the market acquired their market power illegally, such as through a cartel.[20] However, some authority in the U.S. suggests that buyer sophistication or market power might be relevant to assessing the *extent* of market power possessed by defendants.[21] This does not matter for per se claims that exclude evidence of market power, but might be important for antitrust claims where the existence or degree of market power is an element.

Some scholars have argued that antitrust law should be altered to include a countervailing power defense.[22] They can draw some support from the economic theory of the second best, which demonstrates that if a market is inefficient along any dimension, it is indeterminate whether creating another inefficiency will decrease or increase market efficiency.[23] What do you think should be the law on countervailing power? Consider the following hypothetical.

Suppose there are ten local miners of vermiculite, a mineral found in the ground that must be transported to a local processor because it is too heavy to transport long distances before processing. These miners face one local processor who takes advantage of his buyer market power by offering subcompetitive prices. The miners thus decide to form a joint sales agency to bargain as a unified group to increase prices. Is this undesirable? To analyze the issue clearly, it is best to break it down based on the possible sources of the market power that the seller cartel seeks to countervail.

1. Countervailing Illegal Market Power. Take first the case where the miners seek to countervail buyer market power that is illegal because it was acquired in violation of the antitrust laws. This might seem the most attractive case for allowing a miner cartel. But in this case, the best remedy is antitrust enforcement against the buyer. If a seller cartel were allowed then the courts will have to allow a buyer cartel to countervail it if buyer entry occurred in the future, thus leading to cartels on both sides, rather than the competition on both sides that otherwise would have existed in the future.

2. Countervailing Market Power That Is Legal but Correctable by Market Forces. Now suppose the buyer market power is legal but correctable by market forces, such as by entry encouraged by supracompetitive prices. In this case, it would be better to prohibit the

---

[20] *See* Joseph F. Brodley, *Joint Ventures and Antitrust Policy*, 95 HARV. L. REV. 1521, 1569 (1982); Joel Davidow, *Antitrust, Foreign Policy, and International Buying Cooperation*, 84 YALE L.J. 268, 270–71 (1974); LAWRENCE SULLIVAN, HANDBOOK OF THE LAW OF ANTITRUST § 75, at 204 (1977).

[21] *See* Chapter 7.B.6.

[22] *See* Warren S. Grimes, *The Sherman Act's Unintended Bias Against Lilliputians*, 69 ANTITRUST L.J. 195 (2001); Barbara Ann White, *Countervailing Power—Different Rules for Different Markets?*, 41 DUKE L.J. 1045 (1992).

[23] R.G. Lipsey & Kelvin Lancaster, *The General Theory of Second Best*, 24 REV. ECON. STUD. 11 (1956).

seller cartel and to allow market forces to remedy the buyer power, rather than allow a cartel that would entrench market power on the seller side.

3. Countervailing Market Power That Is Legal but Uncorrectable by Market Forces. Now suppose the buyer market power was acquired legally through investment (such as building the processing plant) but is uncorrectable by market forces. If that is so, then the buyer must be a natural monopoly, which could be the case if given the minimum efficient scale for a processing plant, there is not enough vermiculite to supply two plants in the area. In that case, it is better to remedy the natural monopoly with utility-type rate regulation, rather than to entrench an avoidable market power on the other side that would have to be supervised via antitrust litigation. Antitrust adjudicators cannot reasonably provide the sort of prospective and constantly updated guidance on pricing that utility rate regulators provide. Moreover, if the government has declined to adopt utility rate-regulation, then presumably it had some reason for that choice (including perhaps some disagreement about whether it is really a natural monopoly). If so, antitrust adjudicators do not have any warrant to permit a form of vigilante utility rate regulation by allowing the creation of a cartel with market power in the hopes that the cartel will impose a form of rate regulation on their own. That would amount to allowing an anticompetitive agreement that furthers an objective that had been rejected by the government.

4. Countervailing Market Power That Is Legal but Uncorrectable by Market Forces or Utility Rate Regulation. Finally, consider the case where buyer market power is legal, reflects a natural monopoly uncorrectable by market forces, and for some reason is not amendable to utility-type rate regulation. Here, the case is stronger for creating a countervailing market power, but still problematic.

Ex Ante Effects. To begin with, even in such a case, the ex ante effects of permitting a countervailing cartel are likely to be undesirable. The extra returns resulting from buyer market power here reflect a desirable return for the investment in the local area that created that market power. Forcing the buyer to share those returns with miners who did not make that investment necessarily discourages such local investments at the margin, by preventing firms from building costly processing plants in areas that can only support one plant and where the costs of that investment can be recouped only if the builder is allowed to exploit the resulting local market power it earned by its investment. Ultimately, there should be some distinction between market power earned through productive investments and market power create by anticompetitive combinations that reduce market options. We want to promote the former and condemn the latter.

Uncertainty Will Countervail Rather than Collude. Even if we assume away all of those ex ante effects, we cannot know for sure that sellers allowed to use a cartel to create market power will actually exercise it to try to countervail the buyer. The vermiculite miners in this example have incentives to instead collude with the vermiculite processor to enhance their mutual market power against downstream buyers of processed vermiculite and split the supracompetitive profits. *See* Chapter 4.

Ex Post Effects. Even if we assume that all of the above problems did not apply, the ex post efficiency effects of permitting a cartel that tries to exercise countervailing power are at best indeterminate under the theory of the second best. That is, even in this best case scenario, a countervailing cartel might increase or decrease market output. This makes the case for allowing a countervailing power defense even weaker in light of all the aforementioned problems.

Conclusion. Given all the above, the antitrust doctrine of not allowing the countervailing power defense appears preferable. The underdeterrence created by mistakenly allowing the defense in the first several situations considered above is likely to be greater than the overdeterrence created by denying the defense in the last, ambiguous situation. Even in the rare and ambiguous situation, any change in industry costs, technology or demand could end the buyer's "natural" monopoly and thus allow correction by market forces. Thus, even in this case, future market results would probably be worsened by entrenching anticompetitive market power on both sides. Moreover, in that situation, we still have the offsetting inefficiency that a seller cartel will have to allocate mining production in a way that reduces productive efficiency and decreases miner incentives to increase their productive efficiency in the future.

Further, the underdeterrence problem created by allowing the defense would be even greater if we take into account the litigation costs and likely inaccurate conclusions about ascertaining whether buyer market power exists at all. Allowing such a defense would lead all cartels to claim there is buyer market power whenever that is at all plausible. That would certainly lessen the certainty of the per se rule and thus reduce the rule's ability to deter undesirable cartels. Such a defense would also require antitrust courts to decide when countervailing power improves the market outcome, which is difficult to distinguish from asking antitrust courts to inquire into the reasonableness of prices. Antitrust courts are simply ill-equipped to make accurate judgments in these scenarios. Nor do such courts have the administrative capacity to keep updating those judgments as market conditions change over time and for each new bargain struck between the seller cartel and powerful buyer.

To be sure, these problems would not exist if adjudicators could perfectly and costlessly determine and constantly update conclusions about: (1) the existence of market power, (2) which cases fell within the residual category where allocative efficiency gains are possible, and (3) which exercises of countervailing market power increased overall market efficiency notwithstanding the creation of seller productive inefficiencies and the possibility that changing market conditions would alter the analysis. But do we enjoy such a world?

California Dental Ass'n v. FTC

526 U.S. 756 (1999).

■ JUSTICE SOUTER delivered the opinion of the Court.

[About 75% of California dentists belonged to the California Dental Association (CDA), and agreed to abide by its code of ethics. The CDA interpreted its provision against false or misleading advertising to prohibit: (1) advertising the quality of services, on the ground that those services are not susceptible to measurement or verification; and (2) price advertising that uses vague terms like "low fees" or "as low as" and does not fully disclose all variables, like the dollar amount of the undiscounted fee for each service, the amount of the discount, the length of time the discount is offered, and any other limitations. The FTC found that the disclosure required by the price rule was so voluminous that it would not be feasible in advertising, so that the price rule amounted to a prohibition on any advertising that offered of "across the board discounts" or said a dentist's fees were "low, reasonable or affordable." Legally, the FTC concluded that CDA's position constituted an agreement to restrain advertising of quality and price that violated Sherman Act § 1, and thus violated FTC Act § 5, and the Court of Appeals affirmed under a truncated rule of reason analysis.]

We hold that . . . where, as here, any anticompetitive effects of given restraints are far from intuitively obvious, the rule of reason demands a more thorough enquiry into the consequences of those restraints than the Court of Appeals performed. . . .[24]

In *NCAA* we held that a "naked restraint on price and output requires some competitive justification even in the absence of a detailed market analysis." Elsewhere, we held that "no elaborate industry analysis is required to demonstrate the anticompetitive character of" horizontal agreements among competitors to refuse to discuss prices, *Professional Engineers*, or to withhold a particular desired service, *Indiana Dentists*. In each of these cases, which have formed the basis for what has come to be called abbreviated or "quick-look" analysis under the rule of reason, an observer with even a rudimentary understanding of economics could conclude that the arrangements in question would have an anticompetitive effect on customers and markets. In *NCAA*, the league's television plan expressly limited output (the number of games that could be televised) and fixed a minimum price. In *Professional Engineers*, the restraint was "an absolute ban on competitive bidding." In

[24] [Editor's Note: The FTC Act covers (1) for-profits and (2) nonprofits that carry on business for the profit of their members. The Supreme Court also concluded the CDA fell into the latter category because it "provides substantial economic benefit to its for-profit members."]

Indiana Dentists, the restraint was "a horizontal agreement among the participating dentists to withhold from their customers a particular service that they desire." As in such cases, quick-look analysis carries the day when the great likelihood of anticompetitive effects can easily be ascertained.

The case before us, however, fails to present a situation in which the likelihood of anticompetitive effects is comparably obvious. Even on JUSTICE BREYER'S view that bars on truthful and verifiable price and quality advertising are prima facie anticompetitive, and place the burden of procompetitive justification on those who agree to adopt them, the very issue at the threshold of this case is whether professional price and quality advertising is sufficiently verifiable in theory and in fact to fall within such a general rule. Ultimately our disagreement with JUSTICE BREYER turns on our different responses to this issue. Whereas he accepts, as the Ninth Circuit seems to have done, that the restrictions here were like restrictions on advertisement of price and quality generally, it seems to us that the CDA's advertising restrictions might plausibly be thought to have a net procompetitive effect, or possibly no effect at all on competition. The restrictions on both discount and nondiscount advertising are, at least on their face, designed to avoid false or deceptive advertising in a market characterized by striking disparities between the information available to the professional and the patient.[10] Cf. Carr & Mathewson, The Economics of Law Firms: A Study in the Legal Organization of the Firm, 33 J. Law & Econ. 307, 309 (1990) (explaining that in a market for complex professional services, "inherent asymmetry of knowledge about the product" arises because "professionals supplying the good are knowledgeable [whereas] consumers demanding the good are uninformed"); Akerlof, The Market for "Lemons": Quality Uncertainty and the Market Mechanism, 84 Q.J. Econ. 488 (1970) (pointing out quality problems in market characterized by asymmetrical information). In a market for professional services, in which advertising is relatively rare and the comparability of service packages not easily established, the difficulty for customers or potential competitors to get and verify information about the price and availability of services magnifies the dangers to competition associated with misleading advertising.

What is more, the quality of professional services tends to resist either calibration or monitoring by individual patients or clients, partly because of the specialized knowledge required to evaluate the services, and partly because of the difficulty in determining whether, and the

10 "The fact that a restraint operates upon a profession as distinguished from a business is, of course, relevant in determining whether that particular restraint violates the Sherman Act. It would be unrealistic to view the practice of professions as interchangeable with other business activities, and automatically to apply to the professions antitrust concepts which originated in other areas. The public service aspect, and other features of the professions, may require that a particular practice, which could properly be viewed as a violation of the Sherman Act in another context, be treated differently." Goldfarb v. Virginia State Bar, 421 U.S. 773, 788–789, n.17 (1975).

degree to which, an outcome is attributable to the quality of services (like a poor job of tooth-filling) or to something else (like a very tough walnut). Patients' attachments to particular professionals, the rationality of which is difficult to assess, complicate the picture even further. The existence of such significant challenges to informed decisionmaking by the customer for professional services immediately suggests that advertising restrictions arguably protecting patients from misleading or irrelevant advertising call for more than cursory treatment as obviously comparable to classic horizontal agreements to limit output or price competition.

The explanation proffered by the Court of Appeals for the likely anticompetitive effect of the CDA's restrictions on discount advertising began with the unexceptionable statements that "price advertising is fundamental to price competition," and that "[r]estrictions on the ability to advertise prices normally make it more difficult for consumers to find a lower price and for dentists to compete on the basis of price." The court then acknowledged that, according to the CDA, the restrictions nonetheless furthered the "legitimate, indeed procompetitive, goal of preventing false and misleading price advertising." The Court of Appeals might, at this juncture, have recognized that the restrictions at issue here are very far from a total ban on price or discount advertising, and might have considered the possibility that the particular restrictions on professional advertising could have different effects from those "normally" found in the commercial world, even to the point of promoting competition by reducing the occurrence of unverifiable and misleading across-the-board discount advertising. Instead, the Court of Appeals confined itself to the brief assertion that the "CDA's disclosure requirements appear to prohibit across-the-board discounts because it is simply infeasible to disclose all of the information that is required," followed by the observation that "the record provides no evidence that the rule has in fact led to increased disclosure and transparency of dental pricing."

But these observations brush over the professional context and describe no anticompetitive effects. Assuming that the record in fact supports the conclusion that the CDA disclosure rules essentially bar advertisement of across-the-board discounts, it does not obviously follow that such a ban would have a net anticompetitive effect here.

Whether advertisements that announced discounts for, say, first-time customers, would be less effective at conveying information relevant to competition if they listed the original and discounted prices for checkups, x rays, and fillings, than they would be if they simply specified a percentage discount across the board, seems to us a question susceptible to empirical but not a priori analysis. In a suspicious world, the discipline of specific example may well be a necessary condition of plausibility for professional claims that for all practical purposes defy comparison shopping. It is also possible in principle that, even if across-the-board discount advertisements were more effective in drawing customers in the short run, the recurrence of some measure of intentional or accidental misstatement due to the breadth of their claims might leak out over time to make potential patients skeptical of any such across-the-board advertising, so undercutting the method's effectiveness. Cf. Akerlof, 84 Q.J. Econ., at 495 (explaining that "dishonest dealings tend to drive honest dealings out of the market"). It might be, too, that across-the-board discount advertisements would continue to attract business indefinitely, but might work precisely because they were misleading customers, and thus just because their effect would be anticompetitive, not procompetitive. Put another way, the CDA's rule appears to reflect the prediction that any costs to competition associated with the elimination of across-the-board advertising will be outweighed by gains to consumer information (and hence competition) created by discount advertising that is exact, accurate, and more easily verifiable (at least by regulators). As a matter of economics this view may or may not be correct, but it is not implausible, and neither a court nor the Commission may initially dismiss it as presumptively wrong.[12]

In theory, it is true, the Court of Appeals neither ruled out the plausibility of some procompetitive support for the CDA's requirements nor foreclosed the utility of an evidentiary discussion on the point. The court indirectly acknowledged the plausibility of procompetitive justifications for the CDA's position when it stated that "the record provides no evidence that the rule has in fact led to increased disclosure and transparency of dental pricing." But because petitioner alone would have had the incentive to introduce such evidence, the statement sounds as though the Court of Appeals may have thought it was justified without further analysis to shift a burden to the CDA to adduce hard evidence of the procompetitive nature of its policy; the court's adversion to empirical evidence at the moment of this implicit burden-shifting underscores the leniency of its enquiry into evidence of the restrictions' anticompetitive effects.

The Court of Appeals was comparably tolerant in accepting the sufficiency of abbreviated rule-of-reason analysis as to the nonprice advertising restrictions. The court began with the argument that "[t]hese restrictions are in effect a form of output limitation, as they restrict the supply of information about individual dentists' services." Although this

---

[12] JUSTICE BREYER suggests that our analysis is "of limited relevance" because "the basic question is whether this . . . theoretically redeeming virtue in fact offsets the restrictions' anticompetitive effects in this case." He thinks that the Commission and the Court of Appeals "adequately answered that question," but the absence of any empirical evidence on this point indicates that the question was not answered, merely avoided by implicit burden-shifting of the kind accepted by JUSTICE BREYER. The point is that before a theoretical claim of anticompetitive effects can justify shifting to a defendant the burden to show empirical evidence of procompetitive effects, as quick-look analysis in effect requires, there must be some indication that the court making the decision has properly identified the theoretical basis for the anticompetitive effects and considered whether the effects actually are anticompetitive. Where, as here, the circumstances of the restriction are somewhat complex, assumption alone will not do.

sentence does indeed appear as cited, it is puzzling, given that the relevant output for antitrust purposes here is presumably not information or advertising, but dental services themselves. The question is not whether the universe of possible advertisements has been limited (as assuredly it has), but whether the limitation on advertisements obviously tends to limit the total delivery of dental services. The court came closest to addressing this latter question when it went on to assert that limiting advertisements regarding quality and safety "prevents dentists from fully describing the package of services they offer," adding that "[t]he restrictions may also affect output more directly, as quality and comfort advertising may induce some customers to obtain nonemergency care when they might not otherwise do so." This suggestion about output is also puzzling. If quality advertising actually induces some patients to obtain more care than they would in its absence, then restricting such advertising would reduce the demand for dental services, not the supply; and it is of course the producers' supply of a good in relation to demand that is normally relevant in determining whether a producer-imposed output limitation has the anticompetitive effect of artificially raising prices.[13]

Although the Court of Appeals acknowledged the CDA's view that "claims about quality are inherently unverifiable and therefore misleading," it responded that this concern "does not justify banning all quality claims without regard to whether they are, in fact, false or misleading." As a result, the court said, "the restriction is a sufficiently naked restraint on output to justify quick look analysis." The court assumed, in these words, that some dental quality claims may escape justifiable censure, because they are both verifiable and true. But its implicit assumption fails to explain why it gave no weight to the countervailing, and at least equally plausible, suggestion that restricting difficult-to-verify claims about quality or patient comfort would have a procompetitive effect by preventing misleading or false claims that distort the market. It is, indeed, entirely possible to understand the CDA's restrictions on unverifiable quality and comfort advertising as nothing more than a procompetitive ban on puffery, cf. *Bates*, 433 U.S., at 366 (claims relating to the quality of legal services "probably are not susceptible of precise measurement or verification and, under some circumstances, might well be deceptive or misleading to the public, or even false"); id., at 383–384, ("[A]dvertising claims as to the quality of services . . . are not susceptible of measurement or verification;

[13] JUSTICE BREYER wonders if we "mea[n] this statement as an argument against the anticompetitive tendencies that flow from an agreement not to advertise service quality." But as the preceding sentence shows, we intend simply to question the logic of the Court of Appeals's suggestion that the restrictions are anticompetitive because they somehow "affect output," presumably with the intent to raise prices by limiting supply while demand remains constant. We do not mean to deny that an agreement not to advertise service quality might have anticompetitive effects. We merely mean that, absent further analysis of the kind JUSTICE BREYER undertakes, it is not possible to conclude that the net effect of this particular restriction is anticompetitive.

accordingly, such claims may be so likely to be misleading as to warrant restriction") . . .

The point is not that the CDA's restrictions necessarily have the procompetitive effect claimed by the CDA; it is possible that banning quality claims might have no effect at all on competitiveness if, for example, many dentists made very much the same sort of claims. And it is also of course possible that the restrictions might in the final analysis be anticompetitive. The point, rather, is that the plausibility of competing claims about the effects of the professional advertising restrictions rules out the indulgently abbreviated review to which the Commission's order was treated. The obvious anticompetitive effect that triggers abbreviated analysis has not been shown.

In light of our focus on the adequacy of the Court of Appeals's analysis, JUSTICE BREYER'S thorough-going, de novo antitrust analysis contains much to impress on its own merits but little to demonstrate the sufficiency of the Court of Appeals's review. The obligation to give a more deliberate look than a quick one does not arise at the door of this Court and should not be satisfied here in the first instance. Had the Court of Appeals engaged in a painstaking discussion in a league with JUSTICE BREYER'S (compare his 14 pages with the Ninth Circuit's 8), and had it confronted the comparability of these restrictions to bars on clearly verifiable advertising, its reasoning might have sufficed to justify its conclusion. Certainly JUSTICE BREYER'S treatment of the antitrust issues here is no "quick look." Lingering is more like it, and indeed JUSTICE BREYER, not surprisingly, stops short of endorsing the Court of Appeals's discussion as adequate to the task at hand.

Saying here that the Court of Appeals's conclusion at least required a more extended examination of the possible factual underpinnings than it received is not, of course, necessarily to call for the fullest market analysis. Although we have said that a challenge to a "naked restraint on price and output" need not be supported by "a detailed market analysis" in order to "requir[e] some competitive justification," *NCAA*, it does not follow that every case attacking a less obviously anticompetitive restraint (like this one) is a candidate for plenary market examination. The truth is that our categories of analysis of anticompetitive effect are less fixed than terms like "per se," "quick look," and "rule of reason" tend to make them appear. We have recognized, for example, that "there is often no bright line separating per se from Rule of Reason analysis," since "considerable inquiry into market conditions" may be required before the application of any so-called "per se" condemnation is justified. *Id.* . . . As the circumstances here demonstrate, there is generally no categorical line to be drawn between restraints that give rise to an intuitively obvious inference of anticompetitive effect and those that call for more detailed treatment. What is required, rather, is an enquiry meet for the case, looking to the circumstances, details, and logic of a restraint. The object is to see whether the experience of the market has been so clear, or necessarily will be, that a confident conclusion about the principal tendency of a restriction will follow from a quick (or at least quicker) look, in place of a more sedulous one. And of course what we see may vary over time, if rule-of-reason analyses in case after case reach identical conclusions. For now, at least, a less quick look was required for the initial assessment of the tendency of these professional advertising restrictions. Because the Court of Appeals did not scrutinize the assumption of relative anticompetitive tendencies, we vacate the judgment and remand the case for a fuller consideration of the issue. . . .

NOTES AND QUESTIONS ON *CALIFORNIA DENTAL*

1. ***What is the Court's test for determining whether a restraint is "naked" and thus summarily condemned under the abbreviated rule of reason?*** The Court indicated that the restraint here was not a naked restraint, and thus was not subject to abbreviated rule of reason scrutiny, because here the anticompetitive effects were not "intuitively obvious." This cannot mean that anticompetitive effects must be empirically proven, for that would mean that abbreviated rule of reason condemnation would never apply, and the Court made clear it thought it often did apply. Instead, what the Court stressed was that a naked restraint must be devoid of any theoretically plausible procompetitive justification: that is, devoid of any theory of how the restraint might increase market output or reduce prices. If an agreement has no theoretically plausible procompetitive justification, then, to the extent the agreement has any effect at all, it would necessarily harm output or price, and thus the anticompetitive effects would be intuitively obvious. Summary condemnation under the abbreviated rule of reason would in such cases not produce any overdeterrence of desirable conduct. Does this seem like a sensible way to define which restraints are naked and thus summarily condemned under the abbreviated rule of reason?

2. ***Was there a plausible procompetitive justification here?*** The Court concluded that the restraint here did have a theoretically plausible procompetitive justification, which meant it was not "intuitively obvious" that any effects would be anticompetitive, and thus the restraint should not be deemed a naked restraint subject to abbreviated rule of reason scrutiny. The plausible procompetitive justification was that the agreement reduced a "market for lemons" problem that would have otherwise led to unverifiable and misleading advertising on price and quality.

The market for lemons theory was originally developed to explain why markets for used cars seemed to have a disproportionate number of "lemons", slang for defective used cars. The basic idea is as follows. Suppose sellers know whether their used cars are good, but buyers do not. (This is called asymmetric information because the sellers have more information than the buyers). Suppose the market starts out with used cars that are worth between $2,000–$10,000. Because the buyers don't know which cars are worth more, they pay no more than the average value of $6,000. But then sellers with cars worth over $6,000 will drop out of the market because sellers know whether their cars are worth more. The new range will be

$2,000–$6,000, which will make buyers willing to pay no more than the new average of $4,000, leading sellers with cars worth over $4,000 to drop out. And so forth, until only $2,000 lemons are left, leaving us with a market for lemons.

A similar problem could arise with advertising. If sellers know which advertising is accurate but buyers do not, then buyers will assume an average level of accuracy, leading the more accurate sellers to drop out (or adopt more deceptive advertising to gain business), until the inaccurate advertising drives out the accurate advertising. This can be particularly problematic for professional services, where there is a large informational asymmetry between the sellers and buyers, and the buyers may not be able to judge the services they received. The Court did not hold this theory was empirically correct in the case at hand. Rather, the Court held that it was a sufficiently plausible justification in theory that adjudication must consider fuller rule-of-reason review of the actual empirical effects before condemning the restraint. Do you agree this was a plausible justification?

3. ***Was this justification ancillary to any productive business collaboration?*** No, this justification was not ancillary to a productive business collaboration because the dental association was not jointly producing anything for sale, but rather was simply engaged in regulating a perceived market failure. That is the big issue: in other cases (like *Fashion Originators*), the Court condemns restraints that are not ancillary to a productive business collaboration without considering valid procompetitive justifications. Such cases suggest a more thorough sense of nakedness: naked of not only a procompetitive justification but also of any business collaboration.

How can we square these cases? The Court stressed that here the dental association restraint was imposed by a professional organization to regulate an information asymmetry and was not directly on price or output. The resulting doctrine thus seems to be that, unlike ordinary businesses, professionals can impose nonancillary restraints to try to regulate market failures, subject to rule-of-reason review, as long they do not involve direct restraints on price or output of the sort at issue in cases like *Maricopa*.

Do you find this distinction persuasive? On the one hand, traditionally the government has effectively delegated to professional groups the power to self-regulate. Moreover, professionals have expertise, and a core reason to instill professional norms and ethics is to police informational asymmetries between professionals and customers, which is what this professional regulation directly affects. On the other hand, the dentists here are financially interested and politically unaccountable, so one might wonder whether they are really likely to behave differently than other self-regulating businesses, and the government seems a preferable regulator because it is disinterested and politically accountable. One might also conclude that the regulation involved questions more of economics than of dental expertise.

4. ***Why isn't there a less restrictive alternative for advancing this procompetitive justification?*** Would it be a less restrictive alternative to have the Association give consumers more information, such as giving a seal of approval for non-deceptive dentists? While this might work, the problem is that other dentists could create their own seal. Because consumers lack information, they may not know which seal to trust. Thus, assessing this alternative seems to require the sort of empirical assessment that requires full rule-of-reason review.

Would it be a less restrictive alternative to have the voluminous disclosures made to the Association, so that the Association could determine whether the price and quality claims made in advertisements were accurate? The problem is that this alternative might be even more restrictive because it would involve the Association picking and choosing which price and quality claims could be made. This alternative could also be administratively difficult and time-consuming.

5. ***Is the holding here distinguishable from* Indiana Dentists *and* Professional Engineers?** The most important distinction is that the defendants in *Indiana Dentists* and *Professional Engineers* did not offer any procompetitive justification for their restraints. In *Indiana Dentists,* one might also argue that the restraint was on the output of a service, whereas here it was only on advertising. Even though both x rays and advertising are information, x rays are a dental service that one pays for (and thus a dental market output), whereas advertising is something used to get someone to pay for a service (and thus not output in the dental market). On the other hand, the restraint was not directly on price or output in *Professional Engineers*, and there all that was restrained was pre-bid information on pricing, so the lack of procompetitive justification seems the stronger distinction.

6. ***The disagreement with the dissent.*** The dissent agreed with the majority that the dental association restraints in theory had both anticompetitive potential and a plausible procompetitive justification. They disagreed about the order of burden of production of evidence. Both the majority and dissent agreed that the plaintiff must first come forward with theoretically plausible anticompetitive effects. The majority held that when the defendants respond to this by offering a theoretically plausible procompetitive justification, then the plaintiffs must provide empirical proof of anticompetitive effects (like market power) *before* the defendants have to offer empirical proof supporting their procompetitive theory. The dissent effectively said the defendants should have to rebut the anticompetitive theory with empirical evidence of the procompetitive justification before the plaintiff needs to provide empirical evidence supporting the anticompetitive effects. With whom do you agree?

Burdens and Orders of Theory and Proof After *California Dental*

After *California Dental,* the U.S. caselaw appears to adopt the following complex order in which theoretical and empirical claims must be made under Sherman Act § 1.

Step 1. Plaintiff must allege an agreement that theoretically has anticompetitive potential. If it does, the court goes to step 2.

Step 2. Defendants must respond by articulating a theoretically plausible claim that there exists a procompetitive justification for which the restraint was reasonably necessary.

a. If the defendants fail to do so, they lose summarily, and it doesn't really matter whether we call it a per se violation or a naked restraint under the rule of reason. *See Trenton Potteries; Klor's; Professional Engineers; Indiana Dentists; Trial Lawyers.*

b. If the defendants can articulate a theoretically plausible procompetitive justification for which the restraint is reasonably necessary, then treatment varies depending on other factors:

i. If the restraint at issue is reasonably necessary to advance the procompetitive purposes of productive business collaboration among those defendants (that is, a collaboration that actually has some business product), then the court moves to step 3, which is the beginning of full-scale rule-of-reason review. *See BMI; Northwest Stationers; Dagher.*

ii. If the restraint is not alleged to be reasonably necessary to advance the procompetitive purposes of any productive business collaboration *and* the restraint is on price (or on a output level that would affect price), then the procompetitive justification is inadmissible, and the agreement is condemned under the per se rule. *See Maricopa.*

iii. For other restraints that are not reasonably necessary for any productive business collaboration, treatment likely varies depending on whether the defendants are professionals that traditionally engage in market self-regulation or are financially disinterested in the restraint.

(1) Professionals apparently get rule-of-reason review for such self-regulation even when they have a financial self-interest, at least when the regulation is directed at informational market defects, and thus can get to step 3 by articulating a procompetitive justification for which their restraint is reasonably necessary. *See California Dental.*

(2) Nonprofessionals probably do not enjoy the same rule-of-reason review for self-regulation unrelated to productive business collaborations, at least not if they are financially interested, and instead the agreement is summarily condemned. *See Fashion Originators.* But they may well enjoy rule-of-reason review and be able to go onto step 3 when they are financially disinterested in their restraint.

Step 3. If both sides have articulated theoretically plausible anti- and procompetitive effects in a way that triggers full-scale rule-of-reason review, then the plaintiff has the burden of producing empirical evidence of the anticompetitive effects under the rule of reason. *See California Dental.* Such anticompetitive effects can be shown by direct evidence or inferred from market power. *See Indiana Dentists.* If the plaintiff does prove anticompetitive effects, then the court moves to step 4.

Step 4. Given evidence of actual anticompetitive effects, the defendant has the burden of producing empirical evidence to support the claimed procompetitive effects and to show that less restrictive alternatives could not equally achieve those procompetitive effects. *See California Dental.* If the defendant does, then the court moves to step 5.

Step 5. In the final stage, the tribunal weighs the anticompetitive and procompetitive evidence to determine which is greater. The plaintiff has the burden of persuasion on whether the net effect is anticompetitive.

Less Restrictive Alternatives. The issue of whether a less restrictive alternative exists is often considered a separate step, but really it can come up at both steps 2 and 4, because it bears on whether theoretically or empirically the restraint was reasonably necessary to advance the claimed procompetitive justification. Step 2 should be used to consider theoretical arguments that the restraint is not reasonably necessary to advance the procompetitive justification because a less restrictive alternative exists that could equally advance that justification. But often such arguments are controverted by theoretical arguments that the posited alternative was not feasible, would not equally advance the justification, or would not be less restrictive. Such a theoretical conflict suffices to show a plausible enough theoretical relationship between the justification and the restraint to survive step 2. Step 4 should be used to resolve such a theoretical conflict with empirical evidence about whether the posited alternatives are in fact feasible, useful and less restrictive.

Appropriate Litigation Stage. Although lower courts have not been entirely consistent, generally steps 1 and 2 should be conducted at the motion to dismiss stage, given that they are purely theoretical and do not require the costly development of evidence. Steps 3 and 4 should be conducted at the stage of summary judgment, because they turn on whether the empirical evidence demonstrates sufficient evidence of anti- and procompetitive effects. Step 5 should be conducted at trial because it turns on how that evidence is weighed by the factfinder.

The Policy Relevance of Nonprofit Status

It is sometimes argued that nonprofit firms should, like professionals, be treated more deferentially by antitrust law. Proper consideration of this issue requires us to put aside two misconceptions. First, notwithstanding their name, nonprofit firms *can* make a profit. Their organizational form bars them from *distributing* profits to investors, not from making profits, and they might spend those profits in ways that benefit their members or employees. Second, nonprofits *can* run a business. Indeed, most nonprofits are commercial (e.g., hospitals) in the sense that they get most of their revenue from sales. Some nonprofits are donative; that is, they get virtually all their revenue from donations, like the Red Cross. Others are mixed, like universities, which both charge for education and raise money through donations.

The argument for treating nonprofits differently than other firms turns on the premise that they evidence a behavioral difference that merits different treatment. One theory is that nonprofits are different because they don't run their businesses to maximize profits. This has been disputed factually, with the extent of the behavioral difference sufficiently unclear that vigorous debate has developed in the empirical literature about whether nonprofit hospitals act any differently than for-profit hospitals, with some studies suggesting they provide similar amounts of uncompensated care. If the premise is factually accurate, then the implications for antitrust review remain disputed. Should the courts apply more lax antitrust scrutiny because nonprofits are less motivated by profit-maximization? Or should courts apply tougher antitrust scrutiny because nonprofits remain financially interested in reducing competition and may dislike competition on ideological grounds as well as selfish grounds?

Another theory is that nonprofits do run businesses to maximize profits, but should be subjected to less strict antitrust scrutiny because they use their revenue more charitably. One question this raises is whether this is true, or whether they effectively distribute profits to members or employees. A prominent theory of nonprofit hospitals, for example, claims they are run to maximize the financial interests of medical staff. Even if empirically true, the issue remains whether on principle this justifies different treatment. Many firms could claim that their owners or stockholders use their profits charitably. Indeed, the famous *Standard Oil* case involved a corporation owned by John Rockefeller, who was famous for donating his profits to foundations and worthy causes. Likewise, the fact that Bill Gates has become a great philanthropist has not caused any different standards to be applied in this generation's *Microsoft* litigation. One might also think that this theory relies on social welfare justifications of the sort rejected in *Professional Engineers*.

The Legal Treatment of Nonprofits Under U.S. Law

Under U.S. law, the Sherman Act applies to nonprofits. *See NCAA*. The Supreme Court has declined to adopt any presumption that nonprofits are not maximizing revenue, *id.*, and while some demonstrable behavioral difference might bear on the legality of their conduct, the Supreme Court has repeatedly made clear that good motives are insufficient, and the inquiry remains limited to competitive concerns. *Id.; Professional Engineers*. The Sherman Act, however, applies only to restraints on "trade or commerce." Thus, while the Act fully governs restraints a nonprofit might impose on any commercial activity involving the sale of products or services, it does not cover restraints on donative activities.

Other U.S. antitrust statutes do treat nonprofits differently. As explained in *California Dental*, the FTC Act doesn't cover a nonprofit unless it is carrying on activities that profit its members. The Robinson Patman Act exempts purchases by nonprofits for their own use.[25] Clayton Act § 7, the merger statute, refers to the FTC jurisdictional limitation, and thus might not apply to nonprofits, but most courts have held it does because it refers only to a jurisdictional limit in Clayton Act § 11 that excludes business regulated by other agencies.[26] In any event, Sherman Act § 1 probably provides the same merger review standards as Clayton Act § 7.[27]

United States v. Brown University

5 F.3d 658 (3d Cir. 1993).

■ COWEN, CIRCUIT JUDGE. . . .

I. FACTUAL AND PROCEDURAL BACKGROUND

. . . In 1958, MIT and the eight Ivy League schools formed the "Ivy Overlap Group" to collectively determine the amount of financial assistance to award to commonly admitted students. The facts concerning this Agreement are essentially undisputed. The Ivy Overlap Group expressly agreed that they would award financial aid only on the basis of demonstrated need. Thus, merit-based aid was prohibited. To ensure that aid packages would be comparable, the participants agreed to share financial information concerning admitted candidates and to jointly develop and apply a uniform needs analysis for assessing family contributions. . . .

[Congress has promulgated a method for calculating family contributions, from which schools may deviate as long as a student receiving federal aid does not receive more than under the Congressional Methodology]. The Ivy Overlap group . . . differed from the Congressional Methodology in several significant respects. . . . Each deviation resulted in less generous aid packages than under the Congressional Methodology.

Although each Ivy Overlap institution employed the same analysis to compute family contributions, discrepancies in the contribution figures still arose. To eliminate these discrepancies, the Overlap members agreed to meet in early April each year to jointly determine the amount

---

25 *See* 15 U.S.C. § 13c.

26 United States v. Rockford Memorial Corp., 898 F.2d 1278, 1280 (7th Cir.1990); FTC v. University Health, 938 F.2d 1206, 1214–17 (11th Cir.1991).

27 898 F.2d at 1281–82.

of the family contribution for each commonly admitted student. Prior to this conference, the Overlap schools independently determined the family contribution of each student they admitted. . . .

At the two-day spring Overlap conference, the schools compared their family contribution figures for each commonly admitted student. Family contribution differences of less than $500 were ignored. When there was a disparity in excess of $500, the schools would either agree to use one school's figure or meet somewhere in the middle. Due to time constraints, the schools spent only a few minutes discussing an individual and the agreed upon figures were more a result of compromise than of a genuine effort to accurately assess the student's financial circumstances.

All Ivy Overlap Group institutions understood that failing to comply with the Overlap Agreement would result in retaliatory sanctions. Consequently, noncompliance was rare and quickly remedied. For example, in 1986, Princeton began awarding $1,000 research grants to undergraduates based on academic merit. After a series of complaints from other Overlap institutions who viewed these grants as a form of scholarship, Princeton terminated this program.

Stanford represented the Overlap schools' only meaningful competition for students. The Ivy Overlap Group, fearful that Stanford would lure a disproportionate number of the highest caliber students with merit scholarships, attempted to recruit Stanford into the group. Stanford declined this invitation.

In 1991, the Antitrust Division of the Justice Department brought this civil suit alleging that the Ivy Overlap Group unlawfully conspired to restrain trade in violation of section one of the Sherman Act, by (1) agreeing to award financial aid exclusively on the basis of need; (2) agreeing to utilize a common formula to calculate need; and (3) collectively setting, with only insignificant discrepancies, each commonly admitted students' family contribution toward the price of tuition. The Division sought only injunctive relief. All of the Ivy League institutions signed a consent decree with the United States, and only MIT proceeded to trial. . . .

The district court entered judgment in favor of the Division. . . .

II. TRADE OR COMMERCE

. . . Section one, by its terms, does not apply to all conspiracies, but only to those which restrain "trade or commerce. . . ."

The exchange of money for services, even by a nonprofit organization, is a quintessential commercial transaction. Therefore, the payment of tuition in return for educational services constitutes commerce. MIT concedes as much by acknowledging that its determination of the full tuition amount is a commercial decision.

We thus come to the crux of the issue—is providing financial assistance solely to needy students a selective reduction or "discount" from the full tuition amount, or a charitable gift? If this financial aid is a component of the process of setting tuition prices, it is commerce. *See* Catalano, Inc. v. Target Sales, Inc., 446 U.S. 643, 648 (1980) (agreement to eliminate discounts violates section one). If it is pure charity, it is not.

When MIT admits an affluent student, that student must pay approximately $25,000 annually (tuition plus room, board and incidental expenses) if he or she wishes to enroll at MIT. If MIT accepts a needy student and calculates that it will extend $10,000 in financial aid to that student, the student must pay approximately $15,000 to attend MIT. The student certainly is not free to take the $10,000 and apply it toward attendance at a different college. The assistance package is only available in conjunction with a complementary payment of approximately $15,000 to MIT. The amount of financial aid not only impacts, but directly determines the amount that a needy student must pay to receive an education at MIT. The financial aid therefore is part of the commercial process of setting tuition.

MIT suggests that providing aid exclusively to needy students and setting the amount of that aid is not commercial because the price needy students are charged is substantially below the marginal cost of supplying a year of education to an undergraduate student. Because profit maximizing companies would not engage in such economically abnormal behavior, MIT concludes that such activity must be noncommercial. MIT's concession, however, that setting the full tuition amount is a commercial decision subject to antitrust scrutiny undermines this argument. The full tuition figure, like the varying amounts charged to needy students, is significantly below MIT's marginal cost. Therefore, whether the price charged for educational services is below marginal cost is not probative of the commercial or noncommercial nature of the methodology utilized to determine financial aid packages.

The fact that MIT is not obligated to provide any financial aid does not transform that aid into charity. Similarly, discounting the price of educational services for needy students is not charity when a university receives tangible benefits in exchange. Regardless of whether MIT's motive is altruism, self-enhancement or a combination of the two, MIT benefits from providing financial aid. MIT admits that it competes with other Overlap members for outstanding students. By distributing aid, MIT enables exceptional students to attend its school who otherwise could not afford to attend. The resulting expansion in MIT's pool of exceptional applicants increases the quality of MIT's student body. MIT then enjoys enhanced prestige by virtue of its ability to attract a greater portion of the "cream of the crop." The Supreme Court has recognized that nonprofit organizations derive significant benefit from increased prestige and influence. *See* American Society of Mechanical Engineers,

Inc. v. Hydrolevel Corp., 456 U.S. 556, 576. Although MIT could fill its class with students able to pay the full tuition, the caliber of its student body, and consequently the institution's reputation, obviously would suffer. Overlap affords MIT the benefit of an overrepresentation of high caliber students, with the concomitant institutional prestige, without forcing MIT to be responsive to market forces in terms of its tuition costs. By immunizing itself through the Overlap from competition for students based on a price/quality ratio, MIT achieves certain institutional benefits at a bargain. . . .

III. RESTRAINT OF TRADE . . .

A. *Is Overlap Illegal Per Se?*

The district court found that the "Ivy Overlap Group members, which are horizontal competitors, agreed upon the price which aid applicants and their families would have to pay to attend a member institution to which that student had been accepted." Based on this finding, the Division argues that MIT's conduct was per se unlawful price fixing. We disagree. . . .

Per se rules of illegality are judicial constructs, and are based in large part on economic predictions that certain types of activity will more often than not unreasonably restrain competition. The economic models of behavior that spawn these predictions are not equally applicable in all situations. The fact that Overlap may be said to involve price-fixing in "a literal sense," therefore, does not mean that it automatically qualifies as per se illegal price-fixing. *BMI*. . . .

Antitrust analysis is based largely on price theory, which "assures us that economic behavior . . . is primarily directed toward the maximization of profits." R. Bork, The Antitrust Paradox 116 (1978). The rationale for treating professional organizations differently is that they tend to vary somewhat from this economic model. Specifically, while professional organizations aim to enhance the profits of their members, they and the professionals they represent may have greater incentives to pursue ethical, charitable, or other non-economic objectives that conflict with the goal of pure profit maximization. While it is well settled that good motives themselves "will not validate an otherwise anticompetitive practice," *NCAA*, courts often look at a party's intent to help it judge the likely effects of challenged conduct. Thus, when bona fide, non-profit professional associations adopt a restraint which they claim is motivated by "public service or ethical norms," economic harm to consumers may be viewed as less predictable and certain. In such circumstances, it is proper to entertain and weigh procompetitive justifications proffered in defense of an alleged restraint before declaring it to be unreasonable.

The same rationale counsels against declaring Overlap per se unreasonable. As a qualified charitable organization under 26 U.S.C. § 501(c)(3), MIT deviates even further from the profit-maximizing prototype than do professional associations. While non-profit professional associations advance the commercial interests of their for-profit constituents, MIT is, as its 501(c)(3) status suggests, an organization "operated exclusively for . . . educational purposes . . . no part of the net earnings of which inures to the benefit of any private shareholder or individual." 26 U.S.C. § 501(c)(3). This does not mean, of course, that MIT and other bona fide charitable organizations lack incentives to increase revenues. Nor does it necessarily mean that commercially motivated conduct of such organizations should be immune from per se treatment. Like the defendant associations in *Indiana Dentists* and *Professional Engineers*, however, MIT vigorously maintains that Overlap was the product of a concern for the public interest, here the undisputed public interest in equality of educational access and opportunity, and alleges the absence of any revenue maximizing purpose.

This alleged pure altruistic motive and alleged absence of a revenue maximizing purpose contribute to our uncertainty with regard to Overlap's anti-competitiveness, and thus prompts us to give careful scrutiny to the nature of Overlap, and to refrain from declaring Overlap per se unreasonable. We thus agree with the district court that Overlap must be judged under the rule of reason.

B. *The Rule of Reason*

. . . MIT does not dispute that the stated purpose of Overlap is to eliminate price competition for talented students among member institutions. Indeed, the intent to eliminate price competition among the Overlap schools for commonly admitted students appears on the face of the Agreement itself. In addition to agreeing to offer financial aid solely on the basis of need and to develop a common system of needs analysis, the Overlap members agreed to meet each spring to compare data and to conform one another's aid packages to the greatest possible extent. Because the Overlap Agreement aims to restrain "competitive bidding" and deprive prospective students of "the ability to utilize and compare prices" in selecting among schools, it is anticompetitive "on its face." *Professional Engineers*. . . . We therefore agree [with the district court] that Overlap initially "requires some competitive justification even in the absence of a detailed market analysis." *Indiana Dentists* (quoting *NCAA*); *see Professional Engineers*. . . .

At trial, MIT maintained that Overlap had the following procompetitive effects: (1) it improved the quality of the educational program at the Overlap schools; (2) it increased consumer choice by making an Overlap education more accessible to a greater number of students; and (3) it promoted competition for students among Overlap schools in areas other than price. The district court rejected each of these alleged competitive virtues, summarily concluding that they amounted to no more than non-economic social welfare justifications.

On appeal, MIT first contends that by promoting socio-economic diversity at member institutions, Overlap improved the quality of the education offered by the schools and therefore enhanced the consumer appeal of an Overlap education. The Supreme Court has recognized improvement in the quality of a product or service that enhances the public's desire for that product or service as one possible procompetitive virtue. *See NCAA*. The district court itself noted that it cannot be denied "that cultural and economic diversity contributes to the quality of education and enhances the vitality of student life". . . .

MIT also contends that by increasing the financial aid available to needy students, Overlap provided some students who otherwise would not have been able to afford an Overlap education the opportunity to have one. In this respect, MIT argues, Overlap enhanced consumer choice. The policy of allocating financial aid solely on the basis of demonstrated need has two obvious consequences. First, available resources are spread among more needy students than would be the case if some students received aid in excess of their need. Second, as a consequence of the fact that more students receive the aid they require, the number of students able to afford an Overlap education is maximized. In short, removing financial obstacles for the greatest number of talented but needy students increases educational access, thereby widening consumer choice. Enhancement of consumer choice is a traditional objective of the antitrust laws and has also been acknowledged as a procompetitive benefit. *See NCAA*.

Finally, MIT argues that by eliminating price competition among participating schools, Overlap channelled competition into areas such as curriculum, campus activities, and student-faculty interaction. As the Division correctly notes, however, any competition that survives a horizontal price restraint naturally will focus on attributes other than price. This is not the kind of procompetitive virtue contemplated under the Act, but rather one mere consequence of limiting price competition.

MIT next claims that beyond ignoring the procompetitive effects of Overlap, the district court erroneously refused to consider compelling social welfare justifications. MIT argues that by enabling member schools to maintain a steadfast policy of need-blind admissions and full need-based aid, Overlap promoted the social ideal of equality of educational access and opportunity. . . .

The district court was not persuaded by the alleged social welfare values proffered for Overlap because it believed the Supreme Court's decisions in *Professional Engineers* and *Indiana Dentists* required a persuasive procompetitive justification, or a showing of necessity, neither of which it believed that MIT demonstrated. . . . Both the public safety justification rejected by the Supreme Court in *Professional Engineers* and the public health justification rejected by the Court in *Indiana Dentists* were based on the defendants' faulty premise that consumer choices made under competitive market conditions are "unwise" or "dangerous." Here MIT argues that participation in the Overlap arrangement provided some consumers, the needy, with additional choices which an entirely free market would deny them. The facts and arguments before us may suggest some significant areas of distinction from those in *Professional Engineers* and *Indiana Dentists* in that MIT is asserting that Overlap not only serves a social benefit, but actually enhances consumer choice. Overlap is not an attempt to withhold a particular desirable service from customers, as was the professional combination in Indiana Dentists, but rather it purports only to seek to extend a service to qualified students who are financially "needy" and would not otherwise be able to afford the high cost of education at MIT. Further, while Overlap resembles the ban on competitive bidding at issue in *Professional Engineers*, MIT alleges that Overlap enhances competition by broadening the socio-economic sphere of its potential student body. Thus, rather than suppress competition, Overlap may in fact merely regulate competition in order to enhance it, while also deriving certain social benefits. If the rule of reason analysis leads to this conclusion, then indeed Overlap will be beyond the scope of the prohibitions of the Sherman Act.

We note the unfortunate fact that financial aid resources are limited even at the Ivy League schools. A trade-off may need to be made between providing some financial aid to a large number of the most needy students or allowing the free market to bestow the limited financial aid on the very few most talented who may not need financial aid to attain their academic goals. Under such circumstances, if this trade-off is proven to be worthy in terms of obtaining a more diverse student body (or other legitimate institutional goals), the limitation on the choices of the most talented students might not be so egregious as to trigger the obvious concerns which led the Court to reject the "public interest" justifications in *Professional Engineers* and *Indiana Dentists*. However, we leave it for the district court to decide whether full funding of need may be continued on an individual institutional basis, absent Overlap, whether tuition could be lowered as a way to compete for qualified "needy" students, or whether there are other imaginable creative alternatives to implement MIT's professed social welfare goal.

We note too, however, that another aspect of the agreements condemned in *Professional Engineers* and *Indiana Dentists* was that those agreements embodied a strong economic self-interest of the parties to them. In *Professional Engineers*, the undisputed objective of the ban on competitive bidding was to maintain higher prices for engineering services than a free competitive market would sustain. The engineers' public safety justification "rest[ed] on the assumption that the agreement [would] tend to maintain price level; if it had no such effect, it would not serve its intended purpose." Likewise, the Court in *Indiana Dentists* characterized the dentists' agreement to withhold x rays as an "attempt to thwart" the goal of "choosing the least expensive adequate course of dental treatment." Though not singled out by the Court in these two cases, the nature of the agreements made any public interest argument greatly suspect. To the extent that economic self-interest or revenue maximization is operative in Overlap, it too renders MIT's public interest justification suspect. . . . In the case sub judice, the quest for economic self-interest is professed to be absent, as it is alleged that the Overlap agreement was intended, not to obtain an economic profit in the form of greater revenue for the participating schools, but rather to benefit talented but needy prospective students who otherwise could not attend the school of their choice.

The nature of higher education, and the asserted procompetitive and pro-consumer features of the Overlap, convince us that a full rule of reason analysis is in order here. . . .

It is most desirable that schools achieve equality of educational access and opportunity in order that more people enjoy the benefits of a worthy higher education. There is no doubt, too, that enhancing the quality of our educational system redounds to the general good. To the extent that higher education endeavors to foster vitality of the mind, to promote free exchange between bodies of thought and truths, and better communication among a broad spectrum of individuals, as well as prepares individuals for the intellectual demands of responsible citizenship, it is a common good that should be extended to as wide a range of individuals from as broad a range of socio-economic backgrounds as possible. It is with this in mind that the Overlap Agreement should be submitted to the rule of reason scrutiny under the Sherman Act.

We conclude that the district court was obliged to more fully investigate the procompetitive and noneconomic justifications proffered by MIT than it did when it performed the truncated rule of reason analysis. Accordingly, we will remand this case to the district court with instructions to evaluate Overlap using the full-scale rule of reason analysis outlined above. . . .

Even if an anticompetitive restraint is intended to achieve a legitimate objective, the restraint only survives a rule of reason analysis if it is reasonably necessary to achieve the legitimate objectives proffered by the defendant. . . . The district court "questioned" whether the Overlap Agreement was "a necessary ingredient" to achieve the social welfare objectives offered by MIT. The district court implicitly concluded, and we agree, that to some extent the Overlap Agreement promoted equality of access to higher education and economic and cultural diversity. It thus turned directly to the second inquiry—whether a substantially less restrictive alternative, the free market coupled with MIT's institutional resolve, could achieve the same benefits. In a conclusory statement, the court found "no evidence supporting MIT's fatalistic prediction that the end of the Ivy Overlap Group necessarily would sound the death knell of need-blind admissions or need-based aid." Although the district court acknowledged that the end of Overlap could herald the end of full need-based aid at MIT, it also observed that this was not an inevitability if indeed MIT counted full need-based aid among its priority institutional goals.

On remand if the district court, under a full scale rule of reason analysis, finds that MIT has proffered a persuasive justification for the Overlap Agreement, then the Antitrust Division of the Justice Department, the plaintiff in this case, must prove that a reasonable less restrictive alternative exists. The district court should consider, if and when the issue arises, whether the Antitrust Division has shown, by a preponderance of the evidence, that another viable option, perhaps the free market, can achieve the same benefits as Overlap.

NOTES AND QUESTIONS ON *UNITED STATES V. BROWN*

1. ***Why is this a restraint on trade or commerce rather than on the distribution of charitable aid?*** Commerce involves the exchange of money for services, and MIT admitted that its determination of full tuition prices was commercial. The court concluded that financial aid is really a discount from the full price, rather than charity, because the financial aid cannot be used at any other college. In other words, financial aid really just amounts to price discrimination, in which colleges charge wealthier students higher prices than others, just like airlines charge business passengers higher prices than others. MIT argued it was still charity because the cost of college is less than the price charged, but the court rejected that argument because that was also true of full tuition, which MIT conceded was commercial.

Suppose MIT had not made that concession and argued that even its full tuition constituted charity because its price is below cost. Would that argument be persuasive? When a medical clinic charges only a small fee for health care that is far less than its costs, that might well constitute charity. But here the court suggested the answer would still be no because MIT competed with other colleges for outstanding students to gain prestige and was trying to minimize the costs of obtaining them. Although the court did not explain why this made the transaction commercial, this understanding of college motivation does suggest that students are less consumers than inputs. In other words, colleges effectively pay a net price for students (given that the students pay less than the costs) and good students (like good faculty) help colleges achieve prestige, which is what colleges maximize instead of profits. This motivation suggests that colleges have incentives to fix monopsonistic low prices when buying great students, and that the restraint is just as commercial as if colleges tried to fix low prices for faculty salaries or library books.

Another way to challenge the claim that tuition charges constitute charity might be to argue that college faculty are less employees than de facto owners of the colleges. If one views faculty as de facto owners, then the money that colleges pay to faculty is a de facto profit distribution rather than a true cost, in which case the tuition price may exceed the true cost of providing education. Some have similarly argued that nonprofit hospitals should be viewed as de facto owned by their medical staff. *See* Mark V. Pauly & Martin Redisch, *The Not-for-Profit Hospital as a Physicians Cooperative*, 63 AM. ECON. REV. 87 (1973).

Do you think providing financial aid should be understood as charity or as commercial discount? Does your conclusion turn on what we accept as the correct theory of how colleges operate?

2. Why doesn't the per se rule apply? Because the agreement prohibited merit-based financial aid, the effect and undisputed purpose of the agreement was "to eliminate price competition for talented students." Moreover, the agreement also collectively fixed the net price (which equals tuition minus aid) to each student who received financial aid as well, so also eliminated price competition for students on financial aid.

Why, then, didn't the court apply the per se rule against horizontal price-fixing? The court noted that *BMI* held that not all price-fixing was per se illegal, but here (unlike in *BMI*) the agreement was not ancillary to any productive collaboration. The court nonetheless reasoned the per se rule did not apply because, like professionals, nonprofits do not necessarily maximize profits. But unlike nonprofits, professionals have claims to expertise and a tradition of self-regulation. Further, even professionals, are subject to the per se rule when they engage in price-fixing that is not ancillary to any productive collaboration. *See Maricopa; Goldfarb*. Likewise, *California Dental* later indicated that the per se rule would apply to professionals if they directly restrained price. Do you agree with the court's decision not to apply the per se rule?

Would the court reach the same conclusion if Cambridge apartment owners agree to form cartel that price discriminates based on the wealth of tenants in order to maximize the number of tenants who can afford apartments? Presumably not, because the Cambridge apartment owners are not nonprofit institutions. However, their alleged procompetitive justification of maximizing the number of tenants who can afford apartments would be the same as the alleged justification here of maximizing the number of students who can afford college. Should the cases be treated any differently?

3. Does this agreement increase consumer choice or educational quality by making college accessible to more students? MIT argued that, by making education at these elite colleges accessible to more students, the agreement procompetitively increased consumer choice and educational quality. The court concluded this procompetitive justification was sufficiently plausible that full-scale rule-of-reason review was required. But precisely how does this procompetitive justification work?

a. Consumer choice. MIT did not argue that the agreement increased total financial aid or decreased the average net college price. Such an argument would have faced the problem that, without the agreement, the incentives of colleges to compete for students would likely drive them to cut net prices by increasing aid. Instead, the claim was that the agreement reallocated scarce aid dollars away from merit-based aid for the best students and towards financial aid for needier students in a way that made education at these elite colleges accessible to more students.

Assuming that the agreement actually had this effect, it would increase net prices for the former set of students and decrease net prices to the latter set of students. The latter would enjoy increased consumer choice, but the former would have decreased consumer choice because they would be left with less money and thus less freedom to buy other non-educational products. The former may also not be wealthier; they could be superstar underprivileged students who would otherwise have gotten full merit-based scholarships rather than an aid package that includes student loans. Should we call such mixed effects an increase in consumer choice?

One might also wonder whether the agreement really decreased net prices to students receiving financial aid in a way that increased accessibility. After all, the agreement collectively fixed the net price to each student on financial aid in a way that prevented the colleges from offering more aid to compete for these students as well. Rather than reallocating some fixed pot of revenue from merit-based students toward needy students, the agreement may have simply amounted to a horizontal agreement to exercise a collective market power to engage in price discrimination that squeezed more revenue out of all students by pricing to each student based on the maximum net price that could be extracted from that student.

Indeed, as the Court noted, the way the agreement calculated the net price (i.e., family contribution) for each student on financial aid deviated from the Congressional Methodology in various ways, each of which resulted in a *higher* net price. To be sure, a federal statute provided that, for students receiving federal aid, the combined effect of the various college deviations from the Congressional Methodology could not result in a net price that was lower than the Congressional Methodology would have provided. But that statute did not apply to students who were not receiving federal aid. Nor did the statute explain why each and every deviation in methodology always moved toward an increase in net price to students receiving federal aid.

b. Educational quality. If one assumes the agreement did reallocate aid in a way that lowered the net price to students on financial aid, then the agreement would increase the number of students who could afford college. MIT stressed that this increased educational quality by increasing socio-economic diversity. However, if diversity increases quality, then that just means that diversity is part of merit. This argument thus does not explain why, without any agreement, colleges pursuing quality would not have every incentive to purse a diverse class by offering greater merit scholarships to diverse candidates, just as they do for those with high test scores or athletic ability. This argument also would suggest that diverse candidates are not necessarily better off with this agreement, which may instead just allow colleges to buy diversity more cheaply.

An alternative argument is that the agreement increases the overall quality of the student body—including all measures of quality from diversity, SATs, GPAs, sports ability or anything else viewed as contributing to quality—because any expansion in the number of students who can afford college means that the colleges can fill their student body by setting quality thresholds at a higher level. If so, one could argue that the agreement increased the quality of the student body, and thus increased the quality of education purchased by students in a way that benefited students (as well as benefitting the colleges to the extent one views them as prestige-maximizers).

Still, one might wonder why an agreement is necessary if allocating aid in this way increases the quality of the student body. Colleges have their own incentives to offer aid in a way that increases the quality of their student body and thus increases the quality of the educational product they offer. One possibility is that colleges acting individually assess student quality differently than they do collectively, and thus without an agreement would allocate aid to different sets of students. However, that is not really a procompetitive justification because it suggests that the colleges are collectively imposing a quality judgment that deviates from the competitive quality judgment, which is similar to what was condemned in *Professional Engineers*.

The stronger argument would be that, without the agreement, the colleges would use up all their aid on competing for the very best students. Having used up all their aid on those students, they would have to fill the rest of the class with students who were not financially needy, even if their academic credentials or socio-economic contributions are lower than students who were financially needy. The expenditure of aid on the very best students does not increase the quality of the student body at elite colleges because they would go to one of those colleges with or without the agreement. But the quality of the student body is enhanced by spending aid to fill the rest of the class with financially needy students who are better than the less needy students who would otherwise be admitted.

This argument depends on the debatable premise that the agreement lowered net prices to financially needy students. It also depends on the premise that the colleges that were party to the agreement (MIT and the Ivy League colleges) had sufficient collective market power that they would get the very best students either with or without an agreement. If Stanford, which declined to join the agreement, used merit-based aid to take away the very best students, then quality at the defendant colleges might suffer.

However, if the premises are valid, it could provide an explanation why the agreement could benefit even the very best students. To be sure, the very best students would end up paying higher net prices, which harms them. However, the very best students would also end up with higher quality average fellow students, which increases the quality of their education. If the quality benefit exceeds the price harm, then the net effect might be good for the very best students, or at least mixed. Further, under these premises, students on financial aid would enjoy both lower prices and higher quality.

4. Could colleges agree to fix faculty salaries to lower expenditures so the colleges could devote more resources to financial aid to increase student choice and quality? Clearly not. Such an agreement would be per se illegal, eliminating price competition for faculty and setting subcompetitive faculty salaries, thus lowering faculty quality and/or output. But why should this hypothetical be treated any differently from the agreement in this case? One possible distinction is that faculty are more clearly inputs, so it would be more obvious that fixing their salaries would constitute a buyer cartel. However, it may be more accurate to view students as inputs, too, given that colleges pay a net price for students and buy both talented faculty and talented students to increase college prestige.

Another possible distinction is that faculty are in a different market than students, so it would be clear that such a scheme was just harming one market to help another. Generally antitrust does not allow anticompetitive effects in one market to be justified by procompetitive effects in another market, as we will explore in Chapter 7. However, it is not clear why harming one market to benefit another should be treated different from harming some consumers in a market to benefit others. To be sure, one could argue that the difference is that in this case the students who pay more because of the agreement get higher quality education and thus do not suffer a net harm. But one could also argue in this hypothetical that the faculty who suffer from lower salaries benefit from higher quality students and thus also do not suffer a net harm. Perhaps the answer is that, if that were true, then without any agreement individual colleges would have incentives to compete for by offering lower salaries and a higher quality student body funded by using the salary savings on more student aid. In contrast, in this case, it may be that without the agreement individual colleges that cut merit-based aid to fund need-based aid would lose the very best students to other colleges and thus might not increase the overall quality of the class even if they increased the quality of the rest of the class.

Do you think this case should be treated any differently from a college agreement to fix faculty salaries?

5. ***Is it procompetitive to make students pick solely on educational grounds?*** MIT also argued that agreement was procompetitive because it assured students would pick their college on solely on educational grounds, rather than being influenced by prices. The court rejected this argument without any difficulty. It is hard to see why students shouldn't have the same right to trade off price and quality as, for example, the buyers of engineering services. Further, all price fixing leaves only non-price competition, and we normally think that limiting competition to only non-price dimensions is anticompetitive, not procompetitive.

Epilogue to *United States v. Brown*

This case was originally brought under the first Bush Administration. After the Third Circuit's decision, it was settled under the Clinton Administration. Under the settlement, MIT and the Ivy League schools could not discuss or agree with other schools on the financial aid offered individual students, but could exchange financial data about each applicant, agree on general principles for determining financial aid, and have independent auditors review awards and report any gross disparities that might indicate a college was deviating from those principles. However, colleges could only enter into the latter sorts of agreements if they adopted "need-blind and full-need" admission and aid policies, which at the time Harvard President Rudenstine complained would include only "a very small handful" of colleges, excluding Brown and perhaps other Ivy League colleges. *See* William Honan, "M.I.T. Wins Right to Share Financial Aid Data in Antitrust Accord," N.Y. Times Dec. 23, 1993 at A13. President Rudenstine's stated concern that the settlement would increase aid expenditures tends to confirm that the original agreement was not increasing total expenditures on financial aid.

Do you think this settlement was desirable? The settlement did not significantly reduce the restraint on price competition because, even without agreeing on the price charged to each individual customer, allowing an agreement on a general pricing policy and on providing independent audits to identify any deviating participant would normally suffice for a cartel. However, to the extent one agrees with the argument that such an agreement could increase quality if it lowers net prices to financially needy students, then the conditions requiring that the colleges adopt need-blind and full-need policies could help assure that any future agreement advances this procompetitive justification, rather than increasing the net prices to all students.

After this settlement, Congress enacted a statute that gave colleges that admit all students on a need-blind basis an antitrust exemption for agreeing to: (1) award aid only based on need; (2) use a common methodology to determine need, as long as the colleges do not agree on the financial aid award of any individual student; (3) use a common financial aid application, as long as the colleges are free to request additional information; and/or (4) exchange financial aid information about each student with other colleges through a third party. *See* Improving America's Schools Act of 1994 § 568, Pub. L. 103–382, 108 Stat. 4060 (1994). The 1994 statute thus effectively extended the antitrust exemption beyond the settlement to include agreements among colleges with need-blind admissions that did not fully fund all need, which thus weakens the assurance that such agreements lower net prices to financially need students and makes it less likely that such agreements increase student quality. The initial three-year provision was renewed for four years in 1997, for 7 more years in 2001, and for 7 more years in 2008. *See* Pub. L. 110–327, 122 Stat. 3566 (2008). In 2015, the provision was again renewed for 7 years, but this time the permission to exchange financial data about individual students was removed. Pub. L. 114–44, § 2, 129 Stat. 472 (Aug. 6, 2015). Should this antitrust exemption continue to be renewed and, if so, with what conditions?

G. DOES INTELLECTUAL PROPERTY LAW JUSTIFY AN ANTICOMPETITIVE RESTRAINT?

Many commentators on the patent-antitrust intersection frame the issue as raising an inherent tension because antitrust law aims to protect competition, whereas patent law creates monopolies that aim to

patent law v. antitrust law

eliminate competition in order to reward invention.[28] Under this framing, adjudicators must reconcile this tension as best they can, by determining which restraints desirably increase the reward the patent holder gets for its innovation, and whether that benefit offsets any anticompetitive effect.[29] This approach presumes that patent rights merit special treatment compared to other property rights.

This approach raises internal difficulties. The extent to which patent rewards are necessary to incentivize invention is unclear, and it is even less clear what incentive effect comes from any incremental increase in reward that would be produced by restraints associated with patents. One thus might doubt whether adjudicators have the capacity to balance any incremental incentives to innovate against the anticompetitive effects of the restraints at issue. Further, the actual doctrinal distinctions are often unclear or poorly related to such policy concerns. For example, why does U.S. law (as we shall see) treat licensing a patent with price conditions differently than selling the patented product with price conditions? Why does it treat licensing a patent with a price condition differently than licensing with a tying condition?

More fundamentally, one might dispute this entire way of framing the issue and instead conclude that patents are just another form of property right and should be treated no better or worse than any other property right.[30] Patent rights in fact do not necessarily create economic monopolies or ban competition. They merely provide a right to exclude others from a particular innovation. Such patent rights often compete with other patents or methods of accomplishing the same goal, and thus may or may not enjoy any monopoly or market power. Whether a patent confers monopoly power depends entirely on how much value the patent has compared to other market options. This is likewise true for other intellectual property rights, like copyright. The copyright to prevent others from copying this book, for example, confers no monopoly power on its authors (much as we wish it did), as long as competing antitrust books are regarded as reasonable substitutes by a sufficient number of buyers (hard as that possibility may be to fathom for our loyal reader).

One could say precisely the same about physical property rights, like the right to exclude rivals from a firm's plant. Such rights to exclude may or may not preclude competition or confer monopoly power, depending on how valuable that plant is compared to other market options. Whichever sort of property right we are talking about, its ability to preclude competition or create monopoly power turns on its economic value compared to the property rights held by others, not on some metaphysical distinction between the natures of the property rights. If a firm has one

---

[28] *See, e.g.*, Louis Kaplow, *The Patent-Antitrust Intersection: A Reappraisal*, 97 HARV. L. REV. 1813, 1817 (1984).

[29] *Id.* at 1816.

[30] *See* Elhauge, *Defining Better Monopolization Standards*, 56 STANFORD LAW REVIEW 253, 304–05 (2003); U.S. DOJ/FTC, Antitrust Guidelines for the Licensing of Intellectual Property § 2 (1995).

of the 50 patents that exist for making widgets, it will have no market power. If a firm owns the only plant capable of making widgets in the world, it likely has monopoly power.

To be sure, it may be the case that some patent restrictions have greater procompetitive effect or less anticompetitive effect than a comparable restriction on other property rights because of particular facts regarding the patent. But those facts must be identified rather than assumed. The courts have, however, sometimes struggled with this problem.

United States v. General Electric

272 U.S. 476 (1926).

■ MR. CHIEF JUSTICE TAFT delivered the opinion of the Court.

This is a bill in equity, brought by the United States . . . to enjoin . . . General Electric [and Westinghouse] . . . from further violation of the Anti-Trust Act . . . [T]he case involves the validity of a license granted . . . by [General Electric] to the Westinghouse Company to make, use, and sell lamps under the patents owned by the former. It was charged that the license in effect provided that the Westinghouse Company would follow prices and terms of sale from time to time fixed by [General Electric] and observed by it. . . . The District Court upon a full hearing dismissed the bill. . . .

The General Electric Company is the owner of three patents. . . . These three patents cover completely the making of the modern electric lights with the tungsten filaments, and secure to the General Electric Company the monopoly of their making, using, and vending.

The total business in electric lights for the year 1921 was $68,300,000, and the relative percentages of business done by the companies were: General Electric, 69 percent.; Westinghouse, 16 percent.; other licensees, 8 percent.; and manufacturers not licensed, 7 percent. . . .

. . . Conveying less than title to the patent or part of it, the patentee may grant a license to make, use, and vend articles under the specifications of his patent for any royalty, or upon any condition the performance of which is reasonably within the reward which the patentee by the grant of the patent is entitled to secure. It is well settled . . . that where a patentee makes the patented article, and sells it, he can exercise no future control over what the purchaser may wish to do with the article after his purchase. It has passed beyond the scope of the patentee's rights.

But the question is a different one which arises when we consider what a patentee who grants a license to one to make and vend the patented article may do in limiting the licensee in the exercise of the right to sell. The patentee may make and grant a license to another to make and use the patented articles but withhold his right to sell them. The licensee in such a case acquires an interest in the articles made. He owns the material of them and may use them. But if he sells them he infringes the right of the patentee, and may be held for damages and enjoined. If the patentee goes further and licenses the selling of the articles, may he limit the selling by limiting the method of sale and the price? We think he may do so provided the conditions of sale are normally and reasonably adapted to secure pecuniary reward for the patentee's monopoly. One of the valuable elements of the exclusive right of a patentee is to acquire profit by the price at which the article is sold. The higher the price, the greater the profit, unless it is prohibitory. When the patentee licenses another to make and vend and retains the right to continue to make and vend on his own account, the price at which his licensee will sell will necessarily affect the price at which he can sell his own patented goods. It would seem entirely reasonable that he should say to the licensee, "Yes, you may make and sell articles under my patent but not so as to destroy the profit that I wish to obtain by making them and selling them myself." He does not thereby sell outright to the licensee the articles the latter may make and sell or vest absolute ownership in them. He restricts the property and interest the licensee has in the goods he makes and proposes to sell. . . .

. . . [I]n . . . Motion Picture Patents Co. v. Universal Film Co., 243 U.S. 502, [t]he patent . . . covered a part of the mechanism used in motion picture exhibiting machines for feeding a film through the machine with a regular uniform and accurate movement so as not to expose the film to excessive strain or west. The license agreement contained a covenant on the part of the licensee that every machine sold by it should be sold under the restriction and condition that such exhibiting or projecting machines should be used solely for exhibiting or projecting motion pictures of the Motion Picture Patents Company. The [covenant was invalidated] . . . on the ground that the grant of the patent was of the exclusive right to use the mechanism and produce the result with any appropriate material and that the materials or pictures upon which the machine was operated were no part of the patented machine, or of the combination which produced the patented result.

. . . The price at which a patented article sells is certainly a circumstance having a more direct relation and is more germane to the rights of the patentee than the unpatented material with which the patented article may be used. Indeed, as already said, price fixing is usually the essence of that which secures proper reward to the patentee.

Nor do we think that the decisions of this court holding restrictions as to price of patented articles invalid apply to a contract of license like the one in this case. These cases really are only instances of the application of the principle . . . that a patentee may not attach to the article made by him or with his consent a condition running with the article in the hands of purchasers limiting the price at which one who becomes its owner for full consideration shall part with it. They do not consider or condemn a restriction put by a patentee upon his licensee as to the prices at which the latter shall sell articles which he makes and only can make legally under the license. . . .

For the reasons given, we sustain the validity of the license granted by [General Electric] to the Westinghouse Company. The decree of the District Court dismissing the bill is affirmed.

NOTES AND QUESTIONS ON *GENERAL ELECTRIC*

The *General Electric* opinion appears to create a rule of per se *legality* whenever a patentee licenses its patent on any condition "the performance of which is reasonably within the reward" granted by the patent statute. It also held that General Electric's condition requiring the licensee to charge the same lamp prices as General Electric fell within the reasonable patent reward. But how can we generally know when a condition is reasonably within the patent reward?

*1. **The need for functional analysis.*** It seems like the answer cannot turn on purely formalistic grounds. After all, on purely formal grounds, one could equally say it is within the patent reward to (a) sell patented lamps to dealers on the condition that dealers charge no less than General Electric's dealerships or (b) license patents on the condition that the licensee also buy unpatented items. On (a), both conditions increase the patent reward, and although one could say that the first sale exhausts the patentee's interest in a patent reward, the same logic implies that the first license also exhausts the patentee's interest. On (b), the sale of unpatented items could sometimes be the best way to measure the value of the patent and thus price discriminate in a way increase the reward generated by the patent. *See* Chapter 4. We need some sort of functional analysis to determine which agreements to increase the reward reaped from a patent should be deemed "reasonably within" the patent reward granted by patented law.

Moreover, on purely formal grounds, if conditioning a license to intellectual property on licensees charging the same product price were per se legal because within the reward provided by intellectual property law, then the same logic would suggest that conditioning a lease to real property on lessees charging the same product price should be per se legal because within the reward provided by real property law. This formal logic would thus suggest that it would be per se legal for General Electric to lease one of seven lamp-making plants to Westinghouse on the condition Westinghouse charges the same prices for lamps as General Electric. Yet no one thinks a lease conditioned on a horizontal price-fixing condition would be per se legal, again confirming that something other than formalisms must explain the distinction.

Nor does the notion that the "greater power includes lesser power" explain any of these distinctions. After all, that same logic would imply, contrary to actual doctrine, that: (a) the greater power not to sell should include the lesser power to sell on a condition restricting resale; (b) that the greater power not to license should include the lesser power to license on a tying condition; (c) the greater power not to lease should include the lesser power to lease on a price-fixing condition. It would also imply, contrary to *Palmer v. BRG,* that the greater power not to license copyrights should include the lesser power to license copyrights on the condition that the licensee not compete in the same geographic market as the licensor. What all of these distinctions show is that pure formalisms are unhelpful when determining whether a particular condition is legal. Some functional analysis is necessary.

2. ***What are the possible procompetitive justifications?*** There are several procompetitive justifications for licensing the patent to make lamps. Such licenses can (a) transfer the rights to practice the patent to a firm that can more efficiently exercise it; (b) reduce the financial risks for the innovator; or (c) by increasing downstream competition, lower downstream lamp prices and increase downstream lamp output, which increases the total royalties paid to the innovator in a way that better incentivizes innovation.

Is less clear whether these procompetitive justifications for licensing required the challenged pricing condition. On the one hand, General Electric might not want to license without a pricing condition because it fears competition from a licensee would reduce its profit margin. On the other hand, General Electric might be able to avoid that problem without a price condition, by simply licensing the patent at royalty rate that is at or above General Electric's profit margin. However, it may be hard to not only set such a royalty rate, but also continue to update it over time, in a way that the licensee would find acceptable, because it is hard for it to verify the licensor's profit margins and because such a varying royalty rate creates a lot of cost volatility for the licensee, which may reduce its incentives to invest in making the product. Further, even with such a profitable royalty, General Electric may still fear that a lower cost rival might drive it out of the market, which (given the royalty and increased sales) would be profitable during the patent period, but would prevent General Electric from being able to earn post-patent profits to cover some of its own investments in making the product. If the above are true, then it may be that without a pricing condition, the license would not occur and thus the procompetitive effects of licensing could not be obtained.

3. ***What are the possible anticompetitive effects?*** Whether the pricing condition has anticompetitive effects depends on what the firms would have done if General Electric could not license with the pricing condition. If an inability to impose the pricing condition would have caused General Electric to license without that condition, then the condition eliminates efficient price competition in lamp making with no procompetitive effect on licensing.

If an inability to impose the pricing condition would have caused General Electric not to license at all, then the pricing condition does have a procompetitive effect on licensing and whether the condition has any anticompetitive effects depends on what Westinghouse would have done without a license. If the patent were so valuable that Westinghouse could not have made a competitive lamp without a license, then without the pricing condition Westinghouse would not have produced lamps and we would have had no competition in lamp making at all. In this case, the condition cannot have eliminated any competition that otherwise would have occurred and thus has no anticompetitive effect. If the patent were not that valuable and Westinghouse would thus have made a competitive lamp without a license, then without the pricing condition Westinghouse would have produced lamps and we would have had price competition in lamp making. In this case, the condition eliminates price competition that otherwise would have occurred and thus has a strong anticompetitive effect. Further, the less valuable the patent, the weaker any procompetitive effects to weigh against such anticompetitive effects.

*4. **The implications for when a condition is reasonably within the patent reward.*** The above functional analysis has implications for when a court should deem a condition is reasonably within the patent reward. If the patent was not very valuable and Westinghouse could have made a competitive lamp without the patent, then precluding that competition (and earning extra profits by doing so) is outside the legitimate scope of the patent reward. In contrast, if the patent was so valuable that Westinghouse could not have made competitive lamps without the patent, then any pricing condition was just choosing the profit-maximizing way of exploiting General Electric's patent (and rewarding the investment that created it) and thus within the legitimate scope of the patent reward.

In this case, the Supreme Court indicated that the patent was so valuable that Westinghouse could not have made a competitive lamp without it. The Court stressed that General Electric's "patents cover completely the making of the modern electric lights with the tungsten filaments" and concerned articles that Westinghouse "only can make legally under the license." The case thus provides per se legality to pricing conditions in patent licenses only if the patent is sufficiently valuable that downstream competition would not exist without the license.

*5. **Could we say the same for physical property rights?*** Suppose that General Electric leases one of its seven lamp-making plants to Westinghouse on the condition that Westinghouse charges the same prices for lamps as General Electric. If Westinghouse could make competitive lamps without that plant, then precluding that competition is outside the legitimate scope of the real estate property right. But if Westinghouse could not make competitive lamps without that plant, then any pricing condition is just choosing the profit-maximizing way of exploiting General Electric's real estate property right (and rewarding the investment in that property that made it so valuable). In short, whether attaching a pricing condition to a lease of real estate property rights is anticompetitive turns (as with licenses of intellectual property rights) on whether access to the property right is so valuable that a competitive product could not be made without that access.

We might think that patent rights are generally more likely than real estate rights to be so valuable that competitive products could not be made without access to them. But one cannot make any categorical judgment of that sort; it all turns on the economics of the particular piece of intellectual or physical property. While courts used to assume that any patent necessarily conferred some market power—that is, were uniquely valuable—modern courts recognize that patents often have substitutes and thus need not confer such market power. See Chapter 4 discussion of *Illinois Tool Works*. The next case involves a pricing condition attached to the license of a patent that seemed to have little value.

United States v. New Wrinkle, Inc.

342 U.S. 371 (1952).

■ MR. JUSTICE REED delivered the opinion of the Court.

This suit against New Wrinkle, Inc., and The Kay & Ess Co. was instituted . . . by the United States as a civil proceeding. . . . Defendants are charged with . . . conspiring to fix uniform minimum prices and to eliminate competition throughout substantially all of the wrinkle finish industry[3] of the United States by means of patent license agreements. . . . The District Court . . . entered separate judgments as to each defendant dismissing the complaint. . . .

In granting the motions of defendants, the District Court, of course, treated the allegations of the complaint as true. In substance the complaint charges that prior to and during 1937, defendant Kay & Ess was engaged in litigation with a named coconspirator, the Chadeloid Chemical Co., in regard to certain patents covering manufacture of wrinkle finish enamels, varnishes and paints. Each company claimed it controlled the basic patents on wrinkle finish, contending that the patents of the other were subservient to its own. Negotiations throughout 1937 resulted in a contract entered into by Kay & Ess and Chadeloid on November 2, 1937. This contract made provision for the organization of a new corporation, the defendant New Wrinkle. Both Kay & Ess and Chadeloid agreed to accept stock in the new company in exchange for assignments of their wrinkle finish patents. New Wrinkle was to grant patent licenses, incorporating agreements which fixed the minimum prices at which all licensed manufacturers might sell, to the manufacturers in the wrinkle finish industry, including Kay & Ess and Chadeloid. The price-fixing schedules were not to become operative until twelve of the principal producers of wrinkle finishes had subscribed to the minimum prices prescribed in the license agreements.

[3] " 'Wrinkle' finishes . . . are defined as enamels, varnishes and paints which have been compounded from such materials and by such methods as to produce when applied and dried, a hard wrinkled surface on metal or other material. Wrinkle finishes are widely used as coverings for the surfaces of typewriters, cash registers, motors, adding machines, and many other articles of manufacture. They have the following advantages over smooth finishes such as ordinary enamels and varnishes: a. One coat of wrinkle finish is sufficient for many purposes for which two or more coats of smooth finish would be required; b. Surfaces to which wrinkle finishes are to be applied need not be prepared as carefully as those which are to receive smooth finishes, since the wrinkle finishes cover small imperfections; and c. The original appearance of wrinkle-finished articles can be maintained with less cleaning and polishing than that of smooth-finished articles."

Pursuant to this arrangement, the complaint charges New Wrinkle was incorporated, and the patent rights of Kay & Ess and Chadeloid were transferred to it. In conjunction with other named companies and persons, the defendants and Chadeloid thereafter worked together to induce makers of wrinkle finishes to accept the price-fixing patent licenses which New Wrinkle had to offer. These prospective licensees were advised of the agreed-upon prices, terms and conditions of sale in the New Wrinkle licenses, and they were assured that like advice was being given to other manufacturers "in order to establish minimum prices throughout the industry." After May 7, 1938, when the requisite twelve leading manufacturing companies had accepted New Wrinkle licenses, the price schedules became operative. By September 1948, when the complaint was filed in this action, more than two hundred, or substantially all, manufacturers of wrinkle finishes in the United States held nearly identical ten-year extendable license agreements from New Wrinkle. These agreements required, among other things, that a licensee observe in all sales of products covered by the licensed patents a schedule of minimum prices, discounts and selling terms established by the licensor New Wrinkle. Upon thirty days' notice in writing, New Wrinkle might alter any or all of the terms of the price schedule, but such prices, terms and discounts as New Wrinkle might establish were to bind the licensee only if imposed at the same time and in the same terms upon the licensor and all other licensees. Termination provisions in the agreements required a licensee to give three months' written notice and allowed the licensor to terminate the license if a licensee failed to remedy a violation of the agreement within thirty days after written notice thereof by the licensor. A 5-cent per gallon royalty was made payable on all wrinkle finish sold or used by a licensee, said royalty to be reduced to the same figure as that contained in any subsequent license granted at a lower royalty charge. . . . [Appendix A set forth the minimum prices that New Wrinkle set for the sale of wrinkle finish, which ranged from $2.55–4.00/gallon.]

Appellees argue . . . that the principles of *General Electric* control here. . . . *General Electric* . . . allow[s] a patentee to license a competitor in commerce to make and vend with a price limitation controlled by the patentee. When we examined the rule in 1948, the holding of the *General Electric* case was left as stated above. But it was pointed out that "the possession of a valid patent or patents does not give the patentee any exemption from the provisions of the Sherman Act beyond the limits of the patent monopoly." United States v. Line Material Co., 333 U.S. 287, 310. We said that: "two or more patentees in the same patent field may [not] legally combine their valid patent monopolies to secure mutual benefits for themselves through contractual agreements, between themselves and other licensees, for control of the sale price of the patented devices." Price control through cross-licensing was barred as beyond the patent monopoly.

On the day of the *Line Material* decision, this Court handed down United States v. United States Gypsum Co., 333 U.S. 364. The *Gypsum* case was based on facts similar to those here alleged except that the patent owner was also a manufacturer. . . . [W]e consider the fact that New Wrinkle is exclusively a patent-holding company of no significance as a defense to the alleged violation of the Sherman Act. We said in *Gypsum* that: "industry-wide license agreements, entered into with knowledge on the part of licensor and licensees of the adherence of others, with the control over prices and methods of distribution through the agreements and the bulletins, were sufficient to establish a *prima facie* case of conspiracy."

On remand, the prima facie case resulted in a final judgment, affirmed by this Court. In discussing the *General Electric* case, the Court was unanimous in saying that it:

> "gives no support for a patentee, acting in concert with all members of an industry, to issue substantially identical licenses to all members of the industry under the terms of which the industry is completely regimented, the production of competitive unpatented products suppressed, a class of distributors squeezed out, and prices on unpatented products stabilized. . . . it would be sufficient to show that the defendants, constituting all former competitors in an entire industry, had acted in concert to restrain commerce in an entire industry under patent licenses in order to organize the industry and stabilize prices."

We see no material difference between the situation in *Line Material* and *Gypsum* and the case presented by the allegations of this complaint. An arrangement was made between patent holders to pool their patents and fix prices on the products for themselves and their licensees. The purpose and result plainly violate the Sherman Act. The judgment below must be *Reversed*.

NOTES AND QUESTIONS ON *NEW WRINKLE*

1. ***What can we infer from the provisions?*** One provision in the agreement required that the pricing condition would be binding only if imposed on other licensees. Another required that all licensees would get any lower royalty charged another licensee. It is difficult to infer much from these provisions because, whether the agreement is anticompetitive or procompetitive, every licensee wants terms no worse than other licensees are getting.

More telling is the provision that made the pricing condition effective only when the twelve biggest manufacturers signed up. If the value of the license came from the patent, rather than from the pricing condition, then the licensees would want the *fewest* other manufacturers to sign up. Thus, one could infer from this provision that the participants did not believe the pricing condition was procompetitive. We can infer instead from the provision that the agreement was designed to achieve an anticompetitive effect that could only be achieved if enough large firms joined that the participants would collectively have market power in the wrinkle finish market.

The fact that the royalty rate was quite small (5 cents) compared to the minimum price fixed for wrinkle finish ($2.55–4.00) further suggests that the licensees did not value the patent much. This indicates they would likely have made wrinkle finish without the license and that the main effect was to prevent price competition. This state of affairs is also suggested by the fact that, before obtaining this license, many firms (including the 12 largest producers) did successfully make wrinkle finish in competition with the patent holder.

2. ***How should we reconcile the cases?*** Some read the combination of *General Electric* and *New Wrinkle* as adopting a distinction between individual licensing with pricing conditions, which *General Electric* allows, and multiple licensing with pricing conditions, which *New Wrinkle* prohibits on the theory that a horizontal conspiracy among licensees can be inferred. However, the following cut against understanding the cases in this way.

First, the possible anticompetitive and procompetitive effects turn instead on: (1) the value the patent had and the impact that has on the likelihood that rivals would have competed without it; and (2) whether the parties to the licensing agreement, including both the licensor and licensee(s), had enough market power that the pricing condition could affect market prices. The smaller the value of the patent, and the greater the market power of the parties to the licensing agreement, the greater the anticompetitive impact, irrespective of how many licensees there are. For example, having licenses with price conditions for a valuable license among three small manufacturers with little market share would pose little anticompetitive concern. However, having a license with a price condition for a low value license with a firm's only rival would raise grave anticompetitive concerns.

Second, if General Electric had imposed similar pricing conditions on its other licensees, one could not really infer a horizontal conspiracy among those licensees.[31] The licensees may have all accepted independently simply because they needed the patent. And if Westinghouse and any other licensees could not sell lamps without the patent, then the conditioned licenses would not cause any anticompetitive harm.

Finally, if General Electric had licensed (at 5 cents a lamp) some trivial enamel finish patent to Westinghouse that was not necessary to make lamps on the condition that Westinghouse charged at least $3/lamp, then the *General Electric* case would likely have come out differently. The value of the enamel finish would have been obviously low and not necessary for Westinghouse's production of lamps. Thus, setting a relatively high price

31 In fact, the other General Electric licenses restricted output but not prices. *See* A. BRIGHT, THE ELECTRIC LAMP INDUSTRY Chapter 9 (1949). However, price-fixing and output restraints have similar effects, as noted earlier in this chapter.

condition for such a low-value patent could be condemned as outside the reasonable scope of reward of the patent right.

Accordingly, the better distinction is that licenses with horizontal pricing conditions are legal if the patent is so valuable that the licensee (or licensees) could not make a competitive product without the license, which was true in *General Electric* but demonstrably untrue in *New Wrinkle*. They are illegal when, as in *New Wrinkle*, (1) the patent is not very valuable and (2) the parties to the licensing agreement have enough market power that the pricing condition could have an anticompetitive effect.

FTC v. Actavis, Inc.

133 S.Ct. 2223 (2013).

■ JUSTICE BREYER delivered the opinion of the Court.

Company A sues Company B for patent infringement. The two companies settle under terms that require (1) Company B, the claimed infringer, not to produce the patented product until the patent's term expires, and (2) Company A, the patentee, to pay B many millions of dollars. Because the settlement requires the patentee to pay the alleged infringer, rather than the other way around, this kind of settlement agreement is often called a "reverse payment" settlement agreement. And the basic question here is whether such an agreement can sometimes unreasonably diminish competition in violation of the antitrust laws.

In this case, the Eleventh Circuit . . . stated that a reverse payment settlement agreement generally is "immune from antitrust attack so long as its anticompetitive effects fall within the scope of the exclusionary potential of the patent." FTC v. Watson Pharmaceuticals, Inc., 677 F.3d 1298, 1312 (2012). And since the alleged infringer's promise not to enter the patentee's market expired before the patent's term ended, the Circuit found the agreement legal and dismissed the FTC complaint. Id., at 1315. In our view, however, reverse payment settlements such as the agreement alleged in the complaint before us can sometimes violate the antitrust laws. We consequently hold that the Eleventh Circuit should have allowed the FTC's lawsuit to proceed.

I

A

Apparently most if not all reverse payment settlement agreements arise in the context of pharmaceutical drug regulation, and specifically in the context of suits brought under statutory provisions allowing a generic drug manufacturer (seeking speedy marketing approval) to challenge the validity of a patent owned by an already-approved brand-name drug owner. . . . That Act is commonly known as the Hatch-Waxman Act.

First, a drug manufacturer, wishing to market a new prescription drug, must submit a New Drug Application to the federal Food and Drug

Administration (FDA) and undergo a long, comprehensive, and costly testing process, after which, if successful, the manufacturer will receive marketing approval from the FDA.

Second, once the FDA has approved a brand-name drug for marketing, a manufacturer of a generic drug can obtain similar marketing approval through use of abbreviated procedures. The Hatch-Waxman Act permits a generic manufacturer to file an Abbreviated New Drug Application specifying that the generic has the "same active ingredients as," and is "biologically equivalent" to, the already-approved brand-name drug. In this way the generic manufacturer can obtain approval while avoiding the "costly and time-consuming studies" needed to obtain approval "for a pioneer drug." The Hatch-Waxman process, by allowing the generic to piggy-back on the pioneer's approval efforts, "speed[s] the introduction of low-cost generic drugs to market," thereby furthering drug competition.

Third, the Hatch-Waxman Act sets forth special procedures for identifying, and resolving, related patent disputes. It requires the pioneer brand-name manufacturer to list in its New Drug Application the "number and the expiration date" of any relevant patent. And it requires the generic manufacturer in its Abbreviated New Drug Application to "assure the FDA" that the generic "will not infringe" the brand-name's patents.

The generic can provide this assurance in one of several ways. It can certify that the brand-name manufacturer has not listed any relevant patents. It can certify that any relevant patents have expired. It can request approval to market beginning when any still-in-force patents expire. Or, it can certify that any listed, relevant patent "is invalid or will not be infringed by the manufacture, use, or sale" of the drug described in the Abbreviated New Drug Application. *See* § 355(j)(2)(A)(vii)(IV). Taking this last-mentioned route (called the "paragraph IV" route), automatically counts as patent infringement, and often "means provoking litigation." If the brand-name patentee brings an infringement suit within 45 days, the FDA then must withhold approving the generic, usually for a 30-month period, while the parties litigate patent validity (or infringement) in court. If the courts decide the matter within that period, the FDA follows that determination; if they do not, the FDA may go forward and give approval to market the generic product.

Fourth, Hatch-Waxman provides a special incentive for a generic to be the first to file an Abbreviated New Drug Application taking the paragraph IV route. That applicant will enjoy a period of 180 days of exclusivity (from the first commercial marketing of its drug). *See* § 355(j)(5)(B)(iv) (establishing exclusivity period). During that period of exclusivity no other generic can compete with the brand-name drug. If the first-to-file generic manufacturer can overcome any patent obstacle and bring the generic to market, this 180-day period of exclusivity can prove valuable, possibly "worth several hundred million dollars." Indeed, the Generic Pharmaceutical Association said in 2006 that the "'vast majority of potential profits for a generic drug manufacturer materialize during the 180-day exclusivity period.'" The 180-day exclusivity period, however, can belong only to the first generic to file. Should that first-to-file generic forfeit the exclusivity right in one of the ways specified by statute, no other generic can obtain it. *See* § 355(j)(5)(D).

B

[Solvay Pharmaceuticals had a patent for an FDA-approved drug called AndroGel. In 2003,] Actavis, Inc. (then known as Watson Pharmaceuticals), filed an Abbreviated New Drug Application for a generic drug modeled after AndroGel. [So did Paddock Laboratories, in partnership with Par Pharmaceutical.] Both Actavis and Paddock certified under paragraph IV that Solvay's listed patent was invalid and their drugs did not infringe it. . . .

Solvay initiated paragraph IV patent litigation against Actavis and Paddock. Thirty months later the FDA approved Actavis' first-to-file generic product, but, in 2006, the patent-litigation parties all settled. Under the terms of the settlement Actavis agreed that it would not bring its generic to market until August 31, 2015, 65 months before Solvay's patent expired (unless someone else marketed a generic sooner). Actavis also agreed to promote AndroGel to urologists. The other generic manufacturers made roughly similar promises. And Solvay agreed to pay millions of dollars to each generic—$12 million in total to Paddock; $60 million in total to Par; and an estimated $19–$30 million annually, for nine years, to Actavis. The companies described these payments as compensation for other services the generics promised to perform, but the FTC contends the other services had little value. According to the FTC the true point of the payments was to compensate the generics for agreeing not to compete against AndroGel until 2015. . . .

II

A

Solvay's patent, if valid and infringed, might have permitted it to charge drug prices sufficient to recoup the reverse settlement payments it agreed to make to its potential generic competitors. And we are willing to take this fact as evidence that the agreement's "anticompetitive effects fall within the scope of the exclusionary potential of the patent." But we do not agree that that fact, or characterization, can immunize the agreement from antitrust attack.

For one thing, to refer, as the Circuit referred, simply to what the holder of a valid patent could do does not by itself answer the antitrust question. The patent here may or may not be valid, and may or may not be infringed. "[A] valid patent excludes all except its owner from the use of the protected process or product," United States v. Line Material Co., 333 U.S. 287, 308, 68 S.Ct. 550, 92 L.Ed. 701 (1948) (emphasis added). And that exclusion may permit the patent owner to charge a higher-than-competitive price for the patented product. But an invalidated patent carries with it no such right. And even a valid patent confers no right to exclude products or processes that do not actually infringe. The paragraph IV litigation in this case put the patent's validity at issue, as well as its actual preclusive scope. The parties' settlement ended that litigation. The FTC alleges that in substance, the plaintiff agreed to pay the defendants many millions of dollars to stay out of its market, even though the defendants did not have any claim that the plaintiff was liable to them for damages. That form of settlement is unusual. And, for reasons discussed in Part II-B, infra, there is reason for concern that settlements taking this form tend to have significant adverse effects on competition.

Given these factors, it would be incongruous to determine antitrust legality by measuring the settlement's anticompetitive effects solely against patent law policy, rather than by measuring them against procompetitive antitrust policies as well. And indeed, contrary to the Circuit's view that the only pertinent question is whether "the settlement agreement . . . fall[s] within" the legitimate "scope" of the patent's "exclusionary potential," this Court has indicated that patent and antitrust policies are both relevant in determining the "scope of the patent monopoly"—and consequently antitrust law immunity—that is conferred by a patent.

Thus, the Court in *Line Material* explained that "the improper use of [a patent] monopoly," is "invalid" under the antitrust laws and resolved the antitrust question in that case by seeking an accommodation "between the lawful restraint on trade of the patent monopoly and the illegal restraint prohibited broadly by the Sherman Act." 333 U.S. at 310. To strike that balance, the Court asked questions such as whether "the patent statute specifically gives a right" to restrain competition in the manner challenged; and whether "competition is impeded to a greater degree" by the restraint at issue than other restraints previously approved as reasonable. Id., at 311. *See also* United States v. United States Gypsum Co., 333 U.S. 364, 390–391 (1948) (courts must "balance the privileges of [the patent holder] and its licensees under the patent grants with the prohibitions of the Sherman Act against combinations and attempts to monopolize"); Walker Process Equipment, Inc. v. Food Machinery & Chemical Corp., 382 U.S. 172, 174 (1965) ("[E]nforcement of a patent procured by fraud" may violate the Sherman Act). In short, rather than measure the length or amount of a restriction solely against the length of the patent's term or its earning potential, as the Court of Appeals apparently did here, this Court answered the antitrust question by considering traditional antitrust factors such as likely anticompetitive effects, redeeming virtues, market power, and potentially offsetting legal considerations present in the circumstances, such as here those related to patents. *See* Part II-B, infra. Whether a particular restraint lies "beyond the limits of the patent monopoly" is a ***conclusion*** that flows from that analysis and not, as THE CHIEF JUSTICE suggests, its starting point. *Post*, at 2239, 2241–2242 (dissenting opinion).

For another thing, this Court's precedents make clear that patent-related settlement agreements can sometimes violate the antitrust laws. In United States v. Singer Mfg. Co., 374 U.S. 174 (1963), for example, two sewing machine companies possessed competing patent claims; a third company sought a patent under circumstances where doing so might lead to the disclosure of information that would invalidate the other two firms' patents. All three firms settled their patent-related disagreements while assigning the broadest claims to the firm best able to enforce the patent against yet other potential competitors. Id., at 190–192. The Court did not examine whether, on the assumption that all three patents were valid, patent law would have allowed the patents' holders to do the same. Rather, emphasizing that the Sherman Act "imposes strict limitations on the concerted activities in which patent owners may lawfully engage," id., at 197, it held that the agreements, although settling patent disputes, violated the antitrust laws. Id., at 195, 197. And that, in important part, was because "the public interest in granting patent monopolies" exists only to the extent that "the public is given a novel and useful invention" in "consideration for its grant." Id., at 199 (White, J., concurring). *See also* United States v. New Wrinkle, Inc., 342 U.S. 371, 378 (1952) (applying antitrust scrutiny to patent settlement); Standard Oil Co. (Indiana) v. United States, 283 U.S. 163 (1931) (same).

Similarly, both within the settlement context and without, the Court has struck down overly restrictive patent licensing agreements—irrespective of whether those agreements produced supra-patent-permitted revenues. We concede that in United States v. General Elec. Co., 272 U.S. 476, 489 (1926), the Court permitted a single patentee to grant to a single licensee a license containing a minimum resale price requirement. But in *Line Material, supra,* at 308, 310–311, the Court held that the antitrust laws forbid a group of patentees, each owning one or more patents, to cross-license each other, and, in doing so, to insist that each licensee maintain retail prices set collectively by the patent holders. The Court was willing to presume that the single-patentee practice approved in *General Electric* was a "reasonable restraint" that "accords with the patent monopoly granted by the patent law," 333 U.S., at 312, but declined to extend that conclusion to multiple-patentee agreements: "As the Sherman Act prohibits agreements to fix prices, any arrangement between patentees runs afoul of that prohibition and is outside the patent monopoly." Ibid. In *New Wrinkle*, 342 U.S., at 378, the Court held roughly the same, this time in respect to a similar arrangement in settlement of a litigation between two patentees, each of which contended that its own patent gave it the exclusive right to control production. That one or the other company (we may presume) was right about its patent did not lead the Court to confer antitrust immunity. Far from it, the agreement was found to violate the Sherman Act. Id., at 380.

Finally in *Standard Oil Co. (Indiana)*, the Court upheld cross-licensing agreements among patentees that settled actual and impending patent litigation, 283 U.S., at 168, which agreements set royalty rates to be charged third parties for a license to practice all the patents at issue (and which divided resulting revenues). But, in doing so, Justice Brandeis, writing for the Court, warned that such an arrangement would have violated the Sherman Act had the patent holders thereby "dominate[d]" the industry and "curtail[ed] the manufacture and supply of an unpatented product." Id., at 174. These cases do not simply ask whether a hypothetically valid patent's holder would be able to charge, e.g., the high prices that the challenged patent-related term allowed. Rather, they seek to accommodate patent and antitrust policies, finding challenged terms and conditions unlawful unless patent law policy offsets the antitrust law policy strongly favoring competition.

Thus, contrary to the dissent's suggestion, *post*, at 2228–2230, there is nothing novel about our approach. What does appear novel are the dissent's suggestions that a patent holder may simply "pa[y] a competitor to respect its patent" and quit its patent invalidity or noninfringement claim without any antitrust scrutiny whatever, *post*, at 2228, and that "such settlements . . . are a well-known feature of intellectual property litigation," *post*, at 2243. Closer examination casts doubt on these claims. The dissent does not identify any patent statute that it understands to grant such a right to a patentee, whether expressly or by fair implication. It would be difficult to reconcile the proposed right with the patent-related policy of eliminating unwarranted patent grants so the public will not "continually be required to pay tribute to would-be monopolists without need or justification." Lear, Inc. v. Adkins, 395 U.S. 653, 670 (1969). And the authorities cited for this proposition (none from this Court, and none an antitrust case) are not on point. Some of them say that when Company A sues Company B for patent infringement and demands, say, \$100 million in damages, it is not uncommon for B (the defendant) to pay A (the plaintiff) some amount less than the full demand as part of the settlement—\$40 million, for example. *See* Schildkraut, Patent-Splitting Settlements and the Reverse Payment Fallacy, 71 Antitrust L.J. 1033, 1046 (2004) (suggesting that this hypothetical settlement includes "an implicit net payment" from A to B of \$60 million—i.e., the amount of the settlement discount). The cited authorities also indicate that if B has a counterclaim for damages against A, the original infringement plaintiff, A might end up paying B to settle B's counterclaim. Cf. Metro-Goldwyn Mayer, Inc. v. 007 Safety Prods., Inc., 183 F.3d 10, 13 (C.A.1 1999) (describing trademark dispute and settlement). Insofar as the dissent urges that settlements taking these commonplace forms have not been thought for that reason alone subject to antitrust liability, we agree, and do not intend to alter that understanding. But the dissent appears also to suggest that reverse payment settlements—e.g., in which A, the plaintiff, pays money to defendant B purely so B will give up the patent fight—should be viewed for antitrust purposes in the same light as these familiar settlement forms. *See post*, at 2231–2232. We cannot agree. In the traditional examples cited above, a party with a claim (or counterclaim) for damages receives a sum equal to or less than the value of its claim. In reverse payment settlements, in contrast, a party with no claim for damages (something that is usually true of a paragraph IV litigation defendant) walks away with money simply so it will stay away from the patentee's market. That, we think, is something quite different.

Finally, the Hatch-Waxman Act itself does not embody a statutory policy that supports the Eleventh Circuit's view. Rather, the general procompetitive thrust of the statute, its specific provisions facilitating challenges to a patent's validity, *see* Part I-A, supra, and its later-added provisions requiring parties to a patent dispute triggered by a paragraph IV filing to report settlement terms to the FTC and the Antitrust Division of the Department of Justice, all suggest the contrary. *See* §§ 1112–1113, 117 Stat. 2461–2462. Those interested in legislative history may also wish to examine the statements of individual Members of Congress condemning reverse payment settlements in advance of the 2003 amendments. *See*, e.g., 148 Cong. Rec. 14437 (2002) (remarks of Sen. Hatch) ("It was and is very clear that the [Hatch-Waxman Act] was not designed to allow deals between brand and generic companies to delay competition"); 146 Cong. Rec. 18774 (2000) (remarks of Rep. Waxman) (introducing bill to deter companies from "strik[ing] collusive agreements to trade multimillion dollar payoffs by the brand company for delays in the introduction of lower cost, generic alternatives").

B

The Eleventh Circuit's conclusion finds some degree of support in a general legal policy favoring the settlement of disputes. The Circuit's related underlying practical concern consists of its fear that antitrust scrutiny of a reverse payment agreement would require the parties to litigate the validity of the patent in order to demonstrate what would have happened to competition in the absence of the settlement. Any such litigation will prove time consuming, complex, and expensive. The antitrust game, the Circuit may believe, would not be worth that litigation candle.

We recognize the value of settlements and the patent litigation problem. But we nonetheless conclude that this patent-related factor should not determine the result here. Rather, five sets of considerations lead us to conclude that the FTC should have been given the opportunity to prove its antitrust claim.

First, the specific restraint at issue has the "potential for genuine adverse effects on competition." *Indiana Dentists*. The payment in effect amounts to a purchase by the patentee of the exclusive right to sell its product, a right it already claims but would lose if the patent litigation were to continue and the patent were held invalid or not infringed by the generic product. Suppose, for example, that the exclusive right to sell produces $50 million in supracompetitive profits per year for the patentee. And suppose further that the patent has 10 more years to run. Continued litigation, if it results in patent invalidation or a finding of noninfringement, could cost the patentee $500 million in lost revenues, a sum that then would flow in large part to consumers in the form of lower prices.

We concede that settlement on terms permitting the patent challenger to enter the market before the patent expires would also bring about competition, again to the consumer's benefit. But settlement on the terms said by the FTC to be at issue here—payment in return for staying out of the market—simply keeps prices at patentee-set levels, potentially producing the full patent-related $500 million monopoly return while dividing that return between the challenged patentee and the patent challenger. The patentee and the challenger gain; the consumer loses. Indeed, there are indications that patentees sometimes pay a generic challenger a sum even larger than what the generic would gain in profits if it won the paragraph IV litigation and entered the market. *See* Hemphill, 81 N.Y.U. L.Rev., at 1581. *See also* Brief for 118 Law, Economics, and Business Professors et al. as Amici Curiae 25 (estimating that this is true of the settlement challenged here). The rationale behind a payment of this size cannot in every case be supported by traditional settlement considerations. The payment may instead provide strong evidence that the patentee seeks to induce the generic challenger to abandon its claim with a share of its monopoly profits that would otherwise be lost in the competitive market.

But, one might ask, as a practical matter would the parties be able to enter into such an anticompetitive agreement? Would not a high reverse payment signal to other potential challengers that the patentee lacks confidence in its patent, thereby provoking additional challenges, perhaps too many for the patentee to "buy off?" Two special features of Hatch-Waxman mean that the answer to this question is "not necessarily so." First, under Hatch-Waxman only the first challenger gains the special advantage of 180 days of an exclusive right to sell a generic version of the brand-name product. *See* Part I-A, supra. And as noted, that right has proved valuable—indeed, it can be worth several hundred million dollars. Subsequent challengers cannot secure that exclusivity period, and thus stand to win significantly less than the first if they bring a successful paragraph IV challenge. That is, if subsequent litigation results in invalidation of the patent, or a ruling that the patent is not infringed, that litigation victory will free not just the challenger to compete, but all other potential competitors too (once they obtain FDA approval). The potential reward available to a subsequent challenger being significantly less, the patentee's payment to the initial challenger (in return for not pressing the patent challenge) will not necessarily provoke subsequent challenges. Second, a generic that files a paragraph IV after learning that the first filer has settled will (if sued by the brand-name) have to wait out a stay period of (roughly) 30 months before the FDA may approve its application, just as the first filer did. *See* 21 U.S.C. § 355(j)(5)(B)(iii). These features together mean that a reverse payment settlement with the first filer (or, as in this case, all of the initial filers) "removes from consideration the most motivated challenger, and the one closest to introducing competition." Hemphill, *supra*, at 1586. The dissent may doubt these provisions matter, *post*, at 2234–2236, but scholars in the field tell us that "where only one party owns a patent, it is virtually unheard of outside of pharmaceuticals for that party to pay an accused infringer to settle the lawsuit." 1 H. Hovenkamp, M. Janis, M. Lemley, & C. Leslie, IP and Antitrust § 15.3, p. 15–45, n. 161 (2d ed. Supp. 2011). It may well be that Hatch-Waxman's unique regulatory framework, including the special advantage that the 180-day exclusivity period gives to first filers, does much to explain why in this context, but not others, the patentee's ordinary incentives to resist paying off challengers (i.e., the fear of provoking myriad other challengers) appear to be more frequently overcome.

Second, these anticompetitive consequences will at least sometimes prove unjustified. As the FTC admits, off-setting or redeeming virtues are sometimes present. Brief for Petitioner 37–39. The reverse payment, for example, may amount to no more than a rough approximation of the litigation expenses saved through the settlement. That payment may reflect compensation for other services that the generic has promised to perform—such as distributing the patented item or helping to develop a market for that item. There may be other justifications. Where a reverse payment reflects traditional settlement considerations, such as avoided litigation costs or fair value for services, there is not the same concern that a patentee is using its monopoly profits to avoid the risk of patent invalidation or a finding of noninfringement. In such cases, the parties may have provided for a reverse payment without having sought or brought about the anticompetitive consequences we mentioned above. But that possibility does not justify dismissing the FTC's complaint. An antitrust defendant may show in the antitrust proceeding that legitimate justifications are present, thereby explaining the presence of the challenged term and showing the lawfulness of that term under the rule of reason. *See*, e.g., *Indiana Dentists*; 7 Areeda ¶¶ 1504a–1504b, at 401–404 (3d ed. 2010).

Third, where a reverse payment threatens to work unjustified anticompetitive harm, the patentee likely possesses the power to bring that harm about in practice. *See* id., ¶ 1503, at 392–393. At least, the "size of the payment from a branded drug manufacturer to a prospective generic is itself a strong indicator of power"—namely, the power to charge prices higher than the competitive level. 12 id., ¶ 2046, at 351. An important patent itself helps to assure such power. Neither is a firm without that power likely to pay "large sums" to induce "others to stay out of its market." Ibid. In any event, the Commission has referred to studies showing that reverse payment agreements are associated with the presence of higher-than-competitive profits—a strong indication of market power. *See* Brief for Petitioner 45.

Fourth, an antitrust action is likely to prove more feasible administratively than the Eleventh Circuit believed. The Circuit's holding does avoid the need to litigate the patent's validity (and also, any question of infringement). But to do so, it throws the baby out with the bath water, and there is no need to take that drastic step. That is because it is normally not necessary to litigate patent validity to answer the antitrust question (unless, perhaps, to determine whether the patent litigation is a sham). An unexplained large reverse payment itself would normally suggest that the patentee has serious doubts about the patent's survival. And that fact, in turn, suggests that the payment's objective is to maintain supracompetitive prices to be shared among the patentee and the challenger rather than face what might have been a competitive market—the very anticompetitive consequence that underlies the claim of antitrust unlawfulness. The owner of a particularly valuable patent might contend, of course, that even a small risk of invalidity justifies a large payment. But, be that as it may, the payment (if otherwise unexplained) likely seeks to prevent the risk of competition. And, as we have said, that consequence constitutes the relevant anticompetitive harm. In a word, the size of the unexplained reverse payment can provide a workable surrogate for a patent's weakness, all without forcing a court to conduct a detailed exploration of the validity of the patent itself. 12 Areeda ¶ 2046, at 350–352.

Fifth, the fact that a large, unjustified reverse payment risks antitrust liability does not prevent litigating parties from settling their lawsuit. They may, as in other industries, settle in other ways, for example, by allowing the generic manufacturer to enter the patentee's market prior to the patent's expiration, without the patentee paying the challenger to stay out prior to that point. Although the parties may have reasons to prefer settlements that include reverse payments, the relevant antitrust question is: What are those reasons? If the basic reason is a desire to maintain and to share patent-generated monopoly profits, then, in the absence of some other justification, the antitrust laws are likely to forbid the arrangement.

In sum, a reverse payment, where large and unjustified, can bring with it the risk of significant anticompetitive effects; one who makes such a payment may be unable to explain and to justify it; such a firm or individual may well possess market power derived from the patent; a court, by examining the size of the payment, may well be able to assess its likely anticompetitive effects along with its potential justifications without litigating the validity of the patent; and parties may well find ways to settle patent disputes without the use of reverse payments. In our view, these considerations, taken together, outweigh the single strong consideration—the desirability of settlements—that led the Eleventh Circuit to provide near-automatic antitrust immunity to reverse payment settlements.

III

The FTC urges us to hold that reverse payment settlement agreements are presumptively unlawful and that courts reviewing such agreements should proceed via a "quick look" approach, rather than applying a "rule of reason." *See California Dental* ("Quick-look analysis in effect" shifts to "a defendant the burden to show empirical evidence of procompetitive effects. We decline to do so. In *California Dental*, we held (unanimously) that abandonment of the "rule of reason" in favor of presumptive rules (or a "quick-look" approach) is appropriate only where "an observer with even a rudimentary understanding of economics could conclude that the arrangements in question would have an anticompetitive effect on customers and markets." 526 U.S. at 770; id., at 781 (BREYER, J., concurring in part and dissenting in part). We do not believe that reverse payment settlements, in the context we here discuss, meet this criterion.

That is because the likelihood of a reverse payment bringing about anticompetitive effects depends upon its size, its scale in relation to the payor's anticipated future litigation costs, its independence from other services for which it might represent payment, and the lack of any other convincing justification. The existence and degree of any anticompetitive consequence may also vary as among industries. These complexities lead us to conclude that the FTC must prove its case as in other rule-of-reason cases.

To say this is not to require the courts to insist, contrary to what we have said, that the Commission need litigate the patent's validity, empirically demonstrate the virtues or vices of the patent system, present every possible supporting fact or refute every possible pro-defense theory. As a leading antitrust scholar has pointed out, " '[t]here is always something of a sliding scale in appraising reasonableness,' " and as such " 'the quality of proof required should vary with the circumstances.' " *California Dental* (quoting with approval 7 Areeda ¶ 1507, at 402 (1986)).

As in other areas of law, trial courts can structure antitrust litigation so as to avoid, on the one hand, the use of antitrust theories too abbreviated to permit proper analysis, and, on the other, consideration of every possible fact or theory irrespective of the minimal light it may shed on the basic question—that of the presence of significant unjustified anticompetitive consequences. We therefore leave to the lower courts the structuring of the present rule-of-reason antitrust litigation. We reverse the judgment of the Eleventh Circuit. And we remand the case for further proceedings consistent with this opinion. . . .

NOTES AND QUESTIONS ON *ACTAVIS*[32]

1. ***Should any patent settlement be deemed procompetitive if it allows alleged infringers to enter before the expiration of the patent?*** Although a valid patent entitles a holder to exclude others from infringing the patent, a patent issued by the Patent and Trade Office is not necessarily a valid patent. Studies indicate that 48–73% of issued patents are held invalid in court. A patent holder's entitlement to the monopoly profits that come from excluding entrants thus depends on the expected odds that the patent is valid and infringed. Reverse-payment settlements raise the concern that the entrant (usually a generic-drug company) has been paid to stay out of the market longer than merited by the expected outcome of patent litigation. If that is what happened, then a reverse payment settlement that delays entry effectively divides the market over time in a way that has anticompetitive effects similar to other horizontal market divisions (like geographic divisions) that divide markets at the same point in time.

2. ***How can courts determine whether the settlement exclusion of competition exceeded the expected litigation exclusion?*** The main difficulty that had split the lower courts before *Actavis* was that it seemed difficult to determine whether the settlement exclusion period exceeded the expected litigation exclusion period without engaging in a judicial inquiry into the patent merits, which is not only the very thing that patent settlements seek to avoid, but also produces bimodal results that do not capture the expected patent odds at the time of settlement.[33] Scholarship prior to *Actavis* addressed these concerns by proving that, without any inquiry into the patent merits, a court can determine that the settlement exclusion period exceeds the expected litigation exclusion period whenever the reverse-payment amount exceeds the patent holder's anticipated litigation costs, absent some procompetitive justification for which the settlement was reasonably necessary.[34] The basic intuition is that a patent holder would not pay more than its anticipated litigation costs unless it obtained a longer exclusion period than it could obtain through litigation by incurring those litigation costs. This scholarship also showed that a reverse payment of this size sufficed to show both: (1) market power; and (2) that the settlement exceeded the optimal patent reward for innovation (assuming patent law has been optimized) if the settling entrant is not judgment proof.[35]

Actavis is in accord with this scholarship, holding that "the likelihood of a reverse payment bringing about anticompetitive effects depends upon its size, its scale in relation to the payor's anticipated future litigation costs, its independence from other services for which it might represent payment, and

---

[32] Professor Einer Elhauge has served as both a defense and plaintiff expert on economics in cases involving reverse-payment patent settlements, including the remand of the *Actavis* case. These notes draw on McGuire, Drake, Elhauge, Hartman & Starr, *Resolving Reverse-Payment Settlements With The Smoking Gun Of Stock Price Movements*, 101 IOWA L. REV. 1581 (2016).

[33] Einer Elhauge & Alex Krueger, *Solving the Patent Settlement Puzzle*, 91 TEX. L. REV. 283, 285–89 (2012) (summarizing the prior conflict among the circuits).

[34] *Id.* at 283, 290–92, 297–312.

[35] *Id.* at 293–304, 307–11.

the lack of any other convincing justification."[36] The Court also concluded (like this prior scholarship) that when the net reverse payment (i.e., payment net of the value of any return services) exceeds the patent holder's anticipated litigation costs, that fact: (1) shows market power, (2) obviates the need to inquire into the patent merits, and (3) indicates that the settlement exclusion period exceeds what is merited by the expected patent odds.[37]

*3. **How can courts determine the amount of the net reverse payment?*** Although early reverse-payment settlements involved naked cash payments, more recent reverse payments have involved business side deals that obscure the amount of the net reverse payment. For example, the settling entrant might receive payments that are coupled with co-marketing or manufacturing agreements, so that determining the size of the net payment requires quantifying the extent to which the cash payments exceed the market value of the entrant services. Or the reverse payment might be made in the form of product licenses or intellectual property transfers, requiring quantifying the extent to which the value of those patent holder rights exceed whatever the entrant provides in return.[38] One provision, commonly attached to reverse-payment settlements in drug markets, is for the patent holder to agree not to launch its own "authorized generic" version of the drug during the 180 days that the first-filing generic gets to be the exclusive generic entrant. The absence of the patent holder's authorized generic roughly doubles the first-filing generic's revenue during its generic exclusivity period, allowing the patent holder to make a reverse payment without any money changing hands.[39]

One method that sometimes can avoid the difficulty of proving the amount of the reverse payment would be to show that the patent holder's stock market price jumped in response to the announcement of a reverse-payment settlement, which would indicate that the stock market believed that the settlement produced an unexpected increase in profits. Absent proof that the settlement conferred unexpected procompetitive efficiencies, such a jump in the patent holder stock market price means the stock market must have concluded that the settlement exclusion period exceeded the expected exclusion period that would have resulted from litigation or no-payment

---

36 FTC v. Actavis, Inc., 133 S. Ct. 2223, 2237 (2013). *See also In re Cipro,* 348 P.3d 845, 865–871 (Cal. 2015) (same factors under California state antitrust law). It is not a procompetitive justification that the reverse payment makes settlement possible when the facilitated settlement delays entry relative to the expected entry with patent litigation. *Id.* at 869–70; Elhauge & Krueger, *supra* note 33, at 303–04.

37 *Actavis,* 133 S. Ct. at 2236–37; *Cipro,* 348 P.3d at 867, 869–71; Elhauge & Krueger, *supra* note 33, at 290–91, 310–11.

38 Reverse payments that delay rival entry can be anticompetitive and illegal whether or not the payments are made in cash, and whether or not they are exchanged for return services, as long as they reflect a net transfer of value to the delayed entrant. *See* In re Loestrin 24 Fe Antitrust Litigation, 814 F.3d 538, 549–552 (1st Cir. 2016); King Drug Co. of Florence, Inc. v. Smithkline Beecham Corp., 791 F.3d 388, 403–09 (3d Cir.2015); *Cipro,* 348 P.3d at 865–66.

39 Because the patent holder's agreement not to launch an authorized generic is also an agreement to restrain competition, it can independently be challenged as well. United Food & Commercial Workers v. Teikoku Pharma, 74 F.Supp.3d 1052, 1075 (N.D.Cal. 2014).

settlement.[40] This test is conservative because the patent holder stock price might not increase in response to an anticompetitive reverse-payment settlement if the stock market: (1) expected such an anticompetitive reverse-payment settlement all along; or (2) anticipated a risk of antitrust damages that offset the anticompetitive profits from the settlement. Further, stock market event studies of single events often require very large effects for statistical significance, and may fail to pick up substantial anticompetitive effects. The lack of a spike in a patent holder's stock market price accordingly cannot disprove anticompetitive effects, but the existence of one can prove such effects.

4. Is avoiding patent litigation costs a procompetitive justification? The most common alleged procompetitive efficiency is avoiding patent litigation costs. However, a reverse-payment settlement would be reasonably necessary to achieve such an avoidance of litigation costs only if a no-payment settlement were not possible or expected, which will only be in cases when the settling entrant was unreasonably optimistic about its odds of patent victory. Moreover, a cognizable procompetitive justification requires that any efficiency be passed on to consumers sufficiently to offset any harm to consumer welfare from delaying rival entry and competition. Because avoiding litigation costs lowers a fixed cost rather than a marginal cost, it is unlikely to lower prices in a way that gets passed on to consumers at all. Indeed, if the reverse payment amount exceeds the avoided litigation costs, then the settlement would actually raise patent holder costs, which could (even if passed on) only raise prices. Even if we assume that the settlement lowers costs in a way that is passed on to consumers in the relevant market, such a pass through of avoided litigation costs would have to be large enough to offset the total overcharge that results from delaying entry, which is usually unlikely given the relative magnitudes. We can infer that avoided litigation costs cannot be sufficiently large if they are less than the increase in capitalized stock value for the patent holder.[41]

5. Are business side deals a procompetitive justification? Defendants may claim that business side deals coupled with their settlements have procompetitive efficiencies. However, any such efficiencies can be attributed to the reverse-payment settlement only if the settlement was reasonably necessary for that side deal. In the typical case, this will not be true, because nothing prevents the firms from entering into similar business side deals (either with each other or third parties) separately from any patent settlement. Even when the settlement is reasonably necessary for the business side deal in question, the efficiencies would have to be passed on to consumers in the restrained market and be large enough to offset the price increase that results from delaying entry. This is usually unlikely.

---

[40] McGuire, et al, *supra* note 32, at 1582–83, 1594–96. One might argue that maybe the stock market underestimated the expected exclusion period because it underestimated the patent strength and patent holder bargaining power. But the claim that the stock market underestimates in this way is contradicted by evidence that, without reverse payments, patent holder stock market prices generally do not jump and that, with the reverse-payment settlements, entrant stock market prices generally do not drop. *Id.* at 1583, 1588, 1591–92, 1594–95.

[41] *Id.* at 1596.

Indeed, some business side deals (like agreeing not to sell an authorized generic) affirmatively increase prices by diminishing competition. Also usually unlikely is the possibility that unexpected efficiencies from side deals are large enough to explain a large increase in capitalized stock value for the patent holder.[42] Indeed, many business side deals are concessions to the settling entrant (such as transferring other business rights to the entrant or agreeing not to sell an authorized generic) that can only decrease patent holder profits, and thus could not explain an increase in the patent holder's stock price at all.

6. Is ameliorating managerial risk aversion a procompetitive justification? Defendants often argue that reverse-payment settlements are justified by managerial risk aversion. Supporting scholars argue that the reverse payment could be a "risk premium" that managers at the patent holder are willing to pay in order to avoid the uncertainty associated with litigation.[43] This justification is controversial both factually and normatively.

Factually, active capital markets for large publicly-traded companies should generally enforce profit-maximizing behavior by management on behalf of shareholders, which would deter managers from acting on this form of risk aversion because such action decreases shareholder profits.[44] A reverse-payment settlement that requires a risk aversion motive thus involves managerial risk aversion that deviates from shareholder interest.

Normatively, even if managerial risk aversion did explain a settlement, *Actavis* indicated that eliminating "the risk of patent invalidation or a finding of noninfringement . . . prevent[s] the risk of competition. And, as we have said, that consequence constitutes the relevant anticompetitive harm," not a procompetitive virtue.[45] Some scholars add that risk aversion should not be an admissible justification because allowing reverse payments that foster such risk-averse decisions lowers shareholder returns and thus inefficiently reduces incentives to invest in innovation.[46] Others stress that unless the settling entrant is unreasonably optimistic about its odds of winning the patent trial, the less-restrictive alternative of a no-payment settlement can equally achieve this risk reduction, resulting in a shorter settlement exclusion period and thus less harm to competition.[47] Moreover, entrant risk aversion would offset optimism and make such a no-payment settlement more likely.

---

[42] *Id.* at 1597.

[43] *See, e.g.*, Barry C. Harris et al., *Activating* Actavis*: A More Complete Story*, ANTITRUST, Spring 2014, at 83, 85 & n.16 (2014); Robert D. Willig & John P. Bigelow, *Antitrust Policy Toward Agreements that Settle Patent Litigation*, 49 ANTITRUST BULL. 655, 665–67 (2004).

[44] *See* Elhauge & Krueger, *supra* note 33, at 312; *see also Cipro,* 348 P.3d at 869 ("Attempts to quantitatively estimate the frequency with which risk aversion would produce an efficient settlement despite payment in excess of litigation costs suggest such occurrences would be exceedingly rare").

[45] FTC v. Actavis, Inc., 133 S. Ct. 2223, 2236 (2013); King Drug Co. of Florence, Inc. v. Smithkline Beecham Corp., 791 F.3d 388, 410–11 (3d Cir.2015).

[46] *See* Elhauge & Krueger, *supra* note 33, at 312.

[47] Aaron Edlin et al., Actavis *and Error Costs: A Reply to Critics,* ANTITRUST SOURCE, Oct. 2014, at 1, 4–7; Aaron Edlin et al., Activating Actavis, ANTITRUST, Fall 2013, at 18–20.

If, despite the above, risk aversion were deemed a valid procompetitive justification, its application would properly be limited to cases where two bases are shown. (1) No settlement would have resulted without a reverse payment, because the settling entrant is unreasonably optimistic in a way that was not offset by entrant risk aversion. (2) The risk aversion of patent holder managers is so high that they are willing to sacrifice expected corporate profits by not only paying the reverse payment, but also accepting a settlement exclusion period that is less than the expected litigation exclusion period. However, if those two bases really hold, then the settlement should reduce expected patent holder profits. The risk-aversion explanation would thus be disproven by evidence that its expected profits rose, such as proof that its stock price rose.[48] Further, in such cases, any procompetitive gain would be offset by the fact that allowing such settlements would reduce expected patent holder profits in a way that reduces incentives to invest in innovation.

7. ***How can one calculate damages?*** A reverse-payment settlement causes anticompetitive harm if, without the reverse payment, the parties would have either (a) reached a no-payment settlement with an earlier entry date or (b) continued a patent litigation that would have produced an earlier expected entry date.[49] One can calculate a highly conservative lower bound on the period of delay associated with a reverse-payment settlement if one conservatively assumes all the joint profits from settlement went to the settling entrant. If litigation would have resulted without the reverse-payment settlement, this highly conservative lower bound on delay can be calculated by dividing X, the excess amount of payment (i.e., the amount by which the reverse payment exceeds avoided litigation costs), by M, the extra profits per day the patent holder gains by selling as a monopolist rather than against entrant competition.[50] If a no-payment settlement would have resulted without the reverse-payment settlement, this highly conservative lower bound can instead be calculated by dividing R, the reverse-payment amount, by M.[51] In both cases, this method requires estimating the amount of the reverse payment, which can be difficult for reasons noted above. This method is also highly conservative because it is far more likely that the patent holder profits to some extent from agreeing to the reverse-payment settlement.

48 McGuire, et al, *supra* note 32, at 1596–97.

49 King Drug Co. of Florence, Inc. v. Smithkline Beecham Corp., 791 F.3d 388, 410 (3d Cir.2015) (making clear that either would be anticompetitive).

50 Elhauge and Krueger proved that this was true in a model where litigation had some positive length. *See* Elhauge & Krueger, *supra* note 33, at 299–300. They also proved that if at-risk entry occurred during litigation, or would have occurred without settlement, then the lower bound would be even higher, namely $X/M + \theta L$, where θ is the patent holder's estimate of the patent odds and L is the anticipated length of litigation. *See id.* at 301–02.

51 Elhauge and Krueger proved that for a strong patent (i.e., one with no at-risk entry) the minimum settlement period with a reverse payment is $\theta + (1 - \theta)L + X/M$. Elhauge & Krueger, *supra* note 33, at 299–300. Without a reverse payment, the minimum settlement period is $\theta + (1 - \theta)L + C/M$, where C equals the patent holder's anticipated litigation costs. *See Id.* at 314. Likewise, they proved that for a weak patent (i.e., with at-risk entry) the minimum settlement period with a reverse payment is $\theta + X/M$ and without a reverse payment is $\theta - C/M$. *Id.* at 301, 317. For both strong and weak patents, the difference between the settlement period with and without a reverse payment is $(X + C)/M$, which is the same as R/M.

One can estimate the extent to which the reverse-payment settlement increased the profits of the patent holder by showing how much the settlement increased the patent holder's stock market capitalization.[52] This measure is still conservative because it assumes that before the announcement, the stock market believed there was zero chance of a reverse-payment settlement, and that after the announcement, the stock market believed there was zero chance of antitrust liability. Further, stock market event studies of single events often require very large effects for statistical significance, and may fail to pick up substantial anticompetitive effects. Nonetheless, in cases where one can measure the increased stock market capitalization, *S*, adding it to what is paid to the settling entrant produces a conservative estimate of the total additional anticompetitive profits from the settlement. If patent litigation would have resulted without the reverse-payment settlement, a conservative lower bound of $(S + X)/M$ of anticompetitive delay can be estimated. If a no-payment settlement would have resulted instead, a conservative lower bound of $(S + R)/M$ of anticompetitive delay can be estimated. This method produces damage estimates that are higher than produced by the method described in the preceding paragraph, but are still conservative, and thus come closer to the true amount of damages.

Another possible remedy for an illegal reverse payment settlement is an injunctive claim for disgorgement of any profits resulting from the settlement.[53]

H. BUYER CARTELS

Mandeville Island Farms v. American Crystal Sugar

334 U.S. 219 (1948).

■ MR. JUSTICE RUTLEDGE delivered the opinion of the Court.

[Because of their bulk and perishability, sugar beets grown in northern California could be sold only to one of three refiners located there, which processed those beets into sugar that they then sold on an interstate market. Each refiner had paid beetgrowers based on a formula that combined the beet's sugar content and the refiner's profits per hundred pounds of sugar. Then the three refiners all agreed to instead use their average profits to calculate beet prices, which resulted in all three paying the same price for beets. Respondent was the most efficient refiner, and thus the petitioner-farmers who sold beets to it received lower prices than they would have received if prices were calculated based on individual refiner profits.]

52 McGuire, et al, *supra* note 32, at 1597–99.

53 FTC. v. Cephalon, Inc., 100 F.Supp.3d 433 (E.D.Pa. 2015).

In our judgment the amended complaint states a cause of action arising under the Sherman Act, §§ 1 and 2, and the complaint was improperly dismissed [by the lower courts]. . . .

It is clear that the agreement is the sort of combination condemned by the Act, even though the price-fixing was by purchasers, and the persons specially injured under the treble damage claim are sellers, not customers or consumers. And even if it is assumed that the final aim of the conspiracy was control of the local sugar beet market, it does not follow that it is outside the scope of the Sherman Act. For monopolization of local business, when achieved by restraining interstate commerce, is condemned by the Act. And a conspiracy with the ultimate object of fixing local retail prices is within the Act, if the means adopted for its accomplishment reach beyond the boundaries of one state.

The statute does not confine its protection to consumers, or to purchasers, or to competitors, or to sellers. Nor does it immunize the outlawed acts because they are done by any of these. The Act is comprehensive in its terms and coverage, protecting all who are made victims of the forbidden practices by whomever they may be perpetrated.

Nor is the amount of the nation's sugar industry which the California refiners control relevant, so long as control is exercised effectively in the area concerned . . . Congress' power to keep the interstate market free of goods produced under conditions inimical to the general welfare may be exercised in individual cases without showing any specific effect upon interstate commerce.

. . . [U]nder the facts characterizing this industry's operation and the tightening of controls in this producing area by the new agreements and understandings, there can be no question that their restrictive consequences were projected substantially into the interstate distribution of the sugar, as the amended complaint repeatedly alleges. . . .

Even without the uniform price provision and with full competition among the three refiners, their position is a dominating one. The growers' only competitive outlet is the one which exists when the refiners compete among themselves. There is no other market. The farmers' only alternative to dealing with one of the three refiners is to stop growing beets. They can neither plant nor sell except at the refiners' pleasure and on their terms. The refiners thus effectively control the quantity of beets grown, harvested and marketed, and consequently of sugar sold from the area in interstate commerce, even when they compete with each other. They dominate the entire industry. And their dominant position, together with the obstacles created by the necessity for large capital investment and the time required to make it productive, makes outlet through new competition practically impossible. Upon the allegations, it is absolutely so for any single growing season. A tighter or more all-inclusive monopolistic position hardly can be conceived.

When therefore the refiners cease entirely to compete with each other in all stages of the industry prior to marketing the sugar, the last vestige of local competition is removed and with it the only competitive opportunity for the grower to market his product. Moreover it is inconceivable that the monopoly so created will have no effects for the lessening of competition in the later interstate phases of the over-all activity or that the effects in those phases will have no repercussions upon the prior ones, including the price received by the growers.

There were indeed two distinct effects flowing from the agreement for paying uniform growers' prices, one immediately upon the price received by the grower rendering it devoid of all competitive influence in amount; the other, the necessary and inevitable effect of that agreement, in the setting of the industry as a whole, to reduce competition in the interstate distribution of sugar.

The idea that stabilization of prices paid for the only raw material consumed in an industry has no influence toward reducing competition in the distribution of the finished product, in an integrated industry such as this, is impossible to accept. By their agreement the combination of refiners acquired not only a monopoly of the raw material but also and thereby control of the quantity of sugar manufactured, sold and shipped interstate from the northern California producing area. In substance and roughly, if not precisely, they allocated among themselves the market for California beets substantially upon the basis of quotas competitively established among them at the time the uniform price arrangement was agreed upon. It is hardly likely that any refiner would have entered into an agreement with its only competitors, the effect of which would have been to drive away its growers, or therefore that many of the latter would have good reason to shift their dealings within the closed circle. Thus control of quantity in the interstate market was enhanced.

This effect was further magnified by the fact that the widely scattered location of sugar beet growing regions and their different accessibilities to market give the refiners of each region certainly some advantage over growers and refiners in other regions, and undoubtedly large ones over those most distant from the segment of the interstate market served by reason of being nearest to hand.

Finally, the interdependence and inextricable relationship between the interstate and the intrastate effects of the combination and monopoly are shown perhaps most clearly by the provision of the uniform price agreement which ties in the price paid for beets with the price received for sugar. The percentage factor of interstate receipts from sugar which the grower's contract specifies shall enter his price for beets makes that price dependent upon the price of sugar sold interstate. The uniform agreement's effect, when added to this, is to deprive the grower of the advantage of the individual efficiency of the refiner with which he deals, in this case the most efficient of the three, and of the price that refiner receives. It is also to reflect in the grower's price the consequences of the combination's effects for reducing competition among the refiners in the interstate distribution of sugar.

In sum, the restraint and its monopolistic effects were reflected throughout each stage of the industry, permeating its entire structure. This was the necessary and inevitable effect of the agreement among the refiners to pay uniform prices for beets, in the circumstances of this case. Those monopolistic effects not only deprived the beet growers of any competitive opportunity for disposing of their crops by the immediate operation of the uniform price provision; they also tended to increase control over the quantity of sugar sold interstate; and finally by the tie-in provision they interlaced those interstate effects with the price paid for the beets.

These restrictive and monopolistic effects, resulting necessarily from the practices allegedly intended to produce them, fall squarely within the Sherman Act's prohibitions, creating the very injuries they were designed to prevent, both to the public and to private individuals.

It does not matter, contrary to respondent's view, that the growers contracting with the other two refiners may have been benefited, rather than harmed, by the combination's effects, even if that result is assumed to have followed. It is enough that these petitioners have suffered the injuries for which the statutory remedy is afforded. For the test of the legality and immunity of such a combination, in view of the statute's policy, is not that some others than the members of the combination have profited by its operation. It is rather whether the statute's policy has been violated in a manner to produce the general consequences it forbids for the public and the special consequences for particular individuals essential to the recovery of treble damages. Both types of injury are present in this case, for in addition to the restraints put upon the public interest in the interstate sale of sugar, enhancing the refiner's controls, there are special injuries affecting the petitioners resulting from those effects as well as from the immediate operation of the uniform price arrangement itself . . . [R]eversed.

■ MR. JUSTICE JACKSON, with whom MR. JUSTICE FRANKFURTER joins, dissenting. It appears to me that the Court's opinion is based on assumptions of fact which the petitioner disclaimed in the court below. . . . On hearing, the trial judge apparently considered that a cause of action would be stated only if the complaint alleged that the growing contracts affected the price of sugar in interstate commerce. But the contracts accompanying the pleadings indicated that the effects ran in the other direction. The market price of interstate sugar was the base on which the price of beets was to be figured. The latter price was derived from the income which respondent and others received from sugar sold in the open market over the period of a year. The trial judge therefore suggested that the references to restraint of trade in sugar in interstate commerce created an ambiguity in the complaint. Accordingly, the plaintiff, at the suggestion of the court and for the specific purpose of this appeal, filed an amended complaint which completely eliminated the charge that the agreements complained of affected the price of sugar in interstate commerce. . . . Despite the deletion from the complaint of the allegation concerning the price of sugar, the Court assumes, without allegation or evidence, that the price of sugar is affected and on that basis builds its thesis that the Sherman Act has been violated. . . . I would affirm the judgment of the District Court.

NOTES AND QUESTIONS ON *MANDEVILLE*

1. ***Should buyer cartels be illegal only when harm to downstream consumer welfare is proven?*** Much of the opinion focuses on whether the interstate commerce requirement of the statute has been met, an issue that has largely receded into unimportance as subsequent Supreme Court decisions made that requirement trivial to prove. *See* Chapter 1. But the issue of continuing relevance is that here the adverse intrastate effects were only on the sugar beet producers who sold in the local market, and consumers could not be harmed unless there were some adverse effect on the national (interstate) market for buying sugar. Should the statute be interpreted to require some adverse effect on consumers?

Given that the antitrust laws adopt a consumer welfare standard, it might seem that proof of harm to consumers should be required. But the antitrust laws do not require such proof. A simple justification is that: (a) to the extent the buyer cartel has any effect at all on the downstream market, it would be harmful to consumers; and (b) if the buyer cartel has no effect on the downstream market, it harms upstream producers with no benefit to consumers.

Suppose the local buying cartel had simply set a subcompetitive low price for sugar beets. This would result in lower local output of sugar beets, which would consequently lower the downstream sugar output of the California sugar beet refiners. If California sugar beet refiners produce a significant share of the nation's sugar or if other national sugar refiners could not easily and immediately expand production at the same cost to offset any reduction in California sugar output, a lowering of California sugar output would lower national sugar output and thus raise downstream sugar prices. This means that downstream consumers would be hurt by the upstream buying cartel. If instead California sugar beet refiners produce an insignificant share of the nation's sugar and other national sugar refiners could easily and immediately expand production at the same cost to offset any reduction in California sugar output, than a change in the sugar output of California sugar beet refiners would not alter national sugar prices. But even in this case, the California sugar beet refiners would still have incentives to fix subcompetitive low prices for sugar beets because that would increase their profit margin per beet.

Thus, to the extent buying cartel had any effect on downstream consumers, it would be negative. Requiring proof of harm to consumers would thus increase underdeterrence and harm to consumers (because errors will be made assessing that proof and the costs of such prove will result in fewer challenges) without any gain to consumers. Further, even in the best case scenario of no effect on consumers, the buyer cartel still harms upstream producers. It makes sense to protect producers from anticompetitive conduct when doing so causes no harm to consumer welfare. To be sure, the U.S. courts stress that antitrust law protects "competition, not competitors," but what this means is that antitrust law does not protect competitors at the *expense* of consumer welfare, which would clearly conflict with the consumer welfare standard. But antitrust law does protect producers from anticompetitive conduct that has no benefit to consumers.

2. ***Does the fact that beets prices were fixed based on downstream profits require inquiring into cartel's effect on downstream prices?*** The above analysis assumed a buying cartel that simply set a subcompetitive low price for sugar beets. However, here the challenged buyer agreement fixed California sugar beet prices based on a share of the refiner's sugar profits, which in turn depended on national sugar prices. Does that mean, as Justices Jackson and Frankfurter argued, that the plaintiffs should have had to prove that the restraint had an effect on national sugar price? To consider the issue, suppose that sugar beet producers were initially getting competitive prices that gave them 50% of national sugar profits. Suppose further that the California sugar beet refiners agreed that from now on, the price to sugar beet producers would be set at only 1% of national sugar profits. Even if that restraint did not alter national sugar prices, it would clearly lower the upstream price for California sugar beets and thus lower local California sugar beet output, with all the possible effects noted above for a cartel that simply set a subcompetitive price for California sugar beets.

3. ***Does the fact that beets were fixed based on average profits eliminate any adverse effect?*** Are the above conclusions altered by the fact that here the buying cartel apparently did not lower the share of sugar profits given to sugar beet producers, but rather fixed sugar beet prices based on an *average* of the sugar profits of all three local sugar beet refiners? Although that feature means the agreement did not lower the average price paid for sugar beets in California, any effects it did have are still likely to be anticompetitive for the following reasons. By basing prices on average refiner profits, the agreement necessarily made the sugar beet purchase price lower for the most profitable refiner and higher for the other two refiners. Because all the refiners were selling sugar in a national market, presumably the sugar prices they received were the same, and thus the most profitable refiner must have had lower costs and been more efficient. Lowering the price paid by the most efficient refiner and raising the price paid by the less efficient refiners would at the margin decrease the sugar beet output sold to the more efficient refiner and increase the sugar beet output sold to the less efficient refiners. The effect of this shifting of output from the most efficient to the less efficient refiner would increase average California sugar refiner costs, which, to the extent it had any downstream effect, would likely increase sugar prices.

One might wonder why the California sugar refiners would want to enter into an agreement that would raise the prices two of them paid and take away the ability of the more efficient third firm to pay a higher price to reflect the higher profits it could earn on sugar beets. It is hard to see how this could make economic sense for all the refiners unless an agreement to pay the same sugar beet price helped them to maintain some sort of collusion on downstream sugar prices or output. One reason this might be the case is that it is much easier to set and maintain a common downstream collusion price if the firms' costs are similar because then the profit-maximizing downstream price is similar for all the firms. *See* Chapter 7 for further details.

CHAPTER 3

WHAT UNILATERAL CONDUCT IS ILLEGAL?

A. RELEVANT LAWS & BASIC LEGAL ELEMENTS

Three U.S. statutes cover anticompetitive unilateral conduct. The most important is Sherman Act § 2 because it is both general and enforceable by private parties who can seek big damages and bring most of the U.S. lawsuits.

Sherman Act § 2, 15 U.S.C. § 2

> "Every person who shall monopolize, or attempt to monopolize, or combine or conspire with any other person or persons, to monopolize any part of the trade or commerce among the several States, or with foreign nations, shall be deemed guilty of a felony. . . ."

Later provisions add to this criminal penalty the standard set of damage and injunctive claims, including private actions for treble damages. *See* Chapter 1. Courts have interpreted this statute to embody three separate offenses. All of them require an effect on interstate commerce that is trivial to prove and rarely relevant, as well as sufficient effects on U.S. commerce. *See* Chapter 1.

Monopolization. The offense of monopolization "has two elements: (1) the possession of monopoly power in the relevant market and (2) the willful acquisition or maintenance of that power as distinguished from growth or development as a consequence of a superior product, business acumen, or historic accident."[1] This is generally simplified to say the two elements are (1) monopoly power and (2) anticompetitive or exclusionary conduct.[2] Although this standard covers any horizontal agreement to combine into a monopoly,[3] what it adds to Sherman Act § 1 is that it covers unilateral conduct as well. The result is a very general substantive rule forbidding a firm with monopoly power from engaging in any anticompetitive unilateral conduct to obtain, maintain, or enhance that power.

---

1 United States v. Grinnell Corp., 384 U.S. 563, 570–571 (1966).

2 *See* Verizon Communications v. Law Offices of Curtis V. Trinko, 540 U.S. 398, 407 (2004); Aspen Skiing Co. v. Aspen Highlands Skiing Corp., 472 U.S. 585, 595–96, 602, 605 & n.32 (1985).

3 *See, e.g.*, *Grinnell*, 384 U.S. at 576; American Tobacco Co. v. United States, 328 U.S. 781, 783–84, 808–09, 813–14 (1946); Standard Oil Co. v. United States, 221 U.S. 1, 70–75 (1911) (same).

Attempted Monopolization. The offense of attempted monopolization requires proof "(1) that the defendant has engaged in predatory or anticompetitive conduct with (2) a specific intent to monopolize and (3) a dangerous probability of achieving monopoly power."[4] This offense thus adds a specific intent element but lowers the monopoly power requirement to a dangerous probability of obtaining such power. Further, specific intent is understood to be an objective intent inferable from conduct that is palpably anticompetitive. The result is to provide a general substantive rule banning palpably anticompetitive unilateral conduct that might realistically lead to monopoly power.

Conspiracy to Monopolize. The offense of a conspiracy to monopolize requires evidence of (1) a conspiracy (2) a specific intent to monopolize and (3) an overt act in furtherance of the conspiracy.[5] Although this provision does not regulate unilateral conduct, it covers the overlapping issue of agreements that seek to create the sort of monopoly power that is the target of the regulations of unilateral conduct. This provision is not limited to the sort of per se violations covered by Sherman Act § 1, and its elements do not require proof of actual market power or the existence of anticompetitive effects. Many courts have thus concluded that, with the requisite specific intent to monopolize, an agreement might violate Sherman Act § 2 even though it doesn't violate Sherman Act § 1.[6] However, the Supreme Court has more recently suggested the possibility that a dismissal of a Sherman Act § 1 claim for failure to allege a per se violation or anticompetitive effects might require dismissal of a conspiracy to monopolize claim, though it remanded the issue for further consideration.[7]

Unfair Trade Practices. Another U.S. statute governing unilateral conduct is Federal Trade Commission Act § 5, whose language is even more general but whose enforcement is more limited.

Federal Trade Commission Act § 5, 15 U.S.C. § 45

"Unfair methods of competition in or affecting commerce . . . are hereby declared unlawful."

This provision is more general because it covers unilateral anticompetitive conduct even by a firm without monopoly power. As discussed in Chapter 6, this helps cover unilateral conduct that

---

4 Spectrum Sports v. McQuillan, 506 U.S. 447 (1993).

5 United States v. Yellow Cab Co., 332 U.S. 218, 225–26 (1947); *American Tobacco Co.*, 328 U.S. at 789.

6 *See* International Distribution Centers, Inc. v. Walsh Trucking Co., 812 F.2d 786, 795 (2d Cir. 1987); United States v. Consolidated Laundries Corp., 291 F.2d 563, 573 (2d Cir. 1961); Stewart Glass & Mirror v. U.S. Auto Glass Disc. Ctrs., 200 F.3d 307, 316 (5th Cir. 2000); United States v. National City Lines, Inc., 186 F.2d 562, 566–68 (7th Cir. 1951); Baxley-DeLamar Monuments, Inc. v. American Cemetery Ass'n, 843 F.2d 1154, 1157 (8th Cir. 1988); Alexander v. National Farmers Organization, 687 F.2d 1173, 1182 (8th Cir.1982); Monument Builders of Greater Kansas City, Inc. v. American Cemetery Ass'n, 891 F.2d 1473, 1484 (10th Cir.1989); Levine v. Central Florida Medical Affiliates, Inc., 72 F.3d 1538, 1555–56 (11th Cir.1996).

7 NYNEX Corp. v. Discon, Inc., 525 U.S. 128, 139 (1998).

facilitates oligopolistic coordination. More relevant here, this language covers unilateral anticompetitive conduct by firms that have enough market power to create unilateral anticompetitive effects, but not enough power to find monopoly power or a dangerous probability of obtaining it. However, this provision can be enforced only through actions for prospective relief brought by the Federal Trade Commission. *See* Chapter 1. The net result is that, compared to Sherman Act § 2, the FTC Act lowers the power requirement and makes any anticompetitive conduct by a firm with market power potentially actionable, but also limits enforcement to prospective relief sought by a disinterested government agency.

Anticompetitive Price Discrimination. Finally, the Robinson-Patman Act prohibits one particular type of unilateral conduct—anticompetitive price discrimination.

Robinson-Patman Act, 15 U.S.C. § 13(a)

> "It shall be unlawful for any person engaged in commerce, in the course of such commerce, either directly or indirectly, to discriminate in price between different purchasers of commodities of like grade and quality . . . where the effect of such discrimination may be substantially to lessen competition or tend to create a monopoly in any line of commerce, or to injure, destroy, or prevent competition with any person who either grants or knowingly receives the benefit of such discrimination, or with customers of either of them."

This statute does not prohibit all price discrimination, but only price discrimination that threatens anticompetitive effects either in the defendant's market or to downstream markets. Brooke Group Ltd. v. Brown & Williamson Tobacco, 509 U.S. 209, 220 (1993). Such anticompetitive effects are proven if there is "a reasonable possibility" of substantial injury to competition. *Id.* at 222. The statute also has exceptions for where the price discrimination is justified by cost differences, changing market conditions, or good faith efforts to meet competition. *Id.*; 15 U.S.C. § 13. The result is to provide a lower standard of proving anticompetitive effects than Sherman Act § 2 but for a much more limited range of conduct. This chapter addresses only the application of this Act to conduct that causes anticompetitive effects in the defendant's market, deferring claims based on downstream effects until Chapter 5.

The Mix of Regulatory Strategies. One might wonder why a single nation would have antitrust laws with multiple differing standards for judging anticompetitive unilateral conduct. Presumably, there is a better reason than deep indecisiveness. To begin to see the answer, consider whether it would be any better to simply have one statute that created a private action for treble damages against any unilateral anticompetitive conduct by any firm, or at least by any firm with market power. Such a statute would certainly deter more anticompetitive unilateral conduct than does existing U.S. law. However, it would also deter more procompetitive unilateral conduct that might mistakenly be judged to be anticompetitive, which is a particular concern because a rule that covers unilateral conduct would include any conduct a firm might engage in and thus is harder for firms to avoid. The decision by the U.S. (and other nations) not to adopt such a uniformly sweeping rule with treble damages is consistent with a belief that any reduction in underdeterrence of anticompetitive conduct from such a rule would not be worth the increase in overdeterrence of procompetitive conduct.

The question then becomes what set of legal rules would achieve the optimal result by minimizing the total harm from underdeterrence and overdeterrence.[8] If we have a rule limited to firms with some high degree of market power, then it excludes the bulk of firms that have less power and might otherwise be overdeterred and focuses on the set of firms for which the concern about underdeterring undesirable conduct is greatest. For this set of firms, a sweeping rule that covers any of their anticompetitive conduct and imposes high penalties might minimize the total under-and overdeterrence, which would justify the U.S. law on monopolization. If we have another rule that extends to firms with medium levels of market power, then our concern about overdeterrence increases and our concern about underdeterrence decreases. It thus might make sense to reduce overdeterrence concerns by adding an intent requirement to limit the rule to the most palpably anticompetitive conduct, which would fit U.S. law on attempted monopolization. Another strategy might be to limit the rule to specifically defined anticompetitive conduct that is undesirable and can easily be avoided, which arguably fits U.S. law on price discrimination that causes anticompetitive effects in the defendant's market. However, we might still be concerned that firms with modest degrees of market power might remain underdeterred from engaging in anticompetitive unilateral conduct. To address this concern without unduly increasing overdeterrence concerns, we might want a standard (like the FTC Act) that covers any such conduct, but that limits enforcement to prospective relief by a financially disinterested government agency, which (unlike private parties) should exercise its discretion to avoid attacking desirable conduct and when it errs will not create the chilling risk of treble damages or retroactive penalties.

As the above suggests, it may be best to employ a mix of strategies to fully optimize the tradeoff between over-and underdeterrence. If so, it makes sense not to define one single offense of anticompetitive unilateral conduct, but rather to have various offenses, each of which adopts a different strategy. We can understand the separate provisions regulating

---

[8] For a general discussion of the various possible legal strategies for optimizing the tradeoff between overdeterrence and underdeterrence, including using rules versus standards or varying the type or level of sanctions, *see* Elhauge, *Sacrificing Corporate Profits in the Public Interest,* 80 N.Y.U. LAW REVIEW 733, 747–56 (2005); Stephen Bundy & Einer Elhauge, *Knowledge About Legal Sanctions*, 92 MICH. L. REV. 261, 267–79 (1993).

agreements and unilateral conduct as further evidencing such a mixed strategy.

How the Conspiracy to Monopolize Offense Fits Into the Mix. Where the offense of a conspiracy to monopoly fits into this mix of strategies is an interesting question. As noted above, one recent case suggested that failure to prove a § 1 claim dictates dismissal of a conspiracy to monopolize claim, which would make the "conspiracy to monopolize" provision entirely superfluous. This would effectively eliminate the conspiracy to monopolize offense from the U.S. statute and override a lot of prior precedent. However, even if that might be sound antitrust policy, such an interpretation would violate the canon of statutory construction that, if possible, courts should not interpret statutes in a way that renders some statutory language superfluous.[9]

Under that canon, the issue would seem to be whether, when we do not have an ordinary conspiracy but one with the specific intent of monopolizing a market, Congress might have reasonably thought that the mix of overdeterence/underdeterrence concerns was sufficiently different that it makes sense to drop the proof of market power or anticompetitive effects typically necessary to prove a conspiracy was unreasonable. This seems possible because, compared to ordinary agreements, such a conspiracy to monopolize would seem to raise (a) fewer overdeterrence concerns given the specific intent and the goal and (b) greater underdeterrence concerns because, if successful, the harm is greater. Likewise, Congress might have reasonably thought that, where we do not have an ordinary attempt to monopolize but a conspiracy to further it, the overdeterrence/underdeterrence concerns are sufficiently different to drop the proof of a dangerous probability of acquiring a monopoly that is necessary to show attempted monopolization. Overdeterrence concerns would be different because it is easier to avoid a conspiracy than to avoid unilateral conduct, and underdeterrence concerns would be greater because conspiracies are generally more dangerous than unilateral conduct.

One might thus make a reasonable argument for a separate conspiracy to monopolize claim. However, one might instead think that the lack of any need to prove market power or anticompetitive effects creates such overdeterrence problems, and the underdeterrence problems are sufficiently small given the other antitrust provisions regulating this area, that no separate conspiracy to monopolize claim should exist. Even if one thinks the latter, though, it may not be a reasonable reading of the statute because it effectively requires reading some words out of the enactment.

Assuming a conspiracy to monopolize claim does not require the same level of proof on anticompetitive effects or market power as is

---

9 South Carolina v. Catawba Indian Tribe, Inc., 476 U.S. 498, 510 n.22 (1986) (collecting sources).

required for a § 1 claim or an attempted monopolization claim, a separate issue is whether such a claim requires some evidence of market definition. Many courts have indicated that a conspiracy to monopolize claim does not even require proof of market definition.[10] These cases implicitly hold it suffices that the conspirators believed that there was a market they were trying to monopolize and that they could cause the anticompetitive effect of monopolizing it. Other courts have held that proof of market definition is required.[11] The latter cases thus implicitly hold that there must be objective proof that there was a properly defined market that the defendants could have intended to monopolize, thus providing some objective basis for thinking that a successful conspiracy could have created some monopoly power and anticompetitive harm. This legal conflict may not matter much because a factfinder is unlikely to find specific intent to monopolize if the market and any potential for causing anticompetitive harm seem implausible. The main practical impact is thus likely to be which side bears the costly burden of producing sufficient evidence to survive summary judgment on the issue of market definition. Although the burdens of proof on market definition are normally borne by antitrust plaintiffs, one could conclude that the burden of production on that issue should be satisfied by proof that the defendants conspired with the specific intent of having the enormous anticompetitive effect of monopolizing a market, thus justifying a shift in the burden of production onto the defendants.

B. THE POWER ELEMENT

Why ever require proof of some degree of market power for an antitrust claim? After all, if the conduct had no anticompetitive effect, then it would not merit condemnation regardless of how much market power the defendant possessed. And if conduct does have an anticompetitive effect, it should be condemned and an inquiry into whether defendant market power existed seems superfluous.

The answer is that it is often difficult to determine whether conduct had an anticompetitive effect, so that adjudication of that issue is often costly or erroneous, and sometimes both. If every act by every firm were subject to potential antitrust liability if it were later determined to have had an anticompetitive effect, then firms would be deterred from engaging in much desirable conduct that they fear would lead to costly antitrust scrutiny and a risk of mistaken antitrust liability. Legal review of business conduct would also be ubiquitous, imposing a large burden on adjudicators.

---

[10] *See* cases cited *supra* note 6.

[11] *See* Doctor's Hosp. of Jefferson, Inc. v. Southeast Med. Alliance, Inc., 123 F.3d 301, 311 (5th Cir.1997); Bill Beasley Farms, Inc. v. Hubbard Farms, 695 F.2d 1341, 1343 (11th Cir.1983). These decisions may, however, have been superseded by subsequent decisions in those circuits. *See* sources cited *supra* note 6.

Thus, one important reason for a market power requirement is to provide a screen on antitrust review, limiting it to the cases where firms are most likely to impose anticompetitive effects. Such a legal screen is most useful when the biggest concern is mistaken or costly appraisal of conduct. Accordingly, the market power screen is especially important for unilateral conduct cases because without any screen every firm would face an omnipresent risk of antitrust review for all its business conduct.

The legal screen imposed by a market power requirement is most harmful when the biggest concern is instead mistaken or costly appraisals of market power, for then firms might engage in anticompetitive conduct either because they know the enforcement costs of proving market power will prevent them from being sued, or because they figure that the odds of mistaken conclusions that they lack market power make the liability risk lower than the anticompetitive gain. Thus, such a screen is least important for agreements that have no conceivable procompetitive purpose because there is little downside to deterring such conduct, a big downside to underdeterring such conduct when it is anticompetitive, and firms can easily avoid entering into such conduct.

In addition to being a screen, though, market power can also be a sword. Again, the root reason lies in the costs or difficulties of proving anticompetitive effects. Because direct proof of anticompetitive effects is so difficult, courts generally conclude that anticompetitive effects can also be inferred from the combination of defendant market power with conduct that is likely to have anticompetitive effects when engaged in by an actor with such power. This alternative is likely to be more attractive the more costly or erroneous direct proof of anticompetitive effects is, and the more confidence we have in conclusions about market power. In short, the utility of market power as a screen or sword depends on a relative assessment of whether it is more difficult to determine market power or anticompetitive effects.

1. ECONOMIC AND LEGAL TESTS OF MARKET POWER GENERALLY

Before we get into the degree of market power necessary to trigger the above antitrust laws, it is useful to first identify what constitutes market power at all. Perhaps the most common definition used by economists is that market power is a power to raise prices above marginal cost, which is the incremental cost of producing the last unit of output.[12] This definition is normally useful. In a perfectly competitive market, all

[12] *See* PHILLIP AREEDA & LOUIS KAPLOW, ANTITRUST ANALYSIS 556 (5th ed. 1997); CARLTON & PERLOF, MODERN INDUSTRIAL ORGANIZATION 92 (3d ed. 1999); JEAN TIROLE, THE THEORY OF INDUSTRIAL ORGANIZATION 284 (1988); DON E. WALDMAN & ELIZABETH J. JENSEN, INDUSTRIAL ORGANIZATION 40, 437, 667 (2d ed. 2001); William M. Landes & Richard A. Posner, *Market Power in Antitrust Cases*, 94 HARV. L. REV. 937, 939 (1981); Krattenmaker, Lande & Salop, *Monopoly Power and Market Power in Antitrust Law*, 76 GEO. L.J. 241, 247 (1987).

products are sold at marginal cost. An inability to profitably increase prices above marginal cost would certainly indicate the absence of market power, and a persistent ability to charge above long-run marginal costs would typically indicate market power. The degree of market power under this definition is often measured by the Lerner Index, which is the difference between price and marginal cost divided by price.[13] And yet, despite this intuitive appeal and support by economists, courts and enforcement agencies have not adopted the above marginal cost test as the definition of market power.[14] Why?

The main reason usually cited is the notorious difficulty of accurately measuring true marginal costs. But a moment's thought reveals some serious theoretical limitations as well. Suppose, for example, we have a competitive market with numerous sellers with small output who cannot expand quickly, and there is a sudden increase in market demand. Prices will increase sharply, above marginal and average costs, and yet each individual seller is a price taker that cannot itself significantly affect market output or prices. Instead, the price premium they earn over their costs is called an economic rent. Such situations may call for rent control—indeed, the New York rent control laws were initially enacted to deal with the increase in housing demand during World War II. But whether or not rent control is merited, these situations do not suggest an anticompetitive market or that any seller has market power.

Further, firms on competitive markets have constant incentives to improve their products or efficiency of production. Whenever a firm succeeds in doing so, the fact that it has cheaper production or offers a better product than rivals will give it some discretion to price above marginal cost. But if other firms are also constantly improving their own products or efficiency, such an advantage might be short-lived or overcome through competition. Such back-and-forth competition in obtaining efficiency advantages is generally viewed as the essence of competition, rather than as an indication of the sort of market or monopoly power that triggers antitrust concerns.

The above problems suggest we may have to add a duration element requiring that any ability to price above marginal cost persist over time. But even a long-lasting ability to price above marginal cost raises conceptual difficulties. If production requires not just marginal costs but fixed costs to be in the market at all, economic models show that firms will price above marginal cost because new firms will not enter unless they can earn enough to cover fixed and marginal costs.[15] Likewise, if firms have differentiated products with varying attributes, brand image,

[13] Or to put it mathematically, the Lerner Index = (P – MC)/P, where P is price and MC is marginal cost.

[14] *See* Elhauge, *Why Above-Cost Price Cuts to Drive out Entrants Do Not Signal Predation or Even Market Power—and the Implications for Defining Costs,* 112 YALE L.J. 681, 727 n.137 (2003).

[15] *See* Carlton & Perloff, *supra* note 12, at 201–206.

or location of sale, then each firm can have some local market power to charge above marginal cost to customers who are close to it in location or quality or brand preferences.[16] Economists call both sorts of situations cases of "monopolistic competition," to distinguish them from our ideal case of perfect competition, but since fixed costs or product differentiation are a reality in most markets, this is the type of competition the law typically means and can at most aspire to have. Moreover, in such markets, firms can be numerous and prices will equal average cost in the long run. One can call these cases of market power, and perhaps they may usefully be regulated in some affirmative fashion. However, assuming prices equal long-run costs, this is not the sort of power that usefully invites antitrust scrutiny to prevent conduct that might exclude or impede competition, and thus not the sort of market power we mean in antitrust law.[17]

For example, brands of orange juice, coffee, beer and similar products have prices that are 25–67% higher than marginal cost, which would indicate monopoly power by this definition, yet these are understood to be competitive rather than monopoly markets by antitrust law and even by proponents of a marginal cost-based definition of market power.[18] Likewise, economics concludes that price discrimination must signal some degree of economic market power because it means the firm must have a downward sloping demand curve and be pricing some sales above cost.[19] Yet, because such price discrimination is ubiquitous on markets that antitrust deems competitive, it does not alone suffice to prove market power for antitrust purposes.[20]

Another common definition, used in many cases, is that market power is the power to price above competitive levels.[21] This definition

---

[16] *Id.* at 215–225.

[17] *See* United States v. E.I. du Pont de Nemours & Co., 351 U.S. 377, 392–93 (1956) (concluding that cases where firms engage in "monopolistic competition" do not involve "the power that makes an illegal monopoly" even though each firm may enjoy "power over the price and production of his own product" and "may have in one sense a monopoly on certain trade because of location, as an isolated country store or filling station, or because no one else makes a product of just the quality or attractiveness of his product, as for example in cigarettes.")

[18] *See* Elhauge, *Defining Better Monopolization Standards*, 56 STANFORD LAW REVIEW 253, 260 (2003).

[19] *See* Carlton & Perloff, *supra* note 12, at 277; Waldman & Jensen, *supra* note 12, at 436; Hal R. Varian, Price Discrimination, in 1 Handbook of Industrial Organization 599 (Richard Schmalensee & Robert D. Willig eds., 1989).

[20] *See* Illinois Tool Works Inc. v. Independent Ink, Inc., 547 U.S. 28, 44–45 (2006) (concluding that price discrimination does not necessarily indicate market power for antitrust purposes because it often exists on competitive markets). For various theoretical explanations of why firms on competitive markets often engage in price discrimination that entails some prices above marginal cost even though total revenue does not exceed total costs, *see* Elhauge, *supra* note 14, at 735–43.

[21] For cases using this sort of definition, *see* Jefferson Parish Hospital v. Hyde, 466 U.S. 2, 27 n.46 (1984); NCAA v. Board of Regents of the Univ. of Okla., 468 U.S. 85, 109 n.38 (1984); Brooke Group Ltd. v. Brown & Williamson Tobacco Corp., 509 U.S. 209, 235 (1993). *See also* United States Steel Corp. v. Fortner Enterprises, 429 U.S. 610, 620 (1977) (defining market power as the power to "to raise prices or to require purchasers to accept burdensome terms that could not be exacted in a completely competitive market. In short, the question is whether the seller has some advantage not shared by his competitors . . .").

may be more apt for antitrust purposes because it posits a more competitive baseline world where prices would be lower if some diminishment of competition were prevented. But there remain conceptual and practical problems.

One conceptual problem is that a firm might have achieved market power *through* competitive behavior, such as making a better or cheaper product than other firms and driving them out of the market. The resulting prices it charges could thus in a sense be said to reflect a competitive level, and yet the firm would have the sort of power over market prices and output we typically mean by market power. We might instead define a competitive market to be what the market would look like with many firms, but this raises other conceptual problems: if there are economies of scale or other efficiencies to large size, then a competitive market with many firms might have higher costs and prices even at the same output level. The use of a competitive price baseline is thus hard to disentangle from questions about just what degree of competition is optimal.

We could define the competitive baseline as what market prices would have been without the anticompetitive conduct being challenged. This seems more promising, but unfortunately conflates the market power element into the supposedly separate element of whether the defendant engaged in anticompetitive conduct that made prices worse than they would have been but for that misconduct. Such a conflation would eliminate any screening benefit the market power element is meant to provide.

The practical problem is that we generally cannot observe the competitive baseline in monopoly cases because, by definition, the hypothesis under investigation is that we do not have a competitive market. We may thus have to guess what those competitive prices would have been based on prices in analogous competitive markets or what prices were back when the market was more competitive. But either contemporaneous or historical analogies will be inapt to the extent costs differ between those analogous markets and the current one. Further, if, as typical, marginal costs for an industry increase with output, then a competitive market that expands output will have higher marginal costs than an equally efficient monopolist that produces lower output. Comparing current prices to competitive price levels would thus understate market power relative to a comparison between current prices and current marginal costs. To avoid these problems, one might instead infer the competitive baseline from costs in the current market. But then we are back at the problems with a test that asks whether prices are above marginal cost.

A final definition, used in other cases, is that market power is the power to constrain total market output in order to raise market prices and profits.[22] This definition focuses less on whether prices are above some baseline than on the causal connection between defendant output decisions and market price levels. If a defendant's output is a sufficiently small share of the market, or rivals would expand or enter quickly to make up for any constraint in defendant output, then the defendant lacks the requisite market power. If the contrary is true, then a defendant output restriction would predictably increase not only defendant prices but rival prices as well.

This sort of test often best captures the relevant concerns. But it too faces difficulties. The practical difficulty is that, if the defendant is already at the monopoly price, then any further output restriction would lead sufficient buyers to switch to other products to make any output restriction and price increase unprofitable and thus constrain it. Thus, if we are already at the monopoly price and output, we would not see any current evidence of the defendant raising market prices by restricting output. But we might be able to infer such a power by evidence that the firm's output decisions do affect market prices and that it varies output accordingly.

The conceptual difficulty is that this definition presupposes we know what the "market" is so that we can determine not just whether the defendant can change its own output and prices but whether it can change total market output and prices. If a market is characterized by monopolistic competition, then one could imagine defining the market to be just the defendant's brand because it has some short-term discretion to alter its prices by altering its output. Here the economic literature provides little assistance because: "The issue of how markets should be defined from the viewpoint of economic theory has never been answered definitively. Economic theorists generally take the market as a given."[23] This is not so surprising because the question of how best to define markets is a question not just of economics but of legal policy, which depends on both the functional goals that antitrust law is trying to accomplish and judgments about which rules are most administrable. As we shall see, functional and administrative concerns heavily influence the way antitrust law defines a market, but market definition is often bedeviled by the same sort of baseline issues that bedevil efforts to measure market power.

Whichever way we use to define the existence of market power, one way often used to measure the *degree* of that market power is with the elasticity of demand for the defendant's products.[24] Demand is more "elastic" the more that the quantity demanded changes in response to a change in price, and more "inelastic" the less that the quantity demanded

[22] For cases using this sort of definition, *see* Eastman Kodak Co. v. Image Technical Servs., Inc., 504 U.S. 451, 464 (1992); Fortner Enters. v. United States Steel Corp., 394 U.S. 495, 503 (1969); *see also* Benjamin Klein, *Market Power in Antitrust: Economic Analysis After Kodak*, 3 SUP. CT. ECON. REV. 43, 44, 71–85, 88–92 (1993).

[23] *See* Carlton & Perloff, *supra* note 12, at 146.

[24] *Kodak*, 504 U.S. at 469 n.15.

changes if prices are increased. That is, the more inelastic demand is, the less that buyers are willing to change what they buy in response to price increases. In the usual graphs that plot quantity on the X-axis and price on the Y-axis, a steeper demand curve is more inelastic, and a flatter demand curve is more elastic. More precisely, elasticity is the percentage change in quantity divided by the percentage change in price that produces that quantity change. If a 1% price increase changes output by more than 1%, then elasticity is greater than 1, and demand is defined to be "elastic." If a 1% price increase changes output by less than 1%, then elasticity is lower than 1, and demand is defined to be "inelastic."

Firm-specific demand elasticity, the extent to which a firm's own output responds to an increase in its prices, should be sharply distinguished from market-price demand elasticity. Firm-specific demand elasticity helps measure a single-firm's market power, whereas market-price demand elasticity helps measure the extent to which all the firms on the market combined could raise prices. Marketwide demand for a product can be quite inelastic, so that any reduction in marketwide output sharply raises market prices, even though each firm in that market has highly elastic demand, so that any effort by it to reduce output will not significantly raise prices but simply cause buyers to buy elsewhere. On the other hand, if marketwide demand for a product is highly elastic, so that any increase in market prices for that product would cause buyers to purchase other products, then the firm-specific demand elasticities for every firm in that market must also be highly elastic because no single firm that only sells some of the product in that market can enjoy more power than the whole market would. That is, firm-specific demand elasticity can be much higher than marketwide demand elasticity, but not lower.

In a perfectly competitive market, each firm faces an absolutely flat, perfectly elastic, demand curve, so that none can raise prices without losing all its customers. No firm in such a market has market power, and the firm-specific demand elasticity of each is infinite. This does not necessarily mean that we can identify market power and determine its degree by simply measuring a firm's current firm-specific demand elasticity. To begin with, under the conditions of monopolistic competition that probably constitute most workable competition we actually see, every firm has a downward sloping demand curve, at least in the short run. In such a market, each firm faces a somewhat inelastic demand curve, even though none may have the sort of market power that antitrust law seeks to regulate.

Further, demand elasticity generally is different at different price and output levels. This point is often obscured by the tendency to measure elasticity at current prices and output and then apply it to other price and output levels. In fact, demand elasticity varies with price and output, which is highly important because economic analysis shows that even an absolute monopolist would never set a price that leaves it on the inelastic portion of its demand curve.[25] The reason is simple: if a monopolist were on the inelastic portion of its demand curve, then by definition a 1% price increase would reduce its output by less than 1%. This has to be profitable even if its output is entirely costless, and thus surely would be profitable under the more reasonable assumption that there are some marginal costs of production that it avoided by reducing output. Accordingly, a monopolist on the inelastic portion of its demand curve would keep profitably increasing prices (and thus lowering output) until it reached a portion of its demand curve where demand was sufficiently elastic to make further price increases unprofitable. Elastic demand at current levels of price and output is precisely what we would expect from an absolute monopoly that was pricing at the monopoly price. We thus cannot infer an absence of market or monopoly power from the fact that demand is elastic at current prices.

We can conclude that a firm will tend to have greater market power the greater the proportion of its demand curve that is inelastic, and the more inelastic its demand is for that portion. Unfortunately, since a firm with market power will not operate on any inelastic portion of its demand curve, this generally cannot be observed directly, but will have to be inferred from other means.

However, if we assume each firm is pricing at the short-run profit-maximizing level, we can use firm-specific demand elasticity at current prices to determine the degree to which a firm is pricing over its marginal costs because a profit-maximizing firm will raise prices until the marginal revenue lost from diminished sales equals the marginal revenue gained from an increased margin between prices and costs. Indeed, a profit-maximizing firm's Lerner Index equals the inverse of its firm-specific demand elasticity.[26] Thus, to the extent that the Lerner Index is relevant to measuring market power, firm-specific demand elasticity can be used to derive it and, given that prices are generally known, to indirectly determine marginal costs. For example, if firm-specific demand elasticity is 2, then the Lerner index is 1/2, which means the firm's prices are double its marginal cost.[27] A current firm-specific demand elasticity of 2 thus should be regarded as low, and indicative of market power for antitrust purposes where cost-based tests seem appropriate, even though standard economics calls such demand "elastic."

While legal tests often focus on whether the degree of market power suffices to constitute monopoly power, economic models do not really

---

[25] *See* Carlton & Perloff, *supra* note 12, at 93.

[26] A firm that takes into account only its own costs and demand curve will maximize profits by setting price so that $(P - MC)/P = -1/\varepsilon$, where ε is the firm-specific demand elasticity.

[27] Mathematically, a firm-specific demand elasticity of 2 means $(P - MC)/P = 1/2$, which means $P = 2MC$. Note that demand elasticities are almost always negative because an increase in price decreases quantity, but are generally expressed without bothering to express the negative sign. So an "elasticity of 2" generally means -2 must be used in a mathematical formula.

define monopoly power in that way. Rather, in economic models a monopolist is a firm that is literally the only producer of a product for which there are no substitutes that it need ever take into account when setting prices or output. A dominant firm is a firm that faces some rivals, but whose rivals are much smaller and less efficient. Economic models show that such a dominant firm is effectively a monopolist with respect to the "residual" demand curve that is derived by taking the total market demand curve and subtracting from it the output that would be produced by the rivals at each price.[28] Thus, while a dominant firm is somewhat constrained by the existence of rivals, it will still price above its marginal costs and restrict market output below efficient levels. Such a dominant firm is generally what antitrust law means by a monopolist.

Using such a dominant firm model, one can derive the firm-specific demand elasticity of a dominant firm (which can be difficult to ascertain directly) from the marketwide elasticity of demand, the market share of the firm being assessed, and the elasticity of rival supply, which is the percentage change in output supplied by rivals in response to a 1% increase in price. Basically a firm's ability to raise prices will be constrained by both the tendency of buyers to exit the market (the marketwide demand elasticity) and their ability to shift purchases to any increased output supplied by its rivals (which reflects a combination of rival elasticity of supply and their initial market share.)[29] The higher the marketwide demand elasticity or the supply elasticity of rivals, the higher the firm-specific elasticity of demand for the dominant firm, and thus the lower its market power.

Further, if we hold marketwide demand elasticity and rival supply elasticity constant, then the higher a firm's market share, the lower its firm-specific demand elasticity and thus the higher its market power. The reason is twofold. A high firm market share reduces the proportion of its output that it must reduce to create a decrease in marketwide output: a firm with 50% of the market must reduce its output by 20% to reduce market output by 10%, whereas a firm with 90% market share can do so by reducing its output by 11%. A high firm market share also leaves a lower market share to rivals and thus reduces the output expansion they can produce with a given supply elasticity: if a firm lowers

---

[28] *See* Carlton & Perloff, *supra* note 12, at 107–118.

[29] Mathematically, if we call ε_{dom} the firm-specific demand elasticity of the dominant firm, call ε_{mkt} the marketwide demand elasticity, call $\varepsilon_{rivsupp}$ the supply elasticity of rivals, and call S the share of the dominant firm (which of course means $1 - S$ is the share of all the other firms), then it can be shown that $\varepsilon_{dom} = \varepsilon_{mkt}/S + \varepsilon_{rivsupp}(1 - S)/S$. *See* Landes & Posner, *supra* note 12, at 944–45, 985–86. If rivals cannot expand output over the relevant period, or if each firm sets prices under the Cournot assumption that the output of rivals is fixed, then $\varepsilon_{rivsupp} = 0$ and the equation reduces to $\varepsilon_{dom} = \varepsilon_{mkt}/S$. *See id.* at 952 n.30, 954 n.32; *see* also Chapter 7 (discussing Cournot competition). Thus, under fixed rival output or Cournot competition, $1/\varepsilon_{dom} = S\varepsilon_{mkt}$, and because $1/\varepsilon_{dom}$ equals the Lerner index, this means $S/\varepsilon_{mkt} = (P - MC)/P$. This formula provides a way of calculating marginal cost from market price, share and demand elasticity where rival output is fixed or firms set their output under the assumption it is. It also provides a way to calculate how changes in market shares or the various elasticities would alter the price-cost margin.

market output by 10%, rivals with a market share of 50% can offset that by increasing their output by 20% whereas rivals with a market share of 10% must increase their output by 100% to do so. Unfortunately, it may be hard to ascertain the marketwide demand elasticity and rival supply elasticity necessary to know what inference about market power to make from market shares.

2. LEGAL TESTS OF MONOPOLY POWER

The U.S. Supreme Court defines "monopoly power" as "the power to control prices or exclude competition."[30] Given that the economic definitions of any "market power" all involve some discretion over pricing, one might think that any firm with market power necessarily has "control" over its prices and thus must be a monopolist. But this is not what the Court in fact means because it has stressed: "Monopoly power under § 2 requires, of course, something greater than market power under § 1."[31] The Court appears to mean that monopoly power is a relatively high degree of market power, though it has left undefined just what that degree is.

The portion of this test about the power to "exclude competition" is problematic because the second element of monopolization is exclusionary conduct. Thus, in any case where a firm has in fact engaged in exclusionary conduct satisfying the second element, one would think that would necessarily mean that the firm must have had the power to exclude rivals, thus satisfying the first element. Such a conclusion could logically be defended. If a firm engages in inefficient exclusionary conduct, one could reasonably infer that it must have market power from which it derives gains because otherwise such inefficient conduct would be unprofitable. But adopting that logic would largely conflate what are supposed to be separate legal elements, thus eliminating any screening effect from the market power element.[32] The Court, however, appears to define such a power to exclude rivals to exist only when such exclusion allows the firm to raise prices, thus suggesting that some degree of pricing discretion must also be shown.[33] One possible reconciliation is that an ability to raise price might result from constricting either (1) a

---

[30] *Kodak*, 504 U.S. at 481 (quoting United States v. E.I. du Pont de Nemours & Co., 351 U.S. 377, 391 (1956)); *Grinnell*, 384 U.S. at 571 (same).

[31] *See Kodak*, 504 U.S. at 481.

[32] It would not completely conflate those two elements because, as we will see, exclusionary conduct satisfying the second element must be improper or anticompetitive, whereas the power to exclude rivals that satisfies the first element need not be. For example, a firm may enjoy patents that it earned through productive investments and that enable it to exclude all rivals from a product market. Such a firm would have a power to exclude and thus have monopoly power. But the exercise of its patents would not constitute improper exclusionary conduct that satisfies the second element. Still, the problem remains that when conduct does satisfy the second element, it would seem the first element would always be satisfied.

[33] *See duPont*, 351 U.S. at 392 ("Price and competition are so intimately entwined that any discussion of theory must treat them as one. It is inconceivable that price could be controlled without power over competition or vice versa.")

firm's own output or (2) other firms' outputs (by excluding rivals or impairing their efficiency), and that the "control prices" test refers to the former and the "exclude competition" test refers to latter alternative.[34]

In actual practice, though, U.S. courts tend to determine the existence of monopoly or market power without requiring direct evidence of control over pricing *or* power to exclude rivals. Instead, U.S. courts tend to use the alternative of inferring monopoly or market power from firm market shares, at least when coupled with evidence that entry barriers to that market are relatively high.[35] The precise dividing line is unclear. The Supreme Court has indicated that market shares above 66% indicate monopoly power without clearly specifying the lower bound.[36] Lower court cases have generally required a market share of at least 50% to constitute monopoly power.[37] As for market power, the Supreme Court has held that, standing alone, a 30% market share was insufficient to establish the kind of market power necessary to trigger the per se rule against tying, but stressed this differed from general notions of market power because in a tying case finding market power would preclude further inquiry into actual anticompetitive effects.[38]

3. MARKET DEFINITION

Because courts and regulators largely rely on market shares, they must define the relevant markets in order to determine the share of that market that a defendant possesses. This raises two sorts of general framing questions. First, how does the law define markets? Second, why does the law rely on evidence of market share rather than just relying on direct evidence of pricing discretion or market power? As we will see, one important economic concept that courts utilize in defining markets is the cross-elasticity of demand, which is the extent to which a price increase in one item leads to increased sales of another item. Again, an important but often obscured issue is what baseline price one should use. If the cross-elasticity of demand is very high for small price increases over costs or the competitive level, then the two items can be grouped in the same

---

[34] *See* Krattenmaker, Lande & Salop, *supra* note 12, at 248–49.

[35] *See Jefferson Parish*, 466 U.S. at 17; *Kodak*, 504 U.S. at 469 n.15; United States v. Grinnell Corp., 384 U.S. 563, 571 (1966); United States v. Microsoft, 253 F.3d 34, 51 (D.C. Cir. 2001) (en banc).

[36] *See duPont*, 351 U.S. at 379 (observing that "du Pont produced almost 75% of the cellophane sold in the United States" and that "If cellophane is the 'market' . . . , it may be assumed it does have monopoly power over that 'market' under its test"); *Kodak*, 504 U.S. at 481 (holding that proving a 80–95% market share is enough to survive summary judgment, and describing a prior case as holding that "over two-thirds of a market is a monopoly"); *Grinnell*, 384 U.S. at 571 ("The existence of such [monopoly] power ordinarily may be inferred from the predominant share of the market. . . ." In *American Tobacco,* we said that "over two-thirds of the entire domestic field of cigarettes, and . . . over 80% of the field of comparable cigarettes" constituted "a substantial monopoly." In the present case, 87% [share of the business] leaves no doubt that . . . defendants have monopoly power . . . if that business is the relevant market.).

[37] *See* Elhauge, supra note 18, at 336.

[38] *See Jefferson Parish*, 466 U.S. at 26–29.

product market because no monopolist in one of the items could exploit it by charging prices significantly above costs or the competitive level without causing a large amount of buyers to switch to the other item. But can we assume the same if the cross-elasticity of demand is high for small price increases over current levels, where those current prices are themselves alleged to be produced by monopoly power? And if we can't rely on current levels as our baseline, can we independently derive a reliable baseline for costs or what the competitive level would be? Consider the following.

United States v. du Pont & Co. (The Cellophane Case)

351 U.S. 377 (1956).

■ MR. JUSTICE REED delivered the opinion of the Court. . . .

. . . du Pont produced almost 75% of the cellophane sold in the United States, and cellophane constituted less than 20% of all "flexible packaging material" sales. . . . The court below found that the "relevant market for determining the extent of du Pont's market control is the market for flexible packaging materials," and that competition from those other materials prevented du Pont from possessing monopoly powers in its sales of cellophane.

The Government asserts that cellophane and other wrapping materials are neither substantially fungible nor like priced. For these reasons, it argues that the market for other wrappings is distinct from the market for cellophane and that the competition afforded cellophane by other wrappings is not strong enough to be considered in determining whether du Pont has monopoly powers. Market delimitation is necessary under du Pont's theory to determine whether an alleged monopolist violates § 2. The ultimate consideration in such a determination is whether the defendants control the price and competition in the market for such part of trade or commerce as they are charged with monopolizing. Every manufacturer is the sole producer of the particular commodity it makes but its control in the above sense of the relevant market depends upon the availability of alternative commodities for buyers: i.e., whether there is a cross-elasticity of demand between cellophane and the other wrappings. This interchangeability is largely gauged by the purchase of competing products for similar uses considering the price, characteristics and adaptability of the competing commodities. The court below found that the flexible wrappings afforded such alternatives. This Court must determine whether the trial court erred in its estimate of the competition afforded cellophane by other materials.

The burden of proof, of course, was upon the Government to establish monopoly. This the trial court held the Government failed to do . . . For the United States to succeed in this Court now, it must show that erroneous legal tests were applied to essential findings of fact or that the findings themselves were "clearly erroneous" . . . We do not try the facts of cases de novo. . . .

[The court below also found that du Pont did not obtain its market position through exclusionary conduct, but the Supreme Court never reached that issue because it concluded the evidence did not prove monopoly power.]

Our cases determine that a party has monopoly power if it has, over "any part of the trade or commerce among the several states", a power of controlling prices or unreasonably restricting competition. . . . If cellophane is the "market" that du Pont is found to dominate, it may be assumed it does have monopoly power over that "market." Monopoly power is the power to control prices or exclude competition. It seems apparent that du Pont's power to set the price of cellophane has been limited only by the competition afforded by other flexible packaging materials. Moreover, it may be practically impossible for anyone to commence manufacturing cellophane without full access to du Pont's technique [over which it held patents]. However, du Pont has no power to prevent competition from other wrapping materials. The trial court consequently had to determine whether competition from the other wrappings prevented du Pont from possessing monopoly power in violation of § 2. Price and competition are so intimately entwined that any discussion of theory must treat them as one. It is inconceivable that price could be controlled without power over competition or vice versa. . . .

If a large number of buyers and sellers deal freely in a standardized product, such as salt or wheat, we have complete or pure competition. Patents, on the other hand, furnish the most familiar type of classic monopoly. As the producers of a standardized product bring about significant differentiations of quality, designed, or packaging in the product that permit differences of use, competition becomes to a greater or less degree incomplete and the producer's power over price and competition greater over his article and its use, according to the differentiation he is able to create and maintain. A retail seller may have in one sense a monopoly on certain trade because of location, as an isolated country store or filling station, or because no one else makes a product of just the quality or attractiveness of his product, as for example in cigarettes. Thus one can theorize that we have monopolistic competition in every nonstandardized commodity with each manufacturer having power over the price and production of his own product. However, this power that, let us say, automobile or soft-drink manufactures have over their trademarked products is not the power that makes an illegal monopoly. Illegal power must be appraised in terms of the competitive market for the product.

Determination of the competitive market for commodities depends on how different from one another are the offered commodities in character or use, how far buyers will go to substitute one commodity for another. For example, one can think of building materials as in commodity competition but one could hardly say that brick competed with steel or wood or cement or stone in the meaning of Sherman Act litigation; the products are too different. This is the interindustry competition emphasized by some economists. On the other hand, there are certain differences in the formulae for soft drinks but one can hardly say that each one is an illegal monopoly. Whatever the market may be, we hold that control of price or competition establishes the existence of monopoly power under § 2. . . . Our next step is to determine whether du Pont has monopoly power over cellophane: that is, power over its price in relation to or competition with other commodities. . . .

When a product is controlled by one interest, without substitutes available in the market, there is monopoly power. Because most products have possible substitutes, we cannot . . . give "that infinite range" to the definition of substitutes. Nor is it a proper interpretation of the Sherman Act to require that products be fungible to be considered in the relevant market.

The Government argues:

> "we do not here urge that in no circumstances may competition of substitutes negative possession of monopolistic power over trade in a product. The decisions make it clear at the least that the courts will not consider substitutes other than those which are substantially fungible with the monopolized product and sell at substantially the same price."

But where there are market alternatives that buyers may readily use for their purposes, illegal monopoly does not exist merely because the product said to be monopolized differs from others. If it were not so, only physically identical products would be a part of the market. To accept the Government's argument, we would have to conclude that the manufactures of plain as well as moistureproof cellophane were monopolists, and so with films such as Pliofilm, foil, glassine, polyethylene, and Saran, for each of these wrapping materials is distinguishable. These were all exhibits in the case. New wrappings appear, generally similar to cellophane, is each a monopoly? What is called for is an appraisal of the "cross-elasticity" of demand in the trade. . . . In considering what is the relevant market for determining the control of price and competition, no more definite rule can be declared than that commodities reasonably interchangeable by consumers for the same purposes make up that "part of the trade or commerce", monopolization of which may be illegal. As respects flexible packaging materials, the market geographically is nationwide.

. . . Illegal monopolies under § 2 may well exist over limited products in narrow fields where competition is eliminated. . . . In determining the market under the Sherman Act, it is the use or uses to which the commodity is put that control. The selling price between commodities with similar uses and different characteristics may vary, so that the cheaper product can drive out the more expensive. Or, the superior quality of higher priced articles may make dominant the more desirable. Cellophane costs more than many competing products and less than a few. But whatever the price, there are various flexible wrapping materials that are bought by manufacturers for packaging their goods in their own plants or are sold to converters who shape and print them for use in the packaging of the commodities to be wrapped.

Cellophane differs from other flexible packaging materials. From some it differs more than from others. The basic materials from which the wrappings are made . . . are aluminum, cellulose acetate, chlorides, wood pulp, rubber hydrochloride, and ethylene gas. It will adequately illustrate the similarity in characteristics of the various products by noting here Finding 62 as to glassine. Its use is almost as extensive as cellophane, and many of its characteristics equally or more satisfactory to users.[25]

It may be admitted that cellophane combines the desirable elements of transparency, strength and cheapness more definitely than any of the others. Comparative characteristics have been noted thus:

> "Moistureproof cellophane is highly transparent, tears readily but has high bursting strength, is highly impervious to moisture and gases, and is resistant to grease and oils. Heat sealable, printable, and adapted to use on wrapping machines, it makes an excellent packaging material for both display and protection of commodities.
>
> "Other flexible wrapping materials fall into four major categories: (1) opaque nonmoistureproof wrapping paper designed primarily for convenience and protection in handling packages; (2) moistureproof films of varying degrees of transparency designed primarily either to protect, or to display and protect, the products they encompass; (3) nonmoistureproof transparent films designed primarily to display and to some extent protect, but which obviously do a poor protecting job where exclusion or retention of moisture is important; and (4) moistureproof materials other than films of varying degrees of transparency (foils and paper products) designed to protect and display." . . .

---

[25] . . . "Glassine is, in some types, about 90% transparent, so printing is legible through it. Glassine affords low cost transparency. Moisture protection afforded by waxed or lacquered glassine is as good as that or moistureproof cellophane. Glassine has greater resistance to tearing and breakage than cellophane. Glassine runs on packaging machinery with ease equal to that of cellophane. Glassine can be printed faster than cellophane, and can be run faster than moistureproof cellophane on bag machines. Glassine has greater resistance than cellophane to rancidity-inducing ultraviolet rays. Glassine has dimensional stability superior to cellophane. Glassine is more durable in cold weather than cellophane. Printed glassine can be sold against cellophane on the basis of appearance. Glassine may be more easily laminated than cellophane. Glassine is cheaper than cellophane in some types, comparable in others."

But, despite cellophane's advantages it has to meet competition from other materials in every one of its uses. . . . Food products are the chief outlet, with cigarettes next. The Government makes no challenge to Finding 283 that cellophane furnishes less than 7% of wrappings for bakery products, 25% for candy, 32% for snacks, 35% for meats and poultry, 27% for crackers and biscuits, 47% for fresh produce, and 34% for frozen foods. Seventy-five to eighty percent of cigarettes are wrapped in cellophane. Thus, cellophane shares the packaging market with others. The over-all result is that cellophane accounts for 17.9% of flexible wrapping materials, measured by the wrapping surface.

Moreover a very considerable degree of functional interchangeability exists between these products . . . [E]xcept as to permeability to gases, cellophane has no qualities that are not possessed by a number of other materials. Meat will do as an example of interchangeability. Although du Pont's sales to the meat industry have reached 19,000,000 pounds annually, nearly 35%, this volume is attributed "to the rise of self-service retailing of fresh meat." In fact, since the popularity of self-service meats, du Pont has lost "a considerable proportion" of this packaging business to Pliofilm. Pliofilm is more expensive than cellophane, but its superior physical characteristics apparently offset cellophane's price advantage. While retailers shift continually between the two, the trial court found that Pliofilm is increasing its share of the business. One further example is worth noting. Before World War II, du Pont cellophane wrapped between 5 and 10% of baked and smoked meats. The peak year was 1933. Thereafter du Pont was unable to meet the competition of Sylvania and of greaseproof paper. Its sales declined and the 1933 volume was not reached again until 1947. It will be noted that greaseproof paper, glassine, waxed paper, foil and Pliofilm are used as well as cellophane. . . .

An element for consideration as to cross-elasticity of demand between products is the responsiveness of the sales of one product to price changes of the other. If a slight decrease in the price of cellophane causes a considerable number of customers of other flexible wrappings to switch to cellophane, it would be an indication that a high cross-elasticity of demand exists between them; that the products compete in the same market. The court below held that the "(g)reat sensitivity of customers in the flexible packaging markets to price or quality changes" prevented du Pont from possessing monopoly control over price. The record sustains these findings . . .

We conclude that cellophane's interchangeability with the other materials mentioned suffices to make it a part of this flexible packaging material market.

The Government stresses the fact that the variation in price between cellophane and other materials demonstrates they are noncompetitive. . . . Cellophane costs two or three times as much, surface measure, as its chief competitors for the flexible wrapping market, glassine and greaseproof papers. Other forms of cellulose wrappings and those from other chemical or mineral substances, with the exception of aluminum foil, are more expensive. The uses of these materials . . . are largely to wrap small packages for retail distribution. The wrapping is a relatively small proportion of the entire cost of the article. Different producers need different qualities in wrappings and their need may vary from time to time as their products undergo change. But the necessity for flexible wrappings is the central and unchanging demand. We cannot say that these differences in cost gave du Pont monopoly power over prices in view of the findings of fact . . . [that: (1) du Pont lowered cellophane prices to compete with cheaper wrapping materials like glassine and wax paper; (2) some customers switched between types of materials in response to price changes; and (3) du Pont prices tended to track changes in its cost.]

The facts above considered dispose also of any contention that competitors have been excluded by du Pont from the packaging material market. That market has many producers and there is no proof du Pont ever has possessed power to exclude any of them from the rapidly expanding flexible packaging market. . . . The record shows the multiplicity of competitors and the financial strength of some with individual assets running to the hundreds of millions. Indeed, the trial court found that du Pont could not exclude competitors even from the manufacture of cellophane, an immaterial matter if the market is flexible packaging material. Nor can we say that du Pont's profits, while liberal (according to the Government 15.9% net after taxes on the 1937—1947 average), demonstrate the existence of a monopoly without proof of lack of comparable profits during those years in other prosperous industries. Cellophane was a leader over 17%, in the flexible packaging materials market. There is no showing that du Pont's rate of return was greater or less than that of other producers of flexible packaging materials.

The "market" which one must study to determine when a producer has monopoly power will vary with the part of commerce under consideration. The tests are constant. That market is composed of products that have reasonable interchangeability for the purposes for which they are produced—price, use and qualities considered. While the application of the tests remains uncertain, it seems to us that du Pont should not be found to monopolize cellophane when that product has the competition and interchangeability with other wrappings that this record shows. . . .

■ MR. CHIEF JUSTICE WARREN, with whom MR. JUSTICE BLACK and MR. JUSTICE DOUGLAS join, dissenting. . . . The majority . . . admit that "cellophane combines the desirable elements of transparency, strength and cheapness more definitely than any of" a host of other packaging materials. . . .

During the period covered by the complaint (1923–1947) cellophane enjoyed phenomenal growth. . . . Yet throughout this period the price of cellophane was far greater than that of glassine, waxed paper or sulphite paper. . . . We cannot believe that buyers, practical businessmen, would have bought cellophane in increasing amounts over a quarter of a century if close substitutes were available at from one-seventh to one-half cellophane's price. That they did so is testimony to cellophane's distinctiveness.

The inference yielded by the conduct of cellophane buyers is reinforced by the conduct of sellers other than du Pont. . . . Sylvania, the only other cellophane producer, absolutely and immediately followed every du Pont price change, even dating back its price list to the effective date of du Pont's change. Producers of glassine and waxed paper, on the other hand, displayed apparent indifference to du Pont's repeated and substantial price cuts. . . . [F]rom 1924 to 1932 du Pont dropped the price of plain cellophane 84%, while the price of glassine remained constant. And during the period 1933–1946 the prices for glassine and waxed paper actually increased in the face of a further 21% decline in the price of cellophane. . . .

Certainly du Pont itself shared our view. From the first, du Pont [documents indicated] that it need not concern itself with competition from other packaging materials. . . . In 1929, while it was still the sole domestic producer of cellophane, du Pont won its long struggle to raise the tariff from 25% to 60%, ad valorem, on cellophane imports, substantially foreclosing foreign competition. . . . If close substitutes for cellophane had been commercially available, du Pont, an enlightened enterprise, would not have gone to such lengths to control cellophane. . . .

A confidential du Pont report shows that during the period 1937–1947, despite great expansion of sales, du Pont's "operative return" (before taxes) averaged 31%, while its average "net return" (after deduction of taxes, bonuses, and fundamental research expenditures) was 15.9%. [The dissent cited an article showing that du Pont's returns in rayon were 32% when the rayon market had two firms like cellophane, but that average market returns were only 5% when the rayon market had 20 firms.]

. . . The trial judge thought that, if du Pont raised its price, the market would "penalize" it with smaller profits as well as lower sales. Du Pont proved him wrong. When 1947 operating earnings dropped below 26% for the first time in 10 years, it increased cellophane's price 7% and boosted its earnings in 1948. Du Pont's division manager then reported that "If an operative return of 31% is considered inadequate then an upward revision in prices will be necessary to improve the return." It is this latitude with respect to price, this broad power of choice, that the antitrust laws forbid. Du Pont's independent pricing policy and the great profits consistently yielded by that policy leave no room for doubt that it had power to control the price of cellophane. The findings of fact cited by the majority cannot affect this conclusion. For they merely demonstrate, that during the period covered by the complaint, du Pont was a "good monopolist," i.e., . . . that it chose to maximize profits by lowering price and expanding sales. Proof of enlightened exercise of monopoly power certainly does not refute the existence of that power.

The majority opinion purports to reject the theory of "interindustry competition." Brick, steel, wood, cement and stone, it says, are "too different" to be placed in the same market. But cellophane, glassine, wax papers, sulphite papers, greaseproof and vegetable parchment papers, aluminum foil, cellulose acetate, Pliofilm and other films are not "too different," the opinion concludes. The majority approach would apparently enable a monopolist of motion picture exhibition to avoid Sherman Act consequences by showing that motion pictures compete in substantial measure with legitimate theater, television, radio, sporting events and other forms of entertainment. Here, too, "shifts of business" undoubtedly accompany fluctuations in price and "there are market alternatives that buyers may readily use for their purposes". . . .

The majority hold in effect that, because cellophane meets competition for many end uses, those buyers for other uses who need or want only cellophane are not entitled to the benefits of competition within the cellophane industry. For example, . . . the largest single use of cellophane in 1951 was for wrapping cigarettes, and . . . 75 to 80% of all cigarettes are wrapped with cellophane. . . .

du Pont (The Cellophane Case) and Various Bases for Defining Markets

The *du Pont* case, usually called the *Cellophane* case, has two major legal holdings. First, it held that "Monopoly power is the power to control prices or exclude competition." Issues regarding that test have already been discussed in the introduction. Second, the case held that the test of whether two items are in the same market is whether they are "reasonably interchangeable" by buyers. Issues about how to apply this "reasonably interchangeable" test are discussed next.

*1. **Physical/Functional Differences and Similarities.*** The Court held that the fact that cellophane and other flexible wrapping materials had physical differences that conferred different functional advantages did not alone prove a separate product market. This holding makes economic sense because such differences and advantages would not necessarily prevent customers from switching between the items if a monopolist in one item tried to raise prices for one of the items above competitive levels. Physical or functional differences are thus not alone enough to show that power over the item would confer any power to raise prices.

On the other hand, one also cannot infer a single product market from evidence that two items have enough functional similarities that there is a substantial overlap in end uses. If one could, that would lead to odd conclusions, like that bricks and wood are in the same market because both are used for construction or that televisions and radios are in the same market because both are used for entertainment. The reason one cannot infer a single market is that the existence of an overlap in end uses does not necessarily mean that the degree of buyer substitution between the items is high enough to restrain a monopolist in one of the items from raising prices above competitive levels. Thus, an overlap in end use cannot alone disprove the possibility that power over one item would confer power to raise prices.

But does a high *degree* of physical difference determine the issue? The Court seemed to think so when, in dicta, the Court stated that bricks and wood could not be in the same market regardless of substitution between them because they are "too different." This statement suggests the holding may have turned in part on court intuitions about whether cellophane feels more like other flexible packaging materials than bricks feel like wood, suggesting that if cellophane looked more different (like, say, tupperware) the conclusion might have been different even if the cross-elasticities were the same. However, such a reliance on intuitions about physical differences makes little economic sense because items can physically be very different even though substitution between them constrains any power to raise prices in one of the items.

Likewise, the Court suggested in dicta that different retailers or brands of a product that was very physically similar could not be in different markets even if substitution between them does not suffice to prevent each retailer or brand from having pricing discretion. As we shall see, this dicta was later disapproved by the Supreme Court in *Kodak*. Whether the dicta makes economic sense may depend on the reason for the pricing discretion. On the one hand, suppose the firms are engaged in monopolistic competition, where each firm has discretion to price above marginal cost, but recurring fixed costs mean that no firm makes supracompetitive profits. In such a case, it makes antitrust policy sense to conclude that no firm has monopoly power (even though market power exists in a technical economic sense) because the situation does not mean a firm can raise prices over the more competitive levels we might hope for without exclusionary conduct. One the other hand, if the market is differentiated, so that each retailer or brand has discretion to charge not only above marginal cost, but also above average costs, then it is not clear why the law should regard their market power as less than those of other firms with similar demand curves, just because the products or brands are physically similar or even identical. A firm with such retailer or brand power might still be able to raise prices above competitive levels if it can impair rivals with exclusionary conduct.

The functional power to charge above the competitive level that a well-functioning market could achieve is the relevant policy concern, and thus the real question is what effect any physical differences or similarities have on buyer willingness to substitute in response to price increases over competitive levels. Absent empirical evidence, courts may rely on intuitions about whether physical differences or similarities seem

likely to lead to a degree of buyer substitution that would prove or disprove separate markets, but such intuitions should be rejected if they are contrary to empirical evidence about actual buyer substitution rates. Although the occasional court still gets misled by intuitions about physical characteristics, modern courts (and certainly expert agencies) generally focus instead on whether actual buyer substitution rates would eliminate any significant discretion to raise prices above competitive levels. Absent such empirical evidence, should courts at least presume that high degrees of physical/functional differences indicate separate markets and high degrees of physical/functional similarities indicate a single market, as long as that presumption can be rebutted?

*2. **Price Differences.*** The Court also held that evidence that cellophane sold for a significantly higher price than many of the alleged substitutes did not alone prove separate markets. This holding also makes economic sense because a price difference between two items does not necessarily mean a monopolist in one item would have power to raise prices above competitive levels. Suppose, for example, the price for cellophane is 2 cents and the price for wax paper is 1 cent. Suppose further that cellophane costs 2 cents to make and that any price increase over 2 cents would lead all buyers to switch to 1 cent wax paper. Then, cellophane and wax paper should be considered to be in the same market because the possibility of substitution to wax paper would constrain a nominal monopolist in cellophane to price at cost.

Likewise, the Court rejected the claim that separate products are proven if one item has a significantly lower price than substitutes that are alleged to have advantages over it. To see why this also makes economic sense, suppose the price and cost for cellophane is again 2 cents, the price for Pilofilm is 4 cents, and Pilofilm has functional advantages over cellophane that would cause all buyers to switch to Pilofilm if cellophane prices ever exceeded 2 cents. Then cellophane and Pilofilm should be deemed in the same market because substitution to Pilofilm would constrain a nominal monopolist in cellophane to price at cost.

In short, while a price difference indicates that buyers value the items differently, a price difference may not necessarily mean monopoly power if the price difference equals the cost difference between the items. Thus, a price difference does not necessarily show separate products. On the other hand, it may make sense to conclude that price differences should be deemed presumptive evidence of separate products absent evidence that the price difference equaled the cost difference. Would you favor such a presumption?

*3. **Cross-Elasticities at Current Prices: The*** **Cellophane** ***Fallacy.*** Although the above analysis indicates the Court was right to focus on buyer substitution rather than physical or price differences, the Court committed a now well-known economic error when it held that one could infer a single product market from evidence that the cross-elasticities of demand are high at *current* prices. The problem is that current prices may already be at monopoly levels, which are where the monopolist maximizes profits and thus by definition mean a monopolist could not profitably raise prices any further. For example, suppose cellophane prices were 2 cents and any further increase in price would lead to rapid switching to wax paper or Pilofilm, thus indicating a high cross-elasticity of demand, but that cellophane actually costs 0.1 cent to make. This high cross-elasticity at current prices would not mean a monopolist in cellophane had no market power, because the possibility of substituting to wax paper or Pilofilm did not prevent the firm from pricing twenty times its costs. More generally, a monopolist would predictably keep increasing prices until its prices did create significant substitution to other products.

Inferring a single product from substitution at current prices was thus a major error in the Court analysis, which is now so well-recognized that it is commonly referred to as "the Cellophane fallacy." What we really want to know is what buyer substitution rates would be if prices were elevated from competitive levels, which will differ from current levels if monopoly power actually exists. Given this, high cross-elasticities at current prices cannot really disprove the possibility that a separate market exists in which a firm is already exercising monopoly power. As we will see, modern agency guidelines and the later Supreme Court decision in *Kodak* now reject the Cellophane fallacy.

A high cross-elasticity at *competitive* price levels would indicate a single market. Unfortunately, buyer substitution rates at competitive prices are not directly observable in the market at issue whenever market power is already being exercised. Still, sometimes the same product was in the past sold under competitive conditions or is now sold in another geographic market that is competitive. Buyer substitution rates in such competitive baselines can provide a more reliable indicator that avoids the Cellophane fallacy, if one can adjust for differences in demand and costs between the baselines and the actual market at issue.

While a high cross-elasticity can prove a single market only if measured at competitive prices, a *low* cross-elasticity could prove separate markets whether measured at current or competitive prices. A low cross-elasticity at current prices would suggest that prices could be increased significantly if greater market power were obtained in one of those markets, although it would also suggest that much of that potential market power is not being exercised currently. A low cross-elasticity at competitive prices that does not exist at current prices would suggest that monopoly power is already being exercised in the market at issue.

4. Price Trends. Another method for defining markets focuses on the extent to which prices for the items moved in the same way over time. For example, one might think one can infer separate products from evidence that prices for two items failed to move in the same way over time. If A and B are in the same market, a decrease in prices for A would cause buyers to switch to A, thus decreasing demand for B unless

characterizations by employees also raises the issue of whether characterization by any du Pont employee should suffice or whether we need evidence that characterization was approved at the highest firm levels. The involves the usual difficulty with relying on firm admissions: it is often unclear who speaks for the firm. Given these considerations, courts generally hold that such self-characterizations do not dictate a separate markets conclusion, but are relevant and admissible on the issue.

Should courts infer a single market from internal documents that declared cellophane was in a broader market? The problem is that, if courts did so, then firms will in the future start writing internal documents with broad market definitions in order to minimize antitrust scrutiny. Thus, usually courts put greater weight on internal documents that "admit" narrow market definitions than on documents that embrace broad ones. A one-way ratchet ends up being the effect, where internal documents can hurt defendants but rarely help them. Such a one-way ratchet may seem somewhat unfair to defendants, but in practice it results in very bland internal documents that refer to "market segments" rather than "markets."

*8. **Inferring Market from Conduct.*** A more solid basis than mere self-characterization would be evidence that the firm engaged in conduct that makes economic sense only if the firm believed a separate market existed. For example, here the dissent cited evidence that du Pont invested in lobbying for higher import tariffs on foreign cellophane. However, the relevance of this evidence may turn on how large the lobbying costs were. If lobbying costs were very high, such a lobbying investment would probably be economically irrational if du Pont did not have some degree of market power. If lobbying costs are relatively low, then even a firm in a locally competitive market might fear being undercut by foreign cellophane makers that had lower costs. However, if du Pont did not think cellophane was a separate market, it probably makes little economic sense for du Pont to seek tariffs on only foreign cellophane rather than on all foreign flexible packaging materials, unless foreign cellophane was the only low-cost foreign producer of flexible packaging materials. This evidence thus does support a separate market. However, such lobbying need not indicate monopoly power, as long as the firm has sufficient market power to realize enough gain from the reduced competition to cover the lobbying costs.

*9. **How Markets Are Currently Defined.*** There is widespread current recognition that the ultimate conceptual issue for market definition is whether the rate of buyer substitution to other items would constrain a monopolist in the posited market from significantly raising prices above competitive levels. This is the right conceptual issue because the purpose of market definition is functional: to help determine whether it is likely that prices could be raised significantly by a high share within that market or by a restraint on competition within that market. If buyer substitution would constrain even an absolute monopolist in a posited "market" from significantly raising prices, then high shares or restraints within that posited market can have at most an insignificant effect on prices, thus making the market definition functionally unhelpful. Instead, proper market definition should be broadened until buyer substitution to other markets would not constrain a significant price increase, which would indicate that a high share or restraint of that market could have some significant effect on prices.

The *du Pont* Court recognized that all the above eight factors were relevant to this ultimate conceptual issue for market definition. But the Court also recognized that, leaving aside the third factor, each factor was at most a presumptive indicator of such buyer substitution rates. In the end, the Court concluded that all the other factors must give way to the third factor because the Court believed that the third factor directly resolved the ultimate issue. Unfortunately, the Court's belief incorrectly conflated the buyer substitution rate at current prices (which is what the third factor measures) with the rate at competitive prices (which is the ultimate issue). This was the Cellophane fallacy, which has now been rejected as fallacious by the Supreme Court in *Kodak,* as well as in the modern agency guidelines that follow next.

But where does that leave current methods of market definition? It means that the courts and agencies now recognize that when assessing whether firms are already exercising market power, all eight of the factors, including cross-elasticity at current prices, are imperfect proxies for the ultimate question. That ultimate conceptual question is whether buyer substitution rates would prevent a monopolist in the posited market from significantly raising prices above competitive levels, but such buyer substitution rates in that posited market cannot be directly observed if market power is already being exercised. We thus now have conceptual clarity on the ultimate issue, but we lack any direct evidence on that issue in any case alleging that market power already existed. Instead, in modern cases, all eight factors continue to be cited as relevant, perhaps presumptive, but imperfect proxies on that ultimate issue. Adjudicators are left to determine the ultimate issue at best they can from case-specific arguments about the applicability, relevance, and limits of those imperfect proxies.

U.S. DOJ/FTC, Horizontal Merger Guidelines

(2010).

[Although U.S. enforcement agencies have not issued guidelines on how to determine monopoly power or define markets in a monopolization case, they have issued influential guidelines on how they define markets for purposes of merger enforcement, which are also relevant to monopolization cases. The main difference is that in a merger case the question is whether the merger will increase prices from the levels that would prevail without the merger, whereas in a monopolization case the question is whether market power already exists.]

4. ***Market Definition . . .*** Market definition focuses solely on demand substitution factors, i.e., on customers' ability and willingness to substitute away from one product to another in response to a price increase or a corresponding non-price change such as a reduction in product quality or service. The responsive actions of suppliers are also important in competitive analysis. They are considered in these Guidelines in the sections addressing the identification of market participants, the measurement of market shares, the analysis of competitive effects, and entry.

Customers often confront a range of possible substitutes for the products of the merging firms. Some substitutes may be closer, and others more distant, either geographically or in terms of product attributes and perceptions. Additionally, customers may assess the proximity of different products differently. When products or suppliers in different geographic areas are substitutes for one another to varying degrees, defining a market to include some substitutes and exclude others is inevitably a simplification that cannot capture the full variation in the extent to which different products compete against each other. The principles of market definition outlined below seek to make this inevitable simplification as useful and informative as is practically possible. Relevant markets need not have precise metes and bounds.

Defining a market broadly to include relatively distant product or geographic substitutes can lead to misleading market shares. This is because the competitive significance of distant substitutes is unlikely to be commensurate with their shares in a broad market. Although excluding more distant substitutes from the market inevitably understates their competitive significance to some degree, doing so often provides a more accurate indicator of the competitive effects of the merger than would the alternative of including them and overstating their competitive significance as proportional to their shares in an expanded market.

> *Example 4:* Firms A and B, sellers of two leading brands of motorcycles, propose to merge. If Brand A motorcycle prices were to rise, some buyers would substitute to Brand B, and some others would substitute to cars. However, motorcycle buyers see Brand B motorcycles as much more similar to Brand A motorcycles than are cars. Far more cars are sold than motorcycles. Evaluating shares in a market that includes cars would greatly underestimate the competitive significance of Brand B motorcycles in constraining Brand A's prices and greatly overestimate the significance of cars.

Market shares of different products in narrowly defined markets are more likely to capture the relative competitive significance of these products, and often more accurately reflect competition between close substitutes. As a result, properly defined antitrust markets often exclude some substitutes to which some customers might turn in the face of a price increase even if such substitutes provide alternatives for those customers. However, a group of products is too narrow to constitute a relevant market if competition from products outside that group is so ample that even the complete elimination of competition within the group would not significantly harm either direct customers or downstream consumers. The hypothetical monopolist test (*see* Section 4.1.1) is designed to ensure that candidate markets are not overly narrow in this respect.

The Agencies implement these principles of market definition flexibly when evaluating different possible candidate markets. Relevant antitrust markets defined according to the hypothetical monopolist test are not always intuitive and may not align with how industry members use the term "market."

Section 4.1 describes the principles that apply to product market definition, and gives guidance on how the Agencies most often apply those principles. Section 4.2 describes how the same principles apply to geographic market definition. Although discussed separately for simplicity of exposition, the principles described in Sections 4.1 and 4.2 are combined to define a relevant market, which has both a product and a geographic dimension. In particular, the hypothetical monopolist test is applied to a group of products together with a geographic region to determine a relevant market.

4.1 Product Market Definition. When a product sold by one merging firm (Product A) competes against one or more products sold by the other merging firm, the Agencies define a relevant product market around Product A to evaluate the importance of that competition. Such a relevant product market consists of a group of substitute products including Product A. Multiple relevant product markets may thus be identified.

4.1.1 The Hypothetical Monopolist Test. The Agencies employ the hypothetical monopolist test to evaluate whether groups of products in candidate markets are sufficiently broad to constitute relevant antitrust markets. The Agencies use the hypothetical monopolist test to identify a set of products that are reasonably interchangeable with a product sold by one of the merging firms.

The hypothetical monopolist test requires that a product market contain enough substitute products so that it could be subject to post-merger exercise of market power significantly exceeding that existing absent the merger. Specifically, the test requires that a hypothetical profit-maximizing firm, not subject to price regulation, that was the only present and future seller of those products ("hypothetical monopolist") likely would impose at least a small but significant and non-transitory increase in price ("SSNIP") on at least one product in the market, including at least one product sold by one of the merging firms. For the purpose of analyzing this issue, the terms of sale of products outside the candidate market are held constant. The SSNIP is employed solely as a methodological tool for performing the hypothetical monopolist test; it is not a tolerance level for price increases resulting from a merger.

Groups of products may satisfy the hypothetical monopolist test without including the full range of substitutes from which customers choose. The hypothetical monopolist test may identify a group of products as a relevant market even if customers would substitute significantly to products outside that group in response to a price increase.

> *Example 5:* Products A and B are being tested as a candidate market. Each sells for $100, has an incremental cost of $60, and sells 1200 units. For every dollar increase in the price of Product A, for any given price of Product B, Product A loses twenty units of sales to products outside the candidate market and ten units of sales to Product B, and likewise for Product B. Under these conditions, economic analysis shows that a hypothetical profit-maximizing monopolist controlling Products A and B would raise both of their prices by ten percent, to $110. Therefore, Products A and B satisfy the hypothetical monopolist test using a five percent SSNIP, and indeed for any SSNIP size up to ten percent. This is true even though two-thirds of the sales lost by one product when it raises its price are diverted to products outside the relevant market.

When applying the hypothetical monopolist test to define a market around a product offered by one of the merging firms, if the market includes a second product, the Agencies will normally also include a third product if that third product is a closer substitute for the first product than is the second product. The third product is a closer substitute if, in response to a SSNIP on the first product, greater revenues are diverted to the third product than to the second product.

> *Example 6:* In Example 5, suppose that half of the unit sales lost by Product A when it raises its price are diverted to Product C, which also has a price of $100, while one-third are diverted to Product B. Product C is a closer substitute for Product A than is Product B. Thus Product C will normally be included in the relevant market, even though Products A and B together satisfy the hypothetical monopolist test.

The hypothetical monopolist test ensures that markets are not defined too narrowly, but it does not lead to a single relevant market. The Agencies may evaluate a merger in any relevant market satisfying the test, guided by the overarching principle that the purpose of defining the market and measuring market shares is to illuminate the evaluation of competitive effects. Because the relative competitive significance of more distant substitutes is apt to be overstated by their share of sales, when the Agencies rely on market shares and concentration, they usually do so in the smallest relevant market satisfying the hypothetical monopolist test. . .

4.1.2 ***Benchmark Prices and SSNIP Size.*** The Agencies apply the SSNIP starting from prices that would likely prevail absent the merger. If prices are not likely to change absent the merger, these benchmark prices can reasonably be taken to be the prices prevailing prior to the merger.[5] If prices are likely to change absent the merger, e.g., because of innovation or entry, the Agencies may use anticipated future prices as the benchmark for the test. If prices might fall absent the merger due to the breakdown of pre-merger coordination, the Agencies may use those lower prices as the benchmark for the test. In some cases, the techniques employed by the Agencies to implement the hypothetical monopolist test focus on the difference in incentives between pre-merger firms and the hypothetical monopolist and do not require specifying the benchmark prices.

The SSNIP is intended to represent a "small but significant" increase in the prices charged by firms in the candidate market for the value they contribute to the products or services used by customers. This properly directs attention to the effects of price changes commensurate with those that might result from a significant lessening of competition caused by the merger. This methodology is used because normally it is possible to quantify "small but significant" adverse price effects on customers and analyze their likely reactions, not because price effects are more important than non-price effects.

The Agencies most often use a SSNIP of five percent of the price paid by customers for the products or services to which the merging firms contribute value. However, what constitutes a "small but significant" increase in price, commensurate with a significant loss of competition caused by the merger, depends upon the nature of the industry and the merging firms' positions in it, and the Agencies may accordingly use a price increase that is larger or smaller than five percent. Where explicit or implicit prices for the firms' specific contribution to value can be identified with reasonable clarity, the Agencies may base the SSNIP on those prices.

> *Example 8:* In a merger between two oil pipelines, the SSNIP would be based on the price charged for transporting the oil, not on the price of the oil itself. If pipelines buy the oil at one end and sell it at the other, the price charged for transporting the oil is implicit, equal to the difference between the price paid for oil at the input end and the price charged for oil at the output end. The relevant product sold by the pipelines is better described as

[5] Market definition for the evaluation of non-merger antitrust concerns such as monopolization or facilitating practices will differ in this respect if the effects resulting from the conduct of concern are already occurring at the time of evaluation.

"pipeline transportation of oil from point A to point B" than as "oil at point B."

Example 9: In a merger between two firms that install computers purchased from third parties, the SSNIP would be based on their fees, not on the price of installed computers. If these firms purchase the computers and charge their customers one package price, the implicit installation fee is equal to the package charge to customers less the price of the computers.

Example 10: In Example 9, suppose that the prices paid by the merging firms to purchase computers are opaque, but account for at least ninety-five percent of the prices they charge for installed computers, with profits or implicit fees making up five percent of those prices at most. A five percent SSNIP on the total price paid by customers would at least double those fees or profits. Even if that would be unprofitable for a hypothetical monopolist, a significant increase in fees might well be profitable. If the SSNIP is based on the total price paid by customers, a lower percentage will be used.

4.1.3 Implementing the Hypothetical Monopolist Test. The hypothetical monopolist's incentive to raise prices depends both on the extent to which customers would likely substitute away from the products in the candidate market in response to such a price increase and on the profit margins earned on those products. The profit margin on incremental units is the difference between price and incremental cost on those units. The Agencies often estimate incremental costs, for example using merging parties' documents or data the merging parties use to make business decisions. Incremental cost is measured over the change in output that would be caused by the price increase under consideration.

In considering customers' likely responses to higher prices, the Agencies take into account any reasonably available and reliable evidence, including, but not limited to:

- how customers have shifted purchases in the past in response to relative changes in price or other terms and conditions;
- information from buyers, including surveys, concerning how they would respond to price changes;
- the conduct of industry participants, notably:
- sellers' business decisions or business documents indicating sellers' informed beliefs concerning how customers would substitute among products in response to relative changes in price;
- industry participants' behavior in tracking and responding to price changes by some or all rivals;

- objective information about product characteristics and the costs and delays of switching products, especially switching from products in the candidate market to products outside the candidate market;
- the percentage of sales lost by one product in the candidate market, when its price alone rises, that is recaptured by other products in the candidate market, with a higher recapture percentage making a price increase more profitable for the hypothetical monopolist;
- evidence from other industry participants, such as sellers of complementary products;
- legal or regulatory requirements; and
- the influence of downstream competition faced by customers in their output markets.

When the necessary data are available, the Agencies also may consider a "critical loss analysis" to assess the extent to which it corroborates inferences drawn from the evidence noted above. Critical loss analysis asks whether imposing at least a SSNIP on one or more products in a candidate market would raise or lower the hypothetical monopolist's profits. While this "breakeven" analysis differs from the profit-maximizing analysis called for by the hypothetical monopolist test in Section 4.1.1, merging parties sometimes present this type of analysis to the Agencies. A price increase raises profits on sales made at the higher price, but this will be offset to the extent customers substitute away from products in the candidate market. Critical loss analysis compares the magnitude of these two offsetting effects resulting from the price increase. The "critical loss" is defined as the number of lost unit sales that would leave profits unchanged. The "predicted loss" is defined as the number of unit sales that the hypothetical monopolist is predicted to lose due to the price increase. The price increase raises the hypothetical monopolist's profits if the predicted loss is less than the critical loss.

The Agencies consider all of the evidence of customer substitution noted above in assessing the predicted loss. The Agencies require that estimates of the predicted loss be consistent with that evidence, including the pre-merger margins of products in the candidate market used to calculate the critical loss. Unless the firms are engaging in coordinated interaction (*see* Section 7), high pre-merger margins normally indicate that each firm's product individually faces demand that is not highly sensitive to price.[6] Higher pre-merger margins thus indicate a smaller predicted loss as well as a smaller critical loss. The higher the pre-merger margin, the smaller the recapture percentage necessary for the candidate market to satisfy the hypothetical monopolist test.

[6] While margins are important for implementing the hypothetical monopolist test, high margins are not in themselves of antitrust concern.

Even when the evidence necessary to perform the hypothetical monopolist test quantitatively is not available, the conceptual framework of the test provides a useful methodological tool for gathering and analyzing evidence pertinent to customer substitution and to market definition. The Agencies follow the hypothetical monopolist test to the extent possible given the available evidence, bearing in mind that the ultimate goal of market is to help determine whether the merger may substantially lessen competition.

4.1.4 Product Market Definition with Targeted Customers. If a hypothetical monopolist could profitably target a subset of customers for price increases, the Agencies may identify relevant markets defined around those targeted customers, to whom a hypothetical monopolist would profitably and separately impose at least a SSNIP. Markets to serve targeted customers are also known as price discrimination markets. In practice, the Agencies identify price discrimination markets only where they believe there is a realistic prospect of an adverse competitive effect on a group of targeted customers.

> *Example 11:* Glass containers have many uses. In response to a price increase for glass containers, some users would substitute substantially to plastic or metal containers, but baby food manufacturers would not. If a hypothetical monopolist could price separately and limit arbitrage, baby food manufacturers would be vulnerable to a targeted increase in the price of glass containers. The Agencies could define a distinct market for glass containers used to package baby food.

The Agencies also often consider markets for targeted customers when prices are individually negotiated and suppliers have information about customers that would allow a hypothetical monopolist to identify customers that are likely to pay a higher price for the relevant product. If prices are negotiated individually with customers, the hypothetical monopolist test may suggest relevant markets that are as narrow as individual customers (*see also* Section 6.2 on bargaining and auctions). Nonetheless, the Agencies often define markets for groups of targeted customers, i.e., by type of customer, rather than by individual customer. By so doing, the Agencies are able to rely on aggregated market shares that can be more helpful in predicting the competitive effects of the merger.

4.2 Geographic Market Definition. The arena of competition affected by the merger may be geographically bounded if geography limits some customers' willingness or ability to substitute to some products, or some suppliers' willingness or ability to serve some customers. Both supplier and customer locations can affect this. The Agencies apply the principles of market definition described here and in Section 4.1 to define a relevant market with a geographic dimension as well as a product dimension.

The scope of geographic markets often depends on transportation costs. Other factors such as language, regulation, tariff and non-tariff trade barriers, custom and familiarity, reputation, and service availability may impede long-distance or international transactions. The competitive significance of foreign firms may be assessed at various exchange rates, especially if exchange rates have fluctuated in the recent past.

In the absence of price discrimination based on customer location, the Agencies normally define geographic markets based on the locations of suppliers, as explained in subsection 4.2.1. In other cases, notably if price discrimination based on customer location is feasible as is often the case when delivered pricing is commonly used in the industry, the Agencies may define geographic markets based on the locations of customers, as explained in subsection 4.2.2.

4.2.1 Geographic Markets Based on the Locations of Suppliers. Geographic markets based on the locations of suppliers encompass the region from which sales are made. Geographic markets of this type often apply when customers receive goods or services at suppliers' locations. Competitors in the market are firms with relevant production, sales, or service facilities in that region. Some customers who buy from these firms may be located outside the boundaries of the geographic market.

The hypothetical monopolist test requires that a hypothetical profit-maximizing firm that was the only present or future producer of the relevant product(s) located in the region would impose at least a SSNIP from at least one location, including at least one location of one of the merging firms. In this exercise the terms of sale for all products produced elsewhere are held constant. A single firm may operate in a number of different geographic markets, even for a single product.

> *Example 12:* The merging parties both have manufacturing plants in City X. The relevant product is expensive to transport and suppliers price their products for pickup at their locations. Rival plants are some distance away in City Y. A hypothetical monopolist controlling all plants in City X could profitably impose a SSNIP at these plants. Competition from more distant plants would not defeat the price increase because supplies coming from more distant plants require expensive transportation. The relevant geographic market is defined around the plants in City X.

When the geographic market is defined based on supplier locations, sales made by suppliers located in the geographic market are counted, regardless of the location of the customer making the purchase.

In considering likely reactions of customers to price increases for the relevant product(s) imposed in a candidate geographic market, the Agencies consider any reasonably available and reliable evidence, including:

- how customers have shifted purchases in the past between different geographic locations in response to relative changes in price or other terms and conditions;

- the cost and difficulty of transporting the product (or the cost and difficulty of a customer traveling to a seller's location), in relation to its price;
- whether suppliers need a presence near customers to provide service or support;
- evidence on whether sellers base business decisions on the prospect of customers switching between geographic locations in response to relative changes in price or other competitive variables;
- the costs and delays of switching from suppliers in the candidate geographic market to suppliers outside the candidate geographic market; and
- the influence of downstream competition faced by customers in their output markets.

4.2.2 Geographic Markets Based on the Locations of Customers. When the hypothetical monopolist could discriminate based on customer location, the Agencies may define geographic markets based on the locations of targeted customers.[7] Geographic markets of this type often apply when suppliers deliver their products or services to customers' locations. Geographic markets of this type encompass the region into which sales are made. Competitors in the market are firms that sell to customers in the specified region. Some suppliers that sell into the relevant market may be located outside the boundaries of the geographic market.

The hypothetical monopolist test requires that a hypothetical profit-maximizing firm that was the only present or future seller of the relevant product(s) to customers in the region would impose at least a SSNIP on some customers in that region. A region forms a relevant geographic market if this price increase would not be defeated by substitution away from the relevant product or by arbitrage, e.g., customers in the region travelling outside it to purchase the relevant product. In this exercise, the terms of sale for products sold to all customers outside the region are held constant.

Example 13: Customers require local sales and support. Suppliers have sales and service operations in many geographic areas and can discriminate based on customer location. The geographic market can be defined around the locations of customers.

Example 14: Each merging firm has a single manufacturing plant and delivers the relevant product to customers in City X and in City Y. The relevant product is expensive to transport. The merging firms' plants are by far the closest to City X, but

[7] For customers operating in multiple locations, only those customer locations within the targeted zone are included in the market.

> no closer to City Y than are numerous rival plants. This fact pattern suggests that customers in City X may be harmed by the merger even if customers in City Y are not. For that reason, the Agencies consider a relevant geographic market defined around customers in City X. Such a market could be defined even if the region around the merging firms' plants would not be a relevant geographic market defined based on the location of sellers because a hypothetical monopolist controlling all plants in that region would find a SSNIP imposed on all of its customers unprofitable due to the loss of sales to customers in City Y.

When the geographic market is defined based on customer locations, sales made to those customers are counted, regardless of the location of the supplier making those sales.

> *Example 15:* Customers in the United States must use products approved by U.S. regulators. Foreign customers use products not approved by U.S. regulators. The relevant product market consists of products approved by U.S. regulators. The geographic market is defined around U.S. customers. Any sales made to U.S. customers by foreign suppliers are included in the market, and those foreign suppliers are participants in the U.S. market even though located outside it. . . .

5. Market Participants, Market Shares, and Market Concentration . . . Market shares can directly influence firms' competitive incentives. For example, if a price reduction to gain new customers would also apply to a firm's existing customers, a firm with a large market share may be more reluctant to implement a price reduction than one with a small share. Likewise, a firm with a large market share may not feel pressure to reduce price even if a smaller rival does. Market shares also can reflect firms' capabilities. For example, a firm with a large market share may be able to expand output rapidly by a larger absolute amount than can a small firm. Similarly, a large market share tends to indicate low costs, an attractive product, or both.

5.1 Market Participants. All firms that currently earn revenues in the relevant market are considered market participants. Vertically integrated firms are also included to the extent that their inclusion accurately reflects their competitive significance. Firms not currently earning revenues in the relevant market, but that have committed to entering the market in the near future, are also considered market participants.

Firms that are not current producers in a relevant market, but that would very likely provide rapid supply responses with direct competitive impact in the event of a SSNIP, without incurring significant sunk costs, are also considered market participants. These firms are termed "rapid entrants." Sunk costs are entry or exit costs that cannot be recovered outside the relevant market. Entry that would take place more slowly in response to adverse competitive effects, or that requires firms to incur significant sunk costs, is considered in Section 9.

Firms that produce the relevant product but do not sell it in the relevant geographic market may be rapid entrants. Other things equal, such firms are most likely to be rapid entrants if they are close to the geographic market.

> *Example 16:* Farm A grows tomatoes halfway between Cities X and Y. Currently, it ships its tomatoes to City X because prices there are two percent higher. Previously it has varied the destination of its shipments in response to small price variations. Farm A would likely be a rapid entrant participant in a market for tomatoes in City Y.

> *Example 17:* Firm B has bid multiple times to supply milk to School District S, and actually supplies milk to schools in some adjacent areas. It has never won a bid in School District S, but is well qualified to serve that district and has often nearly won. Firm B would be counted as a rapid entrant in a market for school milk in School District S.

More generally, if the relevant market is defined around targeted customers, firms that produce relevant products but do not sell them to those customers may be rapid entrants if they can easily and rapidly begin selling to the targeted customers.

Firms that clearly possess the necessary assets to supply into the relevant market rapidly may also be rapid entrants. In markets for relatively homogeneous goods where a supplier's ability to compete depends predominantly on its costs and its capacity, and not on other factors such as experience or reputation in the relevant market, a supplier with efficient idle capacity, or readily available "swing" capacity currently used in adjacent markets that can easily and profitably be shifted to serve the relevant market, may be a rapid entrant.[8] However, idle capacity may be inefficient, and capacity used in adjacent markets may not be available, so a firm's possession of idle or swing capacity alone does not make that firm a rapid entrant.

5.2 Market Shares. The Agencies normally calculate market shares for all firms that currently produce products in the relevant market, subject to the availability of data. The Agencies also calculate market shares for other market participants if this can be done to reliably reflect their competitive significance.

Market concentration and market share data are normally based on historical evidence. However, recent or ongoing changes in market conditions may indicate that the current market share of a particular firm either understates or overstates the firm's future competitive

---

[8] If this type of supply side substitution is nearly universal among the firms selling one or more of a group of products, the Agencies may use an aggregate description of markets for those products as a matter of convenience.

significance. The Agencies consider reasonably predictable effects of recent or ongoing changes in market conditions when calculating and interpreting market share data. For example, if a new technology that is important to long-term competitive viability is available to other firms in the market, but is not available to a particular firm, the Agencies may conclude that that firm's historical market share overstates its future competitive significance. The Agencies may project historical market shares into the foreseeable future when this can be done reliably.

The Agencies measure market shares based on the best available indicator of firms' future competitive significance in the relevant market. This may depend upon the type of competitive effect being considered, and on the availability of data. Typically, annual data are used, but where individual transactions are large and infrequent so annual data may be unrepresentative, the Agencies may measure market shares over a longer period of time.

In most contexts, the Agencies measure each firm's market share based on its actual or projected revenues in the relevant market. Revenues in the relevant market tend to be the best measure of attractiveness to customers, since they reflect the real-world ability of firms to surmount all of the obstacles necessary to offer products on terms and conditions that are attractive to customers. In cases where one unit of a low-priced product can substitute for one unit of a higher-priced product, unit sales may measure competitive significance better than revenues. For example, a new, much less expensive product may have great competitive significance if it substantially erodes the revenues earned by older, higher-priced products, even if it earns relatively few revenues. In cases where customers sign long-term contracts, face switching costs, or tend to re-evaluate their suppliers only occasionally, revenues earned from recently acquired customers may better reflect the competitive significance of suppliers than do total revenues.

In markets for homogeneous products, a firm's competitive significance may derive principally from its ability and incentive to rapidly expand production in the relevant market in response to a price increase or output reduction by others in that market. As a result, a firm's competitive significance may depend upon its level of readily available capacity to serve the relevant market if that capacity is efficient enough to make such expansion profitable. In such markets, capacities or reserves may better reflect the future competitive significance of suppliers than revenues, and the Agencies may calculate market shares using those measures. Market participants that are not current producers may then be assigned positive market shares, but only if a measure of their competitive significance properly comparable to that of current producers is available. When market shares are measured based on firms' readily available capacities, the Agencies do not include capacity that is committed or so profitably employed outside the relevant market, or so high-cost, that it would not likely be used to respond to a SSNIP in the relevant market.

> *Example 18:* The geographic market is defined around customers in the United States. Firm X produces the relevant product outside the United States, and most of its sales are made to customers outside the United States. In most contexts, Firm X's market share will be based on its sales to U.S. customers, not its total sales or total capacity. However, if the relevant product is homogeneous, and if Firm X would significantly expand sales to U.S. customers rapidly and without incurring significant sunk costs in response to a SSNIP, the Agencies may base Firm X's market share on its readily available capacity to serve U.S. customers.

When the Agencies define markets serving targeted customers, these same principles are used to measure market shares, as they apply to those customers. In most contexts, each firm's market share is based on its actual or projected revenues from the targeted customers. However, the Agencies may instead measure market shares based on revenues from a broader group of customers if doing so would more accurately reflect the competitive significance of different suppliers in the relevant market. Revenues earned from a broader group of customers may also be used when better data are thereby available.

NOTE ON THE U.S. MARKET DEFINITION GUIDELINES

To simplify, the Guidelines conclude that a proposed market is sufficiently broad if an absolute monopolist of the posited market would likely find it profit-maximizing to impose a nontransitory price increase of at least 5%, though other percentages can be used as the SSNIP benchmark. Market definition requires defining both the product market and the geographic market. (For example, even if we know the relevant product market is cellophane, we have to determine whether it is a global, national, or subnational cellophane market.) To assess this issue, one must assess *buyer* substitution (the extent to which buyers would turn to other products or regions in response to a price increase) and profit margins (the amount of profits the firm would lose from buyer substitution compared to the profits it would gain from the price increase). The fact that *some* buyer substitution (to other products or regions) occurs is not enough to conclude the posited market should be broadened. If a hypothetical monopolist in the posited market would find it profit-maximizing to increase prices by at least 5%, then the market definition is sufficiently broad. If not, then the market definition must be broadened to include the closest products or regions to which buyers substitute, until we get a posited product and geographic market that satisfies the test.

The Guidelines make clear that: "The hypothetical monopolist test ensures that markets are not defined too narrowly, but it does not lead to a single relevant market." Instead, agency analysis can use "any relevant market satisfying the test, guided by the overarching principle that the purpose of defining the market and measuring market shares is to illuminate the evaluation of competitive effects." For example, suppose that a monopolist in town A would likely increase prices by 10% before being constrained by suppliers in town B, but a monopolist in both towns A and B would likely increase prices by 20% before being constrained by suppliers outside of A or B. In assessing a merger between firms in town A, then town A would be the relevant geographic market. But in assessing a merger between firms in town A and town B, then A-B would be the relevant geographic market because here the merger could produce a significant price increase even though a merger in an even smaller market could also produce a significant price increase. There is no single, inherently correct, market definition; it all depends on the anticompetitive effects theory that the market definition is trying to illuminate.

Even more counterintuitively, the proper market definition may not run equally in both directions if either the substitution rates or baseline profit margins differ. For example, suppose a monopolist in A would profitably raise prices by 6% given substitution to B, but a monopolist in B could profitably raise prices by only 4% given substitution to A. Then in assessing conduct in A, the proper market definition is A, but in assessing conduct in B, the proper market definition is A-B combined. Again, the reason is that the focus is functional, on the degree of actual power to raise prices that might be created by anticompetitive conduct or mergers.

The Guidelines also clarify that the focus is on the price increase a hypothetical monopolist would likely impose. For example, it could well be that a hypothetical monopolist in a posited market would find a price increase of 5% unprofitable but would find a price increase of 20% profitable. (This might be true if demand is elastic for a 5% price increase because it affects the decisions of relatively elastic buyers, but for price increases greater than 5%, the demand elasticity declines because the remaining buyers have inelastic demand.) In that case, the posited market is valid, even though a 5% price increase is unprofitable, because a 20% price increase would profitably be imposed. This is why the agencies focus on the price increases that would likely be profitable, rather than on "critical loss" analysis of the profitability of a 5% price increase.

Supply substitution is taken into account not in market definition, but rather in defining which firms and capacity are in that defined market. Such firms are deemed to include not only firms that already operate in the posited market, but also firms who operate in another market *if* they would likely enter the posited market rapidly without incurring significant sunk costs in response to any SSNIP. Thus, a similar SSNIP test is used to assess supply substitution.

One might wonder why supply substitution is not simply deemed part of market definition. After all, if the practical import of supply substitution considerations is that sales of product B are being included in market A, aren't the market shares the same as if we defined the market to include A and B? The answer is "no" if only some of the production of B could be easily switched to making A. Further, even if the market share numbers would be the same, the competitive analysis of those share numbers might differ depending on the market definition.

Suppose, for example, the relevant anticompetitive concern was whether a merger would increase the risk of oligopolistic coordination by leaving product market A with three firms, but a fourth firm that makes product B could easily switch to making product A. Then, all four firms should be deemed part of product market A for purposes of considering whether four such firms are likely to oligopolistically coordinate. But one should not dismiss that likelihood on the ground that a product market that includes both A and B is not sufficiently homogeneous to allow such coordination to succeed; the reason is that the inability of buyers to reasonably interchange A and B means that coordination on A will be enough.

Likewise, suppose the anticompetitive concern was instead that a defendant with a very high share of product market A was foreclosing rivals by requiring buyers to buy all their product A from the defendant. Then one should take into account the fact that makers of product B can easily switch to make product A in order to determine whether the defendant has market power in market A. But the relevant *foreclosure* share is not undermined if the defendant allows buyers to buy product B from others because buyers (by definition) do not find product B reasonably interchangeable for A.

Because the Guidelines are focused on whether proposed mergers would worsen market performance, rather than on whether monopoly or market power already exists, the Guidelines "apply the SSNIP starting from prices that would likely prevail absent the merger," which usually "can reasonably be taken to be the prices prevailing prior to the merger." However, in footnote 5, the Guidelines acknowledge that this approach is inappropriate to assess "monopolization or facilitating practices" where monopoly power or anticompetitive effects already exist. Thus, the Guidelines reject the "Cellophane fallacy" of relying on substitution rates at price levels that already reflect monopoly power. In such a case, one must instead ask whether a hypothetical monopolist could impose a SSNIP above a "competitive price" baseline. As discussed in the notes after the *du Pont* case, data on that issue cannot be directly observed in any case where a firm or firms are already exercising market power. In such cases, the lack of direct data on the hypothetical monopolist issue means that issue must be addressed using factors that provide indirect evidence on the issue. However, the Guidelines stress that even when data "to perform the hypothetical monopolist test quantitatively is not available, the conceptual framework of the test provides a useful methodological tool for gathering and analyzing evidence pertinent to customer substitution and to market definition."

Is Market Definition Necessary?

The normal rationale for relying on market share is that market power is difficult to measure directly and that market share data coupled with evidence of significant barriers to entry provides a reasonable proxy for market power. But this rationale is undermined by three considerations.

(1) If we think it is difficult to determine whether an *actual* alleged monopolist can raise prices significantly over competitive levels, it is unclear why we would think it easier to calculate market shares that require us to define a market by determining whether a *hypothetical* monopolist could raise prices significantly above competitive levels. For some market definitions, the answer might be that it is obvious that no reasonable substitute exists and thus obvious that a hypothetical monopolist would thus have significant pricing discretion. But the hypothetical monopolist test arguably provides no help in any monopolization case where there is a genuine conflict about the market definition.

(2) Market share is a fairly unreliable proxy for market power. If a firm has 75% of a market, but rivals would expand immediately to make up for any output restriction, the firm has no pricing discretion. If a firm has 18% of a market, but rivals are completely unable to expand or enter, the firm has substantial pricing discretion. Thus, we at least also need to know the rival supply elasticity.

(3) Market share conclusions are distorted by the all-or-nothing judgments used to define markets. Suppose, for example, that substitution to other flexible packaging materials means a cellophane monopolist would maximize profits by increasing prices by 4% over competitive levels. Then, under the Guidelines, flexible packaging materials would be included in the product market definition, producing a market share of 18%. But 18% understates du Pont's market power compared to the power du Pont would have if the other 82% were really perfect substitutes, because in the latter case du Pont could not increase prices by even 1%.

Likewise, suppose instead that there is slightly less substitution to flexible packaging materials, so that a cellophane monopolist would maximize profits by increasing prices by 6% over competitive levels. Then, under the Guidelines, flexible packaging materials would be excluded from the product market, producing a market share of 75%. But 75% overstates du Pont's market power compared to what it would be if there were no flexible materials to turn to no matter how much du Pont raised prices.

Accordingly, in these cases the real answer seems to be neither 18% and 75%, but something in between. More precisely, to assess the degree of market power we really need to know the marketwide demand elasticity, which will reflect the precise degree of switching to possible substitutes, and not make categorical judgments about whether that demand elasticity will lead to prices increases that are higher or lower than some SSNIP threshold.

Varying the Weight Given to Market Shares. Some argue that courts should respond to these problems by adjusting the weight they attach to market shares based on both (1) judgments about the likely expandability of rivals and (2) awareness about any judgment calls made in defining the market. However, this approach would seem to undermine any apparent precision from market share data and make cases turn really on intuitive judgments. Further, we would need to measure the rival supply elasticity and the marketwide demand elasticity to really determine the degree of market power suggested by any market shares. And if we had that information for any posited market, we could calculate the degree of such pricing discretion from market shares without ever resolving whether the posited market was in some abstract sense "correct." Defining the market narrowly would increase the market share, but that would not matter because a narrow definition would also increase the market demand elasticity (by increasing the likelihood of demand substitution out of the market) and increase rival supply elasticity (by making it more likely other firms would enter into the market to expand supply).[39] Likewise, a broad market definition would have the offsetting effect of lowering market demand elasticity and rival supply elasticity. As long as one takes into account that the market definition alters not only market share, but also market demand elasticity and rival supply elasticity, then one should reach the same conclusion no matter what market definition one uses.

Moreover, there seems to be little reason to think we are generally more likely to have data on rival supply elasticity and the marketwide demand elasticity than on more direct measures of defendant pricing discretion, such as the degree to which defendant prices exceed their costs or competitive levels, defendant's firm-specific demand elasticity, or defendant behavior that makes economic sense only if market power exists. We might thus be better off focusing on those direct measures. As we will see in Chapter 7, in other portions of the Merger Guidelines, the U.S. agencies stress that in merger analysis they often focus on direct measures of anticompetitive effects rather than on market definition and inferences from market shares.

Other Reasons Why Market Shares Might Have Economic Significance. Market shares provide such an imperfect proxy for market power and pricing discretion that one might wonder why market shares are used at all.[40] However, market shares might have economic significance for other reasons.[41] The fact that one firm has a dominant share of a market can help indicate whether that firm is likely to be able to act as a unitary actor who either can exploit collective action problems among buyers or enter into a collusive agreement with a powerful buyer that exploits buyers further downstream. Market shares can also help indicate whether a firm is likely to be able to foreclose enough of the

---

[39] *See* Landes & Posner, *supra* note 12, at 962–63. Recall that $\varepsilon_{dom} = \varepsilon_{mkt}/S + \varepsilon_{rivsupp}(1 - S)/S$. *See supra* note 29. Thus, anything that increases or decreases S in parallel with ε_{mkt} and $\varepsilon_{rivsupp}$ will have offsetting effects. Further, this equation holds true no matter what market definition is used as long as one takes into account that S, ε_{mkt} and $\varepsilon_{rivsupp}$ are all functions of how the market is defined.

[40] Louis Kaplow, *Why (Ever) Define Markets?*, 124 HARVARD LAW REVIEW 437 (2010).

[41] *See* Elhauge, *supra* note 18, at 334–337.

market to create anticompetitive effects, to have incentives to invest in such foreclosure, and/or whether it is likely to have efficiency justifications for foreclosing such a large share of the market. This might help explain why high market shares are used in assessing exclusionary conduct in Chapters 3 and 4.

Further, high market shares held by a few firms can help indicate whether a market has few enough firms to make possible oligopolistic coordination on prices. This might explain why market shares are used when considering oligopolistic coordination in Chapters 6 and 7.

Technical Methods Used in Market Definition

Critical Elasticity of Demand. A popular method of defining markets involves calculating a critical elasticity of demand. This is the highest marketwide elasticity that would make it profitable for a hypothetical monopolist to raise prices by the SSNIP amount of 5% under the U.S. guidelines. If this critical elasticity is higher than the actual elasticity of demand for the posited market, then that supports the market definition, for it suggests a monopolist could raise prices by the SSNIP amount over competitive prices. If the critical elasticity is lower than actual elasticity, then that cuts against the market definition.

As with other methods, the difficulties concern the right baselines to use when conducting such an analysis, here most importantly at what price levels to measure the critical and actual elasticities. The typical approach is to go where the data is: using current prices and profit margins as the baseline from which to consider whether a 5% price increase would be profitable to a hypothetical monopolist given the sales it would lose. The higher current profit margins are, the smaller the critical elasticity will be because a hypothetical monopolist would lose more profits from any lost sales resulting from a given price increase, making rejection of the posited market definition more likely because it is less likely that the current elasticity would be below that figure.[42]

This approach raises several conceptual issues. The first is that the more a market already reflects an anticompetitive market structure, the higher current prices and profit margins will be, which will both lower

[42] To define this mathematically, let m be the current profit margin = (P – MC)/P, which is .5 if prices are twice marginal costs and .75 if prices are 4 times marginal costs. Let t be the SSNIP test percentage used, which is .05 if the test is 5%. Then, assuming a linear demand curve and constant marginal costs, it can be shown that a hypothetical monopolist could increase prices by t without losing profits if the current demand elasticity is at least $1/(m + t)$ and that a price increase of t or greater would be profit-maximizing for the hypothetical monopolist if the current demand elasticity is $1/(m + 2t)$ or greater. Thus, if the current profit margin is 50% and the test percentage is 5%, the critical demand elasticity would be 1/.55 = 1.82 if the question is whether a monopolist could profitably impose a 5% price increase and 1/.6 = 1.67 if the question is whether a profit-maximizing monopolist would impose a price increase of at least 5%. If instead the current profit margin is 75%, then the critical demand elasticity would be 1/.8 = 1.25 if the question is whether a 5% increase would be profitable and 1/.85 = 1.18 if the question is whether a profit-maximizing monopolist would impose at least a 5% increase. Thus, the higher current profit margins, the lower the critical demand elasticity, and the harder it will be to show that current elasticity is low enough to support the market definition under this approach.

the calculated critical elasticity of demand and make it likely that prices have already been raised until demand is elastic. For example, if a monopolist already dominates a market, its profit margins will be high, and it will already be pricing at a monopoly price, which by definition is its profit-maximizing price, thus making any further price increase unprofitable. Literal application of such a method would thus indicate that a monopoly market could never be defined. More generally, high profit margins mean a high Lerner Index and likely market power, which indicates the more narrow market is meaningful, yet under this test high profit margins are used to define the market more broadly and to infer a likely absence of market power.

The U.S. guidelines indicate that competitive price levels should be used as the baseline instead of prevailing prices if the prevailing prices have already been increased by market power or coordination. But because the very reason to do market definition analysis is to help determine whether market power or coordination seems likely, it seems circular to presume that prevailing prices either do or do not reflect such market power or coordination. What we really want to know as a policy matter is what the profit margin and demand elasticity would be at competitive price levels and whether (given that competitive margin and elasticity) a hypothetical monopolist could profitably impose a 5–10% increase above that competitive level. If so, then there is some functional reason to worry about market power or coordination on that market, otherwise not. But we won't have the data on competitive price levels or on what margins or elasticity would be at such levels unless we assume that current prices are competitive, and that assumption assumes away precisely the possibility that is being investigated, which is whether the market is narrow enough that market power or coordination is plausible. Thus critical demand elasticities calculated at current prices will be too low and define markets too narrowly to the extent that markets are not already competitive.

The second issue is that marginal costs are typically unavailable, so that critical demand elasticities are often calculated using *average* profit margins rather than the *marginal* profit margin associated with the final units of output. Average profit margins will reflect the difference between prices and the average variable cost of producing all units, which is the average total cost minus any fixed costs of being in business. But if (as typical) marginal costs increase with increasing output, then marginal costs will likely be higher than average variable costs, meaning that the marginal profit margin will be lower. Using the average profit margin rather than the true marginal profit margin thus likely inflates the profits that a hypothetical monopolist would lose by imposing a 5–10% price increase, and thus makes the critical elasticity of demand lower than it should be. Thus critical demand elasticities calculated using average profit margins will tend to be too low and define markets too narrowly.

The third issue is that critical demand elasticity depends heavily on what assumption one makes about the shape of the demand curve. If one assumes a linear demand curve rather than constant elasticity, then the critical elasticity of demand will be much lower.[43] Indeed, at a profit margin of 50% this seemingly innocuous assumption about the shape of the demand curve can alter the critical elasticity calculated by over 20%.[44] Furthermore, elasticity will sometimes decrease with higher prices because the price increase will drive out marginal customers and leave only customers with very inelastic demand. If so, using the elasticity of demand at current prices will tend to understate the ability of a hypothetical monopolist to profitably impose a 5–10% price increase and thus will tend to make market definition too narrow. Unfortunately, there will often be little information on what the demand curve would look like at prices and output different from the ones that prevailed recently.

Finally, the critical elasticity one calculates turns out to vary depending on whether the question asked is (a) whether a hypothetical monopolist *could* profitably impose a 5–10% price increase, or instead (b) whether a profit-maximizing hypothetical monopolist *would* impose at least a 5–10% price increase. The first asks whether such a price increase would be at least as profitable as the current price. The second asks whether such a price increase would also be more profitable than price increases of less than 5–10%. Since the latter standard is more demanding, it results in a lower critical elasticity and thus leads to more narrow market definitions than the former standard. For example, if the current profit margin is 50%, the latter standard lowers the critical elasticity by 8% under an assumption of linear demand.[45] The U.S. guidelines adopt the latter standard, asking whether a hypothetical "profit-maximizing" monopolist "likely would impose at least" a SSNIP.

Should the standard be whether a hypothetical monopolist could or would impose the relevant price increase? Is there any basis for deciding

---

[43] It might seem that since the slope of a linear demand curve is constant, it must have constant elasticity. But this is not so because the slope (or dQ/dP) measures the extent to which the *amount* of quantity changes in response to a change in the *amount* of price. Elasticity, in contrast, measures the *percentage* change in quantity over the *percentage* change in price, or (dQ/Q)/(dP/P), which is the same as the slope times P/Q. Thus, a linear demand curve is more elastic as Q is small in relation to P (the lefthand side of a linear demand curve) and less elastic as Q is large in relation to P (the righthand side of a linear demand curve). The intuitive way to see this is that, with a constant slope, a $1 price increase will always produce a constant reduction in the *amount* of Q, and this must produce a higher *percentage* reduction in Q as Q gets smaller and a lower *percentage* increase in P as P gets larger, so that the ratio of those percentages will get larger as Q gets smaller and P larger. A demand curve with constant elasticity would have to be a curve that is steep on the lefthand side (where Q is small in relation to P) and flatter on the righthand side (where Q is large in relation to P).

[44] If elasticity is constant, the critical elasticity that would make a price increase of at least t profit-maximizing is $(1 + t)/(m + t)$ whereas it is $1/(m + 2t)$ if demand is linear. Assuming $t = .10$ and the profit margin is 50%, then the critical elasticity is $1.1/.6 = 1.83$ under an assumption of constant elasticity and $1/.7 = 1.43$ under an assumption of linear demand. Both results assume constant marginal costs.

[45] *See supra* note 42.

this issue other than a general policy judgment about how aggressive one wants to make antitrust enforcement? Is this complicated approach to defining markets, in order to calculate a market share that in turn is used to imperfectly infer market power, really any easier or less problematic than directly estimating market power?

Critical Sales Loss. The critical sales loss is the percentage of sales a hypothetical monopolist would have to lose to make a SSNIP unprofitable. If a court concludes that a 5% price increase would cause a higher percentage of sales to switch to other products or areas, then that supports a broader market definition. If a lower percentage would switch, then that supports the more narrow market definition.

This approach raises the four issues noted above for critical elasticities. (1) If prices already reflect market power, then the current price baseline and current profit margin will be inflated. This will misleadingly lower the critical sales loss figure calculated as it inflates profit margins and the predicted percentage of sales that would switch in response to further price increases.[46] (2) Using average rather than marginal profit margins will likewise likely inflate profit margins and thus misleadingly lower the critical sales loss figure. (3) The critical sales loss calculated can turn on the shape of the demand curve assumed, and in any event conclusions about how many sales will be lost with a given price increase will depend on assumptions about the demand curve. (4) The critical sales loss figure calculated will be higher if the question asked is whether the sales loss would make the entire price increase unprofitable than if the question asked is whether the sales loss would suffice to make a lower price increase more profitable.

In addition to these problems, the use of critical sales loss figures can raise a fifth difficulty because, as the U.S. guidelines note, the "breakeven" approach used by critical loss analysis differs from the profit-maximizing approach used by the hypothetical monopolist test. A 5% price increase might produce a critical sales loss figure that is lower than the lost sales that would be produced by such a price increase, yet an even larger price increase (like 25%) might produce a critical sales loss figure that is higher than the lost sales from the larger price increase. That is, a 5% price increase might be unprofitable even though a 25% price increase would be. In that case, a hypothetical monopolist would raise prices by 25%, which would justify the more narrow market definition, and yet the critical sales loss figure calculated for a 5% price increase would indicate the market definition should be broadened.

Assumptions About Effect of Price Increase on Other Products. The current U.S. guidelines ask whether a hypothetical

---

[46] Mathematically, it can be shown that the critical sales loss that would prevent a profit-maximizing monopolist from raising prices by at least t equals $t/(m + 2t)$ if demand is linear but is different under different demand assumptions. The critical sales loss that would make a price increase of t actually lose profits equals $t/(m + t)$ for any demand curve. Again, all these results assume constant marginal costs.

monopolist would likely impose at least a 5% price increase despite substitution to other products or locations *if* one assumes that "the terms of sale of products outside the candidate market are held constant." But in fact, if a price increase leads buyers to switch to other products or locations, that will likely drive up the price of those substitutes to some extent, which will reduce the amount of substitution. Assuming away this effect on substitute prices thus tends to make market definition broader than it otherwise would be.

Summary. While calculations of critical elasticities and critical sales losses may seem merely technical, in fact the methods for their calculation implicate important underlying issues about antitrust policy. Failure to be attentive to those issues can obscure the policy choices being made or produce misleading results in particular cases.

4. AFTERMARKETS

Eastman Kodak v. Image Technical Servs.

504 U.S. 451 (1992).

■ JUSTICE BLACKMUN delivered the opinion of the Court. . . .

The principal issue here is whether a defendant's lack of market power in the primary equipment market precludes—as a matter of law—the possibility of market power in derivative aftermarkets.

Petitioner Eastman Kodak Company manufactures and sells photocopiers and micrographic equipment. Kodak also sells service and replacement parts for its equipment. Respondents are 18 independent service organizations (ISO's) that in the early 1980's began servicing Kodak copying and micrographic equipment. Kodak subsequently adopted policies to limit the availability of parts to ISO's and to make it more difficult for ISO's to compete with Kodak in servicing Kodak equipment. . . . [Respondents conceded Kodak lacked market power in the equipment market, but argued that Kodak had market power in the aftermarket of parts for Kodak equipment.]

Because this case comes to us on petitioner Kodak's motion for summary judgment, "[t]he evidence of [respondents] is to be believed, and all justifiable inferences are to be drawn in [their] favor." . . . Kodak parts are not compatible with other manufacturers' equipment, and vice versa. Kodak equipment, although expensive when new, has little resale value.

Kodak provides service and parts for its machines to its customers. It produces some of the parts itself; the rest are made to order for Kodak by independent original-equipment manufacturers (OEM's). Kodak does not sell a complete system of original equipment, lifetime service, and lifetime parts for a single price. Instead, Kodak provides service after the initial warranty period either through annual service contracts, which include all necessary parts, or on a per-call basis. It charges, through negotiations and bidding, different prices for equipment, service, and parts for different customers. Kodak provides 80% to 95% of the service for Kodak machines. . . .

In 1985 and 1986, Kodak implemented a policy of selling replacement parts for micrographic and copying machines only to buyers of Kodak equipment who use Kodak service or repair their own machines. . . . Kodak intended, through these policies, to make it more difficult for ISOs to sell service for Kodak machines. It succeeded. ISOs were unable to obtain parts from reliable sources, and many were forced out of business, while others lost substantial revenue. Customers were forced to switch to Kodak service even though they preferred ISO service. . . . [The Court concluded this constituted a tying agreement].

Having found sufficient evidence of a tying arrangement, we consider the other necessary feature of an illegal tying arrangement: appreciable economic power in the tying market. Market power is the power "to force a purchaser to do something that he would not do in a competitive market." *Jefferson Parish*. It has been defined as "the ability of a single seller to raise price and restrict output." *Fortner I*. The existence of such power ordinarily is inferred from the seller's possession of a predominant share of the market. *Jefferson Parish; Grinnell; Times-Picayune*.

Respondents contend that Kodak has more than sufficient power in the parts market to force unwanted purchases of the tied market, service. Respondents provide evidence that certain parts are available exclusively through Kodak. Respondents also assert that Kodak has control over the availability of parts it does not manufacture. According to respondents' evidence, Kodak has prohibited independent manufacturers from selling Kodak parts to ISOs, pressured Kodak equipment owners and independent parts distributors to deny ISOs the purchase of Kodak parts, and taken steps to restrict the availability of used machines.

Respondents also allege that Kodak's control over the parts market has excluded service competition, boosted service prices, and forced unwilling consumption of Kodak service. Respondents offer evidence that consumers have switched to Kodak service even though they preferred ISO service, that Kodak service was of higher price and lower quality than the preferred ISO service, and that ISOs were driven out of business by Kodak's policies. Under our prior precedents, this evidence would be sufficient to entitle respondents to a trial on their claim of market power.

Kodak counters that even if it concedes monopoly *share* of the relevant parts market, it cannot actually exercise the necessary market *power* for a Sherman Act violation. This is so, according to Kodak, because competition exists in the equipment market. Kodak argues that it could not have the ability to raise prices of service and parts above the level that would be charged in a competitive market because any increase in profits from a higher price in the aftermarkets at least would be offset by a corresponding loss in profits from lower equipment sales as consumers began purchasing equipment with more attractive service costs.

Kodak does not present any actual data on the equipment, service, or parts markets. Instead, it urges the adoption of a substantive legal rule that "equipment competition precludes any finding of monopoly power in derivative aftermarkets." . . . .

Legal presumptions that rest on formalistic distinctions rather than actual market realities are generally disfavored in antitrust law. This Court has preferred to resolve antitrust claims on a case-by-case basis, focusing on the "particular facts disclosed by the record." *Maple Flooring*. In determining the existence of market power, and specifically the "responsiveness of the sales of one product to price changes of the other," *du Pont*, this Court has examined closely the economic reality of the market at issue.

Kodak contends that there is no need to examine the facts when the issue is market power in the aftermarkets. A legal presumption against a finding of market power is warranted in this situation, according to Kodak, because the existence of market power in the service and parts markets absent power in the equipment market "simply makes no economic sense," and the absence of a legal presumption would deter procompetitive behavior. . . .

The extent to which one market prevents exploitation of another market depends on the extent to which consumers will change their consumption of one product in response to a price change in another, i.e., the "cross-elasticity of demand." Kodak's proposed rule rests on a factual assumption about the cross-elasticity of demand in the equipment and aftermarkets: "If Kodak raised its parts or service prices above competitive levels, potential customers would simply stop buying Kodak equipment. Perhaps Kodak would be able to increase short term profits through such a strategy, but at a devastating cost to its long term interests." Kodak argues that the Court should accept, as a matter of law, this "basic economic reality," that competition in the equipment market necessarily prevents market power in the aftermarkets.[17]

Even if Kodak could not raise the price of service and parts one cent without losing equipment sales, that fact would not disprove market power in the aftermarkets. The sales of even a monopolist are reduced when it sells goods at a monopoly price, but the higher price more than compensates for the loss in sales. Kodak's claim that charging more for service and parts would be a "short-run game," is based on the false dichotomy that there are only two prices that can be charged—a

17 It is clearly true . . . that Kodak "cannot set service or parts prices without regard to the impact on the market for equipment." The fact that the cross-elasticity of demand is not zero proves nothing; the disputed issue is how much of an impact an increase in parts and service prices has on equipment sales and on Kodak's profits.

competitive price or a ruinous one. But there could easily be a middle, optimum price at which the increased revenues from the higher-priced sales of service and parts would more than compensate for the lower revenues from lost equipment sales. The fact that the equipment market imposes a restraint on prices in the aftermarkets by no means disproves the existence of power in those markets. *See* Areeda & Kaplow, at ¶ 340(b) ("The existence of significant substitution in the event of *further* price increases or even at the *current* price does not tell us whether the defendant *already* exercises significant market power") (emphasis in original). Thus, contrary to Kodak's assertion, there is no immutable physical law—no "basic economic reality"—insisting that competition in the equipment market cannot coexist with market power in the aftermarkets.

We next consider the more narrowly drawn question: Does Kodak's theory describe actual market behavior so accurately that respondents' assertion of Kodak market power in the aftermarkets, if not impossible, is at least unreasonable?

To review Kodak's theory, it contends that higher service prices will lead to a disastrous drop in equipment sales. Presumably, the theory's corollary is to the effect that low service prices lead to a dramatic increase in equipment sales. According to the theory, one would have expected Kodak to take advantage of lower-priced ISO service as an opportunity to expand equipment sales. Instead, Kodak adopted a restrictive sales policy consciously designed to eliminate the lower-priced ISO service, an act that would be expected to devastate either Kodak's equipment sales or Kodak's faith in its theory. Yet, according to the record, it has done neither. Service prices have risen for Kodak customers, but there is no evidence or assertion that Kodak equipment sales have dropped.

Kodak and the United States attempt to reconcile Kodak's theory with the contrary actual results by describing a "marketing strategy of spreading over time the total cost to the buyer of Kodak equipment." In other words, Kodak could charge subcompetitive prices for equipment and make up the difference with supracompetitive prices for service, resulting in an overall competitive price. This pricing strategy would provide an explanation for the theory's descriptive failings—if Kodak in fact had adopted it. But Kodak never has asserted that it prices its equipment or parts subcompetitively and recoups its profits through service. Instead, it claims that it prices its equipment comparably to its competitors, and intends that both its equipment sales and service divisions be profitable. Moreover, this hypothetical pricing strategy is inconsistent with Kodak's policy toward its self-service customers. If Kodak were underpricing its equipment, hoping to lock in customers and recover its losses in the service market, it could not afford to sell customers parts without service. In sum, Kodak's theory does not explain the actual market behavior revealed in the record.

Respondents offer a forceful reason why Kodak's theory, although perhaps intuitively appealing, may not accurately explain the behavior of the primary and derivative markets for complex durable goods: the existence of significant information and switching costs. These costs could create a less responsive connection between service and parts prices and equipment sales.

For the service-market price to affect equipment demand, consumers must inform themselves of the total cost of the "package"—equipment, service and parts—at the time of purchase; that is, consumers must engage in accurate lifecycle pricing. Lifecycle pricing of complex, durable equipment is difficult and costly. In order to arrive at an accurate price, a consumer must acquire a substantial amount of raw data and undertake sophisticated analysis. The necessary information would include data on price, quality, and availability of products needed to operate, upgrade, or enhance the initial equipment, as well as service and repair costs, including estimates of breakdown frequency, nature of repairs, price of service and parts, length of "down-time" and losses incurred from down-time.

Much of this information is difficult—some of it impossible—to acquire at the time of purchase. During the life of a product, companies may change the service and parts prices, and develop products with more advanced features, a decreased need for repair, or new warranties. In addition, the information is likely to be customer-specific; lifecycle costs will vary from customer to customer with the type of equipment, degrees of equipment use, and costs of downtime.

Kodak acknowledges the cost of information, but suggests, again without evidentiary support, that customer information needs will be satisfied by competitors in the equipment markets. It is a question of fact, however, whether competitors would provide the necessary information. A competitor in the equipment market may not have reliable information about the lifecycle costs of complex equipment it does not service or the needs of customers it does not serve. Even if competitors had the relevant information, it is not clear that their interests would be advanced by providing such information to consumers.[21]

Moreover, even if consumers were capable of acquiring and processing the complex body of information, they may choose not to do so.

---

[21] To inform consumers about Kodak, the competitor must be willing to forgo the opportunity to reap supracompetitive prices in its own service and parts markets. The competitor may anticipate that charging lower service and parts prices and informing consumers about Kodak in the hopes of gaining future equipment sales will cause Kodak to lower the price on its service and parts, cancelling any gains in equipment sales to the competitor and leaving both worse off. Thus, in an equipment market with relatively few sellers, competitors may find it more profitable to adopt Kodak's service and parts policy than to inform the consumers. *See* 2 P. Areeda & D. Turner, Antitrust Law ¶ 404b1 (1978); App. 177 (Kodak, Xerox, and IBM together have nearly 100% of relevant market). Even in a market with many sellers, any one competitor may not have sufficient incentive to inform consumers because the increased patronage attributable to the corrected consumer beliefs will be shared among other competitors.

Acquiring the information is expensive. If the costs of service are small relative to the equipment price, or if consumers are more concerned about equipment capabilities than service costs, they may not find it cost-efficient to compile the information. Similarly, some consumers, such as the Federal Government, have purchasing systems that make it difficult to consider the complete cost of the "package" at the time of purchase. State and local governments often treat service as an operating expense and equipment as a capital expense, delegating each to a different department. These governmental entities do not lifecycle price, but rather choose the lowest price in each market.

As Kodak notes, there likely will be some large-volume, sophisticated purchasers who will undertake the comparative studies and insist, in return for their patronage, that Kodak charge them competitive lifecycle prices. Kodak contends that these knowledgeable customers will hold down the package price for all other customers. There are reasons, however, to doubt that sophisticated purchasers will ensure that competitive prices are charged to unsophisticated purchasers, too. As an initial matter, if the number of sophisticated customers is relatively small, the amount of profits to be gained by supracompetitive pricing in the service market could make it profitable to let the knowledgeable consumers take their business elsewhere. More importantly, if a company is able to price-discriminate between sophisticated and unsophisticated consumers, the sophisticated will be unable to prevent the exploitation of the uninformed. A seller could easily price-discriminate by varying the equipment/parts/service package, developing different warranties, or offering price discounts on different components.

Given the potentially high cost of information and the possibility a seller may be able to price-discriminate between knowledgeable and unsophisticated consumers, it makes little sense to assume, in the absence of any evidentiary support, that equipment-purchasing decisions are based on an accurate assessment of the total cost of equipment, service, and parts over the lifetime of the machine.

Indeed, respondents have presented evidence that Kodak practices price-discrimination by selling parts to customers who service their own equipment, but refusing to sell parts to customers who hire third-party service companies. Companies that have their own service staff are likely to be high-volume users, the same companies for whom it is most likely to be economically worthwhile to acquire the complex information needed for comparative lifecycle pricing.

A second factor undermining Kodak's claim that supracompetitive prices in the service market lead to ruinous losses in equipment sales is the cost to current owners of switching to a different product. If the cost of switching is high, consumers who already have purchased the equipment, and are thus "locked-in," will tolerate some level of service-price increases before changing equipment brands. Under this scenario, a seller profitably could maintain supracompetitive prices in the aftermarket if the switching costs were high relative to the increase in service prices, and the number of locked-in customers were high relative to the number of new purchasers.

Moreover, if the seller can price-discriminate between its locked-in customers and potential new customers, this strategy is even more likely to prove profitable. The seller could simply charge new customers below-marginal cost on the equipment and recoup the charges in service, or offer packages with life-time warranties or long-term service agreements that are not available to locked-in customers.

Respondents have offered evidence that the heavy initial outlay for Kodak equipment, combined with the required support material that works only with Kodak equipment, makes switching costs very high for existing Kodak customers. And Kodak's own evidence confirms that it varies the package price of equipment/parts/service for different customers.

In sum, there is a question of fact whether information costs and switching costs foil the simple assumption that the equipment and service markets act as pure complements to one another.[24]

We conclude, then, that Kodak has failed to demonstrate that respondents' inference of market power in the service and parts markets is unreasonable, and that, consequently, Kodak is entitled to summary judgment. It is clearly reasonable to infer that Kodak has market power to raise prices and drive out competition in the aftermarkets, since respondents offer direct evidence that Kodak did so. It is also plausible, as discussed above, to infer that Kodak chose to gain immediate profits by exerting that market power where locked-in customers, high information costs, and discriminatory pricing limited and perhaps eliminated any long-term loss. Viewing the evidence in the light most favorable to respondents, their allegations of market power "make . . . economic sense.". . . .

Respondents also claim that they have presented genuine issues for trial as to whether Kodak has monopolized or attempted to monopolize the service and parts markets in violation of § 2 of the Sherman Act. . . . The existence of the first element, possession of monopoly power, is easily resolved. As has been noted, respondents have presented a triable claim that service and parts are separate markets, and that Kodak has the "power to control prices or exclude competition" in service and parts. *du Pont*. Monopoly power under § 2 requires, of course, something greater

---

[24] The dissent disagrees based on its hypothetical case of a tie between equipment and service. "The only thing lacking" to bring this case within the hypothetical case, states the dissent, "is concrete evidence that the restrictive parts policy was . . . generally known." But the dissent's "only thing lacking" is the crucial thing lacking—evidence. Whether a tie between parts and service should be treated identically to a tie between equipment and service, as the dissent and Kodak argue, depends on whether the equipment market prevents the exertion of market power in the parts market. Far from being "anomalous," requiring Kodak to provide evidence on this factual question is completely consistent with our prior precedent.

than market power under § 1. *See Fortner I.* Respondents' evidence that Kodak controls nearly 100% of the parts market and 80% to 95% of the service market, with no readily available substitutes, is, however, sufficient to survive summary judgment under the more stringent monopoly standard of § 2. *See NCAA. Cf. Grinnell* (87% of the market is a monopoly); *American Tobacco* (over 2/3 of the market is a monopoly).

Kodak also contends that, as a matter of law, a single brand of a product or service can never be a relevant market under the Sherman Act. We disagree. The relevant market for antitrust purposes is determined by the choices available to Kodak equipment owners. *See Jefferson Parish.* Because service and parts for Kodak equipment are not interchangeable with other manufacturers' service and parts, the relevant market from the Kodak-equipment owner's perspective is composed of only those companies that service Kodak machines. *See du Pont* (the "market is composed of products that have reasonable interchangeability").[30] . . .

■ JUSTICE SCALIA, with whom JUSTICES O'CONNOR and THOMAS join, dissenting. . . . In the absence of interbrand power, a seller's predominant or monopoly share of its single-brand derivative markets does not connote the power to raise derivative market prices *generally* by reducing quantity. . . . [A] rational consumer considering the purchase of Kodak equipment will inevitably factor into his purchasing decision the expected cost of aftermarket support. . . . If Kodak set generally supracompetitive prices for either spare parts or repair services without making an offsetting reduction in the price of its machines, rational consumers would simply turn to Kodak's competitors for photocopying and micrographic systems. True, there are—as the Court notes—the occasional irrational consumers that consider only the hardware cost at the time of purchase (a category that regrettably includes the Federal Government, whose "purchasing system," we are told, assigns foremarket purchases and aftermarket purchases to different entities). But we have never before premised the application of antitrust doctrine on the lowest common denominator of consumer.

The Court attempts to counter this theoretical point with theory of its own. It says that there are "information costs"—the costs and inconvenience to the consumer of acquiring and processing life-cycle pricing data for Kodak machines—that "could create a less responsive connection between service and parts prices and equipment sales." But this truism about the functioning of markets for sophisticated equipment cannot create "market power" of concern to the antitrust laws where otherwise there is none. "Information costs," or, more accurately, gaps in the availability and quality of consumer information, pervade real-world

[30] Kodak erroneously contends that this Court in *du Pont* rejected the notion that a relevant market could be limited to one brand. The Court simply held in *du Pont* that one brand does not *necessarily* constitute a relevant market if substitutes are available. Here respondents contend there are no substitutes.

markets; and because consumers generally make do with "rough cut" judgments about price in such circumstances, in virtually any market there are zones within which otherwise competitive suppliers may overprice their products without losing appreciable market share. We have never suggested that the principal players in a market with such commonplace informational deficiencies (and, thus, bands of apparent consumer pricing indifference) exercise market power in any sense relevant to the antitrust laws. . . .

Respondents suggest that, even if the existence of interbrand competition prevents Kodak from raising prices *generally* in its single-brand aftermarkets, there remain certain consumers who are necessarily subject to abusive Kodak pricing behavior by reason of their being "locked in" to their investments in Kodak machines. . . . But this "circumstantial" leverage created by consumer investment regularly crops up in smoothly functioning, even perfectly competitive, markets, and in most—if not all—of its manifestations, it is of no concern to the antitrust laws. The leverage held by the manufacturer of a malfunctioning refrigerator (which is measured by the consumer's reluctance to walk away from his initial investment in that device) is no different in kind or degree from the leverage held by the swimming pool contractor when he discovers a 5-ton boulder in his customer's backyard and demands an additional sum of money to remove it; or the leverage held by an airplane manufacturer over an airline that has "standardized" its fleet around the manufacturer's models; or the leverage held by a drill press manufacturer whose customers have built their production lines around the manufacturer's particular style of drill press; the leverage held by an insurance company over its independent sales force that has invested in company-specific paraphernalia; or the leverage held by a mobile home park owner over his tenants, who are unable to transfer their homes to a different park except at great expense. Leverage, in the form of *circumstantial* power, plays a role in each of these relationships; but in none of them is the leverage attributable to the dominant party's *market* power in any relevant sense. Though that power can plainly work to the injury of certain consumers, it produces only "a brief perturbation in competitive conditions—not the sort of thing the antitrust laws do or should worry about."

NOTES AND QUESTIONS ON *KODAK*

*1. **Overruling the*** **Cellophane** ***fallacy.*** One important feature of *Kodak* is that it overrules the *Cellophane* holding that a high cross-elasticity of demand at current prices negates a narrow market definition. As the Court pointed out, the existence of significant substitution if the price were raised above its current level is irrelevant to the question of whether the firm already exercised market power in raising prices up to that current level.

*2. **The timing of market power.*** Does the case really turn on the right time for assessing market power? If the question is whether Kodak had market power in parts at the time of equipment sales, then the answer is clearly no because Kodak was conceded to lack market power in equipment, and buyers could at that stage avoid its power over parts by just buying the equipment from some other firm. But is that the right time to assess market power? The Court's implicit answer is no: the right time to measure market power is instead the time when the consumer is subjected to the aftermarket tying, which came later. At that time, Kodak customers were locked into Kodak parts because they could not switch to non-Kodak parts to fix or maintain their equipment.

To be sure, at the time they bought the Kodak equipment, customers could have anticipated that Kodak would have market power in Kodak parts. But that does not mean customers would have anticipated the alleged tie of Kodak parts to Kodak service. When one enters a market in which a firm has monopoly power, one does not consent to any illegal monopolizing conduct that firm might choose to engage in. One rather enters under the assumption that the firm will comply with antitrust law.

Would Kodak have been deemed to have relevant market power if it had sold Kodak equipment at a price that included lifetime parts and service? Presumably not because then the tie would have occurred at a time when Kodak had no market power over the relevant customers. The lock-in problem would not apply. Nor would the information cost problem apply because the purchase price would clearly reflect lifetime parts and service.

Would Kodak have been deemed to have relevant market power if it had (1) required all purchasers of Kodak equipment to buy parts and service from Kodak or (2) told purchasers at the time they purchased Kodak equipment that they would not be able to get Kodak parts without taking Kodak service? Probably not because again the tie would have occurred at a time when Kodak had no market power over the relevant customers, so they could have avoided the tie by simply purchasing from another firm. The purchasers would thus have no lock-in problem. To be sure, the purchasers would still have an information cost problem because they might have a hard time estimating how much need they will have for Kodak parts and service. But that is true for the typical tie, and tying doctrine nonetheless requires proof of tying market power. If one thinks the right answer in this hypothetical is that market power would be assessed at the time of equipment purchase, that indicates that the court holding either (a) really rests on the lock-in problem rather than on the information cost argument or (b) that the key piece of missing information is being informed at the time of purchase that a tie of Kodak parts to service will be imposed.

3. ***The widgetium hypothetical.*** Suppose there are ten mines in the world that can produce widgetium, a heavy raw ingredient that, given high transportation costs, must be transported to a local plant to be transformed into widgets. Each mine is owned by a different firm. Before a widget producer moves close to a particular mine, none of the widgetium mines have any market power over it. But once a widget producer moves close to a particular mine, then the producer cannot turn to any other mine for widgetium.

The dissent's logic would suggest that no mine can have market power in a local widgetium market because the mines lack any market power on the worldwide market before producers enter a local market. Because the producer would have entered the local market knowing that such entry would thereafter subject the producer to the mine's market power, the dissent suggests that the producer should have priced in the costs before it entered. But the fact that a producer enters a market knowing there will be seller market power does not mean it has implicitly agreed to any subsequent anticompetitive conduct that the local mine might engage in. Instead, it is more reasonable to think each entrant entered the local market assuming that antitrust law would prevent any subsequent anticompetitive conduct. To be sure, prior to entering a local market, a producer could have bargained to get the local mine to sign a contract promising not to violate the antitrust laws. But a rational producer would not bargain for such contract provisions if it believed doing so was unnecessary because antitrust law would protect it from those abuses. In other words, if antitrust law is part of the background conditions under which the contract is formed, then purchasers cannot be blamed for having failed to negotiate a redundant set of contractual protections against antitrust violations.

On the other hand, suppose that, before the producers entered a local market, the local mine informed the producers that the mine did not sell widgetium to any producer who did not also pay the mine for transportation from the local mine to the producer's local plant. In that case, the tie (of widgetium to transportation) is imposed before producers enter, and thus the right time to assess market power is when the producers are deciding whether to move close to the local mine, at which time the mine has no market power. This conclusion does not mean there is some "coming to the nuisance" rule that precludes suits by firms who enter into markets where anticompetitive practices are known to be used. Rather, it simply means that assessments of market power should occur at the time of entry when the conduct is known before entry. If the mine owner instead owned every widgetium mine in the world, then it would have market power over mining at the time of entry, and thus its tie would be problematic even if were known at the time of entry. Likewise, if the relevant conduct were instead something (like a local mine cartel) that violates the antitrust laws regardless of market power, then the fact that producers might know about the cartel before they enter a local market would not provide the local mine cartel with any immunity. But here the relevant conduct is tying, which requires proof of tying market power, and thus the fact that there was no tying market power at the time the producers chose to subject themselves to the tie means there was no antitrust violation. The fact that tying market power did not exist at the time the tie was imposed also suggests that the tie was likely motivated by efficiencies rather than by anticompetitive effects.

In short, the right time to assess market power is generally when the alleged anticompetitive conduct is imposed on the plaintiff. Because the purpose of market definition is inferring the existence of market power, determining the right time to assess market power also has implications for how to define the market. In particular, cases like *Kodak* and the widgetium hypothetical indicate that sometimes market definition requires defining not only the geographic market but also the right temporal market. In other words, market definition sometimes requires assessing not only the three dimensions of space, but also the fourth dimension of time.

*4. **Contract v. antitrust remedies.*** Consider the following argument. Purchasers of Kodak equipment could have asked for contractual terms protecting them against post-purchase practices like ties of parts to service if they wanted such protection. On the other hand, Kodak could have used contractual terms that explicitly authorized such post-purchase practices if it really wanted to engage in such practices. If the contract has not specified a result either way, should we conclude that all we have is a midstream contract problem that should be resolved by whatever default rules might be provided by contract law or perhaps laws against consumer deception, rather than be resolved through antitrust actions? Probably not because normally people contract on the assumption that other substantive laws remain in place, rather than assuming they have to contract to retain those substantive legal protections. To put it another way, even if one used a default rule, the typical default rule assumption would be that antitrust law would govern. The alternative view is that problems raised by the sort of market power created by midstream contract lock-ins involve conduct that is less likely to be seriously anticompetitive and that contractual penalties (being single damages and more easily modifiable) are better suited to deal with such problems without creating overdeterrence. How would you resolve *Kodak* and the general issue of anticompetitive uses of aftermarket power?

C. SECOND ELEMENT: ANTICOMPETITIVE CONDUCT

U.S. monopolization doctrine requires some form of anticompetitive conduct in addition to the requisite level of market power. Such conduct can include various forms of agreements, like exclusionary vertical agreements or conditioned sale agreements whose terms or conditions may foreclose rivals in ways that enhance monopoly power, such as exclusive dealing, tying, loyalty discounts, and bundled loyalty discounts. Those sorts of conditioned agreements are considered separately in Chapter 4, which also considers other bodies of law that bear on such agreements, given that they implicate a common body of economic analysis. This Chapter considers only unilateral conduct that does not require the agreement or compliance of others with any terms or conditions about how they will interact with other market actors.

1. GENERAL STANDARDS

We have seen above that the U.S. Supreme Court has held monopolization has two components: (1) the possession of monopoly power in the relevant market, and (2) "the willful acquisition or maintenance of that power as distinguished from growth or development as a consequence of a superior product, business acumen, or historic accident."[47] It is to this second element that we turn in this section.

The problem is that firms often willfully acquire or maintain monopoly power precisely through business acumen or developing a superior product. The two are not at all mutually exclusive concepts. And while cases of historic accident can be distinguished because they are not willful, it is hard to think of cases where a firm really has a monopoly thrust upon it without the aid of any willful conduct. Further, this test never defines what it means by "business acumen." One would think such acumen might well include any business strategy that reaps supracompetitive profits that isn't prohibited by antitrust law. If so, then the term ultimately turns on the unarticulated criterion for prohibition. The definition of a "superior product" seems more inherently meaningful. But this test does not tell us what to do when the product is sold on terms that tend to exclude rivals—should those terms be deemed anticompetitive or to indicate superior product terms? Further, the Supreme Court has held on multiple occasions that sometimes a firm cannot deny its superior product to its rivals, meaning that there are some occasions where it is illegal to acquire or maintain a monopoly as a consequence of a superior product.[48]

Notwithstanding the use of the word "willful," it is clear that this second element does not require any proof about the subjective intent of the defendant. To the contrary, the Court has repeatedly stressed that "no monopolist monopolizes unconscious of what he is doing."[49] In other words, its references to intent do not refer to subjective intent but rather the *objective* intent that can be inferred from the firm's conduct. Courts do often examine proof of subjective intent in monopolization cases, but not because it is dispositive in its own right—rather they do so because evidence of a subjective intent can help the court to *interpret* otherwise ambiguous conduct and effects. But the ultimate question is an assessment of the conduct and its effects.

Inquiries into intent in any event cannot be divorced from assessments of conduct, given that an improper intent cannot simply be an intent to eliminate competition, which can underlie desirable acts like innovating to make a superior product that will drive one's rivals out of the market. Rather, an improper intent would be an intent to eliminate competition *improperly*, which again requires some normative assessment of conduct in question.

---

[47] *Grinnell*, 384 U.S. at 570–571. This test has continued to be used in more recent Supreme Court cases. *See Trinko*, 540 U.S. at 407; *Kodak*, 504 U.S. at 481; *Aspen*, 472 U.S. at 596 n.19.

[48] *See Kodak*, 504 U.S. at 483 & n.32; *Aspen*, 472 U.S. at 600–11; Otter Tail Power Co. v. United States, 410 U.S. 366 (1973).

[49] *See Aspen*, 472 U.S. at 602; United States v. Griffith, 334 U.S. 100, 105 (1948); *Am. Tobacco* 328 U.S. at 814; Times-Picayune Publishing Co. v. United States, 345 U.S. 594, 626 (1953).

So what type of conduct is deemed improper? Much of the U.S. caselaw focuses on whether the conduct excludes rivals from the market.[50] The problem is that some conduct that tends to exclude rivals and eliminate competition, such as achieving greater efficiency, is highly desirable. Thus, we need some test to sort out which exclusionary conduct should be legal and which illegal.

One set of formulations stresses that conduct that excludes rivals does not constitute monopolization if the monopolist is motivated by "valid business reasons," a "normal business purpose," or "legitimate competitive reasons."[51] Again, the Court means not subjective intent but the objective purposes one can infer from the nature of the challenged conduct. But the problem is that these tests do not specify the criteria used to distinguish the invalid, abnormal, or illegitimate, so that each of these formulations turns on what content one gives to the key placeholder term—"valid," "normal," or "legitimate." The same is true for other formulations that try to distinguish between "improper conduct" and "honestly industrial" conduct,[52] and for attempted monopolization cases, which have defined the prohibited conduct as "conduct which *unfairly* tends to destroy competition" but neglected to define just what fairness means.[53]

Other U.S. caselaw more helpfully adds the word "anticompetitive" to the description of the illicit exclusionary conduct. *Aspen Skiing* described it as "the willful acquisition or maintenance of [monopoly] power by anticompetitive or exclusionary means," which the Court indicated was "conduct that '(1) tends to impair the opportunities of rivals, but also (2) either does not further competition on the merits or does so in an unnecessarily restrictive way.' "[54] And *Trinko* stated "the possession of monopoly power will not be found unlawful unless it is accompanied by an element of anticompetitive *conduct*."[55]

In short, under U.S. law, a monopolist's unilateral conduct is governed by the same rule of reason to judge whether it is anticompetitive as is concerted action by firms that lack monopoly power or any reasonable probability of acquiring it.[56] But as with concerted action, the term "anticompetitive" is not self-defining. Indeed, here the problem is somewhat worse because the doctrine by definition includes

---

50 *Kodak*, 504 U.S. at 482–83 (monopoly power used to "to foreclose competition, to gain a competitive advantage, or to destroy a competitor."); *Otter Tail*, 410 U.S. at 377 (same); *Griffith*, 334 U.S. at 107 (same); *Standard Oil*, 221 U.S. at 75 ("excluding others from the trade"); United States v. American Tobacco, 221 U.S. 106, 181 (1911) ("driving competitors out of business"); United States v. United Shoe Mach. Corp., 110 F.Supp. 295, 342 (D. Mass. 1953), aff'd per curiam, 347 U.S. 521 (1954) ("to exclude competition").

51 *Kodak*, 504 U.S. at 483 & n.32; *Aspen*, 472 U.S. at 605, 608.

52 *Aspen*, 472 U.S. at 596 (quoting jury instructions).

53 *Spectrum Sports*, 506 U.S. at 458 (emphasis added); *see also id.* at 459 (defining prohibited conduct as " 'unfair' or 'predatory' tactics").

54 *Aspen*, 472 U.S. at 595–96, 605 n.32.

55 *Trinko*, 540 U.S. at 407 (emphasis in original).

56 *Standard Oil*, 221 U.S. at 61–62.

unilateral conduct, and thus cannot equate being anticompetitive with using means that reduce market rivalry by increasing coordination with rivals. Further, the Court has held that sometimes a monopolist is affirmatively obliged to diminish market rivalry through cooperation with rivals by giving them access to its product, thus indicating that at least sometimes vigorously competing with rivals by refusing to share its product can be characterized as "anticompetitive or exclusionary." Nor can "anticompetitive" conduct mean whatever conduct results in an outcome that diminishes market rivalry, for that would preclude the very possibility the Court is trying to distinguish—the possibility that desirable conduct can achieve or maintain a monopoly that extinguishes competition.

General standards thus provide little guidance. To get a concrete sense of what conduct is deemed anticompetitive, one needs to examine the standards used to evaluate specific conduct. The following sections in this chapter and Chapter 4 focus on that inquiry.

2. PREDATORY PRICING

The concern about predatory pricing is that firms might strategically cut prices to unprofitable levels in the short term in order to eliminate or discipline rivals and then raise long run prices to supracompetitive levels, inflicting a net long term injury on consumers. The problem is that such harmful predatory pricing is often hard to distinguish from desirable competitive price-cutting, so that attempts to condemn the former may mistakenly condemn and deter the latter. The pervasive concern of predatory pricing doctrine is thus to fashion a rule that adequately deters harmful predatory pricing without overly deterring competitive price-cutting.

Such overdeterrence raises a serious problem both because competitive price-cutting is among the most desirable business activities and because rivals have a heavy anticompetitive incentive to stop it. The last thing one would want would be to enable firms to use antitrust law to discipline rival price cuts. This concern about overdeterrence plays out in many doctrinal ways. It leads some courts to set high criteria for proving predatory pricing. The U.S. courts have done so by concluding that an intent to have such a predatory effect does not suffice and by requiring proof both of below-cost pricing and likely supra-competitive recoupment. It also leads some courts to impose higher standards of sufficient evidence for proving those elements, or to be less willing to infer a conspiracy to predatorily price.

The reciprocal problem is that all such efforts to reduce the overdeterrence of desirable competitive pricing by making predatory pricing harder to prove also necessarily increase the *under*deterrence of undesirable predatory pricing. The overarching question is thus what doctrine would achieve the optimal tradeoff that minimizes the total harm from the underdeterrence of predatory pricing and the overdeterrence of competitive price-cutting.

a. BELOW-COST PREDATORY PRICING

Brooke Group Ltd. (Liggett) v. Brown & Williamson Tobacco Corp.

509 U.S. 209 (1993).

■ JUSTICE KENNEDY delivered the opinion of the Court . . .

. . . . Cigarette manufacturing has long been one of America's most concentrated industries, and for decades, production has been dominated by six firms: R.J. Reynolds, Philip Morris, American Brands, Lorillard, and the two litigants involved here, Liggett and Brown & Williamson. R.J. Reynolds and Philip Morris, the two industry leaders, enjoyed respective market shares of about 28% and 40% at the time of trial. Brown & Williamson ran a distant third, its market share never exceeding 12% at any time relevant to this dispute. Liggett's share of the market was even less, from a low of just over 2% in 1980 to a high of just over 5% in 1984.

The cigarette industry also has long been one of America's most profitable, in part because for many years there was no significant price competition among the rival firms. List prices for cigarettes increased in lock-step, twice a year, for a number of years, irrespective of the rate of inflation, changes in the costs of production, or shifts in consumer demand. Substantial evidence suggests that in recent decades, the industry reaped the benefits of prices above a competitive level . . .

[In 1980, Liggett decided to introduce a line of black and white generic cigarettes that were offered to consumers at list prices 30% below branded cigarettes and promoted to wholesalers with volume rebates. This hit Brown & Williamson especially hard because its brands were favored by price-sensitive consumers. Brown & Williamson responded by introducing its own line of generics with even larger volume rebates. Liggett alleged that Brown & Williamson's volume rebates violated the Robinson-Patman Act because they resulted in prices that were both discriminatory and below average variable costs, and were designed to pressure it to raise generic cigarette prices so they were closer to branded prices.]

. . . The jury awarded Liggett $49.6 million in damages, which the District Court trebled to $148.8 million. After reviewing the record, however, the District Court held that Brown & Williamson was entitled to judgment as a matter of law . . . The United States Court of Appeals for the Fourth Circuit affirmed. . . .

We . . . affirm.

II. A

. . . By its terms, the Robinson-Patman Act condemns price discrimination only to the extent that it threatens to injure competition. . . . Thus, "the Robinson-Patman Act should be construed consistently with broader policies of the antitrust laws." . . .

Liggett contends that Brown & Williamson's discriminatory volume rebates to wholesalers threatened substantial competitive injury by furthering a predatory pricing scheme designed to purge competition from the economy segment of the cigarette market. This type of injury, which harms direct competitors of the discriminating seller, is known as primary-line injury . . . .

. . . [P]rimary line competitive injury under the Robinson-Patman Act is of the same general character as the injury inflicted by predatory pricing schemes actionable under § 2 of the Sherman Act. There are, to be sure, differences between the two statutes. For example, we interpret § 2 of the Sherman Act to condemn predatory pricing when it poses "a dangerous probability of actual monopolization," *Spectrum Sports*, whereas the Robinson-Patman Act requires only that there be "a reasonable possibility" of substantial injury to competition before its protections are triggered. Falls City Industries, Inc. v. Vanco Beverage, Inc., 460 U.S. 428, 434 (1983). But whatever additional flexibility the Robinson-Patman Act standard may imply, the essence of the claim under either statute is the same: A business rival has priced its products in an unfair manner with an object to eliminate or retard competition and thereby gain and exercise control over prices in the relevant market.

Accordingly, whether the claim alleges predatory pricing under § 2 of the Sherman Act or primary-line price discrimination under the Robinson-Patman Act, two prerequisites to recovery remain the same. First, a plaintiff seeking to establish competitive injury resulting from a rival's low prices must prove that the prices complained of are below an appropriate measure of its rival's costs.[1] Although *Cargill* and *Matsushita* reserved as a formal matter the question " 'whether recovery should *ever* be available . . . when the pricing in question is above some measure of incremental cost,' " *Cargill* (quoting *Matsushita*), the reasoning in both opinions suggests that only below-cost prices should suffice, and we have rejected elsewhere the notion that above-cost prices that are below general market levels or the costs of a firm's competitors inflict injury to competition cognizable under the antitrust laws. *See* Atlantic Richfield Co. v. USA Petroleum Co., 495 U.S. 328, 340 (1990). "Low prices benefit consumers regardless of how those prices are set, and so long as they are above predatory levels, they do not threaten competition. . . . We have adhered to this principle regardless of the type of antitrust claim involved." Ibid. As a general rule, the exclusionary

1 Because the parties in this case agree that the relevant measure of cost is average variable cost, however, we again decline to resolve the conflict among the lower courts over the appropriate measure of cost.

effect of prices above a relevant measure of cost either reflects the lower cost structure of the alleged predator, and so represents competition on the merits, or is beyond the practical ability of a judicial tribunal to control without courting intolerable risks of chilling legitimate price-cutting. "To hold that the antitrust laws protect competitors from the loss of profits due to such price competition would, in effect, render illegal any decision by a firm to cut prices in order to increase market share. The antitrust laws require no such perverse result." *Cargill.*

Even in an oligopolistic market, when a firm drops its prices to a competitive level to demonstrate to a maverick the unprofitability of straying from the group, it would be illogical to condemn the price cut: The antitrust laws then would be an obstacle to the chain of events most conducive to a breakdown of oligopoly pricing and the onset of competition. Even if the ultimate effect of the cut is to induce or reestablish supracompetitive pricing, discouraging a price cut and forcing firms to maintain supracompetitive prices, thus depriving consumers of the benefits of lower prices in the interim, does not constitute sound antitrust policy.

The second prerequisite to holding a competitor liable under the antitrust laws for charging low prices is a demonstration that the competitor had a reasonable prospect, or, under § 2 of the Sherman Act, a dangerous probability, of recouping its investment in below-cost prices. *See Matsushita; Cargill.* "For the investment to be rational, the [predator] must have a reasonable expectation of recovering, in the form of later monopoly profits, more than the losses suffered." *Matsushita.* Recoupment is the ultimate object of an unlawful predatory pricing scheme; it is the means by which a predator profits from predation. Without it, predatory pricing produces lower aggregate prices in the market, and consumer welfare is enhanced. Although unsuccessful predatory pricing may encourage some inefficient substitution toward the product being sold at less than its cost, unsuccessful predation is in general a boon to consumers.

That below-cost pricing may impose painful losses on its target is of no moment to the antitrust laws if competition is not injured: It is axiomatic that the antitrust laws were passed for "the protection of competition, not competitors." *Brown Shoe.* . . . Even an act of pure malice by one business competitor against another does not, without more, state a claim under the federal antitrust laws; those laws do not create a federal law of unfair competition or "purport to afford remedies for all torts committed by or against persons engaged in interstate commerce." Hunt v. Crumboch, 325 U.S. 821, 826 (1945).

For recoupment to occur, below-cost pricing must be capable, as a threshold matter, of producing the intended effects on the firm's rivals, whether driving them from the market, or, as was alleged to be the goal here, causing them to raise their prices to supracompetitive levels within a disciplined oligopoly. This requires an understanding of the extent and duration of the alleged predation, the relative financial strength of the predator and its intended victim, and their respective incentives and will. The inquiry is whether, given the aggregate losses caused by the below-cost pricing, the intended target would likely succumb.

If circumstances indicate that below-cost pricing could likely produce its intended effect on the target, there is still the further question whether it would likely injure competition in the relevant market. The plaintiff must demonstrate that there is a likelihood that the predatory scheme alleged would cause a rise in prices above a competitive level that would be sufficient to compensate for the amounts expended on the predation, including the time value of the money invested in it. . . .

Evidence of below-cost pricing is not alone sufficient to permit an inference of probable recoupment and injury to competition. Determining whether recoupment of predatory losses is likely requires an estimate of the cost of the alleged predation and a close analysis of both the scheme alleged by the plaintiff and the structure and conditions of the relevant market. If market circumstances or deficiencies in proof would bar a reasonable jury from finding that the scheme alleged would likely result in sustained supracompetitive pricing, the plaintiff's case has failed. In certain situations—for example, where the market is highly diffuse and competitive, or where new entry is easy, or the defendant lacks adequate excess capacity to absorb the market shares of his rivals and cannot quickly create or purchase new capacity—summary disposition of the case is appropriate. *See*, e.g., *Cargill*.

These prerequisites to recovery are not easy to establish, but they are not artificial obstacles to recovery; rather, they are essential components of real market injury. As we have said in the Sherman Act context, "predatory pricing schemes are rarely tried, and even more rarely successful," *Matsushita*, and the costs of an erroneous finding of liability are high. "[T]he mechanism by which a firm engages in predatory pricing—lowering prices—is the same mechanism by which a firm stimulates competition; because 'cutting prices in order to increase business often is the very essence of competition . . . [;] mistaken inferences . . . are especially costly, because they chill the very conduct the antitrust laws are designed to protect.'" *Cargill* (quoting *Matsushita*). It would be ironic indeed if the standards for predatory pricing liability were so low that antitrust suits themselves became a tool for keeping prices high.

B

Liggett does not allege that Brown & Williamson sought to drive it from the market but that Brown & Williamson sought to preserve supracompetitive profits on branded cigarettes by pressuring Liggett to raise its generic cigarette prices through a process of tacit collusion with the other cigarette companies. Tacit collusion, sometimes called oligopolistic price coordination or conscious parallelism, describes the process, not in itself unlawful, by which firms in a concentrated market might in effect share monopoly power, setting their prices at a profit-maximizing, supracompetitive level by recognizing their shared economic interests and their interdependence with respect to price and output decisions.

In *Matsushita*, we remarked upon the general implausibility of predatory pricing. Matsushita observed that such schemes are even more improbable when they require coordinated action among several firms. Matsushita involved an allegation of an express conspiracy to engage in predatory pricing. The Court noted that in addition to the usual difficulties that face a single firm attempting to recoup predatory losses, other problems render a conspiracy "incalculably more difficult to execute." In order to succeed, the conspirators must agree on how to allocate present losses and future gains among the firms involved, and each firm must resist powerful incentives to cheat on whatever agreement is reached.

However unlikely predatory pricing by multiple firms may be when they conspire, it is even less likely when, as here, there is no express coordination. Firms that seek to recoup predatory losses through the conscious parallelism of oligopoly must rely on uncertain and ambiguous signals to achieve concerted action. The signals are subject to misinterpretation and are a blunt and imprecise means of ensuring smooth cooperation, especially in the context of changing or unprecedented market circumstances. This anticompetitive minuet is most difficult to compose and to perform, even for a disciplined oligopoly.

From one standpoint, recoupment through oligopolistic price coordination could be thought more feasible than recoupment through monopoly: In the oligopoly setting, the victim itself has an economic incentive to acquiesce in the scheme. If forced to choose between cutting prices and sustaining losses, maintaining prices and losing market share, or raising prices and enjoying a share of supracompetitive profits, a firm may yield to the last alternative. Yet on the whole, tacit cooperation among oligopolists must be considered the least likely means of recouping predatory losses. In addition to the difficulty of achieving effective tacit coordination and the high likelihood that any attempt to discipline will produce an outbreak of competition, the predator's present losses in a case like this fall on it alone, while the later supracompetitive profits must be shared with every other oligopolist in proportion to its market share, including the intended victim. In this case, for example, Brown & Williamson, with its 11–12% share of the cigarette market, would have had to generate around \$9 in supracompetitive profits for each \$1 invested in predation; the remaining \$8 would belong to its competitors, who had taken no risk. . . .

To the extent that the Court of Appeals may have held that the interdependent pricing of an oligopoly may never provide a means for achieving recoupment and so may not form the basis of a primary-line injury claim, we disagree. A predatory pricing scheme designed to preserve or create a stable oligopoly, if successful, can injure consumers in the same way, and to the same extent, as one designed to bring about a monopoly. However unlikely that possibility may be as a general matter, when the realities of the market and the record facts indicate that it has occurred and was likely to have succeeded, theory will not stand in the way of liability. *See Eastman Kodak.*

The Robinson-Patman Act . . . suggests no exclusion from coverage when primary-line injury occurs in an oligopoly setting. Unlike the provisions of the Sherman Act, which speak only of various forms of express agreement and monopoly, the Robinson-Patman Act is phrased in broader, disjunctive terms, prohibiting price discrimination "where the effect of such discrimination may be substantially to lessen competition or tend to create a monopoly." For all the words of the Act to carry adequate meaning, competitive injury under the Act must extend beyond the monopoly setting. The language referring to a substantial lessening of competition was part of the original Clayton Act § 2, and the same phrasing appears in § 7 of that Act. In the § 7 context, it has long been settled that excessive concentration, and the oligopolistic price coordination it portends, may be the injury to competition the Act prohibits. *See*, e.g., *Philadelphia National Bank.* We adhere to "the normal rule of statutory construction that identical words used in different parts of the same act are intended to have the same meaning." We decline to create a per se rule of nonliability for predatory price discrimination when recoupment is alleged to take place through supracompetitive oligopoly pricing.

III

Although Liggett's theory of liability, as an abstract matter, is within the reach of the statute, . . . Liggett [lacked sufficient evidence] to submit its case to the jury. . . .

A

. . . [T]he record contains sufficient evidence from which a reasonable jury could conclude that Brown & Williamson envisioned or intended [to pressure Liggett to raise generic process.] There is also sufficient evidence in the record from which a reasonable jury could conclude that for a period of approximately 18 months, Brown & Williamson's prices on its generic cigarettes were below its costs, and that this below-cost pricing imposed losses on Liggett that Liggett was unwilling to sustain, given its corporate parent's effort to locate a buyer for the company. . . . The evidence is inadequate to show that in pursuing this scheme, Brown & Williamson had a reasonable prospect of recovering its losses from below-cost pricing through slowing the growth of generics. . . .

No inference of recoupment is sustainable on this record, because no evidence suggests that Brown & Williamson—whatever its intent in introducing black and whites may have been—was likely to obtain the power to raise the prices for generic cigarettes above a competitive level.

Recoupment through supracompetitive pricing in the economy segment of the cigarette market is an indispensable aspect of Liggett's own proffered theory, because a slowing of growth in the economy segment, even if it results from an increase in generic prices, is not itself anticompetitive. Only if those higher prices are a product of nonmarket forces has competition suffered. If prices rise in response to an excess of demand over supply, or segment growth slows as patterns of consumer preference become stable, the market is functioning in a competitive manner. . . . Because relying on tacit coordination among oligopolists as a means of recouping losses from predatory pricing is "highly speculative," competent evidence is necessary to allow a reasonable inference that it poses an authentic threat to competition. The evidence in this case is insufficient to demonstrate the danger of Brown & Williamson's alleged scheme.

B

Based on Liggett's theory of the case and the record it created, there are two means by which one might infer that Brown & Williamson had a reasonable prospect of producing sustained supracompetitive pricing in the generic segment adequate to recoup its predatory losses: first, if generic output or price information indicates that oligopolistic price coordination in fact produced supracompetitive prices in the generic segment; or second, if evidence about the market and Brown & Williamson's conduct indicate that the alleged scheme was likely to have brought about tacit coordination and oligopoly pricing in the generic segment, even if it did not actually do so.

1

In this case, the price and output data do not support a reasonable inference that Brown & Williamson and the other cigarette companies elevated prices above a competitive level for generic cigarettes. Supracompetitive pricing entails a restriction in output. In the present setting, in which output expanded at a rapid rate following Brown & Williamson's alleged predation, output in the generic segment can only have been restricted in the sense that it expanded at a slower rate than it would have absent Brown & Williamson's intervention. Such a counterfactual proposition is difficult to prove in the best of circumstances; here, the record evidence does not permit a reasonable inference that output would have been greater without Brown & Williamson's entry into the generic segment.

Following Brown & Williamson's entry, the rate at which generic cigarettes were capturing market share did not slow; indeed, the average rate of growth doubled. During the four years from 1980 to 1984 in which Liggett was alone in the generic segment, the segment gained market share at an average rate of 1% of the overall market per year, from .4% in 1980 to slightly more than 4% of the cigarette market in 1984. In the next five years, following the alleged predation, the generic segment expanded from 4% to more than 15% of the domestic cigarette market, or greater than 2% per year.

While this evidence tends to show that Brown & Williamson's participation in the economy segment did not restrict output, it is not dispositive. One could speculate, for example, that the rate of segment growth would have tripled, instead of doubled, without Brown & Williamson's alleged predation. But there is no concrete evidence of this. Indeed, the only industry projection in the record estimating what the segment's growth would have been without Brown & Williamson's entry supports the opposite inference. In 1984, Brown & Williamson forecast in an important planning document that the economy segment would account for 10% of the total cigarette market by 1988 if it did not enter the segment. In fact, in 1988, after what Liggett alleges was a sustained and dangerous anticompetitive campaign by Brown & Williamson, the generic segment accounted for over 12% of the total market. Thus the segment's output expanded more robustly than Brown & Williamson had estimated it would had Brown & Williamson never entered. . . .

Liggett places its principal reliance on direct evidence of price behavior. This evidence demonstrates that the list prices on all cigarettes, generic and branded alike, rose to a significant degree during the late 1980's. From 1986 to 1989, list prices on both generic and branded cigarettes increased twice a year by similar amounts. Liggett's economic expert testified that these price increases outpaced increases in costs, taxes, and promotional expenditures. The list prices of generics, moreover, rose at a faster rate than the prices of branded cigarettes, thus narrowing the list price differential between branded and generic products. Liggett argues that this would permit a reasonable jury to find that Brown & Williamson succeeded in bringing about oligopolistic price coordination and supracompetitive prices in the generic category sufficient to slow its growth, thereby preserving supracompetitive branded profits and recouping its predatory losses.

A reasonable jury, however, could not have drawn the inferences Liggett proposes. All of Liggett's data is based upon the list prices of various categories of cigarettes. Yet the jury had before it undisputed evidence that during the period in question, list prices were not the actual prices paid by consumers. As the market became unsettled in the mid-1980s, the cigarette companies invested substantial sums in promotional schemes, including coupons, stickers, and giveaways, that reduced the actual cost of cigarettes to consumers below list prices. This promotional activity accelerated as the decade progressed. Many wholesalers also passed portions of their volume rebates on to the consumer, which had the effect of further undermining the significance of the retail list prices. Especially in an oligopoly setting, in which price competition is most likely to take place through less observable and less regulable means than list prices, it would be unreasonable to draw conclusions about the existence of tacit coordination or supracompetitive pricing from data that reflects only list prices.

Even on its own terms, the list price data relied upon by Liggett to demonstrate a narrowing of the price differential between generic and full-priced branded cigarettes could not support the conclusion that supracompetitive pricing had been introduced into the generic segment. Liggett's gap data ignores the effect of "subgeneric" cigarettes, which were priced at discounts of 50% or more from the list prices of normal branded cigarettes. Liggett itself, while supposedly under the sway of oligopoly power, pioneered this development in 1988 with the introduction of its "Pyramid" brand. By the time of trial, five of the six major manufacturers offered a cigarette in this category at a discount from the full list price of at least 50%. Thus, the price difference between the highest priced branded cigarette and the lowest price cigarettes in the economy segment, instead of narrowing over the course of the period of alleged predation as Liggett would argue, grew to a substantial extent. . . .

It may be that a reasonable jury could conclude that the cumulative discounts attributable to subgenerics and the various consumer promotions did not cancel out the full effect of the increases in list prices, and that actual prices to the consumer did indeed rise, but rising prices do not themselves permit an inference of a collusive market dynamic. . . . Where, as here, output is expanding at the same time prices are increasing, rising prices are equally consistent with growing product demand. Under these conditions, a jury may not infer competitive injury from price and output data absent some evidence that tends to prove that output was restricted or prices were above a competitive level. *Cf. Monsanto*.

Quite apart from the absence of any evidence of that sort, an inference of supracompetitive pricing would be particularly anomalous in this case, as the very party alleged to have been coerced into pricing through oligopolistic coordination denied that such coordination existed: Liggett's own officers and directors consistently denied that they or other firms in the industry priced their cigarettes through tacit collusion or reaped supracompetitive profits. . . .

2

Not only does the evidence fail to show actual supracompetitive pricing in the generic segment, it also does not demonstrate its likelihood. At the time Brown & Williamson entered the generic segment, the cigarette industry as a whole faced declining demand and possessed substantial excess capacity. These circumstances tend to break down patterns of oligopoly pricing and produce price competition. . . . Tacit coordination is facilitated by a stable market environment, fungible products, and a small number of variables upon which the firms seeking to coordinate their pricing may focus. Uncertainty is an oligopoly's greatest enemy. By 1984, however, the cigarette market was in an obvious state of flux. The introduction of generic cigarettes in 1980 represented the first serious price competition in the cigarette market since the 1930's. This development was bound to unsettle previous expectations and patterns of market conduct and to reduce the cigarette firms' ability to predict each other's behavior.

The larger number of product types and pricing variables also decreased the probability of effective parallel pricing. When Brown & Williamson entered the economy segment in 1984, the segment included value-25s, black and whites, and branded generics. With respect to each product, the net price in the market was determined not only by list prices, but also by a wide variety of discounts and promotions to consumers, and by rebates to wholesalers. In order to coordinate in an effective manner and eliminate price competition, the cigarette companies would have been required, without communicating, to establish parallel practices with respect to each of these variables, many of which, like consumer stickers or coupons, were difficult to monitor. Liggett has not even alleged parallel behavior with respect to these other variables, and the inherent limitations of tacit collusion suggest that such multivariable coordination is improbable. . . .

Even if all the cigarette companies were willing to participate in a scheme to restrain the growth of the generic segment, they would not have been able to coordinate their actions and raise prices above a competitive level unless they understood that Brown & Williamson's entry into the segment was not a genuine effort to compete with Liggett. If even one other firm misinterpreted Brown & Williamson's entry as an effort to expand share, a chain reaction of competitive responses would almost certainly have resulted, and oligopoly discipline would have broken down, perhaps irretrievably. "[O]nce the trust among rivals breaks down, it is as hard to put back together again as was Humpty-Dumpty, and non-collusive behavior is likely to take over." . . .

NOTES AND QUESTIONS ON *BROOKE*

Brooke holds that pricing is predatory only if it: (1) disciplines or eliminates a competitor; (2) the price is below "an appropriate measure of costs"; and (3) recoupment is likely. The last element requires evidence that there is a "reasonable prospect" (in a price discrimination case) or "dangerous probability" (in a straight predatory pricing case) that it will produce supracompetitive profits down the road that exceed the losses from the below-cost pricing. The first element is fairly standard. The second element is slightly more controversial, but let us leave discussion of it until the next section, which addresses whether above-cost pricing should ever be deemed predatory. It is the third element of recoupment that *Brooke* added and that raises the most significant questions.

1. ***Why doesn't pricing below cost suffice to make the pricing predatory?*** One might reasonably conclude that pricing below cost should suffice to make pricing predatory because such pricing would be irrational

unless the defendant intended an anticompetitive effect. However, that inference assumes costs will be adjudicated with perfect accuracy. If one considers the possibility that the judge or jury will sometimes erroneously conclude that costs are higher than they really are, then a pure cost-based test might deter firms from offering low prices that are close to their true cost because such erroneous adjudications of cost mean that pricing close to true cost will create a risk of antitrust liability and treble damages. That would create a serious overdeterrence problem because pricing at cost maximizes allocative efficiency.

Some also argue that offering prices below true costs is legitimate when monopolists are simply meeting a competitor's price. However, when the monopolist product has higher quality, matching nominal prices would mean charging a lower quality-adjusted price than the rival. Even without a quality difference, if the prices are the same then buyers are likely to go with the better-known brand name; entrants generally have to offer a lower promotional price to compensate customers for incurring the information costs of trying out their product. Some argue that monopolists themselves should be able to offer low promotional prices that are below cost, but a firm with monopoly power over a product should not need to offer a promotional price for it, given that a monopolist is by definition already well-known in the market. Even if one did consider meeting competition or promotional pricing to be legitimate defenses for below-cost pricing, it makes sense to allow such defenses only when proven, given that many below-cost prices may not involve meeting competition or promotional prices.

2. ***Should below-cost pricing suffice when coupled with evidence of anticompetitive intent?*** The existence of anticompetitive intent would help resolve ambiguities about whether the defendant thought it was pricing below cost and whether it had any legitimate reason for a below-cost price. However, an anticompetitive intent test would create problems about erroneous adjudications of intent, especially given the ambiguous nature of intent and the risk of punishing companies for the frivolous or ill-considered statements of a few employees. Thus, coupling below-cost pricing with an anticompetitive-intent test can still result in serious overdeterrence.

Moreover, if proof of anticompetitive intent were made a requirement, it would create a big underdeterrence problem because firms would just stop expressing their intent in their documents. Indeed, this problem is always a concern when relying on subjective intent in antitrust law. As a result, evidence on intent tends to be assessed by antitrust law under one-way ratchet, where intent evidence counts against a defendant but the absence of intent evidence does not count for it. Because intent-based tests often simply result in bland documents, the long run effects of adding an intent-based element may not be to add much useful factual information.

3. ***Why add a recoupment element?*** Without recoupment, harm to consumers would not be possible, given that consumers will gain from the low predatory prices without ever suffering a latter price increase. To be sure, below-cost pricing and/or anticompetitive intent mean that the defendant must have thought recoupment was likely, and one might

reasonably conclude that the defendant was best placed to decide whether recoupment is likely or not. But inferring likely recoupment from the defendant's below-cost pricing or intent assumes that findings about costs and intent are found without error. If such findings are not error-free, the overdeterrence problem resurfaces. Requiring independent proof of recoupment thus reduces the overdeterrence problem. It is like wearing both a belt and suspenders to make really sure your pants won't fall down.

However, just as a court can err on costs or intent, so too a court might mistakenly find recoupment unlikely when it was in fact likely. Thus, a recoupment test reduces the overdeterrence problem at the cost of increasing the underdeterrence problem. Whether the decline in overdeterrence is worth the increase in underdeterrence depends on how big one thinks their relative magnitudes are. Because predatory pricing is so close to good competitive pricing, the overdeterrence concerns tend to loom particularly large, especially given treble damages, so U.S. courts have concluded that adding the recoupment element is desirable.

4. ***Isn't recoupment always likely if a firm really has monopoly power or enough market power to have a dangerous probability of acquiring it?*** Yes, because the firm will be able to exercise that market power to raise prices. To be sure, recoupment may not be possible if entry barriers are low or rivals can quickly expand if prices go up, but both those factors should also rebut findings of market or monopoly power. Given this, the recoupment element does not really add much to the market power element in a Sherman Act § 2 case. The recoupment element in such cases might serve as an error-correction mechanism: if we are worried that our methods of assessing market power fail to consider properly the likelihood of rival entry or expansion, then perhaps courts can compensate by requiring a greater showing of likely recoupment. But if courts correctly did the analysis of market power, this inquiry should largely just be duplicative.

The recoupment requirement is more meaningful in cases, like *Brooke*, that involve claims under the Robinson-Patman Act, which does not require proof of market power. Thus, the addition of the recoupment element effectively adds a market power element to Robinson-Patman Act cases that are based on below-cost primary level pricing, albeit an element that turns on future collective market power rather than on current individual market power.

When the defendant is in multiple markets, the recoupment might be in markets other than the one where below-cost pricing is occurring. In such multiple-market cases, losses incurred by the rivals in a market with below-cost pricing may deter their entry into, or drive them out, other markets. In such cases, the recoupment could be in those other markets.

5. ***Was the Court right that recoupment was plausible but unlikely in an oligopoly market?*** Probably. Oligopolists are less likely to engage in predatory pricing because each firm bears all the losses of its below-cost pricing but shares the recoupment benefits with the other oligopolists. Coordination is hard to maintain when it requires incurring such losses, and it is difficult to coordinate both on sharing losses and on the distribution of recoupment profits. Moreover, the overdeterrence concern with deterring competitive price cutting is generally larger in oligopoly markets than monopoly markets because such price cuts are more likely in oligopoly markets and can cause the whole oligopoly to unravel. On the other hand, it might be the case that predatory pricing can effectively be used to discipline deviations from oligopoly pricing, and it is easier to induce rivals to go along with oligopolistic coordination than to drive them out. Thus, the court is probably correct that, although recoupment is unlikely in an oligopoly market, it is not so implausible that it should be categorically rejected.

6. ***Why wasn't recoupment established here?*** *Brooke* indicated that, although unlikely, recoupment could still be proven in an oligopoly market by showing either (a) direct evidence that prices or output were adversely affected by oligopolistic coordination or (b) evidence that market structure made oligopolistic coordination likely. But the Court found that neither showing was made in this case.

a. ***Output and prices showed actual oligopolistic coordination?*** The Court concluded that coordination was not supported by the output data, which showed that output and the rate of growth increased. To be sure, successful oligopolistic coordination might have prevented output from increasing as much as it otherwise would have given other factors, such as perhaps increasing demand. The proper question is thus whether output was lower than it would have been "but for" the challenged conduct (often called the "but-for" level). But the Court noted that the plaintiffs provided no concrete evidence that but-for output would have been higher.

Why wasn't coordination shown by the pricing evidence that, after the alleged predatory pricing, generic list prices increased lock-step, twice a year, in ways unrelated to costs or demand? The lock-step increase was not sufficient because list prices do not reflect actual prices paid after discounts. The dissent thought the lock-step increase was sufficient evidence for the jury to conclude prices rose, which does seem likely, though greater discounts could have offset the price increase. But showing a price increase does not prove oligopoly pricing because it could simply mean demand or costs increased over this period. Thus, the key issue was whether the evidence showed the sort of uniform pricing that indicated oligopoly pricing, and the discounts indicated no such price uniformity. Further, the introduction of subgenerics at lower prices does seem to indicate both lower prices and a deviation from oligopolistic coordination. The Court also noted that the plaintiff denied any oligopolistic pricing was actually going on, though that denial might have reflected the fear that courts have sometimes inferred horizontal price-fixing from oligopolistic coordination that seemed too perfect. *See American Tobacco*, discussed in Chapter 6.

b. ***Market structure suggested likely oligopoly pricing?*** Although market concentration levels were consistent with oligopolistic coordination, the Court thought coordination was unlikely because of declining demand and substantial excess capacity. However, it may well be that competitors are more likely to resort to oligopolistic coordination to preserve profit levels in the face of adverse conditions like declining demand.

Further, substantial excess capacity is actually a predictable effect of oligopolistic coordination because such coordination reduces output, leaving excess capacity. The more telling point was that the likelihood of oligopolistic coordination was undermined by the uncertainty created by new generics, varieties of cigarettes, and price discounts from list prices.

7. ***Wasn't this case really about recoupment on a differentiated market?*** The facts suggest that maybe what was really going on was not oligopolistic coordination across the whole cigarette market, but rather that Brown & Williamson was protecting its position in the cheap cigarette segment of a differentiated market. In such a differentiated market, cheap cigarettes would compete much more against each other than against regular or premium cigarettes. If so, Brown & Williamson might have expected to recoup in a differentiated segment of the market that only it and Liggett occupied, even without any prospect of general oligopolistic coordination. Brown & Williamson would also not be sharing the rewards or costs of predatory pricing with other firms in other segments, which would make recoupment more likely than in a coordination case. However, the case was not litigated on such a theory, so the Court did not address it. Since *Brooke,* differentiated market analysis has become much more prominent, *see* Chapter 7, so one might expect this alternative theory to be more prominent in the future.

The U.S. Conflict on the Proper Cost Measure

Before *Brooke,* the lower U.S. appellate courts held that pricing below some measure of variable cost (like marginal, average variable, or average avoidable cost) was always or presumptively predatory, and pricing above such variable cost measures but below average total cost was presumptively non-predatory, but that the latter presumption could be rebutted by other evidence, such as proof of predatory intent or sacrificing short-term profits.[57] *Brooke* explicitly declined to take any view on the "appropriate" cost measure, and since *Brooke* appellate courts have split on whether *Brooke* thus precludes predation claims alleging prices above any variable cost measure.[58] Plaintiffs often

[57] *See* Northeastern Telephone Co. v. AT & T, 651 F.2d 76, 88 (2d Cir.1981); O. Hommel Co. v. Ferro Corp., 659 F.2d 340, 347–50 (3d Cir.1981); Adjusters Replace-A-Car, Inc. v. Agency Rent-A-Car, Inc., 735 F.2d 884, 889–91 (5th Cir.1984); Arthur S. Langenderfer, Inc. v. S.E. Johnson Co., 729 F.2d 1050, 1056–57 (6th Cir. 1984); Chillicothe Sand & Gravel Co. v. Martin Marietta Corp., 615 F.2d 427, 432 (7th Cir.1980); MCI Communications v. AT & T, 708 F.2d 1081, 1114–23 (7th Cir. 1983) (stressing that long run incremental cost rather than fully distributed cost is the right way to measure average total cost); Morgan v. Ponder, 892 F.2d 1355, 1360 (8th Cir.1989); William Inglis & Sons Baking Co. v. ITT Continental Baking Co., 668 F.2d 1014, 1034–36 (9th Cir.1981); Instructional Sys. Dev. Corp. v. Aetna Casualty & Sur. Co., 817 F.2d 639, 648 (10th Cir.1987); McGahee v. Propane Gas Co., 858 F.2d 1487, 1503 (11th Cir.1988); Southern Pacific Communications Co. v. AT & T, 740 F.2d 980, 1005–07 (D.C.Cir.1984).

[58] *Compare* Stearns Airport Equip. Co. v. FMC Corp., 170 F.3d 518, 532 (5th Cir.1999) (*Brooke* requires overruling prior cases holding that prices above incremental cost could sometimes be predatory if below average total cost); Advo, Inc. v. Philadelphia Newspapers, Inc., 51 F.3d 1191, 1198 (3d Cir.1995) (relying only on incremental costs despite pre-*Brooke* authority to the contrary); United States v. AMR Corp., 335 F.3d 1109, 1116–17 (10th Cir.2003) (relying only on incremental costs despite pre-*Brooke* authority to the contrary), *with* Spirit Airlines v. Northwest Airlines, 431 F.3d 917, 937–38 (6th Cir.2005) (sticking with pre-*Brooke* precedent

effectively concede the issue by basing their claims solely on the theory that the prices were below some measure of variable cost even in circuits that, before *Brooke,* embraced the latter sort of theory.[59]

The precise sort of variable cost measure to use also remains in doubt. Several circuits have stated that the correct measure is marginal cost, but that average variable cost can be used as a surrogate where marginal cost cannot be determined.[60] In contrast, the First Circuit, including in some opinions by now-Justice Breyer, instead refer to the "avoidable" or "incremental" cost of producing the "additional output" it can sell at the alleged predatory price, although it also allows usage of average variable costs when this measure is unavailable.[61] However, no circuit has really made a holding either way since no appellate case has yet raised the distinction between these incremental cost measures. The following analysis provides theoretical support for Justice Breyer's test over one that focuses on marginal or average variable cost.

Elhauge, *Why Above-Cost Price Cuts to Drive Out Entrants Do Not Signal Predation or Even Market Power—And the Implications for Defining Costs*

112 Yale L.J. 681 (2003).

. . . [T]he correct time period for judging whether costs are variable or avoidable is the time period of the alleged predatory pricing. . . . Until the alleged predatory price lasts long enough to be exceeded by those costs that were *variable for that period*, an equally efficient entrant cannot have suffered any loss it could have avoided by exit, and thus cannot have had any incentive to exit. . . . One implication of this is that, for purposes of predatory pricing law, one should thus not distinguish between sunk, fixed, avoidable, and variable costs with general definitions about whether they are escapable in a limited period, or need to be incurred to produce any output or to produce anything beyond the first unit of output. Rather, the question of whether (and what) costs to consider should depend *solely* on whether they could be varied during the time period of the alleged predation. . . .

What is the concern of those who favor using long-term costs even when the predatory pricing period is short? One theory is that predatory pricing at the "rival's variable costs" can induce their exit because "[t]he rival, who also incurs fixed costs, exhausts its financial resources and

---

that prices above average variable costs could be predatory if a contrary presumption were rebutted); Concord Boat Corp. v. Brunswick Corp., 207 F.3d 1039, 1061 (8th Cir.2000) (same).

[59] *See* Vollrath Co. v. Sammi Corp., 9 F.3d 1455, 1461 (9th Cir.1993); Rebel Oil Co., Inc. v. Atlantic Richfield Co., 146 F.3d 1088, 1094 (9th Cir.1998).

[60] *AMR*, 335 F.3d at 1116–17; *Stearns*, 170 F.3d at 532; *Advo*, 51 F.3d at 1198; *Northeastern Telephone*, 651 F.2d at 88 (2d Cir.1981).

[61] *See* Clamp-All Corp. v. Cast Iron Soil Pipe Inst., 851 F.2d 478, 483 (1st Cir.1988) (Breyer, J.); Barry Wright Corp. v. ITT Grinnell Corp., 724 F.2d 227, 232 (1st Cir.1983) (Breyer, J.).

leaves the market." But this is wrong. As long as the price exceeds the costs a rival could vary during the relevant time period, the rival would lose money from leaving the market. . . .

What do we do with software whose marginal or variable cost of production is near zero? The usual answer is that the "new economy" has to be treated differently because marginal or variable costs are so low. But this creation of an ad hoc exception is hardly satisfactory. In the old economy, marginal or variable costs are also often below average or long-term costs. Indeed, the distinction between these cost measures only matters because they sometimes diverge. If this divergence presents a big problem when it is large, it must present at least a small problem when it is small. Our theory for how to deal with that divergence should be able to address the full range of possible magnitudes rather than having ad hoc exceptions, especially since those exceptions create ambiguity about just what the vague dividing line might be.

The better answer is, instead, that it all depends on how long the pricing lasts. If pricing at a near-zero level occurs for a short time, it cannot persuade any equally efficient software rivals to exit, since they also will have near-zero marginal costs and thus retain a profit from operating during that period. If instead such pricing lasts for years, then it could be predatory because it would not allow an equally efficient software rival to recoup the software development costs of updating that software to stay in the market. The latter costs become variable to the rival if the predatory pricing is lengthy, but not if it is brief. Paradox solved. . . .

Another common concern is that equally efficient firms might have different ratios of fixed and variable costs. For example, Williamson observes that more capital-intensive firms can have lower variable costs even when they are less efficient than more labor-intensive firms. He thus advocates using average total costs as a better means of sorting out the efficiencies of firms.

This is a reasonable concern with using the average variable costs of making the predator's *entire* output because that measure is by definition lower than average total costs. Thus, if allowed to price at this measure of average variable costs, even a firm exceeding its optimal capacity could price at a level that is lower than its marginal or average total costs, and thus lower than the costs of an equally efficient firm at providing that incremental output. An average variable cost test can thus offer inadequate protection to an equally efficient rival *if* it is based on an average of the costs that are variable for the predator's entire output.

But this. . . . simply means one must be more precise in defining the relevant output whose costs can be varied. Since our purpose is to determine what cost measure would prevent a firm from excluding an equally efficient rival, the relevant costs that are variable are not the costs of producing the predator's entire output. They are rather the variable costs of the alleged predatory *increase* in output that displaces the *rival's* output. This is because the concern is rival exit (or nonentry), and thus the question is which firm is more efficient at producing the rival's output. . . . This measure of variable costs, in effect, is the sum of the marginal costs for the predatory increase in output, but can be measured more simply by comparing the costs at the higher output to the costs at the lower output, rather than by trying to calculate the marginal costs of producing the last item at each output level. Assuming marginal costs are increasing, this total variable cost figure (when divided by the increased output to give a per-unit figure) will give an average variable cost that is lower than the marginal cost of producing the *last* item that the alleged predator makes, but will still protect a rival that is equally efficient at making the relevant increment of output.

Accordingly, if the capital-intensive firm has increased output to displace its rival's output, we should look only to the higher variable costs of the allegedly predatory increase in output, not to the lower variable costs of producing the predator's entire output. Prices at or above those higher average variable costs cannot drive out a rival that is equally efficient at making that increment of output. If the capital-intensive firm's variable costs of increasing its output enough to displace the rival are lower than the rival's own variable costs of producing that output, then the rival is in fact not equally efficient at making its output. Rather, the rival output can more efficiently be supplied by an increase in the capital-intensive firm's output, even though it may be exceeding its optimal capacity. . . .

[T]his analysis . . . greatly simplifies the cost inquiry. Courts need not determine marginal costs or make complex judgment calls about which costs should be considered variable and which fixed and when to use one cost measure over another. . . . Instead, the relevant incremental costs are simply the difference between the actual total costs the incumbent incurred during the period of alleged predation and the total costs it would have incurred without the alleged predatory increase in output. Unless there has been some exogenous increase in input costs, this can often be determined by simply comparing total costs before and after the alleged predatory behavior. Dividing this by the alleged predatory increase in output converts this into a per-unit incremental cost, which then simply can be compared to the per-unit price the predator charged during the alleged period of predation. . . .

b. ABOVE-COST PREDATORY PRICING

Although it might seem intuitive that predatory prices must be below-cost, in fact some lawmakers and scholars have concluded that certain above-cost price cuts should also be unlawful, whether or not we call them "predatory." Usually, the concern arises in markets where an incumbent dominant firm sells at a price well above its costs. Periodically, a new firm enters the market at a lower price. The incumbent dominant firm then lowers its price to beat (or match) the entrant. The incumbent never prices below its own costs. But because the entrant has higher costs (or lower quality), it cannot compete at the new price and is driven out of the market. Once the less efficient entrant is safely gone, the incumbent reestablishes the old price.

The concern is that such reactive temporary price cuts will not only drive out entrants, but deter similar entry in the future, and thus allow the more efficient incumbent to perpetuate monopoly prices that exceed the price the next most efficient firm would charge. If so, the supposedly certain gains from short-run post-entry price competition never arrive because the entry never occurs, and the long-term loss is experienced with certainty every day. This concern can exist in any industry where incumbent firms are more efficient than potential entrants and exploit their market power (when entrants are not present) to charge prices well above incumbent costs. Indeed, if valid, this concern would overturn a general current skepticism based on the presumption that predatory pricing is rare because it requires the incumbent to sustain losses on a large number of sales. If harmful predation involved profitable above-cost pricing, it would be far more plausible and prevalent.

In academic scholarship, this has led to proposals by prominent economists to either (1) prevent monopolists from cutting price or raising output in response to entry at all, (2) ban such price cuts or output increases when they would not maximize short run profits, or (3) require that any price cut be maintained even after entrants left the market.[62] In the U.S., so far these sorts of arguments have been taken most seriously in airline regulation.

Enforcement Policy Regarding Unfair Exclusionary Conduct in the Air Transportation Industry

63 Fed. Reg. 17,919 (proposed Apr. 10, 1998).

. . . Following Congress's deregulation of the air transportation industry in 1978, all of the major air carriers restructured their route systems into "hub-and-spoke" networks. Major carriers have long charged considerably higher fares in most of their "spoke" city-pairs, or the "local hub markets," than in other city-pairs of comparable distance and density. In recent years, when small, new-entrant carriers have instituted new low-fare service in major carriers' local hub markets, the major carriers have increasingly responded with strategies of price reductions and capacity increases designed not to maximize their own profits but rather to deprive the new entrants of vital traffic and revenues. Once a new entrant has ceased its service, the major carrier will typically retrench its capacity in the market or raise its fares to at

[62] Elhauge, *supra* note 14, at 684–85 (collecting sources).

least their pre-entry levels, or both. The major carrier thus accepts lower profits in the short run in order to secure higher profits in the long run. This strategy can benefit the major carrier prospectively as well, in that it dissuades other carriers from attempting low-fare entry. It can hurt consumers in the long run by depriving them of the benefits of competition. In those instances where the major carrier's strategy amounts to unfair competition, we must take enforcement action in order to preserve the competitive process.

We hereby put all air carriers on notice, therefore, that as a matter of policy, we propose to consider that a major carrier is engaging in unfair exclusionary practices in violation of 49 U.S.C. 41712 if, in response to new entry into one or more of its local hub markets, it pursues a strategy of price cuts or capacity increases, or both, that either (1) causes it to forego more revenue than all of the new entrant's capacity could have diverted from it or (2) results in substantially lower operating profits—or greater operating losses—in the short run than would a reasonable alternative strategy for competing with the new entrant. Any strategy this costly to the major carrier in the short term is economically rational only if it eventually forces the new entrant to exit the market, after which the major carrier can readily recoup the revenues it has sacrificed to achieve this end. . . .

The Department's Mandate

Our mandate under 49 U.S.C. 41712 to prohibit unfair methods of competition authorizes us to stop air carriers from engaging in conduct that can be characterized as anticompetitive under antitrust principles even if it does not amount to a violation of the antitrust laws. The unfair exclusionary behavior we address here is analogous to (and may amount to) predation within the meaning of the federal antitrust laws.

Although the Supreme Court has said that predation rarely occurs and is even more rarely successful, our informal investigations suggest that the nature of the air transportation industry can at a minimum allow unfair exclusionary practices to succeed. Compared to firms in other industries, a major air carrier can price-discriminate to a much greater extent, adjust prices much faster, and shift resources between markets much more readily. Through booking and other data generated by computer reservations systems and other sources, air carriers have access to comprehensive, "real time" information on their competitors' activities and can thus respond to competitive initiatives more precisely and swiftly than firms in other industries. In addition, a major carrier's ability to shift assets quickly between markets allows it to increase service frequency and capture a disproportionate share of traffic, thereby reaping the competitive advantage of the S-Curve effect. These characteristics of the air transportation industry allow the major carrier to drive a new entrant from a local hub market. Having observed this behavior, other potential new entrants refrain from entering, leaving the major carrier free to reap greater profits indefinitely.

Enforcement Action

> We will determine whether major carriers have engaged in unfair exclusionary practices on a case-by-case basis . . . We anticipate that in the absence of strong reasons to believe that a major carrier's response to competition from a new entrant does not violate 49 U.S.C. 41712, we will institute enforcement proceedings to determine whether the carrier has engaged in unfair exclusionary practices when one or more of the following occurs:
>
> (1) The major carrier adds capacity and sells such a large number of seats at very low fares that the ensuing self-diversion of revenue results in lower local revenue than would a reasonable alternative response,
>
> (2) The number of local passengers that the major carrier carries at the new entrant's low fares (or at similar fares that are substantially below the major carrier's previous fares) exceeds the new entrant's total seat capacity, resulting, through self-diversion, in lower local revenue than would a reasonable alternative response, or
>
> (3) The number of local passengers that the major carrier carries at the new entrant's low fares (or at similar fares that are substantially below the major carrier's previous fares) exceeds the number of low-fare passengers carried by the new entrant, resulting, through self-diversion, in lower local revenue than would a reasonable alternative response.

As the term "reasonable alternative response" suggests, we by no means intend to discourage major carriers from competing aggressively against new entrants in their hub markets. A major carrier can minimize or even avoid self-diversion of local revenues, for example, by matching the new entrant's low fares on a restricted basis (and without significantly increasing capacity) and relying on its own service advantages to retain high-fare traffic. We have seen that major carriers can operate profitably in the same markets as low-fare carriers. As noted, major carriers are competing with Southwest, the most successful low-fare carrier, on a broad scale and are nevertheless reporting record or near-record earnings. We will consider whether a major carrier's response to new entry is consistent with its behavior in markets where it competes with other new-entrant carriers or with Southwest. Conceivably, a major carrier could both lower its fares and add capacity in response to competition from a new entrant without any inordinate sacrifice in local revenues. If the new entrant remained in the market, consumers would reap great benefits from the resulting competition, and we would not intercede. Conceivably, too, a new entrant's service might fail for legitimate competitive reasons: our enforcement policy will not guarantee new entrants success or even survival. Optimally, it will give them a level playing field. . . .

NOTES AND QUESTIONS ON THE PROPOSED U.S. DEPARTMENT OF TRANSPORTATION ENFORCEMENT POLICY

In the final days of the Clinton Administration, the Department of Transportation decided not to adopt the above proposed enforcement guidelines and to instead develop standards by proceeding on a case-by-case basis with enforcement actions. The Bush Administration named as its Transportation Secretary Norman Mineta, who had filed comments opposing the proposed enforcement policy, and the proposed policy appears not to have been pursued. Who was right on this issue, the Clinton Administration or the Bush Administration?

The basic argument against a prohibition on reacting to entry with above-cost predatory price cuts is that such a prohibition would (a) raise post-entry prices for any entrant that would have entered anyway because it is equally efficient; (b) do little to change the odds of entry because less efficient entrants cannot survive long term anyway; and (c) raises big administrative problems in defining the moment of entry and what to do when market conditions or product quality change over time after entry.[63]

The proposed U.S. Department of Transportation enforcement policy would have prohibited reactive above-cost price cuts only if they failed to maximize short-run profits. An advantage of this test is that, if a firm decision would sacrifice profits unless it drove out the entrant, we could infer that its price cut must have been intended to drive out the entrant. However, one might doubt the ability of judges and juries to ascertain the profit-maximizing price level, or of firms to predict what they might hold, especially since the price level will change with changing market conditions. Requiring evidence that prices are "substantially" below the profit-maximizing level might seem to help, but such a requirement simply changes an uncertain line to a different point, compounding it with the vagueness of what counts as "substantially." Moreover, price cuts that do maximize short-run profits still have the same adverse effects of driving out entrants and allowing the incumbent to restore monopoly prices that are higher than the costs of the next-most efficient firm. Some argue the law should instead ban any monopolist price cut or output increase in response to entry if one wants to maximize encouragement to entry and everyday low pricing.[64] But doing so would exacerbate inefficiencies as market conditions change.

Regardless of what one thinks about the general desirability of regulating reactive above-cost price cuts, there are features of the airline industry that might make it a relatively better target than other industries. Namely incumbent airlines frequently engage in reactive above-cost price cuts that drives out entrants, and they can do so quickly and easily because they just need to shift planes to the routes where entry has occurred and

---

[63] Elhauge, *supra* note 14.

[64] Aaron S. Edlin, *Stopping Above-Cost Predatory Pricing*, 111 YALE L.J. 941, 945–46 (2002).

planes are (by definition) highly mobile assets. This makes it more likely that, without any regulation, entry would be deterred by rapid post-entry price cuts. This might explain why the issue has come up most for airlines and other transportation industries with similar features. Do you think antitrust law should prohibit some reactive above-cost price cuts by monopolists, and if so which ones and would you apply the rule to all industries or just some?

United States v. AMR Corp.

335 F.3d 1109 (10th Cir. 2003).

This case involves the nature of permissible competitive practices in the airline industry under the antitrust laws of this country, centered around the hub-and-spoke system of American Airlines. The United States brought this suit against . . . American Airlines . . . , alleging monopolization and attempted monopolization through predatory pricing in violation of § 2 of the Sherman Act. In essence, the government alleges that American engaged in multiple episodes of price predation in four city-pair airline markets, all connected to American's hub at Dallas/Fort Worth International Airport ("DFW"), with the ultimate purpose of using the reputation for predatory pricing it earned in those four markets to defend a monopoly at its DFW hub. At its root, the government's complaint alleges that American: (1) priced its product on the routes in question below cost; and (2) intended to recoup these losses by charging supracompetitive prices either on the four core routes themselves, or on those routes where it stands to exclude competition by means of its "reputation for predation." Finding that the government failed to demonstrate the existence of a genuine issue of material fact as to either of these allegations, the district court granted summary judgment in favor of American, . . . [W]e . . . affirm. . . .

Airlines are predominantly organized in a hub-and-spoke system, with traffic routed such that passengers leave their origin city for an intermediate hub airport. Passengers traveling to a concentrated hub tend to pay higher average fares than those traveling on comparable routes that do not include a concentrated hub as an endpoint. This is known as the "hub premium" and a major airline's hub is often an important profit center. Entry of low cost carriers ("LCCs") into a hub market tends to drive down the fares charged by major carriers. Consequently, major carriers generally enjoy higher margins on routes where they do not face LCC competition.

Both American and Delta . . . maintain hubs at DFW, though Delta's presence is considerably smaller than American's. As of May 2000, American's share of passengers boarded at DFW was 70.2%, Delta's share was roughly 18%, and LCC share was 2.4%. . . .

LCCs generally enjoy the advantage of having lower costs than major carriers, allowing them to offer lower fares than their major-airline competitors.[3] During the period between 1995 and 1997, a number of LCCs, including Vanguard, Western Pacific, and Sunjet, began to take advantage of these lower costs by entering certain city-pair routes serving DFW and charging lower fares than American. The instant case primarily involves DFW-Kansas City, DFW-Wichita, DFW-Colorado Springs, and DFW-Long Beach.

American responded to lower LCC fares on these routes with changes in: (1) pricing (matching LCC prices); (2) capacity (adding flights or switching to larger planes); and (3) yield management (making more seats available at the new, lower prices). By increasing capacity, American overrode its own internal capacity-planning models for each route, which had previously indicated that such increases would be unprofitable. In each instance, American's response produced the same result: the competing LCC failed to establish a presence, moved its operations, or ceased its separate existence entirely. Once the LCC ceased or moved its operations, American generally resumed its prior marketing strategy, reducing flights and raising prices to levels roughly comparable to those prior to the period of low-fare competition. Capacity was reduced after LCC exit, but usually remained higher than prior to the alleged episode of predatory activity.

. . . In the instant case, the anticompetitive conduct at issue is predatory pricing. The crux of the government's argument is that the "incremental" revenues and costs specifically associated with American's capacity additions show a loss. Because American spent more to add capacity than the revenues generated by the capacity additions, such capacity additions made no economic sense unless American intended to drive LCCs out of the market. Under the government's theory, American attempted to monopolize the four city-pair routes in question in order to develop a reputation as an exceedingly aggressive competitor and set an example to all potential competitors. Fearing American's predatory response, the theory goes, future potential competitors will decline to enter other DFW market routes and compete. If American succeeds in preventing or at least forestalling the formation of an LCC hub at DFW, it will then be able to charge higher prices on other DFW routes and thereby recoup the losses it incurred from its "capacity dumping" on the four core routes . . .

"Predatory pricing means pricing below some appropriate measure of cost." *Matsushita*.[6] Despite a great deal of debate on the subject, no

[3] For example, in 1994, American calculated ValuJet's stage-length adjusted cost per available seat mile to be 4.32 cents, and American's to be 8.54 cents. Southwest has costs that are 30% lower than American's.

[6] The government notes in its brief that the "gravamen of the complaint is not limited to American's pricing." Rather, the complained of behavior includes American's capacity additions. However, as the district court correctly noted, prices and productive output are "two sides of the same coin." While the specific behavior complained of in the instant case is an increase in output or frequency, these actions must be analyzed in terms of their effect on price and cost. Thus, in order to succeed in the present action, the government must meet the standards of proof for predatory pricing cases established in *Brooke Group*.

consensus has emerged as to what the most "appropriate" measure of cost is in predatory pricing cases. Costs can generally be divided into those that are "fixed" and do not vary with the level of output (management expenses, interest on bonded debt, property taxes, depreciation, and other irreducible overhead) and those that are "variable" and do vary with the level of output (materials, fuel, labor used to produce the product). Marginal cost, the cost that results from producing an additional increment of output, is primarily a function of variable cost because fixed costs, as the name would imply, are largely unaffected by changes in output. For predatory pricing cases, especially those involving allegedly predatory production increases, the ideal measure of cost would be marginal cost because "[a]s long as a firm's prices exceed its marginal cost, each additional sale decreases losses or increases profits." However, marginal cost, an economic abstraction, is notoriously difficult to measure and "cannot be determined from conventional accounting methods." Economists, therefore, must resort to proxies for marginal cost. A commonly accepted proxy for marginal cost in predatory pricing cases is Average Variable Cost ("AVC"), the average of those costs that vary with the level of output.

The Supreme Court has declined to state which of the various cost measures is definitive. . . . Because there may be times when courts need the flexibility to examine both AVC as well as other proxies for marginal cost in order to evaluate an alleged predatory pricing scheme, we again decline to dictate a definitive cost measure for all cases. . . .

Conceding that AVC is a good proxy for marginal cost in most cases, the government nevertheless argues that there may be times when looking only to a market-wide AVC test will disguise the nature of the predatory conduct at issue. Where there is a challenge to well-defined incremental conduct, and where incremental costs may be directly and confidently measured utilizing alternative proxies to AVC, argues the government, the market-wide AVC test is inappropriate.

Considering this to be the situation in the instant case, the government proffers four tests that purport to measure reliably incremental costs—the precise costs associated with the capacity additions at issue. . . . Because Tests Two and Three rely on fully allocated costs and include many fixed costs, the district court held that utilizing these cost measures would be the equivalent of applying an average total cost test, implicitly ruled out by *Brooke Group*'s mention of incremental costs only. . . . We agree with this conclusion. While we will accept alternative proxies to marginal cost beyond AVC, Tests Two and Three are simply not proxies for marginal or incremental cost. . . .

[R]ather than determining whether the added capacity itself was priced below an appropriate measure of cost, Test One effectively treats forgone or "sacrificed" profits as costs, and condemns activity that may have been profitable as predatory.[13] Rather than isolating the costs actually associated with the capacity additions the government purports to measure directly, Test One simply performs a "before-and-after" comparison of the route as a whole, looking to whether profits on the route as a whole decline after capacity was added, not to whether the challenged capacity additions were done below cost. In the end, Test One indicates only that a company has failed to maximize short-run profits on the route as a whole. Such a pricing standard could lead to a strangling of competition, as it would condemn nearly all output expansions, and harm to consumers. We conclude that Test One is invalid as a matter of law. . . .

Test Four attempts to reveal American's predatory conduct by measuring and comparing the incremental costs incurred by American when it added capacity to the city-pair routes in question to the incremental revenue it received from the additional capacity. . . . The costs included in [Test Four] include variable costs American incurs with respect to all of its operations at DFW. Because some of those variable costs do not vary proportionately with the level of flight activity, they are allocated arbitrarily to a flight or route. . . . American identifies these variable, non-proportional common costs as: (1) airport ticket agents, (2) arrival agents, (3) ramp workers, and (4) security. . . . Because the cost component of Test Four includes arbitrarily allocated variable costs, it does not compare incremental revenue to average avoidable cost. Instead, it compares incremental revenue to a measure of both average variable cost and average avoidable cost. Therefore, Test Four does not measure only the avoidable or incremental cost of the capacity additions and cannot be used to satisfy the government's burden in this case.

We conclude that all four proxies are invalid as a matter of law. . . . Because it is uncontested that American did not price below AVC for any route as a whole, . . . the government has not succeeded in establishing the first element of *Brooke Group,* pricing below an appropriate measure of cost.[15] . . .

---

[13] For example, if an airline earned $20.6 million on a route that cost $18 million to operate, it would have $2.6 million in profit. If the airline then added a flight to the route that would cost $500,000 to operate, but brought in an additional $1 million in revenue from passengers, the airline would make $500,000 profit. If adding this extra capacity to the route reduced the profitability of other flights on that route, reducing revenue for the rest of the route by $600,000 down to $20 million, under Test One, this conduct would be considered predatory because rather than comparing the additional flight's $1 million in revenue to its $500,000 in costs, Test One looks only to the reduction in profits on the route as a whole from $2.6 million to $2.5 million. Thus, this conduct would be labeled predatory because the profits for the route as a whole declined, even though the capacity additions themselves were profitable and the route as a whole was still profitable. *See* Einer Elhauge, *Why Above-Cost Price Cuts to Drive Out Entrants Are Not Predatory—and the Implications for Defining Costs and Market Power,* 112 Yale L.J. 681, 694 (2003).

[15] The district court also stated that even if American had priced below an appropriate measure of cost, it was nevertheless entitled to summary judgment because "American's prices only matched, and never undercut, the fares of the new entrant, low cost carriers on the four core routes." . . . However, unlike in the Robinson-Patman Act, such a defense is not expressly provided for by the terms of the Sherman Act. The Supreme Court has never mentioned the

NOTES AND QUESTIONS ON *AMERICAN AIRLINES*

1. ***Should incremental costs include incremental lost revenue?*** Was the court right that the incremental costs of adding capacity should not include the loss of revenue from lower prices on the nonincremental flights? Cutting the other way is the fact that economists often define costs to include opportunity costs like lost profits from alternative uses. But economic models of monopoly pricing distinguish the effect on incremental revenue from marginal cost. Moreover, redefining incremental costs to include foregone profits would effectively convert any cost-based test into a profit-sacrifice test. Thus, regardless of which test on thinks is best, avoiding such a redefinition seems necessary in order to maintain intellectual clarity of what the alternative tests are.

2. ***Relevance to cost measure.*** If above-cost pricing cannot be called predatory under U.S. law, should the same sort of concerns that animate proposals to ban reactive above-cost price cuts nonetheless influence decisions about what cost measure to use? That appears to be occurring in lower U.S. courts, where cutting prices in reaction to entry is often deemed evidence of an anticompetitive intent that is cited as a reason to make the cost measure average total cost rather than variable or marginal costs. *See* Chapter 3.C.2.a. But that would seem to be a valid approach only if the underlying concerns about above-cost price cuts are valid.

3. PREDATORY OVERPAYING BY A MONOPSONIST

Weyerhaeuser Co. v. Ross-Simmons Hardwood Lumber

549 U.S. 312 (2007).

■ MR. JUSTICE THOMAS delivered the opinion of the Court.

Respondent Ross-Simmons, a sawmill, sued petitioner Weyerhaeuser, alleging that Weyerhaeuser drove it out of business by bidding up the price of sawlogs to a level that prevented Ross-Simmons from being profitable. A jury returned a verdict in favor of Ross-Simmons on its monopolization claim, and the Ninth Circuit affirmed. We granted certiorari to decide whether the test we applied to claims of predatory pricing in *Brooke*, also applies to claims of predatory bidding. We hold that it does. Accordingly, we vacate the judgment of the Court of Appeals.

I

This antitrust case concerns the acquisition of red alder sawlogs by the mills that process those logs in the Pacific Northwest. . . . By 2001, Weyerhaeuser's mills were acquiring approximately 65 percent of the alder logs available for sale in the region. . . . From 1990 to 2000,

---

possibility of such a defense under the Sherman Act. We therefore decline to rule that the "meeting competition" defense applies in the § 2 context.

Weyerhaeuser made more than $75 million in capital investments in its hardwood mills in the Pacific Northwest [to improve their efficiency]. By contrast, Ross-Simmons appears to have engaged in little efficiency-enhancing investment.

Logs represent up to 75 percent of a sawmill's total costs. And from 1998 to 2001, the price of alder sawlogs increased while prices for finished hardwood lumber fell. These divergent trends in input and output prices cut into the mills' profit margins, and Ross-Simmons suffered heavy losses during this time. Saddled with several million dollars in debt, Ross-Simmons shut down its mill completely in May 2001. . . .

The District Court . . . instructed the jury that Ross-Simmons could prove that Weyerhaeuser's bidding practices were anticompetitive acts if the jury concluded that Weyerhaeuser "purchased more logs than it needed, or paid a higher price for logs than necessary, in order to prevent [Ross-Simmons] from obtaining the logs they needed at a fair price." . . .

III

Predatory bidding, which Ross-Simmons alleges in this case, involves the exercise of market power on the buy side or input side of a market. In a predatory-bidding scheme, a purchaser of inputs "bids up the market price of a critical input to such high levels that rival buyers cannot survive (or compete as vigorously) and, as a result, the predating buyer acquires (or maintains or increases its) monopsony power." Kirkwood, Buyer Power and Exclusionary Conduct, 72 Antitrust L.J. 625, 652 (2005) (hereinafter Kirkwood). Monopsony power is market power on the buy side of the market. As such, a monopsony is to the buy side of the market what a monopoly is to the sell side and is sometimes colloquially called a "buyer's monopoly."

A predatory bidder ultimately aims to exercise the monopsony power gained from bidding up input prices. To that end, once the predatory bidder has caused competing buyers to exit the market for purchasing inputs, it will seek to "restrict its input purchases below the competitive level," thus "reduc[ing] the unit price for the remaining input[s] it purchases." Salop, Anticompetitive Overbuying by Power Buyers, 72 Antitrust L.J. 669, 672 (2005) (hereinafter Salop). The reduction in input prices will lead to "a significant cost saving that more than offsets the profit[s] that would have been earned on the output." If all goes as planned, the predatory bidder will reap monopsonistic profits that will offset any losses suffered in bidding up input prices.[2] (In this case, the plaintiff was the defendant's competitor in the input-purchasing market. Thus, this case does not present a situation of suppliers suing a monopsonist buyer under § 2 of the Sherman Act, nor does it present a

[2] If the predatory firm's competitors in the input market and the output market are the same, then predatory bidding can also lead to the bidder's acquisition of monopoly power in the output market. In that case, which does not appear to be present here, the monopsonist could, under certain market conditions, also recoup its losses by raising output prices to monopolistic levels.

risk of significantly increased concentration in the market in which the monopsonist sells, *i.e.,* the market for finished lumber.)

IV

A

Predatory-pricing and predatory-bidding claims are analytically similar. This similarity results from the close theoretical connection between monopoly and monopsony. *See* Kirkwood 653 (describing monopsony as the "mirror image" of monopoly); *Khan v. State Oil Co.,* 93 F.3d 1358, 1361 (C.A.7 1996) ("[M]onopsony pricing . . . is analytically the same as monopoly or cartel pricing and [is] so treated by the law"), vacated and remanded on other grounds, 522 U.S. 3 (1997); *Vogel v. American Soc. of Appraisers,* 744 F.2d 598, 601 (C.A.7 1984) ("[M]onopoly and monopsony are symmetrical distortions of competition from an economic standpoint"); *see also* Hearing on Monopsony Issues in Agriculture: Buying Power of Processors in Our Nation's Agricultural Markets before the Senate Committee on the Judiciary, 108th Cong., 1st Sess., 3 (2004). The kinship between monopoly and monopsony suggests that similar legal standards should apply to claims of monopolization and to claims of monopsonization. Cf. Noll, "Buyer Power" and Economic Policy, 72 Antitrust L.J. 589, 591 (2005) ("[A]symmetric treatment of monopoly and monopsony has no basis in economic analysis").

Tracking the economic similarity between monopoly and monopsony, predatory-pricing plaintiffs and predatory-bidding plaintiffs make strikingly similar allegations. A predatory-pricing plaintiff alleges that a predator cut prices to drive the plaintiff out of business and, thereby, to reap monopoly profits from the output market. In parallel fashion, a predatory-bidding plaintiff alleges that a predator raised prices for a key input to drive the plaintiff out of business and, thereby, to reap monopsony profits in the input market. Both claims involve the deliberate use of unilateral pricing measures for anticompetitive purposes.[3] And both claims logically require firms to incur short-term losses on the chance that they might reap supracompetitive profits in the future.

B

More importantly, predatory bidding mirrors predatory pricing in respects that we deemed significant to our analysis in *Brooke Group.* In *Brooke Group,* we noted that " 'predatory pricing schemes are rarely tried, and even more rarely successful.' " Predatory pricing requires a

3 Predatory bidding on inputs is not analytically different from predatory overbuying of inputs. Both practices fall under the rubric of monopsony predation and involve an input purchaser's use of input prices in an attempt to exclude rival input purchasers. The economic effect of the practices is identical: input prices rise. In a predatory-bidding scheme, the purchaser causes prices to rise by offering to pay more for inputs. In a predatory-overbuying scheme, the purchaser causes prices to rise by demanding more of the input. Either way, input prices increase. Our use of the term "predatory bidding" is not meant to suggest that different legal treatment is appropriate for the economically identical practice of "predatory overbuying."

firm to suffer certain losses in the short term on the chance of reaping supracompetitive profits in the future. A rational business will rarely make this sacrifice. The same reasoning applies to predatory bidding. A predatory-bidding scheme requires a buyer of inputs to suffer losses today on the chance that it will reap supracompetitive profits in the future. For this reason, "[s]uccessful monopsony predation is probably as unlikely as successful monopoly predation." R. Blair & J. Harrison, Monopsony 66 (1993).

And like the predatory conduct alleged in *Brooke Group,* actions taken in a predatory-bidding scheme are often " ' "the very essence of competition." ' " Just as sellers use output prices to compete for purchasers, buyers use bid prices to compete for scarce inputs. There are myriad legitimate reasons—ranging from benign to affirmatively procompetitive—why a buyer might bid up input prices. A firm might bid up inputs as a result of miscalculation of its input needs or as a response to increased consumer demand for its outputs. A more efficient firm might bid up input prices to acquire more inputs as a part of a procompetitive strategy to gain market share in the output market. A firm that has adopted an input-intensive production process might bid up inputs to acquire the inputs necessary for its process. Or a firm might bid up input prices to acquire excess inputs as a hedge against the risk of future rises in input costs or future input shortages. There is nothing illicit about these bidding decisions. Indeed, this sort of high bidding is essential to competition and innovation on the buy side of the market.[4]

Brooke Group also noted that a failed predatory-pricing scheme may benefit consumers. The potential benefit results from the difficulty an aspiring predator faces in recouping losses suffered from below-cost pricing. Without successful recoupment, "predatory pricing produces lower aggregate prices in the market, and consumer welfare is enhanced." Failed predatory-bidding schemes can also, but will not necessarily, benefit consumers. *See* Salop 677–678. In the first stage of a predatory-bidding scheme, the predator's high bidding will likely lead to its acquisition of more inputs. Usually, the acquisition of more inputs leads to the manufacture of more outputs. And increases in output generally result in lower prices to consumers.[5] *Id.,* at 677; R. Blair & J. Harrison, *supra,* at 66–67. Thus, a failed predatory-bidding scheme can be a "boon to consumers" in the same way that we considered a predatory-pricing scheme to be.

In addition, predatory bidding presents less of a direct threat of consumer harm than predatory pricing. A predatory-pricing scheme

[4] Higher prices for inputs obviously benefit existing sellers of inputs and encourage new firms to enter the market for input sales as well.

[5] Consumer benefit does not necessarily result at the first stage because the predator might not use its excess inputs to manufacture additional outputs. It might instead destroy the excess inputs. *See* Salop 677, n. 22. Also, if the same firms compete in the input and output markets, any increase in outputs by the predator could be offset by decreases in outputs from the predator's struggling competitors.

ultimately achieves success by charging higher prices to consumers. By contrast, a predatory-bidding scheme could succeed with little or no effect on consumer prices because a predatory bidder does not necessarily rely on raising prices in the output market to recoup its losses. Salop 676. Even if output prices remain constant, a predatory bidder can use its power as the predominant buyer of inputs to force down input prices and capture monopsony profits. *Ibid.*

C

The general theoretical similarities of monopoly and monopsony combined with the theoretical and practical similarities of predatory pricing and predatory bidding convince us that our two-pronged *Brooke Group* test should apply to predatory-bidding claims.

The first prong of *Brooke Group's* test requires little adaptation for the predatory-bidding context. A plaintiff must prove that the alleged predatory bidding led to below-cost pricing of the predator's outputs. That is, the predator's bidding on the buy side must have caused the cost of the relevant output to rise above the revenues generated in the sale of those outputs. As with predatory pricing, the exclusionary effect of higher bidding that does not result in below-cost output pricing "is beyond the practical ability of a judicial tribunal to control without courting intolerable risks of chilling legitimate" procompetitive conduct. Given the multitude of procompetitive ends served by higher bidding for inputs, the risk of chilling procompetitive behavior with too lax a liability standard is as serious here as it was in *Brooke Group*. Consequently, only higher bidding that leads to below-cost pricing in the relevant output market will suffice as a basis for liability for predatory bidding.

A predatory-bidding plaintiff also must prove that the defendant has a dangerous probability of recouping the losses incurred in bidding up input prices through the exercise of monopsony power. Absent proof of likely recoupment, a strategy of predatory bidding makes no economic sense because it would involve short-term losses with no likelihood of offsetting long-term gains. As with predatory pricing, making a showing on the recoupment prong will require "a close analysis of both the scheme alleged by the plaintiff and the structure and conditions of the relevant market."

Ross-Simmons has conceded that it has not satisfied the *Brooke Group* standard. Therefore, its predatory-bidding theory of liability cannot support the jury's verdict. . . .

NOTES AND QUESTIONS ON *WEYERHAEUSER*

1. ***If the complaint is that the defendant has paid too much for inputs, how can a below-cost test be applied?*** The Court's answer was to look at whether the price of the predator's *output* was below cost given its overpaying for inputs. Specifically, the Court's test was whether the downstream price was lower than the total cost of the downstream output, which equals the sum of the upstream price (for the logs) plus the downstream processing cost (to convert logs to lumber). Call the upstream price P_u, the downstream price P_d, and the cost of the downstream processing (here of logs into finished lumber) C_d. Then, the Court's test was basically whether $P_d < P_u + C_d$. This makes sense because the more the upstream price (P_u) is inflated by overpaying, the more likely it is that the downstream price is lower than the total cost of the downstream output.

2. ***Does this holding eliminate any distinctive claim for predatory overbidding because any claim for below-cost pricing of output was already covered by straight predatory pricing claim?*** Not quite because, in a straight predatory pricing claim, the issue would be whether the defendant has monopoly power in the output market, lowered prices in the output market, and could recoup lost profits in the output market. In contrast, in a predatory overbidding case, the defendant must have monopsony power in the input market, have raised prices in the input market, and be able to recoup profits in that input market.

For example, here the input market for logs was regional, whereas the output market for finished lumber seems to have been national. In the national output market, Weyerhaeuser may not have had any monopoly power or ability to affect national lumber prices, and eliminating one small output rival like Ross-Simmons might be unlikely to lead to recoupment of any lost profits in the national lumber market. In contrast, in the regional input market for Northwestern logs, Weyerhaeuser had a 65% buyer share and plausible monopsony power, had allegedly driven up log prices by overbidding, and driving rival purchasers out of that regional log market might allow Weyerhaeuser to recoup lost profits by paying the regional mills a low monopsony price for logs in the future.

4. THE ECONOMICS OF PRICE DISCRIMINATION

Price discrimination is simply charging different prices for the same item. While this may sound bad, it is often legal and can sometimes efficiently expand output. If a firm with market power charges a *uniform* price, it has to take into account that any price reduction it makes to get a marginal customer will lose it profits from the inframarginal customers who are willing to pay a higher rate. Thus, a firm with market power that can charge only a uniform price maximizes profits by charging a price that many marginal customers will not pay, even though they value the product more than the incremental cost of producing it. This is why such firms produce a subcompetitive level of output and allocative inefficiency.

In contrast, suppose a firm with market power engages in *perfect* price discrimination, lowering prices to marginal buyers while charging higher prices to inframarginal buyers, and charging each buyer precisely the amount that that buyer values the product. (In economic theory, such perfect price discrimination is called first-degree price discrimination.) With perfect price discrimination, the firm will produce the perfectly competitive level of output because it has incentives to sell to the marginal buyer at any price that exceeds its incremental cost. This will eliminate any allocative inefficiency. However, perfect price discrimination will also eliminate the consumer surplus that otherwise would result under any uniform price from the fact that inframarginal buyers value the product more than the price they pay. In short, compared to uniform pricing, perfect price discrimination lowers consumer welfare but raises efficiency and total welfare ex post.[65] U.S. antitrust law appears to embrace a consumer welfare standard, although some argue that antitrust law should embrace an efficiency/total welfare standard.[66]

However, truly perfect price discrimination is usually not possible. Suppose instead the firm can only engage in *imperfect* price discrimination. Such imperfect price discrimination usually involves charging different categories of buyers different prices that roughly correlate to the value that buyers in each category put on the product. (This is called third-degree price discrimination). Or imperfect price discrimination can involve offering a menu of product options and prices that causes buyers to self-select in ways that imperfectly correlate with their willingness to pay. (This called second-degree price discrimination).

Compared to the alternative of uniform pricing, such imperfect price discrimination can conceivably increase *or* decrease output, efficiency, consumer welfare, and total welfare ex post. However, it has been proven that, *unless* imperfect price discrimination increases total output, imperfect price discrimination *always reduces* efficiency, consumer welfare, and total welfare ex post.[67] The reason is that imperfect price discrimination reallocates some output from buyers who valued the product more to buyers who valued the product less, which harms

[65] "Total welfare" is the sum of consumer welfare (the difference between consumer valuations and prices charged) and producer welfare (which is the difference between prices and costs, i.e., producer profits). "Total welfare" is thus equivalent to efficiency (the total difference between value and cost) and equal to the sum of consumer welfare and producer profits. If price discrimination increases producer profits by more than it decreases in consumer welfare, then it increases total welfare. This is why price discrimination can increase total welfare but reduce consumer welfare. In contrast, if price discrimination reduces total welfare, then it necessarily also reduces consumer welfare, which equals total welfare minus the profits the firm reaped from price discrimination. (Those profits must be positive or the firm would not price discriminate).

"Ex post" means that the welfare measures are comparing welfare after the price discrimination to welfare right before the price discrimination. Ex post total welfare thus does not take into account that an ability to engage in price discrimination may (because it increases the producer profits anticipated from gaining market power) have ex ante effects on the extent to which firms invest to obtain that market power. If the total welfare measure considers such ex ante effects (on top of the ex post effects), then it is called ex ante total welfare.

[66] *See* Chapter 2.A; John B. Kirkwood & Robert H. Lande, *The Fundamental Goal of Antitrust: Protecting Consumers, Not Increasing Efficiency*, 84 NOTRE DAME L. REV. 191 (2008); Elhauge, *Tying, Bundled Discounts, and the Death of the Single Monopoly Profit Theory*, 123 HARVARD LAW REVIEW 397, 436–442 (2009) (summarizing case law and arguments favoring a consumer welfare standard); Elhauge, *The Failed Resurrection of the Single Monopoly Profit Theory*, 6(1) COMPETITION POLICY INTERNATIONAL 155, 167–172 (Spring 2010) (same).

[67] Hal R. Varian, Price Discrimination, in 1 HANDBOOK OF INDUSTRIAL ORGANIZATION 597, 622–623 (Richard Schmalensee & Robert D. Willig eds., 1989); Elhauge & Nalebuff, *The Welfare Effects of Metering Ties,* 33 J. L. ECON. & ORG. (2017).

consumer and total welfare unless the adverse welfare effects of this reallocation are offset by an output increase. Further, increasing output is necessary, but not sufficient, for price discrimination to increase ex post total welfare. Even if it increases output, price discrimination will increase ex post total welfare *only* if the welfare gains from the output increase (among categories of buyers who would not buy absent price discrimination) are large enough to exceed the welfare loss from the output misallocation (among categories of buyers who would buy whether prices were uniform or discriminatory). For a lognormal distribution of buyer preferences and marginal costs of zero, the output increase would have to be 37% or more.[68]

Further, under a linear, normal, or lognormal distribution of consumer preferences, imperfect price discrimination always reduces consumer welfare.[69] It also reduces ex post total welfare unless the dispersion of customer preferences is large.[70] This makes sense because the greater the dispersion of preferences, the greater the share of potential customers that would not buy at a uniform price, and thus the greater the efficiency advantage of price discrimination.

If the buyers are not final consumers, but instead are intermediaries who resell to consumers, then imperfect price discrimination reduces output and total welfare, other than in cases where the price discrimination discourages inefficient integration.[71] The reason is that the disfavored intermediary paying a higher price will resell at a higher downstream price that tends to drive consumers to the favored intermediary, which will tend to drive up the profits of the favored intermediary and allow the price-discriminating supplier to increase prices to it as well. This effect will harm output and total welfare unless the efficiency and welfare benefits of avoiding inefficient integration are sufficiently large to offset those harms.

Ex ante effects also matter. Because price discrimination increases the profits that a producer can anticipate reaping from market power, allowing price discrimination increases ex ante incentives to invest in activities that might garner market power. Where those activities involve obtaining anticompetitive regulations that hamper rival competition, such investments would be undesirable. When the activities involve innovating to create some product or production process that is sufficiently better or cheaper than rival options to enjoy market power, the innovation is desirable but the investments may not be if their costs are excessive compared to the innovation gain. Such investments can be excessive because firms competing for a market power position have

---

[68] Elhauge & Nalebuff, *supra* note 67; Elhauge, *Rehabilitating Jefferson Parish: Why Ties Without a Substantial Foreclosure Share Should Not Be Per Se Legal*, 80 ANTITRUST L.J. 463, 478 (2016).

[69] *See sources* cited in immediately preceding note.

[70] *See sources* cited in immediately preceding note.

[71] Michael L. Katz, *The Welfare Effects of Third-Degree Price Discrimination in Intermediate Goods Markets,* 77 Amer. Econ. Rev. 154, 161–165 (1987).

incentives to incur costs that dissipate the monopoly profits they expect to earn from that market power. Judge Posner has argued that firms will dissipate all the monopoly profits ex ante (assuming that the long run costs to seeking market power are constant), whereas Professor Fisher has argued that they will only dissipate some of those monopoly profits (assuming instead that that obtaining market power has rising marginal costs).[72] Under Judge Posner's assumption, all ex post producer profits wash out ex ante, so that the ex ante total welfare effects are equal to the consumer welfare effects, which means perfect price discrimination reduces ex ante total welfare and imperfect price discrimination does so as well in the usual case where it reduces consumer welfare. Under Professor Fisher's assumption, the dissipated share will be less than 100%, but this still means that price discrimination that increases ex post total welfare might decrease ex ante total welfare.

Further, the patent race literature proves that, if firms anticipate obtaining 100% of the total surplus created by their innovations, they will invest excessively in innovation, creating an inefficient decrease in ex ante total welfare.[73] Because perfect price discrimination does give a firm 100% of total surplus, this literature proves that perfect price discrimination reduces ex ante total welfare even though it increases ex post total welfare. More generally, this patent race literature proves that investments will be excessive whenever firms obtain more than a certain fraction of the total surplus created by their innovation. This means that, to assure optimal investment, the remaining fraction of total surplus must go to consumers as consumer surplus. If we assume that patent law has already been designed to try to award innovators the optimal fraction of total surplus by allowing patent holders a normal monopoly profit during their patent term, then any price discrimination that allows innovators to extract more than that normal patent award will induce excessive investment and reduce ex ante total welfare.[74]

Another complication is that price discrimination is also ubiquitous in many markets where firms have no market power in the antitrust sense, including hotels, movie theaters, airlines, computers, automobiles, books, clothing, groceries, and a vast array of other products that offer various discounts, rebates and coupons.[75] Such firms may be engaged in monopolistic competition because of fixed costs or brand differentiation,

---

[72] Richard A. Posner, *The Social Costs of Monopoly and Regulation*, 83 J. POL. ECON. 807, 807–09, 812, 822 (1975); Franklin M. Fisher, *The Social Costs of Monopoly and Regulation: Posner Reconsidered*, 93 J. POL. ECON. 410 (1985); Elhauge, *Tying*, *supra* note 66, at 441–42 (summarizing the debate).

[73] *See* SUZANNE SCOTCHMER, INNOVATION AND INCENTIVES 100–03 (2004); Partha Dasgupta & Joseph Stiglitz, *Uncertainty, Industrial Structure, and the Speed of R & D*, 11 BELL J. ECON. 1, 18 (1980); Pankaj Tandon, *Rivalry and the Excessive Allocation of Resources to Research*, 14 BELL J. ECON. 152, 152, 156–57 (1983); Elhauge, *Tying*, *supra* note 66, at 440.

[74] Elhauge, *Tying*, *supra* note 66, at 440; Elhauge, *Failed Resurrection*, *supra* note 66, at 170–72.

[75] Elhauge, *Why Above-Cost Price Cuts*, *supra* note 14, at 732–33; Illinois Tool Works Inc. v. Independent Ink, Inc., 547 U.S. 28, 44–45 (2006).

and thus have downward sloping demand curves that permit price discrimination.[76] Yet because others would enter their market or product space if they earned supracompetitive profits, they will at best be able to use the profits from such price discrimination to cover their fixed costs and the common costs of producing goods for buyers who place different values on that good.[77] Because each firm is disciplined by competition from charging a price-discrimination schedule whose total revenue exceeds its total costs, such price discrimination should permit firms to incur greater fixed and common costs, and thus increase market output and efficiency.[78]

A recurring obstacle to price discrimination is that the seller must not only be able to identify which buyers are willing to pay more for the product, but also must prevent resales from the buyers who are buying at low prices to the buyers whom the seller wishes to charge high prices. Identifying buyer types can sometimes be accomplished by charging buyers according to the intensity of their use. If buyers value a copying machine more the more copies they make, a seller might price discriminate by charging buyers a base rate for the machine plus a metered rate per copy. Other techniques include advertising price discounts in ways more likely to reach only less wealthy customers, or requiring effort to obtain the discounts that high income buyers who value their time more highly are less likely to exert. Preventing resales may sometimes require contractual restrictions, whose enforceability itself may raise antitrust issues. But in some industries, preventing resales is easy because the product does not lend itself to resale, such as personal services or serving hot perishable food.

In the United States, the Robinson-Patman Act regulates price discrimination in goods. The statute does not cover price discrimination that simply reaps higher profits from buyers but rather prohibits price discrimination only if it is reasonably likely to harm competition. *See* Chapters 3.a & 5.c. The Act has been interpreted to cover two sorts of price discrimination.

Primary-line price discrimination is price discrimination that adversely affects *competition at the seller's level*. Here the concern is that the seller might use high prices in one area to fund predatory prices in another area. This sort of price discrimination has been subsumed by predatory pricing doctrine, with the main effect being (as discussed above) that U.S. courts are willing to apply more aggressive tests of predatory pricing when pricing is discriminatory or selective.

---

[76] *See* Chapter 3.A. Price discrimination without market power may also be possible if there is some demand discontinuity and buyers who are willing to pay a higher price select sellers either at random (because they are uninformed or price insensitive) or in proportion to the common costs incurred (such as when more flights or retail outlets offer greater convenience). *See* Elhauge, *Why Above-Cost Price Cuts, supra* note 14, at 736–43. Both types of price discrimination should be output-expanding. *Id.*

[77] Elhauge, *Why Above-Cost Price Cuts, supra* note 14, at 732–54.

[78] *Id.*

Secondary-line price discrimination is price discrimination that adversely affects *competition at the buyers' level*. Here the concern is that the buyers who bought at the higher price will be at a competitive disadvantage in their downstream markets. This topic will be covered in Chapter 5, which addresses conduct or agreements that arguably distort downstream competition. The ubiquitous issue there, as we shall see, is that sellers generally would seem to have little incentive to distort downstream competition, given that sellers benefit from a competitive downstream market for distributing their goods.

5. EXCLUSIONS FROM OWNED PROPERTY—UNILATERAL REFUSALS TO DEAL

A firm that lacks dominant market power may be unable to agree with other firms to engage in a concerted refusal to deal, but can unilaterally choose with whom they deal without fear of antitrust liability. For a firm that has monopoly power, the law is more complicated. Such a firm has no general duty to cooperate with its rivals. But it also has no privilege not to deal. The doctrinal question this raises is: just when is such a firm's unilateral refusal to deal illegal? The underlying policy issue this raises is: to what extent should antitrust law restrict rights to exclude created by various types of property law?

Otter Tail Power Company v. United States

410 U.S. 366 (1973).

■ MR. JUSTICE DOUGLAS delivered the opinion of the Court. . . .

[T]he District Court found that Otter Tail had attempted to monopolize and had monopolized the retail distribution of electric power in its service area in violation of § 2 of the Sherman Act. The District Court found that Otter Tail had attempted to prevent communities in which its retail distribution franchise had expired from replacing it with a municipal distribution system. The principal means employed were (1) refusals to sell power at wholesale to proposed municipal systems in the communities where it had been retailing power; (2) refusals to "wheel" power to such systems, that is to say, to transfer by direct transmission or displacement electric power from one utility to another over the facilities of an intermediate utility. . . .[79]

Otter Tail sells electric power at retail in 465 towns in Minnesota, North Dakota, and South Dakota. . . . In towns where Otter Tail distributes at retail, it operates under municipally granted franchises which are limited from 10 to 20 years. Each town in Otter Tail's service

[79] [Editor's Note: Otter Tail did wholesale and wheel electric power to electric systems that it had not previously served at retail. *See* United States v. Otter Tail Power Co., 331 F. Supp. 54, 57–58 (D. Minn. 1971).]

area generally can accommodate only one distribution system, making each town a natural monopoly market for the distribution and sale of electric power at retail. The aggregate of towns in Otter Tail's service area is the geographic market in which Otter Tail competes for the right to serve the towns at retail. That competition is generally for the right to serve the entire retail market within the composite limits of a town, and that competition is generally between Otter Tail and a prospective or existing municipal system. These towns number 510 and of those Otter Tail serves 91%, or 465.

. . . Between 1945 and 1970, there were contests in 12 towns served by Otter Tail over proposals to replace it with municipal systems. In only three . . . municipal systems actually established. Proposed municipal systems have great obstacles; they must purchase the electric power at wholesale. To do so they must have access to existing transmission lines. The only ones available [to the relevant towns] belong to Otter Tail. . . . Otter Tail refused to sell the new systems energy at wholesale and refused to agree to wheel power from other suppliers of wholesale energy.

. . . As respects Elbow Lake and Hankinson, Otter Tail simply refused to deal, although according to the findings it had the ability to do so. Elbow Lake, cut off from all sources of wholesale power, constructed its own generating plant. Both Elbow Lake and Hankinson requested the Bureau of Reclamation and various cooperatives to furnish them with wholesale power; they were willing to supply it if Otter Tail would wheel it. But Otter Tail refused, relying on provisions in its contracts which barred the use of its lines for wheeling power to towns which it had served at retail. Elbow Lake after completing its plant asked the Federal Power Commission, under § 202(b) of the Federal Power Act, to require Otter Tail to interconnect with the town and sell it power at wholesale.[80] The Federal Power Commission ordered first a temporary and then a permanent connection. Hankinson tried unsuccessfully to get relief from the North Dakota Commission and then filed a complaint with the federal commission seeking an order to compel Otter Tail to wheel. While the application was pending, the town council voted to withdraw it and subsequently renewed Otter Tail's franchise. . . .

I

Otter Tail contends that by reason of the Federal Power Act it is not subject to antitrust regulation with respect to its refusal to deal. We disagree with that position.

"Repeals of the antitrust laws by implication from a regulatory statute are strongly disfavored, and have only been found in cases of

---

[80] [Editor's Note: This request was for standby power to supplement Elbow Lake's new generating plant. 331 F. Supp. at 60. The Court below found that it was economically unfeasible for anyone to build new transmission facilities to wheel electricity to Elbow Lake or Hankinson. *Id.* at 60–61. Further, the area's major generator of electricity, the Bureau of Reclamation, was forbidden to construct new transmission facilities to serve towns where wheeling arrangements could be negotiated. *See* Brief for the United States at 13.]

plain repugnancy between the antitrust and regulatory provisions." Activities which come under the jurisdiction of a regulatory agency nevertheless may be subject to scrutiny under the antitrust laws. . . .

The District Court determined that Otter Tail's consistent refusals to wholesale or wheel power to its municipal customers constituted illegal monopolization. Otter Tail maintains here that its refusals to deal should be immune from antitrust prosecution because the Federal Power Commission has the authority to compel involuntary interconnections of power pursuant to § 202(b) of the Federal Power Act. The essential thrust of § 202, however, is to encourage voluntary interconnections of power. Only if a power company refuses to interconnect voluntarily may the Federal Power Commission, subject to limitations unrelated to antitrust considerations, order the interconnection. The standard which governs its decision is whether such action is "necessary or appropriate in the public interest." Although antitrust considerations may be relevant, they are not determinative.

There is nothing in the legislative history which reveals a purpose to insulate electric power companies from the operation of the antitrust laws. To the contrary, the history of Part II of the Federal Power Act indicates an overriding policy of maintaining competition to the maximum extent possible consistent with the public interest. As originally conceived, Part II would have included a "common carrier" provision making it "the duty of every public utility to . . . transmit energy for any person upon reasonable request . . ." In addition, it would have empowered the Federal Power Commission to order wheeling if it found such action to be "necessary or desirable in the public interest." H.R. 5423, 74th Cong., 1st Sess.; S. 1725, 74th Cong., 1st Sess. These provisions were eliminated to preserve "the voluntary action of the utilities." S.Rep.No.621, 74th Cong., 1st Sess., 19.

It is clear, then, that Congress rejected a pervasive regulatory scheme for controlling the interstate distribution of power in favor of voluntary commercial relationships.[81] When these relationships are governed in the first instance by business judgment and not regulatory coercion, courts must be hesitant to conclude that Congress intended to override the fundamental national policies embodied in the antitrust laws. . . .

Thus, there is no basis for concluding that the limited authority of the Federal Power Commission to order interconnections was intended to be a substitute for, or to immunize Otter Tail from, antitrust regulation for refusing to deal with municipal corporations.

---

81 [Editor's Note: In addition to the powers noted in the text, the Federal Power Commission (FPC) had the power to regulate the rates charged for wheeling or for wholesale electricity. *See* Brief for the United States at 15–16. Retail rates were not subject to FPC regulation, and the states and municipalities in which Otter Tail operated tended not to regulate them either. *Id.* at 15.]

II

The decree of the District Court enjoins Otter Tail from "(r)efusing to sell electric power at wholesale to existing or proposed municipal electric power systems in cities and towns located in (its service area)" and from refusing to wheel electric power over its transmission lines from other electric power lines to such cities and towns. But the decree goes on to provide:

> "The defendant shall not be compelled by the Judgment in this case to furnish wholesale electric service or wheeling service to a municipality except at rates which are compensatory and under terms and conditions which are filed with and subject to approval by the Federal Power Commission."

So far as wheeling is concerned, there is no authority granted the Commission under Part II of the Federal Power Act to order it, for the bills originally introduced contained common carrier provisions which were deleted. The Act as passed contained only the interconnection provision set forth in § 202(b). The common carrier provision in the original bill and the power to direct wheeling were left to the "voluntary coordination of electric facilities." Insofar as the District Court ordered wheeling to correct anticompetitive and monopolistic practices of Otter Tail, there is no conflict with the authority of the Federal Power Commission.

As respects the ordering of interconnections, there is no conflict on the present record. Elbow Lake applied to the Federal Power Commission for an interconnection with Otter Tail and, as we have said, obtained it. Hankinson renewed Otter Tail's franchise. So the decree of the District Court, as far as the present record is concerned, presents no actual conflict between the federal judicial decree and an order of the Federal Power Commission. . . . It will be time enough to consider whether the antitrust remedy may override the power of the Commission under § 202(b) as, if, and when the Commission denies the interconnection and the District Court nevertheless undertakes to direct it. At present, there is only a potential conflict, not a present concrete case or controversy concerning it.

III

The record makes abundantly clear that Otter Tail used its monopoly power in the towns in its service area to foreclose competition or gain a competitive advantage, or to destroy a competitor, all in violation of the antitrust laws. *See Griffith*. The District Court determined that Otter Tail has "a strategic dominance in the transmission of power in most of its service area" and that it used this dominance to foreclose potential entrants into the retail area from obtaining electric power from outside sources of supply. Use of monopoly power "to destroy threatened competition" is a violation of the "attempt to monopolize" clause of § 2 of the Sherman Act. *Lorain Journal*. . . .

When a community serviced by Otter Tail decides not to renew Otter Tail's retail franchise when it expires, it may generate, transmit, and distribute its own electric power. We recently described the difficulties and problems of those isolated electric power systems. Interconnection with other utilities is frequently the only solution. That is what Elbow Lake in the present case did. There were no engineering factors that prevented Otter Tail from selling power at wholesale to those towns that wanted municipal plants or wheeling the power. The District Court found—and its findings are supported—that Otter Tail's refusals to sell at wholesale or to wheel were solely to prevent municipal power systems from eroding its monopolistic position. . . .

V

Otter Tail argues that, without the weapons which it used, more and more municipalities will turn to public power and Otter Tail will go downhill. . . . "The promotion of self-interest alone does not invoke the rule of reason to immunize otherwise illegal conduct." The . . . Sherman Act . . . assumes that an enterprise will protect itself against loss by operating with superior service, lower costs, and improved efficiency. Otter Tail's theory collided with the Sherman Act as it sought to substitute for competition anticompetitive uses of its dominant economic power.

The fact that three municipalities which Otter Tail opposed finally got their municipal systems does not excuse Otter Tail's conduct. That fact does not condone the antitrust tactics which Otter Tail sought to impose. . . . The proclivity for predatory practices has always been a consideration for the District Court in fashioning its antitrust decree.

We do not suggest, however, that the District Court, concluding that Otter Tail violated the antitrust laws, should be impervious to Otter Tail's assertion that compulsory interconnection or wheeling will erode its integrated system and threaten its capacity to serve adequately the public. As the dissent properly notes, the Commission may not order interconnection if to do so "would impair (the utility's) ability to render adequate service to its customers." 16 U.S.C. s 824a(b). The District Court in this case found that the "pessimistic view" advanced in Otter Tail's "erosion study" "is not supported by the record." . . . Affirmed.

■ MR. JUSTICE STEWART, with whom THE CHIEF JUSTICE and MR. JUSTICE REHNQUIST join, concurring in part and dissenting in part. . . .[1] In the face of natural monopolies at retail and similar economies of scale in the subtransmission of power, Congress was forced to address the very

---

1 The District Court looked to Otter Tail's service area, and measured market dominance in terms of the number of towns within that area served by Otter Tail. Computed this way, Otter Tail provides 91% of the retail market. As the appellant points out, however, these towns vary in size from more than 29,000 to 20 inhabitants. If Otter Tail's size were measured by actual retail sales, its market share would be only 28.9% of the electricity sold at retail within its geographic market area. It is important to note that another reasonable geographical market unit might be each individual municipality. Viewed this way, whichever power company sells electricity at retail in a town has a complete monopoly.

problem raised by this case—use of the lines of one company by another. One obvious solution would have been to impose the obligations of a common carrier upon power companies owning lines capable of the wholesale transmission of electricity. Such a provision was originally included in the bill. . . . Yet, after substantial debate, the Congress declined to follow this path. . . .

This legislative history, especially when viewed in the light of repeated subsequent congressional refusals to impose common carrier obligations in this area, indicates a clear congressional purpose to allow electric utilities to decide for themselves whether to wheel or sell at wholesale as they see fit. This freedom is qualified by a grant of authority to the Commission to order interconnection (but not wheeling) in certain circumstances. But the exercise of even that power is limited by a consideration of the ability of the regulated utility to function. . . .

As the District Court found, Otter Tail is a vertically integrated power company. But the bulk of its business—some 90% of its income—derives from sales of power at retail. . . . As a retailer of power, Otter Tail asserted a legitimate business interest in keeping its lines free for its own power sales and in refusing to lend a hand in its own demise by wheeling cheaper power from the Bureau of Reclamation to municipal consumers which might otherwise purchase power at retail from Otter Tail itself. . . .

Here, . . . a monopoly is sure to result either way. If the consumers of Elbow Lake receive their electric power from a municipally owned company or from Otter Tail, there will be a monopoly at the retail level, for there will in any event be only one supplier. The very reason for the regulation of private utility rates—by state bodies and by the Commission—is the inevitability of a monopoly that requires price control to take the place of price competition. . . .

NOTES AND QUESTIONS ON *OTTER TAIL*

1. ***Property rights and ex ante investment incentives.*** Why shouldn't Otter Tail be able to refuse municipalities access to its electricity or its ability to transmit electricity from other suppliers? Isn't that right to exclude others part and parcel of its property rights over its electricity and transmission lines?

One might argue that a refusal to deal should not be deemed legally exclusionary because any adverse effects on rivals are simply a consequence of Otter Tail's "superior product" in the market for wholesale electricity and transmission services. United States v. Grinnell Corp., 384 U.S. 563, 570–571 (1966). But having a superior product in those upstream markets does not mean Otter Tail has a superior product downstream in retail, and the retail market is the one that is allegedly being monopolized by the refusal to deal in the upstream product.

A more serious concern is that imposing a duty to share Otter Tail's electricity and transmission wires with rivals might decrease (1) Otter Tail's incentives to invest in creating facilities that make or transmit (wheel) electricity and (2) the incentives of other firms to invest in creating competitive facilities that make or transmit electricity. In theory, those concerns can be solved by setting the price at which sharing is required sufficiently high, which would reward Otter Tail for investing and incentivize rivals to create their own facilities when feasible. However, that solution requires a reliable and administrable method for courts to determine the prices at which the monopolist must deal. As we shall see, the courts have imposed duties to deal only in cases where such a method can be based on prices set either by a regulator or by the monopolist itself.

Ex ante incentive concerns might arguably also be weaker in some cases. For example, suppose a firm did not earn its upstream monopoly through investment or innovation, but rather acquired it through dumb luck or because government regulations excluded rivals. Then there is less concern that a duty to share will undermine incentives to create the facility that enjoys monopoly power. Further, if regulations exclude upstream rivals, then denying a duty to deal cannot lead to upstream competition. Such possibilities may suggest that perhaps any antitrust duty to deal should turn on the source of the monopoly power over the facility for which sharing is sought, and in particular on whether the source involved investment or innovation that needs to be rewarded to be encouraged. However, usually there are multiple sources of monopoly power that would be hard to sort out in court, and even a monopoly acquired without investment usually takes investment to keep up. Should the duty to deal doctrine depend on inquiries into the extent to which the upstream monopoly power was earned by investment or not?

The concern that a duty to deal might undermine rival incentives to create competitive upstream facilities might also be weak if the upstream firm forecloses so much of the downstream market that an upstream rival would have a hard time making sales if it entered. For example, here one might argue that it is unlikely any other firm would have invested in entering the markets to make or transmit electricity because Otter Tail was the retailer in 91% of the towns that would buy wholesale electricity or transmission services. However, what matters more for that argument is that (as the dissent pointed out) those towns only account for 28.9% of the electricity sales in the area, because 71.1% of downstream purchases would still be available to upstream rivals. Still, if the defendant does foreclose a large share of the downstream market, that would discourage rivals from entering the upstream market, and a refusal to deal can lead to even greater foreclosure that exacerbates the problem.

2. ***Ex post efficiencies.*** Is it clear that providing rivals with access to Otter Tail's wholesale electricity or transmission wires would be efficient, even if we assume no ex ante effect on the incentives to create the facilities? Not necessarily. There may instead be operational efficiencies to having the wheeling, wholesaling, and retailing of electricity done by one vertically-integrated firm such as Otter Tail. Having multiple firms with conflicting financial incentives involved can create management and incentive issues. Where the two firms are jointly responsible for something that keeps the system working well, each has an incentive to shirk, which could lead to conflict over how to manage matters rather than cooperation. For example, the firms would have to manage the problem of which town gets how much electricity in times of high-demand when electricity and transmission line capacity may be scarce. However, this efficiency may not justify a refusal to deal that forces vertical integration if a less restrictive alternative, like rules for allocating scarce capacity, could also achieve operational efficiencies.

A refusal to deal that leads to vertical integration might also increase allocative efficiencies by eliminating the following successive monopolies problem. Assuming no price regulation, an integrated monopolist would charge a downstream retail monopoly price based on the total true marginal costs of getting electricity to the town and then distributing it to retail customers. But if there are successive monopolies—one at wholesale and the other at retail—then the wholesaler would charge a monopoly price based on the true marginal cost of bringing the electricity to the city, and then the retailer would charge a monopoly price based on an inflated marginal cost that includes the wholesale monopoly profits. For example, suppose wholesaling electricity to retailers has a constant marginal cost of 5 cents/kilowatt hour (kwh) and that retailing electricity has a constant marginal cost of 2 cents/kwh. Suppose further that both markets have a constant demand elasticity of 2, so that a monopolist (not subject to price regulation) would maximize profits by pricing at double its marginal cost.[82] Then an integrated monopolist would have a total marginal cost of 7 cents/kwh and maximize its profits by charging a price of 14 cents/kwh. In contrast, if they are separate, a wholesale monopolist would maximize its profits by charging a monopoly price of 10 cents, and then the retail monopolist would have marginal costs of 12 cents (10 cents for the wholesale electricity plus 2 cents of retailing costs) and thus maximize its profits by charging 24 cents. Allowing the wholesale monopolist to integrate downstream would thus both lower prices to consumers and raise the integrated firm's profits because output would increase at lower prices and because it would now earn profits of 7 (rather than 5) cents/kwh. Two monopolies in succession can thus result in higher prices to consumers than one vertically-integrated monopoly.

However, solving the successive monopolies problem may not justify a refusal to deal that forces vertical integration. A less restrictive alternative that may achieve the same efficiency could be for the defendant to condition upstream access on the downstream firm charging a downstream price that does not exceed the efficient integrated-firm price.[83] Another alternative might be for the upstream firm to not only sell the upstream product to its downstream rival, but also sell the downstream product itself at the efficient integrated-firm price in the same market in which its downstream rival operates, which would effectively cap the downstream price that the rival could charge because otherwise it would lose customers. However, while this latter alternative is available in many cases, it was likely unavailable in Otter Tail because local electricity retailing was a natural monopoly.

[82] *See supra* Chapter 3.B.1 for explanation of why a monopolist would price at double its marginal cost with this posited demand elasticity.

[83] This justification for vertical maximum price-fixing agreements is discussed below in Chapter 5.B.2.

Does either type of efficiency from forced vertical integration seem plausible given that Otter Tail did wholesale and wheel electric power to electric systems that it had *not* previously served at retail? If splitting retailing from wheeling and wholesaling were inefficient for operational or successive-monopolies reasons, it would seem equally inefficient if the local system had not competed with Otter Tail for the retail contract. It is less plausible that refusals to split the functions are efficient only when they cut off rivals in the downstream market.

3. Is there only a single monopoly profit that means an upstream monopolist lacks any anticompetitive incentive to exclude efficient downstream rivals? Under the single monopoly theory, there is only one monopoly profit and thus an upstream monopolist has no incentive to monopolize the downstream market unless doing so is efficient. For example, if Otter Tail has monopoly power over the sale and transmission of wholesale electricity, and we ignore any price regulation, it would maximize profits by fostering the most efficient means of retailing electricity with the lowest retail markup, so it could charge a higher monopoly price for the sale or transmission of wholesale electricity. To illustrate, suppose that if it were vertically integrated, Otter Tail's profit-maximizing monopoly retail price would be 14 cents/kwh given consumer demand and that Otter Tail's downstream cost of retailing was 2 cents/kwh. If downstream retail competition were more efficient and would be provided at a cost and retail markup of 1 cent/kwh, then Otter Tail would make more money if it allowed downstream retail competition and sold at wholesale for 13 cents/kwh, resulting in the same 14 cents/kwh price to consumers. Under the single monopoly profit theory, Otter Tail would have an incentive to refuse to deal and drive out downstream retailers only if they were less efficient than Otter Tail would be downstream.

A key premise for this argument is the absence of price regulation. If, instead, regulations capped the upstream wholesale price at 8 cents/kwh but did not regulate the downstream retail price, then Otter Tail would make more money by using a refusal to offer the wholesale electricity to monopolize the retail level and then sell retail electricity at 14 cents/kwh. In this way, using refusals to deal to monopolize another market can be a way of evading price regulation in the upstream market. That may have been going on here because the Federal Power Commission regulated only upstream prices, while downstream retail prices were generally unregulated. However, one might argue that the proper remedy for evading price regulation is not an antitrust lawsuit, but instead an administrative proceeding before the government agency that imposed the regulation, which might be better placed to decide when its regulation is being evaded and how best to remedy any evasion. Should the antitrust duty to deal be used to police the evasion of upstream price regulation?

The more fundamental problem with the single monopoly profit theory is that it depends on various key assumptions that might not hold in specific cases.[84] The assumption that is most likely to be questionable in a refusal to

84 A full set of these assumptions is cataloged below in the section on tying, Chapter 4C. Some of them, like a fixed ratio of products and strong demand correlation between them, seem

deal case is the assumption that the degree of upstream monopoly power is fixed. The single monopoly profit theory implicitly adopts this assumption when it assumes that, with downstream competition, the firm will have no constraint on raising the wholesale price. However, the reality may be that the degree of upstream monopoly could be lessened in the future if downstream competition were allowed. The barriers to entering the upstream electricity markets might be lowered if independent retailers either (a) would give upstream entrants someone to whom to sell or (b) might themselves develop industry expertise that makes it easier for them to enter the upstream electricity markets. If so, then a refusal to deal that prevented downstream retail competition might prevent the degree of upstream monopoly power from being eroded by future competition, and the anticompetitive profits the firm gains from protecting the upstream monopoly might exceed any profits it would gain from allowing efficient downstream retail competition.

This anticompetitive theory depends on the premise that the barriers to entering at two levels (upstream and downstream) are substantially higher than the barriers to entering at the one level upstream. Otherwise, the refusal to deal cannot increase entry barriers and thus cannot increase the degree of monopoly power. If the barrier to entering the downstream market is negligible, then two-level entry will not be meaningfully harder than single-level entry. At the other extreme, if the barrier to entering the upstream market is so high that entering it would be unfeasible regardless of the state of downstream competition, then two-level entry will not be meaningfully harder than single-level upstream entry, given that both are unfeasible. In this case, the degree of upstream monopoly power really is fixed. In between those two extremes, two-level entry can be meaningfully harder than one-level entry, and refusals to deal that extend the upstream monopoly to the downstream level can thus raise entry barriers and increase the degree of monopoly power in anticompetitive ways.

In *Otter Tail*, upstream entry into electricity generation was not impossible because Elbow Lake did build its own electricity generating plant and retail it to itself. But such upstream entry was apparently difficult because other towns did not do so. Moreover, the lower court found it was economically unfeasible for another firm to build new transmission lines to other towns, so that, without access to Otter Tail wheeling, any entering electricity generator would have limited scale and lack access to standby power from other generators, which might make entering the upstream electricity generation market inefficient without access to wheeling. This might make the case the sort of intermediate case where the single monopoly profit theory does not apply. On the other hand, suppose the inefficiencies of generating electricity without wheeling access were so high that viable entry into electricity generation was not generally feasible without access to wheeling, which itself could not feasibly be duplicated. In that case, the barriers to one-level entry (for the combination of generation and

---

unlikely to be an issue for many refusals to deal. For example, wholesale electricity and its retail have a fixed ratio, and there is a strong demand correlation between them because consumers want them both together.

transmission) would be so high that the degree of upstream monopoly power really was fixed, and the barriers to two-level entry (at retail and generation/transmission) would not be meaningfully higher. Then the single monopoly profit theory would apply, and the case would turn on whether evading upstream price regulation was a sound antitrust theory. Do you think the single monopoly profit theory applies to this case?

4. ***How to set the price and other terms of dealing.*** In order to impose a duty to deal, courts must figure out how to set the price and other terms of the required dealing. Otherwise, a firm could easily evade any duty to deal by simply setting the price arbitrarily high. For example, a duty to deal would not be meaningful if Otter Tail could comply with it by offering to sell at $1 billion/kilowatt. Such an extreme price would doubtless be deemed a constructive refusal to deal, but that raises the question: just how high a price can the defendant charge without being deemed to have refused to deal? Requiring the monopolist to price at marginal cost may seem efficient ex post, but it would destroy the ex ante incentives to invest to create facilities valuable enough to have monopoly power, given that pricing at cost would eliminate any return on that investment. Requiring such pricing would also legally conflict with the fact that U.S. antitrust law does not ban excessive or monopoly pricing.

So the monopolist has to be able to charge some price above marginal cost, but how are judges and juries supposed to figure out just how high that price can be, especially given that market conditions that will continually change with time? Further, to influence firm behavior, firms would have to be able to predict what the judge or jury they eventually will draw will say were the terms they had to offer. Open-ended review of the reasonableness of monopolist prices through antitrust litigation thus raises administrability issues similar to reviewing the reasonableness of cartel prices, a sea of doubt on which the courts have refused to sail. *See* Chapter 2.B. In practice, courts avoid this problem by imposing an antitrust duty to deal only when courts can rely on prices set either by a regulator (as in *Otter Tail*) or by the monopolist itself (as in other cases discussed below).

In *Otter Tail,* the Federal Power Commission stood ready to regulate wholesale and wheeling prices, thus providing expert guidance on appropriate pricing levels that was prospective and updated for changing market conditions. Accordingly, the Supreme Court in *Otter Tail* did not need to address the question of what the terms of required dealing would be because the Commission set those terms.

For wholesale electricity, the Commission also had the power to impose a duty to deal itself by ordering wholesale interconnections. Otter Tail argued that this regulatory power should be deemed to preclude an antitrust duty to deal, which might potentially conflict with the regulatory duty if regulators differed from antitrust judges or juries on whether to impose a duty to deal. The Supreme Court rejected this argument on two grounds. First, the regulatory standard differed from the antitrust standard, so there was no necessary conflict if the regulator imposed no duty to deal but the antitrust courts did. Second, there was no actual conflict because the regulator had imposed the same duty to wholesale as the antitrust court, and any potential conflicts could be addressed later. As we shall see, this part of the holding seems to have later been overruled in *Trinko*, which concluded instead that when a regulatory power to impose a duty to deal exists, an antitrust duty is unnecessary and should be avoided when it could lead to potential conflicts between expert agencies and judges and juries about whether a duty should be imposed. Which approach do you think is right?

For wheeling, there was a regulatory gap because the Act did not give the Commission the power order wheeling, even though the Commission could regulate wheeling rates. Thus, for wheeling, an antitrust duty to deal was not redundant and did not raise potential conflicts with Commission judgments about when to impose a duty, and courts imposing an antitrust duty to deal could rely on the Commission to set the terms of the required dealing. One might argue that, even here, an antitrust duty would conflict with the judgment of Congress not to include a wheeling duty to deal in the Federal Power Act. However, non-inclusion of a regulatory duty to deal could just as easily indicate a Congressional intent to leave such refusals to deal subject to other sources of law, like antitrust. Do you think an antitrust duty to deal should be imposed in cases with such a regulatory gap?

Should Natural Monopolies Be Immune from Monopolization Liability?

The *Otter Tail* Court implicitly rejected the dissent argument that, given that retailing electricity is a natural monopoly, the anticompetitive conduct could not constitute monopolization because it could not lead to the acquisition or maintenance of monopoly power that would not otherwise exist. One might argue that this argument is economically irrelevant because the real concern was not the retail monopoly against consumers, but rather that the defendant's conduct would mean all the towns would be controlled by the same entity, and thus foreclosed to a possible rival in the upstream market for wholesaling and wheeling electricity, which was not a natural monopoly. But the legal claim was monopolization of the retail market, so the court did implicitly reject the argument that there should be a natural-monopoly defense to a monopolization claim. Three major reasons support such a conclusion.[85] First, even if the market is a natural monopoly, anticompetitive conduct might adversely affect *which firm* acquires or maintains that monopoly power. It is thus desirable to maintain unimpeded competition to help assure the most efficient firm becomes the natural monopolist. Second, whether a market is a natural monopoly is often uncertain, and unimpeded competition helps provide a market test that the market really is a natural monopoly. Such unimpeded competition seems likely to be more accurate than antitrust courts and juries at determining whether the market is a natural monopoly and who should be the natural monopolist. Third, changing technologies, market conditions, or firm efficiencies may alter whether the market is a natural monopoly and/or

[85] *See* Elhauge, *Defining Better Monopolization Standards,* supra note 18, at, 325–26.

which firm would be the best natural monopolist. A process of unimpeded market competition seems better suited than litigation to adjust either sort of conclusion with such changing conditions.

Aspen Skiing Co. v. Aspen Highlands Skiing Corp.

472 U.S. 585 (1985).

■ JUSTICE STEVENS delivered the opinion of the Court. . . .

[Aspen is a destination ski resort with four mountains. Defendant Ski Co. owned 3 of those 4 mountains, having developed one mountain, bought another in 1964 after it was already developed, and purchased and developed a third in 1967 after others obtained the land and permits. Plaintiff Highlands owned the fourth mountain. Developing another ski mountain in Aspen was difficult because it generally required approval both by the U.S. Forest Service, which was contingent on environmental concerns, and by the county, which had an anti-growth policy.]

[Starting in 1962, the competing Aspen ski mountains jointly offered all-Aspen six-day passes that were useable by skiers on any Aspen mountain, usually sold at a discount from the price for six daily lift ticket prices, with the revenue from the pass distributed to the firms in proportion to the number of skiers who used its mountains. This] provided convenience to the vast majority of skiers who visited the resort for weekly periods, but preferred to remain flexible about what mountain they might ski each day during the visit. . . .

Highlands' share of the revenues from the [all-Aspen] ticket was 17.5% in 1973–1974, 18.5% in 1974–1975, 16.8% in 1975–1976, and 13.2% in 1976–1977.[8] During these four seasons, Ski Co. did not offer its own 3-area, multi-day ticket in competition with the all-Aspen ticket.[9] By 1977, multiarea tickets accounted for nearly 35% of the total market. Holders of multiarea passes also accounted for additional daily ticket sales to persons skiing with them.

. . . [F]or the 1977–1978 season, Ski Co. offered to continue the all-Aspen ticket only if Highlands would accept a 13.2% fixed share of the ticket's revenues. [Highlands resisted on the grounds that the 1976–77 share was an outlier because of weather conditions that year, but when Ski company continued to refuse to divide revenue based on actual usage] Highlands eventually accepted a fixed percentage of 15% for the 1977–1978 season. No survey was made during that season of actual usage of the 4-area ticket at the two competitors' mountains.

---

8 Highlands' share of the total market during those seasons, as measured in skier visits was 15.8% in 1973–1974, 17.1% in 1974–1975, 17.4% in 1975–1976, and 20.5% in 1976–1977.

9 In 1975, the Colorado Attorney General filed a complaint against Ski Co. and Highlands alleging, in part, that the negotiations over the 4-area ticket had provided them with a forum for price fixing in violation of § 1 of the Sherman Act. . . . In 1977, the case was settled by a consent decree that permitted the parties to continue to offer the 4-area ticket provided that they set their own ticket prices unilaterally before negotiating its terms.

In the 1970's the management of Ski Co. increasingly expressed their dislike for the all-Aspen ticket. They complained that a coupon method of monitoring usage was administratively cumbersome. They doubted the accuracy of the survey and decried the "appearance, deportment, [and] attitude" of the college students who were conducting it. In addition, Ski Co.'s president had expressed the view that the 4-area ticket was siphoning off revenues that could be recaptured by Ski Co. if the ticket was discontinued. In fact, Ski Co. had reinstated its 3-area, 6-day ticket during the 1977–1978 season, but that ticket had been outsold by the 4-area, 6-day ticket nearly two to one.

In March 1978, the Ski Co. management recommended to the board of directors that the 4-area ticket be discontinued for the 1978–1979 season. The board decided to offer Highlands a 4-area ticket provided that Highlands would agree to receive a 12.5% fixed percentage of the revenue—considerably below Highlands' historical average based on usage. Later in the 1978–1979 season, a member of Ski Co.'s board of directors candidly informed a Highlands official that he had advocated making Highlands "an offer that [it] could not accept."

Finding the proposal unacceptable, Highlands suggested a distribution of the revenues based on usage to be monitored by coupons, electronic counting, or random sample surveys. If Ski Co. was concerned about who was to conduct the survey, Highlands proposed to hire disinterested ticket counters at its own expense—"somebody like Price Waterhouse"—to count or survey usage of the 4-area ticket at Highlands. Ski Co. refused to consider any counterproposals, and Highlands finally rejected the offer of the fixed percentage. . . .

Ski Co. took additional actions that made it extremely difficult for Highlands to market its own multiarea package to replace the joint offering. Ski Co. discontinued the 3-day, 3-area pass for the 1978–1979 season,[13] and also refused to sell Highlands any lift tickets, either at the tour operator's discount or at retail. Highlands finally developed an alternative product, the "Adventure Pack," which consisted of a 3-day pass at Highlands and three vouchers, each equal to the price of a daily lift ticket at a Ski Co. mountain. The vouchers were guaranteed by funds on deposit in an Aspen bank, and were redeemed by Aspen merchants at full value. Ski Co., however, refused to accept them.

Later, Highlands redesigned the Adventure Pack to contain American Express Traveler's Checks or money orders instead of vouchers. Ski Co. eventually accepted these negotiable instruments in exchange for daily lift tickets.[15] Despite some strengths of the product,

[13] . . . "with the three day ticket, a person could ski on the . . . Aspen Skiing Corporation mountains for three days and then there would be three days in which he could ski on our mountain; but with the six-day ticket, we are absolutely locked out of those people." As a result of "tremendous consumer demand" for a 3-day ticket, Ski Co. reinstated it late in the 1978–1979 season, but without publicity or a discount off the daily rate.

[15] Of course, there was nothing to identify Highlands as the source of these instruments, unless someone saw the skier "taking it out of an Adventure Pack envelope." For the 1981–1982

the Adventure Pack met considerable resistance from tour operators and consumers who had grown accustomed to the convenience and flexibility provided by the all-Aspen ticket.

Without a convenient all-Aspen ticket, Highlands basically "becomes a day ski area in a destination resort." Highlands' share of the market for downhill skiing services in Aspen declined steadily after the 4-area ticket based on usage was abolished in 1977: from 20.5% in 1976–1977, to 15.7% in 1977–1978, to 13.1% in 1978–1979, to 12.5% in 1979–1980, to 11% in 1980–1981. . . .

. . . . In her instructions to the jury, the District Judge explained that the offense of monopolization under § 2 of the Sherman Act has two elements: (1) the possession of monopoly power in a relevant market, and (2) the willful acquisition, maintenance, or use of that power by anticompetitive or exclusionary means or for anticompetitive or exclusionary purposes.[19] Although the first element was vigorously disputed at the trial and in the Court of Appeals, in this Court Ski Co. does not challenge the jury's special verdict finding that it possessed monopoly power. Nor does Ski Co. criticize the trial court's instructions to the jury concerning the second element of the § 2 offense. . . .

Ski Co. filed a motion for judgment notwithstanding the verdict, contending that the evidence was insufficient to support a § 2 violation as a matter of law. . . .[22] . . . The District Court denied Ski Co.'s motion and entered a judgment awarding Highlands treble damages of $7,500,000, costs and attorney's fees.[23]

The Court of Appeals affirmed in all respects. . . .

III

. . . . "The central message of the Sherman Act is that a business entity must find new customers and higher profits through internal expansion—that is, by competing successfully rather than by arranging treaties with its competitors." Ski Co., therefore, is surely correct in

season, Ski Co. set its single ticket price at $22 and discounted the 3-area, 6-day ticket to $114. According to Highlands, this price structure made the Adventure Pack unprofitable.

19 In *Grinnell* we explained: "The offense of monopoly under § 2 of the Sherman Act has two elements: (1) the possession of monopoly power in the relevant market and (2) the willful acquisition or maintenance of that power as distinguished from growth or development as a consequence of a superior product, business acumen, or historic accident."

22 Counsel also appears to have argued that Ski Co. was under a legal obligation to refuse to participate in any joint marketing arrangement with Highlands . . . In this Court, Ski Co. does not question the validity of the joint marketing arrangement under § 1 of the Sherman Act. Thus, we have no occasion to consider the circumstances that might permit such combinations in the skiing industry. *See* generally *NCAA*; *BMI*; *GTE Sylvania*.

23 The District Court also entered an injunction requiring the parties to offer jointly a 4-area, 6-out-of-7-day coupon booklet substantially identical to the "Ski the Summit" booklet accepted by Ski Co. at its Breckenridge resort in Summit County, Colorado. The injunction was initially for a 3-year period, but was later extended through the 1984–1985 season by stipulation of the parties. Highlands represents that "it will not seek an extension of the injunction." No question is raised concerning the character of the injunctive relief ordered by the District Court.

submitting that even a firm with monopoly power has no general duty to engage in a joint marketing program with a competitor. . . .

The absence of an unqualified duty to cooperate does not mean that every time a firm declines to participate in a particular cooperative venture, that decision may not have evidentiary significance, or that it may not give rise to liability in certain circumstances. The absence of a duty to transact business with another firm is, in some respects, merely the counterpart of the independent businessman's cherished right to select his customers and his associates. The high value that we have placed on the right to refuse to deal with other firms does not mean that the right is unqualified.

In *Lorain Journal,* we squarely held that this right was not unqualified. Between 1933 and 1948 the publisher of the Lorain Journal, a newspaper, was the only local business disseminating news and advertising in that Ohio town. In 1948, a small radio station was established in a nearby community. In an effort to destroy its small competitor, . . . the Journal refused to sell advertising to persons that patronized the radio station.

In holding that this conduct violated § 2 of the Sherman Act, the Court dispatched the same argument raised by the monopolist here:

> "The publisher claims a right as a private business concern to select its customers and to refuse to accept advertisements from whomever it pleases. We do not dispute that general right. 'But the word "right" is one of the most deceptive of pitfalls; it is so easy to slip from a qualified meaning in the premise to an unqualified one in the conclusion. Most rights are qualified.' The right claimed by the publisher is neither absolute nor exempt from regulation. Its exercise as a purposeful means of monopolizing interstate commerce is prohibited by the Sherman Act. . . .

In *Lorain Journal,* the violation of § 2 was an "attempt to monopolize," rather than monopolization, but the question of intent is relevant to both offenses. In the former case it is necessary to prove a "specific intent" to accomplish the forbidden objective—as Judge Hand explained, "an intent which goes beyond the mere intent to do the act." *United States v. Aluminum Co. of America,* 148 F.2d 416, 432 (CA2 1945). In the latter case evidence of intent is merely relevant to the question whether the challenged conduct is fairly characterized as "exclusionary" or "anticompetitive"—to use the words in the trial court's instructions—or "predatory," to use a word that scholars seem to favor. Whichever label is used, there is agreement on the proposition that "no monopolist monopolizes unconscious of what he is doing." As Judge Bork stated more recently: "Improper exclusion (exclusion not the result of superior efficiency) is always deliberately intended."

The qualification on the right of a monopolist to deal with whom he pleases is not so narrow that it encompasses no more than the circumstances of *Lorain Journal*. In the actual case that we must decide, the monopolist did not merely reject a novel offer to participate in a cooperative venture that had been proposed by a competitor. Rather, the monopolist elected to make an important change in a pattern of distribution that had originated in a competitive market and had persisted for several years. The all-Aspen, 6-day ticket with revenues allocated on the basis of usage was first developed when three independent companies operated three different ski mountains in the Aspen area. It continued to provide a desirable option for skiers when the market was enlarged to include four mountains, and when the character of the market was changed by Ski Co.'s acquisition of monopoly power. Moreover, since the record discloses that interchangeable tickets are used in other multimountain areas which apparently are competitive,[30] it seems appropriate to infer that such tickets satisfy consumer demand in free competitive markets.

Ski Co.'s decision to terminate the all-Aspen ticket was thus a decision by a monopolist to make an important change in the character of the market.[31] Such a decision is not necessarily anticompetitive, and Ski Co. contends that neither its decision, nor the conduct in which it engaged to implement that decision, can fairly be characterized as exclusionary in this case. . . .

[W]e must assume that the jury followed the court's instructions. The jury must, therefore, have drawn a distinction "between practices which tend to exclude or restrict competition on the one hand, and the success of a business which reflects only a superior product, a well-run business, or luck, on the other." Since the jury was unambiguously instructed that Ski Co.'s refusal to deal with Highlands "does not violate Section 2 if valid business reasons exist for that refusal," we must assume that the jury concluded that there were no valid business reasons for the refusal. The question then is whether that conclusion finds support in the record.

IV

The question whether Ski Co.'s conduct may properly be characterized as exclusionary cannot be answered by simply considering its effect on Highlands. In addition, it is relevant to consider its impact

30 Ski Co. itself participates in interchangeable ticket programs in at least two other markets. . . . Interchangeable lift tickets apparently are also available in some European skiing areas.

31 "In any business, patterns of distribution develop over time; these may reasonably be thought to be more efficient than alternative patterns of distribution that do not develop. The patterns that do develop and persist we may call the optimal patterns. By disturbing optimal distribution patterns one rival can impose costs upon another, that is, force the other to accept higher costs." Bork 156. In § 1 cases where this Court has applied the *per se* approach to invalidity to concerted refusals to deal, "the boycott often cut off access to a supply, facility or market necessary to enable the boycotted firm to compete, . . . and frequently the boycotting firms possessed a dominant position in the relevant market." *Northwest Stationers*.

on consumers and whether it has impaired competition in an unnecessarily restrictive way.[32] If a firm has been "attempting to exclude rivals on some basis other than efficiency," it is fair to characterize its behavior as predatory. It is, accordingly, appropriate to examine the effect of the challenged pattern of conduct on consumers, on Ski Co.'s smaller rival, and on Ski Co. itself.

Superior Quality of the All-Aspen Ticket . . .

Over 80% of the skiers visiting the resort each year have been there before—40% of these repeat visitors have skied Aspen at least five times. Over the years, they developed a strong demand for the 6-day, all-Aspen ticket in its various refinements. Most experienced skiers quite logically prefer to purchase their tickets at once for the whole period that they will spend at the resort; they can then spend more time on the slopes and enjoying après-ski amenities and less time standing in ticket lines. The 4-area attribute of the ticket allowed the skier to purchase his 6-day ticket in advance while reserving the right to decide in his own time and for his own reasons which mountain he would ski on each day. It provided convenience and flexibility, and expanded the vistas and the number of challenging runs available to him during the week's vacation.

While the 3-area, 6-day ticket offered by Ski Co. possessed some of these attributes, the evidence supports a conclusion that consumers were adversely affected by the elimination of the 4-area ticket. In the first place, the actual record of competition between a 3-area ticket and the all-Aspen ticket in the years after 1967 indicated that skiers demonstrably preferred four mountains to three. . . . A consumer survey undertaken in the 1979–1980 season indicated that 53.7% of the respondents wanted to ski Highlands, but would not; 39.9% said that they would not be skiing at the mountain of their choice because their ticket would not permit it. . . . A major wholesale tour operator asserted that he would not even consider marketing a 3-area ticket if a 4-area ticket were available. . . .

Highlands' Ability to Compete

The adverse impact of Ski Co.'s pattern of conduct on Highlands is not disputed in this Court. . . . The evidence concerning its attempt to develop a substitute product either by buying Ski Co.'s daily tickets in bulk, or by marketing its own Adventure Pack, demonstrates that it tried to protect itself from the loss of its share of the patrons of the all-Aspen ticket. The development of a new distribution system for providing the experience that skiers had learned to expect in Aspen proved to be prohibitively expensive. As a result, Highlands' share of the relevant market steadily declined after the 4-area ticket was terminated. The size

[32] "Thus, 'exclusionary' comprehends at the most behavior that not only (1) tends to impair the opportunities of rivals, but also (2) either does not further competition on the merits or does so in an unnecessarily restrictive way." 3 P. Areeda & D. Turner, Antitrust Law 78 (1978).

of the damages award also confirms the substantial character of the effect of Ski Co.'s conduct upon Highlands.[38]

Ski Co.'s Business Justification

Perhaps most significant, however, is the evidence relating to Ski Co. itself, for Ski Co. did not persuade the jury that its conduct was justified by any normal business purpose. Ski Co. was apparently willing to forgo daily ticket sales both to skiers who sought to exchange the coupons contained in Highlands' Adventure Pack, and to those who would have purchased Ski Co. daily lift tickets from Highlands if Highlands had been permitted to purchase them in bulk. The jury may well have concluded that Ski Co. elected to forgo these short-run benefits because it was more interested in reducing competition in the Aspen market over the long run by harming its smaller competitor.

That conclusion is strongly supported by Ski Co.'s failure to offer any efficiency justification whatever for its pattern of conduct.[39] In defending the decision to terminate the jointly offered ticket, Ski Co. claimed that usage could not be properly monitored. The evidence, however, established that Ski Co. itself monitored the use of the 3-area passes based on a count taken by lift operators, and distributed the revenues among its mountains on that basis. Ski Co. contended that coupons were administratively cumbersome, and that the survey takers had been disruptive and their work inaccurate. Coupons, however, were no more burdensome than the credit cards accepted at Ski Co. ticket windows. Moreover, in other markets Ski Co. itself participated in interchangeable lift tickets using coupons. As for the survey, its own manager testified that the problems were much overemphasized by Ski Co. officials, and were mostly resolved as they arose. Ski Co.'s explanation for the rejection of Highlands' offer to hire—at its own expense—a reputable national accounting firm to audit usage of the 4-area tickets at Highlands' mountain, was that there was no way to "control" the audit.

In the end, Ski Co. was pressed to justify its pattern of conduct on a desire to disassociate itself from—what it considered—the inferior skiing services offered at Highlands. The all-Aspen ticket based on usage, however, allowed consumers to make their own choice on these matters of quality. Ski Co.'s purported concern for the relative quality of Highlands' product was supported in the record by little more than vague

[38] In considering the competitive effect of Ski Co.'s refusal to deal or cooperate with Highlands, it is not irrelevant to note that similar conduct carried out by the concerted action of three independent rivals with a similar share of the market would constitute a *per se* violation of § 1 of the Sherman Act. *See Northwest Stationers*; Cf. *Lorain Journal*.

[39] "The law can usefully attack this form of predation only when there is evidence of specific intent to drive others from the market by means other than superior efficiency and when the predator has overwhelming market size, perhaps 80 or 90 percent. Proof of specific intent to engage in predation may be in the form of statements made by the officers or agents of the company, evidence that the conduct was used threateningly and did not continue when a rival capitulated, or *evidence that the conduct was not related to any apparent efficiency*. These matters are not so difficult of proof as to render the test overly hard to meet." Bork 157 (emphasis added).

insinuations, and was sharply contested by numerous witnesses. Moreover, Ski Co. admitted that it was willing to associate with what it considered to be inferior products in other markets.

Although Ski Co.'s pattern of conduct may not have been as " 'bold, relentless, and predatory' " as the publisher's actions in *Lorain Journal,* the record in this case comfortably supports an inference that the monopolist made a deliberate effort to discourage its customers from doing business with its smaller rival. The sale of its 3-area, 6-day ticket, particularly when it was discounted below the daily ticket price, deterred the ticket holders from skiing at Highlands. The refusal to accept the Adventure Pack coupons in exchange for daily tickets was apparently motivated entirely by a decision to avoid providing any benefit to Highlands even though accepting the coupons would have entailed no cost to Ski Co. itself, would have provided it with immediate benefits, and would have satisfied its potential customers. Thus the evidence supports an inference that Ski Co. was not motivated by efficiency concerns and that it was willing to sacrifice short-run benefits and consumer goodwill in exchange for a perceived long-run impact on its smaller rival.

Because we are satisfied that the evidence in the record,[44] construed most favorably in support of Highlands' position, is adequate to support the verdict under the instructions given by the trial court, the judgment of the Court of Appeals is *Affirmed.*

NOTES AND QUESTIONS ON *ASPEN SKIING*

1. ***Does* Lorain Journal *support an antitrust duty to deal with rivals?*** So the Court seemed to say, but in *Lorain Journal* the complaint was not that the defendant simply refused to deal; rather, the complaint was that the defendant newspaper company sold advertising space on the condition that the advertisers not buy advertising time from the paper's rival, a radio station. Prohibiting such exclusive dealing (considered in Chapter 4.B) differs from requiring a firm to sell to its rival. Among other things, a prohibition on exclusive dealing conditions neither restricts a firm's freedom to choose to whom it wants to make unconditioned sales nor requires courts to review the prices of unconditioned sales or offers.

2. ***Was there a refusal to deal?*** Ski Co. did not categorically refuse to deal; instead, it offered Highlands access to its mountains for the joint pass if Highlands would give Ski Co. 87.5% of the joint pass revenue. The Court thus effectively held that demanding such a high price was a constructive refusal to deal. This raises the question of just how courts are supposed to determine what price is so high that it amounts to a refusal to

---

[44] Given our conclusion that the evidence amply supports the verdict under the instructions as given by the trial court, we find it unnecessary to consider the possible relevance of the "essential facilities" doctrine, or the somewhat hypothetical question whether nonexclusionary conduct could ever constitute an abuse of monopoly power if motivated by an anticompetitive purpose. If, as we have assumed, no monopolist monopolizes unconscious of what he is doing, that case is unlikely to arise.

deal. It is the same issue as the one of determining what price the defendant must charge to comply with any duty to deal.

The Court suggested that part of the problem might be that 87.5% was substantially higher than Ski Co.'s historical average based on usage. But 87.5% is not much higher than the 86.8% that was measured in 1976–77, the last year when measurements were made. Nor is it clear why pricing should be proportional to usage. One might think Ski Co. deserves a disproportionate share of joint pass revenue because it owned three-quarters of the mountains and thus created the lion's share of the special convenience that made the four-mountain pass valuable. Perhaps because of this, the Court focused on two prices that the defendant had voluntarily set.

a. Terms in prior dealings with the rival. The Court suggested that one strong reason to impose a duty to deal was that the defendant was terminating the terms of prior dealing with its rival. Such past dealing has two useful features. First, the terms of past dealing provides a ready benchmark to set the terms of required dealing. Courts need not abstractly determine what the correct price is. They can just rely on the fact that the defendant itself thought that price was sufficiently rewarding in the past and that there was no change in circumstances that justified a different conclusion. Second, past dealing suggests that the defendant itself thought such dealing with the rival was efficient, absent some change in circumstances.

The prior dealing benchmark has two drawbacks. First, it can become outmoded as market conditions change over time. Unless courts can adjust for any changed market conditions, it may be hard to update the prior dealing benchmark. However, here that problem was lessened because: (a) the prior dealing benchmark was a formula—charging proportional to customer usage—that could be maintained over time because the formula naturally adjusts for changes in customer preferences; and (b) the plaintiff did not seek any extension of the injunction beyond four years. Second, if the termination of prior dealing were a *necessary* condition for a refusal to deal violation, then it might discourage monopolists from initially giving access to their rivals, even in cases where such access is essential for rivals to enter a downstream market. For this reason, it makes sense not to deem a termination of prior dealing as necessary for a refusal to deal violation, and to instead also consider the simultaneous prices that the defendant charges to others.[86]

b. Terms simultaneously offered to nonrivals. The Court also stressed that Ski Co. refused to sell lift tickets to Highlands at the same retail rate that Ski Co. charged consumers. (Highlands wanted to use those lift tickets so it could offer a joint pass itself). Such simultaneous dealing with nonrivals has two useful features. First, the terms of simultaneous dealing with nonrivals provides a ready benchmark to set the terms of required dealing with the rival. The defendant itself must think that price

[86] Making the termination of prior dealing a necessary condition for a duty to deal would also conflict with *Otter Tail*, which imposed an antitrust duty to supply wholesale electricity and electrical transmission to new electricity retailers whom the defendant had never before supplied.

was sufficiently rewarding, and because the benchmark is simultaneous it automatically changes with changing market conditions. Second, the fact that the defendant is voluntarily offering access to its facility to nonrivals suggests that doing so is efficient under simultaneous market conditions.

Using the simultaneous terms offered to nonrivals has two drawbacks. First, it might sometimes be the case that it is more costly to deal with the rival than with nonrivals. If so, the price offered to nonrivals provides too low a benchmark, and offering the product to nonrivals does not necessarily indicate offering it to the rival is efficient. But that seems unlikely on the facts of *Aspen Skiing* and such cost/efficiency variations could be shown in particular cases. Second, if simultaneously offering some input to nonrivals were a *necessary* condition for a refusal to deal violation, then it might encourage monopolists to stop offering an upstream product to nonrivals so that it could also refuse to deal with rivals. This factor was not much of a concern in *Aspen Skiing* because the defendant could not make any money unless it sold lift tickets to someone. However, there are cases (like *Otter Tail*) where a firm has monopoly power over some upstream input and also makes a downstream product that requires that essential upstream input. In such cases, one could imagine a firm refusing to sell the upstream product to nonrivals in order to be able to refuse to sell it to rivals. For example, Otter Tail could have cut off the supply of wholesale electricity and transmission to towns where Otter Tail had no retailer, so as to provide no simultaneous benchmark. In *Otter Tail*, the regulated rate provided a benchmark, but sometimes there is no regulated rate to use. For this reason, it makes sense not to treat simultaneous discrimination as necessary for a refusal to deal violation, which may explain why *Aspen Skiing* indicates that the more general test is whether the defendant's refusal to sell on certain terms indicates it is sacrificing "short-run benefits."

c. ***The general test of whether the refusal to sell on certain terms indicated the firm is sacrificing "short-run benefits."*** Suppose courts held that a necessary condition to show a refusal to deal violation was either the termination of prior dealing or refusing to offer terms that are simultaneously offered to nonrivals. Then, in some markets, a firm might engage in inefficient vertical integration from the get go, refusing to provide the upstream product to rivals or nonrivals, and instead just selling the downstream product, despite the inefficiency, in order to keep entry barriers high. Could one address such cases with the more general test of whether the defendant's refusal to sell on certain terms indicates it is sacrificing short-run benefits in the upstream market? In theory, yes. The price that the defendant voluntarily charged to downstream customers would still indicate a price that the defendant itself must think is sufficiently rewarding. If one subtracts from that downstream price the cost of operating downstream, then the difference would equal the upstream price that would provide the same monopoly profits as the downstream price the defendant is charging. Demanding more than that upstream price from downstream rivals would sacrifice short-run profits in the upstream product and thus indicate a constructive refusal to deal. As we shall see, this theory comes up later in the *Linkline* case.

3. ***The connection between voluntary pricing tests and ex ante investment incentives.*** The refusal to deal benchmarks used in *Aspen Skiing* rely heavily on prices voluntarily set by the defendant either in the past to the rival or simultaneously to nonrivals.[87] Relying on such voluntarily-set prices helps address the administrability concerns that would be raised if courts had to engage in open-ended review of the reasonableness of the prices demanded. Relying on such voluntarily-set prices also addresses the serious concerns that a duty to deal might discourage ex ante investment in creating a facility valuable enough to enjoy monopoly power. Using the voluntary-price benchmarks leaves the defendant free to charge the independent monopoly price for the upstream product: that is, the upstream price that it would have found profit-maximizing if it were not considering any gains from monopolizing the downstream level. Allowing such independent monopoly pricing also provides powerful incentives for downstream rivals to try to duplicate that upstream facility to avoid paying monopoly prices or for others to duplicate that facility so they could also charge supracompetitive prices.[88] It would also be consistent with the legal permission to charge monopoly pricing.

Charging more than the independent monopoly price for the upstream product would, in contrast, indicate that the firm is sacrificing short-run upstream profits in order to achieve some strategic gain downstream by effectively refusing to deal. The strategic gain could be anticompetitive, like monopolizing the downstream market to prevent a long-run erosion of upstream monopoly power. But it could also be procompetitive, like forcing vertical integration in order to achieve efficiencies. Either way, it would be a constructive refusal to deal, which does not necessarily mean it is illegal, but instead means the anticompetitive and procompetitive effects would have to be assessed.

4. ***The required anticompetitive effects.*** Ski Co.'s constructive refusal to deal did not drive its rival out of the market, nor was it likely to do so. Instead, the anticompetitive effect was two-fold. First, the refusal hampered the rival's competitiveness, driving its market share down from 20.5% to 11% over four years, which enhanced the degree of Ski Co.'s monopoly power and would likely increase consumer prices. Second, the

87 Similar past and simultaneous benchmarks for determining the terms of required dealing were also available in Eastman Kodak v. Image Technical Servs., 504 U.S. 451 (1992), where the defendant terminated the prior supply of parts to rival service providers and simultaneously sold parts to self-service buyers who were not rivals with Kodak in the market for selling service.

88 In *Aspen Skiing,* ex ante investment concerns might be weaker because the denied product was access to ski mountains that were largely made by nature. Rivals could never duplicate such mountains, so one need not worry that requiring mountain access would discourage rival efforts to duplicate them. One might also be less concerned that requiring access would undermine the defendant's ex ante incentives to create the facility because the ski mountains were largely created by nature rather than by its efforts. However, developing and maintaining a ski resort on a mountain does require significant investment, and one might still be worried about discouraging such investments. More generally, it would be hard to sort out in each case how much of the upstream monopoly power was earned or not. Perhaps because of this, the courts have not made unearned monopoly power an element of duty to deal doctrine, but instead have focused on the existence of a price benchmark that is voluntarily set by the defendant or set by a regulator.

refusal deprived consumers of a downstream option (the joint pass) that many preferred. *Aspen Skiing* thus establishes that such anticompetitive effects suffice for a refusal to deal claim, even though the denied product is not essential for the rival to stay in the market.

5. ***Why isn't the joint pass an illegal horizontal agreement?*** In most refusal to deal cases, the two firms competitively set the downstream price. In this case, a problematic feature was that the joint pass required the two firms to set a price together for that joint pass. Does a duty to deal here thus perversely require the firms to engage in an illegal horizontal agreement to fix prices? Probably not, because the price for the joint pass was set at a discount from the individual lift ticket prices that the firms independently set. As long as they set those individual prices separately, adding a joint pass would procompetitively add a desired market option, like the blanket license in *BMI,* and make setting the joint pass price legal as a restraint reasonably ancillary to the joint venture. Indeed, the restraint had been approved in a consent decree with Colorado. Still, such a consent decree would not bar the U.S. or consumers from bring suit against the joint pass, and there was some antitrust risk that another court might have found the procompetitive virtues of the joint pass weaker than the anticompetitive concern that firm discussions and agreements on the joint price would indirectly inflate individual prices.

6. ***Efficiency justifications.*** The Court stressed that the refusal would be legal if the defendant had a legitimate efficiency justification, but the Court found that none was proven. Why did the Court reject the claimed justification that Ski Co. did not want to be associated with inferior mountains? Because consumers liked the joint pass and could choose for themselves which mountain to go to. Why did the Court reject the claim that the refusal to deal was not justified by administrative problems, like the difficulties of monitoring? Because prior experience with the joint pass in Aspen indicated few administrative problems, and Ski Co. participated in joint passes in other ski towns. Further, Ski Co. refused to accept even Highland's checks for lift tickets, which does not seem hard to administer. The past and simultaneous dealing thus provided concrete evidence on efficiency that might be harder to establish in a case where such dealing is absent. However, these justifications were rejected on their facts, not on principle, and in other cases defendants might well have valid efficiency justifications for a refusal to deal.

Verizon Commun. v. Law Offices of Curtis V. Trinko

540 U.S. 398 (2004).

■ JUSTICE SCALIA delivered the opinion of the Court.

The Telecommunications Act of 1996 imposes certain duties upon incumbent local telephone companies in order to facilitate market entry by competitors, and establishes a complex regime for monitoring and enforcement. In this case we consider whether a complaint alleging breach of the incumbent's duty under the 1996 Act to share its network with competitors states a claim under § 2 of the Sherman Act.

I

Petitioner Verizon Communications Inc. is the incumbent local exchange carrier (LEC) serving New York State. Before the 1996 Act, Verizon, like other incumbent LECs, enjoyed an exclusive franchise within its local service area. The 1996 Act sought to "uproo[t]" the incumbent LECs' monopoly and to introduce competition in its place. Central to the scheme of the Act is the incumbent LEC's obligation under 47 U.S.C. § 251(c) to share its network with competitors, including provision of access to individual elements of the network on an "unbundled" basis. New entrants, so-called competitive LECs, resell these unbundled network elements (UNEs), recombined with each other or with elements belonging to the LECs.

Verizon . . . has signed interconnection agreements with rivals such as AT & T, as it is obliged to do under § 252, detailing the terms on which it will make its network elements available. (Because Verizon and AT & T could not agree upon terms, the open issues were subjected to compulsory arbitration under §§ 252(b) and (c).) . . . Part of Verizon's UNE obligation under § 251(c)(3) is the provision of access to operations support systems (OSS), a set of systems used by incumbent LECs to provide services to customers and ensure quality. Verizon's interconnection agreement and long-distance authorization each specified the mechanics by which its OSS obligation would be met. As relevant here, a competitive LEC sends orders for service through an electronic interface with Verizon's ordering system, and as Verizon completes certain steps in filling the order, it sends confirmation back through the same interface. Without OSS access a rival cannot fill its customers' orders.

In late 1999, competitive LECs complained to regulators that many orders were going unfilled, in violation of Verizon's obligation to provide access to OSS functions. The PSC and FCC opened parallel investigations, which led to a series of orders by the PSC and a consent decree with the FCC. Under the FCC consent decree, Verizon undertook to make a "voluntary contribution" to the U.S. Treasury in the amount of $3 million; under the PSC orders, Verizon incurred liability to the competitive LECs in the amount of $10 million. Under the consent decree and orders, Verizon was subjected to new performance measurements and new reporting requirements to the FCC and PSC, with additional penalties for continued noncompliance. In June 2000, the FCC terminated the consent decree. The next month the PSC relieved Verizon of the heightened reporting requirement.

Respondent Law Offices of Curtis V. Trinko, LLP, a New York City law firm, was a local telephone service customer of AT & T. The day after Verizon entered its consent decree with the FCC, respondent filed a complaint . . . on behalf of itself and a class of similarly situated customers. The complaint . . . alleged that Verizon had filled rivals' orders on a discriminatory basis as part of an anticompetitive scheme to discourage customers from becoming or remaining customers of competitive LECs, thus impeding the competitive LECs' ability to enter and compete in the market for local telephone service. . . . The complaint sought damages and injunctive relief for violation of § 2 of the Sherman Act. . . . We granted certiorari, limited to the question whether the Court of Appeals erred in reversing the District Court's dismissal of respondent's antitrust claims.

II

To decide this case, we must first determine what effect (if any) the 1996 Act has upon the application of traditional antitrust principles. . . . Under the sharing duties of § 251(c), incumbent LECs are required to offer three kinds of access. . . . [P]erhaps most intrusive, is the duty to offer access to UNEs on "just, reasonable, and nondiscriminatory" terms, a phrase that the FCC has interpreted to mean a price reflecting long-run incremental cost. A rival can interconnect its own facilities with those of the incumbent LEC, or it can simply purchase services at wholesale from the incumbent and resell them to consumers. The Act also imposes upon incumbents the duty to allow physical "collocation"—that is, to permit a competitor to locate and install its equipment on the incumbent's premises—which makes feasible interconnection and access to UNEs.

That Congress created these duties, however, does not automatically lead to the conclusion that they can be enforced by means of an antitrust claim. Indeed, a detailed regulatory scheme such as that created by the 1996 Act ordinarily raises the question whether the regulated entities are not shielded from antitrust scrutiny altogether by the doctrine of implied immunity. In some respects the enforcement scheme set up by the 1996 Act is a good candidate for implication of antitrust immunity, to avoid the real possibility of judgments conflicting with the agency's regulatory scheme "that might be voiced by courts exercising jurisdiction under the antitrust laws."

Congress, however, precluded that interpretation. Section 601(b)(1) of the 1996 Act is an antitrust-specific saving clause providing that "nothing in this Act or the amendments made by this Act shall be construed to modify, impair, or supersede the applicability of any of the antitrust laws." This bars a finding of implied immunity. As the FCC has put the point, the saving clause preserves those "claims that satisfy established antitrust standards."

But just as the 1996 Act preserves claims that satisfy existing antitrust standards, it does not create new claims that go beyond existing antitrust standards; that would be equally inconsistent with the saving clause's mandate that nothing in the Act "modify, impair, or supersede the applicability" of the antitrust laws. We turn, then, to whether the activity of which respondent complains violates preexisting antitrust standards.

III

The complaint alleges that Verizon denied interconnection services to rivals in order to limit entry. If that allegation states an antitrust claim at all, it does so under § 2 of the Sherman Act, which declares that a firm shall not "monopolize" or "attempt to monopolize." It is settled law that this offense requires, in addition to the possession of monopoly power in the relevant market, "the willful acquisition or maintenance of that power as distinguished from growth or development as a consequence of a superior product, business acumen, or historic accident." *Grinnell.* The mere possession of monopoly power, and the concomitant charging of monopoly prices, is not only not unlawful; it is an important element of the free-market system. The opportunity to charge monopoly prices—at least for a short period—is what attracts "business acumen" in the first place; it induces risk taking that produces innovation and economic growth. To safeguard the incentive to innovate, the possession of monopoly power will not be found unlawful unless it is accompanied by an element of anticompetitive *conduct.*

Firms may acquire monopoly power by establishing an infrastructure that renders them uniquely suited to serve their customers. Compelling such firms to share the source of their advantage is in some tension with the underlying purpose of antitrust law, since it may lessen the incentive for the monopolist, the rival, or both to invest in those economically beneficial facilities. Enforced sharing also requires antitrust courts to act as central planners, identifying the proper price, quantity, and other terms of dealing—a role for which they are ill-suited. Moreover, compelling negotiation between competitors may facilitate the supreme evil of antitrust: collusion. Thus, as a general matter, the Sherman Act "does not restrict the long recognized right of [a] trader or manufacturer engaged in an entirely private business, freely to exercise his own independent discretion as to parties with whom he will deal." United States v. Colgate & Co., 250 U.S. 300, 307 (1919).

However, "[t]he high value that we have placed on the right to refuse to deal with other firms does not mean that the right is unqualified." *Aspen Skiing.* Under certain circumstances, a refusal to cooperate with rivals can constitute anticompetitive conduct and violate § 2. We have been very cautious in recognizing such exceptions, because of the uncertain virtue of forced sharing and the difficulty of identifying and remedying anticompetitive conduct by a single firm. The question before us today is whether the allegations of respondent's complaint fit within existing exceptions or provide a basis, under traditional antitrust principles, for recognizing a new one.

The leading case for § 2 liability based on refusal to cooperate with a rival, and the case upon which respondent understandably places greatest reliance, is *Aspen Skiing.* . . . *Aspen Skiing* is at or near the outer boundary of § 2 liability. The Court there found significance in the defendant's decision to cease participation in a cooperative venture. The unilateral termination of a voluntary (*and thus presumably profitable*) course of dealing suggested a willingness to forsake short-term profits to achieve an anticompetitive end. Similarly, the defendant's unwillingness to renew the ticket *even if compensated at retail price* revealed a distinctly anticompetitive bent.

The refusal to deal alleged in the present case does not fit within the limited exception recognized in Aspen Skiing. The complaint does not allege that Verizon voluntarily engaged in a course of dealing with its rivals, or would ever have done so absent statutory compulsion. Here, therefore, the defendant's prior conduct sheds no light upon the motivation of its refusal to deal—upon whether its regulatory lapses were prompted not by competitive zeal but by anticompetitive malice. The contrast between the cases is heightened by the difference in pricing behavior. In *Aspen Skiing*, the defendant turned down a proposal to sell at its own retail price, suggesting a calculation that its future monopoly retail price would be higher. Verizon's reluctance to interconnect at the cost-based rate of compensation available under § 251(c)(3) tells us nothing about dreams of monopoly.

The specific nature of what the 1996 Act compels makes this case different from *Aspen Skiing* in a more fundamental way. In *Aspen Skiing*, what the defendant refused to provide to its competitor was a product that it already sold at retail—to oversimplify slightly, lift tickets representing a bundle of services to skiers. Similarly, in *Otter Tail*, another case relied upon by respondent, the defendant was already in the business of providing a service to certain customers (power transmission over its network), and refused to provide the same service to certain other customers. In the present case, by contrast, the services allegedly withheld are not otherwise marketed or available to the public. The sharing obligation imposed by the 1996 Act created "something brand new"—"the wholesale market for leasing network elements." The unbundled elements offered pursuant to § 251(c)(3) exist only deep within the bowels of Verizon; they are brought out on compulsion of the 1996 Act and offered not to consumers but to rivals, and at considerable expense and effort. New systems must be designed and implemented simply to make that access possible—indeed, it is the failure of one of those systems that prompted the present complaint.[3]

We conclude that Verizon's alleged insufficient assistance in the provision of service to rivals is not a recognized antitrust claim under this Court's existing refusal-to-deal precedents. This conclusion would be unchanged even if we considered to be established law the "essential

[3] Respondent also relies upon *Terminal Railroad* and *Associated Press*. These cases involved *concerted* action, which presents greater anticompetitive concerns and is amenable to a remedy that does not require judicial estimation of free-market forces: simply requiring that the outsider be granted nondiscriminatory admission to the club.

facilities" doctrine crafted by some lower courts, under which the Court of Appeals concluded respondent's allegations might state a claim. We have never recognized such a doctrine, *see Aspen Skiing*; and we find no need either to recognize it or to repudiate it here. It suffices for present purposes to note that the indispensable requirement for invoking the doctrine is the unavailability of access to the "essential facilities"; where access exists, the doctrine serves no purpose. Thus, it is said that "essential facility claims should . . . be denied where a state or federal agency has effective power to compel sharing and to regulate its scope and terms." P. Areeda & H. Hovenkamp, Antitrust Law, p. 150, ¶ 773e (2003 Supp.). Respondent believes that the existence of sharing duties under the 1996 Act supports its case. We think the opposite: The 1996 Act's extensive provision for access makes it unnecessary to impose a judicial doctrine of forced access. To the extent respondent's "essential facilities" argument is distinct from its general § 2 argument, we reject it.

IV

Finally, we do not believe that traditional antitrust principles justify adding the present case to the few existing exceptions from the proposition that there is no duty to aid competitors. . . .

One factor of particular importance is the existence of a regulatory structure designed to deter and remedy anticompetitive harm. Where such a structure exists, the additional benefit to competition provided by antitrust enforcement will tend to be small, and it will be less plausible that the antitrust laws contemplate such additional scrutiny. . . . The regulatory framework that exists in this case demonstrates how, in certain circumstances, "regulation significantly diminishes the likelihood of major antitrust harm." *Town of Concord*. Consider, for example, the statutory restrictions upon Verizon's entry into the potentially lucrative market for long-distance service. To be allowed to enter the long-distance market in the first place, an incumbent LEC must be on good behavior in its local market. Authorization by the FCC requires state-by-state satisfaction of § 271's competitive checklist, which as we have noted includes the nondiscriminatory provision of access to UNEs. . . . The FCC's § 271 authorization order for Verizon to provide long-distance service in New York discussed at great length Verizon's commitments to provide access to UNEs, including the provision of OSS. Those commitments are enforceable by the FCC through continuing oversight; a failure to meet an authorization condition can result in an order that the deficiency be corrected, in the imposition of penalties, or in the suspension or revocation of long-distance approval. . . .

The regulatory response to the OSS failure complained of in respondent's suit provides a vivid example of how the regulatory regime operates. When several competitive LECs complained about deficiencies in Verizon's servicing of orders, the FCC and PSC responded. The FCC soon concluded that Verizon was in breach of its sharing duties under

§ 251(c), imposed a substantial fine, and set up sophisticated measurements to gauge remediation, with weekly reporting requirements and specific penalties for failure. The PSC found Verizon in violation of the PAP even earlier, and imposed additional financial penalties and measurements with daily reporting requirements. In short, the regime was an effective steward of the antitrust function.

Against the slight benefits of antitrust intervention here, we must weigh a realistic assessment of its costs. Under the best of circumstances, applying the requirements of § 2 "can be difficult" because "the means of illicit exclusion, like the means of legitimate competition, are myriad." United States v. Microsoft Corp., 253 F. 3d 34, 58 (CADC 2001) (en banc) (per curiam). Mistaken inferences and the resulting false condemnations "are especially costly, because they chill the very conduct the antitrust laws are designed to protect." *Matsushita.* The cost of false positives counsels against an undue expansion of § 2 liability. One false-positive risk is that an incumbent LEC's failure to provide a service with sufficient alacrity might have nothing to do with exclusion. Allegations of violations of § 251(c)(3) duties are difficult for antitrust courts to evaluate, not only because they are highly technical, but also because they are likely to be extremely numerous, given the incessant, complex, and constantly changing interaction of competitive and incumbent LECs implementing the sharing and interconnection obligations. Amici States have filed a brief asserting that competitive LECs are threatened with "death by a thousand cuts"—the identification of which would surely be a daunting task for a generalist antitrust court. Judicial oversight under the Sherman Act would seem destined to distort investment and lead to a new layer of interminable litigation, atop the variety of litigation routes already available to and actively pursued by competitive LECs.

Even if the problem of false positives did not exist, conduct consisting of anticompetitive violations of § 251 may be, as we have concluded with respect to above-cost predatory pricing schemes, "beyond the practical ability of a judicial tribunal to control." *Brooke Group.* Effective remediation of violations of regulatory sharing requirements will ordinarily require continuing supervision of a highly detailed decree. We think that Professor Areeda got it exactly right: "No court should impose a duty to deal that it cannot explain or adequately and reasonably supervise. The problem should be deemed irremedia[ble] by antitrust law when compulsory access requires the court to assume the day-to-day controls characteristic of a regulatory agency." Areeda, 58 Antitrust L. J., at 853. In this case, respondent has requested an equitable decree to "[p]reliminarily and permanently enjoi[n] [Verizon] from providing access to the local loop market . . . to [rivals] on terms and conditions that are not as favorable" as those that Verizon enjoys. An antitrust court is unlikely to be an effective day-to-day enforcer of these detailed sharing obligations . . .

Accordingly, the judgment of the Court of Appeals is reversed . . .

NOTES AND QUESTIONS ON *VERIZON V. TRINKO*[89]

In *Trinko,* the Court first decided whether a refusal-to-deal antitrust violation would exist if there were no regulation and then considered whether the existence of the regulation changed that conclusion.

1. ***Absent any regulation, why do antitrust principles not support a duty to deal?*** The Court concluded that *Aspen Skiing* is "at or near the outer boundary" of when the antitrust duty to deal applied. The Court thus affirmed the continuing validity of *Aspen Skiing* and indicated that the antitrust duty to deal might even lie a little beyond it, but not very far beyond. The Court pointed to two key features that were present in *Aspen* but missing here: (1) termination of voluntary prior dealing; and (2) refusing to sell the product to the rival at the price simultaneously offered to nonrivals. It stressed those factors indicated that the defendant in *Aspen* was sacrificing "short-term profits to achieve an anticompetitive end."

a. ***Did not Verizon terminate prior dealing by altering a prior system of filling rival orders promptly?*** It did, but the difference is that in *Aspen* the terminated prior dealing was *voluntarily* engaged in by the defendant, whereas here the prior dealing was involuntarily imposed by regulation. The reason that matters is that only voluntary prior dealing indicates that the defendant itself thought that sharing was efficient ex post and that the price of the prior dealing provided sufficient reward for ex ante investments. To be sure, one might argue that the fact that Congress and an expert agency imposed a regulatory duty to deal, and set the terms for required dealing, should give an antitrust court sufficient confidence that sharing access is efficient and that the terms will provide adequate incentives to build facilities. But in this part of the opinion, the Court is assessing how this case would be decided without any agency regulation. Later in the opinion, the Court assesses whether the presence of the regulation changes matters, which is considered below.

b. ***Did not Verizon discriminate against rival orders by treating them worse than orders for Verizon service?*** Yes, but treating rivals worse than the property owner treats itself is not the same as treating rivals worse than it treats nonrivals. "Discrimination" in favor of a property owner is inherent in the property right to exclude, and such discrimination is also necessary to further ex ante incentives to invest in property. Discrimination in favor of nonrivals over rivals is not inherent in the property right and is usually unnecessary to preserve ex ante incentives to invest in creating valuable property. There was no evidence that Verizon provided more favorable wholesale leases of its telephone network to nonrival outsiders than to rivals.

2. ***Why is this a refusal to deal at all given that access was provided?*** Access was provided, but on an allegedly dilatory basis. The Court implicitly accepted the plaintiff's claim that such slow dealing could constitute a constructive refusal to deal. This makes sense because a duty to deal would be meaningless if it were not accompanied by some sort of time

[89] Disclosure: Professor Elhauge was counsel for Verizon before the Supreme Court.

requirement. Otherwise, firms could promise to provide access so far in the future that none of the firms or products would likely exist then. However, setting the right amount of time seems hard unless one has some reliable benchmark, such as the time to process orders in past or simultaneous dealing. As this suggests, past or simultaneous dealing can provide a benchmark for all sorts of terms other than price, including timing.

3. Does the regulation change the antitrust conclusion? The Court begins by holding that the Telecommunications Act's antitrust savings clause means that the regulatory statute can neither add nor subtract from baseline antitrust standards.

a. Does not the Court effectively reverse this initial holding in its later analysis of whether the regulation changes antitrust standards? One could argue that the Court does effectively reverse this initial holding when it later concludes that the regulatory duty to deal does narrow antitrust standards by (1) precluding application of the essential facility doctrine and (2) cutting against any other antitrust duty to deal because the regulatory authorities can always impose one when it is desirable. But the Court's position is that the antitrust standard always remains the same—weighing procompetitive and anticompetitive effects—and the regulation simply alters what those effects are. This is not uncommon in antitrust cases, because regulation often creates entry barriers or market power or other economically relevant factors that must be considered when doing antitrust analysis. In any event, here the Court already held there would be no antitrust duty without the regulation, so it is simply holding that the regulation is no reason to add a further duty, although its dicta indicates that it viewed the regulation as a reason not to have a duty.

***b. Why does the regulation not cut for an antitrust duty to deal like it did in* Otter Tail?** The regulation does mean that a unitary expert agency stands ready to consistently set, monitor and update the terms of dealing, which makes an antitrust duty to deal more administrable. But the Court feared that antitrust courts might reach different conclusions than the expert agency about whether to impose a duty to deal. To avoid such potential conflicts, courts could also piggyback on agency judgments about when to impose a duty to deal. But if all the antitrust duty does is piggyback on the regulatory duty, then the antitrust duty adds nothing to the regulatory scheme other than treble damages and possible class actions. This would increase enforcement of the regulatory duties, but would also arguably disrupt the regulatory tradeoff struck about the right duties and remedies.

The conclusion in *Verizon* that the regulatory duty to deal cuts against an antitrust duty to deal seems to effectively overrule the part of *Otter Tail* finding an antitrust duty to provide wholesale electricity despite an agency power to impose such a duty. *Verizon* probably leaves intact the other part of *Otter Tail* finding an antitrust duty to provide wheeling where a regulatory gap left the agency unable to impose that duty even though it regulated prices. In such cases of a regulatory gap, one might argue that such gaps reflect deliberate tradeoffs that would be disrupted by an antitrust duty, but that argument seems dubious in cases (like this one) where the regulatory statute includes an antitrust savings clause that indicates the regulatory tradeoff did not mean to preclude any antitrust duties.

Pacific Bell Telephone v. Linkline Communications

555 U.S. 438 (2009).

■ CHIEF JUSTICE ROBERTS delivered the opinion of the Court.

The plaintiffs in this case, respondents here, allege that a competitor subjected them to a "price squeeze" in violation of § 2 of the Sherman Act. They assert that such a claim can arise when a vertically integrated firm sells inputs at wholesale and also sells finished goods or services at retail. If that firm has power in the wholesale market, it can simultaneously raise the wholesale price of inputs and cut the retail price of the finished good. This will have the effect of "squeezing" the profit margins of any competitors in the retail market. Those firms will have to pay more for the inputs they need; at the same time, they will have to cut their retail prices to match the other firm's prices. The question before us is whether such a price-squeeze claim may be brought under § 2 of the Sherman Act when the defendant is under no antitrust obligation to sell the inputs to the plaintiff in the first place. We hold that no such claim may be brought.

I

This case involves the market for digital subscriber line (DSL) service, which is a method of connecting to the Internet at high speeds over telephone lines. AT & T owns much of the infrastructure and facilities needed to provide DSL service in California. In particular, AT & T controls most of what is known as the "last mile"—the lines that connect homes and businesses to the telephone network. Competing DSL providers must generally obtain access to AT & T's facilities in order to serve their customers.

Until recently, the Federal Communications Commission (FCC) required incumbent phone companies such as AT & T to sell transmission service to independent DSL providers, under the theory that this would spur competition. In 2005, the Commission largely abandoned this forced-sharing requirement in light of the emergence of a competitive market beyond DSL for high-speed Internet service; DSL now faces robust competition from cable companies and wireless and satellite services. As a condition for a recent merger, however, AT & T remains bound by the mandatory interconnection requirements, and is obligated to provide wholesale "DSL transport" service to independent firms at a price no greater than the retail price of AT & T's DSL service.

The plaintiffs are four independent Internet service providers (ISPs) that compete with AT & T in the retail DSL market. Plaintiffs do not own all the facilities needed to supply their customers with this service. They instead lease DSL transport service from AT & T pursuant to the merger conditions described above. AT & T thus participates in the DSL market at both the wholesale and retail levels; it provides plaintiffs and other independent ISPs with wholesale DSL transport service, and it also sells DSL service directly to consumers at retail.

In July 2003, the plaintiffs brought suit in District Court, alleging that AT & T violated § 2 of the Sherman Act by monopolizing the DSL market in California. The complaint alleges that AT & T refused to deal with the plaintiffs, denied the plaintiffs access to essential facilities, and engaged in a "price squeeze." Specifically, plaintiffs contend that AT & T squeezed their profit margins by setting a high wholesale price for DSL transport and a low retail price for DSL Internet service. . . . The District Court held that AT & T had no antitrust duty to deal with the plaintiffs, but it denied the motion to dismiss with respect to the price-squeeze claims . . . On interlocutory appeal, the Court of Appeals for the Ninth Circuit affirmed the District Court's denial of AT & T's motion for judgment on the pleadings on the price-squeeze claims . . .

We granted certiorari, to resolve a conflict over whether a plaintiff can bring price-squeeze claims under § 2 of the Sherman Act when the defendant has no antitrust duty to deal with the plaintiff. *See* Covad Communications Co. v. Bell Atlantic Corp., 398 F.3d 666, 673–674 (C.A.D.C.2005) (holding that *Trinko* bars such claims). We reverse.

III

A

. . . As a general rule, businesses are free to choose the parties with whom they will deal, as well as the prices, terms, and conditions of that dealing. *See* United States v. Colgate & Co., 250 U.S. 300, 307 (1919). But there are rare instances in which a dominant firm may incur antitrust liability for purely unilateral conduct. For example, we have ruled that firms may not charge "predatory" prices-below-cost prices that drive rivals out of the market and allow the monopolist to raise its prices later and recoup its losses. *Brooke Group*. Here, however, the complaint at issue does not contain allegations meeting those requirements.

There are also limited circumstances in which a firm's unilateral refusal to deal with its rivals can give rise to antitrust liability. *See Aspen*. Here, however, the District Court held that AT & T had no such antitrust duty to deal with its competitors, and this holding was not challenged on appeal.[2]

The challenge here focuses on retail prices—where there is no predatory pricing—and the terms of dealing—where there is no duty to deal. Plaintiffs' price-squeeze claims challenge a different type of unilateral conduct in which a firm "squeezes" the profit margins of its competitors. This requires the defendant to be operating in two markets,

[2] The Court of Appeals assumed that any duty to deal arose only from FCC regulations, and the question on which we granted certiorari made the same assumption. Even aside from the District Court's reasoning, it seems quite unlikely that AT & T would have an antitrust duty to deal with the plaintiffs. Such a duty requires a showing of monopoly power, but—as the FCC has recognized—the market for high-speed Internet service is now quite competitive; DSL providers face stiff competition from cable companies and wireless and satellite providers.

a wholesale ("upstream") market and a retail ("downstream") market. A firm with market power in the upstream market can squeeze its downstream competitors by raising the wholesale price of inputs while cutting its own retail prices. This will raise competitors' costs (because they will have to pay more for their inputs) and lower their revenues (because they will have to match the dominant firm's low retail price). Price-squeeze plaintiffs assert that defendants must leave them a "fair" or "adequate" margin between the wholesale price and the retail price. In this case, we consider whether a plaintiff can state a price-squeeze claim when the defendant has no obligation under the antitrust laws to deal with the plaintiff at wholesale.

B

1. A straightforward application of our recent decision in *Trinko* forecloses any challenge to AT & T's wholesale prices. In *Trinko*, Verizon was required by statute to lease its network elements to competing firms at wholesale rates. The plaintiff—a customer of one of Verizon's rivals—asserted that Verizon denied its competitors access to interconnection support services, making it difficult for those competitors to fill their customers' orders . . .

We held that the plaintiff's claims were not actionable under § 2. Given that Verizon had no antitrust duty to deal with its rivals at all, we concluded that "Verizon's alleged insufficient assistance in the provision of service to rivals" did not violate the Sherman Act. *Trinko* thus makes clear that if a firm has no antitrust duty to deal with its competitors at wholesale, it certainly has no duty to deal under terms and conditions that the rivals find commercially advantageous.

In this case, as in *Trinko*, the defendant has no antitrust duty to deal with its rivals at wholesale; any such duty arises only from FCC regulations, not from the Sherman Act. There is no meaningful distinction between the "insufficient assistance" claims we rejected in *Trinko* and the plaintiffs' price-squeeze claims in the instant case. The *Trinko* plaintiffs challenged the quality of Verizon's interconnection service, while this case involves a challenge to AT & T's pricing structure. But for antitrust purposes, there is no reason to distinguish between price and nonprice components of a transaction. *See*, e.g., American Telephone & Telegraph Co. v. Central Office Telephone, Inc., 524 U.S. 214, 223 (1998) ("Any claim for excessive rates can be couched as a claim for inadequate services and vice versa"). The nub of the complaint in both *Trinko* and this case is identical—the plaintiffs alleged that the defendants (upstream monopolists) abused their power in the wholesale market to prevent rival firms from competing effectively in the retail market. *Trinko* holds that such claims are not cognizable under the Sherman Act in the absence of an antitrust duty to deal.

The District Court and the Court of Appeals did not regard *Trinko* as controlling because that case did not directly address price-squeeze claims. This is technically true, but the reasoning of *Trinko* applies with equal force to price-squeeze claims. AT & T could have squeezed its competitors' profits just as effectively by providing poor-quality interconnection service to the plaintiffs, as Verizon allegedly did in *Trinko*. But a firm with no duty to deal in the wholesale market has no obligation to deal under terms and conditions favorable to its competitors. If AT & T had simply stopped providing DSL transport service to the plaintiffs, it would not have run afoul of the Sherman Act. Under these circumstances, AT & T was not required to offer this service at the wholesale prices the plaintiffs would have preferred.

2. The other component of a price-squeeze claim is the assertion that the defendant's retail prices are "too low." Here too plaintiffs' claims find no support in our existing antitrust doctrine.

"[C]utting prices in order to increase business often is the very essence of competition." *Matsushita*. In cases seeking to impose antitrust liability for prices that are too low, mistaken inferences are "especially costly, because they chill the very conduct the antitrust laws are designed to protect." *Ibid.*; *see also Brooke Group*. To avoid chilling aggressive price competition, we have carefully limited the circumstances under which plaintiffs can state a Sherman Act claim by alleging that prices are too low. Specifically, to prevail on a predatory pricing claim, a plaintiff must demonstrate that: (1) "the prices complained of are below an appropriate measure of its rival's costs"; and (2) there is a "dangerous probability" that the defendant will be able to recoup its "investment" in below-cost prices. *Brooke Group*. "Low prices benefit consumers regardless of how those prices are set, and so long as they are above predatory levels, they do not threaten competition." Atlantic Richfield Co. v. USA Petroleum Co., 495 U.S. 328, 340 (1990).

In the complaint at issue in this interlocutory appeal, there is no allegation that AT & T's conduct met either of the Brooke Group requirements. Recognizing a price-squeeze claim where the defendant's retail price remains above cost would invite the precise harm we sought to avoid in *Brooke Group*: Firms might raise their retail prices or refrain from aggressive price competition to avoid potential antitrust liability.

3. Plaintiffs' price-squeeze claim, looking to the relation between retail and wholesale prices, is thus nothing more than an amalgamation of a meritless claim at the retail level and a meritless claim at the wholesale level. If there is no duty to deal at the wholesale level and no predatory pricing at the retail level, then a firm is certainly not required to price both of these services in a manner that preserves its rivals' profit margins.

C

1. Institutional concerns also counsel against recognition of such claims. We have repeatedly emphasized the importance of clear rules in antitrust law. Courts are ill suited "to act as central planners, identifying the proper price, quantity, and other terms of dealing." *Trinko*. " 'No court

should impose a duty to deal that it cannot explain or adequately and reasonably supervise. The problem should be deemed irremedia[ble] by antitrust law when compulsory access requires the court to assume the day-to-day controls characteristic of a regulatory agency.' " *Id.; see also* Town of Concord v. Boston Edison Co., 915 F.2d 17, 25 (C.A.1 1990) (Breyer, C.J.) ("[A]ntitrust courts normally avoid direct price administration, relying on rules and remedies . . . that are easier to administer").

It is difficult enough for courts to identify and remedy an alleged anticompetitive practice at one level, such as predatory pricing in retail markets or a violation of the duty-to-deal doctrine at the wholesale level. Recognizing price-squeeze claims would require courts simultaneously to police both the wholesale and retail prices to ensure that rival firms are not being squeezed. And courts would be aiming at a moving target, since it is the interaction between these two prices that may result in a squeeze.

Perhaps most troubling, firms that seek to avoid price-squeeze liability will have no safe harbor for their pricing practices. *See Town of Concord* (antitrust rules "must be clear enough for lawyers to explain them to clients"). At least in the predatory pricing context, firms know they will not incur liability as long as their retail prices are above cost. No such guidance is available for price-squeeze claims.

The most commonly articulated standard for price squeezes is that the defendant must leave its rivals a "fair" or "adequate" margin between the wholesale price and the retail price. One of our colleagues has highlighted the flaws of this test in Socratic fashion:

> "[H]ow is a judge or jury to determine a 'fair price?' Is it the price charged by other suppliers of the primary product? None exist. Is it the price that competition 'would have set' were the primary level not monopolized? How can the court determine this price without examining costs and demands, indeed without acting like a rate-setting regulatory agency, the rate-setting proceedings of which often last for several years? Further, how is the court to decide the proper size of the price 'gap?' Must it be large enough for all independent competing firms to make a 'living profit,' no matter how inefficient they may be? . . . And how should the court respond when costs or demands change over time, as they inevitably will?" *Town of Concord.*

Some amici respond to these concerns by proposing a "transfer price test" for identifying an unlawful price squeeze: A price squeeze should be presumed if the upstream monopolist could not have made a profit by selling at its retail rates if it purchased inputs at its own wholesale rates. Whether or not that test is administrable, it lacks any grounding in our antitrust jurisprudence. An upstream monopolist with no duty to deal is free to charge whatever wholesale price it would like; antitrust law does not forbid lawfully obtained monopolies from charging monopoly prices.

Similarly, the Sherman Act does not forbid—indeed, it encourages—aggressive price competition at the retail level, as long as the prices being charged are not predatory. If both the wholesale price and the retail price are independently lawful, there is no basis for imposing antitrust liability simply because a vertically integrated firm's wholesale price happens to be greater than or equal to its retail price.

2. Amici assert that there are circumstances in which price squeezes may harm competition. For example, they assert that price squeezes may raise entry barriers that fortify the upstream monopolist's position; they also contend that price squeezes may impair nonprice competition and innovation in the downstream market by driving independent firms out of business.

The problem, however, is that amici have not identified any independent competitive harm caused by price squeezes above and beyond the harm that would result from a duty-to-deal violation at the wholesale level or predatory pricing at the retail level. To the extent a monopolist violates one of these doctrines, the plaintiffs have a remedy under existing law. We do not need to endorse a new theory of liability to prevent such harm.

IV

. . . Plaintiffs have also filed an amended complaint, and the District Court concluded that this complaint, generously construed, could be read as alleging conduct that met the *Brooke Group* requirements for predatory pricing.[90] That order, however, applied the "no set of facts" pleading standard that we have since rejected as too lenient. *See* Bell Atlantic Corp. v. Twombly, 550 U.S. 544, 561–563 (2007). It is for the District Court on remand to consider whether the amended complaint states a claim upon which relief may be granted in light of the new pleading standard we articulated in *Twombly*, whether plaintiffs should be given leave to amend their complaint to bring a claim under *Brooke Group*, and such other matters properly before it. Even if the amended complaint is further amended to add a *Brooke Group* claim, it may not survive a motion to dismiss. For if AT & T can bankrupt the plaintiffs by refusing to deal altogether, the plaintiffs must demonstrate why the law prevents AT & T from putting them out of business by pricing them out of the market. Nevertheless, such questions are for the District Court to decide in the first instance. We do not address these issues here, as they

---

[90] [Editor's Note: The District Court held that the amended complaint could be interpreted to allege that the defendant charged rivals and the defendant's retail affiliates a wholesale price that was high enough that its affiliates' retail prices were below the combination of those affiliates' wholesale and retail costs. App. to Pet. for Cert. 48a–50a. It concluded that this allegation satisfied the *Brooke Group* standard as interpreted in *Covad*. *Id.* 39a–40a, 47a–48a. *Covad* held that an "appropriate measure" of costs under *Brooke Group* could include a combination of the upstream price that the defendant charged downstream firms and the defendant's own costs of operating downstream. *See* Covad Communications v. BellSouth, 374 F.3d 1044, 1050–51 (11th Cir. 2004). This standard effectively compares the upstream-downstream price differential to the defendant's costs of operating downstream, rather than comparing the downstream price to the defendant's combined upstream-downstream costs.]

are outside the scope of the question presented and were not addressed by the Court of Appeals in the decision below.

* * *

Trinko holds that a defendant with no antitrust duty to deal with its rivals has no duty to deal under the terms and conditions preferred by those rivals. *Brooke Group* holds that low prices are only actionable under the Sherman Act when the prices are below cost and there is a dangerous probability that the predator will be able to recoup the profits it loses from the low prices. In this case, plaintiffs have not stated a duty-to-deal claim under *Trinko* and have not stated a predatory pricing claim under *Brooke Group*. They have nonetheless tried to join a wholesale claim that cannot succeed with a retail claim that cannot succeed, and alchemize them into a new form of antitrust liability never before recognized by this Court. We decline the invitation to recognize such claims. Two wrong claims do not make one that is right . . .

NOTES AND QUESTIONS ON *LINKLINE*

1. ***Why should a price-squeeze claim be limited to cases where an antitrust duty to deal applies?*** A price-squeeze claim alleges that the defendant has set the upstream price too high relative to the downstream price that the defendant itself charges. The problem cannot be that the downstream price is too low; by hypothesis it exceeds the combined upstream-downstream cost of provision. (If the downstream price were below the defendant's combined upstream-downstream cost, then one could simply rely on predatory pricing doctrine without need to resort to any doctrine on price squeezes, but the plaintiff made no such predatory pricing claim.) Further, a doctrine that encouraged firms to avoid committing a price squeeze by raising the downstream price would clearly harm consumer welfare and allocative efficiency.

The concern with price squeezes is instead that the defendant has raised the upstream price in a way that creates a constructive refusal to deal in the upstream product. Indeed, if the law condemned price squeezes in cases where no antitrust duty to deal applied, that would simply encourage firms to take the even more onerous step of refusing to supply the upstream product to the downstream firm at all. However, the Court's conclusion that price-squeeze claims could amount to a constructive refusal to deal (when the other conditions for a duty to deal are met) has the interesting implication that a refusal to deal can be proven by demanding an upstream price that is too high relative to a downstream price. This effectively adds a third voluntary-price benchmark to the other two benchmarks recognized in *Aspen Skiing* and *Trinko*: (1) past dealing in the upstream product with the rival; and (2) simultaneous dealing in the upstream product with nonrivals.

2. ***If an antitrust duty to deal does apply, when would a price squeeze amount to a constructive refusal to deal?*** The *Linkline* Court did not expressly resolve this question. However, price-squeeze claims have traditionally required a showing that the difference between the upstream price and the downstream price was too low to cover the costs of operating

essential-facility doctrine. Much of the critique appears to reflect the misimpression that the essential-facility doctrine imposes a duty to deal even when refusing to do so would be more efficient and justified by legitimate business reasons. But in fact lower courts applying the essential-facility doctrine have interpreted the feasibility element to serve the same function, holding that sharing a facility is not feasible if denying access serves legitimate business reasons like efficiency, customer satisfaction, cost reduction, service quality, avoiding free riding, or maintaining the defendant's capacity to serve its own customers.[93] Accordingly, both the lower court essential-facility doctrine and the Supreme Court duty-to-deal doctrine require the absence of any sound ex post efficiency justification for the refusal to deal.

Other elements of the lower court essential-facility doctrine are actually narrower than the Supreme Court doctrine. The first element of the essential-facility doctrine requires evidence that the denied facility is "essential" for rivals to compete: in other words, rivals will be driven out of the market without it. In contrast, the Supreme Court doctrine recognizes a refusal-to-deal violation even when the rival clearly can and does survive without access to the facility. *See Aspen*. The Supreme Court approach makes sense because a refusal to deal can have anticompetitive effects even when a rival is not entirely driven from the market.

The third element of the essential-facility doctrine requires evidence that the facility cannot practically be duplicated. The Supreme Court has not required such evidence, and indeed has found refusal-to-deal violations in cases, like *Otter Tail,* where a downstream firm (Elbow Lake) did create its own upstream facility. The Supreme Court approach makes sense because, if the upstream facility is truly nonduplicable, then the degree of upstream monopoly power is fixed and thus the single monopoly profit theory likely applies, making anticompetitive effects impossible. However, the lower courts may mean that the upstream facility is nonduplicable only in the short run. That would leave open the possibility that the upstream facility could be duplicated in the long run if a competitive downstream market existed, which would suffice to negate the single monopoly profit theory and make anticompetitive effects possible.

The difference cutting the other way is that the lower court doctrine does not clearly define the terms at which a defendant must refuse to deal. The Supreme Court doctrine is arguably narrower in that it requires a benchmark provided either by a regulated price or some voluntarily-set defendant price. The lower court doctrine may thus (a) require courts to undertake the administrative burden of determining what the terms of dealing should be and to update those terms as market

---

[93] *See* Illinois v. Panhandle Eastern Pipe Line, 935 F.2d 1469, 1483 (7th Cir. 1991); Abcor Corp. v. AM Int'l, 916 F.2d 924 (4th Cir. 1990); Oahu Gas v. Pacific Resources, 838 F.2d 360, 368–70 (9th Cir. 1988); *MCI,* 708 F.2d at 1132, 1137–38; *Laurel Sand,* 924 F.2d at 545; *Willman,* 34 F.3d at 613; Southern Pacific v. AT & T, 740 F.2d 980, 1009 (D.C. Cir. 1984).

conditions change and (b) create the risk that tribunal errors in setting that price might deter rivals from creating a similar facility and deter firms from investing to create facilities that are so societally valuable that they are essential for a downstream market to exist at all. Because of the overdeterrence problems created by such a doctrine, one might want to limit it to cases where the facility is particularly essential for rival competition and hard for rivals to duplicate in the short run, because those are the cases where underdeterrence problems are highest. Still, one might wonder how, even in such cases, courts would be able to set and modify prices over time in a way that firms could predict without excessively discouraging ex ante investment. This may explain why the Supreme Court has repeatedly expressed hostility toward the lower court's essential-facility doctrine. However, because all the lower courts have adopted this essential-facility doctrine, there has been no circuit conflict about it to prompt Supreme Court review. Should the lower court essential-facility doctrine be overruled now that the Supreme Court has developed its own duty-to-deal doctrine or is a mixed strategy of using both doctrines optimal?

The Application of U.S. Antitrust Duties to Deal to Intellectual Property

Two U.S. appellate circuits hold that antitrust duties to deal can apply to intellectual property as long as the plaintiff establishes the same elements that are necessary to rebut the presumption that any property owner is justified in excluding others.[94] In contrast, the Federal Circuit rejected case-by-case inquiry into the justification for exclusion, finding that absent proof of fraud, sham litigation or illegal tying, antitrust duties to deal are inapplicable "so long as that anticompetitive effect is not illegally extended beyond the statutory patent grant".[95] However, the Federal Circuit test is consistent with the Supreme Court duty to deal, which limits it to cases where the defendant constructively refuses to deal by demanding a price that exceeds the independent monopoly price for the upstream product and thus seeks to extend its reward beyond the scope of that upstream property (here patent) right, generally to monopolize some other market that uses that property as an input. Nor does there seem to be any categorical reason to treat intellectual property differently than other property rights to exclude, which raise similar issues about administrability and tradeoffs between ex ante incentives to make the property valuable and ex post efficiencies in sharing valuable

---

[94] *See* Image Technical Servs., Inc. v. Eastman Kodak Co., 125 F.3d 1195, 1218–20 (9th Cir. 1997) (owners of patents and copyrights must provide access to them if the plaintiff can rebut the presumption that they have a valid business justification for denying access); Data Gen. Corp. v. Grumman Sys. Support Corp., 36 F.3d 1147, 1184–87 & n.64 (1st Cir. 1994) (same for copyrights).

[95] *See* In re Independent Service Organizations Antitrust Litigation, 203 F.3d 1322, 1325–30 (Fed. Cir. 2000).

property.[96] The U.S. Supreme Court has yet to explicitly adjudicate the extent to which antitrust duties to deal apply to intellectual property, but *Eastman Kodak v. Image Technical Servs.*, 504 U.S. 451 (1992), implicitly did so by applying the duty to deal doctrine to a refusal to sell patented parts to rival service organizations. Should any antitrust duty-to-deal doctrine apply equally to any property that meets the elements of that doctrine, whether that property is intellectual property or not?

D. CAUSAL CONNECTION BETWEEN FIRST AND SECOND ELEMENTS REQUIRED?

Einer Elhauge, *Defining Better Monopolization Standards*

56 Stanford Law Review 253 (2003).

. . . U.S. antitrust law does not merely require "monopoly power" in the abstract, but a causal connection between the challenged exclusionary conduct and the acquisition or maintenance of that power. Such a causal connection is implicit in the language of § 2, which makes it illegal to "monopolize," "attempt to monopolize," or "conspire . . . to monopolize." The "-ize" suffix proves crucial, for it indicates that the gravamen of the offense is the illicit creation or maintenance of a monopoly power that otherwise would not exist, at least not to the same degree. Thus, the statutory language calls for proof of some causal connection between the illicit conduct and the extent of monopoly power, or in the case of attempted monopolization, at least a dangerous threat of such a causal connection.

Of course, it will often be unclear just how the market would have developed but for the defendant's misconduct, especially when a monopolist is squelching the development of a new firm or technology. Courts have resolved that problem by holding that, because the wrongdoer appropriately bears the burden of any uncertainty caused by its misconduct, a plaintiff need only prove the exclusionary conduct was reasonably capable of making a significant causal contribution to the acquisition or maintenance of monopoly power. But the underlying basis for liability remains the reasonable likelihood of some causal link

[96] *See* Chapter 2.G; Elhauge, *supra* note 18, at 304–05. This conclusion is consistent with 35 U.S.C. § 271(d)(4), which bars treating a refusal to license as a patent misuse (which can invalidate the patent and effectively impose a business death penalty) but does not bar treating it as an antitrust violation (which can lead only to damages or perhaps compulsory licensing rather than invalidation because the patent would not be a fruit of any antitrust violation, *see* Chapter 1.). *See also Image Technical Servs.*, 125 F.3d at 1214 n.7 (legislative history does not indicate any intent to eliminate antitrust duty); Grid Systems Corp. v. Texas Instruments Inc., 771 F.Supp. 1033, 1037 n.2 (N.D. Cal. 1991) (§ 271(d) only relates to patent misuse not antitrust violations).

between the exclusionary conduct and the extent of the defendant's monopoly power. . . .

This need [under U.S. law] to prove a causal connection between the exclusionary conduct and the acquisition or maintenance of monopoly power might seem inconsistent with language in *Kodak* that resurrected a sentence from *Griffith* defining monopolization as "the use of monopoly power 'to foreclose competition, to gain a competitive advantage, or to destroy a competitor.' " Literally read, this language seems to condemn the use of monopoly power to gain a competitive advantage or to disadvantage rivals in some other market in which the defendant never had monopoly power. But this language in *Kodak* was dicta. Indeed, the *Kodak* Court immediately followed this language with a sentence indicating that *Kodak* would be liable only "[i]f Kodak adopted its parts and service policies as part of a scheme of willful acquisition or maintenance of monopoly power." This sentence appears to reverse any implication that the first language eliminated the need to prove a causal connection to the initial or continued existence of monopoly power. Further reversing any such implication was the later statement in *Spectrum Sports* that § 2 condemns unilateral conduct "only when it actually monopolizes or dangerously threatens to do so."

. . . A causal link between exclusionary conduct and monopoly power is not at all disproved by evidence that the alleged monopolist's prices, profits, or market share declined during the period of exclusionary conduct. Monopolizing activities are frequently undertaken not to create monopoly power but rather to maintain and slow down the erosion of existing monopoly power. In fact, it is precisely when a monopolist sees its monopoly power waning because of a new market threat or technology that it is most desperate to cling to that power, and thus most tempted to use anticompetitive conduct to slow down that erosion and maintain some degree of monopoly power for as long as possible. Thus, there is no reason to assume exclusionary conduct will typically increase monopoly prices, profits, or shares. Rather its anticompetitive effect may typically be to prevent monopoly prices, profits, or shares from dropping further and faster, often by slowing down a market shift to a better or cheaper rival or new product. This is why the Court's monopolization test correctly condemns not just the acquisition but also the "maintenance" of monopoly power with exclusionary conduct, which includes conduct that simply slows down the erosion of monopoly power. . . .

NOTE ON MONOPOLY LEVERAGING

The *Griffith* language noted above had led some U.S. lower courts to approve a theory of monopoly leveraging that covered the use of monopoly power to gain a *non-monopoly* competitive advantage in another market.[97]

[97] *See* Berkey Photo, Inc. v. Eastman Kodak Co., 603 F.2d 263 (2d Cir. 1979); Covad Commun. v. BellSouth, 299 F.3d 1272, 1284–85 (11th Cir.2002); Kerasotes Michigan Theatres v. National Amusements, 854 F.2d 135, 136–38 (6th Cir.1988).

But other lower courts had rejected any monopoly leveraging theory that claims to find monopolization without any proof that defendant's conduct helped it obtain or maintain a monopoly in some market.[98] Subsequent to the Elhauge article above, the U.S. Supreme Court has squarely resolved this split in lower court authority in favor of the latter position.[99] This does not mean no monopoly-leveraging cases can be brought under U.S. law, just that a monopolization case utilizing such a theory would have to prove the monopoly power was leveraged to gain or maintain monopoly power in the other market. In other words, under current U.S. law, monopoly leveraging may explain the source of the power to engage in anticompetitive conduct in another market, but does not dispense with the requirement to prove the causal connection between that anticompetitive conduct and the degree of market power in that other market required by the relevant antitrust statute.

E. ATTEMPTED MONOPOLIZATION

Lorain Journal v. United States

342 U.S. 143 (1951).

■ JUSTICE BURTON delivered the opinion of the Court.

The principal question here is whether a newspaper publisher's conduct constituted an attempt to monopolize . . . , justifying the injunction issued against it [by the district court]. . . .

The [Lorain Journal,] here called the publisher . . . enjoyed a substantial monopoly in Lorain of the mass dissemination of news and advertising, both of a local and national character.

However, in 1948 . . . a corporation independent of the publisher, was licensed . . . to establish and operate in Elyria, Ohio, eight miles south of Lorain, a radio station . . . [with the] call letters, WEOL. . . . Since then it has operated its principal studio in Elyria and a branch studio in Lorain. Lorain has about twice the population of Elyria and is by far the largest community in the station's immediate area. . . . Substantially all of the station's income is derived from its broadcasts of advertisements of goods or services. About 16% of its income comes from national advertising under contracts with advertisers outside of Ohio. . . .

The court below found that appellants knew that a substantial number of Journal advertisers wished to use the facilities of the radio station as well. For some of them it found that advertising in the Journal was essential for the promotion of their sales in Lorain County. It found

[98] *See* Fineman v. Armstrong World Indus., 980 F.2d 171, 206 (3d Cir. 1992); Alaska Airlines v. United Airlines, 948 F.2d 536, 548 (9th Cir. 1991); Virgin Atl. Airways v. British Airways PLC, 257 F.3d 256, 272 (2d Cir. 2001).

[99] *See* Verizon Communications v. Law Offices of Curtis V. Trinko, 540 U.S. 398, 415 n.4 (2004).

that at all times since WEOL commenced broadcasting, appellants had executed a plan conceived to eliminate the threat of competition from the station. Under this plan the publisher refused to accept local advertisements in the Journal from any Lorain County advertiser who advertised or who appellants believed to be about to advertise over WEOL. The court found expressly that the purpose and intent of this procedure was to destroy the broadcasting company.

. . . To carry out appellants' plan, the publisher monitored WEOL programs to determine the identity of the station's local Lorain advertisers. Those using the station's facilities had their contracts with the publisher terminated and were able to renew them only after ceasing to advertise through WEOL. The program was effective. Numerous Lorain County merchants testified that, as a result of the publisher's policy, they either ceased or abandoned their plans to advertise over WEOL. . . .

Because of the Journal's complete daily newspaper monopoly of local advertising in Lorain and its practically indispensable coverage of 99% of the Lorain families, this practice forced numerous advertisers to refrain from using WEOL for local advertising. That result not only reduced the number of customers available to WEOL in the field of local Lorain advertising and strengthened the Journal's monopoly in that field, but more significantly tended to destroy and eliminate WEOL altogether. Attainment of that sought-for elimination would automatically restore to the publisher of the Journal its substantial monopoly in Lorain of the mass dissemination of all news and advertising, interstate and national, as well as local. It would deprive not merely Lorain but Elyria and all surrounding communities of their only nearby radio station. . . . Numerous Lorain advertisers wished to supplement their local newspaper advertising with local radio advertising but could not afford to discontinue their newspaper advertising in order to use the radio.

WEOL's greatest potential source of income was local Lorain advertising. Loss of that was a major threat to its existence. The court below found unequivocally that appellants' conduct amounted to an attempt by the publisher to destroy WEOL and, at the same time, to regain the publisher's pre-1948 substantial monopoly over the mass dissemination of all news and advertising.

To establish this violation of § 2 as charged, it was not necessary to show that success rewarded appellants' attempt to monopolize. The injunctive relief . . . sought to forestall that success. While appellants' attempt to monopolize did succeed insofar as it deprived WEOL of income, WEOL has not yet been eliminated. The injunction may save it. "[W]hen that intent [to monopolize] and the consequent dangerous probability exist, this statute [the Sherman Act], like many others and like the common law in some cases, directs itself against that dangerous probability as well as against the completed result." Swift & Co. v. United States, 196 U.S. 375, 396.

. . . [I]t seems clear that if all the newspapers in a city, in order to monopolize the dissemination of news and advertising by eliminating a competing radio station, conspired to accept no advertisements from anyone who advertised over that station, they would violate §§ 1 and 2 of the Sherman Act. *Cf. Fashion Originators'.* It is consistent with that result to hold here that a single newspaper, already enjoying a substantial monopoly in its area, violates the "attempt to monopolize" clause of § 2 when it uses its monopoly to destroy threatened competition.

The publisher claims a right as a private business concern to select its customers and to refuse to accept advertisements from whomever it pleases. We do not dispute that general right. "But the word 'right' is one of the most deceptive of pitfalls; it is so easy to slip from a qualified meaning in the premise to an unqualified one in the conclusion. Most rights are qualified." The right claimed by the publisher is neither absolute nor exempt from regulation. Its exercise as a purposeful means of monopolizing interstate commerce is prohibited by the Sherman Act. The operator of the radio station, equally with the publisher of the newspaper, is entitled to the protection of that Act. *"In the absence of any purpose to create or maintain a monopoly*, the act does not restrict the long recognized right of trader or manufacturer engaged in an entirely private business, freely to exercise his own independent discretion as to parties with whom he will deal." (Emphasis supplied.) United States v. Colgate & Co., 250 U.S. 300, 307. *See Associated Press* . . .

The judgment accordingly is Affirmed.

NOTES AND QUESTIONS ON *LORAIN JOURNAL*

1. ***Is there any procompetitive justification the conduct in this case might have?*** It is hard to think of one, and the Journal failed to articulate any procompetitive justification.

2. ***If this conduct is anticompetitive and thus harmful to advertisers, why would they agree to buy from Lorain Journal under such an anticompetitive condition?*** Each advertiser would agree because individually it figures its individual decision will determine whether or not it loses Journal access but have little impact on whether the collective result is that enough advertisers agree to drive out the radio station. The advertisers thus have a collective action problem. They are better off if all refuse, but none has individual incentives to refuse.

3. ***Would it be better for the law to wait until the conduct actually restored Lorain Journal's monopoly power in the local advertising market to make sure the anticompetitive effect materialized?*** No. In the interim, competition would be distorted with fewer radio ads than are efficient. Further, if law allows the radio station to be driven out of the market, it may be hard to get it back in the market, leading to a long run reduction in competition. Nor is anything possibly

desirable lost by prohibiting the conduct in the meantime because the conduct had no procompetitive justification.

United States v. American Airlines

743 F.2d 1114 (5th Cir. 1984).

■ W. EUGENE DAVIS, CIRCUIT JUDGE:

The question presented in this antitrust case is whether the government's complaint states a claim of attempted monopolization under section 2 of the Sherman Act against the defendants, American Airlines, and its president Robert L. Crandall, for Crandall's proposal to the president of Braniff Airlines that the two airlines control the market and set prices. The district court dismissed the complaint for failure to state a claim . . . We disagree and reverse. . . .

In February 1982, American and Braniff together enjoyed a market share of more than ninety percent of the passengers on non-stop flights between DFW and eight major cities, and more than sixty percent of the passengers on flights between DFW and seven other cities. The two airlines had more than ninety percent of the passengers on many flights connecting at DFW, when no non-stop service was available between the cities in question. Overall, American and Braniff accounted for seventy-six percent of monthly enplanements at DFW.

For some time before February 1982, American and Braniff were competing fiercely for passengers flying to, from and through DFW, by offering lower fares and better service. During a telephone conversation between Robert Crandall, American's president, and Howard Putnam, Braniff's president, the following exchange occurred:

> Crandall: I think it's dumb as hell for Christ's sake, all right, to sit here and pound the * * * out of each other and neither one of us making a * * * * * * dime.
>
> Putnam: Well—
>
> Crandall: I mean, you know, goddamn, what the * * * * is the point of it? . . .
>
> Putnam: Do you have a suggestion for me?
>
> Crandall: Yes. I have a suggestion for you. Raise your goddamn fares twenty percent. I'll raise mine the next morning.
>
> Putnam: Robert, we—
>
> Crandall: You'll make more money and I will too.
>
> Putnam: We can't talk about pricing.
>
> Crandall: Oh bull * * *, Howard. We can talk about any goddamn thing we want to talk about.

Putnam did not raise Braniff's fares in response to Crandall's proposal; instead he presented the government with a tape recording of the conversation.

The United States subsequently sought an injunction . . . against American Airlines and Crandall based on . . . attempted monopolization.[100] On a motion by the defendants, the district court dismissed the government's complaint for failure to state a claim . . .

Our first step in the analysis of the requisites of attempted monopolization is a consideration of the elements of the completed offense of monopolization.

To establish illegal monopolization two elements must be shown: (1) the possession of monopoly power in the relevant market, and (2) "the willful acquisition or maintenance of that power as distinguished from growth or development as a consequence of a superior product, business acumen, or historic accident." *Grinnell*. Monopoly power is "the power to control price or exclude competition." *du Pont*. If these two elements are shown, the offense of actual monopolization is complete; it is well established that there is no additional requirement that the power actually be exercised. *United States v. Griffith,* 334 U.S. 100, 107 (1948); *American Tobacco Co. v. United States,* 328 U.S. 781, 810–13 (1946). . . .

Applying these principles to the case at hand, we conclude that if Putnam had accepted Crandall's offer, the two airlines, at the moment of acceptance, would have acquired monopoly power. At that same moment, the offense of joint monopolization would have been complete. . . .

Both Crandall and Putnam were the chief executive officers of their airlines; each arguably had the power to implement Crandall's plan. The airlines jointly had a high market share in a market with high barriers to entry. American and Braniff, at the moment of Putnam's acceptance, would have monopolized the market. Under the facts alleged, it follows that Crandall's proposal was an act that was the most proximate to the commission of the completed offense that Crandall was capable of committing. Considering the alleged market share of American and Braniff, the barriers to entry by other airlines, and the authority of Crandall and Putnam, the complaint sufficiently alleged that Crandall's proposal had a dangerous probability of success. . . . In sum, our decision that the government has stated a claim does not add attempt to violations of Section 1 of the Sherman Act or lower the incipiency gate of Section 2.

Finally, we note one final consequence of our reasoning. If a defendant had the requisite intent and capacity, and his plan if executed would have had the prohibited market result, it is no defense that the plan proved to be impossible to execute. As applied here, if Putnam from the beginning never intended to agree such fact would be of no aid to Crandall and American. . . .

Our decision that the government's complaint states a claim of attempted monopolization is consistent with the Act's language and purpose. The application of section 2 principles to defendants' conduct will

---

[100] [Editor's Note: "The Government [sought] as relief to enjoin American from employing Crandall for a period of twenty-four months and to enjoin American from communicating any price information with a competitor for a period of ten years." United States v. American Airlines, Inc., 570 F.Supp. 654, 657 (N.D.Tex.1983).]

deter the formation of monopolies at their outset when the unlawful schemes are proposed, and thus, will strengthen the Act.

Under appellees' construction of the Act, an individual is given a strong incentive to propose the formation of cartels. If the proposal is accepted, monopoly power is achieved; if the proposal is declined, no antitrust liability attaches. If section 2 liability attaches to conduct such as that alleged against Crandall, naked proposals for the formation of cartels are discouraged and competition is promoted.[15]

Appellees argue that price fixing is an offense under section 1 of the Sherman Act and since the government charges that Crandall sought to have American and Braniff fix prices, the government's complaint in reality seeks to have us write an attempt provision into section 1. This argument is meritless. Appellees confuse the section 1 offense of price fixing with the power to control price following acquisition of monopoly power under section 2. Under the facts alleged in the complaint, Crandall wanted both to obtain joint monopoly power and to engage in price fixing. That he was not able to price fix and thus, has no liability under section 1, has no effect on whether his unsuccessful efforts to monopolize constitute attempted monopolization. . . .

We hold that an agreement is not an absolute prerequisite for the offense of attempted joint monopolization and that the government's complaint sufficiently alleged facts that if proved would permit a finding of attempted monopolization by defendants. We therefore vacate the dismissal of the complaint and remand for further proceedings consistent with this opinion.

NOTES AND QUESTIONS ON *AMERICAN AIRLINES* ATTEMPTED CARTEL CASE

1. ***Why didn't the government allege a violation of Sherman Act § 1 or a conspiracy to monopolize under § 2?*** Because Braniff Airlines never agreed to fix prices. Thus, there was no agreement under § 1 nor any conspiracy to monopolize under § 2. Neither provision covers an attempted agreement or attempted conspiracy.

2. ***Was the Court right that American Airlines' attempt to fix prices could nonetheless be condemned as attempted monopolization?*** One can certainly make a reasonable legal argument that because both statutory provisions cover agreements/conspiracies without covering attempted

[15] We disagree with the appellees' contention that our application of § 2 would discourage discussion among potential partners in mergers and joint ventures. Parties who wish to engage in substantial mergers or joint ventures, under the pre-screening procedures of the Hart-Scott-Rodino . . . Act, must notify the Justice Department's Antitrust Division and the Federal Trade Commission before consummating the transaction. The government may have no objection to the transaction, or it may sue to block the transaction . . . Chances that such a transaction would raise a dangerous probability of successful monopolization, are extremely remote.

Transactions that are too small to be subject to the Hart-Scott-Rodino Act will rarely pose a dangerous probability of successful monopolization. If there are such cases, however, and if in such cases the firm proposing the transaction acts with a specific intent to monopolize, then we see no reason why § 2 liability should not attach.

agreements/conspiracies, the statute should be interpreted to exclude such attempts. However, an agreement to form a monopoly cartel had long been held to constitute not only an agreement that violates § 1 and a conspiracy to monopolize that violates § 2, but also monopolization that violates the provision of § 2 against monopolization.[101] Given that successful agreements to form a monopoly cartel constitute monopolization, attempts to form a monopoly cartel can reasonably be understood to constitute attempted monopolization. Do you agree with the Court's interpretation?

3. ***Given that no anticompetitive effects can occur unless another firm accepts an offer to form a price-fixing cartel, why not wait until there is an actual agreement?*** A doctrine that waited for actual agreements would create underdeterrence concerns. Once the other firm agrees, both firms have incentives not to reveal their conspiracy, which may never be detected. We would like to deter even the attempt with legal penalties, given that attempts are necessary for successful agreements. Thus, deterring the attempts will deter successful price-fixing agreements. Nor is there anything possibly procompetitive about an attempt to form a price-fixing agreement. A legal ban on attempts to create a monopoly cartel thus reduces underdeterrence concerns without any creating any offsetting overdeterrence problem.

4. ***If there were three equally-sized firms in a market, would a call offering to fix prices from one firm to a second firm constitute attempted monopolization? What if there were four or five or ten equally-sized firms in a market?*** Because attempted price-fixing agreements are only covered as attempted monopolization, the prohibition does not apply unless the attempt has a dangerous probability of creating monopoly power. If there are only three equally-sized firms, the first attempt probably would create a dangerous probability because acceptance would mean a cartel that covers 67% of the market. As the number of firms in the market increases, it will become less and less likely that the first call from one to another would constitute attempted monopolization, given that the probability of achieving monopoly power would diminish. However, every attempt to cartelize an industry with several firms must begin with this first communication, and one might be inclined to draw the line at a fairly low probability because underdeterrence concerns dominate overdeterrence ones for this sort of conduct.

5. ***Is it appropriate that, instead of seeking criminal penalties, the government sought an injunction banning American Airlines from keeping Robert Crandall as CEO and from communicating any price information with a rival?*** Neither having Crandall as CEO nor price communications with rivals are inherently anticompetitive. However, both sorts of conduct made anticompetitive conduct more likely given this history, and an injunction that just prohibited offering to enter into a price-fixing agreement would add nothing to the statutory prohibition on attempted monopolization. So it is common for antitrust to go beyond prohibiting illegal conduct. A criminal penalty might seem appropriate, but there was (before this decision) a good argument that the law was unclear that attempted monopoly cartels were a crime, so the rule of lenity argues against criminal sanctions. Criminal penalties might be better for future cases now that this is the clear interpretation. Further, an

---

[101] *See*, e.g., United States v. Grinnell Corp., 384 U.S. 563, 576 (1966); Am. Tobacco Co. v. United States, 328 U.S. 781, 783–84, 808–09, 813–14 (1946); Standard Oil Co. v. United States, 221 U.S. 1, 70–75 (1911); *Lorain Journal.*

injunction requiring a company to fire its CEO is likely to be an especially strong deterrent against conduct taken by that CEO. Aggressive injunctive or (in future cases) criminal penalties might be more appropriate because rejected price-fixing agreements cannot be deterred by damage remedies, given that the cartel never took place and thus never created damages.

Spectrum Sports v. McQuillan

506 U.S. 447 (1993).

■ JUSTICE WHITE delivered the opinion of the Court.

[The sole manufacturer of Sorbothane, a shock-absorbing polymer useful in medical, athletic, and equestrian products, had five regional distributors in 1981, one of which was McQuillan and another of which was Spectrum Sports. In 1982, the manufacturer decided to shift medical products to one national distributor, and informed McQuillan that it must give up its athletic shoe distributorship if it wanted to retain its right to distribute equestrian products. When McQuillan refused to stop distributing athletic shoe products, the manufacturer terminated McQuillan as a distributor of all sorbothane products, appointed another company national distributor of equestrian products, and appointed Spectrum Sports national distributor of athletic shoe products. McQuillan sued, alleging among other things attempted monopolization, and won $1 million in attorney fees and $1.7 million in compensatory damages, which were trebled.]

On the § 2 issue that petitioners present here, the Court of Appeals. . . . rejected petitioners' argument that attempted monopolization had not been established because respondents had failed to prove that petitioners had a specific intent to monopolize a relevant market. The court also held that in order to show that respondents' attempt to monopolize was likely to succeed it was not necessary to present evidence of the relevant market or of the defendants' market power. In so doing, the Ninth Circuit relied on *Lessig v. Tidewater Oil Co.,* 327 F.2d 459 (9th Cir. 1964), and its progeny. The Court of Appeals noted that these cases, in dealing with attempt to monopolize claims, had ruled that "if evidence of unfair or predatory conduct is presented, it may satisfy both the specific intent and dangerous probability elements of the offense, without any proof of relevant market or the defendant's market power." If, however, there is insufficient evidence of unfair or predatory conduct, there must be a showing of "relevant market or the defendant's marketpower.". . . .

This Court first addressed the meaning of attempt to monopolize under § 2 in *Swift.* The Court's opinion, written by Justice Holmes, contained the following passage:

> "Where acts are not sufficient in themselves to produce a result which the law seeks to prevent—for instance, the monopoly—but require further acts in addition to the mere forces of nature to bring that result to pass, an intent to bring it to pass is necessary in order to produce a dangerous probability that it will happen. But when that intent and the consequent dangerous probability exist, this statute, like many others and like the common law in some cases,

> directs itself against that dangerous probability as well as against the completed result.

The Court went on to explain, however, that not every act done with intent to produce an unlawful result constitutes an attempt. "It is a question of proximity and degree." *Swift* thus indicated that intent is necessary, but alone is not sufficient, to establish the dangerous probability of success that is the object of § 2's prohibition of attempts.

The Court's decisions since *Swift* have reflected the view that the plaintiff charging attempted monopolization must prove a dangerous probability of actual monopolization, which has generally required a definition of the relevant market and examination of market power. In *Walker Process*, we found that enforcement of a fraudulently obtained patent claim could violate the Sherman Act. We stated that, to establish monopolization or attempt to monopolize under § 2 of the Sherman Act, it would be necessary to appraise the exclusionary power of the illegal patent claim in terms of the relevant market for the product involved. The reason was that "[w]ithout a definition of that market there is no way to measure [the defendant's] ability to lessen or destroy competition."

Similarly, this Court reaffirmed in *Copperweld* that "Congress authorized Sherman Act scrutiny of single firms only when they pose a danger of monopolization. Judging unilateral conduct in this manner reduces the risk that the antitrust laws will dampen the competitive zeal of a single aggressive entrepreneur." Thus, the conduct of a single firm, governed by § 2, "is unlawful only when it threatens actual monopolization." *Id. See also Lorain Journal; Griffith; American Tobacco.*

The Courts of Appeals other than the Ninth Circuit have followed this approach. Consistent with our cases, it is generally required that to demonstrate attempted monopolization a plaintiff must prove (1) that the defendant has engaged in predatory or anticompetitive conduct with (2) a specific intent to monopolize and (3) a dangerous probability of achieving monopoly power. In order to determine whether there is a dangerous probability of monopolization, courts have found it necessary to consider the relevant market and the defendant's ability to lessen or destroy competition in that market.

. . . . We are not at all inclined . . . to embrace *Lessig*'s interpretation of § 2, for there is little if any support for it in the statute or the case law, and the notion that proof of unfair or predatory conduct alone is sufficient to make out the offense of attempted monopolization is contrary to the purpose and policy of the Sherman Act . . . The purpose of the Act is not to protect businesses from the working of the market; it is to protect the public from the failure of the market. The law directs itself not against conduct which is competitive, even severely so, but against conduct which unfairly tends to destroy competition itself. It does so not out of solicitude for private concerns but out of concern for the public interest. Thus, this Court and other courts have been careful to avoid constructions of § 2 which might chill competition, rather than foster it. It is sometimes difficult to distinguish robust competition from conduct with long-term anticompetitive effects; moreover, single-firm activity is unlike concerted activity covered by § 1, which "inherently is fraught with anticompetitive risk." *Copperweld*. For these reasons, § 2 makes the conduct of a single firm unlawful only when it actually monopolizes or dangerously threatens to do so. The concern that § 2 might be applied so as to further anticompetitive ends is plainly not met by inquiring only whether the defendant has engaged in "unfair" or "predatory" tactics. Such conduct may be sufficient to prove the necessary intent to monopolize, which is something more than an intent to compete vigorously, but demonstrating the dangerous probability of monopolization in an attempt case also requires inquiry into the relevant product and geographic market and the defendant's economic power in that market.

We hold that petitioners may not be liable for attempted monopolization under § 2 of the Sherman Act absent proof of a dangerous probability that they would monopolize a particular market and specific intent to monopolize. In this case, the trial instructions allowed the jury to infer specific intent and dangerous probability of success from the defendants' predatory conduct, without any proof of the relevant market or of a realistic probability that the defendants could achieve monopoly power in that market. In this respect, the instructions misconstrued § 2, as did the Court of Appeals in affirming the judgment of the District Court . . .

NOTES AND QUESTIONS ON *SPECTRUM SPORTS*

Spectrum Sports holds that the elements of attempted monopolization are: (1) anticompetitive conduct; (2) a specific intent to monopolize; and (3) a dangerous probability of achieving monopoly power. It further holds that: (a) a court cannot infer the last two elements from the first; and (b) proof of dangerous probability requires some definition of the market and proof that the defendant has a realistic probability of obtaining monopoly power in that market.

1. ***Why not infer an intent to monopolize and a dangerous probability of success from anticompetitive conduct?*** Arguably, one should make that inference, particularly if the defendant offers no other explanation for its conduct. A defendant would not engage in anticompetitive conduct unless it wanted to gain market power and believed it had a dangerous probability of succeeding. Absent such beliefs, a defendant would avoid anticompetitive conduct because it would cause the defendant to lose sales given the inefficiency of such conduct.

The Court, however, is worried about overdeterrence from possible adjudication errors. If courts often have difficulty distinguishing anticompetitive conduct from procompetitive conduct, there will be an overdeterrence problem from basing the entire test on proof of anticompetitive conduct. This overdeterrence problem is bigger here than in § 1 agreement cases because, in agreement cases, antitrust scrutiny can always be avoided by not entering into the agreement. In contrast, purely unilateral conduct, like setting prices or deciding what to sell and to whom, is unavoidable. Adding the last two elements to prove attempted monopolization lowers the overdeterrence problem by requiring proof that the conduct seemed obviously intended to lead to monopoly and that the defendant in fact had enough market power to make that a dangerous probability given its conduct.

On the other hand, adding the last two elements does increase underdeterrence problems because courts will sometimes make mistakes in assessing intent, defining markets, or assessing whether monopoly power is a dangerous probability. Also, the sheer expense or uncertainty of proving those elements will sometimes deter litigants from bringing otherwise meritorious cases. The tradeoff is worth it if the harms from such increased underdeterrence are outweighed by the benefits of decreasing overdeterrence. Do you think the Court has struck the optimal tradeoff of overdeterrence and underdeterrence? Why not instead allow the last two elements to be inferred from anticompetitive conduct when that conduct is unambiguous or egregious?

2. ***How much market power is needed to show a dangerous probability of success?*** The required level of market power must be less than monopoly power, otherwise an attempted monopolization claim would be superfluous and a monopolization claim would always be brought instead because it requires no showing of intent. Monopoly power generally requires a market share over 50% and is usually in the 60–90% range. *See* Chapter 3.B.2. For attempted monopolization, less than 30% is probably insufficient, while 30–50% may be enough, and 50% probably suffices. But we have no clear Supreme Court authority on the topic.

3. ***Does an intent to get a monopoly suffice and, if not, what does the specific intent element add to the other elements?*** It would not suffice to show an intent to get a monopoly by making the best product on the market. The required intent must be an intent to get a monopoly through anticompetitive conduct. But if the required intent is to get a monopoly through anticompetitive conduct, what does the intent requirement add to the other elements? Any firm that engages in anticompetitive conduct necessarily intends the conduct it engaged in. Accordingly, if the specific intent element merely required an intent to engage in the same sort of conduct that is deemed anticompetitive for a monopolization claim, that would make the monopolization claim superfluous because attempted monopolization would always cover the same conduct with a weaker market power requirement.

The answer would seem to be that the specific intent element requires that the anticompetitive conduct must be either palpably anticompetitive on its face or designed by the defendant to be anticompetitive. This standard would exclude conduct that had a procompetitive purpose but had anticompetitive effects that outweighed any procompetitive effects, unless the imbalance was sufficiently large to make it obvious that the conduct was mainly anticompetitive or designed to be so. The specific intent element thus effectively means that proving attempted monopolization requires worse anticompetitive conduct than that needed to prove monopolization. Doing so helps address the increased overdeterrence problem that otherwise would result because attempted monopolization requires less market power than monopolization does.

4. ***Should courts instead use a full sliding scale?*** As the above suggests, attempted monopolization requires worse anticompetitive conduct but less market power than monopolization. The two claims thus offer distinctive ways of optimizing the tradeoff between overdeterrence and underdeterrence. Should courts instead adopt a full sliding scale, requiring stronger proof of anticompetitive conduct the weaker the degree of market power, and vice versa? The problem is that a full sliding scale would create a lot of vagueness, which might make it inadministrable for courts or make it hard for businesses to plan their conduct, which would undermine the ability of the law to influence behavior. So in practice a two-tier scale—one for monopolization claims and another for attempted monopolization—may be the best way to achieve the benefits of different scales without creating excessive vagueness.

CHAPTER 4

VERTICAL AGREEMENTS THAT RESTRICT DEALING WITH RIVALS

A. INTRODUCTION

This chapter concerns exclusionary agreements. Most are downstream agreements between a defendant and its buyers that restrict the ability of those buyers to buy from the defendant's rivals. But the analysis applies equally to upstream agreements between a defendant and its suppliers that restrict the ability of those suppliers to supply the defendant's rivals. Indeed, to some extent, the distinction collapses because any agreement between a manufacturer and the distributors who buy and resell its products could equally be thought of as an agreement for the supply of distribution services. The incidence of payment and formality of title transfers generally does not affect the relevant antitrust inquiry. For simplicity, the following discussion will refer to exclusionary agreements between defendants and their buyers, but throughout it should be understood that it could equally apply to their upstream variant. The dominant concern is that such agreements will foreclose a sufficient share of the downstream (or upstream) market to impede the competitiveness of the defendant's rivals.

Some exclusionary agreements sell a product on the condition that buyers not buy that same product from the defendant's rivals. Such agreements are called exclusive dealing, and they are the topic of Section B.

Other exclusionary agreements involve tying, whereby a seller agrees to sell one product only on the condition that the buyer also take a second product from the seller. This is the topic of Section C. Sometimes tying restricts the buyer from buying the other product from rivals; sometimes it just requires purchasing a certain amount of that product from the defendant and thus has the practical effect of reducing sales by rivals.

Both exclusive dealing and tying agreements also exist in less absolute forms. Loyalty discounts or rebates are like exclusive dealing agreements that are less absolute in form. Rather than imposing an absolute obligation not to deal with rivals, they can condition discounts or rebates on buyers buying all or a high percentage of their purchases from the defendant. Likewise, tying can take the less absolute form of bundled discounts or rebates, which make discounts or rebates conditional on the buyer purchasing both product *A* and product *B* from the defendant. Loyalty and bundled discounts are considered in Section D.

Legally, such vertical exclusionary agreements can be challenged under multiple statutes. In the United States, they can be challenged under Sherman Act § 1 because they involve agreements that constitute restraints of trade if they are on balance anticompetitive. But they can also be challenged under Sherman Act § 2 if the defendant has monopoly power (or a dangerous probability of acquiring it) and the exclusionary agreements anticompetitively help obtain or maintain such monopoly power. Or the FTC can challenge them under FTC Act § 5 if they are anticompetitive. Finally, they can be challenged under another statute that we have not yet introduced:

Clayton Act § 3, 15 U.S.C. § 14

> It shall be unlawful for any person . . . to lease or make a sale . . . of goods . . . , whether patented or unpatented, . . . or fix a price charged therefor, or discount from, or rebate upon, such price, on the condition, agreement, or understanding that the lessee or purchaser thereof shall not use or deal in the goods . . . of a competitor or competitors of the lessor or seller, where the effect . . . may be to substantially lessen competition or tend to create a monopoly in any line of commerce.

This statute effectively requires two elements: (1) sales or pricing of goods conditioned on the buyer not dealing with the seller's rivals; and (2) proof that the effect may be to substantially lessen competition. The latter may be proven in a case-by-case manner or, as we shall see in the case of tying, inferred from the nature of the agreement.

Whichever U.S. statute is invoked, the underlying economics of the relevant agreement is the same, and each statute effectively imposes the same requirement of proving the agreement is anticompetitive. Thus, it is fruitful to analyze them together when considering their application to exclusionary agreements. Further, limitations specific to one of the statutes may not matter much as a practical matter given the existence of the others. For example, the fact that Clayton Act § 3 is limited to goods means that it does not govern similar agreements that involve sales or discounts on services or land, and the fact that it is limited to sales or leases means it does not cover upstream exclusive dealing that forecloses inputs. But neither limitation matters much because such agreements would remain covered by Sherman Act § 1.[1] Likewise, the

[1] Because Congress enacted Clayton Act § 3 in 1914, twenty-four years after the Sherman Act, one might be tempted by the argument that it must have been intended to extend more broadly or there would have been no point in enacting it. But the statute was largely a reaction to Congressional fears that the courts were interpreting (or might interpret) the Sherman Act unduly narrowly in 1914. Thus, while Congress must have intended Clayton Act § 3 to be broader than the 1914 interpretation it feared courts were giving (or might give) the Sherman Act, it did not necessarily intend Clayton Act § 3 to extend beyond the broader interpretation given by modern courts to the Sherman Act. A stronger argument for finding

fact that Sherman Act § 2 is limited to defendants with monopoly or near-monopoly power may not matter much because Sherman Act § 1 remains available to cover cases where defendants have some lesser amount of market power. The degree of market power, or of market foreclosure, may well be relevant to assessing the likelihood or size of anticompetitive effects, but that is equally true under any of the statutes.

B. EXCLUSIVE DEALING

Exclusive dealing agreements are agreements to sell a product on the condition that the buyer takes all (or effectively all) of its requirements of that product from the seller. Such agreements have possible anticompetitive effects, but may also have possible redeeming efficiencies.

Possible Anticompetitive Effects. The major anticompetitive concern is that such agreements might foreclosure enough of the market to rivals as to impair competition. Such foreclosure might impede rival efficiency, entry, existence, or expandability, any of which can anticompetitively increase the market power of the foreclosing firm.

In most industries, there are economies of scale, so that firms can lower their costs by expanding until they reach the output level that minimizes their costs, which is called the minimum efficient scale. If foreclosure prevents a competitive number of rivals from maintaining this scale, or from expanding their operations to reach it, then it impairs their efficiency.[2] Foreclosure can similarly deprive rivals of economies of scope if, without the foreclosure, rival expansion would have enabled them to offer a variety of products that can be more efficiently produced or sold together than separately. Further, even if rivals are able to achieve their minimum efficient scale and scope of production, foreclosure that bars rivals from the most efficient suppliers[3] or means of distribution[4] can also impair rival efficiency by increasing their costs.

Clayton Act § 3 broader might rest simply on its text, which requires proof only that the agreement "may" substantially lessen competition, whereas the Sherman Act generally requires evidence that anticompetitive effects are likely. Courts have not tended to hold that the § 3 language relieves a plaintiff of its obligation to show that anticompetitive effects were more likely than not. Still, some modern courts appear to treat Clayton Act § 3 claims more generously at the margins.

[2] This anticompetitive effect is not necessarily eliminated if the unforeclosed market can sustain merely one rival, for if one rival exists it would be less likely to undercut monopoly pricing, given that it knows it will make less profit in the long run if it did. Rather, to avoid this anticompetitive effect, the unforeclosed market must be large enough to sustain the number of rivals at their minimum efficient scale that is sufficient to prevent such coordination.

[3] *See* Krattenmaker & Salop, Anticompetitive Exclusion, 96 Yale L.J., 234–45 (1986); Stephen C. Salop & David T. Scheffman, *Raising Rivals' Costs*, 73 AM. ECON. REV. 267 (1983) (Special Issue).

[4] *See* LePage's v. 3M, 324 F.3d 141, 159–60 & n.14 (3d Cir. 2003) (en banc); United States v. Microsoft, 253 F.3d 34, 70–71 (D.C. Cir. 2001) (en banc); HOVENKAMP, FEDERAL ANTITRUST POLICY 431 (2d ed. 1999). Although such distributors are nominally buyers, one can conceptualize their foreclosure as effectively a foreclosure of the most efficient suppliers of a necessary input called distribution services.

Most industries are also characterized by a learning curve,[5] so that substantial foreclosure of the market can impair rival efficiency by simply slowing down rival expansion even though it does not outright prevent that expansion.

If rival efficiency is impaired in any of these ways, then rivals will have to cover their now-higher costs by charging higher prices than they otherwise would have. In the extreme case, these higher prices will be unsustainable, and thus rival entry will be deterred and existing rivals will be eliminated. But even if foreclosure reduced rival efficiency without outright eliminating them, it will worsen the market options available to consumers, and mean that these rivals will impose less of a constraint on the defendant's market power than they otherwise would have. This can thus enhance or maintain that market power even if it does not eliminate rivals or bar their entry.

Many modern industries are also characterized by network effects, which means that one seller's product is more valuable to buyers the more that other buyers have purchased the same good from that seller. Where network effects exist, foreclosure can impair rival efficiency by denying rivals access to the number of buyers they need to make their products more valuable to all buyers. Rather than raising rivals' costs, this strategy succeeds by lowering the value of rivals' products. This also worsens the market options available to consumers and lessens the ability of rivals to constrain the monopolist's market power.

In markets where competition by innovation is important, foreclosure can deny rivals economies of scale in recouping investments in research. If firms are foreclosed from a significant share of the market, then successful innovations will have a smaller payoff than they otherwise would have, which will discourage efficient investments in research and innovation.

Foreclosure might also enhance defendant market power by impairing rival expandability even if it does not affect rival efficiency. Standard economic models calculate market power to be directly proportional to defendant market share and inversely proportional to the market share and elasticity of supply of rivals, with the latter measured by the percentage increase in rival supply that will be made in response to a certain percentage increase in price. These standard models effectively assume rivals' ability to expand depends in part on how large they already are. Thus, if a firm can through foreclosure obtain a high share of the market and relegate its rivals to a small share, it can lessen the ability of rivals to constrain its prices given a constant elasticity of supply and thus increase its prices even if it has not lessened the

[5] *See*, e.g., James E. Hodder & Yael A. Ilan, *Declining Prices and Optimality When Costs Follow an Experience Curve*, 7 MANAGERIAL & DECISION ECON. 229 (1986); A. Michael Spence, *The Learning Curve and Competition*, 12 BELL J. ECON. 49 (1981).

efficiency of rivals.[6] Exclusive dealing might also increase buyer switching costs, for example, by preventing buyers from trying rival products for some of their purchases and requiring the more costly or risky decision to do a wholehouse conversion. Such an increase in buyer switching costs will reduce the ability of rivals to expand sales in response to a firm's price increase. In short, it can in this way reduce rival supply elasticity (without reducing rival efficiency) and thus increase the firm's market power.

When exclusive dealing agreements are obtained by seller commitments to give exclusive buyers a discount from the price available to nonexclusive buyers, then exclusive dealing agreements can also effectively divide markets and discourage price competition with rivals.[7] The exclusive dealing condition gives the firm less incentive to lower prices to exclusive buyers (because they cannot buy from the rival) or to nonexclusive buyers (because price reduction to them would, given the exclusivity discount, require lowering prices to captive exclusive buyers). The condition also reduces the ability or incentive for the rival to win sales by cutting prices to exclusive buyers (because they cannot buy from the rival) or to nonexclusive buyers (because the rival need only undercut the inflated price that the firm charges nonexclusive buyers given the exclusivity discount). The effective market division is that the firm's pricing focuses on sales to exclusive buyers, whereas the rival's pricing focuses on sales to nonexclusive buyers. The discouragement to price competition is stronger the higher the foreclosure share, the greater the discount, and the more that rivals also use exclusive dealing agreements. This effect does not depend on rival efficiency being impaired.

Similarly, in an oligopolistic market, exclusive dealing agreements might aid oligopolistic coordination by effectively allocating the market among oligopolists, making it difficult to increase market share by decreasing prices.

Finally, foreclosure can take the form of seller-buyer collaboration to exploit downstream buyers by precluding rival competition. Suppose, for example, that a seller of widgets on a national market pays the only ten retailers in a regional market $1 million each to agree to exclusively sell the seller's product, thus foreclosing competition from rival widget makers. With a regional monopoly, the seller can now raise prices on its

---

6 To put the point mathematically, if e_{def} is the firm-specific demand elasticity of the defendant, then under standard economic measures the degree of its market power is determined by the equation $(P - MC)/P = -1/e_{def}$. *See* Chapter 3. Further, if we call e_{mkt} the marketwide demand elasticity, call $e_{rivsupp}$ the supply elasticity of rivals, and call S the share of the defendant (which of course means $1 - S$ is the share of all the other firms), then it can be shown that $e_{def} = e_{mkt}/S + e_{rivsupp}(1 - S)/S$. *See* Chapter 3. The result is that enhancing defendant market share in ways unrelated to product merits (such as through foreclosure) is anticompetitive, even if it does not lower rival efficiency, because increasing S lowers the defendant's firm-specific demand elasticity, e_{def}, and thus increases its market power, even if the foreclosure does not alter rival supply elasticity or market demand elasticity.

7 Elhauge, *How Loyalty Discounts Can Perversely Discourage Discounting*, 5 JOURNAL OF COMPETITION LAW & ECONOMICS 189 (2009); Elhauge & Wickelgren, *Robust Exclusion and Market Division Through Loyalty Discounts*, 43 INT'L J. INDUS. ORG. 111 (2015).

widgets to supracompetitive levels to retailers in that market, which those retailers will pass on without fear that the higher prices will cause them to lose market share to other retailers because they all have the same agreement. In effect, the exclusionary agreements here allow the seller to serve as a regional cartel ringmaster, splitting the resulting supracompetitive profits with the retailers.[8] This anticompetitive effect does not require that the foreclosure impair rival efficiency in any of the other ways indicated above. It suffices that the foreclosure precludes competition that would otherwise have constrained market power in a downstream regional market.

All the above theories require not only substantial foreclosure of some properly defined market, but some significant barriers to entry and expansion in the foreclosed market. For example, suppose the foreclosed buyers are dealers who merely resell the product to ultimate consumers, entry barriers to being a dealer are zero, and any entrant can immediately and costlessly expand sales to any extent necessary. In that case, foreclosure of dealers cannot effectively foreclose rivals because they can simply create a new entrant who can immediately access the entire consumer market. Or, if the foreclosure covered say 50% of the retail market, the retailers covering the other 50% could instantly expand their purchases of any superior rival product and then resell that increased amount to the consumers, assuming they can easily switch from one type of retailer to another. But foreclosure can limit rival sales if barriers to dealer entry and expandability are significant. Nor are the above factors likely to be an issue if the foreclosed buyers do not merely resell the product, but use it in some fashion. This is clearest when buyers are the ultimate consumers of the product, for then a rival could not possibly overcome foreclosure by creating new buyers and having them expand to make all market purchases.

Possible Redeeming Efficiencies. Although exclusive dealing agreements can have many possible anticompetitive effects, they also have many possible redeeming efficiencies that help explain why they are often used even by firms without market power who are not foreclosing a substantial share of any market. They might reduce uncertainty about whether future sales will occur at the contractually set price. This can lower risk-bearing costs or inventory costs, or give firms the contractual commitments they need to invest in expanding their capacity in a way that achieves economies of scale. One might wonder why sellers could not achieve even greater certainty by specifying not just the contractual price but the future volume of sales. The problem is that where the buyer is a firm that either distributes the product or uses it as an input in some downstream market, specifying future volume might impose excessive risks on the buyer that market demand for the product will collapse, costs

[8] *See generally* Krattenmaker & Salop, *supra* note 3, at 238–40; Elizabeth Granitz & Benjamin Klein, *Monopolization by Raising Rivals' Costs: The Standard Oil Case*, 39 J.L. & ECON. 1 (1996); Hovenkamp, *Mergers & Buyers*, 77 VA. L. REV. 1369 (1991); IV AREEDA, HOVENKAMP & SOLOW, ANTITRUST LAW ¶ 943b, 204–06 & n.4 (1998).

that grow greater the longer the term of the contractual relationship. Exclusivity avoids this risk while still providing the seller with at least the assurance that the buyer will take all it can profitably use.

Exclusive dealing might also encourage relation-specific investments between the seller and buyer that increase their efficiency only with each other. For example, suppose sellers *A*, *B*, and *C* all have plants in a central location equidistant from buyers *X*, *Y* and *Z*, who are located in various directions away from that central location. The sellers can supply all the buyers equally well, but in addition to manufacturing costs of $100 per unit, must incur transportation costs of $20 per unit to supply any of the buyers, bringing the total cost to $120. Suppose, further, that it is efficient for the seller *A* to build its new plant next to buyer *X* in order to eliminate those transportation costs, but if it did so, *A* would have to charge $110 per unit in order to cover the costs of the plant move. If *A* did not secure an exclusive dealing agreement with *X* at a price over $110, then *A* might fear that *X* would expropriate *A*'s investment in the plant move by insisting on a price of $100 after *A* made the move. After the plant move, *A* could not respond by threatening to instead supply *Y* and *Z* because now its costs of supplying *Y* and *Z* are $135 and it cannot compete with *B* and *C* who can sell to them at $120. To avoid this problem, *A* and X might then agree on an exclusive dealing agreement at a price of $115, which splits the joint surplus of $10 created by the plant move. This is better for both *A* and X because *A* gets $5 more per unit, and *X* saves $5 per unit. But if exclusive dealing were not possible, that might deter *A* from ever moving the plant, which would be inefficient because the saved transportation costs exceed the costs of moving the plant.

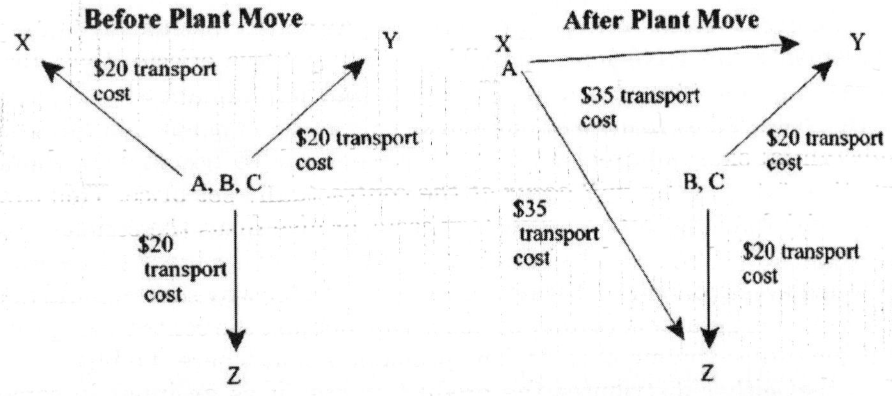

In this example, the plant move is a relationship-specific investment because it creates additional value only if *A* stays related to *X*. This is only one of a myriad relationship-specific investments that might be made, such as tailoring product characteristics or marketing to particular buyers, or training employees to develop special knowledge in the needs of a particular buyer or the product of particular seller. Any of these sorts of relationship-specific investments might be efficiently encouraged by exclusive dealing arrangements. For example, when the buyers are distributors, exclusive dealing might encourage manufacturers to spend on things like advertising that will increases foot traffic to its distributors without fear that customers will be diverted to other brands.[9] In this example, the advertising is a relationship-specific investment encouraged by exclusive dealing.

Another possible efficiency justification might reflect the economics of contracting. Modern economic theory on contracts emphasizes that often the optimal performance that contracting parties want to specify is not verifiable in the sense that parties cannot have high confidence that deviations will be detected and proven in a court of law.[10] In such cases, the most efficient contract will not be one that just tries to specify the desired performance but will instead be one that structures incentives or contractual powers in a way that minimizes the likelihood the contracting parties will want to deviate from optimal performance or that puts the power in the hands of the party with the least incentive to do so. And sometimes the most efficient way to structure incentives or powers might be to adopt an exclusive dealing term.

For example, suppose a manufacturer wants to contract to get a distributor to expend efforts marketing the manufacturer's brand in a given territory. The contract could specify the desired marketing efforts, but it might be difficult to specify precisely what is desired (especially given constantly changing market conditions) or to verify whether the specified performance was given. How, for example, could one verify whether the distributor's sales pitches for the manufacturer were sufficiently enthusiastic? To avoid this problem, one might want to define a more verifiable benchmark, such as a requirement to resell a minimum volume. But that not only might impose excessive risk on the distributor that market demand for the product will collapse, but it will also create insufficient incentives to sell more than the minimum when market demand exceeds expectations. Thus, the parties may instead want to rely on an exclusive dealing term that prohibits the distributor from carrying other brands because that naturally gives the dealer incentives to want to market the manufacturers' brands (because it cannot make money on another brand) and because deviations from such an exclusive dealing term are much easier to verify than insufficiently enthusiastic marketing efforts.

In short, exclusive dealing can have procompetitive efficiencies. Thus, the general modern view in antitrust economics is that exclusive dealing arrangements have sufficient mixed effects that they should be neither per se illegal nor per se legal. Instead, they should be judged

---

9 *See* Howard P. Marvel, *Exclusive Dealing*, 25 J.L. & ECON. 1 (1982).

10 *See generally* PATRICK BOLTON & MATHIAS DEWATRIPONT, CONTRACT THEORY (2005).

under a rule of reason that weighs the likely or actual anticompetitive effects against any efficiency justifications.

United States v. Griffith

334 U.S. 100 (1948).

■ MR. JUSTICE DOUGLAS delivered the opinion of the Court. . . .

[The appellees were a chain of affiliated movie theaters that in April 1939 operated in 85 towns across Oklahoma, Texas, and New Mexico.] Fifty-three of the towns (62 percent) were closed towns, i.e., towns in which there were no competing theatres. Five years earlier the . . . appellees had theatres in approximately 37 towns, 18 of which were competitive and 19 of which (51 per cent) were closed. It was during that five-year period that the acts and practices occurred which, according to the allegations of the complaint, constitute violations of §§ 1 and 2 of the Sherman Act.

[The chain negotiated agreements with each distributor that generally licensed first-run exhibitions of all that distributor's films that season in all the chain's towns, with the rental specified often a fixed minimum paid by the chain as a whole.[11]]. . . . The complaint charged that certain exclusive privileges which these agreement granted the appellee exhibitors over their competitors unreasonably restrained competition by preventing their competitors from obtaining enough first- or second-run films from the distributors[6] to operate successfully. . . .

The District Court . . . found that . . . appellees did not condition the licensing of films in any competitive situation on the licensing of such films in a non-competitive situation, or vice versa. . . .

In United States v. Crescent Amusement Co., 323 U.S. 173, a group of affiliated exhibitors, such as we have in the present case, were found to have violated §§ 1 and 2 of the Sherman Act by the pooling of their buying power and the negotiation of master agreements similar to those we have here. A difference between that case and the present one, which the District Court deemed to be vital, was that in the former the buying power was used for the avowed purpose of eliminating competition and of acquiring a monopoly of theatres in the several towns, while no such purpose was found to exist here. To be more specific, the defendants in the former case through the pooling of their buying power increased their leverage over their competitive situations by insisting that they be given monopoly rights in towns where they had competition, else they would give a distributor no business in their closed towns.

---

[11] [Editor's Note: Although the Court did not mention it, sometimes the film rental charged was a percentage of theater revenues. *See* 68 F. Supp. at 186.]

[6] . . . The charge that these distributors conspired with each other was eliminated from the complaint . . . But the charge that each of the distributors had conspired with the appellee exhibitors was retained.

It is, however, not always necessary to find a specific intent to restrain trade or to build a monopoly in order to find that the anti-trust laws have been violated. It is sufficient that a restraint of trade or monopoly results as the consequence of a defendant's conduct or business arrangements. To require a greater showing would cripple the Act. As stated in *Alcoa*, "no monopolist monopolizes unconscious of what he is doing." Specific intent in the sense in which the common law used the term is necessary only where the acts fall short of the results condemned by the Act. . . . And so, even if we accept the District Court's findings that appellees had no intent or purpose unreasonably to restrain trade or to monopolize, we are left with the question whether a necessary and direct result of the master agreements was the restraining or monopolizing of trade within the meaning of the Sherman Act.

Anyone who owns and operates the single theatre in a town, or who acquires the exclusive right to exhibit a film, has a monopoly in the popular sense. But he usually does not violate § 2 of the Sherman Act unless he has acquired or maintained his strategic position, or sought to expand his monopoly, or expanded it by means of those restraints of trade which are cognizable under § 1. . . . [T]he existence of power "to exclude competition when it is desired to do so" is itself a violation of § 2, provided it is coupled with the purpose or intent to exercise that power. *American Tobacco*. It is indeed "unreasonable, per se, to foreclose competitors from any substantial market." *International Salt*. The anti-trust laws are as much violated by the prevention of competition as by its destruction. It follows a fortiori that the use of monopoly power, however lawfully acquired, to foreclose competition, to gain a competitive advantage, or to destroy a competitor, is unlawful.

A man with a monopoly of theatres in any one town commands the entrance for all films into that area. If he uses that strategic position to acquire exclusive privileges in a city where he has competitors, he is employing his monopoly power as a trade weapon against his competitors. It may be a feeble, ineffective weapon where he has only one closed or monopoly town. But as those towns increase in number throughout a region, his monopoly power in them may be used with crushing effect on competitors in other places. He need not be as crass as the exhibitors in *Crescent*, in order to make his monopoly power effective in his competitive situations. Though he makes no threat to withhold the business of his closed or monopoly towns unless the distributors give him the exclusive film rights in the towns where he has competitors, the effect is likely to be the same where the two are joined. When the buying power of the entire circuit is used to negotiate films for his competitive as well as his closed towns, he is using monopoly power to expand his empire. And even if we assume that a specific intent to accomplish that result is absent, he is chargeable in legal contemplation with that purpose since the end result is the necessary and direct consequence of what he did.

The consequence of such a use of monopoly power is that films are licensed on a non-competitive basis in what would otherwise be competitive situations. That is the effect whether one exhibitor makes the bargain with the distributor or whether two or more exhibitors lump together their buying power, as appellees did here. It is in either case a misuse of monopoly power under the Sherman Act. If monopoly power can be used to beget monopoly, the Act becomes a feeble instrument indeed. Large-scale buying is not, of course, unlawful per se. It may yield price or other lawful advantages to the buyer. It may not, however, be used to monopolize or to attempt to monopolize interstate trade or commerce. Nor, as we hold in United States v. Paramount Pictures, Inc., 334 U.S. 131, may it be used to stifle competition by denying competitors less favorably situated access to the market.

Appellees were concededly using their circuit buying power to obtain films. Their closed towns were linked with their competitive towns. No effort of concealment was made as evidenced by the fact that the rental specified was at times the total minimum amount required to be paid by the circuit as a whole. Monopoly rights in the form of certain exclusive privileges were bargained for and obtained. These exclusive privileges, being acquired by the use of monopoly power, were unlawfully acquired. The appellees, having combined with each other and with the distributors to obtain those monopoly rights, formed a conspiracy in violation of §§ 1 and 2 of the Act. . . .

What effect these practices actually had on the competitors of appellee exhibitors or on the growth of the Griffith circuit we do not know. The District Court, having started with the assumption that the use of circuit buying power was wholly lawful, naturally attributed no evil to it and thus treated the master agreements as legitimate weapons of competition. Since it found that no competitors were driven out of business, or acquired by appellees, or impeded in their business by threats or coercion, it concluded that appellees had not violated the Sherman Act in any of the ways charged in the complaint. These findings are plainly inadequate if we start, as we must, from the premise that the circuit buying power was unlawfully employed. On the record as we read it, it cannot be doubted that the monopoly power of appellees had some effect on their competitors and on the growth of the Griffith circuit. Its extent must be determined on a remand of the cause. We remit to the District Court not only that problem but also the fashioning of a decree which will undo as near as may be the wrongs that were done and prevent their recurrence in the future. . . . Reversed.

NOTES AND QUESTIONS ON *GRIFFITH*

*1. **Why would movie distributors agree to exclusionary agreements that create theater monopoly power?*** There are two main theories to explain this: which theory seems more likely in this case to you?

a. Splitting downstream monopoly profits. Exclusionary agreements that gave the theater chain monopolies in additional towns would raise ticket prices and harm consumers in those towns. However, creating these additional downstream local monopolies might not harm the movie distributors if the theater chain split the additional supracompetitive profits from higher ticket prices with the distributors.[12] Such a split might have been created by the fact that movie rental fees were to some extent based on a percentage of theater revenue. This is similar to a cartel ringmaster theory.

b. Collective action problem. Suppose (contrary to the prior theory) that all the movie distributors would be harmed if enough distributors agreed to exclusionary agreements that create additional downstream theater monopolies, because that would give the theater chain additional market power to pay the distributors lower movie rental fees than the theater chain would pay without the exclusionary scheme. Distributors might still agree if those who agree get somewhat higher rental fees than those who do not agree. If one of many distributors thought the other distributors were going to agree to the exclusionary conditions, then that distributor would conclude that the new harmful monopolies will result and depress movies rental fees regardless of what it decides. Accordingly, it might as well agree so that its rental fee reduction is not quite as bad as it would be without its agreement. If one of many distributors thought the other distributors would refuse to agree to the exclusionary conditions, the distributor would conclude that it will avoid the new harmful monopolies regardless of what it decides, so it still might as well agree to get somewhat higher rental fees. Thus, no matter what each distributor thinks the other distributors will do, each distributor has incentives to agree, which means each will agree and create the exclusion that harms them all. The underlying problem is that the benefits of avoiding the new theater monopolies are enjoyed by all distributors, regardless of whether the individual distributor agrees to the exclusionary agreement, but the costs of resisting the new theater monopolies are incurred only by those who refuse to agree to the exclusionary conditions. Further, each distributor knows that its individual decision makes little difference to whether the new theater monopolies result but definitely determines whether it gets worse terms for refusing to agree.

2. *The irrelevance of whether the monopolist demanded the condition.* The Court held that an antitrust violation was shown even though there was no evidence that the theater chain ever threatened to withhold business in monopoly towns to get exclusive rights in nonmonopoly towns. Was the Court right not to require proof that the monopolist demanded the exclusionary condition? Yes. Under the monopoly profit-sharing theory, the distributors as a group benefit from the exclusion and thus they have every incentive to propose it. Even under the collective-action-problem theory, the incentives that make it profitable for each individual distributor to agree to exclusion (for relatively higher fees than

---

[12] *See* Elhauge, *Defining Better Monopolization Standards*, 56 STANFORD L.REV. 253, 288–292 (2003) (explaining how firms upstream can use exclusionary scheme that creates supracompetitive profits against downstream buyers and splits them among the upstream firms).

those paid to those who do not agree) would also make it profitable for each to propose such exclusion to the theater chain (to get relatively higher fees). To consider an analogy: it is well known that a collective action problem can lead each individual to initiate polluting for individual benefits, even if they are all worse off if everyone pollutes.

But if a monopolist can be liable even if it does not demand the exclusionary condition, what can it do to avoid liability? It has to refrain from agreeing to anticompetitive exclusionary restraints even if other parties request them.

Standard Oil and Standard Stations v. United States

337 U.S. 293 (1949).

■ MR. JUSTICE FRANKFURTER delivered the opinion of the Court. . . .

Standard Oil . . . sells through its own service stations, to the operators of independent service stations, and to industrial users. It is the largest seller of gasoline in [Western U.S.]. In 1946 its combined sales amounted to 23% of the total taxable gallonage sold there in that year: sales by company-owned service stations constituted 6.8% of the total, sales under exclusive dealing contracts with independent service stations, 6.7% of the total; the remainder were sales to industrial users. Retail service-station sales by Standard's six leading competitors absorbed 42.5% of the total taxable gallonage; the remaining retail sales were divided between more than seventy small companies. It is undisputed that Standard's major competitors employ similar exclusive dealing arrangements. In 1948 only 1.6% of retail outlets were what is known as "split-pump" stations, that is, sold the gasoline of more than one supplier.

Exclusive supply contracts with Standard had been entered . . . by the operators of 5,937 independent stations, or 16% of the retail gasoline outlets in the Western area . . . It was also found that independent dealers had entered 742 oral contracts by which they agreed to sell only Standard's gasoline. . . . Of the written agreements, 2,712 were for varying specified terms; the rest were effective from year to year but terminable "at the end of the first 6 months of any contract year, or at the end of any such year, by giving to the other at least 30 days prior thereto written notice. . . ."

Since § 3 of the Clayton Act was directed to prohibiting specific practices even though not covered by the broad terms of the Sherman Act,[4] it is appropriate to consider first whether the enjoined contracts fall

4 After the Clayton Bill, H.R. 15657, had passed the House, the Senate struck § 4, [the equivalent of what became § 3 in the Act], on the ground that such practices were subject to condemnation by the Federal Trade Commission under the then pending Trade Commission Bill. In support of a motion to reconsider this vote, Senator Reed of Missouri argued that the Trade Commission would be unlikely to outlaw agreements of a type held by this Court, in

within the prohibition of the narrower Act. . . . The District Court held that the requirement of showing an actual or potential lessening of competition . . . was adequately met by proof that the contracts covered "a substantial number of outlets and a substantial amount of products, whether considered comparatively or not." Given such quantitative substantiality, the substantial lessening of competition—so the court reasoned—is an automatic result, for the very existence of such contracts denies dealers opportunity to deal in the products of competing suppliers and excludes suppliers from access to the outlets controlled by those dealers. Having adopted this standard of proof, the court excluded as immaterial testimony bearing on "the commercial merits or demerits of the present system as contrasted with a system which prevailed prior to its establishment and which would prevail if the court declared the present arrangement (invalid)." The court likewise deemed it unnecessary to make findings, on the basis of evidence that was admitted, whether the number of Standard's competitors had increased or decreased since the inauguration of the requirements-contract system, whether the number of their dealers had increased or decreased, and as to other matters which would have shed light on the comparative status of Standard and its competitors before and after the adoption of that system. . . .

The issue before us, therefore, is whether the requirement of showing that the effect of the agreements "may be to substantially lessen competition" may be met simply by proof that a substantial portion of commerce is affected or whether it must also be demonstrated that competitive activity has actually diminished or probably will diminish.

The *Standard Fashion* case . . . settled one question of interpretation of § 3. The Court said: ". . . we do not think that the purpose in using the word 'may' was to prohibit the mere possibility of the consequences described. It was intended to prevent such agreements as would under the circumstances disclosed probably lessen competition, or create an actual tendency to monopoly." The Court went on to add that the fact that the Section "was not intended to reach every remote lessening of competition is shown in the requirement that such lessening must be substantial", but because it deemed the finding of two lower courts that the contracts in question did substantially lessen competition and tend to create monopoly amply supported by evidence that the defendant controlled two-fifths of the nation's pattern agencies, it did not pause to indicate where the line between a "remote" and a "substantial" lessening should be drawn.

. . . *International Salt*, at least as to contracts tying the sale of a nonpatented to a patented product, rejected the necessity of demonstrating economic consequences once it has been established that "the volume of business affected" is not "insignificant or insubstantial"

Henry v. A. B. Dick Co., 224 U.S. 1, not to be in violation of the Sherman Act. *See* 51 Cong.Rec. 14088, 14090–92. The motion was agreed to. Id. at 14223.

and that the effect of the contracts is to "foreclose competitors from (a) substantial market." . . . It is clear, therefore, that unless a distinction is to be drawn for purposes of the applicability of § 3 between requirements contracts and contracts tying the sale of a nonpatented to a patented product, the showing that Standard's requirements contracts affected a gross business of $58,000,000 comprising 6.7% of the total in the area goes far toward supporting the inference that competition has been or probably will be substantially lessened.

In favor of confining the standard laid down by the *International Salt* case to tying agreements, important economic differences may be noted. Tying agreements serve hardly any purpose beyond the suppression of competition. The justification most often advanced in their defense—the protection of the good will of the manufacturer of the tying device—fails in the usual situation because specification of the type and quality of the product to be used in connection with the tying device is protection enough. If the manufacturer's brand of the tied product is in fact superior to that of competitors, the buyer will presumably choose it anyway. The only situation, indeed, in which the protection of good will may necessitate the use of tying clauses is where specifications for a substitute would be so detailed that they could not practicably be supplied. In the usual case only the prospect of reducing competition would persuade a seller to adopt such a contract and only his control of the supply of the tying device, whether conferred by patent monopoly or otherwise obtained, could induce a buyer to enter one. The existence of market control of the tying device, therefore, affords a strong foundation for the presumption that it has been or probably will be used to limit competition in the tied product also.

Requirements contracts, on the other hand, may well be of economic advantage to buyers as well as to sellers, and thus indirectly of advantage to the consuming public. In the case of the buyer, they may assure supply, afford protection against rises in price, enable long-term planning on the basis of known costs,[9] and obviate the expense and risk of storage in the quantity necessary for a commodity having a fluctuating demand. From the seller's point of view, requirements contracts may make possible the substantial reduction of selling expenses, give protection against price fluctuations, and—of particular advantage to a newcomer to the field to whom it is important to know what capital expenditures are justified—offer the possibility of a predictable market. They may be useful, moreover, to a seller trying to establish a foothold against the counterattacks of entrenched competitors. Since these advantages of requirements contracts may often be sufficient to account for their use, the coverage by such contracts of a substantial amount of business affords a weaker basis for the inference that competition may be lessened

9 This advantage is not conferred by Standard's contracts, each of which provides that the price to be paid by the dealer is to be the "Company's posted price to its dealers generally at time and place of delivery."

than would similar coverage by tying clauses, especially where use of the latter is combined with market control of the tying device. . . .

Thus, even though the qualifying clause of § 3 is appended without distinction of terms equally to the prohibition of tying clauses and of requirements contracts, pertinent considerations support, certainly as a matter of economic reasoning, varying standards as to each for the proof necessary to fulfill the conditions of that clause. If this distinction were accepted, various tests of the economic usefulness or restrictive effect of requirements contracts would become relevant. Among them would be evidence that competition has flourished despite use of the contracts, and under this test much of the evidence tendered by appellant in this case would be important. Likewise bearing on whether or not the contracts were being used to suppress competition, would be the conformity of the length of their term to the reasonable requirements of the field of commerce in which they were used. Still another test would be the status of the defendant as a struggling newcomer or an established competitor. Perhaps most important, however, would be the defendant's degree of market control, for the greater the dominance of his position, the stronger the inference that an important factor in attaining and maintaining that position has been the use of requirements contracts to stifle competition rather than to serve legitimate economic needs.

Yet serious difficulties would attend the attempt to apply these tests. We may assume, as did the court below, that no improvement of Standard's competitive position has coincided with the period during which the requirements-contract system of distribution has been in effect. We may assume further that the duration of the contracts is not excessive and that Standard does not by itself dominate the market. But Standard was a major competitor when the present system was adopted, and it is possible that its position would have deteriorated but for the adoption of that system. When it is remembered that all the other major suppliers have also been using requirements contracts, and when it is noted that the relative share of the business which fell to each has remained about the same during the period of their use, it would not be farfetched to infer that their effect has been to enable the established suppliers individually to maintain their own standing and at the same time collectively, even though not collusively, to prevent a late arrival from wresting away more than an insignificant portion of the market. If, indeed, this were a result of the system, it would seem unimportant that a short-run by-product of stability may have been greater efficiency and lower costs, for it is the theory of the antitrust laws that the long-run advantage of the community depends upon the removal of restraints upon competition.

Moreover, to demand that bare inference be supported by evidence as to what would have happened but for the adoption of the practice that was in fact adopted or to require firm prediction of an increase of competition as a probable result of ordering the abandonment of the practice, would be a standard of proof if not virtually impossible to meet, at least most ill-suited for ascertainment by courts.[13] Before the system of requirements contracts was instituted, Standard sold gasoline through independent service-station operators as its agents, and it might revert to this system if the judgment below were sustained. Or it might, as opportunity presented itself, add service stations now operated independently to the number managed by its subsidiary, Standard Stations, Inc. From the point of view of maintaining or extending competitive advantage, either of these alternatives would be just as effective as the use of requirements contracts, although of course insofar as they resulted in a tendency to monopoly they might encounter the anti-monopoly provisions of the Sherman Act. As appellant points out, dealers might order petroleum products in quantities sufficient to meet their estimated needs for the period during which requirements contracts are now effective, and even that would foreclose competition to some degree. So long as these diverse ways of restricting competition remain open, therefore, there can be no conclusive proof that the use of requirements contracts has actually reduced competition below the level which it would otherwise have reached or maintained.

We are dealing here with a particular form of agreement specified by § 3 and not with different arrangements, by way of integration or otherwise, that may tend to lessen competition. To interpret that section as requiring proof that competition has actually diminished would make its very explicitness a means of conferring immunity upon the practices which it singles out. Congress has authoritatively determined that those practices are detrimental where their effect may be to lessen competition. It has not left at large for determination in each case the ultimate demands of the "public interest" . . . Though it may be that such an alternative to the present system as buying out independent dealers and making them dependent employees of Standard Stations, Inc., would be a greater detriment to the public interest than perpetuation of the system, this is an issue, like the choice between greater efficiency and freer competition, that has not been submitted to our decision. We are faced, not with a broadly phrased expression of general policy, but merely a broadly phrased qualification of an otherwise narrowly directed statutory provision.

In this connection it is significant that the qualifying language was not added until after the House and Senate bills reached Conference. The conferees responsible for adding that language were at pains, in answering protestations that the qualifying clause seriously weakened the Section, to disclaim any intention seriously to augment the burden of

[13] The dual system of enforcement provided for by the Clayton Act must have contemplated standards of proof capable of administration by the courts as well as by the Federal Trade Commission and other designated agencies. Our interpretation of the Act, therefore, should recognize that an appraisal of economic data which might be practicable if only the latter were faced with the task may be quite otherwise for judges unequipped for it either by experience or by the availability of skilled assistance.

proof to be sustained in establishing violation of it.[15] It seems hardly likely that, having with one hand set up an express prohibition against a practice thought to be beyond the reach of the Sherman Act, Congress meant, with the other hand, to reestablish the necessity of meeting the same tests of detriment to the public interest as that Act had been interpreted as requiring. Yet the economic investigation which appellant would have us require is of the same broad scope as was adumbrated with reference to unreasonable restraints of trade. . . . To insist upon such an investigation would be to stultify the force of Congress' declaration that requirements contracts are to be prohibited wherever their effect "may be" to substantially lessen competition. If in fact it is economically desirable for service stations to confine themselves to the sale of the petroleum products of a single supplier, they will continue to do so though not bound by contract, and if in fact it is important to retail dealers to assure the supply of their requirements by obtaining the commitment of a single supplier to fulfill them, competition for their patronage should enable them to insist upon such an arrangement without binding them to refrain from looking elsewhere.

We conclude, therefore, that the qualifying clause of § 3 is satisfied by proof that competition has been foreclosed in a substantial share of the line of commerce affected. It cannot be gainsaid that observance by a dealer of his requirements contract with Standard does effectively foreclose whatever opportunity there might be for competing suppliers to attract his patronage, and it is clear that the affected proportion of retail sales of petroleum products is substantial. In view of the widespread adoption of such contracts by Standard's competitors and the availability of alternative ways of obtaining an assured market, evidence that competitive activity has not actually declined is inconclusive. Standard's use of the contracts creates just such a potential clog on competition as it was the purpose of § 3 to remove wherever, were it to become actual, it would impede a substantial amount of competitive activity.

Since the decree below is sustained by our interpretation of § 3 of the Clayton Act, we need not go on to consider whether it might also be sustained by § 1 of the Sherman Act. . . . Affirmed.

---

[15] Representative Floyd of Arkansas, one of the managers on the part of the House, explained the use of the word "substantially" as deriving from the opinion of this Court in Addyston Pipe & Steel Co. v. United States, 175 U.S. 211, and quoted the passage . . . in which it is said that "the power of Congress to regulate interstate commerce comprises the right to enact a law prohibiting a citizen from entering into these private contracts which directly and substantially, and not merely indirectly, remotely, incidentally and collaterally, regulate to a greater or less degree commerce among the States." 51 Cong.Rec. 16317–18. Senator Chilton, one of the managers on the part of the Senate, denying that the clause weakened the bill, stated that the words "where the effect may be" mean "where it is possible for the effect to be." Id. at 16002. Senator Overman, also a Senate conferee, argued that even the elimination of competition in a single town would substantially lessen competition. Id. at 15935.

NOTES AND QUESTIONS ON *STANDARD STATIONS*

1. ***Interpreting "may" to mean "probably".*** As the Supreme Court noted, in its earlier decision in *Standard Fashion,* the Court interpreted the language "may" lessen competition in Clayton Act § 3 to mean "probably" lessens competition. One could argue that this reading should be rejected as a rewrite of the statute. However, the Court was concerned that anything "may" have an anticompetitive effect, and it thought Congress was unlikely to have intended anything so sweeping.

2. ***Inferring probable anticompetitive effects from a substantial foreclosure share.*** The Court holds that probable anticompetitive effects are established by proving that exclusive dealing forecloses a substantial *share* of the relevant market.[13] Some critique this holding because a substantial foreclosure share does not directly prove anticompetitive effects. However, the holding does parallel the *Indiana Dentists* position that anticompetitive effects can either be proven directly or inferred to be likely because of a large affected market share. Do you think showing a substantial foreclosure share should suffice to infer likely anticompetitive effects, at least absent persuasive evidence that the exclusive dealing was reasonably necessary for procompetitive efficiencies?

Was the Court right that it should not infer likely anticompetitive effects from the fact that exclusive dealing forecloses a substantial *amount* of sales, even though that is the test the Court uses when judging tying agreements under Clayton Act § 3? The Court reasoned that the difference was that tying hardly ever has procompetitive justifications, whereas exclusive dealing often does. As we will see below in Chapter 4.C, the premise that tying hardly ever has efficiencies is incorrect. However, the distinction can be justified because the anticompetitive effects from exclusive dealing usually require foreclosing a substantial enough market share to impair rival competitiveness. In contrast, tying can create anticompetitive effects that reduce consumer welfare when tying market power is coupled with the foreclosure of a substantial amount of tied sales, which we shall see is when tying is presumptively condemned under the quasi-per se rule.

3. ***Refusing to consider procompetitive justifications.*** Despite acknowledging the existence of possible procompetitive efficiencies for exclusive dealing, the Court held that exclusive dealing that forecloses a substantial market share should be condemned without considering whether any procompetitive effects outweighed the likely anticompetitive effects. Do you agree with this holding?

The Court's main argument was that determining whether the net effects were procompetitive would be an inadministrable test for courts. This holding was consistent with Justice Frankfurter's general jurisprudential concern about keeping courts within their areas of institutional competence. In effect, the Court concluded that an overinclusive rule (condemning any exclusive dealing that creates a substantial foreclosure share, even though

---

[13] The Court focused on the *cumulative* foreclosure share produced by the defendant and other major firms using exclusive dealing. The appropriateness of using a cumulative foreclosure share is considered below in the discussion of the *Motion Pictures* case.

it might sometimes be efficient) would be more accurate than an open-ended standard (weighing the relevant effects case by case), because courts will make too many errors when applying the open-ended standard. Modern antitrust law has gone in a different direction, requiring courts to weigh such effects under the Rule of Reason when judging all sorts of restraints, including (as we shall see below) exclusive dealing. But one might well wonder how accurate judges and juries are in weighing such effects. If one thought the over- and underdeterrence created by inaccurate applications of the rule of reason exceeded the overdeterrence created by an overinclusive rule, then we would get better effects with an overinclusive rule. Do you think Justice Frankfurter was right to prefer a categorical rule over case-by-case Rule of Reason review, at least given the statutory language and legislative history of Clayton Act § 3?

The Court also reasoned that if dealing exclusively with one supplier were efficient, then buyers "will continue to do so though not bound by contract." However, this argument ignored at least two reasons why buyers might want to deviate from an efficient exclusive dealing term. First, the contract price might have become less advantageous to the buyer because of a change in market prices. Second, relationship-specific investments might make it profitable for buyers to deviate from an efficient agreement that was mutually beneficial ex ante. Consider, for example, a supplier who wants to build a distribution center near a major client's premises in order to efficiently lower delivery costs. If the distribution center is built without any exclusive dealing agreement, the client might expropriate those efficiency gains by threatening to switch suppliers unless the client gets a lower price. To avoid such opportunistic threats, the supplier might be willing to make the efficient investment in the nearby distribution center only with an exclusive dealing agreement that prevents the client from switching later. Modern antitrust analysis thus recognizes that exclusive dealing can sometimes be reasonably necessary to achieve efficiencies.

The Court also argued that it would be very difficult to determine whether, without exclusive dealing, Standard Oil might instead acquire service stations. But does the fact that banning exclusive dealing might encourage firms to vertically integrate support the Court's holding? When economic reality makes relationship-specific investments efficient, firms that are banned from using exclusive dealing agreements might predictably instead protect such investments by integrating downstream, given that efficiencies can be introduced to defend vertical mergers. Refusing to consider efficiencies from exclusive dealing would thus predictably induce additional vertical integration, which may be less efficient and more permanently foreclosing of rival suppliers.

4. ***Ascertaining net anticompetitive effects.*** When exclusive dealing is proven to be reasonably necessary to achieve procompetitive efficiencies, determining whether net anticompetitive effects exist requires weighing those procompetitive effects against the likely anticompetitive effects that are inferred from the substantial foreclosure share. Is this an administrable task for judges and juries?

The Court noted that one could not infer the absence of net anticompetitive effects from the fact that the market share of Standard Oil and other large firms using exclusive dealing remained flat, reasoning that their market shares might have "deteriorated but for" the adoption of the exclusive dealing. An even bigger problem with a market share test is that, even if we knew defendant market shares were higher than they would have been without the exclusive dealing, that market share finding could reflect either procompetitive effects that improved defendant efficiency or anticompetitive effects that impaired rivals. A showing that exclusive dealing made defendant market shares higher than but-for levels thus does not tell us whether the exclusive dealing is procompetitive or anticompetitive.

A better approach would be to focus on how the exclusive dealing affected market prices or output. Net anticompetitive effects would not be disproven by evidence that prices dropped (or output rose) from past levels; it may be that prices would have dropped more (or output risen higher) but for the exclusive dealing. The Court's conclusion that the relevant baseline for judging anticompetitive effects is not the historical baseline, but rather the "but for" baseline of what would have happened but for the restraint, thus endures as an important part of modern antitrust analysis. However, the Court's conclusion that it would be "virtually impossible" to determine "what would have happened but for the adoption of the practice" is belied by modern antitrust cases, where this sort of analysis is done all the time by having economics experts offer statistical analysis or modeling to determine what would have occurred but for the restraint. *See* Chapter 1. Still, one might wonder whether judges and juries are sufficiently accurate in assessing such expert testimony to produce results that are better than those produced by the overinclusive rule of *Standard Stations*. What do you think?

FTC v. Motion Picture Advertising Service

344 U.S. 392 (1953).

■ MR. JUSTICE DOUGLAS delivered the opinion of the Court.

Respondent is a producer and distributor of advertising motion pictures which depict and describe commodities offered for sale by commercial establishments. Respondent contracts with theatre owners for the display of these advertising films . . . These contracts run for terms up to five years, the majority being for one or two years. A substantial number of them contains a provision that the theatre owner will display only advertising films furnished by respondent, with the exception of films for charities or for governmental organizations, or announcements of coming attractions. Respondent and three other companies in the same business (against which proceedings were also brought) together had exclusive arrangements for advertising films with approximately three-fourths of the total number of theatres in the United States which display advertising films for compensation. Respondent had exclusive contracts with almost 40 percent of the theatres in the area where it operates.

The Federal Trade Commission, the petitioner, filed a complaint charging respondent with the use of "Unfair methods of competition" in violation of § 5 of the Federal Trade Commission Act. The Commission found that . . . [the] exclusive contracts have limited the outlets for films of competitors and has forced some competitors out of business because of their inability to obtain outlets for their advertising films. . . . The Court of Appeals reversed. . . .

The Commission found in the present case that respondent's exclusive contracts unreasonably restrain competition and tend to monopoly. Those findings are supported by substantial evidence. This is not a situation where by the nature of the market there is room for newcomers, irrespective of the existing restrictive practices. The number of outlets for the films is quite limited. And due to the exclusive contracts, respondent and the three other major companies have foreclosed to competitors 75 percent of all available outlets for this business throughout the United States. It is, we think, plain from the Commission's findings that a device which has sewed up a market so tightly for the benefit of a few falls within the prohibitions of the Sherman Act and is therefore an "unfair method of competition" within the meaning of § 5(a) of the Federal Trade Commission Act.

An attack is made on that part of the order which restricts the exclusive contracts to one-year terms. It is argued that one-year contracts will not be practicable. It is said that the expenses of securing these screening contracts do not warrant one-year agreements, that investment of capital in the business would not be justified without assurance of a market for more than one year, that theatres frequently demand guarantees for more than a year or otherwise refuse to exhibit advertising films. . . . The Commission considered this argument and concluded that, although the exclusive contracts were beneficial to the distributor and preferred by the theatre owners, their use should be restricted in the public interest. The Commission found that the term of one year had become a standard practice and that the continuance of exclusive contracts so limited would not be an undue restraint upon competition, in view of the compelling business reasons for some exclusive arrangement.[2] The precise impact of a particular practice on the trade is for the Commission, not the courts, to determine. The point where a method of competition becomes "unfair" within the meaning of the Act will often turn on the exigencies of a particular situation, trade

[2] . . . "In contacting the theater it is necessary for the respondent to estimate the amount of space it will be able to sell to advertisers. Since film advertising space in theaters is limited to four, five, or six advertisements, it is not unreasonable for respondent to contract for all space available in such theaters, particularly in territories canvassed by its salesmen at regular and frequent intervals. It is therefore the conclusion of the Commission in the circumstances here that an exclusive screening agreement for a period of one year is not an undue restraint upon competition." 47 F.T.C. 389.

practices, or the practical requirements of the business in question. Certainly we cannot say that exclusive contracts in this field should have been banned in their entirety or not at all, that the Commission exceeded the limits of its allowable judgment. . . . Reversed.

■ MR. JUSTICE FRANKFURTER, whom MR. JUSTICE BURTON joins, dissenting. . . . Although we are told that respondent and three other companies have exclusive exhibition contracts with three-quarters of the theaters in the country that accept advertising, there are no findings indicating how many of these contracts extend beyond the one-year period which the Commission finds not unduly restrictive. We do have an indication from the record that more than half of respondent's exclusive contracts run for only one year; if that is so, that part of respondent's hold on the market found unreasonable by the Commission boils down to exclusion of other competitors from something like 1,250 theaters, or about 6%, of the some 20,000 theaters in the country. The hold is on about 10% of the theaters that accept advertising.

The Court's opinion . . . states without discussion that such exclusion from a market without more "falls within the prohibitions of the Sherman Act" because, taken with exclusive contracts of other competitors, 75% of the market is shut off. But there is no reliance here on conspiracy or concerted action to foreclose the market, a charge that would of course warrant action under the Sherman Law. Indeed, we must assume that respondent and the other three companies are complying with an earlier order of the Commission directed at concerted action. While the existence of the other exclusive contracts is, of course, not irrelevant in a market analysis, *see Standard Stations*, this Court has never decided that they may, in the absence of conspiracy, be aggregated to support a charge of Sherman Law violation. . . . And although we are not told in this case whether the pressure for exclusive contracts comes mainly from the distributor or the theater, there are indications that theaters often insist on exclusive provisions. . . . I would have the Court of Appeals remand this case to the Commission.

Cumulative Foreclosure

Motion Picture Advertising holds that, in an exclusive dealing case under Sherman Act § 1 and FTC Act § 5, the foreclosure share should be measured by aggregating the foreclosure produced by the leading sellers: here aggregating the four leading firms to get a foreclosure of 75%. The conclusion that the relevant foreclosure share is cumulative is also supported *Standard Stations,* which cited the cumulative foreclosure share produced by the defendant and six other large firms to support finding substantial foreclosure under Clayton Act § 3.[14] Neither case

[14] Subsequent cases have confirmed the understanding that aggregating foreclosure is appropriate. Tampa Electric v. Nashville Coal, 365 U.S. 320, 334 (1961) (describing and distinguishing *Standard Stations* as a case where there was an "industry-wide practice of relying upon exclusive contracts"); United States v. Philadelphia Nat'l Bank, 374 U.S. 321, 365–66 (1963) ("In [*Standard Stations*], this Court held violative of § 3 of the Clayton Act exclusive

required any evidence that the sellers conspired with each other to impose exclusive dealing. Any conspiracy requirement would in any event be met by the vertical agreements between sellers and buyers.

But does aggregating the foreclosure of nonconspiring sellers to assess anticompetitive effects make economic sense? The answer largely turns on whether the cumulative foreclosure has deprived the market of a competitive number of efficient rivals by barring some firms from achieving their minimum efficient size. If a market had twenty equal-sized firms, all of whom had exclusionary agreements, then the aggregate foreclosure would be 100%, but the agreements would not deprive the market of a competitive number of firms (assuming twenty firms suffices to achieve full competitiveness) and thus would have no anticompetitive effect. But suppose instead two manufacturers use exclusive agreements that, in aggregate, foreclose enough of the market to preclude rivals from achieving their minimum efficient size, but that neither firm's agreements alone would result in sufficient foreclosure to do so. If the market is large enough to sustain more than two firms at their minimum efficient size, then the cumulative foreclosure is the relevant measure of whether the exclusionary agreements have an anticompetitive effect. Such cumulative foreclosure creates an effective duopoly where

contracts whereby the defendant company, which accounted for 23% of the sales in the relevant market and, together with six other firms, accounted for 65% of such sales, maintained control over outlets through which approximately 7% of the sales were made. In [*Motion Picture*] we held unlawful, under § 1 of the Sherman Act and § 5 of the Federal Trade Commission Act, rather than under § 3 of the Clayton Act, exclusive arrangements whereby the four major firms in the industry had foreclosed 75% of the relevant market"); Jefferson Parish v. Hyde, 466 U.S. 2, 30 n.51 (1984) (favorably citing both *Standard Stations* and *Tampa Electric* on the appropriate foreclosure measure under exclusive dealing doctrine); Stop & Shop Supermarket Co. v. Blue Cross & Blue Shield of R.I., 373 F.3d 57, 66 (1st Cir. 2004) (concluding that the relevant "extent of foreclosure" includes that resulting from defendant's exclusionary contracts and "other existing foreclosures" such as by another seller's exclusionary contracts). *See also* IX AREEDA, ANTITRUST LAW 94, 103–04 (1991) ("the relevant foreclosure aggregates those of the defendant and of his rivals."); XI HOVENKAMP, ANTITRUST LAW 160 (1998) ("When exclusive dealing is used to facilitate collusion . . . the relevant foreclosure becomes the *aggregate* foreclosure imposed by the upstream firms in the collusive group.")

A contrary conclusion was reached in Paddock Publ'ns. v. Chicago Tribune, 103 F.3d 42 (7th Cir. 1996), but that decision was based on the erroneous premise that the *Motion Picture* decision rested on a distinction between the Sherman and FTC Act's requirements on concerted action. Further, *Paddock* also ignored all the other Supreme Court precedent noted above and the fact that vertical agreements can also satisfy the concerted action requirement. Even more clearly in conflict with binding Supreme Court precedent is the odd decision in Dickson v. Microsoft Corp., 309 F.3d 193, 212 (4th Cir. 2002), which holds that even a single seller's exclusionary agreements with multiple buyers cannot be aggregated, and that substantial foreclosure can thus be proven only if a single seller's exclusionary agreement with an *individual* buyer alone forecloses a substantial share of the market. This holding is contrary to Standard Fashion Co. v. Magrane-Houston Co., 258 U.S. 346, 352 (1922), which aggregated the manufacturer's exclusive contracts with 20,800 different merchants to conclude 40% of the market was foreclosed. *Standard Stations* and *Motion Picture* likewise aggregated not only foreclosure by different sellers, but exclusionary agreements those sellers had with thousands of different buyers. Further, many Supreme Court cases have found illegal monopolization when a monopolist agrees to do business with many different firms—none of whom alone forecloses a significant share of the market—on the condition that they not deal with the monopolist's rivals. *See Kodak; Lorain Journal; Griffith;* United Shoe Machinery v. United States, 258 U.S. 451 (1922), In all these cases, the Supreme Court has aggregated the monopolist's exclusionary agreements with many different firms to ascertain their exclusionary effect on the monopolist's rivals.

consumers would have otherwise enjoyed a more competitive market with more firms.

Likewise, exclusive dealing agreements by four sellers that foreclose a fifth seller from reaching the minimum efficient size would be anticompetitive if the market (a) could sustain five sellers at their minimum efficient size and (b) would behave more competitively with five firms than with four firms. Further, even if the relevant market could sustain only four firms at their minimum efficient size, such foreclosure can anticompetitively keep out a firm that would have been more efficient if it had been allowed to compete openly and achieve its own economies of size. In short, foreclosure can anticompetitively affect the identity of firms in the market as well as the number of them.

What is the minimum number of firms that assures competitive behavior? That depends on the particulars of each market, including whether the market is differentiated or conducive to oligopolistic coordination. *See* Chapters 6–7. The current U.S. merger guidelines suggest that the normal presumption is that reducing the number of firms is unlikely to have anticompetitive effects if there are more than five major firms in a market. *See* Chapter 7. Professor Areeda concludes that the test of whether foreclosure is "substantial" should be "that foreclosure be presumed unreasonable when it reaches 20 percent for an individual seller or a total of 50 percent for five or fewer sellers."[15]

Because the anticompetitive concern is foreclosing other firms from reaching their minimum efficient size, the aggregation should include exclusive dealing agreements only by large manufacturers that reduce the number of firms below the competitive level (or preclude more efficient firms from the market) by preventing rivals from achieving their minimum efficient size. The cumulative foreclosure share should not include exclusive dealing agreements entered into by minor firms whose market shares are well below the minimum efficient size. Such agreements (a) cannot contribute to preventing a greater number of firms from operating at the minimum efficient size in the market and (b) are likely to have the procompetitive effect of helping those minor firms achieve their own economies of size.

Even if one did not simply aggregate the foreclosure share produced by different manufacturers, the existence of other factors foreclosing the rest of the market to rivals would remain highly relevant to determining the anticompetitive effect of any single firm's exclusionary agreements. For example, suppose one firm had exclusionary agreements foreclosing 60% of the market, and the other 40% could be shown to be unavailable due to regulation. Proper economic analysis would take into account that this regulation means that the single firm's exclusionary agreements foreclosed all the market that would otherwise be available to rivals. The

---

[15] *See* AREEDA, *supra* note 14, at 375, 377, 387. *See also* HOVENKAMP, *supra* note 14, at 152, 160 (single firm foreclosure of 20% and evidence that the selling market concentration has an HHI of at least 1800.)

same follows if the other 40% is instead foreclosed by another firm's exclusionary agreements. This fact would still mean that the single firm's exclusionary agreements foreclosed all of the market that would otherwise be available to rivals. In short, even if not simply aggregated, the anticompetitive effect of one firm's exclusionary agreements can depend on whether other firms have similar exclusionary agreements.[16] Indeed, in *Motion Picture,* while Justice Frankfurter's dissent opposed simply aggregating foreclosure, he acknowledged that "the existence of the other exclusive contracts is, of course, not irrelevant in a market analysis."

Given cumulative foreclosure, the anticompetitive effect (and thus legality) of one firm's exclusionary agreements can change over time if other firms adopt similar agreements. Suppose a market has five major firms, each with 19% of the market. The first major firm to adopt exclusive dealing may not foreclose a substantial share of the market. But if the other four major firms follow suit, then the aggregate foreclosure of 95% will be substantial, which would turn all the agreements invalid, assuming that redeeming efficiencies did not exist or were inadmissible. This is not as odd as it seems because antitrust "legality usually depends upon market circumstances as they exist from time to time; a reasonable restraint in today's environment can become unreasonable when market conditions change. [Thus], if cumulative foreclosure affects the competitive threat, we must weigh it when judging the legality of a restraint."[17]

But the fact that other firms adopt the same exclusive dealing arrangements may also suggest those arrangements are efficient. Are such efficiencies rendered admissible by the next case?

Tampa Electric v. Nashville Coal

365 U.S. 320 (1961).

■ MR. JUSTICE CLARK delivered the opinion of the Court.

We granted certiorari to review a declaratory judgment holding illegal under § 3 of the Clayton Act a requirements contract between the parties providing for the purchase by petitioner of all the coal it would require as boiler fuel at its Gannon Station in Tampa, Florida, over a 20-year period. Both the District court and the Court of Appeals . . . agreed with respondents that the contract fell within the proscription of § 3 and therefore was illegal and unenforceable. We cannot agree that the contract suffers the claimed anti-trust illegality . . .

[16] *See* United States v. General Dynamics, 415 U.S. 486 (1974) (when assessing the competitive significance of a merger, a court should exclude production that has already been committed by contract).

[17] IX AREEDA, ANTITRUST LAW 388 (1991).

The Facts

Petitioner Tampa Electric Company is a public utility located in Tampa, Florida. It produces and sells electric energy to a service area, including the city, extending from Tampa Bay eastward 60 miles to the center of the State, and some 30 miles in width. As of 1954 petitioner operated two electrical generating plants comprising a total of 11 individual generating units, all of which consumed oil in their burners. In 1955 Tampa Electric decided to expand its facilities by the construction of an additional generating plant to be comprised ultimately of six generating units, and to be known as the "Francis J. Gannon Station." Although every electrical generating plant in peninsular Florida burned oil at that time, Tampa Electric decided to try coal as boiler fuel in the first two units constructed at the Gannon Station. Accordingly, it contracted with the respondents to furnish the expected coal requirements for the units. The agreement, dated May 23, 1955, embraced Tampa Electric's "total requirements of fuel . . . for the operation of its first two units to be installed at the Gannon Station . . . not less than 225,000 tons of coal per unit per year," for a period of 20 years. The contract further provided that "if during the first 10 years of the term . . . the Buyer constructs additional units (at Gannon) in which coal is used as the fuel, it shall give the Seller notice thereof two years prior to the completion of such unit or units and upon completion of same the fuel requirements thereof shall be added to this contract." It was understood and agreed, however, that "the Buyer has the option to be exercised two years prior to completion of said unit or units of determining whether coal or some other fuel shall be used in same." Tampa Electric had the further option of reducing, up to 15%, the amount of its coal purchases covered by the contract after giving six months' notice of an intention to use as fuel a by-product of any of its local customers. The minimum price was set at $6.40 per ton delivered, subject to an escalation clause based on labor cost and other factors. Deliveries were originally expected to begin in March 1957, for the first unit, and for the second unit at the completion of its construction.

In April 1957, soon before the first coal was actually to be delivered and after Tampa Electric, in order to equip its first two Gannon units for the use of coal, had expended some $3,000,000 more than the cost of constructing oil-burning units, and after respondents had expended approximately $7,500,000 readying themselves to perform the contract, the latter advised petitioner that the contract was illegal under the antitrust laws, would therefore not be performed, and no coal would be delivered. . . . [Tampa Electric then had to buy the coal from other coal producers at prices of up to $8.80 per ton.]

Application of § 3 of the Clayton Act

. . . United Shoe Machinery Corp. v. United States, 1922, 258 U.S. 451, . . . held that even though a contract does "not contain specific agreements not to use the (goods) of a competitor," if "the practical effect

* * * is to prevent such use," it comes within the condition of the section as to exclusivity. The Court also held, as it had in *Standard Fashion*, that a finding of domination of the relevant market by the lessor or seller was sufficient to support the inference that competition had or would be substantially lessened by the contracts involved there. . . . *Standard Stations* . . . again considered § 3 and its application to exclusive supply or, as they are commonly known, requirements contracts. It held that such contracts are proscribed by § 3 if their practical effect is to prevent lessees or purchasers from using or dealing in the goods, etc., of a competitor or competitors of the lessor or seller and thereby "competition has been foreclosed in a substantial share of the line of commerce affected."

In practical application, even though a contract is found to be an exclusive-dealing arrangement, it does not violate the section unless the court believes it probable that performance of the contract will foreclose competition in a substantial share of the line of commerce affected. Following the guidelines of earlier decisions, certain considerations must be taken. First, the line of commerce, i.e., the type of goods, wares, or merchandise, etc., involved must be determined, where it is in controversy, on the basis of the facts peculiar to the case. Second, the area of effective competition in the known line of commerce must be charted by careful selection of the market area in which the seller operates, and to which the purchaser can practicably turn for supplies. In short, the threatened foreclosure of competition must be in relation to the market affected. . . .

Third, and last, the competition foreclosed by the contract must be found to constitute a substantial share of the relevant market. That is to say, the opportunities for other traders to enter into or remain in that market must be significantly limited. . . .

To determine substantiality in a given case, it is necessary to weigh the probable effect of the contract on the relevant area of effective competition, taking into account the relative strength of the parties, the proportionate volume of commerce involved in relation to the total volume of commerce in the relevant market area, and the probable immediate and future effects which pre-emption of that share of the market might have on effective competition therein. It follows that a mere showing that the contract itself involves a substantial number of dollars is ordinarily of little consequence.

The Application of § 3 Here

. . . We . . . , for the purposes of this case, assume, but do not decide, that the contract is an exclusive-dealing arrangement within the compass of § 3, and that the line of commerce is bituminous coal.

Relevant Market of Effective Competition

Neither the Court of Appeals nor the District Court considered in detail the question of the relevant market. They do seem, however, to have been satisfied with inquiring only as to competition within "Peninsular Florida." . . . Respondents contend that the coal tonnage covered by the contract must be weighed against either the total consumption of coal in peninsular Florida, or all of Florida, . . . or, at most, all of Florida and Georgia. If the latter area were considered the relevant market, Tampa Electric's proposed requirements would be 18% of the tonnage sold therein. . . .

We are persuaded that . . . neither peninsular Florida, nor the entire State of Florida, nor Florida and Georgia combined constituted the relevant market of effective competition. . . . By far the bulk of the overwhelming tonnage marketed from the same producing area as serves Tampa is sold outside of Georgia and Florida, and the producers were "eager" to sell more coal in those States. While the relevant competitive market is not ordinarily susceptible to a "metes and bounds" definition, it is of course the area in which respondents and the other 700 producers effectively compete. The record shows that, like the respondents, they sold bituminous coal "suitable for (Tampa's) requirements," mined in parts of Pennsylvania, Virginia, West Virginia, Kentucky, Tennessee, Alabama, Ohio and Illinois. We take notice of the fact that the approximate total bituminous coal (and lignite) product in the year 1954 from the districts in which these 700 producers are located was 359,289,000 tons, of which some 290,567,000 tons were sold on the open market. . . . [The coal consumed in Florida and Georgia came from seven states.] From these statistics it clearly appears that the proportionate volume of the total relevant coal product as to which the challenged contract pre-empted competition, less than 1%, is, conservatively speaking, quite insubstantial. A more accurate figure, even assuming pre-emption to the extent of the maximum anticipated total requirements, 2,250,000 tons a year, would be .77%.

Effect on Competition in the Relevant Market

It may well be that in the context of antitrust legislation protracted requirements contracts are suspect, but they have not been declared illegal per se. Even though a single contract between single traders may fall within the initial broad proscription of the section, it must also suffer the qualifying disability, tendency to work a substantial—not remote—lessening of competition in the relevant competitive market. It is urged that the present contract pre-empts competition to the extent of purchases worth perhaps $128,000,000, and that this "is, of course, not insignificant or insubstantial." While $128,000,000 is a considerable sum of money, even in these days, the dollar volume, by itself, is not the test, as we have already pointed out.

The remaining determination, therefore, is whether the pre-emption of competition to the extent of the tonnage involved tends to substantially foreclose competition in the relevant coal market. We think not. That market sees an annual trade in excess of 250,000,000 tons of coal and over a billion dollars—multiplied by 20 years it runs into astronomical figures. There is here neither a seller with a dominant position in the market as in *Standard Fashions*; nor myriad outlets with substantial sales volume, coupled with an industry-wide practice of relying upon exclusive contracts, as in *Standard Stations*, nor a plainly restrictive tying arrangement as in *International Salt*. On the contrary, we seem to have only that type of contract which "may well be of economic advantage to buyers as well as to sellers." *Standard Stations*. In the case of the buyer it "may assure supply," while on the part of the seller it "may make possible the substantial reduction of selling expenses, give protection against price fluctuations, and . . . offer the possibility of a predictable market." *Id.* The 20-year period of the contract is singled out as the principal vice, but at least in the case of public utilities the assurance of a steady and ample supply of fuel is necessary in the public interest. Otherwise consumers are left unprotected against service failures owing to shutdowns; and increasingly unjustified costs might result in more burdensome rate structures eventually to be reflected in the consumer's bill. . . . This is not to say that utilities are immunized from Clayton Act proscriptions, but merely that, in judging the term of a requirements contract in relation to the substantiality of the foreclosure of competition, particularized considerations of the parties' operations are not irrelevant. In weighing the various factors, we have decided that in the competitive bituminous coal marketing area involved here the contract sued upon does not tend to foreclose a substantial volume of competition.

We need not discuss the respondents' further contention that the contract also violates § 1 and § 2 of the Sherman Act, for if it does not fall within the broader proscription of § 3 of the Clayton Act it follows that it is not forbidden by those of the former.

The judgment is reversed and the case remanded to the District Court for further proceedings not inconsistent with this opinion.

NOTES AND QUESTIONS ON *TAMPA ELECTRIC*

1. *The adoption of rule of reason review.* *Standard Stations* and *Motion Picture Advertising* held that a substantial foreclosure share sufficed to show exclusive dealing was illegal, without inquiring into efficiencies. *Tampa Electric* states that in practice a substantial foreclosure share is necessary to show illegality, but that determining "substantiality" turns not only on the foreclosure share number, but also on "the probable and immediate effects" that flow from that foreclosure share. Given that it cites *Standard Stations* favorably, *Tampa Electric* may have meant that efficiencies can save exclusive dealing only when the foreclosure share is small. That is how the Supreme Court itself seemed to interpret *Tampa Electric* the next year.[18] Indeed, on this view, the remarkable thing is that

[18] *See* Brown Shoe v. United States, 370 U.S. 294, 330 (1962) (describing *Tampa Electric* as holding that "a requirement contract may escape censure if only a small share of the market is involved, if the purpose of the agreement is to insure to the customer a sufficient supply of a commodity vital to the customer's trade or to insure to the supplier a market for his output and if there is no trend toward concentration in the industry").

the Court was willing to require evidence of some procompetitive justification even when the foreclosure share was only 0.77%. But modern appellate courts, including four justices in 1984, and one appellate judge who has become a Supreme Court justice, instead read *Tampa Electric* to adopt a general Rule of Reason for exclusive dealing agreements.[19] Under this Rule of Reason, modern courts require that anticompetitive effects be either directly proven or inferred as likely because of a large substantial foreclosure share, and courts allow defendants to rebut any anticompetitive effects with proof of procompetitive justifications. Modern courts thus read *Tampa Electric* to overrule *Standard Stations'* exclusion of procompetitive justifications, even when the foreclosure share is large.

Although perhaps not justified by a literal parsing of the precedent, this conclusion fits a more general policy judgment being made by the courts after the 1960s that antitrust economics did not support the categorical hostility of various legal rules on vertical agreements. But this interpretation seems to make Clayton Act § 3 superfluous because Sherman Act § 1 already condemns agreements that violate the Rule of Reason. Does this interpretation thus violate the canon against reading statutory provisions to be superfluous? The argument to the contrary is that the 1914 Congress feared that *Standard Oil v. United States*, 221 U.S. 1 (1911), had adopted a narrower interpretation of the Rule of Reason under Sherman Act § 1. If so, the 1914 Congress would not have thought that a provision that required courts to weigh anticompetitive and procompetitive effects was superfluous then, even though subsequent court interpretations of the Rule of Reason under Sherman Act § 1 have rendered it superfluous now. Still, some lower courts seem uncomfortable with this conclusion, concluding that Clayton Act § 3 requires a lower foreclosure share than Sherman Act § 1. How do you think Clayton Act § 3 should be interpreted?

*2. **Defining the relevant foreclosure market.*** The Court held that the relevant geographic market for measuring the foreclosure share was not the Florida-Georgia area (in which the foreclosure share would have been 18%) but the Appalachian Coal area (in which the foreclosure share was only 0.77%). Why should the Appalachian Coal area be the relevant market? The reason is that the relevant market depends on the anticompetitive concern, which here was that exclusive dealing might impair the competitiveness of rival coal companies by foreclosing them from a big share of the market. Given that concern, the relevant market for measuring foreclosure is the market to which rival coal companies could turn. Because coal was here being shipped from Nashville to Tampa, clearly the defendant's coal came from beyond Florida and Georgia, and the evidence showed that defendant's coal rivals could turn to buyers in states throughout the Appalachian Coal area if they were foreclosed from selling to Tampa Electric.

If instead the anticompetitive theory were that the exclusive dealing effectively created a local cartel or monopoly, as possibly in *Griffith* or under a cartel ringmaster theory, then the relevant market might instead be the

---

19 *See Jefferson Parish*, 466 U.S. at 44–45 (O'Connor, J, concurring in the judgment, joined by Burger, C.J., and Powell & Rehnquist J.J.); Barry Wright v. ITT Grinnell Corp., 724 F.2d 227, 236 (1st Cir. 1983) (Breyer, J.).

local Florida market to which Tampa Electric's buyers could turn. However, such a theory did not apply here, not only because the exclusive dealing here was just between one seller and one buyer, but also because Tampa Electric was a public utility that already had a local electricity monopoly.

3. ***The efficiency.*** In this case, Nashville Coal spent $7.5 million getting ready to supply the coal covered by the contract, and Tampa Electric spent more than $3 million getting ready to use that coal. These are relationship-specific investments that might justify the terms that required (a) Tampa Electric to buy exclusively from Nashville Coal and (b) Nashville Coal to supply all of Tampa Electric's coal requirements. But if the term requiring that Tampa Electric exclusively buy from Nashville Coal was efficient and protected Nashville Coal's relationship-specific investment, why did Nashville Coal object to it? Apparently because coal market prices had risen to $8.80/ton, far above the $6.40 contract price, making it more attractive for Nashville Coal to seek to have the contract voided as illegal, so that it could sell the coal to someone else at market prices.

Why should courts ever allow a seller to void a contract based on an exclusivity term that favors the seller? After all, it seems likely that a seller would do so only when shifts in market prices give the seller an opportunistic incentive to snake out of the contract price. But when exclusive dealing contracts are anticompetitive because of large foreclosure shares without offsetting efficiencies, deeming such contracts voidable helps deter parties from entering into them, precisely because voidability subjects parties to the risk that the other side will opportunistically snake out of the contracts if market prices move in their favor.

United States v. Microsoft

253 F.3d 34 (D.C. Cir. 2001) (en banc).

■ PER CURIAM. . . . The District Court determined that Microsoft had maintained a monopoly in the market for Intel-compatible PC operating systems in violation of § 2. . . . Defining the market as Intel-compatible PC operating systems, the District Court found that Microsoft has a greater than 95% share. It also found the company's market position protected by a substantial entry barrier. . . .

Operating systems perform many functions, including allocating computer memory and controlling peripherals such as printers and keyboards. Operating systems also function as platforms for software applications. They do this by "exposing"—*i.e.,* making available to software developers—routines or protocols that perform certain widely-used functions. These are known as Application Programming Interfaces, or "APIs." For example, Windows contains an API that enables users to draw a box on the screen. Software developers wishing to include that function in an application need not duplicate it in their own code. Instead, they can "call"—*i.e.,* use—the Windows API. Windows contains thousands of APIs, controlling everything from data storage to font display.

Every operating system has different APIs. Accordingly, a developer who writes an application for one operating system and wishes to sell the application to users of another must modify, or "port," the application to the second operating system. This process is both time-consuming and expensive.

"Middleware" refers to software products that expose their own APIs. Because of this, a middleware product written for Windows could take over some or all of Windows's valuable platform functions—that is, developers might begin to rely upon APIs exposed by the middleware for basic routines rather than relying upon the API set included in Windows. If middleware were written for multiple operating systems, its impact could be even greater. The more developers could rely upon APIs exposed by such middleware, the less expensive porting to different operating systems would be. Ultimately, if developers could write applications relying exclusively on APIs exposed by middleware, their applications would run on any operating system on which the middleware was also present. Netscape Navigator and Java—both at issue in this case—are middleware products written for multiple operating systems.

. . . Microsoft argues that . . . [a] contradiction lies between plaintiffs' § 2 theory, under which Microsoft preserved its monopoly against middleware technologies that threatened to become viable substitutes for Windows, and its theory of the relevant market, under which middleware is not presently a viable substitute for Windows. Because middleware's threat is only nascent, however, no contradiction exists. Nothing in § 2 of the Sherman Act limits its prohibition to actions taken against threats that are already well-developed enough to serve as present substitutes. Because market definition is meant to identify products "reasonably interchangeable by consumers," and because middleware is not now interchangeable with Windows, the District Court had good reason for excluding middleware from the relevant market.

. . . [A]fter concluding that Microsoft had monopoly power, the District Court held that Microsoft had violated § 2 by engaging in a variety of exclusionary acts (not including predatory pricing), to maintain its monopoly by preventing the effective distribution and use of products that might threaten that monopoly. Specifically, the District Court held Microsoft liable for: (1) the way in which it integrated IE into Windows; (2) its various dealings with Original Equipment Manufacturers ("OEMs"), Internet Access Providers ("IAPs"), Internet Content Providers ("ICPs"), Independent Software Vendors ("ISVs"), and Apple Computer; (3) its efforts to contain and to subvert Java technologies; and (4) its course of conduct as a whole. Upon appeal, Microsoft argues that it did not engage in any exclusionary conduct. . . .

From a century of case law on monopolization under § 2 . . . several principles do emerge. First, to be condemned as exclusionary, a monopolist's act must have an "anticompetitive effect." That is, it must harm the competitive *process* and thereby harm consumers. In contrast, harm to one or more *competitors* will not suffice. . . .

Second, the plaintiff, on whom the burden of proof of course rests, must demonstrate that the monopolist's conduct indeed has the requisite anticompetitive effect. . . .

Third, if a plaintiff successfully establishes a *prima facie* case under § 2 by demonstrating anticompetitive effect, then the monopolist may proffer a "procompetitive justification" for its conduct. If the monopolist asserts a procompetitive justification—a nonpretextual claim that its conduct is indeed a form of competition on the merits because it involves, for example, greater efficiency or enhanced consumer appeal—then the burden shifts back to the plaintiff to rebut that claim.

Fourth, if the monopolist's procompetitive justification stands unrebutted, then the plaintiff must demonstrate that the anticompetitive harm of the conduct outweighs the procompetitive benefit. In cases arising under § 1 of the Sherman Act, the courts routinely apply a similar balancing approach under the rubric of the "rule of reason." The source of the rule of reason is *Standard Oil Co. v. United States,* 221 U.S. 1 (1911), in which the Supreme Court used that term to describe the proper inquiry under both sections of the Act. . . .

Finally, in considering whether the monopolist's conduct on balance harms competition and is therefore condemned as exclusionary for purposes of § 2, our focus is upon the effect of that conduct, not upon the intent behind it. Evidence of the intent behind the conduct of a monopolist is relevant only to the extent it helps us understand the likely effect of the monopolist's conduct. . . .

[The court concluded that various bundles foreclosed OEMs (original equipment manufacturers), which it described as one of the two most efficient methods of distribution (the second being IAPs). The portions of the opinion dealing with such bundling are excerpted in Chapter 4.B].

3. Agreements With Internet Access Providers [IAPs]. The District Court . . . condemned as exclusionary Microsoft's agreements with various IAPs . . . to provide easy access to IAPs' services from the Windows desktop in return for the IAPs' agreement to promote IE exclusively and to keep shipments of internet access software using Navigator under a specific percentage, typically 25%. . . . Microsoft concluded these exclusive agreements with all "the leading IAPs," including the major OLSs [Online Services]. The most significant of the OLS deals is with AOL, which, when the deal was reached, "accounted for a substantial portion of all existing Internet access subscriptions and . . . attracted a very large percentage of new IAP subscribers." Under that agreement Microsoft puts the AOL icon in the OLS folder on the Windows desktop and AOL does not promote any non-Microsoft browser, nor provide software using any non-Microsoft browser except at the customer's request, and even then AOL will not supply more than 15% of its subscribers with a browser other than IE. . . .

Following *Tampa Electric,* courts considering antitrust challenges to exclusive contracts have taken care to identify the share of the market foreclosed. Some courts have indicated that § 3 of the Clayton Act and § 1 of the Sherman Act require an equal degree of foreclosure before prohibiting exclusive contracts. *See, e.g., Roland Mach. Co. v. Dresser Indus., Inc.,* 749 F.2d 380, 393 (7th Cir.1984) (Posner, J.). Other courts, however, have held that a higher market share must be foreclosed in order to establish a violation of the Sherman Act as compared to the Clayton Act. *See, e.g., Barr Labs. v. Abbott Labs.,* 978 F.2d 98, 110 (3d Cir.1992); 11 HERBERT HOVENKAMP, ANTITRUST LAW ¶ 1800c4 (1998) ("[T]he cases are divided, with a likely majority stating that the Clayton Act requires a smaller showing of anticompetitive effects."). . . .

In this case, plaintiffs challenged Microsoft's exclusive dealing arrangements with the IAPs under both §§ 1 and 2 of the Sherman Act. The District Court, in analyzing the § 1 claim, stated, "unless the evidence demonstrates that Microsoft's agreements excluded Netscape altogether from access to roughly forty percent of the browser market, the Court should decline to find such agreements in violation of § 1." The court recognized that Microsoft had substantially excluded Netscape from "the most efficient channels for Navigator to achieve browser usage share," and had relegated it to more costly and less effective methods (such as mass mailing its browser on a disk or offering it for download over the internet); but because Microsoft has not "completely excluded Netscape" from reaching any potential user by some means of distribution, however ineffective, the court concluded the agreements do not violate § 1. Plaintiffs did not cross-appeal this holding.

Turning to § 2, the court stated: "the fact that Microsoft's arrangements with various [IAPs and other] firms did not foreclose enough of the relevant market to constitute a § 1 violation in no way detracts from the Court's assignment of liability for the same arrangements under § 2. . . . [A]ll of Microsoft's agreements, including the non-exclusive ones, severely restricted Netscape's access to those distribution channels leading most efficiently to the acquisition of browser usage share."

On appeal Microsoft argues that "courts have applied the same standard to alleged exclusive dealing agreements under both Section 1 *and* Section 2," and it argues that the District Court's holding of no liability under § 1 necessarily precludes holding it liable under § 2. The District Court appears to have based its holding with respect to § 1 upon a "total exclusion test" rather than the 40% standard drawn from the caselaw. Even assuming the holding is correct, however, we nonetheless reject Microsoft's contention.

The basic prudential concerns relevant to §§ 1 and 2 are admittedly the same: exclusive contracts are commonplace—particularly in the field of distribution—in our competitive, market economy, and imposing upon a firm with market power the risk of an antitrust suit every time it enters into such a contract, no matter how small the effect, would create an unacceptable and unjustified burden upon any such firm. At the same time, however, we agree with plaintiffs that a monopolist's use of exclusive contracts, in certain circumstances, may give rise to a § 2 violation even though the contracts foreclose less than the roughly 40% or 50% share usually required in order to establish a § 1 violation.

In this case, plaintiffs allege that, by closing to rivals a substantial percentage of the available opportunities for browser distribution, Microsoft managed to preserve its monopoly in the market for operating systems. The IAPs constitute one of the two major channels by which browsers can be distributed. Microsoft has exclusive deals with "fourteen of the top fifteen access providers in North America[, which] account for a large majority of all Internet access subscriptions in this part of the world." By ensuring that the "majority" of all IAP subscribers are offered IE either as the default browser or as the only browser, Microsoft's deals with the IAPs clearly have a significant effect in preserving its monopoly; they help keep usage of Navigator below the critical level necessary for Navigator or any other rival to pose a real threat to Microsoft's monopoly.

Plaintiffs having demonstrated a harm to competition, the burden falls upon Microsoft to defend its exclusive dealing contracts with IAPs by providing a procompetitive justification for them. Significantly, Microsoft's only explanation for its exclusive dealing is that it wants to keep developers focused upon its APIs—which is to say, it wants to preserve its power in the operating system market. That is not an unlawful end, but neither is it a procompetitive justification for the specific means here in question, namely exclusive dealing contracts with IAPs. Accordingly, we affirm the District Court's decision holding that Microsoft's exclusive contracts with IAPs are exclusionary devices, in violation of § 2 of the Sherman Act.

4. Dealings with Internet Content Providers [ICPs], Independent Software Vendors [ISVs], and Apple Computer . . . The District Court described Microsoft's deals with ISVs as follows:

> . . . Microsoft has promised to give preferential support, in the form of early Windows 98 and Windows NT betas, other technical information, and the right to use certain Microsoft seals of approval, to important ISVs that agree to certain conditions. One of these conditions is that the ISVs use Internet Explorer as the default browsing software for any software they develop with a hypertext-based user interface. Another condition is that the ISVs use Microsoft's "HTML Help," which is accessible only with Internet Explorer, to implement their applications' help systems.

The District Court further found that the effect of these deals is to "ensure [ ] that many of the most popular Web-centric applications will rely on browsing technologies found only in Windows," and that Microsoft's deals with ISVs therefore "increase[ ] the likelihood that the millions of consumers using [applications designed by ISVs that entered into agreements with Microsoft] will use Internet Explorer rather than Navigator."

The District Court did not specifically identify what share of the market for browser distribution the exclusive deals with the ISVs foreclose. Although the ISVs are a relatively small channel for browser distribution, they take on greater significance because, as discussed above, Microsoft had largely foreclosed the two primary channels to its rivals. In that light, one can tell from the record that by affecting the applications used by "millions" of consumers, Microsoft's exclusive deals with the ISVs had a substantial effect in further foreclosing rival browsers from the market. . . . Because, by keeping rival browsers from gaining widespread distribution (and potentially attracting the attention of developers away from the APIs in Windows), the deals have a substantial effect in preserving Microsoft's monopoly, we hold that plaintiffs have made a *prima facie* showing that the deals have an anticompetitive effect.

Of course, that Microsoft's exclusive deals have the anticompetitive effect of preserving Microsoft's monopoly does not, in itself, make them unlawful. A monopolist, like a competitive firm, may have a perfectly legitimate reason for wanting an exclusive arrangement with its distributors. Accordingly, Microsoft had an opportunity to, but did not, present the District Court with evidence demonstrating that the exclusivity provisions have some such procompetitive justification. On appeal Microsoft likewise does not claim that the exclusivity required by the deals serves any legitimate purpose; instead, it states only that its ISV agreements reflect an attempt "to persuade ISVs to utilize Internet-related system services in Windows rather than Navigator." As we explained before, however, keeping developers focused upon Windows—that is, preserving the Windows monopoly—is a competitively neutral goal. Microsoft having offered no procompetitive justification for its exclusive dealing arrangements with the ISVs, we hold that those arrangements violate § 2 of the Sherman Act.

Finally, the District Court held that Microsoft's dealings with Apple violated the Sherman Act. . . . The District Court found that "ninety percent of [Apple's] Mac OS users running a suite of office productivity applications [use] Microsoft's Mac Office." Further, the District Court found that:

> In 1997, Apple's business was in steep decline, and many doubted that the company would survive much longer. . . . [M]any ISVs questioned the wisdom of continuing to spend time and money developing applications for the Mac OS. Had Microsoft announced in the midst of this atmosphere that it was ceasing to develop new versions of Mac Office, a great number

> of ISVs, customers, developers, and investors would have interpreted the announcement as Apple's death notice.

Microsoft recognized the importance to Apple of its continued support of Mac Office. In June 1997 Microsoft Chairman Bill Gates determined that the company's negotiations with Apple " 'have not been going well at all. . . . Apple let us down on the browser by making Netscape the standard install.' Gates then reported that he had already called Apple's CEO . . . to ask 'how we should announce the cancellation of Mac Office. . . .' " The District Court further found that, within a month of Gates' call, Apple and Microsoft had reached an agreement pursuant to which

> Microsoft's primary obligation is to continue releasing up-to-date versions of Mac Office for at least five years. . . . [and] Apple has agreed . . . to "bundle the most current version of [IE] . . . with [Mac OS]" . . . [and to] "make [IE] the default [browser]". . . . Navigator is not installed on the computer hard drive during the default installation, which is the type of installation most users elect to employ. . . . [The] Agreement further provides that . . . Apple may not position icons for nonMicrosoft browsing software on the desktop of new Macintosh PC systems or Mac OS upgrades.

The agreement also prohibits Apple from encouraging users to substitute another browser for IE, and states that Apple will "encourage its employees to use [IE]."

This exclusive deal between Microsoft and Apple has a substantial effect upon the distribution of rival browsers. If a browser developer ports its product to a second operating system, such as the Mac OS, it can continue to display a common set of APIs. Thus, usage share, not the underlying operating system, is the primary determinant of the platform challenge a browser may pose. Pre-installation of a browser (which can be accomplished either by including the browser with the operating system or by the OEM installing the browser) is one of the two most important methods of browser distribution, and Apple had a not insignificant share of worldwide sales of operating systems. Because Microsoft's exclusive contract with Apple has a substantial effect in restricting distribution of rival browsers, and because (as we have described several times above) reducing usage share of rival browsers serves to protect Microsoft's monopoly, its deal with Apple must be regarded as anticompetitive.

Microsoft offers no procompetitive justification for the exclusive dealing arrangement. It makes only the irrelevant claim that the IE-for-Mac Office deal is part of a multifaceted set of agreements between itself and Apple, that does not mean it has any procompetitive justification. Accordingly, we hold that the exclusive deal with Apple is exclusionary, in violation of § 2 of the Sherman Act. . . .

NOTES AND QUESTIONS ON *MICROSOFT*

1. ***The foreclosure share threshold.*** The *Microsoft* district court held that Sherman Act § 1 requires a substantial foreclosure share of at least 40%. However, the lower courts are actually split on the minimum share necessary to infer likely anticompetitive effects from a foreclosure share. Some courts have held that 24% suffices.[20] Other courts have indicated that 30–40% is usually necessary.[21] Moreover, as the *Microsoft* appellate opinion indicates, courts generally hold that Sherman Act § 2 requires a significantly lower foreclosure share than Sherman Act § 1, and courts are split about whether Clayton § 3 requires an equal or lower foreclosure share than Sherman Act § 1.

Should the foreclosure share threshold differ for these different statutory provisions? It is not clear why they should. If the foreclosure share is insufficient to create anticompetitive effects, it should be insufficient whether or not the defendant has monopoly power or sells goods. If the foreclosure share suffices to create anticompetitive effects, that should suffice to require some procompetitive justification under the rule of reason, regardless of the statutory provision.

However, it makes sense to vary the required foreclosure share threshold depending on (1) what share the alleged anticompetitive theory indicates is necessary to produce anticompetitive effects given the industry facts and (2) the existence and proven strength of any offsetting procompetitive justifications.

To illustrate the first point, if the relevant anticompetitive theory were depriving rivals of economies of scale, then the appropriate foreclosure share threshold should be higher with lower economies of scale. With small economies of scale, even a large foreclosure share would not prevent the market from having a competitive number of efficient rivals. This is similar to the point that the market share threshold for inferring market power should higher with higher rival elasticity of supply. In this case, however, the anticompetitive theory was instead that preventing Netscape's browser from becoming ubiquitous on computers would prevent Netscape from, in the future, being able to compete with Microsoft's operating system by modifying Netscape's browser to run applications. Given this theory, an anticompetitive effect could exist even if Netscape were foreclosed from a relatively small share of the browser market, because such foreclosure could suffice to prevent a modified Netscape browser from later becoming reasonably interchangeable with Microsoft's operating system to software developers or computer makers. But this conclusion reflects the theory of anticompetitive harm, rather than the level of Microsoft's market power.

---

[20] Twin City Sportservice, Inc. v. Charles O. Finley & Co., Inc., 676 F.2d 1291, 1298, 1304 (9th Cir. 1982).

[21] Stop & Shop Supermarket Co. v. Blue Cross & Blue Shield of R.I., 373 F.3d 57, 68 (1st Cir. 2004) (generally need at least 30–40%). *See id. at* 66 (making clear that the relevant "extent of foreclosure" includes that resulting from defendant's exclusionary contracts and "other existing foreclosures," such as by another seller's exclusionary contracts).

On the second point, if no procompetitive justification is asserted or proven, then it does not take much likelihood of anticompetitive effects to conclude that any net effects must be anticompetitive. Thus, in such cases, it makes sense to use a lower foreclosure share threshold because inferring a relatively low likelihood of anticompetitive effects suffices to infer net anticompetitive effects. The fact that the appellate court concluded that Microsoft failed even to assert a valid procompetitive justification helps explain why the court required showing only a foreclosure of some major distribution channels, rather than the calculation of a foreclosure share.

2. ***What counts as foreclosure.*** The district court thought that proving X% foreclosure required proof that the exclusive dealing "completely excluded Netscape" from reaching X% of users, which could not be satisfied by evidence that the exclusive dealing foreclosed some distributors if Netscape could potentially access users through other distributors. The appellate court disagreed on two grounds.

First, the appellate court held it sufficed that rivals were foreclosed from major distribution channels, because that would lower Netscape usage. Foreclosing some distributors thus counts as foreclosing even though rivals might be able to reach users through other distributors, as long as foreclosing rivals from those distributors would decrease their market share. This could be the case if, for example, the foreclosed distributors were more efficient or more effective than other distributors at obtaining usage at certain potential users.

Second, the appellate court held that foreclosure need not "completely exclude" rivals from anyone. Here the appellate court found foreclosure of Internet Access Providers even though the challenged agreement provided only that they would not "promote" rival browsers nor supply more than 15–25% of their customers with a rival browser. The holding thus indicates that it sufficed that the agreement foreclosed these distributor's promotional services, assuming that access to promotional services could have increased rival usage. The holding also indicates that foreclosing 75–85% of a distributor's sales suffices even though such foreclosure is not 100% and thus not totally exclusive. This makes sense because foreclosing most of a distributor's sales can still suffice to restrain rival sales in a way that could create anticompetitive effects.

The appellate court also concluded that it sufficed that the agreement required Apple and Independent Software Vendors to use Microsoft's browser as their default browser. The holding thus again indicates that it suffices if an agreement forecloses a particular service—here the service of making a browser the default in software—where access to that service could have increased rival usage.

In short, the appellate court concluded that foreclosure need not be total. It suffices that the exclusionary agreement restrains rival sales. This is consistent with Supreme Court precedent that has equated "foreclosure" with a "restraint" on buying from rivals.[22] It also fits the relevant economics

---

[22] *See* Int'l Salt Co. v. United States, 332 U.S. 392, 396–97 (1947); *see also* N. Pac. Ry. Co. v. United States, 356 U.S. 1, 9, 11–12 (1958).

because the possible anticompetitive effects depend on the extent to which rival sales were restrained, not on whether the foreclosure was total at any particular distributor or end-user.

Another issue that has often arisen is whether exclusionary agreements can be foreclosing when they are terminable. Although the relevant Supreme Court cases condemn exclusionary agreements even when they are terminable,[23] there has not been a Supreme Court case on the topic since 1966, and lower courts have since split on this issue. Some lower courts continue to adhere to the older Supreme Court cases by holding that terminability does not undermine the foreclosing effect of an exclusionary agreement.[24] Other lower courts have instead suggested that an ability to terminate (or not renew) exclusionary agreements in less than one year indicates that those agreements presumptively or probably lack any substantial foreclosing effect.[25] The latter cases do not typically explain their deviation from Supreme Court precedent. Nor do they explain how such a presumption could be consistent with the economic explanations for why buyer have incentives to enter into those exclusionary agreements in the first place.[26] The same collective action or supracompetitive-profit-splitting theories that might explain why buyers have individual incentives to agree to anticompetitive exclusionary agreements would also mean they would lack incentives to terminate such agreements, so that terminability would not alter their effects.

C. TYING

Tying is a refusal to sell one product unless the buyer also takes another product from the seller. The product that will not be sold without the other is called the tying product, and generally it is the product in which the defendant has the greatest market power. The tied product is the one that buyers have to take from the seller to get its tying product.

Possible Anticompetitive Effects. The claim that tying can be anticompetitive has been strongly critiqued by the single monopoly profit theory, which argued that (as with the upstream firm who vertically

[23] *See* FTC v. Brown Shoe, 384 U.S. 316, 318–19 & n.13 (1966) (condemning agreement even though buyers could "voluntarily withdraw" at any time), *rev'g* 339 F.2d 45, 53 (8th Cir. 1964) (sustaining agreement in part because "[r]etailers were free to abandon the arrangement at any time they saw it to their advantage so to do"); Standard Oil Co. v. United States, 337 U.S. 293, 296 (1949) (invalidating exclusive dealing agreements that lasted only one year and were terminable upon thirty days notice); Standard Fashion Co. v. Magrane-Houston Co., 258 U.S. 346, 352 (1922) (invalidating exclusive dealing agreements that were terminable upon three months notice).

[24] *See* United States v. Dentsply, Intl., 399 F.3d 181, 193 (3d Cir. 2005); *LePage's*, 324 F.3d at 157 n.11; Minnesota Mining & Manuf. Co. v. Appleton Papers, Inc., 35 F. Supp. 2d 1138 (D. Minn.1999); American Express Travel v. Visa, 2005 WL 1515399, at *6–7 (S.D.N.Y.); Masimo Corp. v. Tyco Health Care, 2006 WL 1236666 (C.D.Cal.).

[25] *See* Omega Envtl. v. Gilbarco, Inc., 127 F.3d 1157, 1163–64 (9th Cir. 1997); Thompson Everett, Inc. v. National Cable Adver., 57 F.3d 1317, 1326 (4th Cir. 1995); U.S. Healthcare, Inc. v. Healthsource, Inc., 986 F.2d 589, 596 (1st Cir. 1993); Roland Mach. Co. v. Dresser Indus., Inc., 749 F.2d 380, 395 (7th Cir. 1984).

[26] *See* Elhauge, *supra* note 12, at 340–342 (explaining the economic error in any presumption favoring exclusionary agreements shorter than one year).

integrates into downstream markets) there was only a single monopoly profit that could not be increased by tying.[27] Their classic example was a monopolist in nuts who tried to tie nuts to bolts. Suppose nuts and bolts each cost 10 cents to make and thus would be priced at 10 cents each if the market for both was competitive. Suppose further that the profit-maximizing price for a combined monopolist in both nuts and bolts would be 40 cents for the nut-bolt set that consumers need. If we have a nut monopolist and a competitive market in bolts, then the nut monopolist would simply charge 30 cents for nuts, with the customers paying 10 cents for bolts on a competitive market to arrive at 40 cents for the nut-bolt set. The nut monopolist would earn monopoly profits of 20 cents per set used. It would earn no additional monopoly profits by tying its sale of nuts to bolts because if it did so the monopoly price would be 40 cents and the cost 20 cents, leaving it with profits of 20 cents a set. In fact, if a competitive market were more efficient and would lower the price of bolts down to 5 cents, the monopolist in nuts would prefer that, because then it could sell nuts for 35 cents and earn 25 cents a set. Thus, the single monopoly profit theory suggested a firm would use tying only if there were some efficiency to doing so.

However, the models indicating a single monopoly profit depended on five key assumptions: (1) buyers do not use varying amounts of the tied product with the tying product; (2) buyer demand for the two products has a strong positive correlation; (3) buyers do not use varying amounts of the tying product; (4) the competitiveness of the tied market is fixed; *and* (5) the competitiveness of the tying market is fixed.[28] Modern antitrust economics scholarship proves that relaxing any *one* of these assumptions invalidates the single monopoly profit theory, and that each relaxed assumption makes possible a distinctive anticompetitive result.

(1) Intraproduct Price Discrimination. If buyers use varying amounts of the tied product with the tying product, then tying may allow a form of price discrimination on the tying product that increases monopoly profits.[29] Suppose that a monopolist sells some capital product that is used with a consumable product: for example, printers that are used with paper. Suppose further that usage of the consumable varies for different buyers in a way that correlates to the total value of the capital product to each buyer. Buyers who use more paper are using their printers more often and thus tend to derive more total value from their

[27] *See* Ward S. Bowman, Jr., *Tying Arrangements and the Leverage Problem*, 67 YALE L.J. 19, 21–23 (1957); Aaron Director & Edward H. Levi, *Law and the Future: Trade Regulation*, 51 NW. U. L. REV. 281, 290, 292–94 (1956); Robert Bork, The Antitrust Paradox (1978); Richard Posner, Antitrust Law: An Economic Perspective (2001).

[28] Elhauge, *Tying, Bundled Discounts, and the Death of the Single Monopoly Profit Theory*, 123 HARVARD LAW REVIEW 397, 400, 404–420 (2009).

[29] This was first shown in Ward S. Bowman, Jr., *Tying Arrangements and the Leverage Problem*, 67 YALE L.J. 19, 23–24, 33 (1957); *see also Jefferson Parish*, 466 U.S. at 15 & n.23 (citing Bowman and treating such intraproduct price discrimination as an anticompetitive effect).

printers, though this correlation is imperfect because some lower-using buyers might get higher per-usage value. If usage is correlated with total value, the monopolist could lower the price for its printer down to marginal cost, contingent on buyers taking all their paper from the seller, with the paper price set well above marginal cost. Then buyers who use more paper will pay more, allowing the monopolist to price discriminate among buyers of printers. This may be the most effective means of price discrimination if the monopolist could not otherwise tell which buyer is more likely to use its printer, and if the monopolist could not otherwise meter usage of its machine in an easy to monitor way.[30]

Tying that produces intra-product price discrimination decreases both consumer welfare and total welfare unless it increases tying product output.[31] Moreover, putting aside possible productive efficiencies or inefficiencies,[32] such ties also have the following effects. If the rate at which consumers desire to use the tying product is distributed uniformly, normally, or log-normally, then such ties always lower consumer welfare even when they increase output.[33] This is significant because consumer welfare is the legal standard in antitrust.[34]

The immediate effect of such ties also lowers total welfare (even when it increases output) unless the dispersion of usage is relatively high.[35] The reason is that ties price discriminate imperfectly and thus inefficiently reallocate some output from buyers whose per-usage valuation is low to those for whom it is high, even when the former buyers use the tying product more heavily and derive more total value from the tying product. This inefficiency will be offset only to the extent the tie increases sales to low-usage buyers, and proportionally more low-usage buyers exist if the dispersion of usage is relatively flat than if it has a log-normal or normal distribution. For example, for log-normal distributions

---

[30] Difficulties in monitoring which paper a buyer uses might cause a seller to instead engage in technological tying that does not require monitoring. For example, it might design its printer so it can only work with its printer cartridges, which it sells at far above marginal costs.

[31] Elhauge & Nalebuff, *The Welfare Effects of Metering Ties*, 33 J.L. ECON. & ORG. (2016) (providing a formal proof); Elhauge, *Tying*, *supra* note 28, at 431 & n.89 (making the same point conceptually without a formal proof).

[32] Productive efficiencies concern the possibility that tying might decrease costs or increase product value, and productive inefficiencies concern the opposite possibility (such as when tying requires incurring additional monitoring costs or altering product design for the worse). The former might offset adverse welfare effects; the latter might make the welfare effects worse.

[33] Elhauge & Nalebuff, *supra* note 31 (providing formal proof for log-normal and uniform distributions); Elhauge, *Rehabilitating Jefferson Parish: Why Ties Without a Substantial Foreclosure Share Should Not Be Per Se Legal*, 80 ANTITRUST L.J. 463, 478–79, 516–19 (2016); (summarizing economic literature and providing formal proof for normal distributions); Elhauge, *Tying*, *supra* note 28, at 433, 481 (proof with uniform distribution).

[34] Elhauge, *Tying*, *supra* note 28, at 436–42 (collecting cases showing that the legal standard is consumer welfare and reasons why that standard makes policy sense); *see also infra* Chapter 7 (summarizing literature indicating that the total welfare objective can actually be advanced better by applying a consumer welfare test than a total welfare test).

[35] Elhauge & Nalebuff, *supra* note 31 (providing formal proof for log-normal and uniform distributions); Elhauge, *Rehabilitating*, *supra* note 33, at 478–79, 516–19 (summarizing economic literature and providing formal proof for normal distributions).

and a tying product marginal cost of zero, the immediate effects of such ties would lower total welfare unless they increase tying product output by more than 37%, which would occur only if the dispersion of desired usage exceeded the dispersion of U.S. income.[36]

Moreover, even if the immediate effects of such ties increase total welfare, overall total welfare can decrease if the additional monopoly profits are somewhat dissipated by the implementation costs of imposing a tie or by the increased managerial inefficiency or ex ante costs induced by those additional supracompetitive profits.[37] Indeed, even if a normal or log-normal distribution had a very high dispersion rate, a profit dissipation of 5% of the additional profits created by such ties would suffice to make such ties reduce overall total welfare.[38]

Tying that produces intra-product price discrimination requires tying market power and causes significant effects only if the tie forecloses a substantial *amount* of tied sales, but it does not require a substantial foreclosure *share*.[39] It would not matter if, for example, the tie affects only 1 percent of the tied market. However, a tie can have this effect only if buyers purchase varying amounts of the tied product and usage of the tied product positively correlates with valuation of the tying product. A fixed-ratio tie thus cannot have this effect.

(2) Interproduct Price Discrimination. If buyer demand for two products does not have a strong positive correlation, then tying can also profitably permit price discrimination across buyers of both products.[40] This is true even if the products are used or bundled in a fixed ratio. This form of tying can increase profits without any substantial tied foreclosure share, but it does require some degree of market power in both products, and it cannot have significant effects unless it forecloses a substantial amount of sales.[41]

To illustrate, suppose there are ten million consumers whose valuations of the Reality Television Network and the Highbrow Television Network range linearly from $0 to $10, but are negatively

---

36 Elhauge & Nalebuff, *supra* note 31.

37 Elhauge, *Rehabilitating*, *supra* note 33, at 486–89.

38 *Id.* at 488, 520; Elhauge & Nalebuff, *supra* note 31.

39 Elhauge, *Rehabilitating*, *supra* note 33, at 476, 480.

40 This was first shown for negatively-correlated demand in George J. Stigler, *United States v. Loew's Inc.: A Note on Block-Booking,* 1963 SUP. CT. REV. 152; *see also Jefferson Parish,* 466 U.S. at 15 & n.23 (citing Stigler and treating such interproduct price discrimination as an anticompetitive effect). Later work demonstrated the effect held as long as demand did not have a strong positive correlation. *See* William James Adams & Janet L. Yellen, *Commodity Bundling and the Burden of Monopoly,* 90 Q.J. ECON. 475, 485 (1976); R. Preston McAfee et al., *Multiproduct Monopoly, Commodity Bundling, and Correlation of Values,* 104 Q.J. ECON. 371, 372–73, 377 (1989); Richard Schmalensee, *Gaussian Demand and Commodity Bundling,* 57 J. BUS. S211, S220 (1984). If the strength of demand relative to cost is high enough, then bundling can increase monopoly profits for anything other than a perfect positive correlation. *Id.* at S215, S220. For lower demand-to-cost ratios, strong but imperfect positive correlations may defeat this strategy.

41 *See* Richard Schmalensee, *Commodity Bundling by Single-Product Monopolies,* 25 J.L. & ECON. 67, 67–69 (1982); Elhauge, *Rehabilitating*, *supra* note 33, at 472, 474.

correlated.[42] Consumers who value one network at $10 value the other at $0, consumers who value one network at $9 value the other at $1, and so on, with the sum of each consumer's valuation for both networks always adding up to $10. Assume a constant marginal cost of zero. Without tying, the firm would maximize profits by setting the price for each network at $5, and the five million consumers who valued each network above $5 would buy it and get positive consumer surplus, adding up to a total of $25 million in consumer surplus across both networks. With tying, the firm would instead charge $10 for a bundle of the two networks, leaving each consumer with zero consumer surplus and reducing consumer welfare by $25 million.

This effect is called inter-product price discrimination because it aims to achieve results similar to price discrimination across both products. Tying that produces inter-product price discrimination decreases both consumer welfare and total welfare unless it produces some output-increasing efficiency.[43] Further, if we put aside possible productive efficiencies or inefficiencies, such ties will (assuming a normal distribution of buyer valuations) always decrease consumer welfare even when they increase output.[44] If the two bundled products have symmetric demand curves, the immediate effects of such ties also reduces total welfare standard unless the strength of demand relative to cost is "especially high."[45] Moreover, if the bundled products have asymmetric demand curves, such ties are even *more* likely to reduce total welfare.[46] It thus seems likely that the immediate effects of such ties usually lower total welfare. Even when they do not, overall total welfare will likely decrease if the additional supracompetitive profits are partly dissipated.[47]

(3) Extracting Individual Consumer Surplus. If buyers use varying amounts of the tying product, then tying can extract individual consumer surplus. The basic reason is that, even at a monopoly price for the tying product, each multi-unit buyer enjoys some consumer surplus because it values the last unit it purchases at the monopoly price and values the prior (or inframarginal) units at something more, given that any buyer rationally uses its initial units to meet its greatest needs first. The difference between each buyer's valuation of those inframarginal units and the monopoly price will be the consumer surplus enjoyed by each buyer at the monopoly price. A tying firm can expropriate that consumer surplus by allowing buyers to purchase the tying product at the monopoly price only if buyers agree to purchase their needs of some tied product at supracompetitive prices. Each buyer will accept the tie as long as the

[42] This example comes from Elhauge, *Rehabilitating, supra* note 33, at 473.

[43] Adams & Yellen, *supra* note 40, at 482–83, 491–92; Elhauge, *Tying, supra* note 28, at 406–07.

[44] Schmalensee, *Gaussian Demand, supra* note 40, at S221–22, S229.

[45] *Id.* at S221.

[46] *Id.* at S218, S223.

[47] Elhauge, *Rehabilitating, supra* note 33, at 486–89.

burden of paying supracompetitive prices on the tied product is less than the consumer surplus that buyer would lose by being unable to buy the tying product at the monopoly price.[48]

Tying that extracts individual consumer welfare always reduces consumer welfare.[49] The immediate effects of such ties also reduce total welfare whenever the buyers who are subject to the tie value the tying product significantly more than the tied product.[50] This condition is likely met for most litigated ties, which generally involve a tying product that the buyers value significantly more than the tied product. Even when it is not met, overall total welfare will still likely decrease if the additional supracompetitive profits are partly dissipated.[51]

This form of tying can increase profits without a substantial tied foreclosure share, but does require tying market power, and it cannot extract significant amounts of consumer surplus unless it forecloses a substantial amount of sales.[52] However, such a tie is possible only when buyers purchase multiple units of the tying product and do not purchase the two products in a fixed ratio.

(4) *Increased Tied Market Power.* If the tied market is not perfectly competitive, then tying that forecloses a substantial share of the tied market can reduce rival competitiveness by impairing rival efficiency, entry, existence, aggressiveness, or expandability.[53] Any one of these adverse effects on rival competitiveness can in turn anticompetitively increase the tying firm's market power in the tied market, thus raising prices and harming consumers.

Consider first situations where tying can reduce tied rival efficiency. If there are costs to entering the tied market, tying can profitably deter entry by an equally efficient rival by foreclosing enough of the tied market to make entry profits lower than entry costs.[54] Likewise, if there are fixed costs to operating in the tied market, tying can cause equally efficient rivals in the tied market to exit (or deter their entry) and thus

---

[48] This was first shown in M. L. Burstein, *The Economics of Tie-In Sales*, 42 REVIEW OF ECONOMICS & STATISTICS 68, 68–69 (1960); M.L. Burstein, *A Theory of Full-Line Forcing*, 55 NORTHWESTERN LAW REVIEW 62, 73–91 (1960). Burstein's theory that tying could be used to squeeze out consumer surplus on the tying product was distinguished from price discrimination and cited favorably in Fortner Enter. v. United States Steel, 394 U.S. 495, 513–514 & n.8 (1969) (White, J., dissenting) ("they may be used to force a full line of products on the customer so as to extract more easily from him a monopoly return on one unique product in the line") (citing Burstein), which was in turn cited favorably as an explanation for the quasi-per se rule against tying both in *Jefferson Parish*, 466 U.S. at 13 n.19; *see also id.* at 15 & n.23 (citing Burstein's theory as showing an anticompetitive effect), and in the dissenting opinion in Eastman Kodak v. Image Technical Servs., 504 U.S. 451, 487 (1992) (Scalia, J., joined by O'Connor & Thomas, JJ., dissenting) (same).

[49] Elhauge, *Tying, supra* note 28, at 412.

[50] *Id.* at 412, 435; Elhauge, *Rehabilitating, supra* note 33, at 470–71.

[51] Elhauge, *Rehabilitating, supra* note 33, at 486–89.

[52] Elhauge, *Tying, supra* note 28, at 412–13; Elhauge, *Rehabilitating, supra* note 33, at 471.

[53] Elhauge, *Tying, supra* note 28, at 413–417.

[54] *See* Barry Nalebuff, *Bundling as an Entry Barrier*, 119 Q.J. ECON. 159, 160–61, 168–70 (2004).

enable the tying firm to obtain a monopoly in the tied market.[55] More generally, for the same reasons discussed in Section B for exclusive dealing, foreclosing the tied market can create anticompetitive effects by depriving tied market rivals of economies of scale, scope, distribution, supply, research, learning, and/or network effects. If tied market foreclosure decreases rival efficiency in any of those ways, it will worsen the market options available to buyers and lessen the constraint on the tying firm's market power in the tied market, thus enabling it to raise prices in the tied market even though rivals are not completely eliminated.

Even if tying does not impair rival efficiency, foreclosure can also impair rival competitiveness by decreasing rival aggressiveness or expandability. Tying can decrease rival aggressiveness in at least two scenarios. First, if firms in the tied market engage in Cournot competition, which means each firm sets output in response to the output choices of others, then tying can encourage tied product rivals to reduce output and charge higher prices.[56] Second, if the tied market is concentrated, but (absent tying) would be undifferentiated and result in Bertrand competition that drives prices down to cost, tying can effectively differentiate the tied market (because buyer valuations for the tying product vary) and induce the rival to charge higher tied product prices.[57] Tying in both scenarios will increase profits for the tying firm if, absent tying, tying product revenue would exceed tied product revenue, which is typical in tying cases. Tying in both scenarios will also harm consumer welfare.[58]

Tying can also decrease rival expandability and increase tied prices if the tying firm has market power in the tied market. Standard economic models calculate market power to be directly proportional to a firm's market share and inversely proportional to its rivals' supply elasticity, which is the percentage increase in rival supply that would result from a one percent increase in market price.[59] These standard models reasonably assume rivals' ability to expand depends on how large they already are. Thus, if a tying firm can through foreclosure obtain a higher

---

[55] *See* Michael D. Whinston, *Tying Foreclosure, and Exclusion,* 80 AM. ECON. REV. 837, 840, 846 (1990).

[56] *See* José Carbajo et al., *A Strategic Motivation for Commodity Bundling*, 38 J. INDUS. ECON. 283, 285–86, 290–92 (1990). The reason is that tying effectively commits the tying firm to increase its share of tied product output, which makes it profitable for rivals to lower output and increase prices, reducing total output of the tied product. *Id.*

[57] *See id.* at 285, 287–89. Without tying, the tied market would be undifferentiated because, even though buyer valuations of the tied product vary, buyers consider the tied products of the firm and its rival to be fungible. With tying, however, the varying buyer valuations of the tying and tied products will differentiate buyers in their willingness to shift from the rival tied product to the tied bundle in response to a rival price increase.

[58] *Id.* at 289, 292.

[59] Define P as price, C as marginal cost, S as the firm's market share, e_{rs} as the rival supply elasticity, and e_m as the market demand elasticity (the percentage reduction in market output that would result from a one percent increase in market price). Then the firm's degree of market power (as measured its ability to raise prices above cost) is determined by the equation $(P - C)/P = S/[e_m + e_{rs}(1 - S)]$. *See* William M. Landes & Richard A. Posner, *Market Power in Antitrust Cases*, 94 HARV. L. REV. 937, 945 (1981).

share of the tied market for reasons unrelated to product merits, it will lower rivals' share of the tied market and thus lessen rival expandability and the constraint on tied product prices.

However, tying that impairs tied rival competitiveness *without* increasing the degree of tying market power cannot increase monopoly profits if (1) the products are used or bundled in a fixed ratio *and* (2) the tied product has no utility without the tying product.[60] The reason is that buyers of the tying product would interpret any premium on the tied product as a per-unit price increase on the tying product. Thus, a firm using a tie cannot reap any additional profits from those buyers that the firm could not have achieved without a tie by simply exercising its power to increase the tying product price, a tying market power which by hypothesis was not increased.

On the other hand, even without affecting tying market power, tying to impair tied market rivals can increase monopoly profits if only *one* of the above two conditions holds. If the products are used or bundled in a fixed ratio, but the tied product also has separate utility when not used with the tying product, then the firm can reap additional profits because it can (given diminished rival competitiveness) charge higher than but-for prices on purchases of the tied product that are not used with the tying product. Likewise, if the products are always used together, but in varying ratios, then tying that impairs tied market rival competitiveness can increase monopoly profits because the tie reduces the consumer surplus that buyers can get by rejecting the tie. Each buyer will accept the tie if the consumer surplus they would get by rejecting the tie and buying only the tied product is lower than the consumer surplus they would get from buying both the tying product at monopoly prices and the tied product at elevated prices. The tie that impairs tied market rivals will lower the former consumer surplus and thus allow the tying firm to extract more consumer surplus with a tie.

(5) Increased Tying Market Power. If one relaxes the assumption that the degree of tying market power is fixed, then tying can create additional anticompetitive effects by making the degree of tying market power higher than it would have been without tying.[61] Tying can increase tying power above but-for levels by either (1) foreclosing enough of the tied market to deter or delay later entry into the tying market, (2) raising the costs of a partial substitute that constrains tying market power, or (3) transferring market power from a waning technology to the next-generation technology. Let's take each scenario in turn.

First, suppose that a firm's tying market power is vulnerable to an increased threat of future entry if successful rival producers exist in the tied market. If so, then the firm has incentives to engage in defensive leveraging, foreclosing the tied market in order to deter or delay later entry into the tying market, thus maintaining its tying market power for

60 *See* Whinston, *supra* note 55, at 840, 850; Elhauge, *Tying*, *supra* note 28, at 416.

61 Elhauge, *Tying*, *supra* note 28, at 417–419.

a longer time or at a higher degree than it would have without tying. For example, recent literature shows that successful tied product makers are often more likely to evolve into tying product makers in future periods, in which case a firm has incentives to foreclose rivals in the tied market in order to prevent or reduce the erosion of its tying market power over time.[62] Alternatively, a firm's tying market power might be vulnerable to future entry or expansion by a single-market rival. Such a rival is often more likely to enter the tying market if buyers have attractive rival options in the tied market, especially if both products are essential inputs into some larger operation.[63]

Second, defensive leveraging has even stronger—and more immediate—anticompetitive effects if a firm's tying market power is otherwise constrained by the fact that the tied product is a partial substitute for the tying product. Foreclosing the market for the tied partial substitute can immediately protect or enhance the firm's tying market power, even if such foreclosure does not deter or delay entry into the tying market.[64]

Third, defensive leveraging also has even stronger—and more permanent—anticompetitive effects if the technological trend is from the market where the firm has market power to the market where the foreclosure is occurring. In such a case, a firm can use foreclosure not just to delay the erosion of its current market power over a waning technology, but to develop new market power over the technology of the future.[65] Such tying can have long-lasting adverse effects by creating market power in the new technology that otherwise might not have existed or by preventing the most efficient firm from winning the new market.

Conditions Necessary for the Possible Anticompetitive Effects. The extraction and price discrimination effects require tying market power, and can be significant in size only if they foreclose a substantial dollar *amount* of sales but do not require a substantial foreclosure *share* in the tied market. Tying agreements producing any of those three effects—intraproduct price discrimination, interproduct price discrimination, and extracting individual consumer surplus—all reduce consumer and total welfare absent some output-increasing efficiency. However, tying agreements having only such effects do not increase the

62 *See, e.g.,* Dennis W. Carlton & Michael Waldman, *The Strategic Use of Tying to Preserve and Create Market Power in Evolving Industries*, 33 RAND J. ECON. 194, 194–96, 198–212 (2002); Dennis W. Carlton, *A General Analysis of Exclusionary Conduct and Refusal to Deal*, 68 ANTITRUST L.J. 659, 668–70 (2001); Feldman, *Defensive Leveraging in Antitrust*, 87 GEO. L.J. 2079 (1999).

63 *See* Choi & Stefanandis, *Bundling, Entry Deterrence, and Specialist Innovators*, 79 J. BUSINESS 2575 (2006); Choi & Stefanandis, *Tying, Investment, and the Dynamic Leverage Theory*, 32 RAND J. Econ. 52 (2001); Barry Nalebuff, *Exclusionary Bundling,* 50 ANTITRUST BULLETIN 321, 324–327 (2005).

64 *See* Ordover & Willing, *An Economic Definition of Predation*, 91 YALE L.J. 8, 38–41 (1981); Whinston, *supra* note 55, at 852–54.

65 *See* Carlton & Waldman, *supra* note 62, at 194, 196–97, 212–15; Carlton, *supra* note 62, at 670–71.

degree of market power in the tied or tying market, and thus might not fit within monopolization doctrine to the extent that enhancing market power is a legal element.

The last two possible anticompetitive effects—increasing tied or tying market power—do require a substantial tied foreclosure share.[66] These two effects are also reinforced by the extraction and price discrimination effects, which prove that a foreclosing tie need not require any short-term profit sacrifice by the tying firm.[67] Likewise, any anticompetitive profits from the last two anticompetitive effects makes the extraction and price discrimination effects all the more attractive to tying firms and exacerbates the anticompetitive effects.

When the tied products are used in a fixed ratio, buyers cannot use varying amounts of the tied or tying products, which knocks out the possibility of intraproduct price discrimination or individual consumer surplus extraction. When the products cannot be used separately, demand for them will generally have a strong positive correlation that knocks out interproduct price discrimination. Further, if the products both (1) have a fixed ratio and (2) lack separate utility, that also knocks out the possibility of increasing profits by increasing tied market power. Thus, the combination of (1) a fixed ratio and (2) no separate utility precludes any of the first four possible anticompetitive effects, leaving only the possibility that a substantial tied foreclosure share might increase the degree of tying market power. The combination of (1) a fixed ratio, (2) no separate utility, and (3) no substantial tied foreclosure share precludes all five of the possible anticompetitive effects. When those three conditions are met, the single monopoly profit theory holds.[68]

Possible Redeeming Efficiencies. Tying also has possible redeeming efficiencies. For the extraction and price discrimination anticompetitive effects, tying can sometimes create output-increasing allocative efficiencies by cutting the price for the tying product and allowing sales to categories of buyers who otherwise would not buy the tying product. However, as noted above, such ties are also likely to reduce consumer welfare and overall total welfare, although the opposite welfare effects might obtain in particular cases. In addition, tying can have the following productive efficiencies, which might be large enough to offset any anticompetitive effects. Indeed, when there is neither tying market power nor substantial tied market foreclosure, then some productive efficiency must explain the tie.

(1) When Bundling Lowers Costs or Increases Value. Two products may be cheaper to make or distribute together, or they may be more valuable to the buyer if the seller bundles them than if the buyer does. For example, it is presumably more efficient to sell cars with the tires on

---

66 The foreclosure produced by a tie should be aggregated with any foreclosure produced by other exclusionary agreements like exclusive dealing.

67 Elhauge, *Tying*, *supra* note 28, at 404, 415–16.

68 *Id.* at 400–02.

than to sell them without tires and have consumers buy and install the tires separately. As this example suggests, such efficiency arguments can often instead be framed as arguments that the two items are really components of a single product, rather than separate products at all. When package cost-savings are asserted as a justification, often plaintiffs respond that a less restrictive alternative would be to offer the products separately and then at a package discount that is no greater than the cost-savings. But this test may be difficult for courts to administer, and the possibility of court error may discourage price cutting down to the full amount of the cost-savings. Likewise, when the bundle is justified as more valuable, the less restrictive alternative might be to offer them both separately and then together. But it may sometimes be too costly to make separate offerings for which there is little consumer demand. For example, while shoe manufacturers could be required to carry shoes both in pairs and separately, that may not be worth the inventory costs because consumers generally only want shoes in pairs, leaving aside the few consumers who have one foot, lost one shoe, or have two feet that are significantly different in size.

(2) When Bundling Improves Quality. Sometimes the seller of the tying product might require that buyers use its tied product with it because they worry that buyers will otherwise use an inferior substitute that will make the tying product work less well and lower its brand reputation. A less restrictive alternative might be simply informing the buyer about the quality issue. But buyers may have free rider problems if they do not bear the full cost of the loss in brand reputation. For example, a fast food franchisor might sell its franchise (the tying product) to the franchisees who own the individual fast food restaurants on the condition that the franchisees buy their chicken (the tied product) only from the franchisor. The franchisor might worry that simply informing the buyer of the quality issue would not suffice because franchisees might free ride off of the brand's reputation to get walk-in traffic and skimp on costs by buying inferior chicken. If all the franchisees do this, the value of the franchise will be diminished for all of them, but each franchisee may figure that it alone will have little impact on the overall brand reputation. Thus, each may have incentives to underweigh quality relative to costs. Another less restrictive alternative might be to specify the relevant quality of the associated product that buyers can use. But it may be difficult to specify that quality (what is tasty chicken?) or hard to monitor compliance with a general quality standard (it may be easier to see who is delivering chicken to the restaurant than to determine the quality of the chicken that others are delivering).

(3) Metering to Shift Financing or Risk-Bearing Costs to the Firm That Can Minimize Them. Sometimes tying might allow a form of price metering that could be understood not as price discrimination, but as an efficient way of shifting financing or risk-bearing costs from buyers to a seller that can bear them more cheaply. Suppose, for example, that it

would be more costly for small buyers to finance the costs of capital equipment than for the seller. Then it might be efficient for the seller to effectively provide financing to buyers by selling the capital equipment below cost, with the buyer repaying the seller with supracompetitive payments on the associated consumable. The seller might accomplish the same by leasing the equipment, but the transaction costs of leasing might be higher.

Or suppose the problem is that the buyers are small businesses who do not vary *ex ante* in the value they attach to the capital equipment but who face the risk that some of them will do badly (and end up not needing the equipment) whereas others will do well (and end up using them a lot). Then it might make sense for the seller to sell the capital equipment very cheaply and make its profits in supracompetitive prices on the consumable. This will reduce the business risks to the buyers because those who will pay less will be those who have done badly in business. It will shift those risks to the seller, who may well face lower risk-bearing costs because it has many buyers, giving it a diversified portfolio that protects it against buyer-specific business declines. Again, leasing the equipment with payments dependent on usage might well be a less restrictive alternative, but perhaps transaction costs would impede that result.

U.S. Law on Tying. Under U.S. antitrust law, a so-called "quasi-per se" rule applies to tying under Sherman Act § 1 and Clayton Act § 3. This rule condemns tying without requiring a showing that any substantial share of the tied market has been foreclosed. Rather, it suffices that the defendant has tying market power and the tie covers a nontrivial dollar amount of tied product.[69] In short, the elements of the quasi per se rule match the elements necessary to have the price discrimination and extraction effects described above, which indicates a judicial policy judgment that those effects deserve antitrust condemnation.[70]

Efficiency justifications are also probably admissible under the quasi-per se rule. This is not entirely clear because the U.S. Supreme Court has so far rejected every efficiency justification that has been offered for tying, and often has done so using language indicating that it believes that generally no justification for tying exists that does not have a less restrictive alternative.[71] However, the Supreme Court has also

[69] Jefferson Parish Hosp. Dist. No. 2 v. Hyde, 466 U.S. 2 (1984); United States v. Loew's, Inc., 371 U.S. 38 (1962); N. Pac. Ry. Co. v. United States, 356 U.S. 1 (1958); Int'l Salt Co. v. United States, 332 U.S. 392 (1947).

[70] Elhauge, *Tying*, *supra* note 28, at 420–26; Elhauge, *Rehabilitating*, *supra* note 33, at 489–90, 497–501.

[71] *See International Salt*, 332 U.S. at 397–98; *Standard Stations,* 337 U.S. at 305–06; Times-Picayune Publishing v. United States, 345 U.S. 594, 605 (1953); *Northern Pacific*, 356 U.S. at 5–6 & n.5; *Loew's*, 371 U.S. at 44; *Jefferson Parish*, 466 U.S. at 9–10 & n.14, 25 n.42; IBM v. United States, 298 U.S. 131, 138–39 (1936).

consistently considered justifications before rejecting them.[72] Further, its most recent tying case states that the "view that tying arrangements may well be procompetitive ultimately prevailed" in its caselaw, which it categorized as rejecting the prior view that ties have no "legitimate business purpose" or "serve hardly any purpose beyond the suppression of competition."[73] This was dicta because the case concerned when market power existed, and the language could be read to mean only that ties have sufficient procompetitive virtues to require some showing of market power, but the case probably signals a willingness to consider a defense of procompetitive justifications even when market power exists. Moreover, efficiencies play a role in determining what counts as separate products that are capable of being tied together at all. However, unless the combination is a new product,[74] the Court seems to prefer to infer such efficiencies from competitive market practices rather than having them proven directly.[75] For example, competitive markets at one time sold cars without bumpers or wipers but later sold cars with bumpers and wipers included, thus indicating there were efficiencies to selling them together that changed them from separate products to a single car product.

In short, calling current U.S. tying doctrine a "quasi-per se" rule is really a misnomer. Rather, the doctrine provides for a bifurcated rule of reason review that requires proving either (a) tying market power and a substantial foreclosure amount or (b) a substantial tied foreclosure share, and then weighs any anticompetitive effects against any offered efficiency justifications.[76] Proving tying market power and a substantial dollar amount of foreclosure allows one to infer one of the three extraction or price discrimination effects absent any efficiency justification, and proving a substantial tied foreclosure share allows one to infer one of the other two anticompetitive effects absent an efficiency justification. The fact that the Court condemns ties based on tying market power and substantial dollar foreclosure, absent an efficiency justification, simply confirms that the Court views the extraction and price discrimination effects as sufficient to condemn ties under Sherman Act § 1 and Clayton Act § 3.[77]

---

72 *See* sources cited in last note; *Kodak*, 504 U.S. at 479–80 & n.27, 485–86; *Fortner I*, 394 U.S. at 506. *See also NCAA,* 468 U.S. at 104 n.26 (although the Court "has spoken of a 'per se' rule against tying arrangements, it has also recognized that tying may have procompetitive justifications that make it inappropriate to condemn without considerable market analysis.")

73 Illinois Tool Works v. Independent Ink, 547 U.S. 28, 36 (2006).

74 *See* United States v. Jerrold Electronics, 187 F.Supp. 545 (E.D. Pa. 1960), *aff'd per curiam*, 365 U.S. 567 (1961).

75 *See Jefferson Parish*, 466 U.S. at 19–24; *Kodak*, 504 U.S. at 462.

76 Elhauge, *Tying*, *supra* note 28, at 425–26; Elhauge, *Rehabilitating*, *supra* note 33, at 466–67.

77 Elhauge, *Tying*, *supra* note 28, at 420–26; Elhauge, *Rehabilitating*, *supra* note 33, at 489–90, 497–501. The extraction and price discrimination effects would presumably not suffice under Sherman Act § 2, because they would not show a causal connection between the tie and the degree of market power. *See* Elhauge, *Tying*, *supra* note 28, at 439 n.112; Chapter 3.D.

Whether we call it a quasi-per se rule or simply a specific form of rule of reason analysis, current U.S. tying doctrine has five elements:

(1) Separate Tying and Tied Products. The allegedly tied items cannot be mere components of a single product, like pens and pen caps. As noted, courts normally infer a single product from competitive market practices.[78] However, courts will also find a single product where the bundle combines components into a new product that operates better when bundled together by the defendant than when bundled together by the end user.[79] Two items (like aluminum ingot and manufacturing services) are also deemed parts of a single product if the buyers to whom the defendant sells only want them as a single finished product (say as aluminum tubes).[80] In such a case, a rival who seeks to have the defendant unbundle one of the items (say aluminum ingot) so the rival can make the same finished product as the defendant really is asserting not a tie but an antitrust duty to deal, which is subject to the limitations on that duty noted in Chapter 3.[81] Two items might also be deemed parts of a single product if intellectual property law encourages bundling them together.[82] Finally, rather than being components of a single product, two items might fail to be separate because they are really the same product.[83] Selling a product on the condition that the buyer purchase more of the same product is addressed not by tying doctrine but rather by doctrines involving exclusionary agreements on single products, like exclusive dealing.

(2) Tying Condition. The defendant must have sold the tying product on the condition that the purchaser take the seller's tied product. Such a condition might take the form of altering the tying product technologically to make rival products operate worse with it, when the technological alternation does not improve performance.[84] It might also take the form of coercive pricing, which charges buyers a higher price for the tying product unless the buyer accepts the tie. Such pricing is often called a bundled "discount," but can more aptly be described as an unbundled "penalty" whenever the unbundled price exceeds the but-for

---

78 *See* X AREEDA, ELHAUGE & HOVENKAMP, ANTITRUST LAW ¶ 1744–45 (1996).

79 *See id.* ¶ 1746.

80 *Id.* ¶ 1748.

81 As noted in Chapter 3.C.5, finished products are likely to involve (1) a fixed ratio of the components that make up the product and (2) strong demand correlation between the components given that buyers want to purchase them together as a finished product. For example, aluminum tubes involve a fixed ratio of aluminum ingot and manufacturing services, and buyers of tubes only want them together, so they have a perfect positive demand correlation. In such a case, the only likely anticompetitive effect is that refusing to sell aluminum ingot to the rival separately from manufacturing services might increase the degree of market power in the "tying" upstream market for aluminum ingot, which is the anticompetitive concern addressed by the antitrust doctrine on refusals to deal.

82 *See id.* ¶ 1749.

83 *See id.* ¶ 1747; *Times-Picayune*, 345 U.S. at 613–14.

84 *See id.* ¶ 1757 (but concluding this is true only for rule of reason review, and requires in addition proof of substantial foreclosure of the tied market and evidence that less than 10–25% of the complementary product used with the defendant's primary product comes from its rivals).

price that would have been charged without bundled pricing. Such an unbundled penalty can have the same extraction and price discrimination effects as a tie and thus should be condemnable based on tying market power and substantial dollar foreclosure, absent an efficiency justification, just as the quasi-per se rule does for ties.[85] Indeed, tying is really just a special case of unbundled penalty, where the unbundled price on the tying product is set at infinity. But, as Section 4.D will show, U.S. law on bundled pricing remains quite unclear.

(3) Non-Trivial Tied Sales. There must be a non-trivial dollar amount of sales in the tied product. A plaintiff need not show that a substantial share of the tied product is foreclosed, although four justices were ready to add that requirement in 1984.[86] However, proving a substantial foreclosure share would seem necessary if the theory of the case were that the tie anticompetitively increased tied or tying market power.

(4) Tying Market Power. The defendant must have market power in the tying product. Although past cases inferred this on thin grounds, more recent cases emphasize the need for real economic market power, with one recent U.S. Supreme Court case holding that a market share of 30% standing alone was not enough and another declining to infer such power from the mere existence of a patent.[87]

(5) No Offsetting Efficiencies. When the first four elements are proven, then a tie can probably still escape condemnation in cases where the defendant can prove the tie was the least restrictive means of producing offsetting efficiencies that were passed on to consumers to an extent large enough to eliminate any harm to consumer welfare.

If quasi-per se illegal tying cannot be proven, bundling can generally still be challenged under the other branch of the bifurcated rule of reason.[88] This branch would apply if the tying and tied products are not deemed separate or if the defendant lacks tying market power against the buyers of the tied products. Under this alternative branch, the plaintiff must show either proof of substantial foreclosure of some market or direct proof of the sort of anticompetitive effects that likely reflect substantial foreclosure.

[85] Elhauge, *Tying, supra* note 28, at 402–03, 450–455, 468–69. If the unbundled price does not exceed the but-for price, then the bundled discount cannot be anticompetitive unless a substantial foreclosure share exists and thus should not be treated the same as a tie under the quasi per se rule. *Id.* at 403, 451, 469–70.

[86] *See Jefferson Parish*, 466 U.S. 2 (O'Connor, J. joined by Burger, C.J., Powell and Rehnquist, JJ., concurring in the judgment).

[87] *See Jefferson Parish*, 466 U.S. 2; *Illinois Tool Works*, 547 U.S. 28.

[88] *See* Areeda, Elhauge & Hovenkamp, Antitrust Law ¶ 1742 (1996); *Times-Picayune*, 345 U.S. at 614–15; *Fortner I,* 394 U.S. at 499–500; *Jefferson Parish*, 466 U.S. at 18, 29–30.

Jefferson Parish Hospital v. Hyde

466 U.S. 2 (1984).

■ JUSTICE STEVENS delivered the opinion of the Court. . . .

In July 1977, respondent Edwin G. Hyde, a board certified anesthesiologist, applied for admission to the medical staff of East Jefferson Hospital. The credentials committee and the medical staff executive committee recommended approval, but the hospital board denied the application because the hospital was a party to a contract providing that all anesthesiological services required by the hospital's patients would be performed by Roux & Associates . . . Respondent then commenced this action seeking a declaratory judgment that the contract is unlawful and an injunction ordering petitioners to appoint him to the hospital staff . . .[4] . . . .

The Court of Appeals held that the case involves a "tying arrangement" because the "users of the hospital's operating rooms (the tying product) are also compelled to purchase the hospital's chosen anesthesia service (the tied product)." Having defined the relevant geographic market for the tying product as the East Bank of Jefferson Parish, the court held that the hospital possessed "sufficient market power in the tying market to coerce purchasers of the tied product." Since the purchase of the tied product constituted a "not insubstantial amount of interstate commerce," . . . the tying arrangement was therefore illegal "per se."

II

. . . It is far too late in the history of our antitrust jurisprudence to question the proposition that certain tying arrangements pose an unacceptable risk of stifling competition and therefore are unreasonable "per se." The rule was first enunciated in International Salt Co. v. United States, 332 U.S. 392, 396 (1947), and has been endorsed by this Court many times since. The rule also reflects congressional policies underlying the antitrust laws. In enacting § 3 of the Clayton Act, Congress expressed great concern about the anticompetitive character of tying arrangements. While this case does not arise under the Clayton Act, the congressional finding made therein concerning the competitive consequences of tying is illuminating, and must be respected.

It is clear, however, that every refusal to sell two products separately cannot be said to restrain competition. If each of the products may be purchased separately in a competitive market, one seller's decision to sell the two in a single package imposes no unreasonable restraint on either market, particularly if competing suppliers are free to sell either the

[4] . . . The fees for anesthesiological services are billed separately to the patients by the hospital. They cover the hospital's costs and the professional services provided by Roux. After a deduction of eight percent to provide a reserve for uncollectible accounts, the fees are divided equally between Roux and the hospital.

entire package or its several parts.[17] For example, we have written that "if one of a dozen food stores in a community were to refuse to sell flour unless the buyer also took sugar it would hardly tend to restrain competition if its competitors were ready and able to sell flour by itself." Northern Pac. R. Co. v. United States, 356 U.S. 1, 7 (1958). Buyers often find package sales attractive; a seller's decision to offer such packages can merely be an attempt to compete effectively—conduct that is entirely consistent with the Sherman Act.

Our cases have concluded that the essential characteristic of an invalid tying arrangement lies in the seller's exploitation of its control over the tying product to force the buyer into the purchase of a tied product that the buyer either did not want at all, or might have preferred to purchase elsewhere on different terms. When such "forcing" is present, competition on the merits in the market for the tied item is restrained and the Sherman Act is violated.

> ". . . By conditioning his sale of one commodity on the purchase of another, a seller coerces the abdication of buyers' independent judgment as to the 'tied' product's merits and insulates it from the competitive stresses of the open market. But any intrinsic superiority of the 'tied' product would convince freely choosing buyers to select it over others anyway." Times-Picayune Publishing Co. v. United States, 345 U.S. 594, 605 (1953).[19]

Accordingly, we have condemned tying arrangements when the seller has some special ability—usually called "market power"—to force a purchaser to do something that he would not do in a competitive

---

[17] "Of course where the buyer is free to take either product by itself there is no tying problem even though the seller may also offer the two items as a unit at a single price." Northern Pac. R. Co. v. United States, 356 U.S. 1, 6 n.4 (1958).

[19] . . . For example, Justice WHITE has written: "There is general agreement in the cases and among the commentators that the fundamental restraint against which the tying proscription is meant to guard is the use of power over one product to attain power over another, or otherwise to distort freedom of trade and competition in the second product. This distortion injures the buyers of the second product, who because of their preference for the seller's brand of the first are artificially forced to make a less than optimal choice in the second. And even if the customer is indifferent among brands of the second product and therefore loses nothing by agreeing to use the seller's brand of the second in order to get his brand of the first, such tying agreements may work significant restraints on competition in the tied product. The tying seller may be working toward a monopoly position in the tied product and, even if he is not, the practice of tying forecloses other sellers of the tied product and makes it more difficult for new firms to enter that market. They must be prepared not only to match existing sellers of the tied product in price and quality, but to offset the attraction of the tying product itself. Even if this is possible through simultaneous entry into production of the tying product, entry into both markets is significantly more expensive than simple entry into the tied market, and shifting buying habits in the tied product is considerably more cumbersome and less responsive to variations in competitive offers. In addition to these anticompetitive effects in the tied product, tying arrangements may be used to evade price control in the tying product through clandestine transfer of the profit to the tied product; they may be used as a counting device to effect price discrimination; and they may be used to force a full line of products on the customer so as to extract more easily from him a monopoly return on one unique product in the line." Fortner Enterprises v. United States Steel Corp. (Fortner I), 394 U.S. 495, 512–514 (1969) (dissenting opinion) (footnotes omitted).

market.[20] When "forcing" occurs, our cases have found the tying arrangement to be unlawful.

Thus, the law draws a distinction between the exploitation of market power by merely enhancing the price of the tying product, on the one hand, and by attempting to impose restraints on competition in the market for a tied product, on the other. When the seller's power is just used to maximize its return in the tying product market, where presumably its product enjoys some justifiable advantage over its competitors, the competitive ideal of the Sherman Act is not necessarily compromised. But if that power is used to impair competition on the merits in another market, a potentially inferior product may be insulated from competitive pressures. This impairment could either harm existing competitors or create barriers to entry of new competitors in the market for the tied product, and can increase the social costs of market power by facilitating price discrimination, thereby increasing monopoly profits over what they would be absent the tie.[23] And from the standpoint of the consumer—whose interests the statute was especially intended to serve—the freedom to select the best bargain in the second market is impaired by his need to purchase the tying product, and perhaps by an inability to evaluate the true cost of either product when they are available only as a package. . . .

Per se condemnation—condemnation without inquiry into actual market conditions—is only appropriate if the existence of forcing is probable. Thus, application of the per se rule focuses on the probability of anticompetitive consequences. Of course, as a threshold matter there must be a substantial potential for impact on competition in order to justify per se condemnation. If only a single purchaser were "forced" with respect to the purchase of a tied item, the resultant impact on competition would not be sufficient to warrant the concern of antitrust law. It is for this reason that we have refused to condemn tying arrangements unless a substantial volume of commerce is foreclosed thereby. Similarly, when a purchaser is "forced" to buy a product he would not have otherwise bought even from another seller in the tied product market, there can be no adverse impact on competition because no portion of the market which would otherwise have been available to other sellers has been foreclosed.

Once this threshold is surmounted, per se prohibition is appropriate if anticompetitive forcing is likely. For example, if the government has

[20] This type of market power has sometimes been referred to as "leverage." Professors Areeda and Turner provide a definition that suits present purposes. " 'Leverage' is loosely defined here as a supplier's ability to induce his customer for one product to buy a second product from him that would not otherwise be purchased solely on the merit of that second product." V. P. Areeda & D. Turner, Antitrust Law ¶ 1134a at 202 (1980).

[23] Sales of the tied item can be used to measure demand for the tying item; purchasers with greater needs for the tied item make larger purchases and in effect must pay a higher price to obtain the tying item. . . . Bowman, Tying Arrangements and the Leverage Problem, 67 Yale L.J. 19 (1957); Burstein, A Theory of Full-Line Forcing, 55 Nw.U.L.Rev. 62 (1960); . . . Stigler, United States v. Loew's Inc.: A Note on Block Booking, 1963 Sup.Ct.Rev. 152.

granted the seller a patent or similar monopoly over a product, it is fair to presume that the inability to buy the product elsewhere gives the seller market power. Any effort to enlarge the scope of the patent monopoly by using the market power it confers to restrain competition in the market for a second product will undermine competition on the merits in that second market. Thus, the sale or lease of a patented item on condition that the buyer make all his purchases of a separate tied product from the patentee is unlawful.

The same strict rule is appropriate in other situations in which the existence of market power is probable. When the seller's share of the market is high, or when the seller offers a unique product that competitors are not able to offer, the Court has held that the likelihood that market power exists and is being used to restrain competition in a separate market is sufficient to make per se condemnation appropriate. Thus, in *Northern Pac.*, we held that the railroad's control over vast tracts of western real estate, although not itself unlawful, gave the railroad a unique kind of bargaining power that enabled it to tie the sales of that land to exclusive, long term commitments that fenced out competition in the transportation market over a protracted period. When, however, the seller does not have either the degree or the kind of market power that enables him to force customers to purchase a second, unwanted product in order to obtain the tying product, an antitrust violation can be established only by evidence of an unreasonable restraint on competition in the relevant market.

In sum, any inquiry into the validity of a tying arrangement must focus on the market or markets in which the two products are sold, for that is where the anticompetitive forcing has its impact. Thus, in this case our analysis of the tying issue must focus on the hospital's sale of services to its patients, rather than its contractual arrangements with the providers of anesthesiological services. In making that analysis, we must consider whether petitioners are selling two separate products that may be tied together, and, if so, whether they have used their market power to force their patients to accept the tying arrangement.

III

The hospital has provided its patients with a package that includes the range of facilities and services required for a variety of surgical operations. At East Jefferson Hospital the package includes the services of the anesthesiologist.[28] Petitioners argue that the package does not involve a tying arrangement at all—that they are merely providing a functionally integrated package of services. . . .

---

[28] It is essential to differentiate between the Roux contract and the legality of the contract between the hospital and its patients. The Roux contract is nothing more than an arrangement whereby Roux supplies all of the hospital's needs for anesthesiological services. That contract raises only an exclusive dealing question. The issue here is whether the hospital's insistence that its patients purchase anesthesiological services from Roux creates a tying arrangement.

Our cases indicate, however, that the answer to the question whether one or two products are involved turns not on the functional relation between them, but rather on the character of the demand for the two items.[30] In *Times-Picayune,* the Court held that a tying arrangement was not present because the arrangement did not link two distinct markets for products that were distinguishable in the eyes of buyers. . . .

The requirement that two distinguishable product markets be involved follows from the underlying rationale of the rule against tying. The definitional question depends on whether the arrangement may have the type of competitive consequences addressed by the rule. The answer to the question whether petitioners have utilized a tying arrangement must be based on whether there is a possibility that the economic effect of the arrangement is that condemned by the rule against tying—that petitioners have foreclosed competition on the merits in a product market distinct from the market for the tying item.[34] Thus, in this case no tying arrangement can exist unless there is a sufficient demand for the purchase of anesthesiological services separate from hospital services to identify a distinct product market in which it is efficient to offer anesthesiological services separately from hospital services.

Unquestionably, the anesthesiological component of the package offered by the hospital could be provided separately and could be selected either by the individual patient or by one of the patient's doctors if the hospital did not insist on including anesthesiological services in the package it offers to its customers. As a matter of actual practice, anesthesiological services are billed separately from the hospital services petitioners provide. There was ample and uncontroverted testimony that patients or surgeons often request specific anesthesiologists to come to a hospital and provide anesthesia, and that the choice of an individual anesthesiologist separate from the choice of a hospital is particularly

[30] The fact that anesthesiological services are functionally linked to the other services provided by the hospital is not in itself sufficient to remove the Roux contract from the realm of tying arrangements. We have often found arrangements involving functionally linked products at least one of which is useless without the other to be prohibited tying devices. *See Mercoid Corp. v. Mid-Continent Co.,* 320 U.S. 661 (1944) (heating system and stoker switch); *Morton Salt Co. v. Suppiger Co.,* 314 U.S. 488 (1942) (salt machine and salt); *International Salt, supra* (same); *Leitch Mfg. Co. v. Barber Co.,* 302 U.S. 458 (1938) (process patent and material used in the patented process); *IBM v. United States,* 298 U.S. 131 (1936) (computer and computer punch cards); *Carbice Corp. v. American Patents Corp.,* 283 U.S. 27 (1931) (ice cream transportation package and coolant); *FTC v. Sinclair Refining Co.,* 261 U.S. 463 (1923) (gasoline and underground tanks and pumps); *United Shoe Mach. Co. v. United States,* 258 U.S. 451 (1921) (shoe machinery and supplies, maintenance, and peripheral machinery); *United States v. Jerrold Electronics Corp.,* 187 F.Supp. 545, 558–560 (E.D. Pa.1960) (components of television antennas), aff'd, 365 U.S. 567 (1961) (*per curiam*). In fact, in some situations the functional link between the two items may enable the seller to maximize its monopoly return on the tying item as a means of charging a higher rent or purchase price to a larger user of the tying item. *See* n. 23, *supra.*

[34] Of course, the Sherman Act does not prohibit "tying," it prohibits "contracts . . . in restraint of trade." Thus, in a sense the question whether this case involves "tying" is beside the point. The legality of petitioners' conduct depends on its competitive consequences, not whether it can be labeled "tying." If the competitive consequences of this arrangement are not those to which the per se rule is addressed, then it should not be condemned irrespective of its label.

frequent in respondent's specialty, obstetric anesthesiology.[36] . . . The record amply supports the conclusion that consumers differentiate between anesthesiological services and the other hospital services provided by petitioners.[39]

Thus, the hospital's requirement that its patients obtain necessary anesthesiological services from Roux combined the purchase of two distinguishable services in a single transaction. Nevertheless, the fact that this case involves a required purchase of two services that would otherwise be purchased separately does not make the Roux contract illegal. As noted above, there is nothing inherently anticompetitive about packaged sales. Only if patients are forced to purchase Roux's services as a result of the hospital's market power would the arrangement have anticompetitive consequences. If no forcing is present, patients are free to enter a competing hospital and to use another anesthesiologist instead of Roux.[41] The fact that petitioners' patients are required to purchase two separate items is only the beginning of the appropriate inquiry.[42]

---

36 . . . As a statistical matter, only 27 per cent of anesthesiologists have financial relationships with hospitals. . . .

39 One of the most frequently cited statements on this subject was made by Judge Van Dusen in *United States v. Jerrold Electronics Corp.,* 187 F.Supp. 545 (E.D. Pa.1960), aff'd, 365 U.S. 567 (1961) (*per curiam*). While this statement was specifically made with respect to § 3 of the Clayton Act, its analysis is also applicable to § 1 of the Sherman Act, since with respect to the definition of tying the standards used by the two statutes are the same. *See Times-Picayune.*

"There are several facts presented in this record which tend to show that a community television antenna system cannot properly be characterized as a single product. Others who entered the community antenna field offered all the equipment necessary for a complete system, but none of them sold their gear exclusively as a single package as did Jerrold. The record also establishes that the number of pieces in each system varied considerably so that hardly any two versions of the alleged product were the same. Furthermore, the customer was charged for each item of equipment and not a lump sum for total payment. Finally, while Jerrold had cable and antennas to sell which were manufactured by other concerns, it required that the electronic equipment in the system be bought from it." 187 F.Supp., at 559.

The record here shows that other hospitals often permit anesthesiological services to be purchased separately, that anesthesiologists are not fungible in that the services provided by each are not precisely the same, that anesthesiological services are billed separately, and that the hospital required purchases from Roux even though other anesthesiologists were available and Roux had no objection to their receiving staff privileges at East Jefferson. Therefore, the *Jerrold* analysis indicates that there was a tying arrangement here. *Jerrold* also indicates that tying may be permissible when necessary to enable a new business to break into the market. *See id.,* at 555–558. Assuming this defense exists, and assuming it justified the 1971 Roux contract in order to give Roux an incentive to go to work at a new hospital with an uncertain future, that justification is inapplicable to the 1976 contract, since by then Roux was willing to continue to service the hospital without a tying arrangement.

41 An examination of the reason or reasons why petitioners denied respondent staff privileges will not provide the answer to the question whether the package of services they offered to their patients is an illegal tying arrangement. As a matter of antitrust law, petitioners may give their anesthesiology business to Roux because he is the best doctor available, because he is willing to work long hours, or because he is the son-in-law of the hospital administrator without violating the per se rule against tying. Without evidence that petitioners are using market power to force Roux upon patients there is no basis to view the arrangement as unreasonably restraining competition whatever the reasons for its creation. Conversely, with such evidence, the per se rule against tying may apply. Thus, we reject the view of the District Court that the legality of an arrangement of this kind turns on whether it was adopted for the purpose of improving patient care.

42 Petitioners argue and the District Court found that the exclusive contract had what it characterized as procompetitive justifications in that an exclusive contract ensures 24-hour anesthesiology coverage, enables flexible scheduling, and facilitates work routine, professional

IV

The question remains whether this arrangement involves the use of market power to force patients to buy services they would not otherwise purchase. Respondent's only basis for invoking the per se rule against tying and thereby avoiding analysis of actual market conditions is by relying on the preference of persons residing in Jefferson Parish to go to East Jefferson, the closest hospital. A preference of this kind, however, is not necessarily probative of significant market power.

Seventy per cent of the patients residing in Jefferson Parish enter hospitals other than East Jefferson. Thus East Jefferson's "dominance" over persons residing in Jefferson Parish is far from overwhelming.[43] The fact that a substantial majority of the parish's residents elect not to enter East Jefferson means that the geographic data does not establish the kind of dominant market position that obviates the need for further inquiry into actual competitive conditions. The Court of Appeals acknowledged as much; it recognized that East Jefferson's market share alone was insufficient as a basis to infer market power, and buttressed its conclusion by relying on "market imperfections" that permit petitioners to charge noncompetitive prices for hospital services: the prevalence of third party payment for health care costs reduces price competition, and a lack of adequate information renders consumers unable to evaluate the quality of the medical care provided by competing hospitals. While these factors may generate "market power" in some abstract sense,[46] they do not generate the kind of market power that justifies condemnation of tying.

Tying arrangements need only be condemned if they restrain competition on the merits by forcing purchases that would not otherwise be made. A lack of price or quality competition does not create this type of forcing. If consumers lack price consciousness, that fact will not force them to take an anesthesiologist whose services they do not want—their indifference to price will have no impact on their willingness or ability to

standards and maintenance of equipment. The Court of Appeals held these findings to be clearly erroneous since the exclusive contract was not necessary to achieve these ends. Roux was willing to provide 24-hour coverage even without an exclusive contract and the credentials committee of the hospital could impose standards for staff privileges that would ensure staff would comply with the demands of scheduling, maintenance, and professional standards. In the past, we have refused to tolerate manifestly anticompetitive conduct simply because the health care industry is involved. *See Maricopa.* Petitioners seek no special solicitude. We have also uniformly rejected similar "goodwill" defenses for tying arrangements, finding that the use of contractual quality specifications are generally sufficient to protect quality without the use of a tying arrangement. *See Standard Stations; International Salt; IBM v. United States,* 298 U.S. 131, 138–140 (1936). Since the District Court made no finding as to why contractual quality specifications would not protect the hospital, there is no basis for departing from our prior cases here.

[43] In fact its position in this market is not dissimilar from the market share at issue in *Times-Picayune,* which the Court found insufficient as a basis for inferring market power. Moreover, in other antitrust contexts this Court has found that market shares comparable to that present here do not create an unacceptable likelihood of anticompetitive conduct. *See United States v. Connecticut National Bank,* 418 U.S. 656 (1974); *du Pont.*

[46] As an economic matter, market power exists whenever prices can be raised above the levels that would be charged in a competitive market. *See Fortner II,* 429 U.S., at 620; *Fortner I,* 394 U.S., at 503–504.

go to another hospital where they can utilize the services of the anesthesiologist of their choice. Similarly, if consumers cannot evaluate the quality of anesthesiological services, it follows that they are indifferent between certified anesthesioligists even in the absence of a tying arrangement—such an arrangement cannot be said to have foreclosed a choice that would have otherwise been made "on the merits."

Thus, neither of the "market imperfections" relied upon by the Court of Appeals forces consumers to take anesthesiological services they would not select in the absence of a tie. It is safe to assume that every patient undergoing a surgical operation needs the services of an anesthesiologist; at least this record contains no evidence that the hospital "forced" any such services on unwilling patients.[47] The record therefore does not provide a basis for applying the per se rule against tying to this arrangement.

V

In order to prevail in the absence of per se liability, respondent has the burden of proving that the Roux contract violated the Sherman Act because it unreasonably restrained competition. That burden necessarily involves an inquiry into the actual effect of the exclusive contract on competition among anesthesiologists. This competition takes place in a market that has not been defined. The market is not necessarily the same as the market in which hospitals compete in offering services to patients; it may encompass competition among anesthesiologists for exclusive contracts such as the Roux contract and might be statewide or merely local.[48] There is, however, insufficient evidence in this record to provide

---

[47] Nor is there an indication in the record that respondents' practices have increased the social costs of its market power. Since patients' anesthesiological needs are fixed by medical judgment, respondent does not argue that the tying arrangement facilitates price discrimination. Where variable-quantity purchasing is unavailable as a means to enable price discrimination, commentators have seen less justification for condemning tying. While tying arrangements like the one at issue here are unlikely to be used to facilitate price discrimination, they could have the similar effect of enabling hospitals "to evade price control in the tying product through clandestine transfer of the profit to the tied product. . . ." *Fortner I,* 394 U.S., at 513 (WHITE, J., dissenting). Insurance companies are the principal source of price restraint in the hospital industry; they place some limitations on the ability of hospitals to exploit their market power. Through this arrangement, petitioners may be able to evade that restraint by obtaining a portion of the anesthesioligists' fees and therefore realize a greater return than they could in the absence of the arrangement. This could also have an adverse effect on the anesthesiology market since it is possible that only less able anesthesiologists would be willing to give up part of their fees in return for the security of an exclusive contract. However, there are no findings of either the District Court or the Court of Appeals which indicate that this type of exploitation of market power has occurred here. The Court of Appeals found only that Roux's use of nurse anesthetists increased its and the hospital's profits, but there was no finding that nurse anesthetists might not be used with equal frequency absent the exclusive contract. Indeed, the District Court found that nurse anesthetists are utilized in all hospitals in the area. Moreover, there is nothing in the record which details whether this arrangement has enhanced the value of East Jefferson's market power or harmed quality competition in the anesthesiology market.

[48] While there was some rather impressionistic testimony that the prevalence of exclusive contracts tended to discourage young doctors from entering the market, the evidence was equivocal and neither the District Court nor the Court of Appeals made any findings concerning the contract's effect on entry barriers. Respondent does not press the point before this Court. It is possible that under some circumstances an exclusive contract could raise entry barriers since

a basis for finding that the Roux contract, as it actually operates in the market, has unreasonably restrained competition. The record sheds little light on how this arrangement affected consumer demand for separate arrangements with a specific anesthesiologist. The evidence indicates that some surgeons and patients preferred respondent's services to those of Roux, but there is no evidence that any patient who was sophisticated enough to know the difference between two anesthesiologists was not also able to go to a hospital that would provide him with the anesthesiologist of his choice.[50]

In sum, all that the record establishes is that the choice of anesthesiologists at East Jefferson has been limited to one of the four doctors who are associated with Roux and therefore have staff privileges.[51] Even if Roux did not have an exclusive contract, the range of alternatives open to the patient would be severely limited by the nature of the transaction and the hospital's unquestioned right to exercise some control over the identity and the number of doctors to whom it accords staff privileges. If respondent is admitted to the staff of East Jefferson, the range of choice will be enlarged from four to five doctors, but the most significant restraints on the patient's freedom to select a specific anesthesiologist will nevertheless remain.[52] Without a showing of actual adverse effect on competition, respondent cannot make out a case under the antitrust laws, and no such showing has been made. . . . [R]eversed.

■ JUSTICE BRENNAN, with whom JUSTICE MARSHALL joins, concurring. As the opinion for the Court demonstrates, we have long held that tying arrangements are subject to evaluation for *per se* illegality under § 1 of the Sherman Act. Whatever merit the policy arguments against this longstanding construction of the Act might have, Congress, presumably aware of our decisions, has never changed the rule by amending the Act. In such circumstances, our practice usually has been to stand by a settled statutory interpretation and leave the task of modifying the statute's

anesthesioligists could not compete for the contract without raising the capital necessary to run a hospital-wide operation. However, since the hospital has provided most of the capital for the exclusive contractor in this case, that problem does not appear to be present.

[50] If, as is likely, it is the patient's doctor and not the patient who selects an anesthesiologist, the doctor can simply take the patient elsewhere if he is dissatisfied with Roux. The District Court found that most doctors in the area have staff privileges at more than one hospital.

[51] The effect of the contract has, of course, been to remove the East Jefferson Hospital from the market open to Roux's competitors. Like any exclusive requirements contract, this contract could be unlawful if it foreclosed so much of the market from penetration by Roux's competitors as to unreasonably restrain competition in the affected market, the market for anesthesiological services. *See* generally *Tampa Electric*; *Standard Stations.* However, respondent has not attempted to make this showing.

[52] The record simply tells us little if anything about the effect of this arrangement on price or quality of anesthesiological services. As to price, the arrangement did not lead to an increase in the price charged to the patient. As to quality, the record indicates little more than that there have never been any complaints about the quality of Roux's services, and no contention that his services are in any respect inferior to those of respondent. Moreover, the self interest of the hospital, as well as the ethical and professional norms under which it operates, presumably protect the quality of anesthesiological services.

reach to Congress. I see no reason to depart from that principle in this case and therefore join the opinion and judgment of the Court.

■ JUSTICE O'CONNOR, with whom CHIEF JUSTICE BURGER, JUSTICE POWELL, and JUSTICE REHNQUIST join, concurring in the judgment. . . . I concur in the Court's decision to reverse but write separately to explain why I believe the Hospital-Roux contract, whether treated as effecting a tie between services provided to patients, or as an exclusive dealing arrangement between the Hospital and certain anesthesiologists, is properly analyzed under the Rule of Reason.

. . . The Court has on occasion applied a *per se* rule of illegality in actions alleging tying in violation of § 1 of the Sherman Act. Under the usual logic of the *per se* rule, a restraint on trade that rarely serves any purposes other than to restrain competition is illegal without proof of market power or anti-competitive effect. . . . Some of our earlier cases did indeed declare that tying arrangements serve "hardly any purpose beyond the suppression of competition." *Standard Stations.* However, this declaration was not taken literally even by the cases that purported to rely upon it. In practice, a tie has been illegal only if the seller is shown to have "sufficient economic power with respect to the tying product to appreciably restrain free competition in the market for the tied product. . . ." *Northern Pacific,* . . . . The Court has never been willing to say of tying arrangements, as it has of price-fixing, division of markets and other agreements subject to *per se* analysis, that they are always illegal, without proof of market power or anticompetitive effect.

The "*per se*" doctrine in tying cases has thus always required an elaborate inquiry into the economic effects of the tying arrangement.[1] As a result, tying doctrine incurs the costs of a rule of reason approach without achieving its benefits: the doctrine calls for the extensive and time-consuming economic analysis characteristic of the rule of reason, but then may be interpreted to prohibit arrangements that economic analysis would show to be beneficial. . . . The time has therefore come to abandon the "*per se*" label and refocus the inquiry on the adverse economic effects, and the potential economic benefits, that the tie may have. . . .

For products to be treated as distinct, the tied product must, at a minimum, be one that some consumers might wish to purchase separately *without also purchasing the tying product.* When the tied product has no use other than in conjunction with the tying product, a seller of the tying product can acquire no *additional* market power by selling the two products together. . . . [T]here is no sound economic reason for treating surgery and anesthesia as separate services. Patients

---

1 This inquiry has been required in analyzing both the prima facie case and affirmative defenses. Most notably, *Jerrold Electronics Corp.*, upheld a requirement that buyers of television systems purchase the complete system, as well as installation and repair service, on the grounds that the tie assured that the systems would operate and thereby protected the seller's business reputation.

are interested in purchasing anesthesia only in conjunction with hospital services, so the Hospital can acquire no *additional* market power by selling the two services together. Accordingly, the link between the Hospital's services and anesthesia administered by Roux will affect neither the amount of anesthesia provided nor the combined price of anesthesia and surgery for those who choose to become the Hospital's patients. In these circumstances, anesthesia and surgical services should probably not be characterized as distinct products for tying purposes.

Even if they are, the tying should not be considered a violation of § 1 of the Sherman Act because tying here cannot increase the seller's already absolute power over the volume of production of the tied product, which is an inevitable consequence of the fact that very few patients will choose to undergo surgery without receiving anesthesia. The Hospital-Roux contract therefore has little potential to harm the patients. On the other side of the balance, the District Court found, and the Court of Appeals did not dispute, that the tie-in conferred significant benefits upon the hospital and the patients that it served. . . .

Whether or not the Hospital-Roux contract is characterized as a tie between distinct products, the contract unquestionably does constitute exclusive dealing. Exclusive dealing arrangements are independently subject to scrutiny under § 1 of the Sherman Act, and are also analyzed under the Rule of Reason. *Tampa Electric*. . . . At issue here is an exclusive dealing arrangement between a firm of four anesthesiologists and one relatively small hospital. . . . Plainly . . . the arrangement forecloses only a small fraction of the markets in which anesthesiologists may sell their services, and a still smaller fraction of the market in which hospitals may secure anesthesiological services. The contract therefore survives scrutiny under the Rule of Reason. . . .

NOTES AND QUESTIONS ON *JEFFERSON PARISH*

1. ***Is the Court correct that it is too late to question the quasi-per se rule against tying?*** The general rule is that *stare decisis* is particularly strong for interpretations of statutes, on the ground that the legislature could have overridden the interpretation if it wanted.[89] However, the antitrust statute uses common law language about "restraints of trade" and has long been interpreted in a common law fashion. Using that approach, the Court had for decades been modifying elements to tying doctrine, especially requiring stronger evidence of tying market power. Further, the Court has narrowed or abandoned many other previous per se rules. This includes not only the *BMI* and *Northwest Stationers* cases on horizontal price-fixing and boycotts, *see* Chapter 2, but also overruling three per se rules on vertical distributional restraints. *See* Chapter 5.

Although the Court stressed legislative history showing that the Congress that enacted Clayton Act § 3 was opposed to tying, it is not clear why that should affect the interpretation of Sherman Act § 1 in this non-

---

[89] ELHAUGE, STATUTORY DEFAULT RULES 211–223 (Harvard University Press 2008).

goods case. Nor does that legislative history seem to dictate the result here given that the text of Clayton Act § 3 requires a showing that "the effect . . . may be to substantially lessen competition". In any event, the Court did not ultimately rest on this legislative history, but instead went on to explain why ties that satisfied the quasi per se rule did have anticompetitive effects.

2. ***What does the Court say justifies the quasi-per se rule?*** The quasi per se rule on tying is not really a per se rule because it requires evidence of tying market power and a substantial dollar amount of foreclosure, and it allows defendants to offer procompetitive efficiencies. As noted in the introduction to this section, tying market power and a substantial dollar amount of foreclosure are sufficient for tying to facilitate price discrimination or extract consumer welfare that harms consumer welfare, but insufficient for tying to increase the degree of market power in the tying or tied markets. The quasi per se rule thus amounts to a form of rule of reason review that fits with the conclusion that it is anticompetitive to reduce consumer welfare by using ties to restrain competition in ways that increase price discrimination or extract consumer surplus. Indeed, the Court stressed that the illegitimate impairment of competition could either be to competitors and barriers to entry or could involve "facilitating price discrimination," and in support of the latter the Court cited the seminal articles for each of the three theories for how tying could harm consumer welfare by facilitating price discrimination or extraction.

The concurring view that the doctrine should require a substantial foreclosure share assumes instead that not all restraints that lower consumer welfare are anticompetitive, but rather that a restraint is anticompetitive only if it increases the degree of market power in some market. Which do you think makes more sense? Why should any restraints of trade that reduce consumer welfare be allowed?

3. ***Does it seem likely that the tie here had price discrimination or extraction effects?*** No. As the Court stressed, "It is safe to assume that every patient undergoing a surgical operation needs the services of an anesthesiologist." Thus, the products lacked separate utility. The Court also stressed in footnote 47 that "patients' anesthesiological needs are fixed by medical judgment." This statement indicates that the tied services were also used in fixed proportions. As noted in the introduction, tying cannot facilitate price discrimination or extraction when the tied products have a fixed ratio and lack separate utility. The Court seemed to recognize this, stating in support of its conclusion that the quasi per se rule should not apply to this particular restraint that: "Where variable-quantity purchasing is unavailable as a means to enable price discrimination, commentators have seen less justification for condemning tying." *See* n.47.

The implausibility of price discrimination or extraction effects here is probably part of what influenced the concurrence to call for requiring a substantial foreclosure share. But the majority concluded that, while that conclusion was appropriate for this particular tie given the fixed ratio and lack of separate utility, that conclusion should not be generalized to all ties.

4. ***What does the Court require to show the necessary "forcing" for a tying agreement?*** The Court equated forcing or coercion with the existence of a tying condition by a firm with tying market power, stating, "By conditioning his sale of one commodity on the purchase of another, a seller coerces the abdication of buyers' independent judgment as to the 'tied' product's merits." The Court did not purport to overrule the holdings in United Shoe Machinery v. United States, 258 U.S. 451 (1922), that it is irrelevant whether (a) the tie was frequently unenforced and (b) the buyers would have bought the defendant's tied product without the tie. To the contrary, *Jefferson Parish* stressed that the requisite forcing existed if the buyer bought a tied product that it "might have preferred to purchase elsewhere on different terms" and that distorting buyers' independent judgment sufficed.

This conclusion makes sense because a buyer's willingness to buy the tied product from the defendant even without a tie would not prevent any of the extraction or price discrimination effects from increasing the prices buyers would pay for the combination of tying and tied products. Buyers who would have bought the same product from the defendant would also still suffer from any foreclosure share effects because, absent that foreclosure, they would have been able to buy the defendant's product at a lower price. Moreover, rational firms would not bother having a tying agreement unless they expected it to alter buyer choices.

5. ***Does it make sense that the Court states that a tie would not be illegal if the tie foreclosed only a single low-volume purchaser or only a purchaser who did not want to buy the tied product from anyone?*** Yes. A tie that forecloses only a single low-volume purchaser cannot have the feared anticompetitive effects. Price discrimination effects by definition require discriminating among *multiple* buyers. Further, regardless of the number of purchasers, foreclosing a low dollar volume cannot create significant price discrimination or extraction effects nor create the substantial foreclosure share necessary to increase the degree of market power in the tied or tying markets.

A tie that forecloses a purchaser who did not want to buy the tied product from anyone also cannot have price discrimination effects, which require some buyer demand for the tied product that is either correlated with demand for the tying product (for intra-product price discrimination) or not too correlated (for inter-product price discrimination). Extraction effects generally involve a requirements tie, which cannot extract anything if the buyer does not buy the tied product at all, and requiring the purchase of a fixed amount of unwanted tied product would never be more advantageous to the seller than instead requiring buyers to pay a lump sum for the right to purchase the tying product, given that the latter option avoids the cost of making the tied product. Foreclosing unwanted purchases also cannot lessen the competitiveness of tied product rivals or increase tying market power, because those unwanted purchases would not be made from anyone without the tie.

6. ***Does the Court's separate products test make sense?*** The Court stated "no tying arrangement can exist unless there is sufficient

demand for the purchase of [the tied product] separate from [the tying product] to identify a distinct product market in which it is efficient to offer [the tied product] separately from [the tying product]." However, the Court did not directly examine the extent of such demand and existence of such efficiencies. Instead, the Court inferred them from actual market practices in competitive markets. The Court found that anesthesiological services were often unbundled from hospital services in other markets, which indicated there must be sufficient demand to make it efficient to offer them separately, making them separate products. Likewise, one can infer from the fact that left and right shoes are *not* unbundled in competitive markets that there must not be sufficient demand to make it efficient to sell them separately, making a pair of shoes is a single product.

While such an inference can be made from competitive market practices, the same inference could not be made if in uncompetitive markets a monopolist prevented any separate sale of the tied product. Such bundling could be profitable because of anticompetitive profits rather than because of efficiencies.

Why infer separate products from competitive market practices, rather than based on direct inquiry into the efficiencies of unbundling? Mainly because the single-product test is supposed to operate as a screen that can avoid further expensive litigation. If competitive market practices show it is inefficient to offer the products unbundled, then we need no further inquiry to conclude the bundle should be allowed categorically, which is achieved by saying it involves a single product and thus no tie at all. When competitive market practices fail to show this, or we have no baseline other than uncompetitive market practices, no categorical inference can be drawn. Instead, the courts must directly inquire not only about whether the defendant's tie has efficiencies, but also about whether less restrictive alternatives exist and whether any efficiencies are sufficiently passed on to consumers to offset any anticompetitive effects.

Jefferson Parish's conclusion that no tie can exist without enough demand to efficiently offer the tied product separately means that such a showing is necessary to declare separate products, but does not mean it *suffices* to do so. For example, in competitive markets, mufflers are often sold separately from cars, but that does not mean that a firm that sells cars with mufflers installed has tied together two products. The reason is that on competitive markets there is no general market practice of selling cars without mufflers, presumably because it is not efficient to do so. Thus, for competitive market practices to indicate separate products, they must show that both the tying and tied products are often sold unbundled. That was true in *Jefferson Parish*, so the Court was not focused on the fact that in other markets the separate provision of the tied product might not necessarily mean separate provision of the tying product.

While the Court relied in part on the separate billing of anesthesiological services from hospital services, such separate billing of components will not always be a reliable indicator that separate provision is efficient. For example, suppose certain factory-installed car options are priced separately, but are hardly ever sold separately. Buyers may for example have the option of buying plastic or wood paneling, but hardly never purchase cars without paneling and get paneling from other manufacturer. Such separate billing may reflect a customer preference for customized products, without necessarily indicating that it is efficient for customers to buy the products from separate manufacturers.

Was the Court right to reject the concurring opinion's test that products cannot be separate if the tied product cannot function without the tying product? As the Court pointed out, such a test would be inconsistent with precedent. *See* n.29. Nor would such a test accurately identify cases where no anticompetitive effects are possible. It would show the products lack separate utility, which would preclude inter-product price discrimination for reasons noted in this Section's introduction. However, it would not show a fixed ratio, and thus could not preclude any of the other anticompetitive effects.

Moreover, the concurrence's single-product test would perversely focus tying doctrine on the cases with the lowest foreclosure shares, because separate uses for the tying product will reduce the percentage of the tied market that could be possibly foreclosed by tying. In contrast, in cases where there is no separate use for the tied product, the concurrence's test would immunize a tying product monopolist who forecloses the tied market completely. For example, under the concurrence's test, tying doctrine would apply to a tie of salt-injection machines to salt, even though the foreclosure share there would be trivial given alternative uses of salt. In contrast, the concurrence's test would immunize a can-closing machine monopolist who ties those machines to cans, even though the foreclosure share there would be nearly 100% given that cans are almost always sold to be closed.

7. Is the Court right that there was insufficient evidence of tying market power to trigger the quasi-per se rule? The Court held that a 30% market share among patients going to hospitals in Jefferson Parish was not alone sufficient to show tying market power that triggers the quasi-per se. The Court recognized market power could be proven with evidence other than market share, but held that such evidence was not shown. The Court of Appeals had concluded that market power was shown by evidence that consumers are price insensitive because of insurance and lack of information. But the Supreme Court reasoned that although such price insensitivity means consumers might be willing to pay more than the competitive price, it is not the type of market power that raises tying concerns, given that it is equally applicable in all hospitals and thus does not bear on how free consumers are to switch to a non-tying seller. Another way to put the point is that such evidence merely shows a general market price inelasticity, which does not bear on whether a particular firm has more power than other firms in the market.

8. Did the Court reject procompetitive justifications on principle for tying agreements or because the facts of this case do not support them? The Court said in footnote 42 that its past cases had uniformly rejected similar quality justifications for tying because specifications were generally a less restrictive alternative, and that there was no basis for departing from these cases, because the district court made no finding about why specifications would not suffice. This suggests that the Court either views its case law as establishing only a presumptive rejection of such justifications that can be rebutted, or is inviting a court to make factual findings that might justify overruling this precedent.

The claimed justification was that the tie "ensures 24-hour anesthesiology coverage, enables flexible scheduling, and facilitates work routine, professional standards and maintenance of equipment." *See* n.42. There are reasons to doubt that justifications could always be equally advanced through "contractual quality specifications" because such specifications could create monitoring costs and incentive problems. If multiple anesthesiologists were using the hospital, then a hospital would, for example, have to (a) monitor them to see who failed to maintain the equipment and (b) figure out how to overcome their incentives to free ride on the maintenance efforts of others. Granting exclusivity to one team of anesthesiologists could reduce the incentive and monitoring problems that might be raised by specifications. For example, with one team, it would be easy to tell which team failed to maintain the equipment, and the team would have greater incentive to maintain it, given that the team would be the only user and could not free ride on others. But the Court did not address such issues because the district court failed to make findings necessary to show contractual specifications were not a less restrictive alternative.

9. Why did the Court conclude that the relevant market was different for the exclusive dealing claim than for the quasi-per se tying claim? The relevant market differs because the relevant market definition turns on the relevant anticompetitive theory. The quasi-per se claims require that the defendant have sufficient tying market power over buyers for price discrimination or extraction effects. Thus, for that claim, market definition turns on whether buyers (here, patients) would find alternative suppliers of the tying product sufficiently interchangeable to prevent such price discrimination or extraction effects. Accordingly, for that claim, the Court considered the extent to which patients in Jefferson Parish would find other hospitals reasonably interchangeable.

In contrast, the exclusive dealing claim and the other branch of tying doctrine require that the foreclosure share be large enough to impede rival competitiveness. Thus, for that claim, market definition turns on whether rival sellers (here, anesthesiologists) would find alternative buyers of their services sufficiently interchangeable. Accordingly, for that claim, all the justices agreed that the relevant inquiry was instead the extent to which anesthesiologists would find other hospitals reasonably interchangeable.

In short, for claims turning on increasing the social costs of tying market power against consumers, the correct market to consider is the market for selling hospital services to consumers. In contrast, for claims turning on foreclosure share effects, the correct market to consider is the market for selling anesthesiologist services to hospitals. Patients in Jefferson Parish might reasonably be limited to alternative hospitals in their locality if foreclosed from using their favorite anesthesiologist, so their geographic market is likely local, as the Court concluded. In contrast, the marginal anesthesiologist foreclosed from one hospital in Jefferson Parish could seek alternative employment in hospitals in a much wider area, perhaps the nation, so their geographic market is much larger. Given the different market definitions, the Court concluded that the foreclosure share was much smaller than the market share that was relevant to the quasi-per se tying claims.

Eastman Kodak v. Image Technical Servs.

504 U.S. 451 (1992).

■ JUSTICE BLACKMUN delivered the opinion of the Court.

[Portions of the opinion relating to market definition and power were excerpted in Chapter 3.] . . .

In 1985 and 1986, Kodak implemented a policy of selling replacement parts for micrographic and copying machines only to buyers of Kodak equipment who use Kodak service or repair their own machines. . . . Customers were forced to switch to Kodak service even though they preferred ISO service. . . . In 1987, the ISO's filed the present action in the District Court, alleging, *inter alia,* that Kodak had unlawfully tied the sale of service for Kodak machines to the sale of parts, in violation of § 1 of the Sherman Act . . .

A tying arrangement is "an agreement by a party to sell one product but only on the condition that the buyer also purchases a different (or tied) product, or at least agrees that he will not purchase that product from any other supplier." *Northern Pacific.* Such an arrangement violates § 1 of the Sherman Act if the seller has "appreciable economic power" in the tying product market and if the arrangement affects a substantial volume of commerce in the tied market. . . .

For service and parts to be considered two distinct products, there must be sufficient consumer demand so that it is efficient for a firm to provide service separately from parts. *Jefferson Parish.* Evidence in the record indicates that service and parts have been sold separately in the past and still are sold separately to self-service equipment owners. Indeed, the development of the entire high-technology service industry is evidence of the efficiency of a separate market for service.

Kodak insists that because there is no demand for parts separate from service, there cannot be separate markets for service and parts. By that logic, we would be forced to conclude that there can never be separate markets, for example, for cameras and film, computers and software, or automobiles and tires. That is an assumption we are unwilling to make. "We have often found arrangements involving functionally linked products at least one of which is useless without the other to be prohibited tying devices." *Jefferson Parish.*

Kodak's assertion also appears to be incorrect as a factual matter. At least some consumers would purchase service without parts, because some service does not require parts, and some consumers, those who self-service for example, would purchase parts without service. Enough doubt is cast on Kodak's claim of a unified market that it should be resolved by the trier of fact.

Finally, respondents have presented sufficient evidence of a tie between service and parts. The record indicates that Kodak would sell parts to third parties only if they agreed not to buy service from ISO's.[8]

Having found sufficient evidence of a tying arrangement, we consider the other necessary feature of an illegal tying arrangement: appreciable economic power in the tying market. . . . [The Court found such market power in the portions excerpted in Chapter 3.A.]

Nor are we persuaded by Kodak's contention that it is entitled to a legal presumption on the lack of market power because . . . there is a significant risk of deterring procompetitive conduct. . . . The alleged conduct—higher service prices and market foreclosure—is facially anticompetitive and exactly the harm that antitrust laws aim to prevent. . . . Kodak contends that, despite the appearance of anti-competitiveness, its behavior actually favors competition because its ability to pursue innovative marketing plans will allow it to compete more effectively in the equipment market. A pricing strategy based on lower equipment prices and higher aftermarket prices could enhance equipment sales by making it easier for the buyer to finance the initial purchase.[26] It is undisputed that competition is enhanced when a firm is able to offer various marketing options, including bundling of support and maintenance service with the sale of equipment. Nor do such actions run afoul of the antitrust laws.[27] But the procompetitive effect of the specific conduct challenged here, eliminating all consumer parts and service options, is far less clear.[28]

We need not decide whether Kodak's behavior has any procompetitive effects and, if so, whether they outweigh the anticompetitive effects. We note only that Kodak's service and parts policy is simply not one that appears always or almost always to enhance competition, and therefore to warrant a legal presumption without any evidence of its actual economic impact. In this case, when we weigh the risk of deterring procompetitive behavior by proceeding to trial against

---

[8] In a footnote, Kodak contends that this practice is only a unilateral refusal to deal, which does not violate the antitrust laws. Assuming, *arguendo,* that Kodak's refusal to sell parts to any company providing service can be characterized as a unilateral refusal to deal, its alleged sale of parts to third parties on condition that they buy service from Kodak is not.

[26] It bears repeating that in this case Kodak has never claimed that it is in fact pursuing such a pricing strategy.

[27] *See Jefferson Parish* ("Buyers often find package sales attractive; a seller's decision to offer such packages can merely be an attempt to compete effectively—conduct that is entirely consistent with the Sherman Act"). *See* also Yates & DiResta, Software Support and Hardware Maintenance Practices: Tying Considerations, The Computer Lawyer, Vol. 8, No. 6, p. 17 (1991) (describing various service and parts policies that enhance quality and sales but do not violate the antitrust laws).

[28] Two of the largest consumers of service and parts contend that they are worse off when the equipment manufacturer also controls service and parts.

the risk that illegal behavior will go unpunished, the balance tips against summary judgment.

For the foregoing reasons, we . . . affirm the denial of summary judgment on respondents' § 1 claim.[29]

■ JUSTICE SCALIA, with whom JUSTICE O'CONNOR and JUSTICE THOMAS join, dissenting. . . . *Per se* rules of antitrust illegality are reserved for those situations where logic and experience show that the risk of injury to competition from the defendant's behavior is so pronounced that it is needless and wasteful to conduct the usual judicial inquiry into the balance between the behavior's procompetitive benefits and its anticompetitive costs. . . . The *per se* rule against tying is just such a rule: Where the conditions precedent to application of the rule are met, *i.e.,* where the tying arrangement is backed up by the defendant's market power in the "tying" product, the arrangement is adjudged in violation of § 1 of the Sherman Act, without *any* inquiry into the practice's actual effect on competition and consumer welfare. But *see Jerrold* (accepting affirmative defense to *per se* tying allegation).

Despite intense criticism of the tying doctrine in academic circles, the stated rationale for our *per se* rule has varied little over the years. When the defendant has genuine "market power" in the tying product—the power to raise price by reducing output—the tie potentially enables

---

[29] The dissent urges a radical departure in this Court's antitrust law. It argues that because Kodak has only an "inherent" monopoly in parts for its equipment, the antitrust laws do not apply to its efforts to expand that power into other markets. The dissent's proposal to grant *per se* immunity to manufacturers competing in the service market would exempt a vast and growing sector of the economy from antitrust laws. Leaving aside the question whether the Court has the authority to make such a policy decision, there is no support for it in our jurisprudence or the evidence in this case.

Even assuming, despite the absence of any proof from the dissent, that all manufacturers possess some inherent market power in the parts market, it is not clear why that should immunize them from the antitrust laws in another market. The Court has held many times that power gained through some natural and legal advantage such as a patent, copyright, or business acumen can give rise to liability if "a seller exploits his dominant position in one market to expand his empire into the next." *Times-Picayune.* Moreover, on the occasions when the Court has considered tying in derivative aftermarkets by manufacturers, it has not adopted any exception to the usual antitrust analysis, treating derivative aftermarkets as it has every other separate market. *See International Salt; IBM v. United States,* 298 U.S. 131 (1936); *United Shoe Machinery Corp. v. United States,* 258 U.S. 451 (1922). . . .

Nor does the record in this case support the dissent's proposed exemption for aftermarkets. The dissent urges its exemption because the tie here "does not permit the manufacturer to project power over a class of consumers distinct from that which it is already able to exploit (and fully) without the inconvenience of the tie." Beyond the dissent's obvious difficulty in explaining why Kodak would adopt this expensive tying policy if it could achieve the same profits more conveniently through some other means, respondents offer an alternative theory, supported by the record, that suggests Kodak *is* able to exploit some customers who in the absence of the tie would be protected from increases in parts prices by knowledgeable customers.

At bottom, whatever the ultimate merits of the dissent's theory, at this point it is mere conjecture. Neither Kodak nor the dissent have provided any evidence refuting respondents' theory of forced unwanted purchases at higher prices and price discrimination. While it may be, as the dissent predicts, that the equipment market will prevent any harms to consumers in the aftermarkets, the dissent never makes plain why the Court should accept that theory on faith rather than requiring the usual evidence needed to win a summary judgment motion.

him to extend that power into a second distinct market, enhancing barriers to entry in each. In addition:

> "[T]ying arrangements may be used to evade price control in the tying product through clandestine transfer of the profit to the tied product; they may be used as a counting device to effect price discrimination; and they may be used to force a full line of products on the customer so as to extract more easily from him a monopoly return on one unique product in the line." *Fortner I* (WHITE, J., dissenting. . . .)

For these reasons, as we explained in *Jefferson Parish*, "the law draws a distinction between the exploitation of market power by merely enhancing the price of the tying product, on the one hand, and by attempting to impose restraints on competition in the market for a tied product, on the other." . . .

[W]ith respect to tying, we have recognized that bundling arrangements not coerced by the heavy hand of market power can serve the procompetitive functions of facilitating new entry into certain markets, *see, e.g., Brown Shoe Co. v. United States,* 370 U.S. 294, 330 (1962), permitting "clandestine price cutting in products which otherwise would have no price competition at all because of fear of retaliation from the few other producers dealing in the market," *Fortner I* (WHITE, J., dissenting), assuring quality control, *see, e.g., Standard Stations,* and, where "the tied and tying products are functionally related, . . . reduc[ing] costs through economies of joint production and distribution." *Fortner I* (WHITE, J., dissenting). "Accordingly, we have [only] condemned tying arrangements [under the *per se* rule] when the seller has some special ability—usually called 'market power'—to force a purchaser to do something that he would not do in a competitive market." *Jefferson Parish*. . . .

It is quite simply anomalous that a manufacturer functioning in a competitive equipment market should be exempt from the *per se* rule when it bundles equipment with parts and service, but not when it bundles parts with service. . . . Under the Court's analysis, the *per se* rule may now be applied to single-brand ties effected by the most insignificant players in fully competitive interbrand markets, as long as the arrangement forecloses aftermarket competitors from more than a *de minimis* amount of business. This seems to me quite wrong. A tying arrangement "forced" through the exercise of such power no more implicates the leveraging and price discrimination concerns behind the *per se* tying prohibition than does a tie of the foremarket brand to its aftermarket derivatives, which . . . would not be subject to *per se* condemnation [because of the lack of interbrand market power in equipment].[2] . . .

---

[2] Even *with* interbrand power, I may observe, it is unlikely that Kodak could have incrementally exploited its position through the tie of parts to service alleged here. Most of the "service" at issue is inherently associated with the parts, *i.e.,* that service involved in

The Court . . . says that there are "information costs"—the costs and inconvenience to the consumer of acquiring and processing life-cycle pricing data for Kodak machines—that "could create a less responsive connection between service and parts prices and equipment sales." But this truism about the functioning of markets for sophisticated equipment cannot create "market power" of concern to the antitrust laws where otherwise there is none. "Information costs," or, more accurately, gaps in the availability and quality of consumer information, pervade real-world markets; and because consumers generally make do with "rough cut" judgments about price in such circumstances, in virtually any market there are zones within which otherwise competitive suppliers may overprice their products without losing appreciable market share. We have never suggested that the principal players in a market with such commonplace informational deficiencies (and, thus, bands of apparent consumer pricing indifference) exercise market power in any sense relevant to the antitrust laws. "While [such] factors may generate 'market power' in some abstract sense, they do not generate the kind of market power that justifies condemnation of tying." *Jefferson Parish.*

. . . [W]hen a manufacturer uses its control over single-branded parts to acquire influence in single-branded service, the monopoly "leverage" is almost invariably of no practical consequence, because of perfect identity between the consumers in each of the subject aftermarkets (those who need replacement parts for Kodak equipment and those who need servicing of Kodak equipment). When that condition exists, the tie does not permit the manufacturer to project power over a class of consumers distinct from that which it is already able to exploit (and fully) without the inconvenience of the tie. Cf., *e.g.*, Bowman, Tying Arrangements and the Leverage Problem, 67 Yale L.J. 19, 21–27 (1957).

We have never before accepted the thesis the Court today embraces: that a seller's inherent control over the unique parts for its own brand amounts to "market power" of a character sufficient to permit invocation of the *per se* rule against tying. As the Court observes, we have applied the *per se* rule to manufacturer ties of *foremarket* equipment to aftermarket derivatives—but only when the manufacturer's monopoly power in the equipment, coupled with the use of derivative sales as "counting devices" to measure the intensity of customer equipment usage, enabled the manufacturer to engage in price discrimination, and thereby more fully exploit its interbrand power. *See International Salt*; *IBM v. United States,* 298 U.S. 131 (1936); *United Shoe Machinery Corp. v. United States,* 258 U.S. 451 (1922). That sort of enduring opportunity

incorporating the parts into Kodak equipment, and the two items tend to be demanded by customers in fixed proportions (one part with one unit of service necessary to install the part). When that situation obtains, " 'no revenue can be derived from setting a higher price for the tied product which could not have been made by setting the optimum price for the tying product.' " P. Areeda & L. Kaplow, Antitrust Analysis ¶ 426(a), p. 706 (4th ed. 1988) (quoting Bowman, Tying Arrangements and the Leverage Problem, 67 Yale L.J. 19 (1957)). These observations strongly suggest that Kodak parts and the service involved in installing them should not be treated as distinct products for antitrust tying purposes.

to engage in price discrimination is unavailable to a manufacturer—like Kodak—that lacks power at the interbrand level. A tie between two aftermarket derivatives does next to nothing to improve a competitive manufacturer's ability to extract monopoly rents from its consumers.[3] . . .

We have recognized in closely related contexts that the deterrent effect of *inter*brand competition on the exploitation of *intra*brand market power should make courts exceedingly reluctant to apply rules of *per se* illegality to intrabrand restraints. For instance, we have refused to apply a rule of *per se* illegality to vertical nonprice restraints "because of their potential for a simultaneous reduction of intrabrand competition and stimulation of interbrand competition," *GTE Sylvania*, the latter of which we described as "the primary concern of antitrust law,". . . . In the absence of interbrand power, a manufacturer's bundling of aftermarket products may serve a multitude of legitimate purposes: It may facilitate manufacturer efforts to ensure that the equipment remains operable and thus protect the seller's business reputation, *see Jerrold*; it may create the conditions for implicit consumer financing of the acquisition cost of the tying equipment through supracompetitively-priced aftermarket purchases, *see, e.g.,* A. Oxenfeldt, Industrial Pricing and Market

---

[3] The Court insists that the record in this case suggests otherwise, *i.e.,* that a tie between parts and service somehow *does* enable Kodak to increase overall monopoly profits. Although the Court does not identify the record evidence on which it relies, the suggestion, apparently, is that such a tie facilitates price discrimination between sophisticated, "high-volume" users of Kodak equipment and their unsophisticated counterparts. The sophisticated users (who, the Court presumes, invariably self-service their equipment) are permitted to buy Kodak parts without also purchasing supracompetitively priced Kodak service, while the unsophisticated are—through the imposition of the tie—compelled to buy both.

While superficially appealing, at bottom this explanation lacks coherence. Whether they self-service their equipment or not, rational foremarket consumers (those consumers who are not yet "locked in" to Kodak hardware) will be driven to Kodak's competitors if the price of Kodak equipment, together with the expected cost of aftermarket support, exceeds competitive levels. This will be true no matter how Kodak distributes the total system price among equipment, parts, and service. Thus, as to these consumers, Kodak's lack of interbrand power wholly prevents it from employing a tie between parts and service as a vehicle for price discrimination. Nor does a tie between parts and service offer Kodak incremental exploitative power over those consumers—sophisticated or not—who have the supposed misfortune of being "locked in" to Kodak equipment. If Kodak desired to exploit its circumstantial power over this wretched class by pressing them up to the point where the cost to each consumer of switching equipment brands barely exceeded the cost of retaining Kodak equipment and remaining subject to Kodak's abusive practices, it could plainly do so without the inconvenience of a tie, through supracompetitive parts pricing alone. Since the locked-in *sophisticated* parts purchaser is as helpless as the locked-in *unsophisticated* one, I see nothing to be gained by price discrimination in favor of the former. If such price discrimination were desired, however, it would not have to be accomplished indirectly, through a tie of parts to service. Section 2(a) of the Robinson-Patman Act would prevent giving lower parts prices to the sophisticated customers only "where the effect of such discrimination may be substantially to lessen competition or tend to create a monopoly in any line of commerce, or to injure, destroy, or prevent competition with any person who either grants or knowingly receives the benefit of such discrimination, or with customers of either of them. . . ." *Ibid.; see, e.g., Falls City Industries, Inc. v. Vanco Beverage, Inc.,* 460 U.S. 428, 434–435 (1983). That prohibited effect often occurs when price-discriminated goods are sold for resale (*i.e.,* to purchasers who are necessarily in competition with one another). *E.g., FTC v. Morton Salt Co.,* 334 U.S. 37, 47 (1948); *see* P. Areeda & L. Kaplow, Antitrust Analysis ¶ 600, p. 923 (1988) ("Secondary-line injury arises [under the Robinson-Patman Act] when a powerful firm buying supplies at favorable prices thereby gains a decisive advantage over its competitors that are forced to pay higher prices for their supplies"). It rarely occurs where, as would be the case here, the price-discriminated goods are sold to various businesses for consumption.

Practices 378 (1951); and it may, through the resultant manufacturer control of aftermarket activity, "yield valuable information about component or design weaknesses that will materially contribute to product improvement," 3 Areeda & Turner ¶ 733c, at 258–259; *see also id.,* ¶ 829d, at 331–332. Because the interbrand market will generally punish intrabrand restraints that consumers do not find in their interest, we should not—under the guise of a *per se* rule—condemn such potentially procompetitive arrangements simply because of the antitrust defendant's inherent power over the unique parts for its own brand.

I would instead evaluate the aftermarket tie alleged in this case under the rule of reason, where the tie's *actual* anticompetitive effect in the tied product market, together with its potential economic benefits, can be fully captured in the analysis, Disposition of this case does not require such an examination, however, as respondents apparently waived any rule-of-reason claim they may have had in the District Court. I would thus reverse the Ninth Circuit's judgment on the tying claim outright. . . .

NOTES AND QUESTIONS ON *KODAK*

1. ***Does* Kodak *effectively end the possibility that the quasi-per se rule against tying might be overruled?*** It seems to because even the conservative dissenters stated that, "Despite intense criticism of the tying doctrine in academic circles," they were sticking to "the stated rationale" that ties with tying market power were anticompetitive when they caused either foreclosure share effects *or* price discrimination and extraction effects. The dissent also reaffirmed that it was because of these effects that antitrust law distinguishes between exploiting market power by simply raising the tying product price versus by using tying agreements.

Further, the dissent's argument against finding sufficient tying market power was that it was not the sort of tying market power that "implicates the leveraging and price discrimination concerns behind the per se tying prohibition." Thus, even these conservative dissenters recognized that price discrimination concerns underlie the quasi-per se rule. Although the dissenters thought market definition was lacking, they acknowledged that the quasi-per se rule prohibits ties "when the manufacturer's monopoly power in the equipment, coupled with the use of derivative sales as 'counting devices' to measure the intensity of customer equipment usage, enabled the manufacturer to engage in price discrimination, and thereby more fully exploit its interbrand power." The dissenters also argued that even with tying market power, it was "unlikely that Kodak could have incrementally exploited" its market power in this harmful way because the tying and tied products (the dissenters presumed) had no separate utility and a fixed ratio. As we shall see, that premise was factually dubious, but, if valid, would indeed have disproven price discrimination and extraction effects. The key point here, however, is that the dissenters felt obliged to disprove such price discrimination effects on the case facts, indicating that even they regarded the incremental exploitation of tying market power through such effects as anticompetitive.

2. *Should Kodak parts and service be deemed separate products?* The Court adopts the same separate products test as *Jefferson Parish*, again inferring the efficiency of separate provision from actual market practices, and again rejecting the alternative test that there must be some demand to use the tied product without the tying product. The Court thus found that the tying product (Kodak parts) was separate from the tied product (service).

a. Suppose the dissent were right that service is not only useless without parts, but also that service and parts are used only in fixed proportions. Is the dissent right that those factors would eliminate all anticompetitive effects? As discussed in the introduction to this section, those two factors would eliminate anticompetitive concerns that any market profits in parts might be increased by intraproduct or interproduct price discrimination among those subject to the tie or by extracting individual consumer surplus. Those two factors would also eliminate the possibility that foreclosing a substantial share of the tied service market could create tied market power that the defendant could exploit against tied product purchases that otherwise would not have been subject to its tying market power in parts. Those two factors thus (if true) knock out four of the five possible anticompetitive effects from tying.

However, those two factors would not eliminate the fifth possibility: that tied market foreclosure might enhance tying market power. Suppose, though, we add a third premise, which the dissent probably assumed: that Kodak had patents over parts for its own machines, which presumably is how Kodak prevented others from making those parts. If so, the patents probably would bar rivals from entering the parts market even without any tie, so that the tie was unlikely to reduce rival entry into the parts market, and thus unlikely to increase tying market power. True, even without affecting parts entry, foreclosing rival service providers might enhance tying market power if service were a partial substitute for parts. But partial substitutes by definition can be used in varying ratios, so partial substitutability would be inconsistent with the Kodak dissenters' factual premise that parts and services are used in fixed ratios.

Moreover, *Kodak* had the unusual feature that one of the alleged anticompetitive effects flowed not from the tie itself, but from alleged discrimination between buyers who were and were not subject to the tie. A fixed ratio and lack of separate utility failed to eliminate the possibility that the fact that the tie was *not* used with self-service buyers created harmful price discrimination between self-service buyers and service-purchasing buyers.

b. Is the dissent right about its factual assumptions that the tie here involved fixed ratios and no separate utility? As the Court pointed out, service is sometimes purchased without parts, and those who self-service buy parts without buying service. Thus, the ratio of usage varies. This variability reintroduces all the possible anticompetitive effects. It also seems quite likely that service is a partial substitute for parts. After all, firms that use more service to maintain their machines tend to have them break down less often, and thus need fewer parts. Further, firms can sometimes use additional service to repair existing parts without replacing them. This partial substitutability means that foreclosing service could increase tying power over parts.

3. ***Were information costs a proper basis to find tying market power over Kodak parts?*** As discussed in Chapter 3, one source of tying market power was that many buyers were already locked into Kodak machines at the time when Kodak parts were tied to service. But the Court also argued that information costs were another basis for finding tying market power. Was the dissent right that this use of information costs was inconsistent with *Jefferson Parish,* which held that a lack of information might make buyers price insensitive in a way that allows a firm to price above cost, but does not indicate the sort of power that raises tying concerns?

A couple distinctions might be drawn. One difference is that in *Kodak* the lack of information was used to help to rebut the claim that any market power in parts would be constrained by the lack of market power in equipment, whereas in *Jefferson Parish* the claim was that the lack of information was the source of market power itself. The other difference is that in *Jefferson Parish* the lack of information was alleged to operate when decisions to buy the tied product were made, which meant the tie could not distort buyer choices on the merits about from whom to purchase the tied product. In contrast, in *Kodak,* the lack of information was claimed to operate only at the equipment purchase stage, which was consistent with the proposition that without the tie buyers could have made informed choices to buy service from someone else.

4. ***Does the tie have a valid procompetitive justification?*** The Court did not rule on whether the defendant had a valid efficiency justification, holding simply that any justification could not support giving summary judgment to the defendant. This holding seems to confirm that when a valid procompetitive justifications does exist, it is admissible notwithstanding the quasi-per se rule against tying. The proffered justification was that the tie efficiently made it easier for buyers to finance equipment purchases. However, that justification did not seem plausible here because it would require that the tie be known at the time the equipment was bought. Moreover, such a procompetitive justification necessarily depends on the premise that the tie between parts and service permitted higher aftermarket prices, which was just what Kodak was denying. The justification thus inherently admitted the existence of some possible anticompetitive effects, which would require balancing the two against each other.

Illinois Tool Works Inc. v. Independent Ink, Inc.

547 U.S. 28 (2006).

■ JUSTICE STEVENS delivered the opinion of the Court.

In *Jefferson Parish*, we repeated the well-settled proposition that "if the Government has granted the seller a patent or similar monopoly over a product, it is fair to presume that the inability to buy the product elsewhere gives the seller market power." This presumption of market power, applicable in the antitrust context when a seller conditions its sale of a patented product (the "tying" product) on the purchase of a second product (the "tied" product), has its foundation in the judicially created patent misuse doctrine. In 1988, Congress substantially undermined that foundation, amending the Patent Act to eliminate the market power presumption in patent misuse cases. *See* 35 U.S.C. § 271(d). The question presented to us today is whether the presumption of market power in a patented product should survive as a matter of antitrust law despite its demise in patent law. We conclude that the mere fact that a tying product is patented does not support such a presumption. . . .

American courts first encountered tying arrangements in the course of patent infringement litigation. . . . In the years since . . . , four different rules of law have supported challenges to tying arrangements. They have been condemned as improper extensions of the patent monopoly under the patent misuse doctrine, as unfair methods of competition under § 5 of the Federal Trade Commission Act, as contracts tending to create a monopoly under § 3 of the Clayton Act, and as contracts in restraint of trade under § 1 of the Sherman Act. . . .

[The case involved a tying claim wherein the tying product was a patented printhead used to print barcodes on cartons and the tied product was unpatented ink].

Over the years, however, this Court's strong disapproval of tying arrangements has substantially diminished. Rather than relying on assumptions, in its more recent opinions the Court has required a showing of market power in the tying product. Our early opinions consistently assumed that "[t]ying arrangements serve hardly any purpose beyond the suppression of competition." *Standard Stations*. In 1962, in *Loew's*, the Court relied on this assumption despite evidence of significant competition in the market for the tying product. . . .

The assumption that "[t]ying arrangements serve hardly any purpose beyond the suppression of competition," rejected in *Fortner II*, has not been endorsed in any opinion since. Instead, it was again rejected just seven years later in *Jefferson Parish*, where, as in *Fortner II*, we unanimously reversed a Court of Appeals judgment holding that an alleged tying arrangement constituted a per se violation of § 1 of the Sherman Act. Like the product at issue in the Fortner cases, the tying product in Jefferson Parish-hospital services—was unpatented, and our holding again rested on the conclusion that the plaintiff had failed to prove sufficient power in the tying product market to restrain competition in the market for the tied product-services of anesthesiologists. . . .

. . . [T]he presumption that a patent confers market power arose outside the antitrust context as part of the patent misuse doctrine . . . , [which provides] a patent misuse defense to infringement claims when a patentee uses its patent "as the effective means of restraining competition with its sale of an unpatented article." . . . The presumption that a patent confers market power migrated from patent law to antitrust law in *International Salt*. . . .

Although the patent misuse doctrine and our antitrust jurisprudence became intertwined in *International Salt*, subsequent events initiated their untwining. . . . Three years before we decided *International Salt*, this Court had expanded the scope of the patent misuse doctrine to include not only supplies or materials used by a patented device, but also tying arrangements involving a combination patent and "unpatented material or [a] device [that] is itself an integral part of the structure embodying the patent." *Mercoid*, 320 U.S. at 665; *see also* Dawson Chemical Co. v. Rohm & Haas Co., 448 U.S. 176, 188–198 (1980) (describing in detail *Mercoid* and the cases leading up to it). In reaching this conclusion, the Court explained that it could see "no difference in principle" between cases involving elements essential to the inventive character of the patent and elements peripheral to it; both, in the Court's view, were attempts to "expan[d] the patent beyond the legitimate scope of its monopoly."

Shortly thereafter, Congress codified the patent laws for the first time. At least partly in response to our *Mercoid* decision, Congress included a provision in its codification that excluded some conduct, such as a tying arrangement involving the sale of a patented product tied to an "essential" or "nonstaple" product that has no use except as part of the patented product or method, from the scope of the patent misuse doctrine. § 271(d); *see also Dawson*, 448 U.S., at 214. Thus, at the same time that our antitrust jurisprudence continued to rely on the assumption that "tying arrangements generally serve no legitimate business purpose," *Fortner I*, Congress began chipping away at the assumption in the patent misuse context from whence it came.

It is Congress' most recent narrowing of the patent misuse defense, however, that is directly relevant to this case. Four years after our decision in *Jefferson Parish* repeated the patent-equals-market-power presumption, Congress amended the Patent Code to eliminate that presumption in the patent misuse context. The relevant provision reads:

> "(d) No patent owner otherwise entitled to relief for infringement or contributory infringement of a patent shall be denied relief or deemed guilty of misuse or illegal extension of the patent right by reason of his having done one or more of the following: . . . (5) conditioned the license of any rights to the

> patent or the sale of the patented product on the acquisition of a license to rights in another patent or purchase of a separate product, *unless, in view of the circumstances, the patent owner has market power in the relevant market for the patent or patented product on which the license or sale is conditioned.*" 35 U.S.C. § 271(d)(5) (emphasis added).

The italicized clause makes it clear that Congress did not intend the mere existence of a patent to constitute the requisite "market power." Indeed, fairly read, it provides that without proof that [the patent holder] had market power in the relevant market, its conduct at issue in this case was neither "misuse" nor an "illegal extension of the patent right."

While the 1988 amendment does not expressly refer to the antitrust laws, it certainly invites a reappraisal of the per se rule announced in *International Salt*. A rule denying a patentee the right to enjoin an infringer is significantly less severe than a rule that makes the conduct at issue a federal crime punishable by up to 10 years in prison. *See* 15 U.S.C. § 1. It would be absurd to assume that Congress intended to provide that the use of a patent that merited punishment as a felony would not constitute "misuse." Moreover, given the fact that the patent misuse doctrine provided the basis for the market power presumption, it would be anomalous to preserve the presumption in antitrust after Congress has eliminated its foundation. Cf. 10 P. AREEDA, H. HOVENKAMP, & E. ELHAUGE, ANTITRUST LAW ¶ 1737c (2d ed.2004) (hereinafter Areeda).

After considering the congressional judgment reflected in the 1988 amendment, we conclude that tying arrangements involving patented products should be evaluated under the standards applied in cases like *Fortner II* and *Jefferson Parish* rather than under the per se rule applied in [old patent misuse cases]. While some such arrangements are still unlawful, such as those that are the product of a true monopoly or a marketwide conspiracy, *see*, e.g., United States v. Paramount Pictures, Inc., 334 U.S. 131, 145–146 (1948), that conclusion must be supported by proof of power in the relevant market rather than by a mere presumption thereof. . . .

Rather than arguing that we should retain the rule of per se illegality, respondent contends that we should endorse a rebuttable presumption that patentees possess market power when they condition the purchase of the patented product on an agreement to buy unpatented goods exclusively from the patentee. Respondent recognizes that a large number of valid patents have little, if any, commercial significance, but submits that those that are used to impose tying arrangements on unwilling purchasers likely do exert significant market power. Hence, in respondent's view, the presumption would have no impact on patents of only slight value and would be justified, subject to being rebutted by evidence offered by the patentee, in cases in which the patent has sufficient value to enable the patentee to insist on acceptance of the tie.

Respondent also offers a narrower alternative, suggesting that we differentiate between tying arrangements involving the simultaneous purchase of two products that are arguably two components of a single product—such as the provision of surgical services and anesthesiology in the same operation, *Jefferson Parish*, or the licensing of one copyrighted film on condition that the licensee take a package of several films in the same transaction, *Loew's*—and a tying arrangement involving the purchase of unpatented goods over a period of time, a so-called "requirements tie." According to respondent, we should recognize a presumption of market power when faced with the latter type of arrangements because they provide a means for charging large volume purchasers a higher royalty for use of the patent than small purchasers must pay, a form of discrimination that "is strong evidence of market power."

The opinion that imported the "patent equals market power" presumption into our antitrust jurisprudence, however, provides no support for respondent's proposed alternative. In *International Salt*, it was the existence of the patent on the tying product, rather than the use of a requirements tie, that led the Court to presume market power. Moreover, the requirements tie in that case did not involve any price discrimination between large volume and small volume purchasers or evidence of noncompetitive pricing. Instead, the leases at issue provided that if any competitor offered salt, the tied product, at a lower price, "the lessee should be free to buy in the open market, unless appellant would furnish the salt at an equal price."

... [T]he vast majority of academic literature recognizes that a patent does not necessarily confer market power. Similarly, while price discrimination may provide evidence of market power, particularly if buttressed by evidence that the patentee has charged an above-market price for the tied package, *see*, e.g., 10 Areeda ¶ 1769c, it is generally recognized that it also occurs in fully competitive markets, *see*, e.g., Baumol & Swanson, The New Economy and Ubiquitous Competitive Price Discrimination: Identifying Defensible Criteria of Market Power, 70 Antitrust L.J. 661, 666 (2003); 9 Areeda ¶ 1711; Landes & Posner 374–375. We are not persuaded that the combination of these two factors should give rise to a presumption of market power when neither is sufficient to do so standing alone. Rather, the lesson to be learned from *International Salt* and the academic commentary is the same: Many tying arrangements, even those involving patents and requirements ties, are fully consistent with a free, competitive market. For this reason, we reject both respondent's proposed rebuttable presumption and their narrower alternative.

It is no doubt the virtual consensus among economists that has persuaded the enforcement agencies to reject the position that the Government took when it supported the per se rule that the Court adopted in the 1940's. In antitrust guidelines issued jointly by the

Department of Justice and the Federal Trade Commission in 1995, the enforcement agencies stated that in the exercise of their prosecutorial discretion they "will not presume that a patent, copyright, or trade secret necessarily confers market power upon its owner." U.S. Dept. of Justice and FTC, Antitrust Guidelines for the Licensing of Intellectual Property § 2.2 (Apr. 6, 1995). While that choice is not binding on the Court, it would be unusual for the Judiciary to replace the normal rule of lenity that is applied in criminal cases with a rule of severity for a special category of antitrust cases.

Congress, the antitrust enforcement agencies, and most economists have all reached the conclusion that a patent does not necessarily confer market power upon the patentee. Today, we reach the same conclusion, and therefore hold that, in all cases involving a tying arrangement, the plaintiff must prove that the defendant has market power in the tying product. . . .

NOTES AND QUESTIONS ON *ILLINOIS TOOL WORKS*

1. ***Does* Illinois Tool Works *confirm the continuing validity of the quasi-per se rule?*** It seems so. The Court stated, "we conclude that tying arrangements involving patented products should be evaluated under the standards applied in cases like . . . *Jefferson Parish* rather than under the per se rule". This statement made clear that the Court thought *Jefferson Parish's* quasi per rule should continue to apply, and that the Court considered it a form of rule of reason analysis "rather than" a per se rule. The Court described *Jefferson Parish* as "rejecting the application of a per se rule" because it required proof of market power and rejected the "assumption that '[t]ying arrangements serve hardly any purpose beyond the suppression of competition' ". In short, it deemed the quasi per se rule a form of rule of reason review that required evidence of tying market power and considered procompetitive justifications. The Court also made clear, through both its articulation of the governing legal rule for tying and its remand instructions, that liability turned on proof of tying market power without requiring any evidence of a substantial foreclosure share. Indeed, a substantial foreclosure share seemed implausible on the facts, given that the ink used for one specialized sort of printhead used to print bar codes on cartons is hardly likely to be a big share of the entire ink market.

2. ***Does the fact that market power must be proven in a patent misuse tying case necessarily imply it should also have to be proven in an antitrust tying case?*** The Court seemed to think so because antitrust liability could lead to criminal sanctions, whereas patent misuse could not. However, no one has been criminally prosecuted for tying for a long time (if ever), and the Department of Justice, which has the sole power to criminally prosecute antitrust violations, itself indicates that it requires market power even when the tying product is patented. Accordingly, a finding of antitrust tying realistically would lead at most to damages or injunctions against tying. In contrast, a finding of patent misuse means that others can infringe the patent, which is tantamount to invalidating it, which can be a business "death penalty." For example, the defendant here would almost certainly fear invalidation of its printhead patent far more than a prohibition on tying those printheads to ink. Thus, the realistic penalties for a patent misuse are generally much higher than for antitrust tying, so it could thus be rational to have higher standards of proof for market power in a patent misuse case.

3. ***Putting aside patent misuse doctrine, did the antitrust presumption that a patent confers market power ever make sense?*** Although patents confer a legal monopoly over an idea, that idea may not necessarily enjoy any economic market power over competing ideas, in the same way that a legal monopoly over the use of a particular plant does not necessarily confer market power if other plants can provide the same or better functionality. *See* Chapter 2.G. Still, while it would be wrong to always assume that patents imply market power, it may be that they provide market power frequently enough that a rebuttable presumption would be warranted. Another argument for such a presumption would be that, compared to plaintiffs, defendants are likely to have greater access to evidence on whether or not their patents enjoy market power.

4. ***Does a presumption of market power at least make sense in a case where the patent is tied to another product, thus indicating enough power to impose the tie?*** No. Presuming market power from the tie in this way would make sense only if there are no procompetitive efficiencies to tying, which the Court clearly thinks are common enough to require a market power screen under the per se rule. If there are such efficiencies, a seller without any tying market power could successfully use efficient ties. Moreover, the logic for rejecting or accepting such a presumption would apply equally whether the tying product was patented or not.

However, it might make sense to presume tying market power from the tie in a case where the defendant cannot even articulate any procompetitive justification. Whether to do so depends on whether a court thinks the underdeterrence that would otherwise be created by erroneous failures to find tying market power outweighs the overdeterrence created by erroneous conclusions that the defendants have offered no procompetitive efficiency.

5. ***Does a presumption of market power at least make sense in a case where the patent is tied to a requirements contract for some consumable in a way that suggests price discrimination?*** No. First, using a requirements contract does not necessarily imply the tie is being used to price discriminate, rather than to advance some procompetitive efficiency, like quality control or to shift financing and risk-bearing costs. Second, although price discrimination always indicates some economic market power, it does not necessarily indicate market power in the antitrust sense given that it often exists on markets that antitrust would regard as competitive. *See* Chapter 3. Moreover, the logic for rejecting or accepting such a presumption again has nothing to do with the existence of a patent.

6. ***Where market power is shown, does this case indicate that procompetitive justifications are admissible?*** The case doesn't explicitly hold that procompetitive justifications are admissible. However, it indicates that the Court thinks procompetitive justifications are sufficiently likely that the law should require demonstrable proof of market power. That means the Court thinks there are procompetitive justifications, which suggests it would admit them.

United States v. Microsoft

253 F.3d 34 (D.C. Cir. 2001) (en banc).

■ Opinion for the Court filed PER CURIAM. . . .

The District Court determined that Microsoft had maintained a monopoly in the market for Intel-compatible PC operating systems in violation of § 2 . . . and illegally tied two purportedly separate products, Windows and Internet Explorer ("IE"), in violation of § 1. . . .

II. MONOPOLIZATION

[Portions addressing monopoly power and framing the inquiry into exclusionary conduct are excerpted above.] . . .

1. Licenses Issued to Original Equipment Manufacturers [OEMs]

The District Court condemned a number of provisions in Microsoft's agreements licensing Windows to OEMs, because it found that Microsoft's imposition of those provisions (like many of Microsoft's other actions at issue in this case) serves to reduce usage share of Netscape's browser and, hence, protect Microsoft's operating system monopoly. . . . Browser usage share is important because . . . a browser (or any middleware product, for that matter) must have a critical mass of users in order to attract software developers to write applications relying upon the APIs it exposes, and away from the APIs exposed by Windows. Applications written to a particular browser's APIs, however, would run on any computer with that browser, regardless of the underlying operating system. . . . If a consumer could have access to the applications he desired—regardless of the operating system he uses—simply by installing a particular browser on his computer, then he would no longer feel compelled to select Windows in order to have access to those applications; he could select an operating system other than Windows based solely upon its quality and price. In other words, the market for operating systems would be competitive. Therefore, Microsoft's efforts to gain market share in one market (browsers) served to meet the threat to Microsoft's monopoly in another market (operating systems) by keeping rival browsers from gaining the critical mass of users necessary to attract developer attention away from Windows as the platform for software development. . . .

a. *Anticompetitive effect of the license restrictions* . . .

The District Court concluded that the first license restriction—the prohibition upon the removal of desktop icons, folders, and Start menu entries—thwarts the distribution of a rival browser by preventing OEMs from removing visible means of user access to IE. The OEMs cannot practically install a second browser in addition to IE, the court found, in part because . . . a certain number of novice computer users, seeing two browser icons, will wonder which to use when and will call the OEM's support line. Support calls are extremely expensive and, in the highly competitive original equipment market, firms have a strong incentive to minimize costs. . . .

[T]he OEM channel is one of the two primary channels for distribution of browsers. By preventing OEMs from removing visible means of user access to IE, the license restriction prevents many OEMs from pre-installing a rival browser and, therefore, protects Microsoft's monopoly from the competition that middleware might otherwise present. Therefore, we conclude that the license restriction at issue is anticompetitive. . . .

The second license provision at issue prohibits OEMs from modifying the initial boot sequence—the process that occurs the first time a consumer turns on the computer. . . . Microsoft's prohibition on any alteration of the boot sequence . . . prevents OEMs from using that process to promote the services of IAPs, many of which—at least at the time Microsoft imposed the restriction—used Navigator rather than IE in their internet access software. . . . Because this prohibition has a substantial effect in protecting Microsoft's market power, and does so through a means other than competition on the merits, it is anticompetitive. . . .

Finally, . . . Microsoft prohibits OEMs from causing any user interface other than the Windows desktop to launch automatically, from adding icons or folders different in size or shape from those supplied by Microsoft, and from using the "Active Desktop" feature to promote third-party brands. These restrictions impose significant costs upon the OEMs; prior to Microsoft's prohibiting the practice, many OEMs would change the appearance of the desktop in ways they found beneficial.

The dissatisfaction of the OEM customers does not, of course, mean the restrictions are anticompetitive. The anticompetitive effect of the license restrictions is, as Microsoft itself recognizes, that OEMs are not able to promote rival browsers, which keeps developers focused upon the APIs in Windows. This kind of promotion is not a zero-sum game; but for the restrictions in their licenses to use Windows, OEMs could promote multiple IAPs and browsers. By preventing the OEMs from doing so, this type of license restriction, like the first two restrictions, is anticompetitive: Microsoft reduced rival browsers' usage share not by improving its own product but, rather, by preventing OEMs from taking actions that could increase rivals' share of usage.

b. *Microsoft's justifications for the license restrictions* . . .

Microsoft's primary copyright argument borders upon the frivolous. The company claims an absolute and unfettered right to use its intellectual property as it wishes: "[I]f intellectual property rights have been lawfully acquired," it says, then "their subsequent exercise cannot give rise to antitrust liability." That is no more correct than the proposition that use of one's personal property, such as a baseball bat, cannot give rise to tort liability. As the Federal Circuit succinctly stated: "Intellectual property rights do not confer a privilege to violate the antitrust laws." *In re Indep. Serv. Orgs. Antitrust Litig.,* 203 F.3d 1322, 1325 (Fed.Cir.2000).

Although Microsoft never overtly retreats from its bold and incorrect position on the law, it also makes two arguments to the effect that it is not exercising its copyright in an unreasonable manner, despite the anticompetitive consequences of the license restrictions discussed above. In the first variation upon its unqualified copyright defense, Microsoft cites two cases indicating that a copyright holder may limit a licensee's ability to engage in significant and deleterious alterations of a copyrighted work. . . . The only license restriction Microsoft seriously defends as necessary to prevent a "substantial alteration" of its copyrighted work is the prohibition on OEMs automatically launching a substitute user interface upon completion of the boot process. We agree that a shell that automatically prevents the Windows desktop from ever being seen by the user is a drastic alteration of Microsoft's copyrighted work, and outweighs the marginal anticompetitive effect of prohibiting the OEMs from substituting a different interface automatically upon completion of the initial boot process. We therefore hold that this particular restriction is not an exclusionary practice that violates § 2 of the Sherman Act.

In a second variation upon its copyright defense, Microsoft argues that the license restrictions merely prevent OEMs from taking actions that would reduce substantially the value of Microsoft's copyrighted work: that is, Microsoft claims each license restriction in question is necessary to prevent OEMs from so altering Windows as to undermine "the principal value of Windows as a stable and consistent platform that supports a broad range of applications and that is familiar to users." Microsoft, however, never substantiates this claim, and, because an OEM's altering the appearance of the desktop or promoting programs in the boot sequence does not affect the code already in the product, the practice does not self-evidently affect either the "stability" or the "consistency" of the platform. . . . Therefore, we conclude Microsoft has not shown that the OEMs' liberality reduces the value of Windows except in the sense that their promotion of rival browsers undermines Microsoft's monopoly—and that is not a permissible justification for the license restrictions.

Apart from copyright, Microsoft raises one other defense of the OEM license agreements: It argues that, despite the restrictions in the OEM license, Netscape is not completely blocked from distributing its product. That claim is insufficient to shield Microsoft from liability for those restrictions because, although Microsoft did not bar its rivals from all means of distribution, it did bar them from the cost-efficient ones.

In sum, we hold that with the exception of the one restriction prohibiting automatically launched alternative interfaces, all the OEM license restrictions at issue represent uses of Microsoft's market power to protect its monopoly, unredeemed by any legitimate justification. The restrictions therefore violate § 2 of the Sherman Act.

2. Integration of IE and Windows . . .

a. *Anticompetitive effect of integration*

As a general rule, courts are properly very skeptical about claims that competition has been harmed by a dominant firm's product design changes. *See, e.g., Foremost Pro Color, Inc. v. Eastman Kodak Co.,* 703 F.2d 534, 544–45 (9th Cir.1983). In a competitive market, firms routinely innovate in the hope of appealing to consumers, sometimes in the process making their products incompatible with those of rivals; the imposition of liability when a monopolist does the same thing will inevitably deter a certain amount of innovation. This is all the more true in a market, such as this one, in which the product itself is rapidly changing. Judicial deference to product innovation, however, does not mean that a monopolist's product design decisions are per se lawful. *See Foremost Pro Color,* 703 F.2d at 545; *see also Cal. Computer Prods.,* 613 F.2d at 739, 744; *In re IBM Peripheral EDP Devices Antitrust Litig.,* 481 F.Supp. 965, 1007–08 (N.D.Cal.1979).

The District Court first condemned as anticompetitive Microsoft's decision to exclude IE from the "Add/Remove Programs" utility in Windows 98. . . . This change reduces the usage share of rival browsers not by making Microsoft's own browser more attractive to consumers but, rather, by discouraging OEMs from distributing rival products. Because Microsoft's conduct, through something other than competition on the merits, has the effect of significantly reducing usage of rivals' products and hence protecting its own operating system monopoly, it is anticompetitive . . .

Second, the District Court found that Microsoft designed Windows 98 [to sometimes override] . . . the user's choice of a browser other than IE as his or her default browser. . . . Because the override reduces rivals' usage share and protects Microsoft's monopoly, it too is anticompetitive.

Finally, the District Court condemned Microsoft's decision to bind IE to Windows 98 "by placing code specific to Web browsing in the same files as code that provided operating system functions." Putting code supplying browsing functionality into a file with code supplying operating system functionality "ensure[s] that the deletion of any file containing browsing-specific routines would also delete vital operating system routines and thus cripple Windows. . . ." As noted above, preventing an OEM from removing IE deters it from installing a second browser because doing so increases the OEM's product testing and support costs; by contrast, had OEMs been able to remove IE, they might have chosen to pre-install Navigator alone. . . . [S]uch commingling has an anticompetitive effect . . .

b. *Microsoft's justifications for integration*

Microsoft proffers no justification for two of the three challenged actions that it took in integrating IE into Windows—excluding IE from the Add/Remove Programs utility and commingling browser and operating system code. . . . Accordingly, we hold that Microsoft's exclusion of IE from the Add/Remove Programs utility and its commingling of browser and operating system code constitute exclusionary conduct, in violation of § 2.

. . . Microsoft claims that it was necessary to design Windows to override the user's preferences when he or she invokes one of "a few" out "of the nearly 30 means of accessing the Internet." According to Microsoft:

> The Windows 98 Help system and Windows Update feature depend on ActiveX controls not supported by Navigator, and the now-discontinued Channel Bar utilized Microsoft's Channel Definition Format, which Navigator also did not support. Lastly, Windows 98 does not invoke Navigator if a user accesses the Internet through "My Computer" or "Windows Explorer" because doing so would defeat one of the purposes of those features—enabling users to move seamlessly from local storage devices to the Web *in the same browsing window*.

The . . . plaintiffs offer no rebuttal whatsoever. Accordingly, Microsoft may not be held liable for this aspect of its product design. . . .

IV. TYING

Microsoft also contests the District Court's determination of liability under § 1 of the Sherman Act. The District Court concluded that Microsoft's contractual and technological bundling of the IE web browser (the "tied" product) with its Windows operating system ("OS") (the "tying" product) resulted in a tying arrangement that was per se unlawful. . . .

There is no doubt that "[i]t is far too late in the history of our antitrust jurisprudence to question the proposition that *certain* tying arrangements pose an unacceptable risk of stifling competition and therefore are unreasonable '*per se*.'" *Jefferson Parish* (emphasis added). But there are strong reasons to doubt that the integration of additional software functionality into an OS falls among these arrangements. Applying per se analysis to such an amalgamation creates undue risks of error and of deterring welfare-enhancing innovation.

The Supreme Court has warned that "'[i]t is only after considerable experience with certain business relationships that courts classify them as *per se* violations. . . .'" *BMI*. Yet the sort of tying arrangement attacked here is unlike any the Supreme Court has considered. The early Supreme Court cases on tying dealt with arrangements whereby the sale or lease of a patented product was conditioned on the purchase of certain unpatented products from the patentee. Later Supreme Court tying cases did not involve market power derived from patents, but continued to involve contractual ties.

In none of these cases was the tied good physically and technologically integrated with the tying good. Nor did the defendants ever argue that their tie improved the value of the tying product to users *and* to makers of complementary goods. In those cases where the defendant claimed that use of the tied good made the tying good more valuable to users, the Court ruled that the same result could be achieved via quality standards for substitutes of the tied good. Here Microsoft argues that IE and Windows are an integrated physical product and that the bundling of IE APIs with Windows makes the latter a better applications platform for third-party software. It is unclear how the benefits from IE APIs could be achieved by quality standards for different browser manufacturers. We do not pass judgment on Microsoft's claims regarding the benefits from integration of its APIs. We merely note that these and other novel, purported efficiencies suggest that judicial "experience" provides little basis for believing that, "because of their pernicious effect on competition and lack of *any* redeeming virtue," a software firm's decisions to sell multiple functionalities as a package should be "conclusively presumed to be unreasonable and therefore illegal without elaborate inquiry as to the precise harm they have caused or the business excuse for their use." *N. Pac. Ry.*, 356 U.S. at 5 (emphasis added).

Nor have we found much insight into software integration among the decisions of lower federal courts. . . . While the paucity of cases examining software bundling suggests a high risk that per se analysis may produce inaccurate results, the nature of the platform software market affirmatively suggests that per se rules might stunt valuable innovation. We have in mind two reasons.

First, . . . the separate-products test is a poor proxy for net efficiency from newly integrated products. Under per se analysis the first firm to merge previously distinct functionalities (*e.g.*, the inclusion of starter motors in automobiles) or to eliminate entirely the need for a second function (*e.g.*, the invention of the stain-resistant carpet) risks being condemned as having tied two separate products because at the moment of integration there will appear to be a robust "distinct" market for the tied product. *See* 10 AREEDA, ELHAUGE & HOVENKAMP, ANTITRUST LAW ¶ 1746, at 224. Rule of reason analysis, however, affords the first mover an opportunity to demonstrate that an efficiency gain from its "tie" adequately offsets any distortion of consumer choice.

The failure of the separate-products test to screen out certain cases of productive integration is particularly troubling in platform software markets such as that in which the defendant competes. Not only is integration common in such markets, but it is common among firms without market power. We have already reviewed evidence that nearly all competitive OS vendors also bundle browsers. Moreover, plaintiffs do not dispute that OS vendors can and do incorporate basic internet plumbing and other useful functionality into their OSs. Firms without market power have no incentive to package different pieces of software together unless there are efficiency gains from doing so. The ubiquity of bundling in competitive platform software markets should give courts reason to pause before condemning such behavior in less competitive markets.

Second, because of the pervasively innovative character of platform software markets, tying in such markets may produce efficiencies that courts have not previously encountered and thus the Supreme Court had not factored into the per se rule as originally conceived. For example, the bundling of a browser with OSs enables an independent software developer to count on the presence of the browser's APIs, if any, on consumers' machines and thus to omit them from its own package. . . . Of course, these arguments may not justify Microsoft's decision to bundle APIs in this case, particularly because Microsoft did not merely bundle with Windows the APIs from IE, but an entire browser application (sometimes even without APIs). . . . Furthermore, the interest in efficient API diffusion obviously supplies a far stronger justification for simple price-bundling than for Microsoft's contractual or technological bars to subsequent *removal* of functionality. But our qualms about redefining the boundaries of a defendant's product and the possibility of consumer gains from simplifying the work of applications developers makes us question any hard and fast approach to tying in OS software markets.

There may also be a number of efficiencies that, although very real, have been ignored in the calculations underlying the adoption of a per se rule for tying. We fear that these efficiencies are common in technologically dynamic markets where product development is especially unlikely to follow an easily foreseen linear pattern. . . .

These arguments all point to one conclusion: we cannot comfortably say that bundling in platform software markets has so little "redeeming virtue," and that there would be so "very little loss to society" from its ban, that "an inquiry into its costs in the individual case [can be] considered [ ] unnecessary." We . . . [thus] vacate the District Court's finding of per se tying liability under Sherman Act § 1. We remand the case for evaluation of Microsoft's tying arrangements under the rule of reason. . . .

Our judgment regarding the comparative merits of the per se rule and the rule of reason is confined to the tying arrangement before us, where the tying product is software whose major purpose is to serve as a platform for third-party applications and the tied product is complementary software functionality. . . .

[T]he fact that we have already considered some of the behavior plaintiffs allege to constitute tying violations in the monopoly maintenance section does not resolve the § 1 inquiry. . . . In order for the District Court to conclude these practices also constitute § 1 tying violations, plaintiffs must demonstrate that their benefits—if any—are outweighed by the harms in the *tied product* market. . . .

NOTES AND QUESTIONS ON *MICROSOFT* HOLDINGS ON TYING

1. ***Why should any of the conduct be deemed a tie or foreclosing, given that OEMs could install a second browser as long as they were willing to incur customer technical support calls?*** The answer turns on the practical effects. If the costs of such technical support calls are enough to in fact decrease demand for rival browsers, then the tie has the requisite restraining effect on buyer demand for rival goods to raise the anticompetitive concerns.

2. ***Is the court correct that being barred from the most efficient means of distribution suffices to create an anticompetitive effect, even if other means of distribution remain open so that rivals are not completely foreclosed from reaching any users?*** Yes. Being barred from the most efficient means of distribution means rivals face higher costs and thus are less able to constrain monopoly pricing by the defendant. Complete foreclosure or elimination is unnecessary to create anticompetitive effects.

3. ***Of the various theories for why tying might be anticompetitive, which seems most applicable here?*** The theory that applies best here is that foreclosing the tied market might increase tying market power, because of the fear that customers would in the future start running applications on browsers, which would make browsers competitive with operating systems. Given the fixed ratio of browser to operating system and the fact that a browser is useless without some operating system, the other anticompetitive theories seem inapplicable, for reasons discussed in the introduction to this section.

4. ***Why were Microsoft's procompetitive justifications rejected?*** Microsoft argued that all its restrictions were justified to prevent alterations to its copyrighted software. Although it can prevent substantial alterations to its copyrighted software (which justified one of its license restrictions), the court deemed copyright law insufficient to justify an ability to prevent any alterations at all. Basically, copyright law was deemed to be functional here rather than expressive. If an author said publishers could not publish her book and change the last chapter, that restriction would likely be sustained. Here, the court thought the functional essence of the software was not being changed; Microsoft was rather bundling software features that did not need to be bundled.

Microsoft also claimed that OEM alterations might produce quality problems. However, the court did not think this claim was factually founded.

5. ***Why does the quasi-per se rule not apply to this tie?*** The *Microsoft* court's rationale was that platform services as an industry raised distinctive issues, such as innovation and a history of integrating previously separate products into single products. However, the Supreme Court has rejected the claim that different antitrust rules should apply to different

industries, as opposed to different sorts of agreement. *See, e.g., Maricopa.* Moreover, these issues are not unique to the platform software market, since many other industries also involve innovation and histories of integrating elements into products over time. For example, in the car industry, windshield wipers were once not included, but now are included in all new car sales. Nor does the great plasticity of software—which makes it easy to bundle or unbundle countless functionalities—suggest that a per se tying rule might be inappropriate, given that such plasticity makes it easier to manipulate bundling for anticompetitive reasons.

A better rationale would be that here the physical integration indicated a fixed ratio, and at the time browsers lacked any separate utility without an operating system. Accordingly, none of the anticompetitive effects that explain the quasi per se rule were applicable. Instead, the only applicable antitrust theory was that tying might increase tying market power, which requires that the tie foreclose a sufficient share of the tied market to have this effect. Because the quasi per se rule does not require proof of a substantial foreclosure share, it would not be suited to identify when this anticompetitive effect applied.

6. ***Is the Court right that the tying inquiry is different under § 1 because it must focus on whether procompetitive justifications offset anticompetitive effects in the tied market?*** No, because a § 1 tying claim could be based on anticompetitive effects in the tying market. However, here such a tying claim would not add anything to the monopolization claim, which already found anticompetitive effects in the tying operating system market, so there would have been no point proceeding with such a theory on remand.

D. LOYALTY AND BUNDLED DISCOUNTS

Loyalty Discounts and Their Similarities to Exclusive Dealing. Loyalty discounts are agreements whereby a seller gives buyers a price discount if buyers remain loyal to the seller by buying all, or some high percentage, of the relevant product from the seller. Loyalty rebates are the same, except that a rebate check is sent later to compliant buyers rather than having the discount taken off the price the buyer pays for the product. Loyalty programs may also provide other benefits that are not given on a per unit basis but are conditional on the buyer maintaining loyalty.

The terminology of "discount" or "rebates" can be misleading because it suggests that these agreements reflect lower prices, which may not be true when they are anticompetitive. All we know from the mere fact of a loyalty "discount" or "rebate" is that there is a price difference between the noncompliant price charged to buyers who decline to comply with the loyalty condition and the lower price charged to those who do. Sometimes, such a price difference might reflect a real discount from the but-for price that would have been paid without any loyalty program. However, if the defendant has raised that noncompliant price above the but-for price it would have charged without any loyalty program, or if its prices have generally been inflated by the foreclosure effects generated by the loyalty program, then the "discounted" price paid by loyal buyers may well be higher than the but-for price. Without some comparison to but-for prices, any loyalty discount or rebate could equally be called a disloyalty penalty imposed on buyers who refuse to restrict purchases from the seller's rivals. Rather than call them either loyalty discounts or disloyalty penalties, it would be more neutral to call them price differences conditioned on loyalty, because an important question is precisely whether the prices charged to those who refuse to abide by those conditions are above but-for prices (in which case they are really penalties) or below but-for prices (in which case they are really discounts). Because the terminology of loyalty discounts and rebates is so prevalent, we shall use it to refer to all price differences conditioned on loyalty, but it should not be understood to indicate that they reflect prices lower than but-for prices.

Loyalty discounts and rebates can differ in form from traditional exclusive dealing agreements in two ways. First, many loyalty discounts or rebates do not impose an absolute obligation to avoid dealing with rivals, but rather only condition the receipt of discounts or rebates on buyers restricting their purchases from rivals. When loyalty discounts and rebates do not require an affirmative buyer commitment, they are less absolute in form than exclusive dealing because they permit buyers a continual choice between complying with the loyalty condition and forgoing the discounts or rebates.

But this distinction may be more formal than real. Although exclusive dealing agreements are absolute in form, in fact under contract law any contractual obligation is a promise to either comply with the obligation or pay expectation damages, so that really such agreements continue to leave buyers with an ongoing choice. Obtaining expectation damages for violating an exclusive dealing agreement may also be difficult because it requires bringing a successful lawsuit and the amount of damages is often hard to establish. Moreover, because any exclusive dealing agreement that violates antitrust law is unenforceable under contract law, an absolute contractual obligation that violated antitrust law would not actually trigger any contractual penalties for noncompliance. Thus, often the only real penalty firms impose on buyers (or suppliers) who do not comply with an absolute exclusive dealing contract is terminating dealing with that buyer in the future. And the main penalty that such termination may impose is the loss of discounts that were given in exchange for the buyer agreement to the exclusivity term.

Similarly, even without buyer commitments, loyalty discounts or rebates could be understood as an absolute obligation that sets the financial penalty at the amount of the forgone discounts or rebates. Indeed, one can understand loyalty discounts or rebates as a way of making loyalty agreements more enforceable because it is easy for a seller to self-enforce such an agreement by withholding discounts or rebates, whereas an absolute obligation would generally require litigation and more uncertain proof of damages. Further, the amount of discounts and rebates can be set well above expectation damages, which would be impermissible under the standard contracts rule against penalty clauses.[90] In any event, under U.S. law, Clayton Act § 3 expressly treats discounts conditioned on not dealing with a rival as equivalent to agreements not to deal with a rival.

Second, loyalty discounts or rebates are often less than 100% exclusive. They may, for example, make the receipt of discounts or rebates conditional on buyers making 80% or 90% of their purchases from the defendant, thus restricting rivals to 10–20% of sales to those buyers. Because the anticompetitive effects generally turn on the total share of the market foreclosed, such agreements raise very similar issues to exclusive dealing.[91] For example, if the loyalty agreements foreclose 90% of sales to buyers who make 80% of purchases, then they achieve 72% marketwide foreclosure. This is likely to be even more anticompetitive than 100% exclusive dealing agreements with buyers who make 70% of purchases, which forecloses only 70% of the market.

Because they are based on the share of purchases made from the defendant, loyalty discounts also differ from volume-based discounts, which provide buyers with financial inducements if they purchase a given volume of product from the defendant. Compared to share-based discounts, volume-based discounts are generally less restrictive because they do not restrain the buyer from buying any volume they wish from the defendant's rivals, and they are more closely related to possible volume-based efficiencies. But when the volume is set in a way that covers all or most of each buyer's needs, the practical effect of volume-based discounts can be much the same as loyalty discounts.

Loyalty discounts can raise the same anticompetitive concerns as exclusive dealing. The main concern remains that they will foreclose a sufficient market share to impede the competitiveness of rivals, and thus increase the seller's market power in the foreclosed market. Further, while loyalty discounts may sometimes involve real discounts, there may also be cases where the noncompliant price exceeds the but-for price that would be charged without any loyalty program, in which case the loyalty discount is really a disloyalty penalty, which makes the coercive effect

[90] Although standard contract law forbids imposing financial penalties for breach that exceed a reasonable estimate of the harm caused by that breach, the same result can generally be obtained by reframing penalties as a bonus for performance because contract law generally refuses to second-guess the adequacy of consideration, which is the value the parties were willing to pay for performance. Loyalty discounts and rebates can exploit this distinction to convert contractually unenforceable penalties for failing to perform a loyalty condition into enforceable bonuses for performing them.

[91] Indeed, in United States v. Microsoft, 253 F.3d 34, 70–71 (D.C. Cir. 2001) (en banc), the court treated an agreement that foreclosed 75–85% of the covered distributors as exclusive dealing agreements.

quite similar to the coercive threat under exclusive dealing. Indeed, one can think of exclusive dealing as simply a special case of loyalty discounts where the disloyal price is set at infinity. But a disloyal price of less than infinity can have the same economic effect. For example, suppose a firm with market power, which sells a product for $100 without any loyalty condition, decides to raise the noncompliant price to $150 with a "discount" of $50, bringing the price back to $100, for any buyer who agrees to take 100% of the product from the firm. For buyers who do not value any units of the product more than $150, such a loyalty "discount" has precisely the same economic impact as absolute exclusive dealing because the threat is to deprive them of all the consumer surplus they would enjoy from buying that firm's product for $100, unless they agree to loyalty condition. Such examples do not mean all loyalty discounts reflect disloyalty penalties, but they mean that some could. Whether actual loyalty discounts reflect disloyalty penalties depends on whether the actual prices charged to disloyal buyers exceed but-for levels.

In those cases where loyalty discounts are really disloyalty penalties, the coercive effect can be smaller in degree than exclusive dealing for some buyers, but is similar in kind. In the above example, for buyers who value at least some units of the product more than $150, the threatened loss of consumer surplus is somewhat less with the loyalty discount than with exclusive dealing because such buyers could retain *some* of that consumer surplus by rejecting the loyalty discount and buying some units at $150, whereas they would get none of it if they rejected exclusive dealing. However, the threatened loss of consumer surplus is similar in kind, and can create the same externality problem. To avoid such an individual penalty, each buyer can have incentives to agree to a loyalty condition that (when many buyers agree) impairs rival competitiveness and raises prices, because most of the harm of each individual agreement is externalized onto the rest of the market (other than for an individual buyer that has more than a 50% market share).

Further, even if the loyalty discount (or exclusive dealing) offers a real short-term discount from but-for prices to compliant buyers, the buyers can all be harmed by accepting such a loyalty discount when the long-term effects of impairing rival competitiveness are higher prices. Indeed, an interesting body of economic literature finds that, because of externality problems, each buyer in a market with many buyers (who do not coordinate with each other) would have incentives to agree to anticompetitive loyalty discounts for a trivial short-term discount, even though the collective effect of all of them doing so is to create a substantial foreclosure share that impairs rival competitiveness in a way that greatly increases long-term prices above but-for levels.[92] Their

[92] MICHAEL D. WHINSTON, LECTURES ON ANTITRUST ECONOMICS 144–47, 166 (2006); Elhauge, *Defining Better*, *supra* note 12, at 284–92; Elhauge, *How Loyalty Discounts*, *supra* note 7, at 190, 217–19; Joseph Farrell, *Deconstructing Chicago on Exclusive Dealing*, 50 ANTITRUST BULL. 465, 476 (2005); Louis Kaplow & Carl Shapiro, *Antitrust*, in 2 HANDBOOK OF LAW & ECONOMICS 1073, 1203–10 (A. Mitchell Polinsky & Steven Shavell eds., 2007);

analysis indicates that if, for example, there are 10,000 equal-sized buyers of a product, and each individual buyer's agreement to a loyalty commitment contributes to a marketwide foreclosure that produces a marketwide price increase, then each individual buyer agreement externalizes 99.99% of the harm caused by that buyer's contribution to the market price increase. Such an externality would mean each buyer has incentives to agree to a loyalty commitment in exchange for any individual discount (or avoided price penalty) that exceeded 0.01% of that buyer's contribution to the marketwide price increase.

In a market with only one buyer, that buyer could not externalize any of the anticompetitive costs onto other buyers in the same market. Likewise, the externality problem across buyers in the same market could be defeated if a market has only a few concentrated buyers who can coordinate on a policy of rejecting anticompetitive loyalty discounts. However, externality problems can be worsened when the relevant buyers are not consumers, but intermediaries who resell to others. Such intermediate buyers might be able to externalize an even higher percentage of the harm by passing much or all of the price increase on to downstream buyers. Thus, some economic literature indicates that intermediate buyers are even more likely to agree to loyalty commitments that lead to a substantial foreclosure share that has anticompetitive effects on rival competitiveness.[93]

One often observes sophisticated buyers initiating requests for loyalty discounts. Some might conclude that such sophisticated buyer initiation likely indicates that the loyalty discounts benefit buyers. Sometimes this will be true, especially in cases where the loyalty discount reflects a real discount and forecloses only a small market share or in other cases where there is no externality problem. However, in cases where buyer decisions are driven by the above externality problem, then even the most sophisticated individual buyer has incentives to initiate a request for an anticompetitive loyalty discount, because each buyer individually benefits from receiving one given that most of the cost of its individual loyalty commitment is externalized onto others, even though the collective effect of all of them initiating a request for loyalty discounts is that all buyers are harmed. Where buyer decisions are driven by the externality problem, the fact that buyers initiate a request for loyalty discounts is similar to the fact that (before the adoption of laws that banned littering) individuals often initiated littering, even though the collective result of all of them doing so was to harm everyone. Moreover,

Eric B. Rasmusen, J. Mark Ramseyer & John S. Wiley, Jr., *Naked Exclusion,* 81 AM. ECON. REV. 1137 (1991); Ilya R. Segal & Michael D. Whinston, Comment, *Naked Exclusion,* 90 AM. ECON. REV. 296 (2000).

93 Jose Miguel Abito & Julian Wright, *Exclusive Dealing with Imperfect Downstream Competition*, 26 INT'L J. INDUS. ORG. 227 (2008); Elhauge, *Defining Better, supra* note 12, at 288–92; Farrell, *supra* note 92, at 475–77; John Simpson & Abraham L. Wickelgren, *Naked Exclusion, Efficient Breach, and Downstream Competition*, 97 AM. ECON. REV. 1305, 1306 (2007); Christodoulos Stefanadis, *Selective Contracts, Foreclosure, and the Chicago School View*, 41 J.L. & ECON. 429 (1998).

sophisticated intermediate buyers might have incentives to request loyalty rebates that give them a share of supracompetitive upstream profits, or loyalty discounts that give them a special discount unavailable to rivals, in order to gain a competitive advantage in the downstream market.[94]

None of this means that all loyalty discounts have such anticompetitive effects or that any per se rule is appropriate. Many loyalty discounts involve true discounts and small foreclosure shares that are unlikely to create anticompetitive effects, and as we shall see below, loyalty discounts can have efficiencies that offset their anticompetitive effects. Rule of reason analysis is thus appropriate, as with exclusive dealing, to determine which loyalty discounts have net anticompetitive effects and which do not.

Where market conditions create the above sort of externality problems, loyalty discounts that create a substantial foreclosure share that impairs rival competitiveness can produce anticompetitive harm even though all the prices are above cost, as prices are with exclusive dealing. For example, suppose a monopolist charges $200 for a product that costs $100 to make, which it sells to thousands of buyers. Other firms stand poised to enter the market, or to expand until they achieve sufficient scale to reduce their costs to $100, in which case competition will drive prices down to $100. To prevent this competitive outcome, the monopolist announces a loyalty program under which its price is $210 unless buyers agree to be loyal and buy 90% of their needs from the monopolist, in which case buyers get a nominal "discount" of $10. The externality theory predicts that all the buyers have incentives to agree because each individual decision to agree gets each buyer all of the nominal $10 "discount" but externalizes the vast bulk of each buyer agreement's marginal contribution to marketwide foreclosure onto the rest of the market. The result can thus be a 90% foreclosure share that prevents rivals from entering or expanding enough to achieve economies of scale, so that the buyers all continue to pay the monopoly price of $200, which is double the $100 price they would have paid but for the loyalty program.

The above example assumed a disloyalty penalty, but similar results could follow with a real loyalty discount. To illustrate, take the hypothetical above, but now instead assume the firm maintains the noncompliant price at $200, giving a true $10 discount (to $190) to buyers who agree to the loyalty condition. Then the externality theory predicts that all buyers still have individual incentives to agree to get the $10 discount, even though the collective result is to create a 90% foreclosure share that prevents rivals from entering and lowering long-term prices to $100. The buyers here get the short-term benefit of a $10 price reduction, but suffer a long-term price increase of $90 over but-for levels (continuing to pay the loyalty discount price of $190, rather than the $100

[94] Elhauge, *Defining Better*, *supra* note 12, at 288–92.

they would have paid without a loyalty program). However, in other cases, rule of reason analysis might reveal that the short-term price cut exceeded the long-term price increase.

Loyalty discounts can also perversely discourage discounting by effectively dividing markets even when they have no effect on rival efficiency.[95] Firms using loyalty discounts have less incentive to lower prices to loyal customers (because they are restrained from dealing with rivals) or to disloyal buyers (because any price reduction to them will, given the loyalty discount, also lower prices to loyal buyers). The condition also reduces the ability or incentive for the rival to win sales by cutting prices to loyal customers (because they are restrained from dealing with the rival) or to disloyal buyers (because the rival need only undercut the inflated disloyalty price charged to them by the firm using loyalty discounts). The effective market division is that the firm's pricing focuses on sales to loyal buyers, whereas the rival's pricing focuses on sales to disloyal buyers. The discouragement to price competition is worse the greater the discount level, the stronger the buyer loyalty commitment, and the greater the cumulative share of the market covered by loyalty discounts. However, the discouragement to price competition can persist in smaller degrees even without buyer loyalty commitments and even at low discount and foreclosure levels.

Bundled Discounts and Their Similarities to Tying. Bundled discounts are agreements to charge a buyer less if he takes both product *A* and *B* from the seller than if the buyer were to buy *A* and *B* separately. The product over which the firm has market power is the "linking" product and the other product is the "linked" product. When the buyer has to buy a high percentage of their linked product purchases from the seller to get the bundled discount, the bundled discount is a bundled loyalty discount. Bundled discounts can have all the same anticompetitive effects as tying whenever the unbundled price for the linking product (the product over which the firm has market power) exceeds the but-for price for that product (the price the firm would charge "but for" the bundling).[96] In other words, bundled "discounts" have all the same effects as tying whenever the price difference really reflects an unbundled penalty. Indeed, one can think of absolute tying as simply a special case of bundled discounts where the unbundled price for *A* is set at infinity.

Suppose, for example, a seller has market power in *A*, which sells independently for $100, and no market power in *B*, which sells at a competitive price of $50. He then raises the unbundled price for *A* to $140 but offers to sell the *A*-*B* bundle for a price of $160. The penalty for rejecting the bundle is that the buyer has to pay $40 extra for *A*, which

[95] *See* Elhauge, *How Loyalty Discounts*, *supra* note 7; Elhauge & Wickelgren, *supra* note 7. This effect does not require 100% exclusion nor any buyer commitment to the loyalty condition, though the size of the effect is great if those factors are present.

[96] Elhauge, *Tying*, *supra* note 28, at 402–03, 450–55.

may be less than the penalty for rejecting a classic tie if the buyer values some units of *A* at more than \$140. But in either case, rejection would entail a loss of consumer surplus on product A that can cause buyers to accept the bundle/tie if that loss would exceed the consumer surplus they lose from buying *B* for \$10 over competitive market rates.

If the unbundled price does not exceed the but-for price, then bundled discounts cannot have three of the possible anticompetitive effects created by tying: increasing intraproduct or interproduct price discrimination or extracting individual consumer surplus.[97] However, when they create a substantial foreclosure share, such bundled discounts can still have the other two anticompetitive effects of increasing the degree of tied or tying market power.[98] Further, the same externality problems that exist for loyalty discounts also apply to bundled discounts, and thus give buyers incentives to accept trivial discounts for agreeing to anticompetitive bundled discounts whose contribution to the creation of a substantial foreclosure share inflicts a marketwide harm that is mainly externalized onto others.[99]

None of these anticompetitive effects depends on any price being below cost. However, the ability of bundled discounts to produce anticompetitive effects depends on the same conditions that limit the ability of ties to do so. As with ties, a fixed product ratio (such as exist for unit-to-unit bundled discounts) means bundled discounts cannot increase intraproduct price discrimination or extract individual consumer surplus. A strong positive demand correlation (usually present when the products lack separate utility) knocks out the possibility of increasing interproduct price discrimination. The absence of a substantial foreclosure share means the bundle cannot increase the degree of tied or tying market power. Thus, the possibility of any anticompetitive effect is precluded by a combination of (1) a fixed ratio, (2) no separate utility, and (3) no substantial foreclosure share.

Cost-Based Tests of Possible Predatory Pricing Impact. For reasons noted above, the ability of loyalty and bundled discounts to achieve anticompetitive effects similar to exclusive dealing and tying does not depend on the discounted prices being below cost, any more than they did for exclusive dealing or tying. However, cost-based tests can tell us when loyalty and bundled discounts can achieve the same anticompetitive effects as predatory pricing.

For bundled discounts, the appropriate cost-based test defines the incremental price for the linked product as the bundled price minus the unbundled price for the linking product. If this incremental price for the linked product is below the defendant's cost of producing the linked product, then the cost test is flunked. (The same results can be obtained by applying the whole bundled discount to the linked product price).

---

97 *Id.*

98 *Id.* at 456–59.

99 *Id.*

For loyalty discounts, the cost-based inquiry turns on the extent to which buyer preferences would allow switching 100% to the rival. If buyer demand for the defendant's product is entirely contestable, then the inquiry would simply be whether the loyalty discount results in prices that are below the defendant's costs. However, suppose instead buyer demand for the defendant's product is partly contestable but partly incontestable. This might be true, for example, if some amount of the product must be bought to use with an installed base of capital or if the buyer is a distributor who has some downstream customers with an inelastic preference for the defendant's product. If so, loyalty discounts that cover both the contestable and incontestable portion of buyer demand amount to intraproduct bundled discounts. The appropriate cost-based test would then define the incremental price on the contestable portion as the total discounted price on the amount needed to meet the loyalty condition minus the undiscounted price on the incontestable portion of that amount. If this incremental price is below the defendant's cost of serving the contestable portion of demand, then the cost test is flunked.

The proper cost measure used in a cost-based test must take account of the fact that bundled and loyalty discounts can often last a long period because, unlike predatory pricing, they are profitable for the defendant. Because the relevant measure of cost includes all costs that are variable over the period of the alleged violation, *see* Chapter 3.C.2.a, if that period lasts a long time that may include something close to what is typically considered average total costs.

Some think that in practice most bundled or loyalty discounts are procompetitive and thus worry more about overdeterrence than underdeterrence, which they argue counsels for a cost-based test that lessens overdeterrence by offering a clearer safe harbor. However, a cost-based test is a poor choice to optimize the balance between overdeterrence and underdeterrence, because a cost-based test perversely exempts the most anticompetitive bundled and loyalty discounts—those that raise price well above costs—and because a cost-based test has the following defects.

First, if the anticompetitive concern is that loyalty or bundled discounts will create marketwide foreclosure that impairs rival efficiency, then such a cost-based foreclosure test assumes away the very anticompetitive concern being tested. Rivals that are equally efficient (in the sense of having a long run cost curve that is as low as the defendant) might be unable to achieve a price as low as the defendant's costs precisely because the foreclosure has relegated them to the high-cost portion of their cost curve. It would seem to be bootstrapping to allow a dominant seller to use loyalty or bundled discounts that impair the efficiency of its rivals, and then cite the rivals' lower efficiency as proof that those agreements cannot have an anticompetitive effect.[100]

Second, unlike in a straight case of low pricing, an equally efficient rival may have very little incentive to lower its price to its costs to try to overcome a bundled discount or a loyalty discount. One reason is that, as noted above, loyalty discounts or bundled loyalty discounts can perversely divide markets in a way that discourages rivals from cutting prices. This effect persists even though rival prices exceed costs, and indeed the problem is that the loyalty discount can affirmatively give rivals incentives to set prices further above costs than they otherwise would.[101] Another reason is that rivals can lack incentives to cut prices to costs even when there is no effective market division. In the bundled discount case, the rival will know that no matter how much profit it sacrifices by lowering its "tied" product price down towards costs, an equally efficient defendant with market power can always offset that rival price cut by simply *raising* the defendant's unbundled price for the "tying" product, without any defendant price cut or profit sacrifice being necessary. Anticipating this, the rival will be reluctant to cut prices at all. Likewise, for loyalty discounts, a rival for the contestable portion of demand will know that no matter how much the rival sacrifices profits by lowering its prices down towards costs, the defendant can always offset that rival price cut by raising the defendant's noncompliant price on the incontestable portion of demand, without any defendant price cut or profit sacrifice being necessary. Using a price-cost test that assumes rivals will price down towards cost in such cases will amount to assuming economically irrational behavior that we are unlikely to see even when the bundled or loyalty discounts are highly anticompetitive.

Third, a cost-based test bears no relationship to whether the bundled discounts are producing the same anticompetitive effects as tying can without a substantial foreclosure share. Because antitrust doctrine condemns ties that increase interproduct and intraproduct price discrimination and extract individual consumer surplus, bundled discounts that create the same effects would seem equally subject to condemnation. But those effects turn on whether the unbundled price for the less-competitive product exceeds its but-for price, which has no necessary connection to whether the effective price for the more-competitive product is below its cost. Indeed, in the case of interproduct price discrimination, the harm flows from market power over both

---

[100] One approach to try to deal with this problem is to compare the incremental price instead to the *rival's* price or costs (including a fair rate of return). *See* X AREEDA, ELHAUGE & HOVENKAMP, ANTITRUST LAW ¶ 1758e, at 350 (1996). However, this approach has several problems. First, the defendant and rival products might differ in features or quality in a way that means a price comparison would require determining quality-adjusted prices, whose magnitude is difficult to assess and could vary across customers with varying preferences. Second, this sort of approach rewards inefficiency by giving greater rights to less efficient rivals. Third, using rival costs would make it difficult for firms to gauge when their bundled or loyalty discounts are illegal because they cannot observe rival costs.

[101] *See* Elhauge, Loyalty Discounts, *supra* note 7; Elhauge & Wickelgren, *supra* note 7.

products, so it is hard to know how to apply an incremental price-cost test at all.

Fourth, a cost-based test also fails to capture the concern that intermediate buyers might collude with sellers to create a foreclosure that helps exploit downstream buyers, and then divide up the supracompetitive profits.[102] In such cases, it may not be possible for rivals to offset the benefits to intermediate buyers by just offering prices at the seller's costs, because rivals would also have to offer a share of supracompetitive profits that are unavailable to them.

Fifth, a cost-based test would not capture the concern that foreclosure might impair rival expandability or aid oligopolistic coordination.

Sixth, unlike with predatory pricing, what requires justification in the case of loyalty and bundled discounts is not the pricing, but the loyalty or bundled condition attached to the pricing. Such conditions create anticompetitive problems that are not raised by mere low pricing. They discourage discounting to unconditioned buyers. Loyalty conditions attached to low prices also prevent rivals from winning sales by matching prices one purchase at a time, but instead require the rival to be able to replace all the units a purchaser has, which may be difficult, especially if some of the purchases are hard to contest, such as when some are used with some installed base of capital equipment. Bundled discounts in addition require rivals to overcome discounts on other products.

Seventh, it is not clear why antitrust concerns should be limited to equally efficient rivals, because impairing or excluding less efficient rivals can also have anticompetitive effects by removing a constraint on the defendant's market power. Suppose, for example, a monopolist has costs of $100 and could charge a monopoly price of $200 but for the existence of a less efficient rival that has costs of $150. Then driving out that less efficient rival with loyalty or bundled discounts will harm consumer welfare.

To be sure, above-cost price cuts could also drive out less efficient rivals. But there are special reasons to limit predatory pricing doctrine to prices that are below cost that do not apply when those prices are conditioned on requirements of loyalty or bundled purchases.[103] Firms can easily avoid using loyalty or bundled conditions, and those conditions may not involve any true discount that benefits consumers even in the short run. Nor is there is anything undesirable about deterring firms from using such conditions when they lack any procompetitive justification, because in that case the firm could always cut prices without that condition. In contrast, predatory pricing doctrine must take into account that firms cannot avoid setting some price, and above-cost price cutting necessarily benefits consumers at least in the short run.

---

[102] *See* Chapter 4.B.

[103] *See* Elhauge, *Tying, supra* note 28, at 464 n.198, 474.

Further, a rule against above-cost price cuts would deter desirable price cuts (a) when entrants are equally or more efficient and (b) when less efficient entrants would enter despite the prospect of above-cost price cuts, given the short-run profits they can earn before those price cuts kick in. Restraining above-cost price cuts also provides only weak encouragement to entry by other less efficient rivals, because in the long run the incumbent will lose enough market share that it can cut prices and drive out the less efficient entrant, and anyway the effects in such cases are mixed because some consumers will pay higher prices to the incumbent than they otherwise would have.

Finally, price-cost tests are difficult to administer. Cost data is very hard to assess, and decades after *Brooke* we still do not even have any clear resolution of what the right cost test is. Further, it is often very hard to get reliable cost data at all. To be sure, the problem also plagues predatory pricing doctrine, but when judging pure pricing, courts do not have the alternative of addressing the issue by simply voiding a condition that lacks any procompetitive justification to offset its restraining effect. There is no such condition in a predatory pricing case, and courts can hardly ban a firm from pricing; courts have to indicate what price the firm could set. Moreover, applying a price-cost test to bundled or loyalty discounts adds the difficult task of calculating the incremental price, which may not only be difficult but impossible for loyalty discounts, given that the data may not exist to quantify incontestable demand. Thus, although price-cost tests may superficially look clearer than applying the rule of reason in hypotheticals where the incremental prices and costs are specified, in actual cases both the price and cost are hard to ascertain, often unclear, and perhaps unknowable.

Possible Efficiencies. Loyalty and bundled discounts raise some, but not all, of the same possible efficiencies as exclusive dealing and tying agreements. It is generally hard to argue that loyalty and bundled discounts are designed to improve quality because they do not guarantee 100% usage of the allegedly higher-quality product. It is also generally hard to argue that they increase value to the buyer, because that would make it be unnecessary to give a discount to get buyers to comply. Further, to the extent the justification is to provide certainty that lowers the sellers' risk-bearing or inventory costs or that encourages relationship-specific investment by the seller, the problem is that loyalty and bundled discounts often lack commitments that prohibit the buyer from changing its purchases, and thus do not create the requisite seller certainty in the way that exclusive dealing obligations might.

Loyalty and bundled discounts might be justified by cost savings, but this raises two issues. First, if the discount amount exceeds any cost savings, then such discounts go beyond this justification and suggest a foreclosing purpose. Perhaps such discounts can be justified as an effective cut in a supracompetitive price (if the discounted price remains above cost), but what requires justification is linking the discount to a loyalty or bundled condition. On the other hand, if firms fear tribunals will later erroneously decide costs are higher than they really are, a prohibition on discounts that exceed the cost savings might deter desirable price-cutting.

Second, if cost-savings are related to volume-based efficiencies, volume-based discounts would generally be an alternative that is not only less restrictive but more effective, thus suggesting share-based discounts must be meant to achieve some nonefficiency goal. After all, a share-based discount gives a greater discount to a compliant small buyer than to a noncompliant large buyer even if the latter purchases a greater total volume and generates more efficiencies. At least presumptively, then, volume-based efficiencies support only volume-based discounts that are uniform in the sense that every buyer can get the same discount if it buys the same volume.

Perhaps one explanation for using share-based discounts to achieve volume-based efficiencies is that, in volatile industries, it may be too risky for the buyer to make volume-based commitments. This is especially likely to be the case when the buyer is distributing a product whose local demand fluctuates; the seller might be able to assess that risk more accurately than the buyer and to spread the localized risk among multiple distributors. If so, share-based commitments might be the best alternative to accomplish similar efficiencies with lower risk-bearing costs. True, volume-based discounts do not require any contractual commitment to buy a fixed volume. But to the extent buyers have to make effective commitments (such as to market the seller's product or to design their own product to use the seller's product as an input), they may be unwilling to make those commitments unless they know they can get a low price no matter how well the product does. Still, this efficiency seems unlikely in industries where purchase requirements are relatively stable, such as hospitals buying medical devices whose volume is determined by patient need.

Another possibility is that loyalty and bundled discounts might sometimes efficiently resolve problems with the verifiability of effort.[104]  One could, for example, imagine them incentivizing marketing efforts in a way that other legal duties could not. And they might do so in a way that is less anticompetitive, and less risky for the distributor, than an exclusive dealing obligation. For example, suppose a seller wants to pay for $1 million in marketing effort by a distributor. However, it knows that if it just hands over the cash, it will have a hard time verifying the effectiveness of that marketing effort. It also knows that specifying marketing duties might not be efficient, because the type of marketing effort that will be the most effective will turn on local and future conditions that the distributor is best placed to judge. One way to avoid such problems might be to use share-based or volume-based discounts or rebates, so that the distributor earns the $1 million (in the form of

[104] *See* Chapter 4.B.

discounts or rebates) only if their efforts actually effectively moved enough of the product. This gives the distributor natural incentives to engage in marketing efforts and exercise its best judgment to make those efforts effective. And share-based discounts might be more efficient than volume-based discounts where the latter seem too risky for the distributor.

Conclusion. In short, loyalty and bundled discounts seem to have enough possible efficiencies and anticompetitive potential to be judged under some form of rule of reason review, rather than being deemed per se legal or illegal.

United States v. Loew's Inc.

371 U.S. 38 (1962).

■ MR. JUSTICE GOLDBERG delivered the opinion of the Court.

These consolidated appeals present as a key question the validity under § 1 of the Sherman Act of block booking of copyrighted feature motion pictures for television exhibition. We hold that the tying agreements here are illegal and in violation of the Act.

The United States brought separate civil antitrust actions . . . against six major distributors . . . alleging that each defendant . . . had, in selling to television stations, conditioned the license or sale of one or more feature films upon the acceptance by the station of a package or block containing one or more unwanted or inferior films. . . .

The court entered separate final judgments against the defendants, wherein each was enjoined from [(a) conditioning the sale of a film on the purchase of another or (b) offering package discounts that had the effect of imposing such a condition.]

. . . The requisite economic power is presumed when the tying product is patented or copyrighted . . . The district judge found that each copyrighted film block booked by appellants for television use "was in itself a unique product"; that feature films "varied in theme, in artistic performance, in stars, in audience appeal, etc.," and were not fungible; and that since each defendant by reason of its copyright had a "monopolistic" position as to each tying product, "sufficient economic power" to impose an appreciable restraint on free competition in the tied product was present. . .[6] We agree. These findings of the district judge, supported by the record, confirm the presumption of uniqueness resulting from the existence of the copyright itself.

Moreover, there can be no question in this case of the adverse effects on free competition resulting from appellants' illegal block booking contracts. Television stations forced by appellants to take unwanted

[6] To use the trial court's apt example, forcing a television station which wants "Gone With The Wind" to take "Getting Gertie's Garter" as well is taking undue advantage of the fact that to television as well as motion picture viewers there is but one "Gone With The Wind."

films were denied access to films marketed by other distributors who, in turn, were foreclosed from selling to the stations. Nor can there be any question as to the substantiality of the commerce involved. The 25 contracts found to have been illegally block booked involved payments to appellants ranging from $60,800 in the case of Screen Gems to over $2,500,000 in the case of Associated Artists. A substantial portion of the licensing fees represented the cost of the inferior films which the stations were required to accept. These anticompetitive consequences are an apt illustration of the reasons underlying our recognition that the mere presence of competing substitutes for the tying product, here taking the form of other programming material as well as other feature films, is insufficient to destroy the legal, and indeed the economic, distinctiveness of the copyrighted product. By the same token, the distinctiveness of the copyrighted tied product is not inconsistent with the fact of competition, in the form of other programming material and other films, which is suppressed by the tying arrangements. . . .

Appellants (other than C & C) make the additional argument that each of them was found to have entered into such a small number of illegal contracts as to make it improper to enter injunctive relief. Appellants urge that their over-all sales policies were to allow selective purchasing of films, and that in light of this, the fact that a few contracts were found to be illegal does not justify the entering of injunctive relief. We disagree. Illegality having been properly found, appellants cannot now complain that its incidence was too scattered to warrant injunctive relief. . . . There is no reason to disturb the judge's legal conclusions and decree merely because he did not find more illegal agreements when, as here, the illegal behavior of each defendant had substantial anticompetitive effects. . . .

The United States contends that the relief afforded by the final judgments is inadequate and that to be adequate it must also: (1) require the defendants to price the films individually and offer them on a picture-by-picture basis; (2) prohibit noncost-justified differentials in price between a film when sold individually and when sold as part of a package . . . Some of the practices which the Government seeks to have enjoined with its requested modifications are acts which may be entirely proper when viewed alone. To ensure, however, that relief is effectual, otherwise permissible practices connected with the acts found to be illegal must sometimes be enjoined. . . .

The final judgments as entered only prohibit a price differential between a film offered individually and as part of a package which "has the effect of conditioning the sale or license of such film upon the sale or license of one or more other films." The Government contends that this provision appearing by itself is too vague and will lead to unnecessary litigation. Differentials unjustified by cost savings may already be prohibited under the decree as it now appears. Nevertheless, the addition of a specific provision to prevent such differentials will prevent uncertainty in the operation of the decree. To ensure that litigation over the scope and application of the decrees is not left until a contempt proceeding is brought, the second requested modification should be added. The Government, however, seeks to make distribution costs the only saving which can legitimately be the basis of a discount. We would not so limit the relevant cost justifications. To prevent definitional arguments, and to ensure that all proper bases of quantity discount may be used, the modification should be worded in terms of allowing all legitimate cost justifications. . . .

NOTES AND QUESTIONS ON *LOEW'S*

1. ***Was there a substantial foreclosure share and tying market power?*** If we define each film as a separate market, then it would seem that there could be no foreclosure of any market since each market necessarily has only one seller under copyright law. But here the situation is best characterized as competition between films that are partial substitutes, for which there are common economies of scale in production. Thus, there might be a theoretical concern that film distributors could foreclose enough of the market for all films to impair rival competitiveness. However, here there were only 25 tying contracts that constituted a limited dollar amount of sales, so it seems unlikely that the ties foreclosed a share of all films that was large enough to achieve such anticompetitive effects. Further, the Court relied only on the dollar foreclosure, requiring no evidence of substantial foreclosure share. It thus seems that the anticompetitive theory that persuaded the Court must have involved something other than foreclosing a substantial enough market share to impair rival competitiveness.

A single film probably also lacks enough market power to impose a tie that could substantially foreclose the market for all films. While perhaps a group of desirable films might have such market power, this issue was not addressed. This may have been because the Court just inferred market power from the copyright on each film, an inference that is no longer permitted after *Illinois Tool Works. See* Chapter 4.C. It may also have reflected the fact that the Court was assuming a different anticompetitive theory, as discussed next.

2. ***Might the tying agreements have facilitated price discrimination?*** They may well have. Suppose there are two television stations. One values "Gone With the Wind" at $200,000 and "Getting Gertie's Garter" at $50,000. The other values "Gone With the Wind" at $180,000 and "Getting Gertie's Garter" at $70,000. If a distributor with both films charged separate prices that were low enough to sell both films to both stations, it would have to charge $180,000 for "Gone With The Wind" and $50,000 for "Getting Gertie's Garter". The distributor would get $230,000 from each television station, for a total of $460,000 across both stations. Because each station would get one of the films for $20,000 less than its value to that station, each would enjoy a consumer surplus of $20,000, for a total consumer welfare of $40,000. If the distributor instead sold both films only as a package, it could get $250,000 per package from each station, thus getting a

total of $500,000 across both stations. Each station would value the package just at what they paid ($250,000), and thus they would now get $0 in consumer welfare.

Such a tie would thus be more profitable for the distributor, and more harmful to consumer welfare, than the alternative of separately pricing the films at levels that would sell both films to both stations. The tie would also be more profitable (and more harmful to consumer welfare) than the alternatives of separately pricing one or both films at higher levels that would sell the film(s) to only one television station, as the following table shows.

Block-Booking as Price Discrimination (W = Gone With the Wind; G = Getting Gertie's Garter)			
Seller Price Options	**Station A (Valuations: W $200K, G $50K)**	**Station B (Valuations: W $180K, G $70K)**	**Firm Revenue & Consumer Welfare (CW)**
W $200K G $70K	Buy W No Buy G	No Buy W Buy G	Revenue $270K CW = $0
W $200K G $50K	Buy W Buy G	No Buy W Buy G	Revenue $300K CW = $20K
W $180K G $70K	Buy W No Buy G	Buy W Buy G	Revenue $430K CW = $20K
W $180K G $50K	Buy W Buy G	Buy W Buy G	Revenue $460K CW = $40K
Package $250K	Buy Package	Buy Package	Revenue $500K CW = $0

The identical effect could be achieved by offering the films at high unbundled prices and then offering a "bundled discount" for the package at $250,000. For example, suppose the distributor instead sold "Gone With the Wind" at an unbundled price of $201,000, "Getting Gertie's Garter" at an unbundled price of "$71,000" and a package of both for $250,000. Then no station would find it desirable to buy either film separately and each would buy the package.

In short, *Loew's* may be an example of a case where a tie or bundle achieves inter-product price discrimination. Such an effect applies to more general and continuous demand curves among buyers, as long as the demands for the two films do not have a strong positive correlation.[105] This effect does not require foreclosing a substantial share of all films, and thus it does not require having sufficient market power across all films to create such a substantial foreclosure share. It suffices for this effect that each film is sufficiently distinctive that it has some film-specific downward sloping

[105] *See supra* text accompanying notes 40–47.

demand curve, a weaker form of market power that might well be conferred by the copyright on each commercially marketable film. This theory thus fits the facts that the Court required no evidence of a substantial foreclosure share and inferred the requisite market power so readily from individual film copyrights.

3. ***Must package discounts be cost justified?*** The Court modified the injunction in two ways. It allowed packaged discounts that are cost-justified—i.e., no larger than the cost savings created by packaging the products—even if the package discounts induce buyers to accept the bundle. This holding seems to establish that package cost savings can be a redeeming procompetitive justification for package discounts that do not exceed the package cost savings.

The Court also modified the injunction to preclude any package discounts that exceed package cost savings. This holding does not necessarily mean that all such package discounts would necessarily be illegal, because the Court also stressed that injunctive relief can go beyond condemning illegal conduct. Banning all package discounts that exceed package cost savings might undesirably deter companies from lowering their package prices if they are uncertain about the degree of cost savings or about how courts might quantify those cost savings. Such uncertainties can create overdeterrence concerns that counsel against a legal prohibition on all package discounts that exceed package cost savings. In contrast, when a defendant has already been found to have acted illegality and the issue is fashioning injunctive relief, underdeterrence concerns get more weight and are thus likely to override such overdeterrence concerns.

Although injunctive remedies can extend beyond illegal conduct for these reasons, the Court would not have designed its injunctive relief in such a way that, even if adjudicated with perfect accuracy, the injunction would interfere with bundled discounts that the Court deemed procompetitive. This point is significant because a package discount could easily exceed the package cost-savings even though the package discount resulted in a bundled price that exceeded the cost of making the bundle or an effective price for the tied product that exceeded the cost of making that product. Indeed, bundled discounts that do not violate such price-cost tests would necessarily exceed package cost savings in any case where no package cost savings exist. Thus, *Loew's* implicitly holds that not all bundled discounts that result in bundled or effective prices above cost are procompetitive.

The U.S. Lower Court Splits on Loyalty Discounts and Bundled Discounts

Clayton Act § 3 explicitly makes it unlawful to substantially lessen competition by selling goods with a "discount" that is conditioned on the buyer not buying from rivals, which has been read to cover bundled or unbundled agreements of this sort whenever they have the practical effect of inducing such loyalty. Supreme Court cases have also established that it is not an antitrust defense that buyers were not 100%

precluded by the loyalty condition,[106] could have avoided a loyalty or bundled condition by paying more,[107] or could have terminated a loyalty condition at will by foregoing such benefits.[108] Nor has any Supreme Court antitrust case finding loyalty discounts illegal required a below-cost price. But these cases all were before 1967, and the lack of recent Supreme Court cases has led to splits by modern lower courts on both single-product loyalty discounts and bundled discounts.

Single-Product Loyalty Discounts. The Eighth Circuit court has held that single-product loyalty discounts are judged under standard rule-of-reason analysis under Sherman Act § 1, but under a price-cost test under Sherman Act § 2.[109] The Third Circuit at first held en banc that, under Sherman Act § 2, single-product loyalty discounts are governed by normal rule-of-reason analysis, rather than by a price-cost test.[110] More recently, two three-judge panels of the Third Circuit have instead held that (under any antitrust provision) a price-cost test applies to single-product loyalty discounts "only when 'price is the clearly predominant mechanism of exclusion.' "[111]

Bundled Discounts. The Third Circuit has held that (under Sherman Act § 1 or § 2) bundled discounts are not judged under a price-cost test but instead under standard rule-of-reason analysis, which makes them illegal when they have anticompetitive effects that are not

[106] *See* FTC v. Brown Shoe, 384 U.S. 316, 318 (1966) (condemning discounts conditioned on obligation to "concentrate" dealer business on the defendant's shoes, which in practice meant 75% of purchases).

[107] *See* Standard Fashion v. Magrane-Houston, 258 U.S. 346, 351–52 (1922) (loyalty condition); United Shoe Machinery v. United States, 258 U.S. 451, 464 (1922) (bundled condition).

[108] *See* FTC v. Brown Shoe, 384 U.S. 316, 318–19 & n.13 (1966) (condemning loyalty discount even though buyers could "voluntarily withdraw" at any time), *rev'g* 339 F.2d 45, 53 (8th Cir. 1964) (sustaining agreement in part because "[r]etailers were free to abandon the arrangement at any time they saw it to their advantage so to do").

[109] Concord Boat v. Brunswick Corp., 207 F.3d 1039, 1058–1060 (8th Cir. 2000) (deeming the challenged "market share discounts" legal under Sherman Act § 1 because plaintiffs failed to show that the loyalty discounts "had foreclosed a substantial share of the . . . market" or required any loyalty commitment or that the market had "significant barriers to entry"); *id.* at 1060–1062 (deeming the "market share discounts" legal under Sherman Act § 2 because they were above cost). Although the First and Sixth Circuits are sometimes wrongly interpreted as holding that loyalty discounts are subject to a price-cost test, in fact they so held only when addressing a separate claim against the discounts themselves. Barry Wright Corp. v. ITT Grinnell Corp., 724 F.2d 227, 230–236 (1st Cir.1983); NicSand, Inc. v. 3M Co., 507 F.3d 442, 451–453 (6th Cir.2007) (en banc). On the alleged loyalty condition attached to those prices, neither court held they were governed by a price-cost test. The First Circuit instead rejected a Sherman Act § 2 challenge to the alleged loyalty discount because (1) there was no actual loyalty condition, just a fixed volume attached to the discounts; (2) there were legitimate business justifications, and (3) the discounts were demanded by a dominant buyer with a 43–52% buyer market share. 724 F.2d at 229, 236–238. The Sixth Circuit held that, while buyers would have a claim against the challenged loyalty discounts if they led to monopoly prices, *id.* at 454, the complaining rival lacked antitrust injury on the unique facts of that case because the rival had 67% of the market and the defendant's loyalty discounts were demanded by buyers and used to overcome the dominant rival's own exclusive dealing agreements. *Id.* at 453–459.

[110] LePage's v. 3M, 324 F.3d 141, 147–52, 157–164 (3d Cir. 2003) (en banc).

[111] Eisai, Inc. v. Sanofi Aventis U.S., LLC, 821 F.3d 394, 402, 409 (2016); ZF Meritor, LLC v. Eaton Corp., 696 F.3d 254, 269 n.9, 275 (3d Cir.2012).

offset by any procompetitive efficiencies.[112] The Ninth Circuit has instead held that bundled discounts are illegal under Sherman Act § 2 only if they violate a discount attribution price-cost test, which asks whether, after attributing all the bundled discount to the more-competitive product, its effective price is below the defendant's cost.[113] Under Sherman Act § 1, the Ninth Circuit did not apply this price-cost test but instead held that bundled discounts could be an illegal tie if either (a) the proportion of separate sales to bundled sales is low (with 14% being low enough) or (b) the defendant is able to sell the tied product at a price that exceeds the rival price for that product.[114] The Sixth Circuit has instead held that the discount attribution price-cost test also determines whether a bundled discount constitutes a tie under Sherman Act § 1.[115]

The cases below illustrate the currently contested issues.

LePage's Inc. v. 3M

324 F.3d 141 (3d Cir. 2003) (en banc).

■ SLOVITER, CIRCUIT JUDGE, with whom BECKER, CHIEF JUDGE, NYGAARD, MCKEE, AMBRO, FUENTES, and SMITH, CIRCUIT JUDGES, join:

Minnesota Mining and Manufacturing Company ("3M") appeals from the District Court's order . . . declining to overturn the jury's verdict for LePage's in its suit against 3M under Section 2 of the Sherman Act ("§ 2"). 3M raises various objections to the trial court's decision but essentially its position is a legal one: it contends that a plaintiff cannot succeed in a § 2 monopolization case unless it shows that the conceded monopolist sold its product below cost. Because we conclude that exclusionary conduct, such as the exclusive dealing and bundled rebates proven here, can sustain a verdict under § 2 against a monopolist and because we find no other reversible error, we will affirm.

I. Factual Background

3M, which manufactures Scotch tape for home and office use, dominated the United States transparent tape market with a market share above 90% until the early 1990s. It has conceded that it has a monopoly in that market. LePage's . . . around 1980, decided to sell "second brand" and private label transparent tape, *i.e.*, tape sold under the retailer's name rather than under the name of the manufacturer. By 1992, LePage's sold 88% of private label tape sales in the United States, which represented but a small portion of the transparent tape market. Private label tape sold at a lower price to the retailer and the customer than branded tape.

---

[112] *LePage's*, 324 F.3d at 147–52, 154–157, 159–164 (under Sherman Act § 2); *Eisai*, 821 F.3d at 405–406 (confirming rejection of price-cost test for bundled discounts under § 1 or § 2); *ZF Meritor*, 696 F.3d at 274 n. 11 (same).

[113] *See* Cascade Health Solutions v. PeaceHealth, 502 F.3d 895, 920–921 (9th Cir. 2007).

[114] *See id.* at 928–929.

[115] *See* Collins Inkjet Corp. v. Eastman Kodak Co., 781 F.3d 264, 270–273 (6th Cir. 2015).

Distribution patterns and consumer acceptance accounted for a shift of some tape sales from branded tape to private label tape. With the rapid growth of office superstores, such as Staples and Office Depot, and mass merchandisers, such as Wal-Mart and Kmart, distribution patterns for second brand and private label tape changed as many of the large retailers wanted to use their "brand names" to sell stationery products, including transparent tape. 3M also entered the private label business during the early 1990s and sold its own second brand under the name "Highland."

LePage's claims that, in response to the growth of this competitive market, 3M engaged in a series of related, anticompetitive acts aimed at restricting the availability of lower-priced transparent tape to consumers. It also claims that 3M devised programs that prevented LePage's and the other domestic company in the business, Tesa Tuck, Inc., from gaining or maintaining large volume sales and that 3M maintained its monopoly by stifling growth of private label tape and by coordinating efforts aimed at large distributors to keep retail prices for Scotch tape high. LePage's claims that it barely was surviving at the time of trial and that it suffered large operating losses from 1996 through 1999.

LePage's brought this antitrust action asserting that 3M used its monopoly over its Scotch tape brand to gain a competitive advantage in the private label tape portion of the transparent tape market in the United States through the use of 3M's multi-tiered "bundled rebate" structure, which offered higher rebates when customers purchased products in a number of 3M's different product lines. LePage's also alleges that 3M offered to some of LePage's customers large lump-sum cash payments, promotional allowances and other cash incentives to encourage them to enter into exclusive dealing arrangements with 3M. . . .

[T]he jury returned its verdict for LePage's on . . . its monopolization . . . clai[m]. . . .

III. Monopolization—Applicable Legal Principles

. . . In this case, the parties agreed that the relevant product market is transparent tape and the relevant geographic market is the United States. . . . LePage's argues that 3M willfully maintained its monopoly in the transparent tape market through exclusionary conduct, primarily by bundling its rebates and entering into contracts that expressly or effectively required dealing virtually exclusively with 3M, which LePage's characterizes as *de facto* exclusive. 3M does not argue that it did not engage in this conduct. It agrees that it offered bundled rebates and entered into some exclusive dealing contracts, although it argues that only the few contracts that are expressly exclusive may be considered as such. Instead, 3M argues that its conduct was legal as a matter of law because it never priced its transparent tape below its cost. . . . For this proposition it relies on the Supreme Court's decision in *Brooke Group*. . . .

It is therefore necessary for us, at the outset, to examine whether we must accept 3M's legal theory that after *Brooke Group,* no conduct by a monopolist who sells its product above cost—no matter how exclusionary the conduct—can constitute monopolization in violation of § 2 of the Sherman Act. . . . LePage's, unlike the plaintiff in *Brooke Group,* does not make a predatory pricing claim. . . . Nothing in any of the Supreme Court's opinions in the decade since the *Brooke Group* decision suggested that the opinion overturned decades of Supreme Court precedent that evaluated a monopolist's liability under § 2 by examining its exclusionary, i.e., predatory, conduct. . . . Thus, nothing that the Supreme Court has written since *Brooke Group* dilutes the Court's consistent holdings that a monopolist will be found to violate § 2 of the Sherman Act if it engages in exclusionary or predatory conduct without a valid business justification.

IV. Monopolization—Exclusionary Conduct . . .

B. *Bundled Rebates*

. . . 3M offered many of LePage's major customers substantial rebates to induce them to eliminate or reduce their purchases of tape from LePage's. Rather than competing by offering volume discounts which are concededly legal and often reflect cost savings, 3M's rebate programs offered discounts to certain customers conditioned on purchases spanning six of 3M's diverse product lines. The product lines covered by the rebate program were: Health Care Products, Home Care Products, Home Improvement Products, Stationery Products (including transparent tape), Retail Auto Products, and Leisure Time. In addition to bundling the rebates, both of 3M's rebate programs set customer-specific target growth rates in each product line. The size of the rebate was linked to the number of product lines in which targets were met, and the number of targets met by the buyer determined the rebate it would receive on all of its purchases. If a customer failed to meet the target for any one product, its failure would cause it to lose the rebate across the line. This created a substantial incentive for each customer to meet the targets across all product lines to maximize its rebates.

The rebates were considerable, not "modest" as 3M states. For example, Kmart, which had constituted 10% of LePage's business, received $926,287 in 1997, and in 1996 Wal-Mart received more than $1.5 million, Sam's Club received $666,620, and Target received $482,001. Just as significant as the amounts received is the powerful incentive they provided to customers to purchase 3M tape rather than LePage's in order not to forego the maximum rebate 3M offered. The penalty would have been $264,000 for Sam's Club, $450,000 for Kmart, and $200,000 to $310,000 for American Stores. . . .

[O]ne of the leading treatises notes that "the great majority of bundled rebate programs yield aggregate prices above cost. Rather than analogizing them to predatory pricing, they are best compared with tying, whose foreclosure effects are similar. Indeed, the 'package discount' is often a close analogy." Phillip E. Areeda & Herbert Hovenkamp, Antitrust Law ¶ 794, at 83 (Supp.2002). The treatise then discusses the anticompetitive effect as follows:

> The anticompetitive feature of package discounting is the strong incentive it gives buyers to take increasing amounts or even all of a product in order to take advantage of a discount aggregated across multiple products. In the anticompetitive case, which we presume is in the minority, the defendant rewards the customer for buying its product *B* rather than the plaintiff's *B*, not because defendant's *B* is better or even cheaper. Rather, the customer buys the defendant's *B* in order to receive a greater discount on *A*, which the plaintiff does not produce. In that case the rival can compete in *B* only by giving the customer a price that compensates it for the foregone *A* discount.

Id. The authors then conclude: "Depending on the number of products that are aggregated and the customer's relative purchases of each, even an equally efficient rival may find it impossible to compensate for lost discounts on products that it does not produce." *Id.* at 83–84.

The principal anticompetitive effect of bundled rebates as offered by 3M is that when offered by a monopolist they may foreclose portions of the market to a potential competitor who does not manufacture an equally diverse group of products and who therefore cannot make a comparable offer . . . . . LePage's private-label and second-tier tapes are . . . less expensive but otherwise of similar quality to Scotch-brand tape. Indeed, before 3M instituted its rebate program, LePage's had begun to enjoy a small but rapidly expanding toehold in the transparent tape market. 3M's incentive was thus . . . to preserve the market position of Scotch-brand tape by discouraging widespread acceptance of the cheaper, but substantially similar, tape produced by LePage's. . . . [T]he bundled rebates reflected an exploitation of the seller's monopoly power. . . . [T]he evidence in this case shows that Scotch-brand tape is indispensable to any retailer in the transparent tape market. . . . 3M's rebates required purchases bridging 3M's extensive product lines. In some cases, these magnified rebates to a particular customer were as much as half of LePage's entire prior tape sales to that customer. . . .

C. *Exclusive Dealing*

The second prong of LePage's claim of exclusionary conduct by 3M was its actions in entering into exclusive dealing contracts with large customers. 3M acknowledges only the expressly exclusive dealing contracts with Venture and Pamida which conditioned discounts on exclusivity. It minimizes these because they represent only a small portion of the market. However, LePage's claims that 3M made payments to many of the larger customers that were designed to achieve sole-source supplier status. . . .

3M also disclaims as exclusive dealing any arrangement that contained no express exclusivity requirement. . . . [T]he law is to the contrary. No less an authority than the United States Supreme Court has so stated. In *Tampa Elec.*, . . . the Court took cognizance of arrangements which, albeit not expressly exclusive, effectively foreclosed the business of competitors.

LePage's introduced powerful evidence that could have led the jury to believe that rebates and discounts to Kmart, Staples, Sam's Club, National Office Buyers and "UDI" were designed to induce them to award business to 3M to the exclusion of LePage's. Many of LePage's former customers refused even to meet with LePage's sales representatives. A buyer for Kmart, LePage's largest customer which accounted for 10% of its business, told LePage's: "I can't talk to you about tape products for the next three years" and "don't bring me anything 3M makes." Kmart switched to 3M following 3M's offer of a $1 million "growth" reward which the jury could have understood to require that 3M be its sole supplier. Similarly, Staples was offered an extra 1% bonus rebate if it gave LePage's business to 3M. . . .

The foreclosure of markets through exclusive dealing contracts is of concern under the antitrust laws. As one of the leading treatises states:

> unilaterally imposed quantity discounts can foreclose the opportunities of rivals when a dealer can obtain its best discount only by dealing exclusively with the dominant firm. For example, discounts might be cumulated over lengthy periods of time, such as a calendar year, when no obvious economies result.

3A Phillip E. Areeda & Herbert Hovenkamp, *Antitrust Law* ¶ 768b2, at 148 (2d Ed.2002); *see also* 11 Herbert Hovenkamp, *Antitrust Law* ¶ 1807a, at 115–16 (1998) (quantity discounts may foreclose a substantial portion of the market). Discounts conditioned on exclusivity are "problematic" "when the defendant is a dominant firm in a position to force manufacturers to make an all-or-nothing choice." *Id.* at 117 n. 7. . . .

LePage's produced evidence that the foreclosure caused by exclusive dealing practices was magnified by 3M's discount practices, as some of 3M's rebates were "all-or-nothing" discounts, leading customers to maximize their discounts by dealing exclusively with the dominant market player, 3M, to avoid being severely penalized financially for failing to meet their quota in a single product line. Only by dealing exclusively with 3M in as many product lines as possible could customers enjoy the substantial discounts. Accordingly, the jury could reasonably find that 3M's exclusionary conduct violated § 2.

V. Anticompetitive Effect

It has been LePage's position in pursuing its § 2 claim that 3M's exclusionary "tactics foreclosed the competitive process by preventing rivals from competing to gain (or maintain) a presence in the market." When a monopolist's actions are designed to prevent one or more new or potential competitors from gaining a foothold in the market by exclusionary, i.e. predatory, conduct, its success in that goal is not only injurious to the potential competitor but also to competition in general. It has been recognized, albeit in a somewhat different context, that even the foreclosure of "one significant competitor" from the market may lead to higher prices and reduced output. *Roland Mach. Co. v. Dresser Indus., Inc.,* 749 F.2d 380, 394 (7th Cir.1984). . . .

[I]n this case, the jury could have reasonably found that 3M's exclusionary conduct cut LePage's off from key retail pipelines necessary to permit it to compete profitably.[14] It was only after LePage's entry into the market that 3M introduced the bundled rebates programs. If 3M were successful in eliminating competition from LePage's second-tier or private-label tape, 3M could exercise its monopoly power unchallenged, as Tesa Tuck was no longer in the market. . . . "Plaintiff introduced evidence that . . . 3M's bundled rebate programs caused distributors to displace Le Page's entirely, or in some cases, drastically reduce purchases from Le Page's." . . . [These were often customized for particular buyers to cause them to drop LePage's and Tesa in favor of 3M.]

. . . [T]he District Court found that "[LePage's] introduced substantial evidence that the anticompetitive effects of 3M's rebate programs caused Le Page's losses." The jury was capable of calculating from the evidence the amount of rebate a customer of 3M would lose if it failed to meet 3M's quota of sales in even one of the bundled products. The discount that LePage's would have had to provide to match the discounts offered by 3M through its bundled rebates can be measured by the discounts 3M gave or offered. For example, LePage's points out that in 1993 Sam's Club would have stood to lose $264,900, and Kmart $450,000 for failure to meet one of 3M's growth targets in a single product line. Moreover, the effect of 3M's rebates on LePage's earnings, if LePage's had attempted to match 3M's discounts, can be calculated by comparing the discount that LePage's would have been required to provide. That amount would represent the impact of 3M's bundled rebates on LePage's ability to compete, and that is what is relevant under § 2 of the Sherman Act.

The impact of 3M's discounts was apparent from the chart introduced by LePage's showing that LePage's earnings as a percentage

---

14 In the transparent tape market, superstores like Kmart and Wal-Mart provide a crucial facility to any manufacturer—they supply high volume sales with the concomitant substantially reduced distribution costs. By wielding its monopoly power in transparent tape and its vast array of product lines, 3M foreclosed LePage's from that critical bridge to consumers that superstores provide, namely, cheap, high volume supply lines.

of sales plummeted to below zero—to negative 10%—during 3M's rebate program. Demand for LePage's tape, especially its private-label tape, decreased significantly following the introduction of 3M's rebates.... Prior to the introduction of 3M's rebate program, LePage's sales had been skyrocketing. Its sales to Staples increased by 440% from 1990 to 1993. Following the introduction of 3M's rebate program which bundled its private-label tape with its other products, 3M's private-label tape sales increased 478% from 1992 to 1997. LePage's in turn lost a proportional amount of sales. It lost key large volume customers, such as Kmart, Staples, American Drugstores, Office Max, and Sam's Club. Other large customers, like Wal-Mart, drastically cut back their purchases.

As a result, LePage's manufacturing process became less efficient and its profit margins declined. In transparent tape manufacturing, large volume customers are essential to achieving efficiencies of scale. As 3M concedes, "'large customers were extremely important to [LePage's], to everyone.' ... Large volumes ... permitted 'long runs,' making the manufacturing process more economical and predictable."

There was a comparable effect on LePage's share of the transparent tape market. In the agreed upon relevant market for transparent tape in the United States, LePage's market share dropped 35% from 1992 to 1997. In 1992, LePage's net sales constituted 14.44% of the total transparent tape market. By 1997, LePage's sales had fallen to 9.35%. Finally, in March of 1997, LePage's was forced to close one of its two plants. That same year, the only other domestic transparent tape manufacturer, Tesa Tuck, Inc., bowed out of the transparent tape business entirely in the United States. Had 3M continued with its program it could have eventually forced LePage's out of the market.

The relevant inquiry is the anticompetitive effect of 3M's exclusionary practices considered together. [*See*] *Cont'l Ore Co. v. Union Carbide & Carbon Corp.*, 370 U.S. 690, 699 (1962).... The anticompetitive effect of 3M's exclusive dealing arrangements, whether explicit or inferred, cannot be separated from the effect of its bundled rebates. 3M's bundling of its products via its rebate programs reinforced the exclusionary effect of those programs.

3M's exclusionary conduct not only impeded LePage's ability to compete, but also it harmed competition itself, a *sine qua non* for a § 2 violation. LePage's presented powerful evidence that competition itself was harmed by 3M's actions. The District Court recognized this in its opinion, when it said:

> The jury could reasonably infer that 3M's planned elimination of the lower priced private label tape, as well as the lower priced Highland brand, would channel consumer selection to the higher priced Scotch brand and lead to higher profits for 3M. Indeed, Defendant concedes that "3M could later recoup the profits it has forsaken on Scotch tape and private label tape by selling more higher priced Scotch tape ... if there would be no

> competition by others in the private label tape segment when 3M abandoned that part of the market to sell only higher-priced Scotch tape."

3M could effectuate such a plan because there was no ease of entry. The District Court found that there was "substantial evidence at trial that significant entry barriers prevent competitors from entering the . . . tape market in the United States. . . ."

There was evidence from which the jury could have determined that 3M intended to force LePage's from the market, and then cease or severely curtail its own private-label and second-tier tape lines. . . . LePage's expert testified that the price of Scotch-brand tape increased since 1994, after 3M instituted its rebate program. In its opinion, the District Court cited the deposition testimony of a 3M employee acknowledging that the payment of the rebates after the end of the year discouraged passing the rebate on to the ultimate customers. The District Court thus observed, "the record amply reflects that 3M's rebate programs did not benefit the ultimate consumer."

As the foregoing review of the evidence makes clear, there was sufficient evidence for the jury to conclude the long-term effects of 3M's conduct were anticompetitive. We must therefore uphold its verdict on liability unless 3M has shown adequate business justification for its practices.

VI. Business Reasons Justification

. . . The defendant bears the burden of "persuad[ing] the jury that its conduct was justified by any normal business purpose." *Aspen Skiing*. Although 3M alludes to its customers' desire to have single invoices and single shipments in defense of its bundled rebates, 3M cites to no testimony or evidence . . . that would support any actual economic efficiencies in having single invoices and/or single shipments. It is highly unlikely that 3M shipped transparent tape along with retail auto products or home improvement products to customers such as Staples or that, if it did, the savings stemming from the joint shipment approaches the millions of dollars 3M returned to customers in bundled rebates.

There is considerable evidence in the record that 3M entered the private-label market only to "kill it." That is precisely what § 2 of the Sherman Act prohibits by covering conduct that maintains a monopoly. Maintaining a monopoly is not the type of valid business reason that will excuse exclusionary conduct. . . .

NOTES AND QUESTIONS ON *LEPAGE'S*

1. ***Was the court right to reject a price-cost test for judging bundled discounts?*** The court rejected 3M's argument that LePage's should have been required to show that the bundled rebates resulted in an incremental price for tape that was below the cost of making tape. This rejection was logical because the relevant anticompetitive effects for bundled discounts are the same as for tying, and none of those effects require showing an effective price for the tied product that is below cost. *See* Introduction to this Section. Although *Brooke* held a price-cost test applied to unconditioned pricing of a single product, that holding does not apply when the pricing of one product is conditioned on taking another product.

2. ***What is the court's test for determining when bundled discounts are anticompetitive?*** The court effectively held that bundled discounts by a monopolist violate § 2 when the bundling lacks any efficiency justification and direct evidence shows that the bundled discounts caused an anticompetitive effect. The court concluded that the direct evidence showed that the bundle (a) impaired rival efficiency by depriving LePage's of economies of scale and requiring it to close one of its two plants and (b) inflicted large losses on LePage's that would have required it to close its other plant and exit the market if the bundle had continued.

This is basically ordinary rule-of-reason inquiry. Similar to *Indiana Dentists,* the direct evidence of anticompetitive effects obviates the need to show that the foreclosure share was large enough to infer likely anticompetitive effects. The advantage this traditional rule-of-reason approach has over a price-cost test is that it directly examines whether any procompetitive efficiencies outweigh the anticompetitive effects. In contrast, failing a price-cost test is a very imperfect proxy for anticompetitive effects and passing it need not indicate any procompetitive efficiencies.

3. ***What is the court's test for determining when loyalty discounts given for exclusivity are anticompetitive?*** As with the bundled discounts, the court seemed to find the loyalty discounts illegal when they created anticompetitive effects on rival efficiency and lacked any procompetitive efficiency. The court did not require any showing that an equally efficient firm could not match the loyalty discount. Nor did the court require showing any foreclosure share. Again, this has the advantage of directly enquiring into anticompetitive and procompetitive effects, whereas a price-cost test is a very imperfect proxy for either.

Cascade Health Solutions v. PeaceHealth

502 F.3d 895 (9th Cir. 2007).

■ GOULD, CIRCUIT JUDGE: . . .

I

McKenzie and PeaceHealth are the only two providers of hospital care in Lane County, Oregon. The . . . relevant market in this case is the market for primary and secondary acute care hospital services in Lane County. Primary and secondary acute care hospital services are common medical services like setting a broken bone and performing a tonsillectomy. Some hospitals also provide what the parties call "tertiary care," which includes more complex services like invasive cardiovascular surgery and intensive neonatal care. . . . In Lane County, PeaceHealth operates three hospitals while McKenzie operates one. McKenzie's . . . hospital . . . offers primary and secondary acute care . . . [but] does not provide tertiary care. . . . In Lane County, PeaceHealth has a 90% market share of tertiary neonatal services, a 93% market share of tertiary cardiovascular services, and a roughly 75% market share of primary and secondary care services. . . .

II

We address initially the attempted monopolization claim. . . PeaceHealth offered bundled discounts to Regence and other insurers in this case. Specifically, PeaceHealth offered insurers discounts if the insurers made PeaceHealth their exclusive preferred provider for primary, secondary, and tertiary care.

Bundled discounts are pervasive, and examples abound. Season tickets, fast food value meals, all-in-one home theater systems—all are bundled discounts. Like individual consumers, institutional purchasers seek and obtain bundled discounts, too. . . . Bundled discounts generally benefit buyers because the discounts allow the buyer to get more for less. Bundling can also result in savings to the seller because it usually costs a firm less to sell multiple products to one customer at the same time than it does to sell the products individually. . . .

However, it is possible, at least in theory, for a firm to use a bundled discount to exclude an equally or more efficient competitor and thereby reduce consumer welfare in the long run. For example, a competitor who sells only a single product in the bundle (and who produces that single product at a lower cost than the defendant) might not be able to match profitably the price created by the multi-product bundled discount. *See* Ortho Diagnostic Sys., Inc. v. Abbott Labs., Inc., 920 F.Supp. 455, 467 (S.D.N.Y.1996). This is true even if the post-discount prices for both the entire bundle and each product in the bundle are above the seller's cost. Judge Kaplan's opinion in *Ortho* provides an example of such a situation:

> Assume for the sake of simplicity that the case involved the sale of two hair products, shampoo and conditioner, the latter made only by A and the former by both A and B. Assume as well that both must be used to wash one's hair. Assume further that A's average variable cost for conditioner is $2.50, that its average variable cost for shampoo is $1.50, and that B's average variable cost for shampoo is $1.25. B therefore is the more efficient producer of shampoo. Finally, assume that A prices conditioner and shampoo at $5 and $3, respectively, if bought separately but at $3 and $2.25 if bought as part of a package. Absent the package pricing, A's price for both products is $8. B therefore must price its shampoo at or below $3 in order to compete effectively with A, given that the customer will be paying A $5 for conditioner irrespective of which shampoo supplier it chooses. With the package pricing, the customer can purchase both products from A for $5.25, a price above the sum of A's average variable cost for both products. In order for B to compete, however, it must persuade the customer to buy B's

> shampoo while purchasing its conditioner from A for $5. In order to do that, B cannot charge more than $0.25 for shampoo, as the customer otherwise will find A's package cheaper than buying conditioner from A and shampoo from B. On these assumptions, A would force B out of the shampoo market, notwithstanding that B is the more efficient producer of shampoo, without pricing either of A's products below average variable cost.

It is worth reiterating that, as the example above shows, a bundled discounter can exclude rivals who do not sell as great a number of product lines without pricing its products below its cost to produce them. Thus, a bundled discounter can achieve exclusion without sacrificing any short-run profits.

In this case, McKenzie asserts it could provide primary and secondary services at a lower cost than PeaceHealth. Thus, the principal anticompetitive danger of the bundled discounts offered by PeaceHealth is that the discounts could freeze McKenzie out of the market for primary and secondary services because McKenzie, like seller B in Judge Kaplan's example, does not provide the same array of services as PeaceHealth and therefore could possibly not be able to match the discount PeaceHealth offers insurers.

. . . [T]he district court based its jury instruction regarding the anticompetitive effect of bundled discounting on the Third Circuit's en banc decision in *LePage's*. . . . As the bipartisan Antitrust Modernization Commission ("AMC") recently noted, the . . . *LePage's* standard . . . asks the jury to consider whether the plaintiff has been excluded from the market, but does not require the jury to consider whether the plaintiff was at least as efficient of a producer as the defendant. Thus, the *LePage's* standard could protect a less efficient competitor at the expense of consumer welfare. . . . The AMC also lamented that *LePage's* "offers no clear standards by which firms can assess whether their bundled rebates are likely to pass antitrust muster." The Commission noted that efficiencies, and not schemes to acquire or maintain monopoly power, likely explain the use of bundled discounts because many firms without market power offer them. . . . The AMC proposed that:

> Courts should adopt a three-part test to determine whether bundled discounts or rebates violate Section 2 of the Sherman Act. To prove a violation of Section 2, a plaintiff should be required to show each one of the following elements (as well as other elements of a Section 2 claim): (1) after allocating all discounts and rebates attributable to the entire bundle of products to the competitive product, the defendant sold the competitive product below its incremental cost for the competitive product; (2) the defendant is likely to recoup these short-term losses; and (3) the bundled discount or rebate program has had or is likely to have an adverse effect on competition.

The AMC reasoned that the first element would (1) subject bundled discounts to antitrust scrutiny only if they could exclude a hypothetical equally efficient competitor and (2) provide sufficient clarity for businesses to determine whether their bundled discounting practices run afoul of § 2. . . .

. . . [I]n neither *Brooke Group* nor *Weyerhaeuser* did the Court go so far as to hold that in every case in which a plaintiff challenges low prices as exclusionary conduct the plaintiff must prove that those prices were below cost. But the Court's opinions strongly suggest that, in the normal case, above-cost pricing will not be considered exclusionary conduct for antitrust purposes, and the Court's reasoning poses a strong caution against condemning bundled discounts that result in prices above a relevant measure of costs.

. . . [W]e hold that the exclusionary conduct element of a claim arising under § 2 of the Sherman Act cannot be satisfied by reference to bundled discounts unless the discounts result in prices that are below an appropriate measure of the defendant's costs. . . . The next question we must address is how we define the appropriate measure of the defendant's costs in bundled discounting cases and how we determine whether discounted prices fall below that mark. . . .

PeaceHealth and some amici urge us to adopt a rule they term the "aggregate discount" rule. This rule condemns bundled discounts as anticompetitive only in the narrow cases in which the discounted price of the entire bundle does not exceed the bundling firm's incremental cost to produce the entire bundle. PeaceHealth and amici argue that support for such a rule can be found in the Supreme Court's single product predation cases-*Brooke Group* and *Weyerhaeuser*.

We are not persuaded that those cases require us to adopt an aggregate discount rule in multi-product discounting cases. As we discussed above, bundled discounts present one potential threat to consumer welfare that single product discounts do not: A competitor who produces fewer products than the defendant but produces the competitive product at or below the defendant's cost to produce that product may nevertheless be excluded from the market because the competitor cannot match the discount the defendant offers over its numerous product lines. This possibility exists even when the defendant's prices are above cost for each individual product and for the bundle as a whole. Under a discount aggregation rule, anticompetitive bundled discounting schemes that harm competition may too easily escape liability.

Additionally, as commentators have pointed out, *Brooke Group*'s safe harbor for above-cost discounting in the single product discount context is not based on a theory that above-cost pricing strategies can never be anticompetitive, but rather on a cost-benefit rejection of a more nuanced rule. That is, the safe harbor rests on the premise that "any consumer benefit created by a rule that permits inquiry into above-cost, single-product discounts, but allows judicial condemnation of those deemed legitimately exclusionary, would likely be outweighed by the consumer harm occasioned by overdeterring nonexclusionary discounts." Lambert, 89 Minn. L.Rev. at 1705. So, in adopting an appropriate cost-based test for bundled discounting cases, we should not adopt an aggregate discount rule without inquiring whether a rule exists that is more likely to identify anticompetitive bundled discounting practices while at the same time resulting in little harm to competition.

The first potential alternative cost-based standard we consider derives from the district court's opinion in *Ortho*. This standard deems a bundled discount exclusionary if the plaintiff can show that it was an equally efficient producer of the competitive product, but the defendant's bundled discount made it impossible for the plaintiff to continue to produce profitably the competitive product. As the district court in Ortho phrased the standard: a plaintiff basing a § 2 claim on an anticompetitive bundled discount "must allege and prove either that (a) the monopolist has priced below its average variable cost or (b) the plaintiff is at least as efficient a producer of the competitive product as the defendant, but that the defendant's pricing makes it unprofitable for the plaintiff to continue to produce." . . .

However, one downside of *Ortho*'s standard is that it does not provide adequate guidance to sellers who wish to offer procompetitive bundled discounts because the standard looks to the costs of the actual plaintiff. A potential defendant who is considering offering a bundled discount will likely not have access to information about its competitors' costs, thus making it hard for that potential discounter, under the *Ortho* standard, to determine whether the discount it wishes to offer complies with the antitrust laws. Also, the *Ortho* standard, which asks whether the actual plaintiff is as efficient a producer as the defendant, could require multiple suits to determine the legality of a single bundled discount. While it might turn out that the plaintiff in one particular case is not as efficient a producer of the competitive product as the defendant, another rival might be. This second rival would have to bring another suit under the *Ortho* approach. We decline to adopt a rule that might encourage more antitrust litigation than is reasonably necessary to ferret out anticompetitive practices. Accordingly, we do not adopt *Ortho*'s approach, which we believe would be unduly cumbersome for sellers to assess and thus might chill procompetitive bundled discounting.

Instead, as our cost-based rule, we adopt what amici refer to as a "discount attribution" standard. Under this standard, the full amount of the discounts given by the defendant on the bundle are allocated to the competitive product or products. If the resulting price of the competitive product or products is below the defendant's incremental cost to produce them, the trier of fact may find that the bundled discount is exclusionary for the purpose of § 2. This standard makes the defendant's bundled discounts legal unless the discounts have the potential to exclude a hypothetical equally efficient producer of the competitive product . . . . .

The discount attribution standard provides clear guidance for sellers that engage in bundled discounting practices. A seller can easily ascertain its own prices and costs of production and calculate whether its discounting practices run afoul of the rule we have outlined. Unlike under the *Ortho* standard, under the discount attribution standard a bundled discounter need not fret over and predict or determine its rivals' cost structure . . .

The next issue before us is the appropriate measure of incremental costs in a bundled discounting case. . . . We have . . . held that a plaintiff can establish a prima facie case of predatory pricing by proving that the defendant's prices were below average variable cost. We see no reason to depart from these principles in the bundled discounting context, and we hold that the appropriate measure of costs for our cost-based standard is average variable cost. . . .

In summary, we hold the following: To prove that a bundled discount was exclusionary or predatory for the purposes of a monopolization or attempted monopolization claim under § 2 of the Sherman Act, the plaintiff must establish that, after allocating the discount given by the defendant on the entire bundle of products to the competitive product or products, the defendant sold the competitive product or products below its average variable cost of producing them. . . .[21] . . .

[21] . . . [T]he AMC's proposed standard in bundled discounting cases, in addition to requiring below-cost pricing, also contains two further proposed elements.

The second element proposed by the AMC is that there is a dangerous probability that the defendant will recoup its investment in the bundled discounting program. This requirement . . . is imported from the single product predatory pricing context, but we think imported incorrectly. We do not believe that the recoupment requirement from single product cases translates to multi-product discounting cases. Single-product predatory pricing, unlike bundling, necessarily involves a loss for the defendant. For a period of time, the defendant must sell below its cost, with the intent to eliminate its competitors so that, when its competition is eliminated, the defendant can charge supracompetitive prices, recouping its losses and potentially more. By contrast, as discussed above, exclusionary bundling does not necessarily involve any loss of profits for the bundled discounter. As the example from *Ortho* illustrates, a bundled discounter can exclude its rivals who do not sell as many product lines even when the bundle as a whole, and the individual products within it, are priced above the discounter's incremental cost to produce them. The trier of fact can identify cases that present this possibility for anticompetitive exclusion by applying the discount attribution standard outlined above. Under that standard, the ultimate question is whether the bundled discount would exclude an equally efficient rival. But because discounts on all products in the bundle have been allocated to the competitive product in issue, a conclusion of below-cost sales under the discount attribution standard may occur in some cases even where there is not an actual loss because the bundle is sold at a price exceeding incremental cost. In such a case, we do not think it is analytically helpful to think in terms of recoupment of a loss that did not occur.

The third element proposed by the AMC is that "the bundled discount or rebate program has had or is likely to have an adverse effect on competition." We view this final element as redundant because it is no different than the general requirement of "antitrust injury" that a plaintiff must prove in any private antitrust action.

For these reasons, while adopting the AMC's proposal to require below-cost sales to prove exclusionary conduct, we do not adopt the element of recoupment, which we think may be inapplicable in some cases, and we do not adopt the element of "adverse effect on competition" as we think that is superfluous in light of the general and pre-existing requirement of antitrust injury . . .

III

Before trial, the district court granted PeaceHealth summary judgment on McKenzie's claim that PeaceHealth illegally tied primary and secondary services to its provision of tertiary services in violation of § 1 of the Sherman Act, . . . because McKenzie presented no evidence that the insurers were coerced into taking the tied product . . . As evidence that no coercion was present in this case, the district court, in granting summary judgment to PeaceHealth, relied heavily on the deposition testimony of Farzenah Whyte, Regence's contract negotiator, who testified that Regence "voluntarily" entered into its contracts with PeaceHealth. PeaceHealth also points out that some insurers contracted to purchase PeaceHealth's services without exclusivity, indicating that PeaceHealth did not force those who wanted tertiary services to purchase primary and secondary services from PeaceHealth also. However, when all justifiable factual inferences are drawn in McKenzie's favor, there is no doubt that PeaceHealth's practice of giving a larger discount to insurers who dealt with it as an exclusive preferred provider may have coerced some insurers to purchase primary and secondary services from PeaceHealth rather than from McKenzie. We conclude that, as a whole, the evidence shows genuine factual disputes about whether PeaceHealth forced insurers either as an implied condition of dealing or as a matter of economic imperative through its bundled discounting, to take its primary and secondary services if the insurers wanted tertiary services.

First, while Whyte testified that Regence was not explicitly forced to deal exclusively with PeaceHealth, Whyte also testified that the higher prices PeaceHealth would have charged Regence had McKenzie been admitted to Regence's PPP would have had a "large impact" on Regence. Also, Whyte stated that she had been "held hostage" by PeaceHealth's pricing practices.

Standing alone, the fact that a customer would end up paying higher prices to purchase the tied products separately does not necessarily create a fact issue on coercion. However, the record contains additional evidence of economic coercion. For example, while PeaceHealth emphasizes that four insurers in Lane County purchased PeaceHealth's services separately, "a trivial proportion of separate sales shows that the package discount is as effective as an outright refusal to sell [the tying product] separately." 10 Areeda & Hovenkamp, supra, ¶ 1758b at 327 (2d ed.2004). In this case, there are twenty-eight insurers operating in Lane County. The fact that only four of them, or about 14% percent, made a separate purchase may indicate some degree of coercion, placing this issue in the realm of disputed facts that must be tendered to a jury. *See* id. at 328 (suggesting that a less than 10% proportion of separate sales indicates an illegal tie). Additionally, McKenzie provided some evidence that its prices on primary and secondary services were lower than PeaceHealth's prices on those services. Again, while not dispositive evidence of an illegal tie, it is a permissible inference that a rational customer would not purchase PeaceHealth's allegedly overpriced product in the absence of a tie. McKenzie also offered expert testimony that Regence's exclusive relationship with PeaceHealth made no economic sense, evidencing coercion . . .

NOTES AND QUESTIONS ON *PEACEHEALTH*

1. ***Are bundled loyalty discounts common?*** The court began its analysis by stressing that bundled discounts, such as fast-food value meals, are pervasive. The court also relied on the AMC claim that the use of bundled discounts by firms lacking market power presumptively suggests that bundled discounts usually have efficiencies. But common forms of bundled discounts are just unit-to-unit bundles, for example requiring buying one hamburger and one order of fries to get the discount. They do not require buyers to make all or a high share of purchases from the seller. For example, McDonald's does not require its customers to make 90% of their annual purchases of hamburgers or fries from McDonald's to get a discount. Thus, while bundled discounts might be common, bundled loyalty discounts might not be. *PeaceHealth* involved a bundled loyalty discount that required insurers to make PeaceHealth its exclusive preferred provider for all the bundled services. Do you commonly observe such bundled loyalty discounts used by firms lacking any market power?

2. ***Do bundled prices necessarily mean a bundled discount?*** The court also opened with the premise that "Bundled discounts generally benefit buyers because the discounts allow the buyer to get more for less." If true, this premise suggests that bundled discounts are presumptively desirable. But unfortunately this premise begs the question whether the bundled pricing reflects a true discount, where the bundled prices are below but-for prices, rather than a penalty, where the unbundled prices are set above but-for prices to penalize noncompliance. To avoid making the *PeaceHealth* opinion conclusory on this topic, should one interpret its holdings as limited to cases where the evidence shows that the bundled pricing reflects a true "bundled discount," rather than a bundled penalty?

3. ***Was the court right to adopt a discount attribution test under Sherman § 2?*** Contrary to *LePage's*, the *PeaceHealth* court held that a bundled discount can violate Sherman Act § 2 only if it flunks a discount attribution test. That discount attribution test asks whether, if the whole bundled discount is attributed to the unbundled price for the more-competitive product (here nontertiary care), the effective price for the more-competitive product is below the defendant's cost of making that product. For example, in the Court's shampoo-conditioner hypothetical, the unbundled prices are respectively \$5 and \$3, totaling \$8, while the bundled prices are \$3 and \$2.25, totaling \$5.25. Thus, the total bundled discount is \$8 – \$5.25 = \$2.75. Attributing all that bundled discount to the unbundled \$3 price for the more-competitive product (conditioner) results in an effective price of \$3 – \$2.75 = \$0.25. Another (mathematically simpler) way of phrasing the same test is to ask whether the difference between the total price for the bundle and the unbundled price for the less-competitive product is below the cost of making the more-competitive product. For example, in this hypothetical, the

total price for the bundle is $5.25 and the unbundled price for the monopoly shampoo is $5, making the difference $5.25 – $5 = $0.25. Both methods recognize that, because anyone buying shampoo from the defendant must pay at least $5, the $5.25 total price for taking the bundle means the effective incremental price for adding a purchase of conditioner from the defendant is $0.25, regardless of how the defendant nominally allocates the bundled discount and pricing across the products. To illustrate, the analysis would be no different if (with the same unbundled prices) the defendant said the bundled prices were instead $2.25 for shampoo and $3 for conditioner, or $4 for shampoo and $1.25 for conditioner, because either way the total price for the bundle is $5.25. All that matters are the two unbundled prices and the total price for taking the bundle because the only three options available to buyers are buying only the first product, only the second product, or both products, and each option has a price associated with it.

Unfortunately, the discount attribution test has various weaknesses, as noted in the Introduction to this Section. First, the discount attribution test allows bundled discounts that drive out less-efficient rivals, which lessens the pricing constraint on the remaining firm in a way that worsens consumer welfare and allocative efficiency. Second, the discount attribution test allows bundled discounts whose effective price exceeds the defendant's costs, even when the rival cannot match that price precisely because the bundled discount foreclosed enough of the market to raise the rival's cost above the defendant's cost. The test thus seems to allow a defendant to bootstrap itself into immunity from antitrust liability by inflicting the anticompetitive effect of making the rival less efficient than itself. Third, the discount attribution test assumes that equally efficient rivals will always have incentives to price down to cost to match the defendant's effective price. But a bundled discount can affirmatively discourage such rival price-cutting for two reasons. (a) Under the discount attribution test, the bundler can respond to any rival price cut by raising the unbundled price on the less-competitive product while keeping the bundled prices the same, which sacrifices no bundled profits but can lower the effective price on the more-competitive product enough to match any above-cost price cut by an equally efficient rival. The prospect of this bundler response will deter the rival from making such price cuts that gain the rival no sales and lose the rival profits without the defendant losing any profits. (b) A bundled loyalty condition can effectively divide the market in a way that is profitable for defendant and its rival. Fourth, the discount attribution test allows bundled discounts that have the price discrimination and extraction effects condemned as anticompetitive by tying law, because those effects turn on whether the unbundled price for the less-competitive product exceeds its but-for price, rather than on whether the effective price for the more-competitive product is below its cost. Moreover, the discount attribution test allows bundled discounts with all the above four types of anticompetitive effects even when the bundling has no efficiency justification and thus must necessarily imposes a net anticompetitive harm.

The *PeaceHealth* court did not consider such anticompetitive effects, and thus it gave no reason why the antitrust test should permit bundled discounts with such anticompetitive effects even when the bundling has no efficiency. Instead, the court relied on three claims by the AMC. The first claim was that the *LePage's* alternative "offers no clear standards." But the *LePage's* holding was simply that bundled discounts by a firm with market power are illegal when they lack any efficiency and have proven anticompetitive effects (there, raising rivals' costs), which is just the standard rule-of-reason that courts apply all the time. Such a test may indeed be easier to apply than a discount attribution test that requires courts to engage in the difficult task of accurately measuring incremental prices and costs. The second AMC claim was that the *LePage's* standard "could protect a less efficient competitor at the expense of consumer welfare." But the *LePage's* standard would condemn bundled discounts only if they have anticompetitive effects and no efficiencies, which by definition means that the prohibited bundled discounts could not benefit consumer welfare. Further, as discussed in the prior paragraph, protecting a less-efficient rival often benefits consumer welfare, and the discount attribution test protects bundled discounts that harm consumer welfare. The third AMC claim was that the use of bundled discounts by firms lacking market power suggests that bundled discounts are usually efficient. However, as noted above, bundled *loyalty* discounts are actually uncommon on competitive markets, suggesting the opposite inference. Nor would the usual efficiency of bundled discounts in competitive markets indicate that antitrust law should allow the subset of bundled discounts that lack any efficiency, are used by firms with market power, and have demonstrable anticompetitive effects. By that flawed logic, one would wrongly conclude that because driving is usually desirable, the law should also allow the subset of driving that occurs under the influence of alcohol.

The *PeaceHealth* court also reasoned that, although *Brooke Group* and *Weyerhaeuser* did not necessarily govern, they strongly suggested that "above-cost pricing will not be considered exclusionary conduct for antitrust purposes." But the complaint about bundled discounts is not about the prices, but rather about the condition linked to those prices. If low prices were the aim, PeaceHealth could have just cut prices on each service without bundling, unless the bundling provided some efficiency that could not otherwise be achieved. The court provides no reason to allow bundling conditions that lack any efficiency justification just because the prices are above cost.

4. Was the court right to reject the aggregate discount test? The aggregate discount test would require showing that the price for the entire bundle exceeded the cost of making the entire bundle. All the above arguments against a discount-attribution test also apply against an aggregate discount test. The possible anticompetitive effects from bundled pricing are the same as from tying, and thus, as with tying, none of the possible anticompetitive effects require proving that the price for the bundle is below the cost of the bundle. An aggregate discount test would also allow bundled pricing even though the effective price for the more-competitive product was well below cost and thus would allow the additional anticompetitive effect of driving equally-efficient rivals out of the market.

5. ***Was the court right to reject the* Ortho *test?*** The Court also rejected the *Ortho* test, which uses a discount attribution test but asks whether the resulting effective price is below the cost of an actual rival that is at least as efficient, rather than asking whether it is below the defendant's cost. As the *PeaceHealth* court reasoned, one problem with the *Ortho* test is that a firm cannot observe the costs of its rivals and thus cannot know how to make its bundled discounts conform to the *Ortho* test. A legal prohibition cannot induce compliance with a legal standard if firms do not know when they are violating that standard.

The *Ortho* test also has other problems compared to the *PeaceHealth* test, even if one favors less-efficient rival tests. First, suppose the rival is equally efficient but has higher costs and prices because it offers a higher-quality product. Then the *Ortho* test would require a defendant with lower quality and costs to price above its rival costs, even though the defendant product would not be competitive at such prices given its lower quality but would, if the defendant priced at its own cost, be attractive to customers who prefer the combination of lower prices and quality. One could try to account for this by adjusting prices for relative quality, but doing so is extremely difficult and the quality-adjusted price would vary for different customers with different preferences on quality. Comparing a defendant's price to its own cost cuts through these issues by leaving each buyer to make the price-quality tradeoff for itself.

Second, whenever the rival is less efficient, the *Ortho* test allows a defendant to use bundled discounts that do result in an effective price below its own costs. Even if one favors less-efficient rival tests, there seems no good reason why a defendant engaged in conduct that would exclude even an equally-efficient rival should be immunized just because its actual rival is less efficient. If such bundling has no efficiencies, then there is nothing positive to outweigh the anticompetitive effects of excluding less-efficient rivals, and thus there is no reason to allow the bundled discount.

However, the *Ortho* test does a better job than the *PeaceHealth* test when the rival has the same cost curve as the defendant and the bundled discount forecloses enough of the market to relegate the rival to the higher-cost portion of its curve. As noted above, the *PeaceHealth* test can allow such bundled discounts, even though they anticompetitively raise rival's costs, when the effective price is above the defendant's cost but below the rival cost that was inflated by the bundle. In contrast, the *Ortho* test would condemn such bundled discounts because having the same cost curve would mean the rival is as efficient and the effective price would be below the rival's inflated cost.

6. ***Was the court right that the appropriate measure of incremental cost was average variable cost?*** Using average variable cost is appropriate as long as it includes all costs that are variable during the period of allegedly illegal bundled discounts. *See* Chapter 3. As the court stressed, "a bundled discounter can achieve exclusion without sacrificing any short-run profits," which means that bundled discounts that violate the discount attribution test can last much longer than below-cost predatory pricing on a single product, which necessarily sacrifices short-run profits.

The costs that are variable during the period of bundled discounts are thus more likely to include recurring fixed costs (which become variable over longer periods because firms have to decide whether to incur them again) and thus come close to forward-looking average total costs.

7. ***Was the court right to reject the AMC elements requiring recoupment and anticompetitive effects?*** The court correctly rejected requiring proof of recoupment because (unlike predatory pricing) bundled discounts require no short term loss of profits that needs to be recouped. The court also rejected requiring proof of anticompetitive effect on the ground that it was duplicative of antitrust injury. But that is not so clear, because given that the court defines the violation as using a bundled discount that violates the discount attribution test in a way that excludes rivals, it would seem a rival that loses sales from such a bundle would show antitrust injury, even if it does not show any anticompetitive effect to consumer welfare. In any event, even if the court's reasoning for declining to inquire into anticompetitive effects makes sense in a private suit, it would not apply to a government suit, which requires no proof of antitrust injury. Because any substantive standard for judging bundled discounts must also apply to government suits, it would seem it should require proof of anticompetitive effects, as *LePage's* does, or a substantial enough foreclosure share to infer such anticompetitive effects.

8. ***What about procompetitive justifications?*** The *PeaceHealth* test not only requires no proof of anticompetitive effects, but also finds a violation when the discount attribution test is violated regardless of whether the defendant had a procompetitive justification for the bundle. In that regard, the test seems quite overinclusive. After all, absolute tying sets the unbundled price for the tying product at effectively infinity, so absolute tying by definition always violates the discount attribution test. Yet, absolute tying often does have procompetitive justifications that seem admissible under modern tying doctrine. *See* Chapter 4.B. Ignoring those same justifications under the discount attribution test means that it will often condemn desirable bundled discounts. It would thus seem that, as in as *LePage's*, procompetitive justifications should be considered as well. But if the test were modified to consider both procompetitive justifications and anticompetitive effects, then we are simply back to the *LePage's* rule-of-reason inquiry that *PeaceHealth* claimed was too vague.

9. ***Should the legal test for bundled discounts differ under Sherman Act § 1 and § 2?*** Although the court applied the discount attribution test to determine when a bundled discount constitutes exclusionary conduct under Sherman Act § 2, Part III of its opinion applied a different test to determine when a bundled discount constitutes a tie under Sherman Act § 1. On the latter issue, the court concluded that a bundled discount could be an illegal tie if either (a) the proportion of separate sales to bundled sales is low (with 14% being low enough) or (b) the defendant is able to sell the tied product at a price that exceeds the rival price for that product. Another circuit has instead concluded that the discount attribution test should also determine when bundled discounts constitute a tie. *See* Collins Inkjet Corp. v. Eastman Kodak Co., 781 F.3d 264, 273 (6th Cir. 2015).

Should the test for bundled discounts differ under Sherman § 1 and § 2? One possible reason it might is that Sherman Act § 1 condemns any restraint of trade that harms consumer welfare, whereas § 2 condemns only exclusionary conduct that increases the degree of monopoly power above but-for levels. *See* Chapter 3. However, neither the discount attribution test nor the low-separate-sales test actually identifies when bundled discounts have either such exclusionary or welfare-reducing effects. If one wants a test that correctly identifies when bundled discounts have exclusionary effects, one should ask (as the *LePage's* test does) whether the bundled discount lowered rival competitiveness in a way that was not offset by efficiencies. If one wants a test that correctly identifies when bundled discounts have the same welfare-reducing extraction and price discrimination effects as tying, one should ask whether the unbundled price for the less-competitive product exceeds its but-for price (i.e., the price that would be charged for that product in a world without the bundle).[116] Such a bundled discount has the same effects as a tie for all buyers who value the less-competitive product below the unbundled price, because an unbundled price that exceeds their valuation will prevent them from buying the less-competitive product outside of the bundle, just like an absolute tie would.

As discussed above, the discount attribution test fails to identify when bundled discounts create either exclusionary effects or the other anticompetitive effects from tying. As for the low-separate-sales test, it has two problems. First, it wrongly condemns bundled discounts when the unbundled price does not exceed the but-for price (meaning the bundled pricing provides real discounts and cannot create the price discrimination or extraction effects of tying) and the proportion of separate sales is low because the bundle is efficient and attractive.[117] Second, the low-separate-sales test wrongly allows bundled discounts when the unbundled price exceeds the but-for price but is not high enough to choke off almost all separate sales, even though such a bundled discount can create the same effects as tying for all buyers who do value the less-competitive product below the unbundled price.[118]

Eisai, Inc. v. Sanofi Aventis U.S., LLC

821 F.3d 394 (3rd Cir. 2016).

■ ROTH, CIRCUIT JUDGE. . . .

I.

Lovenox is an anticoagulant drug used in the treatment and prevention of deep vein thrombosis (DVT), a condition in which blood

[116] Elhauge, *Tying, Bundled Discounts, and the Death of the Single Monopoly Profit Theory*, 123 HARVARD LAW REVIEW 397, 450–455, 468–69 (2009). When the unbundled price is not above the but-for price, bundled discounts can still impair rival competitiveness, increase market power over the less-competitive product, or (with a loyalty condition) divide markets, *id.* at 456–61, but those theories require proving factors additional to those required by the quasi-per se rule on tying, such as showing a substantial foreclosure share or direct proof of anticompetitive effects. *Id.* at 469–77.

[117] *Id.* at 467.

[118] *Id.* at 467–68.

clots develop in a person's veins. Lovenox belongs to a category of injectable, anticoagulant drugs known as low molecular weight heparin (LMWH). Lovenox was the first LMWH approved by the Food and Drug Administration and has been sold by Sanofi in the United States since 1993. Lovenox has at least seven FDA-approved uses (known as indications), including the treatment of certain severe forms of heart attack.

Fragmin is a competing injectable LMWH [sold by] Eisai . . . in the United States. Fragmin has five FDA-approved indications, some of which overlap Lovenox's indications. Fragmin is also indicated to reduce the reoccurrence of symptomatic venous thromboembolism in cancer patients, while Lovenox is not. Lovenox, however, is indicated for treating certain more severe forms of heart attack, an indication that Fragmin does not have.

The relevant product market also consists of two other injectable anticoagulant drugs, Innohep and Arixtra. . . . Lovenox had the most indications of the four drugs, the largest sales force, and maintained a market share of 81.5% to 92.3%. Fragmin had the second largest market share at 4.3% to 8.2%.

. . . When a hospital's purchases of Lovenox were below 75% of its total purchases of LMWHs, it received a flat 1% discount regardless of the volume of Lovenox purchased. But when a hospital increased its market share above that threshold, it would receive an increasingly higher discount based on a combination of the volume purchased and the market share. For example, in 2008, the discount ranged from 9% to 30% of the wholesale price. Additionally, if certain criteria were met, a multi-hospital system could have the hospitals' volumes and market shares calculated as one entity. For a multi-hospital system, the discount started at 15% for a market share meeting the threshold, and increased to 30%. . . .

Eisai commenced this action. . . , asserting (1) willful and unlawful monopolization and attempted monopolization in violation of Section 2 of the Sherman Act; (2) *de facto* exclusive dealing in violation of Section 3 of the Clayton Act; [and] (3) an unreasonable restraint of trade in violation of Section 1 of the Sherman Act. . .

Both parties . . . moved for summary judgment. Eisai relied largely on an expert report by Professor Einer Elhauge, who determined that customers occupying a certain spectrum of market share would not save money by partially switching to a rival drug, even if the rival drug was cheaper than Lovenox. According to Professor Elhauge, the Lovenox Program restricted rival sales by bundling each customer's contestable demand for Lovenox (the units that the customer is willing to switch to rival products) with the customer's incontestable demand for Lovenox (the units that the customer is less willing to switch to rival products). The incontestable demand for Lovenox was based, at least partially, on its unique cardiology indication, which no other anticoagulant in the market possessed and which hospitals needed to treat certain of their patients. Based on Lovenox's and Fragmin's April 2007 prices, Professor Elhauge determined that bundling resulted in an enormous "dead zone" spanning Fragmin's market share: For any system choosing to increase its Fragmin market share from 10% to any amount less than 62%, it would actually cost hospitals more to switch from Lovenox to Fragmin despite Fragmin's lower price. Professor Elhauge also determined that the Program foreclosed between 68% and 84% of the relevant market.

. . . [T]he District Court granted Sanofi's motion for summary judgment. . . .

III.

A.

One form of potentially anticompetitive conduct is an exclusive dealing arrangement, which is an express or *de facto* "agreement in which a buyer agrees to purchase certain goods or services only from a particular seller for a certain period of time." . . . Eisai argues that Sanofi's conduct, as a whole, operated as a *de facto* exclusive dealing arrangement that unlawfully hindered competition. An exclusive dealing agreement is illegal under the rule of reason "only if the 'probable effect' of the arrangement is to substantially lessen competition, rather than merely disadvantage rivals." While there is no set formula for making this determination, we must consider whether a plaintiff has shown substantial foreclosure of the market for the relevant product. We also analyze the likely or actual anticompetitive effects of the exclusive dealing arrangement, including whether there was reduced output, increased price, or reduced quality in goods or services.

. . . Professor Elhauge's examples of foreclosure ultimately derive from a theory of bundling of Lovenox demand. But a bundling arrangement generally involves discounted rebates or prices for the purchase of multiple products. For example, in *LePage's,* the plaintiffs alleged that 3M, a dominant seller of transparent tape in the United States, used its monopoly to gain a competitive advantage in the private label tape portion of the transparent market by offering a "multi-tiered 'bundled rebate' structure, which offered higher rebates when customers purchased products in a number of 3M's different product lines." Analogizing this practice to tying, which is *per se* illegal, we found such bundling anticompetitive because it could "foreclose portions of the market to a potential competitor who does not manufacture an equally diverse group of products and who therefore cannot make a comparable offer." In *ZF Meritor,* we limited the reasoning in *LePage's* "to cases in which a single-product producer is excluded through a bundled rebate program offered by a producer of multiple products, which conditions the rebates on purchases across multiple different product lines." Significantly, Eisai does not claim that Sanofi conditioned discounts on purchases across various product lines, but on different types of demand for the same product. Such conduct does not present the same antitrust concerns as in *LePage's*, and we are aware of no court that has credited this novel theory.

We are not inclined to extend the rationale of *LePage's* based on the facts presented here. Even if bundling of different types of demand for the same product could, in the abstract, foreclose competition, nothing in the record indicates that an equally efficient competitor was unable to compete with Sanofi. Professor Elhauge defines incontestable demand as the "units that the customer is less willing to switch to rival products" because of "unique indications, departmental preferences, and doctor habit." Of course, obtaining an FDA indication requires investing a significant amount of time and resources in clinical trials. But Eisai does not offer evidence demonstrating that fixed costs were so high that competitors entering the market were unable to obtain a cardiology indication. In fact, Eisai has its own unique cancer indication, which it presumably obtained because of its calculated decision to focus on that area, above others. Nor does Eisai explain what percentage of incontestable demand for Lovenox was based on its unique cardiology indication as opposed to the other factors. While Professor Elhauge certainly explains why, in theory, a customer might hesitate to switch from Lovenox to one of its lower priced competitors, Eisai fails to tie Professor Elhauge's model to concrete examples of anticompetitive consequences in the record. Accordingly, we cannot credit Eisai's bundling claims, at least on the facts before us.

. . . Sanofi's conduct is distinguishable from the anticompetitive practices at issue in *ZF Meritor* and *Dentsply*. In *ZF Meritor,* the plaintiff "introduced evidence that compliance with the market penetration targets was mandatory because failing to meet such targets would jeopardize the [customers'] relationships with the dominant manufacturer of transmissions in the market." If customers did not comply with the targets for one year, they had to repay all contractual savings. We observed that the situation was similar to *Dentsply,* where we applied an exclusive dealing analysis because "the defendant threatened to refuse to continue dealing with customers if customers purchased rival's products." The threat to cut off supply ultimately provided customers with no choice but to continue purchasing from the defendants.

Here, Lovenox customers did not risk penalties or supply shortages for terminating the Lovenox Program or violating its terms. The consequence of not obtaining the 75% market share threshold or meeting the formulary requirements was not contract termination; rather, it was receiving the base 1% discount. If a customer chose to terminate the contract entirely, it could still obtain Lovenox at the wholesale price. In fact, nothing in the record demonstrates that a hospital's supply of Lovenox would be jeopardized in any way or that discounts already paid would have to be refunded. Attempting to draw a comparison with *ZF Meritor,* Eisai argues that the threat of not obtaining a higher discount (ranging up to 30% off) "handcuffed" hospitals to the Lovenox Program. Yet, Eisai points to no evidence of this. Moreover, the threat of a lost discount is a far cry from the anticompetitive conduct at issue in *ZF Meritor* or *Dentsply.* On the record before us, Eisai has failed to point to evidence suggesting the kind of clear-cut harm to competition that was present in these earlier cases. Accordingly, Eisai fails to demonstrate that hospitals were foreclosed from purchasing competing drugs as a result of Sanofi's conduct. . . .

[The court also found the direct evidence of anticompetitive effects insufficient.] Without evidence of substantial foreclosure or anticompetitive effects, Eisai has failed to demonstrate that the probable effect of Sanofi's conduct was to substantially lessen competition in the relevant market, rather than to merely disadvantage rivals. Unlike in *LePage's, Dentsply*, and *ZF Meritor,* Lovenox customers had the ability to switch to competing products. They simply chose not to do so. We will therefore affirm the District Court's grant of summary judgment in favor of Sanofi under a rule of reason analysis.

B.

Turning to Sanofi's argument that its discounts amounted to no more than price-based competition and Eisai's suit must be dismissed under the so-called price-cost test, we disagree. We are not persuaded that Eisai's claims fundamentally relate to pricing practices. . . .

When a competitor complains that a rival's sales program violates the antitrust laws, we must consider whether the conduct constitutes an exclusive dealing arrangement or simply a pricing practice. Defendants may argue that the challenged conduct is fundamentally an above-cost pricing scheme and therefore the price-cost test applies, ultimately dooming a plaintiff's claims. But not all contractual practices involving above-cost prices are *per se* legal under the antitrust laws. We previously explained in *ZF Meritor* that the price-cost test may be utilized as a "specific application of the 'rule of reason' " only when "price is the clearly predominant mechanism of exclusion." There, the defendant urged us to apply the price-cost test because the plaintiff's claims were, "at their core, no more than objections to . . . offering prices . . . through its rebate program." We declined to adopt this "unduly narrow characterization of the case as a 'pricing practices' case." We explained that price itself did not function as the exclusionary tool: "Where, as here, a dominant supplier enters into *de facto* exclusive dealing arrangements with every customer in the market, other firms may be driven out not because they cannot compete on a price basis, but because they are never given an opportunity to compete, despite their ability to offer products with significant customer demand."

Under *ZF Meritor,* when pricing predominates over other means of exclusivity, the price-cost test applies. This is usually the case when a firm uses a single-product loyalty discount or rebate to compete with similar products. In that situation, an equally efficient competitor can match the loyalty price and the firms can compete on the merits. More in-depth factual analysis is unnecessary because we know that "the balance always tips in favor of allowing above-cost pricing practices to stand." As a result, we apply the price-cost test as an application of the rule of reason in those circumstances and conclude that the above-cost pricing at issue is *per se* legal. But our conclusion may be different under different factual circumstances. Here, for example, Eisai alleges that its rival, having obtained a unique FDA indication, offered a discount that bundled incontestable and contestable demand. On Eisai's telling, the bundling—not the price—served as the primary exclusionary tool. Because we have concluded that Eisai's claims are not substantiated and that they fail a rule of reason analysis, we will not opine on when, if ever, the price-cost test applies to this type of claim. . . .

V.

For the foregoing reasons, we will affirm the District Court's order, granting summary judgment in favor of Sanofi. . .

NOTES AND QUESTIONS ON *EISAI*

In Part III.B of its opinion, the *Eisai* court rejected applying a price-cost test, suggesting that price is not "the predominant mechanism of exclusion" when a single-product loyalty discount bundles contestable and incontestable demand. In Part III.A, the court held that, under the rule-of-reason analysis that applies when the price-cost test does not, the plaintiff had to show either a substantial foreclosure share or anticompetitive effects. The court further held that bundling contestable and incontestable demand was not automatically foreclosing under *LePage*'s, because *LePage's* applies only to the bundling of different products. Nor was Sanofi's loyalty discount automatically foreclosing under *Meritor*, because the Sanofi customers did not "risk penalties or supply shortages." The court recognized that a single-product loyalty discount without any buyer commitment could "in theory" foreclose by bundling contestable and incontestable demand. However, the court concluded that such foreclosure could not be demonstrated absent evidence either: (1) showing fixed costs were too high for the rival to offer the indications necessary to serve incontestable demand; (2) showing the defendant's incontestable demand was not offset by the rival's incontestable demand for other indications; (3) quantifying the percentage of incontestable demand; or (4) providing concrete examples of buyers deterred from switching because of the bundling of contestable and incontestable demand.

1. ***Is* LePage's *really distinguished?*** Although bundling separate products differs from an intraproduct bundling of contestable and incontestable demand, the economic theory of why such bundling can create anticompetitive harm is not much different, and the *Eisai* court never explains why the distinction should lead to different substantive results. Moreover, Part IV.C of *LePage's* did treat a single-product loyalty discount on tape as foreclosing without requiring any concrete evidence about bundling of contestable and incontestable demand. Perhaps the court thought it more obvious that the single-product loyalty discount in *LePage's* bundled incontestable Scotch brand name tape to contestable private label tape in a way that would be hard to overcome. But one might reasonably think the contrary: that Lovenox was likely to have even stronger incontestable demand among some physicians at hospitals given that Lovenox possessed the only indications to treat some conditions, including serious heart attacks, on top of being the product physicians have the most experience using for medical treatments. In contrast, in *LePage's* the brandname tape was physically identical to the private label tape, and the incontestable demand resulted only from the fact that some consumers prefer to buy a brand name.

2. Is* Meritor *really distinguished? The *Eisai* court distinguished ZF Meritor, LLC v. Eaton Corp., 696 F.3d 254 (3d Cir.2012), on the ground that there the buyers risked "penalties or supply shortages." On the penalties, the court reasoned that in *Meritor*: "If customers did not comply with the targets for one year, they had to repay all contractual savings." But the economic effects of that are very similar to the fact that, if Lovenox buyers did not comply with the loyalty target, they lost their contractual discounts. Either way, failing to comply with the loyalty condition meant losing the discounts. Perhaps the *Eisai* court meant that there was no evidence that the disloyal Lovenox price was a true "penalty"—i.e., above but-for levels. If so, then the court might treat a proven disloyalty penalty as automatically foreclosing. Accordingly, perhaps just as *PeaceHealth* might be limited to cases of true bundled "discounts," where the unbundled price does not exceed but-for levels, *Eisai* might be limited to cases of true loyalty "discounts," where the disloyal price does not exceed but-for levels. However, this is a weak ground to distinguish *Meritor,* which did not rely on any evidence that the disloyal prices were penalties set above but-for prices.

On the threat of shortages, the *Eisai* court reasoned that in *Meritor* failing to meet the loyalty target "could jeopardize the [customers'] relationships with the dominant manufacturer of transmissions in the market." However, in *Meritor* the evidence on that topic showed only that some buyers perceived such a risk of supply cutoff, not that the defendant ever threatened it. 696 F.3d at 277–78. Further, only two of the four loyalty contracts in *Meritor* were subject to any such risk, because the other two were not terminable by the seller, *id.* at 265, and no buyer had ever actually been terminated for noncompliance, *id.* at 282–83.

Moreover, in *Meritor* the loyalty contracts affirmatively permitted customers to buy from any rival that offered a lower price or better product. *Id.* at 266, 287. So there was no financial penalty or termination risk from dealing with the rival if the rival priced at least one penny below what the defendant was willing to charge. This holding in *Meritor* is consistent with Supreme Court cases that equate "foreclosing" a buyer with "restraining" the buyer's choice and deem a buyer to be restrained/foreclosed by a tying condition that requires dealing with the defendant only if the rival is not charging at least 1 penny less for the tied product than the defendant is willing to charge.[119] But this holding in *Meritor* conflicts with any claim that

[119] Int'l Salt Co. v. United States, 332 U.S. 392, 396–97 (1947) (reasoning that a clause freeing buyers if the rival priced lower than the defendant: "does not avoid the stifling effect of

a loyalty condition is foreclosing only if it threatens such large penalties or crippling terminations of supply that a buyer has no choice but to continue buying from the defendant.

The *Eisai* court also simply ignored the portions of *Meritor* that actually relied instead on a general claim that the loyalty discount there bundled contestable to incontestable demand. *Meritor*, 696 F.3d at 278 ("even if an OEM decided to forgo the rebates and purchase a significant portion of its requirements from another supplier, there would still have been a significant demand from truck buyers for Eaton product"); *id.* at 283 ("no OEM could satisfy customer demand without at least some Eaton products"). In *Meritor*, this claim was no more quantified or specified than the similar claim in *Eisai*.

3. Why should any tax on dealing with rivals be permitted when it has no efficiency justification? The *Eisai* court did not deny the plaintiff was right that Sanofi's loyalty condition had no efficiency justification.[120] The court also did not deny that the loyalty discount created a tax on dealing with rivals that meant that at equivalent prices (or even with the rival at way-lower prices), the defendant would get sales it did not deserve on the merits. In tax policy, no one denies that taxes distort economic choices even though they do not mean persons have "no choice" but to avoid the taxed option. Why should such a tax on free market choice be permitted when it affects the lion's share of the market and has no offsetting procompetitive justification?

Indeed, the court acknowledged that the tax imposed by Sanofi's loyalty conditions created a dead zone that prevented buyers from switching to Eisai (despite Eisai offering an equivalent product at way-lower prices) whenever buyers wanted to purchase anything between 10–62% of its product needs from Eisai. Nor did the court deny that Eisai's market share in the U.S. market with the loyalty condition was way lower than in the Canadian market without the loyalty condition, and that Eisai's share was way lower in the portion of the U.S. market affected by the loyalty condition than in the portion of the U.S. market unaffected by the loyalty condition.[121] Why should such large distortions on free market choice be permitted when the loyalty condition has no offsetting efficiencies?

The *Eisai* court also never explains how its holding is consistent with Supreme Court cases that have condemned single-product loyalty discounts without requiring evidence either that (a) the rival could not overcome that discount with price cuts, (b) buyers feared the defendant would cut off supply, (c) the disloyal prices were penalties above but-for levels, or (d) contestable and incontestable demand were bundled and quantified. FTC v. Brown Shoe, 384 U.S. 316, 318 (1966) (condemning discounts conditioned on

---

the agreement on competition. The appellant had at all times a priority on the business at equal prices. A competitor would have to undercut appellant's price to have any hope of capturing the market, while appellant could hold that market by merely meeting competition. We do not think this concession relieves the contract of being a restraint of trade. . ."); N. Pac. Ry. Co. v. United States, 356 U.S. 1, 9, 11–12 (1958) (similar logic).

[120] *See* Redacted Brief for Plaintiff-Appellant, Eisai v. Sanofi-Aventis, No. 14–2017, Third Circuit 49–50 (July 30, 2014).

[121] *See id* at 32.

obligation to "concentrate" dealer business on the defendant's shoes, which in practice meant 75% of purchases); Standard Fashion v. Magrane-Houston, 258 U.S. 346, 351–52 (1922) (condemning loyalty condition given for 50% discount).

4. ***What does* Eisai *require to show that a loyalty discount's bundle of contestable to incontestable demand is foreclosing?*** At points, the *Eisai* court suggests that it requires evidence that the loyalty discount's bundle of contestable to incontestable demand made it impossible for an equally efficient rival to compete, as shown either generally through quantitative data or at least in some concrete examples. One might think this language suggests that the court is requiring evidence that the intra-product bundle, either generally or for at least some specific buyers, makes the effective price for the contestable demand below cost, so that an equally-efficient rival could not overcome it.[122] However, the *Eisai* court also suggests that a price-cost test should not be applied to loyalty discounts that bundle contestable and incontestable demand. Given that, what is the alternative through which a plaintiff can under *Eisai* show (through data or examples) that a loyalty discount that bundles contestable and incontestable demand is foreclosing?

One possibility is that perhaps plaintiffs can establish foreclosure by showing that the tax is significant given the loyalty threshold, loyalty discount, and the contestable share of demand. Professor Fiona Scott Morton and Zachary Abrahamson show that a loyalty discount means that, to compete for all contestable demand, a rival cannot simply match the loyal price, but rather must charge a price that is discounted from the defendant's disloyal price by the loyalty threshold times the loyalty discount divided by the contestable share of demand.[123] The difference between that figure and the loyalty discount tell us the tax on rival sales that the loyalty condition is imposing beyond any effect of the loyalty pricing itself. For example, suppose the threshold for receiving a loyalty discount is 90% of purchases, the loyalty discount is 20%, and 30% of demand is contestable. Then the rival cannot compete by discounting its price to match the loyalty discount of 20%, but rather would have to charge a price that reflects a (.9)(.2)/.3 = 60% discount from the defendant's disloyal price. The difference between 60% and 20% indicates that a 40% tax on rival sales is being imposed by the loyalty condition itself, separate from the effect of the loyal pricing. Given that standard market definition methodology deems a 5% price difference

---

[122] Such an approach would apply the intra-product equivalent of *PeaceHealth*'s discount attribution test, only here it would ask whether the cost of making the contestable portion of demand covered by the loyalty condition exceeds the difference between the total discounted price on the amount needed to meet the loyalty condition and the total disloyal price on the incontestable portion of that amount. For example, suppose a buyer purchases 80 incontestable units and 20 contestable units of a product. The defendant's loyalty condition charges $10/unit if the buyer purchases 100% from it and $11/unit if the buyer does not. Then the total discounted price for the 100 units needed to meet the loyalty condition is 100 time $10 = $1000. If a buyer does not meet the loyalty condition, the total disloyal price for the 80 incontestable units is 80 times $11 = $880. The difference is $1000 – $880 =$120, which is the effective price for taking the 20 contestable units from the defendant. Because $120 for 20 units comes to $6/unit, such a loyalty condition would fail a discount attribution test if the defendant's cost were above $6/unit.

[123] Scott Morton, Fiona M. and Abrahamson, Zachary G, *A Unifying Analytical Framework for Loyalty Rebates* 49 (September 1, 2016), https://ssrn.com/abstract=2833563.

significant enough to define an entirely different market, *see* Chapter 3, any tax above 5% would seem significant because it requires the a rival to price more than 5% below the defendant's loyal price to compete for all contestable sales.

But instead of directly calculating the share of contestable demand in order to calculate such a tax, could not one infer that the bundle of contestable and incontestable demand created by Sanofi's loyalty discount must have imposed a significant tax because it was able to demonstrably prevent sales by a rival selling an equivalent product at a price way lower than Sanofi's discounted loyal price? Is not this evidence similar to the evidence in *PeaceHealth* that the bundled discount there enabled the defendant to sell a product priced above the rival price, which *PeaceHealth* treated as sufficient to treat that bundled discount as coercive like a tie? Is not this evidence of a foreclosing effect also far stronger than in *Meritor,* where the rival was treated as foreclosed even though its prices were higher than the defendant's? 696 F.3d at 266. *Meritor* dismissed the evidence that the rival's prices were higher, reasoning that the loyalty discount produced a marketwide foreclosure that raised the rival's costs in a way that prevented it from pricing at the defendant's level.[124] *Meritor*'s logic is sound on this point, but it (a) applies even if a loyalty discount does not bundle contestable and incontestable demand and (b) conflicts with any notion that loyalty discounts should be deemed illegal only when they make competition impossible for a rival that actually had the same costs as the defendant.

Deeming loyalty discounts anticompetitive only when they flunk a price-cost test or bundle contestable and incontestable demand would also have other problems. First, it would ignore the fact that excluding less-efficient rivals also harms allocative efficiency and consumer welfare. Second, it would ignore the reality that loyalty discounts can restrain a rival's ability and incentive to win sales with price cuts if (a) the loyalty discount divides the market or (b) the rival realizes that the defendant can respond to any cut in rival prices by raising the disloyal price (rather than lowering the loyal one), which could match any rival price cut by lowering the defendant's effective price for contestable demand without sacrificing any defendant profits. The *Eisai* court does not consider those effects or give any reason why such anticompetitive possibilities should be permitted even when the loyalty discount has zero procompetitive efficiency.

5. When is price the clearly predominant mechanism of exclusion? The *Eisai* court made clear that price is not the predominant mechanism of exclusion in certain circumstances. The first is when, like in *LePage's*, a loyalty condition is bundled to prices on a separate product. The second is when, as with classic exclusive dealing, the buyer commits to being loyal to the defendant. The third is when, as in *Meritor,* buyers feared that failing to meet a loyalty condition would risk the defendant cutting off supply altogether. The fourth is when, as in *Meritor*, failing to meet a loyalty

[124] *Meritor*, 696 F.3d at 287 (buyer freedom to buy from lower priced rival did not matter "because [the defendant] had assured that there would be no other supplier that could fulfill the [buyer's] needs or offer a lower price."); *id.* at 281 (treating the exclusion of rivals the same whether they were currently or "potentially" equally efficient).

condition would result in "penalties." Although the *Eisai* court did not make clear what it meant by "penalties", the court could not have meant simply a loss of loyalty discounts, because the court stated that pricing usually predominates "when a firm uses a single-product loyalty discount or rebate to compete with similar products." As noted above, perhaps the court meant cases where the disloyal price was a penalty because it was set above but-for levels. Indeed, it would seem the court must implicitly be using some such test, because otherwise it would be holding that a defendant could avoid antitrust review with a loyalty condition that sets the disloyal price at $1 billion, or any other level buyers would be unwilling to pay for any units, even though setting the disloyal price at such penalty levels would be economically identical to a classic exclusive dealing refusal to supply the product at all to buyers who do not meet a loyalty condition.

The *Eisai* court also suggested, without affirmatively holding, that pricing does not predominate when a single-product loyalty discount bundles contestable and incontestable demand. This makes sense because such intraproduct bundles are similar to the interproduct bundle and intraproduct bundle at issue in *LePage's*. Moreover, for intraproduct bundles, it is clear that the loyalty condition imposes a restraint on rival sales that could not be achieved by the pricing itself, because the restraining effect depends on the fact that the loyalty condition requires the buyer to take contestable purchases from the defendant to avoid adverse pricing on incontestable purchases. Indeed, as noted in the prior section, one can mathematically show that in such cases the loyalty condition imposes a restraining tax on purchases from the rival over and above the effect of the loyal pricing itself, so that the mechanism of exclusion for that tax is clearly the loyalty condition rather than the price.

Pricing also might not predominate when a single-product loyalty discount raises rival's costs in a way that makes the rival unable to match the defendant's price. This conclusion seems necessary to explain the *Meritor* condemnation of a loyalty discount that allowed buyers to purchase from the rival if it offered a lower price or better product. It also makes sense because a test that compares price to the defendant's cost cannot capture the anticompetitive effects created by raising the rival's cost above the defendant's costs. But the *Eisai* court did not consider this possibility because it found no anticompetitive effects.[125]

Pricing would also seem not to predominate when a single-product loyalty discount divides a market in a way that elevates prices. In such cases, applying a price-cost test would make no sense because the market division results from the fact that the loyalty condition (a) reduces the ability of the rival to win sales from loyal buyers, which inflates defendant prices to loyal buyers and (b) requires the defendant to charge an even higher price to disloyal buyers than the inflated price it charges to loyal buyers, resulting in a super-inflated defendant price to disloyal buyers that eliminates any rival incentive to cut prices down towards cost. But this market-division possibility was not raised in *Eisai,* which involved a suit by a rival who would

[125] For a case that did raise the concern that a loyalty discount divided a market, *see* Castro v. Sanofi Pasteur Inc., 134 F. Supp. 3d 820 (D.N.J. 2015).

likely benefit from any market division, rather than by buyers who would be harmed by a market division that raised prices for both the defendant and its rival.

More generally, it would seem that pricing is not the predominant mechanism of exclusion for the conduct being challenged whenever a plaintiff makes clear that it raises no challenge to the pricing itself, only to the loyalty condition attached to that pricing. In such a case, the plaintiff acknowledges that the defendant could lawfully charge the discounted price without any loyalty condition. The plaintiff's harm would thus flow only from the incremental effects of attaching a loyalty condition to those price discounts, which is necessarily an effect that is not predominantly created by the pricing itself.

CHAPTER 5

DISTORTING DOWNSTREAM DISTRIBUTION OF A SUPPLIER'S PRODUCTS

A. INTRODUCTION

Like Chapters 3–4, this chapter addresses vertical agreements and conduct, but the concern is at a different level of competition. Chapters 3–4 addressed the concern that such vertical agreements and conduct might restrict competition from the rivals of a powerful upstream firm in a way that creates anticompetitive effects on the upstream market which benefit the powerful firm. This chapter instead addresses the concern that vertical agreements and conduct might distort downstream competition in distributing a supplier's own products.

Vertical *intra*brand distributional agreements restrain the prices at which dealers can resell the upstream firm's own product or where or to whom the dealers can sell that firm's product. For them, the distortion concern is generally that the restraint might lessen price or nonprice competition among the downstream dealers. For vertical conduct like secondary-line price discrimination, the distortion concern is that supplying some input at different prices to different downstream firms might give an unfair competitive advantage downstream to the downstream firms that get to pay lower prices.

In either sort of situation, legal doctrines designed to address such distortion concerns have confronted the following sort of critique. An upstream firm that is engaging in the challenged vertical agreement or conduct has no financial incentive to raise retail markups by lessening downstream competition in the distribution of its products. Quite the opposite: a manufacturer's interest is normally in decreasing the retail markup. Suppose, for example, that a manufacturer has a product that it wholesales for $80 to retailers who resell it for $100, thus reaping a $20 markup. If the manufacturer can reduce the retail markup to $10 through increased retail competition, then the manufacturer can increase its wholesale price to $90 and still sell the same quantity because retail consumers will still be paying $100. Or the manufacturer might increase its wholesale price to $85, resulting in a retail price of $95 and increased sales because consumers will be paying less. Standing alone, a decreased retail markup should benefit a manufacturer with some combination of increased wholesale prices and sales.

Thus, the critique continues, if the upstream firm has agreed to restrain downstream competition in the distribution of its products, then it must believe that any increased retail markup is offset by some improvement in the efficiency of distribution, such as reducing dealer free riding on the service or advertising of others. The manufacturer's own incentives thus indicate that any vertical distributional restraint that has some anticompetitive effect on the downstream market must have an offsetting procompetitive justification.[1] Accordingly, we should deem such conduct per se legal or at least presumptively reasonable.

The responses to this critique are usually of four sorts. First, it may be that the restraint indirectly does have some anticompetitive effect upstream. Vertical agreements that fix resale prices might, for example, facilitate oligopolistic coordination among upstream manufacturers because retail prices are easier for each other to monitor than wholesale prices. However, such a theory would seem to require proof that in fact the relevant market was oligopolistic, that all the coordinating oligopolists used similar agreements, and that those agreements facilitated their oligopolistic coordination. This concern might thus be thought better covered by the law on agreements or conduct alleged to facilitate oligopolistic coordination, which is addressed in Chapter 6.

Second, it may be that the vertical restraint reflects the market power of a downstream cartel or firm, and is thus imposed on the upstream firms against their interests. For example, if the dealers agree among themselves that they will distribute products only if the manufacturers fix their resale prices at a certain level, that is effectively the same thing as a buyer cartel. Or if the dealers agree amongst themselves to distribute only if the manufacturers divide their territories in a certain way, that is effectively the same thing as a horizontal market division among dealers. Such horizontal agreements among dealers may force manufacturers to agree to restraints that are contrary to manufacturer interests. Likewise, if a downstream dealer with buyer market power insists on being the only outlet for a supplier in a given area, that is effectively a form of exclusive dealing that forecloses rival downstream dealers from access to that supplier.[2] If the foreclosure of suppliers is extensive enough to impair the ability of other downstream

---

[1] The situation would be different if, instead of just restraining the distribution of its own goods, the manufacturer restrained the terms on which all competing goods were distributed as well. Suppose, for example, a widget manufacturer entered into vertical agreements with every retailer, providing that each would not sell *anyone's* widgets for less than \$100. Then the manufacturer would essentially be organizing a horizontal cartel through these vertical agreements that would create a supracompetitive surplus, and could reach some mutually beneficial agreement with retailers that would split that surplus in a way that benefited both the manufacturers and retailers but harmed downstream consumers. Such a case could be addressed as monopolization or as an implicit horizontal agreement. *See Griffith* in Chapter 4 (holding that an upstream version of such cartel ringmastering constituted monopolization); *Interstate Circuit* in Chapter 6 (holding that an upstream version of such cartel ringmastering constituted a horizontal agreement). This chapter, however, addresses only vertical restraints that are limited to the distribution of the manufacturer's own product; that is, this chapter addresses intrabrand restraints, not interbrand restraints.

[2] *See, e.g., Griffith.*

dealers to compete, then there is no reason to treat this form of upstream exclusive dealing differently than the downstream variant. However, these sorts of theories would seem to require evidence that there was either a downstream horizontal agreement or a downstream dealer with market power. And if such proof were available, then a case could instead proceed under the doctrines discussed respectively in Chapters 2 and 4.

Third, vertical restraints may be designed to get dealers to push the manufacturer's brand irrespective of its merits. For example, a manufacturer might impose high resale prices on all its dealers, so that its brand has a high retail markup that makes it more profitable for dealers to push its brand over the brands of other manufacturers. Brand pushing might take overt forms, like outright recommendations to buyers. Or it might take more subtle forms, like placing the favored brand on shelves that are at eye-level or at the end of aisles that customers notice most. If only some manufacturers use vertical price-fixing to encourage dealers to push their brands, then the effect will be to distort dealer recommendations to consumers and thus harm consumer welfare. *See* VIII AREEDA, ANTITRUST LAW ¶ 1614, at 194–198 (1989). Alternatively, other manufacturers might feel obliged to respond by also using vertical price-fixing to prevent dealers from disfavoring their products, with the end result that none of the manufacturers gains any advantage, but all of them suffer the costs of excessive retail markups and unresponsive retail prices. *Id.* at 197–98. One might think manufacturers could achieve the same sort of brand pushing by simply paying dealers a bonus for increased sales. However, such a bonus would effectively be the same as reducing the wholesale price, which if intrabrand retail competition is high, would lower retail prices and bring retailer profit markups back to competitive levels, eliminating the incentive to push. *Id.* at 195.

On the other hand, the brand-pushing theory cannot explain a ban on all vertical price-fixing or restraints because the theory applies only to multibrand dealers that can influence consumer choice. Some also argue that brand pushing is not an illegitimate effort to distort dealer advice, but instead amounts to desirable competition for promotional services. *See* Benjamin Klein, *Assessing Resale Price Maintenance After* Leegin, *in* HANDBOOK OF ANTITRUST ECONOMICS 174, 179–184 (ed. Einer Elhauge 2011). The critics of brand pushing respond that, although bidding for promotional services is involved, such bidding is not procompetitive when the promotional service consists of retailer efforts to mislead consumers. AREEDA, *supra*, at 197.

Fourth, vertical restraints (like many tying agreements) may facilitate downstream price discrimination. For example, a supplier might sell at a higher wholesale price in geographic markets where consumers are richer. If retailers in the poorer markets can buy at the low wholesale price and resell the product in the richer markets, they will undercut the supplier's higher price in the latter. To stop this, a manufacturer might impose vertical territorial restraints to prevent retailers in the poorer markets from reselling to the richer markets. Or the manufacturer might impose vertical price restraints that prevent anyone from selling in the richer markets below some minimum price. This sort of facilitation of price discrimination may have been at issue in the *Dr. Miles* case that originally made vertical price-fixing per se illegal.

Such vertical distributional restraints can thus increase price discrimination, which reduces consumer welfare (the antitrust standard) for any linear, normal, or lognormal distribution of consumer preferences.[3] Because such price discrimination is imperfect, it also reduces total welfare unless the dispersion of consumer preferences is relatively wide, such as a lognormal or normal distribution that is relatively flat.[4] Further, with vertical distributional restraints, the buyers are almost intermediaries, not final consumers, and in such cases imperfect price discrimination reduces both consumer welfare and total welfare, other than in cases where the price discrimination discourages inefficient integration.[5] But if facilitating price discrimination is the anticompetitive theory, one might think liability should turn on proof that the vertical restraints actually did increase price discrimination, and the defendant should have the opportunity to show that, in its particular case, such price discrimination did not lower consumer welfare.

Even to the extent anticompetitive effects exist, one might think they are offset by possible procompetitive justifications. For example, restricting resale prices might encourage retailers to provide important services, like explaining complicated products, without fear that customers will first go to the full-service retailer (to figure out what they want to buy) and then buy the product from a discount retailer (which can sell at a low price because it provides no services). Such free riding might discourage all retailers from providing a valuable service to consumers.

However, some commentators argue that the alleged procompetitive purposes for some forms of vertical restraints, like agreements fixing resale prices, are not really advanced by those agreements, at least not in any way that a less restrictive alternative could not equally achieve.[6] For example, some argue that free riding on services is often inapplicable, either because the retailers do not offer the type of services on which others could free ride or because the terminated retailers provide the same services as other retailers. Further, some argue that, when such free-riding would occur, the manufacturer could avoid free-riding by either providing the services itself, requiring that dealers provide the

---

[3] *See* Chapter 3.C4, Chapter 4.C.

[4] *See* Chapter 3.C4, Chapter 4.C.

[5] *See* Chapter 3.C4.

[6] *See, e.g.*, Robert Pitofsky, *In Defense of Discounters: The No-Frills Case for a Per Se Rule Against Vertical Price Fixing*, 71 GEORGETOWN L J 1487 (1983).

services, or paying dealers separately for the services. If one were confident in this conclusion, one might conclude that the absence of any real procompetitive justification means that some anticompetitive theory must in fact explain the conduct.

In the United States, vertical agreements that restrain the distribution of a supplier's goods are governed by the same Sherman Act § 1 that governs horizontal agreements, but the caselaw that elaborates when such vertical agreements are judged under the rule of reason or per se rule differs considerably from the caselaw described in Chapter 2. Price discrimination in commodities that may distort downstream competition is instead governed by the Robinson-Patman Act, which as detailed below has exceptions when the price discrimination is justified by cost differences, changing market conditions, or good faith efforts to meet competition. 15 U.S.C. § 13.

B. INTRABRAND DISTRIBUTIONAL RESTRAINTS ON RESALE

A vertical minimum price-fixing agreement is an agreement between a manufacturer and dealer that fixes the minimum prices at which the dealer can resell the manufacturer's brand. A vertical maximum price-fixing agreement instead fixes the maximum price of dealer resale of that brand. A vertical nonprice agreement restrains distribution of a manufacturer's brand in some way other than price, usually by limiting where or to whom the dealer can resell that brand.

All three types of vertical agreements were once per se illegal in the United States. Then the Supreme Court in succession overruled the per se rules against vertical nonprice restraints (in 1977), vertical maximum price-fixing (in 1997), and vertical minimum price-fixing (in 2007). The following covers that evolution, which in part reflects the growing influence of antitrust economics on U.S. antitrust law.

1. VERTICAL NONPRICE RESTRAINTS ON DISTRIBUTION

Vertical agreements to restrain distribution of a manufacturer's brand in ways other than price have a lot of similarities with vertical restraints that set minimum prices, but have many significant differences as well. The most important type of vertical nonprice agreements are those that limit to whom a dealer can resell the manufacturer's product. Sometimes these take the form of vertical territorial restraints, which limit dealers to a particular geographic area. Other times they reflect customer limitations, such as limiting one dealer to reselling to commercial users and another to reselling to consumers. Either should be distinguished from exclusive dealing or other similar exclusionary agreements, which limit the manufacturers the dealer can carry, and thus have possible foreclosing effects that may impede interbrand competition between manufacturers. *See* Chapter 4.[7]

Such vertical nonprice restraints are similar to vertical minimum price-fixing in that either might procompetitively curb free riding in services. Likewise, either might anticompetitively reflect (a) coercion by a dealer cartel or by a dealer with market power, (b) a manufacturer desire for brand pushing by multibrand dealers, or (c) the pursuit of a price discrimination scheme that usually decreases consumer welfare. Both types of agreements are also likely to have, and be intended to have, similar effects on retail prices, though resale price maintenance is more likely to totally preclude the possibility of a dealer with low prices and high volume. More important, for either sort of agreement, manufacturers may have incentives to efficiently trade off the procompetitive benefits of increasing retailing efforts against the anticompetitive effects of reducing retail competition.

The differences in possible anticompetitive effects are various. Unlike vertical minimum price-fixing, vertical nonprice restraints do not have the possible adverse *inter*brand effect of impeding the ability of retailers to adjust prices in response to competition from other brands. Vertical limits on territories and customers also don't facilitate oligopolistic coordination between manufacturers, although a nonprice agreement on something like standard delivery terms might. On the other hand, especially when dealers are made the sole outlets in an area, such agreements impose a more severe restraint on *intra*brand competition because they curb price *and* nonprice competition between retailers in distributing that brand.

Vertical nonprice restraints that limit the number of retailers that can sell a given manufacturer's products to certain customers also have possible additional procompetitive benefits compared to vertical price fixing. First, such vertical territorial restraints might encourage dealer investments to develop demand for that manufacturer's product in that area, and in an extreme case such a restraint might be necessary to encourage dealers to carry that manufacturer's product all. A price restraint could not accomplish the same goal, because the manufacturer

---

7 The terminology can be somewhat confusing because an agreement that makes a dealer the "exclusive dealer" in a territory for a particular manufacturer is generally considered a vertical nonprice restraint on distribution, rather than "exclusive dealing" within the meaning of Chapter 4. The reason is that such an agreement does not bar that dealer from carrying the products of other manufacturers and thus has intrabrand effects but not interbrand effects, where the manufacturers are the relevant competing "brands." To minimize confusion, we will call such dealers "sole outlets" rather than "exclusive dealers."

However, if the relevant anticompetitive concern is that the sole outlet dealer is using its market power to foreclose a substantial share of vital suppliers in a way that impairs the competitiveness of rival dealers, then that would raise a claim of upstream exclusive dealing under the methodology of Chapter 4. *See Griffith.* In the latter sort of case, the dealer would not have incentives to trade off procompetitive and anticompetitive effects, but it must be shown that the dealer has the requisite market power to set terms and that it has procured a substantial foreclosure of suppliers that indicates likely anticompetitive effects in the dealer market. In a traditional vertical distributional restraint case, dealer market power and substantial supplier foreclosure are not elements.

could later add extra dealers who could free ride on the investment and erode it with nonprice competition or the manufacturer might adjust (or fail to adjust) future resale prices. Second, vertical nonprice restraints might be designed to assure that dealers resell only to those qualified to carry or use the product. For example, a wholesaler might be limited to reselling to dealers who are qualified to handle the product, or a retailer might be limited to reselling to customers who have the knowledge to safely use that version of the product. Third, vertical nonprice restraints might usefully encourage specialization. One might want each dealer to specialize in a particular type of customer because that makes dealers more effective in assessing and serving their customer's needs.

Again, all these procompetitive justifications resonate as persuasive with courts only because the manufacturer's incentives give us more confidence they are actually being pursued. After all, one could in theory offer all the same justifications in a horizontal case involving market division among retailers—the difference is that there the retailers would be affirmatively motivated by the additional profits they would reap if the agreement did have anticompetitive effects at retail, whereas a manufacturer is harmed by such anticompetitive effects and thus should not voluntarily incur them unless they are offset by improved manufacturer distribution, which may be procompetitive.

Continental T.V. v. GTE Sylvania

433 U.S. 36 (1977).

■ MR. JUSTICE POWELL delivered the opinion of the Court. . . .

Respondent GTE Sylvania Inc. (Sylvania) manufactures and sells television sets. . . . Prompted by a decline in its market share to a relatively insignificant 1% to 2% of national television sales,[1] Sylvania conducted an intensive reassessment of its marketing strategy, and in 1962 adopted the franchise plan challenged here. Sylvania phased out its wholesale distributors and began to sell its televisions directly to a smaller and more select group of franchised retailers. An acknowledged purpose of the change was to decrease the number of competing Sylvania retailers in the hope of attracting the more aggressive and competent retailers thought necessary to the improvement of the company's market position.[2] To this end, Sylvania limited the number of franchises granted for any given area and required each franchisee to sell his Sylvania products only from the location or locations at which he was franchised.[3] A franchise did not constitute an exclusive territory, and Sylvania

[1] RCA at that time was the dominant firm with as much as 60% to 70% of national television sales in an industry with more than 100 manufacturers.

[2] The number of retailers selling Sylvania products declined significantly as a result of the change, but in 1965 there were at least two franchised Sylvania retailers in each metropolitan center of more than 100,000 population.

[3] Sylvania imposed no restrictions on the right of the franchisee to sell the products of competing manufacturers.

retained sole discretion to increase the number of retailers in an area in light of the success or failure of existing retailers in developing their market. The revised marketing strategy appears to have been successful during the period at issue here, for by 1965 Sylvania's share of national television sales had increased to approximately 5%, and the company ranked as the Nation's eighth largest manufacturer of color television sets.

[Because Sylvania's share of San Francisco sales were half its national average, Sylvania added another retailer in San Francisco close to its existing retailer, Continental TV. Continental responded by asking to open a store in Sacramento. Sylvania denied this request because its existing retailers there already had its share of Sacramento sales at triple its national average. Continental TV opened a store in Sacramento anyway, and Sylvania enforced its locational agreement by terminating Continental's franchise to sell Sylvania televisions. The District Court instructed the jury that a vertical agreement restricting the location of a dealer was illegal per se under United States v. Arnold, Schwinn & Co., 388 U.S. 365 (1967), and the jury found Sylvania liable for trebled damages of $1,774,515. The Court of Appeals reversed.]

II

[*Schwinn* held that vertical restraints on the customers a dealer can sell to are per se violation of Sherman § 1 if title to the goods has passed from the manufacturer to the dealer, but are governed by the rule of reason if title, dominion and risk have not passed so that the dealer is acting as an agent of the manufacturer.]. . . . In the present case, it is undisputed that title to the television sets passed from Sylvania to Continental. Thus, the *Schwinn* per se rule applies unless Sylvania's restriction on locations falls outside *Schwinn*'s prohibition against a manufacturer's attempting to restrict a "retailer's freedom as to where and to whom it will resell the products." . . . In intent and competitive impact, the retail-customer restriction in *Schwinn* is indistinguishable from the location restriction in the present case. In both cases the restrictions limited the freedom of the retailer to dispose of the purchased products as he desired. The fact that one restriction was addressed to territory and the other to customers is irrelevant to functional anti-trust analysis, and indeed, to the language and broad thrust of the opinion in *Schwinn* . . .

III

Sylvania argues that if *Schwinn* cannot be distinguished, it should be reconsidered. Although *Schwinn* is supported by the principle of stare decisis, we are convinced that the need for clarification of the law in this area justifies reconsideration. *Schwinn* itself was an abrupt and largely unexplained departure from White Motor Co. v. United States, 372 U.S. 253 (1963), where only four years earlier the Court had refused to endorse a per se rule for vertical restrictions. Since its announcement, *Schwinn* has been the subject of continuing controversy and confusion, both in the scholarly journals and in the federal courts. The great weight of scholarly opinion has been critical of the decision, and a number of the federal courts confronted with analogous vertical restrictions have sought to limit its reach. In our view, the experience of the past 10 years should be brought to bear on this subject of considerable commercial importance.

. . . Per se rules of illegality are appropriate only when they relate to conduct that is manifestly anticompetitive. As the Court explained in Northern Pacific R. Co. v. United States, 356 U.S. 1, 5 (1958), "there are certain agreements or practices which because of their pernicious effect on competition and lack of any redeeming virtue are conclusively presumed to be unreasonable and therefore illegal without elaborate inquiry as to the precise harm they have caused or the business excuse for their use."[16] In essence, the issue before us is whether *Schwinn*'s per se rule can be justified under the demanding standards of *Northern Pacific*. . . .

The market impact of vertical restrictions[18] is complex because of their potential for a simultaneous reduction of intrabrand competition and stimulation of interbrand competition.[19] Significantly, the Court in

---

16 Per se rules thus require the Court to make broad generalizations about the social utility of particular commercial practices. The probability that anticompetitive consequences will result from a practice and the severity of those consequences must be balanced against its pro-competitive consequences. Cases that do not fit the generalization may arise, but a per se rule reflects the judgment that such cases are not sufficiently common or important to justify the time and expense necessary to identify them. Once established, per se rules tend to provide guidance to the business community and to minimize the burdens on litigants and the judicial system of the more complex rule-of-reason trials, but those advantages are not sufficient in themselves to justify the creation of per se rules. If it were otherwise, all of antitrust law would be reduced to per se rules, thus introducing an unintended and undesirable rigidity in the law.

18 As in *Schwinn*, we are concerned here only with nonprice vertical restrictions. The per se illegality of price restrictions has been established firmly for many years and involves significantly different questions of analysis and policy. As Mr. Justice White notes, some commentators have argued that the manufacturer's motivation for imposing vertical price restrictions may be the same as for nonprice restrictions. There are, however, significant differences that could easily justify different treatment. In his concurring opinion in *White Motor*, Mr. Justice Brennan noted that, unlike nonprice restrictions, "[r]esale price maintenance is not only designed to, but almost invariably does in fact, reduce price competition not only *among* sellers of the affected product, but quite as much *between* that product and competing brands." Professor Posner also recognized that "industry-wide resale price maintenance might facilitate cartelizing." Furthermore, Congress recently has expressed its approval of a per se analysis of vertical price restrictions by repealing those provisions of the Miller-Tydings and McGuire Acts allowing fair trade pricing at the option of the individual States. Consumer Goods Pricing Act of 1975, 89 Stat. 801, amending 15 U.S.C. §§ 1, 45(a). No similar expression of congressional intent exists for nonprice restrictions.

19 Interbrand competition is the competition among the manufacturers of the same generic product television sets in this case and is the primary concern of antitrust law. The extreme example of a deficiency of interbrand competition is monopoly, where there is only one manufacturer. In contrast, intrabrand competition is the competition between the distributors wholesale or retail of the product of a particular manufacturer.

The degree of intrabrand competition is wholly independent of the level of interbrand competition confronting the manufacturer. Thus, there may be fierce intrabrand competition among the distributors of a product produced by a monopolist and no intrabrand competition among the distributors of a product produced by a firm in a highly competitive industry. But when interbrand competition exists, as it does among television manufacturers, it provides a significant check on the exploitation of intrabrand market power because of the ability of consumers to substitute a different brand of the same product.

Schwinn did not distinguish among the challenged restrictions on the basis of their individual potential for intrabrand harm or interbrand benefit. Restrictions that completely eliminated intrabrand competition among Schwinn distributors were analyzed no differently from those that merely moderated intrabrand competition among retailers. The pivotal factor was the passage of title: All restrictions were held to be per se illegal where title had passed, and all were evaluated and sustained under the rule of reason where it had not. The location restriction at issue here would be subject to the same pattern of analysis under *Schwinn.*

It appears that this distinction between sale and nonsale transactions resulted from the Court's effort to accommodate the perceived intrabrand harm and interbrand benefit of vertical restrictions. The per se rule for sale transactions reflected the view that vertical restrictions are "so obviously destructive" of intrabrand competition that their use would "open the door to exclusivity of outlets and limitation of territory further than prudence permits."[21] Conversely, the continued adherence to the traditional rule of reason for nonsale transactions reflected the view that the restrictions have too great a potential for the promotion of interbrand competition to justify complete prohibition. The Court's opinion provides no analytical support for these contrasting positions. Nor is there even an assertion in the opinion that the competitive impact of vertical restrictions is significantly affected by the form of the transaction. Non-sale transactions appear to be excluded from the per se rule, not because of a greater danger of intrabrand harm or a greater promise of interbrand benefit, but rather because of the Court's unexplained belief that a complete per se prohibition would be too "inflexibl[e]."

Vertical restrictions reduce intrabrand competition by limiting the number of sellers of a particular product competing for the business of a given group of buyers. Location restrictions have this effect because of practical constraints on the effective marketing area of retail outlets. Although intrabrand competition may be reduced, the ability of retailers to exploit the resulting market may be limited both by the ability of

---

[21] The Court also stated that to impose vertical restrictions in sale transactions would "violate the ancient rule against restraints on alienation." The isolated reference has provoked sharp criticism from virtually all of the commentators on the decision, most of whom have regarded the Court's apparent reliance on the "ancient rule" as both a misreading of legal history and a perversion of antitrust analysis. We quite agree with Mr. Justice Stewart's dissenting comment in *Schwinn* that "the state of the common law 400 or even 100 years ago is irrelevant to the issue before us: the effect of the antitrust laws upon vertical distributional restraints in the American economy today." We are similarly unable to accept Judge Browning's interpretation of *Schwinn*. In this dissent below he argued that the decision reflects the view that the Sherman Act was intended to prohibit restrictions on the autonomy of independent businessmen even though they have no impact on "price, quality, and quantity of goods and services." This view is certainly not explicit in *Schwinn*, which purports to be based on an examination of the "impact (of the restrictions) upon the marketplace." Competitive economies have social and political as well as economic advantages, but an antitrust policy divorced from market considerations would lack any objective benchmarks. As Mr. Justice Brandeis reminded us: "Every agreement concerning trade, every regulation of trade, restrains. To bind, to restrain, is of their very essence." *Chicago Board of Trade*. . . .

consumers to travel to other franchised locations and, perhaps more importantly, to purchase the competing products of other manufacturers. None of these key variables, however, is affected by the form of the transaction by which a manufacturer conveys his products to the retailers.

Vertical restrictions promote interbrand competition by allowing the manufacturer to achieve certain efficiencies in the distribution of his products. These "redeeming virtues" are implicit in every decision sustaining vertical restrictions under the rule of reason. Economists have identified a number of ways in which manufacturers can use such restrictions to compete more effectively against other manufacturers. *See*, e.g., Preston, Restrictive Distribution Arrangements: Economic Analysis and Public Policy Standards, 30 Law & Contemp.Prob. 506, 511 (1965).[23] For example, new manufacturers and manufacturers entering new markets can use the restrictions in order to induce competent and aggressive retailers to make the kind of investment of capital and labor that is often required in the distribution of products unknown to the consumer. Established manufacturers can use them to induce retailers to engage in promotional activities or to provide service and repair facilities necessary to the efficient marketing of their products. Service and repair are vital for many products, such as automobiles and major household appliances. The availability and quality of such services affect a manufacturer's goodwill and the competitiveness of his product. Because of market imperfections such as the so-called "free rider" effect, these services might not be provided by retailers in a purely competitive situation, despite the fact that each retailer's benefit would be greater if all provided the services than if none did.

Economists also have argued that manufacturers have an economic interest in maintaining as much intrabrand competition as is consistent with the efficient distribution of their products. Bork, The Rule of Reason and the Per Se Concept: Price Fixing and the Market Division (II), 75 Yale L.J. 373, 403 (1966); Posner, supra, n. 13, at 283, 287–288.[24] Although the view that the manufacturer's interest necessarily corresponds with that of the public is not universally shared, even the leading critic of vertical restrictions concedes that *Schwinn*'s distinction

---

[23] Marketing efficiency is not the only legitimate reason for a manufacturer's desire to exert control over the manner in which his products are sold and serviced. As a result of statutory and common-law developments, society increasingly demands that manufacturers assume direct responsibility for the safety and quality of their products. For example, at the federal level, apart from more specialized requirements, manufacturers of consumer products have safety responsibilities under the Consumer Product Safety Act, and obligations for warranties under the Consumer Product Warranties Act. Similar obligations are imposed by state law. The legitimacy of these concerns has been recognized in cases involving vertical restrictions. *See*, e.g., Tripoli Co. v. Wella Corp., 425 F.2d 932 (CA3 1970).

[24] "Generally a manufacturer would prefer the lowest retail price possible, once its price to dealers has been set, because a lower retail price means increased sales and higher manufacturer revenues." Note, 88 Harv.L.Rev. 636, 641 (1975). In this context, a manufacturer is likely to view the difference between the price at which it sells to its retailers and their price to the consumer as his "cost of distribution," which it would prefer to minimize. Posner, *supra*, n. 13, at 283.

between sale and nonsale transactions is essentially unrelated to any relevant economic impact. Comanor, Vertical Territorial and Customer Restrictions: White Motor and Its Aftermath, 81 Harv.L.Rev. 1419, 1422 (1968).[25] Indeed, to the extent that the form of the transaction is related to interbrand benefits, the Court's distinction is inconsistent with its articulated concern for the ability of smaller firms to compete effectively with larger ones. Capital requirements and administrative expenses may prevent smaller firms from using the exception for nonsale transactions.[26]

We conclude that the distinction drawn in *Schwinn* between sale and nonsale transactions is not sufficient to justify the application of a per se rule in one situation and a rule of reason in the other. The question remains whether the per se rule stated in *Schwinn* should be expanded to include non-sale transactions or abandoned in favor of a return to the rule of reason. We have found no persuasive support for expanding the per se rule. As noted above, the *Schwinn* Court recognized the undesirability of "prohibit[ing] all vertical restrictions of territory and all franchising. . . ."[27] And even Continental does not urge us to hold that all such restrictions are per se illegal.

We revert to the standard articulated in *Northern Pacific* . . . for determining whether vertical restrictions must be "conclusively presumed to be unreasonable and therefore illegal without elaborate inquiry as to the precise harm they have caused or the business excuse for their use." Such restrictions, in varying forms, are widely used in our free market economy. As indicated above, there is substantial scholarly and judicial authority supporting their economic utility. There is relatively little authority to the contrary.[28] Certainly, there has been no showing in this case, either generally or with respect to Sylvania's agreements, that vertical restrictions have or are likely to have a "pernicious effect on competition" or that they "lack . . . any redeeming virtue." Accordingly, we conclude that the per se rule stated in *Schwinn*

---

[25] Professor Comanor argues that the promotional activities encouraged by vertical restrictions result in product differentiation and, therefore, a decrease in interbrand competition. This argument is flawed by its necessary assumption that a large part of the promotional efforts resulting from vertical restrictions will not convey socially desirable information about product availability, price, quality, and services. Nor is it clear that a per se rule would result in anything more than a shift to less efficient methods of obtaining the same promotional effects.

[26] We also note that per se rules in this area may work to the ultimate detriment of the small businessmen who operate as franchisees. To the extent that a per se rule prevents a firm from using the franchise system to achieve efficiencies that it perceives as important to its successful operation, the rule creates an incentive for vertical integration into the distribution system, thereby eliminating to that extent the role of independent businessmen.

[27] Continental's contention that balancing intrabrand and interbrand competitive effects of vertical restrictions is not a "proper part of the judicial function," is refuted by *Schwinn* itself. *Topco* is not to the contrary, for it involved a horizontal restriction among ostensible competitors.

[28] There may be occasional problems in differentiating vertical restrictions from horizontal restrictions originating in agreements among the retailers. There is no doubt that restrictions in the latter category would be illegal per se, *see*, e.g., *General Motors*; *Topco*, but we do not regard the problems of proof as sufficiently great to justify a per se rule.

must be overruled.[30] In so holding we do not foreclose the possibility that particular applications of vertical restrictions might justify per se prohibition under *Northern Pacific*. But we do make clear that departure from the rule-of-reason standard must be based upon demonstrable economic effect rather than as in *Schwinn* upon formalistic line drawing.

In sum, we conclude that the appropriate decision is to return to the rule of reason that governed vertical restrictions prior to *Schwinn*. When anticompetitive effects are shown to result from particular vertical restrictions they can be adequately policed under the rule of reason, the standard traditionally applied for the majority of anticompetitive practices challenged under § 1 of the Act. Accordingly, the decision of the Court of Appeals is *Affirmed*.

■ MR. JUSTICE WHITE, concurring in the judgment. . . . It is common ground among the leading advocates of a purely economic approach to the question of distribution restraints that the economic arguments in favor of allowing vertical nonprice restraints generally apply to vertical price restraints as well. Although the majority asserts that "the per se illegality of price restrictions . . . involves significantly different questions of analysis and policy," I suspect this purported distinction may be as difficult to justify as that of *Schwinn* under the terms of the majority's analysis. . . . The effect, if not the intention, of the Court's opinion is necessarily to call into question the firmly established per se rule against price restraints. . . .

NOTES AND QUESTIONS ON *SYLVANIA*

1. ***Did* Schwinn's *sale/nonsale distinction make sense?*** *Schwinn* held that vertical nonprice restraints were per se illegal when (as in *Sylvania*) title passed from the manufacturer to the dealer, but subject to the rule of reason if title, dominion and risk did not pass to the dealer. The existence of a sale with title transfer was an odd basis for determining whether the restraint was anticompetitive or should be per se illegal. As we will see in Chapter 6, the sale/nonsale distinction relates more to whether the parties are actually separate entities capable of reaching an agreement or whether instead (because of the absence of a sale) the downstream dealer is merely an agent of the upstream manufacturer.

2. ***Was* Sylvania *right to hold that the rule of reason applied?*** Under the *Northern Pacific* test, the *Sylvania* Court decision is clearly correct because, given manufacturer incentives to minimize retail markups and possible procompetitive efficiencies, it is not the case that vertical nonprice agreements categorically have a "pernicious effect on competition" and lack "any redeeming virtue." However, it is less clear that the *Sylvania* decision is correct if the appropriate test is instead whether a per se rule

30 The importance of stare decisis is, of course, unquestioned, but as Mr. Justice Frankfurter stated in Helvering v. Hallock, 309 U.S. 106, 119 (1940), "stare decisis is a principle of policy and not a mechanical formula of adherence to the latest decision, however recent and questionable, when such adherence involves collision with a prior doctrine more embracing in its scope, intrinsically sounder, and verified by experience."

would reduce the aggregate harm from overdeterrence and underdeterrence. Adopting a rule of reason increases underdeterrence because courts may erroneously fail to find actual anticompetitive effects or accept justifications that do not really apply. Nonetheless, the odds of overdeterring with a per se rule are likely higher than the odds of underdeterring with a rule of reason, especially where, as here, the vertical territorial restraint covers a market share of only 1–2% and clearly was not structured to benefit retailers (given that the restraint provided for more than one dealer per territory and allowed the manufacturer to add additional dealers per territory).

3. ***Should the Court instead have adopted a quasi-per se rule that presumptively condemned vertical nonprice restraints when the manufacturer has market power?*** Probably not, because manufacturer market power is not a great proxy for the anticompetitive concerns raised by vertical restraints on dealer distribution. Higher manufacturer market power actually makes it *less* likely that the restraint was imposed by a retail cartel or retail market power. A manufacturer monopoly would also decrease the likelihood of oligopolistic coordination. On the other hand, a manufacturer's high market share might (a) increase the likelihood of manufacturer coordination if there were other manufacturers with relatively high shares with whom it could coordinate, (b) indicate a power to induce brand pushing, or (c) be relevant to whether the restraint could facilitate price discrimination, which requires market power. But manufacturer market power is not so generally linked to the relevant anticompetitive concerns as to make it a reliable presumptive indicator of anticompetitive effects.

4. ***Did this holding necessarily imply that the Court should also overrule the per se rule against vertical minimum price-fixing?*** Justice White's concurrence concluded that implication was valid, which seems correct under the *Northern Pacific* test. However, the same implication does not necessarily follow if the per se rule is based instead on what optimizes the mix of overdeterrence and underdeterrence. Compared to vertical minimum price-fixing, vertical territorial restraints are less likely to be an effective means of facilitating oligopolistic coordination, and thus their anticompetitive effects are a bit less worrisome. And vertical territorial restraints have the additional procompetitive virtues that they might encourage dealers to make manufacturer-specific investments to develop demand or might assure dealer qualifications or specialization. So a per se rule against vertical territorial restraints raises greater overdeterrence concerns and creates lower benefits in reducing underdeterrence. Three decades later, the Court did overturn the per se rule against vertical minimum price-fixing, but that conclusion was not inevitable, and one reason for the 5–4 split in that later decision was a split on whether to apply the *Northern Pacific* test or a general test of optimizing rule deterrence.

5. ***Should the rule on vertical nonprice restraints be per se <u>legality</u>?*** One could argue that per se *legality* is appropriate because manufacturers have the right incentives to trade off any anticompetitive effects against any procompetitive efficiencies. But such restraints might be used to advance dealer market power or a dealer cartel, allow manufacturers to coordinate on dividing territories, or implement some scheme of vertical exclusionary agreements, so a rule of per se legality could create serious underdeterrence. One could argue that this underdeterrence risk is not worth the overdeterrence created by the rule of reason, but since *Sylvania* the rule of reason has hardly ever led to condemnation of vertical territorial restraints, which suggests that any overdeterrence is limited.

*6. **Why doesn't the Court's logic apply equally to horizontal market divisions?*** A horizontal agreement dividing territories among dealers could have precisely the same procompetitive justifications as vertical territorial restraints. But that does not mean the Court should overrule the per se rule against horizontal market divisions among dealers. The difference is that horizontal restraints require agreement only by dealers who have clear incentives to anticompetitively maximize their profits. In contrast, a vertical restraint requires agreement by a manufacturer who has incentives to minimize the retail markup unless the agreement has an offsetting procompetitive virtue.

*7. **Even if** **Schwinn** ***was wrongly decided, should the Court overrule statutory precedent that Congress has let stand?*** In overruling *Schwinn*, the *Sylvania* decision cut against the principle of *stare decisis*, which is conventionally at its strongest in statutory cases on the ground that Congress could have overridden any statutory precedent that conflicted with legislative views. But because antitrust statutes use open-ended terms that incorporate common law concepts, they are generally deemed to delegate to the courts the power to develop antitrust law in a common law fashion. Accordingly, as we shall see, the Supreme Court has felt free to overrule antitrust precedent when the Court later concludes that precedent conflicts with modern antitrust economics, not only in this case, but in other cases as well.

2. VERTICAL MAXIMUM PRICE-FIXING

With other vertical distributional restraints, the manufacturer's interest in minimizing retailer profit margin is normally invoked to support the claim that the manufacturer must believe that distributional efficiencies (like reducing free riding in services) offset any anticompetitive effects generated by the restraints. In contrast, vertical maximum price-fixing cannot further the reduction of free riding in dealer services. Instead, it seems to reflect quite directly the manufacturer's procompetitive interest in minimizing the retail profit margin. Vertical agreements that fix maximum prices also don't raise the same anticompetitive concerns as agreements that set minimum prices because they can't induce dealers to engage in brand pushing and are unlikely to reflect dealer market power or to help facilitate oligopolistic coordination by manufacturers. The only exception would seem to be the case where the maximum is really a minimum.

Why wouldn't retail competition be a better way of determining the optimal retail profit margin than having the supplier set it? Generally two sorts of reasons are invoked. First, a supplier might develop a brand reputation for low or fair prices that helps bring in customers, but be worried that individual dealers will have incentives to free ride on that brand reputation by charging higher prices. For example, consider a McDonald's restaurant on a highway. Many people will pull off the highway to eat there because the McDonald's brand reputation causes them to expect low prices. If the franchisee who owns that store charges prices that are somewhat higher than normal McDonald's prices, those people will probably just go ahead and buy rather than bother leaving and stopping at another place. But they will leave the restaurant expecting higher prices from the brand than they did before. Because any loss of brand reputation for low prices will mostly be externalized onto the other McDonald's restaurants at which these people will be less likely to stop in the future, each restaurant has incentives to free ride on the brand reputation by charging higher prices. This can harm all the restaurants in the end because they will be unable to offer the brand reputation that maximizes their clientele and profitability. An agreement imposed by the supplier (here franchisor) that fixes maximum prices can curb such free riding. One can generalize this beyond the McDonald's sort of case: all brands have some reputational position and need to get customers to overcome the transaction costs of going to a store or looking at their brand within a store. They may thus need to set maximum prices to avoid free riding on their reputation for a particular price level because such free-riding will diminish customer willingness to go to their stores or examine their brand.

Second, the most efficient means of distribution may be for a supplier to just have one dealer in a given area, such as having one newspaper delivery firm to cover a certain city. Or it might simply be that the local market is too thin to efficiently support a large enough number of dealers to produce retail competition. If the supplier's product enjoys any market power, this will give that dealer a certain degree of local market power, which was effectively created by the manufacturer. This creates a successive market power problem that will lead the retailer to mark up the prices to levels that are inefficiently high and decrease supplier profits. *See* Chapter 3. The supplier might thus try to curb this by fixing maximum resale prices.

One might wonder why the latter problem could not be solved by simply charging the retailer the optimal price plus a lump sum franchise fee per year that equals the expected monopoly profits.[8] This would effectively auction off the rights to this local market power. But this strategy raises various problems. (1) The manufacturer may have difficulty accurately projecting expected monopoly profits that vary over time with changing local retailing costs and demand. (2) The risk-bearing costs of entering into such an arrangement may be higher for retailers because if local retailing costs are higher (or demand lower) than

---

[8] *See, e.g.*, JEAN TIROLE, THE THEORY OF INDUSTRIAL ORGANIZATION 176 (1988).

expected, then the retailer loses out. (3) Exploiting local market power may diminish brand traffic by lessening the brand reputation for low or at least nonexploitative prices. For all these reasons, a manufacturer may find it more attractive to fix maximum resale prices and alter them with changing market conditions.

Alternatively, a manufacturer could accomplish the same control over dealer market power by simply engaging in vertical integration. But such vertical integration may be inefficient compared to using separate dealers. Further, vertical integration would be a more (rather than less) restrictive alternative to having independent dealers with discretion over how they do their business as long as they do not exceed maximum prices.

State Oil Co. v. Khan

522 U.S. 3 (1997).

■ O'CONNOR, J., delivered the opinion for a unanimous Court.

. . . In *Albrecht v. Herald*, 390 U.S. 145 (1968), this Court held that vertical maximum price fixing is a per se violation of [Sherman Act § 1]. In this case, we are asked to reconsider that decision in light of subsequent decisions of this Court. We conclude that *Albrecht* should be overruled. . . .

A review of this Court's decisions leading up to and beyond *Albrecht* is relevant to our assessment of the continuing validity of the per se rule established in Albrecht. Beginning with *Dr. Miles,* the Court recognized the illegality of agreements under which manufacturers or suppliers set the minimum resale prices to be charged by their distributors. By 1940, the Court broadly declared all business combinations "formed for the purpose and with the effect of raising, depressing, fixing, pegging, or stabilizing the price of a commodity in interstate or foreign commerce" illegal per se. *Socony*. Accordingly, the Court condemned an agreement between two affiliated liquor distillers to limit the maximum price charged by retailers in Kiefer-Stewart Co. v. Joseph E. Seagram & Sons, 340 U.S. 211 (1951), noting that agreements to fix maximum prices, "no less than those to fix minimum prices, cripple the freedom of traders and thereby restrain their ability to sell in accordance with their own judgment." Id. at 213.

In subsequent cases, the Court's attention turned to arrangements through which suppliers imposed restrictions on dealers with respect to matters other than resale price. In . . . *Schwinn*, the Court . . . held that, upon the transfer of title to goods to a distributor, a supplier's imposition of territorial restrictions on the distributor was "so obviously destructive of competition" as to constitute a per se violation of the Sherman Act. . . .

Albrecht, decided the following Term, involved a newspaper publisher who had granted exclusive territories to independent carriers subject to their adherence to a maximum price on resale of the newspapers to the public. Influenced by its decisions in *Socony*, *Kiefer-Stewart*, and *Schwinn*, the Court concluded that it was per se unlawful for the publisher to fix the maximum resale price of its newspapers. The Court acknowledged that "[m]aximum and minimum price fixing may have different consequences in many situations," but nonetheless condemned maximum price fixing for "substituting the perhaps erroneous judgment of a seller for the forces of the competitive market."

Albrecht was animated in part by the fear that vertical maximum price fixing could allow suppliers to discriminate against certain dealers, restrict the services that dealers could afford to offer customers, or disguise minimum price fixing schemes. The Court rejected the notion (both on the record of that case and in the abstract) that, because the newspaper publisher "granted exclusive territories, a price ceiling was necessary to protect the public from price gouging by dealers who had monopoly power in their own territories."

In a vigorous dissent, Justice Harlan asserted that the majority had erred in equating the effects of maximum and minimum price fixing. Justice Harlan pointed out that, because the majority was establishing a per se rule, the proper inquiry was "not whether dictation of maximum prices is ever illegal, but whether it is always illegal." He also faulted the majority for conclusively listing "certain unfortunate consequences that maximum price dictation might have in other cases," even as it rejected evidence that the publisher's practice of fixing maximum prices counteracted potentially anticompetitive actions by its distributors. Justice Stewart also dissented, asserting that the publisher's maximum price fixing scheme should be properly viewed as promoting competition, because it protected consumers from dealers such as Albrecht, who, as "the only person who could sell for home delivery the city's only daily morning newspaper," was "a monopolist within his own territory."

Nine years later, in *Sylvania*, the Court overruled *Schwinn*, thereby rejecting application of a per se rule in the context of vertical nonprice restrictions. . . .

In *Sylvania*, the Court declined to comment on *Albrecht*'s per se treatment of vertical maximum price restrictions, noting that the issue "involve[d] significantly different questions of analysis and policy." Subsequent decisions of the Court, however, have hinted that the analytical underpinnings of *Albrecht* were substantially weakened by *Sylvania*. . . .

Most recently, in *ARCO*, although *Albrecht*'s continuing validity was not squarely before the Court, some disfavor with that decision was signaled by our statement that we would "assume, arguendo, that *Albrecht* correctly held that vertical, maximum price fixing is subject to the per se rule." More significantly, we specifically acknowledged that vertical maximum price fixing "may have procompetitive interbrand effects," and pointed out that, in the wake of *Sylvania*, "[t]he procompetitive potential of a vertical maximum price restraint is more evident . . . than it was when *Albrecht* was decided, because exclusive territorial arrangements and other nonprice restrictions were unlawful per se in 1968."

Thus, our reconsideration of *Albrecht*'s continuing validity is informed by several of our decisions, as well as a considerable body of scholarship discussing the effects of vertical restraints. Our analysis is also guided by our general view that the primary purpose of the antitrust laws is to protect interbrand competition. *See*, e.g., *Business Electronics*. "Low prices," we have explained, "benefit consumers regardless of how those prices are set, and so long as they are above predatory levels, they do not threaten competition." *ARCO*. Our interpretation of the Sherman Act also incorporates the notion that condemnation of practices resulting in lower prices to consumers is "especially costly" because "cutting prices in order to increase business often is the very essence of competition." *Matsushita*.

So informed, we find it difficult to maintain that vertically-imposed maximum prices could harm consumers or competition to the extent necessary to justify their per se invalidation. As Chief Judge Posner wrote for the Court of Appeals in this case:

> "As for maximum resale price fixing, unless the supplier is a monopolist he cannot squeeze his dealers' margins below a competitive level; the attempt to do so would just drive the dealers into the arms of a competing supplier. A supplier might, however, fix a maximum resale price in order to prevent his dealers from exploiting a monopoly position. . . . [S]uppose that State Oil, perhaps to encourage . . . dealer services . . . has spaced its dealers sufficiently far apart to limit competition among them (or even given each of them an exclusive territory); and suppose further that Union 76 is a sufficiently distinctive and popular brand to give the dealers in it at least a modicum of monopoly power. Then State Oil might want to place a ceiling on the dealers' resale prices in order to prevent them from exploiting that monopoly power fully. It would do this not out of disinterested malice, but in its commercial self-interest. The higher the price at which gasoline is resold, the smaller the volume sold, and so the lower the profit to the supplier if the higher profit per gallon at the higher price is being snared by the dealer." 93 F.3d, at 1362.

See also R. BORK, THE ANTITRUST PARADOX 281–282 (1978) ("There could, of course, be no anticonsumer effect from [the type of price fixing considered in *Albrecht*], and one suspects that the paper has a legitimate interest in keeping subscriber prices down in order to increase circulation and maximize revenues from advertising").

We recognize that the *Albrecht* decision presented a number of theoretical justifications for a per se rule against vertical maximum price fixing. But criticism of those premises abounds. The *Albrecht* decision was grounded in the fear that maximum price fixing by suppliers could interfere with dealer freedom. In response, as one commentator has pointed out, "the ban on maximum resale price limitations declared in *Albrecht* in the name of 'dealer freedom' has actually prompted many suppliers to integrate forward into distribution, thus eliminating the very independent trader for whom *Albrecht* professed solicitude." 7 P. AREEDA, ANTITRUST LAW ¶ 1635, p. 395 (1989). For example, integration in the newspaper industry since *Albrecht* has given rise to litigation between independent distributors and publishers.

The *Albrecht* Court also expressed the concern that maximum prices may be set too low for dealers to offer consumers essential or desired services. But such conduct, by driving away customers, would seem likely to harm manufacturers as well as dealers and consumers, making it unlikely that a supplier would set such a price as a matter of business judgment. In addition, *Albrecht* noted that vertical maximum price fixing could effectively channel distribution through large or specially-advantaged dealers. It is unclear, however, that a supplier would profit from limiting its market by excluding potential dealers. Further, although vertical maximum price fixing might limit the viability of inefficient dealers, that consequence is not necessarily harmful to competition and consumers.

Finally, *Albrecht* reflected the Court's fear that maximum price fixing could be used to disguise arrangements to fix minimum prices, which remain illegal per se. Although we have acknowledged the possibility that maximum pricing might mask minimum pricing, *see Maricopa County*, we believe that such conduct as with the other concerns articulated in *Albrecht* can be appropriately recognized and punished under the rule of reason.

Not only are the potential injuries cited in *Albrecht* less serious than the Court imagined, the per se rule established therein could in fact exacerbate problems related to the unrestrained exercise of market power by monopolist-dealers. Indeed, both courts and antitrust scholars have noted that *Albrecht*'s rule may actually harm consumers and manufacturers. Other commentators have also explained that *Albrecht*'s per se rule has even more potential for deleterious effect on competition after our decision in *Sylvania*, because, now that vertical nonprice restrictions are not unlawful per se, the likelihood of dealer monopoly power is increased. We do not intend to suggest that dealers generally possess sufficient market power to exploit a monopoly situation. Such retail market power may in fact be uncommon. *See*, e.g., *Business Electronics*; *Sylvania*. Nor do we hold that a ban on vertical maximum price fixing inevitably has anticompetitive consequences in the exclusive dealer context.

After reconsidering *Albrecht*'s rationale and the substantial criticism the decision has received, however, we conclude that there is insufficient economic justification for per se invalidation of vertical maximum price fixing. That is so not only because it is difficult to accept the assumptions underlying *Albrecht*, but also because *Albrecht* has little or no relevance to ongoing enforcement of the Sherman Act. *See Copperweld*. Moreover, neither the parties nor any of the amici curiae have called our attention to any cases in which enforcement efforts have been directed solely against the conduct encompassed by *Albrecht*'s per se rule.

Respondents argue that reconsideration of *Albrecht* should require "persuasive, expert testimony establishing that the per se rule has distorted the market." Their reasoning ignores the fact that *Albrecht* itself relied solely upon hypothetical effects of vertical maximum price fixing. Further, *Albrecht*'s dire predictions have not been borne out, even though manufacturers and suppliers appear to have fashioned schemes to get around the per se rule against vertical maximum price fixing. In these circumstances, it is the retention of the rule of *Albrecht*, and not, as respondents would have it, the rule's elimination, that lacks adequate justification. *See*, e.g., *Sylvania*.

. . . In the context of this case, we infer little meaning from the fact that Congress has not reacted legislatively to *Albrecht*. In any event, the history of various legislative proposals regarding price fixing seems neither clearly to support nor to denounce the per se rule of *Albrecht*. Respondents are of course free to seek legislative protection from gasoline suppliers of the sort embodied in the Petroleum Marketing Practices Act, 92 Stat. 322, 15 U.S.C. § 2801 et seq. For the reasons we have noted, however, the remedy for respondents' dispute with State Oil should not come in the form of a per se rule affecting the conduct of the entire marketplace.

Despite what Chief Judge Posner aptly described as *Albrecht*'s "infirmities, [and] its increasingly wobbly, moth-eaten foundations," 93 F.3d at 1363, there remains the question whether *Albrecht* deserves continuing respect under the doctrine of stare decisis. The Court of Appeals was correct in applying that principle despite disagreement with *Albrecht*, for it is this Court's prerogative alone to overrule one of its precedents.

We approach the reconsideration of decisions of this Court with the utmost caution. Stare decisis reflects "a policy judgment that 'in most matters it is more important that the applicable rule of law be settled than that it be settled right.'" Agostini v. Felton, 117 S.Ct. 1997, 2016 (1997). It "is the preferred course because it promotes the evenhanded, predictable, and consistent development of legal principles, fosters reliance on judicial decisions, and contributes to the actual and perceived integrity of the judicial process." Payne v. Tennessee, 501 U.S. 808, 827 (1991). . . .

But "[s]tare decisis is not an inexorable command." *Ibid.* In the area of antitrust law, there is a competing interest, well-represented in this Court's decisions, in recognizing and adapting to changed circumstances and the lessons of accumulated experience. Thus, the general presumption that legislative changes should be left to Congress has less force with respect to the Sherman Act in light of the accepted view that Congress "expected the courts to give shape to the statute's broad mandate by drawing on common-law tradition." *Professional Engineers.* As we have explained, the term "restraint of trade," as used in § 1, also "invokes the common law itself, and not merely the static content that the common law had assigned to the term in 1890." *Business Electronics; see also Sylvania.* Accordingly, this Court has reconsidered its decisions construing the Sherman Act when the theoretical underpinnings of those decisions are called into serious question. *See*, e.g., *Copperweld; Sylvania.*

Although we do not "lightly assume that the economic realities underlying earlier decisions have changed, or that earlier judicial perceptions of those realities were in error," we have noted that "different sorts of agreements" may amount to restraints of trade "in varying times and circumstances," and "[i]t would make no sense to create out of the single term 'restraint of trade' a chronologically schizoid statute, in which a 'rule of reason' evolves with new circumstances and new wisdom, but a line of per se illegality remains forever fixed where it was." *Business Electronics.* Just as *Schwinn* was "the subject of continuing controversy and confusion" under the "great weight" of scholarly criticism, *Sylvania*, *Albrecht* has been widely criticized since its inception. With the views underlying *Albrecht* eroded by this Court's precedent, there is not much of that decision to salvage.

Although the rule of *Albrecht* has been in effect for some time, the inquiry we must undertake requires considering " 'the effect of the antitrust laws upon vertical distributional restraints in the American economy today.' " *Sylvania.* As the Court noted in *ARCO*, there has not been another case since *Albrecht* in which this Court has "confronted an unadulterated vertical, maximum-price-fixing arrangement." Now that we confront *Albrecht* directly, we find its conceptual foundations gravely weakened.

In overruling *Albrecht*, we of course do not hold that all vertical maximum price fixing is per se lawful. Instead, vertical maximum price fixing, like the majority of commercial arrangements subject to the antitrust laws, should be evaluated under the rule of reason. In our view, rule-of-reason analysis will effectively identify those situations in which vertical maximum price fixing amounts to anticompetitive conduct. . . .

NOTES AND QUESTIONS ON *STATE OIL V. KHAN*

1. ***Should vertical maximum price-fixing be judged under a rule of reason?*** The Court seems correct that rule-of-reason review makes more sense than a rule of per se illegality. But should vertical maximum price-fixing be per se *legal?* Arguably, yes, given the strong procompetitive justifications, weak anticompetitive effects, and desirable manufacturer incentives. After all, if the fixed price really is just a maximum (and not a hidden minimum), then vertical maximum price-fixing directly reflects the manufacturer interest in minimizing the retail markup and has the powerful procompetitive justification of curbing any dealer market power (or cartel). Nor can true vertical maximum price-fixing facilitate oligopolistic coordination (because it cannot prevent undercutting the oligopoly price), encourage dealer brand pushing (because it cannot confer a greater markup to dealers who push), or facilitate price discrimination by preventing arbitrage (because those who buy low could resell below any maximum).

However, one might be worried that per se legality would create immunity in cases where the nominal maximum is really a hidden minimum, in which case the agreement could have any of the anticompetitive effects described in the previous paragraph, because the agreement would really be vertical minimum price-fixing. Still, one might think that any such claim should require proof that the maximum is really a minimum and that, when such proof exists, the restraint could be judged under the doctrine applicable to vertical minimum price-fixing.

2. ***Why differentiate maximum and minimum price-fixing in the vertical context when both are deemed per se illegal in the horizontal context?*** There are several reasons. First, the potential justifications differ because vertical maximum price-fixing can directly restrain dealer market power (power that the manufacturer itself might have created by appointing a local dealer) or can curb free riding on a brand reputation for low prices (as in the McDonald's highway franchise hypothetical in this Chapter's introduction). Second, the anticompetitive concerns also differ. Vertical maximum price-fixing is less likely to have anticompetitive effects because it does not eliminate any interbrand competition. In contrast, horizontal maximum price-fixing does affect interbrand competition, so it is more likely to serve as a veiled price minimum or (if it really is just a maximum) to impede market entry or quality. Third, the incentives of the relevant business decisionmakers differ greatly. For vertical maximum price-fixing, manufacturers have incentives to minimize any anticompetitive retail markups. For horizontal maximum price-fixing, none of the agreeing parties have incentives to minimize their own profits.

3. ***Who should have overruled* Albrecht?** The Supreme Court assumed, as in *Sylvania,* that it should overrule its antitrust precedent, even though Congress had declined to do so. But does this stance suggest that the lower court should also have felt free to overrule *Albrecht,* given the erosion of its economic foundations? Consider the following argument: "The main reason the Supreme Court should ever overrule statutory precedent is that Congress is too busy to rectify every interpretive mistake the Supreme Court makes. Thus, the Supreme Court itself should correct misinterpretations when the Court is confident Congress would agree if Congress were to consider the issue. But it is also true that the Supreme Court is too busy to rectify every interpretive mistake it makes. Thus, when a lower court feels confident that the Supreme Court would overrule a precedent if it were to consider the issue, then the lower court should no longer feel itself bound by that precedent."

Of course, Supreme Court precedents are binding in the lower courts, but then again Congressional statutes are binding in the Supreme Court. And the argument here that the Supreme Court is too busy to fix all its precedents is much like the argument that Congress is too busy to override precedent it does not like. The more telling differences are the following. First, in the statutory case, the Congressional instruction is itself ambiguous, whereas here there was no ambiguity about the meaning of the Supreme Court precedent; that precedent is just now thought to be incorrect. Second, while the language of antitrust statutes could be understood as broad enough to "delegate" common law authority to the courts, Supreme Court decisions cannot plausibly be thought to delegate to lower courts the authority to override Supreme Court decisions.

3. VERTICAL AGREEMENTS FIXING MINIMUM RESALE PRICES

Leegin Creative Leather Products v. PSKS, Inc.

551 U.S. 877 (2007).

■ JUSTICE KENNEDY delivered the opinion of the Court.

In *Dr. Miles Medical Co.* v. *John D. Park & Sons Co.*, 220 U.S. 373 (1911), the Court established the rule that it is *per se* illegal under § 1 of the Sherman Act for a manufacturer to agree with its distributor to set the minimum price the distributor can charge for the manufacturer's goods. The question presented by the instant case is whether the Court should overrule the *per se* rule and allow resale price maintenance agreements to be judged by the rule of reason, the usual standard applied to determine if there is a violation of § 1. The Court has abandoned the rule of *per se* illegality for other vertical restraints a manufacturer imposes on its distributors. Respected economic analysts, furthermore, conclude that vertical price restraints can have procompetitive effects. We now hold that *Dr. Miles* should be overruled and that vertical price restraints are to be judged by the rule of reason.

I

[Leegin made Brighton brand leather goods and accessories. The jury found that Leegin had entered into agreements with its retailers that fixed the minimum prices they could charge, a finding that Leegin did not dispute on appeal. On the ground that such agreements are *per se* illegal, the District Court excluded expert defense testimony describing the procompetitive effects of Leegin's pricing policy. The jury awarded $1.2 million in damages to PSKS, a retailer terminated for undercutting Leegin's minimum retail prices, which after trebling and attorney fees came to almost $4 million. The Fifth Circuit affirmed.]

II

. . . The rule of reason is the accepted standard for testing whether a practice restrains trade in violation of § 1. . . . Resort to *per se* rules is confined to restraints . . . "that would always or almost always tend to restrict competition and decrease output." *Business Electronics Corp.* v. *Sharp Electronics Corp.*, 485 U.S. 717, 723. To justify a *per se* prohibition a restraint must have "manifestly anticompetitive" effects, *GTE Sylvania*, and "lack . . . any redeeming virtue," *Northwest Stationers.*

As a consequence, the *per se* rule is appropriate only after courts have had considerable experience with the type of restraint at issue, *see BMI,* and only if courts can predict with confidence that it would be invalidated in all or almost all instances under the rule of reason, *see Maricopa.* It should come as no surprise, then, that "we have expressed reluctance to adopt *per se* rules with regard to restraints imposed in the context of business relationships where the economic impact of certain practices is not immediately obvious." *Khan.* And, as we have stated, a "departure from the rule-of-reason standard must be based upon demonstrable economic effect rather than . . . upon formalistic line drawing." *GTE Sylvania.*

III

. . . The reasoning of the Court's more recent jurisprudence has rejected the rationales on which *Dr. Miles* was based. By relying on the common-law rule against restraints on alienation, the Court justified its decision based on "formalistic" legal doctrine rather than "demonstrable economic effect," *GTE Sylvania.* The Court in *Dr. Miles* relied on a treatise published in 1628, but failed to discuss in detail the business reasons that would motivate a manufacturer situated in 1911 to make use of vertical price restraints. Yet the Sherman Act's use of "restraint of trade" "invokes the common law itself, . . . not merely the static content that the common law had assigned to the term in 1890." *Business Electronics.* The general restraint on alienation, especially in the age when then-Justice Hughes used the term, tended to evoke policy concerns extraneous to the question that controls here. Usually associated with land, not chattels, the rule arose from restrictions removing real property from the stream of commerce for generations. The Court should be cautious about putting dispositive weight on doctrines from antiquity but of slight relevance. We reaffirm that "the state of the common law 400 or even 100 years ago is irrelevant to the issue before us: the effect of the antitrust laws upon vertical distributional restraints in the American economy today." *GTE Sylvania.*

Dr. Miles, furthermore, treated vertical agreements a manufacturer makes with its distributors as analogous to a horizontal combination among competing distributors. In later cases, however, the Court rejected the approach of reliance on rules governing horizontal restraints when defining rules applicable to vertical ones. *See, e.g., Business Electronics* (disclaiming the "notion of equivalence between the scope of horizontal *per se* illegality and that of vertical *per se* illegality"); *Maricopa* (noting that "horizontal restraints are generally less defensible than vertical restraints"). Our recent cases formulate antitrust principles in accordance with the appreciated differences in economic effect between vertical and horizontal agreements, differences the *Dr. Miles* Court failed to consider.

The reasons upon which *Dr. Miles* relied do not justify a *per se* rule. As a consequence, it is necessary to examine, in the first instance, the economic effects of vertical agreements to fix minimum resale prices, and to determine whether the *per se* rule is nonetheless appropriate.

A

Though each side of the debate can find sources to support its position, it suffices to say here that economics literature is replete with procompetitive justifications for a manufacturer's use of resale price maintenance. Even those more skeptical of resale price maintenance acknowledge it can have procompetitive effects. The few recent studies documenting the competitive effects of resale price maintenance also cast doubt on the conclusion that the practice meets the criteria for a *per se* rule. *See* T. Overstreet, Resale Price Maintenance: Economic Theories and Empirical Evidence 170 (1983) (hereinafter Overstreet) (noting that "[e]fficient uses of [resale price maintenance] are evidently not unusual or rare"); *see also* Ippolito, Resale Price Maintenance: Empirical Evidence From Litigation, 34 J. Law & Econ. 263, 292–293 (1991) (hereinafter Ippolito).

The justifications for vertical price restraints are similar to those for other vertical restraints. *See GTE Sylvania*. Minimum resale price maintenance can stimulate interbrand competition—the competition among manufacturers selling different brands of the same type of product—by reducing intrabrand competition—the competition among retailers selling the same brand. The promotion of interbrand competition is important because "the primary purpose of the antitrust laws is to protect [this type of] competition." *Khan*. A single manufacturer's use of vertical price restraints tends to eliminate intrabrand price competition; this in turn encourages retailers to invest in tangible or intangible services or promotional efforts that aid the manufacturer's position as against rival manufacturers. Resale price maintenance also has the potential to give consumers more options so that they can choose among low-price, low-service brands; high-price, high-service brands; and brands that fall in between.

Absent vertical price restraints, the retail services that enhance interbrand competition might be underprovided. This is because discounting retailers can free ride on retailers who furnish services and then capture some of the increased demand those services generate. *GTE Sylvania*. Consumers might learn, for example, about the benefits of a manufacturer's product from a retailer that invests in fine showrooms, offers product demonstrations, or hires and trains knowledgeable employees. Or consumers might decide to buy the product because they see it in a retail establishment that has a reputation for selling high-quality merchandise. Marvel & McCafferty, Resale Price Maintenance and Quality Certification, 15 Rand J. Econ. 346, 347–349 (1984) (hereinafter Marvel & McCafferty). If the consumer can then buy the product from a retailer that discounts because it has not spent capital providing services or developing a quality reputation, the high-service retailer will lose sales to the discounter, forcing it to cut back its services to a level lower than consumers would otherwise prefer. Minimum resale price maintenance alleviates the problem because it prevents the discounter from undercutting the service provider. With price competition decreased, the manufacturer's retailers compete among themselves over services.

Resale price maintenance, in addition, can increase interbrand competition by facilitating market entry for new firms and brands. "[N]ew manufacturers and manufacturers entering new markets can use the restrictions in order to induce competent and aggressive retailers to make the kind of investment of capital and labor that is often required in the distribution of products unknown to the consumer." *GTE Sylvania*; *see* Marvel & McCafferty 349 (noting that reliance on a retailer's reputation "will decline as the manufacturer's brand becomes better known, so that [resale price maintenance] may be particularly important as a competitive device for new entrants"). New products and new brands are essential to a dynamic economy, and if markets can be penetrated by using resale price maintenance there is a procompetitive effect.

Resale price maintenance can also increase interbrand competition by encouraging retailer services that would not be provided even absent free riding. It may be difficult and inefficient for a manufacturer to make and enforce a contract with a retailer specifying the different services the retailer must perform. Offering the retailer a guaranteed margin and threatening termination if it does not live up to expectations may be the most efficient way to expand the manufacturer's market share by inducing the retailer's performance and allowing it to use its own initiative and experience in providing valuable services. *See* Mathewson & Winter, The Law and Economics of Resale Price Maintenance, 13 Rev. Indus. Org. 57, 74–75 (1998) (hereinafter Mathewson & Winter); Klein & Murphy, Vertical Restraints as Contract Enforcement Mechanisms, 31 J. Law & Econ. 265, 295 (1988); *see also* Deneckere, Marvel, & Peck, Demand Uncertainty, Inventories, and Resale Price Maintenance, 111 Q. J. Econ. 885, 911 (1996) (noting that resale price maintenance may be beneficial to motivate retailers to stock adequate inventories of a manufacturer's goods in the face of uncertain consumer demand).

B

While vertical agreements setting minimum resale prices can have procompetitive justifications, they may have anticompetitive effects in other cases; and unlawful price fixing, designed solely to obtain monopoly profits, is an ever present temptation. Resale price maintenance may, for example, facilitate a manufacturer cartel. *See Business Electronics*. An unlawful cartel will seek to discover if some manufacturers are undercutting the cartel's fixed prices. Resale price maintenance could assist the cartel in identifying price-cutting manufacturers who benefit from the lower prices they offer. Resale price maintenance, furthermore, could discourage a manufacturer from cutting prices to retailers with the concomitant benefit of cheaper prices to consumers.

Vertical price restraints also "might be used to organize cartels at the retailer level." *Business Electronics*. A group of retailers might collude to fix prices to consumers and then compel a manufacturer to aid the unlawful arrangement with resale price maintenance. In that instance the manufacturer does not establish the practice to stimulate services or to promote its brand but to give inefficient retailers higher profits. Retailers with better distribution systems and lower cost structures would be prevented from charging lower prices by the agreement. Historical examples suggest this possibility is a legitimate concern. *See, e.g.,* Marvel & McCafferty, The Welfare Effects of Resale Price Maintenance, 28 J. Law & Econ. 363, 373 (1985) (hereinafter Marvel) (providing an example of the power of the National Association of Retail Druggists to compel manufacturers to use resale price maintenance); Hovenkamp 186 (suggesting that the retail druggists in *Dr. Miles* formed a cartel and used manufacturers to enforce it).

A horizontal cartel among competing manufacturers or competing retailers that decreases output or reduces competition in order to increase price is, and ought to be, *per se* unlawful. *See Texaco*; *GTE Sylvania*. To the extent a vertical agreement setting minimum resale prices is entered upon to facilitate either type of cartel, it, too, would need to be held unlawful under the rule of reason. This type of agreement may also be useful evidence for a plaintiff attempting to prove the existence of a horizontal cartel.

Resale price maintenance, furthermore, can be abused by a powerful manufacturer or retailer. A dominant retailer, for example, might request resale price maintenance to forestall innovation in distribution that decreases costs. A manufacturer might consider it has little choice but to accommodate the retailer's demands for vertical price restraints if the manufacturer believes it needs access to the retailer's distribution network. A manufacturer with market power, by comparison, might use resale price maintenance to give retailers an incentive not to sell the products of smaller rivals or new entrants. *See, e.g.,* Marvel 366–368. As should be evident, the potential anticompetitive consequences of vertical price restraints must not be ignored or underestimated.

C

Notwithstanding the risks of unlawful conduct, it cannot be stated with any degree of confidence that resale price maintenance "always or almost always tend[s] to restrict competition and decrease output."

Business Electronics. Vertical agreements establishing minimum resale prices can have either procompetitive or anticompetitive effects, depending upon the circumstances in which they are formed. And although the empirical evidence on the topic is limited, it does not suggest efficient uses of the agreements are infrequent or hypothetical. *See* Overstreet 170; *see also id.*, at 80 (noting that for the majority of enforcement actions brought by the Federal Trade Commission between 1965 and 1982, "the use of [resale price maintenance] was not likely motivated by collusive dealers who had successfully coerced their suppliers"); Ippolito 292 (reaching a similar conclusion). As the rule would proscribe a significant amount of procompetitive conduct, these agreements appear ill suited for *per se* condemnation.

Respondent [PSKS] contends, nonetheless, that vertical price restraints should be *per se* unlawful because of the administrative convenience of *per se* rules. *See, e.g., GTE Sylvania* (noting "*per se* rules tend to provide guidance to the business community and to minimize the burdens on litigants and the judicial system"). That argument suggests *per se* illegality is the rule rather than the exception. This misinterprets our antitrust law. *Per se* rules may decrease administrative costs, but that is only part of the equation. Those rules can be counterproductive. They can increase the total cost of the antitrust system by prohibiting procompetitive conduct the antitrust laws should encourage. They also may increase litigation costs by promoting frivolous suits against legitimate practices. The Court has thus explained that administrative "advantages are not sufficient in themselves to justify the creation of *per se* rules," *GTE Sylvania*, and has relegated their use to restraints that are "manifestly anticompetitive," *id.* Were the Court now to conclude that vertical price restraints should be *per se* illegal based on administrative costs, we would undermine, if not overrule, the traditional "demanding standards" for adopting *per se* rules. Any possible reduction in administrative costs cannot alone justify the *Dr. Miles* rule.

Respondent also argues the *per se* rule is justified because a vertical price restraint can lead to higher prices for the manufacturer's goods. *See also* Overstreet 160 (noting that "price surveys indicate that [resale price maintenance] in most cases increased the prices of products sold"). Respondent is mistaken in relying on pricing effects absent a further showing of anticompetitive conduct. Cf. *id.*, at 106 (explaining that price surveys "do not necessarily tell us anything conclusive about the welfare effects of [resale price maintenance] because the results are generally consistent with both procompetitive and anticompetitive theories"). For, as has been indicated already, the antitrust laws are designed primarily to protect interbrand competition, from which lower prices can later result. *See Khan*. The Court, moreover, has evaluated other vertical restraints under the rule of reason even though prices can be increased in the course of promoting procompetitive effects. *See, e.g., Business Electronics*. And resale price maintenance may reduce prices if manufacturers have resorted to costlier alternatives of controlling resale prices that are not *per se* unlawful. *See infra*; *see also* Marvel 371.

Respondent's argument, furthermore, overlooks that, in general, the interests of manufacturers and consumers are aligned with respect to retailer profit margins. The difference between the price a manufacturer charges retailers and the price retailers charge consumers represents part of the manufacturer's cost of distribution, which, like any other cost, the manufacturer usually desires to minimize. *See GTE Sylvania* ("Economists . . . have argued that manufacturers have an economic interest in maintaining as much intrabrand competition as is consistent with the efficient distribution of their products"). A manufacturer has no incentive to overcompensate retailers with unjustified margins. The retailers, not the manufacturer, gain from higher retail prices. The manufacturer often loses; interbrand competition reduces its competitiveness and market share because consumers will "substitute a different brand of the same product." *Id.*; *see Business Electronics*. As a general matter, therefore, a single manufacturer will desire to set minimum resale prices only if the "increase in demand resulting from enhanced service . . . will more than offset a negative impact on demand of a higher retail price." Mathewson & Winter 67.

The implications of respondent's position are far reaching. Many decisions a manufacturer makes and carries out through concerted action can lead to higher prices. A manufacturer might, for example, contract with different suppliers to obtain better inputs that improve product quality. Or it might hire an advertising agency to promote awareness of its goods. Yet no one would think these actions violate the Sherman Act because they lead to higher prices. The antitrust laws do not require manufacturers to produce generic goods that consumers do not know about or want. The manufacturer strives to improve its product quality or to promote its brand because it believes this conduct will lead to increased demand despite higher prices. The same can hold true for resale price maintenance.

Resale price maintenance, it is true, does have economic dangers. If the rule of reason were to apply to vertical price restraints, courts would have to be diligent in eliminating their anticompetitive uses from the market. This is a realistic objective, and certain factors are relevant to the inquiry. For example, the number of manufacturers that make use of the practice in a given industry can provide important instruction. When only a few manufacturers lacking market power adopt the practice, there is little likelihood it is facilitating a manufacturer cartel, for a cartel then can be undercut by rival manufacturers. Likewise, a retailer cartel is unlikely when only a single manufacturer in a competitive market uses resale price maintenance. Interbrand competition would divert consumers to lower priced substitutes and eliminate any gains to retailers from their price-fixing agreement over a single brand. Resale price maintenance should be subject to more careful scrutiny, by contrast, if many competing manufacturers adopt the practice. Cf. F.M. Scherer & D. Ross, Industrial Market Structure and Economic Performance 558 (3d ed. 1990) (noting that "except when [resale price maintenance] spreads to cover the bulk of an industry's output, depriving consumers of a meaningful choice between high-service and low-price outlets, most [resale price maintenance arrangements] are probably innocuous"); Easterbrook, Vertical Arrangements and the Rule of Reason, 53 Antitrust L.J. 135, 162 (1984) (suggesting that "every one of the potentially-anticompetitive outcomes of vertical arrangements depends on the uniformity of the practice").

The source of the restraint may also be an important consideration. If there is evidence retailers were the impetus for a vertical price restraint, there is a greater likelihood that the restraint facilitates a retailer cartel or supports a dominant, inefficient retailer. If, by contrast, a manufacturer adopted the policy independent of retailer pressure, the restraint is less likely to promote anticompetitive conduct. A manufacturer also has an incentive to protest inefficient retailer-induced price restraints because they can harm its competitive position.

As a final matter, that a dominant manufacturer or retailer can abuse resale price maintenance for anticompetitive purposes may not be a serious concern unless the relevant entity has market power. If a retailer lacks market power, manufacturers likely can sell their goods through rival retailers. *See also Business Electronics* (noting "[r]etail market power is rare, because of the usual presence of interbrand competition and other dealers"). And if a manufacturer lacks market power, there is less likelihood it can use the practice to keep competitors away from distribution outlets.

The rule of reason is designed and used to eliminate anticompetitive transactions from the market. This standard principle applies to vertical price restraints. A party alleging injury from a vertical agreement setting minimum resale prices will have, as a general matter, the information and resources available to show the existence of the agreement and its scope of operation. As courts gain experience considering the effects of these restraints by applying the rule of reason over the course of decisions, they can establish the litigation structure to ensure the rule operates to eliminate anticompetitive restraints from the market and to provide more guidance to businesses. Courts can, for example, devise rules over time for offering proof, or even presumptions where justified, to make the rule of reason a fair and efficient way to prohibit anticompetitive restraints and to promote procompetitive ones.

For all of the foregoing reasons, we think that were the Court considering the issue as an original matter, the rule of reason, not a *per se* rule of unlawfulness, would be the appropriate standard to judge vertical price restraints.

IV

We do not write on a clean slate, for the decision in *Dr. Miles* is almost a century old. So there is an argument for its retention on the basis of *stare decisis* alone. Even if *Dr. Miles* established an erroneous rule, "*[s]tare decisis* reflects a policy judgment that in most matters it is more important that the applicable rule of law be settled than that it be settled right." *Khan.* And concerns about maintaining settled law are strong when the question is one of statutory interpretation. *See, e.g., Hohn* v. *United States*, 524 U.S. 236, 251 (1998).

Stare decisis is not as significant in this case, however, because the issue before us is the scope of the Sherman Act. *Khan* ("[T]he general presumption that legislative changes should be left to Congress has less force with respect to the Sherman Act"). From the beginning the Court has treated the Sherman Act as a common-law statute. *See Professional Engineers.* Just as the common law adapts to modern understanding and greater experience, so too does the Sherman Act's prohibition on "restraint[s] of trade" evolve to meet the dynamics of present economic conditions. The case-by-case adjudication contemplated by the rule of reason has implemented this common-law approach. Likewise, the boundaries of the doctrine of *per se* illegality should not be immovable. For "[i]t would make no sense to create out of the single term 'restraint of trade' a chronologically schizoid statute, in which a 'rule of reason' evolves with new circumstance and new wisdom, but a line of *per se* illegality remains forever fixed where it was." *Business Electronics*

A

Stare decisis, we conclude, does not compel our continued adherence to the *per se* rule against vertical price restraints. As discussed earlier, respected authorities in the economics literature suggest the *per se* rule is inappropriate, and there is now widespread agreement that resale price maintenance can have procompetitive effects. It is also significant that both the Department of Justice and the Federal Trade Commission—the antitrust enforcement agencies with the ability to assess the long-term impacts of resale price maintenance—have recommended that this Court replace the *per se* rule with the traditional rule of reason. In the antitrust context the fact that a decision has been "called into serious question" justifies our reevaluation of it. *Khan.*

Other considerations reinforce the conclusion that *Dr. Miles* should be overturned. Of most relevance, "we have overruled our precedents when subsequent cases have undermined their doctrinal underpinnings." *Dickerson* v. *United States*, 530 U.S. 428, 443 (2000). The Court's treatment of vertical restraints has progressed away from *Dr. Miles*' strict approach. We have distanced ourselves from the opinion's rationales. This is unsurprising, for the case was decided not long after enactment of the Sherman Act when the Court had little experience with antitrust analysis. Only eight years after *Dr. Miles*, moreover, the Court reined in the decision by holding that a manufacturer can announce suggested resale prices and refuse to deal with distributors who do not follow them. *Colgate.*

In more recent cases the Court, following a common-law approach, has continued to temper, limit, or overrule once strict prohibitions on vertical restraints. In 1977, the Court overturned the *per se* rule for vertical nonprice restraints, adopting the rule of reason in its stead. *GTE Sylvania.* While the Court in a footnote in *GTE Sylvania* suggested that differences between vertical price and nonprice restraints could support different legal treatment, the central part of the opinion relied on authorities and arguments that find unequal treatment "difficult to justify," *id.* (White, J., concurring in judgment).

Continuing in this direction, in two cases in the 1980's the Court defined legal rules to limit the reach of *Dr. Miles* and to accommodate the doctrines enunciated in *GTE Sylvania* and *Colgate.* In *Monsanto*, the Court required that antitrust plaintiffs alleging a § 1 price-fixing conspiracy must present evidence tending to exclude the possibility a manufacturer and its distributors acted in an independent manner. Unlike Justice Brennan's concurrence, which rejected arguments that *Dr. Miles* should be overruled, the Court "decline[d] to reach the question" whether vertical agreements fixing resale prices always should be unlawful because neither party suggested otherwise. In *Business Electronics* the Court further narrowed the scope of *Dr. Miles.* It held that the *per se* rule applied only to specific agreements over price levels and not to an agreement between a manufacturer and a distributor to terminate a price-cutting distributor.

Most recently, in 1997, after examining the issue of vertical maximum price-fixing agreements in light of commentary and real experience, the Court overruled a 29-year-old precedent treating those agreements as *per se* illegal. *Khan* . . . . . Our continued limiting of the reach of the decision in *Dr. Miles* and our recent treatment of other vertical restraints justify the conclusion that *Dr. Miles* should not be retained.

The *Dr. Miles* rule is also inconsistent with a principled framework, for it makes little economic sense when analyzed with our other cases on vertical restraints. If we were to decide the procompetitive effects of resale price maintenance were insufficient to overrule *Dr. Miles*, then cases such as *Colgate* and *GTE Sylvania* themselves would be called into question. These later decisions, while they may result in less intrabrand competition, can be justified because they permit manufacturers to secure the procompetitive benefits associated with vertical price restraints through other methods. The other methods, however, could be less efficient for a particular manufacturer to establish and sustain. The end result hinders competition and consumer welfare because manufacturers are forced to engage in second-best alternatives and because consumers are required to shoulder the increased expense of the inferior practices.

The manufacturer has a number of legitimate options to achieve benefits similar to those provided by vertical price restraints. A manufacturer can exercise its *Colgate* right to refuse to deal with retailers that do not follow its suggested prices. The economic effects of unilateral and concerted price setting are in general the same. *See, e.g., Monsanto.* The problem for the manufacturer is that a jury might conclude its unilateral policy was really a vertical agreement, subjecting it to treble damages and potential criminal liability. *Ibid.; Business Electronics.* Even with the stringent standards in *Monsanto* and *Business Electronics*, this danger can lead, and has led, rational manufacturers to take wasteful measures. A manufacturer might refuse to discuss its pricing policy with its distributors except through counsel knowledgeable of the subtle intricacies of the law. Or it might terminate longstanding distributors for minor violations without seeking an explanation. The increased costs these burdensome measures generate flow to consumers in the form of higher prices.

Furthermore, depending on the type of product it sells, a manufacturer might be able to achieve the procompetitive benefits of resale price maintenance by integrating downstream and selling its products directly to consumers. *Dr. Miles* tilts the relative costs of vertical integration and vertical agreement by making the former more attractive based on the *per se* rule, not on real market conditions. *See Business Electronics*; *see generally* Coase, The Nature of the Firm, 4 Economica, New Series 386 (1937). This distortion might lead to inefficient integration that would not otherwise take place, so that consumers must again suffer the consequences of the suboptimal distribution strategy. And integration, unlike vertical price restraints, eliminates all intrabrand competition. *See, e.g., GTE Sylvania.*

There is yet another consideration. A manufacturer can impose territorial restrictions on distributors and allow only one distributor to sell its goods in a given region. Our cases have recognized, and the economics literature confirms, that these vertical nonprice restraints have impacts similar to those of vertical price restraints; both reduce intrabrand competition and can stimulate retailer services. *See, e.g., Business Electronics*; *Monsanto.* Cf. Scherer & Ross 560 (noting that vertical nonprice restraints "can engender inefficiencies at least as serious as those imposed upon the consumer by resale price maintenance"); Steiner, How Manufacturers Deal with the Price-Cutting Retailer: When Are Vertical Restraints Efficient?, 65 Antitrust L. J. 407, 446–447 (1997) (indicating that "antitrust law should recognize that the consumer interest is often better served by [resale price maintenance]—contrary to its per se illegality and the rule-of-reason status of vertical nonprice restraints"). The same legal standard (*per se* unlawfulness) applies to horizontal market division and horizontal price fixing because both have similar economic effect. There is likewise little economic justification for the current differential treatment of vertical price and nonprice restraints. Furthermore, vertical nonprice restraints may prove less efficient for inducing desired services, and they reduce intrabrand competition more than vertical price restraints by eliminating both price and service competition.

In sum, it is a flawed antitrust doctrine that serves the interests of lawyers—by creating legal distinctions that operate as traps for the unwary—more than the interests of consumers—by requiring manufacturers to choose second-best options to achieve sound business objectives.

B

Respondent's arguments for reaffirming *Dr. Miles* on the basis of *stare decisis* do not require a different result. Respondent looks to congressional action concerning vertical price restraints. In 1937, Congress passed the Miller-Tydings Fair Trade Act, 50 Stat. 693, which made vertical price restraints legal if authorized by a fair trade law enacted by a State. Fifteen years later, Congress expanded the exemption to permit vertical price-setting agreements between a manufacturer and a distributor to be enforced against other distributors not involved in the agreement. McGuire Act, 66 Stat. 632. In 1975, however, Congress repealed both Acts. Consumer Goods Pricing Act, 89 Stat. 801. That the *Dr. Miles* rule applied to vertical price restraints in 1975, according to respondent, shows Congress ratified the rule.

This is not so. The text of the Consumer Goods Pricing Act did not codify the rule of *per se* illegality for vertical price restraints. It rescinded statutory provisions that made them *per se* legal. Congress once again placed these restraints within the ambit of § 1 of the Sherman Act. And, as has been discussed, Congress intended § 1 to give courts the ability "to develop governing principles of law" in the common-law tradition. *Texas Industries, Inc.* v. *Radcliff Materials, Inc.*, 451 U.S. 630, 643 (1981); *see Business Electronics* ("The changing content of the term 'restraint of trade' was well recognized at the time the Sherman Act was enacted"). Congress could have set the *Dr. Miles* rule in stone, but it chose a more flexible option. We respect its decision by analyzing vertical price restraints, like all restraints, in conformance with traditional § 1 principles, including the principle that our antitrust doctrines "evolv[e] with new circumstances and new wisdom." *Business Electronics.*

The rule of reason, furthermore, is not inconsistent with the Consumer Goods Pricing Act. Unlike the earlier congressional exemption, it does not treat vertical price restraints as *per se* legal. In this respect, the justifications for the prior exemption are illuminating. Its goal "was to allow the States to protect small retail establishments that Congress thought might otherwise be driven from the marketplace by large-volume discounters." *California Retail Liquor Dealers Assn.* v. *Midcal Aluminum, Inc.*, 445 U.S. 97, 102 (1980). The state fair trade laws also appear to have been justified on similar grounds. The rationales for these provisions are foreign to the Sherman Act. Divorced from competition and consumer welfare, they were designed to save inefficient small retailers from their inability to compete. The purpose of the antitrust laws, by contrast, is "the protection of *competition*, not *competitors*." *Atlantic Richfield Co.* v. *USA Petroleum Co.*, 495 U.S. 328, 338 (1990) (internal quotation marks omitted). To the extent Congress repealed the exemption for some vertical price restraints to end its prior practice of encouraging anticompetitive conduct, the rule of reason promotes the same objective.

Respondent also relies on several congressional appropriations in the mid-1980's in which Congress did not permit the Department of Justice or the Federal Trade Commission to use funds to advocate overturning *Dr. Miles*. *See, e.g.,* 97 Stat. 1071. We need not pause long in addressing this argument. The conditions on funding are no longer in place, and they were ambiguous at best. As much as they might show congressional approval for *Dr. Miles*, they might demonstrate a different proposition: that Congress could not pass legislation codifying the rule and reached a short-term compromise instead.

Reliance interests do not require us to reaffirm *Dr. Miles*. To be sure, reliance on a judicial opinion is a significant reason to adhere to it, *Payne* v. *Tennessee*, 501 U.S. 808, 828 (1991), especially "in cases involving property and contract rights," *Khan*. The reliance interests here, however, like the reliance interests in *Khan*, cannot justify an inefficient rule, especially because the narrowness of the rule has allowed manufacturers to set minimum resale prices in other ways. And while the *Dr. Miles* rule is longstanding, resale price maintenance was legal under fair trade laws in a majority of States for a large part of the past century up until 1975.

It is also of note that during this time "when the legal environment in the [United States] was most favorable for [resale price maintenance], no more than a tiny fraction of manufacturers ever employed [resale price maintenance] contracts." Overstreet 6; *see also id.,* at 169 (noting that "no more than one percent of manufacturers, accounting for no more than ten percent of consumer goods purchases, ever employed [resale price maintenance] in any single year in the [United States]"); Scherer & Ross 549 (noting that "[t]he fraction of U.S. retail sales covered by [resale price maintenance] in its heyday has been variously estimated at from 4 to 10 percent"). To the extent consumers demand cheap goods, judging vertical price restraints under the rule of reason will not prevent the market from providing them. Cf. Easterbrook 152–153 (noting that "S.S. Kresge (the old K-Mart) flourished during the days of manufacturers' greatest freedom" because "discount stores offer a combination of price and service that many customers value" and that "[n]othing in restricted dealing threatens the ability of consumers to find low prices"); Scherer & Ross 557 (noting that "for the most part, the effects of the [Consumer Goods Pricing Act] were imperceptible because the forces of competition had already repealed the [previous antitrust exemption] in their own quiet way").

For these reasons the Court's decision in *Dr. Miles* is now overruled. Vertical price restraints are to be judged according to the rule of reason.

V

Noting that Leegin's president has an ownership interest in retail stores that sell Brighton, respondent claims Leegin participated in an unlawful horizontal cartel with competing retailers. Respondent did not make this allegation in the lower courts, and we do not consider it here.

The judgment of the Court of Appeals is reversed, and the case is remanded for proceedings consistent with this opinion. . . .

■ JUSTICE BREYER, with whom JUSTICE STEVENS, JUSTICE SOUTER, and JUSTICE GINSBURG join, dissenting.

. . . On the one hand, agreements setting minimum resale prices may have serious anticompetitive consequence. . . .

Those who express concern about the potential anticompetitive effects find empirical support in the behavior of prices before, and then after, Congress in 1975 repealed the Miller-Tydings Fair Trade Act, and the McGuire Act. Those Acts had permitted (but not required) individual States to enact "fair trade" laws authorizing minimum resale price maintenance. At the time of repeal minimum resale price maintenance was lawful in 36 States; it was unlawful in 14 States. Comparing prices in the former States with prices in the latter States, the Department of Justice argued that minimum resale price maintenance had raised prices by 19% to 27%.

After repeal, minimum resale price maintenance agreements were unlawful *per se* in every State. The Federal Trade Commission (FTC) staff, after studying numerous price surveys, wrote that collectively the surveys "indicate[d] that [resale price maintenance] in most cases increased the prices of products sold with [resale price maintenance]." Most economists today agree that, in the words of a prominent antitrust treatise, "resale price maintenance tends to produce higher consumer prices than would otherwise be the case."

On the other hand, those favoring resale price maintenance have long argued that resale price maintenance agreements can provide important consumer benefits. The upshot is, as many economists suggest, sometimes resale price maintenance can prove harmful; sometimes it can bring benefits. But before concluding that courts should consequently apply a rule of reason, I would ask such questions as, how often are harms or benefits likely to occur? How easy is it to separate the beneficial sheep from the antitrust goats? . . . .

I have already described studies and analyses that suggest (though they cannot prove) that resale price maintenance can cause harms with some regularity—and certainly when dealers are the driving force. But what about benefits? How often, for example, will the benefits to which the Court points occur in practice? I can find no economic consensus on this point. There is a consensus in the literature that "free riding" takes place. But "free riding" often takes place in the economy without any legal effort to stop it. Many visitors to California take free rides on the Pacific Coast Highway. We all benefit freely from ideas, such as that of creating the first supermarket. Dealers often take a "free ride" on investments that others have made in building a product's name and reputation. The question is how often the "free riding" problem is serious enough significantly to deter dealer investment.

To be more specific, one can easily *imagine* a dealer who refuses to provide important presale services, say a detailed explanation of how a product works (or who fails to provide a proper atmosphere in which to sell expensive perfume or alligator billfolds), lest customers use that "free" service (or enjoy the psychological benefit arising when a high-priced retailer stocks a particular brand of billfold or handbag) and then buy from another dealer at a lower price. Sometimes this must happen in reality. But does it happen often? We do, after all, live in an economy where firms, despite *Dr. Miles' per se* rule, still sell complex technical equipment (as well as expensive perfume and alligator billfolds) to consumers.

All this is to say that the ultimate question is not whether, but *how much,* "free riding" of this sort takes place. And, after reading the briefs, I must answer that question with an uncertain "sometimes."

How easily can courts identify instances in which the benefits are likely to outweigh potential harms? My own answer is, *not very easily*. . . .

Given the uncertainties that surround key items in the overall balance sheet, particularly in respect to the "administrative" questions, I can concede to the majority that the problem is difficult. And, if forced to decide now, at most I might agree that the *per se* rule should be slightly modified to allow an exception for the more easily identifiable and temporary condition of "new entry." But I am not now forced to decide this question. The question before us is not what should be the rule, starting from scratch. . . .

We write, not on a blank slate, but on a slate that begins with *Dr. Miles* and goes on to list a century's worth of similar cases, massive amounts of advice that lawyers have provided their clients, and untold numbers of business decisions those clients have taken in reliance upon that advice. Indeed a Westlaw search shows that *Dr. Miles* itself has been cited dozens of times in this Court and hundreds of times in lower courts. Those who wish this Court to change so well-established a legal precedent bear a heavy burden of proof. I am not aware of any case in which this Court has overturned so well-established a statutory precedent. Regardless, I do not see how the Court can claim that ordinary criteria for over-ruling an earlier case have been met. . . .

I can find no change in circumstances in the past several decades that helps the majority's position. In fact, there has been one important change that argues strongly to the contrary. In 1975, Congress repealed the McGuire and Miller-Tydings Acts. And it thereby consciously *extended Dr. Miles' per se* rule. Indeed, at that time the Department of Justice and the FTC, then urging application of the *per se* rule, discussed virtually every argument presented now to this Court as well as others not here presented. And they explained to Congress why Congress should reject them. Congress fully understood, and consequently intended, that the result of its repeal of McGuire and Miller-Tydings would be to make minimum resale price maintenance *per se* unlawful.

Congress did not prohibit this Court from reconsidering the *per se* rule. But enacting major legislation premised upon the existence of that rule constitutes important public reliance upon that rule. . . .

With the preceding discussion in mind, I would consult the list of factors that our case law indicates are relevant when we consider overruling an earlier case. . . .

First, the Court applies *stare decisis* more "rigidly" in statutory than in constitutional cases. This is a statutory case.

Second, the Court does sometimes overrule cases that it decided wrongly only a reasonably short time ago. . . . We here overrule one *statutory* case, *Dr. Miles*, decided 100 years ago, and we overrule the cases that reaffirmed its *per se* rule in the intervening years.

Third, the fact that a decision creates an "unworkable" legal regime argues in favor of overruling. Implementation of the *per se* rule, even with the complications attendant the exception allowed for in *Colgate,* has proved practical over the course of the last century, particularly when compared with the many complexities of litigating a case under the "rule of reason" regime. No one has shown how moving from the *Dr. Miles* regime to "rule of reason" analysis would make the legal regime governing minimum resale price maintenance more "administrable," particularly since *Colgate* would remain good law with respect to *unreasonable* price maintenance.

Fourth, the fact that a decision "unsettles" the law may argue in favor of overruling. The *per se* rule is well-settled law, as the Court itself has previously recognized. *Sylvania.* It is the majority's change here that will unsettle the law.

Fifth, the fact that a case involves property rights or contract rights, where reliance interests are involved, argues against overruling. This case involves contract rights and perhaps property rights (consider shopping malls). And there has been considerable reliance upon the *per se* rule. As I have said, Congress relied upon the continued vitality of *Dr. Miles* when it repealed Miller-Tydings and McGuire. The Executive Branch argued for repeal on the assumption that *Dr. Miles* stated the law. Moreover, whole sectors of the economy have come to rely upon the *per se* rule. A factory outlet store tells us that the rule "form[s] an essential part of the regulatory background against which [that firm] and many other discount retailers have financed, structured, and operated their businesses." . . .

This Court's overruling of the *per se* rule jeopardizes this reliance, and more. What about malls built on the assumption that a discount distributor will remain an anchor tenant? What about home buyers who have taken a home's distance from such a mall into account? What about Americans, producers, distributors, and consumers, who have understandably assumed, at least for the last 30 years, that price competition is a legally guaranteed way of life? The majority denies none of this. It simply says that these "reliance interests . . . , like the reliance interests in *Khan*, cannot justify an inefficient rule."

The Court minimizes the importance of this reliance, adding that it "is also of note" that at the time resale price maintenance contracts were lawful " 'no more than a tiny fraction of manufacturers ever employed' " the practice. By "tiny" the Court means manufacturers that accounted for up to " 'ten percent of consumer goods purchases' " annually. That figure in today's economy equals just over $300 billion. Putting the Court's estimate together with the Justice Department's early 1970's study translates a legal regime that permits all resale price maintenance into retail bills that are higher by an average of roughly $750 to $1000 annually for an American family of four. Just how much higher retail bills will be after the Court's decision today, of course, depends upon what is now unknown, namely how courts will decide future cases under a "rule of reason." But these figures indicate that the amounts involved are important to American families and cannot be dismissed as "tiny."

Sixth, the fact that a rule of law has become "embedded" in our "national culture" argues strongly against overruling. The *per se* rule forbidding minimum resale price maintenance agreements has long been "embedded" in the law of antitrust. It involves price, the economy's " 'central nervous system.' " It reflects a basic antitrust assumption (that consumers often prefer lower prices to more service). It embodies a basic antitrust objective (providing consumers with a free choice about such matters). And it creates an easily administered and enforceable bright line, "Do not agree about price," that businesses as well as lawyers have long understood.

The only contrary *stare decisis* factor that the majority mentions consists of its claim that this Court has "[f]rom the beginning . . . treated the Sherman Act as a common-law statute," and has previously overruled antitrust precedent. It points in support to *Khan*, . . . and to *Sylvania* . . . The Court decided *Khan*, however, 29 years after *Albrecht*—still a significant period, but nowhere close to the century *Dr. Miles* has stood. The Court specifically noted the *lack* of any significant reliance upon *Albrecht*. *Khan* (*Albrecht* has had "little or no relevance to ongoing enforcement of the Sherman Act"). *Albrecht* had far less support in traditional antitrust principles than did *Dr. Miles*. And Congress had nowhere expressed support for *Albrecht's* rule.

In *Sylvania*, the Court, in overruling *Schwinn*, explicitly distinguished *Dr. Miles* on the ground that while Congress had "recently . . . expressed its approval of a *per se* analysis of vertical price restrictions" by repealing the Miller-Tydings and McGuire Acts, "[n]o similar expression of congressional intent exists for nonprice restrictions." Moreover, the Court decided *Sylvania* only a decade after *Schwinn*. And it based its overruling on a generally perceived need to avoid "confusion" in the law, a factor totally absent here. . . .

NOTES AND QUESTIONS ON *LEEGIN*

1. ***What should be the standard for determining when to have a per se rule?*** Both the majority and dissent essentially conceded that economic theory was mixed on vertical minimum price-fixing, with procompetitive and anticompetitive effects both possible. The majority stressed that, given this mixed theory, the traditional standard for a per se rule was not met. That traditional standard asks whether the type of agreement almost always has anticompetitive effects and hardly ever has procompetitive ones, which amounts to asking whether a per se rule would hardly ever cause overdeterrence. The dissent instead implicitly adopted a standard that asks whether any greater overdeterrence created by the per se rule would be offset by the greater underdeterrence created by the rule of reason, stressing the high risk of underdeterrence created by erroneous applications of the rule of reason.

The dissent standard has the advantage that it directly focuses on which rule would optimize behavior by minimizing the combination of overdeterrence and underdeterrence. Perhaps one could justify the traditional standard on the ground that overdeterrence concerns should get greater weight because they are magnified by treble damages. However, as indicated in Chapter 1, it is not actually clear that treble damages are overcompensatory once one considers (a) the odds of nondetection or nonadjudication, (b) the lack of prejudgment interest, and (c) the lack of recovery for deadweight losses or umbrella effects on rival pricing. Still, for reasons noted below, litigation against vertical minimum price-fixing will almost always be brought by a terminated dealer, and the odds of detection and adjudication may be relatively high in cases involving terminated dealers, increasing overdeterrence concerns. Further, the deadweight losses and effects on rival pricing might be slight in such cases, lessening underdeterrence concerns. Which standard do you think is best for deciding when to adopt a per se rule, either generally or specifically for vertical minimum price-fixing?

2. ***Did the empirical evidence support continuing the rule of per se illegality?*** The dissent suggested that the mixed theory could be resolved by empirical evidence about the effects of the Fair Trade Acts, which allowed (but did not require) states to legalize vertical minimum price-fixing. This empirical evidence showed that, while those Acts were in force, prices

were higher in states that allowed (and enforced) vertical minimum price-fixing than in states that did not. It also showed that, in states that had allowed vertical minimum price-fixing under these Acts, prices dropped after the repeal of those Acts restored the rule of per se illegality. The majority responded by stressing that higher prices might be procompetitive if they were coupled with more services that consumers wanted. But the simpler problem with this empirical evidence was that it compared prices under a rule of per se illegality to prices under a rule of per se *legality*. A rule of per se legality is likely to have more anticompetitive effects than a rule of reason that remains available to redress anticompetitive forms of the conduct, and thus the comparative effects are not the same as switching from a rule of per se illegality to a rule of reason, which was the relevant issue in *Leegin*. So the empirical data cited by the dissent provided powerful evidence against a rule of per se *legality*, but not compelling evidence against a rule of reason.

However, empirical data since *Leegin* seems to provide stronger evidence for favoring per se illegality over a rule of reason. This empirical data shows that, after *Leegin,* prices were higher in states whose state antitrust laws followed *Leegin*'s switch to a rule of reason than in states whose state antitrust laws instead maintained per se rules against vertical minimum price-fixing. Alexander MacKay & David Aron Smith, The Empirical Effects of Minimum Resale Price Maintenance (SSRN June 16, 2014). There remains the issue of whether the increased prices were offset by increased retail services that consumers valued more than the price increases, but if that were so, then vertical minimum price-fixing should result in a net increase in output, and instead this empirical data showed that output was lower in states that followed *Leegin*'s switch to a rule of reason. Do these empirical findings support restoring per se illegality? Do they support at least requiring the defendant to prove a procompetitive justification before the plaintiff must provide empirical evidence of anticompetitive effects?

3. ***Did* stare decisis *require maintaining per se illegality?*** The dissent stressed that, given the empirical evidence and the mixed theory, one should go with *stare decisis*. But do the standard rules on *stare decisis* really apply in antitrust? As a matter of practice, given cases like *Sylvania* and *Khan,* the Court seems to overrule antitrust decisions in common law fashion all the time. Further, the text of the Sherman Act incorporates capacious common law language that might be thought to effectively delegate antitrust issues to the courts for ongoing common law development.

But even if, generally, the Court exercises common law power over antitrust doctrine, one might argue that the Court in *Leegin* should have treated vertical minimum price-fixing differently, given that Congress had specifically repealed the Fair Trade Acts. The dissent argued that this repeal indicated a legislative preference for bringing back the rule of per se illegality. The majority argued that this repeal instead indicated a legislative preference for returning the issue to the federal courts for continued common law development. Which seems correct to you?

Assuming the issue was delegated for common law development, a key issue was the fit with other doctrines. The majority stressed how anomalous the per se rule against vertical minimum price-fixing was, given that *Sylvania* and *Khan* had already overruled the per se rules against vertical nonprice restraints and vertical maximum price-fixing. The dissent stressed that the different treatment made sense because (a) vertical minimum price-fixing was somewhat more likely to be anticompetitive than the other two varieties of vertical intrabrand restraints and (b) any implications from the Fair Trade Act repeal only applied to vertical minimum price-fixing. But amidst this dispute, neither side addressed the bigger problem of common law fit—namely that, given *BMI*, the per se rule against *horizontal* price fixing no longer applies in cases when it advances a procompetitive justification ancillary to a productive relationship. Given *BMI*, adhering to *Dr. Miles* would have meant having antitrust law treat vertical minimum price-fixing that is ancillary to a productive business relation between a supplier and distributor *worse* than the law treats horizontal price-fixing that is ancillary to productive business relations like joint ventures between rivals. That would be anomalous, to say the least.

Another key issue for *stare decisis* was whether reliance interests weighed against overruling *Dr. Miles*. The dissent argued that it did because *Dr. Miles* had been binding precedent for 96 years. But does any reliance really differ depending on whether the overruled doctrine was around for 96 years, rather than for 10 or 29 years, as in *Sylvania* and *Khan*? It seems likely that any meaningful current reliance would have been incurred within the ten years or so running up the decision.

Further, it is not clear that any reliance here would counsel against legal change. Reliance can be an important reason not to change the law when reliance increases the costs of legal change (or reduces the benefits of such legal change), such as when a technological investment made in reliance on prior pollution laws makes a legal change to new pollution laws more costly or less beneficial.[9] But when reliance does not alter the costs or benefits of the legal change, then the more efficient doctrine would require parties to bear the risk of legal change, rather than making their reliance a reason to avoid that legal change.[10] While parties may have relied on *Dr. Miles* by not using vertical minimum price-fixing, does it seem likely that such reliance would alter the desirability of overruling *Dr. Miles*?

Finally, it is unclear how much reliance there really was on *Dr. Miles*. Although the dissent suggested that overruling *Dr. Miles* would create a sea change in legal practice, many factors had already limited the actual enforcement of *Dr. Miles* by the time of the *Leegin* decision. First, under the *Business Electronics* case discussed by the Court, ambiguous agreements (including even a vertical agreement to terminate a retailer because of price-fixing) were interpreted to constitute a vertical nonprice agreement, thus already making them subject to rule-of-reason scrutiny. Second, as will be discussed in Chapter 6, under *Colgate* and *Monsanto,* if a supplier "unilaterally" demanded that its dealers adhere to minimum resale prices

---

[9] *See* ELHAUGE, STATUTORY DEFAULT RULES 307–308 (2008); Steven Shavell, *On Optimal Legal Change, Past Behavior, and Grandfathering*, 37 J. LEGAL STUDIES 37 (2008).

[10] *See* ELHAUGE, STATUTORY DEFAULT RULES 306–307 (2008); Louis Kaplow, *An Economic Analysis of Legal Transitions*, 99 HARVARD LAW REVIEW 509, 522–536 (1986).

and those dealers acquiesced by complying with the minimum resale prices, it was not deemed a vertical agreement at all, thus meaning it was effectively per se legal. Third, U.S. enforcement agencies rarely, if ever, brought actions against vertical minimum price-fixing, mainly because they were persuaded by the economic critique of *Dr. Miles*. Fourth, rival manufacturers or retailers usually cannot bring suit against vertical minimum price-fixing because they cannot show antitrust injury, given that they would only benefit if such an agreement caused other manufacturers or retailers to charge anticompetitively high prices. *See* Chapter 1. Fifth, while consumers do have antitrust standing, to prove injury and damages, they must prove a net anticompetitive effect, which requires satisfying an effective rule of reason that negated the practical advantage of any per se rule on liability. Perhaps for this reason, consumers hardly ever actually brought suit against vertical minimum price-fixing. The upshot was that the per se rule against vertical minimum price-fixing was generally invoked only, as in *Leegin*, by retailers subject to the vertical price-fixing agreement, either in a suit brought to challenge their termination for noncompliance or defensively to avoid enforcement of such an agreement. The per se rule thus provided little incremental enforcement whenever retailers were willing participants. Ending such suits might not have been that big of a change.

*4. **How should courts conduct rule-of-reason scrutiny of vertical minimum price-fixing?*** The Court recognized at least four theories as to why manufacturers might agree to anticompetitive vertical minimum price-fixing despite ordinary manufacturer incentives to minimize retail markups. Covered in more detail in the introduction to this chapter, the theories are that vertical price-fixing might: (1) reflect a cartel among retailers; (2) facilitate oligopolistic coordination among manufacturers; (3) be imposed by a powerful retailer to impede competition by an efficient retail rival; or (4) be used by a powerful manufacturer "to give retailers an incentive not to sell the products of smaller rivals or new entrants" (i.e., for brand pushing).

Each anticompetitive theory suggests requiring different sorts of evidence. Theory (1) requires evidence of an agreement among dealers. Theory (2) requires evidence that (a) market structure and other market factors suggest that oligopoly pricing among manufacturers is feasible and (b) a large enough number of competing manufacturers adopted vertical minimum price-fixing that it could help them facilitate oligopolistic coordination. The Court's language on the latter point suggests that courts should aggregate the shares of the manufacturers in concentrated markets, much as the Court's exclusive dealing precedents do when assessing cumulative foreclosure. Theory (3) requires evidence of retailer market power and an effect on rival retail competition. Finally, theory (4) requires evidence that dealers carry multiple brands and can influence decisionmaking. The Court suggested that manufacturer market power might be necessary for anticompetitive brand pushing. However, without manufacturer market power, a collective action problem could drive multiple manufacturers to use vertical minimum price-fixing, both to get their brands pushed and to protect against dealers pushing other brands over their brands. Although the end result could be that all the manufacturers use vertical minimum price-fixing, so that the efforts to seek brand pushing cancel each other out and leave no manufacturer pushed over the others, all the manufacturers (and consumers) would suffer the anticompetitive effects of excessive retail markups and unresponsive retail prices.

The Court also suggested that a restraint is more likely to be anticompetitive if it was initiated by a dealer than if it was initiated by a manufacturer. Such dealer initiation could indicate that powerful downstream retailers or retailer cartels were anticompetitively forcing minimum prices on reluctant manufacturers. However, dealers also have incentives to offer terms they think manufacturers would find efficient and profitable, so dealer initiation may simply indicate that they are pursuing those procompetitive objectives in order to better compete with other dealers. Likewise, manufacturer initiation does not necessarily indicate that the restraint does not reflect the interests of powerful dealers or dealer cartels, because manufacturers have incentives to get retailers to carry their products by offering terms they know powerful dealers or dealer cartels will find profitable, even if those profits come at the expense of consumer welfare. Further, manufacturers have their own anticompetitive incentives to initiate restraints that encourage brand pushing or that facilitate oligopolistic coordination or price discrimination. Thus, *who* initiated the transaction has little bearing on whether it is procompetitive or anticompetitive. Indeed, dealer initiation will have even less bearing if the doctrine signals to the market that culpability may turn on it, as dealers will simply make sure to have manufacturers initiate any anticompetitive restraints that may benefit dealers.

4. HOW TO CHARACTERIZE AGREEMENTS

a. ARE DUAL DISTRIBUTION AGREEMENTS VERTICAL OR HORIZONTAL OR NEITHER?

Often a manufacturer chooses to use independent distributors in some locations, but to distribute on its own in other locations. This is generally called a dual distribution arrangement. For example, the *Leegin* manufacturer also operated at retail, but the Court declined to address whether this meant that the agreement restraining retail prices should be deemed horizontal, rather than vertical. The precedent on how to classify such dual distribution restraints has centered on vertical nonprice restraints, because for them the distinction in legal treatment between vertical and horizontal agreements has existed the longest. For example, suppose that, in the *Sylvania* case, Sylvania had operated its own retailer in Sacramento. Would that mean its agreements restricting the locations of its retailers should be deemed vertical (because Sylvania supplies the retailers as a manufacturer) or horizontal (because Sylvania is a competing retailer)?

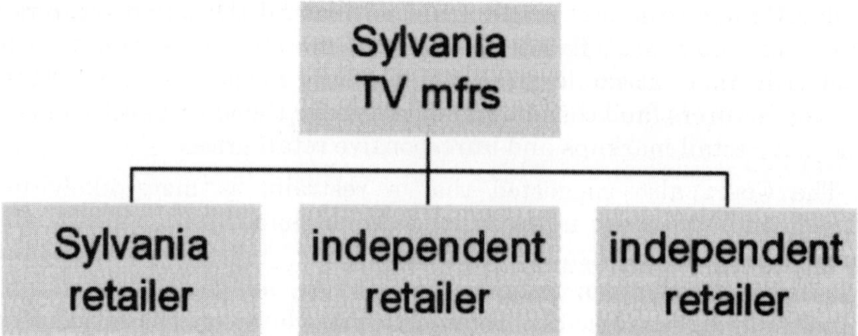

The U.S. Supreme Court has not yet addressed this question post-*Sylvania*, and its pre-*Sylvania* decisions were in conflict on this issue.[11] Most circuit courts have held that dual distribution restraints on territories are categorically vertical and governed by ordinary rule-of-reason scrutiny.[12] But several circuit courts classify dual distribution restraints as vertical when they serve manufacturer interests, but horizontal when they serve retailer interests.[13] Which position is correct?

1. Does dual distribution alter the likely effects or incentives? The fact that the manufacturer, rather than an independent retailer, owns one of the retail locations does not make the restraint any less competitive, nor any less justifiable. Nor does it alter the existence of a manufacturer incentive to minimize the retail markup. After all, the manufacturer would still want to minimize the markup charged by other, independent dealers. Still, the fact that the manufacturer owns one of its retailers may somewhat attenuate the magnitude of that incentive, given that the manufacturer now would earn any higher retail markup on those sales taking place in the manufacturer's own retail location. On the other hand, dual distribution decreases the likelihood that the restraint was coerced by a dealer cartel or a dealer with market power, because dual distribution means a manufacturer can opt for self-distribution if dealers try to impose an unwanted restraint on dealer competition.

2. Does it make sense to judge dual-distribution restraints by whether they are primarily in the interests of dealers or manufacturers? The courts that do not categorically classify dual

---

[11] *Compare* United States v. McKesson & Robbins, Inc., 351 U.S. 305, 312–13 (1956) (horizontal); Schwegmann Bros. v. Calvert Corp., 341 U.S. 384, 389 (1951) (same), *with* White Motor Co. v. United States, 372 U.S. 253, 261 (1963) (vertical); United States v. Arnold Schwinn & Co., 388 U.S. 365, 370, 372 (1967) (vertical).

[12] Electronics Communications v. Toshiba America Consumer Products, Inc., 129 F.3d 240, 243 (2d Cir. 1997); AT & T v. JMC Telecom, 470 F.3d 525, 531 (3d Cir. 2006); PSKS, Inc. v. Leegin Creative Leather Prods., Inc., 615 F.3d 412, 420–21 (5th Cir. 2010); International Logistics v. Chrysler, 884 F.2d 904, 906 (6th Cir. 1989); Illinois Corporate Travel v. American Airlines, 889 F.2d 751, 753 (7th Cir. 1989); Smalley & Co. v. Emerson & Cuming, 13 F.3d 366, 368 (10th Cir. 1993).

[13] Donald B. Rice Tire v. Michelin Tire, 638 F.2d 15, 16 (4th Cir. 1981); Hampton Audio Electronics v. Contel Cellular, 1992 WL 131169, at *3 (4th Cir. 1992); Ryko Manufacturing v. Eden Services, 823 F.2d 1215, 1231 (8th Cir. 1987); Krehl v. Baskin-Robbins, 664 F.2d 1348, 1356–57 (9th Cir. 1982); Midwestern Waffles v. Waffle House, 734 F.2d 705, 711, 720 (11th Cir. 1984).

distribution restraints as vertical instead make the classification turn on whether the restraint primarily furthers the interests of dealers or manufacturers. But how are courts supposed to determine whose interest is primarily served by a restraint? The cases suggest three possibilities.

One possibility is to focus on who initiated the restraint. But for reasons noted above in the Notes on *Leegin*, who initiated the restraint has little bearing on whether it is anticompetitive. Initiation does not even provide any reliable indicator of whose interests the restraint serves. One party may initiate a restraint because serving the *counter-party's* interests puts it in a better position, either with regards to negotiating with that counter-party or in persuading that counter-party to deal with it rather than with its rivals.

Even if initiation could tell us whose interests are being served, that would still fail to bear on whether the agreement was likely to be procompetitive or anticompetitive. Suppose the agreement is procompetitive, increasing retail markups in order to incentivize valuable distribution services. If so, the agreement would advance the interests of both dealers and manufacturers alike, so both might equally initiate it. Or suppose the agreement anticompetitively creates supracompetitive downstream profits that are split between the manufacturer and dealers through some arrangement. If so, the agreement would again advance the interests of both dealers and manufacturers alike, so both might equally initiate it. Accordingly, one cannot tell much about whether an agreement is procompetitive or anticompetitive by whether it serves the interests of dealers or manufacturers or both.

Another possibility would be to judge whether a restraint primarily served the interests of dealers or manufacturers by asking whether it primarily had anticompetitive effects on retail markups (which primarily benefit retailers) or procompetitive effects on distribution (which primarily benefit manufacturers). However, such an inquiry would effectively ask whether anticompetitive effects outweigh procompetitive effects, which would replicate rule-of-reason review. It would not make much sense to conduct rule-of-reason review to decide whether to apply a per se rule or rule of reason. Further, as noted above, a restraint may serve the interests of both manufacturers and dealers, and the way it serves those mutual interests might be procompetitive or anticompetitive.

A third possibility would conclude that manufacturer interests are being served whenever a procompetitive justification exists. Under this approach, a dual distribution restraint would never really be per se illegal, given that the existence of any procompetitive justification would always trigger rule-of-reason scrutiny. However, this approach would mean dual distribution restraints would be condemned without inquiry into anticompetitive effects whenever the defendant lacks any procompetitive justification, thus making the restraint subject to abbreviated rule-of-reason review. This possibility would make this interest-served test more coherent. Whether this approach would really subject dual distribution restraints to a tougher test than vertical restraints turns on whether abbreviated rule-of-reason scrutiny would also apply even to a purely vertical distributional restraint when the defendant has no procompetitive justification. The Supreme Court has yet to resolve that issue. If this possibility did result in a tougher test for dual distribution restraints, the best explanation would seem to be that dual distribution attenuates the manufacturer incentive to minimize retail markups that drives the more lenient test that applies to purely vertical distributional restraints.

3. ***Does* Topco *survive* Sylvania?** In United States v. Topco Associates, 405 U.S. 596 (1972), various small stores that averaged a 6% market share in their regional markets created an entity called Topco to buy, transport, warehouse, and distribute goods under the Topco label to the member stores, which agreed to sell the Topco products only in their designated territories. The Court held this territorial agreement involved a horizontal market division that was per se illegal. It is unclear whether *Topco* survives *Sylvania.* After all, Topco did involve a vertical supply relationship, so one could have classified it as a vertical territorial restraint like *Sylvania* or perhaps as a dual distribution restraint that should be treated as vertical. Cutting against this classification is the fact that, unlike for typical vertical or dual distribution restraints, the *Topco* supplier was created by the dealers, so the supplier did not have an independent incentive to minimize dealer markups. Cutting for this classification is the fact that, given the small market share covered by the restraint, adverse effects on interbrand competition or dealer markups seemed unlikely in either *Topco* or *Sylvania.*

4. ***Should the agreement in* Palmer v. BRG *have been treated as a dual distribution restraint subject to rule-of-reason review?*** *Palmer v. BRG* did involve a dual distribution agreement, whereby Harcourt Brace supplied bar materials for BRG to use in Georgia and Harcourt Brace used the same bar materials itself outside of Georgia. However, the *Palmer* restraint arguably differed from classic dual distribution restraints in terms of likely incentives and the probability of interbrand effects. The reason is that, in *Palmer,* the restraint ended vigorous interbrand competition, and the profit-sharing term meant that the supplier would directly share in any inflated downstream retail profits. These differences likely explain why, as discussed in Chapter 2, the Court treated the vertical aspects as a fig leaf that failed to alter what was really a horizontal market division. But *Palmer* would likely have been decided differently if the facts had indicated the restraint eliminated competition between only two of many different bar review courses, which would have made anticompetitive interbrand effects unlikely.

b. VERTICAL AGREEMENTS TO "BOYCOTT" THE RIVAL OF A DEALER WITHOUT ANY PROCOMPETITIVE JUSTIFICATION

NYNEX v. Discon

525 U.S. 128 (1998).

■ JUSTICE BREYER delivered the opinion of the Court.

In this case we ask whether the antitrust rule that group boycotts are illegal per se as set forth in *Klor's*, applies to a buyer's decision to buy from one seller rather than another, when that decision cannot be justified in terms of ordinary competitive objectives. We hold that the per se group boycott rule does not apply. . . .

This case involves the business of removing . . . obsolete telephone equipment . . .—a business called "removal services." Discon, Inc., the respondent, sold removal services used by New York Telephone . . . a subsidiary of NYNEX Corporation. NYNEX also owns Materiel Enterprises Company, a purchasing entity that bought removal services for New York Telephone. . . . [Discon] claims . . . that Materiel Enterprises had switched its purchases from Discon to Discon's competitor, AT & T Technologies, as part of an attempt to defraud local telephone service customers by hoodwinking regulators. According to Discon, Materiel Enterprises would pay AT & T Technologies more than Discon would have charged for similar removal services. It did so because it could pass the higher prices on to New York Telephone, which in turn could pass those prices on to telephone consumers in the form of higher regulatory-agency-approved telephone service charges. At the end of the year, Materiel Enterprises would receive a special rebate from AT & T Technologies, which Materiel Enterprises would share with its parent, NYNEX. Discon added that it refused to participate in this fraudulent scheme, with the result that Materiel Enterprises would not buy from Discon, and Discon went out of business.

. . . The case before us involves *Klor's*. The Second Circuit did not forbid the defendants to introduce evidence of "justification." To the contrary, it invited the defendants to do so, for it said that the "per se rule" would apply only if no "pro-competitive justification" were to be found. Thus, the specific legal question before us is whether an antitrust court considering an agreement by a buyer to purchase goods or services from one supplier rather than another should (after examining the buyer's reasons or justifications) apply the per se rule if it finds no legitimate business reason for that purchasing decision. We conclude no boycott-related per se rule applies and that the plaintiff here must allege and prove harm, not just to a single competitor, but to the competitive process, i.e., to competition itself.

Our conclusion rests in large part upon precedent, for precedent limits the per se rule in the boycott context to cases involving horizontal agreements among direct competitors. . . . Although *Klor's* involved a threat made by a single powerful firm, it also involved a horizontal agreement among those threatened, namely, the appliance suppliers, to hurt a competitor of the retailer who made the threat. This Court emphasized in *Klor's* that the agreement at issue was

> "not a case of a single trader refusing to deal with another, nor even of a manufacturer and a dealer agreeing to an exclusive distributorship. Alleged in this complaint is a wide combination consisting of manufacturers, distributors and a retailer." *Klor's.*

This Court subsequently pointed out specifically that *Klor's* was a case involving not simply a "vertical" agreement between supplier and customer, but a case that also involved a "horizontal" agreement among competitors. *See Business Electronics.* And in doing so, the Court held that a "vertical restraint is not illegal per se unless it includes some agreement on price or price levels." This precedent makes the per se rule inapplicable, for the case before us concerns only a vertical agreement and a vertical restraint, a restraint that takes the form of depriving a supplier of a potential customer.

Nor have we found any special feature of this case that could distinguish it from the precedent we have just discussed. We concede Discon's claim that the petitioners' behavior hurt consumers by raising telephone service rates. But that consumer injury naturally flowed not so much from a less competitive market for removal services, as from the exercise of market power that is lawfully in the hands of a monopolist, namely, New York Telephone, combined with a deception worked upon the regulatory agency that prevented the agency from controlling New York Telephone's exercise of its monopoly power.

To apply the per se rule here—where the buyer's decision, though not made for competitive reasons, composes part of a regulatory fraud—would transform cases involving business behavior that is improper for various reasons, say, cases involving nepotism or personal pique, into treble-damages antitrust cases. And that per se rule would discourage firms from changing suppliers—even where the competitive process itself does not suffer harm.

The freedom to switch suppliers lies close to the heart of the competitive process that the antitrust laws seek to encourage. At the same time, other laws, for example, "unfair competition" laws, business tort laws, or regulatory laws, provide remedies for various "competitive practices thought to be offensive to proper standards of business morality." Thus, this Court has refused to apply per se reasoning in cases involving that kind of activity.

Discon points to another special feature of its complaint, namely, its claim that Materiel Enterprises hoped to drive Discon from the market lest Discon reveal its behavior to New York Telephone or to the relevant regulatory agency. That hope, says Discon, amounts to a special anticompetitive motive.

We do not see how the presence of this special motive, however, could make a significant difference. That motive does not turn Materiel Enterprises' actions into a "boycott" within the meaning of this Court's precedents. Nor, for that matter, do we understand how Discon believes the motive affected Materiel Enterprises' behavior. Why would Discon's demise have made Discon's employees less likely, rather than more likely, to report the overcharge/rebate scheme to telephone regulators? Regardless, a per se rule that would turn upon a showing that a defendant not only knew about but also hoped for a firm's demise would create a legal distinction—between corporate knowledge and corporate motive—that does not necessarily correspond to behavioral differences and which would be difficult to prove, making the resolution of already complex antitrust cases yet more difficult. We cannot find a convincing reason why the presence of this special motive should lead to the application of the per se rule.

Finally, we shall consider an argument that is related tangentially to Discon's per se claims. The complaint alleges that New York Telephone (through Materiel Enterprises) was the largest buyer of removal services in New York State, and that only AT & T Technologies competed for New York Telephone's business. One might ask whether these accompanying allegations are sufficient to warrant application of a *Klor's*-type presumption of consequent harm to the competitive process itself.

We believe that these allegations do not do so, for, as we have said, antitrust law does not permit the application of the per se rule in the boycott context in the absence of a horizontal agreement. (Though in other contexts, say, vertical price fixing, conduct may fall within the scope of a per se rule not at issue here.) The complaint itself explains why any such presumption would be particularly inappropriate here, for it suggests the presence of other potential or actual competitors, which fact, in the circumstances, could argue against the likelihood of anticompetitive harm. The complaint says, for example, that New York Telephone itself was a potential competitor in that New York Telephone considered removing its equipment by itself, and in fact did perform a few jobs itself. The complaint also suggests that other nearby small local telephone companies needing removal services must have worked out some way to supply them. The complaint's description of the removal business suggests that entry was easy, perhaps to the point where other firms, employing workers who knew how to remove a switch and sell it for scrap, might have entered that business almost at will. To that extent, the complaint suggests other actual or potential competitors might have provided roughly similar checks upon "equipment removal" prices and services with or without Discon. At the least, the complaint provides no sound basis for assuming the contrary. Its simple allegation of harm to Discon does not automatically show injury to competition. . . .

NOTES AND QUESTIONS ON *NYNEX V. DISCON*

1. ***Distinguishing* Klor's.** Why should this vertical "boycott" be treated any differently than the horizontal boycott organized by the dealer in *Klor's*, in which the court held it unnecessary to prove market power or harm to competition? The answer is that vertical and horizontal agreements not to deal with others raise very different overdeterrence and underdeterrence concerns. Any firm has to choose its suppliers, which necessarily requires decisions *not* to buy from other suppliers. Vertical agreements not to deal with others are thus unavoidable and ubiquitous, and in general involve procompetitive free market choices. In contrast, horizontal agreements not to deal with others are usually avoidable, relatively rare, and less likely to have procompetitive purposes. Antitrust review of vertical "boycotts" without any proof of market power or anticompetitive effects would thus create far greater overdeterrence concerns, because it would require judicial second-guessing of ubiquitous, unavoidable business decisions that usually involve procompetitive free market choices. Applying the rule of reason, as *NYNEX* did, to vertical "boycotts" reduces overdeterrence by limiting antitrust review to the subset of cases where there is market power or direct proof of anticompetitive effects. Further, it is in that subset of cases where underdeterrence concerns are clearest and strongest.

2. ***Why does this alleged vertical agreement survive the rule of reason?*** Even accepting that *Klor's* per se treatment should not apply, the question remains why the alleged vertical agreement in *NYNEX* was not invalidated under the rule of reason. The complaint, after all, alleges an agreement lacking any procompetitive justification. Would not proving those allegations make the challenged agreement a naked restraint that should be summarily condemned under the rule of reason, even if anticompetitive effects are not proven? The *NYNEX* Court holds otherwise, thus effectively ruling that the naked restraint doctrine does not apply to ordinary vertical agreements not to deal with another firm. The reason for this holding seems related to the same overdeterrence and underdeterrence concerns noted above. If merely alleging the absence of a procompetitive justification for choosing one supplier over another sufficed to trigger antitrust scrutiny into the merits of that decision, courts could be called upon to second guess each and every purchase decision to determine whether it was justified. Such ubiquitous court review would be costly, often erroneous, and could deter ordinary efficient decisions to change suppliers, as the buyer may fear that terminated suppliers would bring suit in antitrust.

But even if the inapplicability of the naked restraint doctrine requires full-scale rule-of-reason review, why was the requisite anticompetitive effect not alleged by the allegations that consumers were harmed by increased telephone fees? The answer is that the allegation was that telephone fees were raised because regulators were deceived, rather than because the alleged vertical "boycott" created or worsened market power by suppressing competition. Deceiving regulators may well harm consumers and give rise to a cause of action under telecommunications law, but such deception would not cause the type of anticompetitive harm that antitrust law seeks to remedy.

3. Does* NYNEX *mean that <u>no</u> vertical agreement can ever constitute a boycott that is illegal as a naked restraint? Probably not. *NYNEX* limited its affirmative holding to a buyer decision to purchase from one supplier rather than another, and the Court indicated that "special features" might distinguish other vertical agreements. For example, consider a vertical agreement with the following special features. Suppose that a supplier pays a buyer not to buy a product from the supplier's rival, but the supplier itself does not supply that product to the buyer. Such a case might well be deemed a naked restraint that can be condemned without proof of anticompetitive effects, because condemning that sort of agreement raises lower overdeterrence concerns and failing to condemn it raises greater underdeterrence concerns. Overdeterrence concerns are lower because such agreements are rare, easily avoidable, distinguishable from other ubiquitous business decisions, and seem to lack any plausible procompetitive purpose. Underdeterrence concerns are greater because it is hard to see how a seller could hope to profit from such an agreement unless harming its rival has anticompetitive effects in the seller's market. In contrast, agreements to choose one supplier over another raise far greater overdeterrence concerns and far lower underdeterrence concerns.

C. PRICE DISCRIMINATION THAT ARGUABLY DISTORTS DOWNSTREAM COMPETITION

Primary-line price discrimination involves cases where the concern is that the lower price is targeted at customers of the seller's rivals and will discipline the rivals or drive them out of the market. Such cases were addressed in Chapter 3. Secondary-line price discrimination instead involves cases where the concern is that the businesses that buy at the higher price will be at a competitive disadvantage, thus distorting competition in the downstream market where those businesses compete. Secondary-line price discrimination also differs from what one might call "pure" price discrimination against consumers, which is designed to maximize the seller's profits but cannot impede competition among buyers, because consumers do not compete on any market that is further downstream. Tertiary-line price discrimination raises the same concern as secondary-line price discrimination, only one level further downstream. The tertiary-line concern is that the firms that buy upstream at the higher price will incur higher costs that require them in turn to sell their own product further downstream at higher prices than the firms that buy upstream at lower prices, so that the businesses supplied further downstream by the first set of firms will be at a competitive disadvantage.

Prohibitions on the above forms of price discrimination do not prevent sellers from charging different prices to different types of ultimate consumers, such as the movie theater that charges different prices for adults and children, because those consumers do not compete in a downstream market. Of course, different retailers might have different sets of customers, so that a supplier might want to achieve such consumer price discrimination by charging different prices to retailers with different sets of customers, such as charging higher prices to retailers who operate in high-income areas than to retailers who operate in low-income areas. But prohibitions on primary, secondary, or tertiary price discrimination are unlikely to impede such price discrimination, because those prohibitions require a showing that the buyers who were charged different prices themselves compete downstream in some market, which generally requires showing that they are reselling in a market with some common set of consumers.

Under U.S. law, price discrimination is regulated by the Robinson-Patman Act. It has three affirmative elements, making it prima facie illegal to (1) price discriminate between different buyers, (2) of like goods, (3) where the effect may be substantially to lessen competition or to injure competition with any person. It also offers three defenses, allowing the defendant to rebut illegality by showing that the price difference is justified by (1) a cost difference, (2) changing market conditions over time, or (3) a good faith effort to meet the differing terms of competitors.

Robinson-Patman Act § 2

15 U.S.C. § 13.[14]

(a) Price; selection of customers. It shall be unlawful for any person . . . either directly or indirectly, to discriminate in price between different purchasers of commodities of like grade and quality . . . where the effect of such discrimination may be substantially to lessen competition or tend to create a monopoly in any line of commerce, or to injure, destroy, or prevent competition with any person who either grants or knowingly receives the benefit of such discrimination, or with customers of either of them: *Provided*, That nothing herein contained shall prevent differentials which make only due allowance for differences in the cost of manufacture, sale, or delivery resulting from the differing methods or quantities in which such commodities are to such purchasers sold or delivered: *Provided, however*, That the Federal Trade Commission may fix and establish quantity limits, and revise the same as it finds necessary, as to particular commodities or classes of commodities, where it finds that available purchasers in greater quantities are so few as to render differentials on account thereof unjustly discriminatory or promotive of monopoly in any line of commerce; and the foregoing shall then not be construed to permit differentials based on differences in quantities greater than those so fixed and established: *And provided*

[14] The Robinson-Patman Act was a 1936 amendment of former Clayton Act § 2, which had previously prohibited anticompetitive price discrimination but exempted price differences based on quantity and arguably had an narrower definition of the requisite anticompetitive effects.

further, That nothing herein contained shall prevent persons engaged in selling goods, wares, or merchandise in commerce from selecting their own customers in bona fide transactions and not in restraint of trade: *And provided further*, That nothing herein contained shall prevent price changes from time to time where in response to changing conditions affecting the market for or the marketability of the goods concerned, such as but not limited to actual or imminent deterioration of perishable goods, obsolescence of seasonal goods, distress sales under court process, or sales in good faith in discontinuance of business in the goods concerned.

(b) Burden of rebutting prima-facie case of discrimination. Upon proof being made . . . that there has been discrimination in price or services or facilities furnished, the burden of rebutting the prima-facie case thus made by showing justification shall be upon the person charged with a violation of this section, and unless justification shall be affirmatively shown, the Commission is authorized to issue an order terminating the discrimination: *Provided, however*, That nothing herein contained shall prevent a seller rebutting the prima-facie case thus made by showing that his lower price or the furnishing of services or facilities to any purchaser or purchasers was made in good faith to meet an equally low price of a competitor, or the services or facilities furnished by a competitor.

FTC v. Morton Salt Co.

334 U.S. 37 (1948).

■ MR. JUSTICE BLACK delivered the opinion of the Court. . . .

[The Court of Appeals set aside an FTC decision finding that Respondent had violated the Robinson-Patman Act.] . . . Respondent sells its finest brand of table salt, known as Blue Label, on what it terms a standard quantity discount system available to all customers. Under this system the purchasers pay a delivered price and the cost to both wholesale and retail purchasers of this brand differs according to the quantities bought. These prices are as follows, after making allowance for rebates and discounts:

	Per case
Less-than-carload purchases	$1.60
Carload purchases	1.50
5,000-case purchases in any consecutive 12 months	1.40
50,000-case purchases in any consecutive 12 months	1.35

Only five companies have ever bought sufficient quantities of respondent's salt to obtain the $1.35 per case price. These companies could buy in such quantities because they operate large chains of retail stores in various parts of the country. As a result of this low price these five companies have been able to sell Blue Label salt at retail cheaper than wholesale purchasers from respondent could reasonably sell the same brand of salt to independently operated retail stores, many of whom competed with the local outlets of the five chain stores . . .

First. Respondent's basic contention . . . is that its "standard quantity discounts, available to all on equal terms, as contrasted for example, to hidden or special rebates, allowances, prices or discounts, are not discriminatory, within the meaning of the Robinson-Patman Act." Theoretically, these discounts are equally available to all, but functionally they are not. For as the record indicates . . . no single independent retail grocery store, and probably no single wholesaler, bought as many as 50,000 cases or as much as $50,000 worth of table salt in one year. Furthermore, the record shows that, while certain purchasers were enjoying one or more of respondent's standard quantity discounts, some of their competitors made purchases in such small quantities that they could not qualify for any of respondent's discounts, even those based on carload shipments. The legislative history of the Robinson-Patman Act makes it abundantly clear that Congress considered it to be an evil that a large buyer could secure a competitive advantage over a small buyer solely because of the large buyer's quantity purchasing ability. The Robinson-Patman Act was passed to deprive a large buyer of such advantages except to the extent that a lower price could be justified by reason of a seller's diminished costs due to quantity manufacture, delivery or sale, or by reason of the seller's good faith effort to meet a competitor's equally low price.

Section 2 of the original Clayton Act had included a proviso that nothing contained in it should prevent "discrimination in price * * * on account of differences in the grade, quality, or quantity of the commodity sold, or that makes only due allowance for difference in the cost of selling or transportation * * *." That section has been construed as permitting quantity discounts, such as those here, without regard to the amount of the seller's actual savings in cost attributable to quantity sales or quantity deliveries. The House Committee Report on the Robinson-Patman Act considered that the Clayton Act's proviso allowing quantity discounts so weakened § 2 "as to render it inadequate, if not almost a nullity." The Committee considered the present Robinson-Patman amendment to § 2 "of great importance." Its purpose was to limit "the use of quantity price differentials to the sphere of actual cost differences. Otherwise," the report continued, "such differentials would become instruments of favor and privilege and weapons of competitive oppression." The Senate Committee reporting the bill emphasized the same purpose, as did the Congressman in charge of the Conference Report when explaining it to the House just before final passage. And it was in furtherance of this avowed purpose—to protect competition from all price differentials except those based in full on cost savings—that § 2(a) of the amendment provided "That nothing herein contained shall prevent differentials which make only due allowance for differences in the cost of manufacture, sale, or delivery resulting from the differing methods or quantities in which such commodities are to such purchasers sold or delivered."

The foregoing references, without regard to others which could be mentioned, establish that respondent's standard quantity discounts are discriminatory within the meaning of the Act, and are prohibited by it whenever they have the defined effect on competition.

Second. [The respondent had the burden of proving that cost savings justified its quantity discount differentials.] First, the general rule of statutory construction that the burden of proving justification or exemption under a special exception to the prohibitions of a statute generally rests on one who claims its benefits, requires that respondent undertake this proof under the proviso of § 2(a). Secondly, § 2(b) of the Act specifically imposes the burden of showing justification upon one who is shown to have discriminated in prices. And the Senate committee report on the bill explained that the provisos of § 2(a) throw "upon any who claims the benefit of those exceptions the burden of showing that their case falls within them." We think that the language of the Act, and the legislative history just cited, show that Congress meant by using the words "discrimination in price" in § 2 that in a case involving competitive injury between a seller's customers the Commission need only prove that a seller had charged one purchaser a higher price for like goods than he had charged one or more of the purchaser's competitors. . . .

Third. . . . [T]he statute does not require the Commission to find that injury has actually resulted. The statute requires no more than that the effect of the prohibited price discriminations "may be substantially to lessen competition . . . or to injure, destroy, or prevent competition." After a careful consideration of this provision of the Robinson-Patman Act, we have said that "the statute does not require that the discriminations must in fact have harmed competition, but only that there is a reasonable possibility that they 'may' have such an effect." Corn Products v. FTC, 324 U.S. 726, 742.[14] Here the Commission found what would appear to be obvious, that the competitive opportunities of certain merchants were injured when they had to pay respondent substantially more for their goods than their competitors had to pay. The findings are adequate.

Fourth. It is urged that the evidence is inadequate to support the Commission's findings of injury to competition. As we have pointed out, however, the Commission is authorized by the Act to bar discriminatory

[14] This language is to be read also in the light of the following statement in the same case.

"... But as was held in the *Standard Fashion* case, with respect to the like provisions of § 3 of the Clayton Act . . . the use of the word 'may' was not to prohibit discriminations having 'the mere possibility' of those consequences, but to reach those which would probably have the defined effect on competition."

324 U.S. at page 738. The Committee Reports and Congressional debate on this provision of the Robinson-Patman Act indicate that it was intended to have a broader scope than the corresponding provision of the old Clayton Act. *See* note 18 *infra*.

prices upon the "reasonable possibility" that different prices for like goods to competing purchasers may have the defined effect on competition. That respondent's quantity discounts did result in price differentials between competing purchasers sufficient in amount to influence their resale price of salt was shown by evidence. This showing in itself is adequate to support the Commission's appropriate findings that the effect of such price discriminations "may be substantially to lessen competition . . . and to injure, destroy and prevent competition." . . .

It is also argued that respondent's less-than-carload sales are very small in comparison with the total volume of its business and for that reason we should reject the Commission's finding that the effect of the carload discrimination may substantially lessen competition and may injure competition between purchasers who are granted and those who are denied this discriminatory discount. To support this argument, reference is made to the fact that salt is a small item in most wholesale and retail businesses and in consumers' budgets. For several reasons we cannot accept this contention.

There are many articles in a grocery store that, considered separately, are comparatively small parts of a merchant's stock. Congress intended to protect a merchant from competitive injury attributable to discriminatory prices on any or all goods sold in interstate commerce, whether the particular goods constituted a major or minor portion of his stock. Since a grocery store consists of many comparatively small articles, there is no possible way effectively to protect a grocer from discriminatory prices except by applying the prohibitions of the Act to each individual article in the store.

Furthermore, in enacting the Robinson-Patman Act Congress was especially concerned with protecting small businesses which were unable to buy in quantities, such as the merchants here who purchased in less-than-carload lots. To this end it undertook to strengthen this very phase of the old Clayton Act. The committee reports on the Robinson-Patman Act emphasized a belief that § 2 of the Clayton Act had "been too restrictive in requiring a showing of general injury to competitive conditions. . . ." The new provision, here controlling, was intended to justify a finding of injury to competition by a showing of "injury to the competitor victimized by the discrimination."[18] Since there was evidence

---

[18] In explaining this clause of the proposed Robinson-Patman Act, the Senate Judiciary Committee said:

"This clause . . . tends to exclude from the bill otherwise harmless violations of its letter, but accomplishes a substantial broadening of a similar clause now contained in section 2 of the Clayton Act. The latter has in practice been too restrictive, in requiring a showing of general injury to competitive conditions in the line of commerce concerned; whereas the more immediately important concern is in injury to the competitor victimized by the discrimination. Only through such injuries, in fact, can the larger general injury result, and to catch the weed in the seed will keep it from coming to flower." S.Rep. No.1502, 74th Cong., 2d Sess. 4. *See* also H.Rep.No.2287, 74th Cong., 2d Sess. 8; 80 Cong.Rec. 9417.

sufficient to show that the less-than-carload purchasers might have been handicapped in competing with the more favored carload purchasers by the differential in price established by respondent, the Commission was justified in finding that competition might have thereby been substantially lessened or have been injured within the meaning of the Act.

Apprehension is expressed in this Court that enforcement of the Commission's order against respondent's continued violations of the Robinson-Patman Act might lead respondent to raise table salt prices to its carload purchasers. Such a conceivable, though, we think, highly improbable contingency, could afford us no reason for upsetting the Commission's findings and declining to direct compliance with a statute passed by Congress.

. . . It would greatly handicap effective enforcement of the Act to require testimony to show that which we believe to be self-evident, namely, that there is a "reasonable possibility" that competition may be adversely affected by a practice under which manufacturers and producers sell their goods to some customers substantially cheaper than they sell like goods to the competitors of these customers. This showing in itself is sufficient to justify our conclusion that the Commission's findings of injury to competition were adequately supported by evidence. . . .

The judgment of the Circuit Court of Appeals is reversed . . .

NOTES AND QUESTIONS ON *MORTON SALT*

1. Should a quantity discount that is available to all buyers who buy that quantity be deemed price discrimination? The Court held that a quantity discount that is available to all buyers who buy that quantity constituted price discrimination under the Act. Such a quantity discount is formally nondiscriminatory in the sense that it offers the same terms to all buyers. However, the Court stressed that, in practice, only some buyers could buy the requisite quantity, so the quantity discount was functionally discriminatory. If a quantity discount is functionally discriminatory and the amount of the discount exceeds any quantity-based cost savings, then such pricing would discriminate in favor of bigger buyers relative to an efficiency baseline.

The issue was debatable because one could interpret the statutory term "discriminate" to require formal discrimination and thus not be satisfied when a defendant offers the same terms to everyone, even if those equal terms have a discriminatory impact. But cutting for the Court's holding is the fact that the statute bans price discrimination in goods of "like grade and quality," without limiting such a ban to cases of "like quantity." Further, the statute has a special exception for price differentials that are justified by cost differences that result from different quantities, which would be unnecessary if charging different prices for different quantities did not count as price discrimination at all. The legislative history also expressly indicates a desire to prevent quantity discounts that could not be cost justified, owing mainly to Congress' concern that such discounts in excess of cost savings favored powerful buyers.

Does the Court's holding mean that all quantity discounts that cannot be cost justified constitute price discrimination under the Act? Not necessarily. It surely would not be price discrimination to offer quantity discounts if all buyers bought the same quantity and thus paid the same price. It may also not be price discrimination to offer quantity discounts that all buyers *could* obtain given the quantities they buy of the relevant product, even though some buyers chose to buy lower quantities from the defendant and thus paid a higher price. On the one hand, the Court stressed that in *Morton Salt* some buyers did not buy enough of the relevant product to ever qualify for some or all quantity discounts, thus suggesting such functional discrimination was necessary for its holding. On the other hand, the Court did in dicta state that it interpreted the Act to mean that price discrimination required showing only "that a seller had charged one purchaser a higher price for like goods than he had charged one or more of the purchaser's competitors." This statement that any price difference equals price discrimination has been repeated in other cases, but one could image a modern court reading the case more narrowly to apply only to quantity discounts that were functionally discriminatory.

2. ***Should a sufficient likelihood of anticompetitive effects be inferred from the price difference itself?*** The Court held that courts could infer a sufficient likelihood of anticompetitive effects from the existence of a price difference substantial enough to influence the resale prices of competing purchasers. This statutory interpretation is problematic because it effectively reads the anticompetitive effects element out of the statute by allowing it to be inferred from the price discrimination itself.

The Court reasoned that it had previously read the language of the anticompetitive effects provision as not requiring proof of actual anticompetitive injury, but rather as requiring only a "reasonable possibility" that the price discrimination may have an anticompetitive injury. However, that reading hardly seems inevitable because, as the Court itself noted, it has also read similar "may" language in Clayton Act § 3 to require evidence that the conduct would "probably" lessen competition. Moreover, it is not clear why the mere existence of a substantial price difference affecting some competing buyers (out of perhaps many) should suffice to show even a reasonable possibility of anticompetitive injury.

The Court reasoned that the Robinson-Patman Act's legislative history indicated a Congressional intent to protect small businesses by broadening the effects provision to include any injury to an *individual* competitor harmed by price competition. But even if some legislators had that view, it was reflected in the statutory text only to the extent that provision covered price discrimination that may injure "competition with any person" who received the lower price, which still seems to require some injury to competition, rather than just to a competitor. Given that the Court now often rejects using legislative history to change the meaning of otherwise clear statutory text, the current Court might well find this interpretation unpersuasive, especially given that it conflicts with the usual principle that antitrust statutes should be read to protect competition, not competitors.

Moreover, it seems clear that the Congress that enacted the Robinson-Patman Act could not have had an unlimited intent to protect small businesses that could not buy in big quantities. If Congress had had that intent, then the statute would not allow a cost justification defense at all, because small buyers might also be injured by quantity discounts that *were* cost justified. Rather, the Congressional intent could at most be to protect small buyers from quantity discounts that could *not* be cost justified. But a manufacturer like Morton Salt has no apparent incentive to harm small buyers with price discrimination that is not cost justified. To the contrary, if a manufacturer eliminates small buyers, then the remaining large buyers might end up with buyer market power that would reduce manufacturer profits. Thus, absent any anticompetitive effects on the market, it would seem that a manufacturer would offer a quantity discount only if it were cost justified. If that is the case, the Court's interpretation has the odd feature that it effectively protects small businesses only in cases where a cost justification likely exists (given manufacturer incentives) but cannot be proven. It would make more sense to read the statute to require the defendant to prove its quantity discounts were cost justified only *after* the plaintiff shows likely anticompetitive effects, just as the statute on its face seems to do.

To be sure, Congress may have been concerned that big buyers with market power would force manufacturers to charge the powerful buyers lower prices that were not cost justified, even when such discriminatory prices were not in the interests of the manufacturers. But if that were the concern, then the focus of liability should be on *buyers* who insist on price discrimination that is not cost justified, a concern that is already addressed by a different provision, Robinson Patman Act 2(f), which makes buyers liable for knowingly inducing or receiving a prohibited price discrimination.

Nor did the evidence show likely anticompetitive effects. A manufacturer like Morton Salt usually has no incentive to diminish competition among its wholesalers and retailers. Instead, it generally wants to maximize competition among its customers, so that it can decrease the retail markup as much as possible. There was no evidence that Morton Salt's lower prices to some buyers foreclosed enough of the downstream market to impair rival efficiency. Nor was any evidence offered to show that the individual wholesalers and retailers that bought the larger quantities had sufficient buyer market power to induce Morton Salt to give them a lower price despite anticompetitive effects on downstream competition. Accordingly, Morton Salt had no apparent reason to offer a quantity discount unless it was indeed cost justified.

Finally, one might wonder whether the price difference sufficed to show even a reasonable likelihood of injury to individual buyers, given the evidence that salt was a small share of the buyers' overall costs. However, the Court seems right that as long as the price difference suffices to influence buyers' resale price for salt, then the price difference would deprive those buyers who paid higher sale prices of some downstream sales in the downstream salt market. That injury might not be a large share of the buyers' overall profits, but it would be an injury to individual buyers, which is all the statute requires under the Court's reading.

3. ***Does it make sense that the Act is limited to commodities?*** To the extent that price discrimination is an economic concern, there does not appear to be much reason to limit that concern to price discrimination about commodities, as the Robinson-Patman Act does. The explanation may be that, when the statute was enacted in 1936, Congress was most concerned about the competitive advantage of large manufacturers over their smaller counterparts, perhaps because there was not then similar evidence of significant competitive advantages between large and small sellers of services or other non-commodities.

Texaco v. Hasbrouck

496 U.S. 543 (1990).

■ JUSTICE STEVENS delivered the opinion of the Court.

Petitioner (Texaco) sold gasoline directly to respondents and several other retailers in Spokane, Washington, at its retail tank wagon prices (RTW) while it granted substantial discounts to two distributors. [The two distributors, Gull and Dompier, acted both as wholesalers, reselling some gas to independent stations, and as retailers, selling some gas in their own stations. Neither maintained any significant storage facilities and Dompier was reimbursed for hauling the gas to its stations.] . . . [T]he stations supplied by the two distributors increased their sales volume dramatically, while respondents' sales suffered a corresponding decline. Respondents filed an action against Texaco . . . alleging that the distributor discounts violated § 2(a) of the [Robinson-Patman] Act. Respondents recovered treble damages, and the Court of Appeals for the Ninth Circuit affirmed the judgment. We granted certiorari to consider Texaco's contention that legitimate functional discounts do not violate the Act because a seller is not responsible for its customers' independent resale pricing decisions. While we agree with the basic thrust of Texaco's argument, we conclude that in this case it is foreclosed by the facts of record. . . .

It is appropriate to begin our consideration of the legal status of functional discounts[11] by examining the language of the Act. . . . The Act contains no express reference to functional discounts. It does contain two affirmative defenses that provide protection for two categories of discounts—those that are justified by savings in the seller's cost of manufacture, delivery or sale, and those that represent a good faith response to the equally low prices of a competitor. As the case comes to us, neither of those defenses is available to Texaco.

---

[11] . . . "A functional discount is one given to a purchaser based on its role in the supplier's distributive system, reflecting, at least in a generalized sense, the services performed by the purchaser for the supplier."

In order to establish a violation of the Act, respondents had the burden of proving four facts: (1) that Texaco's sales to Gull and Dompier were made in interstate commerce; (2) that the gasoline sold to them was of the same grade and quality as that sold to respondents; (3) that Texaco discriminated in price as between Gull and Dompier on the one hand and respondents on the other; and (4) that the discrimination had a prohibited effect on competition. Moreover, for each respondent to recover damages, he had the burden of proving the extent of his actual injuries. J. Truett Payne Co. v. Chrysler Motors Corp., 451 U.S. 557 (1981).

The first two elements of respondents' case are not disputed in this Court,[14] and we do not understand Texaco to be challenging the sufficiency of respondents' proof of damages. Texaco does argue, however, that although it charged different prices, it did not "discriminate in price" within the meaning of the Act, and that, at least to the extent that Gull and Dompier acted as wholesalers, the price differentials did not injure competition. We consider the two arguments separately.

Texaco's first argument would create a blanket exemption for all functional discounts. Indeed carried to its logical conclusion, it would exempt all price differentials except those given to competing purchasers. . . . Although [some legislative history] does support Texaco's argument, we remain persuaded that the argument is foreclosed by the text of the Act itself. In the context of a statute that plainly reveals a concern with competitive consequences at different levels of distribution, and carefully defines specific affirmative defenses, it would be anomalous to assume that the Congress intended the term "discriminate" to have such a limited meaning. . . . The reasons we gave for our decision in *Anheuser-Busch* apply here as well. . . .

> "the statute itself spells out the conditions which make a price difference illegal or legal, and we would derange this integrated statutory scheme were we to read other conditions into the law by means of the nondirective phrase, 'discriminate in price.' Not only would such action be contrary to what we conceive to be the meaning of the statute, but, perhaps because of this, it would be thoroughly undesirable. As one commentator has succinctly put it, 'Inevitably every legal controversy over any price difference would shift from the detailed governing provisions—"injury," ' cost justification, 'meeting competition,' etc.—over into the 'discrimination' concept of ad hoc resolution divorced from specifically pertinent statutory text."

[14] Texaco has not contested here the proposition that branded gas and unbranded gas are of like grade and quality. *See* FTC v. Borden Co., 383 U.S. 637, 645–646 (1966) ("the economic factors inherent in brand names and national advertising should not be considered in the jurisdictional inquiry under the statutory 'like grade and quality' test").

Since we have already decided that a price discrimination within the meaning of § 2(a) "is merely a price difference," we must reject Texaco's first argument. . . .

In *Morton Salt*, we held that a injury to competition may be inferred from evidence that some purchasers had to pay their supplier "substantially more for their goods than their competitors had to pay." *See also* Falls City Industries, Inc. v. Vanco Beverage, Inc., 460 U.S. 428, 435–436 (1983). Texaco, supported by the United States and the Federal Trade Commission as amici curiae, (the Government), argues that this presumption should not apply to differences between prices charged to wholesalers and these charged to retailers. Moreover, they argue that it would be inconsistent with fundamental antitrust policies to construe the Act as requiring a seller to control his customers' resale prices. The seller should not be held liable for the independent pricing decisions of his customers. As the Government correctly notes, this argument endorses the position advocated 35 years ago in the Report of the Attorney General's National Committee to Study the Antitrust Laws (1955).

After observing that suppliers ought not to be held liable for the independent pricing decisions of their buyers,[16] and that without functional discounts distributors might go uncompensated for services they performed,[17] the Committee wrote:

> "The Committee recommends, therefore, that suppliers granting functional discounts either to single-function or to integrated buyers should not be held responsible for any consequences of their customers' pricing tactics. Price cutting at the resale level is not in fact, and should not be held in law, "the effect of" a differential that merely accords due recognition and reimbursement for actual marketing functions. The price cutting of a customer who receives this type of differential results from his own independent decision to lower price and operate at a lower profit margin per unit. The legality or illegality of this price cutting must be judged by the usual legal tests. In any event, consequent injury or lack of injury should not be the supplier's legal concern.

---

[16] "In the Committee's view, imposing on any dual supplier a legal responsibility for the resale policies and prices of his independent distributors contradicts basic antitrust policies. Resale-price fixing is incompatible with the tenets of a free and competitive economy. . . . And even short of such arrangements, a conscious adherence in a supplier's sales to retail customers to the price quotations by independent competing distributors is hardly feasible as a matter of business operation, or safe as a matter of law."

[17] "In our view, to relate discounts or prices solely to the purchaser's resale activities without recognition of his buying functions thwarts competition and efficiency in marketing. It compels affirmative discrimination against a substantial class of distributors, and hence serves as a penalty on integration. If a businessman actually fulfills the wholesale function by relieving his suppliers of risk, storage, transportation, administration, etc., his performance, his capital investment, and the saving to his suppliers, are unaffected by whether he also performs the retailing function, or any number of other functions. A legal rule disqualifying him from discounts recognizing wholesaling functions actually performed compels him to render these functions free of charge."

"On the other hand, the law should tolerate no subterfuge. For instance, where a wholesaler-retailer buys only part of his goods as a wholesaler, he must not claim a functional discount on all. Only to the extent that a buyer actually performs certain functions, assuming all the risk, investment, and costs involved, should he legally qualify for a functional discount. Hence a distributor should be eligible for a discount corresponding to any part of the function he actually performs on that part of the goods for which he performs it."

We generally agree with this description of the legal status of functional discounts. A supplier need not satisfy the rigorous requirements of the cost justification defense in order to prove that a particular functional discount is reasonable and accordingly did not cause any substantial lessening of competition between a wholesaler's customers and the supplier's direct customers.[18] The record in this case, however, adequately supports the finding that Texaco violated the Act.

The hypothetical predicate for the Committee's entire discussion of functional discounts is a price differential "that merely accords due recognition and reimbursement for actual marketing functions." Such a discount is not illegal. In this case, however, . . . there was no substantial evidence indicating that the discounts to Gull and Dompier constituted a reasonable reimbursement for the value to Texaco of their actual marketing functions. Indeed, Dompier was separately compensated for its hauling function, and neither Gull and Dompier maintained any significant storage facilities. . . .

As we have already observed, the "due recognition and reimbursement" concept endorsed in the Attorney General's Committee's study would not countenance a functional discount completely untethered to either the supplier's savings or the wholesaler's costs. The

---

[18] In theory, a supplier could try to defend a functional discount by invoking the Act's cost justification defense, but the burden of proof with respect to the defense is upon the supplier, and interposing the defense "has proven difficult, expensive, and often unsuccessful." 3 E. Kintner & J. Bauer, Federal Antitrust Law, § 23.19, pp. 366–367 (1983). Moreover, to establish the defense a "seller must show that the price reductions given did not exceed the actual cost savings," *id.*, § 23.10, p. 345, and this requirement of exactitude is ill-suited to the defense of discounts set by reference to legitimate, but less precisely measured, market factors.

Discounters will therefore likely find it more useful to defend against claims under the Act by negating the causation element in the case against them: a legitimate functional discount will not cause any substantial lessening of competition. The concept of substantiality permits the causation inquiry to accommodate a notion of economic reasonableness with respect to the pass-through effects of functional discounts, and so provides a latitude denied by the cost-justification defense. We thus find ourselves in substantial agreement with the view that:

> "Conceived as a vehicle for allowing differential pricing to reward distributive efficiencies among customers operating at the same level, the cost justification defense focuses on narrowly defined savings to the seller derived from the different method or quantities in which goods are sold or delivered to different buyers. . . . Moreover, the burden of proof as to the cost justification defense is on the seller charged with violating the Act, whereas the burden of proof remains with the enforcement agency or plaintiff in circumstances involving functional discounts since functional pricing negates the probability of competitive injury, an element of a prima facie case of violation."

Rill, Availability and Functional Discounts Justifying Discriminatory Pricing, 53 Antitrust L. J. 929, 935 (1985).

longstanding principle that functional discounts provide no safe harbor from the Act is likewise evident from the practice of the Federal Trade Commission, which has, while permitting legitimate functional discounts, proceeded against those discounts which appeared to be subterfuges to avoid the Act's restrictions. . . .[21]. . . .

Both Gull and Dompier received the full discount on all their purchases even though most of their volume was resold directly to consumers. The extra margin on those sales obviously enabled them to price aggressively in both their retail and their wholesale marketing. To the extent that Dompier and Gull competed with respondents in the retail market, the presumption of adverse effect on competition recognized in the *Morton Salt* case becomes all the more appropriate. Their competitive advantage in that market also constitutes evidence tending to rebut any presumption of legality that would otherwise apply to their wholesale sales.

The evidence indicates, moreover, that Texaco affirmatively encouraged Dompier to expand its retail business and that Texaco was fully informed about the persistent and marketwide consequences of its own pricing policies. Indeed, its own executives recognized that the dramatic impact on the market was almost entirely attributable to the magnitude of the distributor discount and the hauling allowance. Yet at the same time that Texaco was encouraging Dompier to integrate downward, and supplying Dompier with a generous discount useful to such integration, Texaco was inhibiting upward integration by the respondents: two of the respondents sought permission from Texaco to haul their own fuel using their own tankwagons, but Texaco refused. The special facts of this case thus make it peculiarly difficult for Texaco to claim that it is being held liable for the independent pricing decisions of Gull or Dompier. . . .

Such indirect competitive effects surely may not be presumed automatically in every functional discount setting, and, indeed, one would expect that most functional discounts will be legitimate discounts which do not cause harm to competition. At the least, a functional discount that constitutes a reasonable reimbursement for the purchasers' actual marketing functions will not violate the Act. When a functional discount is legitimate, the inference of injury to competition recognized

---

[21] *See* also In re Mueller Co., 60 F.T.C. 120, 127–128 (1962) (refusing to make allowance for functional discounts in any way that would "add a defense to a prima facie violation of Section 2(a) which is not included in either Section 2(a) or Section 2(b)"). The FTC in *Mueller* expressly disavowed dicta from Doubleday and Co., 52 F.T.C. 169 (1955) suggesting that functional discounts are per se legal if justified by the buyer's costs. *Mueller* held that the discounts were controlled instead by the reasoning propounded in In re General Foods Corp., 52 F.T.C. 798 (1956), which refers to the value of the services to the supplier giving the discount.

We need not address the relative merits of *Mueller* and *Doubleday* in order to resolve the case before us. We do, however, reject the requirement of exactitude which might be inferred from *Doubleday's* dictum that a functional discount offered to a buyer "should not exceed the cost of that part of the function he actually performs on that part of the goods for which he performs it." As already noted, a causation defense in a functional discount case does not demand the rigorous accounting associated with a cost justification defense.

in the Morton Salt case will simply not arise. Yet it is also true that not every functional discount is entitled to a judgment of legitimacy, and that it will sometimes be possible to produce evidence showing that a particular functional discount caused a price discrimination of the sort the Act prohibits. When such anti-competitive effects are proved—as we believe they were in this case—they are covered by the Act.[30] . . .

The judgment is affirmed.

■ JUSTICE WHITE, concurring in the result. . . . [T]he Court not only declares that a price differential that merely accords due recognition and reimbursement for actual marketing functions does not trigger the presumption of an injury to competition, but also announces that "[s]uch a discount is not illegal." There is nothing in the Act to suggest such a defense . . .

■ JUSTICE SCALIA, with whom JUSTICE KENNEDY joins, concurring in the judgment. . . . [P]etitioner argues at length that even if petitioner's discounts to Gull and Dompier cannot be shown to be cost based they should be exempted, because the "functional discount" is an efficient and legitimate commercial practice that is ordinarily cost based, though it is all but impossible to establish cost justification in a particular case. The short answer to this argument is that it should be addressed to Congress.

The Court does not, however, provide that response, but accepts this last argument in somewhat modified form. . . . Relying on a mass of extratextual materials, the Court concludes that the Act permits such "reasonable" functional discounts even if the supplier cannot satisfy the "rigorous requirements of the cost justification defense." I find this conclusion quite puzzling. The language of the Act is straightforward: Any price discrimination whose effect "may be substantially . . . to injure, destroy, or prevent competition" is prohibited, unless it is immunized by the "cost justification" defense, *i.e.,* unless it "make[s] only due allowance for differences in the cost of manufacture, sale, or delivery resulting from the differing methods or quantities in which [the] commodities are . . . sold or delivered." 15 U.S.C. § 13(a). There is no exception for "reasonable" functional discounts that do not meet this requirement. Indeed, I am at a loss to understand what *makes* a functional discount "reasonable" *unless* it meets this requirement. It does not have to meet it penny for penny, of course: The "rigorous requirements of the cost justification defense" to which the Court refers, are not the rigors of mathematical precision, but the rigors of *proof* that the amount of the discount and the amount of the cost saving are close enough that the difference cannot produce any *substantial* lessening of competition. How is one to determine that a functional discount is "reasonable" except by proving (through the normally, alas, "rigorous" means) that it meets this test? Shall we use a nationwide average?

---

[30] The parties do not raise, and we therefore need not address, the question whether the inference of injury to competition might also be negated by evidence that disfavored buyers could make purchases at a reasonable discount from favored buyers.

I suppose a functional discount can be "reasonable" (in the relevant sense of being unlikely to subvert the purposes of the Act) if it is not commensurate with the supplier's costs *saved* (as the cost justification defense requires), but is commensurate with the wholesaler's costs *incurred* in performing services for the supplier. Such a discount would not produce the proscribed effect upon competition, since if it constitutes only reimbursement for the wholesaler one would not expect him to pass it on. The relevant measure of the discount in order to determine "reasonableness" on that basis, however, is not the measure the Court applies to Texaco ("value to [the supplier] of [the distributor's] actual marketing functions"), but rather "cost to the distributor of the distributor's actual marketing functions"—which is of course not necessarily the same thing. I am therefore quite unable to understand what the Court has in mind by its "reasonable" functional discount that is not cost justified.

To my mind, there is one plausible argument for the proposition that a functional basis for differential pricing *ipso facto*—cost justification or not—negates the probability of competitive injury, thus destroying an element of the plaintiff's prima facie case: In a market that is really functionally divided, retailers are in competition with one another, not with wholesalers. That competition among retailers cannot be injured by the supplier's giving lower prices to wholesalers—because if the price differential is passed on, all retailers will simply purchase from wholesalers instead of from the supplier. Or, to put it differently, when the market is functionally divided all competing retailers have the opportunity of obtaining the same price from wholesalers, and the supplier's functional price discrimination alone does not cause any injury to competition. Therefore (the argument goes), if functional division of the market is established, it should be up to the complaining retailer to show that some special factor (*e.g.,* an agreement between the supplier and the wholesaler that the latter will not sell to the former's retailer-customers) prevents this normal market mechanism from operating. As the Court notes, this argument was not raised by the parties here or below, and it calls forth a number of issues that would benefit from briefing and factual development. I agree that we should not decide the merit of this argument in the first instance.

NOTES AND QUESTIONS ON *TEXACO V. HASBROUCK*

1. ***Should charging different prices to wholesalers than to retailers count as price discrimination always, sometimes, or never?*** The Court held that any price difference is price discrimination under the Act, so a price difference between wholesalers and retailers *always* counts as price discrimination. But that conclusion is debatable. The statutory language does not specify what it means by "discriminate," and one might reasonably conclude that it is not "discrimination" to treat unlike buyers differently. To be sure, one could reject this conclusion on the ground that the statute bans price discrimination between different purchasers in goods

of "like grade and quality," without limiting it to cases of "like buyers." But such a conclusion is not supported by other evidence from the statutory structure and legislative history of the sort that *Morton Salt* cited to treat quantity discounts as price discrimination. Indeed, as the Court noted, some legislative history supported the contrary conclusion that pricing differently to wholesalers and retailers did not necessarily constitute price discrimination.

On the other hand, even if one thought it was not *always* discriminatory to treat unlike buyers differently, it would be discriminatory to give a bigger discount to wholesalers than their services warrant. Thus, even this conclusion would reject the conclusion that price differences between wholesalers and retailers can *never* constitute price discrimination.

2. ***When should a sufficient likelihood of anticompetitive effects be inferred from price discrimination between wholesalers and retailers?*** The Court concluded that, even though *Morton Salt* held one could infer the requisite anticompetitive effects from the price discrimination itself, that inference is invalid when the purchasers operate at different market levels, unless the plaintiff can show the wholesale discount was not a reasonable reimbursement for the value of the wholesaler's services.

Why adopt a test that focuses on the reasonable relation to reimbursement for services test? The main reason is that if sellers could not give a lower price to those performing wholesale services, then wholesalers would not be compensated for the costs of those services, which would effectively bar suppliers from selling to both wholesalers and retailers. Further, if the discount equals the value of the wholesale services, then the retailers supplied by those wholesalers are not likely to have a competitive advantage over the retailers supplied directly by the defendant, unless the wholesaler can provide that value at lower cost than the supplier selling directly, in which case any injury to the direct-purchasing retailers really reflects the wholesaler's greater efficiency rather than the price discrimination. (One might also reasonably argue that it is not discriminatory to charge different prices to wholesalers and retailers if the difference is reasonably related to functional differences, but the Court did not rely on that logic.)

Another reason for this test is that firms often have mixed wholesale-retail functions, so one must determine the extent to which they are actually offering wholesale services. The Court does not want to disqualify a business that performs a wholesale function from being compensated for those wholesale services simply because that business also performs a retailing function. Thus, to the extent that a distributor is responsible for certain wholesale functions and assumes all the risk, investment, and necessary costs of doing so, then that distributor may receive a functional discount, but only on those goods for performs such wholesale functions and proportional to the value of those wholesale services.

3. ***Should the test instead focus on whether the price discrimination is cost justified?*** Given that the point of allowing the price difference is to compensate wholesalers for the costs of wholesale services, one might wonder why the Court adopts a test that focuses on a difference in value, which is hard to quantify and appears nowhere in the Act, rather than on a difference in cost, which is easier to quantify and right in the statute. After all, when the supplier directly supplies retailers, then it must itself incur a cost of providing wholesale services that it does not incur when supplying a wholesaler, so a discount that equals that cost difference should cover the cost of providing wholesale services.

The Court's answer, in footnote 18, was that using the cost-justification defense would put the burden on the defendant and require showing a strict relation between the price difference and the cost difference. In contrast, the Court's test puts the burden on the plaintiff, rather than on the defendant (by framing the issue as one of likely anticompetitive effects), and requires only a reasonable relation between the price differences and reimbursement for services rather than stringent proof of price-cost matching.[15]

The Court's approach has sound policy reasons. As it indicates in footnote 18, proving the cost savings associated with using a wholesaler may be inexact and difficult due to less precisely measured market factors. A cost test would also require allocating such costs across different products and determining marginal cost with changing market conditions. Given these difficulties, courts might often mistakenly measure the cost difference and condemn discounts that did not exceed the true cost difference. The prospect of such errors would mean that a legal test that strictly required that every discount be cost justified would discourage price discounts that come close to the actual cost savings, and discouraging that sort of discounting is anticompetitive. Further, given the lack of evidence that Dompier and Gull had buyer market power, Texaco had no incentive to give them discounts that were disproportionate to the cost or value of their services.

However, this reading arguably conflicts with the statutory text, which specifies that defendants have the burden of strictly proving that price differences do not exceed cost differences. The same policy arguments cited by the Court cut equally against how the statute generally treats cost justifications, so however persuasive those policy arguments might be, they do not seem consistent with the Congressional policy view that animated the Act. The Court could instead have achieved the same result, while being more consistent with the statutory language, by instead concluding that a price difference justified by different buyer services is not really discriminatory because treating unlike cases differently is not discriminatory.

4. Unless something prevents the favored wholesaler from reselling to certain retailers, does any injury to those retailers result from their inability to compete for the business of that wholesaler rather than any pricing decision of the supplier? The answer seems to be yes. If retailers always buy from wholesalers, who only sell to retailers,

[15] Just how loose a relation suffices is unclear because the evidence in this case indicated that the wholesalers (Gull and Dompier) provided no wholesale services for which they were not separately compensated, and they received the wholesale discount even when they just directly resold at retail. Because there was no relation at all between the discounts and services, the case does not tell us anything about just how close a relation must be to be "reasonable."

then really the retailers and wholesalers are not in competition with each other, and thus price differences between them do not affect competition between them. And even if one wholesaler is favored over others, it is unclear why this should harm some retailers unless they are for some reason unable to buy from the favored wholesaler, though the statute's concern with tertiary-line price discrimination seems to assume such an injury can follow.

However, this line of analysis seems weak in this case because the favored wholesalers also operated at retail and had obvious incentives to favor themselves over other retailers. Perhaps, in future cases, the law should require that plaintiffs show they tried to buy from the favored wholesaler and that it either refused to sell to them or demanded higher prices than it charged other retailers. In the last situation, a price discrimination might lie against the wholesaler directly, if it in fact sold to both favored and disfavored retailers at different prices.

5. Should branded and unbranded versions of a physically identical product be deemed "of like grade and quality"? Footnote 14 of *Texaco v. Hasbrouck* cites the *Borden* rule that branded and unbranded products are "of like grade and quality" if they are physically the same. This rule unfortunately ignores the economic reality that brand names can alter consumer willingness to pay as much as physical features do. But if price differences between different brand names were deemed categorically nondiscriminatory, then firms could always evade the statute by adopting different brand names for discriminatorily priced products. If instead price differences between different brands were deemed discriminatory only when they exceeded the difference in the value of the brand names, then courts would become embroiled in difficult adjudications about valuing brand names. Thus, although the *Borden* rule may not always reflect economic reality, the alternatives might be legally inadministrable.

Volvo Trucks N.A. v. Reeder-Simco GMC

546 U.S. 164 (2006).

■ JUSTICE GINSBURG delivered the opinion of the Court.

This case concerns specially ordered products—heavy-duty trucks supplied by Volvo . . . and sold by franchised dealers through a competitive bidding process. In this process, the retail customer states its specifications and invites bids, generally from dealers franchised by different manufacturers. Only when a Volvo dealer's bid proves successful does the dealer arrange to purchase the trucks, which Volvo then builds to meet the customer's specifications.

Reeder . . . , a Volvo dealer located in Fort Smith, Arkansas, commenced suit against Volvo alleging that Reeder's sales and profits declined because Volvo offered other dealers more favorable price concessions than those offered to Reeder. Reeder sought redress for its alleged losses under . . . the . . . Robinson-Patman Act . . . Reeder prevailed at trial and on appeal . . .

We granted review on the federal claim to resolve the question whether a manufacturer offering its dealers different wholesale prices may be held liable for price discrimination proscribed by Robinson-Patman, absent a showing that the manufacturer discriminated between dealers contemporaneously competing to resell to the same retail customer. . . . [T]he Robinson-Patman Act, we hold, does not reach the case Reeder presents. The Act centrally addresses price discrimination in cases involving competition between different purchasers for resale of the purchased product. Competition of that character ordinarily is not involved when a product subject to special order is sold through a customer-specific competitive bidding process.

I

. . . It is common practice in the industry for manufacturers to offer customer-specific discounts to their dealers. Volvo decides on a case-by-case basis whether to offer a discount and, if so, what the discount rate will be, taking account of such factors as industry-wide demand and whether the retail customer has, historically, purchased a different brand of trucks. The dealer then uses the discount offered by Volvo in preparing its bid; it purchases trucks from Volvo only if and when the retail customer accepts its bid.

Reeder was one of many Volvo dealers, each assigned by Volvo to a geographic territory. Reeder's territory encompassed ten counties in Arkansas and two in Oklahoma. Although nothing prohibits a Volvo dealer from bidding outside its territory, Reeder rarely bid against another Volvo dealer. In the atypical event that the same retail customer solicited a bid from more than one Volvo dealer, Volvo's stated policy was to provide the same price concession to each dealer competing head to head for the same sale. . . .

Reeder dominantly relied on comparisons between concessions Volvo offered when Reeder bid against non-Volvo dealers, with concessions accorded to other Volvo dealers similarly bidding against non-Volvo dealers for other sales. Reeder's evidence compared concessions Reeder received on four occasions when it bid successfully against non-Volvo dealers (and thus purchased Volvo trucks), with more favorable concessions other successful Volvo dealers received in connection with bidding processes in which Reeder did not participate. Reeder also compared concessions offered by Volvo on several occasions when Reeder bid unsuccessfully against non-Volvo dealers (and therefore did not purchase Volvo trucks), with more favorable concessions received by other Volvo dealers who gained contracts on which Reeder did not bid.

Reeder's vice-president, Heck, testified that Reeder did not look for instances in which it received a *larger* concession than another Volvo dealer, although he acknowledged it was "quite possible" that such instances occurred. Nor did Reeder endeavor to determine by any statistical analysis whether Reeder was disfavored on average as compared to another dealer or set of dealers. . . .

II . . .

To establish the secondary-line injury of which it complains, Reeder had to show that (1) the relevant Volvo truck sales were made in interstate commerce; (2) the trucks were of "like grade and quality"; (3) Volvo "discriminate[d] in price between" Reeder and another purchaser of Volvo trucks; and (4) "the effect of such discrimination may be . . . to injure, destroy, or prevent competition" to the advantage of a favored purchaser, *i.e.,* one who "receive[d] the benefit of such discrimination." 15 U.S.C. § 13(a). It is undisputed that Reeder has satisfied the first and second requirements. Volvo and the United States, as *amicus curiae,* maintain that Reeder cannot satisfy the third and fourth requirements, because Reeder has not identified any differentially-priced transaction in which it was both a "purchaser" under the Act and "in actual competition" with a favored purchaser for the same customer.

A hallmark of the requisite competitive injury, our decisions indicate, is the diversion of sales or profits from a disfavored purchaser to a favored purchaser. We have also recognized that a permissible inference of competitive injury may arise from evidence that a favored competitor received a significant price reduction over a substantial period of time. *See Morton Salt*; *Falls City Industries,* 460 U.S. at 435. Absent actual competition with a favored Volvo dealer, however, Reeder cannot establish the competitive injury required under the Act.

III

The evidence Reeder offered at trial falls into three categories: (1) comparisons of concessions Reeder received for four successful bids against *non-Volvo* dealers, with larger concessions other successful Volvo dealers received for *different sales* on which Reeder did not bid (purchase-to-purchase comparisons); (2) comparisons of concessions offered to Reeder in connection with several unsuccessful bids against *non-Volvo* dealers, with greater concessions accorded other Volvo dealers who competed successfully for *different sales* on which Reeder did not bid (offer-to-purchase comparisons); and (3) evidence of two occasions on which Reeder bid against another Volvo dealer (head-to-head comparisons). The Court of Appeals concluded that Reeder demonstrated competitive injury under the Act because Reeder competed with favored purchasers "at the same functional level . . . and within the same geographic market." As we see it, however, selective comparisons of the kind Reeder presented do not show the injury to competition targeted by the Robinson-Patman Act. . . .

Both the purchase-to-purchase and the offer-to-purchase comparisons fall short, for in none of the discrete instances on which Reeder relied did Reeder compete with beneficiaries of the alleged discrimination *for the same customer*. Nor did Reeder even attempt to show that the compared dealers were consistently favored vis-à-vis Reeder. Reeder simply paired occasions on which it competed with *non-*

Volvo dealers for a sale to Customer A with instances in which other Volvo dealers competed with *non-Volvo* dealers for a sale to Customer B. The compared incidents were tied to no systematic study and were separated in time by as many as seven months.

We decline to permit an inference of competitive injury from evidence of such a mix-and-match, manipulable quality. No similar risk of manipulation occurs in cases kin to the chain-store paradigm. Here, there is no discrete "favored" dealer comparable to a chain store or a large independent department store—at least, Reeder's evidence is insufficient to support an inference of such a dealer or set of dealers. For all we know, Reeder, on occasion, might have gotten a better deal vis-à-vis one or more of the dealers in its comparisons.

Reeder may have competed with other Volvo dealers for the opportunity to bid on potential sales in a broad geographic area. At that initial stage, however, competition is not affected by differential pricing; a dealer in the competitive bidding process here at issue approaches Volvo for a price concession only after it has been selected by a retail customer to submit a bid. Competition for an opportunity to bid . . . is based on a variety of factors, including the existence *vel non* of a relationship between the potential bidder and the customer, geography, and reputation.[3] . . . That Volvo dealers may bid for sales in the same geographic area does not import that they in fact competed for the same customer-tailored sales. In sum, the purchase-to-purchase and offer-to-purchase comparisons fail to show that Volvo sold at a lower price to Reeder's "competitors," hence those comparisons do not support an inference of competitive injury. . . .

Reeder did offer evidence of two instances in which it competed head to head with another Volvo dealer. When multiple dealers bid for the business of the *same* customer, only one dealer will win the business and thereafter purchase the supplier's product to fulfill its contractual commitment. Because Robinson-Patman "prohibits only discrimination 'between different *purchasers*,'" Volvo and the United States argue, the Act does not reach markets characterized by competitive bidding and special-order sales, as opposed to sales from inventory. We need not decide that question today. Assuming the Act applies to the head-to-head transactions, Reeder did not establish that it was *disfavored* vis-à-vis other Volvo dealers in the rare instances in which they competed for the same sale—let alone that the alleged discrimination was substantial. *See* 1 ABA Section of Antitrust Law, Antitrust Law Developments 478–479 (5th ed. 2002) ("No inference of injury to competition is permitted when the discrimination is not substantial." (collecting cases)).

---

[3] A dealer's reputation for securing favorable concessions, we recognize, may influence the customer's bidding invitations. We do not pursue that point here, however, because Reeder did not present—or even look for—evidence that Volvo consistently disfavored Reeder while it consistently favored certain other dealers.

Reeder's evidence showed loss of only one sale to another Volvo dealer, a sale of 12 trucks that would have generated $30,000 in gross profits for Reeder. Per its policy, Volvo initially offered Reeder and the other dealer the same concession. Volvo ultimately granted a larger concession to the other dealer, but only after it had won the bid. In the only other instance of head-to-head competition Reeder identified, Volvo increased Reeder's initial 17% discount to 18.9%, to match the discount offered to the other competing Volvo dealer; neither dealer won the bid. In short, if price discrimination between two purchasers existed at all, it was not of such magnitude as to affect substantially competition between Reeder and the "favored" Volvo dealer.

IV

Interbrand competition, our opinions affirm, is the "primary concern of antitrust law." *GTE Sylvania.* The Robinson-Patman Act signals no large departure from that main concern. Even if the Act's text could be construed in the manner urged by Reeder and embraced by the Court of Appeals, we would resist interpretation geared more to the protection of existing *competitors* than to the stimulation of *competition.* In the case before us, there is no evidence that any favored purchaser possesses market power, the allegedly favored purchasers are dealers with little resemblance to large independent department stores or chain operations, and the supplier's selective price discounting fosters competition among suppliers of different brands. By declining to extend Robinson-Patman's governance to such cases, we continue to construe the Act "consistently with broader policies of the antitrust laws." *Brooke Group*; *see Automatic Canteen Co. of America v. FTC,* 346 U.S. 61, 63 (1953) (cautioning against Robinson-Patman constructions that "extend beyond the prohibitions of the Act and, in doing so, help give rise to a price uniformity and rigidity in open conflict with the purposes of other antitrust legislation").

[T]he judgment of the Court of Appeals for the Eighth Circuit is reversed . . .

▪ JUSTICE STEVENS, with whom JUSTICE THOMAS joins, dissenting. . . . For decades, juries have routinely inferred the requisite injury to competition under the Robinson-Patman Act from the fact that a manufacturer sells goods to one retailer at a higher price than to its competitors. This rule dates back to . . . *Morton Salt* . . . We have treated as competitors those who sell "in a single, interstate retail market." *Falls City* Under this approach—uncontroversial until today—Reeder would readily prevail. There is ample evidence that Volvo charged Reeder higher prices than it charged to competing dealers in the same market over a period of many months. . . .

Volvo nonetheless argues that no competitive injury could have occurred because it never discriminated against Reeder when Reeder and another Volvo dealer were seeking concessions with regard to the same ultimate customer. In Volvo's view, each transaction was a separate market, one defined by the customer and those dealers whom it had asked for bids. For each specific customer who has solicited bids, Reeder's only "competitors" were the other dealers making bids. Accordingly, if none of these other dealers were Volvo dealers, then Reeder suffered no competitive harm (relative to other Volvo dealers) when Volvo gave it a discriminatorily high price.

. . . Nothing in the statute or in our precedent suggests that "competition" is evaluated by a transaction-specific inquiry, and such an approach makes little sense. It requires us to ignore the fact that competition among truck dealers is a continuing war waged over time rather than a series of wholly discrete events. Each time Reeder managed to resell trucks it had purchased at discriminatorily high prices, it was forced either to accept lower profit margins than were available to favored Volvo dealers or to pass on the higher costs to its customers (who then might well go to a different dealer the next time). And we have long indicated that lost profits relative to a competitor are a proper basis for permitting the *Morton Salt* inference. . . .

The Court appears to hold that, absent head-to-head bidding with a favored dealer, a dealer in a competitive bidding market can suffer no competitive injury.[4] It is unclear whether that holding is limited to franchised dealers who do not maintain inventories, or excludes virtually all franchisees from the effective protection of the Act. In either event, it is not faithful to the statutory text. . . .

NOTES AND QUESTIONS ON *VOLVO*

1. ***Is each specialty customer order a separate market?*** The Court stressed that the Robinson-Patman Act covers secondary-line price discrimination only between purchasing dealers who compete downstream in the same downstream market. But is the Court right that in the case of competitive bidding for specialty customer orders, each customer order is ordinarily a separate market, so that purchasing dealers are not in downstream competition unless they are both bidding for the same customer's order? This conclusion seems dubious because it does not meet the normal standards of market definition discussed in Chapter 3, given that customers could switch to another set of dealers if the dealers they happened to contact tried to charge too much. It also seems dubious even if one's concern is just the competitive disadvantage of some dealers, given that dealers in the same geographic market compete to get customers interested, as well as to win sales from the customers they interest. Dealers who can offer lower prices are more likely to get customers interested and win their sales.

---

[4] Indeed, if Volvo's argument about the meaning of "purchaser" ultimately meets with this Court's approval, then the Robinson-Patman Act will simply not apply in the special-order context. Any time a special-order dealer fails to complete a transaction because the high price drives away its ultimate customer, there will be no Robinson-Patman violation because the dealer will not meet the "purchaser" requirement, and any time the dealer completes the transaction but at a discriminatorily high price, there will be no violation because the dealer has no "competition" (as the majority sees it) for that specific transaction at the moment of purchase.

Perhaps, then, the dissent was correct in arguing that the competing-purchaser element should have been met by showing that the purchasing dealers generally competed in the same geographic market for sales, even though they were not charged different prices when they were both competing for the same customer orders. However, if the market should properly be defined as geographic, rather than customer based, then the plaintiff should have to prove that it received systematically higher quotes than other dealers. The plaintiff did not show that in this case, but rather showed only episodic differences in quotes for particular customer orders. One possible way to understand the Court's designation of the market as customer-based, then, was that it came in response to the plaintiff's order-specific allegations of discrimination, rather than market-wide allegations that might have led the Court to analyze a broader geographic market.

Interestingly, *Volvo* suggests that wholesaler-retailer price differences generally should not be deemed to constitute price discrimination at all because wholesalers and retailers usually do not compete for the same customers. This point was not telling in *Texaco v. Hasbrouck* because the particular wholesalers in *Texaco* also competed at retail with the disfavored retail purchasers, but the point likely applies to most wholesaler-retailer price differences. The alternative view would be that it should suffice that the retailer paying the higher price has difficulty competing with rival retailers who are supplied by a favored wholesaler that cannot or will not supply the disfavored retailer.

2. Even when not bidding for same customer, would not consistent price discrimination between Reeder and other Volvo dealers still harm Reeder's ability to get new customers and compete with both Volvo dealers and non-Volvo dealers? Suppose that whenever they are *not* bidding for the same customer, Volvo offers Volvo trucks to other purchasing dealers at lower prices than Reeder. Then Reeder will tend to make worse bids than other Volvo dealers, with the result that customers are likely to invite future bids less often from Reeder and more often from other Volvo dealers. Reeder would also lose more customers to non-Volvo dealers, with the result that Reeder does less well in the market generally, thus harming Reeder compared not only to other Volvo dealers but also compared to non-Volvo dealers.

However, Reeder did not show that it was systematically disfavored compared to the other Volvo dealers. Instead, Reeder showed only episodic discrimination in quotes in particular cases. Had Reeder shown more systemic price discrimination, the Court in footnote 3 left open the possibility that such a claim might be valid.

3. Is not price discrimination for a specific customer order impossible because only one dealer can win the order and pay a price? Suppose Reeder and another Volvo dealer are bidding for the same customer order, and Volvo offers the other Volvo dealer a lower price. Then only one of the dealers will win the bid and purchase the Volvo trucks for resale, so that Volvo's conduct cannot constitute price discrimination between different "purchasers" under the Act. The dissent pointed out this problem with the Court's approach in footnote 4, but the Court declined to address the point.

Does this mean that, under the Court's approach, selling to dealers who engage in competitive bidding for specialty orders can never be subject to the Robinson-Patman Act? No, that would be true only if we assume episodic discrimination claims. If the plaintiff could show systematic discrimination across all quotes, then the Court leaves open the possibility it could prove a claim. This result makes some sense. For a specialty goods market, prices will vary for each purchase, so it should not be enough to show variation in some quotes; one should have to show systematic variation across all the quotes. Otherwise there cannot be an effect across the geographic market. The problem with the plaintiff's theory of the case is that it uses discrimination examples that assumed customer-specific discrimination rather than marketwide discrimination, but price discrimination is not really provable in a customer-specific way.

*4. **Does simply requiring price discrimination that is systematic and substantial resolve the issues?*** If there were some covered price discrimination, the Court seems to require evidence that the price discrimination (a) systematically disfavored the plaintiff and (b) occurred in a substantial number of cases. These requirements seem sensible. Both elements seem necessary to show a likely anticompetitive effect. Element (a) also bears on whether price discrimination really exists at all. Given that these requirements were not met, it would seem the Court could have avoided reaching any of the other issues in this case.

*5. **Could the Court avoid all these complications by overruling*** **Morton Salt?** It would seem so. The complications are caused by *Morton Salt*'s holding that anticompetitive effects could be inferred from substantial price discrimination involving one dealer on the market. If that holding were overruled, then the Act could be interpreted to require proof of a probable effect on "competition" in the broader geographic market. Such an interpretation would also adhere better to the statutory text, which requires separate proof of price discrimination and a probable effect on competition.

The Court may be hinting it is ready to engage in such an overruling in the end of its opinion, when the Court states that it interprets the Robinson-Patman Act according to the general antitrust principle of protecting interbrand competition rather than intrabrand competition and individual competitors. Ironically, however, the Court's focus on specialty-order competition actually protects Reeder only against intrabrand competition with other Volvo dealers, and not at all against discriminatory prices that hurt Reeder's ability to engage in interbrand competition with non-Volvo dealers.

Other Robinson-Patman Act Provisions

The Robinson-Patman Act also contains a variety of other provisions designed to prevent sellers from evading the basic restriction on unjustified commodity price discrimination by paying brokerage or commission fees for nonexistent services, § 2(c), or giving discriminatory access to allowances or services, § 2(d)–(e). These clauses go beyond the basic restriction in that they require no proof of effects nor permit the defense of cost-justification. § 2(c) also allows no defense of meeting competition, and may not even require discrimination. Finally, § 2(f) makes a buyer liable if it knowingly induces or receives a prohibited price discrimination. All these are codified at 15 U.S.C. § 13(c)–(f). In addition, although rarely enforced, Robinson-Patman Act § 3 does impose criminal penalties for knowing price discrimination with an anticompetitive purpose. *See* 15 U.S.C. § 13a.

CHAPTER 6

PROVING AN AGREEMENT OR CONCERTED ACTION

Sherman Act § 1 condemns anticompetitive agreements even when firms do not have the monopoly power necessary to trigger Sherman Act § 2. This chapter addresses the legal standards for proving such an agreement. It first addresses the foundational issue of how to determine whether the defendants are separate entities capable of having an agreement or instead a single actor whose unilateral conduct can generally be challenged only under the more demanding standards of Sherman Act § 2. It then addresses the legal standards for proving a vertical or horizontal agreement between separate entities, and the extent to which oligopolistic coordination itself can be covered. It leaves until the next chapter a particular class of agreements—mergers that unite what were separate entities into one.

A. ARE THE DEFENDANTS SEPARATE ENTITIES?

Copperweld Corp. v. Independence Tube Corp.

467 U.S. 752 (1984).

■ CHIEF JUSTICE BURGER delivered the opinion of the Court. . . .

Review of this case calls directly into question whether the coordinated acts of a parent and its wholly owned subsidiary can, in the legal sense contemplated by § 1 of the Sherman Act, constitute a combination or conspiracy. The so-called "intra-enterprise conspiracy" doctrine provides that § 1 liability is not foreclosed merely because a parent and its subsidiary are subject to common ownership. . . . In no case has the Court considered the merits of the intra-enterprise conspiracy doctrine in depth . . . Although the Court has expressed approval of the doctrine on a number of occasions, a finding of intra-enterprise conspiracy was in all but perhaps one instance unnecessary to the result. . . .

Petitioners, joined by the United States as amicus curiae, urge us to repudiate the intra-enterprise conspiracy doctrine. The central criticism is that the doctrine gives undue significance to the fact that a subsidiary is separately incorporated and thereby treats as the concerted activity of two entities what is really unilateral behavior flowing from decisions of a single enterprise.

We limit our inquiry to the narrow issue squarely presented: whether a parent and its wholly owned subsidiary are capable of conspiring in violation of § 1 of the Sherman Act. We do not consider under what circumstances, if any, a parent may be liable for conspiring with an affiliated corporation it does not completely own. . . .

The Sherman Act contains a "basic distinction between concerted and independent action." *Monsanto*. The conduct of a single firm is governed by § 2 alone and is unlawful only when it threatens actual monopolization. It is not enough that a single firm appears to "restrain trade" unreasonably, for even a vigorous competitor may leave that impression. . . . In part because it is sometimes difficult to distinguish robust competition from conduct with long-run anti-competitive effects, Congress authorized Sherman Act scrutiny of single firms only when they pose a danger of monopolization. Judging unilateral conduct in this manner reduces the risk that the antitrust laws will dampen the competitive zeal of a single aggressive entrepreneur.

Section 1 of the Sherman Act, in contrast, reaches unreasonable restraints of trade effected by a "contract, combination . . . or conspiracy" between *separate* entities. It does not reach conduct that is "wholly unilateral." Concerted activity subject to § 1 is judged more sternly than unilateral activity under § 2. Certain agreements, such as horizontal price fixing and market allocation, are thought so inherently anticompetitive that each is illegal per se without inquiry into the harm it has actually caused. Other combinations, such as mergers, joint ventures, and various vertical agreements, hold the promise of increasing a firm's efficiency and enabling it to compete more effectively. Accordingly, such combinations are judged under a rule of reason, an inquiry into market power and market structure designed to assess the combination's actual effect. Whatever form the inquiry takes, however, it is not necessary to prove that concerted activity threatens monopolization.

The reason Congress treated concerted behavior more strictly than unilateral behavior is readily appreciated. Concerted activity inherently is fraught with anticompetitive risk. It deprives the marketplace of the independent centers of decisionmaking that competition assumes and demands. In any conspiracy, two or more entities that previously pursued their own interests separately are combining to act as one for their common benefit. This not only reduces the diverse directions in which economic power is aimed but suddenly increases the economic power moving in one particular direction. Of course, such mergings of resources may well lead to efficiencies that benefit consumers, but their anticompetitive potential is sufficient to warrant scrutiny even in the absence of incipient monopoly. . . .

The distinction between unilateral and concerted conduct is necessary for a proper understanding of the terms "contract, combination . . . or conspiracy" in § 1. Nothing in the literal meaning of those terms excludes coordinated conduct among officers or employees of the same company. But it is perfectly plain that an internal "agreement" to implement a single, unitary firm's policies does not raise the antitrust dangers that § 1 was designed to police. The officers of a single firm are not separate economic actors pursuing separate economic interests, so agreements among them do not suddenly bring together economic power that was previously pursuing divergent goals. Coordination within a firm is as likely to result from an effort to compete as from an effort to stifle competition. In the marketplace, such coordination may be necessary if a business enterprise is to compete effectively. For these reasons, officers or employees of the same firm do not provide the plurality of actors imperative for a § 1 conspiracy.

There is also general agreement that § 1 is not violated by the internally coordinated conduct of a corporation and one of its unincorporated divisions. Although this Court has not previously addressed the question, there can be little doubt that the operations of a corporate enterprise organized into divisions must be judged as the conduct of a single actor. The existence of an unincorporated division reflects no more than a firm's decision to adopt an organizational division of labor. A division within a corporate structure pursues the common interests of the whole rather than interests separate from those of the corporation itself; a business enterprise establishes divisions to further its own interests in the most efficient manner. Because coordination between a corporation and its division does not represent a sudden joining of two independent sources of economic power previously pursuing separate interests, it is not an activity that warrants § 1 scrutiny.

Indeed, a rule that punished coordinated conduct simply because a corporation delegated certain responsibilities to autonomous units might well discourage corporations from creating divisions with their presumed benefits. This would serve no useful antitrust purpose but could well deprive consumers of the efficiencies that decentralized management may bring. . . .

For similar reasons, the coordinated activity of a parent and its wholly owned subsidiary must be viewed as that of a single enterprise for purposes of § 1 of the Sherman Act. A parent and its wholly owned subsidiary have a complete unity of interest. Their objectives are common, not disparate; their general corporate actions are guided or determined not by two separate corporate consciousnesses, but one. They are not unlike a multiple team of horses drawing a vehicle under the control of a single driver. With or without a formal "agreement," the subsidiary acts for the benefit of the parent, its sole shareholder. If a parent and a wholly owned subsidiary do "agree" to a course of action, there is no sudden joining of economic resources that had previously served different interests, and there is no justification for § 1 scrutiny.

Indeed, the very notion of an "agreement" in Sherman Act terms between a parent and a wholly owned subsidiary lacks meaning. A § 1 agreement may be found when "the conspirators had a unity of purpose or a common design and understanding, or a meeting of minds in an unlawful arrangement." But in reality a parent and a wholly owned subsidiary always have a "unity of purpose or a common design." They share a common purpose whether or not the parent keeps a tight rein over the subsidiary; the parent may assert full control at any moment if the subsidiary fails to act in the parent's best interests.[18]

The intra-enterprise conspiracy doctrine looks to the form of an enterprise's structure and ignores the reality. Antitrust liability should not depend on whether a corporate subunit is organized as an unincorporated division or a wholly owned subsidiary. A corporation has complete power to maintain a wholly owned subsidiary in either form. The economic, legal, or other considerations that lead corporate management to choose one structure over the other are not relevant to whether the enterprise's conduct seriously threatens competition. Rather, a corporation may adopt the subsidiary form of organization for valid management and related purposes. Separate incorporation may improve management, avoid special tax problems arising from multistate operations, or serve other legitimate interests. Especially in view of the increasing complexity of corporate operations, a business enterprise should be free to structure itself in ways that serve efficiency of control, economy of operations, and other factors dictated by business judgment without increasing its exposure to antitrust liability. Because there is nothing inherently anticompetitive about a corporation's decision to create a subsidiary, the intra-enterprise conspiracy doctrine "impose[s] grave legal consequences upon organizational distinctions that are of de minimis meaning and effect."

If antitrust liability turned on the garb in which a corporate subunit was clothed, parent corporations would be encouraged to convert subsidiaries into unincorporated divisions. . . . Such an incentive serves no valid antitrust goals but merely deprives consumers and producers of the benefits that the subsidiary form may yield. . . .

Any reading of the Sherman Act that remains true to the Act's distinction between unilateral and concerted conduct will necessarily disappoint those who find that distinction arbitrary. It cannot be denied that § 1's focus on concerted behavior leaves a "gap" in the Act's proscription against unreasonable restraints of trade. An unreasonable restraint of trade may be effected not only by two independent firms acting in concert; a single firm may restrain trade to precisely the same extent if it alone possesses the combined market power of those same two

[18] [Some] . . . Courts of Appeals [have used] . . . criteria [that] measure the "separateness" of the subsidiary: whether it has separate control of its day-to-day operations, separate officers, separate corporate headquarters, and so forth. At least when a subsidiary is wholly owned, however, these factors are not sufficient to describe a separate economic entity for purposes of the Sherman Act. The factors simply describe the manner in which the parent chooses to structure a subunit of itself. They cannot overcome the basic fact that the ultimate interests of the subsidiary and the parent are identical, so the parent and the subsidiary must be viewed as a single economic unit.

firms. Because the Sherman Act does not prohibit unreasonable restraints of trade as such—but only restraints effected by a contract, combination, or conspiracy—it leaves untouched a single firm's anticompetitive conduct (short of threatened monopolization) that may be indistinguishable in economic effect from the conduct of two firms subject to § 1 liability.

We have already noted that Congress left this "gap" for eminently sound reasons. Subjecting a single firm's every action to judicial scrutiny for reasonableness would threaten to discourage the competitive enthusiasm that the antitrust laws seek to promote. Moreover, whatever the wisdom of the distinction, the Act's plain language leaves no doubt that Congress made a purposeful choice to accord different treatment to unilateral and concerted conduct. Had Congress intended to outlaw unreasonable restraints of trade as such, § 1's requirement of a contract, combination, or conspiracy would be superfluous, as would the entirety of § 2. . . .

The appropriate inquiry in this case, therefore, is not whether the coordinated conduct of a parent and its wholly owned subsidiary may ever have anticompetitive effects, as the dissent suggests. Nor is it whether the term "conspiracy" will bear a literal construction that includes parent corporations and their wholly owned subsidiaries. For if these were the proper inquiries, a single firm's conduct would be subject to § 1 scrutiny whenever the coordination of two employees was involved. Such a rule would obliterate the Act's distinction between unilateral and concerted conduct, contrary to the clear intent of Congress as interpreted by the weight of judicial authority. Rather, the appropriate inquiry requires us to explain the logic underlying Congress' decision to exempt unilateral conduct from § 1 scrutiny, and to assess whether that logic similarly excludes the conduct of a parent and its wholly owned subsidiary. Unless we second-guess the judgment of Congress to limit § 1 to concerted conduct, we can only conclude that the coordinated behavior of a parent and its wholly owned subsidiary falls outside the reach of that provision.

Although we recognize that any "gap" the Sherman Act leaves is the sensible result of a purposeful policy decision by Congress, we also note that the size of any such gap is open to serious question. Any anticompetitive activities of corporations and their wholly owned subsidiaries meriting antitrust remedies may be policed adequately without resort to an intra-enterprise conspiracy doctrine. A corporation's initial acquisition of control will always be subject to scrutiny under § 1 of the Sherman Act and § 7 of the Clayton Act. Thereafter, the enterprise is fully subject to § 2 of the Sherman Act and § 5 of the Federal Trade Commission Act. That these statutes are adequate to control dangerous anticompetitive conduct is suggested by the fact that not a single holding of antitrust liability by this Court would today be different in the absence of an intra-enterprise conspiracy doctrine. It is further suggested by the fact that the Federal Government, in its administration of the antitrust laws, no longer accepts the concept that a corporation and its wholly owned subsidiaries can "combine" or "conspire" under § 1. Elimination of the intra-enterprise conspiracy doctrine with respect to corporations and their wholly owned subsidiaries will therefore not cripple antitrust enforcement. It will simply eliminate treble damages from private state tort suits masquerading as antitrust actions. . . .

We hold that Copperweld and its wholly owned subsidiary Regal are incapable of conspiring with each other for purposes of § 1 of the Sherman Act. To the extent that prior decisions of this Court are to the contrary, they are disapproved and overruled. . . .

NOTES AND QUESTIONS ON *COPPERWELD*

1. ***Why should Sherman Act § 1 not cover conspiracies between a parent and wholly-owned subsidiary?*** The court stressed that the effect of an alleged "conspiracy" between a parent and wholly-owned subsidiary would be the same as the effect of a "conspiracy" between divisions of a single corporation, and two divisions would clearly be deemed a single entity incapable of conspiring. One might object that one could also say that the end result of the alleged conspiracy is joint decisionmaking, just as with a conspiracy between separately-owned firms, which would clearly be treated as separate entities. But a conspiracy between separately-owned firms has the effect of *worsening* market performance because it removes competitive incentives to act independently that otherwise would operate. In contrast, a parent and wholly-owned subsidiary (like two divisions of a single corporation) would not have incentives to compete with each other even if they did not conspire, so an alleged "conspiracy" between them cannot have the effect of restraining independent competition that otherwise would have existed.

As the Court stressed, antitrust law finds an agreement between separate entities when the conspirators have "a unity of purpose or a common design and understanding." But parents and wholly-owned subsidiaries inherently have such a unity of purpose and common design and understanding. The parent's 100% shareholding in the subsidiary means that the parent gets 100% of the subsidiary's profits, so profits earned by the parent and subsidiary are fungible. Thus, they necessarily have a unity of financial purpose. The parent's 100% shareholding in the subsidiary also means that the parent's management selects and can remove the subsidiary's management. Thus, a parent and wholly-owned subsidiary necessarily have common control that gives them a common design and understanding about what they are doing. Because a parent and wholly-owned subsidiary *always* have a unity of purpose and common understanding, any alleged "agreement" between them cannot lessen their incentives to compete with each other. Such "agreements" are thus not worth deterring under antitrust law. The Court's reasoning indicated that two business units should be deemed a single entity for antitrust purposes whenever their structure (1) gives them "a complete unity of common interest" and (2) puts them under "the control of a single driver."

This antitrust definition differs from corporate law, which treats separately incorporated parents and subsidiaries as separate entities. The difference in definitions reflects different legal purposes. In corporate law, the purpose is to define the proper scope of limited liability (clarifying which assets are available to which creditors) and perhaps to gain advantages under certain regulations or tax laws. In antitrust law, the purpose is to determine when deterring agreements between business units would functionally increase their incentives to compete with each other. Treating separately incorporated but wholly-owned firms as separate entities under antitrust would not advance any antitrust purpose. Instead, it would likely cause many of them to forego separate incorporation and operate as divisions of one corporation, forcing them into an organizational form they regard as less efficient with no antitrust gain and a possible loss of advantages under corporate, tax, or regulatory laws. As with other issues in antitrust, functional considerations trump formalities. Thus, a unity of profits and control always suffices to deem two business units a single entity for antitrust purposes, even if the units are formally separate entities for corporate law purposes.

*2. **Should we concerned about the lack of Sherman Act scrutiny for an unreasonable restraint by a single firm with market power that falls short of monopoly power?*** The Court notes that this decision leaves a "gap" because it means no Sherman Act review for an unreasonable restraint adopted via unilateral conduct by a single firm with market power that falls short of monopoly power, even though the same restraint might be condemned if adopted via agreement by two firms that jointly have the identical degree of market power or via unilateral conduct by a single firm with monopoly power.

However, as the Court suggests, Congress had sound grounds not to make every unilateral decision by a firm with some market power reviewable under the Sherman Act to determine whether it constitutes an unreasonable restraint of trade. Namely, "because it is sometimes difficult to distinguish robust competition from conduct with long-run anti-competitive effects," reviewing unilateral conduct under the Sherman Act creates a significant risk of adjudicative errors that "will dampen the competitive zeal of a single aggressive entrepreneur" and thus raise serious overdeterrence concerns. It thus makes sense that "Congress authorized Sherman Act scrutiny of single firms only when they pose a danger of monopolization," which is when the underdeterrence problem would be greatest and thus most likely to outweigh the overdeterrence problem.

It also makes sense that "Congress treated concerted behavior more strictly than unilateral behavior" involving the same exercise of market power, given that agreements between "independent centers of decisionmaking" reduces competition among them that would otherwise exist, thus raising greater underdeterrence problems. Further, while unilateral conduct cannot generally be avoided, agreements with other entities generally can be, thus lessening overdeterrence concerns. Indeed, we would not be able to maintain the rules of per se illegality for activities like price fixing if unilateral conduct were subjected to § 1 review, given that firms cannot avoid unilaterally setting some price.

Also, although the Sherman Act has this "gap", antitrust law in general does not. As the Court observes, such unilateral conduct by a firm with market power remains subject to FTC Act § 5, which creates less overdeterrence because it poses no risk of treble damages and can be enforced only by a financially-disinterested federal agency. Using a statute that creates less overdeterrence makes sense for unilateral sub-monopoly conduct that poses lower underdeterrence concerns than the agreements or monopoly conduct covered by the Sherman Act. Further, to the extent our real concern is how the single firm grew large enough to have market power, a parent's initial acquisition of a subsidiary (or division) would remain reviewable under not only Sherman Act § 1, but also Clayton Act § 7. If the single firm grew to have market power not by acquisitions, but rather by making a better product and winning sales via internal expansion, then the profits it accrues from its earned market power are not anticompetitive, but rather are a desirable reward for investing in efforts to offer a market option that is better than the options offered by other firms. *See Trinko*.

3. ***Should two subsidiaries that are wholly owned by a common parent or set of shareholders be deemed a single entity?*** Most but not all cases hold that two subsidiaries that are wholly owned by a common parent or set of shareholders should be deemed a single entity that cannot conspire with each other.[1] Although such commonly-owned subsidiaries are not explicitly addressed by *Copperweld*, they do seem to have a unity of profits and control that means they inherently lack independent incentives to compete with each other. Thus, the logic of *Copperweld* supports the courts that hold that such commonly-owned subsidiaries should be deemed a single entity, given that a "conspiracy" between them does not displace any independent incentives to compete that might otherwise exist.[2] Likewise, *Copperweld* suggests that business units should be deemed a single entity whenever joint ownership means completely shared profits and common control.

4. ***Should a parent and majority-owned subsidiary be deemed a single entity?*** *Copperweld* explicitly left open if and when a parent and non-wholly owned subsidiary could be considered a single entity. Suppose, for example, a parent corporation owns 51% of the voting stock in a subsidiary. Then the parent has control because it can select the subsidiary's board and management, indeed perhaps as much normal operational control

---

[1] For cases holding they cannot conspire, *see* Siegel Transfer v. Carrier Express, 54 F.3d 1125 (3d Cir. 1995); Advanced Health-Care Servs. v. Radford Cmty. Hosp., 910 F.2d 139, 146 (4th Cir. 1990); Hood v. Tenneco Texas Life Ins., 739 F.2d 1012 (5th Cir. 1984); Century Oil Tool v. Prod. Specialties, 737 F.2d 1316, 1317 (5th Cir. 1984); Guzowski v. Hartman, 969 F.2d 211, 214 (6th Cir. 1992); Freeman v. San Diego Ass'n of Realtors, 322 F.3d 1133, 1147 (9th Cir. 2003). In contrast, Mitchael v. Intracorp., 179 F.3d 847, 857 (10th Cir. 1999), applied a "complete unity of interest" test and declined to hold that it always meant that two wholly-owned subsidiaries cannot conspire with each other.

[2] Another way to reach the same conclusion would be to conclude that under *Copperweld* the parent and each wholly-owned subsidiary constitute a single entity, and thus both wholly-owned subsidiaries are part of the parental entity, which is a single entity.

as the parent would have over a wholly-owned subsidiary. However, the existence of minority shareholders in the subsidiary means there is not a unity of profits, because the parent gets all the profits from parent sales but only 51% of the profits from subsidiary sales. In short, such situations place the two *Copperweld* factors in tension because there is a unity of control but not a unity of profits. On the one hand, an agreement between a parent and majority-owned subsidiary may undermine incentives to compete that might otherwise be created by the lack of profit unity. On the other hand, the common control and mostly shared profits may sufficiently prevent competition that an agreement would not significantly worsen matters.

Not surprisingly, the circuits are split on this issue. Some hold that parents and majority-owned subsidiaries are a single entity only if the majority share is near 100%.[3] These decisions are consistent with the view that control and a near-unity of profits is necessary to eliminate the risk that an agreement could worsen matters. Other courts hold that parents and majority-owned subsidiaries are always a single entity.[4] These decisions suggest the contrary view that control and mostly-shared profits suffice to prevent competition, so an agreement has no significant effect. Finally, some courts leave it to the factfinder to decide case by case whether the related firms acted as a single entity.[5] Which courts do you think are right?

5. Should a parent and minority-owned subsidiary be deemed a single entity when the parent has working control? Suppose a parent corporation has a 30% stake that is enough to give it working control over a subsidiary, given the smaller stockholdings of the other subsidiary shareholders. Should such a parent and subsidiary be deemed a single entity? One could argue that working control effectively produces the same joint control as with 51% or even 100% control, that the difference between 30% profit sharing and 51% is just a matter of degree, and that 30% profit sharing is enough to undermine incentives to compete with each other. On the other hand, both *Copperweld* factors are weakened because the parent does not have an absolute legal right of control and the 30% stake means there is even less unity of profits. Thus, one might instead conclude that an

---

[3] *See* Tunis Brothers Co. v. Ford Motor, 763 F.2d 1482, 1495 n. 20 (3d Cir. 1985) (finding separate entities even though parent owned 79% of equity and 100% of voting stock), vacated on other grounds, 475 U.S. 1105 (1986); American Vision Centers v. Cohen, 711 F.Supp. 721 (E.D.N.Y. 1989) (finding separate entities where stake was 54%); Aspen Title & Escrow v. Jeld-Wen, Inc., 677 F.Supp. 1477, 1486 (D. Or. 1987) (finding separate entities where stake was 60–75% but not where it was a de minimis amount below 100%, like 97.5%); Leaco Enterprises v. General Electric, 737 F.Supp. 605, 609 (D. Or. 1990) (concluding that 91.9% was de minimis amount less than 100%); *Siegel Transfer*, 54 F.3d at 1134 & n.7 (affirming single entity finding under de minimus standard where parent owned 99.92% and suggesting in dicta it would find a single entity for any share above 80%). *See also* Fishman v. Estate of Wirtz, 807 F.2d 520, 541 n.19 (7th Cir. 1986) (rejecting single entity claim when the common investors were not identical and it was not clear the common investors had majority control over one firm).

[4] *See* Total Benefit Services v. Group Ins. Admin., Inc., 1993–1 Trade Cas. (CCH) ¶ 70,148 (E.D. La. 1993) (85%); Bell Atlantic Business Systems Services v. Hitachi Data Systems, 849 F.Supp. 702, 706 (N.D. Cal. 1994) (parent owned 80% but dicta suggested anything over 50% would suffice); Novatel Communications v. Cellular Telephone, 1986 WL 15507 (N.D. Ga.) (51%).

[5] *See* Computer Identics v. Southern Pacific Co., 756 F.2d 200, 204–05 (1st Cir. 1985); Coast Cities Truck Sales v. Navistar International Transportation, 912 F.Supp. 747, 765–66 (D. N.J. 1995).

agreement is sufficiently likely to worsen incentives to compete to merit scrutiny under Sherman Act § 1. The only case to consider the issue has apparently taken the latter view.[6]

6. ***The relation to review of the initial acquisition.*** The initial acquisition of partial ownership in another corporation can also be challenged under Sherman Act § 1 or Clayton Act § 7, whether it creates a majority or minority stake, on the ground that the acquisition lessens competition by creating influence, sharing information, or changing incentives. *See* Chapter 7. However, such review of the inherent effects of a partial acquisition does not preclude the possibility that a post-acquisition agreement might restrain incentives to compete even further, which would merit separate antitrust review under Sherman Act § 1.

The Relevance of Agency Relations

Copperweld states that "corporations cannot conspire with their own officers" and its logic suggests that a firm cannot conspire with agents that share its economic interest.[7] But the answer can be different under U.S. law if agents have a personal motive to conspire that is independent of the firm's objectives.[8] More generally, the single entity doctrine raises the question of when someone, including another firm, should be considered an "agent" rather than a separate person capable of conspiring. Categorization difficulties come up most often when a firm sells through a dealer using a "consignment contract" where the supplier retains title and gives a fee or commission to the dealer upon sale. If all those arrangements were an agreement between separate entities, then antitrust law on vertical agreements would apply every time a firm used a salesperson on commission or had a delivery person collect the sales price. If all such arrangements were deemed to involve an agency relationship that could not be a conspiracy, then it would be easy to evade scrutiny of any vertical agreement with independent dealers by simply having the manufacturer retain title and pay the dealer a "commission" equal to the difference between the wholesale price and the distributor's resale price.

The basic answer U.S. antitrust law gives is to treat such arrangements as agency relations only when the actors lack the sort of independent economic stake that, without the restraint, would make

---

[6] *See* Sonitrol of Fresno, Inc. v. American Telephone and Telegraph, 1986 WL 953 (D.D.C.) (even if parent had de facto control it was not a single entity with a subsidiary where its stake was below 50% and thus did not confer legal control.).

[7] *See Siegel Transfer*, 54 F.3d 1125; Mann v. Princeton Community Hospital Assn., 1992–1 Trade Cas. (CCH) ¶ 69,738 (4th Cir. 1992); R. Ernest Cohn D.C., D.A.B.C.O. v. Bond, 953 F.2d 154 (4th Cir. 1991); Surgical Care Center v. Hospital Service District No. 1, 309 F.3d 836, 841 (5th Cir. 2002); Ozark Heartland Electronics v. Radio Shack, 278 F.3d 759, 763–64 (8th Cir. 2002); Tiftarea Shopper v. Georgia Shopper, 786 F.2d 1115, 1118 (11th Cir. 1986).

[8] *See* Victorian House v. Fisher Camuto Corp., 769 F.2d 466, 469 (8th Cir. 1985); Motive Parts Warehouse v. Facet Enters., 774 F.2d 380, 387 (10th Cir. 1985). But *see* Nurse Midwifery Ass'n v. Hibbett, 927 F.2d 904 (6th Cir. 1991) (rejecting such a test). The courts are divided on whether a hospital can conspire with its medical staff. *See* Willman v. Heartland Hosp. E., 34 F.3d 605, 610 (8th Cir. 1994) (collecting sources on both sides).

them efficient independent decisionmakers. Thus, in United States v. General Electric, 272 U.S. 476 (1926), the Court found an agency relation, rather than a vertical price-fixing agreement, when the supplier retained not only title but the risk of loss from fire, and dealers received a fixed commission per sale. In contrast, in Simpson v. Union Oil Co., 377 U.S. 13 (1964), the Court found a vertical price-fixing agreement, rather than an agency relation, when the supplier retained title but its dealers were responsible for the risk of loss from fire and received a commission that was somewhat dependent on the resale price. This pattern of results makes sense. In *General Electric,* allowing the dealers to set the sales price would have led to economic disaster because, with a fixed commission/sale, the dealers would have incentives to set the sales price at $0 to maximize the number of sales. In contrast, in *Simpson*, the dealer was responsible for losses and received a commission that depended somewhat on the sales price. Thus, absent a vertical price-fixing agreement, the *Simpson* dealer would, if considering a decision to cut retail prices, have had economic incentives to consider both the upside (increased sales) and downside (decreased revenue per sale).[9]

In short, it makes sense to deem actors selling on consignment nonagents only when antitrust law would want to preserve their ability to make independent decisions. And preserving that ability is desirable only when the actors would have efficient economic incentives to consider both the benefits and costs of price cutting.

American Needle v. National Football League

560 U.S. 183 (2010).

■ JUSTICE STEVENS delivered the opinion of the Court.

. . . The question whether an arrangement is a contract, combination, or conspiracy is different from and antecedent to the question whether it unreasonably restrains trade. This case raises that antecedent question about the business of the 32 teams in the National Football League (NFL) and a corporate entity that they formed to manage their intellectual property. We conclude that the NFL's licensing activities constitute concerted action that is not categorically beyond the coverage of [Sherman Act] § 1. The legality of that concerted action must be judged under the Rule of Reason.

I

Originally organized in 1920, the NFL is an unincorporated association that now includes 32 separately owned professional football

[9] *Simpson* distinguished *General Electric* on the quite different grounds that it involved a patented product, but *General Electric* itself made clear that, if the arrangement had involved independent purchasers rather than agents, it would have deemed it vertical price-fixing, and that its ruling on agents applied whether or not the product was patented. In *American Needle*, the Supreme Court adopted the functional distinction between *Simpson* and *General Electric* that is described in the text above.

teams. Each team has its own name, colors, and logo, and owns related intellectual property. Like each of the other teams in the league, the New Orleans Saints and the Indianapolis Colts, for example, have their own distinctive names, colors, and marks that are well known to millions of sports fans.

Prior to 1963, the teams made their own arrangements for licensing their intellectual property and marketing trademarked items such as caps and jerseys. In 1963, the teams formed National Football League Properties (NFLP) to develop, license, and market their intellectual property. Most, but not all, of the substantial revenues generated by NFLP have either been given to charity or shared equally among the teams. However, the teams are able to and have at times sought to withdraw from this arrangement.

Between 1963 and 2000, NFLP granted nonexclusive licenses to a number of vendors, permitting them to manufacture and sell apparel bearing team insignias. Petitioner, American Needle, Inc., was one of those licensees. In December 2000, the teams voted to authorize NFLP to grant exclusive licenses, and NFLP granted Reebok International Ltd. an exclusive 10-year license to manufacture and sell trademarked headwear for all 32 teams. It thereafter declined to renew American Needle's nonexclusive license.

American Needle [alleged] . . . that the agreements between the NFL, its teams, NFLP, and Reebok violated . . . the Sherman Act. . . . The Court of Appeals for the Seventh Circuit affirmed [a district court decision dismissing the § 1 claims.] The panel observed that "in some contexts, a league seems more aptly described as a single entity immune from antitrust scrutiny, while in others a league appears to be a joint venture between independently owned teams that is subject to review under § 1." Relying on Circuit precedent, the court limited its inquiry to the particular conduct at issue, licensing of teams' intellectual property. The panel agreed with petitioner that "when making a single-entity determination, courts must examine whether the conduct in question deprives the marketplace of the independent sources of economic control that competition assumes." The court, however, discounted the significance of potential competition among the teams regarding the use of their intellectual property because the teams "can function only as one source of economic power when collectively producing NFL football." The court noted that football itself can only be carried out jointly. Moreover, "NFL teams share a vital economic interest in collectively promoting NFL football . . . [to] compet[e] with other forms of entertainment." "It thus follows," the court found, "that only one source of economic power controls the promotion of NFL football," and "it makes little sense to assert that each individual team has the authority, if not the responsibility, to promote the jointly produced NFL football." Recognizing that NFL teams have "license[d] their intellectual property collectively" since 1963, the court held that § 1 did not apply. . . .

II

... The meaning of the term "contract, combination ... or conspiracy" is informed by the " 'basic distinction' " in the Sherman Act " 'between concerted and independent action' " that distinguishes § 1 of the Sherman Act from § 2. *Copperweld*. ... Congress used this distinction between concerted and independent action to deter anticompetitive conduct and compensate its victims, without chilling vigorous competition through ordinary business operations. The distinction also avoids judicial scrutiny of routine, internal business decisions.

Thus, in § 1 Congress "treated concerted behavior more strictly than unilateral behavior." *Id.* This is so because unlike independent action, "[c]oncerted activity inherently is fraught with anticompetitive risk" insofar as it "deprives the marketplace of independent centers of decisionmaking that competition assumes and demands." *Id.* And because concerted action is discrete and distinct, a limit on such activity leaves untouched a vast amount of business conduct. As a result, there is less risk of deterring a firm's necessary conduct; courts need only examine discrete agreements; and such conduct may be remedied simply through prohibition.[2] Concerted activity is thus "judged more sternly than unilateral activity under § 2," *Id.* For these reasons, § 1 prohibits any concerted action "in restraint of trade or commerce," even if the action does not "threate[n] monopolization," *Id.* And therefore, an arrangement must embody concerted action in order to be a "contract, combination ... or conspiracy" under § 1.

III

We have long held that concerted action under § 1 does not turn simply on whether the parties involved are legally distinct entities. Instead, we have eschewed such formalistic distinctions in favor of a functional consideration of how the parties involved in the alleged anticompetitive conduct actually operate.

As a result, we have repeatedly found instances in which members of a legally single entity violated § 1 when the entity was controlled by a group of competitors and served, in essence, as a vehicle for ongoing concerted activity. In *United States v. Sealy, Inc.,* 388 U.S. 350 (1967), for example, a group of mattress manufacturers operated and controlled Sealy, Inc., a company that licensed the Sealy trademark to the manufacturers, and dictated that each operate within a specific geographic area. The Government alleged that the licensees and Sealy were conspiring in violation of § 1, and we agreed. We explained that "[w]e seek the central substance of the situation" and therefore "we are

---

[2] If Congress prohibited independent action that merely restrains trade (even if it does not threaten monopolization), that prohibition could deter perfectly competitive conduct by firms that are fearful of litigation costs and judicial error. Moreover, if every unilateral action that restrained trade were subject to antitrust scrutiny, then courts would be forced to judge almost every internal business decision.

moved by the identity of the persons who act, rather than the label of their hats." *Id.* We thus held that Sealy was not a "separate entity, but . . . an instrumentality of the individual manufacturers." *Id.* In similar circumstances, we have found other formally distinct business organizations covered by § 1. *See, e.g., Northwest Wholesale Stationers; NCAA; United States v. Topco Associates,* 405 U.S. 596, 609 (1972); *Associated Press; Terminal Railroad.* We have similarly looked past the form of a legally "single entity" when competitors were part of professional organizations[3] or trade groups.[4]

Conversely, there is not necessarily concerted action simply because more than one legally distinct entity is involved. Although, under a now-defunct doctrine known as the "intraenterprise conspiracy doctrine," we once treated cooperation between legally separate entities as necessarily covered by § 1, we now embark on a more functional analysis. . . . We finally reexamined the intraenterprise conspiracy doctrine in *Copperweld,* and concluded that it was inconsistent with the " 'basic distinction between concerted and independent action.' " *Id.* Considering it "perfectly plain that an internal agreement to implement a single, unitary firm's policies does not raise the antitrust dangers that § 1 was designed to police," *id.*, we held that a parent corporation and its wholly owned subsidiary "are incapable of conspiring with each other for purposes of § 1 of the Sherman Act," *id.* We explained that although a parent corporation and its wholly owned subsidiary are "separate" for the purposes of incorporation or formal title, they are controlled by a single center of decisionmaking and they control a single aggregation of economic power. Joint conduct by two such entities does not "depriv[e] the marketplace of independent centers of decisionmaking," *id.*, and as a result, an agreement between them does not constitute "a contract, combination . . . or conspiracy" for the purposes of § 1.[5]

IV

As *Copperweld* exemplifies, "substance, not form, should determine whether a[n] . . . entity is capable of conspiring under § 1." *Id.* This inquiry is sometimes described as asking whether the alleged conspirators are a single entity. That is perhaps a misdescription, however, because the question is not whether the defendant is a legally single entity or has a single name; nor is the question whether the parties

---

[3] *See, e.g., Indiana Dentists; Maricopa; Professional Engineers; Goldfarb v. Virginia State Bar,* 421 U.S. 773 (1975).

[4] *See, e.g., Allied Tube & Conduit Corp. v. Indian Head, Inc.,* 486 U.S. 492 (1988); *Radiant Burners v. Peoples Gas Light & Coke,* 364 U.S. 656 (1961) *(per curiam); Fashion Originators.*

[5] This focus on "substance, not, form," *Copperweld,* can also be seen in our cases about whether a company and its agent are capable of conspiring under § 1. *See, e.g., Simpson v. Union Oil Co. of Cal.,* 377 U.S. 13, 20–21, 84 S.Ct. 1051, 12 L.Ed.2d 98 (1964); *see* also E. Elhauge & D. Geradin, Global Antitrust Law and Economics 787–788, and n. 7 (2007) (hereinafter Elhauge & Geradin) (explaining the functional difference between *Simpson* and *United States v. General Elec. Co.,* 272 U.S. 476 (1926), in which we treated a similar agreement as beyond the reach of § 1).

involved "seem" like one firm or multiple firms in any metaphysical sense. The key is whether the alleged "contract, combination . . . , or conspiracy" is concerted action—that is, whether it joins together separate decisionmakers. The relevant inquiry, therefore, is whether there is a contract, "combination . . . or conspiracy" amongst "separate economic actors pursuing separate economic interests," *id.*, such that the agreement "deprives the marketplace of independent centers of decisionmaking," *id.*, and therefore of "diversity of entrepreneurial interests," *Fraser v. Major League Soccer, L.L.C.*, 284 F.3d 47, 57 (C.A.1 2002) (Boudin, C. J.), and thus of actual or potential competition.

Thus, while the president and a vice president of a firm could (and regularly do) act in combination, their joint action generally is not the sort of "combination" that § 1 is intended to cover. Such agreements might be described "as really unilateral behavior flowing from decisions of a single enterprise." *Copperweld*. Nor, for this reason, does § 1 cover "internally coordinated conduct of a corporation and one of its unincorporated divisions," *id.*, because "[a] division within a corporate structure pursues the common interests of the whole," *id.*, and therefore "coordination between a corporation and its division does not represent a sudden joining of two independent sources of economic power previously pursuing separate interests," *id.* Nor, for the same reasons, is "the coordinated activity of a parent and its wholly owned subsidiary" covered. *See id.* They "have a complete unity of interest" and thus "[w]ith or without a formal 'agreement,' the subsidiary acts for the benefit of the parent, its sole shareholder." *Id.*

Because the inquiry is one of competitive reality, it is not determinative that two parties to an alleged § 1 violation are legally distinct entities. Nor, however, is it determinative that two legally distinct entities have organized themselves under a single umbrella or into a structured joint venture. The question is whether the agreement joins together "independent centers of decisionmaking." *Id.* If it does, the entities are capable of conspiring under § 1, and the court must decide whether the restraint of trade is an unreasonable and therefore illegal one.

V

The NFL teams do not possess either the unitary decisionmaking quality or the single aggregation of economic power characteristic of independent action. Each of the teams is a substantial, independently owned, and independently managed business. "[T]heir general corporate actions are guided or determined" by "separate corporate consciousnesses," and "[t]heir objectives are" not "common." *Copperweld*; *see also North American Soccer League v. NFL*, 670 F.2d 1249, 1252 (C.A.2 1982) (discussing ways that "the financial performance of each team, while related to that of the others, does not . . . necessarily rise and fall with that of the others"). The teams compete with one another, not only on the playing field, but to attract fans, for gate receipts and for contracts with managerial and playing personnel.

Directly relevant to this case, the teams compete in the market for intellectual property. To a firm making hats, the Saints and the Colts are two potentially competing suppliers of valuable trademarks. When each NFL team licenses its intellectual property, it is not pursuing the "common interests of the whole" league but is instead pursuing interests of each "corporation itself," *Copperweld*; teams are acting as "separate economic actors pursuing separate economic interests," and each team therefore is a potential "independent cente[r] of decisionmaking," *id.* Decisions by NFL teams to license their separately owned trademarks collectively and to only one vendor are decisions that "depriv[e] the marketplace of independent centers of decisionmaking," *id.,* and therefore of actual or potential competition. *See NCAA* (observing a possible § 1 violation if two separately owned companies sold their separate products through a "single selling agent"); cf. Areeda & Hovenkamp 1478a, at 318 ("Obviously, the most significant competitive threats arise when joint venture participants are actual or potential competitors").

In defense, respondents argue that by forming NFLP, they have formed a single entity, akin to a merger, and market their NFL brands through a single outlet. But it is not dispositive that the teams have organized and own a legally separate entity that centralizes the management of their intellectual property. An ongoing § 1 violation cannot evade § 1 scrutiny simply by giving the ongoing violation a name and label. "Perhaps every agreement and combination in restraint of trade could be so labeled." *Timken Roller Bearing v. United States,* 341 U.S. 593, 598 (1951).

The NFL respondents may be similar in some sense to a single enterprise that owns several pieces of intellectual property and licenses them jointly, but they are not similar in the relevant functional sense. Although NFL teams have common interests such as promoting the NFL brand, they are still separate, profit-maximizing entities, and their interests in licensing team trademarks are not necessarily aligned. Common interests in the NFL brand "*partially* unit[e] the economic interests of the parent firms," Broadley, Joint Ventures and Antitrust Policy, 95 Harv. L.Rev. 1521, 1526 (1982) (emphasis added), but the teams still have distinct, potentially competing interests.

It may be, as respondents argue, that NFLP "has served as the 'single driver' of the teams" "promotional vehicle," " 'pursu[ing] the common interests of the whole.' " Brief for NFL Respondents 28 (quoting *Copperweld*). But illegal restraints often are in the common interests of the parties to the restraint, at the expense of those who are not parties. It is true, as respondents describe, that they have for some time marketed their trademarks jointly. But a history of concerted activity does not immunize conduct from § 1 scrutiny. "Absence of actual competition may simply be a manifestation of the anticompetitive agreement itself." *Freeman,* 322 F.3d, at 1149.

Respondents argue that nonetheless, as the Court of Appeals held, they constitute a single entity because without their cooperation, there would be no NFL football. It is true that "the clubs that make up a professional sports league are not completely independent economic competitors, as they depend upon a degree of cooperation for economic survival." *Brown,* 518 U.S., at 248. But the Court of Appeals' reasoning is unpersuasive.

The justification for cooperation is not relevant to whether that cooperation is concerted or independent action.[6] A "contract, combination . . . or conspiracy," § 1, that is necessary or useful to a joint venture is still a "contract, combination . . . or conspiracy" if it "deprives the marketplace of independent centers of decisionmaking," *Copperweld. See NCAA* ("[J]oint ventures have no immunity from antitrust laws"). Any joint venture involves multiple sources of economic power cooperating to produce a product. And for many such ventures, the participation of others is necessary. But that does not mean that necessity of cooperation transforms concerted action into independent action; a nut and a bolt can only operate together, but an agreement between nut and bolt manufacturers is still subject to § 1 analysis. Nor does it mean that once a group of firms agree to produce a joint product, cooperation amongst those firms must be treated as independent conduct. The mere fact that the teams operate jointly in some sense does not mean that they are immune.[7]

The Court of Appeals carved out a zone of antitrust immunity for conduct arguably related to league operations by reasoning that coordinated team trademark sales are necessary to produce "NFL football," a single NFL brand that competes against other forms of entertainment. But defining the product as "NFL football" puts the cart before the horse: Of course the NFL produces NFL football; but that does not mean that cooperation amongst NFL teams is immune from § 1 scrutiny. Members of any cartel could insist that their cooperation is necessary to produce the "cartel product" and compete with other products.

The question whether NFLP decisions can constitute concerted activity covered by § 1 is closer than whether decisions made directly by the 32 teams are covered by § 1. This is so both because NFLP is a

---

[6] As discussed *infra,* necessity of cooperation is a factor relevant to whether the agreement is subject to the Rule of Reason. *See NCAA* (holding that NCAA restrictions on televising college football games are subject to Rule of Reason analysis for the "critical" reason that "horizontal restraints on competition are essential if the product is to be available at all").

[7] In any event, it simply is not apparent that the alleged conduct was necessary at all. Although two teams are needed to play a football game, not all aspects of elaborate interleague cooperation are necessary to produce a game. Moreover, even if leaguewide agreements are necessary to produce football, it does not follow that concerted activity in marketing intellectual property is necessary to produce football.

separate corporation with its own management and because the record indicates that most of the revenues generated by NFLP are shared by the teams on an equal basis. Nevertheless we think it clear that for the same reasons the 32 teams' conduct is covered by § 1, NFLP's actions also are subject to § 1, at least with regards to its marketing of property owned by the separate teams. NFLP's licensing decisions are made by the 32 potential competitors, and each of them actually owns its share of the jointly managed assets. Cf. *Sealy,* 388 U.S. at 352–354. Apart from their agreement to cooperate in exploiting those assets, including their decisions as the NFLP, there would be nothing to prevent each of the teams from making its own market decisions relating to purchases of apparel and headwear, to the sale of such items, and to the granting of licenses to use its trademarks.

We generally treat agreements within a single firm as independent action on the presumption that the components of the firm will act to maximize the firm's profits. But in rare cases, that presumption does not hold. Agreements made within a firm can constitute concerted action covered by § 1 when the parties to the agreement act on interests separate from those of the firm itself,[8] and the intrafirm agreements may simply be a formalistic shell for ongoing concerted action. *See, e.g., Topco Associates,* 405 U.S. at 609; *Sealy,* 388 U.S. at 352–354.

For that reason, decisions by the NFLP regarding the teams' separately owned intellectual property constitute concerted action. Thirty-two teams operating independently through the vehicle of the NFLP are not like the components of a single firm that act to maximize the firm's profits. The teams remain separately controlled, potential competitors with economic interests that are distinct from NFLP's financial well-being. Unlike typical decisions by corporate shareholders, NFLP licensing decisions effectively require the assent of more than a mere majority of shareholders. And each team's decision reflects not only an interest in NFLP's profits but also an interest in the team's individual profits. The 32 teams capture individual economic benefits separate and apart from NFLP profits as a result of the decisions they make for the NFLP. NFLP's decisions thus affect each team's profits from licensing its own intellectual property. "Although the business interests of" the teams "will *often* coincide with those of the" NFLP "as an entity in itself, that commonality of interest exists in every cartel." *Los Angeles Memorial Coliseum Comm'n v. NFL,* 726 F.2d 1381, 1389 (C.A.9 1984) (emphasis added). In making the relevant licensing decisions, NFLP is therefore "an instrumentality" of the teams. *Sealy,* 388 U.S. at 352–354; *see also Topco Associates,* 405 U.S. at 609.

---

[8] *See* Areeda & Hovenkamp 1471; Elhauge & Geradin 786–787, and n. 6; *see* also *Capital Imaging Assoc. v. Mohawk Valley Medical Assoc., Inc.,* 996 F.2d 537, 544 (C.A.2 1993); *Bolt v. Halifax Hospital Medical Center,* 891 F.2d 810, 819 (C.A.11 1990); *Oksanen v. Page Memorial Hospital,* 945 F.2d 696, 706 (C.A.4 1991); *Motive Parts Warehouse v. Facet Enterprises,* 774 F.2d 380, 387–388 (C.A.10 1985); *Victorian House, Inc. v. Fisher Camuto Corp.,* 769 F.2d 466, 469 (C.A.8 1985); *Weiss v. York Hospital,* 745 F.2d 786, 828 (C.A.3 1984).

If the fact that potential competitors shared in profits or losses from a venture meant that the venture was immune from § 1, then any cartel "could evade the antitrust law simply by creating a 'joint venture' to serve as the exclusive seller of their competing products." *Major League Baseball Properties, Inc. v. Salvino, Inc.,* 542 F.3d 290, 335 (C.A.2 2008) (Sotomayor, J., concurring in judgment). "So long as no agreement," other than one made by the cartelists sitting on the board of the joint venture, "explicitly listed the prices to be charged, the companies could act as monopolies through the 'joint venture.' " *Id.* (Indeed, a joint venture with a single management structure is generally a better way to operate a cartel because it decreases the risks of a party to an illegal agreement defecting from that agreement). However, competitors "cannot simply get around" antitrust liability by acting "through a third-party intermediary or 'joint venture.' " *Id.,* at 336.[9]

VI

Football teams that need to cooperate are not trapped by antitrust law. "[T]he special characteristics of this industry may provide a justification" for many kinds of agreements. *Brown,* 518 U.S. at 252 (STEVENS, J., dissenting). The fact that NFL teams share an interest in making the entire league successful and profitable, and that they must cooperate in the production and scheduling of games, provides a perfectly sensible justification for making a host of collective decisions. But the conduct at issue in this case is still concerted activity under the Sherman Act that is subject to § 1 analysis.

When "restraints on competition are essential if the product is to be available at all," *per se* rules of illegality are inapplicable, and instead the restraint must be judged according to the flexible Rule of Reason. *NCAA* ("Our decision not to apply a *per se* rule to this case rests in large part on our recognition that a certain degree of cooperation is necessary if the type of competition that petitioner and its member institutions seek to market is to be preserved"); *see also Dagher*. In such instances, the agreement is likely to survive the Rule of Reason. *See BMI* ("Joint ventures and other cooperative arrangements are also not usually unlawful . . . where the agreement . . . is necessary to market the product at all"). And depending upon the concerted activity in question, the Rule

[9] For the purposes of resolving this case, there is no need to pass upon the Government's position that entities are incapable of conspiring under § 1 if they have "effectively merged the relevant aspect of their operations, thereby eliminating actual and potential competition . . . in that operational sphere" and "the challenged restraint [does] not significantly affect actual or potential competition . . . outside their merged operations." Brief for United States as *Amicus Curiae* 17. The Government urges that the choices to "offer only a blanket license" and "to have only a single headwear licensee" might not constitute concerted action under its test. *Id.,* at 32. However, because the teams still own their own trademarks and are free to market those trademarks as they see fit, even those two choices were agreements amongst potential competitors and would constitute concerted action under the Government's own standard. At any point, the teams could decide to license their own trademarks. It is significant, moreover, that the teams here control NFLP. The two choices that the Government might treat as independent action, although nominally made by NFLP, are for all functional purposes choices made by the 32 entities with potentially competing interests.

of Reason may not require a detailed analysis; it "can sometimes be applied in the twinkling of an eye." *NCAA.*

Other features of the NFL may also save agreements amongst the teams. We have recognized, for example, "that the interest in maintaining a competitive balance" among "athletic teams is legitimate and important," *NCAA.* While that same interest applies to the teams in the NFL, it does not justify treating them as a single entity for § 1 purposes when it comes to the marketing of the teams' individually owned intellectual property. It is, however, unquestionably an interest that may well justify a variety of collective decisions made by the teams. What role it properly plays in applying the Rule of Reason to the allegations in this case is a matter to be considered on remand. . . .

Accordingly, the judgment of the Court of Appeals is reversed, and the case is remanded for further proceedings consistent with this opinion.

NOTES AND QUESTIONS ON *AMERICAN NEEDLE*

1. ***Formalism v. functionalism.*** The *American Needle* opinion makes clear that whether separate entities exist for antitrust agreement purposes turns not on formalisms but on whether functionally there exist independent economic decisionmakers that could be restricted by an antitrust agreement. If, without the alleged agreement, the actors would still act in the same way because of common control and an identical economic interest, then any "agreement" between them cannot meaningfully restrain their decisions and thus they are treated as a single entity incapable of conspiring. But if, without the alleged agreement, the actors have enough separate control and divergent economic interests that they could make independent economic decisions, then an agreement between them can restrain their decisions and thus they are treated as separate entities capable of conspiring. Actors are particularly likely to be treated as separate entities if they are actual or potential competitors in the market being restrained.

Consistent with its rejection of formalism, the Court makes clear that single entity status could not be established by the mere fact that the joint venture was a separate corporate entity with its own corporate management. Instead, the Court cited two functional factors to support its conclusion that NFLP decisions reflected a horizontal agreement among the NFL team members: (1) the joint venture was subject to ongoing control by team members that have their own independent management and economic interests, and (2) the ongoing ability of those decisionmakers to unilaterally compete in the relevant market, here because the team members were "potentially competing suppliers of valuable trademarks" given that "the teams still own their own trademarks and are free to market those trademarks as they see fit . . . At any point, the teams could decide to license their own trademarks." The first factor (disunity of control and profits) corresponds to the reverse of the elements *Copperweld* deemed sufficed to treat two business units as a single entity. The second factor is whether the business units are potential competitors. The Court's holding makes it clear that joint venture decisions will receive separate entity treatment when both factors are met, but (as discussed below) leaves it unsettled whether the first factor alone should suffice for a separate-entities conclusion.

The Court also made clear that the first factor could not be disproven by showing the members of the joint venture had a *collective* economic interest. As the Court observed, such a collective economic interest generally exists for illegal horizontal agreements, such as with a cartel that maximizes collective profits for it members. What matters is whether the members retained some separate control and economic interest so that, freed from the restraint of the alleged agreement, they might make independent economic decisions that could be contrary to that collective economic interest, such as with cartel members who have independent incentives to undercut the cartel price. The Court further made clear that the second factor could not be disproven by showing that the members had a recent history of not actually competing in the relevant activity (here that they had for some time marketed trademarks only jointly), because that recent history might simply reflect the results of a successful anticompetitive agreement. Instead, the second factor could be met by showing that the members potentially *could* compete by licensing their own trademarks.

2. When the two functional factors point in opposing directions. The Court's decision did not resolve what to do when the two functional factors point in opposing directions. As the Court noted in footnote 9, the Government effectively argued that the second factor should be deemed necessary for separate entity treatment, reasoning that, to the extent the joint venture eliminated actual and potential competition between the members, the joint venture constituted a merger of the members into a single entity. In such a case, the *formation* of the joint venture would itself be a horizontal agreement under the Government standard, and thus subject to antitrust scrutiny under both § 1 and the merger doctrines discussed in Chapter 7. But *subsequent* decisions by the joint venture would be treated as decisions by a single entity (rather than as an agreement among its members) to the extent they were within the scope of merged activities. The Court in footnote 9 declined to hold whether the Government standard was correct because it concluded that the second factor was met in the actual case, as well as in the Government's two hypotheticals. But the Court also emphasized the first factor in response to the government in footnote 9, stating: "It is significant, moreover, that the teams here control NFLP." Thus, the Court's decision left it unresolved whether the first factor might alone suffice for separate entity treatment. Should it?

The first factor would seem to hold for any joint venture, which by definition is an arrangement where firms engage in some joint business activity (the joint venture) but retain independent status and continue to operate separately to some extent (which is what distinguishes a joint venture from a merger). Thus, if meeting the first factor suffices for separate entity treatment, then all decisions by a joint venture involve an agreement between the members. In contrast, if the second factor is necessary for separate entity treatment, then most but not all joint venture decisions would be agreements among their members. Most would be because most joint ventures do not preclude actual or potential competition by their members with the joint venture on most joint venture activities. But not all would be because sometimes joint ventures preclude actual or potential competition by their members on at least some joint venture activities, which under the government approach would be treated as effectively merging those aspects of their business activities. Thus, under the Government's suggested standard, decisions by a joint venture would be decisions by a single entity only to the extent that they involved merged business activities on which the members were not actual or potential competitors.

To see what is potentially at stake in the as-yet unresolved issue, suppose each of the NFL teams had instead irrevocably transferred all their trademark rights to NFLP. An irrevocable transfer of trademark rights would mean that the teams were no longer actual or potential competitors in the licensing market, unless NFLP decided to grant those rights back. The second factor thus would likely be deemed unmet. However, the first factor would still be met because the independent teams would have ongoing control over how NFLP licenses and over whether NFLP grants trademark rights back to the teams. Under the Government's suggested approach, the teams would be treated as having effectively merged their trademark licensing into the joint venture. Thus, while this merger would be a horizontal agreement, subsequent licensing decisions by NFLP would be treated as decisions by a single entity rather than as horizontal agreements among its members.[10] In contrast, if the first factor suffices for separate entity treatment, then not only would the combination of trademark rights into NFLP be a horizontal agreement, but also each licensing decision by NFLP would reflect a *separate* horizontal agreement that was subject to antitrust scrutiny.

How should such a hypothetical irrevocable transfer of trademark rights to NFLP be treated? The answer to this question does not really alter *whether* an antitrust agreement exists, because under the Government approach the merger would still be an agreement. Instead, the answer alters the *timing* and *scope* of the agreement that is subject to antitrust scrutiny. An approach that made the first factor sufficient for separate entity treatment would be less vulnerable to statute of limitations problems and would focus more on specific licensing decisions. An approach (like the Government's) that made the second factor necessary for separate entity treatment means that the effective merger may be hard to challenge after the statute of limitations runs out and would not focus on those specific licensing decisions. The latter approach could be justified by the view that the horizontal combination that created any market power was the irrevocable transfer of rights and that condemning NFLP licensing decisions could not alter that irrevocable combination or create any additional horizontal competition among the members. A possible response is that, while an "irrevocable" rights transfer is irrevocable by an individual team, it

---

[10] Such licensing decisions might still be subject to review as unilateral conduct under the doctrines discussed in Chapter 3 (if the NFLP had monopoly power or a dangerous probability of acquiring it) or as vertical agreements between NFLP and its licenses under the doctrines discussed in Chapters 4–5.

is not irrevocable by the joint venture, which could always transfer those rights back. Thus, the choice between approaches may in part turn on whether one thinks that prohibiting particular licensing agreements by the NFLP might lead the independent teams to exercise their joint control over the NFLP to grant those trademark rights back to the teams. But even if the latter is true, it might seem odd to suggest that a horizontal agreement is invalid because it restrains competition that could not exist unless another horizontal agreement restored that competition. It might be simpler to treat the moment of horizontal combination as the key moment whenever individual firms can no longer unilaterally deviate from it, on the expectation that in the future the joint venture would exercise any collective rights in their collective interests.

Is the actual case that different from this irrevocable transfer hypothetical? As the Court describes the facts, in 2000 the teams authorized the NFLP to grant exclusive rights to the club trademarks and then had NFLP grant exclusive rights on headgear to Reebok. Further, the record indicates that the NFL team resolution authorizing the exclusive Reebok license provided that "the member clubs hereby approve the necessary grant of licenses" and that "the member clubs agree to give their full cooperation as necessary to implement and further the" exclusive license with Reebok.[11] Doesn't this language effectively transfer the team trademark rights to NFLP and then Reebok because the teams approved the necessary grants and an individual team decision to license its trademark would violate the exclusive NFLP license that the team authorized and pledged to support? If so, then the teams' agreement to authorize NFLP to grant this exclusive license would seem to make it a single entity when it did so under the Government approach, but the Court seemed to reject that conclusion in footnote 9. Perhaps the fact that the exclusive license to Reebok was only 10 years might suffice to make the teams potential future competitors under the government approach, and also might make it more realistic that the team members might exercise their joint control to decline to renew the exclusive license in the future, thus making it more sensible to focus on the first factor.

3. ***Justifications and the limited nature of the functional inquiry on single entity status.*** Although the Court focused on a functional analysis, it made clear that this focus did *not* mean an inquiry into whether the alleged agreement furthered some functional goal. For purposes of ascertaining whether separate entities exist, the functional inquiry is simply into whether there exist independent economic decisionmakers whose competitive decisions might be restrained by the alleged agreement. Thus, the Court stressed that the existence of a functional reason for cooperation is not relevant to whether an agreement exists; such a reason just goes to whether the agreement has a *justification* that helps it survive Rule of Reason scrutiny. As the Court stressed, when agreements on issues like the production and scheduling of games are necessary to provide a product at all, such a powerful justification makes the agreement likely to survive Rule of Reason review. Indeed, such a conclusion seems not only likely but

---

11 *See* Joint Appendix in American Needle v. NFL at 465–66.

inevitable, because if there could be no product without the agreement, then the agreement does not restrain any competition. But the Court observed that the need to cooperate to put on football games did not show that the teams needed to cooperate in marketing intellectual property. Another possible justification in sports leagues is that some restraints might improve product quality by increasing the competitive balance between teams. Whether this justification applied to the joint licensing was a matter the Court left to be determined on remand, but it made clear that, even if it applied, it would just be a factor to be considered under the Rule of Reason, and would not justify treating the joint venture as a single entity. How should this justification be treated on remand?

4. ***Relationship to*** **Texaco v. Dagher.** As discussed in Chapter 2, *Texaco v. Dagher* held that, because the formation of the joint venture in that case was not alleged to be anticompetitive, the joint venture's agreement to fix the price of its product could not violate the per se rule or abbreviated rule of reason. Because this holding was about the right standard to apply to the agreement, rather than about the existence of the agreement, it does not conflict with the holding in *American Needle.* But *American Needle* does seem to cut back on dicta in *Texaco v. Dagher* which stated:

> Texaco and Shell Oil formed a joint venture, Equilon, to consolidate their operations in the western United States, thereby ending competition between the two companies . . . Texaco and Shell Oil did not compete with one another in the relevant market—namely, the sale of gasoline to service stations in the western United States . . . In other words, the pricing policy challenged here amounts to little more than price setting by a single entity—albeit within the context of a joint venture—and not a pricing agreement between competing entities with respect to their competing products. . . . When "persons who would otherwise be competitors pool their capital and share the risks of loss as well as the opportunities for profit . . . such joint ventures [are] regarded as a single firm competing with other sellers in the market."

In the *American Needle* joint venture, the teams withdrew from the relevant trademark market, and thus did not compete with each other in that market but instead shared profits in that market through the joint venture. Nonetheless, *American Needle* held that the joint venture should not be deemed a single entity because its members were *potential* competitors and had independent interests and exercised joint control over the joint venture in which they shared profits. But that was also true in *Texaco v. Dagher*, given that Texaco and Shell Oil could have re-entered the market for selling gasoline in the western United States. Thus, the *American Needle* holding conflicts with this single-entity dicta in *Texaco v. Dagher*. Moreover, *Texaco v. Dagher* itself has other language that seems to conflict with its single-entity dicta, stating that the plaintiffs "should have challenged [the joint venture conduct] pursuant to the rule of reason," which would have been impossible if the joint venture were a single entity engaged in above-cost pricing. Perhaps the best explanation for the overbroad single-entity dicta in *Texaco v. Dagher* is that in that case the alleged conduct—fixing prices for the joint venture product—was unavoidable because those prices would also have been fixed if the joint venture set different prices for the different brands. Accordingly, there was no way to separate the legitimacy of price-setting by the joint venture from the legitimacy of the joint venture itself, which had been conceded. Do you find *American Needle* consistent with *Texaco v. Dagher* and, if so, how would you reconcile them?

B. STANDARDS FOR FINDING A VERTICAL AGREEMENT

Vertical agreements raise a distinctive set of tricky issues. The core problem is that because the firms are in some supply relationship, they must necessarily be in some sort of agreement. And because they can generally choose whom to supply, they can effectively reach understandings by simply refusing to deal with buyers who do not comply with announced conditions. When a supplier unilaterally demands compliance with an anticompetitive condition and buyers acquiesce in that demand, should such demand and acquiescence be regarded as an agreement? When the agreement involves some exclusionary condition, like tying or exclusive dealing, the usual answer is "yes" under U.S. antitrust law, on the ground that the sale agreement satisfies any agreement requirement and the announced condition of tying or exclusivity is what makes it a tying or exclusive agreement, a conclusion reinforced by the fact that Clayton Act § 3 simply covers sales that are conditioned on the buyer not dealing with rivals.[12] On the other hand, when the vertical agreement involves some intrabrand restraint on distribution, the usual answer under U.S. antitrust law is "no," on the ground that a nonmonopoly supplier is free to unilaterally choose with whom it wishes to deal. However, we shall see that the last answer can be "yes" under U.S. law when the supplier either (a) seeks and obtains assurances from dealers that they will comply with the condition or (b) engages in individualized exhortation to induce noncomplying dealers back into line.

Monsanto Co. v. Spray-Rite Service Corp.

465 U.S. 752 (1984).

■ JUSTICE POWELL delivered the opinion of the Court.

This case presents a question as to the standard of proof required to find a vertical price-fixing conspiracy in violation of § 1 of the Sherman Act. . . .

Petitioner Monsanto Co. manufactures chemical products, including agricultural herbicides. . . . [I]ts sales accounted for approximately 15% of the corn herbicide market and 3% of the soybean herbicide market. In the corn herbicide market, the market leader commanded a 70% share.

---

12 *See* AREEDA, ELHAUGE & HOVENKAMP, X ANTITRUST LAW ¶¶ 1752f1, 1754 (1996).

In the soybean herbicide market, two other competitors each had between 30% and 40% of the market. Respondent Spray-Rite Service Corp. was engaged in the wholesale distribution of agricultural chemicals from 1955 to 1972. . . . Spray-Rite was a discount operation, buying in large quantities and selling at a low margin. . . . Monsanto declined to renew Spray-Rite's distributorship. . . . Spray-Rite was the 10th largest out of approximately 100 distributors of Monsanto's primary corn herbicide. . . .

Spray-Rite brought this action under § 1 of the Sherman Act. . . . [T]he jury found that . . . the termination of Spray-Rite was pursuant to a conspiracy between Monsanto and one or more of its distributors to set resale prices. . . . The Court of Appeals . . . affirmed. . . . The court stated that "proof of termination following competitor complaints is sufficient to support an inference of concerted action." . . . We reject the statement by the Court of Appeals . . . of the standard of proof required to submit a case to the jury in distributor-termination litigation, but affirm the judgment under the standard we announce today. . . .

This Court has drawn two important distinctions that are at the center of this and any other distributor-termination case. First, there is the basic distinction between concerted and independent action—a distinction not always clearly drawn by parties and courts. Section 1 of the Sherman Act requires that there be a "contract, combination . . . or conspiracy" between the manufacturer and other distributors in order to establish a violation. Independent action is not proscribed. A manufacturer of course generally has a right to deal, or refuse to deal, with whomever it likes, as long as it does so independently. United States v. Colgate & Co., 250 U.S. 300, 307 (1919). Under *Colgate*, the manufacturer can announce its resale prices in advance and refuse to deal with those who fail to comply. And a distributor is free to acquiesce in the manufacturer's demand in order to avoid termination.

The second important distinction in distributor-termination cases is that between concerted action to set prices and concerted action on nonprice restrictions. The former have been *per se* illegal since the early years of national antitrust enforcement. *See Dr. Miles*. The latter are judged under the rule of reason. . . . *See Sylvania*.

While these distinctions in theory are reasonably clear, often they are difficult to apply in practice. . . .[T]he economic effect of all of the conduct described above—unilateral and concerted vertical price setting, agreements on price and nonprice restrictions—is in many, but not all, cases similar or identical. And judged from a distance, the conduct of the parties in the various situations can be indistinguishable. For example, the fact that a manufacturer and its distributors are in constant communication about prices and marketing strategy does not alone show that the distributors are not making independent pricing decisions. A manufacturer and its distributors have legitimate reasons to exchange information about the prices and the reception of their products in the market. Moreover, it is precisely in cases in which the manufacturer attempts to further a particular marketing strategy by means of agreements on often costly nonprice restrictions that it will have the most interest in the distributors' resale prices. The manufacturer often will want to ensure that its distributors earn sufficient profit to pay for programs such as hiring and training additional salesmen or demonstrating the technical features of the product, and will want to see that "free-riders" do not interfere. *See Sylvania.* Thus, the manufacturer's strongly felt concern about resale prices does not necessarily mean that it has done more than the *Colgate* doctrine allows.

Nevertheless, it is of considerable importance that independent action by the manufacturer, and concerted action on nonprice restrictions, be distinguished from price-fixing agreements, since under present law the latter are subject to *per se* treatment and treble damages. On a claim of concerted price fixing, the antitrust plaintiff must present evidence sufficient to carry its burden of proving that there was such an agreement. If an inference of such an agreement may be drawn from highly ambiguous evidence, there is a considerable danger that the doctrines enunciated in *Sylvania* and *Colgate* will be seriously eroded.

The flaw in the evidentiary standard adopted by the Court of Appeals in this case is that it disregards this danger. Permitting an agreement to be inferred merely from the existence of complaints, or even from the fact that termination came about "in response to" complaints, could deter or penalize perfectly legitimate conduct. As Monsanto points out, complaints about price cutters "are natural—and from the manufacturer's perspective, unavoidable—reactions by distributors to the activities of their rivals." Such complaints, particularly where the manufacturer has imposed a costly set of nonprice restrictions, "arise in the normal course of business and do not indicate illegal concerted action." Moreover, distributors are an important source of information for manufacturers. In order to assure an efficient distribution system, manufacturers and distributors constantly must coordinate their activities to assure that their product will reach the consumer persuasively and efficiently. To bar a manufacturer from acting solely because the information upon which it acts originated as a price complaint would create an irrational dislocation in the market. . . .[8]

Thus, something more than evidence of complaints is needed. There must be evidence that tends to exclude the possibility that the manufacturer and nonterminated distributors were acting independently. As Judge Aldisert has written, the antitrust plaintiff should present direct or circumstantial evidence that reasonably tends to prove that the manufacturer and others "had a conscious commitment to a common scheme designed to achieve an unlawful objective." Cf.

---

[8] We do not suggest that evidence of complaints has no probative value at all, but only that the burden remains on the antitrust plaintiff to introduce additional evidence sufficient to support a finding of an unlawful contract, combination, or conspiracy.

American Tobacco Co. v. United States, 328 U.S. 781, 810 (1946) (circumstances must reveal "a unity of purpose or a common design and understanding, or a meeting of minds in an unlawful arrangement").[9] . . .

Applying this standard to the facts of this case, we believe there was sufficient evidence for the jury reasonably to have concluded that Monsanto and some of its distributors were parties to an "agreement" or "conspiracy" to maintain resale prices and terminate price cutters. In fact there was substantial *direct* evidence of agreements to maintain prices. There was testimony from a Monsanto district manager, for example, that Monsanto on at least two occasions in early 1969, about five months after Spray-Rite was terminated, approached price-cutting distributors and advised that if they did not maintain the suggested resale price, they would not receive adequate supplies of Monsanto's new corn herbicide. When one of the distributors did not assent, this information was referred to the Monsanto regional office, and it complained to the distributor's parent company. There was evidence that the parent instructed its subsidiary to comply, and the distributor informed Monsanto that it would charge the suggested price. Evidence of this kind plainly is relevant and persuasive as to a meeting of minds.[10]

An arguably more ambiguous example is a newsletter from one of the distributors to his dealer-customers. The newsletter is dated October 1, 1968, just four weeks before Spray-Rite was terminated. It was written after a meeting between the author and several Monsanto officials, and discusses Monsanto's efforts to "[get] the 'market place in order.'" The newsletter reviews some of Monsanto's incentive and shipping policies, and then states that in addition "every effort will be made to maintain a minimum market price level." The newsletter relates these efforts as follows:

> "In other words, we are assured that Monsanto's company-owned outlets will not retail at less than their suggested retail price to the trade as a whole. Furthermore, those of us on the distributor level are not likely to deviate downward on price to anyone as the idea is implied that doing this possibly could discolor the outlook for continuity as one of the approved distributors during the future upcoming seasons. So, none interested in the retention of this arrangement is likely to risk being deleted from this customer service opportunity. Also, as far as the national accounts are concerned, they are sure to recognize the desirability of retaining Monsanto's favor on a

[9] The concept of "a meeting of the minds" or "a common scheme" in a distributor-termination case includes more than a showing that the distributor conformed to the suggested price. It means as well that evidence must be presented both that the distributor communicated its acquiescence or agreement, and that this was sought by the manufacturer.

[10] In addition, there was circumstantial evidence that Monsanto sought agreement from the distributor to conform to the resale price. The threat to cut off the distributor's supply came during Monsanto's "shipping season" when herbicide was in short supply. The jury could have concluded that Monsanto sought this agreement at a time when it was able to use supply as a lever to force compliance.

continuing basis by respecting the wisdom of participating in the suggested program in a manner assuring order on the retail level 'playground' throughout the entire country. It is elementary that harmony can only come from following the rules of the game and that in case of dispute, the decision of the umpire is final."

It is reasonable to interpret this newsletter as referring to an agreement or understanding that distributors and retailers would maintain prices, and Monsanto would not undercut those prices on the retail level and would terminate competitors who sold at prices below those of complying distributors; these were "the rules of the game."[11] . . .

We conclude that the Court of Appeals applied an incorrect standard to the evidence in this case. The correct standard is that there must be evidence that tends to exclude the possibility of independent action by the manufacturer and distributor. That is, there must be direct or circumstantial evidence that reasonably tends to prove that the manufacturer and others had a conscious commitment to a common scheme designed to achieve an unlawful objective. Under this standard, the evidence in this case created a jury issue as to whether Spray-Rite was terminated pursuant to a price-fixing conspiracy between Monsanto and its distributors. The judgment of the court below is affirmed.

NOTES AND QUESTIONS ON *MONSANTO*

1. ***Should demand and acquiescence be deemed an agreement?*** *Monsanto* held that unilateral supplier demand followed by dealer acquiescence did not suffice to show an antitrust agreement. There are certainly reasons to doubt that distinction. The effects on dealer autonomy and resale decisions are likely to be the same from demand and acquiescence as they would be from a formal agreement. Nor is there even any real difference in penalty for violating the demanded condition, because even a formal contract fixing resale prices would have been unenforceable at the time, which was before *Leegin* overruled the per se rule against vertical price-fixing. Thus, for both a formal contract and for demand and acquiescence, the only enforceable penalty for noncompliance would be the supplier terminating future dealing with the noncomplying dealer.

Nonetheless, the Court's distinction made some policy sense, given that treating resale price demands and acquiescence as an agreement triggered per se illegality at the time. First, categorically condemning such demands and acquiescence had a major overdeterrence concern. Demand and acquiescence might be found when a supplier merely provides valuable

---

[11] The newsletter also is subject to the interpretation that the distributor was merely describing the likely reaction to unilateral Monsanto pronouncements. But Monsanto itself appears to have construed the flyer as reporting a price-fixing understanding. Six weeks after the newsletter was written, a Monsanto official wrote its author a letter urging him to "correct immediately any misconceptions about Monsanto's marketing policies." The letter disavowed any intent to enter into an agreement on resale prices. The interpretation of these documents and the testimony surrounding them properly was left to the jury.

suggestions about the optimal resale price (which could be mistaken for a demand) and then selects and retains the dealers it thinks are best, who might not surprisingly be those more likely to price at optimal levels (which could be mistaken for acquiescence). Deterring those price suggestions and dealer selections could be undesirable.

Second, demand and acquiescence may make certain anticompetitive effects less likely and thus lessens underdeterrence concerns. First, supplier demand following by dealer acquiescence suggests that the supplier is driving the agreement, which may make it less likely that the scheme reflects a dealer cartel or market power. Second, demands followed by a general pattern of dealer acquiescence may be more likely than formal agreements to produce some disuniformity in dealer prices. Such disuniformity makes it less likely that the scheme furthers oligopolistic price coordination, which requires precision on pricing because otherwise price differences can be misinterpreted as deviations from coordination.

None of this reasoning means that demand and acquiescence on prices is always desirable or never creates anticompetitive effects. But such reasoning indicates that, compared to other vertical agreements on price, demand and acquiescence raises greater overdeterrence concerns and lower underdeterrence concerns. That in turns suggests that bad net effects would flow from deeming such demand and acquiescence an agreement that triggered per se illegality.

However, this rationale for the *Monsanto* distinction made more sense at a time when vertical price-fixing was per se illegal. Overdeterrence concerns were greater then because treating price demands and acquiescence as agreements triggered per se illegality. Per se illegality also meant that varying levels of underdeterrence concerns could not be addressed by simply considering the level of anticompetitive effect under the rule of reason. Instead, the *Monsanto* Court had to make the all-or-nothing choice of concluding that price demands and acquiescence were either agreements (and thus categorically illegal) or nonagreements (and thus categorically legal). After *Leegin*, a holding that demand and acquiescence constitutes an agreement would simply trigger a rule-of-reason review that would consider any evidence that anticompetitive effects are weak and procompetitive justifications are likely in the case at hand. Given that, should courts now treat demands and acquiescence as a vertical agreement?

2. ***Should supplier termination in response to dealer complaints about price-cutting suffice to infer an agreement?*** *Monsanto* also held that a vertical price-fixing agreement could not be inferred from a supplier's decision to terminate a dealer in response to complaints by other dealers about that dealer's price-cutting. One reason not to infer an agreement is that suppliers have independent incentives to curb free-riding by dealers, which could lead suppliers to unilaterally decide to terminate a dealer in response to dealer complaints about its price-cutting, even if the supplier never had any price-fixing agreement with dealers. Further, even if there is no price-fixing agreement, dealer complaints about other dealers' pricing are inevitable. When a dealer free rides by offering lower services and cutting prices, other dealers are unlikely to complain

about the lower services, because that is not what takes away their business. Their compliant will likely instead focus on the price cutting that does take away their business. Given the inevitability of dealer complaints about other dealer's pricing, supplier terminations of dealers will often be preceded by such dealer complaints, even when the supplier is actually making a unilateral decision about which dealers it wants to use based on their services or other factors. If any dealer termination that followed another dealer's price complaint sufficed to infer a vertical price-fixing agreement, that could restrain the freedom of suppliers to select their dealers, especially back when such an agreement was per se illegal.

3. ***What was the Court's test for what <u>does</u> suffice to establish an agreement?*** The Court's general standard was that to show an agreement, the evidence cannot be just as consistent with conspiracy as with independent action; rather the evidence must at least tend to exclude the possibility of independent action. However, that general standard would seem to be met by demand and acquiescence. After all, the supplier's view that demanding conformance was necessary, coupled with the evidence that the dealers acquiesced to that demand, tend to exclude independent decisionmaking about resale prices. However, given that the Court concludes that demand and acquiescence is not an agreement, the Court must mean something more specific than this general standard.

The Court suggested a more specific test in footnote 9, stating that, at least in distributor termination cases, proving an agreement required evidence "both that the distributor communicated its acquiescence or agreement, and that this was sought by the manufacturer." Mere demand and acquiescence would not suffice to meet that test, because (1) acquiescence might occur without being communicated or (2) the supplier may not seek any communication about that acquiescence.

However, the Court then found an agreement even though the evidence it cited did not actually meet its footnote 9 test. Much of the evidence showed communication only of the demand, not of the acquiescence. For example, the Court pointed to evidence that the supplier twice told price-cutting distributors that they would not receive adequate supplies if they continued to deviate from suggested retail prices. All that shows is that the supplier communicated the demand, which occurs in all demand and acquiescence cases. It shows no communication of acquiescence. Likewise, the Court relied on evidence that the supplier made a threat to cut off a noncomplying dealer during a time of shortage, thus suggesting that the timing was designed to secure compliance. All that shows is that the demand was intended to be effective, which is true of all demands. It provides no evidence that acquiescence was communicated.

Other evidence indicated that both demand and acquiescence were communicated, but provided no proof that the supplier *sought* communication of the acquiescence. For example, the Court relied on evidence that the supplier made complaints to the parent of one noncomplying dealer, the parent told the dealer to comply, and the dealer informed the supplier that the dealer would charge the suggested retail price. While that shows the dealer communicated acquiescence, it provides no evidence that the supplier sought any communication about acquiescence. The supplier could have been just as happy (if not more) with actual acquiescence without hearing any assurances about that acquiescence, especially since the supplier is likely trying to avoid making a per se illegal agreement. Similarly, the Court cited evidence that a newsletter from a distributor to its dealer-customers stated that the distributor was assured that the supplier's company-owned stores would not retail for less than the suggested retail price and that no distributor was likely to deviate because deviation risked termination. That newsletter suggested there was likely some communication of a demand that led the distributor to conclude that deviation risked termination. That newsletter also arguably suggested communication of acquiescence by at least this one distributor, though that is debatable because the distributor simply predicted compliance was likely without committing to compliance itself. But nothing in that newsletter indicated that the supplier had sought any communication about acquiescence. The Court stressed the additional fact that, after the newsletter was circulated, the supplier immediately sent the author a letter disavowing any agreement and asking the author to correct any misimpression along those lines. The Court argued that this supplier letter indicated that the supplier itself construed the newsletter as reporting a price-fixing understanding. However, the supplier letter could instead simply indicate that the supplier was (it turns out, rightly) worried someone might mistakenly get that impression and wanted to make it crystal clear that the supplier had *not* sought this arguable communication of acquiescence and indeed was annoyed about seeing it communicated.

The Court thus did not seem to take literally its dicta in footnote 9 about finding an agreement in an intrabrand distribution case only when communications about acquiescence both occur and are sought by the supplier. However, the evidence recounted above does establish that Monsanto went beyond general demands followed by dealer acquiescence, showing that Monsanto also engaged in *individualized* exhortation to induce noncomplying dealers back into line. Given that the Court found such evidence sufficient to show an agreement, the Court's actual holding is thus that demand and acquiescence can suffice if coupled with individualized exhortations to comply.

At the time, it made some policy sense to conclude that an agreement could be established by showing either (1) the supplier seeking and obtaining dealer assurances or (2) individualized supplier exhortations to induce dealer compliance. First, as with the seeking and obtaining of assurances, individualized exhortations are less likely than general demands and acquiescence to be confused with mere supplier price suggestions followed by decisions about which dealers to select or retain. Overdeterrence concerns are thus weaker. Second, as with the seeking and obtaining of assurances, individualized exhortations are more likely to assure uniform compliance and thus create the sort of price precision needed to facilitate oligopolistic coordination, which is the biggest anticompetitive concern because it affects interbrand competition. Underdeterrence concerns are thus greater. Accordingly, treating demands and acquiescence as agreements only when there are either individualized exhortations or the seeking and obtaining or assurances would trigger per se illegality in cases where overdeterrence concerns are weaker and underdeterrence concerns are greater.

However, again, this made more sense back when treating a class of conduct as an agreement triggered per se illegality, thus requiring categorical judgments. After *Leegin*, it may make more sense to treat all demands and acquiescence as agreements, whether or not they involve individualized exhortation or seeking and obtaining assurances, given that doing so now triggers a rule-of-reason review that can consider any anticompetitive effects and procompetitive justifications in specific cases.

C. STANDARDS FOR FINDING A HORIZONTAL AGREEMENT OR CONCERTED ACTION

An explicit agreement is clearly covered under U.S. law even without parallel conduct. But because horizontal agreements restraining competition are generally illegal, explicit evidence of them is often hard to come by. Thus, the more usual and more difficult issue is when to infer an agreement or concerted action from circumstances given parallel conduct.

In U.S. caselaw, the terms "agreement" and "concerted action" are generally used interchangeably to refer to the sort of joint decision covered by Sherman Act § 1, as distinguished from the sort of separate decisions covered only by Sherman Act § 2. U.S. law instead focuses on a distinction between (a) parallel separate action and (b) agreement/concerted action. However, the conclusions drawn about this distinction in the cases often seem obscure or conclusory. We can clarify the analysis by breaking down the problem into various sorts of situations, each of which will be illustrated by the excerpted cases that follow below.

(1) In some cases the parallel conduct is at least equally consistent with an independent motive that each firm would pursue regardless of what the other firms did. In such cases, we shall see there is no agreement or concerted action under U.S. law.

(2) In other cases, the parallel conduct would be unprofitable if other firms did not engage in the same conduct. These cases are tricky because firms might engage in such parallel conduct either because they have a hidden express agreement or because they are in an oligopolistic market and recognize their price interdependence. We can break this set down into three further sets of cases. (a) Sometimes, such parallel conduct seems unlikely without a hidden express agreement, in which case an agreement will be inferred under U.S. law. (b) Other times, the parallel conduct follows common invitations or secret meetings, in which case an agreement can again be inferred under U.S. law. (c) Finally, sometimes, such parallel conduct likely reflects separate decisions that take into account price interdependence on oligopolistic markets. U.S.

law holds that pure oligopolistic price coordination does not involve an agreement or concerted action. The basis for this conclusion probably lies less in the belief than such coordination does not involve a joint understanding that could be understood as an agreement, than in the realization that firms on oligopolistic markets cannot avoid knowing their prices are interdependent when they set their prices. Thus, it would be hard to define any prohibition on oligopolistic price coordination in a way that tells firms how to behave.

(3) On the other hand, U.S. law does ban agreements or concerted practices (like bans on secret discounts) that facilitate oligopolistic coordination by making it easier for oligopolists to settle on common price and notice and respond to deviations. Even the interdependent adoption of such facilitating practices has been condemned as an illegal agreement. The reason appears to be that such facilitating agreements or practices can be avoided, and thus condemned in a meaningful way.

Further, avoidable practices that facilitate oligopolistic coordination can be illegal even when purely unilateral under FTC Act § 5.

1. PARALLEL CONDUCT CONSISTENT WITH AN INDEPENDENT MOTIVE

Theatre Enterprises v. Paramount Film Distributing

346 U.S. 537 (1954).

■ MR. JUSTICE CLARK delivered the opinion of the Court.

Petitioner brought this suit ... alleging that respondent motion picture producers and distributors had violated the antitrust laws by conspiring to restrict "first-run" pictures to downtown Baltimore theatres, thus confining its suburban theatre to subsequent runs and unreasonable "clearances."[5] After hearing the evidence a jury returned a general verdict for respondents. The Court of Appeals affirmed ... Petitioner ... urges ... that the trial judge should have directed a verdict in its favor ...

[P]etitioner owns and operates the Crest Theatre, located in a neighborhood shopping district some six miles from the downtown shopping center in Baltimore, Maryland. The Crest, possessing the most modern improvements and appointments, opened on February 26, 1949. Before and after the opening, petitioner, through its president, repeatedly sought to obtain first-run features for the theatre. Petitioner approached each respondent separately, initially requesting exclusive first-runs, later asking for first-runs [at the same time as a downtown

---

[5] "A clearance is the period of time, usually stipulated in license contracts, which must elapse between runs of the same feature within a particular area or in specified theatres."

theatre] . . . But respondents uniformly rebuffed petitioner's efforts and adhered to an established policy of restricting first-runs in Baltimore to the eight downtown theatres. Admittedly there is no direct evidence of illegal agreement between the respondents and no conspiracy is charged as to the independent exhibitors in Baltimore, who account for 63% of first-run exhibitions. The various respondents advanced much the same reasons for denying petitioner's offers. Among other reasons, they asserted that [simultaneous] first-runs are normally granted only to noncompeting theatres. Since the Crest is in "substantial competition" with the downtown theatres, a [simultaneous] arrangement would be economically unfeasible. And even if respondents wished to grant petitioner such a license, no downtown exhibitor would waive his clearance rights over the Crest and agree to a simultaneous showing. As a result, if petitioner were to receive first-runs, the license would have to be an exclusive one. However, an exclusive license would be economically unsound because the Crest is a suburban theatre, located in a small shopping center, and served by limited public transportation facilities; and, with a drawing area of less than one-tenth that of a downtown theatre, it cannot compare with those easily accessible theatres in the power to draw patrons. Hence the downtown theatres offer far greater opportunities for the widespread advertisement and exploitation of newly released features, which is thought necessary to maximize the over-all return from subsequent runs as well as first-runs. The respondents, in the light of these conditions, attacked the guaranteed offers of petitioner, one of which occurred during the trial, as not being made in good faith. Respondents Loew's and Warner refused petitioner an exclusive license because they owned the three downtown theatres receiving their first-run product.

The crucial question is whether respondents' conduct toward petitioner stemmed from independent decision or from an agreement, tacit or express. To be sure, business behavior is admissible circumstantial evidence from which the fact finder may infer agreement. But this Court has never held that proof of parallel business behavior conclusively establishes agreement or, phrased differently, that such behavior itself constitutes a Sherman Act offense. Circumstantial evidence of consciously parallel behavior may have made heavy inroads into the traditional judicial attitude toward conspiracy; but "conscious parallelism" has not yet read conspiracy out of the Sherman Act entirely. Realizing this, petitioner attempts to bolster its argument for a directed verdict by urging that the conscious unanimity of action by respondents should be "measured against the background and findings in the *Paramount* case." In other words, since the same respondents had conspired in the *Paramount* case to impose a uniform system of runs and clearances without adequate explanation to sustain them as reasonable restraints of trade, use of the same device in the present case should be legally equated to conspiracy. But the *Paramount* decrees, even if admissible, were only prima facie evidence of a conspiracy covering the area and existing during the period there involved. Alone or in conjunction with the other proof of the petitioner, they would form no basis for a directed verdict. Here each of the respondents had denied the existence of any collaboration and in addition had introduced evidence of the local conditions surrounding the Crest operation which, they contended, precluded it from being a successful first-run house. They also attacked the good faith of the guaranteed offers of the petitioner for first-run pictures and attributed uniform action to individual business judgment motivated by the desire for maximum revenue. This evidence, together with other testimony of an explanatory nature, raised fact issues requiring the trial judge to submit the issue of conspiracy to the jury . . . *Affirmed.*

NOTES AND QUESTIONS ON *THEATRE ENTERPRISES*

1. ***Was there an independent business reason that would explain the parallel conduct?*** Yes, each film distributor had independent business incentives to refuse first-run rights to the suburban theatre. The downtown theatres insisted on exclusive licenses, and if any individual distributor had to choose between giving an exclusive first-run license to a downtown theatre or to a suburban theatre, the downtown theatre was preferable because it would offer a greater return and provide better advertisement. This business reason is independent because it does not depend on other firms making the same choice. Indeed, if other film distributors decided to instead engage in nonparallel conduct by giving first-run rights to the suburban theatre, an individual distributor would be even better off because that would reduce the competition it faces in the more profitable downtown market. Thus, the film distributors had no economic incentive to form the alleged agreement.

2. ***If this were deemed a horizontal agreement, how could a film distributor avoid entering into one?*** If the parallel refusals to deal were deemed a horizontal agreement, a film distributor could avoid entering into such an agreement only by instead giving first-run rights to the suburban theatre. That would be undesirable because, if they have independent business reasons not to do so, this forces them into inefficient contracts.

3. ***What is the relevance of the prior conspiracy?*** The suburban theatre argued that a conspiracy should be inferred because the same film distributors had previously been found guilty of another conspiracy. However, as the Court ruled, prior conspiracies are relevant, but not determinative of the existence of the new agreement. A prior conspiracy is relevant for several reasons: (1) If the firms have conspired before, that suggests they found conspiring profitable and thus are more likely to have made similar calculations here. (2) It is probably easier to extend existing illegal relationships to other related illegal activities than to create new illegal relationships. (3) A prior conspiracy that has been caught will likely make a firm cautious about creating records, and can thus help explain a lack of documentation about the currently alleged conspiracy. But prior conspiracies cannot be determinative because independent reasons might explain the new parallel conduct. If the law instead provided that, once firms have conspired, all their subsequent parallel behavior would be deemed a conspiracy, then the law would require those firms to avoid efficient parallel behavior that was motivated by independent business reasons. Such a legal requirement would harm consumer welfare. These sorts of concerns thus limit the relevance of prior conspiracies.

Matsushita Electric v. Zenith Radio

475 U.S. 574 (1986).

■ JUSTICE POWELL delivered the opinion of the Court . . .

[Respondents Zenith Radio and Emerson Radio are U.S. television manufacturers. Petitioners are 21 corporations that made or sold Japanese television and other "consumer electronic products" (CEPs). Respondents claimed] that petitioners had illegally conspired to drive American firms from the American CEP market. According to respondents, the gist of this conspiracy was a " 'scheme to raise, fix and maintain artificially *high* prices for television receivers sold by [petitioners] in Japan and, at the same time, to fix and maintain *low* prices for television receivers exported to and sold in the United States.' " These "low prices" were allegedly at levels that produced substantial losses for petitioners. The conspiracy allegedly began as early as 1953, and according to respondents was in full operation by sometime in the late 1960's . . . The District Court . . . court found that the admissible evidence did not raise a genuine issue of material fact as to the existence of the alleged conspiracy . . . The Court of Appeals . . . reversed. . . .

We begin by emphasizing what respondents' claim is *not*. Respondents cannot recover antitrust damages based solely on an alleged cartelization of the Japanese market, because American antitrust laws do not regulate the competitive conditions of other nations' economies.[6] Nor can respondents recover damages for any conspiracy by petitioners to charge higher than competitive prices in the American market. Such conduct would indeed violate the Sherman Act, but it could not injure respondents: as petitioners' competitors, respondents stand to gain from any conspiracy to raise the market price in CEPs. Finally, for the same reason, respondents cannot recover for a conspiracy to impose nonprice restraints that have the effect of either raising market price or limiting output. Such restrictions, though harmful to competition, actually *benefit* competitors by making supra-competitive pricing more attractive . . .

Respondents nevertheless argue that these supposed conspiracies, if not themselves grounds for recovery of antitrust damages, are circumstantial evidence of another conspiracy that *is* cognizable: a conspiracy to monopolize the American market by means of pricing below the market level. The thrust of respondents' argument is that petitioners

[6] The Sherman Act does reach conduct outside our borders, but only when the conduct has an effect on American commerce.

used their monopoly profits from the Japanese market to fund a concerted campaign to price predatorily and thereby drive respondents and other American manufacturers of CEPs out of business. Once successful, according to respondents, petitioners would cartelize the American CEP market, restricting output and raising prices above the level that fair competition would produce. The resulting monopoly profits, respondents contend, would more than compensate petitioners for the losses they incurred through years of pricing below market level.

The Court of Appeals found that respondents' allegation of a horizontal conspiracy to engage in predatory pricing, if proved, would be a *per se* violation of § 1 of the Sherman Act.[8] Petitioners did not appeal from that conclusion. . . .

To survive petitioners' motion for summary judgment, respondents must establish that there is a genuine issue of material fact as to whether petitioners entered into an illegal conspiracy that caused respondents to suffer a cognizable injury . . . [I]f the factual context renders respondents' claim implausible—if the claim is one that simply makes no economic sense—respondents must come forward with more persuasive evidence to support their claim than would otherwise be necessary. . . .

Respondents correctly note that "[on] summary judgment the inferences to be drawn from the underlying facts . . . must be viewed in the light most favorable to the party opposing the motion." But antitrust law limits the range of permissible inferences from ambiguous evidence in a § 1 case. Thus, in *Monsanto,* we held that conduct as consistent with permissible competition as with illegal conspiracy does not, standing alone, support an inference of antitrust conspiracy. To survive a motion for summary judgment or for a directed verdict, a plaintiff seeking damages for a violation of § 1 must present evidence "that tends to exclude the possibility" that the alleged conspirators acted independently. *Monsanto.* Respondents in this case, in other words, must show that the inference of conspiracy is reasonable in light of the competing inferences of independent action or collusive action that could not have harmed respondents. . . .

A predatory pricing conspiracy is by nature speculative. Any agreement to price below the competitive level requires the conspirators to forgo profits that free competition would offer them. The forgone profits may be considered an investment in the future. For the investment to be rational, the conspirators must have a reasonable

---

8 . . . We need not resolve [the] debate [about the right cost measure in § 2 predatory pricing cases] here because unlike the cases cited above, this is a Sherman Act § 1 case. For purposes of this case, it is enough to note that respondents have not suffered an antitrust injury unless petitioners conspired to drive respondents out of the relevant markets by (i) pricing below the level necessary to sell their products, or (ii) pricing below some appropriate measure of cost. An agreement without these features would either leave respondents in the same position as would market forces or would actually benefit respondents by raising market prices. Respondents therefore may not complain of conspiracies that, for example, set maximum prices above market levels, or that set minimum prices at *any* level.

expectation of recovering, in the form of later monopoly profits, more than the losses suffered . . . [T]he success of such schemes is inherently uncertain: the short-run loss is definite, but the long-run gain depends on successfully neutralizing the competition. Moreover, it is not enough simply to achieve monopoly power, as monopoly pricing may breed quick entry by new competitors eager to share in the excess profits. The success of any predatory scheme depends on *maintaining* monopoly power for long enough both to recoup the predator's losses and to harvest some additional gain. Absent some assurance that the hoped-for monopoly will materialize, *and* that it can be sustained for a significant period of time, "[the] predator must make a substantial investment with no assurance that it will pay off." For this reason, there is a consensus among commentators that predatory pricing schemes are rarely tried, and even more rarely successful.

These observations apply even to predatory pricing by a *single firm* seeking monopoly power. In this case, respondents allege that a large number of firms have conspired over a period of many years to charge below-market prices in order to stifle competition. Such a conspiracy is incalculably more difficult to execute than an analogous plan undertaken by a single predator. The conspirators must allocate the losses to be sustained during the conspiracy's operation, and must also allocate any gains to be realized from its success. Precisely because success is speculative and depends on a willingness to endure losses for an indefinite period, each conspirator has a strong incentive to cheat, letting its partners suffer the losses necessary to destroy the competition while sharing in any gains if the conspiracy succeeds. The necessary allocation is therefore difficult to accomplish. Yet if conspirators cheat to any substantial extent, the conspiracy must fail, because its success depends on depressing the market price for *all* buyers of CEPs. If there are too few goods at the artificially low price to satisfy demand, the would-be victims of the conspiracy can continue to sell at the "real" market price, and the conspirators suffer losses to little purpose.

Finally, if predatory pricing conspiracies are generally unlikely to occur, they are especially so where, as here, the prospects of attaining monopoly power seem slight. In order to recoup their losses, petitioners must obtain enough market power to set higher than competitive prices, and then must sustain those prices long enough to earn in excess profits what they earlier gave up in below-cost prices. Two decades after their conspiracy is alleged to have commenced, petitioners appear to be far from achieving this goal: the two largest shares of the retail market in television sets are held by RCA and respondent Zenith, not by any of petitioners. Moreover, those shares, which together approximate 40% of sales, did not decline appreciably during the 1970's. Petitioners' collective share rose rapidly during this period, from one-fifth or less of the relevant markets to close to 50%. Neither the District Court nor the Court of Appeals found, however, that petitioners' share presently allows them to charge monopoly prices; to the contrary, respondents contend that the conspiracy is ongoing—that petitioners are still artificially *depressing* the market price in order to drive Zenith out of the market. The data in the record strongly suggest that that goal is yet far distant.[15]

The alleged conspiracy's failure to achieve its ends in the two decades of its asserted operation is strong evidence that the conspiracy does not in fact exist. Since the losses in such a conspiracy accrue before the gains, they must be "repaid" with interest. And because the alleged losses have accrued over the course of two decades, the conspirators could well require a correspondingly long time to recoup. Maintaining supracompetitive prices in turn depends on the continued cooperation of the conspirators, on the inability of other would-be competitors to enter the market, and (not incidentally) on the conspirators' ability to escape antitrust liability for their *minimum* price-fixing cartel. Each of these factors weighs more heavily as the time needed to recoup losses grows. If the losses have been substantial—as would likely be necessary in order to drive out the competition—petitioners would most likely have to sustain their cartel for years simply to break even.

Nor does the possibility that petitioners have obtained supracompetitive profits in the Japanese market change this calculation. Whether or not petitioners have the *means* to sustain substantial losses in this country over a long period of time, they have no *motive* to sustain such losses absent some strong likelihood that the alleged conspiracy in this country will eventually pay off. . . .

In *Monsanto*, we emphasized that courts should not permit factfinders to infer conspiracies when such inferences are implausible, because the effect of such practices is often to deter procompetitive conduct. Respondents, petitioners' competitors, seek to hold petitioners liable for damages caused by the alleged conspiracy to cut prices. Moreover, they seek to establish this conspiracy indirectly, through evidence of other combinations (such as the check-price agreements and the five company rule) whose natural tendency is to raise prices, and through evidence of rebates and other price-cutting activities that respondents argue tend to prove a combination to suppress prices. [The district court correctly found that an expert report finding below-cost pricing was unsupported by the evidence.] But cutting prices in order to increase business often is the very essence of competition. Thus, mistaken inferences in cases such as this one are especially costly, because they chill the very conduct the antitrust laws are designed to protect . . .

In most cases, this concern must be balanced against the desire that illegal conspiracies be identified and punished. That balance is, however, unusually one-sided in cases such as this one. As we earlier explained,

[15] Respondents offer no reason to suppose that entry into the relevant market is especially difficult, yet without barriers to entry it would presumably be impossible to maintain supracompetitive prices for an extended time. . . .

predatory pricing schemes require conspirators to suffer losses in order eventually to realize their illegal gains; moreover, the gains depend on a host of uncertainties, making such schemes more likely to fail than to succeed. These economic realities tend to make predatory pricing conspiracies self-deterring: unlike most other conduct that violates the antitrust laws, failed predatory pricing schemes are costly to the conspirators. Finally, unlike predatory pricing by a single firm, *successful* predatory pricing conspiracies involving a large number of firms can be identified and punished once they succeed, since some form of minimum price-fixing agreement would be necessary in order to reap the benefits of predation. Thus, there is little reason to be concerned that by granting summary judgment in cases where the evidence of conspiracy is speculative or ambiguous, courts will encourage such conspiracies. . . .

As our discussion . . . shows, petitioners had no motive to enter into the alleged conspiracy. To the contrary, as presumably rational businesses, petitioners had every incentive *not* to engage in the conduct with which they are charged, for its likely effect would be to generate losses for petitioners with no corresponding gains. . . . The Court of Appeals erred in two respects: (i) the "direct evidence" on which the court relied had little, if any, relevance to the alleged predatory pricing conspiracy; and (ii) the court failed to consider the absence of a plausible motive to engage in predatory pricing.

The "direct evidence" on which the court relied was evidence of *other* combinations, not of a predatory pricing conspiracy. Evidence that petitioners conspired to raise prices in Japan provides little, if any, support for respondents' claims: a conspiracy to increase profits in one market does not tend to show a conspiracy to sustain losses in another. Evidence that petitioners agreed to fix *minimum* prices (through the check-price agreements) for the American market actually works in petitioners' favor, because it suggests that petitioners were seeking to place a floor under prices rather than to lower them. The same is true of evidence that petitioners agreed to limit the number of distributors of their products in the American market—the so-called five company rule. That practice may have facilitated a horizontal territorial allocation, but its natural effect would be to raise market prices rather than reduce them. Evidence that tends to support any of these collateral conspiracies thus says little, if anything, about the existence of a conspiracy to charge below-market prices in the American market over a period of two decades.

That being the case, the absence of any plausible motive to engage in the conduct charged is highly relevant to whether a "genuine issue for trial" exists . . . Lack of motive bears on the range of permissible conclusions that might be drawn from ambiguous evidence: if petitioners had no rational economic motive to conspire, and if their conduct is consistent with other, equally plausible explanations, the conduct does not give rise to an inference of conspiracy. Here, the conduct in question consists largely of (i) pricing at levels that succeeded in taking business away from respondents, and (ii) arrangements that may have limited petitioners' ability to compete with each other (and thus kept prices from going even lower). This conduct suggests either that petitioners behaved competitively, or that petitioners conspired to *raise* prices. Neither possibility is consistent with an agreement among 21 companies to price below market levels. Moreover, the predatory pricing scheme that this conduct is said to prove is one that makes no practical sense: it calls for petitioners to destroy companies larger and better established than themselves, a goal that remains far distant more than two decades after the conspiracy's birth. Even had they succeeded in obtaining their monopoly, there is nothing in the record to suggest that they could recover the losses they would need to sustain along the way. In sum, in light of the absence of any rational motive to conspire, neither petitioners' pricing practices, nor their conduct in the Japanese market, nor their agreements respecting prices and distribution in the American market, suffice to create a "genuine issue for trial."[21]

On remand, the Court of Appeals is free to consider whether there is other evidence that is sufficiently unambiguous to permit a trier of fact to find that petitioners conspired to price predatorily for two decades despite the absence of any apparent motive to do so. The evidence must "[tend] to exclude the possibility" that petitioners underpriced respondents to compete for business rather than to implement an economically senseless conspiracy. *Monsanto.* In the absence of such evidence, there is no "genuine issue for trial" under Rule 56(e), and petitioners are entitled to have summary judgment reinstated . . .

The decision of the Court of Appeals is reversed, and the case is remanded for further proceedings consistent with this opinion. *It is so ordered.*

NOTES AND QUESTIONS ON *MATSUSHITA*

1. ***Given the lack of evidence that any prices were below cost, was there parallel conduct and would any conspiracy be illegal?*** Yes, the alleged parallel conduct was charging low prices. Although unilateral above-cost low pricing does not violate the antitrust laws, *see Brooke,* a conspiracy to engage in it would be an antitrust violation because it would involve horizontal price-fixing.

2. ***Why cannot a conspiracy to charge low prices be inferred from the parallel conduct?*** The Court holds that, just as for a vertical agreement, showing a horizontal agreement requires evidence " 'that tends to exclude the possibility' that the alleged conspirators acted independently." This does not mean the evidence must make the possibility of independent

---

[21] We do not imply that, if petitioners had had a plausible reason to conspire, ambiguous conduct could suffice to create a triable issue of conspiracy. Our decision in *Monsanto* establishes that conduct that is as consistent with permissible competition as with illegal conspiracy does not, without more, support even an inference of conspiracy.

action 0%. It just means the evidence cannot be just "as consistent with" independent parallel action as with conspiracy. This holding goes beyond the ordinary burden of proof at trial, because the Court is holding that a plaintiff cannot even survive summary judgment if the alleged supporting evidence is equally consistent with independent action or conspiracy.

Here, the Court held that a collective incentive to engage in a conspiracy was implausible because the alleged conspiracy required (1) incurring two decades of losses with subcompetitive pricing, without end in sight, (2) allocating those losses among 21 conspirators who would want to shirk them; and (3) recouping those losses sometime in the future by successfully shifting to an illegal conspiracy to charge high prices after they drove out the U.S. firms, which would require escaping antitrust liability, preventing new entry, and allocating the gains among the 21 conspirators. It was more plausible that the parallel conduct just reflected individual incentives to charge low prices to get business.

3. ***Should courts infer a conspiracy to charge subcompetitive prices from evidence of either (a) a conspiracy to raise prices in Japan or (b) a conspiracy to fix minimum prices in the U.S.?*** No. (a) Even if the firms have reaped supracompetitive profits from a price-fixing cartel in Japan, that does not suggest a conspiracy to engage in subcompetitive pricing in the U.S. occurred or would be profitable. (b) If anything a conspiracy to fix minimum U.S. prices cuts the other way and helps the plaintiff rivals.

Cement Manufacturers Protective Ass'n v. United States

268 U.S. 588 (1925).

■ MR. JUSTICE STONE, delivered the opinion of the Court.

[The Cement Manufacturers' Protective Association and its member cement makers collected and disseminated to each other information about: (a) whether buyers with requirements contracts for specific jobs were taking more cement than the job required and (b) when buyers were delinquent on obligations to pay for cement. The district court enjoined these activities as a violation of Sherman Act § 1.] . . .

Specific Job Contracts . . .

The specific job contract is a form of contract in common use by manufacturers of cement [whereby contractors had the option to take future deliveries of cement at the contract price up to the quantity required for a specific job.] . . . It enables contractors to bid for future construction work with the assurance that the requisite cement will be available at a definitely ascertained maximum price.

In view of the option features of the contract referred to, the contractor is involved in no business risk if he enter into several specific job contracts with several manufacturers for the delivery of cement for a single specific job. The manufacturer, however, is under no moral or legal obligation to supply cement except such as is required for the specific job. If, therefore, the contractor takes advantage of his position and of the peculiar form of the specific job contract, as modified by the custom of the trade, to secure deliveries from each of several manufacturers of the full amount of cement required for the particular job, he in effect secures the future delivery of cement not required for the particular job, which he is not entitled to receive, which the manufacturer is under no legal or moral obligation to deliver, and which presumably he would not deliver if he had information that it was not to be used in accordance with his contract. The activities of the defendants complained of are directed toward securing this information and communicating it to members, and thus placing them in a position to prevent contractors from securing future deliveries of cement which they are not entitled to receive under their specific job contracts, and which experience shows they endeavor to procure especially in a rising market. . . .

Exchange of Information Concerning Credits

Members of the association render monthly reports of all accounts of customers two months or more over due, giving the name and address of the delinquent debtor; the amount of the overdue account in ledger balance; [and] accounts in hands of attorneys for collection. . . . There were never any comments concerning names appearing on the list of delinquent debtors. The government neither charged nor proved that there was any agreement with respect to the use of this information or with respect to the persons to whom or conditions under which credit should be extended. The evidence falls far short of establishing any understanding on the basis of which credit was to be extended to customers, or that any co-operation resulted from the distribution of this information, or that there were any consequences from it other than such as would naturally ensue from the exercise of the individual judgment of manufacturers in determining, on the basis of available information, whether to extend credit or to require cash or security from any given customer . . .

Legal Consequence of Defendants' Activities

. . . That a consequence of the gathering and dissemination of information with respect to the specific job contracts was to afford, to manufacturers of cement, opportunity and grounds for refusing deliveries of cement which the contractors were not entitled to call for, an opportunity of which manufacturers were prompt to avail themselves, is . . . not open to dispute. We do not see, however, in the activity of the defendants with respect to specific job contracts any basis for the contention that they constitute an unlawful restraint of commerce. The government does not rely on any agreement or understanding among members of the association that members would either make use of the specific job contract, or that they would refuse to deliver "excess" cement under specific job contracts. Members were left free to use this type of contract and to make such deliveries or not as they chose and the evidence . . . shows that in 1920 padded specific job contracts were cut down something less than two-thirds of the total amount of the padding as a result of the of gathering and reporting this information. It may be assumed, however, if manufacturers take the precaution to draw their sales contracts in such form that they are not to be required to deliver cement not needed for the specific jobs described in these contracts, that they would, to a considerable extent, decline to make deliveries, upon receiving information showing that the deliveries claimed were not called for by the contracts.

Unless the provisions in the contract are waived by the manufacturer, demand for and receipt of such deliveries by the contractor would be a fraud on the manufacturer, and in our view the gathering and dissemination of information which will enable sellers to prevent the perpetration of fraud upon them, which information they are free to act upon or not as they choose, cannot be held to be an unlawful restraint upon commerce, even though in the ordinary course of business most sellers would act on the information and refuse to make deliveries for which they were not legally bound . . .

Distribution of information as to credit and responsibility of buyers undoubtedly prevents fraud and cuts down to some degree commercial transactions which would otherwise be induced by fraud. . . . [W]e cannot regard the procuring and dissemination of information which tends to prevent the procuring of fraudulent contracts or to prevent the fraudulent securing of deliveries of merchandise on the pretense that the seller is bound to deliver it by his contract, as an unlawful restraint of trade even though such information be gathered and disseminated by those who are engaged in the trade or business principally concerned . . .

The judgment of the District Court is reversed.

NOTES AND QUESTIONS ON *CEMENT MANUFACTURERS*

1. ***Why would buyers want to buy more cement than they needed on a requirements contract?*** When market prices rise above the contract price, buyers would want to buy more cement than they needed in order to resell the extra cement at a profit. In doing so, they are imposing an option risk on the cement seller that was not contracted for because the contract limited purchases to the buyer's requirements.

2. ***Would an agreement not to sell to bad buyers be illegal?*** Yes, an agreement not to sell cement to bad buyers (here those who had bad credit or overbought cement on requirements contracts) would be a per se illegal horizontal boycott. Firms have good reasons not to deal with bad buyers, but firms have no reason why they could not make such decisions independently rather than collectively.

3. ***Can we infer an agreement not to sell to bad buyers from parallel conduct that followed the distribution of information?*** The parallel conduct here was that cement makers often cancelled contracts with bad buyers after receiving information that those buyers had bad credit or overbought cement on requirements contracts. But this parallel conduct does not suffice to infer an agreement. Any individual cement maker who knew a buyer had bad credit or was overbuying cement would have reasons to cease business with that buyer. These business reasons are independent because they do not depend on other firms making the same choice. Indeed, a cement maker would be even better off if their competitors engaged in nonparallel conduct: continuing to do business with the bad buyers, which would cause competitors to lose money by selling to buyers who were insolvent or overbought cement at below-market prices. Thus, cement makers had no economic incentive to form an agreement to refuse to deal with the bad buyers.

4. ***Was the agreement to circulate a list of bad buyers itself illegal?*** No, it is efficient and procompetitive to give cement makers information about buyer credit and overpurchases on requirements contracts, information that each cement maker can use to make its own independent decisions. Any relevant information that can make pricing more accurate is procompetitive. Disseminating such information also helps good buyers, because without information distinguishing types of buyers, cement sellers would have to charge all buyers higher contract prices to cover the fact that bad buyers impose a higher default rate and risk of overpurchases at below-market price. The dissemination of such information thus allows sellers to lower prices to good buyers and creates efficient incentives for buyers to avoid such inefficient conduct.

2. PARALLEL CONDUCT THAT WOULD BE UNPROFITABLE IF NOT ENGAGED IN BY OTHER FIRMS

a. WHEN THE PARALLEL CONDUCT IS UNLIKELY WITHOUT A HIDDEN EXPRESS AGREEMENT

Eastern States Retail Lumber Dealers' Ass'n v. United States

234 U.S. 600 (1914).

■ MR. JUSTICE DAY delivered the opinion of the court . . .

The defendants are various lumber associations composed largely of retail lumber dealers in New York, New Jersey, Pennsylvania, Connecticut, Massachusetts, Rhode Island, Maryland and the District of Columbia . . . [They collected information from their retailer members about which wholesalers were competing with those retailers by selling directly to consumers and circulated the lists of such wholesalers to each retailer member. The District Court enjoined these activities as a violation of Sherman Act § 1.]

. . . When viewed in the light of the history of these associations and the conflict in which they were engaged to keep the retail trade to themselves and to prevent wholesalers from interfering with what they regarded as their rights in such trade there can be but one purpose in giving the information in this form to the members of the retail associations of the names of all wholesalers who by their attempt to invade the exclusive territory of the retailers, as they regard it, have been guilty of unfair competitive trade. These lists were quite commonly spoken of as blacklists, and when the attention of a retailer was brought to the name of a wholesaler who had acted in this wise it was with the evident purpose that he should know of such conduct and act accordingly. True it is that there is no agreement among the retailers to refrain from dealing with listed wholesalers, nor is there any penalty annexed for the failure so to do, but he is blind indeed who does not see the purpose in the predetermined and periodical circulation of this report to put the ban upon wholesale dealers whose names appear in the list of unfair dealers trying by methods obnoxious to the retail dealers to supply the trade which they regard as their own. Indeed this purpose is practically conceded in the brief of the learned counsel for the appellants:

> "It was and is conceded by defendants and the Court below found that the circulation of this information would have a natural tendency to cause retailers receiving these reports to withhold patronage from listed concerns. That was of course the very object of the defendants in circulating them."

In other words, the circulation of such information among the hundreds of retailers as to the alleged delinquency of a wholesaler with one of their number had and was intended to have the natural effect of causing such retailers to withhold their patronage from the concern listed.

. . . Here are wholesale dealers in large number engaged in interstate trade upon whom it is proposed to impose as a condition of carrying on that trade that they shall not sell in such manner that a local retail dealer may regard such sale as an infringement of his exclusive right to trade, upon pain of being reported as an unfair dealer to a large number of other retail dealers associated with the offended dealer, the purpose being to keep the wholesaler from dealing not only with the particular dealer who reports him but with all others of the class who may be informed of his delinquency . . . This record abounds in instances where the offending dealer was thus reported, the hoped for effect, unless he discontinued the offending practice, realized, and his trade directly and appreciably impaired.

But it is said that in order to show a combination or conspiracy within the Sherman Act some agreement must be shown under which the concerted action is taken. It is elementary, however, that conspiracies are seldom capable of proof by direct testimony and may be inferred from the things actually done, and when in this case by concerted action the names of wholesalers who were reported as having made sales to consumers were periodically reported to the other members of the associations, the conspiracy to accomplish that which was the natural consequence of such action may be readily inferred . . .

NOTES AND QUESTIONS ON *EASTERN STATES LUMBER*

1. ***Could an agreement not to deal with offending firms be inferred from parallel conduct that followed the distribution of information?*** In both this case and *Cement Manufacturers*, the defendants circulated a list of offending firms and then engaged in the parallel conduct of often ceasing business with those offending firms. But no conspiracy not to deal with the offending firms was inferred in *Cement Manufacturers*. What is the difference?

The difference is that, unlike in *Cement Mfrs*, in this case there was no independent incentive to cease dealing with the offending firms. An individual retailer who receives information that a wholesaler is competing at retail has no independent financial incentive to stop doing business with that wholesaler. Whatever the other retailers do, it would be profitable for an individual retailer to keep doing business with such a wholesaler whenever it offers the best price.

Retailers as a group might have a *collective* incentive to boycott the offending wholesalers, because such a boycott might persuade those wholesalers to stop competing at retail. But assuming a large number of retailers, a decision by a single retailer to stop doing business with such wholesalers is unlikely to significantly affect whether those wholesalers compete at retail. Instead, the wholesalers would continue competing at retail unless enough *other* retailers boycott the wholesalers to persuade them otherwise, and if that happens the wholesalers' exit from retail will benefit each retailer regardless of whether that retailer itself participated in the boycott. Thus, given a large number of retailers, it was implausible that collective incentives would motivate the parallel conduct without a hidden express conspiracy to boycott wholesalers who appeared on the list.

2. ***Was the agreement to circulate a list of offending buyers itself illegal?*** It seems so, because while the Court noted that circulating the list often did lead many retailers to stop doing business with the listed wholesalers, the Court mainly stressed that the conspiracy could be inferred from the circulation of the list itself, which the Court enjoined. As the Court stressed, there would have been no purpose in circulating the list unless the associations thought retailers would respond by ceasing to do business with such wholesalers. Further, given the reasoning above, the associations would have had no reason to think that circulating the list would lead retailers to cease doing business with wholesalers on the list unless there were some hidden express agreement to boycott them. Thus, one could infer an agreement to boycott wholesalers on the list from the circulation of the list itself. However, the reason one can draw that inference is not, as the Court seemed to think, that such parallel refusals to deal were a "natural effect" or "natural consequence" of the circulation of the list. To the contrary, the reason is that such parallel refusals to deal were so *unnatural*, given individual incentives, that circulating the list made sense only if there were

an agreement to boycott wholesalers on the list. By contrast, in *Cement Manufacturers* circulating the list did naturally lead to parallel conduct because of individual incentives, so no conspiracy could be inferred.

American Tobacco v. United States

328 U.S. 781 (1946).

■ MR. JUSTICE BURTON delivered the opinion of the Court.

The petitioners are The American Tobacco Company, Liggett & Myers Tobacco Company, R. J. Reynolds Tobacco Company, . . . and certain officials of the respective companies who were convicted by a jury . . . of violating §§ 1 and 2 of the Sherman Anti-Trust Act . . . Each petitioner was fined $5,000 on each of the other counts, making $15,000 for each petitioner and a total of $255,000 . . . The Circuit Court of Appeals . . . affirmed each conviction.

. . . [A]lthough American, Liggett and Reynolds gradually dropped in their percentage of the national domestic cigarette production from 90.7% in 1931 to 73.3%, 71% and 68%, respectively, in 1937, 1938 and 1939, they have accounted at all times for more than 68%, and usually for more than 75%, of the national production. The balance of the cigarette production has come from six other companies. No one of those six ever has produced more than the 10.6% once reached by Brown & Williamson in 1939 . . .

The verdicts show . . . that the jury found that the petitioners conspired to fix prices . . . in the distribution and sale of their principal products. The petitioners sold and distributed their products to jobbers and to selected dealers who bought at list prices, less discounts . . . The list prices charged and the discounts allowed by petitioners have been practically identical since 1923 and absolutely identical since 1928. Since the latter date, only seven changes have been made by the three companies and those have been identical in amount. The increases were first announced by Reynolds. American and Liggett thereupon increased their list prices in identical amounts.

The following record of price changes is circumstantial evidence of the existence of a conspiracy and of a power and intent to exclude competition coming from cheaper grade cigarettes. During the two years preceding June, 1931, the petitioners produced 90% of the total cigarette production in the United States. In that month tobacco farmers were receiving the lowest prices for their crops since 1905. The costs to the petitioners for tobacco leaf, therefore, were lower than usual during the past 25 years, and their manufacturing costs had been declining. It was one of the worst years of financial and economic depression in the history of the country. On June 23, 1931, Reynolds, without previous notification or warning to the trade or public, raised the list price of Camel cigarettes, constituting its leading cigarette brand, from $6.40 to $6.85 a thousand. The same day, American increased the list price for Lucky Strike cigarettes, its leading brand, and Liggett the price for Chesterfield cigarettes, its leading brand, to the identical price of $6.85 a thousand. No economic justification for this raise was demonstrated. The president of Reynolds stated that it was "to express our own courage for the future and our own confidence in our industry." The president of American gave as his reason for the increase, "the opportunity of making some money." He further claimed that because Reynolds had raised its list price, Reynolds would therefore have additional funds for advertising and American had raised its price in order to have a similar amount for advertising. The officials of Liggett claimed that they thought the increase was a mistake as there did not seem to be any reason for making a price advance but they contended that unless they also raised their list price for Chesterfields, the other companies would have greater resources to spend in advertising and thus would put Chesterfield cigarettes at a competitive disadvantage. This general price increase soon resulted in higher retail prices and in a loss in volume of sales. Yet in 1932, in the midst of the national depression with the sales of the petitioners' cigarettes falling off greatly in number, the petitioners still were making tremendous profits as a result of the price increase. Their net profits in that year amounted to more than $100,000,000. This was one of the three biggest years in their history . . .

There was evidence that when dealers received an announcement of the price increase from one of the petitioners and attempted to purchase some of the leading brands of cigarettes from the other petitioners at their unchanged prices before announcement of a similar change, the latter refused to fill such orders until their prices were also raised, thus bringing about the same result as if the changes had been precisely simultaneous . . .

It is not the form of the combination or the particular means used but the result to be achieved that the statute condemns. It is not of importance whether the means used to accomplish the unlawful objective are in themselves lawful or unlawful. Acts done to give effect to the conspiracy may be in themselves wholly innocent acts. Yet, if they are part of the sum of the acts which are relied upon to effectuate the conspiracy which the statute forbids, they come within its prohibition. No formal agreement is necessary to constitute an unlawful conspiracy. Often crimes are a matter of inference deduced from the acts of the person accused and done in pursuance of a criminal purpose . . . The essential combination or conspiracy in violation of the Sherman Act may be found in a course of dealings or other circumstances as well as in any exchange of words. Where the circumstances are such as to warrant a jury in finding that the conspirators had a unity of purpose or a common design and understanding, or a meeting of minds in an unlawful arrangement, the conclusion that a conspiracy is established is justified . . .

NOTES AND QUESTIONS ON *AMERICAN TOBACCO*

1. ***Should oligopolistic price coordination itself be deemed a conspiracy?*** Suppose you are one of three oligopolists, and one firm announces it will raise prices by 10%. If you do not announce you will match that price increase, then it is predictable that the first firm would rescind its price increase. Suppose you take this prediction into account and thus decide to match the first firm's announced price increase without ever discussing anything with the first firm. Should that be deemed an antitrust conspiracy?

As we shall see, the answer under U.S. antitrust law is no, such oligopolistic price coordination is not itself an antitrust conspiracy. But why? Despite formalistic claims that coordination is inherently different from agreement, the oligopolists have reached a mutual understanding that the law could call an "agreement." Further, it seems to make policy sense to condemn such price coordination because it is harmful to efficiency and consumer welfare. However, the problem with trying to condemn price coordination is that firms cannot avoid setting prices and understanding their price interdependence when they choose what prices to set. The law would thus have a hard time defining the violation. What would the law tell firms to do: set prices without thinking about the likely reaction of their rivals? It would be hard for firms to put aside their knowledge or for courts to know when they have done so. The law could instead focus on the price levels, requiring firms to set the prices they would have set if their prices were not interdependent. But that would force courts to set sail on the sea of doubt of deciding on a reasonable price. Even if the courts were willing to do so, there are no clear objective standards for determining how far above cost prices should be.

2. ***Given that pure price coordination is not an agreement, why did the Court infer an agreement in* American Tobacco*?*** The Court does not clearly explain its criteria for inferring an agreement, but its holding has two plausible interpretations. The first is that the Court thought it was unlikely that pure oligopolistic coordination would lead to precisely parallel price increases for decades, often on the same day, despite declining demand and costs and even during the Great Depression. That might be too much precision and effectiveness to expect from mere oligopolistic coordination, given the constant incentives to cheat on the supracompetitive prices. If such precision and effectiveness is unlikely with pure coordination, then it indicates that a hidden express agreement likely existed. Cutting against this interpretation is the fact that, without any hidden express agreement, it would seem rational for American and Liggett to adopt a strategy of immediately matching any price increase by Reynolds. Given that, such precise and effective price matching could be equally consistent with oligopolistic coordination.

The second interpretation is that, given that the parallel pricing was actually consistent with oligopolistic coordination, the Court effectively held that an agreement should be inferred when parallel pricing is equally consistent with a hidden express agreement or oligopolistic coordination. Such an interpretation is consistent with the later decisions in *Matsushita* and *Monsanto*, which held only that an agreement should not be inferred when the evidence is equally consistent with hidden conspiracy or *independent* action. Indeed, if parallel conduct is equally consistent with hidden conspiracy or coordination, then that affirmatively indicates it is more consistent with hidden conspiracy than with independent action, thus satisfying the *Matsushita/Monsanto* standard for finding an agreement.

The distinction can also be explained by the different effects of inferring a conspiracy in these different situations. *Matsushita* and *Monsanto* have the powerful rationale that finding an agreement in such situations would mistakenly overdeter efficient independent action. Further, when the parallel conduct can be explained by independent incentives, the firms have no motive for collective action and thus no reason to want to reach an agreement. Thus, the concern about underdeterring hidden express agreements is low.

In contrast, when the evidence is just as consistent with hidden express agreement as with oligopolistic coordination, finding an agreement would not overdeter any desirable conduct. To be sure, finding an agreement in such cases would deter oligopolistic coordination that was precise and effective enough to resemble the results of a hidden express agreement. But while we cannot quite define a legal offense about coordination, such coordination remains undesirable, so there is no harm from deterring it. The worst that would happen is that, to avoid a finding of agreement, the oligopolists may occasionally avoid price matching to make their coordination more imprecise and less effective, but that consequence would be socially desirable and could help unravel oligopolistic pricing, which generally depends on precision. While some price coordination is unavoidable, really precise price coordination can be avoided.

Moreover, the underdeterrence concerns are also greater in cases where parallel conduct could be explained equally by either hidden express agreement or by oligopolistic coordination. The reason is that, whenever a hidden express agreement does exist in an oligopolistic market, the defendants can typically argue that the parallel conduct could be explained by coordination. Thus, without a doctrine allowing an agreement to be inferred in cases where parallel conduct fits a collective motive that is equally consistent with either hidden express conspiracy or oligopolistic coordination, hidden agreements would be underdeterred. Indeed, without such a doctrine, hidden express agreements would perversely be harder to prove in concentrated markets than in unconcentrated markets.

To put it another way, the holding in *American Tobacco* seems to be that, although oligopolistic coordination is not itself an antitrust violation, it also is not a defense to a claim of horizontal price-fixing. Thus, even though the parallel pricing was just as consistent with oligopolistic coordination as with hidden express conspiracy, *American Tobacco* inferred a conspiracy. This result may seem harsh because the defendant is equally likely to have engaged in price coordination that would not be illegal. But such price coordination actually does involve a mutual understanding that could satisfy the agreement requirement and that has undesirable anticompetitive effects. It is not being treated as such only because some price coordination seems unavoidable. But really precise price coordination is avoidable. Further, here the parallel pricing is equally likely to result from a hidden conspiracy that would constitute a crime.

However, it remains the law that oligopolistic coordination is not alone illegal. Thus, when the parallel conduct involves only the sort of imprecise price matching in an oligopolistic market that is affirmatively more likely to reflect oligopolistic coordination than hidden express agreement, it remains the case that no antitrust violation can be found.

b. WHEN THE PARALLEL CONDUCT FOLLOWS COMMON INVITATIONS OR SECRET MEETINGS

Interstate Circuit v. United States

306 U.S. 208 (1939).

■ MR. JUSTICE STONE delivered the opinion of the Court . . .

[The district court found that appellants agreed with each other to enter into and carry out the contracts that were unreasonable restraints of trade] . . . The [eight] distributor appellants are engaged in the business of distributing in interstate commerce motion picture films, copyrights on which they own or control, for exhibition in theatres throughout the United States. They distribute about 75% of all first-class feature films exhibited in the United States. They solicit from motion picture theatre owners and managers in Texas and other states applications for licenses to exhibit films, and forward the applications, when received from such exhibitors, to their respective New York offices, where they are accepted or rejected . . .

The exhibitor group of appellants consists of Interstate Circuit, Inc., and Texas Consolidated Theatres, Inc., and . . . are affiliated with each other and with Paramount Pictures Distributing Co., Inc., one of the distributor appellants. [Interstate and Texas Consolidated collectively had a monopoly on first-run theatres in many Texas cities, but in many (but not all) of these cities there were rival second-run theatres.]

On July 11, 1934, following a previous communication on the subject to the eight branch managers of the distributor appellants, O'Donnell, the manager of Interstate and Consolidated, sent to each of them a letter on the letterhead of Interstate, each letter naming all of them as addressees, in which he asked compliance with two demands as a condition of Interstate's continued exhibition of the distributors' films in its "A" or first-run theatres at a night admission of 40 cents or more. One demand was that the distributors "agree that in selling their product to subsequent runs, that this 'A' product will never be exhibited at any time or in any theatre at a smaller admission price than 25 cents for adults in the evening." The other was that "on 'A' pictures which are exhibited at a night admission of 40 cents or more—they shall never be exhibited in conjunction with another feature picture under the so-called policy of double features." The letter added that with respect to the "Rio Grande Valley situation," with which Consolidated alone was concerned, "We must insist that all pictures exhibited in our 'A' theatres at a maximum night admission price of 35 cents must also be restricted to subsequent runs in the Valley at 25 cents."

The admission price customarily charged for preferred seats at night in independently operated subsequent-run theatres in Texas at the time of these letters was less than 25 cents . . . In most of them the admission was 15 cents or less. It was also the general practice in those theatres to provide double bills either on certain days of the week or with any feature picture which was weak in drawing power. The distributor appellants had generally provided in their license contracts for a minimum admission price of 10 or 15 cents, and three of them had included provisions restricting double-billing. But none was at any time previously subject to contractual compulsion to continue the restrictions. The trial court found that the proposed restrictions constituted an important departure from prior practice.

The local representatives of the distributors, having no authority to enter into the proposed agreements, communicated the proposal to their home offices. Conferences followed between Hoblitzelle and O'Donnell, acting for Interstate and Consolidated, and the representatives of the various distributors. In these conferences each distributor was represented by its local branch manager and by one or more superior officials from outside the state of Texas. In the course of them each distributor agreed with Interstate for the 1934–35 season to impose both the demanded restrictions upon their subsequent-run licensees in the six Texas cities served by Interstate, except Austin and Galveston. . . . None of the distributors yielded to the demand that subsequent runs in towns in the Rio Grande Valley served by Consolidated should be restricted. One distributor, Paramount, which was affiliated with Consolidated, agreed to impose the restrictions in certain other Texas and New Mexico cities.

The trial court found that the distributor appellants agreed and conspired among themselves to take uniform action upon the proposals made by Interstate, . . . and that the restrictions operated to increase the income of the distributors and of Interstate and to deflect attendance from later-run exhibitors who yielded to the restrictions to the first-run theatres of Interstate. . . .

Although the films were copyrighted, appellants do not deny that the conspiracy charge is established if the distributors agreed among themselves to impose the restrictions upon subsequent-run exhibitors. As is usual in cases of alleged unlawful agreements to restrain commerce, the Government is without the aid of direct testimony that the distributors entered into any agreement with each other to impose the restrictions upon subsequent-run exhibitors. In order to establish agreement it is compelled to rely on inferences drawn from the course of conduct of the alleged conspirators.

The trial court drew the inference of agreement from the nature of the proposals made on behalf of Interstate and Consolidated; from the manner in which they were made; from the substantial unanimity of action taken upon them by the distributors; and from the fact that appellants did not call as witnesses any of the superior officials who negotiated the contracts with Interstate or any official who, in the normal course of business, would have had knowledge of the existence or non-existence of such an agreement among the distributors. This conclusion is challenged by appellants because not supported by subsidiary findings or by the evidence. We think this inference of the trial court was rightly drawn from the evidence . . .

The O'Donnell letter named on its face as addressees the eight local representatives of the distributors, and so from the beginning each of the distributors knew that the proposals were under consideration by the others. Each was aware that all were in active competition and that without substantially unanimous action with respect to the restrictions for any given territory there was risk of a substantial loss of the business and good will of the subsequent-run and independent exhibitors, but that with it there was the prospect of increased profits. There was, therefore, strong motive for concerted action, full advantage of which was taken by Interstate and Consolidated in presenting their demands to all in a single document.

There was risk, too, that without agreement diversity of action would follow. Compliance with the proposals involved a radical departure from the previous business practices of the industry and a drastic increase in admission prices of most of the subsequent-run theatres. Acceptance of the proposals was discouraged by at least three of the distributors' local managers. Independent exhibitors met and organized a futile protest which they presented to the representatives of Interstate and Consolidated. While as a result of independent negotiations either of the two restrictions without the other could have been put into effect by any one or more of the distributors and in any one or more of the Texas cities served by Interstate, the negotiations which ensued and which in fact did result in modifications of the proposals resulted in substantially unanimous action of the distributors, both as to the terms of the restrictions and in the selection of the four cities where they were to operate.

One distributor, it is true, did not agree to impose the restrictions in Houston, but this was evidently because it did not grant licenses to any subsequent-run exhibitor in that city, where its own affiliate operated a first-run theatre. The proposal was unanimously rejected as to Galveston and Austin, as was the request that the restrictions should be extended to the cities of the Rio Grande Valley served by Consolidated. We may infer that Galveston was omitted because in that city there were no subsequent-run theatres in competition with Interstate. But we are unable to find in the record any persuasive explanation, other than agreed concert of action, of the singular unanimity of action on the part of the distributors by which the proposals were carried into effect as written in four Texas cities but not in a fifth or in the Rio Grande Valley. Numerous variations in the form of the provisions in the distributors' license agreements and the fact that in later years two of them extended the restrictions into all six cities, do not weaken the significance or force of the nature of the response to the proposals made by all the distributor appellants. It taxes credulity to believe that the several distributors would, in the circumstances, have accepted and put into operation with substantial unanimity such far-reaching changes in their business methods without some understanding that all were to join, and we reject as beyond the range of probability that it was the result of mere chance . . . [Defendants presented alternative reasons why they each might have independently rejected the proposal in Austin and the Rio Grande Valley, none of which the Court found persuasive.] In the face of this action and similar unanimity with respect to other features of the proposals, and the strong motive for such unanimity of action, we decline to speculate whether there may have been other and more legitimate reasons for such action not disclosed by the record, but which, if they existed, were known to appellants . . . Taken together, the circumstances of the case which we have mentioned, when uncontradicted and with no more explanation than the record affords, justify the inference that the distributors acted in concert and in common agreement in imposing the restrictions upon their licensees in the four Texas cities.

This inference was supported and strengthened when the distributors, with like unanimity, failed to tender the testimony, at their command, of any officer or agent of a distributor who knew, or was in a position to know, whether in fact an agreement had been reached among them for concerted action. When the proof supported, as we think it did, the inference of such concert, the burden rested on appellants of going forward with the evidence to explain away or contradict it. They undertook to carry that burden by calling upon local managers of the distributors to testify that they had acted independently of the other distributors, and that they did not have conferences with or reach agreements with the other distributors or their representatives. The failure under the circumstances to call as witnesses those officers who did have authority to act for the distributors and who were in a position to know whether they had acted in pursuance of agreement is itself persuasive that their testimony, if given, would have been unfavorable to appellants. The production of weak evidence when strong is available can lead only to the conclusion that the strong would have been adverse. Silence then becomes evidence of the most convincing character.

While the District Court's finding of an agreement of the distributors among themselves is supported by the evidence, we think that in the circumstances of this case such agreement for the imposition of the restrictions upon subsequent-run exhibitors was not a prerequisite to an unlawful conspiracy. It was enough that, knowing that concerted action was contemplated and invited, the distributors gave their adherence to the scheme and participated in it. Each distributor was advised that the others were asked to participate; each knew that cooperation was essential to successful operation of the plan. They knew that the plan, if carried out, would result in a restraint of commerce, which, we will presently point out, was unreasonable within the meaning of the Sherman Act, and knowing it, all participated in the plan. The evidence is persuasive that each distributor early became aware that the others had joined. With that knowledge they renewed the arrangement and carried it into effect for the two successive years.

It is elementary that an unlawful conspiracy may be and often is formed without simultaneous action or agreement on the part of the conspirators. Acceptance by competitors, without previous agreement, of an invitation to participate in a plan, the necessary consequence of which, if carried out, is restraint of interstate commerce, is sufficient to establish an unlawful conspiracy under the Sherman Act.

[The Court also held that the vertical agreements between the distributors and Interstate Circuit and Consolidated were unreasonable restraints even where there was no horizontal agreement to enter into those vertical agreements, rejecting the argument that they were a proper exercise of the distributor's copyrights because the agreements were imposed to further Interstate's monopoly power in exhibiting movies in major Texas cities.] *Affirmed.*

■ MR. JUSTICE ROBERTS, dissenting . . . The Government stresses the fact that each of the distributors must have acted with knowledge that some or all of the others would grant or had granted Interstate's demand. But such knowledge was merely notice to each of them that if it was successfully to compete for the first run business in important Texas cities it must meet the terms of competing distributors or lose the business of Interstate . . .

NOTES AND QUESTIONS ON *INTERSTATE CIRCUIT*

1. ***The evidence that parallel conduct was unlikely without a hidden express conspiracy.*** Part of the Court's opinion in *Interstate Circuit* inferred a horizontal agreement among the distributors based on the reasoning that their parallel action would have been unlikely absent some agreement. For example, the Court stressed that the eight distributors simultaneously accepted Interstate's demand for higher second-run prices in the same cities and rejected the demand in the same cities. But was that parallelism unlikely without agreement? After all, the parallel choices could have simply reflected variations in the degree of Interstate's market power in the different cities. Such variations in market power would have applied equally to each distributor and could have led each of them to independently decide to accept the demands in cities where Interstate had more market power and reject the demands in cities where it had less market power.

However, the defendants' ability to offer that argument was limited by the fact that all of the distributors refused to supply witnesses who had been at the negotiating table with Interstate. Such a failure to supply witnesses is suspicious, suggesting that their testimony would not have helped the defendants. This failure to supply witnesses about secret negotiations suggests a hidden express agreement was more likely than independent action, because the distributors would have incentives to supply the witnesses if they had acted independently.

2. ***The* Interstate Circuit *test.*** The more famous part of *Interstate Circuit* indicates that—even if a hidden horizontal agreement could not be inferred—a conspiracy among the distributors would still be established by the facts that: (1) each received an invitation to common action; (2) each knew others were invited; (3) each knew that joint action was necessary for success; and (4) each accepted the invitation. This test raises various questions.

a. Why was joint action necessary for success? One might wonder why the Court thought joint action was necessary for success. After all, one could argue that any individual distributor would be happy to be the only one to accept Interstate's demand and exhibit movies in the major Texas cities. However, it is unlikely that Interstate would have continued with the plan if only one film distributor agreed, because then Interstate would then have lost access to the vast majority of new films. Rather, if only one film distributor agreed to the higher second-run prices, Interstate would have likely negotiated for access to movies from the other distributors on different terms. That would leave the film distributor who agreed to the higher second-run ticket price at a competitive disadvantage because that distributor would have committed to a price that could be undercut by the ticket prices for movies from other distributors. Thus, each distributor would have independent business reasons to want to avoid being the only distributor who contractually committed to higher second-run prices.

On the other hand, it is likely that the distributors would collectively benefit if they *all* agreed to set their exhibition prices for second-run movies at no less than 25 cents. In doing so, they would effectively be allowing Interstate to serve as a cartel ringmaster for the distributors, fixing a high price that all of them would charge and thus avoiding being undercut by rival pricing. But to achieve that goal, it would be necessary for all of them to agree to the new price, which is why joint action was necessary for success. Given this motive for common action and lack of independent motives, the eight distributors were unlikely to agree to the demands without some understanding that all of them were agreeing.

b. Why was this an invitation to common action? The dissent disagreed that this was an invitation to common action. Instead, the dissent thought that Interstate let each distributor know the same proposal had been made to all distributors not as an effort to get the distributors to act together, but rather as an effort to play them off against each other by letting them know they had to compete for the business of Interstate. But the dissent's characterization would make sense only if distributors would want to agree individually even if other distributors did not. If distributors would only want to agree jointly (for reasons noted above), then the dissent's argument does not hold water, because it depends on the distributors wanting to obtain a competitive advantage by agreeing when their rivals would not.

c. Does the* Interstate Circuit *test also condemn ordinary oligopolistic price coordination? Read literally, the *Interstate Circuit* test does seem to condemn ordinary oligopolistic coordination through price leadership. After all, with successful price coordination: (1) the announcement by one firm of a future price increase is an invitation to the common action of matching that price increase; (2) each oligopolist knows the other firms are also invited to match that price increase; (3) each oligopolist knows that joint action is necessary for success, because if one firm does not match the announced price increase, it will be rescinded; and (4) each oligopolist accepts the invitation by matching the price increase.

However, as explained in the Notes following *American Tobacco,* in fact antitrust law does not prohibit pure oligopolistic price coordination. What is the difference? The difference is that the best explanation for why the law does not condemn pure oligopolistic price coordination is that setting a price knowingly is unavoidable conduct, so the law has no way to define the offense in a way that would give oligopolists guidance about how to behavior lawfully. In contrast, in this case, the conspiracy was inferred from parallel conduct that followed secret negotiations and a letter that invited common action, which are entirely avoidable behaviors. Thus, firms can avoid liability by not engaging in such secret negotiations or issuing such common invitations.

Accordingly, the best way to square the *Interstate Circuit* test with the doctrine allowing pure oligopolistic price coordination is to modestly change the first element of the *Interstate Circuit* test to "(1) each received an *avoidable* invitation to common action". Probably the *Interstate Circuit* Court was implicitly assuming such avoidability, given that avoidability was obvious on the facts of the actual case.

3. PARALLEL CONDUCT CONSISTENT WITH INDEPENDENT INCENTIVES OR UNAVOIDABLE INTERDEPENDENCE

Bell Atlantic v. Twombly

550 U.S. 544 (2007).

■ JUSTICE SOUTER delivered the opinion of the Court.

Liability under § 1 of the Sherman Act, requires a "contract, combination . . . , or conspiracy, in restraint of trade or commerce." The question in this putative class action is whether a § 1 complaint can survive a motion to dismiss when it alleges that major telecommunications providers engaged in certain parallel conduct unfavorable to competition, absent some factual context suggesting agreement, as distinct from identical, independent action. We hold that such a complaint should be dismissed.

I

The upshot of the 1984 divestiture of the American Telephone & Telegraph Company's (AT & T) local telephone business was a system of regional service monopolies (. . ."Incumbent Local Exchange Carriers" (ILECs)). . . . More than a decade later, Congress withdrew approval of the ILECs' monopolies by enacting the Telecommunications Act of 1996 (1996 Act), which . . . "subject[ed] [ILECs] to a host of duties intended to facilitate market entry." . . . "Central to the [new] scheme [was each ILEC's] obligation . . . to share its network with competitors," *Trinko*, which came to be known as "competitive local exchange carriers" (CLECs). . . . Owing to the "considerable expense and effort" required to make unbundled network elements available to rivals at wholesale prices, *Trinko*, the ILECs vigorously litigated the scope of the sharing obligation imposed by the 1996 Act, with the result that the Federal Communications Commission (FCC) three times revised its regulations to narrow the range of network elements to be shared with the CLECs. . . .

The complaint alleges that the ILECs conspired to restrain trade in two ways, each supposedly inflating charges for local telephone and high-speed Internet services. Plaintiffs say, first, that the ILECs "engaged in parallel conduct" in their respective service areas to inhibit the growth of upstart CLECs. Their actions allegedly included making unfair agreements with the CLECs for access to ILEC networks, providing inferior connections to the networks, overcharging, and billing in ways designed to sabotage the CLECs' relations with their own customers. According to the complaint, the ILECs' "compelling common motivatio[n]" to thwart the CLECs' competitive efforts naturally led them to form a conspiracy; "[h]ad any one [ILEC] not sought to prevent CLECs . . . from competing effectively . . . , the resulting greater competitive inroads into that [ILEC's] territory would have revealed the degree to which competitive entry by CLECs would have been successful in the other territories in the absence of such conduct."

Second, the complaint charges agreements by the ILECs to refrain from competing against one another. These are to be inferred from the ILECs' common failure "meaningfully [to] pursu[e]" "attractive business opportunit[ies]" in contiguous markets where they possessed "substantial competitive advantages," and from a statement of Richard Notebaert, chief executive officer (CEO) of the ILEC Qwest, that competing in the territory of another ILEC " 'might be a good way to turn a quick dollar but that doesn't make it right.' ". . .

II

. . . "[t]he crucial question" is whether the challenged anticompetitive conduct "stem[s] from independent decision or from an agreement, tacit or express," *Theatre Enterprises*. While a showing of parallel "business behavior is admissible circumstantial evidence from which the fact finder may infer agreement," it falls short of "conclusively establish[ing] agreement or . . . itself constitut[ing] a Sherman Act offense." *Id.* Even "conscious parallelism," a common reaction of "firms in a concentrated market [that] recogniz[e] their shared economic interests and their interdependence with respect to price and output decisions" is "not in itself unlawful." *Brooke*; *see* 6 P. Areeda & H. Hovenkamp, Antitrust Law ¶ 1433a, p. 236 (2d ed.2003) (hereinafter Areeda & Hovenkamp) ("The courts are nearly unanimous in saying that mere interdependent parallelism does not establish the contract, combination, or conspiracy required by Sherman Act § 1"); Turner, The Definition of Agreement Under the Sherman Act: Conscious Parallelism and Refusals to Deal, 75 Harv. L.Rev. 655, 672 (1962) ("[M]ere interdependence of basic price decisions is not conspiracy").

The inadequacy of showing parallel conduct or interdependence, without more, mirrors the ambiguity of the behavior: consistent with conspiracy, but just as much in line with a wide swath of rational and competitive business strategy unilaterally prompted by common perceptions of the market. Accordingly, we have previously hedged against false inferences from identical behavior at a number of points in the trial sequence. An antitrust conspiracy plaintiff with evidence showing nothing beyond parallel conduct is not entitled to a directed verdict, *see Theatre Enterprises*; proof of a § 1 conspiracy must include evidence tending to exclude the possibility of independent action, *see Monsanto*; and at the summary judgment stage a § 1 plaintiff's offer of conspiracy evidence must tend to rule out the possibility that the defendants were acting independently, *see Matsushita*. . . .

This case presents the antecedent question of what a plaintiff must plead in order to state a claim under § 1 of the Sherman Act. . . . [W]e hold that stating such a claim requires a complaint with enough factual matter (taken as true) to suggest that an agreement was made. Asking for plausible grounds to infer an agreement does not impose a probability requirement at the pleading stage; it simply calls for enough fact to raise a reasonable expectation that discovery will reveal evidence of illegal agreement.[4] And, of course, a well-pleaded complaint may proceed even

---

[4] Commentators have offered several examples of parallel conduct allegations that would state a § 1 claim under this standard. *See*, e.g., 6 Areeda & Hovenkamp ¶ 1425, at 167–185 (discussing "parallel behavior that would probably not result from chance, coincidence, independent responses to common stimuli, or mere interdependence unaided by an advance understanding among the parties"); Blechman, Conscious Parallelism, Signalling and Facilitating Devices: The Problem of Tacit Collusion Under the Antitrust Laws, 24 N.Y.L. S. L.Rev. 881, 899 (1979) (describing "conduct [that] indicates the sort of restricted freedom of action and sense of obligation that one generally associates with agreement"). The parties in this case agree that "complex and historically unprecedented changes in pricing structure made

if it strikes a savvy judge that actual proof of those facts is improbable, and "that a recovery is very remote and unlikely." In identifying facts that are suggestive enough to render a § 1 conspiracy plausible, we have the benefit of the prior rulings and considered views of leading commentators, already quoted, that lawful parallel conduct fails to bespeak unlawful agreement. It makes sense to say, therefore, that an allegation of parallel conduct and a bare assertion of conspiracy will not suffice. Without more, parallel conduct does not suggest conspiracy, and a conclusory allegation of agreement at some unidentified point does not supply facts adequate to show illegality. Hence, when allegations of parallel conduct are set out in order to make a § 1 claim, they must be placed in a context that raises a suggestion of a preceding agreement, not merely parallel conduct that could just as well be independent action. . . .

III

When we look for plausibility in this complaint, . . . plaintiffs' claim of conspiracy in restraint of trade comes up short. To begin with, the complaint leaves no doubt that plaintiffs rest their § 1 claim on descriptions of parallel conduct and not on any independent allegation of actual agreement among the ILECs. . . .

We think that nothing contained in the complaint invests either the action or inaction alleged with a plausible suggestion of conspiracy. As to the ILECs' supposed agreement to disobey the 1996 Act and thwart the CLECs' attempts to compete, . . . nothing in the complaint intimates that the resistance to the upstarts was anything more than the natural, unilateral reaction of each ILEC intent on keeping its regional dominance. The 1996 Act did more than just subject the ILECs to competition; it obliged them to subsidize their competitors with their own equipment at wholesale rates. The economic incentive to resist was powerful, but resisting competition is routine market conduct, and even if the ILECs flouted the 1996 Act in all the ways the plaintiffs allege, there is no reason to infer that the companies had agreed among themselves to do what was only natural anyway; so natural, in fact, that if alleging parallel decisions to resist competition were enough to imply an antitrust conspiracy, pleading a § 1 violation against almost any group of competing businesses would be a sure thing.

The complaint makes its closest pass at a predicate for conspiracy with the claim that collusion was necessary because success by even one CLEC in an ILEC's territory "would have revealed the degree to which competitive entry by CLECs would have been successful in the other territories." But, its logic aside, this general premise still fails to answer the point that there was just no need for joint encouragement to resist the 1996 Act; as the District Court said, "each ILEC has reason to want

---

at the very same time by multiple competitors, and made for no other discernible reason," would support a plausible inference of conspiracy.

to avoid dealing with CLECs" and "each ILEC would attempt to keep CLECs out, regardless of the actions of the other ILECs."

Plaintiffs' second conspiracy theory rests on the competitive reticence among the ILECs themselves in the wake of the 1996 Act, which was supposedly passed in the " 'hop[e] that the large incumbent local monopoly companies . . . might attack their neighbors' service areas, as they are the best situated to do so.' " Contrary to hope, the ILECs declined " 'to enter each other's service territories in any significant way,' " and the local telephone and high-speed Internet market remains highly compartmentalized geographically, with minimal competition. Based on this state of affairs, and perceiving the ILECs to be blessed with "especially attractive business opportunities" in surrounding markets dominated by other ILECs, the plaintiffs assert that the ILECs' parallel conduct was "strongly suggestive of conspiracy."

But it was not suggestive of conspiracy, not if history teaches anything. In a traditionally unregulated industry with low barriers to entry, sparse competition among large firms dominating separate geographical segments of the market could very well signify illegal agreement, but here we have an obvious alternative explanation. In the decade preceding the 1996 Act and well before that, monopoly was the norm in telecommunications, not the exception. The ILECs were born in that world, doubtless liked the world the way it was, and surely knew the adage about him who lives by the sword. Hence, a natural explanation for the noncompetition alleged is that the former Government-sanctioned monopolists were sitting tight, expecting their neighbors to do the same thing.

In fact, the complaint itself gives reasons to believe that the ILECs would see their best interests in keeping to their old turf. Although the complaint says generally that the ILECs passed up "especially attractive business opportunit[ies]" by declining to compete as CLECs against other ILECs, it does not allege that competition as CLECs was potentially any more lucrative than other opportunities being pursued by the ILECs during the same period,[13] and the complaint is replete with indications that any CLEC faced nearly insurmountable barriers to profitability owing to the ILECs' flagrant resistance to the network sharing requirements of the 1996 Act. Not only that, but even without a monopolistic tradition and the peculiar difficulty of mandating shared networks, "[f]irms do not expand without limit and none of them enters every market that an outside observer might regard as profitable, or even a small portion of such markets." Areeda & Hovenkamp ¶ 307d, at 155

[13] The complaint quoted a reported statement of Qwest's CEO, Richard Notebaert, to suggest that the ILECs declined to compete against each other despite recognizing that it " 'might be a good way to turn a quick dollar.' " [H]owever, . . . Notebaert was also quoted as saying that entering new markets as a CLEC would not be "a sustainable economic model" because the CLEC pricing model is "just . . . nuts." Another source cited in the complaint quotes Notebaert as saying he thought it "unwise" to "base a business plan" on the privileges accorded to CLECs under the 1996 Act because the regulatory environment was too unstable.

(Supp.2006) (commenting on the case at bar). The upshot is that Congress may have expected some ILECs to become CLECs in the legacy territories of other ILECs, but the disappointment does not make conspiracy plausible. We agree with the District Court's assessment that antitrust conspiracy was not suggested by the facts adduced under either theory of the complaint, which thus fails to state a valid § 1 claim. . . .

NOTES AND QUESTIONS ON *TWOMBLY*

1. ***Why a conspiracy cannot be inferred from parallel resistance to connecting rival carriers.*** In *Twombly*, the plaintiffs alleged that one could infer that the incumbent phone carriers conspired to resist connecting rival carriers to their networks from the fact that all the incumbent carriers did so. The Court concluded that such an inference was improper because such parallel resistance was entirely consistent with independent incentives. As the Court pointed out, any local monopoly has independent incentives to try to resist entry. The lack of independent incentives to connect rival carriers was precisely why the Telecommunications Act compelled the incumbent carriers to offer such connections. Further, the legally-required connections forced the incumbent carriers to "subsidize their competitors with their own equipment at wholesale rates." Each incumbent carrier thus had powerful independent incentives to resist connecting rival carriers and would have resisted "regardless of the actions of the other" incumbent carriers. Perhaps such resistance could be challenged as a violation of the Telecommunications Act, but the independent incentives to resist mean that one cannot infer any conspiracy to resist from parallel resistance.

2. ***Why a conspiracy cannot be inferred from parallel non-entry into each other's territories.*** The plaintiffs also alleged that one could infer that the incumbent carriers conspired not to enter each other's territories from the fact that none of them did so. The Court concluded that this inference was improper because such parallel non-entry could be explained by both independent and interdependent incentives.

One reason the incumbent carriers had independent incentives not to enter each other's territories was precisely because incumbent carriers were so resistant to connecting new entrants that such entry was unprofitable, as the plaintiffs had stressed in alleging the first conspiracy. Sources cited in the complaint indeed indicated that entering incumbent markets was not economically sustainable because the entry pricing model was "just nuts" and because the regulatory protections for entrants were too unstable. Moreover, normal competitive firms making independent decisions fail to enter most markets that others might consider profitable, presumably because the firms declining to enter assess the risks or profitability of entry differently, prefer other business opportunities, or do not want to lose focus on their existing markets.

The Court indicated that the incumbent carriers also had interdependent incentives not to enter each other's territories. The incumbent carriers liked the existing world where each had their own local monopoly and "knew the adage about him who lives by the sword"; i.e., that a firm that entered the markets of other incumbent carriers was likely to have other incumbent carriers enter its own market. The firms were thus "sitting tight, expecting their neighbors to do the same thing." In short, the incumbent carriers might simply be coordinating on a strategy of not invading each other's territories.

In dicta, the Court more generally stated that interdependent parallelism did not suffice to establish an agreement. However, the sources that the Court quoted for this proposition were focused on interdependent price or output decisions. What is distinctive about those decisions is that they are unavoidable. Firms cannot avoid setting some price and making some output, and firms also cannot avoid understanding their interdependence when they decide what price or output to set. Likewise, in *Twombly* itself, the decision about whether to enter other markets was unavoidable. Firms cannot avoid making some decision about whether or not to enter another market, nor can they avoid realizing their interdependence when they make such decisions. Thus, any doctrine that tried to prohibit "interdependent entry decisions" would (like any attempt to prohibit interdependent pricing or output decisions) fail to give firms any guidance about exactly what they are supposed to stop doing.

However, often firms interdependently adopt entirely avoidable practices, like exchanging individuated price information. In those cases, the Court has been willing to infer an agreement to adopt the practice, as we shall see in the next Section. The true distinction is thus not between agreement and interdependence, but rather between interdependence on avoidable conduct (which can be an agreement) and unavoidable conduct (which cannot be). Consistent with this analysis, the lower courts have generally held that a conspiracy can be inferred from parallel conduct and a "plus factor", which they often hold is established by showing a "motivation for common action," that is, a disincentive to engage in the conduct unless others engage in the same conduct.[13] Such a motive for common action exists whenever firms have interdependent incentives, so the lower courts cannot mean that parallel actions explained by interdependence never constitute an agreement. On the other hand, pure oligopolistic coordination on price or output also involves a motive for common action, so the lower courts cannot mean that interdependent actions always constitute an agreement. Rather, a motive for common action should be treated as a plus factor only when the parallel action is avoidable.

3. Is **Twombly** *consistent with* **American Tobacco?** Yes. Recall that there are two interpretations to *American Tobacco*. The first is that a price-fixing conspiracy there was inferred because the price-matching was so precise that it seemed unlikely it could be explained by pure oligopolistic

13 *See* AREEDA, KAPLOW & EDLIN, ANTITRUST ANALYSIS 226–31 (6th ed. 2004).

coordination. That proposition is affirmatively confirmed in footnote 4 of *Twombly*.

The second interpretation of *American Tobacco* is that, given that precise price-matching was actually consistent with coordination in a three-firm market, a price-fixing conspiracy can be inferred when parallel pricing is equally consistent with a hidden express agreement or oligopolistic coordination. That proposition was not disturbed by *Twombly,* in which the alleged evidence did not indicate a type of parallelism that made a hidden express agreement just as likely as oligopolistic coordination. Instead, the *Twombly* Court indicated that the alleged evidence made parallel non-entry equally consistent with *independent* incentives or coordination, and that inferring a hidden express agreement was thus implausible. Indeed, if parallel conduct is equally consistent with independent action or coordination, then that affirmatively indicates it is more consistent with independent action than with hidden conspiracy, thus flunking the *Matsushita/Monsanto* standard for finding an agreement.

The distinction between *Twombly* and *American Tobacco* can also be explained by the different effects of inferring a conspiracy in these different situations. Equal consistency between coordination and *independent* incentives means that condemning the parallel conduct as a conspiracy would raise strong overdeterrence concerns (deterring efficient independent conduct) without strongly reducing underdeterrence (because any agreement is unnecessary and any coordination is unavoidable). In contrast, equal consistency between coordination and hidden conspiracy indicates that condemnation would raise weak overdeterrence concerns (because coordination is not desirable) and strongly reduce underdeterrence (because hidden conspiracies can easily look like coordination).

Indeed, *Twombly* explicitly indicated that in "a traditionally unregulated industry with low barriers to entry, sparse competition among large firms dominating separate geographical segments of the market could very well signify illegal agreement." In that hypothesized case, entry is so individually profitable and easy that parallel non-entry would not be just as consistent with independent incentives as with coordination. However, such parallel non-entry despite clear high profits from easy entry could be as consistent with a hidden express agreement as with oligopolistic coordination. The Court's willingness to infer a conspiracy in such cases thus suggests it is confirming this interpretation of *American Tobacco* as well.

4. AGREEMENTS OR PRACTICES THAT FACILITATE CARTELS OR OLIGOPOLISTIC COORDINATION

For oligopolistic price coordination to work, the oligopolists must have collective market power and be able to coordinate. If the oligopolists do not have collective market power, then they will be unable to raise prices no matter how well they coordinate. Likewise, even if they do have collective market power, they will be unable to raise prices unless they can coordinate amongst themselves sufficiently to act as a collective.

Whether collective market power exists turns on the same factors considered in Chapter 3: market share, rival expandability, barriers to entry, and the extent to which consumers would switch to other markets in response to a price increase. The difference is that because the issue here is whether the oligopolists have collective market power, the first two factors would turn on their collective market share and the expandability of rivals outside the oligopoly.

The ability to coordinate turns on whether the oligopolists can do three things: (1) settle on a cooperative price; (2) detect individual firm defections from that price; and (3) respond to such defections in a way that makes defection unprofitable. Whether those three features exist turns largely on market conditions.

For example, if the firms make homogeneous products and have homogeneous costs of production and delivery, then it will be relatively easy to settle on the same price, detect when other firms have defected, and respond to defections with price cuts targeted at the defector. But when different firms make different products and have varying costs of production or delivery, then all three factors are harder to satisfy. With such varying products and costs, the market price that maximizes profits will vary for different firms, so they will find it harder to settle on a common price. Varying product features or delivery costs can also make it harder to detect whether firms are undercutting the oligopoly price or are instead making an adjustment that accurately reflects the differences in product features or transportation costs. Such variation also makes it harder to punish defections, because any deviating firm will have more attraction to the set of consumers who have product preferences or geographical locations closer to the product features or location of the deviating firm. Finally, when products or associated services vary, each firm will have incentives to engage in nonprice competition (by making its product or associated services better), which can increase costs and eat away the profits from oligopoly pricing.

Likewise, oligopolistic coordination will be easier if the market involves transparent pricing for incremental sales that can be adjusted daily in response to the prices of others. But suppose instead purchases in the market involve secret discounts and/or simultaneous bidding for large contracts. Then it will be harder for the oligopolists to detect each other's defections or respond to them in time. Secret discounts and large contracts also create higher incentives to defect by undercutting the oligopoly price, because such defections are less likely to be detected and because defections that lock in large contracts may produce large enough gains to offset any penalty for defection.

When intrinsic market conditions impede coordination, oligopolists have incentives to enter into agreements that facilitate oligopolistic coordination by making it easier to settle on a common price and notice and respond to deviations. For example, oligopolists may agree to standardize their products or associated services, charge delivery costs from a common basing point rather than their actual locations, eliminate secret discounting, or exchange information about each other's prices.

Even though oligopolistic price coordination itself cannot be challenged as a price-fixing agreement, an agreement to engage in a practice that facilitates oligopolistic coordination can be challenged as an agreement that unreasonably restrains trade because it restrains firms to use the facilitating practice and produces anticompetitive effects. Indeed, even the interdependent parallel adoption of such facilitating practices can be condemned as a tacit agreement that restrains trade, because (unlike with oligopolistic price coordination itself) the illegal interdependent activity can be defined in a way that firms can avoid. Further, the parallel adoption of facilitating practices can, even without any agreement, be condemned as unilateral conduct that has anticompetitive effects under FTC Act § 5. In short, oligopolistic coordination on a facilitating practice can be an antitrust conspiracy or violation even though oligopolistic coordination on price cannot be.

As with oligopolistic coordination, a successful cartel must also be able to agree on a common price, notice individual firm defections from that price, and punish the defectors. Those tasks are generally easier in a cartel because typically the cartel members expressly negotiate the common price and communicate about the monitoring and punishment of defectors. However, even a cartel can have difficulty with those tasks, and agreements on the sort of practices that facilitate oligopolistic coordination can also facilitate cartel formation and enforcement. For example, agreements to suppress cost or quality differences make it easier to agree on the cartel price, and agreements to exchange information about individuated pricing make it easier to detect defections from a cartel price.

When direct proof of the cartel agreement is available, proof of an agreement on such facilitating practices is unnecessary because the cartel agreement is already per se illegal. However, suppose direct proof of a cartel is absent in a market where market conditions or concentration levels make oligopolistic coordination unlikely, but the firms agree to use a facilitating practice that does not further any independent business incentives. Then the agreement to use the facilitating practice can be explained only by a motive for common action, from which one can infer it is facilitating a hidden cartel, given that coordination is unlikely. Indeed, in such a case the parallel adoption of such a facilitating practice allows us to infer both a hidden express agreement to adopt that facilitating practice (because neither coordination or independent actions could explain the parallel adoption) and a hidden cartel that is furthered by that facilitating practice.

American Column & Lumber v. United States

257 U.S. 377 (1921).

■ MR. JUSTICE CLARKE delivered the opinion of the Court.

[The American Hardwood Manufacturers' Association had 400 members, 365 of which participated in the "Open Competition Plan" (the Plan), whereby each member gave the Association daily reports on the terms of each of its sales (including copies of the invoices), monthly reports on its output and inventory, and a list of its prices. The Association then disseminated to members weekly summaries of all sales, including price and purchaser, and monthly summaries of the production, inventory, and price lists of each member, coupled with a report analyzing current market conditions and projecting future market conditions. The Plan also provided for monthly meetings to "afford opportunity for the discussion of all subjects of interest to the members." The participants made 33% of the hardwood produced in the United States. The district court enjoined these activities as a violation of Sherman Act § 1.]

The record shows that the Plan was evolved by a committee, which, in recommending its adoption, said: "The purpose of the plan is to disseminate among members accurate knowledge of production and market conditions so that each member may gauge the market intelligently instead of guessing at it; to make competition open and above board instead of secret and concealed; to substitute, in estimating market conditions, frank and full statements of our competitors for the frequently misleading and colored statements of the buyer."

After stating that the purpose was not to restrict competition or to control prices but to "furnish information to enable each member to intelligently make prices and to intelligently govern his production," the committee continues: "The chief concern of the buyer, as we all know, is to see that the price he pays is no higher than that of his competitors, against whom he must sell his product in the market. The chief concern of the seller is to get as much as anybody else for his lumber; in other words to get what is termed the top of the market for the quality he offers. By making prices known to each other they will gradually tend toward a standard *in harmony with market conditions*, a situation advantageous to both buyer and seller."

. . . [A] further explanation of the objects and purposes of the Plan was made in an appeal to members to join it, in which it is said: "The theoretical proposition at the basis of the Open Competition Plan is that

Knowledge regarding prices actually made is all that is necessary to keep prices at reasonably stable and normal levels. The Open Competition Plan is a central clearing house for information on prices, trade statistics and practices. By keeping all members fully and quickly informed of what the others have done, the work of the Plan results in *a certain uniformity of trade practice.* There is no agreement to follow the practice of others, *although members do follow their most intelligent competitors*, if they know what these competitors have been actually doing." . . .

And in another later and somewhat similar, appeal sent to all the members, this is found: "Competition, blind, vicious, unreasoning, may stimulate trade to abnormal activity, but such condition is no more sound than that medieval spirit some still cling to of taking a club and going out and knocking the other fellow and taking away his bone. The keynote to modern business success is mutual confidence and co-operation. *Co-operative competition, not cutthroat competition.* Co-operation is a matter of business, because it pays, because it enables you to get the best price for your product, because you come into closer *personal contact with the market.* Co-operation will only replace *undesirable competition* as you develop a co-operative spirit. For the first time in the history of the industry, the hardwood manufacturers are organized into one compact, comprehensive body, equipped to serve the whole trade in a thorough and efficient manner . . . More members mean more power to do more good for the industry. With co-operation of this kind we will very soon have enlisted in our efforts practically every producing interest, *and you know what that means.*"

Thus, the Plan proposed a system of cooperation among the members, consisting of the interchange of reports of sales, prices, production, and practices, and in meetings of the members for discussion, for the avowed purpose of substituting "co-operative competition" for cutthroat competition, of keeping "prices at reasonably stable and normal levels," and of improving the "human relations" among the members. But the purpose to agree upon prices or production was always disclaimed . . .

Plainly it would be very difficult to devise a more minute disclosure of everything connected with one's business than is here provided for by this Plan, and very certainly only the most attractive prospect could induce any man to make it to his rivals and competitors . . . This extensive interchange of reports, supplemented as it was by monthly meetings at which an opportunity was afforded for discussion "of all subjects of interest to the members," very certainly constituted an organization through which agreements, actual or implied, could readily be arrived at and maintained, if the members desired to make them.

[In fact, the conduct went beyond the Plan in that: (1) weekly regional meetings were held; (2) the weekly sales report included a forecast of future market conditions that ended up being discussed at practically every meeting; (3) before each meeting members were asked to the output they had last month and estimated they would have next month, and to state their general view of market conditions, which the Association used to provide estimates of actual and future market conditions to all members.]

The Plan on paper provided only for reports of past transactions and much is made of this in the record and in argument—that reporting to one another past transactions cannot fix prices for the future. But . . . [the] questions [directed at members before the meetings] plainly invited an estimate and discussion of future market conditions by each member, and a co-ordination of them by an expert analyst could readily evolve an attractive basis for cooperative, even if unexpressed, "harmony" with respect to future prices . . .

This elaborate plan for the interchange of reports does not simply supply to each member the amount of stock held, the sales made and the prices received, by every other member of the group, thereby furnishing the data for judging the market, on the basis of supply and demand and current prices. It goes much farther. It not only furnishes such information, with respect to stock, sales and prices, but also reports, giving the views of each member as to "market conditions for the next few months"; what the production of each will be for the next "two months"; frequent analyses of the reports by an expert, with, we shall see, significant suggestions as to both future prices and production; and opportunities for future meetings for the interchange of views, which the record shows were very important. It is plain that the only element lacking in this scheme to make it a familiar type of the competition suppressing organization is a definite agreement as to production and prices. But this is supplied: By the disposition of men "to follow their most intelligent competitors," especially when powerful; by the inherent disposition to make all the money possible, joined with the steady cultivation of the value of "harmony" of action; and by the system of reports, which makes the discovery of price reductions inevitable and immediate. The sanctions of the plan obviously are financial interest, intimate personal contact, and business honor, all operating under the restraint of exposure of what would be deemed bad faith and of trade punishment by powerful rivals . . .

[In meetings and reports members were repeatedly advised that increasing production or overproduction would be bad business because there was not enough demand and that business would be good if members did not increase production. This] is sufficient to convincingly show that one of the prime purposes of the meetings . . . and of the various reports, was to induce members to co-operate in restricting production, thereby keeping the supply low and the prices high, and that whenever there was any suggestion of running the mills to an extent which would bring up the supply to a point which might affect prices, the advice against operations which might lead to such result was put in the strongest possible terms. The co-operation is palpable and avowed, its purpose is clear, and we shall see that it was completely realized.

Next, the record shows clearly that the members . . . assiduously cultivated, through the [association] letters . . . speaking for them all, and through the discussions at the meetings, the general conviction that higher and higher price were obtainable and a disposition on the part of all to demand them. [Plan reports repeatedly advised that there was no reason to cut prices because, given the reduced amount of lumber stock on the market, market demand exceeded supply and was leading to increased prices.] To this we must add that constantly throughout the minutes of the various meetings there is shown discussion of the stock and production reports in which the shortage of supply was continually emphasized, with the implication, not disguised, that higher prices must result. Men in general are so easily persuaded to do that which will obviously prove profitable that this reiterated opinion from the analyst of their association, with all obtainable data before him, that higher prices were justified and could easily be obtained, must, inevitably have resulted, as it did result, in concert of action in demanding them.

But not only does the record thus show a persistent purpose to encourage members to unite in pressing for higher and higher prices, without regard to cost, but there are many admissions by members, not only that this was the purpose of the Plan, but that it was fully realized. [The court collected many quotes from members who stated the Plan had enabled them to raise prices.] . . . These quotations are sufficient to show beyond discussion that the purpose of the organization, and especially of the frequent meetings, was to bring about a concerted effort to raise prices regardless of cost or merit, and so was unlawful, and that the members were soon entirely satisfied that the Plan was "carrying out the purpose for which it was intended."

As to the price conditions during the year: Without going into detail, the record shows that the prices of the grades of hardwood in most general use were increased to an unprecedented extent during the year. Thus, the increases in prices of varieties of oak, range from 33.3% to 296% during the year; of gum, 60% to 343%, and of ash, from 55% to 181%. While it is true that 1919 was a year of high and increasing prices generally, and that wet weather may have restricted production to some extent, we cannot but agree with the members of the Plan themselves, as we have quoted them, and with the District Court, in the conclusion that the united action of this large and influential membership of dealers contributed greatly to this extraordinary price increase.

Such close co-operation, between many persons, firms, and corporations controlling a large volume of interstate commerce, as is provided for in this Plan, is plainly in theory, as it proved to be in fact, inconsistent with that free and unrestricted trade which the statute contemplates shall be maintained, and that the persons conducting the association fully realized this is apparent from their protesting so often as they did . . . that they sought only to supplant cutthroat competition with what in their own judgment would be "fair and reasonable competition," . . . and by their repeated insistence that the Sherman Law, "designed to prevent the restraint of trade, is itself one of the greatest restrainers of trade, and should be repealed." . . .

Genuine competitors do not make daily, weekly, and monthly reports of the minutest details of their business to their rivals, as the defendants did; they do not contract, as was done here, to submit their books to the discretionary audit, and their stocks to the discretionary inspection, of their rivals, for the purpose of successfully competing with them; and they do not submit the details of their business to the analysis of an expert, jointly employed, and obtain from him a "harmonized" estimate of the market as it is, and as, in his specially and confidentially informed judgment, it promises to be. This is not the conduct of competitors, but is so clearly that of men united in an agreement, express or implied, to act together and pursue a common purpose under a common guide that, if it did not stand confessed a combination to restrict production and increase prices in interstate commerce, and as, therefore, a direct restraint upon that commerce, as we have seen that it is, that conclusion must inevitably have been inferred from the facts which were proved. To pronounce such abnormal conduct on the part of 365 natural competitors, controlling one-third of the trade of the country in an article of prime necessity, a "new form of competition," and not an old form of combination in restraint of trade, as it so plainly is, would be for this court to confess itself blinded by words and forms to realities which men in general very plainly see, and understand and condemn, as an old evil in a new dress and with a new name.

The Plan is, essentially, simply an expansion of the gentleman's agreement of former days, skillfully devised to evade the law. To call it open competition, because the meetings were nominally open to the public, or because some voluminous reports were transmitted to the Department of Justice, or because no specific agreement to restrict trade or fix prices is proved, cannot conceal the fact that the fundamental purpose of the Plan was to procure "harmonious" individual action among a large number of naturally competing dealers with respect to the volume of production and prices, without having any specific agreement with respect to them, and to rely for maintenance of concerted action in both respects, not upon fines and forfeitures as in earlier days, but upon what experience has shown to be the more potent and dependable restraints, of business honor and social penalties—cautiously reinforced by many and elaborate reports, which would promptly expose to his associates any disposition in any member to deviate from the tacit understanding that all were to act together under the subtle direction of a single interpreter of their common purposes, as evidenced in the minute reports of what they had done and in their expressed purposes as to what they intended to do.

In the presence of this record it is futile to argue that the purpose of the Plan was simply to furnish those engaged in this industry, with widely scattered units, the equivalent of such information as is contained in the newspaper and government publications with respect to the market for commodities sold on Boards of Trade or Stock Exchanges. One distinguishing and sufficient difference is that the published reports go to both seller and buyer, but these reports go to the seller only; and another is that there is no skilled interpreter of the published reports, such as we have in this case, to insistently recommend harmony of action likely to prove profitable in proportion as it is unitedly pursued . . . Affirmed . . .

■ [JUSTICES HOLMES, BRANDEIS and MCKENNA dissented, concluding that any market effects that resulted from better-informed sellers was not anticompetitive. Brandeis and McKenna added that: (1) it was not anticompetitive to give sellers advice about the implications of market facts for decisions they should make about production and prices; (2) that sellers did not keep a uniform portion of their capacity unused, and in fact engaged in strenuous efforts to increase production in the face of difficult weather and labor conditions; and (3) that there was no uniformity in prices, and that the member expectation that the Plan would increase prices simply reflected the belief that better information would lead to that result.]

NOTES AND QUESTIONS ON *AMERICAN COLUMN*

1. ***Aggregated v. individuated information exchanges.*** Firms in a competitive market might have legitimate interests in data on *average* market prices, output, and inventory in order to each make their own independent business plans. For example, information that market prices are high, or market output or inventory are low, can give a firm greater confidence that if it invests in building or maintaining a production plant, it will be able to sell enough output to recoup that investment.

However, here the defendant firms exchanged *individuated* information about what particular firms were charging and producing and what individual buyers were paying. A firm generally has no legitimate independent business reason to give its rivals such individuated information on its prices and output. Sharing such information would just give its rivals the knowledge to barely undercut its prices, which they would have incentives to do unless restrained by some agreement on prices. On the other hand, if there were a cartel, exchanging this sort of individuated information is highly useful because it helps cartel members spot any firm that is deviating from the cartel by charging too little or producing too much, which helps the cartel punish and deter such deviations. One can thus infer that the firms must have had some sort of cartel agreement to be willing to exchange such sensitive individuated information.

2. ***Past information v. future projections.*** While competitive firms have a legitimate interest in exchanging information about average *past* market prices and output, here the defendants also met weekly to discuss each other's projections of *future* market prices and output. Exchanging such projections can be very similar to exchanging proposals to offer the future

prices and outputs that fit that projection, with a discussion about which projection is "right" being much like an agreement to charge that projected price and make that projected output. For example, if firms end up concluding that the best projection is that prices will go up 15% and output will go down 10%, that suggests they are agreeing to charge 15% more and produce 10% less.

3. ***Information v. exhortation.*** The defendants also went beyond the exchange of information. They collectively sent each other exhortations not to expand output or lower prices, and they imposed social sanctions on those who did not follow such exhortations. The use of such collective exhortations and sanctions indicates that the firms were trying to act in concert, rather than rely on independent business decisionmaking.

4. ***Does the evidence that prices rose and output declined indicate an agreement on price or output?*** Such evidence is suggestive, but not alone conclusive on whether an agreement on price or output existed. The price increase and output decrease could be attributable to other causes, such as the end of World War I increasing demand and wet weather decreasing supply. However, such alternative causes would not explain why the defendants were constantly advising each other that increasing production would be bad business. If demand is increasing and the supply of others is decreasing due to wet weather, then that would create strong independent business reasons to increase production for any firms that could do so. The fact that instead the defendants actively discouraged each other from increasing production indicated that they were trying to reduce output more than would be caused by bad weather and independent business decisionmaking alone, which suggests that the price increase was at least in part a result of those collective efforts to suppress output.

5. ***Is the inference of a cartel undermined by the evidence that price and unused capacity were non-uniform?*** No. A lack of price uniformity is consistent with a cartel. Any price cartel creates an incentive to cheat on the cartel price, which can lead to some deviations and disuniformity. Also, a cartel that restricts output could produce different prices because of variations in bargaining, product quality, or local market conditions. Likewise, output restrictions could predictably lead to non-uniform amounts of excess capacity. Nor does the fact that some firms were still adding capacity indicate the lack of a cartel, especially in a market with expanding demand. The cartel may be causing firms to add less capacity than they otherwise would, or some cartel members might add capacity so they have the excess capacity needed to punish deviators from the cartel. Capacity expansions by some firms might also indicate either incentives to cheat on the cartel or that the firms were preparing in case the cartel fell apart in the future.

Maple Flooring Manufacturers Ass'n v. United States

268 U.S. 563 (1925).

■ MR. JUSTICE STONE delivered the opinion of the Court . . .

[The Maple Flooring Manufacturers Association had 22 defendant members that made maple, beech, and birch flooring, generally in Michigan, Minnesota or Wisconsin.] . . . [I]n the year 1922 the defendants produced 70% of the total production of these types of flooring, the percentage having been gradually diminished during the five years preceding, the average for the five years being 74.2% . . . The activities . . . of which the Government complains may be summarized as follows:

(1) The computation and distribution among the members of the association of the average cost to association members of all dimensions and grades of flooring.

(2) The compilation and distribution among members of a booklet showing freight rates on flooring from Cadillac, Michigan, to between five and six thousand points of shipment in the United States.

(3) The gathering of statistics which at frequent intervals are supplied by each member of the Association to the Secretary of the Association giving complete information as to the quantity and kind of flooring sold and prices received by the reporting members, and the amount of stock on hand, which information is summarized by the Secretary and transmitted to members without, however, revealing the identity of the members in connection with any specific information thus transmitted.

(4) Meetings at which the representatives of members congregate and discuss the industry and exchange views as to its problems.

Before considering these phases of the activities of the Association, it should be pointed out that it is neither alleged nor proved that there was any agreement among the members of the Association either affecting production, fixing prices or for price maintenance. Both by the articles of association and in actual practice, members have been left free to sell their product at any price they choose and to conduct their business as they please. Although the bill alleges that the activities of the defendants hereinbefore referred to resulted in the maintenance of practical uniformity of net delivered prices as between the several corporate defendants, the evidence fails to establish such uniformity and it was not seriously urged before this Court that any substantial uniformity in price had in fact resulted from the activities of the Association, although it was conceded by defendants that the dissemination of information as to cost of the product and as to production and prices would tend to bring about uniformity in prices through the operation of economic law. Nor was there any direct proof that the activities of the Association had affected prices adversely to consumers. On the contrary, the defendants offered a great volume of evidence tending to show that the trend of prices of the product of the defendants corresponded to the law of supply and demand and that it evidenced no abnormality when compared with the price of commodities generally. There is undisputed evidence that the prices of members were fair and reasonable and that they were usually lower than the prices of non-members and there is no claim that defendants were guilty of unfair or arbitrary trade practices.

[The Government alleged, and the district court found, that the Association's activities constituted an agreement that restrained trade in violation of Sherman Act § 1.] . . .

It cannot, we think, be questioned that data as to the average cost of flooring circulated among the members of the Association when combined with a calculated freight rate which is either exactly or approximately the freight rate from the point of shipment, plus an arbitrary percentage of profit, could be made the basis for fixing prices or for an agreement for price maintenance . . . But . . . the record is barren of evidence that the published list of costs and the freight-rate book have been so used by the present Association . . .

The names of purchasers were not reported and . . . the identifying number of the mill making the report was omitted. All reports of sales and prices dealt exclusively with past and closed transactions. The statistics gathered by the defendant Association are given wide publicity. They are published in trade journals which are read by from 90 to 95% of the persons who purchase the products of Association members. They are sent to the Department of Commerce which publishes a monthly survey of current business. They are forwarded to the Federal Reserve and other banks and are available to anyone at any time desiring to use them. It is to be noted that the statistics gathered and disseminated do not include current price quotations; information as to employment conditions; geographical distribution of shipments; the names of customers or distribution by classes of purchasers; the details with respect to new orders booked, such as names of customers, geographical origin of orders; or details with respect to unfilled orders, such as names of customers, their geographical location; the names of members having surplus stocks on hand; the amount of rough lumber on hand; or information as to cancellation of orders. Nor do they differ in any essential respect from trade or business statistics which are freely gathered and publicly disseminated in numerous branches of industry producing a standardized product such as grain, cotton, coal oil, and involving interstate commerce, whose statistics disclose volume and material elements affecting costs of production, sales price and stock on hand . . .

[M]eetings appear to have been held monthly . . . Trade conditions generally, as reflected by the statistical information disseminated among members, were discussed; the market prices of rough maple flooring were also discussed, as were also manufacturing and market conditions. . . . There was no occasion to discuss past prices, as those were fully detailed in the statistical reports, and the Association was advised by counsel that future prices were not a proper subject of discussion. It was admitted by several witnesses, however, that upon occasion the trend of prices and future prices became the subject of discussion outside the meeting among individual representatives of the defendants attending the meeting. The Government, however, does not charge, nor is it contended, that there was any understanding or agreement, either express or implied, at the meetings or elsewhere, with respect to prices. . . .

In *Eastern States Retail Lumber* . . . [it] was conceded by the defendants, and the court below found, that the circulation of this information would have a natural tendency to cause retailers receiving these reports to withhold patronage from listed concerns; that it therefore, necessarily, tended to restrain wholesalers from selling to the retail trade, which in itself was an undue and unreasonable restraint of commerce. Moreover, the court said: "This record abounds in instances where the offending dealer was thus reported, the hoped for effect, unless he discontinued the offending practice, realized, and his trade directly and appreciably impaired." There was thus presented a case in which the court could not only see that the combination would necessarily result in a restraint on commerce which was unreasonable, but where in fact such restraints had actually been effected by the concerted action of the defendants.

In American Column the . . . record disclosed a systematic effort, participated in by the members of the Association and led and directed by the secretary of the Association, to cut down production and increase prices. The court not only held that this concerted effort was in itself unlawful, but that it resulted in an actual excessive increase of price to which the court found the "united action of this large and influential membership of dealers contributed greatly." The opinion of the court in that case rests squarely on the ground that there was a combination on the part of the members to secure concerted action in curtailment of production and increase of price, which actually resulted in a restraint of commerce, producing increase of price . . .

It is not, we think, open to question that the dissemination of pertinent information concerning any trade or business tends to stabilize that trade or business and to produce uniformity of price and trade practice. Exchange of price quotations of market commodities tends to produce uniformity of prices in the markets of the world. Knowledge of the supplies of available merchandise tends to prevent over-production and to avoid the economic disturbances produced by business crises resulting from overproduction. But the natural effect of the acquisition of wider and more scientific knowledge of business conditions, on the minds of the individuals engaged in commerce, and its consequent effect in stabilizing production and price, can hardly be deemed a restraint of commerce or if so it cannot, we think, be said to be an unreasonable restraint, or in any respect unlawful.

It is the consensus of opinion of economists and of many of the most important agencies of Government that the public interest is served by the gathering and dissemination, in the widest possible manner, of information with respect to the production and distribution, cost and prices in actual sales, of market commodities, because the making available of such information tends to stabilize trade and industry, to produce fairer price levels and to avoid the waste which inevitably attends the unintelligent conduct of economic enterprise. Free competition means a free and open market among both buyers and sellers for the sale and distribution of commodities. Competition does not become less free merely because the conduct of commercial operations becomes more intelligent through the free distribution of knowledge of all the essential factors entering into the commercial transaction. General knowledge that there is an accumulation of surplus of any market commodity would undoubtedly tend to diminish production, but the dissemination of that information cannot in itself be said to be restraint upon commerce in any legal sense. The manufacturer is free to produce, but prudence and business foresight based on that knowledge influence free choice in favor of more limited production. Restraint upon free competition begins when improper use is made of that information through any concerted action which operates to restrain the freedom of action of those who buy and sell.

It was not the purpose or the intent of the Sherman Anti-Trust Law to inhibit the intelligent conduct of business operations, nor do we conceive that its purpose was to suppress such influences as might affect the operations of interstate commerce through the application to them of the individual intelligence of those engaged in commerce, enlightened by accurate information as to the essential elements of the economics of a trade or business, however gathered or disseminated. Persons who unite in gathering and disseminating information in trade journals and statistical reports on industry; who gather and publish statistics as to the amount of production of commodities in interstate commerce, and who report market prices, are not engaged in unlawful conspiracies in restraint of trade merely because the ultimate result of their efforts may be to stabilize prices or limit production through a better understanding of economic laws and a more general ability to conform to them, for the simple reason that the Sherman Law neither repeals economic laws nor prohibits the gathering and dissemination of information. Sellers of any commodity who guide the daily conduct of their business on the basis of market reports would hardly be deemed to be conspirators engaged in restraint of interstate commerce. They would not be any the more so merely because they became stockholders in a corporation or joint owners of a trade journal, engaged in the business of compiling and publishing such reports.

[N]or do we think that the proper application of the principles of decision of *Eastern States Retail Lumber* or *American Column* . . . leads to any such result. The court held that the defendants in those cases were engaged in conspiracies against interstate trade and commerce because it was found that the character of the information which had been gathered and the use which was made of it led irresistibly to the conclusion that they had resulted, or would necessarily result, in a concerted effort of the defendants to curtail production or raise prices of commodities shipped in interstate commerce. The unlawfulness of the combination arose not from the fact that the defendants had effected a combination to gather and disseminate information, but from the fact that the court inferred from the peculiar circumstances of each case that concerted action had resulted, or would necessarily result, in tending arbitrarily to lessen production or increase prices.

Viewed in this light, can it be said in the present case, that the character of the information gathered by the defendants, or the use which is being made of it, leads to any necessary inference that the defendants either have made or will make any different or other use of it than would normally be made if like statistics were published in a trade journal or were published by the Department of Commerce, to which all the gathered statistics are made available? The cost of production, prompt information as to the cost of transportation, are legitimate subjects of enquiry and knowledge in any industry. So likewise is the production of the commodity in that industry, the aggregate surplus stock, and the prices at which the commodity has actually been sold in the usual course of business.

We realize that such information, gathered and disseminated among the members of a trade or business, may be the basis of agreement or concerted action to lessen production arbitrarily or to raise prices beyond the levels of production and price which would prevail if no such agreement or concerted action ensued and those engaged in commerce were left free to base individual initiative on full information of the essential elements of their business. Such concerted action constitutes a restraint of commerce and is illegal and may be enjoined, as may any other combination or activity necessarily resulting in such concerted action as was the subject of consideration in *American Column*. . . . But in the absence of proof of such agreement or concerted action having been actually reached or actually attempted, under the present plan of operation of defendants we can find no basis in the gathering and dissemination of such information by them or in their activities under their present organization for the inference that such concerted action will necessarily result within the rule laid down in those cases.

We decide only that trade associations or combinations of persons or corporations which openly and fairly gather and disseminate information as to the cost of their product, the volume of production, the actual price which the product has brought in past transactions, stocks of merchandise on hand, approximate cost of transportation from the principal point of shipment to the points of consumption, as did these defendants, and who, as they did, meet and discuss such information and statistics without however reaching or attempting to reach any agreement or any concerted action with respect to prices or production or restraining competition, do not thereby engage in unlawful restraint of commerce . . . *[R]eversed* . . .

NOTES AND QUESTIONS ON *MAPLE FLOORING*

1. ***Aggregate past information v. individuated information and future projections.*** Unlike in *American Column*, in this case the defendants did not share individuated data on prices and output nor discuss projections of future prices and output. Instead, the defendants in *Maple Flooring* exchanged only aggregate or average information about past prices and output. Firms do have independent incentives to use information about aggregate past pricing and output in order to plan their individual production decisions. Indeed, the government produces such aggregate information in order to aid firm decisionmaking in many competitive markets. Further, such aggregate past information is far less likely to facilitate a cartel or coordination than the sort of individuated information exchanged in *American Column*. Individuated information would reveal who might be deviating from the cartel or oligopoly price and thus whom to retaliate against. Future projections would provide a salient adjustable point to jointly set or coordinate on future price increases. Aggregate information about past prices and output is less helpful for cartel enforcement or oligopolistic coordination, though it might help somewhat because aggregate information can revealing when someone must be deviating (without necessarily revealing who) and by providing estimates of past pricing or output that could provide a salient (but less adjustable) point for future collusion.

2. ***Is exchanging aggregate past information per se legal?*** It is unclear whether *Maple Flooring* holds that an agreement to exchange aggregated past information, standing alone,[14] is per se legal, even among oligopolists?[15] Parts of the opinion suggest a per se approval by emphasizing the procompetitive benefits of circulating accurate aggregated information

---

[14] When it does not stand alone, but is used to facilitate a price-fixing cartel, an agreement to exchange such aggregated information has been held per se illegal under EC law, thus making those who participate in such an exchange liable even if they did not participate in the price-fixing cartel itself. *See* Commission Decision of 13 July 1994, Cartonboard, O.J. 1994, L 243/1.

[15] The market in *Maple Flooring* had 22 firms, which back in 1925 the Court likely would have been considered sufficiently oligopolistic for successful coordination. However, modern empirical work indicates that oligopolistic coordination is unlikely to significantly increase prices after there are five firms in the market. *See* Bresnahan & Reiss, *Entry and Competition in Concentrated Markets,* 99 J. POL., ECON. 977 (1991).

about past prices and output to aid individual firm planning, and by stressing the unlikelihood that such information could be used for anticompetitive purposes. Other parts emphasize the lack of any evidence that the exchange of information led to uniform or increased prices. If those later statements were necessary to the holding, then that suggests the Court instead held only that the agreement to exchange this information survived rule of reason review because anticompetitive effects were not proven. Under the latter interpretation, oligopolists that agree to exchange aggregated past information could be liable if that information does produce uniform or higher prices by facilitating oligopolistic coordination. Which interpretation do you think is best?

3. ***Is the Court's decision consistent with its admission that any information exchange tends to make prices uniform and stabilize prices and output?*** Yes, because such a general tendency is the natural result if accurate industry information is given to independent competitive business who use it to individually make more accurate projections when deciding on their own future production. If uninformed competitive firms are more likely to mistakenly fail to project that future market demand will likely exceed market supply, then they will be more likely to find themselves with insufficient production (because they hired too few workers or invested in too little expansion) and see prices go up a lot. If uninformed competitive firms are more likely to mistakenly fail to project that future market supply will likely exceed market demand, then they will be more likely to find themselves with too much production and see prices plummet. Thus, accurate information should reduce price volatility even in highly competitive industries, but that is a procompetitive effect because it results from greater efficiency. Because such price effects come from the independent and procompetitive usage of accurate market information to make individual firm production decisions, it is not the sort of price effect condemned by antitrust law.

United States v. Container Corp.

393 U.S. 333 (1969).

■ MR. JUSTICE DOUGLAS delivered the opinion of the Court.

This is a civil antitrust action charging a price-fixing agreement in violation of § 1 of the Sherman Act. The District Court dismissed the complaint [after conducting a bench trial].

The case as proved is unlike any other price decisions we have rendered. There was here an exchange of price information but no agreement to adhere to a price schedule as in . . . *Socony*. There was here an exchange of information concerning specific sales to identified customers, not a statistical report on the average cost to all members, without identifying the parties to specific transactions, as in *Maple Flooring*. While there was present here, as in *Cement Mfrs.*, an exchange of prices to specific customers, there was absent the controlling circumstance, *viz.*, that cement manufacturers, to protect themselves from delivering to contractors more cement than was needed for a specific job and thus receiving a lower price, exchanged price information as a means of protecting their legal rights from fraudulent inducements to deliver more cement than needed for a specific job.

Here all that was present was a request by each defendant of its competitor for information as to the most recent price charged or quoted, whenever it needed such information and whenever it was not available from another source. Each defendant on receiving that request usually furnished the data with the expectation that it would be furnished reciprocal information when it wanted it. That concerted action is of course sufficient to establish the combination or conspiracy, the initial ingredient of a violation of § 1 of the Sherman Act. There was of course freedom to withdraw from the agreement. But the fact remains that when a defendant requested and received price information, it was affirming its willingness to furnish such information in return.

There was to be sure an infrequency and irregularity of price exchanges between the defendants; and often the data were available from the records of the defendants or from the customers themselves. Yet the essence of the agreement was to furnish price information whenever requested. Moreover, although the most recent price charged or quoted was sometimes fragmentary, each defendant had the manuals with which it could compute the price charged by a competitor on a specific order to a specific customer. Further, the price quoted was the current price which a customer would need to pay in order to obtain products from the defendant furnishing the data.

The defendants account for about 90% of the shipment of corrugated containers from plants in the Southeastern United States. While containers vary as to dimensions, weight, color, and so on, they are substantially identical, no matter who produces them, when made to particular specifications. The prices paid depend on price alternatives. Suppliers when seeking new or additional business or keeping old customers, do not exceed a competitor's price. It is common for purchasers to buy from two or more suppliers concurrently. A defendant supplying a customer with containers would usually quote the same price on additional orders, unless costs had changed. Yet where a competitor was charging a particular price, a defendant would normally quote the same price or even a lower price.

The exchange of price information seemed to have the effect of keeping prices within a fairly narrow ambit. Capacity has exceeded the demand from 1955 to 1963, the period covered by the complaint, and the trend of corrugated container prices has been downward. Yet despite this excess capacity and the downward trend of prices, the industry has expanded in the Southeast from 30 manufacturers with 49 plants to 51 manufacturers with 98 plants. An abundance of raw materials and machinery makes entry into the industry easy with an investment of $50,000 to $75,000.

The result of this reciprocal exchange of prices was to stabilize prices though at a downward level. Knowledge of a competitor's price usually meant matching that price. The continuation of some price competition is not fatal to the Government's case. The limitation or reduction of price competition brings the case within the ban, for as we held in *Socony,* interference with the setting of price by free market forces is unlawful *per se.* Price information exchanged in some markets may have no effect on a truly competitive price. But the corrugated container industry is dominated by relatively few sellers. The product is fungible and the competition for sales is price. The demand is inelastic, as buyers place orders only for immediate, short-run needs. The exchange of price data tends toward price uniformity. For a lower price does not mean a larger share of the available business but a sharing of the existing business at a lower return. Stabilizing prices as well as raising them is within the ban of § 1 of the Sherman Act. As we said in *Socony,* "in terms of market operations stabilization is but one form of manipulation." The inferences are irresistible that the exchange of price information has had an anticompetitive effect in the industry, chilling the vigor of price competition. The agreement in the present case, though somewhat casual, is analogous to those in *American Column,* and *United States v. American Linseed Oil Co.*, 262 U.S. 371.

Price is too critical, too sensitive a control to allow it to be used even in an informal manner to restrain competition. *Reversed.*

■ MR. JUSTICE FORTAS, concurring . . . I join in the judgment and opinion of the Court. I do not understand the Court's opinion to hold that the exchange of specific information among sellers as to prices charged to individual customers, pursuant to mutual arrangement, is a *per se* violation of the Sherman Act.

Absent *per se* violation, proof is essential that the practice resulted in an unreasonable restraint of trade. There is no single test to determine when the record adequately shows an "unreasonable restraint of trade"; but a practice such as that here involved, which is adopted for the purpose of arriving at a determination of prices to be quoted to individual customers, inevitably suggests the probability that it so materially interfered with the operation of the price mechanism of the marketplace as to bring it within the condemnation of this Court's decisions.

Theoretical probability, however, is not enough unless we are to regard mere exchange of current price information as so akin to price-fixing by combination or conspiracy as to deserve the *per se* classification. I am not prepared to do this, nor is it necessary here. In this case, the probability that the exchange of specific price information led to an unlawful effect upon prices is adequately buttressed by evidence in the record. This evidence, although not overwhelming, is sufficient in the special circumstances of this case to show an actual effect on pricing and to compel us to hold that the court below erred in dismissing the Government's complaint.

In summary, the record shows that the defendants sought and obtained from competitors who were part of the arrangement information about the competitors' prices to specific customers. "In the majority of instances," the District Court found, that once a defendant had this information he quoted substantially the same price as the competitor, although a higher or lower price would "occasionally" be quoted. Thus the exchange of prices made it possible for individual defendants confidently to name a price equal to that which their competitors were asking. The obvious effect was to "stabilize" prices by joint arrangement—at least to limit any price cuts to the minimum necessary to meet competition. In addition, there was evidence that, in some instances, during periods when various defendants ceased exchanging prices exceptionally sharp and vigorous price reductions resulted.

On this record, taking into account the specially sensitive function of the price term in the antitrust equation, I cannot see that we would be justified in reaching any conclusion other than that defendants' tacit agreement to exchange information about current prices to specific customers did in fact substantially limit the amount of price competition in the industry. That being so, there is no need to consider the possibility of a *per se* violation.

■ MR. JUSTICE MARSHALL, with whom MR. JUSTICE HARLAN and MR. JUSTICE STEWART join, dissenting. I agree with the Court's holding that there existed an agreement among the defendants to exchange price information whenever requested. However, I cannot agree that that agreement should be condemned, either as illegal *per se*, or as having had the purpose or effect of restricting price competition in the corrugated container industry in the Southeastern United States . . .

I do not believe that the agreement in the present case is so devoid of potential benefit or so inherently harmful that we are justified in condemning it without proof that it was entered into for the purpose of restraining price competition or that it actually had that effect . . . Complete market knowledge is certainly not an evil in perfectly competitive markets. This is not, however, such a market, and there is admittedly some danger that price information will be used for anticompetitive purposes, particularly the maintenance of prices at a high level. If the danger that price information will be so used is particularly high in a given situation, then perhaps exchange of information should be condemned.

I do not think the danger is sufficiently high in the present case. Defendants are only 18 of the 51 producers of corrugated containers in the Southeastern United States. Together, they do make up 90% of the market and the six largest defendants do control 60% of the market. But entry is easy; an investment of $50,000 to $75,000 is ordinarily all that is necessary. In fact, the number of sellers has increased from 30 to the present 51 in the eight-year period covered by the complaint. The size of the market has almost doubled because of increased demand for corrugated containers. Nevertheless, some excess capacity is present. The products produced by defendants are undifferentiated. Industry demand is inelastic, so that price changes will not, up to a certain point, affect the total amount purchased. The only effect of price changes will be to reallocate market shares among sellers.

In a competitive situation, each seller will cut his price in order to increase his share of the market, and prices will ultimately stabilize at a competitive level—*i.e.*, price will equal cost, including a reasonable return on capital. Obviously, it would be to a seller's benefit to avoid such price competition and maintain prices at a higher level, with a corresponding increase in profit. In a market with very few sellers, and detailed knowledge of each other's price, such action is possible. However, I do not think it can be concluded that this particular market is sufficiently oligopolistic, especially in light of the ease of entry, to justify the inference that price information will necessarily be used to stabilize prices. Nor do I think that the danger of such a result is sufficiently high to justify imposing a *per se* rule without actual proof. . . .

The Court does not hold that the agreement in the present case was a deliberate attempt to stabilize prices. The evidence in the case, largely the result of stipulation, would not support such a holding . . . Nor do I believe that the Government has proved that the exchange of price information has in this case had the necessary effect of restraining price competition. . . . The record indicates that defendants have offered voluminous evidence concerning price trends and competitive behavior in the corrugated container market. Their exhibits indicate a downward trend in prices, with substantial price variations among defendants and among their different plants. There was also a great deal of shifting of accounts. The District Court specifically found that the corrugated container market was highly competitive and that each defendant engaged in active price competition. The Government would have us ignore this evidence and these findings, and assume that because we are dealing with an industry with overcapacity and yet continued entry, the new entrants must have been attracted by high profits. The Government then argues that high profits can only result from stabilization of prices at an unduly high level. Yet, the Government did not introduce any evidence about the level of profits in this industry, and no evidence about price levels . . . The Government admits that the price trend was down, but asks the Court to assume that the trend would have been accelerated with less informed, and hence more vigorous, price competition.[3] In the absence of any proof whatsoever, I cannot make such an assumption. It is just as likely that price competition was furthered by the exchange as it is that it was depressed.

---

[3] There was no effort to demonstrate that the price behavior of those manufacturers who did not exchange price information, if any, varied significantly from the price behavior of those who did. In fact, several of the District Court's findings indicate that when certain defendants stopped exchanging price information, their price behavior remained essentially the same, and, in some cases, prices actually increased.

Finally, the Government focuses on the finding of the District Court that in a majority of instances a defendant, when it received what it considered reliable price information, would quote or charge substantially the same price. The Court and my Brother FORTAS also focus on this finding. Such an approach ignores, however, the remainder of the District Court's findings. The trial judge found that price decisions were individual decisions, and that defendants frequently did cut prices in order to obtain a particular order. And, the absence of any price parallelism or price uniformity and the downward trend in the industry undercut the conclusion that price information was used to stabilize prices . . .

NOTES AND QUESTIONS ON *CONTAINER*

1. Is it likely that the firms exchanged individual price quotes in order to undercut each other's prices? No, if that were the expected effect, the firms would not be willing to provide such information to each other. Exchanging individual price quotes would benefit the firms only if they expected that the exchange would help them avoid undercutting each other's prices by mistake. Because undercutting each other's prices would make independent business sense, this expectation indicates an anticompetitive understanding (whether reached by hidden agreement or coordination) that they would not use the information to undercut each other's prices. The expectation that other firms would want to offer lower prices without the exchange also suggests supracompetitive pricing.

2. What sufficed to infer an agreement to exchange individual price quotes? The one point on which all the Justices agreed was that this case involved an agreement to exchange individual price information. But there was not actually any direct evidence of such an agreement. Rather, all of the Justices inferred the agreement from the reciprocal practice of answering requests for price quotes. Such a reciprocal practice could arise from coordination in an oligopolistic market and thus need not indicate any hidden express agreement. Instead, *Container* indicates that the interdependent adoption of a facilitating practice (like exchanging individual price quotes) constitutes an antitrust conspiracy, even though interdependent pricing alone does not.

This distinction makes sense on antitrust policy grounds. As noted above, there is no conceptual problem with treating an interdependent understanding as an agreement. The problem with treating interdependent pricing as an agreement is instead that such pricing is unavoidable. In contrast, the interdependent adoption of facilitating practices like exchanging price quotes is entirely avoidable. Condemning the interdependent adoption of a facilitating practice reduces anticompetitive effects by preventing a facilitation that would otherwise help the oligopoly raise prices more than it otherwise could. Nor does such condemnation create any overdeterrence concerns, because the exchange of specific, individuated price information serves no procompetitive purpose.

3. ***Should an agreement to exchange individual price information be per se illegal?*** It would seem so, because such an agreement has anticompetitive potential with no procompetitive virtue, regardless of market concentration. In a non-oligopolistic market, firms have no incentive to exchange such individuated information unless there is a hidden express agreement to use the information anticompetitively. In an oligopolistic market, firms have no incentive to exchange such individuated information unless there is either a hidden express agreement or oligopolistic coordination on using the information anticompetitively. This may explain why the majority seemed to embrace an effective per se approach, condemning the agreement without inquiring into whether the market was oligopolistic and without requiring any direct evidence of increased prices.

The concurring opinion said it was not yet ready to find per se illegality, because it was not sure an agreement to exchange price quotes inevitably hampered competition. But the defendants would have no incentive to exchange price quotes unless doing so did hamper competition, and the concurring opinion does not give any reason to permit such an agreement without a procompetitive benefit. The dissent rejected per se illegality, adding that it did not think an agreement to exchange price quotes was "devoid of potential benefit". But the dissent did not explain what that procompetitive benefit could be.

Focusing on the agreement to exchange price information can simplify cases like *American Column*. In that case, the Court addressed whether an agreement on price or output existed, which required an inference from circumstantial evidence and proof of parallel conduct on prices or output. The *Container* case makes clear that the *American Column* Court could instead have simply held that the undisputed agreement to exchange the individuated information was itself illegal.

4. ***Was the market oligopolistic?*** While rejecting per se illegality, the dissent indicated that an agreement to exchange individual price information could be illegal when a market is oligopolistic, but the dissent concluded the market was not actually oligopolistic. While that inquiry would not be necessary under a per se rule, it would normally be necessary for any facilitating practice that does have procompetitive effects, in order to show that the likelihood of anticompetitive effects offset those procompetitive benefits under the Rule of Reason.

Was the market oligopolistic? The market factors cut in different ways. Although there were 51 total firms in the market, the 18 defendants controlled 90% of the market, indicating a high collective market share. While 18 is higher than the number of firms that is typically able to coordinate, the six largest defendants controlled 60% of the market and 18 it is not too many firms to effectively monitor. The dissent acknowledged that the products were undifferentiated. After all, corrugated containers are the sort of shipping boxes we all use when moving, which do not vary much among different producers. Such product homogeneity makes oligopolistic coordination easier. The dissent also acknowledged that demand was growing and inelastic, so a price increase was unlikely to reduce market output, which makes collective market power more likely.

Against the above evidence, the dissent stressed that entry was relatively easy and increasing over time and that excess capacity remained in the market. Low entry barriers do cut against a conclusion that the alleged oligopoly had collective market power. However, a trend of increasing entry indicates that new firms were attracted by high prices, which is consistent with supracompetitive pricing. Moreover, the fact that the defendants maintained excess capacity, during a time when demand was growing and other firms found the market prices attractive enough to enter, suggests that the defendants were suppressing their output. After all, the costs of increasing production would seem lower for the defendants, who could simply use their excess capacity to increase production, than for entrants, who had to incur capital costs to enter. Even though the capital costs of entry were only $50–75,000, that is still a cost of expanding output that the entrants faced and the defendants with excess capacity did not. If the prices were high enough to invite entry despite those higher entrant costs, then those prices should have also given the defendants independent incentives to use their excess capacity to expand output. The fact that the defendants did not act on those independent incentives suggests they were instead coordinating (or conspiring) on reducing output.

5. ***Did the evidence directly show anticompetitive effects?*** The evidence showed that prices were decreasing and market output was increasing. This does not negate anticompetitive effects because, as the Government pointed out, the price decrease and output increase could have been faster or sharper without the information exchange. But no affirmative evidence was offered to show that prices and output were higher than those but-for levels. The evidence also showed that, when firms stopped exchanging prices, that sometimes produced sharp price reductions, sometimes produced no change, and sometimes produced a price increase. Such mixed evidence also did not provide much direct evidence of anticompetitive effects. The majority and concurring opinion instead mainly relied on the evidence that, most of the time, a firm who received price information would charge the same price as its rival. This evidence indicated that prices were affected by the information exchange, at least in the sense of narrowing the range of prices. That effect is so likely to follow from any agreement to exchange price information that it is close to a per se rule.

Container thus holds that even that the weak effect of reducing price variation suffices to condemn an agreement to exchange individuated price quotes, even though *Maple Flooring* held that a similar weak effect did not suffice to condemn an agreement to exchange aggregated price information. The difference is that agreements to exchange individuated price information have far greater anticompetitive potential, and far less procompetitive justification, than agreements to exchange aggregate price information.

6. ***Why not just rely on buyers?*** If sellers cannot exchange price quotes, one might wonder why the firms do not just rely on what the buyers tell them about the other prices they have been quoted. The obvious reason is that buyers have incentives to exaggerate how low a quote they are getting from other sellers, hoping that will get them a lower price. Does this suggest the exchange of price quotes among sellers might be justified as necessary to curb buyer deception, just like in *Cement Manufacturers?* No, for two reasons. First, the nature of the buyer deception differs in the two cases in a way that changes the efficiency effects. In *Cement Manufacturers,* the buyer deception inefficiently shifted uncontracted-for risks to sellers and raised contract prices to honest buyers. In *Container*, the buyer deception procompetitively undermined oligopolistic coordination by suggesting that other firms were defecting. Curbing the buyer deception was thus efficient in *Cement Manufacturers* but not in *Container*. Second, the nature of the information differs in ways that changes whether the information exchange implies an agreement on how to use the information. In *Cement Manufacturers,* the defendants had incentives to exchange the information even without an agreement about how to use it, because each defendant had an independent motive to use such information to cease doing business with buyers who imposed additional risks. In *Container,* the defendants had no incentive to exchange the information unless they also had a common understanding that firms would not use that information to undercut each other's prices.

7. ***What if sellers posed as buyers?*** Suppose that sellers decided to pose as buyers and ask other sellers what prices they were quoting. As long as each seller did this on its own and other sellers truly did not know the apparent buyers were actually sellers, a court could not infer agreement. The activity does not involve even the sort of interdependent mutual understanding that was deemed an agreement in *Container*. Each seller would provide price quotes because it is acting on its independent incentive to make sales and a mistaken belief that the request comes from a buyer, rather than because of an interdependent understanding that other sellers will reciprocate later. Thus the activity could not be condemned under Sherman Act § 1. However, if the market were sufficiently oligopolistic, such a unilateral facilitating practice could be condemned under FTC Act § 5, and indeed should be condemned because it has anticompetitive potential and no procompetitive benefit.

United States v. United States Gypsum

438 U.S. 422 (1978).

■ MR. CHIEF JUSTICE BURGER delivered the opinion of the Court.

. . . The gypsum board industry is highly concentrated, with the number of producers ranging from 9 to 15 in the period 1960–1973. The eight largest companies accounted for some 94% of the national sales with the seven "single-plant producers" accounting for the remaining 6%. Most of the major producers and a large number of the single-plant producers are members of the Gypsum Association which since 1930 has served as a trade association of gypsum board manufacturers . . .

The focus of the Government's price-fixing case at trial was interseller price verification—that is, the practice allegedly followed by the gypsum board manufacturers of telephoning a competing producer to determine the price currently being offered on gypsum board to a specific customer . . . [T]he question upon which the Court of Appeals focused [was] whether verification of price concessions with competitors for the sole purpose of taking advantage of the § 2(b) meeting-competition defense should . . . preclud[e] liability under § 1 of the Sherman Act . . .

Section 2(a) of the Clayton Act, as amended by the Robinson-Patman Act, embodies a general prohibition of price discrimination between buyers when an injury to competition is the consequence. The primary exception to the § 2(a) bar is the meeting-competition defense which is incorporated as a proviso to the burden-of-proof requirements set out in § 2(b) . . . [I]n Standard Oil Co. v. FTC, 340 U.S. 231 (1951) . . . we . . . constru[ed] § 2(b) to provide an absolute defense to liability for price discrimination . . .

In FTC v. A. E. Staley Mfg. Co., 324 U.S. 746 (1945), the Court provided the first and still the most complete explanation of the kind of showing which a seller must make in order to satisfy the good-faith requirement of the § 2(b) defense:

> "Section 2(b) does not require the seller to justify price discriminations by showing that in fact they met a competitor's price. But it does place on the seller the burden of showing that the price was made in good faith to meet a competitor's . . . We agree with the Commission that the statute at least requires the seller, who has knowingly discriminated in price, to show the existence of facts which would lead a reasonable and prudent person to believe that the granting of a lower price would in fact meet the equally low price of a competitor." *Id.*, at 759–760.

Application of these standards to the facts in *Staley* led to the conclusion that the § 2(b) defense had not been made out. The record revealed that the lower price had been based simply on reports of salesmen, brokers, or purchasers with no efforts having been made by the seller "to investigate or verify" the reports or the character and reliability of the informants. Similarly, in Corn Products Co. v. FTC, 324 U.S. 726 (1945), decided the same day, the § 2(b) defense was not allowed because "[the] only evidence said to rebut the *prima facie* case . . . of the price discriminations was given by witnesses who had no personal knowledge of the transactions, and was limited to statements of each witness's assumption or conclusion that the price discriminations were justified by competition."

Staley's "investigate or verify" language coupled with *Corn Products'* focus on "personal knowledge of the transactions" have apparently suggested to a number of courts that, at least in certain circumstances, direct verification of discounts between competitors may be necessary to meet the burden-of-proof requirements of the § 2(b) defense . . .

A good-faith belief, rather than absolute certainty, that a price concession is being offered to meet an equally low price offered by a competitor is sufficient to satisfy the § 2(b) defense. While casual reliance on uncorroborated reports of buyers or sales representatives without further investigation may not, as we noted earlier, be sufficient to make the requisite showing of good faith, nothing in the language of § 2(b) or the gloss on that language in *Staley* and *Corn Products* indicates that direct discussions of price between competitors are required . . . On the contrary, the § 2(b) defense has been successfully invoked in the absence of interseller verification on numerous occasions . . . . .

The so-called problem of the untruthful buyer which concerned the Court of Appeals does not in our view call for a different approach to the § 2(b) defense. The good-faith standard remains the benchmark against which the seller's conduct is to be evaluated, and we agree with the Government and the FTC that this standard can be satisfied by efforts falling short of interseller verification in most circumstances where the seller has only vague, generalized doubts about the reliability of its commercial adversary—the buyer.[29] Given the fact-specific nature of the inquiry, it is difficult to predict all the factors the FTC or a court would consider in appraising a seller's good faith in matching a competing offer in these circumstances. Certainly, evidence that a seller had received reports of similar discounts from other customers, or was threatened with a termination of purchases if the discount were not met, would be relevant in this regard. Efforts to corroborate the reported discount by seeking documentary evidence or by appraising its reasonableness in terms of available market data would also be probative as would the seller's past experience with the particular buyer in question.

There remains the possibility that in a limited number of situations a seller may have substantial reasons to doubt the accuracy of reports of a competing offer and may be unable to corroborate such reports in any of the generally accepted ways . . . As an abstract proposition, resort to interseller verification as a means of checking the buyer's reliability seems a possible solution to the seller's plight, but careful examination reveals serious problems with the practice.

Both economic theory and common human experience suggest that interseller verification—if undertaken on an isolated and infrequent basis with no provision for reciprocity or cooperation—will not serve its putative function of corroborating the representations of unreliable buyers regarding the existence of competing offers. Price concessions by oligopolists generally yield competitive advantages only if secrecy can be maintained; when the terms of the concession are made publicly known,

[29] "Although a seller may take advantage of the meeting competition defense only if it has a commercially reasonable belief that its price concession is necessary to meet an equally low price of a competitor, a seller may acquire this belief, and hence perfect its defense, by doing everything reasonably feasible—short of violating some other statute, such as the Sherman Act—to determine the veracity of a customer's statement that he has been offered a lower price. If, after making reasonable, lawful, inquiries, the seller cannot ascertain that the buyer is lying, the seller is entitled to make the sale . . . There is no need for a seller to discuss price with his competitors to take advantage of the meeting competition defense." (Citations omitted.) Brief for United States 86–87, and n. 78.

other competitors are likely to follow and any advantage to the initiator is lost in the process. *See also Container.* Thus, if one seller offers a price concession for the purpose of winning over one of his competitor's customers, it is unlikely that the same seller will freely inform its competitor of the details of the concession so that it can be promptly matched and diffused. Instead, such a seller would appear to have at least as great an incentive to misrepresent the existence or size of the discount as would the buyer who received it. Thus verification, if undertaken on a one-shot basis for the sole purpose of complying with the § 2(b) defense, does not hold out much promise as a means of shoring up buyers' representations.

The other variety of interseller verification is, like the conduct charged in the instant case, undertaken pursuant to an agreement, either tacit or express, providing for reciprocity among competitors in the exchange of price information. Such an agreement would make little economic sense, in our view, if its sole purpose were to guarantee all participants the opportunity to match the secret price concessions of other participants under § 2(b). For in such circumstances, each seller would know that his price concession could not be kept from his competitors and no seller participating in the information-exchange arrangement would, therefore, have any incentive for deviating from the prevailing price level in the industry. *See Container.* Regardless of its putative purpose, the most likely consequence of any such agreement to exchange price information would be the stabilization of industry prices. Instead of facilitating use of the § 2(b) defense, such an agreement would have the effect of eliminating the very price concessions which provide the main element of competition in oligopolistic industries and the primary occasion for resort to the meeting-competition defense. . . .

We are left, therefore, on the one hand, with doubts about both the need for and the efficacy of interseller verification as a means of facilitating compliance with § 2(b), and, on the other, with recognition of the tendency for price discussions between competitors to contribute to the stability of oligopolistic prices and open the way for the growth of prohibited anticompetitive activity. To recognize even a limited . . . exception for interseller verification in such circumstances would be to remove from scrutiny under the Sherman Act conduct falling near its core with no assurance, and indeed with serious doubts, that competing antitrust policies would be served thereby. In Automatic Canteen Co. v. FTC, 346 U.S. 61, 74 (1953), the Court suggested that as a general rule the Robinson-Patman Act should be construed so as to insure its coherence with "the broader antitrust policies that have been laid down by Congress"; that observation buttresses our conclusion that exchanges of price information—even when putatively for purposes of Robinson-

Patman Act compliance—must remain subject to close scrutiny under the Sherman Act.[32]

NOTES AND QUESTIONS ON *GYPSUM*

1. ***Is it sound antitrust policy to prohibit selective price cuts unless they meet competition?*** When a firm selectively offers a price cut to some buyers but not others, it engages in price discrimination. Without cost justifications or changing market conditions, the Robinson-Patman Act (at least as interpreted in *Morton Salt*) prohibits such selective price cuts unless they reflect good faith efforts to meet competition. The Act can thus often require firms to match rival prices, rather than undercut rival prices either in advance or in response to a rival quote. The problem is that this feature of the Robinson-Patman Act effectively helps enforce oligopolistic pricing, prohibiting precisely the sort of undercutting of rival prices that is most likely to cause an unraveling of oligopolistic coordination. This is an important substantive problem with the Robinson-Patman Act, and it creates statutory tension because an agreement to match but not undercut each other's prices would be per se illegal under the Sherman Act.

2. ***Can a seller establish a good faith belief by just relying on what the buyer says?*** Under the Robinson-Patman Act, a seller cannot establish a good faith belief that it is meeting competition by simply relying on buyer statements that other sellers have offered the buyer a low price. The reason is that buyers have incentives to lie and say that a rival seller has offered a lower price when in fact it has not.

3. ***Given that a seller cannot simply rely on buyer statements, why cannot a seller establish a good belief by checking with other sellers?*** The Court reasoned there were two possibilities. The first is that the interseller price verification involves no tacit or express agreement of reciprocity. In that scenario, checking with sellers is no more reliable than checking with buyers because both have incentives to lie. Indeed, no rational seller would share its prices truthfully without some tacit or express agreement that its prices would not be undercut.

The other possibility is that the interseller price verification does involve a tacit or express agreement of reciprocity. But in that case, the agreement to exchange price quotes would itself violate the Sherman Act under the *Container* decision. And such an agreement would be rational only

[32] That the § 2(b) defense may not be available in every situation where a competing offer has in fact been made is not, in our view, a meaningful objection to our holding. The good-faith requirement of the § 2(b) defense implicitly suggests a somewhat imperfect matching between competing offers actually made and those allowed to be met. Unless this requirement is to be abandoned, it seems clear that inadequate information will, in a limited number of cases, deny the defense to some who, if all the facts had been known, would have been entitled to invoke it. For reasons already discussed, interseller verification does not provide a satisfactory solution to this seemingly inevitable problem of inadequate information. Moreover, § 2(b) affords only a defense to liability and not an affirmative right under the Act. While sellers are, of course, entitled to take advantage of the defense when they can satisfy its requirements, efforts to increase its availability at the expense of broader, affirmative antitrust policies must be rejected.

if its purpose was to prevent price concessions, rather than assure they were accurately matched.

*4. **If a seller cannot check with other sellers or simply rely on the buyer, what is a seller supposed to do?*** Although a seller cannot check with other sellers or simply rely on the buyer, it can establish a good faith belief by verifying a buyer's claim to have a lower offer from another seller. The Court suggests that it would suffice if (a) other customers reported similar rival discounts, (b) the buyer in question threatened not to buy if the claimed rival discount was not met, or (c) the buyer provided the seller with documentation of the rival offer.

However, each of these possibilities is problematic. The fact that other buyers are not reporting similar discounts may simply mean that the rival is providing a selective discount to the buyer in question. Also, a seller may hesitate to ask other buyers whether they have received similar discounts from the rival, because a seller will hardly want to run around advertising the discounts of their rivals to other buyers.

The fact that a buyer threatens to buy elsewhere does not really verify the claimed rival price quote. Every negotiation is driven by an implicit threat to buy elsewhere unless contract demands are satisfied. The buyer could be bluffing, so making such a threat does not mean that the buyer actually received a lower price offer from the rival. Moreover, any buyer statement about rival discounts is intended to convey a threat to buy from the rival, or else the buyer statement could not affect the seller's decision whether to discount. Such an implicit threat thus exists whenever a buyer claims rivals are offering a lower price.

As for documentation, it raises two problems. First, if a buyer refuses to provide documentation, another case holds that a seller nonetheless acts in good faith if it relies on the statements of a buyer who threatens to buy elsewhere. Great Atlantic & Pacific Tea v. FTC, 440 U.S. 69 (1979). Thus, documentation is clearly not necessary. The buyer threat to buy from the rival suffices, and such a threat really seems implicit in every case. Second, if a buyer does give the seller documentary proof of the rival offer, that would accomplish much the same as the interseller verification that the Court prohibited.

The fundamental problem is that accurately verifying buyer assertions about rival price quotes is affirmatively harmful under the Sherman Act, which under the *Container* decision seeks to prevent sellers from curbing buyer deceptions that can undermine cartel or oligopolistic pricing. That Sherman Act policy cannot really be squared with a legal requirement of thorough investigation before lowering prices to meet what a buyer says the rivals are offering. Unfortunately, such an investigation is what the Robinson-Patman Act inadvisedly requires. To resolve this tension with the minimum damage to sound antitrust policy, the Court in *Gypsum* effectively cabins the Robinson-Patman Act to its smallest plausible legal scope, prohibiting interseller verification and deeming buyer threats to buy elsewhere adequate verification, even though in fact such buyer threats are unlikely to accurately verify the claimed rival price.

5. ***Buyer liability.*** Robinson-Patman Act § 2(f) makes a buyer liable if it knowingly induces or receives a prohibited price discrimination. Should a buyer be held liable under § 2(f) when it knows the seller's price has beat the competition, even though the seller is not liable because it in good faith thought it was just meeting competition? In *Great Atlantic,* the Court held no because: (1) the § 2(f) language requiring "a prohibited price discrimination" means that buyer liability depends on seller liability under § 2(a); and (2) interpreting § 2(f) to prohibit the knowing receipt of a price cut that did not meet competition would require buyers to inform sellers when they have beaten competition, which would lead to the equivalent of the exchange of price quotes that was prohibited in *Container.*

The Court left open whether a buyer that affirmatively lied about a rival bid should be liable under § 2(f) when the seller relied in good faith on the buyer's representations. Should such a lying buyer be liable given the Court's reasoning? The same two reasons cited in *Great Atlantic* would also seem to suggest no Robinson-Patman Act liability for the lying buyer: (1) the statutory language would still indicate no buyer violation without a seller violation; and (2) imposing antitrust liability for buyer lying about price quotes would increase the likelihood that sellers would receive the sort of accurate information about rival price quotes that decisions like *Container* try to avoid. A Court might hesitate to condone lying, but the reality is that, in oligopolistic markets, buyer lying about rival pricing is procompetitive.

FTC v. Cement Institute

333 U.S. 683 (1948).

■ MR. JUSTICE BLACK delivered the opinion of the Court.

. . . [The FTC charged that respondents, the Cement Institute and its 74 members that made or sold cement, committed an unfair method of competition in violation of FTC Act § 5.] . . . The core of the charge was that the respondents had restrained and hindered competition in the sale and distribution of cement by means of a combination among themselves made effective through mutual understanding or agreement to employ a multiple basing point system of pricing. It was alleged that this system resulted in the quotation of identical terms of sale and identical prices for cement by the respondents at any given point in the United States. This system had worked so successfully, it was further charged, that for many years prior to the filing of the complaint, all cement buyers throughout the nation, with rare exceptions, had been unable to purchase cement for delivery in any given locality from any one of the respondents at a lower price or on more favorable terms than from any of the other respondents . . .

The Commission has jurisdiction to declare that conduct tending to restrain trade is an unfair method of competition even though the selfsame conduct may also violate the Sherman Act . . . [A]lthough all conduct violative of the Sherman Act may likewise come within the unfair trade practice prohibitions of the Trade Commission Act, the converse is not necessarily true. It has long been recognized that there are many unfair methods of competition that do not assume the proportions of Sherman Act violations. Hence a conclusion that respondents' conduct constituted an unfair method of competition does not necessarily mean that their same activities would also be found to violate § 1 of the Sherman Act . . .

The Multiple Basing Point Delivered Price System.—. . . Goods may be sold and delivered to customers at the seller's mill or warehouse door or may be sold free on board (f.o.b.) trucks or railroad cars immediately adjacent to the seller's mill or warehouse. In either event the actual cost of the goods to the purchaser is, broadly speaking, the seller's "mill price" plus the purchaser's cost of transportation. However, if the seller fixes a price at which he undertakes to deliver goods to the purchaser where they are to be used, the cost to the purchaser is the "delivered price." A seller who makes the "mill price" identical for all purchasers of like amount and quality simply delivers his goods at the same place (his mill) and for the same price (price at the mill). He thus receives for all f.o.b. mill sales an identical net amount of money for like goods from all customers. But a "delivered price" system creates complications which may result in a seller's receiving different net returns from the sale of like goods. The cost of transporting 500 miles is almost always more than the cost of transporting 100 miles. Consequently if customers 100 and 500 miles away pay the same "delivered price," the seller's net return is less from the more distant customer . . .

The best known early example of a basing point price system was called "Pittsburgh plus." It related to the price of steel. The Pittsburgh price was the base price, Pittsburgh being therefore called a price basing point. In order for the system to work, sales had to be made only at delivered prices. Under this system the delivered price of steel from anywhere in the United States to a point of delivery anywhere in the United States was in general the Pittsburgh price plus the railroad freight rate from Pittsburgh to the point of delivery. Take Chicago, Illinois, as an illustration of the operation and consequences of the system. A Chicago steel producer was not free to sell his steel at cost plus a reasonable profit. He must sell it at the Pittsburgh price plus the railroad freight rate from Pittsburgh to the point of delivery. Chicago steel customers were by this pricing plan thus arbitrarily required to pay for Chicago produced steel the Pittsburgh base price plus what it would have cost to ship the steel by rail from Pittsburgh to Chicago had it been shipped. The theoretical cost of this fictitious shipment became known as "phantom freight." But had it been economically possible under this plan for a Chicago producer to ship his steel to Pittsburgh, his "delivered price" would have been merely the Pittsburgh price, although he actually would have been required to pay the freight from Chicago to Pittsburgh. Thus the "delivered price" under these latter circumstances required a Chicago (non-basing point) producer to "absorb" freight costs. That is, such a seller's net returns became smaller and smaller as his deliveries approached closer and closer to the basing point.

Several results obviously flow from use of a single basing point system such as "Pittsburgh plus" originally was. One is that the "delivered prices" of all producers in every locality where deliveries are made are always the same regardless of the producers' different freight costs. Another is that sales made by a non-base mill for delivery at different localities result in net receipts to the seller which vary in amounts equivalent to the "phantom freight" included in, or the "freight absorption" taken from the "delivered price."

As commonly employed by respondents, the basing point system is not single but multiple. That is, instead of one basing point, like that in "Pittsburgh plus," a number of basing point localities are used. In the multiple basing point system, just as in the single basing point system, freight absorption or phantom freight is an element of the delivered price on all sales not governed by a basing point actually located at the seller's mill. And all sellers quote identical delivered prices in any given locality regardless of their different costs of production and their different freight expenses. Thus the multiple and single systems function in the same general manner and produce the same consequences—identity of prices and diversity of net returns . . .

This Court's opinion in *Cement Mfrs.* . . . known as the *Old Cement* case, is relied on by the respondents in almost every contention they present. We think it has little relevance, if any at all, to the issues in this case . . . In the first place, unlike the *Old Cement* case, the Commission does here specifically charge a combination to utilize the basing point system as a means to bring about uniform prices and terms of sale . . . In the second place, individual conduct, or concerted conduct, which falls short of being a Sherman Act violation may as a matter of law constitute an "unfair method of competition" prohibited by the Trade Commission Act. A major purpose of that Act, as we have frequently said, was to enable the Commission to restrain practices as "unfair" which, although not yet having grown into Sherman Act dimensions would, most likely do so if left unrestrained. The Commission and the courts were to determine what conduct, even though it might then be short of a Sherman Act violation, was an "unfair method of competition." This general language was deliberately left to the "commission and the courts" for definition because it was thought that "There is no limit to human inventiveness in this field"; that consequently, a definition that fitted practices known to lead towards an unlawful restraint of trade today would not fit tomorrow's new inventions in the field; and that for Congress to try to keep its precise definitions abreast of this course of conduct would be an "endless task."

Findings and Evidence.—. . . [W]e think that the following facts . . . are sufficient to warrant the Commission's finding of concerted action.

When the Commission rendered its decision there were about 80 cement manufacturing companies in the United States operating about 150 mills. Ten companies controlled more than half of the mills and there were substantial corporate affiliations among many of the others. This concentration of productive capacity made concerted action far less difficult than it would otherwise have been. The belief is prevalent in the industry that because of the standardized nature of cement, among other reasons, price competition is wholly unsuited to it. That belief is historic. It has resulted in concerted activities to devise means and measures to do away with competition in the industry. Out of those activities came the multiple basing point delivered price system. Evidence shows it to be a handy instrument to bring about elimination of any kind of price competition. The use of the multiple basing point delivered price system by the cement producers has been coincident with a situation whereby for many years, with rare exceptions, cement has been offered for sale in every given locality at identical prices and terms by all producers. Thousands of secret sealed bids have been received by public agencies which corresponded in prices of cement down to a fractional part of a penny. [The Court cited an example where 11 bidders each submitted identical sealed bids of $3.286854 per barrel with the identical discount of 10 cents per barrel for payment within 15 days.]

Occasionally foreign cement has been imported, and cement dealers have sold it below the delivered price of the domestic product. Dealers who persisted in selling foreign cement were boycotted by the domestic producers. Officers of the Institute took the lead in securing pledges by producers not to permit sales f.o.b. mill to purchasers who furnished their own trucks, a practice regarded as seriously disruptive of the entire delivered price structure of the industry.

During the depression in the 1930's, slow business prompted some producers to deviate from the prices fixed by the delivered price system. Meetings were held by other producers; an effective plan was devised to punish the recalcitrants and bring them into line. The plan was simple but successful. Other producers made the recalcitrant's plant an involuntary base point. The base price was driven down with relatively insignificant losses to the producers who imposed the punitive basing point, but with heavy losses to the recalcitrant who had to make all its sales on this basis. In one instance, where a producer had made a low public bid, a punitive base point price was put on its plant and cement was reduced 10 cents per barrel; further reductions quickly followed until the base price at which this recalcitrant had to sell its cement dropped to 75 cents per barrel, scarcely one-half of its former base price of $1.45. Within six weeks after the base price hit 75 cents capitulation occurred and the recalcitrant joined a Portland cement association. Cement in that locality then bounced back to $1.15, later to $1.35, and finally to $1.75.

The foregoing are but illustrations of the practices shown to have been utilized to maintain the basing point price system. Respondents offered testimony that cement is a standardized product, that "cement is cement," that no differences existed in quality or usefulness, and that purchasers demanded delivered price quotations because of the high cost of transportation from mill to dealer. There was evidence, however, that the Institute and its members had, in the interest of eliminating competition, suppressed information as to the variations in quality that sometimes exist in different cements. Respondents introduced the testimony of economists to the effect that competition alone could lead to the evolution of a multiple basing point system of uniform delivered prices and terms of sale for an industry with a standardized product and with relatively high freight costs. These economists testified that for the above reasons no inferences of collusion, agreement, or understanding could be drawn from the admitted fact that cement prices of all United States producers had for many years almost invariably been the same in every given locality in the country. There was also considerable testimony by other economic experts that the multiple basing point system of delivered prices as employed by respondents contravened accepted economic principles and could only have been maintained through collusion.

The Commission did not adopt the views of the economists produced by the respondents. It decided that even though competition might tend to drive the price of standardized products to a uniform level, such a tendency alone could not account for the almost perfect identity in prices, discounts, and cement containers which had prevailed for so long a time in the cement industry. The Commission held that the uniformity and absence of competition in the industry were the results of understandings or agreements entered into or carried out by concert of the Institute and the other respondents. It may possibly be true, as respondents' economists testified, that cement producers will, without agreement express or implied and without understanding explicit or tacit, always and at all times (for such has been substantially the case here) charge for their cement precisely, to the fractional part of a penny, the price their competitors charge. Certainly it runs counter to what many people have believed, namely, that without agreement, prices will vary—that the desire to sell will sometimes be so strong that a seller will be willing to lower his prices and take his chances. We therefore hold that the Commission was not compelled to accept the views of respondents' economist-witnesses that active competition was bound to produce uniform cement prices. The Commission was authorized to find understanding, express or implied, from evidence that the industry's Institute actively worked, in cooperation with various of its members, to maintain the multiple basing point delivered price system; that this pricing system is calculated to produce, and has produced, uniform prices and terms of sale throughout the country; and that all of the respondents have sold their cement substantially in accord with the pattern required by the multiple basing point system.

Unfair Methods of Competition.—We sustain the Commission's holding that concerted maintenance of the basing point delivered price system is an unfair method of competition prohibited by the Federal Trade Commission Act. In so doing we give great weight to the Commission's conclusion . . . [T]he express intention of Congress [was] to create an agency whose membership would at all times be experienced, so that its conclusions would be the result of an expertness coming from experience . . . The kind of specialized knowledge Congress wanted its agency to have was an expertness that would fit it to stop at the threshold every unfair trade practice—that kind of practice which, if left alone, "destroys competition and establishes monopoly."

We cannot say that the Commission is wrong in concluding that the delivered-price system as here used provides an effective instrument which, if left free for use of the respondents, would result in complete destruction of competition and the establishment of monopoly in the cement industry . . . We uphold the Commission's conclusion that the basing point delivered price system employed by respondents is an unfair trade practice which the Trade Commission may suppress.[19]

NOTES AND QUESTIONS ON *CEMENT INSTITUTE*

1. ***Why can an agreement to use a common basing point be inferred?*** Using a common basing point means that every seller charges each buyer the seller's cement price plus the transportation cost from the common basing point to the buyer, no matter where the seller is actually located. For example, here a common basing point was Pittsburgh. Using a common basing point thus meant that if a seller in Chicago was selling to a buyer in Chicago, the transportation cost from Pittsburgh to Chicago would be added to the seller's price even though that transportation cost is not actually incurred. Without such a common basing point system, each firm would charge a price plus actual transportation costs and thus would have an advantage in selling to customers located near the firm. Adhering to a common basing point system negates that transportation cost advantage and will often prevent each firm from making sales to nearby customers that it otherwise would have won. Thus, firms have no independent incentive to adhere to a basing point system: adherence will frequently lose the firm sales and such a system inefficiently allocates sales in a way that ignores actual transportation costs.

---

[19] While we hold that the Commission's findings of combination were supported by evidence, that does not mean that existence of a "combination" is an indispensable ingredient of an "unfair method of competition" under the Trade Commission Act.

Given the lack of independent incentive, the parallel adherence to a common basing point must reflect a common motive. Adherence could be profitable if other firms also adhere to the basing point system and that system helps the firms collude on higher prices. A common basing point can aid collusion in several ways. First, a common basing point makes it easier to settle on a common price because it suppresses transportation cost differences. Second, a common basing point makes it easier to notice deviations from that common price by eliminating ambiguities about whether changed prices or shifts in sales might reflect changed transportation costs rather than price deviations. Third, a common basing point makes it easier to punish such deviations through the mechanism of making the deviator's city a basing point, which makes all rival charges lower in that city by omitting any transportation cost. Such aids to collusion are important whether the firms are coordinating on price or have a hidden cartel, because even a cartel must solve the problems of settling on a common cartel price and noticing and punishing deviations from that price.

Given that only a collective motive could explain parallel adherence to a common basing point, there must have been either some hidden express agreement or tacit coordination with other firms to use a common basing point. Because 74 firms were involved, tacit coordination seems implausible, suggesting that the parallel adherence must have reflected a hidden express agreement. Further, even if the common basing point were adopted via tacit coordination, adopting an avoidable facilitating practice via tacit coordination suffices to constitute an agreement under the *Container* decision. The Court thus did not need to resolve whether the parallel adherence reflected "mutual understanding or agreement" to affirm the FTC's finding of "concerted action."

2. ***Did other parallel conduct conflict with independent incentives?*** Yes, the firms also engaged in several other forms of parallel conduct that confirmed they were not acting independently. First, the firms pledged not to permit sales free on board (f.o.b.) mill. Selling f.o.b. mill occurs when a seller loads its product for free on board the buyer's truck at the seller's mill, leaving the buyer responsible for transportation costs from the seller's mill to the buyer's location. If it were inefficient for buyers to bear their own transportation costs, there would be no need for sellers to pledge to avoid selling f.o.b. mill; buyers faced with the choice between having transportation costs borne by the seller or buyer would simply choose the more efficient option. Nor is clear why f.o.b. mill pricing would be inefficient, given that such pricing can perfectly reflect the producers' actual production costs, with the buyer bearing the actual transportation costs. Firms thus have no independent incentive to pledge not to sell f.o.b. mill. The only plausible explanation is a collective motive: that firms are making that pledge with an understanding that others will make the same pledge and thus prevent f.o.b. mill sales from allowing a form of pricing where buyers incur their actual transportation costs, which would undermine the basing point scheme.

Second, the firms punished defectors by making their city a basing point with a low base price. The firms had no independent economic motive to participate in such punishment because participation requires sacrificing profits by selling in the defector's city at a price that is not only low but also ignores the cost of transporting goods to that city. Parallel participation in such punishment would be profitable only if (a) other firms participated as well, indicating some agreement (tacit or express) on joint participation, and (b) such punishments deterred defection from a price understanding that was profitable for the firms collectively.

Third, the firms suppressed information on their varying product quality. If a firm has higher quality cement, it has no independent business motive to suppress that information. The only incentive to do so would be the collective one of helping to maintain a collusive price. Suppressing quality information helps maintain collusive pricing because if quality differentials were known, buyers would favor the better cement makers at equal prices. That in turn could cause other rivals to cut prices to maintain sales, which would cause the better firms to match those price cuts, and so forth, which could cause any collusion on a common price to unravel. To prevent this, the firms trying to collude on prices would have to settle on a schedule of price differences that equal the value of the quality differences, but that is much harder than settling on a single common price. Quality differences also impede collusion by creating uncertainty about whether price cuts reflect deviations from the collusive pricing or disagreements about the level or value of quality differences.

Fourth, the firms boycotted dealers who sold foreign cement at prices below the defendant's delivered prices. This boycott is similar to the parallel refusal by retailers in *Eastern States Lumber* to deal with wholesalers who competed at retail. In both cases, firms have no independent incentive to participate in such a boycott, rather than using whichever dealer/wholesaler offers the best combination of service and price. Their only motive would be a collective one: that if other firms joined in boycotting the dealers, that would impede competition from the foreign cement competitors.

In short, the above parallel acts (pledging not to sell f.o.b. mill, punishing defectors by making them basing points with low prices, suppressing quality information, and boycotting dealers who sold foreign cement) are all inconsistent with independent incentives and thus must reflect a collective motive. In theory, firms could tacitly coordinate on such parallel behavior in a concentrated market, and coordinating on such avoidable facilitating practices would be an agreement under *Container*. But given the involvement of 72 firms, such coordination seems implausible, indicating that these parallel behaviors must have reflected a hidden express agreement. Even with such an express cartel, the firms would still have collective incentives to (a) punish defectors from the cartel price and dealers who offered competing foreign cement and (b) suppress variations in transportation costs or product quality that would make it harder to settle on a common cartel price and notice deviations from it.

3. ***Can an agreement be inferred from identical pricing?*** Inferring an agreement from identical prices can be problematic because in a perfectly competitive market for a homogeneous product, independent pricing should produce identical pricing in equilibrium. But no real market is perfectly competitive because there is always some variation in cost and quality, not all of which the firms could eliminate by suppressing variations in transportation costs and information about product quality. Further, here the prices were identical not only in equilibrium after other firms had a chance to respond to each other's pricing, but also in sealed simultaneous bids, which were identical to the sixth decimal point—that is, to one-millionth of a cent. That seems implausible not only with independent bidding but even with tacit coordination, thus suggesting there must have been some hidden express agreement.

4. ***Was inferring an agreement necessary under the FTC Act?*** Finding an agreement is necessary under Sherman Act § 1, but not under FTC Act § 5. Thus, even if one thought the facilitating practices were adopted by parallel independent action, those practices could be condemned under FTC Act § 5 on the grounds that they facilitated anticompetitive pricing. However, if there were independent incentives to engage in the conduct, there may well be a procompetitive justification for the conduct, which would have to be weighed against the anticompetitive effects under some form of rule-of-reason analysis limited to the FTC Act.

Similarly, suppose *Container* were overruled and tacit coordination on a facilitating practice were no longer deemed an agreement. Then the interdependent adoption of the facilitating practices could still be condemned under FTC Act § 5. Indeed, since interdependent adoption would indicate a lack of independent incentives, the particular practices at issue here would have not any procompetitive justification, and thus could be condemned categorically under a per se rule limited to the FTC Act.

The best explanation for why unilateral anticompetitive conduct is covered by the FTC Act, but not the Sherman Act, is a difference in overdeterrence concerns. The concern that mistakes in assessing unilateral conduct might mistakenly overdeter desirable conduct is lower under the FTC Act because it can be enforced only by a financially-disinterested expert agency that can only seek injunctive remedies. In contrast, the Sherman Act is also enforced by financially-interested private parties seeking treble damages and by prosecutors who can seek criminal penalties.

5. ***Could the FTC Act ban pure oligopolistic price coordination?*** Given the lack of an agreement requirement under the FTC Act, one might wonder why it has not been interpreted to ban pure oligopolistic price coordination itself. The answer is that pricing with knowledge of interdependence is unavoidable in oligopolistic markets, so the offense cannot be defined regardless of the Act applied. Indeed, the fact that the FTC does not condemn pure oligopolistic price coordination, even though it is clearly anticompetitive, confirms that the obstacle to antitrust condemnation does not result from the formal agreement requirement under Sherman Act § 1, but rather from the unavoidability of such price coordination. In contrast, when facilitating practices are avoidable (as in this case), they can be condemned under the FTC Act, regardless of whether those practices were adopted independently, interdependently, or by express agreement.

6. ***Was the concerted use of a basing point system per se illegal?*** The Court affirmed the FTC's holding that the concerted maintenance of a basing point was an unfair method of competition without requiring any showing of anticompetitive effects or consideration of procompetitive justifications. Such a rule of per se illegality makes sense. Because the facilitating practices all lacked any independent motive, they also all lacked any procompetitive justification. Indeed, even leaving aside any facilitating effects, using a common basing point with pledges against f.o.b. mill sales leads to inefficient transportation waste, suppressing quality differences leads to inefficient purchase decisions, and boycotting dealers who offer foreign cement leads to inefficient selections of dealers. Such facilitating practices can also have strong anticompetitive effects whether the market is oligopolistic (in which case the practices can facilitate anticompetitive price coordination) or not (in which cases the practices can facilitate cartel formation and enforcement). Indeed, unless the parties thought these facilitating practices had such anticompetitive effects, they would not have adopted them. Thus, the parallel adoption of such facilitating practices, whether by express or tacit agreement, can be condemned per se both under Sherman Act § 1 and FTC Act § 5.

7. ***Should it be illegal for oligopolists to agree to hold a meeting to discuss future prices?*** Yes. Holding such a meeting is likely to lead to anticompetitive effects and has no plausible procompetitive effect. Holding such a meeting is also highly avoidable, so if agreements to hold such meetings are condemned, oligopolists will have no difficulty knowing how to avoid condemnation.

8. ***Should an agreement to discuss oligopoly theory be illegal?*** Suppose five oligopolists agree to hold a meeting to have an antitrust professor lecture to them about oligopoly pricing theory. Should the agreement to hold such an educational seminar itself be condemned as an agreement that facilitates oligopolistic coordination? It would seem so. The agreement to hold the seminar satisfies the agreement requirement, and jointly attending such a seminar is likely to facilitate oligopolistic coordination by making sure each firm shares the same understanding of how coordination works and how to interpret the behavior of other firms. Agreeing to jointly attend such a seminar also has no plausible procompetitive purpose and is easily avoidable.

9. ***Should the parallel adoption of pricing algorithms that facilitate coordination be illegal?*** There is increasing concern that the combination of computer-based pricing algorithms and rich access to pricing data on the Internet is enabling greater coordination, even in markets that were previously viewed as too unconcentrated for coordination.[16] If the parallel adoption of such algorithms is interdependent, then it could be treated as an illegal agreement to adopt the algorithms, because (unlike pricing itself) adopting the facilitating algorithm is avoidable. But what if independent incentives lead firms to parallel adoption of algorithms in order to respond to competitive prices more rapidly, but the end result facilitates coordination by speeding price responses so much that they eliminate or sharply reduce any profits from short-term price cuts? Such parallel independent adoption of facilitating algorithms could not be condemned as a facilitating agreement, but it could be condemned under the FTC Act as a unilateral facilitating practice that leads to anticompetitive results. Should it be? The answer would seem to depend on whether the FTC could define which pricing algorithms facilitate coordination versus which intensify competition.

Summary on Horizontal Agreements and Facilitating Practices

A. ***When Can Horizontal Agreement Be Inferred from Parallel Conduct?*** Parallel conduct has two possible explanations: the parallel conduct either furthers independent incentives or can be explained only by a motive for common action.

1. ***Independent Incentives.*** If the parallel conduct furthers independent incentives (which would motivate the conduct no matter what others did), no agreement can be inferred. *Theatre Enterprises; Cement Manufacturers.*

2. ***Collective Incentives.*** If the parallel conduct is explicable only by a motive for common action (i.e., only if others engage in the same conduct), there are two sub-possibilities. It is either likely or unlikely that coordination could explain the parallel conduct (with that likelihood turning on the number of firms, precision of the parallelism, or other market factors).

16 *See* ARIEL EZRACHI & MAURICE E. STUCKE, THE PROMISE AND PERILS OF THE ALGORITHM-DRIVEN ECONOMY (2016).

a. Coordination Unlikely. If it is unlikely that coordination could explain the parallel conduct, then a court can infer that there was likely a hidden express agreement. *Eastern State Lumber; Interstate Circuit.* The reason is that, because the parallel conduct can be explained only by a motive for common action, an inability to coordinate leaves only a hidden express agreement as a possible explanation for the parallel conduct.

b. Coordination Likely. If interdependent coordination is a likely explanation for the parallel conduct, the legal treatment turns on whether the interdependent conduct is unavoidable or avoidable.

i. Unavoidable Conduct. If the parallel conduct involves unavoidable business conduct (like setting a price or output or deciding where to enter or with whom to deal), then no agreement is inferred. *Twombly.* The reason is that, although such parallel conduct does involve a mutual understanding that has anticompetitive effects, firms cannot avoid the conduct nor avoid recognizing their interdependence when they engage in it. Indeed, because such conduct is unavoidable, it also is not illegal unilateral conduct under the FTC Act despite its anticompetitive effects, thus confirming that the legality rests more on the unavoidability of the conduct than on the absence of a mutual understanding or anticompetitive effects.

ii. Avoidable Conduct. If the parallel conduct involves avoidable conduct (like a common invitation, exchanging price quotes, or using a common basing point), then an agreement can be inferred, even if the parallel conduct results from interdependent coordination, rather than from any hidden express conspiracy. *Interstate Circuit; Container; Cement Institute.* The reason is that such parallel conduct not only involves a mutual understanding that has anticompetitive effects, but also is avoidable, so the offense can be defined and the parallel conduct deterred. The combination of this point with 2a above means that, when avoidable parallel conduct can be explained only by a motive for common action, an agreement on that conduct can be inferred without resolving whether coordination is likely or not. *Container; Cement Institute.*

B. Tiebreakers. No agreement is inferred if the parallel conduct is just as consistent with independent incentives as with either hidden conspiracy, *Matsushita,* or coordination on unavoidable conduct, *Twombly.* But an agreement can be inferred if the parallel conduct is just as consistent with hidden conspiracy as with coordination, even if the conduct is unavoidable. *American Tobacco.*

C. Facilitating Practices. An agreement on practices that facilitate either coordination or cartels (like an agreement to exchange individuated pricing data or to use a common basing point) can be illegal, even if any facilitated coordination would itself be legal, *Container;*

Cement Institute, or no direct proof of any facilitated cartel exists, *American Column.* An agreement on practices that further only independent decisionmaking is generally legal, because furthering such independent decisionmaking usually has procompetitive benefits. *Cement Manufacturers; Maple Flooring.* However, those procompetitive benefits might conceivably be offset if the information also facilitates coordination. *Maple Flooring.*

When firms engage in the parallel adoption of avoidable practices that facilitate coordination or cartels, there are two possible explanations: the parallel adoption of those practices either furthers independent incentives or can be explained only by a motive for common action.

1. ***Independent Incentives.*** If the parallel adoption of the facilitating practices furthers independent incentives, no agreement on the practices can be inferred. The conduct might be illegal under the FTC Act, but the independent incentives indicate a likely procompetitive benefit that would be weighed against any anticompetitive effects.

2. ***Collective Incentives.*** If the parallel adoption of the facilitating practices can be explained only by a motive for common action, there are two sub-possibilities: it is either likely or unlikely that the firms could coordinate.

a. ***Coordination Unlikely.*** If it is unlikely that the firms could coordinate, then a court can infer that there was likely a hidden express agreement on the parallel adoption of the facilitating practice, because that is the only remaining explanation. The inability to coordinate further means that the firms would not have adopted the facilitating practice unless they also had a hidden agreement on the underlying business conduct as well, such as an agreement to use circulated information to boycott rivals or avoid price cuts. *Eastern State Lumber; American Column.* Thus, if coordination is unlikely, a court can infer an agreement not only on the adoption of the facilitating practice, but also on the underlying business conduct.

b. ***Coordination Likely.*** If interdependent coordination is a likely explanation for the parallel adoption of avoidable facilitating practices, then a court can infer an agreement on the avoidable practice, even if it cannot infer an agreement on the unavoidable business conduct that is facilitated. *Container; Cement Institute.* The combination of this point with 2a above means that, when only collective incentives can explain the parallel adoption of an avoidable facilitating practice, an agreement to adopt the practice can be inferred without resolving whether coordination is likely or not. *Container; Cement Institute.* When the agreement to adopt the facilitating practice is itself illegal, this may moot the issue of whether one can also infer an agreement on the underlying business conduct. *Container; Cement Institute.*

CHAPTER 7

MERGERS AND ACQUISITIONS

A. INTRODUCTION

Mergers are the combination of previously independent firms into one firm. For antitrust purposes, it does not matter whether the combination reflects a formal merger of two corporations into a single corporation or instead the acquisition of another firm's assets or stock. Nor does it matter whether, after the merger, the acquired business becomes a subsidiary that continues to be a separate legal entity. All that matters is that what used to be separate businesses pursuing independent profit motives have now been combined into one common ownership structure that gives the businesses a joint profit motive. Thus, like the issue of what constitutes separate entities discussed in Chapter 6.A, the issue of what constitutes a merger is entirely functional under antitrust law.

There are three kinds of mergers. (1) Horizontal mergers combine firms that used to compete in selling or buying in the same market. They raise similar issues to horizontal agreements, except that in addition they raise the concern that they might help create a market concentration that leads to oligopolistic coordination. (2) Vertical mergers combine firms that used to sell and buy on opposite sides of the same market. They raise issues similar to vertical agreements. (3) Conglomerate mergers include any business combination that is not horizontal or vertical. However, one of the concerns conglomerate mergers raise is that, but for the merger, one of the firms might have entered the market of the other, so that the conglomerate merger eliminates potential horizontal competition. Another concern is that a conglomerate merger might enable the merged entity to engage in anticompetitive vertical conduct or agreements. For example, a merger between firms that make different products could enable the merged firm to tie the product sales together. Thus, conglomerate mergers can raise concerns that are horizontal or vertical in nature.

When a stock acquisition gives one firm effective control over another firm, it is generally treated as a merger even if the acquisition is for far less than 100% of the stock. A partial asset acquisition could also be treated as a merger. For example, if a firm that makes lamps purchases another firm's lamp division, it is making a partial asset acquisition that would be treated as an antitrust merger of their lamp businesses, even though there is no corporate merger or stock acquisition.

Partial stock acquisitions can also be condemned as anticompetitive even when they do not confer enough control to constitute a merger. Such noncontrolling acquisitions might be condemned on the theories that they lessen competition by either: (1) giving the acquirer the ability to influence the competitive conduct of the target firm; (2) giving the acquirer confidential information in the target firm; or (3) lessening the financial incentives of the firms to compete with each other. *See* U.S. DOJ/FTC Horizontal Merger Guidelines § 13 (2010).

General Legal Standards on Mergers and Acquisitions. Mergers and acquisitions are covered by Sherman Act § 1 if they anticompetitively restrain trade, because every merger or acquisition involves an agreement. However, although a merger necessarily gives the combined firm a power to jointly fix prices, mergers are not per se illegal. This is because, as long as they involve some economic integration, mergers generally have some plausible efficiency justification to them. Thus, like joint ventures, mergers are judged under the rule of reason unless they are a sham. Mergers are likewise covered by FTC Act § 5, and a merger that created a firm with monopoly power would violate Sherman Act § 2.

More important, mergers and acquisitions are covered by a statute directly specifically at them:

Clayton Act § 7, 15 U.S.C. § 18

> No person engaged in commerce or in any activity affecting commerce shall acquire, directly or indirectly, the whole or any part of the stock or . . . the whole or any part of the assets of another person engaged also in commerce or in any activity affecting commerce, where in any line of commerce or in any activity affecting commerce in any section of the country, the effect of such acquisition may be substantially to lessen competition, or to tend to create a monopoly.
>
> No person shall acquire, directly or indirectly, the whole or any part of the stock or . . . the whole or any part of the assets of one or more persons engaged in commerce or in any activity affecting commerce, where in any line of commerce or in any activity affecting commerce in any section of the country, the effect of such acquisition, of such stocks or assets, or of the use of such stock by the voting or granting of proxies or otherwise, may be substantially to lessen competition, or to tend to create a monopoly.

The term "person" includes not just natural persons, but all legal entities like corporations. Why the seemingly duplicative provisions? The first provision addresses cases where one business acquires stock or assets in another business (i.e., both must be persons engaged in or affecting commerce). The second provision covers cases when any person (whether a business or not) acquires the stock or assets of one or more businesses, thus extending the statute to cases where an investor not engaged in commerce may affect competition by its acquisition in a business. For example, the second provision would apply if an investor bought stock in two competing businesses and the effect may be to lessen competition between those businesses, even though the investor never engages in commerce itself.[1] Under the second provision, it suffices not only if the effect "of such acquisition" may be anticompetitive, but also if the effect "of such stocks or assets, or of the use of such stock" may be anticompetitive. Thus, under the latter provision, the anticompetitive effects do not necessarily have to be traced to the moment of acquisition, but can be from the ongoing existence of the stock or assets itself (which could, say, diminish incentives to compete) or from the post-acquisition use of that stock.

Mergers and acquisitions are normally challenged under Clayton Act § 7 rather than Sherman Act § 1, because historically the former was thought to have more lenient standards. The term "may be substantially to lessen" indeed suggests a purpose to block a merger as long as there is some risk of significant anticompetitive effects. However, the legislative history indicates an intent to require at least proof of some reasonable probability of anticompetitive effects, and the agencies and some courts often seem to read the language to require (like similar language in Clayton Act § 3) a showing that anticompetitive effects are more likely than not.

Whichever statute is used, antitrust law embodies a containment policy against allowing mergers or acquisitions that will create an anticompetitive market structure, on the theory that it is easier to prevent such effects prophylactically, rather than try to undo the market structure or police monopoly or oligopoly pricing directly. Thus, the emphasis is on reviewing mergers and acquisitions before they are consummated and blocking the ones with predicted anticompetitive effects. This prophylactic approach means enforcement agencies and adjudicators must typically forecast the anticompetitive effects before the merger or acquisition actually occurs.

The Exception for Passive Investments That Lack Anticompetitive Effects. Because Clayton Act § 7 prohibits acquiring "any part of the stock" of another firm—voting or nonvoting—when the effect "may be substantially to lessen competition," it can prohibit acquisitions of noncontrolling stakes in a corporation that may substantially lessen competition. 15 U.S.C. § 18. However, Clayton Act § 7 does "not apply to persons purchasing such stock solely for investment and not using the same by voting or otherwise to bring about, or in attempting to bring about, the substantial lessening of competition." 15 U.S.C. § 18. Getting the benefit of this exception thus requires proving both of the following elements: (1) the stock acquisition must be *solely* for

[1] On the anticompetitive concerns with such horizontal shareholding, *see* Elhauge, *Horizontal Shareholding*, 129 HARVARD LAW REVIEW 1267 (2016).

investment, *and* (2) the acquired stock must not *actually* be used to lessen competition substantially or to attempt to do so.

The first prong requires that the investment be purely passive, which excludes not only investments that give working control, but also investments that give the acquirer influence over the target's business decisions or access to the target's sensitive business information. For example, the Supreme Court has held that even if a 23% stake did not confer working control, the passive investment exception did not apply because the investor tried to influence business decisions.[2] The solely-for-investment element has been found to be met only when the investor committed either to not vote its stock or (in what amounts to the same thing) to vote the shares in the same proportion as other shareholders vote, often with the additional requirements that the investor not nominate directors, have any representative on the board, or exert any other form of influence over management.[3] Likewise, agency guidelines make clear that the antitrust agencies consider a partial stock acquisition anticompetitive if it gives the acquirer an ability to influence the target that might produce anticompetitive effects or (even without any influence) gives the acquirer access to the target's confidential business information that might lead to anticompetitive effects.[4]

The second prong provides that, even when an investment is purely passive, it is still subject to review, but under a harder-to-prove standard than Clayton Act § 7 applies to active investments.[5] Whereas an active investment is illegal if it *may* substantially lessen competition, a passive investment is illegal only if it *actually* does so, or was *intended* to do so. For example, one business's purely passive 20% investment in another business might lessen competition because it lessens the incentives of the acquirer to compete with the target, given that the acquirer gets 20% of profits from any lost sales that go to the target.[6] Likewise, if the leading

---

[2] United States v. E.I. du Pont de Nemours & Co., 353 U.S. 586, 597–606 (1957).

[3] United States v. Tracinda Inv. Corp., 477 F.Supp. 1093, 1098 (C.D. Cal. 1979) (solely-for-investment element was met when the investor committed to vote shares proportionately to other shareholders); Anaconda Co. v. Crane Co., 411 F.Supp. 1210, 1218–19 (S.D.N.Y. 1975) (solely-for-investment element was met when the investor committed not to seek representation on board of directors and not to vote shares in any way that might lessen competition); United States v. Gillette Co., 55 Fed. Reg. 28,312, 28,322 (July 10, 1990) (stating that solely-for-investment element was met when the investor committed not to vote its stock, nominate directors, have any representative on the board, deny credit, or exert any influence over management).

[4] U.S. DOJ/FTC Horizontal Merger Guidelines § 13 (2010).

[5] *du Pont*, 353 U.S. at 597–98 ("Even when the purchase is solely for investment, the plain language of § 7 contemplates an action at any time the stock is used to bring about, or in attempting to bring about, the substantial lessening of competition."); *Tracinda*, 477 F.Supp. at 1098–1099 & n.5; *Anaconda*, 411 F.Supp. at 1218–19.

[6] U.S. DOJ/FTC Horizontal Merger Guidelines § 13 (2010); Daniel P. O'Brien & Steven C. Salop, *Competitive Effects of Partial Ownership: Financial Interest and Corporate Control*, 67 ANTITRUST L.J. 559 (2000); David Gilo, *The Anticompetitive Effect of Passive Investment*, 99 MICH. L. REV. 1, 8–28 (2000). Even if Clayton Act § 7 did not apply, a purely passive investment that lessened competitive incentives in a way that was likely to produce anticompetitive effects would be reviewable as an unreasonable restraint of trade or unfair trade practice (and maybe even as monopolization or attempted monopolization if the firms collectively have or threaten

shareholders of two competing business are the same institutional investors, their horizontal shareholdings might lessen the incentives of those firms to compete with each other, even if those institutional investors are purely passive about their investments.[7]

Filing Requirements. In order to better advance antitrust's prophylactic approach to mergers and acquisitions, the Hart-Scott-Rodino Act requires that those who plan to acquire "voting securities or assets" of another firm that meet certain dollar thresholds must (absent an applicable exemption) file information about the acquisition with the federal antitrust agencies. 15 USC § 18a(a). This filing requirement applies if the stock acquisition exceeds $50 million in 2004 dollars and the acquirer and target are sufficiently large.[8]

The filing requirement has its own passive investor exception, which is broader than the substantive exception for passive investments that lack anticompetitive effects. In other words, an acquirer can be a passive investor exempt from filing, even though the acquirer would not be a passive investor for purposes of assessing liability under the substantive provision. The filing requirement's passive investor exception does not apply if the acquired voting securities both (1) are solely for investment purposes and (2) do not give the acquirer more than 10% of the target's voting securities. 15 USC § 18a(c)(9). A DOJ-FTC regulation treats a stock holding as solely for investment only "if the person holding or acquiring such voting securities has no intention of participating in the formulation, determination, or direction of the basic business decisions of the issuer."[9] This regulation on its face seems to deny the filing exemption to investors who influence business decisions via voting, but the agencies' report regarding the purpose of this regulation states:

monopoly power), *see* Chapters 2–5, or as a facilitating agreement or practice if it seems likely to aid oligopolistic coordination by lessening incentives to defect, *see* Chapter 6.C.3.

7 *See* Elhauge, *Horizontal Shareholding*, 129 HARVARD LAW REVIEW 1267, 1307–08 (2016). Holding shares across horizontal competitors is also a combination or agreement that violates Sherman Act § 1 if it has anticompetitive effects, and such anticompetitive effects would also create a violation of FTC Act § 5 even without any agreement. *See id.* at.1304 & p.1308 n.205.

8 15 U.S.C. § 18a(a). The firm-size standard is satisfied if the assets or annual sales of the acquirer and target exceed $10 million for one of them and $100 million for the other, in 2004 dollars. Id. § 18a(a)(2)(B). Filing is also required if the acquisition exceeds $200 million in 2004 dollars regardless of the size of the acquirer or target firm, but it seems likely that an acquisition of that size would usually satisfy the firm-size standard. Id. § 18a(a)(2)(A).

9 16 C.F.R. § 801.1(i)(1). This regulation on its face seems to deny the filing exemption to investors who influence business decisions via voting, but the agencies' report regarding the purpose of this regulation states:

> [M]erely voting the stock will not be considered evidence of an intent inconsistent with investment purpose. However, certain types of conduct could be so viewed. These include but are not limited to: (1) Nominating a candidate for the board of directors of the issuer; (2) proposing corporate action requiring shareholder approval; (3) soliciting proxies; (4) having a controlling shareholder, director, officer or employee simultaneously serving as an officer or director of the issuer; (5) being a competitor of the issuer; or (6) doing any of the foregoing with respect to any entity directly or indirectly controlling the issuer.

43 Fed. Reg. 33,450, 33,465 (1978). Factor (5) indicates that merely owning shares in a competing firm can suffice to lose the solely-for-investment exception to the filing requirement.

"[M]erely voting the stock will not be considered evidence of an intent inconsistent with investment purpose."[10] Treating investors who exercise influence via "mere" voting as passive is broader than the substantive provision, which requires a lack of influence. The filing exemption for passive investors is also broader in the sense that it applies as long as the voting share is less than 10%, even if the stock acquisition is actually likely or intended to create anticompetitive effects, whereas the substantive provision only applies without such actual or intended anticompetitive effects. If the passive investor is an institutional investor, they are exempt from filing if their voting share is less than 15%.[11] Further, no filing is necessary for acquisitions of convertible voting securities that do not presently entitle the holder to vote for directors, although making the conversion would require an advance filing.[12]

In the initial filing about a merger of acquisition, the acquirer must provide the relevant agency with documents and analyses of the effects of the merger. (The DOJ and FTC have divided up merger work by specializing in different industries.) Unless the agencies make a "second request" for additional information within 30 days (15 days for cash tender offers), the parties may consummate their merger. In 95% of cases, the agencies decide no second request is necessary, generally because of low market share and concentration figures, though they may also rely on evidence from prior investigations, public data, and input from market participants, especially buyers.[13] In the 5% of cases where the agency makes a second request, it engages in a detailed analysis to decide whether the merger is likely to have anticompetitive effects. Parties opposed to the merger may also weigh in with their own facts and analyses. If the merger creates anticompetitive effects only in certain markets, like a merger between nationwide retailers that creates excessive market concentration in just a few local markets, then the merging parties often simply agree to divest assets in those local markets. Or firms may offer conduct remedies, like guarantees to refrain from raising prices or to charge the same price as in a competitive market, although the U.S. agencies strongly prefer structural remedies (like divestitures) over conduct remedies.[14]

---

[10] The agency report goes on to state:

However, certain types of conduct could be so viewed. These include but are not limited to: (1) Nominating a candidate for the board of directors of the issuer; (2) proposing corporate action requiring shareholder approval; (3) soliciting proxies; (4) having a controlling shareholder, director, officer or employee simultaneously serving as an officer or director of the issuer; (5) being a competitor of the issuer; or (6) doing any of the foregoing with respect to any entity directly or indirectly controlling the issuer.

43 Fed. Reg. 33,450, 33,465 (1978). Factor (5) indicates that merely owning shares in a competing firm can suffice to lose the solely-for-investment exception to the filing requirement.

[11] *Id.* § 802.64(b).

[12] 16 C.F.R. §§ 802.31, 801.1(f)(2), 801.32.

[13] *See* U.S. DOJ/FTC, Commentary on the Horizontal Merger Guidelines (March 2006).

[14] *See* DOJ, Antitrust Division Policy Guide to Merger Remedies at III.A (Oct. 2004).

Caselaw v. Agency Practice. If the merging parties and the agency cannot come to an agreement, then the agency must go to court to seek a preliminary injunction blocking the merger.[15] Likewise, even if the agency declines to pursue a case, a private litigant is free to go to court to enjoin a merger. Thus, ultimately the decision whether to approve the merger is up to the courts.

However, as a practical matter, many merging parties drop a proposed merger if the agency is opposed, both because it is often difficult to maintain merger financing for the long period that litigation would take and because the agencies enjoy favorable standards of proof on preliminary injunctions that require them to show only a reasonable likelihood of success. In addition, the enforcement agencies have had a narrower view of which mergers are anticompetitive than the available U.S. Supreme Court caselaw. Thus, for most of the last few decades, merging firms were wary of going to court when the Supreme Court precedent was more adverse than agency enforcement policy.

Further, other private parties rarely seek to challenge a merger that the agency has cleared. In part this is because agencies generally do a good job of identifying the anticompetitive mergers. But it also reflects the fact that private parties do not have the benefit of the extensive information collected by the government, and have difficulty conducting discovery quickly enough to block a merger before it occurs. In addition, competitors almost always lack standing to challenge a horizontal merger, and buyers generally have collective action problems in organizing to bring litigation and will not yet have suffered the sort of damages that might attract class action counsel. And after the merger, courts are reluctant to give an injunction to "unscramble the eggs" by undoing the merger, and it is often difficult to prove measurable damages if the claim is one like increased oligopoly pricing.

Thus, in practice, almost all substantive decisions about mergers are made by the enforcement agencies rather than by the courts. Further, when merger cases do get to court, they rarely last long enough to get to the U.S. Supreme Court. Indeed, the Supreme Court has not decided a case about the substantive standards that govern federal merger antitrust law since the 1976 enactment of the Hart-Scott-Rodino Act. The odd result is that we are left with many old Supreme Court cases that have never been overruled yet clearly do not reflect modern merger practice. For example, *Brown Shoe v. United States*, 370 U.S. 294 (1962), condemned a horizontal merger even where the market share of the combined firm was 5% and condemned a vertical merger that foreclosed all of 1.2% of the relevant market, and along the way suggested that efficiencies were grounds to condemn (not justify) the merger. Any effort

---

15 If the FTC obtains such a preliminary injunction, it then itself adjudicates whether the merger violates antitrust law, though that determination is subject to appellate review. *See* Chapter 1. The DOJ would instead proceed to a trial at a district court for such a permanent adjudication. *Id.*

to challenge such a merger today would not only fail but be laughed at by the agencies and probably most courts. Even *United States v. Philadelphia National Bank*, 374 U.S. 321 (1963), which held that a merger was presumptively unlawful if the merger would create a firm with a 30% market share and increase the market share of the two biggest firms from 44% to 59%, is broader and less rigorous than modern agency practice. And *United States v. Von's Grocery*, 384 U.S. 270 (1966), held that this approach also presumptively condemned a merger that created a firm with 7.5% market share and increased the market share of the two largest firms by all of 1.4%, which again brings us back to a claim that would be deemed laughable in modern agency practice. *Brown Shoe* and *Philadelphia National Bank* also reflected a Goldilocks approach to market definition. That is, in both cases one market definition was too broad (because it would have made the market shares of the merging firms small) and another was too narrow (because it would have put the merging firms in separate markets and thus meant there was no horizontal merger that increased market concentration at all), and the Court responded by choosing a medium market definition that was "just right" (big enough to include both firms but not much larger). Modern practice takes a much more rigorous approach to market definition, as we saw in Chapter 3.

This leads to the rather unusual result that "the law in action" on mergers is mainly agency enforcement policy. The inconvenient fact that these old Supreme Court cases would condemn many mergers that are now routinely approved is politely ignored by the agencies and even by the lower courts in the few merger cases that reach them, which instead tend to rely more on the enforcement guidelines issued by the agencies. Further, these guidelines are actually broader than the actual enforcement practices of the agencies. Unfortunately, the U.S. agencies generally do not write opinions to explain their merger decisions, in part because they must render those decisions quickly and those decisions are just about whether to litigate, and the vast bulk of agency decisions are decisions not to bring litigation that under U.S. law are a matter of prosecutorial discretion that is unreviewable by the courts. Thus, to get a sense of what actual merger practice is like in the United States, this book will supplement these guidelines with some empirical data on actual merger practice, and focus on a few lower court cases that (while not authoritative) more accurately reflect actual modern enforcement practice than Supreme Court precedent does.

B. HORIZONTAL MERGERS

Horizontal mergers raise two sorts of general anticompetitive concerns: unilateral effects and oligopolistic effects.

(1) Unilateral effects. A horizontal merger might allow the merged firm to exercise market power unilaterally. Such effects are called unilateral because they do not depend on the merger changing the conduct of the nonmerging firms. There are essentially two theories of how such unilateral effects might occur.

(a) Merger Creates Unilateral Market Power Given Constraints on Rivals. The merger might result in a single firm with significant market power, such as when the merged firm's market share is large and rivals' ability to expand is constrained by capacity or other factors.

(b) Merged Brands Close to Each Other on Differentiated Market. A merger between two firms whose brands are close to each other in a differentiated market might lead to adverse unilateral effects even though their share of the entire market is not great.

(2) Oligopoly Effects. A horizontal merger might create a more concentrated market structure that enables or exacerbates oligopoly pricing. Such effects are called oligopoly effects because (unlike unilateral effects) they do depend on the merger changing the conduct of nonmerging firms. The level of market concentration is generally measured by the Herfindahl-Hirschman Index, which is the sum of the square of each firm's market shares. That is, if a market has *n* firms, with respective market shares of $S_1, S_2 \cdots S_n$, then HHI = $S_1^2 + S_2^2 + S_3^2 + \cdots S_n^2$. For example, if a market had five firms, each with a 20% market share, the HHI would be five times 20^2 = 2000. If two of those firms merged, leaving one merged firm with 40% market share and the other three firms with 20% each, then the post-merger HHI would be 40^2 + three times 20^2 = 2800. The change in HHI (often called ΔHHI) would then be 800. More generally, ΔHHI always equals two times the pre-merger market share of one merging firm times the pre-merger share of the other merging firm.[16] One can express the HHI in decimals (.2000 and .2800 in the above cases), but like baseball batting averages, the decimal is generally dropped in discussion, other than in formulas used to predict price effects, where the decimal matters.

There are essentially two theories about how multiple firms in concentrated markets might elevate prices to supracompetitive levels: uncoordinated Cournot interactions and oligopolistic coordination.

(a) Uncoordinated Cournot Interactions. The Cournot model assumes that each firm chooses whatever output level maximizes its profits, taking the output levels of the other firms as given. If so, and all firms have constant marginal costs and homogeneous products, then it can be shown that the market equilibrium output will result in an aggregate Lerner Index (which measures the aggregate extent to which firm prices exceed marginal cost) that equals the HHI (expressed in

---

16 To see why, suppose firms 1 and 2 merge. Then, the pre-merger HHI = $S_1^2 + S_2^2 + S_3^2 + \cdots S_n^2$. The post-merger HHI = $(S_1 + S_2)^2 + S_3^2 \cdots\cdots S_n^2$. All the market shares from the third firm on are unchanged by the merger, so the change in HHI is $(S_1 + S_2)^2 - S_1^2 - S_2^2 = S_1 + 2S_1S_2 + S_2^2 - S_1^2 - S_2^2 = 2S_1S_2$. Thus, in the example involving the merger of firms with 20% market share each, then ΔHHI = 2(20)(20) = 800, which matches the result if one fully calculates the pre- and post-merger HHIs and subtracts the former from the latter.

decimals) divided by the market demand elasticity.[17] Although the 2010 U.S. Merger Guidelines describe Cournot effects as one of the "coordinated" effects, Cournot effects actually require neither coordinating on common terms nor monitoring and retaliation to deter individually rational efforts to deviate from those terms. Instead, Cournot effects require only that each firm make individually rational decisions, which will reflect the individually rational responses of other firms. Cournot effects thus do not require coordination because firms have no incentive to cheat: rather, they each individually maximize profits by keeping their output at the Cournot equilibrium.

However, Cournot effects depend on the assumption that firms compete by picking an output, rather than by picking a price. If the assumptions are the same, but firms instead compete by picking prices and can instantaneously expand output to supply the whole market, then the Bertrand model shows that (even in a duopoly) firms that are not coordinating their behavior will find it profit-maximizing to choose a price that undercuts the price chosen by the other, until the prices of each are driven down to marginal cost. Thus, uncoordinated Bertrand competition in a homogenous market leads (even for a merger that results in duopoly) to perfectly competitive pricing at marginal cost.[18]

Whether the Cournot or Bertrand model best describes uncoordinated market behavior in a concentrated market may depend on the nature of the industry. In some markets, where producing a given output requires serious advance planning, it may be more accurate to say that firms decide on their output, and then sell that output at whatever price they can get for it. In other markets, it may be more accurate to say that each firm picks a price, and then sells whatever output it can at that price.

(b) Coordinated Oligopoly Behavior. If they can engage in coordinated interaction, then firms in concentrated markets can elevate prices to supracompetitive levels, regardless of whether they compete by picking output, prices, or both. Suppose, for example, a market has two firms, each with 50% market share and costs of $20/unit. One firm announces that next month it will raise its prices from $20 to $25. The other firm knows that if it does not match the $25 price, then the first firm will rescind its price increase and they will each earn less profit. Thus, although in the short run it would be profit-maximizing for the other firm to undercut that price slightly, charging $24.99 and taking market share, it has incentives to instead coordinate with the other firm

---

17 More precisely, if S_i is the market share of firm i (its quantity over the market quantity), and L_i equals the Lerner Index (P – MC)/P)) for firm i, then $\Sigma S_i L_i = HHI/\epsilon$ where ϵ equals the absolute value of the marketwide demand elasticity. *See* CARLTON & PERLOF, MODERN INDUSTRIAL ORGANIZATION 268 (3rd ed. 2000). A market with a 100% monopolist would have an HHI of 1.0000 and thus its Lerner Index = $1/\epsilon$ as noted in Chapter 3. *See* also Chapter 1 on NEIO models.

18 In contrast, on differentiated markets, Bertrand price competition results in prices that exceed costs, which means that a merger can produce unilateral effects.

by matching its price increase. Such pricing requires coordination because it must overcome each firm's individual incentive to cheat on the elevated price.

Through such coordination, firms can price supracompetitively without entering into an actual horizontal agreement that violates the antitrust laws. *See* Chapter 6. Their ability to do so depends on whether the oligopolists (a) have collective market power and (b) can coordinate. Their ability to coordinate on price depends on whether market conditions allow the oligopolists to: (1) settle on a cooperative price; (2) notice defection by other firms from that price; and (3) respond to such defection. *Id.* The greater the number of oligopolists, the harder it is to meet those conditions because more firms make it harder to settle on a common price, to notice defections by a particular firm, and to coordinate any punishment for defections. A smaller number of oligopolists thus tends to increase their ability to coordinate, and a horizontal merger that leaves fewer firms in the market can thus enable or exacerbate oligopolistic price coordination. Some empirical evidence has indicated that adding firms to a market tends to reduce prices until one gets to five significant firms, after which the addition of more firms has little effect on pricing.[19] This evidence suggests that five significant firms is normally sufficient to prevent oligopolistic coordination, but that a merger that leaves a market with four or fewer significant firms would normally increase the likelihood of oligopolistic coordination. A market with four equally-sized firms has an HHI of 2500, which we shall see the U.S. merger guidelines define as the threshold for a highly concentrated market.

Other market factors may also impede oligopolistic price coordination. If the product is not homogeneous, but instead firms offer products with varying quality or characteristics, it will be difficult to settle on a common schedule of prices reflecting those variations and to notice and respond to defections by others, especially since defections may take the form of nonprice competition. If pricing is not public but rather is privately negotiated, or if secret discounts are made from public pricing, then it will be harder to notice or respond to defections by others. If the costs of firms vary, it will be difficult to settle on a common price. If the market consists of infrequent bids for large projects, then firms will have stronger incentives to defect to win the large bids and lock in sales for a long time. Thus, the presence of these sorts of factors make it less likely that a merger would lead to anticompetitive price coordination, whereas their absence makes such coordination more likely. However, some factors that impede oligopolistic price coordination, such as product differentiation, also make unilateral effects more likely.

---

[19] *See* Bresnahan & Reiss, *Entry and Competition in Concentrated Markets,* 99 J. POL. ECON. 977 (1991). However, algorithmic pricing and electronic data may now be increasing the ability to coordinate in markets with a larger number of firms. *See* Chapter 6.

Oligopolistic coordination may also occur on matters other than price. Firms might coordinate on output, market divisions, or innovation. Further, in a differentiated market, coordinating on a policy of not invading the product spaces occupied by other firms can be an effective strategy for maintaining anticompetitive prices. For example, *Twombly* recognizes that firms might coordinate on not invading the market positions of other firms. *See* Chapter 6. Thus, theories of oligopolistic coordination and market differentiation are not mutually exclusive, even though in a differentiated market the coordination will generally not be on price.

(3) The Use of HHI Thresholds. As we shall see, the U.S. merger guidelines heavily rely on HHI thresholds. This is somewhat odd because HHIs have direct economic relevance only to Cournot effects, which are rarely pursued as a theory for challenging mergers. Instead, merger cases and the merger guidelines focus on unilateral and coordinated effects, which have a poor or unreliable connection to HHI levels.

HHIs have little (and often inverse) relevance to unilateral effects. On differentiated markets, unilateral effects can exist even if the merger firm market shares and HHIs are both very low. Even when the concern is that the merger might create conventional single-firm market power, that effect turns on expandability of the non-merging firms, not on their concentration level. For example, suppose two firms with 20% market share each merge. The market power created by their post-merger 40% market share will depend on the supply elasticity of the other 60% of the market, but is not higher if the other 60% consists of three firms with 20% share each rather than six firms with 10% each. Indeed, if rivals with 20% of the market can expand more easily, the single firm market power may be higher in the latter case. Yet, the post-merger HHI will be 2800 in the former case and 2200 in the latter case, wrongly signaling that the former is more anticompetitive and (as we shall see) dropping the latter case below a key HHI threshold used by the U.S. agencies.

HHIs also correlate only loosely (and sometimes inversely) to oligopolistic coordination. As noted above, whether oligopolistic coordination will increase prices turns on two things. The first is whether the oligopolists have collective market power, which does not depend on the concentration of the other firms in the market that nonetheless affect the HHI. Indeed, the oligopolists' collective market power will probably be less constrained if the non-oligopolists consist of minor firms than a large maverick firm, yet the HHI will be higher in the latter case. The second important factor is whether the oligopolists can coordinate with each other. The ability to coordinate does increase with fewer oligopolists, which usefully correlates with higher HHI. But the ability to coordinate also decreases the more varying the oligopolists are from each other, which can perversely correlate with higher HHI.[20] A better quantitative

[20] Holding collective market share and the number of oligopolists constant, the HHI will be lower the more similar their market shares. For example, take the case where a merger

threshold to determine whether coordination seems sufficiently likely would be to simply consider the number of oligopolists and their collective market share. Ironically, that would bring us back to metrics like the 4-firm concentration level, which were once used in merger analysis before the fancier HHI came in vogue.

Perhaps the use of HHI thresholds reflects a view that with high HHIs, it is likely there are either Cournot effects or price coordination effects, thus avoiding any need to hinge the case on a claim about whether firms compete by picking output or price. But that cannot explain using HHIs when the concern is unilateral effects, and it remains the case that HHIs often correlate poorly to coordination effects. Perhaps instead the use of HHI thresholds is a historical holdover from the focus of earlier merger analysis on the connection between concentration levels and Cournot effects, and the use of HHIs has continued because the agencies need some crude metric to screen through a huge number of merger filings before determining the relevant anticompetitive theory. However, if that is the rationale, it suggests that this crude screen should not be the focus of courts when a merger challenge is actually brought.

(4) Offsetting Factors. Proper antitrust analysis does not stop with identification of possible anticompetitive concerns. Such concerns may be offset by low entry barriers, merger-created efficiencies, or because one of the firms was failing and would have exited the market without the merger. U.S. law thus takes those factors into account before blocking a merger. The following will separately discuss each major element of horizontal merger analysis: the two major anticompetitive theories—(1) unilateral effects or (2) oligopoly effects—and the three major offsetting factors—(3) post-merger entry, (4) efficiencies, and (5) the failing firm defense. This Section then ends with factor (6), which considers the extent to which buyer power or views should affect merger analysis.

leaves one firm with 40% market share and the other three firms with 20% each, creating an HHI of 2800. If instead the shares of the three non-merging were respectively 30%, 20% and 10%, the HHI would be $40^2 + 30^2 + 20^2 + 10^2 = 3000$. The HHI would be higher in the latter case, but the greater variation in market share probably suggests greater variation in costs and product attractiveness that would make oligopolistic coordination harder.

1. UNILATERAL EFFECTS

U.S. DOJ/FTC, Horizontal Merger Guidelines

(2010).

1. Overview. . . .

The Agencies seek to identify and challenge competitively harmful mergers while avoiding unnecessary interference with mergers that are either competitively beneficial or neutral. Most merger analysis is necessarily predictive, requiring an assessment of what will likely happen if a merger proceeds as compared to what will likely happen if it does not. Given this inherent need for prediction, these Guidelines reflect the congressional intent that merger enforcement should interdict competitive problems in their incipiency and that certainty about anticompetitive effect is seldom possible and not required for a merger to be illegal.

These Guidelines describe the principal analytical techniques and the main types of evidence on which the Agencies usually rely to predict whether a horizontal merger may substantially lessen competition. They are not intended to describe how the Agencies analyze cases other than horizontal mergers. These Guidelines are intended to assist the business community and antitrust practitioners by increasing the transparency of the analytical process underlying the Agencies' enforcement decisions. They may also assist the courts in developing an appropriate framework for interpreting and applying the antitrust laws in the horizontal merger context. . . .[2]

The unifying theme of these Guidelines is that mergers should not be permitted to create, enhance, or entrench market power or to facilitate its exercise. For simplicity of exposition, these Guidelines generally refer to all of these effects as enhancing market power. A merger enhances market power if it is likely to encourage one or more firms to raise price, reduce output, diminish innovation, or otherwise harm customers as a result of diminished competitive constraints or incentives. In evaluating how a merger will likely change a firm's behavior, the Agencies focus primarily on how the merger affects conduct that would be most profitable for the firm.

A merger can enhance market power simply by eliminating competition between the merging parties. This effect can arise even if the merger causes no changes in the way other firms behave. Adverse competitive effects arising in this manner are referred to as "unilateral effects." A merger also can enhance market power by increasing the risk of coordinated, accommodating, or interdependent behavior among

[2] These Guidelines are not intended to describe how the Agencies will conduct the litigation of cases they decide to bring. Although relevant in that context, these Guidelines neither dictate nor exhaust the range of evidence the Agencies may introduce in litigation.

rivals. Adverse competitive effects arising in this manner are referred to as "coordinated effects." In any given case, either or both types of effects may be present, and the distinction between them may be blurred.

These Guidelines principally describe how the Agencies analyze mergers between rival suppliers that may enhance their market power as sellers. Enhancement of market power by sellers often elevates the prices charged to customers. For simplicity of exposition, these Guidelines generally discuss the analysis in terms of such price effects. Enhanced market power can also be manifested in non-price terms and conditions that adversely affect customers, including reduced product quality, reduced product variety, reduced service, or diminished innovation. Such non-price effects may coexist with price effects, or can arise in their absence. When the Agencies investigate whether a merger may lead to a substantial lessening of non-price competition, they employ an approach analogous to that used to evaluate price competition. Enhanced market power may also make it more likely that the merged entity can profitably and effectively engage in exclusionary conduct. Regardless of how enhanced market power likely would be manifested, the Agencies normally evaluate mergers based on their impact on customers. The Agencies examine effects on either or both of the direct customers and the final consumers. The Agencies presume, absent convincing evidence to the contrary, that adverse effects on direct customers also cause adverse effects on final consumers. . . .

2. Evidence of Adverse Competitive Effects

The Agencies consider any reasonably available and reliable evidence to address the central question of whether a merger may substantially lessen competition. This section discusses several categories and sources of evidence that the Agencies, in their experience, have found most informative in predicting the likely competitive effects of mergers. The list provided here is not exhaustive. In any given case, reliable evidence may be available in only some categories or from some sources. For each category of evidence, the Agencies consider evidence indicating that the merger may enhance competition as well as evidence indicating that it may lessen competition.

2.1 Types of Evidence

2.1.1 Actual Effects Observed in Consummated Mergers

When evaluating a consummated merger, the ultimate issue is not only whether adverse competitive effects have already resulted from the merger, but also whether such effects are likely to arise in the future. Evidence of observed post-merger price increases or other changes adverse to customers is given substantial weight. The Agencies evaluate whether such changes are anticompetitive effects resulting from the merger, in which case they can be dispositive. However, a consummated merger may be anticompetitive even if such effects have not yet been observed, perhaps because the merged firm may be aware of the possibility of post-merger antitrust review and moderating its conduct. Consequently, the Agencies also consider the same types of evidence they consider when evaluating unconsummated mergers.

2.1.2 Direct Comparisons Based on Experience

The Agencies look for historical events, or "natural experiments," that are informative regarding the competitive effects of the merger. For example, the Agencies may examine the impact of recent mergers, entry, expansion, or exit in the relevant market. Effects of analogous events in similar markets may also be informative.

The Agencies also look for reliable evidence based on variations among similar markets. For example, if the merging firms compete in some locales but not others, comparisons of prices charged in regions where they do and do not compete may be informative regarding post-merger prices. In some cases, however, prices are set on such a broad geographic basis that such comparisons are not informative. The Agencies also may examine how prices in similar markets vary with the number of significant competitors in those markets.

2.1.3 Market Shares and Concentration in a Relevant Market

The Agencies give weight to the merging parties' market shares in a relevant market, the level of concentration, and the change in concentration caused by the merger. *See* Sections 4 and 5. Mergers that cause a significant increase in concentration and result in highly concentrated markets are presumed to be likely to enhance market power, but this presumption can be rebutted by persuasive evidence showing that the merger is unlikely to enhance market power.

2.1.4 Substantial Head-to-Head Competition

The Agencies consider whether the merging firms have been, or likely will become absent the merger, substantial head-to-head competitors. Such evidence can be especially relevant for evaluating adverse unilateral effects, which result directly from the loss of that competition. *See* Section 6. This evidence can also inform market definition. *See* Section 4. . . .

2.2 Sources of Evidence

The Agencies consider many sources of evidence in their merger analysis. The most common sources of reasonably available and reliable evidence are the merging parties, customers, other industry participants, and industry observers.

2.2.1 Merging Parties

The Agencies typically obtain substantial information from the merging parties. This information can take the form of documents, testimony, or data, and can consist of descriptions of competitively relevant conditions or reflect actual business conduct and decisions. Documents created in the normal course are more probative than documents created as advocacy materials in merger review. Documents describing industry conditions can be informative regarding the operation of the market and how a firm identifies and assesses its rivals, particularly when business decisions are made in reliance on the accuracy of those descriptions. The business decisions taken by the merging firms also can be informative about industry conditions. For example, if a firm sets price well above incremental cost, that normally indicates either that the firm believes its customers are not highly sensitive to price (not in itself of antitrust concern, *see* Section 4.1.3[3]) or that the firm and its rivals are engaged in coordinated interaction (*see* Section 7). Incremental cost depends on the relevant increment in output as well as on the time period involved, and in the case of large increments and sustained changes in output it may include some costs that would be fixed for smaller increments of output or shorter time periods.

Explicit or implicit evidence that the merging parties intend to raise prices, reduce output or capacity, reduce product quality or variety, withdraw products or delay their introduction, or curtail research and development efforts after the merger, or explicit or implicit evidence that the ability to engage in such conduct motivated the merger, can be highly informative in evaluating the likely effects of a merger. Likewise, the Agencies look for reliable evidence that the merger is likely to result in efficiencies. The Agencies give careful consideration to the views of individuals whose responsibilities, expertise, and experience relating to the issues in question provide particular indicia of reliability. The financial terms of the transaction may also be informative regarding competitive effects. For example, a purchase price in excess of the acquired firm's stand-alone market value may indicate that the acquiring firm is paying a premium because it expects to be able to reduce competition or to achieve efficiencies. . . .

4. Market Definition

When the Agencies identify a potential competitive concern with a horizontal merger, market definition plays two roles. First, market definition helps specify the line of commerce and section of the country in which the competitive concern arises. In any merger enforcement action, the Agencies will normally identify one or more relevant markets in which the merger may substantially lessen competition. Second, market definition allows the Agencies to identify market participants and measure market shares and market concentration. *See* Section 5. The measurement of market shares and market concentration is not an end in itself, but is useful to the extent it illuminates the merger's likely competitive effects.

---

[3] High margins commonly arise for products that are significantly differentiated. Products involving substantial fixed costs typically will be developed only if suppliers expect there to be enough differentiation to support margins sufficient to cover those fixed costs. High margins can be consistent with incumbent firms earning competitive returns.

The Agencies' analysis need not start with market definition. Some of the analytical tools used by the Agencies to assess competitive effects do not rely on market definition, although evaluation of competitive alternatives available to customers is always necessary at some point in the analysis.

Evidence of competitive effects can inform market definition, just as market definition can be informative regarding competitive effects. For example, evidence that a reduction in the number of significant rivals offering a group of products causes prices for those products to rise significantly can itself establish that those products form a relevant market. Such evidence also may more directly predict the competitive effects of a merger, reducing the role of inferences from market definition and market shares. Where analysis suggests alternative and reasonably plausible candidate markets, and where the resulting market shares lead to very different inferences regarding competitive effects, it is particularly valuable to examine more direct forms of evidence concerning those effects. . . .

[Other portions on market definition are excerpted in Chapter 3].

5. Market Participants, Market Shares, and Market Concentration

The Agencies normally consider measures of market shares and market concentration as part of their evaluation of competitive effects. The Agencies evaluate market shares and concentration in conjunction with other reasonably available and reliable evidence for the ultimate purpose of determining whether a merger may substantially lessen competition . . .

[Sections on identifying market participants and calculating market shares are excerpted in Chapter 3.]

5.3 Market Concentration

Market concentration is often one useful indicator of likely competitive effects of a merger. In evaluating market concentration, the Agencies consider both the post-merger level of market concentration and the change in concentration resulting from a merger. Market shares may not fully reflect the competitive significance of firms in the market or the impact of a merger. They are used in conjunction with other evidence of competitive effects. *See* Sections 6 and 7.

In analyzing mergers between an incumbent and a recent or potential entrant, to the extent the Agencies use the change in concentration to evaluate competitive effects, they will do so using projected market shares. A merger between an incumbent and a potential entrant can raise significant competitive concerns. The lessening of competition resulting from such a merger is more likely to be substantial, the larger is the market share of the incumbent, the greater is the competitive significance of the potential entrant, and the greater is the competitive threat posed by this potential entrant relative to others.

The Agencies give more weight to market concentration when market shares have been stable over time, especially in the face of historical changes in relative prices or costs. If a firm has retained its market share even after its price has increased relative to those of its rivals, that firm already faces limited competitive constraints, making it less likely that its remaining rivals will replace the competition lost if one of that firm's important rivals is eliminated due to a merger. By contrast, even a highly concentrated market can be very competitive if market shares fluctuate substantially over short periods of time in response to changes in competitive offerings. However, if competition by one of the merging firms has significantly contributed to these fluctuations, perhaps because it has acted as a maverick, the Agencies will consider whether the merger will enhance market power by combining that firm with one of its significant rivals.

The Agencies may measure market concentration using the number of significant competitors in the market. This measure is most useful when there is a gap in market share between significant competitors and smaller rivals or when it is difficult to measure revenues in the relevant market. The Agencies also may consider the combined market share of the merging firms as an indicator of the extent to which others in the market may not be able readily to replace competition between the merging firms that is lost through the merger.

The Agencies often calculate the Herfindahl-Hirschman Index ("HHI") of market concentration. The HHI is calculated by summing the squares of the individual firms' market shares,[9] and thus gives proportionately greater weight to the larger market shares. When using the HHI, the Agencies consider both the post-merger level of the HHI and the increase in the HHI resulting from the merger. The increase in the HHI is equal to twice the product of the market shares of the merging firms.[10]

Based on their experience, the Agencies generally classify markets into three types:[21]

- *Unconcentrated Markets:* HHI below 1500
- *Moderately Concentrated Markets:* HHI between 1500 and 2500
- *Highly Concentrated Markets:* HHI above 2500

[9] For example, a market consisting of four firms with market shares of thirty percent, thirty percent, twenty percent, and twenty percent has an HHI of 2600 ($30^2 + 30_2 + 20^2 + 20^2 = 2600$). The HHI ranges from 10,000 (in the case of a pure monopoly) to a number approaching zero (in the case of an atomistic market). Although it is desirable to include all firms in the calculation, lack of information about firms with small shares is not critical because such firms do not affect the HHI significantly.

[10] For example, the merger of firms with shares of five percent and ten percent of the market would increase the HHI by 100 ($5 \times 10 \times 2 = 100$).

[21] [Editor's Note: The following changed the prior merger guidelines, which defined markets as unconcentrated for HHI less than 1000, moderately concentrated for HHI between 1000 and 1800, and highly concentrated for HHI over 1800.]

The Agencies employ the following general standards for the relevant markets they have defined:

- *Small Change in Concentration:* Mergers involving an increase in the HHI of less than 100 points are unlikely to have adverse competitive effects and ordinarily require no further analysis.
- *Unconcentrated Markets:* Mergers resulting in unconcentrated markets are unlikely to have adverse competitive effects and ordinarily require no further analysis.
- *Moderately Concentrated Markets:* Mergers resulting in moderately concentrated markets that involve an increase in the HHI of more than 100 points potentially raise significant competitive concerns and often warrant scrutiny.
- *Highly Concentrated Markets:* Mergers resulting in highly concentrated markets that involve an increase in the HHI of between 100 points and 200 points potentially raise significant competitive concerns and often warrant scrutiny. Mergers resulting in highly concentrated markets that involve an increase in the HHI of more than 200 points will be presumed to be likely to enhance market power. The presumption may be rebutted by persuasive evidence showing that the merger is unlikely to enhance market power.[22]

The purpose of these thresholds is not to provide a rigid screen to separate competitively benign mergers from anticompetitive ones, although high levels of concentration do raise concerns. Rather, they provide one way to identify some mergers unlikely to raise competitive concerns and some others for which it is particularly important to examine whether other competitive factors confirm, reinforce, or counteract the potentially harmful effects of increased concentration. The higher the post-merger HHI and the increase in the HHI, the greater are the Agencies' potential competitive concerns and the greater is the likelihood that the Agencies will request additional information to conduct their analysis.

6. Unilateral Effects

The elimination of competition between two firms that results from their merger may alone constitute a substantial lessening of competition. Such unilateral effects are most apparent in a merger to monopoly in a relevant market, but are by no means limited to that case. Whether

---

[22] [Editor's Note: This changed prior merger guidelines, which not only set the highly concentrated threshold at 1800, but also stated that a HHI increase of between 50–100 potentially raised concerns and an HHI increase of over 100 would be presumed to be likely to be anticompetitive.]

cognizable efficiencies resulting from the merger are likely to reduce or reverse adverse unilateral effects is addressed in Section 10.

Several common types of unilateral effects are discussed in this section. Section 6.1 discusses unilateral price effects in markets with differentiated products. Section 6.2 discusses unilateral effects in markets where sellers negotiate with buyers or prices are determined through auctions. Section 6.3 discusses unilateral effects relating to reductions in output or capacity in markets for relatively homogeneous products. Section 6.4 discusses unilateral effects arising from diminished innovation or reduced product variety. These effects do not exhaust the types of possible unilateral effects; for example, exclusionary unilateral effects also can arise.

A merger may result in different unilateral effects along different dimensions of competition. For example, a merger may increase prices in the short term but not raise longer-term concerns about innovation, either because rivals will provide sufficient innovation competition or because the merger will generate cognizable research and development efficiencies. *See* Section 10.

6.1 Pricing of Differentiated Products

In differentiated product industries, some products can be very close substitutes and compete strongly with each other, while other products are more distant substitutes and compete less strongly. For example, one high-end product may compete much more directly with another high-end product than with any low-end product.

A merger between firms selling differentiated products may diminish competition by enabling the merged firm to profit by unilaterally raising the price of one or both products above the pre-merger level. Some of the sales lost due to the price rise will merely be diverted to the product of the merger partner and, depending on relative margins, capturing such sales loss through merger may make the price increase profitable even though it would not have been profitable prior to the merger.

The extent of direct competition between the products sold by the merging parties is central to the evaluation of unilateral price effects. Unilateral price effects are greater, the more the buyers of products sold by one merging firm consider products sold by the other merging firm to be their next choice. The Agencies consider any reasonably available and reliable information to evaluate the extent of direct competition between the products sold by the merging firms. This includes documentary and testimonial evidence, win/loss reports and evidence from discount approval processes, customer switching patterns, and customer surveys. The types of evidence relied on often overlap substantially with the types of evidence of customer substitution relevant to the hypothetical monopolist test. *See* Section 4.1.1.

Substantial unilateral price elevation post-merger for a product formerly sold by one of the merging firms normally requires that a significant fraction of the customers purchasing that product view products formerly sold by the other merging firm as their next-best choice. However, unless pre-merger margins between price and incremental cost are low, that significant fraction need not approach a majority. For this purpose, incremental cost is measured over the change in output that would be caused by the price change considered. A merger may produce significant unilateral effects for a given product even though many more sales are diverted to products sold by non-merging firms than to products previously sold by the merger partner.

> *Example 19:* In Example 5, the merged entity controlling Products A and B would raise prices ten percent, given the product offerings and prices of other firms. In that example, one-third of the sales lost by Product A when its price alone is raised are diverted to Product B. Further analysis is required to account for repositioning, entry, and efficiencies.

In some cases, the Agencies may seek to quantify the extent of direct competition between a product sold by one merging firm and a second product sold by the other merging firm by estimating the diversion ratio from the first product to the second product. The diversion ratio is the fraction of unit sales lost by the first product due to an increase in its price that would be diverted to the second product. Diversion ratios between products sold by one merging firm and products sold by the other merging firm can be very informative for assessing unilateral price effects, with higher diversion ratios indicating a greater likelihood of such effects. Diversion ratios between products sold by merging firms and those sold by non-merging firms have at most secondary predictive value.

Adverse unilateral price effects can arise when the merger gives the merged entity an incentive to raise the price of a product previously sold by one merging firm and thereby divert sales to products previously sold by the other merging firm, boosting the profits on the latter products. Taking as given other prices and product offerings, that boost to profits is equal to the value to the merged firm of the sales diverted to those products. The value of sales diverted to a product is equal to the number of units diverted to that product multiplied by the margin between price and incremental cost on that product. In some cases, where sufficient information is available, the Agencies assess the value of diverted sales, which can serve as an indicator of the upward pricing pressure on the first product resulting from the merger. Diagnosing unilateral price effects based on the value of diverted sales need not rely on market definition or the calculation of market shares and concentration. The Agencies rely much more on the value of diverted sales than on the level of the HHI for diagnosing unilateral price effects in markets with differentiated products. If the value of diverted sales is proportionately small, significant unilateral price effects are unlikely.[11]

Where sufficient data are available, the Agencies may construct economic models designed to quantify the unilateral price effects resulting from the merger. These models often include independent price responses by non-merging firms. They also can incorporate merger-specific efficiencies. These merger simulation methods need not rely on market definition. The Agencies do not treat merger simulation evidence as conclusive in itself, and they place more weight on whether their merger simulations consistently predict substantial price increases than on the precise prediction of any single simulation.

A merger is unlikely to generate substantial unilateral price increases if non-merging parties offer very close substitutes for the products offered by the merging firms. In some cases, non-merging firms may be able to reposition their products to offer close substitutes for the products offered by the merging firms. Repositioning is a supply-side response that is evaluated much like entry, with consideration given to timeliness, likelihood, and sufficiency. *See* Section 9. The Agencies consider whether repositioning would be sufficient to deter or counteract what otherwise would be significant anticompetitive unilateral effects from a differentiated products merger.

6.2 Bargaining and Auctions

In many industries, especially those involving intermediate goods and services, buyers and sellers negotiate to determine prices and other terms of trade. In that process, buyers commonly negotiate with more than one seller, and may play sellers off against one another. Some highly structured forms of such competition are known as auctions. Negotiations often combine aspects of an auction with aspects of one-on-one negotiation, although pure auctions are sometimes used in government procurement and elsewhere.

A merger between two competing sellers prevents buyers from playing those sellers off against each other in negotiations. This alone can significantly enhance the ability and incentive of the merged entity to obtain a result more favorable to it, and less favorable to the buyer, than the merging firms would have offered separately absent the merger. The Agencies analyze unilateral effects of this type using similar approaches to those described in Section 6.1.

Anticompetitive unilateral effects in these settings are likely in proportion to the frequency or probability with which, prior to the merger, one of the merging sellers had been the runner-up when the other won the business. These effects also are likely to be greater, the

[11] For this purpose, the value of diverted sales is measured in proportion to the lost revenues attributable to the reduction in unit sales resulting from the price increase. Those lost revenues equal the reduction in the number of units sold of that product multiplied by that product's price.

greater advantage the runner-up merging firm has over other suppliers in meeting customers' needs. These effects also tend to be greater, the more profitable were the pre-merger winning bids. All of these factors are likely to be small if there are many equally placed bidders.

The mechanisms of these anticompetitive unilateral effects, and the indicia of their likelihood, differ somewhat according to the bargaining practices used, the auction format, and the sellers' information about one another's costs and about buyers' preferences. For example, when the merging sellers are likely to know which buyers they are best and second best placed to serve, any anticompetitive unilateral effects are apt to be targeted at those buyers; when sellers are less well informed, such effects are more apt to be spread over a broader class of buyers.

6.3 Capacity and Output for Homogeneous Products

In markets involving relatively undifferentiated products, the Agencies may evaluate whether the merged firm will find it profitable unilaterally to suppress output and elevate the market price. A firm may leave capacity idle, refrain from building or obtaining capacity that would have been obtained absent the merger, or eliminate pre-existing production capabilities. A firm may also divert the use of capacity away from one relevant market and into another so as to raise the price in the former market. The competitive analyses of these alternative modes of output suppression may differ.

A unilateral output suppression strategy is more likely to be profitable when (1) the merged firm's market share is relatively high; (2) the share of the merged firm's output already committed for sale at prices unaffected by the output suppression is relatively low; (3) the margin on the suppressed output is relatively low; (4) the supply responses of rivals are relatively small; and (5) the market elasticity of demand is relatively low.

A merger may provide the merged firm a larger base of sales on which to benefit from the resulting price rise, or it may eliminate a competitor that otherwise could have expanded its output in response to the price rise.

> *Example 20:* Firms A and B both produce an industrial commodity and propose to merge. The demand for this commodity is insensitive to price. Firm A is the market leader. Firm B produces substantial output, but its operating margins are low because it operates high-cost plants. The other suppliers are operating very near capacity. The merged firm has an incentive to reduce output at the high-cost plants, perhaps shutting down some of that capacity, thus driving up the price it receives on the remainder of its output. The merger harms customers, notwithstanding that the merged firm shifts some output from high-cost plants to low-cost plants.

In some cases, a merger between a firm with a substantial share of the sales in the market and a firm with significant excess capacity to serve that market can make an output suppression strategy profitable.[12] This can occur even if the firm with the excess capacity has a relatively small share of sales, if that firm's ability to expand, and thus keep price from rising, has been making an output suppression strategy unprofitable for the firm with the larger market share.

6.4 Innovation and Product Variety

Competition often spurs firms to innovate. The Agencies may consider whether a merger is likely to diminish innovation competition by encouraging the merged firm to curtail its innovative efforts below the level that would prevail in the absence of the merger. That curtailment of innovation could take the form of reduced incentive to continue with an existing product-development effort or reduced incentive to initiate development of new products.

The first of these effects is most likely to occur if at least one of the merging firms is engaging in efforts to introduce new products that would capture substantial revenues from the other merging firm. The second, longer-run effect is most likely to occur if at least one of the merging firms has capabilities that are likely to lead it to develop new products in the future that would capture substantial revenues from the other merging firm. The Agencies therefore also consider whether a merger will diminish innovation competition by combining two of a very small number of firms with the strongest capabilities to successfully innovate in a specific direction.

The Agencies evaluate the extent to which successful innovation by one merging firm is likely to take sales from the other, and the extent to which post-merger incentives for future innovation will be lower than those that would prevail in the absence of the merger. The Agencies also consider whether the merger is likely to enable innovation that would not otherwise take place, by bringing together complementary capabilities that cannot be otherwise combined or for some other merger-specific reason. *See* Section 10.

The Agencies also consider whether a merger is likely to give the merged firm an incentive to cease offering one of the relevant products sold by the merging parties. Reductions in variety following a merger may or may not be anticompetitive. Mergers can lead to the efficient consolidation of products when variety offers little in value to customers. In other cases, a merger may increase variety by encouraging the merged firm to reposition its products to be more differentiated from one another.

If the merged firm would withdraw a product that a significant number of customers strongly prefer to those products that would remain available, this can constitute a harm to customers over and above any

[12] Such a merger also can cause adverse coordinated effects, especially if the acquired firm with excess capacity was disrupting effective coordination.

effects on the price or quality of any given product. If there is evidence of such an effect, the Agencies may inquire whether the reduction in variety is largely due to a loss of competitive incentives attributable to the merger. An anticompetitive incentive to eliminate a product as a result of the merger is greater and more likely, the larger is the share of profits from that product coming at the expense of profits from products sold by the merger partner. Where a merger substantially reduces competition by bringing two close substitute products under common ownership, and one of those products is eliminated, the merger will often also lead to a price increase on the remaining product, but that is not a necessary condition for anticompetitive effect.

> *Example 21:* Firm A sells a high-end product at a premium price. Firm B sells a mid-range product at a lower price, serving customers who are more price sensitive. Several other firms have low-end products. Firms A and B together have a large share of the relevant market. Firm A proposes to acquire Firm B and discontinue Firm B's product. Firm A expects to retain most of Firm B's customers. Firm A may not find it profitable to raise the price of its high-end product after the merger, because doing so would reduce its ability to retain Firm B's more price-sensitive customers. The Agencies may conclude that the withdrawal of Firm B's product results from a loss of competition and materially harms customers. . . .

NOTES AND QUESTIONS ON THE U.S. GUIDELINES ON UNILATERAL EFFECTS

When assessing unilateral effects in a differentiated market, the 2010 U.S. Merger Guidelines focus more on diversion ratios than on market definition or HHIs. The diversion ratio is the fraction of customers a firm loses from a price increase that go to the other firm. To calculate, one examines situations when firm 1 increased its price. The diversion ratio then equals

$$\frac{\text{purchases that switched to firm 2}}{\text{all purchases firm 1 lost}}$$

If firm 1 and 2 completely merge, then when firm 1 raises prices, for any sales lost firm 1 now also recapture profits equal to the diversion ratio from firm 1 to 2 (call it D_{12}) times the pre-merger profit markup on firm 2's product (which equals firm 2's price minus its cost, call it $P_2 - C_2$). Likewise, when firm 1 lowers price, then for any sales gained, firm 1 now incurs the additional cost of diverting that same amount of profits, $D_{12}(P_2 - C_2)$, from firm 2, which it would own after a merger. Thus, the merger tends to encourage price increases and discourage price decreases.

Indeed, a merger that creates this profit diversion has the same impact on firm 1's pricing as an increase in its marginal cost equal to $D_{12}(P_2 - C_2)$.

The reason is that, after the merger, each successful sale of the firm 1 product now has the additional cost of diverting away that profit on firm 2's product. Accordingly, a merger will create upward pricing pressure when the profit diversion exceeds any cost reduction produced by merger efficiencies, E_1C_1, where E_1 is percentage efficiency gain to firm 1 and C_1 is firm 1's pre-merger cost. In short, the merger will increase firm 1's prices whenever $D_{12}(P_2 - C_2) > E_1C_1$.[23] For a full analysis one would also have to include any merger efficiencies for firm 2, which actually tends to increase the post-merger prices of firm 1 by increasing the profit diversion.[24] If the firms have the same diversion ratios, prices, costs, and merger efficiencies, the merger will increase prices if $(D/(1 - D))(M/(1 - M)) > E$, where M is the pre-merger profit margin.[25]

For example, suppose that if firm 1 raises its price by $1, it loses 100 sales, 40 of which go to firm 2. Then the diversion ratio from firm 1 to 2 is 40/100 = 40%. If firm 2's profit markup were $1, then this 40% diversion ratio means that, after a merger, firm 1 would lose 40 cents (in foregone profits from firm 2 that it now owns) for every sale that firm 1 would gain with a price cut. Accordingly, a merger would have the same impact on firm 1 pricing as a 40 cent increase in its marginal cost. The merger will thus increase prices unless merger efficiencies are at least 40 cents per unit. If firm 1's pre-merger costs were $1/unit, this means the merger will increase prices unless the merger reduces firm 1's costs by 40%. To apply the more general formula for both merged firms, suppose they each had the same diversion ratio (40%) and pre-merger cost ($1) and price ($2, given $1 markup). Then, then M = ($2 – $1)/$2 = 50%, and (D/(1 – D))(M/(1 – M)) = 40%/60% = 67%. Thus the merger will increase prices unless the merger reduces costs by 67%.

The size of such a price increase can be constrained to the extent other firms would respond to a merged-firm price increase by repositioning their brands. After all, the same would be equally true if a firm's in a differentiated market had its marginal costs rose by 40 cents—the degree to which it could raise prices might be constrained by the repositioning of other firms. But such repositioning would be only a feedback effect of a price increase, so repositioning would not alter the fact or direction of the price effect, but only its size.

*1. **Does it make sense to use HHIs a threshold for unilateral or coordinated effects?*** Given that the HHIs are only directly relevant to Cournot effects, it does not make much sense to use them (as the U.S. Guidelines do) as a threshold to determine whether to consider unilateral or coordinated effects, as discussed in the introduction to this Section. HHIs are a particularly poor threshold to use when the concern is unilateral effects,

---

[23] Joseph Farrell & Carl Shapiro, *Antitrust Evaluation of Horizontal Mergers: An Economic Alternative to Market Definition*, B.E. J. THEOR. ECON., vol. 10, no. 1, art. 9, at 11 (2010). Professors Farrell and Shapiro were the chief economists for the FTC and DOJ when these merger guidelines were adopted.

[24] *Id.* at 12–13.

[25] *Id.* at 13. That is, M = (P – C)/P. In this symmetric case, the pre-merger P and C is the same for both firms, so M is the same for both as well.

given that unilateral effects can exist with small HHIs and by definition do not depend on the concentration of the rest of the market. HHIs also correlate only loosely (and sometimes perversely) with coordinated effects. A far more relevant threshold would be the number of oligopolists and their collective market share.

2. ***Is market definition necessary to find unilateral effects on a differentiated market?*** If product offerings are sufficiently differentiated that the merger of firms whose offerings are close to each other can have price effects, it is not clear why we should care about market definition, market shares, or HHIs levels. One might think that, if such price effects are possible, a market should be defined narrowly as the product space right around those firms. However, defining a narrow market will not produce accurate results if the merging firms are not the closest rivals to each other, because even a narrow market definition treats all firms within the product space/market as identical, despite the reality that they are not. In such cases, direct consideration of differentiated market effects is more accurate. Further, intuition often makes courts reluctant to define markets narrowly around certain brands, even when that definition matches economic reality.

FTC v. Staples, Inc.

970 F.Supp. 1066 (D.D.C. 1997).

■ THOMAS F. HOGAN, DISTRICT JUDGE. [The FTC] . . . seeks a preliminary injunction . . . to enjoin the consummation of any acquisition by defendant Staples, Inc., of defendant Office Depot, Inc. . . . Defendants are both corporations which sell office products—including office supplies, business machines, computers and furniture—through retail stores, commonly described as office supply superstores, as well as through direct mail delivery and contract stationer operations. Staples is the second largest office superstore chain in the United States with approximately 550 retail stores located in 28 states and the District of Columbia, primarily in the Northeast and California. In 1996 Staples' revenues from those stores were approximately $4 billion through all operations. Office Depot, the largest office superstore chain, operates over 500 retail office supply superstores that are located in 38 states and the District of Columbia, primarily in the South and Midwest. Office Depot's 1996 sales were approximately $6.1 billion. OfficeMax, Inc., is the only other office supply superstore firm in the United States.

On September 4, 1996, defendants Staples and Office Depot . . . entered into [a merger agreement. The FTC voted to challenge the merger and brought this suit.] . . .

II. The Geographic Market

One of the few issue about which the parties to this case do not disagree is that metropolitan areas are the appropriate geographic markets for analyzing the competitive effects of the proposed merger. . . .

III. The Relevant Product Market

. . . The Commission defines the relevant product market as "the sale of consumable office supplies through office superstores," with "consumable" meaning products that consumers buy recurrently, i.e., items which "get used up" or discarded. For example, under the Commission's definition, "consumable office supplies" would not include capital goods such as computers, fax machines, and other business machines or office furniture, but does include such products as paper, pens, file folders, post-it notes, computer disks, and toner cartridges. The defendants . . . counter that the appropriate product market . . . is simply the overall sale of office products, of which a combined Staples-Office Depot accounted for 5.5% of total sales in North America in 1996. . . . [T]he Court finds that the appropriate relevant product market definition in this case is, as the Commission has argued, the sale of consumable office supplies through office supply superstores.

The general rule when determining a relevant product market is that "[t]he outer boundaries of a product market are determined by the reasonable interchangeability of use [by consumers] or the cross-elasticity of demand between the product itself and substitutes for it." *Brown Shoe,* 370 U.S. at 325; *see also du Pont*. . . . This case, of course, is an example of perfect "functional interchangeability." The consumable office products at issue here are identical whether they are sold by Staples or Office Depot or another seller of office supplies. A legal pad sold by Staples or Office Depot is "functionally interchangeable" with a legal pad sold by Wal-Mart. . . . A computer disk sold by Staples-Office Depot is "functionally interchangeable" with a computer disk sold by CompUSA. . . . However, as the government has argued, functional interchangeability should not end the Court's analysis.

The Supreme Court did not stop after finding a high degree of functional interchangeability between cellophane and other wrapping materials in the *du Pont* case. . . . Following that reasoning in this case, the Commission has argued that a slight but significant increase in Staples-Office Depot's prices will not cause a considerable number of Staples-Office Depot's customers to purchase consumable office supplies from other non-superstore alternatives such as Wal-Mart, Best Buy, Quill, or Viking. On the other hand, the Commission has argued that an increase in price by Staples would result in consumers turning to another office superstore, especially Office Depot, if the consumers had that option. Therefore, the Commission concludes that the sale of consumable office supplies by office supply superstores is the appropriate relevant product market in this case, and products sold by competitors such as Wal-Mart, Best Buy, Viking, Quill, and others should be excluded. . . .

The Court acknowledges that there is, in fact, a broad market encompassing the sale of consumable office supplies by all sellers of such supplies, and that those sellers must, at some level, compete with one another. However, the mere fact that a firm may be termed a competitor in the overall marketplace does not necessarily require that it be included in the relevant product market for antitrust purposes. The Supreme Court has recognized that within a broad market, "well-defined submarkets may exist which, in themselves, constitute product markets for antitrust purposes." *Brown Shoe* . . . There is a possibility, therefore, that the sale of consumable office supplies by office superstores may qualify as a submarket within a larger market of retailers of office supplies in general.

The Court in *Brown Shoe* provided a series of factors or "practical indicia" for determining whether a submarket exists including "industry or public recognition of the submarket as a separate economic entity, the product's peculiar characteristics and uses, unique production facilities, distinct customers, distinct prices, sensitivity to price changes, and specialized vendors." Since the Court described these factors as "practical indicia" rather than requirements, subsequent cases have found that submarkets can exist even if only some of these factors are present. . . .

The Commission discussed several of the *Brown Shoe* "practical indicia" in its case, such as industry recognition, and the special characteristics of superstores which make them different from other sellers of office supplies, including distinct formats, customers, and prices. Primarily, however, the FTC focused on what it termed the "pricing evidence," which the Court finds corresponds with *Brown Shoe's* "sensitivity to price changes" factor. First, the FTC presented evidence comparing Staples' prices in geographic markets where Staples is the only office superstore, to markets where Staples competes with Office Depot or OfficeMax, or both. Based on the FTC's calculations, in markets where Staples faces no office superstore competition at all, something which was termed a one firm market during the hearing, prices are 13% higher than in three firm markets where it competes with both Office Depot and OfficeMax. . . . Similarly, the evidence showed that Office Depot's prices are significantly higher—well over 5% higher,[8] in Depot-only markets than they are in three firm markets. . . .

This evidence all suggests that office superstore prices are affected primarily by other office superstores and not by non-superstore competitors such as mass merchandisers like Wal-Mart, Kmart, or Target, wholesale clubs such as BJ's, Sam's, and Price Costco, computer or electronic stores such as Computer City and Best Buy, independent retail office supply stores, mail orders firms like Quill and Viking, and contract stationers. Though the FTC did not present the Court with evidence regarding the precise amount of non-superstore competition in each of Staples' and Office Depot's one, two, and three firm markets, it is clear to the Court that these competitors, albeit in different combinations and concentrations, are present in every one of these markets. For

[8] . . . The *Merger Guidelines* use 5% as the usual approximation of a "small but significant and nontransitory price increase." For this reason, the Court's analysis will often refer to this 5% number.

example, it is a certainty that the mail order competitors compete in all of the geographic markets at issue in this case. Office products are available through the mail in all 50 states, and have been for approximately 30 years. Despite this mail order competition, however, Staples and Office Depot are still able to charge higher prices in their one firm markets than they do in the two firm markets and the three firm markets without losing a significant number of customers to the mail order firms. The same appears to be true with respect to Wal-Mart. Bill Long, Vice President for Merchandising at Wal-Mart Stores, testifying through declaration, explained that price-checking by Wal-Mart of Staples' prices in areas where both Staples and Wal-Mart exist showed that, on average, Staples' prices were higher where there was a Staples and a Wal-Mart but no other superstore than where there was a Staples, a Wal-Mart, and another superstore.

The evidence with respect to the wholesale club stores is consistent. Mike Atkinson, Vice President, Division Merchandise Manager of BJ's Wholesale Club, testified at the hearing regarding BJ's price checking of Staples and Office Depot in areas where BJ's competes with one or both of those superstores. . . . BJ's price checking found that, in general, office supply superstore prices were lowest where there was both a Staples and an Office Depot. In addition, Staples' own pricing information shows that warehouse clubs have very little effect on Staples' prices. . . . There is also consistent evidence with respect to computer and/or consumer electronics stores such as Best Buy. . . .

There is similar evidence with respect to the defendants' behavior when faced with entry of another competitor. The evidence shows that the defendants change their price zones when faced with entry of another superstore, but do not do so for other retailers. . . .

. . . [T]he Court finds this evidence a compelling showing that a small but significant increase in Staples' prices will not cause a significant number of consumers to turn to non-superstore alternatives for purchasing their consumable office supplies. Despite the high degree of functional interchangeability between consumable office supplies sold by the office superstores and other retailers of office supplies, the evidence presented by the Commission shows that even where Staples and Office Depot charge higher prices, certain consumers do not go elsewhere for their supplies. This further demonstrates that the sale of office supplies by non-superstore retailers are not responsive to the higher prices charged by Staples and Office Depot in the one firm markets. This indicates a low cross-elasticity of demand between the consumable office supplies sold by the superstores and those sold by other sellers.

Turning back to the other *Brown Shoe* "practical indicia" of submarkets . . . the . . . evidence shows that office superstores are, in fact, very different in appearance, physical size, format, the number and variety of SKU's offered, and the type of customers targeted and served than other sellers of office supplies. . . . Office supply superstores are high volume, discount office supply chain stores averaging in excess of 20,000 square feet, with over 11,000 of those square feet devoted to traditional office supplies, and carrying over 5,000 SKUs of consumable office supplies in addition to computers, office furniture, and other non-consumables. In contrast, stores such as Kmart devote approximately 210 square feet to the sale of approximately 250 SKUs of consumable office supplies. Kinko's devotes approximately 50 square feet to the sale of 150 SKUs. Target sells only 400 SKUs. Both Sam's Club and Computer City each sell approximately 200 SKUs. . . . The superstores' customer base overwhelmingly consists of small businesses with fewer than 20 employees and consumers with home offices. In contrast, mail order customers are typically mid-sized companies with more than 20 employees. . . .

Another of the "practical indicia" for determining the presence of a submarket suggested by *Brown Shoe* is "industry or public recognition of the submarket as a separate economic entity." The Commission offered abundant evidence on this factor from Staples' and Office Depot's documents which shows that both Staples and Office Depot focus primarily on competition from other superstores. . . . When assessing key trends and making long range plans, Staples and Office Depot focus on the plans of other superstores. In addition, when determining whether to enter a new metropolitan area, both Staples and Office Depot evaluate the extent of office superstore competition in the market and the number of office superstores the market can support. When selecting sites and markets for new store openings, defendants repeatedly refer to markets without office superstores as "non-competitive," even when the new store is adjacent to or near a warehouse club, consumer electronics store, or a mass merchandiser such as Wal-Mart. . . . In addition, it is clear from the evidence that Staples and Office Depot price check the other office superstores much more frequently and extensively than they price check other retailers such as BJ's or Best Buy, and that Staples and Office Depot are more concerned with keeping their prices in parity with the other office superstores in their geographic areas than in undercutting Best Buy or a warehouse club.

For the reasons set forth in the above analysis, the Court finds that the sale of consumable office supplies through office supply superstores is the appropriate relevant product market for purposes of considering the possible anti-competitive effects of the proposed merger between Staples and Office Depot. The pricing evidence indicates a low cross-elasticity of demand between consumable office products sold by Staples or Office Depot and those same products sold by other sellers of office supplies. This same evidence indicates that non-superstore sellers of office supplies are not able to effectively constrain the superstores prices, because a significant number of superstore customers do not turn to a non-superstore alternative when faced with higher prices in the one firm markets. In addition, the factors or "practical indicia" of *Brown Shoe* support a finding of a "submarket" under the facts of this case, and "submarkets," as *Brown Shoe* established, may themselves be appropriate product markets for antitrust purposes[11]. . . .

IV. Probable Effect on Competition

After accepting the Commission's definition of the relevant product market, the Court next must consider the probable effect of a merger between Staples and Office Depot in the geographic markets previously identified. . . . Currently, the least concentrated market is that of Grand Rapids-Muskegon-Holland, Michigan, with an HHI of 3,597, while the most concentrated is Washington, D.C. with an HHI of 6,944. In contrast, after a merger of Staples and Office Depot, the least concentrated area would be Kalamazoo-Battle Creek Michigan, with an HHI of 5,003, and many areas would have HHIs of 10,000. The average increase in HHI caused by the merger would be 2,715 points. . . . The combined shares of Staples and Office Depot in the office superstore market would be 100% in 15 metropolitan areas. It is in these markets the post-merger HHI would be 10,000. In 27 other metropolitan areas, where the number of office superstore competitors would drop from three to two, the post-merger market shares would range from 45% to 94%, with post-merger HHIs ranging from 5,003 to 9,049. Even the lowest of these HHIs indicates a "highly concentrated" market.

According to the Department of Justice Merger Guidelines, . . . an HHI over 1800 qualifies as "highly concentrated." Further, . . . unless mitigated by other factors . . . an increase in the HHI in excess of 50 points in a post-merger highly concentrated market may raise significant competitive concerns. . . . The *Merger Guidelines,* of course, are not binding on the Court, but, as this Circuit has stated, they do provide "a useful illustration of the application of the HHI," and the Court will use that guidance here. . . . With HHIs of this level, the Commission certainly has shown a "reasonable probability" that the proposed merger would have an anti-competitive effect.

The HHI calculations and market concentration evidence, however, are not the only indications that a merger between Staples and Office Depot may substantially lessen competition. Much of the evidence already discussed with respect to defining the relevant product market also indicates that the merger would likely have an anti-competitive effect. The evidence of the defendants' own current pricing practices, for example, shows that an office superstore chain facing no competition from other superstores has the ability to profitably raise prices for consumable office supplies above competitive levels. . . . Since prices are significantly lower in markets where Staples and Office Depot compete,

[11] As other courts have noted, use of the term "submarket" may be confusing. *See Allen-Myland v. IBM Corp.,* 33 F.3d 194, 208 n. 16 (3d Cir.1994) (finding it less confusing to speak in terms of the relevant product market rather than the submarket). *Olin Corp. v. FTC,* 986 F.2d 1295, 1299 (9th Cir.1993) ("[E]very market that encompasses less than all products is, in a sense, a submarket"). Whatever term is used—market, submarket, relevant product market—the analysis is the same.

eliminating this competition with one another would free the parties to charge higher prices in those markets, especially those in which the combined entity would be the sole office superstore. In addition, allowing the defendants to merge would eliminate significant future competition. Absent the merger, the firms are likely, and in fact have planned, to enter more of each other's markets, leading to a deconcentration of the market and, therefore, increased competition between the superstores.

In addition, direct evidence shows that by eliminating Staples' most significant, and in many markets only, rival, this merger would allow Staples to increase prices or otherwise maintain prices at an anti-competitive level.[14] The merger would eliminate significant head-to-head competition between the two lowest cost and lowest priced firms in the superstore market. Thus, the merger would result in the elimination of a particularly aggressive competitor in a highly concentrated market, a factor which is certainly an important consideration when analyzing possible anti-competitive effects. It is based on all of this evidence as well that the Court finds that the Commission has shown a likelihood of success on the merits and a "reasonable probability" that the proposed transaction will have an anti-competitive effect.

By showing that the proposed transaction between Staples and Office Depot will lead to undue concentration in the market for consumable office supplies sold by office superstores in the geographic markets agreed upon by the parties, the Commission establishes a presumption that the transaction will substantially lessen competition. Once such a presumption has been established, the burden of producing evidence to rebut the presumption shifts to the defendants. *See, e.g., United States v. Marine Bancorporation,* 418 U.S. 602, 631 (1974); *United States v. General Dynamics Corp.,* 415 U.S. 486, 496–504 (1974). To meet this burden, the defendants must show that the market-share statistics give an inaccurate prediction of the proposed acquisition's probable effect on competition. . . .

In their criticism of the Commission's pricing evidence, the defendants accused the FTC of "cherry-picking" its data and pointed to specific examples which contradict the Commission's conclusions. . . . However, the fact that there may be some examples with respect to individual items in individual cities which contradict the FTC's evidence does not overly concern the Court. A few examples of isolated products simply cannot refute the power of the FTC's evidence with respect to the overall trend over time, which is that Staples' and Office Depot's prices are lowest in three firm markets and highest where they do not compete

[14] . . . This does not necessarily mean that prices would rise from the levels they are now. Instead, according to the Commission, prices would simply not decrease as much as they would have on their own absent the merger. . . . Therefore, when the Court discusses "raising" prices it is also with respect to raising prices with respect to where prices would have been absent the merger, not actually an increase from present price levels.

with another office superstore. Neither does the fact that some two superstore areas have lower prices than some three firm markets. . . .

Defendants also argued that the regional price differences set forth in the FTC's pricing evidence do not reflect market power, because the reason for those differentials is not solely the presence or absence of other superstore competition. Instead, argued the defendants, these differentials are the result of a host of factors other than superstore competition. As examples of other factors which cause differences in pricing between geographic markets, the defendants offered sales volume, product mix, marketing or advertising costs, and distribution costs. Defendants also argued that there are differences in wages and rent which cause the differences in pricing between certain stores. The Court, however, cannot find that the evidence submitted by the defendants with respect to other reasons for the differences in pricing between one, two, and three firm markets is sufficient to rebut the Commission's evidence. . . .

[The portions of the opinion on entry, efficiencies, and balancing the equities are excerpted later in this chapter.]

NOTES AND QUESTIONS ON *STAPLES*

1. ***Should the market definition or market shares really matter?*** Most of the case focused on whether the market was "office superstores" or all "consumable office supplies." The court found the former, thus concluding the merging parties were two of only three firms in the market and thus the merger would give them a post-merger share of 45–100%, depending on the locality. Had the court found the latter, their post-merger market share would have been only 5.5%.

But should finding the broader market really change the result? No, because either way, the price evidence would still have shown that a merger between the two firms would significantly increase prices and harm consumers. It does not really matter whether those price effects indicate unilateral effects because (a) the merged firms have big shares in a narrow market or (b) they are close to each other in a broader differentiated market in which their market share is small. Such pricing evidence illustrates why HHI thresholds are really unrelated to the relevant competitive concern, given that firms with small market shares can nonetheless raise prices significantly in a differentiated product space.

2. ***Does the pricing evidence moot the need for any market definition or unilateral effects analysis?*** The price evidence showed that towns with only one office superstore charged higher prices than towns with two or three office super stores. In other words, in towns that had Staples *or* OfficeDepot, prices were high despite any constraint imposed by other stores. In towns that had Staples *and* OfficeDepot and those other stores, prices were lower. Such evidence directly indicates that the merger would raise prices in towns that now had both firms and would, after the merger, have only one of them.

Given this pricing evidence, one does not really need market definition or market share calculations at all, because they are just proxies for trying to imperfectly predict pricing effects. Indeed, when (as in this case) one can ascertain price effects by directly observing price differences across different geographic markets where the merged firms do or do not compete, one also does not need any complicated unilateral effects analysis of diversion ratios or examination of demand and supply elasticities. Although such pricing evidence indicates that there must be unilateral effects (regardless of how the market is defined), the precise mechanism does not really matter, because either way the merger would anticompetitively raise prices and harm consumers.

With the advent of computerized pricing data because of scanning bar codes, do you think antitrust will or should move towards proving cases more with direct evidence of price effects than by defining markets and proving high market shares?

U.S. Agency Enforcement Activity

The 2010 U.S. Guidelines increased the HHI thresholds because actual agency practice indicated that enforcement was not likely at the low levels suggested by the old thresholds. Outside of oil markets, the agencies virtually never challenged mergers that resulted in HHIs below 2000.[26] However, in suggesting that enforcement is presumptive for mergers that significantly increase HHI to a level over 2500, the 2010 Guidelines may still overstate the likelihood of enforcement if past agency enforcement practices continue. FTC data on mergers that significantly increase HHI indicate that, for post-merger HHIs less than 4000, the likelihood of enforcement is below 40% when the market is left with four significant rivals and below 50% when it is left with three.[27] Further, when the merger leaves the market with only two significant rivals, it takes an HHI of over 3000 to make enforcement more likely than not.[28] Overall, the average HHI in a case that the FTC closed without challenge after a second request was 3055–3271 (with an HHI change of 703–825), whereas the average HHI in a case where the FTC did challenge was 5220–5833 (with a change of 1774–1903).[29] Enforcement odds were best predicted by HHIs when the relevant anticompetitive theory is oligopolistic effects and by the number of significant rivals when the relevant theory is unilateral effects.[30]

---

[26] *See* FTC-DOJ, Merger Challenges Data, Fiscal Years 1999–2003, at Tables 3–10.

[27] *See* Coate & Ulrick, *Transparency at the Federal Trade Commission: The Horizontal Merger Review Process 1996–2003*, 73 ANTITRUST L.J. 531, 557 (2006).

[28] *Id.*

[29] *See id.* at 543.

[30] *See* Coate, *Empirical Analysis of Merger Enforcement Under the 1992 Merger Guidelines*, 27 REV. INDUS. ORG. 279 (2005).

2. OLIGOPOLY EFFECTS

U.S. DOJ/FTC, Horizontal Merger Guidelines

(2010).

2.1 Types of Evidence [In addition to types of evidence noted in excerpt under unilateral effects, the agencies also consider the following in a coordinated effects case.] . . .

2.1.5 Disruptive Role of a Merging Party

The Agencies consider whether a merger may lessen competition by eliminating a "maverick" firm, i.e., a firm that plays a disruptive role in the market to the benefit of customers. For example, if one of the merging firms has a strong incumbency position and the other merging firm threatens to disrupt market conditions with a new technology or business model, their merger can involve the loss of actual or potential competition. Likewise, one of the merging firms may have the incentive to take the lead in price cutting or other competitive conduct or to resist increases in industry prices. A firm that may discipline prices based on its ability and incentive to expand production rapidly using available capacity also can be a maverick, as can a firm that has often resisted otherwise prevailing industry norms to cooperate on price setting or other terms of competition. . . .

7. Coordinated Effects

A merger may diminish competition by enabling or encouraging post-merger coordinated interaction among firms in the relevant market that harms customers. Coordinated interaction involves conduct by multiple firms that is profitable for each of them only as a result of the accommodating reactions of the others. These reactions can blunt a firm's incentive to offer customers better deals by undercutting the extent to which such a move would win business away from rivals. They also can enhance a firm's incentive to raise prices, by assuaging the fear that such a move would lose customers to rivals.

Coordinated interaction includes a range of conduct. Coordinated interaction can involve the explicit negotiation of a common understanding of how firms will compete or refrain from competing. Such conduct typically would itself violate the antitrust laws. Coordinated interaction also can involve a similar common understanding that is not explicitly negotiated but would be enforced by the detection and punishment of deviations that would undermine the coordinated interaction. Coordinated interaction alternatively can involve parallel accommodating conduct not pursuant to a prior understanding. Parallel accommodating conduct includes situations in which each rival's response to competitive moves made by others is individually rational, and not motivated by retaliation or deterrence nor intended to sustain an agreed-upon market outcome, but nevertheless emboldens price increases and weakens competitive incentives to reduce prices or offer customers better terms. Coordinated interaction includes conduct not otherwise condemned by the antitrust laws.

The ability of rival firms to engage in coordinated conduct depends on the strength and predictability of rivals' responses to a price change or other competitive initiative. Under some circumstances, a merger can result in market concentration sufficient to strengthen such responses or enable multiple firms in the market to predict them more confidently, thereby affecting the competitive incentives of multiple firms in the market, not just the merged firm.

7.1 Impact of Merger on Coordinated Interaction

The Agencies examine whether a merger is likely to change the manner in which market participants interact, inducing substantially more coordinated interaction. The Agencies seek to identify how a merger might significantly weaken competitive incentives through an increase in the strength, extent, or likelihood of coordinated conduct. There are, however, numerous forms of coordination, and the risk that a merger will induce adverse coordinated effects may not be susceptible to quantification or detailed proof. Therefore, the Agencies evaluate the risk of coordinated effects using measures of market concentration (*see* Section 5) in conjunction with an assessment of whether a market is vulnerable to coordinated conduct. *See* Section 7.2. The analysis in Section 7.2 applies to moderately and highly concentrated markets, as unconcentrated markets are unlikely to be vulnerable to coordinated conduct.

Pursuant to the Clayton Act's incipiency standard, the Agencies may challenge mergers that in their judgment pose a real danger of harm through coordinated effects, even without specific evidence showing precisely how the coordination likely would take place. The Agencies are likely to challenge a merger if the following three conditions are all met: (1) the merger would significantly increase concentration and lead to a moderately or highly concentrated market; (2) that market shows signs of vulnerability to coordinated conduct (*see* Section 7.2); and (3) the Agencies have a credible basis on which to conclude that the merger may enhance that vulnerability. An acquisition eliminating a maverick firm (*see* Section 2.1.5) in a market vulnerable to coordinated conduct is likely to cause adverse coordinated effects.

7.2 Evidence a Market Is Vulnerable to Coordinated Conduct

The Agencies presume that market conditions are conducive to coordinated interaction if firms representing a substantial share in the relevant market appear to have previously engaged in express collusion affecting the relevant market, unless competitive conditions in the market have since changed significantly. Previous express collusion in another geographic market will have the same weight if the salient characteristics of that other market at the time of the collusion are comparable to those in the relevant market. Failed previous attempts at collusion in the relevant market suggest that successful collusion was difficult pre-merger but not so difficult as to deter attempts, and a merger may tend to make success more likely. Previous collusion or attempted collusion in another product market may also be given substantial weight if the salient characteristics of that other market at the time of the collusion are closely comparable to those in the relevant market.

A market typically is more vulnerable to coordinated conduct if each competitively important firm's significant competitive initiatives can be promptly and confidently observed by that firm's rivals. This is more likely to be the case if the terms offered to customers are relatively transparent. Price transparency can be greater for relatively homogeneous products. Even if terms of dealing are not transparent, transparency regarding the identities of the firms serving particular customers can give rise to coordination, e.g., through customer or territorial allocation. Regular monitoring by suppliers of one another's prices or customers can indicate that the terms offered to customers are relatively transparent.

A market typically is more vulnerable to coordinated conduct if a firm's prospective competitive reward from attracting customers away from its rivals will be significantly diminished by likely responses of those rivals. This is more likely to be the case, the stronger and faster are the responses the firm anticipates from its rivals. The firm is more likely to anticipate strong responses if there are few significant competitors, if products in the relevant market are relatively homogeneous, if customers find it relatively easy to switch between suppliers, or if suppliers use meeting-competition clauses.

A firm is more likely to be deterred from making competitive initiatives by whatever responses occur if sales are small and frequent rather than via occasional large and long-term contracts or if relatively few customers will switch to it before rivals are able to respond. A firm is less likely to be deterred by whatever responses occur if the firm has little stake in the status quo. For example, a firm with a small market share that can quickly and dramatically expand, constrained neither by limits on production nor by customer reluctance to switch providers or to entrust business to a historically small provider, is unlikely to be deterred. Firms are also less likely to be deterred by whatever responses occur if competition in the relevant market is marked by leapfrogging technological innovation, so that responses by competitors leave the gains from successful innovation largely intact.

A market is more apt to be vulnerable to coordinated conduct if the firm initiating a price increase will lose relatively few customers after rivals respond to the increase. Similarly, a market is more apt to be vulnerable to coordinated conduct if a firm that first offers a lower price or improved product to customers will retain relatively few customers thus attracted away from its rivals after those rivals respond.

The Agencies regard coordinated interaction as more likely, the more the participants stand to gain from successful coordination. Coordination generally is more profitable, the lower is the market elasticity of demand.

Coordinated conduct can harm customers even if not all firms in the relevant market engage in the coordination, but significant harm normally is likely only if a substantial part of the market is subject to such conduct. The prospect of harm depends on the collective market power, in the relevant market, of firms whose incentives to compete are substantially weakened by coordinated conduct. This collective market power is greater, the lower is the market elasticity of demand. This collective market power is diminished by the presence of other market participants with small market shares and little stake in the outcome resulting from the coordinated conduct, if these firms can rapidly expand their sales in the relevant market.

Buyer characteristics and the nature of the procurement process can affect coordination. For example, sellers may have the incentive to bid aggressively for a large contract even if they expect strong responses by rivals. This is especially the case for sellers with small market shares, if they can realistically win such large contracts. In some cases, a large buyer may be able to strategically undermine coordinated conduct, at least as it pertains to that buyer's needs, by choosing to put up for bid a few large contracts rather than many smaller ones, and by making its procurement decisions opaque to suppliers . . .

NOTES AND QUESTIONS ON U.S. GUIDELINES ON OLIGOPOLY EFFECTS

1. ***Why doesn't the likelihood of oligopolistic coordination turn solely on market concentration?*** The reason is that the likelihood of oligopolistic coordination is also affected by the extent to which market conditions allow firms to settle on common conduct, notice deviations, and respond to deviations in a way that deters them. The factors discussed in the Guidelines bear on such issues. For example, product homogeneity makes it easier to settle on a common price and notice deviations from it, price transparency makes it easier to notice deviations, and having many repeat transactions (rather than large all-or-nothing contracts) make it easier to respond to deviations in a way that can deter them.

2. ***Even if oligopolistic coordination were not possible, could Cournot effects still occur if each firm individually chooses an output level rather than a price?*** Yes, which makes it puzzling that the Guidelines do not have any section discussing uncoordinated oligopoly effects. The conditions necessary to prove such effects turn not on whether firms can coordinate but rather on whether they engage in Cournot competition by picking output levels rather than picking prices. Given that the Cournot model is what best fits the HHI thresholds that the Guidelines use, it is surprising that Guidelines do not have a section discussing when such effects are likely to trigger antitrust enforcement.

*3. **Should Cournot effects be considered "coordinated" even though they do not require settling on common terms or punishment of deviation from such common terms?*** That would be a strained understanding of what coordination means. In any event, even if we call Cournot effects "coordinated", it would not make sense to require evidence of factors that bear on an ability to settle on common terms and to notice and punish rival deviations from common terms, when assessing whether a merger might have anticompetitive Cournot effects, because such an ability is not necessary for Cournot effects.

Qualitative v. Empirical Assessments

The U.S. Guidelines take the approach of looking at the factors that theoretically affect the level of oligopolistic coordination and then reaching some qualitative assessment of how likely coordination seems given those factors. Such qualitative assessments seem to rest largely on subjective judgments about the weight of the factors. One might wonder why, instead of resting on such subjective judgments, agencies and courts don't simply examine directly the empirical evidence about the extent to which firms in the relevant market are able to price above marginal cost. If such evidence existed, then one might be able to infer the degree of coordination or unilateral effects that must be going on in a more rigorous and precise way.

The new empirical industrial organization (NEIO) models take this approach. *See* Chapter 1. Under this approach, the degree to which firms behave competitively is neither assumed nor made the subject of qualitative assessment. Instead, it is put into the equation as a "conduct parameter," which is then calculated by measuring the relevant elasticities, price-cost margins, and market concentration. For example, rather than assuming either Cournot effects or coordination, or their absence, one can use the equation $(P - MC)/P = (1 + K)HHI/\epsilon$, where K is the conduct parameter, P is price, MC is marginal cost, and ϵ is marketwide demand elasticity. Past data on price, costs, market concentration and demand elasticity can then be examined to determine the remaining variable K. If K turns out to equal -1, then that suggests an absence of even Cournot effects. If K is zero, then that is consistent with pure Cournot effects because then the Lerner Index equals HHI/ϵ. If K is positive, it indicates oligopolistic coordination over and above mere Cournot effects.

FTC v. H.J. Heinz Co.

246 F.3d 708 (D.C. Cir. 2001).

■ KAREN LECRAFT HENDERSON, CIRCUIT JUDGE.

On February 28, 2000 H.J. Heinz . . . and . . . Beech-Nut . . . entered into a merger agreement. The . . . FTC . . . sought a preliminary injunction . . . The district court denied the preliminary injunction and the FTC appealed to this court. For the reasons set forth below, we reverse the district court and remand for entry of a preliminary injunction against Heinz and Beech-Nut.

I. Background

Four million infants in the United States consume 80 million cases of jarred baby food annually, representing a domestic market of $865 million to $1 billion. The baby food market is dominated by three firms, Gerber . . . , Heinz and Beech-Nut. Gerber, the industry leader, enjoys a 65 per cent market share while Heinz and Beech-Nut come in second and third, with a 17.4 per cent and a 15.4 per cent share respectively. The district court found that Gerber enjoys unparalleled brand recognition with a brand loyalty greater than any other product sold in the United States. Gerber's products are found in over 90 per cent of all American supermarkets.

By contrast, Heinz is sold in approximately 40 per cent of all supermarkets. Its sales are nationwide but concentrated in northern New England, the Southeast and Deep South and the Midwest. Despite its second-place domestic market share, Heinz is the largest producer of baby food in the world with $1 billion in sales worldwide. Its domestic baby food products with annual net sales of $103 million are manufactured at its Pittsburgh, Pennsylvania plant, which was updated in 1991 at a cost of $120 million. The plant operates at 40 per cent of its production capacity and produces 12 million cases of baby food annually. Its baby food line includes about 130 SKUs (stock keeping units), that is, product varieties (*e.g.*, strained carrots, apple sauce, etc.). Heinz lacks Gerber's brand recognition; it markets itself as a "value brand" with a shelf price several cents below Gerber's.

Beech-Nut has a market share (15.4%) comparable to that of Heinz (17.4%), with $138.7 million in annual sales of baby food, of which 72 per cent is jarred baby food. Its jarred baby food line consists of 128 SKUs. Beech-Nut manufactures all of its baby food in Canajoharie, New York at a manufacturing plant that was built in 1907 and began manufacturing baby food in 1931. Beech-Nut maintains price parity with Gerber, selling at about one penny less. It markets its product as a premium brand. Consumers generally view its product as comparable in quality to Gerber's. Beech-Nut is carried in approximately 45 per cent of all grocery stores. Although its sales are nationwide, they are concentrated in New York, New Jersey, California and Florida.[3]

At the wholesale level Heinz and Beech-Nut both make lump-sum payments called "fixed trade spending" (also known as "slotting fees" or "pay-to-stay" arrangements) to grocery stores to obtain shelf placement.

[3] Although Heinz and Beech-Nut introduced evidence showing that in areas that account for 80% of Beech-Nut sales, Heinz has a market share of about 2% and in areas that account for about 72% of Heinz sales, Beech-Nut's share is about 4%, the FTC introduced evidence that Heinz and Beech-Nut are locked in an intense battle at the wholesale level to gain (and maintain) position as the second brand on retail shelves.

Gerber, with its strong name recognition and brand loyalty, does not make such pay-to-stay payments. The other type of wholesale trade spending is "variable trade spending," which typically consists of manufacturers' discounts and allowances to supermarkets to create retail price differentials that entice the consumer to purchase their product instead of a competitor's. . . .

[T]he district court . . . court concluded that it was "more probable than not that consummation of the Heinz/Beech-Nut merger will actually increase competition in jarred baby food in the United States." . . .

II. Analysis

. . . [In] Section 7 of the Clayton Act . . . "Congress used the words '*may* be substantially to lessen competition' (emphasis supplied), to indicate that its concern was with probabilities, not certainties." *Brown Shoe*, 370 U.S. at 323 (emphasis original); *see* S.Rep. No. 1775, at 6 (1950), U.S. Code Cong. & Admin. News at 4293, 4298 ("The use of these words ['may be'] means that the bill, if enacted, would not apply to the mere possibility but only to the reasonable probability of the pr[o]scribed effect. . . ."). . . .

1. *Likelihood of Success*

To determine likelihood of success on the merits we measure the probability that, after an administrative hearing on the merits, the Commission will succeed in proving that the effect of the Heinz/Beech-Nut merger "may be substantially to lessen competition, or to tend to create a monopoly" in violation of section 7 of the Clayton Act. 15 U.S.C. § 18. This court and others have suggested that the standard for likelihood of success on the merits is met if the FTC "has raised questions going to the merits so serious, substantial, difficult and doubtful as to make them fair ground for thorough investigation, study, deliberation and determination by the FTC in the first instance and ultimately by the Court of Appeals." . . .

In *United States v. Baker Hughes Inc.*, 908 F.2d 981, 982–83 (D.C.Cir.1990), we explained the analytical approach by which the government establishes a section 7 violation. First the government must show that the merger would produce "a firm controlling an undue percentage share of the relevant market, and [would] result[ ] in a significant increase in the concentration of firms in that market." *Philadelphia Nat'l Bank,* 374 U.S. at 363. Such a showing establishes a "presumption" that the merger will substantially lessen competition. *See Baker Hughes,* 908 F.2d at 982. To rebut the presumption, the defendants must produce evidence that "show[s] that the market-share statistics [give] an inaccurate account of the [merger's] probable effects on competition" in the relevant market. *United States v. Citizens & S. Nat'l Bank,* 422 U.S. 86, 120 (1975).[7] "If the defendant successfully rebuts the

this is the test for FTC to establish Clayton Act §7 violation

---

[7] To rebut the defendants may rely on "[n]onstatistical evidence which casts doubt on the persuasive quality of the statistics to predict future anticompetitive consequences" such as "ease

presumption [of illegality], the burden of producing additional evidence of anticompetitive effect shifts to the government, and merges with the ultimate burden of persuasion, which remains with the government at all times." *Baker Hughes Inc.*, 908 F.2d at 983. . . .

a. Prima Facie Case

Merger law "rests upon the theory that, where rivals are few, firms will be able to coordinate their behavior, either by overt collusion or implicit understanding, in order to restrict output and achieve profits above competitive levels." *FTC v. PPG Indus.*, 798 F.2d 1500, 1503 (D.C.Cir.1986). Increases in concentration above certain levels are thought to "raise[ ] a likelihood of 'interdependent anticompetitive conduct.'" *Id.* (quoting *General Dynamics*, 415 U.S. at 497); *see FTC v. Elders Grain*, 868 F.2d 901, 905 (7th Cir.1989). Market concentration, or the lack thereof, is often measured by the Herfindahl-Hirschman Index (HHI).[9]

Sufficiently large HHI figures establish the FTC's prima facie case that a merger is anti-competitive. *See Baker Hughes*, 908 F.2d at 982–83 & n.3; *PPG*, 798 F.2d at 1503. The district court found that the pre-merger HHI "score for the baby food industry is 4775"—indicative of a highly concentrated industry.[10] The merger of Heinz and Beech-Nut will increase the HHI by 510 points. This creates, by a wide margin, a presumption that the merger will lessen competition in the domestic jarred baby food market. *See* Horizontal Merger Guidelines, *supra*, § 1.51 (stating that HHI increase of more than 100 points, where post-merger HHI exceeds 1800, is "presumed . . . likely to create or enhance market power or facilitate its exercise"); *see also Baker Hughes*, 908 F.2d at 982–83 & n.3; *PPG*, 798 F.2d at 1503. Here, the FTC's market concentration statistics[12] are bolstered by the indisputable fact that the merger will

of entry into the market, the trend of the market either toward or away from concentration, and the continuation of active price competition." *Kaiser Aluminum & Chem. Corp. v. FTC*, 652 F.2d 1324, 1341 (7th Cir.1981). In addition, the defendants may demonstrate unique economic circumstances that undermine the predictive value of the government's statistics. *See United States v. General Dynamics Corp.*, 415 U.S. 486, 506–10 (1974) (fundamental changes in structure of coal market made market concentration statistics inaccurate predictors of anticompetitive effect).

[9] "The FTC and the Department of Justice, as well as most economists, consider the measure superior to such cruder measures as the four-or eight-firm concentration ratios which merely sum up the market shares of the largest four or eight firms." *PPG*, 798 F.2d at 1503. The Department of Justice and the FTC rely on the HHI in evaluating proposed horizontal mergers. *See Horizontal Merger Guidelines* §§ 1.5, 1.51. . . . Under the Merger Guidelines a market with a postmerger HHI above 1800 is considered "highly concentrated" and "mergers that increase the HHI in such a market by over . . . 100 points [in such markets] are [presumed] likely to create or enhance market power or facilitate its exercise." Although the Merger Guidelines are not binding on the court, they provide "a useful illustration of the application of the HHI." *PPG*, 798 F.2d at 1503 n. 4.

[10] . . . The [district] court defined the product market as jarred baby food and the geographic market as the United States. The parties do not challenge the court's definition.

[12] The Supreme Court has cautioned that statistics reflecting market share and concentration, while of great significance, are not conclusive indicators of anticompetitive effects. In *General Dynamics* the Supreme Court held that the market share statistics the government used to seek divestiture of the merged firm were insufficient because, in failing to take into account the acquired firm's long-term contractual commitments (coal contracts), the

eliminate competition between the two merging parties at the wholesale level, where they are currently the only competitors for what the district court described as the "second position on the supermarket shelves." Heinz's own documents recognize the wholesale competition and anticipate that the merger will end it. . . .

Finally, the anticompetitive effect of the merger is further enhanced by high barriers to market entry. The district court found that there had been no significant entries in the baby food market in decades and that new entry was "difficult and improbable." This finding largely eliminates the possibility that the reduced competition caused by the merger will be ameliorated by new competition from outsiders and further strengthens the FTC's case.

As far as we can determine, no court has ever approved a merger to duopoly under similar circumstances.

b. Rebuttal Arguments

In response to the FTC's prima facie showing, the appellees make three rebuttal arguments, which the district court accepted . . . For the reasons discussed below, these arguments fail and thus were not a proper basis for denying the FTC injunctive relief.

1. Extent of Pre-Merger Competition. The appellees first contend . . . that Heinz and Beech-Nut do not really compete against each other at the retail level. Consumers do not regard the products of the two companies as substitutes, the appellees claim, and generally only one of the two brands is available on any given store's shelves. Hence, they argue, there is little competitive loss from the merger.

This argument has a number of flaws which render clearly erroneous the court's finding that Heinz and Beech-Nut have not engaged in significant pre-merger competition. First, in accepting the appellees' argument that Heinz and Beech-Nut do not compete, the district court failed to address the record evidence that the two do in fact price against each other, and that, where both are present in the same areas,[14] they depress each other's prices as well as those of Gerber even though they are virtually never all found in the same store. This evidence undermines the district court's factual finding.

Second, the district court's finding is inconsistent with its conclusion that there is a single, national market for jarred baby food in the United States. The Supreme Court has explained that "[t]he outer boundaries of a product market are determined by the reasonable interchangeability of use [by consumers] or the cross-elasticity of demand between the product itself and substitutes for it." *Brown Shoe,* 370 U.S. at 325; *see also du Pont.* The definition of product market thus "focuses solely on demand

statistics overestimated the acquired firm's ability to compete in the relevant market in the future. *General Dynamics,* 415 U.S. at 500–504.

14 There are at least ten metropolitan areas in which Heinz and Beech-Nut both have more than a 10 per cent market share and their combined share exceeds 35 per cent.

substitution factors," *i.e.,* that consumers regard the products as substitutes. Horizontal Merger Guidelines, *supra,* § 1.0. By defining the relevant product market generically as jarred baby food, the district court concluded that in areas where Heinz's and Beech-Nut's products are both sold, consumers will switch between them in response to a "small but significant and nontransitory increase in price (SSNIP)." Horizontal Merger Guidelines, *supra,* § 1.11. . . .

Third, and perhaps most important, the court's conclusion concerning pre-merger competition does not take into account the indisputable fact that the merger will eliminate competition at the wholesale level between the only two competitors for the "second shelf" position. Competition between Heinz and Beech-Nut to gain accounts at the wholesale level is fierce with each contest concluding in a winner-take-all result. The district court regarded this loss of competition as irrelevant because the FTC did not establish to its satisfaction that wholesale competition ultimately benefitted consumers through lower retail prices. The district court concluded that fixed trade spending did not affect consumer prices and that "the FTC's assertion that the proposed merger will affect variable trade spending levels and consumer prices is . . . at best, inconclusive." . . .

In rejecting the FTC's argument regarding the loss of wholesale competition, the court committed two legal errors. First, as the appellees conceded at oral argument, no court has ever held that a reduction in competition for wholesale purchasers is not relevant unless the plaintiff can prove impact at the consumer level. Second, it is, in any event, not the FTC's burden to prove such an impact with "certainty." To the contrary, the antitrust laws assume that a retailer faced with an increase in the cost of one of its inventory items "will try so far as competition allows to pass that cost on to its customers in the form of a higher price for its product."

2. *Post-Merger Efficiencies.* [Excerpted Below.]

3. *Innovation.* [Excerpted Below.]

4. *Structural Barriers to Collusion.* . . . Jonathan B. Baker, a former Director of the Bureau of Economics at the FTC, . . . testified that in order to coordinate successfully, firms must solve "cartel problems" such as reaching a consensus on price and market share and deterring each other from deviating from that consensus by either lowering price or increasing production. He opined that after the merger the merged entity would want to expand its market share at Gerber's expense, thereby decreasing the likelihood of consensus on price and market share. In his report, Baker elaborated on his theory, explaining that the efficiencies created by the merger will give the merged firm the ability and incentive to take on Gerber in price and product improvements. He also predicted that policing and monitoring of any agreement would be more difficult than it is now, due in part to a time lag in the ability of one firm to detect price cuts by another. But the district court made no

finding that any of these "cartel problems" are so much greater in the baby food industry than in other industries that they rebut the normal presumption. In fact, Baker's testimony about "time lag" is refuted by the record which reflects that supermarket prices are available from industry-wide scanner data within 4–8 weeks. His testimony is further undermined by the record evidence of past price leadership in the baby food industry.

The combination of a concentrated market and barriers to entry is a recipe for price coordination. . . . The creation of a durable duopoly affords both the opportunity and incentive for both firms to coordinate to increase prices. . . . Because the district court failed to specify any "structural market barriers to collusion" that are unique to the baby food industry, its conclusion that the ordinary presumption of collusion in a merger to duopoly was rebutted is clearly erroneous. . . .

NOTES AND QUESTIONS ON *FTC V. HEINZ*

1. ***Should the fact that the merger would create a duopoly suffice to infer likely anticompetitive effects?*** Without the merger, the market shares were Gerber 65%, Heinz 17.4%, Beech-Nut 15.4%. With the merger, the market shares would be Gerber 65% and Heinz-BeechNut 32.8%, leaving the market with a duopoly controlling 98% of the market. The opinion reasoned that (1) such a merger to duopoly sufficed to show coordination was likely, and (2) the defendant failed to rebut that likelihood. The presumption rests on the premise that one needs no fancy analysis to conclude that the anticompetitive effects from creating a duopoly are sufficiently likely to justify at least a presumption against a merger, which the defendant could always rebut by showing special reasons to think oligopoly effects will not occur or that there are offsetting efficiencies. Does that premise seem reasonable to you?

2. ***Is this market likely Cournot or Bertrand?*** Because the government brought the case on a theory of price coordination, it does not seem to have disputed that, without coordination, the firms would engage in Bertrand competition. This assumption is consistent with the facts that: (1) the market featured differentiated products, with Heinz at the low end and Gerber and Beech-Nut at the high end; and (2) Heinz had so much excess capacity, which suggests it would likely set a price and then sell whatever output it could at that price.

3. ***Did the evidence suggest it was likely that oligopolistic coordination would occur between Gerber and a merged Heinz-Beech-Nut?*** The defendants argued that it was unlikely the merger would have anticompetitive effects because Heinz and Beech-Nut did not compete at retail. The defendants' expert was Dr. Jonathan Baker, who had been the FTC's chief economist when it brought the *Staples* case, and he conducted an empirical study quite similar to the *Staples* study, showing that retail prices in local markets where all three firms were present were not significantly different than in local markets where only two firms were present. FTC v. H.J. Heinz, Co., 116 F.Supp.2d 190, 196 (D.D.C.2000). He also showed that

the cross-elasticity of demand at retail between Heinz and Beech-Nut was not significant. *Id.* If such empirical evidence was determinative in *Staples,* why not here?

The main answer was that the empirical study examined the wrong market level. In *Staples,* the merging parties all operated stores at retail, so the issue was how the merger would affect local retail prices. But none of the baby food companies sold products at retail. Instead, they all sold on a national wholesale market to retail stores. The issue was thus whether the merger would adversely affect competition in the national wholesale market for selling baby food to retail stores. In that market, the evidence was that Heinz and Beech-Nut did compete vigorously with each other by using "trade spending" to acquire the second shelf space at retail stores, while Gerber was dominant enough that it did not need to expend anything on trade spending to get the first shelf space. Indeed, the evidence at retail seemed explained by the fact that this wholesale competition for the second shelf space meant that Heinz and Beech-Nut were usually not in the same store, so it was unlikely that consumers would switch between them in response to retail price changes. But if Heinz and Beech-Nut merged, they would no longer have to compete with trade spending at wholesale, which would effectively raise the wholesale price paid by their buyers, who were the retail stores.

Still, even if the empirical study did not disprove the proposition that Heinz and Beech-Nut competed in the relevant wholesale market, what exactly was the evidence that the merger would lead to likely price coordination? The defendants argued that it was unlikely that the firms could settle on a common price, monitor each other's prices, and respond to deviations. The appellate court gave two responses. First, the Court noted that retail prices are easily observable using scanner data, and that the firms seemed to have engaged in price leadership in the past, with Beech-Nut's retail price kept just one cent below Gerber's, while Heinz was kept several cents lower. Such coordination on a price differential would indicate price coordination even though the prices were not the same. However, this response was inconsistent with the appellate court's own emphasis on the fact that the relevant market was a national wholesale market, not local retail markets. An ability to coordinate at retail does not necessarily mean an ability to coordinate at wholesale, where prices are much more varied and hard to observe, especially given that they depended on varying trade spending. Indeed, the facts indicated that the firms were not coordinating at wholesale because Gerber was offering no trade spending, thus effectively setting a much higher wholesale price, while Heinz and Beech-Nut were competing vigorously at wholesale with varying levels of trade spending.

Second, the Court stressed that the defendants had not shown that coordination in the baby food market was "so much greater in the baby food industry than in other industries that they rebut the normal presumption" that a duopoly is likely to lead to coordination. This conclusion means that the court implicitly held that the presumption not only shifts the burden of proof to the defendants, but also changes the standard of proof, requiring the defendants to show not just that coordination was unlikely, but that it was less likely in this industry than in the average industry. That makes sense if one believes coordination is likely in the average duopoly. But this logic does not quite explain was a sufficient rebuttal was not provided by the evidence that here it was hard to coordinate at wholesale and that actual trade spending suggested there was no wholesale coordination.

The better answer would seem to be that the relevant question was not whether significant coordination was already occurring, but whether the merger would create or worsen any coordination. Such an effect seemed highly likely because the only competition in trade spending was between Heinz and Beech-Nut. Once they were merged, they would have no need to use trade spending because they would get the second shelf space by default, just like Gerber got the first shelf space by default without any trade spending. The merger thus seemed likely to eliminate trade spending discounts from being given to retail stores, which would raise the effective price they paid at wholesale. Moreover, while the market was differentiated without the merger, with Gerber and Beech-Nut having premium brands and Heinz a low-end brand, the whole merger plan was for the merged firm to make Beech-Nut's recipes in Heinz's facility, which would leave just two premium brands. This would reduce product differentiation in a way that would make coordination easier. The main argument to the contrary was that the merged firm would have lower costs and thus incentives to undercut Gerber's price. But the defendants did not show that this cost difference was likely to get the merged firm to offer trade spending that would be unnecessary after the merger given that it would get the second shelf space by default.

4. Should an effect on consumer prices be required? The defendants also argued that even if the merger would lower trade spending (and thus effectively raise wholesale prices), the merger should not be blocked because there was no evidence that trade spending lowered downstream retail prices to consumers, even in local markets where all three firms were present. 116 F.Supp.2d at 197. The appellate court rejected this argument on principle, holding that an anticompetitive effect on wholesale purchasers sufficed even if no effect on downstream consumers could be shown. This holding is consistent with a consumer welfare standard because if raising wholesale prices has any effect on consumer prices, it would raise them, and if it has no effect on consumer prices, then there is no benefit to consumers that offsets the harm to retail stores. Antitrust law would not protect supermarkets *at the expense of* consumers, but it does bar anticompetitive conduct that harms supermarkets while conferring no benefit (or attenuated harm) on consumers. This point is similar to the analysis in Chapter 2 of the *Mandeville* case, where harm to upstream beet farmers sufficed, given that reducing local beet output could not benefit downstream consumers but might harm them.

The appellate court also concluded that even if it could not be proven with certainty, the antitrust laws assumed that higher wholesale prices would be passed on downstream to consumers. But was this assumption disproven by the empirical evidence that trade spending did not lead to lower prices in markets where all three firms were present? Not really, because trade spending is something offered on a national wholesale market to obtain local shelf-space, so there is no reason to think it would lower prices more in local markets where three firms got shelf-space at stores than in local markets where two firms got shelf-space at stores.

3. POST-MERGER ENTRY

U.S. DOJ/FTC, Horizontal Merger Guidelines

(2010).

9. Entry

The analysis of competitive effects in Sections 6 and 7 focuses on current participants in the relevant market. That analysis may also include some forms of entry. Firms that would rapidly and easily enter the market in response to a SSNIP are market participants and may be assigned market shares. *See* Sections 5.1 and 5.2. Firms that have, prior to the merger, committed to entering the market also will normally be treated as market participants. *See* Section 5.1. This section concerns entry or adjustments to pre-existing entry plans that are induced by the merger.

As part of their full assessment of competitive effects, the Agencies consider entry into the relevant market. The prospect of entry into the relevant market will alleviate concerns about adverse competitive effects only if such entry will deter or counteract any competitive effects of concern so the merger will not substantially harm customers.

The Agencies consider the actual history of entry into the relevant market and give substantial weight to this evidence. Lack of successful and effective entry in the face of non-transitory increases in the margins earned on products in the relevant market tends to suggest that successful entry is slow or difficult. Market values of incumbent firms greatly exceeding the replacement costs of their tangible assets may indicate that these firms have valuable intangible assets, which may be difficult or time consuming for an entrant to replicate.

A merger is not likely to enhance market power if entry into the market is so easy that the merged firm and its remaining rivals in the market, either unilaterally or collectively, could not profitably raise price or otherwise reduce competition compared to the level that would prevail in the absence of the merger. Entry is that easy if entry would be timely, likely, and sufficient in its magnitude, character, and scope to deter or counteract the competitive effects of concern.

The Agencies examine the timeliness, likelihood, and sufficiency of the entry efforts an entrant might practically employ. An entry effort is defined by the actions the firm must undertake to produce and sell in the market. Various elements of the entry effort will be considered. These elements can include: planning, design, and management; permitting, licensing, or other approvals; construction, debugging, and operation of production facilities; and promotion (including necessary introductory discounts), marketing, distribution, and satisfaction of customer testing and qualification requirements. Recent examples of entry, whether successful or unsuccessful, generally provide the starting point for identifying the elements of practical entry efforts. They also can be informative regarding the scale necessary for an entrant to be successful, the presence or absence of entry barriers, the factors that influence the timing of entry, the costs and risk associated with entry, and the sales opportunities realistically available to entrants.

If the assets necessary for an effective and profitable entry effort are widely available, the Agencies will not necessarily attempt to identify which firms might enter. Where an identifiable set of firms appears to have necessary assets that others lack, or to have particularly strong incentives to enter, the Agencies focus their entry analysis on those firms. Firms operating in adjacent or complementary markets, or large customers themselves, may be best placed to enter. However, the Agencies will not presume that a powerful firm in an adjacent market or a large customer will enter the relevant market unless there is reliable evidence supporting that conclusion.

In assessing whether entry will be timely, likely, and sufficient, the Agencies recognize that precise and detailed information may be difficult or impossible to obtain. The Agencies consider reasonably available and reliable evidence bearing on whether entry will satisfy the conditions of timeliness, likelihood, and sufficiency.

9.1 Timeliness

In order to deter the competitive effects of concern, entry must be rapid enough to make unprofitable overall the actions causing those effects and thus leading to entry, even though those actions would be profitable until entry takes effect.

Even if the prospect of entry does not deter the competitive effects of concern, post-merger entry may counteract them. This requires that the impact of entrants in the relevant market be rapid enough that customers are not significantly harmed by the merger, despite any anticompetitive harm that occurs prior to the entry.

The Agencies will not presume that an entrant can have a significant impact on prices before that entrant is ready to provide the relevant product to customers unless there is reliable evidence that anticipated future entry would have such an effect on prices.

9.2 Likelihood

Entry is likely if it would be profitable, accounting for the assets, capabilities, and capital needed and the risks involved, including the need for the entrant to incur costs that would not be recovered if the entrant later exits. Profitability depends upon (a) the output level the entrant is likely to obtain, accounting for the obstacles facing new entrants; (b) the price the entrant would likely obtain in the post-merger market, accounting for the impact of that entry itself on prices; and (c) the cost per unit the entrant would likely incur, which may depend upon the scale at which the entrant would operate.

9.3 Sufficiency

Even where timely and likely, entry may not be sufficient to deter or counteract the competitive effects of concern. For example, in a differentiated product industry, entry may be insufficient because the products offered by entrants are not close enough substitutes to the products offered by the merged firm to render a price increase by the merged firm unprofitable. Entry may also be insufficient due to constraints that limit entrants' competitive effectiveness, such as limitations on the capabilities of the firms best placed to enter or reputational barriers to rapid expansion by new entrants. Entry by a single firm that will replicate at least the scale and strength of one of the merging firms is sufficient. Entry by one or more firms operating at a smaller scale may be sufficient if such firms are not at a significant competitive disadvantage . . .

NOTES AND QUESTIONS ON U.S. GUIDELINES ON ENTRY

1. ***When is entry timely?*** The pre-2010 Guidelines defined entry as timely if it occurs within two years, while the 2010 Guidelines define entry as timely if it is rapid enough to make it unprofitable to engage in the actions that cause the anticompetitive effects of concern. The previous approach was simpler, but it was unrelated to the ultimate policy question and allowed harm to consumers for up to two years. The new approach is less certain, but directly goes to whether the entry can actually prevent the anticompetitive harm, which is the relevant policy question. Which approach seems preferable?

2. ***When is entry likely?*** The pre-2010 Guidelines defined entry as likely if it would be profitable at *pre*-merger prices, whereas the 2010 Guidelines define entry as likely if it would be profitable at the price the entrant would likely obtain in the *post*-merger market. The advantage of the new approach is that it focuses on the price the entrant would actually get if it entered. Moreover, if entry would be profitable at pre-merger prices, one would expect that the firms would already have entered, unless entrant's additional output would depress prices below those pre-merger prices enough to make entry unprofitable. After the proposed merger, if it indeed has anticompetitive effects, the existing firms will constrict output, so that an additional firm might be able supply that missing output without depressing prices below pre-merger prices.

To be sure, if entry were not profitable at pre-merger prices, entry cannot constrain market prices to pre-merger levels. However, conceptually that goes not to the likelihood of entry, but rather to the *sufficiency* of entry, the third and final factor in Guidelines. So the profitability of entry at pre-merger prices may still be necessary to prove low entry barriers under the

2010 Guidelines, albeit under a different factor. Other issues that may make entry insufficient is if the entrant (a) is too far from the merging parties in a differentiated market, (b) has a competitive disadvantage, or (c) is unlikely to produce enough to constrain prices sufficiently.

FTC v. Staples, Inc.

970 F.Supp. 1066 (D.D.C. 1997).

■ THOMAS F. HOGAN, DISTRICT JUDGE. . . . [Portions of the opinion defining the market and finding likely anticompetitive effects are excerpted above.]

V. Entry Into the Market

"The existence and significance of barriers to entry are frequently, of course, crucial considerations in a rebuttal analysis [because] [i]n the absence of significant barriers, a company probably cannot maintain supra-competitive pricing for any length of time." *Baker Hughes, Inc.*, 908 F.2d at 987. . . . If the defendants' evidence regarding entry showed that the Commission's market-share statistics give an incorrect prediction of the proposed acquisition's probable effect on competition because entry into the market would likely avert any anti-competitive effect by acting as a constraint on Staples-Office Depot's prices, the Court would deny the FTC's motion. The Court, however, cannot make such a finding in this case.

. . . [W]hile it is true that all office superstore entrants have entered within the last 11 years, the recent trend for office superstores has actually been toward exiting the market rather than entering. Over the past few years, the number of office superstore chains has dramatically dropped from twenty-three to three. All but Staples, Office Depot, and OfficeMax have either closed or been acquired. The failed office superstore entrants include very large, well-known retail establishments such as Kmart, Montgomery Ward, Ames, and Zayres. A new office superstore would need to open a large number of stores nationally in order to achieve the purchasing and distribution economies of scale enjoyed by the three existing firms. Sunk costs would be extremely high. Economies of scale at the local level, such as in the costs of advertising and distribution, would also be difficult for a new superstore entrant to achieve since the three existing firms have saturated many important local markets. . . .

For the reasons discussed above, the Court finds it extremely unlikely that a new office superstore will enter the market and thereby avert the anti-competitive effects from Staples' acquisition of Office Depot. . . . The Court also finds it unlikely that the expansions by U.S. Office Products and Wal-Mart would avert the anti-competitive effects which would result from the merger.

The problems with the defendants' evidence regarding U.S. Office Products are numerous. In contrast to Staples and Office Depot, U.S.

Office Products is a company which is focused on a contract stationers business servicing primarily the medium corporate segment. The Mailboxes stores recently acquired by U.S. Office Products carry only 50–200 SKUs of office supplies in stores of approximately 1,000–4,000 square feet with no more than half of that area devoted to consumable office supplies. In addition to their small size and limited number of SKUs, the Mailboxes stores would not actually be new entrants. U.S. Office Products is acquiring existing stores, and, besides Mr. Ledecky's plans to put a U.S. Office Products catalogue in every Mailboxes store, there was no testimony regarding plans to expand the number of SKUs available in the retail stores themselves or to increase the size of the average Mailboxes store. Finally, though Mr. Ledecky testified that if Staples and Office Depot were to raise prices after the merger he would look on that as an opportunity to take business away from the combined entity, he later clarified that statement by explaining that he meant in the contract stationer field.

The defendants' evidence regarding Wal-Mart's expansion of Department 3 has similar weaknesses. While the total number of SKUs expected to be carried by the new Department 3 is impressive, Mr. Glass estimated it to be between 2,600 to 3,000 SKUs, the evidence shows that this is only an increase of approximately 400 SKUs. The Court has already found that Wal-Mart's sales of office supplies are outside the relevant product market in this case primarily because the pricing evidence shows that Wal-Mart does not presently effectively constrain the superstores' prices. The Court cannot conclude that an addition of 400 SKUs and reconfigured shelf space will significantly change Wal-Mart's ability to constrain Staples' and Office Depot's prices. The superstores will continue to offer significantly more SKUs of consumable office supplies. For these reasons, the Court cannot find that Wal-Mart's expansion through Department 3 is likely to avert anti-competitive effects resulting from Staples' acquisition of Office Depot.

The defendants' final argument with respect to entry was that existing retailers such as Sam's Club, Kmart, and Best Buy have the capability to reallocate their shelf space to include additional SKUs of office supplies. While stores such as these certainly do have the power to reallocate shelf space, there is no evidence that they will in fact do this if a combined Staples-Office Depot were to raise prices by 5% following a merger. In fact, the evidence indicates that it is more likely that they would not. For example, even in the superstores' anti-competitive zones where either Staples or Office Depot does not compete with other superstores, no retailer has successfully expanded its consumable office supplies to the extent that it constrains superstore pricing. Best Buy attempted such an expansion by creating an office supplies department in 1994, offering 2000 SKUs of office supplies, but found the expansion less profitable than hoped for and gave up after two years. For these reasons, the Court also cannot find that the ability of many sellers of office supplies to reconfigure shelf space and add SKUs of office supplies is likely to avert anti-competitive effects from Staples' acquisition of Office Depot. . . .

[Portions of the opinion addressing alleged efficiencies and balancing the equities are excerpted below.]

NOTES AND QUESTIONS ON *STAPLES*

1. ***Does the history of entry and exit resolve the issue of whether entry barriers are low?*** The fact that all the office superstores entered within the last 11 years does not prove post-merger entry would be likely, because the market may have since reached saturation. Indeed, the court stressed that recent years had not featured entry, which suggests that economies of scale may now be deterring entry. This lack of recent entry coupled with recent exit by all but the 3 office superstores indicates that entry barriers are now relatively high. Still, that does not necessarily prove entry barriers would be high enough to keep out another firm if the *Staples* merger caused prices to rise.

2. ***Do rival plans or abilities to expand office supply offerings show entry is likely?*** There was evidence that Wal-Mart and Mailboxes, Etc., planned to expand their office supply offerings, and that Sam's Club, Kmart, and Best Buy could reallocate shelf space to office supplies. These plans suggest entry of some sort was likely. But such expansion would not be the same as creating an office superstore and thus would not show likely entry into the office superstore market. Nor would such expansion suffice to eliminate any anticompetitive effects, given the conclusion (previously discussed) that office superstores are a separate market, or at least a differentiated product space, for which price increases would not be prevented by the option of switching to non-office superstores for office supplies.

3. ***Does the price evidence suffice to show entry barriers must not be sufficiently low?*** Yes. That evidence showed that prices were higher in markets with one office superstore than in markets with two or three, which alone shows that the threat of entry must not suffice to curb price increases in markets with one office superstore. Given this sort of hard price evidence, courts need not rely on qualitative assessments about the likelihood of entry that inevitable involve some uncertainty.

4. EFFICIENCIES & WEIGHING THE EQUITIES

U.S. DOJ/FTC, Horizontal Merger Guidelines

(2010).

10. Efficiencies

Competition usually spurs firms to achieve efficiencies internally. Nevertheless, a primary benefit of mergers to the economy is their potential to generate significant efficiencies and thus enhance the merged firm's ability and incentive to compete, which may result in lower prices, improved quality, enhanced service, or new products. For example, merger-generated efficiencies may enhance competition by permitting two ineffective competitors to form a more effective competitor, e.g., by combining complementary assets. In a unilateral effects context, incremental cost reductions may reduce or reverse any increases in the merged firm's incentive to elevate price. Efficiencies also may lead to new or improved products, even if they do not immediately and directly affect price. In a coordinated effects context, incremental cost reductions may make coordination less likely or effective by enhancing the incentive of a maverick to lower price or by creating a new maverick firm. Even when efficiencies generated through a merger enhance a firm's ability to compete, however, a merger may have other effects that may lessen competition and make the merger anticompetitive.

The Agencies credit only those efficiencies likely to be accomplished with the proposed merger and unlikely to be accomplished in the absence of either the proposed merger or another means having comparable anticompetitive effects. These are termed merger-specific efficiencies.[13] Only alternatives that are practical in the business situation faced by the merging firms are considered in making this determination. The Agencies do not insist upon a less restrictive alternative that is merely theoretical.

Efficiencies are difficult to verify and quantify, in part because much of the information relating to efficiencies is uniquely in the possession of the merging firms. Moreover, efficiencies projected reasonably and in good faith by the merging firms may not be realized. Therefore, it is incumbent upon the merging firms to substantiate efficiency claims so that the Agencies can verify by reasonable means the likelihood and magnitude of each asserted efficiency, how and when each would be achieved (and any costs of doing so), how each would enhance the merged firm's ability and incentive to compete, and why each would be merger-specific.

Efficiency claims will not be considered if they are vague, speculative, or otherwise cannot be verified by reasonable means. Projections of efficiencies may be viewed with skepticism, particularly when generated outside of the usual business planning process. By contrast, efficiency claims substantiated by analogous past experience are those most likely to be credited.

Cognizable efficiencies are merger-specific efficiencies that have been verified and do not arise from anticompetitive reductions in output

[13] The Agencies will not deem efficiencies to be merger-specific if they could be attained by practical alternatives that mitigate competitive concerns, such as divestiture or licensing. If a merger affects not whether but only when an efficiency would be achieved, only the timing advantage is a merger-specific efficiency.

or service. Cognizable efficiencies are assessed net of costs produced by the merger or incurred in achieving those efficiencies.

The Agencies will not challenge a merger if cognizable efficiencies are of a character and magnitude such that the merger is not likely to be anticompetitive in any relevant market.[14] To make the requisite determination, the Agencies consider whether cognizable efficiencies likely would be sufficient to reverse the merger's potential to harm customers in the relevant market, e.g., by preventing price increases in that market.[15] In conducting this analysis, the Agencies will not simply compare the magnitude of the cognizable efficiencies with the magnitude of the likely harm to competition absent the efficiencies. The greater the potential adverse competitive effect of a merger, the greater must be the cognizable efficiencies, and the more they must be passed through to customers, for the Agencies to conclude that the merger will not have an anticompetitive effect in the relevant market. When the potential adverse competitive effect of a merger is likely to be particularly substantial, extraordinarily great cognizable efficiencies would be necessary to prevent the merger from being anticompetitive. In adhering to this approach, the Agencies are mindful that the antitrust laws give competition, not internal operational efficiency, primacy in protecting customers.

In the Agencies' experience, efficiencies are most likely to make a difference in merger analysis when the likely adverse competitive effects, absent the efficiencies, are not great. Efficiencies almost never justify a merger to monopoly or near-monopoly. Just as adverse competitive effects can arise along multiple dimensions of conduct, such as pricing and new product development, so too can efficiencies operate along multiple dimensions. Similarly, purported efficiency claims based on lower prices can be undermined if they rest on reductions in product quality or variety that customers value.

The Agencies have found that certain types of efficiencies are more likely to be cognizable and substantial than others. For example, efficiencies resulting from shifting production among facilities formerly

14 The Agencies normally assess competition in each relevant market affected by a merger independently and normally will challenge the merger if it is likely to be anticompetitive in any relevant market. In some cases, however, the Agencies in their prosecutorial discretion will consider efficiencies not strictly in the relevant market, but so inextricably linked with it that a partial divestiture or other remedy could not feasibly eliminate the anticompetitive effect in the relevant market without sacrificing the efficiencies in the other market(s). Inextricably linked efficiencies are most likely to make a difference when they are great and the likely anticompetitive effect in the relevant market(s) is small so the merger is likely to benefit customers overall.

15 The Agencies normally give the most weight to the results of this analysis over the short term. The Agencies also may consider the effects of cognizable efficiencies with no short-term, direct effect on prices in the relevant market. Delayed benefits from efficiencies (due to delay in the achievement of, or the realization of customer benefits from, the efficiencies) will be given less weight because they are less proximate and more difficult to predict. Efficiencies relating to costs that are fixed in the short term are unlikely to benefit customers in the short term, but can benefit customers in the longer run, e.g., if they make new product introduction less expensive.

owned separately, which enable the merging firms to reduce the incremental cost of production, are more likely to be susceptible to verification and are less likely to result from anticompetitive reductions in output. Other efficiencies, such as those relating to research and development, are potentially substantial but are generally less susceptible to verification and may be the result of anticompetitive output reductions. Yet others, such as those relating to procurement, management, or capital cost, are less likely to be merger-specific or substantial, or may not be cognizable for other reasons.

When evaluating the effects of a merger on innovation, the Agencies consider the ability of the merged firm to conduct research or development more effectively. Such efficiencies may spur innovation but not affect short-term pricing. The Agencies also consider the ability of the merged firm to appropriate a greater fraction of the benefits resulting from its innovations. Licensing and intellectual property conditions may be important to this enquiry, as they affect the ability of a firm to appropriate the benefits of its innovation. Research and development cost savings may be substantial and yet not be cognizable efficiencies because they are difficult to verify or result from anticompetitive reductions in innovative activities . . .

NOTES AND QUESTIONS ON U.S. GUIDELINES ON EFFICIENCIES

The Guidelines allow efficiency justifications if they are (1) verifiable, (2) merger specific, and (3) sufficiently large and passed on to customers to prevent any price increase from the merger's anticompetitive effects.

1. ***Does the requirement of showing efficiencies are merger specific relate to any other rule of reason concept?*** Yes, it is essentially the same as showing a restraint has no less restrictive alternative under the rule of reason. If an efficiency could be achieved without the merger, then the less restrictive alternative is to achieve that efficiency without any merger.

2. ***Do the Guidelines condemn a merger that decreases producer costs by $100 million but increases consumer prices by $10 million?*** Yes, because the Guidelines require that the efficiencies "be sufficient to reverse the merger's potential to harm customers in the relevant market, e.g., by preventing price increases in that market." The Guidelines thus require evidence that the efficiencies are sufficiently "passed through to customers" to offset any anticompetitive harm to consumer. Accordingly, the Guidelines embrace a consumer welfare standard, rather than a total welfare standard that would instead conclude that the $100 million gain to producers outweighs the $10 million harm to consumers.

3. ***Why are efficiencies that lower fixed costs less likely to justify a merger?*** The reason is that marginal costs are what determine which prices will maximize profits, because varying prices will affect the marginal costs a firm incurs, but will not affect the fixed costs it incurs. Lowering fixed costs thus will benefit producers, but will not lower prices in a way that

benefits consumer welfare in the short run. The treatment of fixed costs in guideline 15 is thus consistent with the consumer welfare approach generally taken in the Guidelines. If fixed costs are recurring, then reducing them could in the long run decrease consumer prices in markets characterized by monopolistic competition, but only if that fixed cost reduction were available to entrants, *see* Chapter 3.B.1, which seems unlikely for a fixed cost reduction that requires a merger. Moreover, it becomes increasingly hard to predict anything the further in the future one goes, and in the short run consumer welfare would definitely be harmed if a merger has anticompetitive effects without any reduction in marginal costs.

4. ***What if a merger benefits consumers in one market, but harms consumers in another market?*** Merging firms often operate in multiple product or geographic markets, so a merger might benefit consumers in one market, but harm them in another. The U.S. Guidelines generally require that efficiencies must benefit consumers in the market where the mergers create anticompetitive concerns, and thus do not allow efficiencies in one market to justify anticompetitive effects in another market. This is consistent with caselaw, *United States v. Philadelphia National Bank*, 374 U.S. 321, 370–71 (1963), and the fact that Clayton Act § 7 bans mergers that substantially lessen competition "in any line of commerce."

This market-by-market approach is unproblematic in the usual case, in which firms can divest assets to avoid harm in particular markets and proceed with the merger in the markets where the merger is beneficial to consumers. However, sometimes the effects in the two markets are inextricably linked with each other because any divestiture necessary to eliminate the anticompetitive effect in one market would prevent the economic integration necessary to achieve the efficiency in the other market. In these cases, Guideline footnote 14 suggests that the agencies might exercise their prosecutorial discretion not to challenge such a merger if the net effect strongly benefits consumer welfare overall. But the explanation that such decisions rest on "prosecutorial discretion" implicitly acknowledges that such a merger would still violate the Clayton Act by harming competition in at least one line of commerce, which could trigger challenges by private parties or states.

5. ***How likely is it that efficiencies would ever justify an otherwise anticompetitive merger?*** Quite unlikely. To begin with, because decisions to merge reflect a calculated risk about merger synergies that often do not pan out in practice, it is generally very hard for merging parties to prove those efficiencies are verifiable and merger-specific. Even if they could do so, it is very hard to show efficiencies that are sufficiently large and passed on to consumers to offset any consumer harm. In fact, to date, it does not appear that the federal antitrust agencies have ever concluded that an efficiency defense saved a merger that the agencies felt would be anticompetitive but for those efficiencies. Thus, although the agencies have often found efficiencies for mergers that they concluded also did not create anticompetitive effects, so far an efficiencies defense has never changed the result.

Merger Efficiencies and Total v. Consumer Welfare

As discussed above, efficiencies that lower fixed costs but not marginal costs will not lower prices charged to consumers in the short run, and are unlikely to do so even in the long run. Moreover, even a merger that lowers marginal costs will usually fail to lower consumer prices if it significantly increases market power. Suppose, for example, the pre-merger firm-specific demand elasticity of a firm is 2 and a proposed merger would increase market power by lowering that elasticity by 10%. Without a marginal cost decrease, it would raise price by 12.5%.[31] Marginal costs would have to drop by over 11% to offset this additional power to raise prices and make the merger benefit consumer welfare.[32] In contrast, if the legal test were instead total welfare, then modest cost decreases could offset larger price increases. For example, if demand elasticity is 2, then a cost decrease of .25% suffices to offset the negative effect on total welfare of a price increase of 5%, and a cost decrease of 9% offsets a price increase of 30%.[33]

In short, efficiencies must be much larger to satisfy a consumer welfare test than a total welfare test. The essential reason is that a cost decrease creates a total welfare gain over the producer's entire output. A price increase, in contrast, creates a total welfare loss only for the marginal output that is lost because some consumers will no longer buy the product. The price increase for the remaining output is a transfer payment from consumers to producers that does not alter total welfare, though it obviously has a distributive effect.

Figure 6 below illustrates the phenomenon. It depicts a merger that creates market power that raises prices from the pre-merger price of P_{pre} to the post-merger price of P_{post} and reduces market quantity from Q_{pre} to Q_{post}, but also generates efficiencies that reduce marginal costs from MC_{pre} to MC_{post}. Producers benefit from both the cost reduction on the quantity they continue to produce, Q_{post} (area A), and from the increased prices on that quantity (area B). Consumers are harmed by those increased prices (same area B) and because the merger causes them to forgo purchases from Q_{pre} to Q_{post} that they valued above the pre-merger price (area C). Under a consumer welfare test, the merger flunks as long as $B + C > 0$, which will always be the case if the merger raises prices. But under a total welfare test, area B can be ignored because it is just a transfer payment, and the merger increases total welfare as long as $A > C$. Visual inspection shows that the total welfare test is clearly met in Figure 6. The main reason the total welfare test is so much easier to meet is that the total welfare loss occurs only over marginal output (Q_{pre} to

---

[31] Recall from Chapter 3 that $(P - MC)/P = 1/e$. An initial elasticity of 2 meant that $P = 2MC$. If elasticity drops to 1.8, then that $(P - MC)/P = 1/1.8$, which implies $P = 2.25MC$.

[32] From the last footnote $P = 2.25MC$. So to make the pre and post-merger prices the same, $2MC_{pre\text{-}merger} = 2.25MC_{post\text{-}merger}$. Thus, $MC_{post\text{-}merger} = 2/2.25MC_{pre\text{-}merger} = .888MC_{pre\text{-}merger}$.

[33] *See* Williamson, *Economies as an Antitrust Defense: The Welfare Tradeoffs*, 58 AMER. ECON. REV. 18, 22–23 (1968).

Q_{post}) but the total welfare gain occurs over all inframarginal output (0 to Q_{post}).

Figure 6. Consumer v Total Welfare Tradeoff

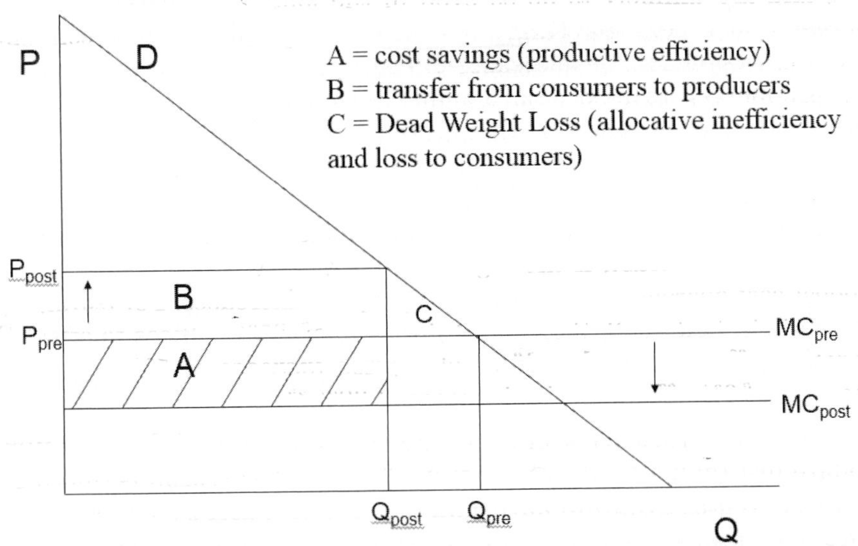

A merger law that prevents any merger that raises prices and harms consumer welfare can thus produce a possible loss of total welfare when the prevented merger would have increased total welfare. As noted above, U.S. antitrust law has adopted consumer welfare as the relevant legal test rather than total welfare. But many argue that antitrust law should be changed to make total welfare the relevant legal test instead. Advocates of this position point out that consumer welfare has an imperfect fit with distributional concerns because antitrust victims are not always poorer than the violator's shareholders. Further, if antitrust law tried to limit the consumer welfare test to cases where antitrust victims were poorer than the violator's shareholders, the result would be added litigation expense and uncertainty. Such a limited consumer welfare test would also mean that marginal gains in income would produce marginal gains in expected liability, creating the same work disincentives as income taxes. It would thus be more efficient to achieve any desired redistribution more efficiently through the tax system, which could avoid the added litigation expense and uncertainty.[34]

On the other hand, if antitrust victims are usually poorer than the shareholders of violators, then a consumer welfare test applied across the board could further redistribution without creating similar work disincentives. The reason is that under such a categorical approach, the

[34] *See* Louis Kaplow & Steven Shavell, *Why the Legal System Is Less Efficient than the Income Tax in Redistributing Income*, 23 J. LEGAL STUD. 667 (1994) (showing that it is more efficient to redistribute income via taxation than by taking into account the income of litigating parties when applying other laws).

income of the litigating parties would not matter (only their status as consumer or producer), so that increases in marginal income would not increase marginal expected liability.[35] This categorical approach may thus be a more efficient at achieving redistributive objectives than using an income tax system that creates greater work disincentives.

Moreover, many of the arguments for a consumer welfare test have nothing to do with distributional effects. Instead, the more interesting arguments for a consumer welfare test indicate that, even if one assumes that total welfare should be the ultimate societal objective, such a total welfare objective may surprisingly be advanced better by using a consumer welfare test. The reasons turn out to be numerous.

First, if society wants to maximize total welfare and a firm has several profitable options that would increase total welfare, then the law should incentivize each firm to choose the option that increases total welfare the most. If the law uses a total welfare test, that will cause firms to choose the most profitable act among the options that increase total welfare, but that will often not be the option that increases total welfare the most.[36] A consumer welfare test can drive firms to choose the profitable option that increases total welfare the most, rather than more profitable options that increase total welfare less. Indeed, the literature finds that, for uniform distributions, if the number of possible actions is four, then a pure consumer welfare test is actually the test that makes firms most likely to choose the options that maximize total welfare. If the number of possible actions is less than four, the test that maximizes total welfare is actually somewhere between total and consumer welfare. If the number of possible actions is more than four, the test that maximizes total welfare actually requires that the gains to consumer welfare not only be positive but increasingly large.

Second, if firms have private information about their efficiencies, then there is an enforcement probability that leads firms to propose mergers only when they increase total welfare, which would make all proposed mergers increase total welfare.[37] But an agency that used a total welfare test would approve all such mergers, which would deviate from the optimal enforcement probability. This second point indicates that deviations from total welfare toward consumer welfare are likely to be optimal, though it does not by itself necessarily support a pure consumer welfare test.

Third, if monopolists dissipate their monopoly profits in efforts to obtain market power, then those monopoly profits wash out ex ante, and thus a consumer welfare test may better maximize ex ante total welfare. An ex post total welfare test would approve actions that increase

---

[35] *See* Elhauge, *The Failed Resurrection of the Single Monopoly Profit Theory*, 6(1) COMPETITION POLICY INTERNATIONAL 155, 168 (Spring 2010).

[36] *See* Abraham Wickelgren, *Issues in Antitrust Enforcement,* in HANDBOOK OF ANTITRUST ECONOMICS (ed. Einer Elhauge 2012) (reviewing the literature).

[37] *Id.*

monopoly profits by more than they harm consumer welfare, but if the increased monopoly profits are totally dissipated ex ante, such actions would harm ex ante total welfare.[38] The greater the share of monopoly profits that are dissipated ex ante, the more likely it is that a consumer welfare test does a better job of advancing ex ante total welfare than an ex post total welfare test would.

Fourth, another theory suggests that monopolists tend to dissipate monopoly profits in greater managerial inefficiency.[39] If so, then this theory indicates that the dissipated portion of those additional monopoly profits will not affect even ex post total welfare. This again suggests that a consumer welfare test may do a better job of maximizing overall total welfare than a total welfare test.

Fifth, a consumer welfare test makes it easier to coordinate international enforcement.[40] The reason is that in our current international system, each nation has concurrent antitrust jurisdiction, which effectively allocates decisive enforcement power to whichever nations are the most aggressive enforcer, which are likely to be the nations that are net importers in the market at issue. Such importing nations have incentives to apply a consumer welfare test correctly, but would have incentives to underweigh producer benefits if they were applying a total welfare test.

Sixth, generally firms should be able to restructure any action that increases total welfare in a way that does not harm consumer welfare.[41] For example, if the dollar gains to the merging parties exceed the dollar losses to consumers, the merging parties could usually devise some mechanism to transfer enough of their gain to consumers to offset any losses to those consumers. One possibility may be simply committing not to raise prices or lower output, though that may raise difficulties if market conditions indicate prices or output should change over time or if there are concerns firms might evade the price commitment by lowering quality and thus effectively raising quality-adjusted prices.

Another possibility would be for firms to create some sort of consumer trust. For example, if the objection to a merger efficiency is that it lowers fixed costs but not marginal costs, then merging firms could use their reduction in fixed costs to fund a trust that will then pay the merged firm a dollar sum for every unit it sells. In this way, the trust could convert a reduction in fixed costs into a reduction in marginal costs. If the concern is that the merged firm will not pass on a sufficient share

---

38 *See* Elhauge, *The Failed Resurrection, supra* note 35, at 169–172; Elhauge, *Tying, Bundled Discounts, and the Death of the Single Monopoly Profit Theory*, 123 HARVARD LAW REVIEW 397, 439–442 (2009).

39 *See* Elhauge, *Defining Better Monopolization Standards*, 56 Stanford Law Review 253, 299–300 (2003) (summarizing X-inefficiency theory that monopolists exhibit greater agency costs and other inefficiencies).

40 Elhauge, *Tying, supra* note 38, at 438.

41 *See* Elhauge, *The Failed Resurrection, supra* note 35, at 168–69; Elhauge, *Tying, supra* note 38, at 438.

of the reduction in its marginal costs to make consumers better off, the trust could instead pay consumers a sum for every unit they purchase, though this would also cause shifts in the demand curve that would have to be taken into account. Whatever the details, one would think merging firms with large net efficiency gains in the offing could put together some sort of Coasian deal that makes the firms better off without harming consumers, unless the transaction costs of doing so are so large they exceed the net efficiency gains.

An additional benefit to a consumer trust approach is that it helps avoid the problem that agencies may have a much harder time than merging firms in assessing the amount of efficiencies. If the merging parties are really confident that the size of their efficiencies offsets the consumer harm, then they should be willing to fund a plan to offset any consumer harm. In other words, a consumer welfare test allows mergers that increase total welfare as long as the merging firms are willing to compensate for any adverse effects on consumers, which usefully forces merging firms to put their money where their mouth is on the claim that efficiency gains offset consumer harm.

This sixth point suggests that a consumer welfare test usually will not block action that increases total welfare, but instead would only induce the restructuring necessary to make sure that consumers benefit as well. This sixth point is related to the first point above, because if manufacturers have to structure their actions to preserve consumer welfare, they might as well choose the action choice that maximizes total welfare because that will generally also maximize firm profits given the lack of harm to consumer welfare.

FTC v. H.J. Heinz Co.

246 F.3d 708 (D.C. Cir. 2001).

■ KAREN LECRAFT HENDERSON, CIRCUIT JUDGE. . . . [Portions of the opinion finding presumptive anticompetitive effects are excerpted above].

b. Rebuttal Arguments . . .

2. *Post-Merger Efficiencies*. The appellees' second attempt to rebut the FTC's prima facie showing is their contention that the anticompetitive effects of the merger will be offset by efficiencies resulting from the union of the two companies, efficiencies which they assert will be used to compete more effectively against Gerber. It is true that a merger's primary benefit to the economy is its potential to generate efficiencies. As the *Merger Guidelines* now recognize, efficiencies "can enhance the merged firm's ability and incentive to compete, which may result in lower prices, improved quality, or new products."

Although the Supreme Court has not sanctioned the use of the efficiencies defense in a section 7 case, *see Procter & Gamble Co.*, 386 U.S.

at 580,[18] the trend among lower courts is to recognize the defense. *See, e.g., FTC v. Tenet Health Care Corp.*, 186 F.3d 1045, 1054 (8th Cir.1999); *University Health*, 938 F.2d at 1222; *FTC v. Cardinal Health, Inc.*, 12 F.Supp.2d 34, 61 (D.D.C.1998); *Staples*, 970 F.Supp. at 1088–89; *see also* ABA Antitrust Section, *Mergers and Acquisitions: Understanding the Antitrust Issues* 152 (2000) ("The majority of courts have considered efficiencies as a means to rebut the government's prima facie case that a merger will lead to restricted output or increased prices. These courts, however, generally have found inadequate proof of efficiencies to sustain a rebuttal of the government's case."). In 1997 the Department of Justice and the FTC revised their Horizontal Merger Guidelines to recognize that "mergers have the potential to generate significant efficiencies by permitting a better utilization of existing assets, enabling the combined firm to achieve lower costs in producing a given quantity and quality than either firm could have achieved without the proposed transaction."

Nevertheless, the high market concentration levels present in this case require, in rebuttal, proof of extraordinary efficiencies, which the appellees failed to supply. *See University Health*, 938 F.2d at 1223 ("[A] defendant who seeks to overcome a presumption that a proposed acquisition would substantially lessen competition must demonstrate that the intended acquisition would result in significant economies and that these economies ultimately would benefit competition and, hence, consumers."); Horizontal Merger Guidelines § 4 (stating that "[e]fficiencies almost never justify a merger to monopoly or near-monopoly"); 4A Areeda, *et al.*, *Antitrust Law* ¶ 971f, at 44 (requiring "extraordinary" efficiencies where the "HHI is well above 1800 and the HHI increase is well above 100"). Moreover, given the high concentration levels, the court must undertake a rigorous analysis of the kinds of efficiencies being urged by the parties in order to ensure that those "efficiencies" represent more than mere speculation and promises about post-merger behavior. The district court did not undertake that analysis here.

In support of its conclusion that post-merger efficiencies will outweigh the merger's anticompetitive effects, the district court found that the consolidation of baby food production in Heinz's under-utilized Pittsburgh plant "will achieve substantial cost savings in salaries and operating costs." The court also credited the appellees' promise of

[18] In *Procter & Gamble Co.*, 386 U.S. at 580 the Supreme Court stated that "[p]ossible economies cannot be used as a defense to illegality" in section 7 merger cases. The issue is, however, not a closed book. *See Staples*, 970 F.Supp. at 1088 (collecting cases). Areeda and Turner explain that "[i]n interpreting the *Clorox* language, moreover, observe that the court referred only to 'possible' economies and to economies that 'may' result from mergers that lessen competition. To reject an economies defense based on mere possibilities does not mean that one should reject such a defense based on more convincing proof." 4 Phillip Areeda & Donald Turner, *Antitrust Law* ¶ 941b, at 154 (1980). They conclude that "[t]he Court's brief and unelaborated language [in *Clorox*] cannot reasonably be taken as a definitive disposition of so important and complex an issue as the role of economies in analyzing legality of a merger." *Id.*

improved product quality as a result of recipe consolidation.[19] The only cost reduction the court quantified as a percentage of pre-merger costs, however, was the so called "variable conversion cost": the cost of processing the volume of baby food now processed by Beech-Nut. The court accepted the appellees' claim that this cost would be reduced by 43% if the Beech-Nut production were shifted to Heinz's plant, a reduction the appellees' expert characterized as "extraordinary."

The district court's analysis falls short of the findings necessary for a successful efficiencies defense in the circumstances of this case. We mention only three of the most important deficiencies here. First, "variable conversion cost" is only a percentage of the total variable manufacturing cost. A large percentage reduction in only a small portion of the company's overall variable manufacturing cost does not necessarily translate into a significant cost advantage to the merger. Thus, for cost reduction to be relevant, we must at least consider the percentage of Beech-Nut's total variable manufacturing cost that would be reduced as a consequence of the merger. At oral argument, the appellees' counsel agreed. This correction immediately cuts the asserted efficiency gain in half since, according to the appellees' evidence, using total variable manufacturing cost as the measure cuts the cost savings from 43% to 22.3%.

Second, the percentage reduction in *Beech-Nut's* cost is still not the relevant figure. After the merger, the two entities will be combined, and to determine whether the merged entity will be a significantly more efficient competitor, cost reductions must be measured across the new entity's combined production—not just across the pre-merger output of Beech-Nut. The district court, however, did not consider the cost reduction over the merged firm's combined output. At oral argument the appellees' counsel was unable to suggest a formula that could be used for determining that cost reduction.

Finally, and as the district court recognized, the asserted efficiencies must be "merger-specific" to be cognizable as a defense. That is, they must be efficiencies that cannot be achieved by either company alone because, if they can, the merger's asserted benefits can be achieved without the concomitant loss of a competitor. Yet the district court never explained why Heinz could not achieve the kind of efficiencies urged without merger. As noted, the principal merger benefit asserted for Heinz is the acquisition of Beech-Nut's better recipes, which will allegedly make its product more attractive and permit expanded sales at prices lower than those charged by Beech-Nut, which produces at an inefficient plant. Yet, neither the district court nor the appellees addressed the question

[19] In addition, the district court described Heinz's distribution network as much more efficient than Beech-Nut's. It failed to find, however, a significant diseconomy of scale in distribution from which either Heinz or Beech-Nut suffers. In other words, although Beech-Nut has an inefficient distribution system, it can make that system more efficient without merger. Heinz's own efficient distribution network illustrates that a firm the size of Beech-Nut does not need to merge in order to attain an efficient distribution system.

whether Heinz could obtain the benefit of better recipes by investing more money in product development and promotion—say, by an amount less than the amount Heinz would spend to acquire Beech-Nut. At oral argument, Heinz's counsel agreed that the taste of Heinz's products was not so bad that no amount of money could improve the brand's consumer appeal. That being the case, the question is how much Heinz would have to spend to make its product equivalent to the Beech-Nut product and hence whether Heinz could achieve the efficiencies of merger without eliminating Beech-Nut as a competitor. The district court, however, undertook no inquiry in this regard. In short, the district court failed to make the kind of factual determinations necessary to render the appellees' efficiency defense sufficiently concrete to offset the FTC's prima facie showing.

3. *Innovation.* The appellees claim next that the merger is required to enable Heinz to innovate, and thus to improve its competitive position against Gerber. Heinz and Beech-Nut asserted, and the district court found, that without the merger the two firms are unable to launch new products to compete with Gerber because they lack a sufficient shelf presence or ACV. This kind of defense is often a speculative proposition. *See* 4A Areeda, *et al., supra,* ¶ 975g (noting "truly formidable" proof problems in determining innovation economies). In this case, given the old-economy nature of the industry as well as Heinz's position as the world's largest baby food manufacturer, it is a particularly difficult defense to prove. The court below accepted the appellees' argument principally on the basis of their expert's testimony that new product launches are cost-effective only when a firm's ACV is 70% or greater (Heinz's is presently 40%; Beech-Nut's is 45%). That testimony, in turn, was based on a graph that plotted revenue against ACV. According to the expert, the graph showed that only four out of 27 new products launched in 1995 had been successful—all for companies with an ACV of 70% or greater.

The chart, however, does not establish this proposition and the court's consequent finding that the merger is necessary for innovation is thus unsupported and clearly erroneous. All the chart plotted was revenue against ACV and hence all it showed was the unsurprising fact that the greater a company's ACV, the greater the revenue it received. Because the graph did not plot the profitability (or any measure of "cost-effectiveness"), there is no way to know whether the expert's claim—that a 70% ACV is required for a launch to be "successful" in an economic sense—is true.[21] Moreover, the number of data points on the chart were few; they were limited to launches in a single year; and they involved launches of all new grocery products rather than of baby food alone. Assessing such data's statistical significance in establishing the

[21] For example, a 5 cent piece of bubble gum introduced with a 90% ACV could appear as a failure on the graph because of low revenue but nonetheless be profitable. On the other hand, a high priced grocery product introduced with the same ACV could generate a lot of revenue (and thus appear as a "success" on the graph) yet be unprofitable.

proposition at issue, *i.e.,* the necessity of 70% ACV penetration, is thus highly speculative. The district court did not even address the question of the data's statistical significance and the appellees' counsel could offer no help at oral argument. In the absence of reliable and significant evidence that the merger will permit innovation that otherwise could not be accomplished, the district court had no basis to conclude that the FTC's showing was rebutted by an innovation defense.

Moreover, Heinz's insistence on a 70-plus ACV before it brings a new product to market may be largely to persuade the court to recognize promotional economies as a defense. Heinz argues that to profitably launch a new product, it must have nationwide market penetration to recoup the money spent on advertising and promotion. It wants to spread advertising costs out among as many product units as possible, thereby lowering the advertising cost per unit. It does not want to "waste" promotional expenditures in markets where its products are not on the shelf or where they are on only a few shelves. For example, in a metropolitan area in which Heinz has a 75 per cent ACV, every dollar spent on advertising is two or three times more "effective" than in a market in which it has only a 25 per cent ACV. As one authority notes, however, "[t]he case for recognizing a defense based on promotional economies is relatively weak." 4A Areeda, *et al., supra,* ¶ 975f, at 77. The district court accepted Heinz's claim that it could not introduce new products without at least a 70 per cent ACV because it would be unable to adequately diffuse its advertising and promotional expenditures. But the court failed to determine whether substantial promotional scale economies exist now and, if they do, whether Heinz and Beech-Nut "for that reason operate at a substantial competitive disadvantage in the market or markets in which they sell" or whether there are effective alternatives to merger by which the disadvantage can be overcome. *Id.* at ¶ 975f2, at 78. . . .

Although we recognize that, post-hearing, the FTC may accept the rebuttal arguments proffered by the appellees, including their efficiencies defense, and permit the merger to proceed, we conclude that the FTC succeeded in "rais[ing] questions going to the merits so serious, substantial, difficult and doubtful as to make them fair ground for thorough investigation, study, deliberation and determination by the FTC." . . .

2. Weighing of the Equities

Although the FTC's showing of likelihood of success creates a presumption in favor of preliminary injunctive relief, we must still weigh the equities in order to decide whether enjoining the merger would be in the public interest. 15 U.S.C. § 53(b); *see PPG,* 798 F.2d at 1507; *Weyerhaeuser,* 665 F.2d at 1081–83. The principal public equity weighing in favor of issuance of preliminary injunctive relief is the public interest in effective enforcement of the antitrust laws. *University Health,* 938 F.2d at 1225. The Congress specifically had this public equity consideration in mind when it enacted section 13(b). *See Food Town Stores,* 539 F.2d at 1346 (Congress enacted section 13(b) to preserve status quo until FTC can perform its function). The district court found, and there is no dispute, that if the merger were allowed to proceed, subsequent administrative and judicial proceedings on the merits "will not matter" because Beech-Nut's manufacturing facility "will be closed, the Beech-Nut distribution channels will be closed, the new label and recipes will be in place, and it will be impossible as a practical matter to undo the transaction." *H.J. Heinz,* 116 F.Supp.2d at 201. Hence, if the merger were ultimately found to violate the Clayton Act, it would be impossible to recreate pre-merger competition. Section 13(b) itself embodies congressional recognition of the fact that divestiture is an inadequate and unsatisfactory remedy in a merger case, 119 Cong. Rec. 36612 (1973), a point that has been emphasized by the United States Supreme Court. *See, e.g., FTC v. Dean Foods Co.,* 384 U.S. 597, 606 n.5 ("Administrative experience shows that the Commission's inability to unscramble merged assets frequently prevents entry of an effective order of divestiture.").

On the other side of the ledger, the appellees claim that the injunction would deny consumers the procompetitive advantages of the merger. The district court found that if the merger were preliminarily enjoined, the injury to competition would also be irreversible, that is, the merger would be abandoned and could not be consummated if ultimately found lawful. By contrast to its first finding, however, for the latter conclusion the court relied not on the facts of this case but on our statement in *Exxon* that—as a general matter—temporarily blocking a tender offer is likely to end an attempted acquisition, "as a result of the short life-span of most tender offers." In their brief in this court, the appellees offer nothing more to support the finding that the merger would never be consummated were an injunction to issue. Indeed, they devote only a single sentence, without any citation, to the point. The district court's finding that an injunction would "kill this merger" is thus not a factual finding supported by record evidence. This case does not involve a short-lived tender offer as did the case cited by the court for its "kill the merger" conclusion. The appellees acknowledge that there is no alternative buyer for Beech-Nut and the court found that it is not a failing company but rather a "profitable and ongoing enterprise." If the merger makes economic sense now, the appellees have offered no reason why it would not do so later. Moreover, Beech-Nut's principal assets of value to Heinz are, assertedly, its recipes and brand name. Nothing in the record leads us to believe that both will not still exist when the FTC completes its work. It may be that Beech-Nut will have to sell its recipes to Heinz at a lower price than the price of today's merger. But that is at best a "private" equity which does not affect our analysis of the impact on the market of the two options now before us and which has not in any event been urged by the appellees.[25]

In sum, weighing of the equities favors the FTC. If the merger is ultimately found to violate section 7 of the Clayton Act, it will be too late to preserve competition if no preliminary injunction has issued. On the other hand, if the merger is found not to lessen competition substantially, the efficiencies that the appellees urge can be reclaimed by a renewed transaction. Our conclusion with respect to the equities necessarily lightens the burden on the FTC to show likelihood of success on the merits, a burden which the FTC has met here. . . .

NOTES AND QUESTIONS ON *FTC V. HEINZ*

1. ***Is there an efficiencies defense?*** Although the agencies routinely consider efficiencies in their merger analysis, there is some uncertainty about whether an efficiency defense exists legally because in *Procter & Gamble* the Supreme Court stated that "[p]ossible economics cannot be used as a defense to illegality in section 7 merger cases." Some courts, like *Heinz,* have suggested this statement excludes only "possible" efficiencies, but it seems unlikely that *Procter & Gamble* meant only that unproven facts could not be a defense. A more plausible interpretation (which would accomplish the same goal of acknowledging the relevance of efficiencies) would be to say that *Procter & Gamble* meant only that proving some efficiencies does not suffice to prove a "defense" because the efficiencies would have be proven to be large enough and passed through sufficiently to overcome the anticompetitive effects in order to meet the statutory standard of not substantially lessening competition. (As we will see with the failing firm "defense", the Court had some reason to be leery of absolute defenses that did not focus on net anticompetitive effects.)

2. ***How can one tell whether sufficient efficiencies are shown?*** The major efficiency defense was that the merged firm could transfer manufacture of Beech-Nut's higher-quality baby food to Heinz's newer more efficient plant, which had 60% unused capacity. The appellate court rejected this argument for several reasons.

First, the appellate court ruled that the district court was wrong that the cost reduction was 43% because it used the wrong denominator (a subset of Beech-Nut's variable costs), when the percentage was 22.3% of all of Beech-Nut's variable costs and the correct denominator was the combined Heinz-BeechNut's variable costs, which would lower this percentage further down to 10–11%. Still, a 10–11% cost saving is pretty high. How can one assess whether it would likely result in a price reduction or not?

---

[25] . . . "While it is proper to consider private equities in deciding whether to enjoin a particular transaction, we must afford such concerns little weight, lest we undermine section 13(b)'s purpose of protecting the "public-at-large, rather than the individual private competitors." *University Health,* 938 F.2d at 1225 (citation omitted); *cf. Weyerhaeuser,* 665 F.2d at 1083 ("Private equities do not outweigh effective enforcement of the antitrust laws. When the Commission demonstrates a likelihood of ultimate success, a countershowing of private equities alone would not suffice to justify denial of a preliminary injunction barring the merger.").

One method is to focus on past pass-through rates of cost savings, and ask whether the price increase is likely to offset that pass through. For example, if in the past 20% of cost savings were passed through in lower prices to customers, one would infer that a 10–11% drop in cost savings would result in a 2–2.2% drop in prices and ask whether the anticompetitive effects of the merger would likely increase prices by more than 2–2.2%.

A more general method would be to estimate prices using the formula $(P - C)/P = (1 + k)HHI/E_d$. Here, the merger increased HHI from .4765 to .5300. Suppose that the market demand elasticity is 2, the pre-merger cost per unit is 10, and that the merger will reduce cost by 10% to 9. Take two possible views about the merger's effect on coordination. First, suppose the merger would significantly increase coordination and thus increase k from 0.2 to 0.4. If so, then before the merger, $(P - 10)/P = (1.2)(.4765)/2$, which simplifies to $P = 14.0$. After the merger, $(P - 9)/P = (1.4)(.5300)/2$, which simplifies to $P = 14.3$. Thus, the merger would increase prices despite a 10% cost savings. Second, suppose the merger would not increase coordination, so would not increase k. Then the price after the merger would be $(P - 9)/P = (1.2)(.5300)/2$, which simplifies to $P = 13.2$. Thus, the merger would decrease prices. In this example, whether the cost savings result in a net price reduction accordingly turns on the extent to which one predicts the merger would increase coordination. (If the cost savings were lower, an increase in HHI alone could suffice for net anticompetitive effects without any increase in coordination.)

The appellate court never reached these tradeoffs because it concluded that this efficiency was also not cognizable on principle because it was not merger-specific. The court reasoned that Heinz could instead develop better baby food recipes itself and make them in its efficient plant. But even if Heinz could improve its quality so easily, it may not be so easy to develop a brand reputation for being nearly equal to Gerber. Indeed, if doing so was so easy, one would think Heinz would have done so already. If such a brand reputation cannot be easily recreated, there would seem to be merger-specific efficiencies from making Beech-Nut brands in Heinz's efficient plant.

On the other hand, one might be concerned that this efficiency defense necessarily meant the merger would eliminate lower-priced baby food and reduce product differentiation, which would facilitate coordination. Further, this efficiency defense also necessarily meant that the plan was to close the existing Beech-Nut plant. Such a reduction in capacity may cap future output in a way that raises prices. To be sure, currently Beech-Nut's whole output could be made in Heinz's unused capacity, so the reduction in capacity might well not cap short term output. In the long run, however, demand might increase in a way that would use all that reduced capacity, in which case the capacity reduction would cap output in a way that would raise prices. Further, the current existence of substantial underutilized capacity might itself suggest that pre-merger the firms were already engaged in oligopolistic coordination.[42] One might also be concerned that allowing

[42] *See* IV AREEDA, ANTITRUST LAW at 217 (a "merger might be even more dangerous with industrywide excess capacity, which can (1) indicate that the firms have already successfully coordinated their prices at high levels and thereby reduced output in relation to existing

mergers because they transfer one firm's output to another firm's excess capacity would create an incentive for firms to build excess capacity in order to justify mergers that eliminate competition.

Finally, the appellate court rejected the defense that the merger would increase innovation because the merged firm would have greater incentives to invest in innovation if it had shelf space at a greater percentage of stores. It is hard to prove such a claim. One might reasonably think that the effect would be the opposite: that a firm handed shelf-space by a merger would have less need to innovate to try to obtain more shelf space. The general claim that increased market power induces more innovation is a long-standing argument made by many firms, but has been very much disputed, with others arguing that competition is more likely to spur innovation. In any event, one might doubt that much significant innovation could really be expected in the baby food industry.

How to Balance the Equities in Merger Cases

Although courts generally talk about balancing the equities, in fact the harm to defendants from blocking a merger is only deemed legitimate if it reflects the denial of a procompetitive benefit. Thus, the real issues on preliminary injunction are the likelihoods and magnitudes of procompetitive versus anticompetitive effects, and which of them would last longer because they would be irreparable at trial. For example, suppose the odds are 50–50 whether a trial will deem a merger to have net procompetitive or anticompetitive effects, each of which is the same in expected magnitude. If a consummated merger could not be undone after trial (because it is too difficult to unscramble the eggs as the *Heinz* courts found), then preliminarily allowing the merger will have a 50% chance of producing anticompetitive effects that last forever. If an unconsummated merger could still be done after trial (as the *Heinz* appellate court found), then preliminarily blocking the merger has a 50% chance of denying procompetitive benefits but only for the period until the trial is completed. On the other hand, if the unconsummated merger could not be done after trial (because it would be abandoned given the difficulty of maintaining financing, as the *Heinz* district court found), then preliminarily blocking the merger has a 50% chance of denying procompetitive benefits forever. Thus, whether preliminarily blocking the merger creates net benefits or harms turns on the likelihoods, magnitudes, and reversibilities of possible anticompetitive effects and denied procompetitive benefits.[43]

---

capacity and (2) deter new entry and thereby shelter incumbents from potential competitors currently outside the market.") (summarizing *FTC v. Elders Grain*, 868 F.2d 901, 905 (7th Cir. 1989)).

[43] Mathematically, a court should preliminarily block a merger if

$$P_{ac}M_{ac\text{-}pre} + P_{ac}P_{ac\text{-}irr}M_{ac\text{-}post} > P_{pc}M_{pc\text{-}pre} + P_{pc}P_{pc\text{-}irr}M_{pc\text{-}post}$$

where P_{ac} is the probability of net anticompetitive effects, $M_{ac\text{-}pre}$ is the expected magnitude of anticompetitive effects pre-trial, $P_{ac\text{-}irr}$ is the probability that anticompetitive effects will be irreversible (eggs cannot be unscrambled), $M_{ac\text{-}post}$ is the expected magnitude of anticompetitive effects post-trial, P_{pc} is the probability of net procompetitive effects, $M_{pc\text{-}pre}$ is the expected

5. THE FAILING FIRM DEFENSE

International Shoe v. FTC

280 U.S. 291 (1930).

■ MR. JUSTICE SUTHERLAND delivered the opinion of the Court.

[International Shoe acquired the capital stock of McElwain Company. The FTC found the merger anticompetitive and ordered divestiture of that capital stock.] . . .

Beginning in 1920 there was a marked falling off in prices and sales of shoes, as there was in other commodities; and, because of excessive commitments which the McElwain Company had made for the purchase of hides as well as the possession of large stocks of shoes and an inability to meet its indebtedness for large sums of borrowed money, the financial condition of the company became such that its officers, after long and careful consideration of the situation, concluded that the company was faced with financial ruin, and that the only alternatives presented were liquidation through a receiver or an outright sale. . . . In the spring of 1921 the company owed approximately $15,000,000 to some 60 or 70 banks and trust companies, and, in addition, nearly $2,000,000 on current account. Its factories, which had a capacity of 38,000 to 40,000 pairs of shoes per day, in 1921 were producing only 6,000 or 7,000 pairs. An examination of its balance sheets and statements and the testimony of its officers and others conversant with the situation, clearly shows that the company had reached the point where it could no longer pay its debts as they became due. In the face of these adverse circumstances it became necessary, under the laws of Massachusetts, to make up its annual financial statement, which, when filed, would disclose a condition of insolvency, as that term is defined by the statute and decisions of the State, and thus bring the company to the point of involuntary liquidation. . . .

The condition of the International Company, on the contrary, notwithstanding these adverse conditions in the shoe trade generally, was excellent. That company had so conducted its affairs that its surplus stock was not excessive, and it was able to reduce prices. Instead of a decrease, it had an increase of business of about 25 per cent in the

---

magnitude of procompetitive effects pre-trial, $P_{pc\text{-}irr}$ is the probability that procompetitive effects will be irreversible (merger will be abandoned), and $M_{pc\text{-}post}$ is the expected magnitude of procompetitive effects post-trial. Given that all the variables are difficult to quantify, such formulas cannot be expected to produce precise answers, but they are useful in helping to frame the analysis and see the tradeoffs. Because the post-trial periods will last much longer, the magnitudes of post-trial effects are likely larger, though they may also be discounted to present value.

If damage remedies were adequate, then even pre-trial harms might be reversible. But for mergers that are procompetitive, there is no mechanism for allowing consumers and defendants to recover any lost procompetitive benefits. And for mergers that are anticompetitive, it is difficult to quantify the anticompetitive harm and distribute any damages to consumers, as the *Staples* court noted.

number of shoes made and sold. During the early months of 1921, orders exceeded the ability of the company to produce, so that approximately one-third of them were necessarily canceled. In this situation, with demands for its products so much in excess of its ability to fill them, the International was approached by officers of the McElwain Company with a view to a sale of its property. After some negotiation, the purchase was agreed upon. The transaction took the form of a sale of the stock instead of the assets, not, as the evidence clearly establishes, because of any desire or intention to thereby affect competition, but because by that means the personnel and organization of the McElwain factories could be retained, which, for reasons that seem satisfactory, was regarded as vitally important. It is perfectly plain from all the evidence that the controlling purpose of the International in making the purchase in question was to secure additional factories, which it could not itself build with sufficient speed to meet the pressing requirements of its business.

Shortly stated, the evidence establishes the case of a corporation in failing circumstances, the recovery of which to a normal condition was, to say the least, in gravest doubt, selling its capital to the only available purchaser in order to avoid what its officers fairly concluded was a more disastrous fate. It was suggested by the court below, and also here in argument, that instead of an outright sale, any one of several alternatives might have been adopted which would have saved the property and preserved competition; but, as it seems to us, all of these may be dismissed as lying wholly within the realm of speculation. The company might, as suggested, have obtained further financial help from the banks, with a resulting increased load of indebtedness which the company might have carried and finally paid, or, on the other hand, by the addition of which, it might more certainly have been crushed. As to that, one guess is as good as the other. It might have availed itself of a receivership, but no one is wise enough to predict with any degree of certainty whether such a course would have meant ultimate recovery or final and complete collapse. If it had proceeded, or been proceeded against, under the Bankruptcy Act, holders of the preferred stock might have paid or assumed the debts and gone forward with the business; or they might have considered it more prudent to accept whatever could be salvaged from the wreck and abandon the enterprise as a bad risk.

As between these and all other alternatives, and the alternative of a sale such as was made, the officers, stockholders and creditors, thoroughly familiar with the factors of a critical situation and more able than commission or court to foresee future contingencies, after much consideration, felt compelled to choose the latter alternative. There is no reason to doubt that in so doing they exercised a judgment which was both honest and well informed; and if aid be needed to fortify their conclusion, it may be found in the familiar presumption of rightfulness which attaches to human conduct in general. Aside from these considerations, the soundness of the conclusion which they reached finds ample confirmation in the facts already discussed and others disclosed by the record.

In the light of the case thus disclosed of a corporation with resources so depleted and the prospect of rehabilitation so remote that it faced the grave probability of a business failure with resulting loss to its stockholders and injury to the communities where its plants were operated, we hold that the purchase of its capital stock by a competitor (there being no other prospective purchaser), not with a purpose to lessen competition, but to facilitate the accumulated business of the purchaser and with the effect of mitigating seriously injurious consequences otherwise probable, is not in contemplation of law prejudicial to the public and does not substantially lessen competition or restrain commerce within the intent of the Clayton Act. . . . *Reversed.*

■ MR. JUSTICE STONE, [joined by JUSTICES HOLMES and BRANDEIS,] dissenting. . . . Nor am I able to say that the McElwain Company, for the stock of which petitioner gave its own stock having a market value of $9,460,000, was then in such financial straits as to preclude the reasonable inference by the Commission that its business, conducted either through a receivership or a reorganized company, would probably continue to compete with that of petitioner. It plainly had large value as a going concern, there was no evidence that it would have been worth more or as much if dismantled, and there was evidence that the depression in the shoe trade in 1920–1921 was then a passing phase of the business. . . .

NOTES AND QUESTIONS ON *INTERNATIONAL SHOE V. FTC*

International Shoe held that two elements suffice to establish a failing company defense: (1) the acquired firm was insolvent; and (2) the acquirer was the only available purchaser. The Court required no evidence that the firm (1) could not have averted liquidation and (2) searched for alternative buyers, concluding that the courts could trust the firm's business judgment on such "speculative" issues.

1. ***Given that the McElwain Company was insolvent, would a merger necessarily only increase market output by preventing the exit of a failing firm?*** No. Without the merger, the company might have sold to another buyer, restructured its debt, or reorganized in bankruptcy to reduce the debt to existing creditors and allow the company to continue as a going concern. If (leaving aside existing debt) the company would make enough net profits to be worth more as a going concern than liquidated, the creditors would rationally prefer to preserve the firm as a going concern so that they could recoup as much of their loans as possible. Even if bankruptcy would instead have led to liquidation of company's assets, any firm that purchased those assets in liquidation would likely use the assets to make shoes.

2. ***Does it seem likely that, absent the merger, the company would have been liquidated?*** Probably not. As the Court itself notes, International Shoe decided to pay almost $10 million for the stock of

McElwain Company, rather than buying its assets, in order to retain "the personnel and organization of the McElwain factories," which suggests the company probably had sufficient going concern value that without the merger it would have been sold to another buyer, restructured, or reorganized, rather than liquidated. However, perhaps the going concern value was much higher to International Shoe than to other shoe manufacturers, either because International Shoe expected anticompetitive profits or had unique problems of undercapacity, given that International Shoe seems to have been the one shoe firm doing well and unable to fill its orders. Still, if other shoe manufacturers were willing to buy the assets at all, those assets would stay in the market without the merger. If, on the other hand, International Shoe were the only shoe manufacturer willing to buy the assets, it would be better to allow it to buy the firm directly, rather than making it purchase the assets in liquidation, because liquidation loses the going concern value of the firm, like an organized management and workforce and existing contracts with suppliers and customers.

3. ***Was the Court right that the corporate participants in the McElwain Company were best placed to decide whether to sell the business to International Shoe, get new loans, or reorganize in bankruptcy?*** No, because those participants have incentives to make the decision that maximizes the value of the McElwain Company, rather than the decision that minimizes the anticompetitive effect. Indeed, making a sale that gives another firm market power will generally be the profit-maximizing move because such a buyer should be willing to pay more than other buyers.

4. ***Would efficiencies have been an economically sounder argument?*** It would seem so. McElwain had unused capacity, and International Shoe was unable to fill its orders, so transferring that unused capacity to International Shoe without losing going concern value seemed likely to efficiently increase output. Such efficiencies could then be weighed against any anticompetitive effects to determine whether the net effects were anticompetitive. However, the failing firm defense has been understood to be absolute, rather than to require such weighing. The problems created by such absolutism probably explain why the failing firm defense has been greatly narrowed over time, as the following materials indicate.

Citizen Publishing v. United States

394 U.S. 131 (1969).

■ MR. JUSTICE DOUGLAS delivered the opinion of the Court.

Tucson, Arizona, has only two daily newspapers of general circulation, the Star and the Citizen. The Citizen . . . is an evening paper published six times a week. The Star . . . has a Sunday as well as a daily issue. Prior to 1940 the two papers vigorously competed with each other. While their circulation was about equal, the Star sold 50% more advertising space than the Citizen and operated at a profit, while the

Citizen sustained losses. Indeed the Star's annual profits averaged about $25,825, while the Citizen's annual losses averaged about $23,550. . . .

[Beginning in 1940, a] joint operating agreement between the two papers . . . provided that each paper should retain its own news and editorial department, as well as its corporate identity. It provided for the formation of Tucson Newspapers, Inc. (TNI), which was to be owned in equal shares by the Star and Citizen and which was to manage all departments of their business except the news and editorial units. The production and distribution equipment of each paper was transferred to TNI. The latter had five directors—two named by the Star, two by the Citizen, and the fifth chosen by the Citizen out of three named by the Star.

The purpose of the agreement was to end any business or commercial competition between the two papers and to that end three types of controls were imposed. First was *price fixing*. The newspapers were sold and distributed by the circulation department of TNI; commercial advertising placed in the papers was sold only by the advertising department of TNI; the subscription and advertising rates were set jointly. Second was *profit pooling*. All profits realized were pooled and distributed to the Star and the Citizen by TNI pursuant to an agreed ratio. Third was a *market control*. It was agreed that neither the Star nor the Citizen nor any of their stockholders, officers, and executives would engage in any other business in Pima County—the metropolitan area of Tucson—in conflict with the agreement. Thus competing publishing operations were foreclosed.

All commercial rivalry between the papers ceased. Combined profits before taxes rose from $27,531 in 1940 to $1,727,217 in 1964.

[The District Court found violations of Sherman Act §§ 1 and 2, and Clayton Act § 7.] . . . The only real defense of appellants was the "failing company" defense—a judicially created doctrine. The facts tendered . . . mak[e] plain that the requirements of the failing company doctrine were not met. That defense was before the Court in *International Shoe* v. *FTC,* where § 7 of the Clayton Act was in issue. The evidence showed that the resources of one company were so depleted and the prospect of rehabilitation so remote that "it faced the grave probability of a business failure." There was, moreover, "no other prospective purchaser." It was in that setting that the Court held that the acquisition of that company by another did not substantially lessen competition within the meaning of § 7.

In the present case the District Court found: "At the time Star Publishing and Citizen Publishing entered into the operating agreement, and at the time the agreement became effective, Citizen Publishing was not then on the verge of going out of business, nor was there a serious probability at that time that Citizen Publishing would terminate its business and liquidate its assets unless Star Publishing and Citizen Publishing entered into the operating agreement." The evidence sustains that finding. There is no indication that the owners of the Citizen were contemplating a liquidation. They never sought to sell the Citizen and there is no evidence that the joint operating agreement was the last straw at which the Citizen grasped. Indeed the Citizen continued to be a significant threat to the Star. How otherwise is one to explain the Star's willingness to enter into an agreement to share its profits with the Citizen? Would that be true if as now claimed the Citizen was on the brink of collapse?

The failing company doctrine plainly cannot be applied in a merger or in any other case unless it is established that the company that acquires the failing company or brings it under dominion is the only available purchaser. For if another person or group could be interested, a unit in the competitive system would be preserved and not lost to monopoly power. So even if we assume, *arguendo*, that in 1940 the then owners of the Citizen could not long keep the enterprise afloat, no effort was made to sell the Citizen; its properties and franchise were not put in the hands of a broker; and the record is silent on what the market, if any, for the Citizen might have been.

Moreover, we know from the broad experience of the business community since 1930, the year when the *International Shoe* case was decided, that companies reorganized through receivership, or through Chapter X or Chapter XI of the Bankruptcy Act often emerged as strong competitive companies. The prospects of reorganization of the Citizen in 1940 would have had to be dim or nonexistent to make the failing company doctrine applicable to this case.

The burden of proving that the conditions of the failing company doctrine[4] have been satisfied is on those who seek refuge under it. That burden has not been satisfied in this case.

We confine the failing company doctrine to its present narrow scope. . . .

NOTES AND QUESTIONS ON *CITIZEN PUBLISHING*

Citizen Publishing re-interpreted *International Shoe* in a way that increased the requirements of the failing company defense. (1) The Court held that insolvency did not suffice unless it would drive the firm to liquidate and go out of business, which the Court held required evidence that the prospects for reorganization were "dim or nonexistent." (2) The lack of an alternative purchaser required proof that reasonable efforts failed to find any alternative purchaser. The Court also made clear that the merging firms

---

[4] Bills were introduced both in the 90th Congress . . . and in the 91st Congress . . . to exempt from the antitrust laws joint operating agreements between newspapers because of economic distress. Extensive hearings were held in 1967 and 1968. The hearings reflect all shades of opinion. As stated by the House Subcommittee: "The antitrust laws embody concepts and principles which long have been considered to be the bedrock of our economic institutions. Piecemeal exemptions from the antitrust laws to cope with problems of particular industries have been given reluctantly and only after there has been a clear showing of overriding need." As of this date Congress has taken no action on any of those bills.

had the burden of proving these elements. These changes from *International Shoe* probably reflect a combination of the increased practice of reorganizing in bankruptcy and growing dissatisfaction with how overinclusive the test of *International Shoe* was. Do you agree with these changes?

In footnote 4, *Citizen Publishing* noted that Congress was considering a bill to create an antitrust exemption for newspaper joint operating agreements in cases of economic distress, but the Court declined to adopt such an exemption judicially. The next year Congress enacted a statute providing an antitrust exemption for a "joint newspaper operating arrangement" if "not more than one of the newspaper publications . . . was likely to remain or become a financially sound publication," and requiring approval by the Attorney General under this standard for future joint newspaper operating arrangements.[44] This statute appears to substantially weaken the general standards for the failing firm defense articulated in *Citizen Publishing* for cases of newspaper joint operating agreements by requiring proof of only insolvency, rather than proof of likely liquidation and the absence of other purchasers.

Is there any sound policy reason to make the failing company defense easier to prove for newspapers than in other industries? Perhaps so, because although weakening the standards may not be desirable as a purely economic matter, the political risks of a news and editorial monopoly might outweigh the economic risks of approving a joint operating agreement that may raise prices but preserve editorial competition.

Given the pending bills, should the Court have tried to anticipate legislative preferences by adopting such a special rule for newspapers via judicial decision? Probably not. It seems better to force Congress to adopt such an exemption if it wants one, both because Congress can better make open-ended tradeoffs between economic and political risks, and because it would have been difficult for the Court to anticipate the precise standard Congress would want and even harder to interpret the Sherman Act to create the sort of administrative approval process Congress ultimately wanted.[45] Thus, by provoking a statutory override, this decision led to a statutory result that reflected legislative preferences more accurately and precisely than could have been achieved by any judicial decision trying to estimate legislative preferences.

U.S. DOJ/FTC, Horizontal Merger Guidelines

(2010).

11. Failure and Exiting Assets

Notwithstanding the analysis above, a merger is not likely to enhance market power if imminent failure, as defined below, of one of the

[44] Newspaper Preservation Act, 84 Stat. 466 (1970), 15 U.S.C. § 1803.

[45] *See* ELHAUGE, STATUTORY DEFAULT RULES 181–183 (Harvard University Press 2008) (arguing that the presumption against antitrust exemptions in cases where legislative preferences are unclear is justified when decisions that conflict with actual legislative preferences are more likely to provoke statutory overrides that make those preferences clear when the decisions deny an exemption than when they recognize an exemption.)

merging firms would cause the assets of that firm to exit the relevant market. This is an extreme instance of the more general circumstance in which the competitive significance of one of the merging firms is declining: the projected market share and significance of the exiting firm is zero. If the relevant assets would otherwise exit the market, customers are not worse off after the merger than they would have been had the merger been enjoined.

The Agencies do not normally credit claims that the assets of the failing firm would exit the relevant market unless all of the following circumstances are met: (1) the allegedly failing firm would be unable to meet its financial obligations in the near future; (2) it would not be able to reorganize successfully under Chapter 11 of the Bankruptcy Act; and (3) it has made unsuccessful good-faith efforts to elicit reasonable alternative offers that would keep its tangible and intangible assets in the relevant market and pose a less severe danger to competition than does the proposed merger.[16]

Similarly, a merger is unlikely to cause competitive harm if the risks to competition arise from the acquisition of a failing division. The Agencies do not normally credit claims that the assets of a division would exit the relevant market in the near future unless both of the following conditions are met: (1) applying cost allocation rules that reflect true economic costs, the division has a persistently negative cash flow on an operating basis, and such negative cash flow is not economically justified for the firm by benefits such as added sales in complementary markets or enhanced customer goodwill;[17] and (2) the owner of the failing division has made unsuccessful good-faith efforts to elicit reasonable alternative offers that would keep its tangible and intangible assets in the relevant market and pose a less severe danger to competition than does the proposed acquisition. . . .

NOTES AND QUESTIONS ON MERGER GUIDELINES ON THE FAILING FIRM DEFENSE

The 2010 Guidelines follow the same test as *Citizen's Publishing*, requiring evidence (1) not only of insolvency but also an inability to reorganize in bankruptcy, and (2) that the firm made unsuccessful good faith efforts to find alternative buyers that would keep the assets in the market. However, the Guidelines also make clear that those elements are just regarded as relevant to the ultimate test, which is whether the assets of the failing firm would otherwise exit the relevant market. If this ultimate test were met, then the projected market share of the failing firm would be 0%.

---

[16] Any offer to purchase the assets of the failing firm for a price above the liquidation value of those assets will be regarded as a reasonable alternative offer. Liquidation value is the highest value the assets could command for use outside the relevant market.

[17] Because the parent firm can allocate costs, revenues, and intra-company transactions among itself and its subsidiaries and divisions, the Agencies require evidence on these two points that is not solely based on management plans that could have been prepared for the purpose of demonstrating negative cash flow or the prospect of exit from the relevant market.

One implication of this ultimate test is that, even if the two elements were met, the failing firm defense would not apply if, without the merger, the firm would be liquidated in a way resulted in its assets being sold piecemeal to firms *within* the market. The justification for this conclusion is that such a liquidation would likely be less anticompetitive than having those assets all transferred to a merged firm that would gain anticompetitive market power. On the other hand, forcing liquidation in such a case might require inefficiently sacrificing the going-concern value of the firm. Why deny the failing firm defense in such cases? Probably the best explanation is that the failing firm defense is absolute, so recognizing it would immunize the merger even if the anticompetitive effects outweigh any efficiencies from preserving going concern value. Given its absolute nature, agencies and courts and agencies sensibly prefer to narrow the failing firm defense to cases where meeting the defense really disproves any possibility of anticompetitive effect, which is only in the extreme case when the assets would otherwise leave the market entirely. Denying the failing firm defense still allows agencies and courts to directly consider failing firm issues as bearing on the extent of anticompetitive effects and efficiencies under a general balancing rule-of-reason approach.

How can one decide what constitutes a good faith effort to obtain a reasonable alternative offer? Good faith cannot just mean selling to the highest bidder, because the buyer who would reap the greatest anticompetitive profits is likely be the highest bidder. But if a firm cannot just sell to the highest bidder, how much below that bid still constitutes a reasonable alternative offer? Reflecting the ultimate test, footnote 16 of the guidelines indicates that an alternative offer is reasonable if it exceeds the value of the assets *outside* the market and would create less anticompetitive effect than the merger.

6. THE RELEVANCE OF BUYER POWER OR VIEWS

a. MERGERS BETWEEN BUYERS THAT CREATE BUYER POWER

It has long been understood that: "The exercise of market power by buyers, or monopsony, can impose social costs equivalent to those imposed by monopoly."[46] This point was strongly reaffirmed in the *Weyerhaeuser* case excerpted for Chapter 3. It is no defense that the creation of monopsony power lowers prices in the purchasing market. Those lower prices are *sub*competitive prices and thus (like *supra*competitive prices) produce a lower and subcompetitive market output. This will be true even if sellers have no fixed costs as long as they have increasing marginal costs.[47] A buyer with market power will maximize profits by paying only a subcompetitive price even though that lowers output because it will take into account the fact that any

[46] IV AREEDA, HOVENKAMP & SOLOW, ANTITRUST LAW ¶ 980 (rev. ed. 1998); *see generally* BLAIR & HARRISON, MONOPSONY (1993).

[47] *See, e.g.*, HOVENKAMP, FEDERAL ANTITRUST POLICY § 1.2b (1994).

additional marginal purchases it can make by increasing the price will increase the market price it pays for all inframarginal purchases.[48]

The adverse effects of buyer market power may seem counter-intuitive because the consequence is lower prices in the purchasing market. But these lower prices are *sub*competitive prices and thus (like *supra*competitive prices) produce a lower and subcompetitive market output and quality. Thus, the intuition proves false for at least three reasons.

(1) Where the firm with buyer market power also has selling market power in a downstream market, the predictable result of upstream monopsony power is lower downstream output, and thus *higher* (supracompetitive) prices in the downstream market in which the powerful buyer sells.[49]

(2) Even without higher prices in a downstream market, the creation of monopsony power remains anticompetitive in the upstream market and harmful to sellers in it.[50]

(3) Even if an upstream exercise of buyer market power did turn out to lower downstream consumer prices, those lower prices would remain *sub*competitive prices that create *sub*competitive levels of market output and quality downstream. These subcompetitive levels of output and quality would remain harmful to consumers, who by definition would have been willing to pay more for the output and quality level that a competitive market would have afforded them.

Further, if price discrimination is possible, then a buyer with market power that wants to gain a competitive advantage downstream may be able to insist on a large discount compared to what the sellers charge

---

[48] For a seller with market power, its marginal revenue is lower than the price it charges to make the marginal sale because it has to take into account that any price cut lowers the prices it makes on the inframarginal sales. Thus, the seller with market power does not produce the output where price equals its marginal costs but rather the lower output where its marginal revenue equals its marginal costs. Likewise, for a buyer with market power, its marginal outlay is higher than the price it pays to make the marginal purchase because it has to take into account that any price increase raises the prices it pays on inframarginal purchases. Thus, the buyer with market power does not offer prices high enough to result in an output where price equals its marginal demand, but rather demands subcompetitive prices that produce a lower output where its marginal outlay equals its marginal demand.

[49] *Id.*; Roger D. Blair & Jeffery L. Harrison, *Antitrust Policy and Monopsony*, 76 CORNELL L. REV. 297, 335 (1991) ("Substantive economic analysis reveals that it is an error to infer that the lower prices a monopsonist obtains translate into lower ultimate prices for the monopsonists' customers.").

[50] *See* Weyerhaeuser Co. v. Ross-Simmons Hardwood Lumber, 549 U.S. 312 (2007) (articulating test for predatory overbuying that imposes liability for enhancing upstream monopsony power in a local market rather than requiring anticompetitive effects in the downstream national market); Mandeville Island Farms v. American Crystal Sugar, 334 U.S. 219 (1948) (condemning a buying cartel in a regional sugar beet market without any proof that it would have a price effect on the downstream national market in refined sugar); United States v. Pennzoil, 252 F.Supp. 962 (W.D.Pa. 1965) (condemning merger that created local monopsony power in Pennsylvania crude oil market even though it seemed unlikely to affect output in downstream worldwide market for refined oil); United States v. Rice Growers Ass'n, 1986–2 Trade Cas. (CCH) ¶ 67,288 (E.D. Cal.) (condemning merger that created local monopsony power in California paddy rice market even though it seemed unlikely to affect output in downstream worldwide market for milled rice).

other buyers who compete with the powerful buyer downstream. This may distort downstream competition. Further, the upstream result can be that the powerful buyer pays a *sub*competitive price on its purchases whereas rival buyers pay a *supra*competitive price for their purchases. Both *sub*competitive and *supra*competitive prices lead to lower output than the competitive price. The *sub*competitive prices will lower output by making sellers less willing to produce for the powerful buyer; the *supra*competitive prices will lower output by making rival buyers less willing to purchase.

U.S. DOJ/FTC, Horizontal Merger Guidelines

(2010).

12. Mergers of Competing Buyers

Mergers of competing buyers can enhance market power on the buying side of the market, just as mergers of competing sellers can enhance market power on the selling side of the market. Buyer market power is sometimes called "monopsony power."

To evaluate whether a merger is likely to enhance market power on the buying side of the market, the Agencies employ essentially the framework described above for evaluating whether a merger is likely to enhance market power on the selling side of the market. In defining relevant markets, the Agencies focus on the alternatives available to sellers in the face of a decrease in the price paid by a hypothetical monopsonist.

Market power on the buying side of the market is not a significant concern if suppliers have numerous attractive outlets for their goods or services. However, when that is not the case, the Agencies may conclude that the merger of competing buyers is likely to lessen competition in a manner harmful to sellers.

The Agencies distinguish between effects on sellers arising from a lessening of competition and effects arising in other ways. A merger that does not enhance market power on the buying side of the market can nevertheless lead to a reduction in prices paid by the merged firm, for example, by reducing transactions costs or allowing the merged firm to take advantage of volume-based discounts. Reduction in prices paid by the merging firms not arising from the enhancement of market power can be significant in the evaluation of efficiencies from a merger, as discussed in Section 10.

The Agencies do not view a short-run reduction in the quantity purchased as the only, or best, indicator of whether a merger enhances buyer market power. Nor do the Agencies evaluate the competitive effects of mergers between competing buyers strictly, or even primarily, on the basis of effects in the downstream markets in which the merging firms sell.

Example 24: Merging Firms A and B are the only two buyers in the relevant geographic market for an agricultural product. Their merger will enhance buyer power and depress the price paid to farmers for this product, causing a transfer of wealth from farmers to the merged firm and inefficiently reducing supply. These effects can arise even if the merger will not lead to any increase in the price charged by the merged firm for its output. . . .

b. SHOULD MERGERS BETWEEN SELLERS BE DEEMED CONSTRAINED BY BUYER POWER?

U.S. DOJ/FTC, Horizontal Merger Guidelines

(2010).

8. Powerful Buyers

Powerful buyers are often able to negotiate favorable terms with their suppliers. Such terms may reflect the lower costs of serving these buyers, but they also can reflect price discrimination in their favor.

The Agencies consider the possibility that powerful buyers may constrain the ability of the merging parties to raise prices. This can occur, for example, if powerful buyers have the ability and incentive to vertically integrate upstream or sponsor entry, or if the conduct or presence of large buyers undermines coordinated effects. However, the Agencies do not presume that the presence of powerful buyers alone forestalls adverse competitive effects flowing from the merger. Even buyers that can negotiate favorable terms may be harmed by an increase in market power. The Agencies examine the choices available to powerful buyers and how those choices likely would change due to the merger. Normally, a merger that eliminates a supplier whose presence contributed significantly to a buyer's negotiating leverage will harm that buyer.

Example 22: Customer C has been able to negotiate lower pre-merger prices than other customers by threatening to shift its large volume of purchases from one merging firm to the other. No other suppliers are as well placed to meet Customer C's needs for volume and reliability. The merger is likely to harm Customer C. In this situation, the Agencies could identify a price discrimination market consisting of Customer C and similarly placed customers. The merger threatens to end previous price discrimination in their favor.

Furthermore, even if some powerful buyers could protect themselves, the Agencies also consider whether market power can be exercised against other buyers.

Example 23: In Example 22, if Customer C instead obtained the lower pre-merger prices based on a credible threat to supply its own needs, or to sponsor new entry, Customer C might not be harmed. However, even in this case, other customers may still be harmed. . . .

c. SHOULD BUYER POWER ALTER ASSESSMENTS OF MERGERS THAT OTHERWISE CREATE SELLER MARKET POWER?

As noted in Chapter 2, countervailing power is generally not a defense to a per se illegal cartel. But for mergers, the issue is different because a rule of reason applies. Thus, here the issue is whether buyer power might sufficiently reduce the *degree* of any seller power created by the merger that it would be offset by any merger-specific efficiencies.

However, there are several reasons to doubt that the existence of buyer market power will prevent an otherwise anticompetitive merger from raising prices or lowering output. As the Guideline note, buyer power may not suffice to offset any increased seller power. Worse, a successive monopolies problem might in fact mean that market power at two levels exacerbates anticompetitive effects. The Guidelines also note that powerful dealers might cut special deals that protect the powerful buyers but harm their less powerful competitors who also purchase in the same market. Indeed, powerful buyers may have incentives not to exercise any countervailing market power to reduce seller maker power at all, but rather to collude with the seller to preserve and enhance seller market power in exchange for a share of the sellers' supracompetitive profits. Even when powerful buyers do try to exercise countervailing market power, it is generally indeterminate whether this will raise or lower prices. It is also generally better to allow the buyer market power to be corrected by market forces rather than to entrench market power on both sides, especially given that buyer power might reflect desirable rewards for investing to create a market option that is so valuable that it enjoys power.

d. SHOULD BUYER VIEWS ALTER ASSESSMENTS OF MERGERS BETWEEN SELLERS?

U.S. DOJ/FTC, Horizontal Merger Guidelines

(2010).

2.2 Sources of Evidence. . . .

2.2.2 Customers

Customers can provide a variety of information to the Agencies, ranging from information about their own purchasing behavior and choices to their views about the effects of the merger itself.

Information from customers about how they would likely respond to a price increase, and the relative attractiveness of different products or suppliers, may be highly relevant, especially when corroborated by other evidence such as historical purchasing patterns and practices. Customers also can provide valuable information about the impact of historical events such as entry by a new supplier.

The conclusions of well-informed and sophisticated customers on the likely impact of the merger itself can also help the Agencies investigate competitive effects, because customers typically feel the consequences of both competitively beneficial and competitively harmful mergers. In evaluating such evidence, the Agencies are mindful that customers may oppose, or favor, a merger for reasons unrelated to the antitrust issues raised by that merger.

When some customers express concerns about the competitive effects of a merger while others view the merger as beneficial or neutral, the Agencies take account of this divergence in using the information provided by customers and consider the likely reasons for such divergence of views. For example, if for regulatory reasons some customers cannot buy imported products, while others can, a merger between domestic suppliers may harm the former customers even if it leaves the more flexible customers unharmed. *See* Section 3.

When direct customers of the merging firms compete against one another in a downstream market, their interests may not be aligned with the interests of final consumers, especially if the direct customers expect to pass on any anticompetitive price increase. A customer that is protected from adverse competitive effects by a long-term contract, or otherwise relatively immune from the merger's harmful effects, may even welcome an anticompetitive merger that provides that customer with a competitive advantage over its downstream rivals.

> *Example 1:* As a result of the merger, Customer C will experience a price increase for an input used in producing its final product, raising its costs. Customer C's rivals use this input more intensively than Customer C, and the same price increase applied to them will raise their costs more than it raises Customer C's costs. On balance, Customer C may benefit from the merger even though the merger involves a substantial lessening of competition.

2.2.3 Other Industry Participants and Observers

Suppliers, indirect customers, distributors, other industry participants, and industry analysts can also provide information helpful to a merger inquiry. The interests of firms selling products complementary to those offered by the merging firms often are well aligned with those of customers, making their informed views valuable.

Information from firms that are rivals to the merging parties can help illuminate how the market operates. The interests of rival firms often diverge from the interests of customers, since customers normally lose, but rival firms gain, if the merged entity raises its prices. For that reason, the Agencies do not routinely rely on the overall views of rival firms regarding the competitive effects of the merger. However, rival firms may provide relevant facts, and even their overall views may be instructive, especially in cases where the Agencies are concerned that the merged entity may engage in exclusionary conduct.

> *Example 2:* Merging Firms A and B operate in a market in which network effects are significant, implying that any firm's product is significantly more valuable if it commands a large market share or if it is interconnected with others that in aggregate command such a share. Prior to the merger, they and their rivals voluntarily interconnect with one another. The merger would create an entity with a large enough share that a strategy of ending voluntary interconnection would have a dangerous probability of creating monopoly power in this market. The interests of rivals and of consumers would be broadly aligned in preventing such a merger.

3. Targeted Customers and Price Discrimination

When examining possible adverse competitive effects from a merger, the Agencies consider whether those effects vary significantly for different customers purchasing the same or similar products. Such differential impacts are possible when sellers can discriminate, e.g., by profitably raising price to certain targeted customers but not to others. The possibility of price discrimination influences market definition (*see* Section 4), the measurement of market shares (*see* Section 5), and the evaluation of competitive effects (*see* Sections 6 and 7).

When price discrimination is feasible, adverse competitive effects on targeted customers can arise, even if such effects will not arise for other customers. A price increase for targeted customers may be profitable even if a price increase for all customers would not be profitable because too many other customers would substitute away. When discrimination is reasonably likely, the Agencies may evaluate competitive effects separately by type of customer. The Agencies may have access to information unavailable to customers that is relevant to evaluating whether discrimination is reasonably likely.

For price discrimination to be feasible, two conditions typically must be met: differential pricing and limited arbitrage.

First, the suppliers engaging in price discrimination must be able to price differently to targeted customers than to other customers. This may involve identification of individual customers to which different prices are offered or offering different prices to different types of customers based on observable characteristics.

> *Example 3:* Suppliers can distinguish large buyers from small buyers. Large buyers are more likely than small buyers to self-supply in response to a significant price increase. The merger may lead to price discrimination against small buyers, harming

them, even if large buyers are not harmed. Such discrimination can occur even if there is no discrete gap in size between the classes of large and small buyers.

In other cases, suppliers may be unable to distinguish among different types of customers but can offer multiple products that sort customers based on their purchase decisions.

Second, the targeted customers must not be able to defeat the price increase of concern by arbitrage, e.g., by purchasing indirectly from or through other customers. Arbitrage may be difficult if it would void warranties or make service more difficult or costly for customers. Arbitrage is inherently impossible for many services. Arbitrage between customers at different geographic locations may be impractical due to transportation costs. Arbitrage on a modest scale may be possible but sufficiently costly or limited that it would not deter or defeat a discriminatory pricing strategy . . .

NOTE ON BUYER NONCOMPLAINTS

In practice, one of the most influential factors in determining whether U.S. enforcement agencies move to block a merger is whether buyers are complaining. For mergers that resulted in a post-merger HHI between 2000–3999, the FTC was 93% likely to challenge the merger if there were strong (that is, economically sophisticated) buyer complaints, but only 32% likely to challenge without them.[51] With strong buyer complaints, the FTC was 100% likely to challenge a merger that left the market with between three to five significant competitors; without such buyer complaints, if the number of significant competitors was three, the likelihood was only 50%; if it was four, the likelihood was only 7%; and if it was five, the likelihood was 0%.[52] Moreover, the latter statistics include mergers where the only buyers are consumers, when the agencies clearly do not expect strong complaints given each buyer's low stake. These statistics thus probably overstate the likelihood of a challenge when a merger has business buyers who have all declined to complain. Other nations also put great weight on the existence or absence of buyer complaints.[53]

Buyers have such strong influence on merger enforcement for three main reasons. First, they often have the information that the agencies need to decide whether a merger is likely to create anticompetitive problems. Second, having buyers as witnesses is often thought necessary to putting on an effective case at trial, though that would seem to depend on whether courts treat their absence as problematic. Third, and most important, buyers are often thought to have incentives that align them well with competitive concerns, unlike rivals of the merging parties, who generally should benefit from an anticompetitive merger and be hurt by an efficient one. If a merger

---

[51] *See* FTC, Horizontal Merger Investigation Data: Fiscal Years 1996–2003, at Tables 7.1–7.2 (2004).

[52] *Id.* at 8.1–8.2. *See also* Coate & Ulrick, *supra* note 27, at 549, 561.

[53] *See* ABA, I COMPETITION LAWS OUTSIDE THE UNITED STATES at Canada-84–85 (2001).

is likely to create unilateral or oligopoly effects that raise prices, then buyers have incentives to complain. If the merger were not likely to create such anticompetitive effects, or generated efficiencies that offset them enough to lower prices, then buyers would not have incentives to complain. Or so the logic goes.

However, buyer noncomplaints may provide a poor signal. One reason is that buyers may be uninformed or unsophisticated about the facts or the substance or procedure of antitrust merger analysis. The more important reason is that their incentives may be skewed. This skew means a buyer may fail to complain even though it does believe the merger is anticompetitive, or would believe so if it expended the resources to investigate the issue.[54]

Where there are many buyers, they face a collective action problem that may prevent buyers from complaining about an inefficient merger. To complain to an antitrust enforcement agency, firms must incur significant individual costs. These include not only the considerable economic cost of doing serious economic and legal analysis, but often more important the cost of possible retaliation or maltreatment by the firms that wish to merge, which those firms will have even more power to do if the merger succeeds. In contrast, the benefits of successfully complaining are collective and nonexclusive because each buyer benefits if an inefficient merger is blocked whether it complained or not. Moreover, each buyer likely realizes that its single decision whether or not to complain is unlikely to affect the outcome. Thus, each buyer has individual incentives to free ride on the possible complaints of other buyers because the costs of complaining are borne individually whereas the benefits are collective. The result can be that no buyer complains even though the merger is in fact inefficient.

Where some buyers are large and have buyer market power, collective action problems may be less important. But this market structure creates other incentive problems. The powerful buyers may figure that their purchasing power will get them discounts from the supracompetitive prices inflicted on rivals or potential entrants.[55] Such special discounts may fully offset any price increase expected from the merger, or go beyond such an offset to give the powerful buyers a share of the seller's supracompetitive profits, but even if they don't, the competitive advantage the powerful buyers gain against their less powerful rivals may give them additional downstream profits that offset the cost of any merger-caused price increase. Indeed, firms seeking to merge are generally advised to go to all their buyers before proposing their merger to give them whatever assurances are necessary to get them to refrain from complaining, which often take the form of special long-term contracts guaranteeing that the prices of such powerful buyers will not be raised if the merger goes through, which effectively guarantees them precisely just a special discount.

---

[54] In contrast, the existence of complaints by a credible buyer (that is not also a rival) provides a stronger signal, for if the buyer really thought the merger was likely to lower prices, it would have no incentive to expend the considerable resources it takes to mount a credible complaint in a merger case.

[55] *See* Elhauge, *Defining Better, supra* note 39, at 288–92.

Further, just as a few firms in an oligopolistic industry can coordinate on price, perhaps a few firms in an industry can also coordinate on a policy of not objecting to each other's mergers. True, this requires coordination across levels of production and over time. But if the firms in the industry are few enough, they can develop a social norm against complaining about each others' mergers. Anecdotal evidence suggests such a norm exists in many industries, and a firm that deviated from it might well expect others to complain about its mergers. Any firm that thinks it might want to merge down the line thus may have incentives not to object to mergers by others.

Further, business buyers are generally corporations, and corporations cannot speak for themselves—only their managers can. A firm's managers may benefit from a short-term price reduction, or by avoiding the costs of complaining, even if the firm's long-term costs increase because the merger enhanced seller market power that harms their successors. That is, agency costs might mean that no corporate buyer complains about an anticompetitive merger.

Finally, other buyers might have special reasons why they might not oppose an inefficient merger. Some buyers may plan to enter the relevant market themselves, like HMOs who do not object to hospital mergers because the HMOs themselves plan to enter the market for providing some medical-surgical services. Increased market concentration makes such entry easier and more profitable for such buyers. Other buyers are governmental actors who do not face market discipline but do face political pressure, and thus may lack sufficient incentives to oppose inefficient mergers. Moreover, to the extent any increased monopoly profits are garnered in-state, whereas much of the anticompetitive costs are externalized outside the state, state buying agencies may have incentives not to oppose inefficient mergers.

One might imagine coupling evidence of a lack of buyer complaints with economic analysis rebutting all the above concerns. But the economic analysis that would be necessary to determine whether buyer noncomplaints are reliable indicators of merger efficiency is probably more complicated and less accurate than the economic analysis employed to analyze directly the merger on structural grounds. Thus, even though buyer noncomplaints may not be irrelevant, they do not appear to offer a useful screen for avoiding traditional analysis of market structure.

C. VERTICAL MERGERS

Vertical mergers have several possible anticompetitive effects. Generally, these effects are similar to the possible anticompetitive effects from exclusive dealing. That is, the concern is that the vertical merger might foreclose a sufficient share of suppliers or buyers to rivals that it impairs the ability of rivals to compete, and may even effectively require two-level entry to compete. If there are few firms in the market, vertical mergers might also facilitate oligopolistic coordination among them by making their pricing more noticeable (such as when a manufacturer merges into retail) or because the merged firm can, as buyer, better monitor rival upstream pricing.

Vertical mergers also raise the concern that they might eliminate potential horizontal competition, such as when the merging firms are likely to have entered each others' market absent the merger. We will, however, defer those issues to the section on conglomerate mergers, which centers more directly on that issue. Finally, vertical integration might facilitate price discrimination if the integrated firm is more able to stop any buyer resales that would otherwise undermine such price discrimination. As usual, such price discrimination usually decreases consumer, also decreases total welfare if the distribution of consumer preferences is not too flat, but increases total welfare if the distribution curve is fairly flat. *See* Chapter 3.

Absent one of those anticompetitive effects, even firms with market power generally have no incentive to use vertical mergers to prevent vigorous competition upstream or downstream because their market power at any given stage is greater if other production or distribution stages are more efficient because that increases the value of the ultimate product to consumers. Vertical mergers can also have affirmatively procompetitive effects. In part, these are similar to the possible procompetitive effects from exclusive dealing. Vertical mergers can reduce uncertainty, eliminate free riding incentives between manufacturers and dealers in promoting a brand, or more generally encourage firm-specific investments, but do so in a way that systematically restricts opportunism rather than being limited to specific deals. Vertical mergers can also create other important additional efficiencies. Like horizontal mergers, vertical mergers can create integrative efficiencies, but they tend to be less economies of size and more economies of scope or synergies (like lowering costs by integrating vertical production). Further, where vertical mergers combine firms that have market or monopoly power in successive markets, they avoid the lower output or inefficient substitution that such successive market power causes.

In the United States, the current law on vertical mergers is obscure. *Brown Shoe* did condemn a vertical merger that foreclosed only 1.2% of the relevant market. But, while that case has never been overruled, it clearly does not reflect modern antitrust practice. The U.S. agencies issued guidelines in 1984 that covered vertical mergers. These certainly come closer to reflecting current law than does *Brown Shoe*. But although the parts of the guidelines dealing with horizontal mergers have repeatedly been updated since 1984, the portions on vertical and conglomerate mergers never have been. Further, former FTC Chairman Professor Pitofsky has stated, "Unlike the horizontal merger guidelines which may be the most influential piece of government regulation in the past fifty years, and the conglomerate merger guidelines which seem to have caught the direction the law was going, the vertical merger guidelines have been widely ignored."[56]

Modern U.S. antitrust enforcement policy clearly deems vertical mergers far less likely than horizontal mergers to raise anticompetitive concerns.[57] From 1996–2003, the FTC's second requests included 17 vertical cases and 162 horizontal cases.[58] Moreover, actual U.S. enforcement action against vertical mergers is nearly non-existent. "The FTC successfully challenged three vertical mergers during the Clinton administration, and the FTC during the second Bush administration has challenged one and closely examined a second. In every one of the challenged cases the merger was abandoned or substantially restructured before it was allowed to proceed so there is no court opinion elaborating on theory."[59] There is thus little concrete guidance available about the content of modern U.S. antitrust law on vertical mergers. Further complicating matters is the fact that, unlike with horizontal mergers, vertical merger enforcement in the U.S. is strongly influenced by whether Democrats or Republicans are in office. For horizontal mergers, the change from the Clinton to Bush Administration had no statistically significant effect on FTC enforcement odds.[60] In contrast, that same shift caused the odds of vertical merger challenges to drop sharply.[61] To reveal where the two varying enforcement policies currently lie, below after the 1984 Guidelines this book excerpts an FTC consent decree on a vertical merger case (called *Cadence*) that produced divided statements by FTC commissioners.

Like horizontal mergers, vertical mergers are also subject to efficiency and failing firm defenses. Entry barriers are also relevant at both the upstream and downstream levels.

U.S. DOJ, Merger Guidelines

(1984).

4.21 Barriers to Entry from Vertical Mergers. In certain circumstances, the vertical integration resulting from vertical mergers could create competitively objectionable barriers to entry. Stated generally, three conditions are necessary (but not sufficient) for this problem to exist. First, the degree of vertical integration between the two markets must be so extensive that entrants to one market (the "primary

---

56 *See* Robert Pitofsky, *Past, Present, and Future of Antitrust Enforcement at the Federal Trade Commission,* 72 U. CHIC. L. REV. 209, 220 (2005).

57 *Id.*

58 *See* FTC, Horizontal Merger Investigation Data: Fiscal Years 1996–2003, at Table 1 (2004). The figure of 162 includes not only the 151 the FTC classified as "horizontal" but also the 11 it classified as involving either buyer power or joint ventures since both of those also involve horizontal combinations.

59 *Id.*

60 *See* Coate & Ulrick, *supra* note 27, at 546–47, 554.

61 *See* Coate, *Twenty Years of Federal Trade Commission Merger Enforcement Activity* (1985–2004), Potomac Working Paper in Law and Economics 05–02, at 4 & Table 1 (Oct. 2005).

market") also would have to enter the other market (the "secondary market")[30] simultaneously. Second, the requirement of entry at the secondary level must make entry at the primary level significantly more difficult and less likely to occur. Finally, the structure and other characteristics of the primary market must be otherwise so conducive to non-competitive performance that the increased difficulty of entry is likely to affect its performance. The following standards state the criteria by which the Department will determine whether these conditions are satisfied.

4.211 Need for Two-Level Entry. If there is sufficient unintegrated capacity in the secondary market, new entrants to the primary market would not have to enter both markets simultaneously. The Department is unlikely to challenge a merger on this ground where post-merger sales (purchases) by unintegrated firms in the secondary market would be sufficient to service two minimum-efficient-scale plants in the primary market. When the other conditions are satisfied, the Department is increasingly likely to challenge a merger as the unintegrated capacity declines below this level.

4.212 Increased Difficulty of Simultaneous Entry to Both Markets. The relevant question is whether the need for simultaneous entry to the secondary market gives rise to a substantial incremental difficulty as compared to entry into the primary market alone. If entry at the secondary level is easy in absolute terms, the requirement of simultaneous entry to that market is unlikely adversely to affect entry to the primary market. Whatever the difficulties of entry into the primary market may be, the Department is unlikely to challenge a merger on this ground if new entry into the secondary market can be accomplished under the conditions stated in Section [3]. When entry is not possible under those conditions, the Department is increasingly concerned about vertical mergers as the difficulty of entering the secondary market increases. The Department, however, will invoke this theory only where the need for secondary market entry significantly increases the costs (which may take the form of risks) of primary market entry.

More capital is necessary to enter two market than to enter one. Standing alone, however, this additional capital requirement does not constitute a barrier to entry to the primary market. If the necessary funds were available at a cost commensurate with the level of risk in the secondary market, there would be no adverse effect. In some cases, however, lenders may doubt that would-be entrants to the primary market have the necessary skills and knowledge to succeed in the secondary market and, therefore, in the primary market. In order to compensate for this risk of failure, lenders might charge a higher rate for

30 This competitive problem could result from either upstream or downstream integration, and could affect competition in either the upstream market or the downstream market. In the text, the term "primary market" refers to the market in which the competitive concerns are being considered, and the term "secondary market" refers to the adjacent market.

the necessary capital. This problem becomes increasingly significant as a higher percentage of the capital assets in the secondary market are long-lived and specialized to that market and, therefore, difficult to recover in the event of failure. In evaluating the likelihood of increased barriers to entry resulting from increased cost of capital, therefore, the Department will consider both the degree of similarity in the essential skills in the primary and secondary markets and the economic life and degree of specialization of the capital assets in the secondary market.

Economies of scale in the secondary market may constitute an additional barrier to entry to the primary market in some situations requiring two-level entry. The problem could arise if the capacities of minimum-efficient-scale plants in the primary and secondary markets differ significantly. For example, if the capacity of a minimum-efficient-scale plant in the secondary market were significantly greater than the needs of a minimum-efficient-scale plant in the primary market, entrants would have to choose between inefficient operation at the secondary level (because of operating an efficient plant at an inefficient output or because of operating an efficiently small plant) or a larger than necessary scale at the primary level. Either of these effects could cause a significant increase in the operating costs of the entering firm.[33]

4.213 Structure and Performance of the Primary Market. Barriers to entry are unlikely to affect performance if the structure of the primary market is otherwise not conducive to monopolization or collusion.[34] The Department is unlikely to challenge a merger on this ground unless overall concentration of the primary market is above 1800 HHI (a somewhat lower concentration will suffice if one or more of the factors discussed in Section [2.1] indicate that effective collusion is particularly likely). Above that threshold, the Department is increasingly likely to challenge a merger that meets the other criteria set forth above as the concentration increases.

4.22 Facilitating Collusion Through Vertical Mergers

4.221 Vertical Integration to the Retail Level. A high level of vertical integration by upstream firms into the associated retail market may facilitate collusion in the upstream market by making it easier to monitor price. Retail prices are generally more visible than prices in upstream markets, and vertical mergers may increase the level of vertical integration to the point at which the monitoring effect becomes significant. Adverse competitive consequences are unlikely unless the upstream market is generally conducive to collusion and a large percentage of the products produced there are sold through vertically integrated retail outlets.

---

33 It is important to note, however, that this problem would not exist if a significant outside market exists at the secondary level. In that case, entrants could enter with the appropriately scaled plants at both levels, and sell or buy in the market as necessary.

34 For example, a market with 100 firms of equal size would perform competitively despite a significant increase in entry barriers.

The Department is unlikely to challenge a merger on this ground unless (1) overall concentration of the upstream market is above 1800 HHI (a somewhat lower concentration will suffice if one or more of the factors discussed in Section [2.1] indicate that effective collusion is particularly likely), and (2) a large percentage of the upstream product would be sold through vertically-integrated retail outlets after the merger. Where the stated thresholds are met or exceeded, the Department's decision whether to challenge a merger on this ground will depend upon an individual evaluation of its likely competitive effect.

4.222 Elimination of a Disruptive Buyer. The elimination by vertical merger of a particularly disruptive buyer in a downstream market may facilitate collusion in the upstream market. If upstream firms view sales to a particular buyer as sufficiently important, they may deviate from the terms of a collusive agreement in an effort to secure that business, thereby disrupting the operation of the agreement. The merger of such a buyer with an upstream firm may eliminate that rivalry, making it easier for the upstream firms to collude effectively. Adverse competitive consequences are unlikely unless the upstream market is generally conducive to collusion and the disruptive firm is significantly more attractive to sellers than the other firms in its market.

The Department is unlikely to challenge a merger on this ground unless (1) overall concentration of the upstream market is 1800 HHI or above (a somewhat lower concentration will suffice if one or more of the factors discussed in Section [2.1] indicate that effective collusion is particularly likely), and (2) the allegedly disruptive firm differs substantially in volume of purchases or other relevant characteristics from the other firms in its market. . . .

4.23 Evasion of Rate Regulation. Non-horizontal mergers may be used by monopoly public utilities subject to rate regulation as a tool for circumventing that regulation. The clearest example is the acquisition by a regulated utility of a supplier of its fixed or variable inputs. After the merger, the utility would be selling to itself and might be able arbitrarily to inflate the prices of internal transactions. Regulators may have great difficulty in policing these practices, particularly if there is no independent market for the product (or service) purchased from the affiliate. As a result, inflated prices could be passed along to consumers as "legitimate" costs. In extreme cases, the regulated firm may effectively preempt the adjacent market, perhaps for the purpose of suppressing observable market transactions, and may distort resource allocation in that adjacent market as well as in the regulated market. In such cases, however, the Department recognizes that genuine economies of integration may be involved. The Department will consider challenging mergers that create substantial opportunities for such abuses.[36]

[36] Where a regulatory agency has the responsibility for approving such mergers, the Department may express its concerns to that agency in its role as competition advocate.

4.24 *Efficiencies.* As in the case of horizontal mergers, the Department will consider expected efficiencies in determining whether to challenge a vertical merger. An extensive pattern of vertical integration may constitute evidence that substantial economies are afforded by vertical integration. Therefore, the Department will give relatively more weight to expected efficiencies in determining whether to challenge a vertical merger than in determining whether to challenge a horizontal merger.

NOTES AND QUESTIONS ON U.S. VERTICAL MERGER GUIDELINES

The 1984 U.S. Guidelines require that the primary market have an HHI above 1800 and that the merger either (1) anticompetitively raises entry barriers because (a) the unforeclosed market could support fewer than two firms at minimum efficient scale and (b) two-level entry is significantly harder than one-level entry into the primary market, *or* (2) facilitates oligopolistic coordination because (a) the upstream market is sufficiently concentrated and a large percentage of the upstream product would be sold through vertically-integrated outlets after the merger or (b) the merger would eliminate a disruptive buyer. Although these Guidelines have not yet been updated, presumably the HHI level would now be increased to 2500 given the 2010 Horizontal Merger Guidelines.

These Guidelines are clearly far narrower than the decision in *Brown Shoe.* The Guidelines approve a merger if the unforeclosed market could support two firms. In *Brown Shoe*, the Supreme Court condemned a merger where the unforeclosed market supported 70,000 other retail outlets. There was no evidence that the merger significantly raised entry barriers in *Brown Shoe,* and the shoe markets there were not oligopolistic but rather highly fragmented. Further, the trend toward vertical mergers that *Brown Shoe* thought increased anticompetitive concerns is taken as a sign that those mergers are efficient in the Guidelines. Suppose one believes that *Brown Shoe* more accurately reflects the intent of the 1950 Congress that amended Clayton Act § 7, given that the 1962 *Brown Shoe* decision was more contemporaneous with that legislature and conducted an extensive analysis of the legislative history.

1. ***Is it legitimate for the Guidelines to take an approach so much narrower than the only Supreme Court authority interpreting the statute's application to vertical mergers?*** The Supreme Court is authoritative on what the statute means. However, the agencies have prosecutorial discretion and are free to choose to exercise it more narrowly than the law would allow. Given that *Brown Shoe* cannot be justified by modern antitrust economics, it seems sensible for the agencies to take a more narrow approach.

But should *Brown Shoe* then be followed in private litigation? Perhaps not, because the statute condemns acquisitions only if "the effect of such acquisition may be substantially to lessen competition", and one might sensibly conclude that application of that constant statutory standard changes with updated economic information about which mergers have the effect of substantially lessening competition. Even if the 1950 Congress had particular ideas about what it thought substantially lessened competition, it may not have wanted those ideas to bind if new information arose about what substantially lessens competition.[62]

*2. **Does the fact that Congress has not overridden the Guidelines mean that the current Congress likes their narrowing of merger policy?*** It could, but it is also consistent with the possibilities that: (1) inertia and decisionmaking costs do not make it worth Congress's time to address the issue; or (2) Congress is divided and has effective committee vetos, supramajority requirements, and Presidential vetos, which may mean Congress could not enact legislation approving or rejecting any agency guidelines. If there were evidence that the agency guidelines reflected the views of the current Congress, but not the enacting one, there is an interesting question about whether that means judicial interpretation should use the agency guidelines to resolve statutory ambiguities.[63]

In the Matter of Cadence Design Systems, Inc.

124 F.T.C. 131 (1997).

[Cadence, which made integrated circuit layout environments, wanted to acquire CCT, which made integrated circuit routing tools. The FTC charged the following in a complaint.] Integrated circuit layout environments are software infrastructures within which integrated circuit designers access integrated circuit layout tools, including . . . routing tools. . . . CCT is currently the only firm with a commercially viable . . . integrated circuit routing tool. At least one other firm with . . . routing-technology is in the process of developing [an] integrated circuit routing tool. Cadence is the dominant supplier of integrated circuit layout environments. Cadence's leading competitor in the supply of integrated circuit layout environments is the Avant! Corporation. Avant! and several of its top executives have been charged criminally with conspiracy and theft of trade secrets from Cadence.

There are substantial barriers to entry in the market for . . . integrated circuit routing tools, [which] . . . are technologically complex and difficult to develop. De novo entry takes approximately two to three and a half years for a company that already possesses certain underlying core technology that can be used to develop [an] integrated circuit router . . . Entry is likely to take even longer for a company that does not possess such technology.

---

[62] *See* Elhauge, *supra* note 45, at 138–143 (pointing out that changed circumstances can justify changing statutory interpretation in order to fulfill the enacting legislature's static preferences).

[63] *See* Elhauge, *supra* note 45, at 10, 41–69 (arguing that when statutory meaning is ambiguous, the enacting legislature itself would prefer that agencies track current legislative preferences because "the enacting legislative polity would prefer *present* influence (while it exists) over *all* the statutes being interpreted, rather than *future* influence (when it no longer exists) over the *subset* of statutes it enacted.")

In order to achieve the necessary compatibility between the integrated circuit layout tools that they use, integrated circuit designers select integrated circuit layout tools that have interfaces to a common integrated circuit layout environment. Since Cadence is the dominant supplier of integrated circuit layout environments, [an] integrated circuit routing tool that lacks an interface into a Cadence integrated circuit layout environment is less likely to be selected by integrated circuit designers than [an] integrated circuit routing tool that possesses an interface into a Cadence integrated circuit layout environment.

An integrated circuit layout environment is not likely to be selected by integrated circuit designers unless a full set of compatible integrated circuit layout tools is available. A full set of integrated circuit layout tools includes at least placement, routing, and analysis and verification tools, each of which must be able to interface into the integrated circuit layout environment that the integrated circuit designer has selected.

It is in Cadence's interest to make available to users of a Cadence integrated circuit layout environment a complete a set of integrated circuit layout tools, because to do so makes the Cadence integrated circuit layout environment more valuable to integrated circuit designers. Cadence historically has provided access to Cadence integrated circuit layout environments to suppliers of complementary integrated circuit layout tools that Cadence does not supply.

Cadence does not, however, have incentives to provide access to a Cadence integrated circuit layout environment to suppliers of integrated circuit layout tools that compete with Cadence products. Cadence historically has been reluctant to provide access to Cadence integrated circuit layout environments to suppliers of integrated circuit layout tools that compete with Cadence products.

Prior to the Proposed Merger, Cadence did not have a commercially viable . . . integrated circuit routing tool. As a result of the Proposed Merger, Cadence will own the only currently available commercially viable . . . integrated circuit routing tool. For this reason, the Proposed Merger will make Cadence less likely to permit potential suppliers of competing . . . integrated circuit routing tools to obtain access to Cadence integrated circuit layout environments. Without access to Cadence integrated circuit layout environments, developers are less likely to gain successful entry into the market for . . . integrated circuit routing tools.

The Proposed Merger will make it more likely that successful entry into the . . . integrated circuit routing tool market would require simultaneous entry into the market for integrated circuit layout environments. This need for dual-level entry will decrease the likelihood of entry into the market for . . . integrated circuit routing tools.

The Proposed Merger may substantially lessen competition or tend to create a monopoly in the market for . . . integrated circuit routing tools.

The Proposed Merger may, among other things, lead to higher prices, reduced service, and less innovation. . . .

DECISION AND ORDER

[Based on the above complaint, the FTC and merging parties entered into a consent order approving the merger on the conditions that for the next ten years Cadence: (1) had to provide other integrated circuit router tool companies with equal access to Cadence's "Connections Program," which provided independent software developers with the interfaces necessary to work with Cadence's integrated circuit layout, and (2) notify the FTC before acquiring another integrated circuit routing tool company.] . . .

■ STATEMENT OF CHAIRMAN ROBERT PITOFSKY & COMMISSIONER JANET D. STEIGER.[64] . . . The Commission's complaint alleges a well-established vertical theory of competitive harm, laid out in the 1984 Merger Guidelines. The Guidelines explain that a vertical merger can produce horizontal anticompetitive effects by making competitive entry less likely if (1) as a result of the merger, there is a need for simultaneous entry into two or more markets and (2) such simultaneous entry would make entry into the single market less likely to occur. While the dissenting Commissioners may take issue in this case with the "dual-level entry" theory of vertical mergers that the 1984 Guidelines articulate, the available evidence suggests that the Cadence/CCT merger, which combines Cadence's dominant position in integrated circuit layout environments with CCT's current monopolistic position in . . . integrated circuit routers, presents a straightforward case of anticompetitive effects caused by vertical integration. We believe that this type of competitive harm merits our attention.[4]

. . . [U]nless a would-be supplier of routing tools had the ability to develop an interface to the Cadence integrated circuit layout environment, it would not be able to market its routing product effectively to the vast majority of potential customers which use the Cadence layout environment. Without an expectation that it could design software compatible with Cadence's installed base, a would-be entrant might well decide not to compete.

After the Cadence/CCT merger, Cadence would have had an incentive to impede attempts by companies developing routing technology competitive with CCT's . . . router technology, IC Craftsman, to gain access to the Cadence integrated circuit layout environment. Following the merger, successful entry into the routing tool market is more likely to require simultaneous entry into the market for integrated

64 [Editor's Note: Commissioner Varney initially joined this statement when it was issued for public comment, but left the FTC before this statement was finalized.]

4 Contrary to Commissioner Starek's assertions that enforcement action here, in the context of a merger, leads logically to enforcement action against internal vertical expansion, . . . such unilateral action has been known to present a completely different set of questions under the antitrust laws for more than one hundred years.

circuit layout environments. Without a consent order that mandates access to Cadence's layout environment, and thus lowers the barriers to entry in the market, a combined Cadence/CCT will face less competitive pressure to innovate or to price aggressively. Thus, competition would likely be reduced as a result of the acquisition.

The remedy in this matter preserves opportunities for new entrants with integrated circuit routers competitive with IC Craftsman by allowing them to interface with Cadence's layout environments on the same terms as developers of complementary design tools. Specifically, the order requires Cadence to allow independent commercial router developers to build interfaces between their design tools and the Cadence layout environment through Cadence's "Connections Program." The Connections Program is in place now and has more than one hundred participants who have all entered a standard form contract with Cadence. . . .

The dissenting statements fail to give full weight to all the incentives at work in the vertical case. It is true that Cadence would be motivated by the entry of new, promising routing technology to allow an interface to its layout environment to sell more of its complementary products. And absent the merger, that would be its only incentive. But with the merger, Cadence clearly also has an incentive to prevent loss of sales in its competing products. And while these two incentives may compete as a theoretical matter, the evidence in this case indicated that Cadence has acted historically according to the latter incentive. There is some reason to believe that Cadence in the past has thwarted attempts by firms offering potentially competitive technology to develop interfaces to its layout environment (including at one point, CCT). Now that it has a satisfactory router to offer its customers, there is no reason to think that absent the consent order, Cadence would treat developers of routers that would compete with IC Craftsman any differently than it once treated CCT.

Commissioner Azcuenaga also suggests that the consent order is unnecessary because a company developing a router to compete with IC Craftsman could proceed, as CCT did, without an interface to Cadence's design layout environment. The evidence showed, however, that CCT's management thought that ensuring compatibility with Cadence's layout environment was critical and that marketing without that compatibility, which it had done, was not sufficient. It took the extreme measure of inducing a third party to write software for CCT to interface IC Craftsman with the Cadence layout environment without Cadence's knowledge. Moreover, despite CCT's success in developing a routing program, its sales of IC Craftsman were quite modest before it obtained an authorized interface with the Cadence environment.

Commissioner Azcuenaga is further concerned that mandating access to the Connections Program for developers of routing software on terms as favorable as for other Connections participants might have unintended consequences. In particular, she is concerned that the order may prompt Cadence to charge higher prices to all Connections partners. But the Connections Program is an existing program with over one hundred members, and Cadence would have significant logistical difficulties, and would risk injuring its reputation, if it suddenly altered the terms of the program. Also, Cadence has good reasons for having so many Connections partners—they offer Cadence customers valuable tools, most of which do not compete with Cadence products. It seems unlikely that Cadence would be motivated to make the Connections Program less appealing to those partners.

Both Commissioners Azcuenaga and Starek suggest that the remedy may be difficult to enforce. Any time this Commission enters an order, it takes upon itself the burden of enforcing the order, which requires use of our scarce resources. However, we think the order, which simply requires Cadence to allow competitors and potential competitors developing routing technology to participate in independent software interface programs on terms no less favorable than the terms applicable to any other participants in such programs, is a workable approach.[11] Connections partners all sign the same standard-form contract and there has been a consistent pattern of conduct with respect to the program to use as a baseline for future comparisons. Moreover, the Commission has had experience with such non-discrimination provisions, and can rely on respondent's compliance reports required under the order as well as complaints from independent software developers to ensure compliance with the consent order. We think the dissenting Commissioners' scenarios about intractable compliance issues are unfounded. . . .

■ STATEMENT OF COMMISSIONER MARY L. AZCUENAGA CONCURRING IN PART AND DISSENTING IN PART. The acquisition of [CCT] by Cadence . . . combines the only firm currently marketing [an] integrated circuit routing tool with a firm that was, at least until the acquisition, on the verge of entry into this market. I find reason to believe that the proposed merger would violate Section 7 of the Clayton Act under a horizontal, potential competition theory [because Cadence was likely to enter the tool market, and thus I concur in the part of the order requiring notification of future acquisitions of tool companies.]. . . .

The vertical theory of violation alleged in the complaint is that the acquisition of [CCT] by Cadence will make it more difficult for another firm to introduce [an] IC router because such an entrant would need its own IC layout environment to enter the market, and that dual level entry is more difficult. Although this is a recognized theory, I question whether it applies in this case and whether a firm needs to enter both the routing and the environment markets simultaneously.

---

11 The language of the consent order is clear in requiring that terms for routing companies be no less favorable than for any other participant in the Connections Program. Thus, we do not understand Commissioner Starek's conclusion that the order could be interpreted to require routing companies to pay a "fee no higher than the highest fee." . . .

[CCT] was successful in developing and marketing its routing program before it gained access to Cadence's environment. In a separate statement, Chairman Pitofsky and Commissioners Varney and Steiger assert that [CCT's] "sales were modest before the merger announcement." I disagree based on [CCT's] penetration of the market. Cadence's willingness to pay more that $400 million in stock for [CCT] also suggests a greater competitive significance than the majority concedes. [CCT's] record indicates that access to a layout environment is not a precondition to successful entry in the market for . . . integrated circuit routers. It appears, based on the available information, that dual level entry theory does not apply in this market.

In addition, although Cadence initially denied [CCT] access to its connections program, it subsequently reversed course and granted the access. This suggests that Cadence capitulated to pressure from customers to grant [CCT] access and that Cadence has little or no power to deny access to its connections program if granting access is the only way to enable its customers to use a product they want to use. Finally, . . . the order is premised on the allegation in . . . the complaint that "Cadence does not, however, have incentives to provide access to a Cadence integrated circuit layout environment to suppliers of integrated circuit layout tools that compete with Cadence products." The incentives appear to be at least as likely to go the other way. If another company develops an innovative, advanced router, one would assume that Cadence would have incentives to welcome the innovative product to its suite of connected design tools, thereby enhancing the suite's utility to customers.

[T]he order [requiring equal access to interfaces] may be counterproductive and may result in substantial enforcement costs for the Commission. Because [this order] bars Cadence from charging developers of "Commercial Integrated Circuit Routing Tools" a higher access fee than developers of other design tools, one possible, unintended consequence of the order is that Cadence may reduce or eliminate discounting of access fees. In addition, enforcement of the provision of the order requiring Cadence to provide access to the connections program to developers of "Commercial Integrated Circuit Routing Tools" on terms "no less favorable than the terms applicable to any other participants" may embroil the Commission unnecessarily in complex commercial disputes. . . .

■ DISSENTING STATEMENT OF COMMISSIONER ROSCOE B. STAREK, III. . . . To justify the complaint and order, the Commission once again invokes the specter of anticompetitive "foreclosure" as a direct consequence of the transaction. As I have made clear on previous occasions, foreclosure theories are generally unconvincing as a rationale for antitrust enforcement. The current case provides scant basis for revising this conclusion. . . .

The logic of the complaint is fundamentally flawed. Even if we assume arguendo—as the complaint in this case does—that Cadence is "dominant" in the supply of software components complementary to the router,[4] the fact remains that it has no incentive to restrict the supply of routers . . .[5] The same is true here: the introduction of a lower-priced or higher-quality routing program increases the value of Cadence's "dominant" position in the sale of software complementary to the router, because it increases the demand for Cadence design software, thereby allowing Cadence to increase the price and/or the output of these programs. Despite the assertions of Chairman Pitofsky and Commissioner Steiger to the contrary,[6] this is true whether or not Cadence has vertically integrated into the sale of routing software, for efficient entry into the production of routing software increases the joint profits of the entrant and Cadence. If the Commission is correct that Cadence is "dominant" in the supply of software components complementary to routers, then of course Cadence may be in a position to expropriate—e.g., via royalties paid to Cadence by the entrant for the right to "connect" to Cadence's software—some or all of the "efficiency rents" that otherwise would accrue to an efficient entrant. This, however, would constitute harm to a competitor, not to competition, and Cadence would have no incentive to set any such rates so high as to preclude entry. . . .

Contrary to the analysis presented above, suppose that somehow Cadence could profit anticompetitively from denying interconnection rights to independent router vendors. If that were so, then it would not be sufficient merely to prevent Cadence from acquiring producers of complementary software. Rather, the Commission would have to take the further step of preventing Cadence from developing its own routers; for

---

4 The anticompetitive theory requires Cadence to have substantial monopoly power: if there were numerous good alternatives to Cadence's suite, other independent vendors of routing software could affiliate with them and there would be no "foreclosure."

5 Moreover, . . . the description of the premerger state of competition set forth in the complaint itself tends to exclude the possibility of substantial postmerger foreclosure. . . . [T]he . . . complaint alleges that there are substantial premerger barriers to entry into the market for the kind of "router" software that CCT produces. But one cannot find both that the premerger supply elasticity of substitutable software is virtually zero and that the merger would result in the substantial postmerger foreclosure of independent software producers. If entry into . . . IC router software is effectively blocked premerger, as the complaint contends, it cannot also be the case that the merger would cause a substantial incremental reduction in entry opportunities.

6 Chairman Pitofsky and Commissioner Steiger assert that "Cadence clearly also has an incentive to prevent loss of sales in its competing products." . . . Because [they never describe] . . . how this conclusion was reached, it is difficult to identify precisely the source of the erroneous reasoning. Chiefly, however, it seems to reflect a manifestation of the "sunk cost fallacy," whereby it is argued that because Cadence has now sunk a large sum of money into acquiring CCT, this in and of itself would provide Cadence with an incentive not to deal with independent vendors of complements. This reasoning, of course, is fallacious: the cost incurred by Cadence in acquiring CCT—whether a large or a small sum—is irrelevant to profit-maximizing behavior once incurred, for bygones are forever bygones. The introduction of a superior new router, even if by an independent vendor, will increase the joint profits of Cadence and this vendor (irrespective of the amount spent in acquiring CCT), and both parties will have a profit incentive to facilitate its introduction.

under the anticompetitive theory advanced in the complaint, any vertical integration by Cadence into routers, whether accomplished by acquisition or through internal expansion, would engender equivalent post-integration incentives to "foreclosure" independent vendors of routing software.[8] Of course, . . . there is likely to be little enthusiasm for such a policy because there is a general predisposition to regard internal capacity expansion as procompetitive.[9]

Not only am I unpersuaded that Cadence's acquisition of CCT is likely to reduce competition in any relevant market, but . . . I would find the order unacceptable even were I convinced as to liability. . . . [T]he Commission imposes a "most favored nations" clause that requires Cadence to allow all independent router developers to participate in its software interface programs on terms that are "no less favorable than the terms applicable to any other participants in" those interface programs. Even apart from the usual problems with "most favored nations" clauses in consent orders,[10] this order . . . will require that the Commission continuously regulate the prices and other conditions of access.

. . . What does it mean to mandate treatment "no less favorable than" that granted to others, when Cadence's current Connections Program—with well over 100 participants—allows access prices to differ substantially across participants and imposes substantial restrictions on the breadth and scope of the permitted connection rights?[11] Does it mean that router vendors pay a connection fee no higher than the highest fee paid by an existing participant? Or would they pay a fee no higher than the current lowest fee? Or does it mean something else? Router vendors surely will argue for the second interpretation—a view also apparently shared by Chairman Pitofsky and Commission Steiger—yet there is no obvious reason why router vendors should be entitled to such a Commission-mandated preferential pricing arrangement . . . Similarly, does the "no less favorable" requirement mandate that the vendors of

[8] Thus, it is unclear how the Commission should respond, under the logic of its complaint, were Cadence to introduce an internally developed software program (now provided by one or more independent vendors) that is complementary to its "dominant" suite of programs. Obviously Cadence would be in a position (similar to that alleged in the Commission's complaint) to block access to the Cadence design software if it wanted to. Even if Cadence did not terminate the independent vendors, consistent application of the economic logic of the present complaint seemingly would require the Commission to seek a prophylactic "open access" order against Cadence similar to the order sought here. This enforcement policy would of course have a number of adverse competitive consequences, including deterrence of Cadence from efficiently entering complementary software lines through internal expansion.

[9] . . . [T]he Commission has alleged the existence of substantial pre-acquisition market power in both vertically related matters (routing software and the rest of the IC layout "suite" . . .). Under these circumstances, there is a straightforward reason why vertical integration is both profitable and procompetitive (i.e., likely to result in lower prices to consumers): vertical integration would yield only one monopoly markup by the integrated firm, rather than separate markups (as in the pre-integration situation) by Cadence and CCT.

[10] . . . [T]hese clauses have the capacity to cause all prices to rise rather than to fall. The Chairman and Commissioner Steiger seem comfortable with this outcome, provided that all vendors pay the same price.

[11] For example, CCT had been permitted to participate in the Connections Program with its printed circuit board router but not with its IC router.

routing software obtain access rights as broad as the broadest rights now granted, or simply no worse than the narrowest now granted? . . .

The preceding suggests strongly that the real (albeit unstated) goal of the order is not to nullify any actual anticompetitive effects from the transaction, but rather to invalidate the principal aspects of Cadence's "Connections Program" (i.e., the ability to charge different connection fees and to terminate vendors at will) without demonstrating that the program's provisions violate the law. There is little reason to believe that this program is harmful to competition, and there are strong efficiency reasons for allowing Cadence to set different fees for different vendors. Moreover, setting a uniform fee would result in price increases to at least some vendors.

Because I do not accept the Commission's theory of liability in this case, and because I find the prescribed remedy at best unenforceable and at worst competitively harmful, I dissent.

NOTES AND QUESTIONS ON *CADENCE*

The proposed vertical merger was between Cadence, which was the dominant supplier of integrated circuit (IC) layouts, and CCT, which was the only firm with a commercially viable IC routing tool. IC tools, including routing tools, required an interface with a compatible IC layout. The anticompetitive concern was that the merged firm would deny Cadence layout interfaces to future entrants into the routing tool market. The consent decree approved the merger on the condition that the merged firm allow other routing tool companies equal access to Cadence's Connections Program, which provided interfaces necessary to work with the Cadence layout to 100 other makers of IC tools.

1. ***Was anticompetitive market foreclosure possible?*** Two doubts were raised about the possibility of foreclosure. First, even if the merger foreclosed routing tool entrants from Cadence's layouts, entrants could try to persuade IC designers to use layouts from Avant, the other firm in the layout market. However, Cadence was dominant in the layout market, which means its layout must have had some significant advantages over other layouts and that IC designers would generally use Cadence layouts. Being foreclosed from access to the dominant layout would thus discourage entry into the IC routing tool market, even if entrants could still sell routing tools to IC designers willing to use other layouts. Moreover, Avant had been criminally charged for stealing trade secrets from Cadence, which indicated Avant might (if the case went badly for it) not be able to supply layouts at all.

Second, Commissioner Azcuenaga argued that a routing tool company must not really need a Cadence layout interface because CCT itself successfully entered the routing tool market without one. However, the majority observed that CCT was unable to make significant sales until Cadence authorized an interface to its IC layout.

2. ***Would the merged firm have incentives to foreclose?*** Commission Starek's dissent argued that the merged firm would have no incentive to deny access to its layout to rival producers of routing tools. If such foreclosure would not increase entry barriers (by requiring rivals to enter both markets to offer a desirable combination of layouts and routing tools), then he would be correct that Cadence's economic incentives would be to maximize the value of its layout by having the most efficient router tools in the market.[65] However, if foreclosure would increase entry barriers in this way, then denying access to the merged firm's layouts could increase the degree of market power it had in either or both markets, which would increase its profits and thus give it an incentive to deny access to its layout.

Perhaps Commissioner Starek ignores the possibility that foreclosure might raise entry barriers because his footnote 5 assumes that the existence of entry barriers to the routing tool market means that the merger cannot increase entry barriers. He would be correct on that point if entry barriers to the routing tool market were infinite, because requiring two-level entry cannot increase entry barriers if they are already infinite. But if entry barriers to routing tools are high but not infinite, then those entry barriers could be raised by requiring two-level entry.

However, even if denying access to layouts would increase entry barriers, the result would be conflicting economic incentives: an incentive to increase entry barriers and a contrary incentive to have the most efficient complementary product. Predicting post-merger foreclosure means concluding that the former incentive will likely outweigh the latter, which can be difficult to determine. Here, the FTC majority concluded that the entry-barrier-increasing incentive would likely win out because in the past Cadence had historically denied layout access to suppliers of competing tools, even though the efficient-complementary-product incentive did cause Cadence to grant access to suppliers of noncompetitive tools.

3. ***Might eliminating successive monopolies be efficient?*** Starek dissent footnote 9 points out that the existence of market power in both the layout and routing tool markets suggests that the merger would eliminate a successive monopoly problem and thus increase efficiency. *See* Chapter 3. This is probably the best argument for Starek's position. Further, such successive market power seems likely to exist for most vertical mergers that meet the Guideline conditions for being potentially anticompetitive, raising difficult questions about how to weigh this potential procompetitive benefit against the possible anticompetitive effects. On the other hand, the successive monopolies problem can often be resolved by using vertical maximum price fixing, which is a less restrictive alternative than eliminating downstream competition. *See* Chapters 3, 5.

4. ***Do the reasons to restrict vertical mergers also apply to vertical expansion?*** The Starek dissent argues that the theory applied to this merger must be wrong because it implies the FTC should also ban internal expansion into vertical markets, which is generally deemed

---

[65] *See* Chapter 3 on refusals to deal. This analysis assumes router tools are useless without layouts and that router tools and layouts are used in a fixed ratio. If routing tools have separate utility or if layouts and routing tools are used in varying proportions, then the other anticompetitive effects from tying could apply and make it profitable to tie layouts and routing tools by denying layout access to rival routing tools. *See* Chapter 4 on tying.

procompetitive. He is right that vertical expansion could create similar anticompetitive incentives to foreclose rivals. However, unlike vertical mergers (which simply acquire existing firms), internal expansion adds new capacity and output, which is more likely to benefit consumer welfare. Also, legally, Clayton Act § 7 applies to acquisitions, not to internal expansions.

5. ***Why not allow the merger and police any anticompetitive post-merger foreclosure under the unilateral refusal to deal doctrine?*** That would be an alternative. Indeed, if any post-merger refusal involved discrimination based on rivalry, such as denying layout interface access to competing tools but not to noncompeting tools, it would seem to violate the refusal to deal doctrine if it created or enhanced monopoly power and lacked any persuasive efficiency justification. *See* Chapter 3. But the refusal to deal doctrine has been narrowly construed, is often uncertain, and requires significant costly litigation. The equal access condition for merger approval effectively provided a nondiscrimination duty that was more easily enforceable because it did not require proving any enhancement of monopoly power or lack of efficiencies. Such a nondiscrimination duty is easier to enforce than an absolute duty to deal because the terms of the required dealing can be ascertained by seeing how the Connections Program treats noncompeting tools.

D. CONGLOMERATE MERGERS

Any merger that is not a horizontal or vertical merger falls by default into the category of conglomerate merger. Conglomerate mergers raise two sorts of concerns: (1) that they might eliminate potential horizontal competition; and (2) that the merger will enable the merged firm to engage in vertical exclusionary conduct post-merger. Like horizontal and vertical mergers, either theory of anticompetitive harm can be rebutted by establishing low entry barriers, offsetting efficiencies, or the failing firm defense.

Eliminating Potential Competition. The acquisition of a potential competitor who is not already in the market might have economic relevance for two sorts of reasons. First, the perception that the potential competitor might enter a market can constrain current market pricing and behavior. Acquiring the potential competitor can lift this constraint and thus directly raise market prices above current levels. Second, it might be that the potential competitor actually would have entered the market. Acquiring the potential competitor then would eliminate actual future competition and market deconcentration that otherwise would have occurred and lowered prices below current levels. The first is known in the literature as the elimination of "perceived potential competition"; the latter as the elimination of "actual potential competition." In the first, what matters is the perception of incumbent firms about the likelihood of entry in response to a price increase. In the second, what matters is the likelihood that the acquired firm actually would have entered at current prices.

To a large extent, the economic theory on mergers that eliminate perceived potential competitors is simply the flip side of economic theory on limit pricing. The theory of limit pricing indicates that the possibility of entry often induces firms with dominant market power to price below the full profit-maximizing monopoly level by setting a limit price that keeps perceived likely entrants out. It follows from this theory that mergers with perceived potential competitors can raise this limit and thus increase prices.

The economic theory on mergers that eliminate actual potential competitors is the same as the general economic theory supporting the proposition that firms with dominant market power will charge more than they would without such power, or the various theories about why concentrated oligopoly markets can have worse economic performance than deconcentrated ones. Because the grounds for concern here are that the acquired firm would (absent the merger) have actually entered and offered independent competition, the theoretical and empirical grounds for thinking such mergers harm the market are the same as that for thinking that mergers that increase market concentration will harm the market. The only grounds for distinction are greater uncertainty about whether the entry would have actually occurred and how extensive it would have been. But similar uncertainties are entertained all the time in considering *defensive* uses of potential competition—that is, in considering the argument that the possibility of supplier entry lessens the anticompetitive concerns one might otherwise have with a merger. *See* Chapter 7.A.3. Under a neutral regulatory approach, there does not appear to be any reason to allow greater uncertainty in such *defensive* uses of the potential competition argument than in *offensive* uses of the potential competition argument to condemn a merger.

The U.S. Supreme Court has sustained blocking a conglomerate merger that eliminated perceived potential competition, but has not yet blocked a merger that eliminated only actual potential competition, although the logic of its opinions would seem to extend to the latter as well. U.S. enforcement guidelines have for decades provided that the elimination of either perceived or actual potential competition can trigger an agency enforcement action. Actual U.S. enforcement is, however, relatively rare. From 1996–2003, the FTC issued second requests in 12 potential competition cases compared to 162 horizontal cases and 17 vertical ones.[66] The willingness to challenge mergers that raise potential competition issues is much lower if the FTC chair is a Republican.[67] Thus, U.S. enforcement of potential competition theories exhibit the same sort of political division that afflicts vertical merger enforcement, rather than the relatively nonpartisan enforcement that governs horizontal mergers.

---

[66] *See* FTC, Horizontal Merger Investigation Data: Fiscal Years 1996–2003, at Table 1 (2004).

[67] *See* Coate, *Twenty Years, supra* note 61, at 5 & Table 1.

Enabling Post-Merger Exclusionary Conduct. Another concern with conglomerate mergers is that they might enable the merged firm to engage in post-merger conduct that anticompetitively forecloses rivals. For example, a merger of a firm that sells product *A* with one that sells product *B* might enable the merged firm to engage in anticompetitive bundling of products *A* and *B*. In several conglomerate merger cases, the concern has instead been the related one that a merger of a firm that *buys* product *A* with a firm that sells product *B* might enable the merged to engage in reciprocity: buying product *A* from other businesses only if they buy product *B* from it. This is similar to tying with the difference that here it is the willingness to buy (rather than sell) product *A* that is conditioned on the other firm buying product *B*.

Although a 1965 U.S. Supreme Court sustained blocking a conglomerate merger on the grounds that it would enable the merged firm to engage in reciprocity,[68] modern U.S. antitrust practice generally refuses to block a conglomerate merger on the theory that it will enable the merged firm to engage in post-merger exclusionary conduct. The typical reason given is that the proper remedy is not to block the merger but to wait to see if the feared post-merger conduct actually occurs, which may resolve uncertainties about whether it is actually anticompetitive, and then to penalize the post-merger conduct directly when appropriate. This is clearest when the post-merger conduct is something like tying, which is covered by Sherman Act § 1 and Clayton Act § 3 and subject to treble damages.

The availability of adequate post-merger penalties is less clear for reciprocity for two reasons. First, reciprocity may not be sufficiently concrete to constitute an agreement, and the merged firm may have market power that falls short of monopoly power. Such reciprocity might still be challengeable under FTC § 5 if it were anticompetitive, but that might be viewed as an insufficient deterrent given its weak penalties. Second, even under FTC Act, it would be hard to define and remedy reciprocity post-merger. Doing so would require ascertaining whether a firm is refusing to buy one product from a seller because the seller does not buy another product from it, or instead is refusing for legitimate reasons regarding the merits of the first product. This may be particularly hard to ascertain when the firm is buying a product from the seller that is made using a component that the first firm sells and believes is the best product on that component market. Moreover, even when reciprocity can be identified, prohibiting it would require obligating the firm to buy from a seller it does not want to buy from, which would require defining how much it has to buy from that seller and at what terms. Thus, it may be hard to police reciprocity post-merger, which argues for trying to prevent the sorts of market structures that create incentives to engage in it.

---

68 *See* FTC v. Consolidated Foods, 380 U.S. 592 (1965).

This probably explains why conglomerate merger cases have been more concerned with reciprocity. However, the theory that a merger should be blocked because it creates an opportunity for reciprocity has not been pursued by modern U.S. enforcement agencies, and it is not clear that current U.S. courts would approve it. Nor does it seem likely that modern U.S. agencies or courts would find reciprocity itself worrisome absent stronger proof than was offered in the 1965 case that the buyer market power and resulting foreclosure were significant enough to have anticompetitive effects that were not outweighed by any procompetitive effects.

U.S. DOJ, Merger Guidelines

(1984).

4.11 The Theory of Potential Competition. In some circumstances, the non-horizontal merger[25] of a firm already in a market (the "acquired firm") with a potential entrant to that market (the "acquiring firm")[26] may adversely affect competition in the market. If the merger effectively removes the acquiring firm from the edge of the market, it could have either of the following effects:

4.111 Harm to "Perceived Potential Competition." By eliminating a significant present competitive threat that constrains the behavior of the firms already in the market, the merger could result in an immediate deterioration in market performance. The economic theory of limit pricing suggests that monopolists and groups of colluding firms may find it profitable to restrain their pricing in order to deter new entry that is likely to push prices even lower by adding capacity to the market. If the acquiring firm had unique advantages in entering the market, the firms in the market might be able to set a new and higher price after the threat of entry by the acquiring firm was eliminated by the merger.

4.112 Harm to "Actual Potential Competition." By eliminating the possibility of entry by the acquiring firm in a more procompetitive manner, the merger could result in a lost opportunity for improvement in market performance resulting from the addition of a significant competitor. The more procompetitive alternatives include both new entry and entry through a "toehold" acquisition of a present small competitor.

4.12 Relation Between Perceived and Actual Potential Competition. If it were always profit-maximizing for incumbent firms to set price in such a way that all entry was deterred and if information and coordination were sufficient to implement this strategy, harm to perceived potential competition would be the only competitive problem to address. In practice, however, actual potential competition has

---

[25] Under traditional usage, such a merger could be characterized as either "vertical" or "conglomerate," but the label adds nothing to the analysis.

[26] The terms "acquired" and "acquiring" refer to the relationship of the firms to the market of interest, not to the way the particular transaction is formally structured.

independent importance. Firms already in the market may not find it optimal to set price low enough to deter all entry; moreover, those firms may misjudge the entry advantages of a particular firm and, therefore, the price necessary to deter its entry.[27]

4.13 Enforcement Standards. Because of the close relationship between perceived potential competition and actual potential competition, the Department will evaluate mergers that raise either type of potential competition concern under a single structural analysis analogous to that applied to horizontal mergers. The Department first will consider a set of objective factors designed to identify cases in which harmful effects are plausible. In such cases, the Department then will conduct a more focused inquiry to determine whether the likelihood and magnitude of the possible harm justify a challenge to the merger. In this context, the Department will consider any specific evidence presented by the merging parties to show that the inferences of competitive harm drawn from the objective factors are unreliable.

The factors that the Department will consider are as follows:

4.131 Market Concentration. Barriers to entry are unlikely to affect market performance if the structure of the market is otherwise not conducive to monopolization or collusion. Adverse competitive effects are likely only if overall concentration, or the largest firms's market share, is high. The Department is unlikely to challenge a potential competition merger unless overall concentration of the acquired firm's market is above 1800 HHI (a somewhat lower concentration will suffice if one or more of the factors discussed in [other parts of the Guidelines] indicate that effective collusion in the market is particularly likely). Other things being equal, the Department is increasingly likely to challenge a merger as this threshold is exceeded.

4.132 Conditions of Entry Generally. If entry to the market is generally easy, the fact that entry is marginally easier for one or more firms is unlikely to affect the behavior of the firms in the market. The Department is unlikely to challenge a potential competition merger when new entry into the acquired firm's market can be accomplished by firms without any specific entry advantages under the conditions stated in [other parts of the Guidelines]. Other things being equal, the Department is increasingly likely to challenge a merger as the difficulty of entry increases above that threshold.

4.133 The Acquiring Firm's Entry Advantage. If more than a few firms have the same or a comparable advantage in entering the acquired firm's market, the elimination of one firm is unlikely to have any adverse competitive effect. The other similarly situated firm(s) would continue to exert a present restraining influence, or, if entry would be profitable, would recognize the opportunity and enter. The Department is unlikely

27 When collusion is only tacit, the problem of arriving at and enforcing the correct limit price is likely to be particularly difficult.

to challenge a potential competition merger if the entry advantage ascribed to the acquiring firm (or another advantage of comparable importance) is also possessed by three or more other firms. Other things being equal, the Department is increasingly likely to challenge a merger as the number of other similarly situated firms decreases below three and as the extent of the entry advantage over non-advantaged firms increases.

If the evidence of likely actual entry by the acquiring firm is particularly strong,[28] however, the Department may challenge a potential competition merger, notwithstanding the presence of three or more firms that are objectively similarly situated. In such cases, the Department will determine the likely scale of entry, using either the firm's own documents or the minimum efficient scale in the industry. The Department will then evaluate the merger much as it would a horizontal merger between a firm the size of the likely scale of entry and the acquired firm.

4.134 The Market Share of the Acquired Firm. Entry through the acquisition of a relatively small firm in the market may have a competitive effect comparable to new entry. Small firms frequently play peripheral roles in collusive interactions, and the particular advantages of the acquiring firm may convert a fringe firm into a significant factor in the market. The Department is unlikely to challenge a potential competition merger when the acquired firm has a market share of five percent or less. Other things being equal, the Department is increasingly likely to challenge a merger as the market share of the acquired firm increases above that threshold. The Department is likely to challenge any merger satisfying the other conditions in which the acquired firm has market share of 20 percent or more.

4.135 Efficiencies. As in the case of horizontal mergers, the Department will consider expected efficiencies in determining whether to challenge a potential competition merger. . . .

U.S. DOJ/FTC, Horizontal Merger Guidelines

(2010).

. . . These Guidelines outline the principal analytical techniques, practices, and the enforcement policy of the Department of Justice and the Federal Trade Commission (the "Agencies") with respect to mergers and acquisitions involving actual or potential competitors ("horizontal mergers") under the federal antitrust laws. . . .

5.1 Market Participants

All firms that currently earn revenues in the relevant market are considered market participants. . . . Firms not currently earning

---

[28] For example, the firm already may have moved beyond the stage of consideration and have made significant investments demonstrating an actual decision to enter.

revenues in the relevant market, but that have committed to entering the market in the near future, are also considered market participants.

Firms that are not current producers in a relevant market, but that would very likely provide rapid supply responses with direct competitive impact in the event of a SSNIP, without incurring significant sunk costs, are also considered market participants. These firms are termed "rapid entrants." Sunk costs are entry or exit costs that cannot be recovered outside the relevant market. Entry that would take place more slowly in response to adverse competitive effects, or that requires firms to incur significant sunk costs, is considered in Section 9.

Firms that produce the relevant product but do not sell it in the relevant geographic market may be rapid entrants. Other things equal, such firms are most likely to be rapid entrants if they are close to the geographic market . . .

5.2 Market Shares

The Agencies normally calculate market shares for all firms that currently produce products in the relevant market, subject to the availability of data. The Agencies also calculate market shares for other market participants if this can be done to reliably reflect their competitive significance . . . The Agencies measure market shares based on the best available indicator of firms' future competitive significance in the relevant market. . . .

In most contexts, the Agencies measure each firm's market share based on its actual or projected revenues in the relevant market. . . .

5.3 Market Concentration . . .

In analyzing mergers between an incumbent and a recent or potential entrant, to the extent the Agencies use the change in concentration to evaluate competitive effects, they will do so using projected market shares. A merger between an incumbent and a potential entrant can raise significant competitive concerns. The lessening of competition resulting from such a merger is more likely to be substantial, the larger is the market share of the incumbent, the greater is the competitive significance of the potential entrant, and the greater is the competitive threat posed by this potential entrant relative to others . . .

NOTES AND QUESTIONS ON U.S. GUIDELINES ON MERGERS AFFECTING POTENTIAL COMPETITION

The 1984 U.S. merger guidelines embrace theories of both potential and perceived competition in highly concentrated markets, and make clear that the DOJ is unlikely to pursue cases where entry barriers are too low and focuses more on whether the acquiring firm has significant entry advantages over all but a few firms. The merger guidelines also presumptively exclude "toehold" mergers with firms holding less than 5% of the market, in part because some cases had condemned conglomerate mergers with larger firms on the grounds that the acquiring firm should instead have acquired a smaller toehold firm.

The 2010 Horizontal Merger Guidelines also address mergers between potential competitors, but take a simpler approach. They simply project a future market share for the potential entrant, and then apply the standard horizontal merger guidelines given those projections. The 1984 Guidelines projected market shares, but only when the likelihood of entry was "particularly strong." The 2010 Guidelines, however, effectively always require strong evidence of likely entry by narrowing who counts as a potential entrant, requiring evidence that the firm either (1) has already "committed" to entry or (2) would very likely enter rapidly in response to a SSNIP without incurring significant sunk costs. Firms already committed to enter seem to correspond to actual potential competition, and firms likely to enter rapidly seem to correspond to perceived potential competition, though on the latter the 2010 Guidelines focus more on actual responsiveness to price increases rather than incumbent perceptions of it. The 2010 Guidelines approach also seems to avoid the 1984 guideline approach of counting how many other firms have similar entry advantages, by simply taking any entry advantages into account in projecting future shares.

1. ***Should the 2010 Guidelines be reviewed as replacing or supplementing the 1984 Guidelines on potential competition?*** The problem is that if the 1984 Guidelines remain operative on potential competition, they would seem to circumvent the 2010 Guidelines limits on how sure entry must be by effectively including in the market firms that have not committed to enter or would not be likely to rapidly enter in response to a price increase because they would have to incur significant sunk costs to enter. Perhaps the 2010 Guidelines meant to narrowly construe only who was in the market (to prevent merging firms from diluting their market shares with less likely entrants), without being so narrow on assessing potential entrants for offensive purposes (to assess whether mergers with potential entrants might have anticompetitive effects). However, the 2010 Guidelines state that they "outline the principal analytical techniques, practices, and the enforcement policy" of the agencies "with respect to mergers and acquisitions involving actual or *potential* competitors ('horizontal mergers')," which seems to define "horizontal" mergers to include conglomerate mergers with potential competitors, and suggests the 2010 Guidelines intend to replace the prior ones.

The differences between the 1984 and 2010 Guidelines boil down to the fact that the former would block mergers with potential entrants who have entry advantages possessed by few other firms if they: (a) have not committed to enter but are actually likely to do so; (b) would have to incur significant sunk costs to enter but are likely enough to enter in response to price increases that they would constrain those price increases from ever occurring; (c) are not actually likely to enter in response to price increases, but are wrongly perceived to be likely to do so by incumbents. Should claims in such cases be pursued? Note that claims (a) and (b) would be consistent with neutral treatment of defensive and offensive uses of potential entry, because the existence of such potential entrants (if not part of the merger) could eliminate anticompetitive concerns under 2010 Guidelines § 9, even though such potential entrants are not quite likely enough to enter to be deemed market participants already.

Even if the 1984 Guidelines on potential competition survive, given that modern U.S. agencies only sometimes challenge mergers that leave three firms in a market, does it seem likely they would ever apply the 1984 guideline approach of challenging a merger that eliminates one of three possible entrants? In practice, it seems unlikely that the potential competition argument will have much impact on current U.S. agency action unless the merger is with a firm that has unique entry advantages or is more likely than others to enter.

2. What about eliminating doubly-potential competition? Suppose two firms form a joint venture to enter into a market that neither of them are in now. Can their combination be challenged on the ground that, without their joint venture, either (a) both of them would have entered that market or (b) one would entered and had its pricing constrained by the perception the other might enter too? Both were held to be viable claims in United States v. Penn-Olin Chemical, 378 U.S. 158 (1964), which remains binding law, though it seems unlikely the agencies would bring such a claim today.

United States v. Marine Bancorporation

418 U.S. 602 (1974).

■ MR. JUSTICE POWELL delivered the opinion of the Court.

The United States brought this civil antitrust action . . . to challenge a proposed merger between two commercial banks. The acquiring bank is a large, nationally chartered bank based in Seattle, Washington, and the acquired bank is a medium-size, state-chartered bank located at the opposite end of the State in Spokane. The banks are not direct competitors to any significant degree in Spokane or any other part of the State. They have no banking offices in each other's home cities. The merger agreement would substitute the acquiring bank for the acquired bank in Spokane and would permit the former for the first time to operate as a direct participant in the Spokane market.

The proposed merger would have no effect on the number of banks in Spokane. The United States bases its case exclusively on the potential-competition doctrine under § 7 of the Clayton Act. It contends that if the merger is prohibited, the acquiring bank would find an alternative and more competitive means for entering the Spokane area and that the acquired bank would ultimately develop by internal expansion or mergers with smaller banks into an actual competitor of the acquiring bank and other large banks in sections of the State outside Spokane. The Government further submits that the merger would terminate the alleged procompetitive influence that the acquiring bank presently exerts over Spokane banks due to the potential for its entry into that market.

After a full trial, the District Court held against the Government on all aspects of the case. We affirm that court's judgment. We hold that in applying the potential-competition doctrine to commercial banking, courts must take into account the extensive federal and state regulation of banks, particularly the legal restraints on entry unique to this line of commerce. The legal barriers to entry in the instant case, notably state-law prohibitions against *de novo* branching, against branching from a branch office, and against multibank holding companies, compel us to conclude that the challenged merger is not in violation of § 7.

I. BACKGROUND . . .

The acquiring bank, National Bank of Commerce (NBC), [has] . . . its principal office in Seattle, [and] . . . is a wholly owned subsidiary of a registered bank holding company, Marine Bancorporation, Inc. (Marine). . . . The target bank, Washington Trust Bank (WTB), . . . [has] . . . headquarters in Spokane. Spokane is located in the extreme eastern part of the State, approximately 280 road miles from Seattle. . . . WTB has seven branch offices, six in the city of Spokane and one in . . . a Spokane suburb. . . . It controls 17.4% of the 46 commercial banking offices in the Spokane metropolitan area. . . . Although WTB has exhibited a pattern of moderate growth, at no time during its 70-year history has it expanded outside the Spokane metropolitan area.

. . . There are six banking organizations operating in the Spokane metropolitan area. One organization, Washington Bancshares, . . . held 42.1% of total deposits in the area. Seattle-First National Bank . . . held 31.6%. The target bank held 18.6% of total deposits at that time, placing it third in the Spokane area . . . Thus, taken together, Washington Bancshares, Seattle-First National Bank, and WTB hold approximately 92% of total deposits in the Spokane area. None of the remaining three commercial banks in Spokane holds a market share larger than 3.1%.

. . . The United States sought to establish that the merger "may . . . substantially . . . lessen competition" within the meaning of § 7 in three ways: by eliminating the prospect that NBC, absent acquisition of the market share represented by WTB, would enter Spokane *de novo* or through acquisition of a smaller bank and thus would assist in deconcentrating that market over the long run; by ending present procompetitive effects allegedly produced in Spokane by NBC's perceived presence on the fringe of the Spokane market; and by terminating the alleged probability that WTB as an independent entity would develop through internal growth or through mergers with other medium-size banks into a regional or ultimately statewide counterweight to the market power of the State's largest banks. The Government's first theory—alleged likelihood of *de novo* or foothold entry by NBC if the challenged merger were blocked—was the primary basis upon which this case was presented to the District Court.

II. THE RELEVANT MARKETS

... The ... relevant product market ... is the "business of commercial banking ..." ... The ... relevant geographic market is the Spokane metropolitan area ...

III. POTENTIAL-COMPETITION DOCTRINE

... The potential-competition doctrine has been defined in major part by ... cases, particularly *United States v. Falstaff Brewing Corp.*, 410 U.S. 526 (1973). Unequivocal proof that an acquiring firm actually would have entered *de novo* but for a merger is rarely available. Thus, as *Falstaff* indicates, the principal focus of the doctrine is on the likely effects of the premerger position of the acquiring firm on the fringe of the target market. In developing and applying the doctrine, the Court has recognized that a market extension merger may be unlawful if the target market is substantially concentrated, if the acquiring firm has the characteristics, capabilities, and economic incentive to render it a perceived potential *de novo* entrant, and if the acquiring firm's premerger presence on the fringe of the target market in fact tempered oligopolistic behavior on the part of existing participants in that market. In other words, the Court has interpreted § 7 as encompassing what is commonly known as the "wings effect"—the probability that the acquiring firm prompted premerger procompetitive effects within the target market by being perceived by the existing firms in that market as likely to enter *de novo*. *Falstaff*. The elimination of such present procompetitive effects may render a merger unlawful under § 7.

Although the concept of perceived potential entry has been accepted in the Court's prior § 7 cases, the potential-competition theory upon which the Government places principal reliance in the instant case has not. The Court has not previously resolved whether the potential-competition doctrine proscribes a market extension merger solely on the ground that such a merger eliminates the prospect for long-term deconcentration of an oligopolistic market that in theory might result if the acquiring firm were forbidden to enter except through a *de novo* undertaking or through the acquisition of a small existing entrant (a so-called foothold or toehold acquisition). *Falstaff* expressly reserved this issue....

B. Structure of the Spokane Market.

... The potential-competition doctrine has meaning only as applied to concentrated markets. That is, the doctrine comes into play only where there are dominant participants in the target market engaging in interdependent or parallel behavior and with the capacity effectively to determine price and total output of goods or services. If the target market performs as a competitive market in traditional antitrust terms, the participants in the market will have no occasion to fashion their behavior to take into account the presence of a potential entrant. The present procompetitive effects that a perceived potential entrant may produce in an oligopolistic market will already have been accomplished if the target market is performing competitively. Likewise, there would be no need for concern about the prospects of long-term deconcentration of a market which is in fact genuinely competitive.

In an effort to establish that the Spokane commercial banking market is oligopolistic, the Government relied primarily on concentration ratios indicating that three banking organizations (including WTB) control approximately 92% of total deposits in Spokane. . . . We conclude that by introducing evidence of concentration ratios of the magnitude of those present here the Government established a prima facie case that the Spokane market was a candidate for the potential-competition doctrine. On this aspect of the case, the burden was then upon appellees to show that the concentration ratios, which can be unreliable indicators of actual market behavior, did not accurately depict the economic characteristics of the Spokane market. In our view, appellees did not carry this burden, and the District Court erred in holding to the contrary. Appellees introduced no significant evidence of the absence of parallel behavior in the pricing or providing of commercial bank services in Spokane. . . .

C. Potential De Novo or Foothold Entry.

. . . . The Government contends that the challenged merger violates § 7 because it eliminates the alleged likelihood that, but for the merger, NBC would enter Spokane *de novo* or through a foothold acquisition. Utilization of one of these methods of entry, it is argued, would be likely to produce deconcentration of the Spokane market over the long run or other procompetitive effects, because NBC would be required to compete vigorously to expand its initially insignificant market share.

Two essential preconditions must exist before it is possible to resolve whether the Government's theory, if proved, establishes a violation of § 7. It must be determined: (i) that in fact NBC has available feasible means for entering the Spokane market other than by acquiring WTB; and (ii) that those means offer a substantial likelihood of ultimately producing deconcentration of that market or other significant procompetitive effects. . . . There is no dispute that NBC possesses the financial capability and incentive to enter. The controversy turns on what methods of entry are realistically possible and on the likely effect of various methods on the characteristics of the Spokane commercial banking market.

It is undisputed that under state law NBC cannot establish *de novo* branches in Spokane and that its parent holding company cannot hold more than 25% of the stock of any other bank. Entry for NBC into Spokane therefore must be by acquisition of an existing bank. The Government contends that NBC has two distinct alternatives for acquisition of banks smaller than WTB and that either alternative would be likely to benefit the Spokane commercial banking market.

First, the Government contends that NBC could arrange for the formation of a new bank (a concept known as "sponsorship"), insure that the stock for such a new bank is placed in friendly hands, and then ultimately acquire that bank. Appellees respond that this approach would violate the spirit if not the letter of state-law restrictions on bank branching. . . . [W]e will assume, *arguendo*, that NBC conceivably could succeed in sponsoring and then acquiring a new bank in Spokane at some indefinite time in the future. It does not follow from this assumption, however, that this method of entry would be reasonably likely to produce any significant procompetitive benefits in the Spokane commercial banking market. To the contrary, it appears likely that such a method of entry would not significantly affect that market.

State law would not allow NBC to branch from a sponsored bank after it was acquired. NBC's entry into Spokane therefore would be frozen at the level of its initial acquisition. Thus, if NBC were to enter Spokane by sponsoring and acquiring a small bank, it would be trapped into a position of operating a single branch office in a large metropolitan area with no reasonable likelihood of developing a significant share of that market.[42] This assumed method of entry therefore would offer little realistic hope of ultimately producing deconcentration of the Spokane market. Moreover, it is unlikely that a single new bank in Spokane with a small market share, and forbidden to branch, would have any other significant procompetitive effect on that market. The Government introduced no evidence, for example, establishing that the three small banks presently in Spokane have had any meaningful effect on the economic behavior of the large Spokane banks. In sum, it blinks reality to conclude that the opportunity for entry through sponsorship, assuming its availability, is comparable to the entry alternatives open to unregulated industries such as those involved in this Court's prior potential-competition cases or would be likely to produce the competitive effects of a truly unfettered method of entry. Since there is no substantial likelihood of procompetitive loss if the challenged merger is undertaken in place of the Government's sponsorship theory, we are unable to conclude that the effect of the former "may be substantially to lessen competition" within the meaning of the Clayton Act.

As a second alternative method of entry, the Government proposed that NBC could enter by a foothold acquisition of one of two small, state-chartered commercial banks that operate in the Spokane metropolitan area. . . . Granting the Government the benefit of the doubt that these

[42] NBC's acquisition of WTB, by comparison, will give it eight banking offices in Spokane and a significant market share. From this position, NBC will be able to have a substantial impact on the Spokane market. The Government suggests that a sponsored bank could create a number of branches before being acquired. The Government offered no proof that this has ever occurred in Washington. Undertaking sponsorship on such a scale is probably unrealistic, and it would multiply the problems of obtaining approval of a sponsorship plan from bank regulatory agencies. In any event, nothing in § 7 of the Clayton Act requires a firm to go to such lengths in order to avoid a merger that has no effect on concentration in the relevant market in the first place.

two small banks were available merger partners for NBC, or were available at some not too distant time, it again does not follow that an acquisition of either would produce the long-term market-structure benefits predicted by the Government. Once NBC acquired either of these banks, it could not branch from the acquired bank. This limitation strongly suggests that NBC would not develop into a significant participant in the Spokane market . . .

In sum, with regard to either of its proposed alternative methods of entry, the Government has offered an unpersuasive case on the first precondition of the question reserved in *Falstaff*—that feasible alternative methods of entry in fact existed. Putting these difficulties aside, the Government simply did not establish the second precondition. It failed to demonstrate that the alternative means offer a reasonable prospect of long-term structural improvement or other benefits in the target market. In fact, insofar as competitive benefits are concerned, the Government is in the anomalous position of opposing a geographic market extension merger that will introduce a third full-service banking organization to the Spokane market, where only two are now operating, in reliance on alternative means of entry that appear unlikely to have any significant procompetitive effect. Accordingly, we cannot hold for the Government on its principal potential-competition theory. Indeed, since the preconditions for that theory are not present, we do not reach it, and therefore we express no view on the appropriate resolution of the question reserved in *Falstaff*. . . .

D. Perceived Potential Entry.

. . . Rational commercial bankers in Spokane, it must be assumed, are aware of the regulatory barriers that render NBC an unlikely or an insignificant potential entrant except by merger with WTB. In light of those barriers, it is improbable that NBC exerts any meaningful procompetitive influence over Spokane banks by "standing in the wings." Moreover, the District Court found as a fact that "the threat of entry by NBC into the Spokane market by any means other than the consummation of the merger, to the extent any such threat exists, does not have any significant effect on the competitive practices of commercial banks in that market nor any significant effect on the level of competition therein." . . .

E. Elimination of WTB's Potential for Growth.

[T]he Government [also] challenges the merger on the ground that it will eliminate the prospect that WTB may expand outside its base in Spokane and eventually develop into a direct competitor with large Washington banks in other areas of the State. The District Court found, however, that the Government had "failed to establish . . . that there is any reasonable probability that WTB will expand into other banking markets. . . ." The record amply supports this finding. At no time in its 70-year history has WTB established branches outside the Spokane metropolitan area. Nor has it ever acquired another bank or received a merger offer other than the one at issue here. In sum, the Government's argument about the elimination of WTB's potential for expansion outside Spokane is little more than speculation. . . .

IV. CONCLUSION

In applying the doctrine of potential competition to commercial banking, courts must, as we have noted, take into account the extensive federal and state regulation of banks. Our affirmance of the District Court's judgment in this case rests primarily on state statutory barriers to *de novo* entry and to expansion following entry into a new geographic market. In States where such stringent barriers exist and in the absence of a likelihood of entrenchment, the potential-competition doctrine—grounded as it is on relative freedom of entry on the part of the acquiring firm—will seldom bar a geographic market extension merger by a commercial bank. In States that permit free branching or multibank holding companies, courts hearing cases involving such mergers should take into account all relevant factors, including the barriers to entry created by state and federal control over the issuance of new bank charters. Testimony by responsible regulatory officials that they will not grant new charters in the target market is entitled to great weight, although it is not determinative. To avoid the danger of subjecting the enforcement of the antitrust laws to the policies of a particular bank regulatory official or agency, courts should look also to the size and growth prospects of the target market, the size and number of banking organizations participating in it, and past practices of regulatory agencies in granting charters. If regulatory restraints are not determinative, courts should consider the factors that are pertinent to any potential-competition case, including the economic feasibility and likelihood of *de novo* entry, the capabilities and expansion history of the acquiring firm, and the performance as well as the structural characteristics of the target market. . . .

NOTES AND QUESTIONS ON *MARINE BANCORP*

While *Marine Bancorp* did not rule on whether a conglomerate merger could be condemned on grounds that it prevented actual potential competition, it did rule that (if valid) any such claim would require proof that: (1) the market was sufficiently concentrated that the elimination of a potential entrant mattered; (2) the potential entrant had the ability and incentives to enter without the merger; and (3) the potential entry would have a substantial likelihood of having a significant procompetitive impact. The latter seems to include inquiry into how timely the entry would have been.

1. ***How could actual and perceived potential entry differ?*** One might think that in general actual potential competition would be correctly perceived, so they usually would not differ. But they can differ for various reasons. There might be a perceived potential competition effect without an actual potential competition effect for two reasons. First, perception might not match reality: firms in the market may think another firm would likely enter, even though it actually would not. Second, there might be a perceived potential competition effect because firms accurately think another firm will enter if they do not constrain their pricing, but no actual potential competition because the fact that the firms are induced to engage in such limit pricing makes the other firm unlikely to actually enter.

Likewise, there might be an actual potential competition effect without a perceived potential competition effect for two reasons. First, perception might not match reality: firms in the market may think another firm is unlikely to enter, even though it actually would. Second, firms may accurately perceive that potential competition will actually occur, but there may be no perceived potential competition effect because this prospect does not constraint current prices, either because firms in the market lack an ability to coordinate on limit pricing or lack sufficient incentives to limit price because the short-term gains of supracompetitive profits outweigh the discounted long-term losses of inviting entry.

Thus, either a perceived or actual potential competition effect could exist without the other, even if perceptions are all accurate. Either effect is harmful without the other. A perceived potential competition effect means the merger would immediately raise current prices. An actual potential competition effect means the merger would raise future prices at whatever time actual entry would otherwise have occurred.

2. ***Does* Marine Bancorp *identify the right three factors for potential competition claims?*** Not quite because the "incentives and ability to enter" factor is both overinclusive and underinclusive. It is overinclusive because, even if an acquired firm has the incentives and ability to enter, entry barriers might be so low that lots of firms have those same incentives and ability to enter. In that case, potential competition theory should not bar the merger because the threat of entry will render the market competitive regardless of whether the merger occurs. The potential competition theory only works for entry barriers that either are lower for the acquired firm or are in a middle range that can be overcome by the acquired firm but not by other potential entrants. Thus, as the 1984 Guidelines stressed, the focus should be not only on the acquired firm's incentives and ability to enter, but on whether it has greater incentives and ability to enter than other potential entrants.

The "incentives and ability to enter" factor is also underinclusive because a firm might not have the ability or incentives to enter but be perceived as likely to enter if prices rose. This might reflect either misperceptions about its abilities or an accurate perception that, although the firm could and would enter if prices rose, current limit pricing eliminated its incentives to actually enter. However, the Court applied the "incentives and ability to enter" factor only to claims of actual potential competition. When rejecting the claim of perceived potential competition effects, the Court relied on (a) the unlikelihood that firms inaccurately perceived publicly known regulations that made entry unlikely or insignificant; and (b) evidence that current pricing was not constrained by any perceptions of potential entry.

When to Block a Merger Based on a Risk of Post-Merger Misconduct

The U.S. agencies have largely abandoned efforts to block mergers based on post-merger misconduct, largely on the theory that other laws can always deter any post-merger misconduct and should be changed or reinterpreted if they do not. However, as we have emphasized throughout this book, uncertainties in information and adjudication mean that any rule that regulates conduct optimally cannot eliminate underdeterrence, but rather can only minimize the sum of harm from under-and overdeterrence. Thus, other laws will, even if optimally designed, always leave some bad post-merger conduct underdeterred, raising the question whether it is better to tackle the problem by blocking the merger that creates the ability or incentives to engage in that misconduct.

If efficiency gains from a merger are shown, an agency that wanted to assess whether to block a merger based on the risk of post-merger misconduct would have to determine whether that efficiency exceeds the likelihood of post-merger misconduct times the magnitude of the anticompetitive harm it would create. Thus, the ultimate question is whether the Merger-Specific Efficiency Gain > (Probability Post-Merger Misconduct is Profitable) × (Probability Post-Merger Misconduct Will Be Undeterred by Other Laws) × (Magnitude of Anticompetitive Harm from Post-Merger Misconduct). Although the relevant variables may not be susceptible of precise quantification, this sort of formula usefully helps to frame analysis. In particular, it shows that merger enforcement is more desirable the more likely it is that the feared post merger-conduct will be (1) profitable, (2) undeterred, and (3) anticompetitive.

Indeed, we can use the above formula and 3 factors to map the general pattern of merger enforcement. It makes sense that the areas of most vigorous merger enforcement are blocking mergers that create unilateral or oligopoly effects, because there the bad post-merger misconduct is high unilateral or oligopoly pricing, which is highly profitable, cannot be regulated post-merger, and causes great anticompetitive harm. *See* Chapters 3, 6. Conglomerate mergers that eliminate potential competition manifest more mixed enforcement, because the potential competition may not be profitable and eliminating it may not be that harmful, but any anticompetitive problem cannot be deterred post-merger because there is no effective way to force the merged firm to enter a market and compete with itself. Vertical mergers manifest even weaker enforcement because there the feared post-merger misconduct is refusing to deal with rivals, which may not be profitable, is subject to at least some (though fairly deferential) antitrust scrutiny under unilateral refusal to deal doctrine, and may not be that anticompetitive when it occurs. Conglomerate mergers that enable post-merger exclusionary conduct manifest the weakest enforcement because there the feared conduct is vertical exclusionary conduct that may not be profitable, is subject to strictest antitrust scrutiny of any post-merger conduct here discussed, and may not be anticompetitive if it occurs. Not surprisingly, conglomerate mergers that enable post-merger exclusionary conduct have historically been challenged mainly when the post-merger conduct is something relatively hard to regulate, like reciprocity, so more likely to go undeterred.

INDEX

References are to Pages